CIVIL RIGHTS in AMERICA

1500

to the

Present

CIVIL RIGHTS in AMERICA

1500
to the
Present

Jay A. Sigler

Preface by
Deval L. Patrick

GALE

DETROIT · NEW YORK · LONDON

CIVIL RIGHTS in AMERICA: 1500 to the PRESENT
Jay A. Sigler

Gale Research Staff

Leslie Joseph, *Project Editor*
Camille Killens, *Associate Editor*
Catherine Goldstein, *Assistant Editor*
Lawrence W. Baker, *Managing Editor*

Maria Franklin, *Permissions Manager*
Michelle Lonoconus, *Permissions Assistant*

Mary Beth Trimper, *Production Director*
Evi Seoud, *Assistant Production Manager*
Shanna P. Heilveil, *Production Assistant*

Pamela A. E. Galbreath, *Senior Art Director*
Cynthia Baldwin, *Production Design Manager*
Barbara J. Yarrow, *Graphic Services Manager*
Randy Bassett, *Image Database Supervisor*
Pamela Reed, *Photography Coordinator*

Kenneth Benson, *Data Entry Coordinator*

Library of Congress Cataloging-in-Publication Data

Sigler, Jay A.
    Civil rights in America : 1500 to the present / Jay A. Sigler.
        p.   cm.
    Includes bibliographical references and index.
    ISBN 0-7876-0612-X (alk. paper)
    1. Civil rights—United States—History.
I. Title.
JC599.U5S53 1988
323'.0973—dc21

98-13951
CIP

While every effort has been made to ensure the reliability of the information presented in this publication, Gale does not guarantee the accuracy of the data contained herein. Gale accepts no payment for listing; and inclusion in the publication of any organization, agency, institution, publication, service, or individual does not imply endorsement of the editors or publisher. Errors brought to the attention of the publisher and verified to the satisfaction of the publisher will be corrected in future editions.

 The paper used in this publication meets the minimum requirements of American National Standard for Information Sciences—Permanence Paper for Printed Library Materials, ANSI Z39.478-1984.

Printed in the United States of America

10 9 8 7 6 5 4 3 2 1

To President Gerald Ford, who said, "Perhaps our country has not always lived up to its ideals. But then no country ever had higher ideals to live up to." (Speech of July 4, 1976, for the nation's Bicentennial Celebration.)

Advisory Board

Charles Boyle
Puerto Rican Legal Defense and Education Fund, Inc.

James Carnes
Southern Poverty Law Center

Lisa Friedman
Constitutional Rights Foundation

Ozell Hudson
Director, Lawyer's Committee for Civil Rights Under Law

Rebecca Jackson
Center for Constitutional Rights

Judith Krug
Director, Office for Intellectual Freedom, American Library Association

Michael Reggio
Director, Law-related Education Programs, Oklahoma State Bar Association

Judge Joseph Rodriguez
United States District Court, District of New Jersey

Frank Wilkinson
Director, First Amendment Foundation

Contributors

Howard Ball
   Professor of Political Science, University of Vermont

Roger A. Barbour
   Attorney

Michael Thomas Bedard
   Governmental Civil Rights Officer, State of New Jersey

Frank De Varona
   Superintendent of Schools, Region 1, Hialiah, Florida

Don Grinde
   Professor, Alana Studies Program, University of Vermont

Bill Hing
   Professor, Stanford Law School, Stanford University

Steve Jenkins
   P.A.S.S. Administrator, Permian High School, Permian, Texas

Michael Reggio
   Director, Law-related Education Programs, Oklahoma State Bar Association

Louis A. Schopfer
   Office of State Treasurer, State of New Jersey

J. Owens Smith
   Head, Afro-Ethnic Studies Department, California State University, Fullerton,
      California

Contents

Preface

This speech given by Deval L. Patrick, former head of the Civil Rights Division of the United States Department of Justice from 1993 until 1996, is a moving and articulate expression of many of the basic ideas presented in these volumes. Because of his official positions, Deval Patrick cannot endorse any particular book, and the printing of his speech is not intended to suggest that he would approve of all elements of this volume. The personal insights provided in this speech reveal a lot about the speaker, but the statement also makes some very important points about the current condition of civil rights in America, and shows that the quest for American rights is never-ending and involves all of us. The speech is printed exactly as it was given.

In 1997 Mr. Patrick returned to the private practice of law, joining a Boston legal firm. However, because of his national reputation as an effective rights advocate, he was selected by a federal judge to head an unprecedented Equality and Fairness Task Force. It was the task force's job to monitor acts of discrimination committed by Texaco against its employees. Mr. Patrick's shining reputation in civil rights was built quietly. During his tenure as head of the Civil Rights Division he had an 87 percent success rate in Justice Department prosecutions for civil rights crimes.

Remarks by Deval L. Patrick
Assistant Attorney General
Civil Rights Division
United States Department of Justice
Before the Town Hall
Los Angeles
October 4, 1994
Los Angeles, California

I came to Milton Academy, a private boarding school in Massachusetts, in 1970, the night before classes began. I had lived until then in a small apartment in an inner-city neighborhood on the south side of Chicago, a life of want, of deeply segregated and ill-equipped schools, of gang violence and limited hope—and I had never seen Milton or any place like it before. When I drove up the main street, I remember thinking of the large green in the center of the campus, that I had never seen so much privately-owned lawn before.

We had a dress code then: boys wore jackets and ties to classes. Now, a jacket on the south side of Chicago is a "windbreaker." So when the clothing list arrived at home, explaining the dress code, my family splurged on a new windbreaker. The first day of classes, when all the other boys were donning their blue blazers and tweed coats, there was I in my windbreaker. I had a lot to learn indeed.

But I figured it out—in time. I learned about the jackets, the rep ties, indeed the whole line of Brooks Brothers merchandise. I learned that peculiar truth about private schools: how the graduates never die, they just turn into buildings. I learned about money, what it could do, how it endowed some people with an extraordinary and often undeserved self-importance. And I learned that none of that mattered.

I learned a few other things that did matter. I learned about the long legacy of achievement that schools like that represent and expect of their graduates. I learned how to make friends across differences, some meaningful but most far less so. And most significant of all, I learned to appreciate education as more than accumulated information and prestige, but instead, to borrow from Robert Frost, as "learning to listen to anything, without losing your temper or your self-confidence."

I did not come to some of these notions until well after I had moved on from that school, long after the uneasiness of those early days in 1970 when I was still trying to find my way around that school in every sense of the term. I didn't discover what really matters until I got a little perspective. And it's the importance of perspective that I want mainly to talk about today.

Perspective is not just distance on your subject, but a different angle, a different lighting, a different way of viewing it. And the more you can vary your perspective—through life experiences and time—the deeper your understanding. Jeremy Knowles made this point beautifully in a speech a while back to the incoming freshmen at Harvard and Radcliffe colleges. Referring to a certain "Henry Moore sculpture on that terrace near Lamont Library," Dean Knowles said that "standing in front of it on the path, or gazing at it from the library, it looks pretty lumpy. A bunch of massive golden shapes, quite attractive, but meaningless, and mostly good for photographing small children in. But go out of the gate onto Quincy Street, and turn left, and look back through the thirty-fourth gap in the second set of railings. Suddenly you will see a splendid and voluptuous work. What is the moral?" he asked. His answer: if you don't understand something, the reason may be that you're simply standing in the wrong place. "So if you don't understand a theorem in physics or a passage from *Ulysses,* or a Schoenberg Trio . . . Or your roommate's politics, remember Henry Moore," said Dean Knowles, "and try a new perspective."

I'm sure you understand the point. The perspectives of each of us change in subtle and not-so-subtle ways, shaped by experience and by time. It happens imperceptibly much of the time. Then again, sometimes you are compelled to try a new perspective. I remember the moment in April of 1974, when college decisions came in. Now, while everyone at Milton is of course expected to go to college, you must understand that no one in my family had ever been. I had applied to five colleges, but there was only one I really wanted. When the letter came on April 15 that I was admitted to that one, I called home and my grandmother picked up the phone. I told her my news, that I was going to Harvard. She told me how proud she was of me, so pleased, so excited. Then she paused and said, "where is that anyway?" That's a different perspective. And I never forgot. Not at Harvard. Not at Harvard Law School. Not through any of the extraordinary experiences or associations I have had since that day. That lesson taught that the beginning of discovering what matters is learning what doesn't. The prestige didn't matter. The opportunity, the reason to hope mattered. That's perspective. In nothing else, as I see it, is the lack of perspective more glaring or the need for it more critical in this country than on the issues of civil rights. For centuries, American ideals of equality, opportunity, and fair play have been confounded by the politics and practices of division and exclusion. Slowly, painstakingly, over many decades, men and women of good will, of perspective—having faced up to the gulf between our reality and our ideals and come down in favor of our ideals—have pressed for, cajoled and demanded progress in closing that gap. But, as a nation, we are not yet truly free.

For it is undeniably true that legions of racial and ethnic minorities feel less of a sense of opportunity, less assured of our equality and less confident of fair treatment today than we have in many, many years. Now, society's collective thinking on the meaning of opportunity seems to begin and end with the topic of affirmative action. Now, we seem to view the demands of political expedience and the specter of opinion polls as more important than basic concepts of fair play and due process. The notion of equality is hardly even mentioned in public discourse, as if avoiding the subject avoids the problem. Some openly question whether the civil rights movement has gone too far and others, including many African Americans, are wondering whether integration was ever a valid goal.

Take, for example, the area of voting rights. The right to vote, and to have that vote mean something, are at the core of our democratic values. A little perspective reminds us of that. We redeemed that principle when we passed the Voting Rights Act, and then the work began: first poll taxes and literacy tests; then, voter harassment and intimidation, a problem we have not solved entirely yet; and then the drawing of district lines to dilute the significance of the minority vote. These issues keep evolving not because minorities keep grasping for more, but because we are dealing with places with persistent ingenuity in keeping minorities down and out of the game.

A little perspective reminds us that these are not mere abstract issues. These are real-life problems. Imagine what it means for a poor person to be able to vote without worrying about whether it costs too much. Imagine what it means for an illiterate citizen or one who doesn't read English well to get help or a translation without shame. Imagine what it means for an elderly black woman who associates a county courthouse with beatings and violence to be able to go down and vote without fear of intimidation and harassment.

And then imagine what it means to cast your vote time and time and time again for a candidate who will never win simply because the white majority won't vote for any candidate you want. Without perspective, we turn away from real people and real problems like these, in favor of abstractions. Abstractions like the Supreme Court's decision in *Shaw* v. *Reno. Shaw* involved a challenge to North Carolina's 1991 congressional redistricting plan, a plan the state legislature adopted in order to comply with the Voting Rights Act. Five white plaintiffs—three of whom didn't even live in the districts—challenged the creation of two of the state's twelve congressional districts, the ones in which blacks were in the majority. Indeed, those two districts sent two black representatives to Congress. But the Court criticized these districts as promoting "segregation." Many casual commentators do, too. But in this, perspective fails us.

We forget that the challenged plan was responsible for desegregating the North Carolina congressional delegation. We forget that, in a state where one in every five citizens is African American, North Carolina had not sent a single African American to Congress in this century. We forget that state's long experience of segregation, exclusion and intentional dilution of minority voting strength, even though it was this very reality that led to the adoption of the Voting Rights Act in the first place.

Our perspective is replaced by hysteria and overheated rhetoric, reducing important and complex problems to political buzzwords, and crowding out reason. We call these districts "bizarrely shaped," as if congressional districts ever lend themselves to anything that could fairly be called a "normal" or "regular" shape. We call these districts "segregating voters by race" or racial "apartheid," as if they were not in fact the most integrated congressional districts in the country.

Lacking perspective, we sometimes even drift into the absurd, such as when a district court in Louisiana described a 63 percent-black district as "segregation of voters by race" when, in the court's own words, it "combin[ed] English-Scotch-Irish, mainline Protestants, traditional rural black Protestants, south Louisiana black Catholics, continental French-Spanish-German Roman Catholics, sui generic creoles, and thoroughly mixed polyglots . . . As never heretofore so extensively agglomerated." By what stretch of imagination is this "segregation"? We are so wrapped up in the rhetoric of "racial gerrymandering" that we cannot see that state legislatures, having made political compromises across racial lines to solve real problems, have created models of the very integration we have so long valued as a nation.

Perspective has returned to the Civil Rights Division today. Knowing the facts about and history of these districts, we have undertaken to defend against these recent attacks on the gains of the Voting Rights Act. We have done so because the right of historically excluded citizens to have an equal opportunity to elect the candidates of their choice is central to ensuring that each and every American is treated as a full and equal member of our civic society. A person who is denied an effective voice in the governance of his nation simply cannot feel the same sense of investment in the affairs of that nation. Congress affirmed this with passage of the Voting Rights Act. And in carrying out Congress's mandate, it sometimes makes sense—especially in jurisdictions with a history of ingenuity in excluding minority voters—to create electoral districts in which African Americans or Latinos form a majority.

So, we who defend—who believe in—civil rights have an obligation to defend these districts. Not because of beliefs in the value of an integrated Congress—though that is a true advantage by any measure of effective, responsible government. And not because of beliefs about whether minorities can or cannot be effectively represented by whites or vice versa—both abstract analysis and practical experience have shown that people are effectively represented by members of other races much of the time. We must defend these districts because, in those places and circumstances where politics is already racially polarized, minorities will never be able to elect candidates of their choice without such districts. To stand by and watch a segment of the community be disempowered because of race would violate our commitment to enforce the Voting Rights Act, and contradict the values our nation holds so dear. This same loss of perspective is evident in the debate over enforcement of the Americans with Disabilities Act as well. After passage of the Act, some in the business community responded almost hysterically—complying with the act will cost too much, they said, and this cost certainly isn't worth it to help such a small minority. Others responded more theoretically—the ADA is unwarranted government intrusion in the marketplace, they said. Or, as some state and local officials put it, the ADA is a so-called "unfunded mandate."

Once again, hysterical reactions and abstract discussions crowd out perspective. The fact is, most compliance with the ADA is simple and inexpensive. And far from being a tiny minority, people with disabilities make up a large segment of our population—one in seven Americans, according to the 1990 census. Indeed, we all have a good chance of becoming disabled with age; and any one of us could become disabled at any time, for any length of time. When the size of this potential market is compared with the relatively insignificant costs of complying with the law, it is clear that opening up our nation's commercial facilities and public accommodations makes good business sense.

But more than good business sense is at stake here. The ADA is a civil rights law, not an "unfunded mandate." We don't put a price on equal opportunity in this country, any more than we do on the value of faith, loyalty or courage. At stake is the opportunity for people with disabilities to live their lives as fully as anyone else, as a part of the whole of society.

These are real challenges for real people. Like the recent experience of Marca Bristo, the new chair of the National Council on Disabilities. Marca, who uses a wheelchair, was visiting a museum with her six-year-old son. Marca's son sat on her lap while she negotiated her wheelchair through the museum's corridors.

She stopped to look at one of the exhibits, and her son got off her lap and began walking around. Just then, a very large tour group came in, blocking her view of her son. She tried to wheel around the group to a place where she could see her child, but to no avail. When the group moved on, her son was nowhere in sight. She could only hear him crying out for her. He was frightened.

She travelled towards the voice, and she soon saw her son at the end of a corridor. But there were a few steps between her and her child, between her and her ability to comfort her child. Such a simple barrier, and so simple to deal with. And yet rather than deal with it, even once the problem was brought to the attention of the museum administration, one official responded by telling Marca that the museum "couldn't be responsible for [her] inability to be a better mother." That's cruel. That's also a loss of perspective.

In countless lives, what seem like little things to many of us—a few steps—can make a profound difference. It only takes perspective to see it. If we are truly committed to ensuring that every American has an equal right to participate fully in all aspects of civic, cultural and political life, then we must commit ourselves to making the promise of the Americans with Disabilities Act a reality.

We must regain our perspective in education, too, and through that commit ourselves to ensuring that every child has an equal opportunity to obtain a quality education. Today, 40 years after the *Brown* v. *Board of Education* decision, the great task of integration remains unfinished. As we continue to strive towards integration, we must remember that assuring educational quality for all children undergirds the whole reason for the struggle leading to and flowing from *Brown*. And so we must address inequalities by race, ethnicity and gender that occur even in nominally desegregated schools, and to help assure that all children get the attention they deserve from their teachers. We need educators who are personally inclined and practically able to pay attention to their students. I went to public schools on the south side of Chicago through junior high school and then, by luck and scholarship, to high school at Milton. That meant I went from an eighth grade class of 40 students per teacher to a typical ninth grade class of twelve students per teacher. Now, as a parent and simply as an observer of human nature, I can see that kids are hungry for the company of adults and that teachers who can and do pay personal attention to their students can and do make profound differences in life after life. To illustrate my point, I want to share a story that Marian Wright Edelman tells about one schoolteacher, Jean Thompson, and one fifth grade boy, Teddy Stollard:

On the first day of school, Jean Thompson told her students, "boys and girls, I love you all the same." Teachers lie. Little Teddy Stollard was a boy Jean Thompson did not like. He slouched in his chair, didn't pay attention, his mouth hung open in a stupor, his eyes were always unfocused, his clothes were mussed, his hair unkempt, and he smelled. He was an unattractive boy and Jean Thompson didn't like him.

Teachers have records. And Jean Thompson had Teddy's. First grade: "Teddy's a good boy. He shows promise in his work and attitude. But he has a poor home situation." Second grade: "Teddy is a good boy. He does what he is told. But he is too serious. His mother is terminally ill." Third grade: "Teddy is falling behind in his work; he needs help. His mother died this year. His father shows no interest." Fourth grade: "Teddy is in deep waters; he is in need of psychiatric help. He is totally withdrawn."

Christmas came, and the boys and girls brought their presents and piled them on her desk. They were all in brightly colored paper except for Teddy's. His was wrapped in brown paper and held together with scotch tape. And on it, scribbled in crayon, were the words, "for Miss Thompson from Teddy." She tore open the brown paper and out fell a rhinestone bracelet with most of the stones missing and a bottle of cheap perfume that was almost empty. When the other boys and girls began to giggle she had enough sense to put some of the perfume on her wrist, put on the bracelet, hold her wrist up to the other children and say, "doesn't it smell lovely? Isn't the bracelet pretty?" And taking their cue from the teacher, they all agreed.

At the end of the day, when all the children had left, Teddy lingered, came over to her desk and said, "Miss Thompson, all day long, you smelled just like my mother. And her bracelet, that's her bracelet, it looks real nice on you, too. I'm really glad you like my presents." And when he left, she got down on her knees and buried her head in her chair and she begged God to forgive her.

The next day when the children came, she was a different teacher. She was a teacher with a heart. And she cared for all the children, but especially those who needed help. Especially Teddy. She tutored him and put herself out for him.

By the end of the year, Teddy had caught up with a lot of the children and was even ahead of some. Several years later, Jean Thompson got this note:

Dear Miss Thompson:

I'm graduating and I'm second in my high school class. I wanted you to be the first to know. Love, Teddy.

Four years later she got another note:

Dear Miss Thompson:

I wanted you to be the first to know. The university has not been easy, but I liked it. Love, Teddy Stollard.

Four years later, there was another note:

Dear Miss Thompson:

As of today, I am Theodore J. Stollard, M.D. How about that? I wanted you to be the first to know. I'm going to be married in July. I want you to come and sit where my mother would have sat, because you're the only family I have. Dad died last year.

And she went and she sat where his mother should have sat because she deserved to be there. She had become a decent and loving human being.

You and I know that there are millions of Teddy Stollards all over this nation, children who are left out and left back—who will never become doctors or lawyers or teachers or police officers or much else—because there was no Jean Thompson. My point is simply that, with perspective on real problems in real people's lives, civil rights today must address our collective responsibility for the attention children get from educators and the practical ability school districts and parents alike have to "reach out for them, speak up for them, vote, lobby and struggle for them" [Edelman] wherever and whenever they can.

I have mentioned just a few of the areas in which the Civil Rights Division is working today. But I am trying, mainly, to emphasize why our work matters. For what we are talking about here, at its essence, isn't just cases and statutes. It is about a fundamental affirmation of the American creed.

Our national creed has its roots in the earliest days of the republic. In the Declaration of Independence, our founders set forth the fundamental principles for which this nation stands. Foremost among these principles is a commitment to one nation, indivisible—a recognition that the fate of each one of us is inextricably bound to that of each other and of society as a whole. Our common ideals tell us that we cannot progress as a society by leaving some of our people behind; we must all advance together.

The second fundamental principle of our national creed follows necessarily from the first: all people are created equal. Abraham Lincoln dedicated our nation to this proposition, and we as a people have borne faith to it ever since. It is a part of our shared American identity. History will ultimately judge us by our efforts to meet this commitment.

It is our faith in affirming these principles—of equality, opportunity and fair play—that makes us Americans. To be sure, we have never fully attained the high ideals to which we are dedicated. But—with a few brief exceptions—our history is a history of reaching for our ideals, of closing the gap between our reality and our ideals. Lincoln explained it well when he said our nation's founders "meant to set up a standard maxim for free society, which should be familiar to all, and revered by all; constantly looked to, constantly labored for, and even though never perfectly attained, constantly approximated, and thereby constantly spreading and deepening its influence, and augmenting the happiness and value of life to people of all colors everywhere."

By fighting to expand opportunities, to promote equality, and to empower all people in our society, we are continuing the process Lincoln spoke of—the constant attempt to approximate our nation's great ideals, to spread and deepen their influence. Martin Luther King, Jr., was right when he said, "the arc of the moral universe is long, but it bends toward justice." All those people of perspective in all walks of American life, who work to ensure that the arc bends forward rather than backward, are engaged in a true act of patriotism.

Some would have us see civil rights as a fight among competing factions for entitlements. Some would have us believe that one group's gain is another's loss, that those who want their rights vindicated are engaged in special pleading, and that civil rights is of concern to only so-called "special interests." Abstract debates about colorblindness and hysterical rhetoric about quotas have been so prominent in public discourse that many people think of civil rights as simply a battleground over who gets what size slice of the pie. In such an atmosphere, is it any wonder that we see groups turning inward and refusing to invest in each other's struggles.

But we all have a stake in the struggle for equality, opportunity and fair play. When an African American stands up for the right to equal educational opportunity, he stands up for all of us. When a Latina stands up for the right to a chance to elect the candidate of her choice, she stands up for all of us. When a Jew stands up against those who vandalize his place of worship, he stands up for all of us. And when a person with a hearing impairment stands up for access to 911 emergency services, she stands up for all of us. For civil rights is not about deciding who gets the spoils. It is about reclaiming our fundamental values and aspirations as a nation.

It is a struggle. It is often hard work. But we must resist this tendency towards the dissolution of our society into mutually isolated and mutually distrustful groups. For if we don't, we will surely perish. And the nation our forebears imagined—and have entrusted now to us—will never come to pass. We must stick together in this struggle: not simply because it is politically correct, but because it is morally correct.

This is a defining point in history: our young people are increasingly alienated from civic society, and too many of the rest of us have let cynicism and selfishness define our lives. But I believe in America still. The president fervently does. And so must you. Diverse a people as we are and have always been—we are still one nation, one people, with one common destiny. And each of us is diminished when any one—on account of a happenstance of birth or chance—experiences anything less than the full measure of his or her dignity and privilege as a human being and an American. So, let us recapture our perspective, set aside our hysterics, and, reclaim the American conscience. Destiny demands of us no less.

Thank you.

Introduction

A New Look at our American Rights

In just 55 words of the Declaration of Independence the basic features of the American creed were stated for all time in terms of our rights.

> We hold these truths to be self-evident, that all men are created equal, that they are endowed by their Creator with certain inalienable Rights, that among these are Life, Liberty, and the pursuit of Happiness. That to secure these rights, Governments are instituted among Men, deriving their just powers from the consent of the governed.

When he was asked, as he often was in later years, what his sources were for these noble words of 1776, Thomas Jefferson replied that his purpose was "not to find out new principles, or new arguments, never before thought of, not merely to say things which have never been said before; but to place before mankind the common sense of the subject, in terms so plain and firm as to command their assent." Those words of the Declaration of Independence, which have inspired our leaders from Abraham Lincoln at Gettysburg to Martin Luther King Jr. on the steps of the Lincoln Memorial, should make it clear to all Americans that our rights are extremely important, and that the protection of those rights is the prime purpose of government.

Our rights as Americans may be among our most important possessions—more important than our cars, our televisions, our computers, or even our homes. In many other nations, where rights are few or fragile, nothing is secure, and individuals must live from day to day wishing that their government and other powerful forces in the society would simply leave them alone. We have seen newspaper and television images of other peoples being driven from their own homes, losing their most valuable possessions to hostile officials without their consent, and being imprisoned without trial. While Americans cannot say that they are able to fully exercise all of their individual rights, we have been fortunate, because we have been protected against the worst kinds of harm that governments can inflict on their own people. Our American rights cannot be taken for granted. They are the gift of several centuries of progress in rights development. However, each generation must renew its awareness of American rights or risk the erosion of those rights.

Our American rights are of fairly recent origin. Before American independence there was no freedom of speech or of the press. Religious freedom was largely unknown. Even the early heroes of American history had only a dim notion of individual rights. Revolutionary War leader Patrick Henry declared: "Give me liberty or give me death" in 1775, just prior to the American Revolution, but he was prepared to vote to outlaw any Virginian who spoke well of the English king. Most of the American colonies tolerated few religions, and some had established religions. The 1791 Bill of Rights began a long, slow process in the growth of American rights.

There is every reason to believe that the Bill of Rights was designed partly to define early American rights and partly to permit the states to adopt their own views of rights. The first major group to challenge this view of individual rights as an aspect of states' rights was the abolitionists who sought to stamp out slavery in America. They believed that slavery, which was tolerated in the Constitution, was opposed to all ideas of human dignity. They believed that the Bill of Rights had to be read in a new way that gave freedom to all Americans and ended slavery.

In 1833 the U.S. Supreme Court held that the Bill of Rights did not apply to the states, but only to the federal government. Women had no constitutional right to vote in the United States until 1920. Native Americans did not receive rights in this country until Congress made them citizens in 1924. Freedom of speech and freedom of the press were not guaranteed against state action until 1931. Public school prayers were constitutional until 1962.

Our Changing Rights

Our American rights are subject to changes, and the alterations in our rights come about through statutes, court decisions, and the practices of government officials.

Most Americans assume, without thinking about it, that they are free to enjoy more individual rights than almost any other people in the world. Some confuse their rights with entitlements, or claims to some sort of government benefit, like a veteran's bonus or a senior citizen discount. There is no "right" to a driver's license or to a hunting or fishing license. There is no "right" to be paid social security in old age. All are privileges that the government can extend to citizens. Many people are confused about their rights and use rights talk loosely, assuming that if they shout loud enough they will be better able to claim their

rights. The truth about American rights is more complicated than that.

On the surface American rights may seem to be simply a long list of items derived from the national Constitution and the Bill of Rights. That is partly true, but there are many other sources of rights in America. American states have constitutions and bills of rights of their own. In addition, both the national Congress and the state legislatures have given specific meaning to American rights by expanding their definition through statutory language.

Most Americans are familiar with the active leadership in civil rights policy taken by the national Supreme Court. Indeed, to a very large extent, our rights today cannot be understood without examining Supreme Court interpretations of various rights documents. But a careful look at the situation reveals that the Supreme Court has been the interpreter and guardian of American rights most actively during the twentieth century. The Court was, with few exceptions, inactive in defending rights during most of the nineteenth century, and, at times, it even defended slavery. A future Supreme Court may choose to play a limited role in defining American rights, leaving the matter to other levels of government, or to the tender mercies of politicians.

Professor Michael J. Sandel, in his 1996 book *Democracy's Discontent,* refers to "procedural liberalism" as a fundamental part of the American public philosophy. Procedural liberalism emphasizes individual rights against the majority and is defined and defended primarily by our courts. It is based upon a concern with neutrality of individual treatment and fairness on the part of the government. It seems that procedural liberalism has become a modern feature of American rights.

Another mistake people make about American rights is to take the phrase "all men are created equal" too literally. To be created equal did not always signify that all Americans had the exact same rights. When Jefferson wrote this language for the American Declaration of Independence it was daring and bold. However, at the time when it was written, women, Native Americans, slaves, and others were clearly not included. In fact, the American Constitution as it was originally written accepted the unequal condition of those groups. The Constitution had to be amended to give women the right to vote. The struggle for women's suffrage took decades, culminating in the ratification of the Nineteenth Amendment in 1920. Similarly, Native Americans were the last group of Americans to be granted voting rights and citizenship, and it took an act of Congress in 1924 to accomplish that.

Still another confusion about rights is the claim sometimes made by reformers for economic equality. Figures reveal that Americans are deeply divided by income. In spite of our nation's modern commitment to political equality, the earnings gap between the richest and the poorest Americans is greater than in any other Western industrialized society. But economic equality is not an American right. Nowhere in the Constitution, the Bill of Rights, or any important statute is the idea of economic equality advanced. Nowadays, it is assumed that we all have the equal right to earn as much as we can, even if some will make much more than others. The jobless, the homeless, and children without parental support are losers in this struggle to make a living.

Economic inequality in the United States has been growing for the past three decades. A 1996 report of the Census Bureau entitled "A Brief Look at Postwar U.S. Income Inequality" revealed that between 1968 and 1994 the share of total income going to the top fifth of American households increased from 40.5 percent to 46.9 percent. Meanwhile, the bottom 80 percent lost income share. The biggest gains of all went to the top 5 percent of households. The widening gap between incomes in America is explained partly by government policies, but more by a worldwide shift to a purer form of competitive capitalism—an economic system that does not aim at producing equality.

A common misunderstanding about rights is that only minorities really care about their rights. Yet most rights in America have little to do with minority status. Rights now belong to all Americans equally. Problems with minority rights arise when some groups are excluded from full enjoyment of their opportunities as Americans and are the victims of discrimination. While affirmative action programs do exist, they benefit women, veterans, and others, not just minority group members.

Slavery was regarded as constitutional until the 1865 Civil War. Racial segregation was lawful in the United States until 1954. Many people date the modern history of civil rights to the 1954 *Brown v. Board of Education* school desegregation decision of the Supreme Court, but that ruling was only part of a great expansion of civil rights in America in this century that has benefited all Americans. The most familiar example of discrimination in America was the institution of slavery. African Americans and some Native Americans were deprived altogether of their rights as human beings. This rights deprivation was one of the major causes of our bloodiest war, the American Civil War.

To a very large extent the course of American rights was changed by the events that followed the Civil War. Some of our rights had been developed out of English history and the experiences of colonial government in America, but the long struggle over slavery was a culminating event in our national history and in the emergence of our modern views of American rights. The Constitution was amended three times to accomplish this major shift in thinking. The Thirteenth, Fourteenth, and Fifteenth Amendments, all ratified after the end of the Civil War, are as critical to our enjoyment of rights today as the Bill of Rights itself. The Supreme Court held in 1833 that the Bill of Rights did not apply to actions of the states of the United States. After the passage of the three Civil War Amendments the Court slowly changed its views, and today *almost* all of the Bill of Rights applies to both federal and state governments.

The Fragility of Our Rights

The most essential fact about American rights is that they are constantly changing. Our rights are not inscribed in stone for all time. Most of this change has been in the direction of rights expansion, but at key moments in American history rights have been reduced or shrunken.

At various times some Americans have been stripped of their rights, not for what they had done, but for belonging to the "wrong" group. The World War II internment of Japanese American citizens behind barbed wire fences was a chilling example of rights deprivation. However, many Japanese American citizens had their lands and rights taken away before, under some state laws. That sad story has always been a symbol of the fragility of our rights during wartime or periods of national fearfulness. There are other examples of American rights that have been lost during periods of stress, but the general movement of our rights is toward recognition of more and more rights for our people.

Students should be alert to the fact that while they have the same protections as other Americans, they do not have them to the same extent. Fourth Amendment rights regarding search and seizure are weaker for minors than for adults. This means that school authorities may, under many circumstances, establish dress codes, censor student newspapers, search student lockers, or even look into notebooks and purses when reasonable suspicions are aroused. Drug testing of student athletes may be permissible even when similar programs are limited for adults. Normally, school officials do not need court warrants to conduct searches. Another example of limited student rights is that schools may limit and punish student tobacco smoking in ways that are not yet permitted for adults.

Rights are real and relevant in many ordinary school situations. School dress codes, prescribing what students are allowed to wear in public schools, have come into dispute all over the nation, raising freedom of expression problems. Another public school practice, the issue of celebrating the Christmas holidays, is affected by First Amendment concerns. What about Christmas? Decisions about what to do in December should begin with the understanding that public schools may not sponsor religious devotions or celebrations, although study about religious holidays is allowed by the First Amendment, as long as it does not extend to religious worship or practice. Public schools must devise holiday programs that serve an educational purpose for all students—programs that make no students feel excluded or identified with a religion not their own. Nativity pageants or plays portraying the Hanukkah miracle are not appropriate in the public school setting, but other kinds of musical and dramatic presentations about the holidays may be acceptable. While recognizing the holiday season, none of the school activities in December should have the purpose, or effect, of promoting or inhibiting religion. The First Amendment, as applied in the public schools, is one example of the complexity of American rights.

Rights issues can make headlines. In June 1994 President Clinton signed into law a bill making it a crime to block access to health clinics, prompting lawsuits to be filed by anti-abortion groups, including Operation Rescue and the American Life League. The law has been challenged by groups that contend that their freedom of assembly and free speech rights under the First Amendment have been violated, but the Supreme Court has yet to be convinced about these assertions. Abortion is a rights battleground area today, as states and the federal government attempt to develop rights policies.

Some rights issues are awaiting action. President Clinton also told lawmakers in 1994 to look into the creation of an Employee Verification Registration card, to help curb the flow of jobs and public financial aid to illegal immigrants. All American immigrants would have one, and the card would include a photograph, vital information on a magnetic strip, and perhaps even the immigrant's fingerprint. The particular approach to immigration has not yet been adopted, although the issue of immigrant rights is being discussed all over the nation. Even now, the issue of government and business access to personal information is unresolved, although a significant problem of individual rights.

In 1996 President Clinton and the U.S. Justice Department became alarmed at the enormous number of church burnings throughout the African American community in the South. The possibility that these acts may have been deliberately caused by racists as an attempt to intimidate African Americans was investigated. That such a series of calamities should occur in our own day shows how some Americans still disregard the rights of others. This kind of threat to American rights must be a concern of government.

Our rights have been expanded gradually through the political process, by elections, the passage of legislation and the ratification of changes in the Constitution, and by Supreme Court interpretations. Presidential leadership also has played a large role in rights expansion. Whatever rights Americans enjoy are the end result of a gradual political agreement on what those rights should be. Ultimately, American democracy has generated all of our rights, even though some of them have been created by our least democratic part of government—the courts.

Some Problems with Rights

Some critics contend that assertion of American rights tends to divide and separate us from one another. Those who would resist change have made that charge many times in the past. At times our vast multicultural society can generate a lot of group and interpersonal hostility, disturbing the calm appearance of our public life, as groups and individuals struggle for their rights. The expansion of rights that has followed these struggles may seem to some members of society as special treatment, rather than simple equality. That is a risk, surely, but as long as some members of society are treated unfairly or denied equal opportunities to enjoy life in America, their rights will be the concern of us all.

The idea of individual rights is central to being an American. Democracy and majority rule are also essential features of American life. Unfortunately, these ideas are not in complete harmony. Democracy requires that government respond to the will of the people, as expressed ultimately in elections. Majority rule usually governs at the polling places and in our legislatures. Individual rights amount to claims against popular majorities. Claims of minorities' rights are obvious examples, but, in a sense, every claim of right is a protest against the will of the majority.

Individual rights are claims to resist the will of popular majorities. People assert their rights against governments and against other individuals who are threatening them. Those who are comfortable with political and economic conditions have little reason to assert their rights. Nonetheless, as Americans we all feel that there may be times when we, too, may express an unpopular opinion or act against the current fashions and political views. Nearly all Americans will, at some time, feel their rights invaded and attempt to assert their own claims. That is why individual and group rights are a vital part of American democracy, while also in opposition to one of its primary aspects: majority rule. Americans always retain the right to be out of step with their fellow Americans.

With the passage of time two classes of rights have appeared in America: "general rights" and "special rights." The rights found in the Bill of Rights and the original version of the American Constitution, considered general rights, are the products of centuries of prior historical experience. These are the backbone of rights in America. The broad-based individual rights such as free speech, freedom of assembly, and freedom of religion are available to all. The same general quality applies to the listed criminal procedural protections available in the American Bill of Rights, in the Fourth through the Eighth Amendments, and elsewhere in the Constitution. The right to be safe against an "unreasonable search and seizure" is one that any American can now claim.

Special rights arise because the enjoyment of American rights has not been equal for all Americans. That is why some of the post-Civil War amendments were made to the Constitution—the rights of ex-slaves became a matter of national concern. Each new immigrant group also suffered from some form of discrimination when they came to these shores, and those who were here all along, the Native Americans, were sometimes the objects of cruel extermination or forceful relocation programs. Because of the actual experiences of various American groups, their story of unequal treatment is a blot on the development of American rights. For many group members special rights have been created to balance the scales of justice somewhat. That is why American women, hardly a minority group at all, have been given so many special protections in recent years. That is also why the second section of this book is devoted to some of those groups.

It would be very divisive if Americans constantly fought over competing claims of rights. Old hatreds and memories divide people in many other parts of the globe. Despite their enormous diversity of culture and historic background, Americans retain a willingness to live within the broad political consensus that forms our democracy. But there are unresolved tensions in American life. Many different minorities feel left out of the political and economic mainstream. American women, who actually are a majority of the population, sometimes identify with these minority feelings because they, too, have been treated in an unequal and unfair way.

Some critics of American rights policies have said that special rights claims tend to divide society and emphasize the differences that separate Americans rather than the ties that bind us together. There is some truth to these observations. Rights talk can encourage hostile attitudes rather than lead to peaceful solutions. Carried to extremes, rights talk can amount to little more than name-calling, and Americans have a rich vocabulary of names to be applied to others in anger. Rights talk can even lead to violence when it blinds people emotionally. In this book we shall attempt to get behind the false front of rights slogans to meet the real world of American rights. As we shall see, American rights are never absolute and total, but are a form of compromise between the lofty language of our abstract claims and the needs of a large, diverse, multicultural, and democratic America.

The Supreme Court does not acknowledge the concept of "special rights." Instead, the Court insists that all Americans must be treated equally and given the "equal protection of the laws" guaranteed by the Fourteenth Amendment to the Constitution. Nonetheless, various federal and state laws have forbid discrimination against the disabled, the elderly, homosexuals, and other unpopular groups. The Supreme Court has sustained this kind of special consideration.

American Rights: Some User's Notes

There are many people writing and talking about rights in America, ranging from extreme racist groups to mainstream long-established and distinguished organizations. Reformers of all persuasions try to use the language of rights as a way to parade their particular complaints about American life. Some rights talk is mere propaganda. For this reason this book is designed to serve as a reliable compass through the subject of American rights, which will help to point the direction our rights are going.

Readers should not assume that American rights can be grasped simply by looking at the Constitution. The words of the Constitution and the Bill of Rights are just a starting point on the journey. Times change and society grows and demands more from the Constitution. New rights are created by our legislatures from time to time. There is also a risk that constitutional rights can be lost, forgotten, or ignored. Indeed, "the price of eternal vigilance is the price of liberty," as Thomas Jefferson said. In modern times we might say, "liberty use it or lose it," but before you can use your rights, you must first understand them.

As mentioned previously the scope and extent of American rights are constantly changing. The exact meaning of our rights depends on our actual use of them and what a public official understands our rights to be at a particular time when we claim them. Each chapter in this book is a springboard to knowledge of your rights. The chapters provide the basics. To keep pace with the changing interpretations you must go deeper.

In the interest of accuracy, official documents are sprinkled throughout. Readers are not asked to rely on the author's interpretations but are allowed to read and judge for themselves as much as possible. Some of the quotations in this book are thick with legal language, providing a barrier to rapid understanding. Readers should resort to the glossary when puzzled by unfamiliar legal terms. With patience, a sufficient understanding of the legal texts can be gained. No one can pretend to be a legal expert on just a glance at this volume, but by patient effort the mysteries of statutes and Supreme Court rulings can be penetrated. You do not have to be a lawyer to enjoy your rights as an American.

Some words and phrases used in civil rights are particularly important, although they are not familiar in every day speech. Three phrases are especially important: "due process of law," "equal protection of the laws," and "state action." Some mention is made of these terms in the glossary, but because these phrases cut across all aspects of American rights, readers should be alerted to their modern meaning.

"Due process of law" occurs twice in the Constitution, in the Fifth and Fourteenth Amendments. The concept dates back to twelfth century England and is probably the oldest portion of civil rights policy in the English-speaking world. The idea first appeared in the Magna Carta of 1215, but the exact phrase, "due process of law" emerged out of later English acts of Parliament. In one form or other every American state has incorporated the idea of "due process of law" into its fundamental law. Many other democratic nations also have adopted some version of "due process," although it is most developed in the United States.

In 1354 Parliament declared that "no man of what estate or condition shall be put out of his land or tenement, nor taken nor imprisoned or disinherited, nor put to death without being brought in to answer by due process of law." In this language lies the kernel of limited government. The absolute powers of the monarch were curtailed in the name of justice for the individual. In a modern democracy this is a key idea. Government cannot arbitrarily strip a person of his property, liberty, or life without some semblance of a "due process procedure." Of course, the question of what "process" is "due" to an individual to ensure fairness is in dispute.

The American judiciary has devoted a lot of its efforts to defining the contents of the phrase, "due process of law," although precise definition may be impossible. Procedural safeguards for individuals are rooted in due process, but the exact scope of these safeguards is found scattered in various court rulings. In various chapters of this book the "due process" clause is given special attention.

Procedural process is most deeply involved in the criminal justice system. Federal and state courts alike are held to the highest standards of fairness required anywhere in the world. Because of the "due process" requirements, illegally seized evidence must be suppressed at a criminal trial, no matter how powerful it may be to implicate a criminal defendant. Because of the due process clause suspects must be given elaborate warning by arresting officers, informing them of their right to remain silent and of their right to counsel. Police and prosecutors are held to very high standards of behavior in the United States, in spite of our high crime rate—all in the name of "due process."

The idea of "equal protection of the laws" is a much more modern idea, and it is more closely tied to the history of this nation. The Fourteenth Amendment to the Constitution was written after the Civil War as a means of correcting the historic shame of slavery. The amendment was designed to wipe out an 1857 Supreme Court ruling which had declared that slaves were not citizens and were not protected by the rights given in the Constitution. In fact, the majority opinion stated that even freed African American slaves "had no right which the white man was bound to respect." Such a racist view of American rights could not long survive, and the Civil War was fought and won partly on the issue of American rights.

The Congress that wrote the Fourteenth Amendment may have had more than the rights of the newly freed slaves in mind. The phrase "equal protection of the laws" does not refer only to African Americans, but to all Americans, and that was how the drafters saw it. Congress intended

that the former slave states would treat all citizens equally, and the amendment made all people "born or naturalized in the United States . . . citizens of the United States and of the state wherein they reside." Rights are a fundamental part of American citizenship.

Courts have made the "equal protection of the laws" portion of the Fourteenth Amendment the cornerstone of American rights policies. The chief use of the phrase is as a standard of review of state legislation. States may not set up classifications for some citizens that do not apply to others. Classifications that are made among citizens must be reasonable, and not arbitrary, "and must rest upon some ground of difference having a fair and substantial relation to the objects of the legislation, so that persons similarly circumstanced shall be treated alike," *(Royster Guano Company* v. *Virginia,* 1920). So the equal protection of the laws clause benefits all Americans, whether women or men, African American or white. However, as indicated by several 1996 decisions, voting districts for representation cannot be racially based, because of the same clause.

Judicial intervention in the name of the "equal protection of the laws" reached its height during the 1950s and 1960s under the leadership of Chief Justice Earl Warren. Beginning with the pivotal 1954 case of *Brown* v. *Board of Education,* the Supreme Court used its powers to declare more and more state laws unconstitutional because of their segregationist effect. Public school desegregation was a special objective of this judicial campaign, but so were other forms of racial discrimination. Today, any state or local legislation that has a racial basis is "suspect" and probably a violation of the "equal protection of the laws."

Other "suspect classifications" may exist, but none are as significant as race. Courts are suspicious of state, federal, and local laws calling for unequal treatment of citizens for any reason. Age, sex, socioeconomic status, religion, and physical condition may all come to mind as ways of making distinctions among American rights. Courts will, in the name of "equal protection of the laws" look closely at all such forms of unequal treatment, but especially if fundamental rights are involved. Free speech, voting, procreation, and travel are examples of fundamental rights given special attention as part of the "equal protection of the laws."

The last unfamiliar, but very important concept, that is sprinkled throughout American rights is the idea of "state action." Most of our civil rights are a protection against state actions rather than the acts of other individuals. Curiously, private racial discrimination may be tolerable in America, if it is nonviolent, but official discrimination by agents of federal, state, or local governments offends the Fourteenth Amendment. That is why private clubs may withhold membership from women or minority group members and not run afoul of the law. Parents can choose to send their children to racially discriminating schools and that is allowed, although the schools may not receive federal or state support, because that would be illegal "state action." In fact, the Supreme Court agrees that private colleges may choose to discriminate on racial, religious, or gender bases, although they may be ineligible for federal funds if they do.

The Fourteenth Amendment does not require states or the federal government to prohibit private discrimination. Even fundamental rights like free speech may be denied to a citizen on private property, as in a shopping mall. But states may not lend their powers to private acts of discrimination. That is why the Supreme Court held that a restrictive contract in a private land deed that prohibited sale to certain minority group members was not illegal. However, if a court attempted to enforce such a restrictive racial or religious clause in a contract it would be a form of prohibited "state action." Frankly, it is not very clear what kind of conduct is purely private in America. After all, the roads and the police and fire services are provided to all, including those who discriminate against others. The best way to understand "state action" is to realize that courts do not want to get involved with purely private acts of discrimination unless there is a strong public interest in doing so. All we know for certain is what the Supreme Court has said on the subject, which is that a state may not "significantly involve itself . . . with invidious discrimination."

A statute can punish private acts of discrimination and eliminate the issue of "state action." By passing the 1964 Civil Rights Act Congress prohibited private discrimination in the fields of employment and public accommodation. This made the dilemma of the 1960s "sit-in" demonstrators purely academic. Before the passage of the Civil Rights Act of 1964 citizens who sought to compel private businesses to desegregate their facilities ran the risk of being sued for trespass. Owners could legally throw out those who sat-in at segregated Southern lunch counters. Private discrimination in such public facilities is now unlawful by statute, and the problem of "state action" does not arise. But there are still many private clubs and strictly private organizations that regularly discriminate against women and minorities. There is insufficient "state action" to reach such private actions.

Obviously, individuals need to pursue these issues in greater depth. A rich explanatory bibliography is provided at the end of this book. Use it. Books and articles give greater detail to complex rights subjects. Videos and Internet sources also are provided in the bibliography in an effort to provide lively commentary to issues in American rights. In addition, a list of leading rights organizations is provided, so you may make contact with groups that share your concern and interests or to clarify your understanding.

The best source for a firm understanding of our rights may be gained by reading opinions of the Supreme Court, many of which are condensed in this book. Yet, even Supreme Court judges, the best and final experts concerning American rights, are not always in agreement about rights. Other rights are found scattered in various state and federal statutes. Some rights are located in administrative regulations or presidential orders. Remember, though, that without some form of official recognition of a right, there is no right. Rights depend on official authorization.

You cannot be expected to know and fully understand everything about rights; no one person does, not even the Chief Justice of the Supreme Court of the United States. Some rights issues are still unresolved. All that this book can do is lead you to a greater knowledge of the substance of the rights that all Americans share. You must decide whether public officials or private parties have acted with due regard for your rights, bearing in mind that they, as Americans, have both rights and responsibilities as citizens, just as you do.

The Plan of this Book

This book is divided into four sections. Section 1 portrays the broad sweep of American rights history. From the arrival of the first white settlers in America until our current time conflicts have arisen that have often resulted in suppression and rarely been converted into rights. Native Americans were the first settlers, and their rights were frequently ignored by those who came after. The Spanish explorers and settlers arrived in the New World during the fifteenth and sixteenth centuries. The English settlements of the seventeenth century came after the Spanish, and about the same time as the French, the Dutch, and other European groups began to make the journey across the Atlantic Ocean. Each group found itself in conflict with the Native Americans and with the other Europeans. Many of these conflicts were translated into war and conquest. Native Americans lost most of their land to American settlers during the nineteenth century. In addition, the United States went to war with Hispanics four times during the nineteenth century, securing large portions of territory, while expelling many of the local inhabitants.

Each European group, at one time or another, used slaves as part of their economic system. Slaves had no rights, and rights for most other citizens were barely discernible before the eighteenth century.

Rights slowly emerged in the eastern seaboard of the United States. In the seventeenth century the small population in the English colonial territories inherited certain rights from the English. The English common law provided a few rights for the protection of the colonists, especially in the area of criminal justice. Because of their distance from England colonists sometimes got away with broader claims of rights than were available in England. Many more rights were added after Independence. American thinkers such as James Madison and Thomas Jefferson also contributed their new, broader vision of rights.

The unique story of American rights begins with the Constitution and the Bill of Rights. At the time they were written the world marveled at the enormous freedom bestowed upon the people of the United States. However, many Americans did not enjoy all the rights promised in those great documents, especially the slaves, the Native Americans, and the immigrants to these shores. Only in the twentieth century were rights extended to many of those Americans. Women, too, obtained new rights.

Section 2 describes the historical experiences of various ethnic, religious, racial, and cultural minorities with regard to their rights. Each of these groups has a different perspective on rights, which is largely unfamiliar to those who are not part of the group. African Americans, Asian Americans, Hispanic Americans, and Native Americans are subdivided into many other groups, each of which have had different encounters with American rights problems. All these deserve attention by those of us who form the comfortable majority and by members of other minority groups.

Some Americans may be a part of an unusual minority, whether it be children, the disabled, the elderly, prisoners, or as gays and lesbians. Women, although a very large element in our society, may be regarded as a sort of "virtual minority," for the purposes of their rights. All these groups have had some experience with discrimination, and all of them have a contrasting variety of rights.

Most readers will be unfamiliar with the rights experiences of American Jews, Arab Americans, Italian Americans, Polish Americans, and other immigrants to our shores. These deserve attention, too. In various ways, all Americans have had a taste of group discrimination or have memories of discrimination, as recounted to them by their parents and grandparents.

Section 3 deals with the general rights that all Americans share. Freedom of speech, religion, and the press are the backbone of our rights as Americans. Voting rights, housing rights, and educational rights have also emerged in recent years as areas of great concern and are given special attention. Employment rights are important to most Americans, although they derive more from recent statutes than from the Bill of Rights. Many of the historical rights acquired by Americans are gathered together in chapter 15 on criminal justice, but many of us enjoy our rights in other ways, unconnected with the criminal law.

Chapter 9 is the first chapter of the section 3, and while it describes the most important civil rights story of the century, the ending of racial segregation in America, it is mainly intended to provide insight into the politics of civil rights in general. This chapter tells about the impact of the states upon our civil rights. It delves into the interest groups, lobbyists, and political campaigns that are concerned with American rights. The derivation of our national rights policies are shown to be subject to a different and peculiar kind of politics in which the federal courts play a featured role within the separation of powers of national government.

Some rights are left out of this book because the topic is so vast. Space limitations impose themselves even in a volume of this size. Among the rights that are not considered at length is the disputable right to bear arms. In spite of the claims of the National Rifle Association that the Second Amendment to the Constitution creates an absolute individual right to bear arms, the law of American rights is to the contrary. Most Americans believe that the Constitution gives them the absolute right to own a gun. They are wrong. Federal judges for more than 50 years have said that no such right exists. The right to bear arms is treated as a potential future right. Similarly, the so-called "right to die" is presented here as a possible future right. Thus, those who choose to end their lives may not, in the future, be regarded as criminals for doing so.

New civil rights are just barely discernible on the horizon. Competing views of differing groups and individuals will eventually reach the attention of our courts and legislatures. Those rights that seem to our leaders as most pressing will gain new recognition. In an electronic age our privacy rights need better definition. Private property, once the key concept in American rights, may be revived again and take new shape. As our lives lengthen due medical discoveries and new technology some Americans will claim the so-called "right-to-die" as an ultimate right. Rights to welfare and to work may become important in the next century as our economy creates new threats and opportunities for American wage earners. Immigrants may be given new rights, and so may the hearing impaired, the blind, and the mentally infirm. These possibilities are explored in the last chapter of section 3.

In this book we shall pay close attention to what the language of statutes and the Constitution actually state, and to how the courts have interpreted that language. Majority opinion does not create American rights. Our rights derive from essential texts and from judicial rulings. Our emphasis in this work is on the legal basis of civil rights, without neglecting their moral foundations. The sources that are supplied are largely legal texts, not philosophical notions or political speculation.

Readers need not guess whether their American rights restrict the government and other citizens in this society. No artificial distinctions are made here between rights and liberties. No philosophical boundaries are drawn to hamper understanding. Rights language is sometimes used to describe relationships inside families or between doctors and patients, lawyers and clients, employers and employees. Whenever it seemed to the editor that a right was generally available to all Americans it was considered seriously, regardless of the social setting.

Rights language used to be largely negative in tone. Men and women traditionally held certain rights against the intrusion of the state. These rights remain. In recent years, rights have been extended to include private acts of discrimination by business or by individuals. In addition to this broader view of rights some newer economic and social rights are emerging. There may not yet be a right to medical care, to social security, or to welfare, but there is a right to political participation, including voting. Gradually, a shift is taking place to expand our thinking about rights, although they still primarily serve as an individual's shield against government.

The final part of this book, section 4, is intended to encourage individual research into and deeper analysis of American rights. Major court decisions are excerpted. The most significant civil rights documents, including speeches, statutes, and administrative decisions are provided for further study. Lastly, for those who want to go beyond the material presented, a list of the best books, articles, videos, motion pictures, and other sources dealing with American rights is provided in the appendix. A brief glossary, explaining unfamiliar terms, is also available for assistance.

The last words on the subject of American rights belong to Thomas Jefferson, one of the chief architects of American rights. In his First Inaugural Address Jefferson alerted Americans to the vital importance of their rights. Jefferson spoke of "exact and equal justice to all men, of whatever state or persuasion, religious or political." He did not speak of the rights of women, African Americans, or Native Americans, because those ideas did not enjoy much support during Jefferson's lifetime. He said that "freedom of religion, freedom of the press, and freedom of the person under the protection of the habeas corpus" were "principles which form the bright constellation which has gone before us, and guided our steps through an age of revolution and reform." These rights, he said, "should be the creed of our political faith, the text of civil instruction, the touchstone by which we try the services of those we trust." Yet Jefferson was keenly aware that nei- ther our Constitution nor our rights were frozen in time when our Constitution was ratified. Rights change and evolve, just as societies change and grow. Our rights of tomorrow will be greater than our rights of the past. That is part of the pride and glory of being an American.

Acknowledgments

I want to be as specific as possible in giving recognition to the many people who have helped make this book possible. No enterprise so ambitious can be completed without the work of many minds and many hearts.

Thanks to Peg Bessette of Gale Research for getting me started in this project. However, it was Leslie Joseph and Terry Murray who did the hard work of reviewing, revising, and improving the text and the coverage of this book. Thanks too to Beth Baker for proofreading and coding contributions.

I am especially grateful for the assistance provided by James Nettleman, documents librarian, Rutgers University. Also very helpful were Barbara Fontana, Librarian of the United States Commission on Civil Rights; the bibliographers at the Balch Institute for Ethnic Studies in Philadel-phia; the Zimmerman Reference Department of the library of the University of New Mexico; and I appreciated the lists provided by such groups as the American Indian Heritage Foundation, the First Amendment Center, and by Anthony Anderson of the Government Documents Department, University of Southern California. The Meiklejohn Civil Liberties Institute provided many useful reference leads.

Artist Neil King worked closely with me to draw my ideas into vivid reality. Scott Tambert, of Public Domain Images provided significant help in locating rare photographic and other sources in the Library of Congress.

Thanks to all of you!

Jay A. Sigler

Credits

In addition to images received from the Library of Congress and the National Archives, photographs and illustrations appearing in *Civil Rights in America* were received from the following sources:

AP/Wide World Photos: pages 151, 272, 320; Bettmann Archive/Newsphotos, Inc.: pages 280, 445; Connecticut State Police page 529; Courtesy of Vine Deloria Jr.: page 237; Courtesy of Kenneth Estell: page 122; Courtesy of Henry B. Gonzalez: page 174; Reproduced by arrangement with the Heirs to the Estate of Martin Luther King, Jr., c/o Writers House Inc. as agent for the proprietor: pages 30, 609–11; Neil R. King: pages 24, 45, 56, 60, 62, 134, 190, 215, 239, 255, 265, 266, 268, 275, 281, 287, 291, 293, 332, 350, 353, 374, 379, 387, 390, 407, 428, 435, 453, 456, 460, 463, 465, 473, 497, 509, 510, 519, 523, 525, 544, 548, 555, 557, 573, 575, 578; Courtesy of Larry Racioppa: page 187; U.S. Aeronautics and Space Administration: page 177.

Chronology

Pre-1600s

5,000–8,000 B.C.: Migrants from Asia arrive in North America, migrate to South and Central America, and found various Native American cultures.

c. A.D. 500: Mayan civilization reaches height.

c. 750: Toltecs establish civilization in Mexico.

c. 1000: Leif Eriksson explores Canadian coastline; founds settlement (called Vinland) at Newfoundland.

1325: Aztecs found city of Tenochtitlán.

1492: Columbus discovers Americas.

1497: John Cabot explores coast of northeastern America, up to Delaware.

1513: Juan Ponce De León explores coast of Florida.

1519: Spanish conquistador Hernán Cortés enters Tenochtitlán with army; Aztec emperor Moctezuma taken prisoner.

1520: Aztecs rebel. Cortés destroys Tenochtitlán, builds new city (present-day Mexico City) and establishes Spanish control.

1527: Estevan sails from Spain to Santo Domingo as part of expedition to conquer and settle Florida.

1534–35: Jacques Cartier explores Gulf of St. Lawrence; establishes Quebec.

1535: Viceroyalty of New Spain erected in South America.

1565: St. Augustine, Florida, founded by Spanish explorer, Pedro Menéndez de Avilés.

1600–1699

1605: French explorer Samuel de Champlain founds Port Royal in Canada. French develop fur trade.

1607: Jamestown colony established by English settlers in Virginia.

1609: Henry Hudson explores Hudson River, establishes Dutch claims.

1614: Dutch found colony of New Amsterdam.

1619: First African laborers in North America arrive as indentured servants in Jamestown.

1620: William Bradford departs Holland and arrives in North America aboard the Mayflower; establishes colony in Massachusetts for the purpose of allowing the Puritan separatists from the Church of England to practice their own version of Christianity.

Roger Williams (c. 1603–1683), founder of Rhode Island colony, made it a haven for heterodoxy.

1623: British establish their first settlement at Nova Scotia.

1626: Dutch buy Manhattan Island from the Native Americans for approximately $24 and name it New Amsterdam.

1630: Boston founded by John Winthrop and other Puritans.

1634: Maryland founded as a Catholic colony with religious tolerance.

1635–36: Roger Williams banished from Massachusetts; enters the wilderness and establishes Providence, a place that practices separation of church and state authority.

1638: Anne Hutchinson is banished from Massachusetts Bay Colony for her independent religious views. She flees to New York and is eventually killed by Native Americans.

1641: The Massachusetts General Court drafts the first broad statement of American liberties called the Massachusetts *Body of Liberties.* The document includes a right to petition and a due process clause.

1647: Peter Stuyvesant becomes governor of New Amsterdam.

1654: First Jews arrive in New Amsterdam.

1663: Rhode Island grants religious freedom. Government of France takes over administration of its North American colonies from chartered company.

1664: British capture New Amsterdam from Dutch; rename it New York.

1670: British establish Hudson's Bay Company.

1675–76: King Philip's War started by Native American leader, Metacom. Ends with killing of many Narragansett Indians and Wompanoag chief, King Philip.

1681: Quaker leader William Penn receives royal charter to Pennsylvania.

1683: William Penn signs treaty with Delaware Indians and makes payments for Native American lands.

1688: Quakers at Germantown, Pennsylvania, adopt the first formal antislavery resolution. The Society of Friends declares on this date that slavery is in opposition to both the principles of Christianity and the rights of man.

1689: Publication of John Locke's letter *Concerning Toleration* provides philosophical basis for George Mason's proposed Article Sixteen of the Virginia Declaration of Rights of 1776.

1692: Salem witchcraft trials are held. Nineteen persons (mostly women) are executed for being witches.

1700–1799

1704: Band of Indians attack settlers in Deerfield, Massachusetts, killing 400 and kidnaping 100. First regular newspaper, *Boston News Letter,* begins in America. The government had suppressed an earlier 1690 newspaper after one issue.

1702–13: British win important victories over French in Canada.

1708: Connecticut grants "full liberty of worship" to Anglicans and Baptists.

1720: Slave revolt breaks out in New York City. Nine whites are slain and twenty-one African Americans are executed as participants. The number of slave crimes punishable by death is increased in New York.

1735: Freedom of the press is established in America, as John Peter Zenger is acquitted of libeling British governor Cosby, whom he had criticized in the newspaper *Weekly Journal.*

1739: First serious slave uprising in South Carolina. More than 25 whites die and more than 30 slaves are killed for alleged participation.

1754–63: French and Indian War takes place. English and Indian allies capture Quebec and defeat French.

1760: American pioneer Daniel Boone crosses Blue Ridge Mountains for first time; explores Tennessee.

1763: Treaty of Paris signed, concluding Seven Years' War; Britain given Canada and all French territory east of the Mississippi River and Florida. Pontiac holds great war council, then attacks Detroit.

1765: British impose Stamp Act upon American colonies as a means of raising tax revenues to help defray the cost of the French and Indian War in North America.

1767: Townshend Acts are passed by British Parliament, imposing an import tax on American colonies and contributing to the revolt against British rule.

1770: Boston Massacre occurs, the first armed skirmish prior to the American Revolution. Crispus Attucks of Framingham, Massachusetts, an escaped slave, dies along with four other American colonists.

Crispus Attucks, an escaped slave, was one of the first men killed in the Revolutionary War, when British troops fired on a crowd of protesters in the Boston Massacre of 1770.

1771: The state of Virginia jails 50 Baptist worshipers for preaching the Gospel contrary to the Anglican Book of Common Prayer.

1773: Samuel Adams arranges and orchestrates the Boston Tea Party, dumping tea into Boston Harbor to protest the British tax on tea.

1774: "Intolerable Acts" of British Parliament curtails the Massachusetts rights of self-rule. Eighteen Baptists are jailed in Massachusetts for their public protest and refusal to pay taxes that support the Congregational Church. A group of Shakers led by Mother Ann Lee set sail from England for America. Quebec Act sets up colonial government of Canada, with special provisions for large French-speaking population.

1775: Benjamin Franklin and Benjamin Rush found the first Abolitionist organization, the Society for the Relief of Free Negroes Unlawfully Held in Bondage. Tom Paine's *Pennsylvania Magazine* publishes the first article supporting women's rights. Ethan Allen seizes Fort Ticonderoga in New York. Patrick Henry presents resolutions to the second Virginia Revolutionary Convention for Arming Militia with famous "give me liberty or give me death" speech.

1775–83: American Revolution is fought. Canada remains loyal to British crown and becomes

In 1776 the Continental Congress adopted the Declaration of Independence of the Thirteen Colonies of North America, the first national independence document in world history.

haven for tens of thousands of American Tories. War for Independence begins at Lexington and Concord, Massachusetts, on April 19, 1775. African Americans were among the Minutemen who fight the British.

1776: Continental Congress adopts Declaration of Independence. A section which states that King George III had forced slavery and the slave trade on the colonists is eliminated from Thomas Jefferson's draft, at the insistence of representatives from Georgia and South Carolina. Virginia's House of Burgesses passes the Virginia Declaration of Rights. The Virginia Declaration is the first bill of rights to be included in a state constitution in America. Colony of New Jersey permits women's suffrage, but that ends in 1807. Mohawk chief Joseph Brant allies with Great Britain.

1777: Articles of Confederation approved by Continental Congress. Vermont (not yet a state) abolishes slavery.

1778: George Washington winters at Valley Forge. George Rogers Clark leads expedition against the Kaskaskia and Cahokia Indians. France offers treaty of alliance with Americans.

1779: Benedict Arnold offers his services to British general Henry Clinton and is declared a traitor by the Americans.

1780: Pennsylvania becomes the first state to abolish slavery.

1781: Annapolis Convention to ratify the Articles of Confederation is held. The ratified Articles do not include a single provision to guarantee personal liberties to Americans. The Senate also defeats James Madison's proposed Fourteenth Amendment, which provides that "No state shall infringe . . . the right of conscience, nor the freedom of speech or press."

1783: Massachusetts Supreme Court outlaws slavery, citing the state's Bill of Rights which declares that "all men are created equal."

1784: First successful American newspaper, *Pennsylvania Packet and General Advertiser,* is published.

1785–88: John Adams serves as first American minister to Britain.

1786: Thomas Jefferson's Virginia Statute for Religious Freedom ("Bill 82") establishes "freedom of conscience" as the underlying basis for subsequent religious freedom protections. Shay's Rebellion, a revolt of indebted poor farmers, erupts in western Massachusetts. Although the revolt is crushed by force, it reveals the weaknesses of the government under the Articles of Confederation.

1787: U.S. Congress drafts new Constitution. Congress also prohibits slavery in the Northwest Territory.

1787–88: Alexander Hamilton publishes a majority of the *Federalist* essays and leads the fight for ratification of a new American Constitution.

1789: Constitution is ratified by 11 of 13 American states. George Washington is chosen as first president of the United States. First Congress meets at Federal Hall in New York City. French Revolution begins.

1790: District of Columbia is created to provide site for new U.S. national capital. Philadelphia becomes the first capital of the United States until federal offices are moved to the District of Columbia in 1800. Benjamin Franklin dies.

1791: U.S. Bill of Rights (the first ten amendments to the Constitution) are ratified. Vermont becomes first new U.S. state created after the original 13. Thomas Paine publishes *The Rights of Man,* spurring agitation for reform and leading the British government to charge him with seditious libel. Slaves revolt in Spanish colony of Louisiana and in French Santo Domingo.

1793: Fugitive Slave Act is passed by Congress, making it a federal crime to harbor an escaped slave or to interfere with his arrest. The cotton gin is invented by Eli Whitney, making slave labor in cotton fields economically attractive.

1793–98: Henri Christophe joins Haitian insurgent forces led by Toussaint Louverture.

1794–95: John Jay negotiates treaty with Great Britain ending the American Revolution. Farmer's Whiskey Rebellion in late 1794 is suppressed by federal troops in western Pennsylvania.

1797: Elizabeth Ann Seton helps found the Society for the Relief of Poor Widows with Children.

1798: The Federalist majority passes the repressive Alien and Sedition Acts in Congress, imposing severe jail sentences and stiff fines for publicly criticizing the government. The Acts are repealed in 1800 by the administration of President Thomas Jefferson. U.S. Navy and Marines ban enlistment of African Americans.

1800–1899

1800: Thomas Jefferson is elected U.S. president by a vote in the House of Representatives, to break tie in electoral votes.

1800: Washington, D.C., becomes the nation's capital city. There are 2,464 free inhabitants and 623 slaves.

1801: John Marshall is appointed as Chief Justice of the Supreme Court. James Madison begins eight-year tenure as Jefferson's secretary of state.

1801–05: U.S. wars against Barbary pirates in Tripolitan War.

1803: John Marshall hands down verdict in *Marbury* v. *Madison* case, which becomes the first decision to void an act of Congress. Louisiana Purchase from France of lands once held by Spain doubles land area of the United States.

1803–15: Napoleonic Wars in Europe become opportunity for revolt in Spanish New World colonies.

1804: Lewis and Clark exploration, ordered by President Jefferson, reaches the Pacific Ocean. Twelfth Amendment to the U.S. Constitution is ratified, providing for election of president by electoral college. This is the last amendment to the federal constitution prior to the Civil War. Ohio becomes the first Northern state to enact "black laws," which limit the liberties of freed African Americans.

1807: Robert Fulton makes first practical steamboat trip from New York City to Albany.

1808: Importation of African slaves into the United States is banned by federal law. Napoleon's French army invades and occupies Spanish-ruled Mexico.

1810: Revolt for independence begins in Venezuela and New Granada (modern Colombia and other territories).

1811: William Henry Harrison, governor of Indiana, defeats Native Americans at Battle of Tippecanoe.

1812–15: British forces in Canada repulse several American invasions in the War of 1812. After 1812 Battle of Tippecanoe in which Harrison destroyed the town of Indian leader, Prophet,

Andrew Jackson "Old Hickory," was the military leader of a campaign to drive the Seminole Indians out of present-day Florida. It was his military success, in part, which led to his election as seventh president of the United States.

many Indians join British side. Indian leader Tecumseh captures Detroit with British General Brock. Oliver Hazard Perry's fleet defeats the British in the 1813 Battle of Lake Erie. British forces burn White House and Capitol in 1814. Star Spangled Banner is written.

1813: Rebels proclaim Mexico a constitutional republic; carry on guerrilla warfare against Spanish rule.

1814: John Quincy Adams and Henry Clay negotiate the Treaty of Ghent, ending the War of 1812. War continues until final Battle of New Orleans in 1815.

1816: Connecticut extends the vote to all white adult males, regardless of property qualifications. Women and African Americans are not included.

1817–18: Andrew Jackson leads campaign in Florida against Seminole Indians. A force of Native Americans and African Americans are defeated in the Battle of the Suwanne in Florida.

1818: Convention of 1818 sets border between the United States and Canada.

1819: Congress passes first immigration statutes. Spain cedes Florida to the United States. James Madison argues for the end of slavery, proposing that special homelands for freed African Americans be founded in the West to ensure racial separation.

1820–21: Henry Clay's Missouri Compromise provides for admission of Missouri as a slave state and Maine as a free state, maintaining balance between free and slave states.

1821: Black Republic of Liberia formed, as African Americans are encouraged to emigrate. In Treaty of Aquala, Mexico's independence formally recognized by Spain. Símon Bolivar gains Venezuelan and Greater Columbian independence from Spain. Peru proclaims independence. Brazil declares independence from Portugal under rule of Pedro I. Emma Willard founds first U.S. women's college, Troy Female Seminary.

1823: James Monroe announces his "Doctrine" on further European colonization in the Western Hemisphere. Mexico established as a federal republic.

1824: Election of John Quincy Adams for president decided in House of Representatives due to lack of majority winner in electoral votes. Pawtucket, Rhode Island, strike by female weavers is first such action by American women.

1827: Cherokee Constitution passed. John Ross elected principal chief.

1829: Spanish military force driven out of Mexico by General Antonio López de Santa Anna.

1830: Joseph Smith finishes *The Book of Mormon*. Mormon church organized.

1831: William Lloyd Garrison publishes first issue of *The Liberator*. Nat Turner's slave rebellion crushed in Virginia, after calling in federal troops.

1832: South Carolina passes Ordinance of Nullification, threatening to withdraw from the Union. Black Hawk Wars against Sauk and Fox Indians push Indians further westward after their defeats.

1833: Supreme Court, in *Barron v. Baltimore*, holds that the Bill of Rights applies only to the national government and is not a restriction upon the states. Oberlin College in Ohio is the first to adopt coeducation of men and women and refuses to bar students because of race. Lucretia Mott founds Philadelphia Female Anti-Slavery Society.

1834: Slavery is abolished in the British Empire.

1835: Americans in the Mexican province of Texas proclaim independence from Mexico. Gold is discovered on Cherokee Indian lands in Georgia. Native Americans are forced to give up their lands and to move across the Mississippi River.

1836: Texas, largely populated by Americans, secedes and successfully turns back Santa Anna's armies attempting to retake the region for Mexico. Sam Houston is victorious at San Jacinto. Davy Crockett dies at the Alamo. Seminole Indians fight to protest their removal from Florida lands. War with Native Americans (largely Seminoles) in Florida begins.

1836–37: Constant warfare results in near starvation for Osceola's Seminoles. Frustrations and deprivations haunt the army fighting the Indians.

1839: Cinque, an African American slave, leads mutiny on slave ship and is taken into custody. Trial begins in Hartford, Connecticut.

1840: Under Act of Union, British unite Upper and Lower Canada.

1841: First immigrant wagon train leaves Independence, Missouri, for California. Frederick Douglass begins antislavery career.

1842: Seminole Indians lose war in Florida and are forced to relocate to Oklahoma. Webster-Ashburton Treaty between Great Britain and U.S. draws the borderlines between the U.S. and Canada.

1842–46: U.S. Army captain John Charles Fremont commands three exploring expeditions into the Trans-Mississippi West.

1844–45: John C. Calhoun serves as U.S. secretary of state and pushes for the annexation of Texas.

1846–48: Mexican War between the United States and Mexico fought over admission of Texas to U.S. and other grievances.

1846: United States declares war on Mexico. Zachary Taylor commands battles of Palo Alto, Resaca de la Palma, and Monterrey in Mexican-American War. Brigham Young begins the Great Mormon trek to Utah. Massacre of 130 Apache in Chihuahua, Mexico, by scalp-hunters; one of the victims is the father of Indian leader Cochise.

1847: Winfield Scott commands army that captures Mexico City and ends Mexican resistance. American slave Dred Scott files his first suit for freedom in Missouri.

1848: Treaty of Guadalupe-Hidalgo signed by U.S. and Mexico, ceding New Mexico and California to the United States. California gold rush begins. Elizabeth Cady Stanton and Lucretia Mott organize first women's rights convention in Seneca Falls, New York.

1850: Compromise of 1850 is effected between pro and antislavery factions in the United States; Daniel Webster supports Compromise; becomes secretary of state. Congress passes harsher Fugitive Slave Law. Sojourner Truth joins abolitionist movement. Harriet Tubman leads her first party of slaves north to freedom.

1852: Harriet Beecher Stowe's *Uncle Tom's Cabin* is published.

1853: National Council of Colored People founded at Rochester, New York, as a permanent body to advance the cause of African Americans.

Zachary Taylor was a war hero in the Mexican-American War before becoming the twelfth president of the United States in 1849.

Santa Anna named Mexican dictator. Gadsden Purchase from Mexico includes pieces of New Mexico and Arizona. William Walker invades Baja California with some armed supporters and declares its independence; they are ejected by Mexican authorities. Commodore Matthew C. Perry negotiates treaty to open Japan to United States ships.

1854: Republican Party is formed at Ripon, Wisconsin.

1856: Abolitionist John Brown leads antislavery revolt against Missourians at Osawatomie, Kansas.

1857: U.S. Supreme Court in *Dred Scott* v. *Sandford* decides that a slave does not become free when he enters a free state because slaves are not citizens. It also rules that Congress cannot bar slavery from a territory, making the Missouri Compromise of 1820–21 unconstitutional.

1859: Abolitionist John Brown seizes arms at Harper's Ferry, Virginia, is captured, and hanged the same year. Publication of John Stuart Mill's essay *On Liberty of Thought and Discussion*. The essay establishes his marketplace of ideas model. The marketplace model later becomes the philosophical basis for Supreme Court Justice Oliver Wendell Holmes's classic dissents of the early twenti-

eth century in favor of increased freedom of speech.

1860: Abraham Lincoln is elected president in a four-way contest for office. The New York state assembly passes the Married Woman's Property Act, which declares that a woman is not subject to control or interference by her husband. The act also allows her to keep her own earnings and have guardianship over her children. This is the first such law in the United States that recognizes the rights of women.

1861: Seven southern states secede from the Union. President Lincoln blockades southern ports and calls for army volunteers. Jefferson Davis resigns from U.S. Senate after Mississippi secedes; elected president of the Confederate States. Secretary of War appoints Dorothy Dix superintendent of nurses. Benito Juárez assumes presidency of Mexico. Joint military expedition by Spain, Great Britain, and France invades Mexico to restore order.

1861–65: American Civil War.

1862: Land grant act passed to benefit agricultural education. Homestead Act passed, granting family farms to western settlers.

1863: Emancipation Proclamation issued by Abraham Lincoln, freeing "all slaves in areas still in rebellion." Ulysses S. Grant, commander of Union forces, captures Vicksburg; wins battle of Chattanooga. Confederate General Stonewall Jackson leads troops at Battle of Chancellorsville. New York City workers riot for four days over Civil War draft law.

1864: Maximilian, Austrian archduke, becomes emperor of newly established French-dominated Empire of Mexico. Grant is made general-in-chief of the army. Philip Sheridan is appointed commander of the cavalry of the Army of the Potomac. "Sheridan's Robbers" clear Jubal Early's Confederate cavalry out of Shenandoah Valley. William Tecumseh Sheridan commands western theater armies that capture Atlanta and devastate much of Georgia. Sand Creek Massacre between the U.S. army and Cheyenne and Arapaho Indians, results in the death of hundreds of people awaiting tribal surrender.

1865: Confederate Army General in Chief Robert E. Lee surrenders at Appomattox Courthouse,

Virginia. Abraham Lincoln is shot and killed by John Wilkes Booth at Ford's Theater in Washington, D.C. Thirteenth Amendment to U.S. Constitution is ratified, prohibiting slavery. Mississippi legislature passes the first of the Southern state "Black Codes," which limit the civil rights of newly freed slaves. African Americans may not attend schools with whites, sit on juries, or testify in court against whites. Unemployed African Americans are treated as vagrants, subject to arrest.

1866: Ku Klux Klan organizes secretly to terrorize African Americans who seek to vote. Congress backs freedmen's rights by statute. Female Anti-Slavery Society reorganized into the Equal Rights Association; Lucretia Mott is elected its first president.

1867: Alaska is sold to the United States by Russia. Mexican empire overthrown; Maximilian captured and shot. Mexican republic is reestablished; liberal leader Benito Juárez in power again as president. British North America Act unites Ontario, Quebec, New Brunswick, and Nova Scotia into Dominion of Canada. Sir John A. Macdonald is made first prime minister

1868: Fourteenth Amendment, making African Americans citizens and giving them constitutional rights, is ratified. Thaddeus Stevens drafts the impeachment of President Andrew Johnson. Ulysses Grant is elected president of the United States. Elizabeth Blackwell founds Women's Medical College.

1869: Susan B. Anthony and Elizabeth Cady Stanton organize National Women's Suffrage Association. First woman's suffrage laws passed in Territory of Wyoming. Knights of Labor formed in Philadelphia as the first national labor organization. U.S. transcontinental railroad completed at Promontory, Utah.

1870: Fifteenth Amendment to the U.S. Constitution, barring denial of the right of citizens (not including women) to vote, is ratified. Ellen H. Richards is the first woman admitted to Massachusetts Institute of Technology (MIT). Women given the vote in Wyoming and Utah Territory.

1871: *U.S.* v. *Cruikshank* decided. The U.S. Supreme Court throws out scores of federal

Abraham Lincoln issued the Emancipation Proclamation in 1863, declaring freedom for all slaves in rebellious areas.

murder indictments for the deaths of over 100 African American citizens on the grounds that no federal murder suits are permitted. Indian Appropriation Act of 1871 is passed. This statute ends treatymaking with Native Americans and also deprives them of the right to counsel. In Los Angeles 23 Chinese are lynched during anti-Chinese riots.

1873: U.S. financial depression begins. Susan B. Anthony is arrested for leading a group of women to the polls in Rochester, New York.

1874: Women from 17 states meet to form the Women's Christian Temperance Union, which will become, under Frances Willard's leadership, the largest association in the world for women. Willard stresses women's suffrage in order to move temperance forward.

1875: Congress passes Civil Rights Act, giving equal rights to African Americans in public accommodations and jury duty. Supreme Court hears *Minor* v. *Happersett,* where a Virginia woman claims that the Missouri state constitution and registration law, limiting the right to vote to men, is a denial of her rights as a citizen under the Fourteenth Amendment. The Court rules against her, declaring "that the Constitution has not added the right of suffrage to the privileges and immunities of citizenship as they existed at the time it was adopted."

In 1876, with backing from the Church, rebel leader Porfirio Díaz leads a military takeover of Mexico City and assumes the presidency of Mexico. He rules the country, with one four-year lapse, until 1911.

1876: Porfirio Díaz, rebel leader in earlier period of unrest, takes up new rebellion against Mexican government. Sitting Bull defeats Custer at Battle of Little Bighorn.

1877: Surrender and subsequent killing of Crazy Horse. Indian chief of Oglala Sioux, who had resisted having his people placed on a reservation, retreat across Yellowstone. President Hayes sends federal troops to suppress nationwide railroad strikes; Sămuel Gompers blacklisted for strike activity. Molly Maguires, Irish terrorist group, broken up by hanging of 11 leaders in Scranton, Pennsylvania.

1878: Elizabeth Cady Stanton persuades California Senator Aaron A. Sargent to introduce a federal amendment for women's suffrage, which is introduced into every succeeding Congress until its adoption in 1920.

1879: California amends state constitution to forbid employment of Chinese laborers. Church of Christ, Scientist, chartered by Mary Baker Eddy. Susette and Francis La Flesche travel to Washington to lobby for Indian rights

1880: Congress ratifies Chinese Exclusion Treaty to limit immigration of Chinese. Although the treaty is vetoed by President Arthur in 1882, Congress overrides the veto.

1881: Booker T. Washington establishes Tuskegee Institute in Alabama. U.S. President James A. Garfield is killed by discontented office-seek-

er. Helen Hunt Jackson publishes *A Century of Dishonor* about the mistreatment of Native Americans. Segregation of public transportation is instated. Tennessee segregates railroad cars, followed by Florida (1887), Mississippi (1888), Texas (1889), Louisiana (1890), Alabama, Kentucky, Arkansas, and Georgia (1891), South Carolina (1898), North Carolina (1899), Virginia (1900), Maryland (1904), and Oklahoma (1907).

1882: Clara Barton becomes president of the American Red Cross. Helen Hunt Jackson is designated special commissioner of Indian Affairs by President Chester Arthur.

1883: On October 15, the Supreme Court declares the Civil Rights Act of 1875 unconstitutional. The Court declares that the Fourteenth Amendment forbids states, but not individual citizens, from discriminating. Pendleton Act passed, reforming federal civil service and ending the "spoils system."

1884: Grover Cleveland is elected president of the United States, defeating Republican James G. Blaine.

1885: First trans-Canadian railway, Canadian Pacific Railway, is completed.

1886: In Haymarket Square riot, anarchist bomb kills 11 during Chicago labor demonstration. American Federation of Labor is formed by 25 craft unions. Apache chief Geronimo's final surrender. *United States* v. *Kagama* decided by the Supreme Court, indicating that Congress can override treaties made with Native Americans.

1887: General Allotment Act passed, forcing American citizenship on American Indians through allotments and a 25-year waiting period.

1889: Hull House is opened by Jane Addams as one of the first community centers for the poor. Johnstown, Pennsylvania, flood kills 2,200 persons.

1890: Ellis Island, New York, opened as an immigration depot. Sherman Antitrust Act passed, beginning the first federal effort to curb monopolies. Battle of Wounded Knee, South Dakota, the last conflict between Indians and American troops, results in 200 Indian and 29 soldier deaths. African Americans are disen-

In Haymarket Square riot, an anarchist bomb kills 7 and injuries several others during Chicago labor demonstration. Eight anarchists are tried for murder and sentenced to death. Four are eventually executed.

franchised in Southern states. The Mississippi Plan, approved on November 1, uses literacy and "understanding" tests to disenfranchise African American citizens. Similar statutes are adopted by South Carolina (1895), Louisiana (1898), North Carolina (1900), Alabama (1901), Virginia (1901), Georgia (1908), and Oklahoma (1910).

1894: William Jennings Bryan fails as Democratic candidate for U.S. Senate; begins "free silver" crusade and campaign for presidency. Jacob Coxey organizes an army of the unemployed for a march on Washington.

1895: Jose Martí orders uprising in Cuba against Spain; killed in battle. Lillian D. Wald establishes "Nurses' Settlement" on Henry Street in New York.

1896: U.S. Supreme Court declares in *Plessy* v. *Ferguson* that "separate but equal" is a constitutionally acceptable race policy. Mary Lease is chosen delegate to Populist convention in St. Louis, Missouri.

1897: Gold rush in Klondike, Alaska.

1898: U.S. battleship *Maine* is blown up in Havana harbor. The United States blockades Cuba, declares war on Spain, and sends fleet to Philippines. Spain agrees to cede Philippines, Puerto Rico, and Guam, and frees Cuba. The United States annexes Hawaii. Eugene V.

Debs helps create the Social Democratic Party (later Socialist Party). Ida B. Wells leads delegation to President William McKinley to protest lynching. Theodore Roosevelt organizes and serves as colonel of "Rough Riders" during the Spanish-American War.

1899: Filipino insurgents rebel against American occupation of the Philippines.

1900–present

1900: Carry Nation, an antisaloon agitator, begins raiding saloons with a hatchet. International Ladies' Garment Workers' Union founded.

1901: President McKinley is assassinated; Vice President Theodore Roosevelt becomes president. Congressman George H. White gives up his seat on March 4. No African American would serve in Congress for the next 28 years. On October 16, after an afternoon meeting at the White House with African American leader Booker T. Washington, President Theodore Roosevelt informally invites Washington to remain and eat dinner with him, making Washington the first African American to dine at the White House with the president. A furor arise over the social implications of Roosevelt's casual act; 105 African Americans are known to have been lynched in 1901.

1903: Treaty between U.S. and Colombia grants U.S. rights to Panama Canal Zone. Mother Jones leads a children's march to protest child labor. Alaska boundary set by joint Canadian-U.S. commission. Wright brothers make first successful airplane flights. Federal law forbids "anarchists" entry into the country. Supreme Court case *Lone Wolf* v. *Hitchcock* deems Congressional "plenary powers" in Indian affairs as not reviewable by the courts.

1905: W. E. B. Du Bois founds the Niagara Movement. Theodore Roosevelt appoints Elihu Root secretary of state. Department of Commerce and Labor created by Congress. U.S. Supreme Court declares maximum hour laws for bakers unconstitutional in *Lochner* v. *New York*.

1905–11: Carlos Montezuma works for creation of a Pan-Indian national organization. San Francisco earthquake hits in 1906. Pure Food and Drug Act passed. Notable Progressive Robert La Follette begins 19 years in U.S. Senate.

1908: U.S. and Japan sign treaty that restricts Japanese immigration. U.S. Supreme Court declares an Oregon law limiting the working hours for women unconstitutional in *Muller* v. *Oregon.*

1909: National Association for the Advancement of Colored People (NAACP) founded. Rose Schneiderman organizes uprising of 20,000 and coordinates garment workers' strikes. Admiral Robert Peary reaches North Pole, accompanied by Matthew Henson, an African American, and three Eskimos.

1909–16: Charlotte Perkins Gilman writes, edits, and publishes the feminist journal, *Forerunner.*

1910: The first issue of *Crisis,* a publication sponsored by the NAACP and edited by W. E. B. Du Bois, appears on November 1. On December 19, the City Council of Baltimore approves the first city ordinance designating the boundaries of African American and white neighborhoods. This ordinance is followed by similar ones in Dallas, Texas; Greensboro, North Carolina; Louisville, Kentucky; Norfolk, Virginia; Oklahoma City, Oklahoma; Richmond, Virginia; Roanoke, Virginia; and St. Louis, Missouri. The Supreme Court declares the Louisville ordi-

nance, and all other forms of official housing segregation, to be unconstitutional in 1917.

1911: In October the National Urban League is organized to help African Americans secure equal employment; professor Kelly Miller is a founding member. Sixty African Americans are known to have been lynched in 1911.

1911: Porfirio Díaz is overthrown as president of Mexico; Francisco I. Madero is elected in his place. Emiliano Zapata revolts in the Mexican state of Morelos.

1912–25: U.S. Marines occupy Nicaragua.

1914: U.S. Marines briefly occupy the Mexican state of Veracruz after Mexicans seize U.S. ship in harbor there. Panama Canal opens. Marcus Garvey founds United Negro Improvement Association in Jamaica.

1914–18: Germany's submarine warfare against merchant shipping helps bring United States into World War I on Allied side. Argentina remains neutral; Brazil joins Allies. Canada also joins Allies, providing substantial troop support and war material.

1915: U.S. troops land in Haiti, as Haiti becomes an American protectorate. Herbert Hoover named chairman of the Commission for Relief in Belgium

1916: Pancho Villa raids Columbus, New Mexico. Army commander John Joseph Pershing leads Mexican expedition. United States buys Virgin Islands from Denmark and establishes military government in Dominican Republic. Jeannette Rankin, a Republican from Montana, is elected to the House of Representatives and becomes the first woman to serve in Congress. Margaret Sanger opens first birth control clinic in the United States and is arrested for "maintaining a public nuisance." Louis Brandeis is appointed to the U.S. Supreme Court as its first Jewish member.

1917: America enters World War I on April 6. 370,000 African Americans serve in military service—more than half in the French war zone. One of the bloodiest race riots in the nation's history takes place in East St. Louis, Illinois, on July 1–3. A Congressional committee reports that 40 to 200 people were killed, hundreds more injured, and 6,000 driven from their homes. Eighteenth Amendment (Prohibition) ratified. New Constitution of Mexico enacted, providing for agrarian reforms and separation of church and state. Unrest erupts in Canada over newly enacted conscription (draft) for WWI, particularly among French-Canadians. The United States begins military conscription. Espionage Act passed in the United States. Eugene Debs, socialist leader, jailed for ten years under the Act, eventually pardoned. One hundred other U.S. labor leaders prosecuted under the Espionage Act. Congress enacts (over President Wilson's veto) an immigration law that imposes literacy tests and severely limits Asian immigration.

1918: World War I ends after one million Americans had served in Europe. President Woodrow Wilson announces his Fourteen Points: a peace proposal advanced at the Paris Peace Conference after WWI.

1919: U.S. Senate refuses to ratify League of Nations Covenant. Boston police strike. About 250 "radicals" are deported to Russia from the United States without trial, following widespread "Red Scare" in the wake of the Russian Revolution. About 2,700 communists and anarchists are arrested in the United States from 1919 to 1920. American Legion founded by Colonel Theodore Roosevelt. *Schenck* v. *U.S.* decided, in which the Supreme Court sets forth its famous "clear and present danger" test, affirming the constitutionality of the Espionage Act. The test defines conditions under which criminal punishment of speech can be justified.

1920: Founding of the American Civil Liberties Bureau (later called the American Civil Liberties Union).

1920: Nineteenth Amendment to U.S. Constitution ratified, giving women the right to vote. League of Women Voters is founded. Five elected members of New York legislature denied seats because they are Socialists. James Weldon Johnson is appointed secretary of the NAACP. First commercial radio station in U.S. begins broadcasts.

1921: Congress sharply curtails immigration to United States. Congress raises U.S. tariff to highest levels. Ku Klux Klan revives in South

President (Thomas) Woodrow Wilson, twenty-eighth president of the United States.

and Middle West. William Howard Taft appointed chief justice of the Supreme Court.

1923: Teapot Dome scandal, which implicates President Harding's cabinet officials in oil dealings and embarrasses the president. The U.S. Supreme Court strikes down a state law that prohibits teaching in any language other than English *(Meyer* v. *Nebraska).* First sound motion picture shown.

1923: Calvin Coolidge takes office as thirtieth U.S. president after Harding dies

1924: Indian Citizenship Act makes all Native Americans citizens of the United States. Japanese and Asian immigration barred by Congress. Nellie Taylor Ross of Wyoming and Miriam Ferguson of Texas become first women to be elected U.S. governors.

1925: In guarded language in the case of *Gitlow* v. *New York,* the Supreme Court indicates that the Bill of Rights applies to the states, beginning a new era in national civil rights policy. John Scopes is found guilty of teaching evolution in a Tennessee public school.

1926: Catholic Church property nationalized in Mexico.

1927: Charles Lindbergh flies the Atlantic Ocean nonstop alone. U.S. Marines land in China to protect American property there.

Aviation legend Amelia Earhart disappeared with her copilot Fred Noonan while attempting an around-the-world flight in 1937

1928: *Olmstead* v. *United States* decided by the Supreme Court. In this famous wiretapping case, Justice Louis Brandeis writes the dissenting opinion in which he argues that "the right to be left alone is the most comprehensive of rights" inherent in American citizenship. U.S. signs Kellogg-Briand Pact, renouncing all war. Alvaro Obregon reelected president of Mexico and is later assassinated. Amelia Earhart becomes first woman to fly the Atlantic Ocean alone.

1929: Stock market crash marks beginning of Great Depression.

1931: In *Stromberg* v. *Carlson* the Supreme Court finally holds that freedom of speech and freedom of the press apply to the states, through the Fourteenth Amendment. Statute of Westminster enacted by Great Britain, establishes Canada as an independent, self-governing member of the British Commonwealth of Nations.

1933: President Franklin D. Roosevelt convenes special congressional session to halt wave of bank failures resulting from Depression; introduces "New Deal." Dorothy Day's *Catholic Worker* published; by year's end circulation is 100,000. As secretary of labor, Frances Perkins becomes the first female cabinet member. Prohibition ends in the United States, as the states ratify the Twenty-first Amendment.

1934: Indian Reorganization Act abandons allotments but reinforces the right to maintain tribal autonomy.

1933–39: Severe drought in U.S. Midwest farming region results in huge dust storms and migration of thousands.

1934–40 Mexican President Lazaro Cardenas institutes land reforms, nationalizes railroads, and seizes foreign-owned oil-producing facilities and mines.

1935: John L. Lewis forms Committee for Industrial Organizations (CIO).

1936: Paraguay installs South America's first fascist regime.

1937: *Palko* v. *Connecticut* ruling of the U.S. Supreme Court holds that the freedom of speech and the freedom of the press represent the "indispensable condition of nearly every other form of freedom."

1938: National minimum wage law for the United States is passed.

1939: The U.S. Justice Department creates the Civil Liberties Unit, predecessor of the Civil Rights Division.

1940: First peacetime military conscription (the "draft") becomes law in the U.S. Smith Act passed, making it illegal to "advocate, abet, advise, or teach the duty, necessity, desirability, or propriety of overthrowing or destroying any government of the United States by force of violence."

1941: Japanese attack Pearl Harbor. Jeannette Rankin begins second term in House of Representatives and casts only vote in either House against American entry into WWII. The United States enters WWII as full-scale belligerent. Chester Nimitz appointed commander-in-chief of the Pacific Fleet.

1943: Dwight Eisenhower designated commander of Operation Overlord, the invasion of France.

1944: U.S. and Allied forces invade Europe at Normandy, France. G.I. Bill of Rights passed, giving substantial aid to military veterans.

1945: Douglas MacArthur appointed commander of all U.S. Army forces in the Pacific. Franklin Roosevelt dies; Harry S Truman becomes president. Eleanor Roosevelt is appointed delegate to United Nation General Assembly. Ralph Bunche, an African American statesman, also serves in U.S. delegation to San Francisco and London conferences on the organization of the United Nations. United States drops atomic bomb on Hiroshima and Nagasaki

1946: Philippines is given independence by the United States.

1947: Jackie Robinson plays for the Brooklyn Dodgers, ending racial segregation in major league baseball by becoming the first African American athlete to play at that level. Secretary of State George C. Marshall outlines the Marshall Plan, providing massive economic aid to war-torn Europe to counter communist expansion.

1948: Harry S Truman submits a civil rights plan to Congress. The United States recognizes the state of Israel. Truman wins electoral upset victory in "whistlestop" campaign. Berlin Airlift starts as an American response to a ground blockade of the city by Soviet authorities.

1949: President Truman issues an executive order that ends racial segregation in the Armed Forces. North Atlantic Treaty Organization (NATO) is formed. Eleven leaders of the U.S. Communist Party are sentenced to prison for teaching and advocating the violent overthrow of the American government. Conviction of top Communists upheld by the Supreme Court, in spite of First Amendment free speech claims.

1950: U.S. Senator Joseph McCarthy launches anti-communist crusade in West Virginia. Ralph J. Bunch, an African American, receives the Nobel Peace Prize.

1950–53: Military intervention to halt communist expansion in Asia erupts into the Korean War.

1952: President Truman orders seizure of U.S. steel mills during Korean War, but action is declared unconstitutional by the Supreme Court. Immigration and Naturalization Act passed, removing prior racial and ethnic features of immigration laws. Fulgencio Batista seizes power in Cuba in military coup. This is

In 1945 First Lady Eleanor Roosevelt was appointed delegate to the United Nations General Assembly. She would later be instrumental in drafting the United Nation's Universal Declaration of Human Rights.

the first year in 71 years that there are no reported racial lynchings in the United States.

1953: Earl Warren is sworn in as the Chief Justice of the U.S. Supreme Court, launching a period of unprecedented judicial activism promoting civil rights.

1954: Thurgood Marshall represents NAACP in *Brown* v. *Board of Education* in which the Supreme Court unanimously rejects public school racial segregation and overrules 1896 case of *Plessy* v. *Ferguson*. The "separate but equal" segregationist doctrine is overthrown.

1955: U.S. Supreme Court declares that public schools must be desegregated "with all deliberate speed." Rosa Parks refuses to give her seat to a white man on a bus in Montgomery, Alabama. Bus segregation ordinance declared unconstitutional. Military coup in Argentina ousts President Juan Peron. Roy Wilkins becomes executive secretary of NAACP.

1956: Massive resistance to Supreme Court desegregation rulings called for by 101 Southern congressmen.

1957: Eisenhower Doctrine announced which allows the United States to offer economic and military aid to any country resisting communist takeover. First civil rights statute passed since just after the Civil War (1875) protects voting rights. National Guard is ordered by President Eisenhower to Little

The 1963 March on Washington brought over 250,000 people to the Lincoln Memorial.

Rock, Arkansas, to assist in the desegregation of the high school.

1958: Japanese Americans who had renounced their citizenship in 1942 and had been placed in "relocation centers" regain full American citizenship, but their homes and property are not restored to them. First U.S. earth satellite goes into orbit. U.S. Marines sent to Lebanon to protect elected government from overthrow. In *NAACP* v. *Alabama* the U.S. Supreme Court validates the right of the NAACP to keep its membership lists secret, ruling that to require otherwise would violate NAACP members' constitutional right to assembly.

1959: Vice President Richard Nixon shares "kitchen" debate with Soviet leader Nikita Khrushchev at U.S. trade show in Moscow. Alaska is admitted as forty-ninth state and Hawaii is admitted as fiftieth state of the union.

1959–61: Fidel Castro seizes power in Cuba and installs communist regime.

1960: Four African American students refuse to leave a segregated lunch counter in the South, starting the "sit-in" protests. Greensboro, North Carolina's, lunch counters are desegregated on July 25. Congress passes stronger voting rights legislation. Supreme Court decides that a state may not change the boundaries of a city to exclude African American voters *(Gomillion* v. *Lightfoot).*

1960–73: Vietnam War, first involving France and after 1963, the United States.

1961: U.S.-backed Bay of Pigs invasion of Cuba fails. Rafael Trujillo, dictator of the Dominican Republic since 1930, is assassinated. Freedom Rides are organized to protest racial segregation in interstate transportation.

1962: James Meredith integrates the University of Mississippi. President John F. Kennedy forces withdrawal of Soviet missiles in Cuba prompting Cuban Missle Crisis. In *Engel* v. *Vitale* the U.S. Supreme Court invalidates a nondenominational prayer composed by New York State Board of Regents and rules that government may not compose official prayers.

1963: Civil Rights leader Medgar Evers is assassinated by a white supremacist in Jackson, Mississippi. President John F. Kennedy submits civil rights bill to Congress. Civil Rights March on Washington brings 250,000 people to the Lincoln Memorial, where Martin Luther King Jr. delivers "I Have a Dream" speech. Nuclear Test Ban Treaty ratified. Ngo Dinh Diem of South Vietnam is assassinated in a military coup. Kennedy is assassinated in Dallas, Texas; succeeded by Lyndon B. Johnson.

1964: Major federal Omnibus Civil Rights Act passed signed by President Lyndon Johnson.

Twenty-fourth Amendment ratified prohibiting use of poll taxes in federal elections. Council of Federated Organizations launch Freedom Summer (a mobilization of youth workers for African American rights in the South). Civil rights workers murdered near Philadelphia, Mississippi. Free Speech Movement begins among University of California Students; campus sit-ins and unrest begins all over the nation in later years.

1964: Twenty-fourth Amendment, which bans the use of the poll tax in elections, takes effect. President Lyndon Johnson signs the Civil Rights Act of 1964 into law.

1965: Martin Luther King Jr. is arrested in Selma, Alabama, during demonstrations asserting the right of African Americans to vote. The Voting Rights Act becomes law. It has two principle provisions: Section 2 provides that "no voting qualification or prerequisite to voting, or standard, practice, or procedure shall be imposed or applied by any state or political subdivision to deny or abridge the right of any citizen of the United States to vote on account of race of color." Section 5 prohibits states and portions of states, in the South and elsewhere, from putting any new voting procedures, including new districts, into effect without first giving the attorney general a chance to object or getting a ruling from U.S. District Court in Washington that the change "does not have the purpose and will not have the effect of denying or abridging the right to vote on account of race or color." Malcolm X is assassinated. Watts riots in Los Angeles, California, last six days, claiming the lives of 35 people.

1966: The Supreme Court finds the Voting Rights Act constitutional against a states' rights challenge in *South Carolina* v. *Katzenbach*. Stokely Carmichael replaces John R. Lewis as head of the Student Nonviolent Coordinating Committee (SNCC), calling for "black power" at rally in Mississippi. Huey P. Newton and Bobby Seale found Black Panther party in Oakland, California. National Organization for Women (NOW) is founded by Betty Friedan. Supreme Court rules, in *Miranda* v. *Arizona,* that the Fifth Amendment self-incrimination clause rules out confessions by persons in police custody unless careful steps are taken to inform suspects of

their rights at the time of arrest. Massachusetts elects first African American senator, Edward Brook.

1967: Justice Thurgood Marshall takes his seat on the Supreme Court as first African American member. Robert Clark is elected becoming the first African American member of the Mississippi legislature in the twentieth century. Equal Employment Opportunity Commission created. Riots in Detroit on July 22 result in the deaths of 43 persons. Riots follow in 127 American cities, killing at least 77 and injuring at least 4,000. Antiwar demonstrators march on the Pentagon; 647 persons are arrested.

1968: Martin Luther King Jr. and Senator Robert F. Kennedy are assassinated. Civil Rights Bill of 1968 is passed, with sweeping housing and antiriot provisions. Representative Shirley Chisholm (D-NY) elected as the first African American woman in the U.S. Congress. Carl B. Stokes is elected mayor of Cleveland, the first African American to hold that office in a major American city. National Advisory Committee on Civil Disorder, headed by Illinois Governor Otto Kerner Jr., concludes: "Our nation is moving towards two societies, one black, one white-separate and unequal." Indian Civil Rights Act enacted, empowering tribal governments and courts to implement tribal governments and communities through "plenary powers."

1969: Nixon begins Strategic Arms Limitation Talks (SALT) with Soviets. Chicago 7 trial begins. Charles Evers becomes mayor of Fayette, Mississippi, first African American mayor of integrated city in the Deep South since Reconstruction. In the case of *Tinker* v. *Des Moines Independent School District* the Supreme Court held that a junior high student has the right to wear a black armband in protest of the Vietnam War. Woodstock music festival, highlight of youth music scene, held in August concert attended by 500,000 young people.

1970: Four students are killed by National Guardsmen in antiwar demonstration at Kent State University in Ohio. Two women generals, the first in American history, appointed by President Nixon.

1971: Twenty-sixth Amendment ratified, lowering the voting age to 18. Classified Pentagon Papers printed by the *New York Times* and the *Washington Post*. President Nixon asks courts to suppress publication during Vietnam War. On June 30, the Supreme Court upholds the right of the newspapers to publish Pentagon Papers in *New York Times* v. *United States.*

1972: Nixon makes historic visit to China and USSR; signs SALT I antiballistic missile treaty. Watergate scandal attempts to cover up Republican burglary of Democratic party headquarters. Equal Rights Amendment approved by U.S. Senate, sent to states. The Amendment, which bans various forms of discrimination against women, is never ratified by the states. Five hundred Native Americans combine in a sit-in protest at the Bureau of Indian Affairs, complaining of denial of rights. In *Wisconsin* v. *Yoder* the Supreme Court overturns the convictions of several Amish parents who were fined for violating compulsory school attendance laws, holding that the attendance laws violated the free exercise of the parents' religious rights.

1973: U.S. troops withdraw from Vietnam. Military draft ends. *Roe* v. *Wade* decided by the Supreme Court, creating a right to abortion during the first trimester of pregnancy. American Indian Movement occupies Wounded Knee, South Dakota (Pine Ridge Sioux Reservation), to protest governmental policies on reservations.

1974: Nixon resigns after impeachment threat. Vietnam Peace Pact signed in Paris. President Gerald Ford pardons Nixon for Watergate crimes. Supreme Court decides *Milliken* v. *Bradley* case, which effectively defeats efforts to racially integrate urban with suburban schools in the United States.

1976: Eskimos file claim asserting rights to over 750,000 square miles of Canadian territory. U.S. celebrates nation's bicentennial.

1977: President Jimmy Carter inaugurated, pardons most Vietnam War protesters who deserted abroad. Panama Canal Treaty returns canal to Panama.

1978: Supreme Court decides *University of California* v. *Bakke,* which limits uses of affirmative action programs. U.S. Senate ratifies Panama Canal treaty, agreeing to turn over the canal to Panama on December 31, 1999. American Indian Religious Freedom Act grants limited religious freedom to native peoples.

1979: First national march on Washington for gay and lesbian rights draws 100,000 participants.

1980: Ronald Reagan is elected as the nation's fortieth president, in a stunning electoral sweep. First woman graduates from a national military academy.

1979–81: Fifty-two Americans are held hostage at the U.S. embassy in Iran. They are eventually freed after being held for 444 days.

1981: President Reagan shot and wounded in assassination attempt. Sandra Day O'Conner appointed to the Supreme Court as its first woman member.

1982: Equal Rights Amendment for women's rights defeated, after a 19-year struggle for state ratification. Argentina seizes British-held Falkland Islands; Margaret Thatcher sends in British troops.

1983: U.S. invades Grenada, overcomes small defense force, and deposes Marxist regime. U.S. Marines sent to Lebanon.

1984: Ronald Reagan reelected as president by the greatest Republican victory in history, carrying 49 states. U.S. Marines are removed from Lebanon.

1985: Top Argentina government leaders, who were involved in 1976 coup, convicted of murder and human rights abuses.

1986: Iran-contra scandal in U.S. On January 20 the U.S. officially observes Martin Luther King Day for the first time. U.S. Senate confirms William Rehnquist as Chief Justice of the Supreme Court.

1987: Reagan signs Intermediate Nuclear Forces (INF) Treaty, providing for dismantling of all U.S. and Soviet intermediate-range nuclear weapons. Quebec provincial government signs Canadian Constitution. Canada and U.S. agree to free trade arrangement.

1988: The United States sends troops to Honduras following border incursion by Nicaraguan troops. George Bush elected as forty-first U.S. President.

In 1980 Ronald Reagan was elected the nation's fortieth president, in a stunning electoral sweep.

1989: End of Berlin Wall separating East and West Germany. Central American peace plan adopted to end warfare in Nicaragua. Drug lords assassinate a presidential candidate in Colombia. Chilean voters end military rule. U.S. troops invade Panama and imprison Manuel Noriega for drug trafficking. Hungary declared a free republic. Failure of Marxist economies all over Eastern Europe.

1990: Reunification of Germany. Free elections held in Nicaragua; procommunist Sandinista President Daniel Ortega ousted by pro-U.S. leader Violeta Barrios de Chamorro. A new Russian state emerges as separate states secede out of the former Soviet Union. Cold War between United States and Russia effectively ends. U.S. President Bush signs Americans With Disabilities Act. Native American Grave Protection and Repatriation Act protects Indian burials and returns burials in museums to qualified descendants. Nelson Mandela released from prison in the Republic of South Africa.

1991: The United States responds to Iraqi invasion of Kuwait touching off the Gulf War. Rodney King police beating controversy erupts. Clarence Thomas approved by U.S. Senate as an associate justice of the Supreme Court, in spite of charges of sexual harassment made against him.

1992: Bill Clinton is elected president. Riots sweep Los Angeles after jury acquits four policemen of all but one charge of beating Rodney King, in spite of videotaped evidence of severe treatment of King.

1993: President Clinton announces expanded rights of gays in the military. Janet Reno is appointed as first woman Attorney General. Family and Medical Leave Act signed into law, permitting workers in larger businesses to take up to 12 weeks of unpaid leave for special needs. Gun Control Act (the Brady Bill) signed into law, creating a five-day waiting period for the purchase of handguns. The Supreme Court rules in *Shaw* v. *Reno* that districts drawn with such "bizarre" shapes that they are unexplainable on grounds other than race are unconstitutional unless they can be shown to be "narrowly tailored" to serve a "compelling state interest."

1994: Republican Party captures both houses of U.S. Congress for the first time since 1952. Byron De La Beckwith is found guilty of the 1963 murder of Medgar Evers. Supreme Court upholds random drug tests for student athletes. *Shaw* v. *Reno* reapportionment decision brings political turmoil across the South, where two dozen majority-African American districts were drawn in the early 1990s, mostly after prodding from the Justice Department.

In 1990 President George Bush signed the Americans With Disabilities Act, providing a comprehensive federal regulatory scheme designed to eliminate both intentional and inadvertent discrimination against Americans who suffer from physical or mental disabilities.

1995: Supreme Court strikes down Colorado's anti-gay Amendment 2 as a denial of the equal protection of the laws guaranteed by the federal constitution.

1996: Supreme Court strikes down voting districts in several Southern states because they are too blatantly based upon race. Congress refuses to pass statute that protects homosexuals against job discrimination.

1997: Religious Freedom Restoration Act of 1993, in which Congress sought to spell out various kinds of permitted and acceptable religious practices, is declared unconstitutional by the Supreme Court.

U.S. District Courts declare some voting districts unconstitutional in Texas, Louisiana, and Georgia. Freedom of Access to Clinics Act is enacted, making it a federal crime to obstruct entrances to reproductive health centers or to threaten anyone providing or receiving such services. *Apartheid,* the policy of racial segregation and discrimination, ends in South Africa. Nelson Mandela is elected president of the Republic of South Africa.

Civil Rights
Throughout U.S. History

Chapter 1

The Origins and the
Limits of American Rights

Jay A. Sigler

The history of American rights is both an old and a new story. The origins of our rights can be said to reach back as far as thirteenth-century England. On the other hand, the nationalization of rights to all American men, women, and children is largely a twentieth-century event. The average citizen may imagine that he has a virtual bag of rights that he carries about, while others have similar bags. Many believe that these rights are unchanging, sprung forth at the time of American independence from England. Those simple views are essentially incorrect. There is no doubt that Americans today have more rights than any people anywhere in the world's history. But our rights are mostly of fairly recent creation, even if their roots lie deep in our history.

The recent evolution of American rights is little understood. Many people are surprised to learn that the Bill of Rights of the national Constitution did not apply to state government actions even as late as 1925. The Supreme Court had long restricted our basic rights to an application against federal laws only. Even then, few federal laws were declared unconstitutional as violations of American rights prior to the 1930s. Until the Supreme Court ruled on those matters in 1931, even freedom of speech and the press were not regarded as fundamental rights against state action. Historically speaking, the Bill of Rights in its original context was largely seen as a means of restricting national powers over individuals, not as a charter of individual rights against all governments.

Of course, for African Americans, full rights were not enjoyed for most of American history. Up until the end of World War II (or perhaps long after that date) America was a society that was deeply segregated by race, denying African Americans their basic rights. Slavery had been ended in 1865, but the principles of equal protection of laws were still undeveloped for 90 years afterwards, in spite of the language of the Fourteenth Amendment to the Constitution. Many other American minority groups also experienced a grudging extension of their full rights of citizenship.

Only by taking a broad, historical view of rights can we understand how far we have come in our enjoyment of rights in America. Rights of one kind or another have existed in many societies. Probably the rights that surround criminal trials are the most ancient in origin. Other older rights have emerged out of the protections given individuals to own, hold, sell, and inherit land and property. Even before American independence many of these rights existed. In 1774 the Continental Congress claimed that all colonists were entitled to "all the rights, liberties and immunities of free and natural born subjects within the realm of England." The colonists had a firm understanding of their rights as Englishmen, and many of those rights were included in their charters.

The colonial conception of civil liberties had little to do with free speech, religion, assembly, or publication. It certainly did not signify that minorities, slaves, Jews, or women had rights. Catholics might be tolerated in some colonies, but not in all. Baptists and Methodists could be—and were—persecuted for their beliefs. Poor people could be sent to debtor's prisons. They had no rights. The more educated of the colonists merely expected that they would enjoy the rights provided by the English common law and by a few great historic documents of English legal history. For many colonists it was also believed that there was a right to be left alone by the mother country. Interference with that right could lead to a right to revolution. Independence could be claimed by the more radical colonists as founded upon a denial of the rights of Englishmen to rule themselves in the New World.

Many scholars trace the roots of American rights to the Magna Carta of 1215. Most of that document has no practical significance today because it dealt with issues of feudalism, but it was a first step in restricting the absolute powers of the English kings. Although written for the benefit of English nobility, the clergy, and some of the English towns, the document does contain language that sounds familiar. Translated from the original Latin, article 39 of the Magna Carta states that:

> No freeman shall be arrested, or detained in prison, or deprived of his freedom, or outlawed, or banished, or in any way molested; and we will not set forth against him nor send any against him, unless by the lawful judgment of his peers and by the law of the land.

This article was a historical landmark not because it created any new rights but because it amounted to a royal admission that certain old rights could not be ignored or suspended at the king's convenience. Charters of liberties had previously been granted by Henry I, Stephen, and Henry II in order to placate the public. However, when King John was forced by his rebellious barons at Runnymede to sign the Magna Carta, it was clear that the king could not be above the law. In later centuries Magna Carta became a symbol of the supremacy of English law and customs over the kings. It cannot be said that Magna Carta granted trial by jury or taxation without representation, although some lawyers made those assertions in the seventeenth century.

For most of human history the law had been subject to the desires of the sovereign power. The decrees of a king, czar, or dictator were lawful automatically. However, no rights of citizens are possible if the king can do as he wills. Without limitations upon the king (or any modern dictator), there is no prospect for individual rights. The first principle needed for the enjoyment of any rights may be called "constitutionalism," which means that there are certain fundamental principles that restrain all officials of government. In America, these principles start from our Constitution. In England, which lacks a written single document constitution, rights derive from the common law, from Magna Carta, and from some important statutes.

The English common law provides some of the sources of American rights. The jury system created in very early times was originally a means of securing twelve senior and trusted local residents to determine what the law and customs required. In its origins, the jury was also used by the English kings as a way to keep the peace, as jurors could inform on their neighbors' misdeeds. Over the centuries the jury became a check on absolute royal powers, but there were times when the king's judges threw the jurors into jail for failing to do the king's will. By the time of the American Revolution the right to trial by jury was established. However, in English history, the jury had been used primarily as a means of determining community sentiment about the laws.

The English common law did not protect free speech or guarantee freedom of the press. It did not eliminate the requirement of a government license prior to publication. A person who published a book or a pamphlet could later be sued for seditious libel,

The U.S. Constitution was drafted by the delegates meeting at the Constitutional Convention of 1787. By 1789 it had been ratified by 11 of the 13 American states.

an offense against the king or his government. The punishment for sedition was exceedingly severe. Even members of Parliament were thrown into the Tower of London for criticizing the king. Ordinary people could have their ears clipped, their tongues pierced by hot irons, or even be sentenced to death for sedition. Libel or slander principles, which also developed under the common law, made it risky to speak out against fellow citizens, for fear of being sued for speech or writings. Anyone who spoke out on a controversial matter in England risked being punished in some way for doing so.

A few procedural developments did lead to greater rights. The common law of crimes permitted an accused person to have a lawyer for minor offenses and for accusations of treason. However, serious crimes were not subject to this right to counsel. Legal assistance for most serious cases was denied on the ground that the king's judges could be trusted to do justice and did not need the help of the defendant's lawyer. Consequently, many Englishmen were sentenced to the gallows, to long prison terms, or to transportation abroad—especially to Australia and America—without having had the benefit of a lawyer to defend them. The right to counsel became important in post-Revolutionary America as a reaction to the limited right under English common law.

The English common law became encrusted with elaborate procedural devices. A case had to be filed with the proper form or paper in the cor-rect tribunal at the right time or else it would fail. The common law was a paradise for lawyers and the judges who controlled the vast, creaky machinery of the law. However, justice was often denied or went astray in the murky depths of the legal procedures. It is true that these elaborate procedures, properly used, could produce important rights for individuals. The writs of habeas corpus, quo warranto, mandamus, certiorari, and similar mysterious documents were sometimes employed by skillful English lawyers against arbitrary government actions. In America new life was breathed into these ancient writs, to the benefit of individual rights. In America the traditions of common law were learned and absorbed by lawyers and judges but turned to new and different uses than they had in England. As Justice Tilghman of Pennsylvania said in 1813: "we adopted English usages, or substituted others better suited to our wants, till at length before the time of the Revolution we had formed a system of our own."

The English Petition of Right of 1628 added to the common law rights available to Englishmen, and by extension, to Americans. The English king Charles was compelled by Parliament to grant new rights to Englishmen. King Charles was short on money because of an unsuccessful war against France, and the Parliament took advantage of his financial needs by petitioning the king about various royal abuses of power. Under pressure, the king gave his consent in 1628.

The Petition of Right, among other matters, condemns the failure to discharge people from unjust imprisonment on a writ of habeas corpus. It also complains of court martials against civilians and of forced quartering of soldiers in private homes. In general, the arbitrary use of martial law is especially condemned in the Petition. These grievances subsequently found their way into the specific language of the American Constitution and into the constitutional law developed by the American Supreme Court. The Petition of Right was even cited by the Supreme Court in condemning one of the actions taken during the Civil War by President Abraham Lincoln.

The Bill of Rights of 1689 added to the growing list of the individual rights of Englishmen. It was the product of the Glorious Revolution of 1688, a parliamentary coup against royal power. The events leading up to the bill of rights began with the return of Charles II to the throne of England in 1660, which was welcomed by Parliament. However, Charles's strong pro-Catholic stands and his frequent violations of established law irritated many prominent figures. Under the subsequent rule of James II (1685–1688) there were even more direct clashes between Parliament and the king. There were direct royal interferences with established political and religious liberties. In reaction, a group of powerful politicians secretly invited Prince William of Orange and his wife Mary, who were Protestants, to become rulers of England. James II fled to France while the new Protestant monarchs took his throne. The Glorious Revolution was over without a shot being fired.

Parliament became more powerful after unseating James II. A series of laws was rapidly passed ensuring the rights of Englishmen against royal authority. The Bill of Rights passed on December 16, 1689, was the culmination of this expansion of rights in England. This English Bill of Rights provided for a jury trial in criminal cases. It specifically condemned "excessive bail," "excessive fines," and "cruel and unusual punishments." All these rights were borrowed and introduced directly into the Eighth Amendment to the American Constitution one century later.

The English Bill of Rights did not create free speech rights, except for members of Parliament. It censured the raising and keeping of a standing army in peacetime but had little to say regarding martial law to suspend rights. It established some sort of right to bear arms, but only for Protestants. Religious liberty was not guaranteed. From the point of view of English history, the most important part of the Bill of Rights was the provision that denied the king the power to suspend the laws of Parliament. To all of this William and Mary agreed.

The American Declaration of Independence was not chiefly designed to proclaim new rights for Americans. Instead, it was directed against the abuses of the English king as a means of justification of separation from the mother country. The Declaration of Independence of the Thirteen Colonies of North America was the first national independence document in world history and deserves fame for that fact. It has inspired revolutionary movements around the world and given hope to those who seek to break the bonds of colonialism. The document itself says little about rights, but what it does say is part of the subsequent legacy or the legend of Thomas Jefferson, its principal author.

The language of the second paragraph of the Declaration of Independence should be familiar to every American: "We hold these truths to be self-evident, that all men are endowed by their creator with unalienable rights, that among these, are life, liberty, and the pursuit of happiness." The simple language makes a far more sweeping statement than Jefferson realized. Yet a passage that Jefferson intended to include in the Declaration was deleted at the insistence of the Continental Congress. Jefferson's original draft condemned the trade in slaves as violating human nature's "most sacred rights of life and liberty." This language was considered too strong by opposing Southern slaveholders and some New England merchants.

Jefferson always denied that he had intended to create or discover new rights when he wrote the Declaration of Independence, although the statement that "all men are created equal" seems today to be extremely powerful. At the time the Declaration was written many Americans had a general understanding about their rights, and Jefferson probably meant to convey those thoughts. However, he used more general language based on the writing of the English philosopher, John Locke (1632–1704). Locke had emphasized life, liberty, and especially property as fundamental rights that government was bound to protect. Jefferson expanded prop-

Thomas Jefferson *(1743–1826)*

Thomas Jefferson is one of the most famous of all American leaders. However, his place in the history of American rights is assured for a number of reasons. Jefferson's authorship of the Declaration of Independence is one of his most significant contributions. Jefferson's championing of church-state separation is another. His views regarding the importance of individual rights are scattered over a lifetime of activity and writing. More than any other philosopher, Jefferson provided the foundation for thinking about the rights of Americans. A student of the theories of John Locke and other French and English political theorists, Jefferson was able to translate their thoughts into an American context in vibrant and living language.

The Declaration of Independence is perhaps the most important of all American documents. When he prepared the first draft of the Declaration of Independence, Jefferson was a tall, freckled Virginia lawyer of 33 years, who was already recognized as a brilliant writer and thinker. Although the section of the draft document that condemned slavery was stricken by the Continental Congress, what remains is still a stirring statement of basic principles. As Jefferson wrote, "all men are created equal," and they are "endowed by their Creator with certain inalienable rights, that among these are life, liberty, and the pursuit of happiness." According to the Declaration, the protection of these rights is the main function of government, which draws its authority "from the consent of the governed." This remains the best statement of the purpose of American rights, although the ideals expressed by the Declaration of Independence are not yet fulfilled.

Jefferson himself was inconsistent in his views on slavery. When he wrote the Declaration of Independence he included an attack upon the slave trade in his list of royal abuses. His draft stated that the king had "waged cruel war against human nature itself, violating its most sacred rights of life and liberty in the persons of a distant people who never offended him, captivating and carrying them into slavery in another hemisphere, or to incur miserable death in their transportation thither." This language was offensive to his fellow southern representatives to the Continental Congress and was removed at their insistence. Jefferson remained alert to the evils of slavery but favored the gradual deportation of slaves as a solution, warning Americans that "the two races, equally free, cannot live in the same government." He feared that freed slaves would take revenge against their former masters. Jefferson kept slaves but was opposed to intermarriage and the "mixture" of African Americans and whites. Obviously, there were some limits to his view that all men were created equal, yet Jefferson was much more generous in his views of minority rights than most Americans of his period. In his Second Inaugural Address he stated that Native Americans, "endowed with the faculties and the rights of men," have a right to freedom and happiness, and he often spoke of the evils of slavery.

Jefferson made many other contributions to the development of American rights. He struggled many years to establish principles of religious toleration and freedom in Virginia and America. He strongly supported the addition of the Bill of Rights to the Constitution. Jefferson opposed John Adams's repressive Alien and Sedition Acts of 1798, which he saw as an attack on freedom of the press. In response to their passage Jefferson drew up the Kentucky and Virginia Resolutions, which took a strict and narrow view of national powers over state governments.

Thomas Jefferson was the third president of the United States, author of the Declaration of Independence, and an apostle of agrarian democracy. He shared the democratic tendencies of his frontier neighbors and opposed the aristocratic tendencies in the new American nation. As president, Jefferson was responsible for the Louisiana Purchase of 1803, which acquired vast, formerly Spanish lands from France. This area of 828,000 square miles doubled the national domain and absorbed into the nation areas that were previously settled by the Spanish and, more especially, by Native Americans.

The list of Jefferson's many accomplishments during his political career is long and extensive, both in Virginia and on the national scene. However, as an architect of American rights, few Americans can match Jefferson's accomplishments. His words and ideas are embedded deep in the American consciousness.

Thomas Jefferson's original draft of the Declaration of Independence condemned the trade in slaves as violating human nature's "most sacred rights of life and liberty," but this passage was deleted at the insistence of some members of the Continental Congress.

erty to include a "pursuit of happiness," which goes beyond life and liberty. Yet many later generations of Americans have found in the language about man's equality, unalienable rights, and the pursuit of happiness the basis for their claims of rights. Only in the past few decades has the equality of American rights hinted at in the Declaration of Independence started to become a reality. In each new generation the language of the Declaration seems to have a new meaning. Life, liberty, and the pursuit of happiness are still goals for the shapers of many rights policies in America.

The Constitution is not a storehouse of all American rights, but it did give expression to some of the rights commonly enjoyed in the freed

American states. It must be pointed out that the Constitution did not ban the slave trade, although Article I, Section 9, clause 1 gave Congress the power to limit the importation of slaves after 1808. Even then, slavery would continue after 1808, and slaves merely became a domestic product. Slaves did not have the constitutional rights of American men.

Another feature of the Constitution shows clearly a shameful disregard for human rights. Under the Constitution's Article I, Section 2, as it was originally written, a slave was counted as three-fifths of a white person for the purposes of taxation and representation. The slaves had no rights, but their bodies counted in the political strength of the slaveholding states. Yet the word

John Locke *(1632–1704)*

The idea that our rights are eternal, unchanging personal possessions, which are superior to any government and beyond the legitimate reach of ordinary politics can be traced to the English political philosopher John Locke. Locke is not the first person to have conceived of individual rights in this way, but he gave the idea of rights its clearest, most classic statement. Locke's writings form the basis for most discussions about rights in America, even for those who never heard of him. Americans live in a Lockean framework of rights, although the meanings of those rights in a modern world are still being discovered and may have changed from their original Lockean context.

Locke insisted that government was originally formed for the purpose of protecting man's individual rights against the incursions of other individuals. In particular, life, liberty, and property were each said by Locke to be basic individual rights whose existence preceded the state itself. Government was obliged to protect these rights as the result of a social contract that gave rise to the state. These natural rights of man could be abused by other individuals or by the government itself. Government was formed to protect those natural rights. If the government severely abused natural, individual rights, the people had an additional right to revolution. This right of revolution was used to justify the American Revolution.

Locke did not live long enough to see the American Revolution. Instead, he used his arguments to justify the English Glorious Revolution of 1688. His most famous work, *Two Treatises on Civil Government*, was written for this purpose. As a result of that book, Locke became the best known exponent of individual freedom. His fame spread throughout Europe for those ideas and for his other important views concerning the nature of human knowledge and experience. While Locke is renowned for his political theory, he also made a deep impression on Western philosophical thinking.

John Locke's views on religious freedom were also quite advanced. He wrote three separate essays on religious toleration, contending that only atheism and Roman Catholicism should be suppressed. Freedom of individual conscience and the right to property ranked highest in Locke's scheme of values.

During his lifetime Locke held several minor diplomatic posts, but for most of his adult life he lectured on Greek, rhetoric, and especially philosophy at Oxford University. For the most part, Locke spent his time delving into the major philosophical issues of the period. However, his radical political views sometimes got him into trouble, and he was forced to leave England for Holland from 1683 to 1689. Many of Locke's ideas entered into American thinking, but Locke was himself only little concerned with events in the English colonies in the New World.

"slave" never appears in the Constitution, showing some slight disturbance over the existence of slavery. These rights denials were eliminated in the text of the Constitution by the ratification of the Thirteenth, Fourteenth, and Fifteenth Amendments after the Civil War.

Native Americans were also scanted by the original Constitution. Although mentioned twice in the text, it seems clear that they are not citizens and perhaps have no rights. Article I, Section 8 gave Congress the power to regulate commerce with "foreign nations, and among the several states, and with the Indian tribes," showing that Native Americans had some sort of special status. However, nothing was required to protect Indian property rights.

The Bill of Rights

Two of the framers of the Constitution, George Mason and Eldridge Gerry, opposed its adoption partly on the ground that it contained no bill of rights. In Virginia Patrick Henry opposed ratification of the Constitution on the same ground. The English common law, colonial charters, and the bills of rights found in the various state constitutions all suggested that a national bill of rights was needed, in addition to the short list of rights found in the Constitution. Many of the drafters of the Constitution at first resisted this pressure, believing that a bill of rights was unneeded, since the states had their own. They also believed that the new national government was one of limited powers and was unlikely to invade individual rights.

The opposition to the Constitution grew, partly because of the absence of a bill of rights. To stem the tide George Mason, Thomas Jefferson, and James Madison prepared a Virginia version of a proposed bill of rights for the national government. The Bill of Rights, which represent the first ten articles of the Amendments to the Constitution of the United States, was framed in its final form largely by James Madison. Much of the language used was based upon George Mason's "Declaration of Rights" for the Virginia Constitution of 1776, a document that is still part of Virginia's current constitution.

James Madison introduced his proposed amendments in the first session of Congress. He reversed his previous opposition to the idea. Most of Madison's propositions were ultimately adopted by Congress on September 25, 1789, and were rapidly submitted to the states for ratification. Ratification was achieved on March 1, 1792, and the fact was announced by the Secretary of State, Thomas Jefferson. The Bill of Rights was born. However, three states—Massachusetts, Connecticut, and Georgia—failed to ratify the amendments, and did not do so until 1939, during the sesquicentennial celebration of the Constitution.

One of the motivations for drafting the Bill of Rights was to place restraints on the powers of the central government. John Roche, a leading scholar, concludes that "rather than being designed as the armor of the free citizen, these first ten amendments to the Constitution were the result of the strong desire of many state governments to eliminate in advance the growth of a national judicial administration patterned on the British model." In fact Jefferson expressed that view in a letter to Madison in March 1789.

The text of the Bill of Rights is curious because the First Amendment is directed only at Congress. The opening phrase of the Bill of Rights states that "Congress shall make no law . . . ." Although Congress is not referred to elsewhere in the Bill of Rights, the states that ratified the amendments understood that Congress was limited by them. Congress, not the executive or judicial branch, was deemed to be the most powerful part of the new constitutional regime. Few people imagined that the judiciary or the president would enlarge the rights stated in the Bill of Rights.

As it stands, the Bill of Rights comprises a mere 413 words. It expressly mentions about 25 assorted rights. The Ninth Amendment says that there may be other rights beyond those listed but which are not enumerated. This expresses Madison's fears that a bill of rights could be a means of denying new rights that were not specifically listed. However, the subsequent history of rights in America made the Bill of Rights a sufficient starting point for a considerable expansion of the rights of the American people, well beyond what was expected when it was ratified.

When the Bill of Rights was written Madison did not intend to set forth new rights not found in the various state constitutions. Even so, the language originally proposed by Madison was often much stronger and clearer than the final text of the Bill of Rights. Congressional debate watered down the original proposals. Consider the changes made to the First Amendment. Madison's original resolution read:

> The civil rights of none shall be abridged on account of religious worship, nor shall any national religion be established nor shall the full and equal rights of conscience be in any manner, or on any pretext infringed.

> The people shall not be deprived or abridged of their right to speak, to write, or to publish their sentiments; and the freedom of the press, as one of the great bulwarks of liberty, shall be inviolable. The people shall not be restrained from peacefully assembling and consulting for the common good; nor from applying to the legislatures by petition, or remonstrances, for redress of grievances.

Compare this with the compressed language of the First Amendment, which, unlike the proposal, is aimed at Congress:

> Congress shall make no law respecting an establishment of religion, or prohibiting the free exercise thereof; or abridging freedom of speech, or of the press; or the right of the people peaceably to assemble, and to petition government for a redress of grievances.

Madison's original language is more absolute and sweeping than in the version adopted. The freedom of conscience, the right of free expression to write and to publish, were obscured. The prominence given to a free press is missing. Madison believed that an independent judiciary would repair many of these changes. In time, he proved to be correct. Still, the language of the First Amendment had been emptied of some its original force.

No new rights were added to the Constitution until the end of the Civil War in 1865. For the years between, the Bill of Rights of the national government and the bills of rights of the states were operative. Slavery was untouched by these rights. States sometimes violated their own bills of rights, especially freedom of the press, which was often sharply restricted. The federal Bill of Rights was rarely used during these years. The Supreme Court did not prove to be a guardian of American rights in this era, so early American rights, while more impressive than in other nations (save for

George Mason (1725–1792)

George Mason was an affluent Virginia planter who became involved in critical events surrounding the American Revolution, the creation of the Constitution, and the emergence of the Bill of Rights. As a member of the Virginia constitutional convention of 1776, Mason drafted the very significant Virginia Declaration of Rights. This document was copied by many American states as a compilation of basic rights. When Thomas Jefferson drew up the Declaration of Independence he borrowed ideas from Mason's Declaration of Rights.

Mason was an active participant in the Constitutional Convention of 1787. He helped draft many of its most important provisions, but he opposed the compromise permitting the slave trade. Mason refused to sign the Constitution because it lacked a Bill of Rights. He and Patrick Henry led the fight in Virginia against constitutional ratification. Eventually, their views prevailed, and a national Bill of Rights, based upon the Virginia Declaration of Rights, was ratified as the first ten amendments to the Constitution in 1791.

the persistence of slavery here) were much more limited than they became after the Civil War.

James Madison believed that the Bill of Rights would be applied to the states and the national government after ratification. The question of the scope of the Bill of Rights was uncertain until 1833. In that year Chief Justice Marshall of the United States Supreme Court ruled that the Bill of Rights did not apply to the states. His logic in the case of *Barron* v. *Baltimore* (1833) was that because only Congress was named in the First Amendment and the states were nowhere mentioned in the Bill of Rights, the document did not apply to them. Up until the Civil War only the specific rights mentioned in the original Constitution applied to the states. The specific rights are the privilege against habeas corpus, the prohibition of bills of attainder and ex post facto laws, the privileges and immunities clause of Article IV, the prohibition against a religious test oath for office, and the requirement not to impair the obligation of contract. All these were binding upon the states, and little else.

James Madison *(1751–1836)*

James Madison was fourth president of the United States from 1809 until 1817. He served as secretary of state to President Thomas Jefferson from 1801 to 1809. Madison was elected in 1789 to the first Congress of the United States. While there he drafted and sponsored the first ten amendments to the national constitution—the Bill of Rights—as it later came to be known. James Madison was one of the greatest political figures and political thinkers in the history of the nation.

When the Constitution was first adopted many opponents criticized the absence of protections for individual rights. A proposal to prepare a Bill of Rights was made at the close of the Constitutional Convention in 1787, but it was not acted upon. Madison in his campaign for his seat in Congress said, "It is my sincere opinion that the Constitution ought to be revised, and that the First Congress meeting under it should ought to prepare and recommend to the states . . . the most satisfactory provision for all essential rights."

On June 8, 1789, Madison placed his proposals before the House of Representatives. Many congressmen opposed his proposal; some urged delay. Madison pushed for immediate action. He warned that if these amendments were postponed ". . . it may occasion suspicions, which, though not well founded, may tend to inflame or prejudice the public against our decisions."

Most of James Madison's original draft of the first ten amendments were preserved without changes. In preparing his draft Madison had borrowed heavily from the Virginia Declaration of Rights, but he added many new features not found in that document. The nucleus of the Bill of Rights provided guarantees for individual rights in matters of speech, religion, petitions, and a free press. Madison lost out on his proposal that the states be prohibited from infringing on individual rights. When submitted to the states on September 25, 1789, the Bill of Rights was ratified fairly rapidly (1791). In most respects, Madison's great work for individual rights was achieved. He deserves the name of the "Father of the Bill of Rights."

Madison's deep knowledge of political philosophy was embodied in the *Federalist Papers,* which he wrote in partnership with Alexander Hamilton and John Jay to explain the underlying theory of the new national constitution. He also applied his knowledge of government and political theory to the draft of the Virginia Constitution in 1776.

Madison's career was long and distinguished. Like George Washington, Thomas Jefferson, and Alexander Hamilton, he was one of the giants of the early years of the American republic. Madison was an active participant in the drafting of the Constitution of the United States. Always a friend of civil rights, Madison attacked repressive measures like the Alien and Sedition Acts (1798) passed during the John Adams administration.

James Madison retired from public office in 1817 to his Virginia home in Montpelier. When he died in 1836 he left a grateful nation a rich heritage of accomplishments, in spite of the unpleasant memories of the War of 1812, which was fought ingloriously during his term as president.

After the Civil War there was a need to abolish slavery and to redefine the rights of the newly freed slaves. In the process all American rights were expanded in a fashion that restricted the powers of state and local governments. The redefinition of American rights was an important milestone in the history of rights in America, not only for African Americans but for all citizens.

The Thirteenth Amendment, ratified in 1865, prohibits slavery and involuntary servitude in America and gives Congress the power to enforce that policy. No state could claim that it had the power to preserve slavery thereafter. This section of the Constitution is still sometimes used against shameful working conditions that approach slavery.

The Fourteenth Amendment gave exslaves national citizenship as well as state citizenship. But the amendment went on to say that "no state shall make or enforce any law which shall abridge the privileges and immunities of citizens of the United States." This language seems to plainly create new rights as an aspect of American citizenship. Some of its drafters clearly intended that, but the matter when disputed in the Supreme Court was given a much narrower interpretation.

The Fourteenth Amendment also forbids the states from depriving "any person of life, liberty or property without due process of law," nor may any state "deny to any person the equal protection of the laws." The language of these two phrases of the Fourteenth Amendment accounts for more than one third of the litigation before the Supreme Court of the United States. However, when it was written into the Constitution few realized how potent a weapon for expanding civil rights these phrases would become.

According to constitutional historian John P. Roche the Fourteenth Amendment "was intended to destroy the right of any state or individual to deny an individual his natural rights." It also provided a constitutional foundation for the statutes that Congress passed to defend the newly freed slaves. The Civil Rights Act of 1866 was designed by the radical reformers in Congress to broaden the rights of African Americans in America. However, the Supreme Court stood in the path of progress by interpreting the statute narrowly. By the end of the century the Court had thoroughly emasculated the Fourteenth Amendment in a series of major decisions. Separate but equal treatment of African Americans was permitted, and Jim Crow discriminatory laws directed against them were allowed to stand.

In general, the Supreme Court of the nineteenth century was not eager to expand American individual rights. In a 1876 case the Court examined the issue of whether trial by jury was a privilege or an immunity of national citizenship that the states are forbidden by the Fourteenth Amendment to abridge. The Court says that it was not, nor was the due process clause of any assistance. (See *Walker* v. *Saurinet,* 1876.) Moreover, with just a few case exceptions, African Americans, Asian Americans, Native Americans, and other underprivileged minorities in America were not protected by the Supreme Court of the last century.

So the Fourteenth Amendment meant less in the last century than it does today. The amendment did not nationalize the Bill of Rights. As late as 1922 the Supreme Court was able to declare that "neither the Fourteenth Amendment nor any other provision of the Constitution of the United States imposes upon the states any restrictions about freedom of speech." (See *Prudential Insurance Company* v. *Cheek,* 1922.) Within ten years of that declaration the First Amendment had been incorporated within the Fourteenth Amendment by virtue of judicial interpretation. Today, much of the Supreme Court's docket is composed of cases that arise out of provisions of the Bill of Rights, as incorporated through the Fourteenth Amendment and applied against actions of state or local governments. Over the course of the past 60 years the Supreme Court has vastly expanded the reach of the Bill of Rights.

Certain provisions of the federal Bill of Rights still have not been extended to the states. The Second (right to bear arms), Third, and Seventh Amendments have not been held to apply to state actions, and the Fifth Amendment's guarantee for indictment by grand jury as well as the Eighth Amendment's ban on excessive fines and bail have also not been mandated for the states. The rest of the Bill of Rights has, by various decisions of the Supreme Court, been made to apply to the state governments.

This remarkable use of the Fourteenth Amendment has placed the Supreme Court at the center of the construction of modern American rights policy. Questions of criminal justice and of individual rights frequently crowd the Court's calendar, creating a close relationship between state and national governments. In time the vehicle of this change in American constitutional law often focused upon the language of the Fourteenth Amendment, which commands that "no state shall . . . deprive any person of life, liberty or property, without due process of law."

Most of the important policy shifts in the application of the Bill of Rights took place in the 1960s and 1970s, when an activist Court, led by Chief Justice Earl Warren, decided to reform many aspects of state criminal procedure. In those same years the Court took on itself the issue of racial desegregation of the public schools. Most of the precedents established in the Warren years still form the law of American rights today. The current Court, although much more conservative on rights policy, has not disturbed the rights revolution accomplished in the 1960s and 1970s. In fact, some expansion of American rights are still taking place, although a few retreats are also evident from Court rulings.

with some exceptions, essential legal equality has been attained. The rights available at first to just a few have been expanded to all citizens. That triumph of American rights is largely a twentieth-century development and is treated in the next chapter. Nonetheless, economic equality still divides the nation. African Americans, Native Americans, and Hispanics Americans are at the bottom of the economic ladder in America. While it is true that Americans enjoy more legal rights than do most other people, it is also true that many of those who live in urban slums and rural poverty do not enjoy the same quality of life.

One explanation for unequal conditions is the different experiences of various immigrant groups in America. Racial and ethnic economic inequality is partly based on differing historical experiences. All immigrants suffered from discrimination when they first arrived, but many have entered the mainstream of American life, while others lag behind. The discrimination that persists in modern America has economic roots.

One of the groups that made some contributions to the new rights of Americans was the Quakers. William Penn established his colony in 1681. Land was purchased from the Indians, not taken away. Penn's proprietary regime was unusually liberal for its age. There was a representative assembly elected by the landowners. There was no tax-supported state church, as in other colonies in America. Freedom of worship was guaranteed, although Penn was pressured by English authorities to deny Catholics and Jews in his colony the privilege of voting or holding office.

While it's true that Americans enjoy more legal rights than do most other people, it is also true that many of those who live in urban slums and rural poverty do not enjoy the same quality of life.

Immigrants and Equal Rights

In a sense all Americans except those who were here as natives are immigrants or the children of immigrants. The Dutch, Swedes, English, Welsh, and a few other European settlers braved the passage to the New World during the seventeenth century to begin a new life in what was for them a new world. They brought with them their few possessions and also their own cultures and ideals. The notion of rights was still just beginning. Few colonists thought of themselves as bearers of rights, except those based on the law of the nations of their origins. American rights began on almost virgin soil.

Over the years Americans have obtained equality before the law. The Fourteenth Amendment commanded it, and in the twentieth century,

The humane Quakers developed a strong dislike for Negro slavery, and made efforts to stop it elsewhere. Immigrants were welcomed, especially religious misfits who were discouraged or repressed elsewhere. In many ways seventeenth-century Pennsylvania was a haven for civil liberty, even if there were "blue laws" aimed at ungodly practices. Gambling, stage plays, May games, and excessive hilarity were frowned upon. Although William Penn suffered greatly for his liberal views, his new commonwealth did establish a form of freedom of conscience and worship almost unknown elsewhere in the world.

By the time of the American Revolution the colonies had become very similar. Population mixes between the colonies had created a basically English nation on the American eastern coast.

Quaker leader William Penn founded his colony in 1681 and established friendly relations with the Native Americans already inhabiting the region.

The English colonists, although separated by geography and differing historical backgrounds, were bound together by some practices and customs that had evolved. All enjoyed some form of religious freedom. They all possessed some degree of self-government, if not democracy, and they all enjoyed some measure of economic opportunity. In addition, there was a heritage of rights drawn from the mother country and embellished in the New World. They enjoyed the freedoms available to Englishmen. As we have seen, these were an important source of rights but not akin to modern American rights.

The America of 1776 was some form of melting pot of populations. Heavily accented Germans formed 6 percent of the population. Many had fled religious persecution, economic oppression, and frequent wars. They settled chiefly in Pennsylvania, forming a third of that colony's population. The German newcomers were the first major immigrant group, becoming known by many as the "Pennsylvania Dutch."

Another non-English group, the Scots, were about as numerous as the Germans. They were descended from the turbulent Scots lowlanders, who had been transplanted by the English to Northern Ireland. In Ireland they had been resented by the dominant Irish Catholics. Beginning in the 1700s many of these Scots (called Scotch-Irish) migrated to America, chiefly to Pennsylvania. They settled on the Pennsylvania western frontier, fighting with the Native Americans for lands there. Many fought bravely in the American Revolution, having little love for the British.

The largest single non-English group was African, predominantly brought as slaves to America. There were about 500,000 involuntary African immigrants to America living here in 1775. That was about 20 percent of the population, far more than any other non-English immigrant group. In some southern states slaves outnumbered the white population. The slaves, being regarded as property, had no rights.

Another large group of immigrants were indentured servants, numbering about 250,000, who had come to America by 1775. These "white slaves" were mainly people who could not afford the price of passage in America. They mortgaged themselves to those who advanced them the money for transportation. Gradually they could become free men, but it took at least five years to pay off the debts. After a period of hardship, these freed men could enjoy the rights of other Americans—rights which slaves could never have. Still, many indentured servants died in servitude or returned propertyless, to England.

In the early 19th century America beckoned to the struggling masses of Europe. It seemed a land of opportunity and freedom. There was plentiful land, low taxes, and no compulsory military service. Religious toleration was generally practiced in America, and no state church was established.

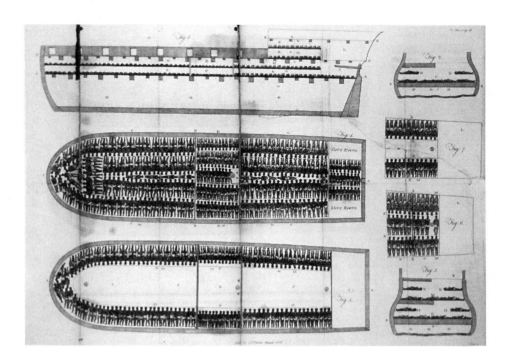

In 1775 the largest single non-English group was African, predominantly brought over to America on slave ships such as this.

Ireland was a particular source of a very large immigrant population. A terrible rot had devastated the potato crop in Ireland, and large numbers of the Irish were killed by disease and hunger. In the 1840s tens of thousands of destitute Irish fled to America and elsewhere for a new start in life. In time there were more Irish in America than in Ireland itself. Many of the Irish settled in Boston and New York City, where they discovered vile slum conditions. The Irish were usually looked down upon by the resident population, and forced to take the most menial kinds of jobs. Sometimes they were confronted by "No Irish Need Apply" signs in shop windows. Many of them encountered anti-Catholic prejudice, since there had been only a small number of Catholics in America. In 1844 a two day anti-Catholic riot broke out in Philadelphia, resulting in the burning of two Catholic churches and the death of 13 people.

German immigration to America also increased during these years. Between 1830 and 1860 1.5 million Germans came to America. They were not as impoverished as the Irish immigrants, but they were mainly poor people, displaced by economic hardship. The Germans tended to regard themselves as cultural superiors to the Irish but were themselves often dubbed as "damned Dutchmen."

The startling rise of immigration frightened many American "nativists." They claimed that foreign "scum" would take jobs away from real Americans. The new immigrants might also outbreed and eventually outvote the real Americans, taking away political power and influence from established groups. Sometimes nativism became a political rallying cry. At other times it was expressed as violence against immigrants.

In 1849 the Know Nothing Party was formed secretly by extreme nativists. This formidable American political group agitated for rigid restrictions on immigration and naturalization and was fiercely anti-Catholic. They fought for laws preventing the immigration of alien paupers. Even many of those who did not join this secret party were deeply sympathetic to their cause. By 1854 the Know Nothings had 43 seats in the U.S. House of Representatives and had elected a governor and controlled both houses of the legislature in the state of Massachusetts.

Asian immigrants came later, and in smaller numbers, but they were even more subject to discriminatory treatment than European immigrants. Chinese workers were imported to America to work on the construction of rails in the American West. About 10,000 pigtailed Chinese coolees provided cheap and willing labor. They helped lay the rails and dig the mountain tunnels for the Union Pacific and Central Pacific railway companies.

Cheap Chinese labor was also used in agricultural work in California. By 1880, 9 percent of Californians (about 75,000 people) were of Chinese origin. In San Francisco some Irish-born workers, fearing the competition of the Chinese,

By 1880, 9 percent of Californians (about 75,000 people) were of Chinese origin. In San Francisco some Irish-born workers, fearing the competition of the Chinese, took direct action against them. Scores of Chinese were abused; others were simply murdered.

took direct action against them. Scores of Chinese were abused. Some had their pigtails cut off; others were simply murdered.

Treaties between China and the United States were written to limit the immigration of Chinese to America. One such treaty accords Chinese in America many of the "rights privileges and immunities" of American citizens, but this provision had little effect on widespread anti-Chinese acts. In 1882 Congress passed the Chinese Exclusion Act, which seemed to close the doors to Chinese immigration. The statute asserted that no state or federal court could admit Chinese to citizenship after 1882. This statute, although declared unconstitutional, was succeeded by the 1884 Chinese Exclusion Treaty, which incorporated most of the same features. For decades thereafter Chinese and Japanese immigra-

tion was severely limited, and access to citizenship was rationed or eliminated at various times. However, Chinese children born in America were citizens, with all the rights of American citizens.

The Supreme Court did interpret the Fourteenth Amendment to protect the rights of Chinese Americans. In 1886 the Court struck down a San Francisco ordinance that made criminal the conduct of a laundry business in any building not made of brick or stone, with such exceptions for wooden structures as administrative officials might make. When it was revealed that 80 wooden laundries owned by whites were licensed while 200 Chinese American applicants were denied licenses, the Court found that the equal protection of the laws clause of the Fourteenth Amendment had been violated (*Yick Wo* v. *Hopkins,* 1886).

Today some newer immigrant groups suffer from discrimination. Newcomers from Haiti, the Dominican Republic, Laos, Cambodia, Korea, Mexico, and other areas of the world have come to America in the past few decades seeking a better life for themselves and their children. Each group has experienced great difficulty in adjusting to American life. Many have been victims of discrimination, yet because of the legal protections now available, acts of discrimination tend to be limited. For many of them economic inequality is quite prevalent. Many new immigrants are poor or close to the poverty line. It must be remembered that our current views of American rights extend only to equal opportunity and nondiscrimination. No group and no individual in America has a right to a high or even a decent standard of living. That concept is beyond the current thinking about rights in America.

Bibliography

Bailey, Thomas B. *The American Pageant.* New York: D. C. Heath, 1996.

Chafee, Zechariah, Jr. *Documents on Fundamental Human Rights.* Boston: Athenaeum Press, 1963.

Glasser, Ira. *Visions of Liberty: The Bill of Rights for All Americans.* Boston: Little Brown, 1991.

Morris, Richard. *Studies in the History of American Law.* New York: Harpers, 1930.

Pacheco, Josephine S. *To Secure the Blessings of Liberty: Rights in American History.* Lanham, Md.: University Press of America, 1993.

Roche, John P. *Courts and Rights.* New York: Random House, 1961.

Stone, Geoffrey R., Richard Epstein, and Cass R. Sunstein. *The Bill of Rights in the Modern State.* Chicago: University of Chicago Press, 1992.

Human Rights
in Twentieth-Century
United States

Michael H. Reggio

The history of human rights in twentieth-century United States generally tracks the progress of human rights. However, as with most advancements, this progress includes gains and losses, positives and negatives, steps forward and steps backward. But the bottom line for United States' citizens is that today they enjoy more human rights than they have in the history of the country. Furthermore, they enjoy more human rights than the citizens of nearly any country in the world.

Every American political party in some way tries to advance human rights ideas. For example, the 1992 Democratic Party Platform, entitled, "A New Covenant with the American People," mentioned human rights frequently. It stated that our "economic strength—indeed our national security—is grounded on a healthy domestic economy. But we cannot be strong at home unless we are part of a vibrant and expanding global economy that recognizes human rights and seeks to improve the living standards of all the world's people." The platform affirmed that standing up for human rights "is a proud tradition of the Democratic Party." On the other side of the political spectrum, right-wing conservative presidential candidate Patrick Buchanan, while speaking at the Republican GOP Party State Convention in San Antonio on June 22, 1996, said of his party, "You know, our party has a great and glorious history. In 1860 we were the party of Mr. Lincoln that extended human rights to a whole segment of Americans who had been denied citizenship and human rights." During World War II, Franklin Delano Roosevelt framed the war ideology around four concepts: freedom of speech, freedom of worship, freedom from want, and freedom from fear. The latter two rights are not even found in the Constitution, but human rights activists would call them human rights.

The use of the phrase "human rights" is fairly new. First used by Henry David Thoreau in his treatise, *Civil Disobedience,* the phrase entered into general usage following World War II and after the founding of the United Nations in

1945. The expression has come to replace the phrases "natural rights" and "rights of man." These terms fell into disfavor because of the intellectual controversy over natural law concepts and because of the use of the term "man" when theorists began to apply human rights universally to include women.

Although the expression "human rights" is fairly recent, the concepts of human rights are not. We find their roots in ancient times, especially in most of the world's religions, which express the concept of individual worth and dignity. The modern concepts of human rights grew most directly out of the natural rights and natural law theories of the seventeenth and eighteenth centuries. The popular theorists of the era, such as Thomas Hobbes, Benedict de Spinoza, John Locke, Charles de Secondat Montesquieu, and Jean-Jacques Rousseau advanced the idea that each human being is born "naturally" with certain rights. Each human being has certain rights, not because of her country's citizenship or the religious or social membership into which he belongs, but because he or she was born as a human being. What those rights are has been hotly debated. Nevertheless, most agree about certain rights. For example, most natural law theorists included values such as respect for life and liberty in their list of natural rights; therefore, they would also probably agree that all should be free from the excess use of force and torture. In fact the term "natural rights" predominated until well into the twentieth century, when as a result of Nazi genocidal atrocities the term "human rights" came into vogue.

Our founding fathers, especially Thomas Jefferson, were well versed in the theories of natural law. The basic concepts that underlie our modern systems of government were founded upon these theories. The Magna Carta, the Petition of Right of 1628, the Glorious Revolution of 1688 and the resulting Bill of Rights, the Virginia Bill of Rights, and the Declaration of Independence all had as their basis the belief in human rights. In the Declaration of Independence, Thomas Jefferson, who relied heavily on Locke and Montesquieu, declared that American colonists were a "free people claiming their rights as derived from the laws of nature and not as the gift of their Chief Magistrate." He went on to pen one of the most recognized proclamations ever; "We hold these truths to be self-evident, that all men are created equal, that they are endowed by their Creator with certain unalienable Rights, that among these are Life, Liberty and the Pursuit of Happiness." President Jimmy Carter in his "Farewell Address to the Nation" in 1981 said, "America did not invent human rights. In a very real sense, it's the other way around. Human rights invented America. Ours was the first nation in the history of the world to be founded explicitly on such an idea. . . . The fundamental force that unites us is not kinship or place of origin or religious preference. The love of liberty is the common blood that flows in our American veins."

The concept of human rights may have its roots in other countries, but since the founding of the republic, the United States has led the world in defining human rights. For example, the Marquis de Lafayette, who fought next to George Washington in the Revolutionary War, took American ideas about human rights back to Europe in the form of the "Declaration of the Rights of Man and of the Citizen of August 26, 1789." This document declared that "men are born and remain free and equal in rights," and that "the aim of every political association is the preservation of the natural and imprescriptible rights of man. . . ." Lafayette defined the rights of man as "liberty, property, safety and resistance to oppression." His definition of "liberty" included the freedoms of speech, religion, and association, and freedom from arbitrary arrest and imprisonment. Leo Tolstoy, Mahatma Gandhi, and Martin Luther King Jr. used American concepts of human rights to set forth their beliefs.

In the last half of the nineteenth century and the first half of the twentieth century, human rights activism moved forward. Political theorists and rights activists argued back and forth about what were human rights. Many thought that human rights were found only in one's imagination. Activists clamored for solutions to deprived individuals and groups, while theorists debated grander themes. For example, Calvin Coolidge, in his speech accepting the Republican vice-presidential nomination in 1920, stated, "Men speak of natural rights, but I challenge anyone to show where in nature any rights existed or were recognized until there was established for their declaration and protection a duly promulgated body of corresponding laws." Political and religious groups called for human rights. During this period

Americans addressed many human rights issues in the United States: slavery, child labor, brutal working conditions, the "Indian Problem," and voting rights. Although reformers did not often solve these problems, profound social, economic, and political changes did occur during this period.

The United Nations

In looking at the human rights movement in the twentieth century, it is difficult to define "human rights." It is even more difficult to categorize what rights to include under the umbrella of human rights. Mid-twentieth century, many scholars looked to the United Nations to determine what rights they would specifically classify as "human rights." After the failure of the League of Nations (1919–1940) and in the aftermath of the bloodbath of the Nazi Holocaust, countries of the world formed the United Nations in 1945. In its charter, the United Nations stated its "faith in fundamental human rights, in the dignity and worth of the human person, in the equal rights of men and women and of nations large and small." According to its charter, one of its goals was "to develop friendly relations among nations based on respect for the principle of equal rights and self-determination of peoples . . . [and] promoting and encouraging respect for human rights and for fundamental freedoms for all without distinction as to race, sex, language, or religion." In 1948, led by First Lady Eleanor Roosevelt, delegates from 14 nations representative of most political systems and geographical areas of the United Nations met together to draft a declaration of human rights for the world. The group of delegates, called the Commission on Human Rights, developed the United Nations Universal Declaration of Human Rights. Forty-eight nations of the United Nations adopted it. Only eight nations abstained (Belarus, Czechoslovakia, Poland, Saudi Arabia, South Africa, Ukraine, the Soviet Union, and Yugoslavia). The adopting countries meant this declaration to be "a common standard of achievement for all peoples and all nations." It listed 30 human rights that covered social, economic, political, and cultural rights. And what did we look for, and do we still look for today, when it comes to human rights? Eleanor Roosevelt gave us some insight when she wrote, "Where, after all, do human rights begin? In small places, close to home—so close and so small that they may not be seen on any maps of the world, yet they are the world of the individual person; the factory, the farm, or the office where he works. Such are the places where every man, woman, and child seeks equal justice, equal opportunity, equal dignity without discrimination. Unless these rights have meaning there, they have little meaning anywhere. Without concerned citizen action close to home, we shall look in vain for progress in the large world." Most scholars generally accept these rights as the basis for the beginning of a list of human rights. Human rights are the seedbed of modern civil rights.

Yet human rights must be broken down into two additional categories: political rights, those the government has the power to grant, and societal rights, those accorded by people within society. For example, the government may codify the right for African Americans to have equal opportunity to a job, and it may be the law of the land, but it will matter little if most of society refuses to grant equal opportunity to African American job applicants.

No single list of human rights will satisfy everyone, and any list changes from person to person. For example, some pro-choice camps declare abortion a human right, whereas some pro-life camps declare a fetus's right to life a human right. Given the limited space in this chapter, this discussion of human rights must necessarily leave out some rights that others may consider essential. In addition, I will not extensively cover human rights discussed in other chapters (e.g., freedom of speech). Specifically, this chapter will cover the civil rights of African Americans, Hispanics and Hispanic Americans, Asians and Asian Americans, women, and workers. I will also cover political and social rights, especially the right to be free from excess government power and the right to work. Both points of view, political (governmental) and social (societal), will be addressed. I also profess that I strongly support human rights and am critical when they are withheld from members of society. The episodes discussed in this chapter reveal some of the major tragedies and triumphs of civil rights in America during the recent past.

African American Civil Rights

The turn of the twentieth century was a time of extreme racism. Our founding fathers established this country on the concept that all men were created equal, but huge inequalities existed, both political and social, depending on the color or race of a person. Between the years 1889 and 1903, on the average, mobs either lynched, hanged, burned, or mutilated two African Americans every week. Between 1900 and 1914 there were more than 1,000 lynchings. At this time, whites usually caused riots by entering and rioting in minority neighborhoods. Such riots raged in both the South and the North. One of the most devastating riots occurred in Brownsville, Texas, in 1906. The Brownsville riot started with several African American soldiers in an interracial clash with police and merchants. Similar race riots broke out elsewhere such as, Atlanta, Georgia, in 1906, and Springfield, Illinois, in 1908.

Reaction to the Philippine War

In 1899, the Filipinos revolted and it took three years for the United States to put down the revolt. Many history books tell us that the Filipinos fired the first shot; however, American soldiers later testified that the United States did so. The Filipinos fought for independence; Americans went to war fervently and for different reasons. Senator Albert Beveridge said that the war was about markets. On January 9, 1900, he pointed out that the Philippines was a base at the door of China. When asked about the severity with which the United States was putting down the revolt, he said, "It has been charged that our conduct of the war has been cruel, Senators, it has been the reverse . . . . Senators must remember that we are not dealing with Americans or Europeans. We are dealing with Orientals." In November 1901 the *Philadelphia Ledger* Manila correspondent wrote that the ". . . Filipino as such was little better than a dog. . . ." Mark Twain, in his usual satirical tongue, said of the Philippine War, "We have pacified some thousands of the islanders and buried them . . . [and] subjugated the remaining ten millions by Benevolent Assimilation, which is the pious new name of the musket." Whites called the brown-skinned Filipino "nigger." One volunteer bragged, "Our fighting blood was up, and we all wanted to kill 'niggers' . . . . This shooting human beings beats rabbit hunting all to pieces." Much of labor opposed the war, while others saw opportunity for new markets. Many labor organizations, especially socialist groups, openly opposed the war, noting that the working man of the United States was no better off than the Filipino laborer.

African Americans had very mixed reactions to the war. On the one hand, some felt a need to show that African Americans were just as "American"—courageous and patriotic—as any whites. On the other hand, many African Americans compared their own treatment in the United States with the treatment of the Filipinos. This seething opposition to racism often bubbled into violence. In Tampa, Florida, a race riot broke out when intoxicated white soldiers used an African American child for target practice (to prepare them to kill Filipinos). In Lakeland, Florida, African Americans beat a white drugstore owner when he refused to serve them drinks. Many African American ministers spoke out against sending African American soldiers to fight a war to "enslave" other peoples. African American soldier William Simms wrote a letter home stating, "I was struck by a question a little Filipino boy asked me, which ran about this way: 'Why does the American Negro come . . . to fight . . . He is the same as me and me all the same as you. Why don't you fight those people in America who burn Negroes, that make a beast of you . . . ?'" Four African American regiments served in the Philippines. Many African Americans deserted during the war. The most famous soldier, David Fagan of the Twenty-fourth Infantry, not only deserted but joined the Philippine insurgency forces. He wrought havoc upon the U.S. forces for two years. Yet most African Americans fought with valor and bravery, believing they would be rewarded as heroes, like white soldiers, when they returned home. White Americans, however, shunned African American soldiers when they returned home. Restaurant owners gave returning white soldiers free meals and greeted them with parades. Store owners often greeted African American soldiers with boos. Instead of free meals, store owners told them that they could not eat at white establishments. Though they fought with valor and courage, the policy of putting white officers in charge of African American soldiers continued until after World War II.

The Early Struggle for African American Civil Rights

Many who follow the rise of human rights in the United States look closely at the African American civil rights movement of the twentieth century. The turn of the century saw African Americans not in legal slavery but definitely in

Though African Americans fought with valor through many American wars, the policy of putting white officers in charge of African American soldiers continued until World War II.

social, cultural, and economic slavery. In 1896, the concept of "separate but equal" established in the *Plessy* v. *Ferguson* case was the law of the land. African Americans could be legally excluded as long as there were equal facilities for them to use; for example, whites could have separate schools from African Americans. Whites could even have separate drinking fountains as long as there was one available for African Americans.

At the turn of the century, both African Americans and whites considered ex-slave Booker T. Washington the most prominent African American leader. He founded the Tuskegee Institute for African Americans in Alabama where he emphasized learning crafts and trades. Washington was willing to accept temporary second-class social status in exchange for later economic and social opportunity. Graduates of his Institute, however, faced economic and social discrimination and were unable to use their training. During Washington's leadership African Americans became more disenfranchised, and segregation became more entrenched. Other African American leaders emerged, such as W. E. B. Du Bois, who attacked the accommodationist philosophies of Washington. These new leaders called for a liberal education rather than a vocational education to develop African American leadership. They also began demanding full civil rights for their brothers. In 1905, in Niagara Falls, Ontario, they founded the Niagara Movement. In 1909, the Niagara group

joined with concerned whites to organize the National Association for the Advancement of Colored People (NAACP). The NAACP led the fight for civil rights within the legal system. Six years later it won its first Supreme Court case when the Court struck down the "grandfather clause," a way to keep minorities from registering to vote.

The Exodus North

In 1910, African American workers made only one third of white workers' salaries. Ninety percent of African Americans lived in the South. Poverty among African Americans was a way of life. Furthermore, in the early 1900s, the South fell into a deepening economic depression due to weather disasters and the boll weevil's attack on Southern agriculture. The African American population began an exodus to the North to search for jobs. They thought wages and working conditions would be better in the North than under the subservient system in which they worked in the South. During World War I, when Congress cut off immigration, labor shortages in the North grew even worse. Factory managers sent labor recruiters to the South to find low-wage-earning African Americans. Between 1910 and 1920, more than 500,000 African Americans moved to the North. The African American population jumped from 5,000 to 41,000 in Detroit, 8,000 to 34,000 in Cleveland, 44,000 to 110,000 in Chicago, and 92,000 to 152,000 in New York. Because of labor shortages,

by 1920, most African Americans worked in factories rather than in domestic and personal service.

Although wages and even job prospects were better in the North than in the economically ravaged South, conditions were still deplorable. Segregation and discrimination ran rampant. Whites forced African Americans to live in overcrowded and run-down houses and apartments. Employers paid them poorly. They were the last hired and the first fired.

Northern newspapers and home owners resisted this "African American invasion." In Chicago, hundreds of whites organized the Hyde Park Improvement Protective Club. It announced that African Americans could live only in certain "districts" and warned real estate agents not to sell homes to African Americans in white neighborhoods. In 1917, the Chicago Real Estate Board complained that African Americans were pouring in at the rate of ten thousand per month and would soon destroy property values. Later that year, bombers destroyed the homes of several African American families. The next year saw more bombs following a letter that stated, "We are going to BLOW these FLATS TO HELL and if you don't want to go with them you had better move at once." In 1919, terrorists bombed offices of real estate agents who sold homes to African Americans in white sections of town. White gangs posted notices promising "to get all niggers on the Fourth of July." African Americans began preparing to defend themselves, but all stayed peaceful until July 27. At a public swimming pool where city officials allowed African Americans to swim in a small section of the pool only, one African American child drowned after drifting into the white side of the pool. African American witnesses testified that white boys hit him with rocks. Upon hearing this, a few African Americans attacked several whites. In retaliation, white gangs beat some African Americans who were walking in a white neighborhood, and a general riot broke out. Whites entered African American neighborhoods and attacked African Americans. White gangs attacked African Americans in sections reserved for them on streetcars. Rioting continued for a week and finally the state militia restored order. Before it was all over, 23 African Americans and 15 whites were killed, while 342 African Americans and 178 whites were injured.

World War I and the Great Depression

Many African American leaders opposed World War I. A. Philip Randolph, an African American socialist, argued that we should first win democracy for all Americans before we fight for democracy for the rest of the world. Under the war fervor of patriotism, the Ku Klux Klan made a comeback, moving extensively into the North for the first time. By 1924, it had over 4.5 million members. African Americans were its main target.

Nevertheless, as in the Philippine War, most African Americans supported the war and volunteered for duty. The military commissioned fourteen hundred African American officers, while two hundred thousand African Americans fought in the war to end all wars.

After the war, the typical postwar depression set in. Veterans needed work, so employers fired African Americans to make room for white workers. White gangs and local Ku Klux Klan chapters helped insure that whites would get preferential treatment. Racists launched a wave of terror against African Americans. Historians have called the summer of 1919 the "Red Summer," as blood flowed in the streets of America. African Americans became more disenchanted with their position in society.

Into this atmosphere stepped Jamaican-born Marcus Garvey. He founded the Universal Negro Improvement Association and established a branch in Harlem, New York. By 1920, U.S. membership had reached several hundred thousand; the association became the largest African American movement up to that time. Garvey called for the return of African Americans to Africa. He pushed forward the idea of "race pride" and the rediscovery of African heritage. He helped develop a race consciousness among young African Americans. He was largely responsible for the "Harlem Renaissance," in which African American talent in music, literature, and arts flowered. African American journals and newspapers began publication. Yet the movement fell apart in 1927 when the government arrested Garvey for mail fraud and deported him back to Jamaica.

The Great Depression and the New Deal

The great depression of the rural areas of the 1920s quickly moved into the cities. It hit African Americans the hardest: their unemployment rate was two to three times that of whites. When governments established public assistance programs, African Americans usually received less than whites. They often had to wait until after whites had eaten in soup lines; and often, if there was not enough food for all, they went hungry. As their economic plight intensified, African American organizations arose to help. One major organization was in St. Louis, where the St. Louis Urban

The administration of Franklin Delano Roosevelt made sure that African Americans shared in New Deal Programs. Yet, for all of the government programs, African Americans were little better-off than before the Depression.

League established a national movement in 1929 called "Jobs for Negroes." The league boycotted department chains that catered to African American customers but only hired white salespeople. In 1936, the National Negro Congress was founded, and the next year the Congress formed the Southern Negro Youth Congress.

In the late 1920s and early 1930s much of America turned away from the Republican Party, not only blaming it for the Great Depression but accusing it of being insensitive to citizens' needs. This reaction was even greater among African Americans, who voted heavily for Democrats for the first time in the 1928 elections. In 1930, President Herbert Hoover blundered politically when he nominated John J. Parker to fill a vacancy on the United States Supreme Court. Parker was a man with acknowledged anti-African American views. In response, Americans, led by the NAACP, loudly condemned his nomination, and the Senate voted it down. The stage was set. The Republican Party became known as "anti-Negro" among African Americans. In the 1932 presidential election, African Americans voted overwhelmingly for Franklin Delano Roosevelt.

President Roosevelt strengthened his positions with African Americans with his administration's seeming attention to their plight. He had an advisory board sometimes called his "black cabinet," which included economist Robert Weaver; executive secretary of the National Urban League;

In 1941 President Roosevelt issued Executive Order 8802, which banned discrimination in government or defense industries.

vants, and migrant workers in the South, African Americans did not qualify for new social entitlements such as social security, minimum wages, or unemployment insurance. In the North, as usual, employers hired whites first and African Americans last. This seemed unfair to African American leaders. A. Phillip Randolph, socialist leader and head of the Brotherhood of Sleeping Car Porters, threatened an African American protest march on Washington in 1941. To head off the march, Roosevelt issued Executive Order 8802, which banned discrimination in government or defense industries. The order also established the Fair Employment Practices Committee (FEPC) to investigate complaints. However, the FEPC was toothless when it came to enforcement.

Wages did go up for some African Americans and some individuals found more jobs during the war. Another mass migration of African Americans from the South began. One and one-half million African Americans journeyed to the North for better jobs and housing. However, serious housing shortages occurred in African American parts of major cities and racial tension increased. Again race riots broke out. One of most serious riots occurred in Detroit in 1943, resulting in several deaths.

World War II

During World War II, many African Americans fought, and although fighting units remained segregated, the U.S. Army began to integrate officer training. Fighting against the racist regime of Adolph Hitler and Nazi Germany caused intellectual conflicts among many Americans, and racism was quickly becoming "un-American." Soon, Benjamin Davis became the United States' first African American general when the U.S. Army promoted him to brigadier general. In 1948, President Harry Truman continued the trend by ordering the integration of all military forces. He also issued an executive order mandating a policy of "fair employment throughout the Federal establishment, without discrimination because of race, color, religion or national origin." At the beginning of the Korean War, African Americans and whites fought and died side by side.

After World War II and after the hideous details of the Holocaust became known, the drive for African American civil and human rights moved forward rapidly in the political and social

Eugene Jones; and National Youth Administration's Director of Negro Affairs, Mary McLeod Bethune. The Roosevelt administration made sure that African Americans shared in New Deal programs. The New Deal provided low-income public housing for African American families as well as white ones. The Works Project Administration (WPA), National Youth Administration (NYA), and the Civilian Conservation Corps (CCC) helped African Americans find jobs, especially young African Americans who wanted to continue their education. The Federal Writers Project supported African American authors as well as white ones. Labor began to make inroads under the Roosevelt administration, and in the 1930s the Congress of Industrial Organizations (CIO) was established. They organized large numbers of African Americans. By 1940, labor had organized over 200,000 African Americans. Yet, for all of the government programs, African Americans were little better-off than they had been before the Depression.

The New Deal did not end the Depression. As a result, race riots exploded across the United States. One of the worst of these riots was in Harlem in 1935. Over ten thousand African Americans took to the streets. The government countered with seven hundred policemen to quell the rioting. Beginning in the early 1940s, World War II did what the New Deal could not do: it jump-started the economy. Jobs became more plentiful, but as sharecroppers, tenant farmers, domestic ser-

African American soldiers,
Buffalo Division, 1945.

arenas. In 1947, Jackie Robinson became the first African American baseball player to break the color, or race, barrier. The race barrier had been broken in some other sports, such as professional basketball and professional football, but at the time most people considered them minor sports. Jesse Owens had allowed Americans to laugh in the face of Hitler and other racists before World War II, as a result of his triumphs at the Berlin Olympics of 1936, and Joe Louis, professional boxer of the 1930s, had shown that an African American could be the best boxer in the world. But, professional baseball was the last bastion of white supremacy in American sports. It would take many years for African Americans to rise in the coaching and administration of sports franchises, but the precedents had been set.

The Demise of "Separate but Equal"

The NAACP continued to win cases in the courts. The association attacked restrictive covenants that prohibited African Americans from living in white neighborhoods and attacked discrimination in public transportation. Their work led to the most important civil rights case in our time, *Brown* v. *Board of Education of Topeka* (Kansas) in 1954. This case overturned the *Plessy* decision of "separate but equal." A young lawyer, Thurgood Marshall, later to become one of the most influential justices of the United States Supreme Court, argued the case for integration of public schools. The Court ruled that "separate but equal" was not equal and began a series of court-ordered integration rulings that would change the face of America. Chief Justice Earl Warren, writing for the majority, said, "To separate . . . [African American children] from others of similar age and qualifications solely because of their race generates a feeling of inferiority as to their status in the community that may affect their hearts and minds in a way unlikely ever to be undone. . . . In the field of public education the doctrine of 'separate but equal' has no place. Separate education facilities are inherently unequal." The next year, in a supplementary ruling, the Court instructed lower courts to enforce the *Brown* decision "with all deliberate speed."

All across America, African Americans rose up against racism and discrimination. They organized strikes, sit-ins, and demonstrations. They created economic pressure through boycotts. Although these measures were extremely effective, African Americans made the most gains locally as some communities ended separation of public facilities, swimming pools, parks, and the like. African Americans were willing to tough it out against the odds, but the opposition was entrenched: As George Wallace, Governor of Alabama, put it, "Segregation now, segregation tomorrow, segregation forever!" Curiously, a media event unrelated to civil rights would have a huge effect on the national impact of the civil rights movement.

The fledgling television networks had been competing against huge movie conglomerates and studios for America's entertainment dollar. Many thought that television could not handle the competition and would soon end in ruin. However, in the 1950s, the networks hit upon an extremely popular format: the game shows. Millions of people sat in front of their televisions watching shows such as "21," "The $64,000 Challenge," and "Dotto." On the show "21," in December 1956, an unlikely hero, Herb Stempel, kept coming back each week to win more and more money. Unbeknownst to the audience, producers rigged the shows, and contestants were prompted with the answers ahead of time. When the producers of the show told Herb that another contestant would replace him, Herb grew angry. He told newspapers of the hoax and ultimately testified before Congress. Scandal hit the networks. Disgusted that they had been duped, millions of people turned off their televisions sets. To counter the hoax that they had perpetrated on the American public, the major networks established

the modern-day evening newscast, vowing that they would hold to the highest standards of integrity. Each night, news reporters in the field reported live and taped newscasts of breaking news. In the late 1950s and the early 1960s, the civil rights movement was the breaking news. The networks beamed news into the homes of millions. Citizens saw pictures of police beating demonstrators as well as peaceful and violent marches for freedom. The civil rights movement and mass media made a powerful and moving team.

On December 1, 1955, Rosa Parks, an African American woman, quietly refused to give up her seat to a white man on a Montgomery, Alabama, bus. This began the famous bus boycott of 1955–1956 led by Martin Luther King Jr., minister of the Dexter Avenue Baptist Church. The boycott ended in November 1956 when the U.S. Supreme Court declared unconstitutional the segregation of public transportation facilities. When asked later why she refused to give up her seat, Ms. Parks said she was tired. King said, "There comes a time when people get tired. We are here . . . to say to those who have mistreated us so long that we are tired— tired of being segregated and humiliated; tired of being kicked about by the brutal feet of oppression." By 1957, King had established the Southern Christian Leadership Conference. The first civil rights legislation passed in the United States since 1875, the Civil Rights Act of 1957, passed both houses of Congress, and President Eisenhower signed it into law. The act gave the national government the power to prevent minorities from being denied the vote. By 1958, over 1 million more African American voters had registered.

In 1960, in Greensboro, North Carolina, the famous Woolworth lunch counter sit-in began. Woolworth managers refused service to African American youths. The youths promised to "sit-in" until the national chain relented. This was not the first time African Americans had used sit-ins at national chain lunch counters; in fact, they had used them successfully in the past to force other national chain stores to serve African Americans. But, this time, the nightly news television cameras beamed the sit-in to television sets all across the country. With the success of this sit-in, student leaders formed the Student Nonviolent Coordinating Committee and began sit-ins all across the country. In 1961, African Americans teamed with sympathetic whites to begin what they called "freedom rides." Freedom riders would board interstate-bound buses in Alabama and Mississippi to force desegregation. Racist mobs violently jerked freedom riders from their buses and brutally clubbed many in front of reporters and television cameras. African Americans, echoing Rosa Parks, decided that they were "tired" and wanted "freedom now." To recognize the Emancipation Proclamation Centennial, they came up with the slogan, "Freedom Now." The civil rights movement also had the support of the administration. In a civil rights message to Congress, John F. Kennedy in 1963 called for equal rights for African Americans and said, "No one has been barred on account of his race from fighting or dying for America—There are no "white" or "colored" signs on the foxholes or graveyards of battle."

In the spring of 1963, Martin Luther King Jr. led a civil rights march in Birmingham, Alabama. Night after night, the evening news showed scenes of police and firemen using vicious guard dogs and fire hoses to break up demonstrations. Police arrested African Americans en masse. In the fall of 1963, terrorists killed four African American girls when they threw a bomb into a Birmingham church.

The March on Washington

The civil rights movement ended with a bang in 1963, when civil rights leader Bayard Rustin organized a march in Washington that included 250,000 people. Here Martin Luther King Jr. stood in front of the Lincoln Memorial and was immortalized as he galvanized America with his "I Have A Dream" speech. Not only were hundreds of thousands of people in attendance but millions of people watched on television. King reminded them that although Lincoln had delivered the Emancipation Proclamation over 100 years before, African Americans were still not free.

The march convinced Congress to pass the Civil Rights Act of 1964. This was one of the most extensive civil rights bills ever to become law. It forbade discrimination in employment, voting, and public facilities and gave the attorney general power to deny federal funds to those practicing discrimination. The states ratified the Twenty-fourth Amendment, banning poll taxes the same year.

Efforts intensified in 1965 to register African Americans to vote. The effort in Selma, Alabama, typified the struggle. Millions of people sat in

The civil rights movement had the support of the Kennedy administration.

front of their television sets and watched as police used whips, tear gas, fire hoses, clubs, and dogs to attack thousands of African Americans demonstrating for equal access to the polls. Police arrested thousands. Nevertheless, the heart of America seemed to soften and the demonstrations led to national sympathy and support. John Lewis of the Student Nonviolent Coordinating Committee and Martin Luther King Jr. led over 40,000 protestors from all across the nation on a march from Selma to Alabama's state capital, Montgomery, to protest their treatment. Congress then passed the 1965 Voting Rights Act, which eliminated all qualifying tests based on discrimination and required the appointment of federal registrars.

The Black Power Movement

Though African Americans advanced politically, in African American inner-city America emotions seethed. While the right to vote was important to them, so too were the issues of poor housing, high unemployment, poor educational facilities, police brutality and insensitivity, and a lack of understanding for inner-city minorities. Beginning in the 1960s, the African American community seemed to develop two classes. Between 1960 and 1982, the percentage of African American families earning the equivalent of $25,000 (in 1982 dollars) went from 10 percent to 25 percent. But an "African American underclass" also developed. In 1980, while African Americans constituted only 12

Martin Luther King Jr.'s "I Have a Dream"

I say to you today, my friends, that in spite of the difficulties and frustrations of the moment, I still have a dream. It is a dream deeply rooted in the American dream.

I have a dream that one day this nation will rise up and live out the true meaning of its creed: "We hold these truths to be self-evident: that all men are created equal."

I have a dream that one day on the red hills of Georgia the sons of former slaves and the sons of former slave owners will be able to sit down together at a table of brotherhood.

I have a dream that one day even the state of Mississippi, a desert state, sweltering with the heat of injustice and oppression, will be transformed into an oasis of freedom and justice.

I have a dream that my four children will one day live in a nation where they will not be judged by the color of their skin but by the content of their character. I have a dream today.

I have a dream that one day the state of Alabama, whose governor's lips are presently dripping with the words of interposition and nullification, will be transformed into a situation where little black boys and black girls will be able to join hands with little white boys and white girls and walk together as sisters and brothers. I have a dream today.

I have a dream that one day every valley shall be exalted, every hill and mountain shall be made low, the rough places will be made plain, and the crooked places will be made straight, and the glory of the Lord shall be revealed, and all flesh shall see it together.

This is our hope. This is the faith with which I return to the South. With this faith we will be able to hew out of the mountain of despair a stone of hope.

With this faith we will be able to transform the jangling discords of our nation into a beautiful symphony of brotherhood. With this faith we will be able to work together, to pray together, to struggle together, to go to jail together, to stand up for freedom together, knowing that we will be free one day.

This will be the day when all of God's children will be able to sing with a new meaning, "My country, 'tis of thee, sweet land of liberty, of thee I sing. Land where my fathers died, land of the pilgrim's pride, from every mountainside, let freedom ring."

And if America is to be a great nation this must become true. So let freedom ring from the prodigious hilltops of New Hampshire. Let freedom ring from the mighty mountains of New York. Let freedom ring from the heightening Alleghenies of Pennsylvania!

Let freedom ring from the snowcapped Rockies of Colorado!

Let freedom ring from the curvaceous peaks of California!

But not only that; let freedom ring from Stone Mountain of Georgia!

Let freedom ring from Lookout Mountain of Tennessee!

Let freedom ring from every hill and every molehill of Mississippi. From every mountainside, let freedom ring.

When we let freedom ring, when we let it ring from every village and every hamlet, from every state and every city, we will be able to speed up that day when all of God's children, black men and white men, Jews and Gentiles, Protestants and Catholics, will be able to join hands and sing in the words of the old Negro spiritual, "Free at last! Free at last! Thank God Almighty, we are free at last!"

percent of the population, 43 percent of all welfare families were African American. The number of single-parent female-headed families between 1960 and 1980 doubled to 40 percent, as compared with 10 to 12 percent for white families. The issues causing the class split seethed to the surface in the summers of 1965 to 1968 as costly riots. Rioters destroyed white-owned as well as African American-owned property. Pitched battles between police and African American youth occurred. They cost hundreds of lives and millions of dollars of property. Riots occurred all across the nation, including

The March on Washington in 1963 united many African Americans in their push for civil rights, but in the years that followed young African American militant leaders began to challenge Martin Luther King Jr.'s nonmilitant views.

Chicago, Newark, Detroit, New York, and Watts (Los Angeles, California). The worst riot was in Watts, where 35 people died and property damage reached 200 million dollars.

Young African American militant leaders began to challenge Martin Luther King Jr.'s non-militant views. They formed organizations such as the Black Panthers, the Deacons for Defense, and the Revolutionary Action Movement. Leaders like Stokely Carmichael and H. Rap Brown called for a more activist role especially among African American youth. Stokely Carmichael called for "black power." The militant leaders accused King of being too soft and of being a lackey of whites wishing to keep African Americans repressed. Malcolm X, a militant minister in the Nation of Islam (Black Muslims), took up the call for black power and advocated violence if necessary to achieve African American aims. In 1964 he declared, "I don't see any American dream. . . . I see an American nightmare." He broke with the leader of the Nation of Islam, Elijah Muhammad, and founded the Organization of Afro-American Unity. He succinctly expressed his goals when he wrote, "The common goal of 22 million Afro-Americans is respect as human beings, the God-given right to be a human being. Our common goal is to obtain the human rights that America has been denying us. We can never get civil rights in America until our human rights are first restored. We will never be recognized as citizens there until we are first recognized as humans." Assassins mysteriously cut him down in early 1965.

Young African American militant leaders formed organizations such as the Black Panthers, the Deacons for Defense, and the Revolutionary Action Movement.

The Vietnam War

Like wars before it, the Vietnam War divided African Americans. Martin Luther King Jr. unpopularly opposed the war. He felt military leaders put African Americans in harm's way more often than whites. He felt that money spent on the war could better be served solving domestic problems. More important, he came to the belief that if he proposed nonviolent means for African Americans to defeat racial injustice, it would be hypocritical to support violent means in Vietnam. On one hand, militant leaders of the civil rights movement attacked him; on the other hand, he was criticized for his views on Vietnam. The relationship between poverty and violence concerned King. He came to believe that without the reduction of poverty, African American gains would be minimal. He began to look at freedom from poverty as a human right. In 1967, he said, "I watched that dream turn into a nightmare as I moved through the ghettos of the nation and saw African American brothers and sisters perishing on a lonely island of poverty in the midst of a vast ocean of material prosperity, and saw the nation doing nothing to grapple with the Negroes' problem of poverty."

The Assassination of Martin Luther King Jr.

In 1968, Reverend King went to Memphis, Tennessee, in support of sanitation workers with labor troubles. The last thing Martin Luther King Jr. did was to help organize the "Poor People's Campaign." This was to be a march in Washington to emphasize the relationship between poverty and interurban violence. But he did not make the march. On April 4, 1968, in Memphis, James Earl Ray cut him down with a sniper's bullet (some dispute over Ray's actual role in the assassination still continues). Tears and blood fell all across the nation as marches and riots broke out in the cities. Mourners buried him in Atlanta. They inscribed part of his "I Have A Dream" speech on his tombstone: "Free at Last, Free at Last, Thank God Almighty, I'm Free at Last." The civil rights movement continued without King, but it did so at a much slower pace. The pace of the strides made under King have not since been duplicated.

By the 1970s, many of the civil rights movement's legislative and political goals had been achieved. President Lyndon B. Johnson's War on Poverty and many state programs had furthered antidiscriminatory goals. Governor Jimmy Carter in 1971 said, "No poor, rural, weak, or black person should ever again have to bear the additional burden of being deprived of the opportunity for an education, a job, or simple justice." Nevertheless, while laws finally put African Americans on an equal footing with whites, opportunities for advancement did not readily materialize. Civil rights statutes took a new direction. Affirmative action programs were set

Martin Luther King Jr. believed that without the reduction of poverty, African American gains would be minimal.

up to achieve the intent of civil rights legislation. These programs, often taking the form of quotas, allowed specific minorities the same opportunities as whites. White America and some in the African American community denounced affirmative action programs, calling them "reverse discrimination" programs and accusing the government of discriminating against whites. However, these programs provided many opportunities for African Americans to move into the middle and upper socioeconomic classes. However, since the *Bakke* decision in 1978 by the Supreme Court, *(Regents of University of California* v. *Bakke),* the courts struck down affirmative action programs.

African American unrest increased. Not all leaders of the civil rights movement were happy. Dick Gregory, activist and comedian, said of

African American civil rights, "What black folks are given in the U.S. on the installment plan, as in civil-rights bills [are] not to be confused with *human rights,* which are the dignity, stature, humanity, respect, and freedom belonging to all people by right of their birth." African Americans proportionately were accused and convicted of more crimes than whites. Many African Americans accused the government of stepping backward in time when required to enforcing their rights.

There was also a white backlash. Vice President Spiro T. Agnew said, "Intellectual and spiritual leaders hailed the cause of civil rights and gave little thought to where the civil disobedience road might end. But defiance of the law, even for the best reasons, opens a tiny hole in the dike and soon a trickle becomes a flood. . . . And while no thinking person denies that social injustice exists, no thinking person can condone any group's, for any reason, taking justice into its own hands. Once this is permitted, democracy dies; for democracy is sustained through one great premise: the premise that civil rights are balanced by civil responsibilities." Many white conservative politicians said that African Americans had become victims of government entitlement programs that encouraged minorities to stay in poverty and become wards of the state. They went on to say that government gave too many advantages to one group of people, that is, African Americans. Neither side seemed to trust the other. This impasse boiled over with the Rodney King incident of March 3, 1991.

Rodney King led police on a high-speed chase and when stopped resisted arrest. Four white Los Angeles policemen subdued him viciously, mostly by beating him with their night sticks, and a witness caught the beating on videotape. The City of Los Angeles charged the officers with assault and brought them to trial. Many African American citizens believed that despite what seemed to be overwhelming evidence of the videotape (shown over and over on television news shows), an American jury would not convict the officers. On April 29, 1992, after a change of venue to a predominantly white community, the jury acquitted the four officers of most charges. Many African Americans claimed to have lost faith in the American system of justice. That evening riots broke out in many cities, but the most severe one occurred in Los Angeles. It lasted for more than two days, and whole neighborhoods were destroyed. Forty-nine people were killed and over 1,400 injured. Rioters set over 4,000 fires and destroyed or damaged nearly 5,300 buildings.

Today, polls show that most African Americans do not believe that government officials, especially police, will treat them fairly or equally. They feel that their votes mean little and often believe that they are not represented at the legislative level. They believe that justice in the courts will not be meted out fairly to African Americans. This belief was evident in the trial of O. J. Simpson, who was accused of murdering his wife and her friend. Many more African Americans viewed Simpson as innocent than did their white counterparts. Proportionately, more African Americans than whites believed that the police actually planted evidence to make Simpson look guilty. Many African Americans have even lost faith in their longtime friend, the Supreme Court. In 1996, it handed down a series of decisions that struck down Congressional districts drawn along racial lines to insure African American representation.

Asian American Civil Rights

Much like African Americans, Asian Americans have fought an uphill battle to have their civil and human rights recognized. For Asian Americans as well, assimilation into the population has been much more difficult because of physical characteristics that set them apart from most European Americans.

Thousands of Chinese fled to the United States for economic security, most during the middle to latter 1800s. Railroad building was critical to Chinese immigration as many immigrants were brought here specifically to work on the railroad construction gangs. Others served as domestic servants, cooks, and cleaners. Racism and discrimination met them at every turn, and by the middle of the 1880s, Congress had passed the Chinese Exclusion Acts, which prohibited the flow of legal immigration to the United States. In the 1890s, Congress passed a law that only allowed "white" people to become naturalized citizens. By the turn of the twentieth century, Chinese Americans had their dreams of assimilation into America's so-called "melting pot" crushed. (These events are explained more fully in chapters 4 and 7.)

In the early 1900s many states passed laws prohibiting Asian Americans from owning land. The first was the California Alien Land Law of 1920. By 1925, twelve other states had passed similar laws (Washington, Arizona, Oregon, Idaho, Nebraska, Texas, Kansas, Louisiana, Montana, New Mexico, Minnesota, and Missouri). During World War II, three more states, Utah, Wyoming, and Arkansas, also passed them. Legislatures mainly aimed these laws at Japanese Americans, but the laws of course, also affected the Chinese. Most Americans, especially those that were hostilely racist, saw no difference between Japanese, Chinese, Korean, or any person of Asian descent. In 1922, the Supreme Court upheld the law prohibiting Asian Americans to become citizens in *Ozawa* v. *United States*. Chinese Americans were mainly segregated into various Chinatowns across the United States, especially in San Francisco, Los Angeles, and New York. They struggled, often at subsistence wages, in sweatshops, restaurants, and laundries, and at other menial-labor jobs.

A small turning point for Chinese Americans came on December 8, 1941, when both the United States and China declared war on Japan and became allies. Young Chinese Americans enthusiastically joined the military. Twenty-two percent of all Chinese males entered the military; 13,449 Chinese either volunteered or were drafted during World War II. As one Chinese American put it: for the first time we "were accepted by Americans as being friends . . ." and finally "we became part of an American dream."

Just as important were labor opportunities that occurred during the war effort. Thousands of Chinese Americans landed defense plant jobs. They found defense jobs at bases in California, Washington, New York, and as far south as Mississippi. For the first time, Chinese women found decent-paying jobs.

Reports of valiant last stands by the Chinese military fighting against the Japanese and the loss of thousands, even millions, of Chinese lives in China reached the American public. Soon Americans were sympathetic to the plight of the "valiant and brave" Chinese American. The Japanese propaganda machine had a field day by pointing out the contradictions between our "separate but equal" positions and the Chinese Exclusion Laws. President Roosevelt supported the repeal of these laws. He wrote, "China is our ally. . . . For many long years she stood alone in the fight against aggression. Today we fight at her side. She has continued her gallant struggle against very great odds." In 1943, Congress agreed and repealed the exclusion laws. President Roosevelt said, "By repeal of the Chinese exclusion laws, we can correct a historic mistake and silence the distorted Japanese propaganda." However, Congress still only allowed 105 Chinese to immigrate to the United States annually. This was a piteously low number; nevertheless, the immigration gates were finally opened a crack. After nearly one hundred years, Chinese not only had a chance to immigrate to the United States but could also become naturalized citizens. Soon after the war, in 1948, the Supreme Court struck down the Alien Land Laws as violating the Fourteenth Amendment equal protection clause. In *Oyama* v. *California* (1948) the Court said that the laws were "nothing more than outright racial discrimination" and pointed to the United Nations' Universal Declaration of Human Rights as it asked the question, How could the United States be faithful to the Declaration if it barred land ownership based on race?

Yet, today, the vast majority of Chinese Americans are little better-off. Fifty-five percent of the Chinese population in New York Chinatown speaks little or no English. Chinese women have become the major source of "seamstress labor" in the New York City garment industry. In San Francisco, Chinese immigrant women produce almost half of all garments manufactured in the American garment industry. Most work for minimum wage in garment sweatshops.

The Japanese American story is even more tragic. They, like the Chinese, came to the United States in large numbers during the late 1800s. A huge influx of Japanese immigrants occurred between 1898 to 1907. They arrived mainly in the western United States and especially in California and Washington State. By 1910, Japanese Americans made up the largest minority group in Washington State. They found only degrading work and faced extreme racial prejudice. They originally came to make money and then return to Japan, but most soon determined that this would be their final home. They tried very hard to integrate into American society. In most cases, this did not occur; however, a few immigrants became very successful. Kinji Ushijima, a labor contractor better known as George Shima, became a millionaire. Before he died in 1926 with an estate worth over $15 million, he purchased a house in a fashionable white residential area in Berkeley, California. Protestors picketed the streets. The local newspapers ran headlines such as "Yellow Peril in College Town" and "Jap Invades Fashionable Quarters." But Kinji refused to move. He lived in his house in white America until his death of natural causes.

Abiko Kyutaro became the largest labor contractor in California and helped found the Japanese American Industrial Corporation. He supplied cheap labor to agriculture, railroads, and mining companies. He became a crusader for the integration of Japanese into American society. In a newspaper he published called the *Nichibei Shimbun,* he encouraged Japanese to settle on farms, be productive, and raise families. He created an actual model of this farming philosophy in 1906, when he began the American Land and Produce Company. The company developed 3,200 acres of desert land in the San Joaquin Valley of California and turned them into farms. He called the settlement the Yamato (or New Japan) Colony. The colony set up irrigation ditches and planted grapes, fruit trees, and alfalfa for hay. By 1917, it was a success. Over 40 farmers settled there. But their hard work and success did not lead to acceptance; rather, it led to a backlash against these new competitive foreigners.

The federal government soon passed exclusion laws directed at Japanese immigration. In 1905, white farmers who felt threatened by the success of Japanese American farmers established the Asiatic Exclusion League in San Francisco. The following year, the San Francisco school board segregated Japanese American children from white children. In 1907, President Theodore Roosevelt, bowing to calls to limit Japanese immigration, pressured Japan to stop allowing Japanese to emigrate from Japan to the United States. This resulted in the "Gentleman's Agreement," in which the Japanese government agreed to stop issuing passports to Japanese laborers wishing to come to the United States. In many states, white farmers burned Japanese farms. In Anacortes, Washington, citizens asked the city council to force companies to replace Japanese cannery workers with white workers. States passed the Alien Land Laws in the 1920s. In 1922, the *Ozawa* case ended the naturalization hopes of Japanese Americans. What was greeted as the final nail in the coffin of Japanese integration into society came in 1924. Congress passed a new immigration law prohibiting the immigration of any group of people ineligible for citizenship. They aimed this at Asian Americans, more specifically at Japanese immigrants. The first generation of Japanese, known as the Issei, believe that there was no future for them in this land of opportunity. They hoped that their children, the second generation, called the Nisei, might have a future.

The Nisei were born in America and therefore were citizens by birth. Because their children, the Nisei, spoke English and understood American customs, the Issei hoped that the Nisei would be their ambassadors to America. But white children sometimes attacked Japanese American children on the streets on their way to school: They kicked, beat, and spat upon them. They told them to go back to Japan and called them "chinks" and "Japs." Never-

theless, the Issei emphasized education and a strong work ethic. Most Nisei graduated from high school and their average educational level was two years of college, yet even those graduating from college could not find jobs in white America. The social system relegated them to finding jobs in Japanese sections of town, such as Little Tokyo in Los Angeles. Few could find jobs that matched their training; instead, they worked in restaurants and as store clerks. The Nisei had the highest educational level of any group of menial laborers in the world. Furthermore, the Nisei were torn between their parents' culture and affinity for Japan and their own cultural identity as Americans. They were Americans. They dressed as Americans. They talked as Americans. Their interests were not haiku and calligraphy but rather big bands, *Life* magazine, Bing Crosby, and Humphrey Bogart. They recognized their ancestry but were truly American patriots. Their world came crashing down on December 7, 1941.

In the 1940 census, there were 126,947 Japanese Americans. Sixty-three percent of these were citizens. In addition there were nearly 158,000 Japanese Americans living in the territory of Hawaii. On December 7, 1941, Japan attacked Pearl Harbor. That day, President Roosevelt ordered the Federal Bureau of Investigation (FBI) to arrest dangerous enemy aliens, including Japanese, German, and Italian nationals. Before the end of the day 737 Japanese Americans had been arrested. Four days later, the FBI detained 1,370 Japanese Americans considered "dangerous enemy aliens."

Immediately after the bombing, racist feelings against the Japanese that had often been hidden below the surface broke out openly. Japanese parents feared sending their children to school. Japanese Americans were beaten on the streets. Calls for the arrest of all Japanese sympathizers grew loud. Most considered all Japanese Americans enemy sympathizers. Many Americans considered all Japanese Americans disloyal and an internal military threat, not because they participated in antiwar efforts but because of the color of their skin. On December 22, the Agriculture Committee of the Los Angeles Chamber of Commerce called for the "absolute federal control" of all Japanese nationals. By year's end, the government ordered all enemy aliens to surrender any "contraband" that they might possess. Americans made more calls for control and even detention of

Japanese Americans. On January 6, 1942, all Japanese Americans registered for selective service were reclassified as 4C (enemy aliens). The military services discharged many Japanese American soldiers already in the military. They transferred others to menial and "safe positions" such as kitchen detail. Leland Ford, congressman from the Los Angeles area district, went to Secretary of State Cordell Hull demanding the removal of all Japanese Americans from the West Coast for fear of aiding and abetting possible invading forces from Japan. He said, "I do not believe that we could be any too strict in our consideration of the Japanese in the face of the treacherous way in which they do things."

Local organizations and newspapers came out opposed to Japanese. Radio stations such as the *Mutual Broadcasting Company* called for their removal from the West and Hawaii. The *Los Angeles Times* racistly editorialized that "a viper is nonetheless a viper wherever the egg is hatched—so a Japanese American, born of Japanese parents—grows up to be a Japanese, not an American."

Two months preceding the bombing of Pearl Harbor, Curtis B. Munson, under orders from President Roosevelt, carried out an investigation on the loyalties of Japanese Americans. He classified them into four separate groups. Of the Issei, the first generation, mainly aged 55 years and older, he wrote that they were:

> considerably weakened in their loyalty to Japan. . . . They expect to die here [in the United States]. They are quite fearful of being put in a concentration camp. Many would take out American citizenship if allowed to do so. . . . The Issei have to break with their religion, their god and Emperor, their family, their ancestors and their after-life in order to be loyal to the United States. . . . Yet they do break, and send their boys off to the Army with pride and tears. They are good neighbors.

Of the second generation "Nisei," those mostly educated in the United States and under the age of 30 years, he wrote:

> . . . in spite of discrimination against them and a certain amount of insults accumulated through the years from irresponsible elements, [they] show a pathetic eagerness to be Americans. They are in constant conflict with the orthodox, well disciplined family life of their elders. . . . There are still Japanese in the United States who will tie dynamite round their waist and make a human bomb out of themselves. We grant this, but today they are few. [The least likely] . . .

World War II anti-Japanese propaganda poster.

from a Japanese standpoint are the Nisei. They are universally estimated from 90 to 98 percent loyal to the United States . . . The Nisei are pathetically eager to show this loyalty. They are not Japanese in culture. They are foreigners to Japan. . . . Some gesture of protection or wholehearted acceptance of this group would go a long way to swinging them away from any last romantic hankering after old Japan. They are not oriental or mysterious, they are very American and are of a proud, self-respecting race suffering from a little inferiority complex and a lack of contact with the white boys they went to school with. They are eager for this contact and to work alongside them.

Others of the second generation were known as Kibei. Kibei received part or all of their education back in Japan. Munson wrote of them:

> . . . the Kibei are considered the most dangerous element and closer to the Issei with special reference to those who received their early education in Japan. It must be noted, however, that many of those who visited Japan subsequent to their early American education come back with added loyalty to the United States. In fact, it is a saying that all a Nisei needs is a trip to Japan to make a loyal American out of him. The American educated Japanese is a boor in Japan and treated as a foreigner. . . .

The third generation, the Sansei, were too young and not a security threat. However, Munson also issued a report on the Hawaiian Japanese. In it he wrote:

> . . . the Hawaiian Japanese does not suffer from the same inferiority complex or feel the same mistrust of the whites that he does on the mainland. While it is seldom on the mainland that

you find even a college-educated Japanese-American citizen who talks to you wholly openly until you have gained his confidence, this is far from the case in Hawaii. Many young Japanese there are fully as open and frank and at ease with a white as white boys are. In a word Hawaii is more of a melting pot because there are more brown skins to melt—Japanese, Hawaiian, Chinese and Filipino. It is interesting to note that there has been absolutely no bad feeling between the Japanese and the Chinese in the islands due to the Japanese-Chinese war. Why should they be any worse toward us?

Munson's conclusions were clear:

The story was all the same. There is no Japanese "problem" on the Coast. There will be no armed uprising of Japanese. There will undoubtedly be some sabotage finance by Japan . . . executed largely by imported agents. . . .There is far more danger from Communists . . . on the Coast than there is from Japanese. The Japanese here is almost exclusively a farmer, a fisherman or a small businessman.

Munson had his own plan. He wanted the government to seize only the Japanese nationals' property, thereby putting the Nisei in control: "It is the aim that the Nisei should police themselves, and as a result police their parents."

J. Edgar Hoover, director of the Federal Bureau of Investigation (FBI), also had a different view. He felt that the FBI had already identified possible Japanese agents and had eliminated the threat. He opposed mass removal of Japanese Americans.

In an atmosphere of the war hysteria, Americans feared another sneak attack by Japan, this time on the western coast of the United States. Accordingly, fear of Japanese Americans increased. More Americans called for their removal. American Legions demanded Japanese American removal from the West Coast.

On January 28, 1942, the California State Personnel Board barred civil service positions to "descendants of natives with whom the United States [is] at war." They enforced this rule only against Japanese Americans. The next day, Attorney General Francis Biddle established zones of land in which he prohibited all enemy aliens. He ordered all enemy aliens out of the San Francisco waterfront areas. In early February, the United States Army set up twelve "restricted areas" in which enemy aliens were under a 9:00 P.M. to 6:00 A.M. curfew. It allowed travel only to and from work, which could not be more than five miles

from their home. Earl Warren was then California's Attorney General and soon to be the Chief Justice of the United States Supreme Court. In fact, because of his leadership in the rulings striking down segregation and racist government policies, he has been called the "most despised Justice" ever to serve on the Supreme Court. Yet in 1942, he also called for something to be done about the Japanese American threat. He said the Japanese Americans in his state were the "Achilles heel of the entire civilian defense effort" and said "unless something is done it may bring about a repetition of Pearl Harbor. . . ." The West Coast Congressional Delegation called on the president to remove "all persons of Japanese lineage . . . aliens and citizens alike, from the strategic areas of California, Oregon and Washington." The California Joint Immigration Committee followed with the same request.

On February 19, 1942, President Roosevelt signed Executive Order 9066, authorizing the definition of military areas in the United States "from which any or all persons may be excluded as deemed necessary or desirable." This order allowed Japanese Americans to be removed from their homes and interned in camps. Only two groups were "unpatriotic" enough to speak out against the order: the Society of Friends (Quakers) and the American Civil Liberties Union (ACLU). Milton Eisenhower, brother of General Dwight D. Eisenhower, headed the civilian branch of the Western Defense Command. The Western Defense Command had the responsibility, if necessary, for the process of notifying and rounding up all persons of Japanese ancestry on the West Coast. Six days later, the United States Navy ordered all Japanese American residents of Terminal Island, San Pedro, California, to leave within 48 hours and to settle elsewhere, wherever they could.

The call for the detention and evacuation of all Japanese Americans fell on the shoulders of two men. Lieutenant General John L. DeWitt of the Western Defense Command was entrusted with the internal security of the western United States. General Delos Emmons was in charge of the military government of Hawaii. Both were required to carry out Executive Order 9066. Each of these men responded in different ways.

General Emmons immediately made a statement that "No person, be he citizen or alien, need worry, provided he is not connected with subversive elements. . . . While we have been subjected to a serious attack by a ruthless and treacherous enemy, we must remember that this is America and we must do things the American Way. We must distinguish between loyalty and disloyalty among our people." The War Department heavily pressured Emmons to intern Japanese Americans, but business leaders and newspapers supported Emmons's statements: Whereas mainland labor perceived Japanese Americans as a threat, in Hawaii they made up most of the labor force. For example, Japanese Americans in Hawaii made up the majority of agricultural workers, nearly all of the transportation force, and even 90 percent of the carpenters. Nonetheless, the War Department continued to pressure Emmons to evacuate the Japanese Americans from Hawaii. He argued in turn that detention of this much of his work force would cripple the rebuilding efforts of the island and destroy the economy. The Honolulu Chamber of Commerce agreed and called for fair treatment of Japanese Americans. Its president said, "The citizens of Japanese blood would fight as loyally for America as any other citizen." Hawaii's congressional delegation urged restraint and advised the military government to do nothing more than find spies. When schools reopened in January 1942, the Superintendent of Schools sent a statement to all teachers saying, "Let us keep constantly in mind that America is not making war on citizens of the United States or on law-abiding aliens within America." For the most part, General Emmons successfully resisted the War Department's pressure. Out of over 158,000 Japanese Americans in Hawaii, he interned only 1,444 Japanese. Most of these were Kibei.

On the mainland General John L. DeWitt produced a totally different result. Some have accused General DeWitt of being a racist. Others have criticized him as being the wrong man in the wrong place at the wrong time. An elderly bureaucrat, his military experience was in supply rather than combat. Military leaders had little respect for him. Critics have accused him of being cautious and easily caving in to pressure from the public and his superiors, and his superiors strongly wanted the removal of Japanese Americans. To the secretary of war, Henry Stimson, he wrote, "In the war in which we are now engaged . . . racial affinities are not severed by migration. The Japanese race is an enemy race, and while many second and third-generation Japanese born on United States soil, pos-

In 1942 President Roosevelt signed Executive Order 9066, which allowed Japanese Americans to be removed from their homes and interned in camps.

sessed of United States citizenship, have become 'Americanized,' the racial strains are undiluted. . . . It therefore follows that along the vital Pacific Coast over 112,000 potential enemies of Japanese extraction are at large today." He later pointed out that, "A Jap's a Jap . . . and that's all there is to it." Despite much military and civilian intelligence to the contrary, on March 2, 1942, DeWitt cited "military necessity" and U.S. security reasons when he issued Public Proclamation No. 1. It created military areas in Arizona, California, Oregon, and Washington from where German, Italian, or Japanese aliens and anyone of "Japanese ancestry" could be removed. Two weeks later he issued Proclamation No. 2, which included Idaho, Montana, Nevada, and Utah. The forcible removal of Japanese Americans from the West Coast began.

Without due process, Japanese Americans, guilty of nothing more than their ancestry, were forced to leave their homes and businesses and report to detention centers throughout the western portions of the United States.

When J. Edgar Hoover of the FBI learned that DeWitt was going to go ahead with his evacuation of Japanese Americans based on his "intelligence," he bluntly remarked that DeWitt's intelligence was based on "hysteria and lack of judgement." He said DeWitt's military necessity was based "primarily upon public and political pressure rather than on factual data."

By the time it was over, more than 110,000 Japanese Americans, 70,000 of them American citizens, had been forced from their homes into hastily set-up camps for them across the western inland part of the United States. Without due process, Japanese Americans, guilty of nothing more than their ancestry, were ordered to leave their homes and report to detention processing centers. Most

reported voluntarily, but those that did not were rounded up and arrested. Often officials gave them less than a few days to gather their belongings and report to detention centers. Most Japanese Americans were forced to sell their property quickly, often, for pennies on the dollar, or risk losing it. A few lucky ones had white friends who kept their property for them while they were gone. The government allowed each detainee one trunkful of clothes and possessions. Detainees were not allowed radios, cameras, or other personal items.

Upon arriving at the assembly centers, detainees were shocked at the conditions that they found. Many of the centers were worse than the worst slums in which they had been economically forced to live. Officials housed them in fair-

Japanese American child
awaiting internment.

grounds, racetracks, and stockyards. One Japanese American remembered that they "were filthy, smelly, and dirty. There were roughly two thousand people packed in one large building. No beds were provided, so they gave us gunny sacks to fill with straw, that was our bed." Another evacuee who slept in a stable sadly reminisced, "Suddenly you realized that human beings were being put behind fences just like on the farm where we had horses and pigs in corrals." Administrators often moved evacuees from one camp to the next. They often began in one of the over twenty "assembly centers" and finally transferred to one of the ten "relocation centers." The relocation centers were located in isolated areas, often in desert areas. Evacuees did not know where they were. The ten relocation centers were Topaz in Utah, Poston and

Gila River in Arizona, Amache in Colorado, Jerome and Rohwer in Arkansas, Minidoka in Idaho, Manzanar and Tule Lake in California, and Heart Mountain in Wyoming.

Conditions in the camps were often terrible. A sign at the Minidoka Relocation Center today reads ". . . Victims of war time hysteria, these people, two-thirds of whom were United States citizens, lived a bleak humiliating life in tar paper barracks behind barbed wire and under armed guard . . ." Milton Eisenhower, testifying before the Senate Appropriations Committee in 1943, said that the camp construction ". . . is so very cheap that, frankly, if it stands up for the duration [of the war] we are going to be lucky." One evacuee remembered that their camp resembled a prison and each family had one 20-by-20 room. It had "a pot bellied stove, a single electric light hanging from the ceiling, an Army cot for each person and a blanket for the bed." One evacuee, a child at the time of internment, recalled that there was school in the detention centers. Each day camp teachers required him to begin the school day by saluting the flag and singing "My country, 'tis of thee, sweet land of liberty" while facing the flagpole. Beyond the flagpole lay barbed wire and guards carrying rifles. One young person said he did not remember much, but he did "remember being afraid."

Although most Japanese Americans reported to assembly centers, some refused. A few tried to stay free. Gordon K. (Kiyoshi) Hirabayashi broke curfew and refused to register for evacuation. Also, police caught Fred T. Korematsu on June 12, 1942, and charged him with violation of the exclusion orders. Both cases went to the Supreme Court. The Court upheld both convictions. In the Korematsu case, the Supreme Court had to decide whether the forced relocation of a U.S. citizen because of his heritage was a violation of his rights. The Court answered no. Justice Hugo Black, speaking for the majority said, ". . . when under conditions of modern warfare our shores are threatened by hostile forces, the power to protect must be commensurate with the threatened danger. . . . There was evidence of disloyalty on the part of some, the military authorities considered that the need for action was great, and the time for action was short." In a passionate dissent, Justice Owen Roberts said, "This is not a case of keeping people off the streets at night as was *Kiyoshi Hirabayashi* v. *United States*. . . . On the contrary, it is the case of convicting a citizen as a punishment for not submitting to imprisonment in a concentration camp, based on his ancestry and solely because of his ancestry, without evidence or inquiry concerning his loyalty and good disposition towards the United States." Justice Frank Murphy, also in dissent wrote, "Racial discrimination in any form and in any degree has no justifiable part whatever in our democratic way of life."

One irony of the Japanese internment came in early 1943 when teams of Army officers came to the detention camps recruiting enlisted men and registering Japanese American citizens for the draft. They asked everyone loyalty questions. Of the 77,957 eligible to register, 87 percent (68,018)

answered positively to the questions. Over 33,000 Nisei soldiers served during the war in Italy, Europe, North Africa, France, and the Pacific Theater. The principal units were the Hawaiian-formed 100th Infantry Battalion; the 442nd Regiment, formed from volunteers from the internment camps; and the secret Nisei Military Intelligence Service. The Nisei showed their courage and heroism time and again. The 442nd fought in places like Luciana, Livorno, and Bruyeres and rescued the famous Texan "Lost Battalion" surrounded by German forces in the Vosges Mountains. During the European war, the unit suffered 9,486 wounded and 600 killed, the highest casualty rate of any American unit during the war. They became the most decorated unit in history. For their heroism, the men of the 442nd won 18,143 individual decorations, including 52 Distinguished Service Crosses, 560 Silver Stars, 810 Bronze Stars, and more than 3,600 Purple Hearts. Private First Class Sadao Munemori received the Congressional Medal of Honor posthumously. The 442nd won 7 coveted Presidential Unit Citations for its performance. The men in the 100th Battalion earned 900 Purple Hearts, 36 Silver Stars, 21 Bronze Stars, and 3 Distinguished Service Crosses. General Joseph Stilwell praised the Nisei soldiers when he said, "They bought an awful hunk of America with their blood. . . . those Nisei boys have a place in the American heart, now and forever." In 1946, President Harry Truman met with the 442nd and praised them by saying, "You fought for the free nations of the world . . . you fought not only the enemy, you fought prejudice—and won." The Nisei also fought in the Pacific, not only dying on the beaches but serving in the intelligence branch as interpreters and translators. General Charles Willoughby, Chief of Intelligence, said that the Nisei contribution shortened the war in the Pacific by two years. In fact, he said it stopped the Japanese landing on Bataan.

On December 17 and 18, 1944, relief finally arrived for the Japanese internees. On December 17, Public Proclamation No. 21, effective January 2, 1945, allowed evacuees to return home. On December 18, the Supreme Court released two decisions: the *Korematsu* decision and an uncelebrated, nearly unknown and unremembered decision. In the latter, the Court granted a writ of habeas corpus to Mitsuye Endo, a Japanese American girl, and ordered her freed from a detention camp. The Court said that these centers had been set up to ascertain citizens' loyalty. After the center had ascertained an individual's loyalty, (and as the relocation center had ascertained Endo's loyalty), the intent should be to resettle the detainee outside the center. The Court took pains to point out that it was not ruling on the constitutionality of the relocation program. From this point on, after a detainee's loyalty had been assured, he or she had to be released.

Gradually the camps emptied. By December 1945, the war with Japan having ended (August 14, 1945), the camps were nearly all abandoned. The government gave each detainee $25 and a train ticket. Most detainees returned home. Many settled elsewhere. But upon returning home, Japanese Americans again faced racial bigotry and discrimination. To prevent Japanese from returning home, many whites formed organizations such as "No Japs Incorporated" or the "San Diego and the Home Front Commandoes in Sacramento." Nearly 8,000 people chose to leave the United States permanently.

In 1948, in *Oyama* v. *California,* the Supreme Court struck down the Alien Land laws. That same year the Evacuation Claims Act authorized payment to Japanese Americans who suffered economic loss during their "detention." The Act allowed a return of ten cents for every dollar lost. Four years later the McCarran-Walter Immigration and Naturalization Act ended the naturalization ban and the Asian exclusion laws.

In 1988, Congress passed a bill that authorized a payment of $20,000 to each survivor of the internment camps. In addition, it extended an apology to Japanese Americans. Ronald Reagan signed the bill, admitting that the United States had committed "a grave wrong." He pointed out the exploits of the 442nd Regiment. He said America needed to end this "sad chapter in American history." Though authorized, Congress has paid little money to survivors.

Hispanic American Civil Rights

The fastest growing minority group in the United States is the Hispanic American population. In 1992, they numbered over 22 million. Nearly 60 percent trace their ancestors to Mexico. Today, 86 percent of all Hispanic Americans make their home in five states: Texas, California, New Mexico, Arizona, and Colorado. While numerous cultural groups have immigrated to the United States, the largest three groups came from Mexico, Puerto Rico, and Cuba. Two thirds of all Puerto Ricans live in New York City. Sixty percent of Cuban Americans live in Florida.

Some may argue that of all minority groups in America, Hispanic Americans have most easily realized the American dream. However, like other minority groups, they fought for their civil and human rights. For a long period, they lost many rights most Americans take for granted.

Most Hispanic immigration occurred for economic and political reasons. Between 1900 and the census of 1930, the Hispanic American population in the Southwest grew from 375,000 to 1,160,000. The majority were Mexican immigrants. They worked at the most menial jobs as sweatshop workers, migrant farm workers, and laborers. The greatest surge occurred during the 1920s, when nearly half a million Mexicans arrived. By 1920, in California, farm labor was 75 percent Mexican. In Texas, by 1928, the Mexican population represented 75 percent of the construction labor force. Together one tenth of Mexico's population migrated to the "northern land of opportunity," mainly owing to poverty and civil war.

Hispanic Americans were considered cheap labor and easily controlled. Employers almost always paid them less than whites, even when they worked in the sweatshops. For example, in one sweat shop, they paid Hispanic Americans $3 per day, while they paid whites $4. In the farming regions of California they were paid $0.50 to $1.00 less per day.

Whites controlled the labor force in many ways; interfering with Hispanic Americans' use of automobiles was one. Employers discouraged Hispanic Americans from owning cars so that they could not move around. Police often ticketed Mexicans on trumped-up charges. Police and local sheriffs usually stopped Hispanic Americans if they saw them driving. In addition, a form of indentured servitude developed. Employers fronted Mexican laborers with money at exorbitant rates to pay for basic necessities. After going into debt on the farm, they found they could never leave. Workers had to work off all debts before they could depart. Most often, employers would have them arrested and jailed if they tried to leave.

Between 1900 and the census of 1930, the Hispanic American population in the Southwest grew from 375,000 to 1,160,000. The majority were Mexican immigrants.

their pay cut from $0.35 per hour to $0.15 per hour. They began organizing. Two prominent Hispanic American unions developed: the Confederation of Mexican Labor Unions and the Imperial Valley Workers' Union. The largest strike occurred in 1933 when workers struck for $1.00 per hundredweight of picked cotton. The farmers offered $0.60 and called in the military and local police. Farmers threatened workers and beat them. In the end, the workers agreed to a compromise of $0.75 cents per hundredweight.

Because of the extreme labor shortages during World War II, the government negotiated the Mexican Farm Labor Supply Program with Mexico. Commonly called the Bracero Program, or the Day Laborer Program, it allowed the importation of Mexican workers into the United States. The program lasted until 1964. During the war years, the federal government appropriated over $100 million for import labor. They recruited thousands of workers as farm laborers, railroad workers, laborers, and low-wage workers to help transport military freight and personnel. In 1942, they imported 4,000 workers; in 1943, 52,000; in 1944, 62,000; and in 1945, 120,000.

Like other loyal American citizens, including all minorities, Hispanic Americans served bravely in the war when called by their country. Half a million Mexican Americans served in the armed forces. Yet, even while Mexican Americans fought for the war effort, at home, racial violence broke out. Often, whites would go into the barrios of Los Angeles and other places to attack Hispanic Americans.

The border between the United States and Mexico stretches nearly 2,000 miles. For many, the border represents the difference between poverty and riches. Since the 1940s, the United States has not been able to stem the flow of immigrants from the south. By 1990, estimates of illegal Hispanic American aliens in the United States ranged as high as 2 million. As did those who came before them, they found jobs at the lowest economic levels. In California, the trend had been to follow the crop harvest and then return to Mexico. Increasingly, many decided to stay.

The lack of education was another way to keep the Hispanic Americans in their place. One sugar beet grower summed up his ideal of the Hispanic American worker: "If I wanted a man I would want one of the more ignorant ones. . . . Educated Mexicans are the hardest to handle. . . . It is all right to educate them no higher then we educate them here in these little towns. I will be frank. They would make more desirable citizens if they would stop about the seventh grade."

Even in those who would allow Hispanics a degree of education, racism was present. A woman on a Texas ranch said, "Let him [the Mexican] have as good an education but still let him know he is not as good as a white man. God did not intend him to be; He would have made them white if he had." In the rare cases that schools allowed Hispanic Americans to attend school, they taught them manual labor training and domestic science "to prepare them for their lot in life."

During World War I, when labor shortages occurred, plant managers often went to Mexico to bring back cheap labor. However, during the Great Depression, when factories no longer needed cheap Mexican labor, 400,000 Mexicans were forcibly "repatriated" back to Mexico. Thousands of these were second-generation Hispanic Americans and now citizens of the United States.

During the late 1920s and early 1930s, many Hispanic Americans fought back for decent wages. Between 1928 and 1932, farm workers had

In the 1960s, the advent of the African American civil rights movement produced a growing cultural awareness among Hispanic Americans. One Mexican American migrant worker named César Chávez helped form the National Farm

Workers Association (NFWA) among Hispanic Americans in 1962. In 1966, the NFWA merged with a branch of the AFL-CIO to form the United Farm Workers (UFW). Chávez had become nationally known in 1965 when he led a strike of grape pickers and organized a grape boycott. He eventually won three-year contracts and a new minimum wage. The UFW fought other farm worker battles against lettuce growers and other "truck farm" businesses, but with less success. In addition, in the 1980s, farm laborers of California, most of whom were Hispanic Americans, began coming down with high rates of cancer, possibly due to exposure to insecticides and other chemicals. To call attention to this plight, Cesar Chávez began a hunger strike in 1988 that lasted 35 days.

Hispanic Americans still fight today for equality. Many schools, mainly populated by Hispanic Americans, are second-rate. According to official figures of the U.S. Labor Department wages are very low among Hispanic American workers. For a more complete overview of Hispanic Americans and their fight for human rights, refer to the chapter in this book on Hispanic Americans.

Proposition 187

The 1990s saw a rise in racism and xenophobia across the United States, with minorities suddenly losing many gains they made in the twentieth century. Equal opportunity programs and affirmative action programs were struck down by the courts in the name of reverse discrimination. There were calls to stop or put moratoriums on immigration. Representative congressional districts drawn to insure minority representation were struck down by courts all across the country.

Calls for "English to be named as the national language," and the disruptions of services to "illegal" immigrants were heard each day. In 1995, California voters passed Proposition 187, which denied government funding of health care, education, and other state benefits to illegal aliens or children of illegal aliens. The Hispanic American population struck back with legal suits: The fight over Proposition 187 as this book went to press was still in the courts. Pat Buchanan, speaking about one of his election-year issues in his more popular-than-expected presidential campaign in 1996, said, "Illegal immigration must be halted, and no illegal alien given welfare. We need a nationwide Proposition 187, a closing of the Southwest border to illegals (with the National Guard, if necessary) and a new immigration law where we Americans decide who comes, and when." He went on to call for a moratorium on all immigration (especially from the south) until time enough passed to assimilate the tens of millions of recent immigrants. He believed this assimilation would take at least a decade; many sociologists say it would take many decades. He opposed the constitutional right of children of aliens born in the United States to receive citizenship automatically. He pointed out time and again his belief that the framers never intended to extend automatic citizenship to children born of illegal immigrants. Many Americans share his views and wish to enact these views into law. Public opinion on immigration is still shifting and uncertain.

Women's Rights

Throughout the world, as well as in the United States, women generally have had fewer rights than their male counterparts. Men and the law saw women mainly in a reproductive capacity. They considered women physically and intellectually inferior and often a source of evil and temptation. The Greeks taught their children that it was a woman, Pandora, who released plagues of evil and unhappiness onto mankind. Early Roman law portrayed women as children and always subject to men. Hinduism in the East, developed after 500 B.C., required women to walk behind their husbands, would not allow women (and children) to own property, would not allow widows to remarry, and forced women into subjugation to men. Western and mid-Eastern religions portrayed women as inferior. St. Jerome of the fourth century said, "Woman is the gate of the devil, the path of wickedness, the sting of the serpent, in a word a perilous object." Thomas Aquinas, thirteenth-century theologian, said women were "created to be man's helpmate, . . ." but, except for reproduction, "men would be better assisted by other men."

That the male-controlled government of the United States considered women inferior and lacking equal rights is an understatement. In 1872, woman activist Susan B. Anthony illegally voted in New York. Police arrested her. The U.S. District Attorney charged her and claimed that Anthony on ". . . the fifth day of November, 1872 . . . voted. . . . At that time she was a woman." The judge did not allow her to testify in federal court because she was a woman. He took the case in his own hands when he instructed the "gentleman of the jury" to find Anthony guilty because the Fourteenth Amendment's equal protection clause did not specifically protect a woman's right to vote. He fined her one hundred dollars. She refused to pay and the judge released her.

Men have long considered women the "weaker sex" and have relegated supposedly "lesser tasks" such as homemaking, child-rearing, and washing clothes, to them. In 1908, for example, the United States ruled that female maximum hour laws were constitutional owing to a woman's "physical structure and . . . maternal functions" (*Muller* v. *Oregon*). Despite the often strenuous and heavy labor required for many of these "lesser tasks," and even though present-day physiological tests indicate that women have a greater tolerance for pain, these traditional beliefs still exist today. Traditionally assigned only the social and biological role of mother, women have often defined themselves in a domestic role. However, this is changing. With the ease of access to contraceptive practices and drugs, and the legalization of abortion, women have often freed themselves from these roles and moved into areas traditionally dominated by men. For example, at the turn of the twentieth century only 19 percent of all college graduates were female. In 1984, nearly one half of all graduates were women. By the mid-eighties, 53 percent of all college students were women.

The fight for women's rights began with the founding of the country. In 1776 Abigail Adams argued strongly with her husband, John Adams, for raising women to the equal status of men. The women's rights movement intertwined itself with the abolitionist movement of the nineteenth century. In 1848, at the Seneca Falls (New York) Convention, women made a strong call for women's suffrage with the passage of the Declaration of Sentiments, a document based on the Declaration of Independence. The word suffrage itself is based on the Latin word for "vote." Oberlin College admitted its first women students in 1834. In 1835 a woman named Angelina Grimké spoke to the Massachusetts legislature—a first in American history. In the twentieth century, the rise of women's rights mainly followed two paths, the fight for the vote and the feminist movement.

Women fought earnestly for women's suffrage in the late nineteenth century but did not realize the dream until the early twentieth. In fact, a constitutional amendment granting suffrage to women was presented to every Congress from 1878 forward. Susan B. Anthony, Elizabeth Cady Stanton, Lucretia Mott, Lucy Stone, Harriet Tubman, Sojourner Truth, and others carried the fight not only to Congress but to the streets of cities all across the country. But by the turn of the modern century, a new leadership arose. In 1900, Susan B. Anthony

resigned as president of the National American Woman Suffrage Association (NAWSA). Carrie Chapman Catt succeeded her. In 1902, Elizabeth Cady Stanton died. In 1906, Susan B. Anthony died. During those same years, women won the vote in Australia and Finland. Harriet Stanton Blatch, daughter of Elizabeth Cady Stanton, followed in her mother's footsteps and founded the Equality League of Self-Supporting Women, later called the Women's Political Union. In 1910 the league held its first suffrage parade in New York City. Alice Paul, only 15 years old in 1900, soon became one of the strongest and most persuasive leaders of the movement.

The suffrage movement moved to the states on a state-by-state basis. By 1900, Wyoming, Utah, Colorado, and Idaho had enfranchised women. These western states had a high regard for women, because of a shortage of females compared to males. In 1912, Arizona, Kansas, and Oregon passed suffrage referendums. The next year, Alice Paul organized a suffrage parade in Washington, D.C., the day of Woodrow Wilson's inauguration. In 1914, Montana and Nevada gave women the right to vote. But while the movement generally moved forward, it had its defeats. The main one was in 1915 when New York State voted down suffrage. However, the next year Jeannette Rankin, a Republican from Montana, became the first female congressperson ever elected to the United States House of Representatives. She immediately

became the leader of the women's movement in Congress. She drafted another women's suffrage amendment. The suffrage movement was gaining steam. In 1916, President Woodrow Wilson even addressed the NAWSA Convention.

Opposition grew. Intense arguments boiled over between anti-suffragettes and suffragettes. Former President Grover Cleveland, in the April 1905 *Ladies' Home Journal,* stated, "Sensible and responsible women do not want to vote. The relative positions to be assumed by man and woman in the working out of our civilization were assigned long ago by a higher intelligence than ours." Helen Keller considered voting and pointed out that there was more to women's rights than just the vote. Speaking in England, she said, ". . . democracy is but a name. We vote? What does that mean? It means that we choose between two bodies of real, though not avowed autocrats. We choose between Tweedledum and Tweedledee . . ." In 1911, opponents of women's suffrage founded the National Association Opposed to Woman Suffrage. In 1913, Virginia historian and author Conway W. Sams wrote the book *Shall Women Vote?: A Book for Men.* In it he attacked the women's movement and echoed the thoughts of many opposed to it. He stated that woman's suffrage was "one of the greatest afflictions which could happen to any State" and the women's movement was "a movement which has as its object the stripping of men of their rights, and the transferring of them to women and

Mary Lease *(1850–1933)*

This radical American politician was an early advocate of the rights and interests of the small farmer and other aggrieved American workers. Mary Lease dramatized the plight of Americans who had been economically left behind by the industrialization of the nation. Lease was a powerful orator for the Farmer's Alliance and the People's Party, two grass-roots political groups strong in the South and West during the 1890s. Later in life Mary Lease turned her attention to the cause of woman's suffrage and was an ardent campaigner in that effort.

children." He said that women's rights advances already made in his state of Virginia "are enough to undermine the family, the home, and society itself; and that, unless they be soon corrected by the several States of this Union, and by the other governments organized by men of our race, they will bring untold evil upon it."

In 1917, the movement grew more violent. Hundreds of women picketed the White House. Police arrested Alice Paul and 96 other suffragists and jailed them for "obstructing traffic." Some were jailed for up to 30 days. The court sentenced Dr. Caroline Spencer and Alice Paul to seven months in prison. They went on a hunger strike to protest their arrest and treatment; as a result, they were brutally force-fed. The government threw Paul into solitary confinement and then transferred her to a mental hospital and dumped her in a locked room with boarded-over windows. Later, on appeal, a court ruled that the government had illegally arrested, convicted, and imprisoned the women.

Yet the mood of the country was changing. Women won the right to vote in North Dakota, Ohio, Indiana, Rhode Island, Nebraska, Michigan, New York, and Arkansas. Women continued to stage round-the-clock picket lines in front of the White House. In 1918, the Republicans took over Congress. It had more liberal views than the former Democratic Congress. The House of Representatives passed a resolution favoring a woman suffrage amendment, but the Senate defeated the resolution.

Finally that year, Congress passed Representative Rankin's amendment to the Constitution giving women the right to vote and sent it to the states for ratification. Twenty-three states, including New York, quickly ratified the amendment. The struggle for ratification by the balance of the necessary three fourths of the states began. Finally, Henry Burn of Tennessee, under heavy pressure from women's groups—and as legend now has it, extreme pressure from his mother—cast the deciding vote that made Tennessee the thirty-sixth and final state needed to ratify the Nineteenth Amendment to the Constitution. The U.S. secretary of state quickly stated that the amendment was in effect.

Women now had the right to vote in national elections, though many Americans, both male and female, disapproved. For example, Edith Bolling Galt Wilson, second wife of President Woodrow Wilson, had her doubts. She said, "We learned today that Dudley Malone had espoused the cause of those detestable suffragette pickets. If anyone had told us that Dudley Malone could be such a traitor we would not have believed it. . . . My precious one did not come home from the office until six-thirty and was so weary it broke my heart to look at him." Some states held out; in fact, it took until 1952 for Virginia to ratify the Nineteenth Amendment.

Women won the right to vote, but they still lagged behind in many other areas, especially in the workplace, in politics, and in legal status. But great strides occurred in the twentieth century. On the seventy-fifth anniversary of the Seneca Falls convention in 1923, Alice Paul proposed an Equal Rights Amendment to remedy inequalities not addressed in the Nineteenth Amendment. A new fight began.

Although they had won the right to vote, women in many states continued to be barred from jury duty and public office. However, there were exceptions, in the late 1920s, two widows succeeded their husbands as governors of Texas and Wyoming. In 1933, President Franklin D. Roosevelt appointed Frances Perkins as the first female Secretary of Labor. At the urging of First Lady Eleanor Roosevelt, many women gained positions in federal social service bureaus in the New Deal era. For example, Mary McLeod Bethune became a director within the National Youth Administration. In 1952, the Democratic and Republican parties finally eliminated women's divisions within the parties.

Congress passed the Nineteenth Amendment to the Constitution in 1918, giving women the right to vote in national elections.

The private sector heavily discriminated against women. For example, in the early 1900s, school administrators still often insisted on rules for female teachers that had been in effect in the late 1800s. For example, the following "Rules for Female Teachers" were enforced in Massachusetts by state regulation:

1. Do not get married.

2. Do not leave town at any time without permission of the school board.

3. Do not keep company with men.

4. Be home between the hours of 8:00 P.M. and 6:00 A.M.

5. Do not loiter downtown in ice cream stores.

6. Do not smoke.

7. Do not get into a carriage or automobile with any man except your father or brother.

8. Do not dress in bright colors.

9. Do not dye your hair.

10. Do not wear any dress more than two inches above the ankle.

Rules such as these lasted until the 1960s. Even then, in some places school boards furloughed female teachers if they became pregnant. Furthermore, often districts would not allow them to return to their classrooms until months had elapsed after the birth of their child.

Politically, women's issues were rather quiet until the 1960s. However, women's rights issues did arise. The American Civil Liberties Union

Jane Addams (1860–1935)

This prominent American social reformer was deeply concerned with the deplorable housing conditions of America's urban poor, and she took steps to change the patterns of housing. Jane Addams was the daughter of an Illinois state senator who was an abolitionist and a friend of Abraham Lincoln. Addams was educated at Rockford Female Seminary and attended the Women's Medical College in Philadelphia, until failing health forced her to withdraw.

In 1883, while touring Europe with her stepmother, Addams became concerned about urban poverty, which she more sharply observed on her return to the United States. After a second visit to Europe in 1887, she decided to found a settlement house, drawn from the example of Toynbee Hall, a university settlement in London. In 1889 Addams and Ellen Starr bought Hull House, a large building in a poor immigrant section of Chicago. They wanted to create an area of protection for these vulnerable people. The mission of Hull House expanded, and a nursery, a dispensary, and a boarding house were added. By 1893 Hull House was running 40 local clubs on behalf of poor residents of Chicago. This was the origin of what Addams regarded as a "settlement house" movement.

The Hull House experience was projected on the national consciousness by the 1895 publication of *Hull House Maps and Papers*, which provided a detailed view of the conditions of the urban poor in Chicago. In 1902 Jane Addams wrote *Democracy and Social Ethics*, a call for reform of the social conditions of the poor. She

emphasized the plight of poor young people in her 1909 book, *The Spirit of Youth and the City Streets*. In the same year Addams became the first woman president of the National Conference of Charities and Corrections.

Her best-known book was an autobiography, *Twenty Years at Hull House*, published in 1910. Her concept of creating community centers for poor people won many admirers around the world. The settlement movement that she started in the United States did improve housing conditions for many poor Americans. The idea of a settlement house as a center for assisting the poor spread to a few other places, but for Addams these settlements were more than housing arrangements: They were springboards for further social reform.

Addams was also active in the women's suffrage movement and in the antiwar movement. During World War I she aroused considerable hostility for her opposition to American involvement. Addams was chairperson of the Women's Peace Party in 1915 and by 1919 presided over the second women's Peace Congress held in Zurich, Switzerland, helping to raise funds for victims of the war.

In 1920 Addams became a founding member of the American Civil Liberties Union. She fought for groups she believed were suffering deprivation, including African Americans and immigrants. In the 1920s the Daughters of the American Revolution called Jane Addams "the most dangerous woman in America today." She was awarded the Nobel Peace Prize in 1931.

(ACLU) began to get involved in the women's movement early and became feministic long before feminism became popular in the 1960s. In fact, suffragists and other women activists such as Jane Addams and Jeannette Rankin helped found the organization in 1920. The ACLU argued more women's rights cases before the United States Supreme Court than any other organization, and it continues to do so. (One recent battle, *United States* v. *Virginia*, 1996, was over admitting woman, Shannon Faulkner, to The Citadel, an all-male, state-funded military academy. The ACLU won the case in early 1996.) In the 1920s, the ACLU successfully

appealed the obscenity conviction of one of its founding mothers, suffragist and sex educator Mary Ware Dennett. The state convicted her of distributing the pamphlet, "The Sex Side of Life"—a sex education primer for adolescents. In 1937, it successfully represented Connecticut schoolteachers in their fight to be reinstated in their jobs following the birth of their children. In the 1940s, the ACLU established the Committee on Discrimination Against Women in Employment to advocate for legislation guaranteeing equal pay for equal work. It was this committee that began opposition to laws prohibiting the use of contraceptives and the distribution of birth

Women began flooding the job market at the turn of the century. In 1900 there were 500,000 female office workers; in 1870, there had been 19,000.

control information. In the next decade, the ACLU lobbied Congress to secure tax deductions for child care for mothers in need.

Women in the Labor Movement

Women fighting for rights in the workplace went hand-in-hand with the labor movement of the twentieth century. (See later in this chapter for an overview of the labor movement.) Women began flooding the job market at the turn of the century. In 1900 there were 500,000 female office workers; in 1870, there had been 19,000. Businesses hired women as switchboard operators and store workers. Hospitals and doctors hired women as nurses. School districts hired half a million women as teachers.

Labor conditions for women in the early twentieth century were horrible. Nearly 80-year-old Mother Mary Jones (Mary Harris Jones), who briefly worked in a Milwaukee brewery, described the working conditions of women in 1910:

Condemned to slave daily in the wash-room in wet shoes and wet clothes, surrounded with foul-mouthed, brutal foremen . . . the poor girls work in the vile smell of sour beer, lifting cases of empty and full bottles weighing from 100 to 150 pounds. . . . Rheumatism is one of the chronic ailments and is closely followed by consumption. . . . The foreman even regulates the time the girls may stay in the toilet room. . . . For this employers paid them $3.00 a week.

In 1909, the Handbook of the Women's Trade Union Industrial League described work conditions in steam laundries:

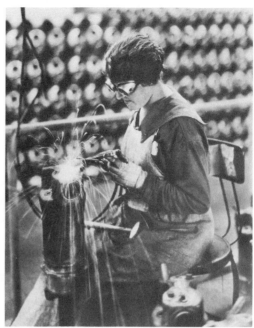

Photo on left: When the United States entered World War I in 1917, thousands of suffragists worked in the war effort.

Photo on right: When the United States entered World War II, industry recruited millions of women for defense industry jobs. They became a significant part of the labor force.

How would you like to iron a shirt a minute? Think of standing at a mangle just above the washroom with the hot steam pouring up through the floor for 10, 12, 14 and sometimes 17 hours a day! Sometimes the floors are made of cement and then it seems as though one were standing on hot coals, and the workers are dripping with perspiration. . . . They . . . [are] breathing air laden with particles of soda, ammonia, and other chemicals!

Days were horribly long and most women worked at least 12 hours per day.

By this time, Great Britain and similar countries of the world had passed ten-hour-day laws for women and children. These restrictions were not enacted in the United States until the 1910s. Action began first at the state level, as states began to pass laws limiting working hours and improving working conditions for women and children. Unfortunately, many laws, in their attempt to improve working conditions, discriminated against women. For example, some states passed laws prohibiting women from lifting weights above a certain amount, often as little as 15 pounds.

Women did not always greet these laws enthusiastically. Times were difficult. Women often felt they had to work more and longer hours just to help their families survive. Soon, some women and lawmakers saw that many of these labor laws restricted the rights of working women. For example, laws prohibiting women from working more than eight-hour days or from working at

night prevented women from holding certain jobs, particularly supervisory jobs, that might have required overtime work. Laws that barred women from lifting certain weights again precluded them from holding certain jobs.

In wartime, women served in the armed forces. When the United States entered World War I in 1917, NAWSA pledged its support. Thousands of suffragists worked in the war effort. Many folded bandages in their local headquarters. Others volunteered in hospitals and government offices. Suffrage leaders hoped that after the war, America would reward women with the vote. But, as war often does to society, it split the women's movement. Many feminist leaders split with the NAWSA over its patriotic support of the war. Alice Paul led the Congressional Union for Women's Suffrage in agitating for the vote during the war. Another group, the New York branch of the Woman's Peace party, led by Crystal Eastman, refused to support the war "to make the world safe for democracy" when American women did not have democratic rights. The National Woman's Peace party, headed by Jane Addams, supported a peace settlement but did not openly oppose the war. Thousands of women went into the workplace to replace young men in the European trenches. However, upon the soldiers' return, many women left the workplace to go back to their homes. Employers forced many to leave, but some women left voluntarily to cre-

Women laborers assembling fighter planes during World War II.

ate job openings for returning veterans. As with many racial minorities, employers readily hired women when they needed workers but quickly replaced them with men when men would work for similar wages.

During World War II almost 300,000 women served in the army and navy, taking performed noncombatant jobs as secretaries, typists, and nurses. When the United States entered World War II, industry recruited millions of women for defense industry jobs. They became a significant part of the labor force. The U.S. Army and Navy established the Women's Army Corp (WAC) and Women Accepted for Volunteer Emergency Service (WAVE) as the first women's military corps. As in World War I, women flocked to war industry

jobs. By 1947, two years after the end of the war, the percentage of women in the labor force had declined as women left jobs to get married and make way for returning soldiers. But by end of the decade, the numbers of working women again began to increase.

During the post–World War II period, the feminist movement waned somewhat. The fight for women's rights continued, mainly through the work of a few feminist groups. The media almost overwhelmingly pronounced the feminist movement dead and celebrated the role of the happy suburban housewife.

In the 1950s, as the civil rights movement escalated in the South, women's issues again became more visible. Women such as Septima

Many African American women found being both a minority and a woman was two strikes against them.

woman in the country, to head it. Although she was in ill health and died the year before the commission issued its report, her name and reputation gave the committee credence and respect. The Commission published its report, *American Women*. Most considered its emphasis and view as extremely moderate. Far from a radical feminist view, it described many problems confronting women, including a desperate need for child care and that "one of the most pervasive limitations is the social climate in which women choose what they prepare themselves to do." The Commission presented the following recommendations:

1. the end of blatant sex discrimination in government employment (where agency heads still specified the preferred sex of applicants to fill a job).

2. an executive order to encourage federal contractors to stop sex discrimination.

3. appointment of women 'of demonstrated ability and political sensitivity' to policy-making positions.

4. improvement and extension of protective labor laws to men, but meanwhile, retention of legislation limiting maximum hours of work for women; such legislation effectively prevented women from earning higher overtime pay.

5. repeal of restrictions that set maximum limits upon weights women could lift; these restrictions barred able women from many higher paying jobs.

6. continuing the prohibition against home work but permitting flexibility for clerical, editorial, and research part-time work for women 'during years of intensive homemaking.'

7. passing equal pay for equal work laws.

8. making a widow's benefit under Social Security equal to the amount her husband would have received (they made no recommendations for changes in the Social Security system for married women workers who paid the tax but received no more than wives who made no payments).

9. paid maternity leave or comparable insurance benefits for women workers.

10. that educational institutions offer part-time study, financial aid, and flexible academic and residency requirements to accommodate the patterns of women's lives. These supportive measures would allow women who followed the traditional role to reenter the labor force when their children had grown.

11. programs to help women prepare for this dual role by teaching child care, family relations, nutrition, family finances, and 'the relation of individuals and families to society'

Clark led sit-ins and demonstrations in support of African American civil rights. As in the abolitionist days, women and others saw contradictions between fighting for African American civil rights and women not having their civil rights. As it did with other minority civil rights movements, the African American civil rights experience affected the feminist movement. (Even in 1970, Robin Morgan in the article "Double Jeopardy: To Be Black and Female," in the book *Sisterhood Is Powerful* declared, "Let me state here and now that the black woman in America can justly be described as a 'slave of a slave.'") In addition, in 1959, three landmark books on women were published. The first book, *A Century of Struggle* by Eleanor Flexner, was the first professional history of the nineteenth-century women's movement. It implicitly called for women to fight for their rights. In the second book, *A Century of Higher Education for American Women,* Mabel Newcomer disclosed that the relative position of women in the academic world was declining. The author of the third book, Robert Smuts, in *Women and Work In America* stated that "the picture of women's occupations outside the home between 1890 and 1950 had changed in only a few essentials."

By 1961, women's organizations and women in his administration openly pressured President John F. Kennedy to establish a President's Commission on the Status of Women. He did so in 1961 and named Eleanor Roosevelt, the most respected

12. imaginative counseling programs to 'lift aspirations beyond stubbornly persistent assumptions about 'women's roles' and 'women's interests' and result in choices that have inner authenticity for their makers.'

Cracks in unity appeared during this period within the women's movement. A large group supported the Equal Rights Amendment (ERA), while others opposed it, mainly because of its anticipated impact on protective labor legislation for women. In fact, in 1963 the hired staff of the Commission on the Status of Women headed by Esther Peterson, who was also Assistant Secretary of Labor, tried to move the emphasis away from the ERA to passing "specific bills for specific ills." However, many feminists opposed the idea. Alice Paul, the aging leader of the National Woman's Party (NWP), who had originated the idea for the ERA in 1923, spoke out against Peterson's approach. She said that the NWP, using the "specific bills" approach, literally framed hundreds of bills but succeeded in passing only a few. She stated that she had devised the Equal Rights Amendment to wipe out all discriminatory laws in a single stroke. Now she and others believed that the Commission was a plot to block the ERA's passage. They expected that opponents would persuade Congress to delay any action on it until the Commission issued a report; this occurred. On the day the Commission released its report, October 11, 1963, Esther Peterson sent a thank-you letter to Senator Carl Hayden for his help in immobilizing the ERA in Congress by attaching a rider that nullified its intent, as "an indispensable safeguard" against its passage. She asked him to continue attaching the rider in the event the ERA was introduced in Congress again, yet despite these conflicts, the ball for women's rights rolled again. The government distributed 83,000 copies of the Commission's report. In 1965, Scribner published it for distribution through bookstores across the nation.

During the 1960s, Congress passed several federal laws that improved the economic status of women. Most important was the Equal Pay Act of 1963. Efforts to pass equal pay legislation—"comparable pay should be given for comparable work"—began at the end of World War II. But the measure failed under both Democratic and Republican administrations. The main argument continually used to defeat the measure was that it was impossible to determine "comparable work." Representative Katherine St. George (R-NY) amended the key clause with compromise language so that it read "equal pay for equal work." From this point on legislators better accepted the bill. In fact, one year the House actually passed the bill by voice vote and without any vocal opposition, but it died in the Senate. The business community strongly opposed it. They mounted an opposition campaign to defeat the effort. Over opposition of the Chamber of Commerce and many corporate executives who testified against it, the Equal Pay Act passed both houses of Congress in May 1963. This was the first federal law to require equal compensation for men and women doing equal work in federal jobs. It amended the Fair Labor Standards Act. It prohibited sexual discrimination in wages for equal work on jobs requiring equal skill, effort, and responsibility, under similar working conditions. To protect men, it prohibited employers from lowering men's wages to achieve this goal. The act exempted wage differentials based on seniority, merit, or piece rate. It barred unions from negotiating wage differences based on sex. The act exempted from coverage executive, administrative, and professional employees, including teachers and academic administrative personnel in educational institutions. It had taken 18 years to achieve this victory, and for the first time, the federal government asserted the right of women to be employed on the same basis as men.

Perhaps the most important bill passed by Congress in the 1960s was the Civil Rights Act of 1964. In June 1963, the Chair of the House Judiciary Committee, Rep. Emanuel Celler (D-NY), who long opposed the Equal Rights Amendment, introduced the civil rights bill. This bill primarily protected African Americans and other racial, religious, or ethnic minorities against discrimination in voting, access to public education, employment, public accommodations, and in federally-assisted programs. After 22 days of hearings, Celler reported the bill out of committee favorably on November 20, 1963, two days before President Kennedy's assassination. In December 1963, the National Council of the National Woman's Party passed a resolution calling for an amendment to the Civil Rights bill to prohibit discrimination based on sex. They protested that the bill "would not even give protection against discrimination because of 'race, color, religion, or national origin' to a White Woman, a Woman of the Christian Religion, or a Woman of United States origin."

An amendment was attached, but the way it came about showed humor in an often humorless arena. The Civil Rights bill passed committee and headed for debate on the House floor. Members of the National Woman's Party contacted Representative Howard W. Smith (D-VA), Chair of the House Rules Committee, to suggest that a ban against sex discrimination be included in the legislation. Smith, a Southern conservative who was also a longtime sponsor of the Equal Rights Amendment, told them he expected such an amendment to be offered on the floor. Though opposed to the Civil Rights bill, he agreed that if it were going to pass it should cover sex discrimination as well so that women would have the same rights as African Americans. Most believe that he supported the amendment to make the bill unacceptable to others in the House and as a way to kill the Civil Rights Act. Female congresswomen Martha Griffiths (D-MI) and Katherine St. George (R-NY), who backed the amendment, planned on introducing the amendment, but they decided to let Smith introduce it himself. They believed Smith's sponsorship of the amendment, as part of a Southern strategy designed to defeat the entire bill, would guarantee the votes of 100 or more Representatives from the deep South, who would otherwise vote against a feminist measure. On February 8, 1964, Smith introduced the amendment to add the word "sex" to the provisions of Title VII of the Civil Rights Act. The debate has since been called the "Ladies' Day in the House."

Many believe that Smith was insincere in introducing the amendment. Though he has denied this, Representative Martha Griffiths said that it was Smith himself who told her he had proposed the amendment as a joke. On the House floor, he began his own arguments in its favor by reading a letter from a woman complaining that the 1960 Census had reported 2,661,000 "extra females" in the United States. He laughingly reported that she asked him to introduce legislation to remedy the shortage of men for women to marry. His reading of the letter brought cackles from the floor and from the gallery. Smith repeatedly had to ask for quiet. He concluded, "I read that letter just to illustrate that women have some real grievances." Representative Emanuel Celler, the leader of the coalition handling the bill, responded in kind: "I can say as a result of forty-nine years of experience—and I celebrate my fiftieth wedding anniversary next year—that women, indeed, are not in the minority in my house. . . . I usually have the last two words, and those words are, 'Yes, dear.'" More seriously, he quoted Esther Peterson, who insisted that adding sex to the Civil Rights bill would "not be to the best advantage of women at this time." While the male representatives were having a grand time, the tone of the debate betrayed a deep-rooted sexism that galvanized many in the hall. Despite the many reservations expressed by many women representatives, every congresswoman but one abruptly rallied to support the amendment in defiance of party disci-

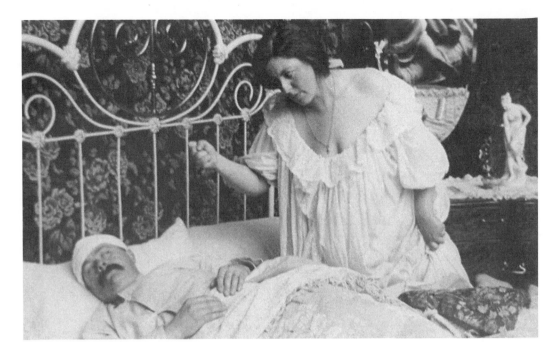

During the struggle for women's rights, opponents showed deep-rooted sexism by joking that women did not need an Equal Rights Amendment because they were already too powerful in their homes.

pline. Martha Griffiths, a supporter of the bill, stood and chastised her male peers. She pointed out that the men's laughter only underscored women's second class citizenship. She said that the bill without the amendment would leave white women without the same protection that African American women would have. She declared that the main function of protective labor laws for women was to protect men's access to the best paying jobs. She concluded by proclaiming that a white man's vote against the amendment was a vote against his wife, his widow, his sister, and his daughter. The Southern strategy backfired and on February 8, 1964, the amendment against sex discrimination passed by a vote of 168 to 133. As the teller announced the vote count, a woman activist from the gallery cried, "We made it! God bless America!" The whole Civil Rights Act passed the House two days later by a vote of 290 to 130. Every man who had spoken in favor of the sex discrimination amendment, except Rep. Ross Bass (D-TN), voted against the Civil Rights Act. The Senate passed its version of the Civil Rights Bill, with the sex discrimination provision included. Two weeks later, the House adopted the Senate version by better than a two-thirds vote. On the same day, President Johnson signed the bill into law. By utilizing reactionary Southern strategists, and without a widespread national women's rights movement, a few feminists pulled off a major political coup. The bill prohibited discrimination against women by any company with 25 or more employees. It also established the Equal Employment Opportunity Commission (EEOC) to address discrimination claims.

The next year, the Senate confirmed President Johnson's five appointees to the EEOC. They were Franklin D. Roosevelt Jr., Luther Holcomb, Richard Graham, Samuel C. Jackson, and Aileen Clarke Hernandez, the only woman. Hernandez, an African American woman with an Hispanic surname, called her appointment a "20 percent nod to more than 50 percent of the population." When the appointees were named, few thought that sexual discrimination would make up many of the cases upon which they would rule. In fact, they named no women to top appointments. Hernandez said that "the Commission was not planning to be an example to industry of the meaning of 'equal opportunity employer.'" In fact, when looking over the hundreds of pages of documents to prepare them for their duties, Hernandez said she found "only limited references to sex discrimination—all of which suggested minimal attention to the entire subject." A government official said that the EEOC would be lenient in enforcing sexist claims "if the women's groups will let us get away with it." Hernandez decried that "Commission meetings produced a sea of male faces, nearly all of which reflected attitudes that ranged from boredom to virulent hostility whenever the issue of sex discrimination was raised." The message came through clearly that the Commission's priority was race discrimination—and apparently only

President Lyndon Johnson signed the Civil Rights Act of 1964, which prohibited certain instances of discrimination against women and established the Equal Employment Opportunity Commission (EEOC) to address discrimination claims. Of the five people appointed to the EEOC, only one was a woman.

as it related to African American men. "There was such insensitivity to sex discrimination," she noted, "that a major meeting with employers in California was arranged at a private club which barred women—even though I was scheduled to accompany the Chairman to the meeting." Although much of the EEOC seemed reluctant to deal with sex discrimination cases, they soon had to. One third of the complaints dealt with sex discrimination.

Attitudes in the press and society were little different. In light of the sex discrimination clause, on June 22, 1965, the Wall Street Journal asked readers to picture "a shapeless, knobby-kneed male 'bunny' serving drinks to a group of stunned businessmen in a Playboy Club" or a "matronly vice-president" chasing her male secretary around a desk. An official of a large airline was quoted asking, "What are we going to do now when a gal walks into our office, demands a job as an airline pilot, and has the credentials to qualify?" The manager of an electronic company who employed only women worried aloud about having to provide "equal opportunity" to men: "I suppose we'll have to advertise for people with small, nimble fingers and hire the first male midget with unusual dexterity."

Government continued to expand women's rights. Presidential Executive Order 17 in 1967 prohibited hiring bias against women by federal government contractors. In 1972, after nearly 50 years

of trying, both houses of Congress passed the Equal Rights Amendment. President Richard Nixon signed it. The 1972 Civil Rights Act passed and banned sex discrimination in employment and education. In that same year Shirley Chisholm became the first African American to run for president.

But sexual discrimination against women persisted. Retail stores often refused to issue independent credit cards to married women. Divorced or single women found it difficult to obtain credit or to purchase a house or a car. Congress, state legislatures, and city councils often passed welfare, crime, prostitution, and abortion laws that displayed bias against women. For example, federal investigators investigated women more often than men concerning welfare claims. Sexual biases were often built into laws. For example, a state would usually charge a woman who shot and killed her husband with homicide, whereas it could charge a man who had shot his wife with a less serious offense, such as assault. It took until 1968 for Pennsylvania courts to void a state law that required a woman convicted of a felony be sentenced to the maximum punishment prescribed by law. Men were not subject to this law. More often than not, city attorneys prosecuted women prostitutes while allowing their male customers to go free.

In February 1963, woman activist Betty Friedan published *The Feminine Mystique,* which rapidly hit the best seller lists with 3 million copies sold. It articulated dissatisfaction about limits on women. The public widely read and discussed it. Friedan claimed that there was a substantial reservoir of educated women, not in the labor force, that remained untapped. It remained untapped because "the feminine mystique" forced them to stay isolated in suburban homes with an "almost mandatory 2.3 children and a largely absentee husband, uniformed in a gray flannel suit and preoccupied with upward mobility on a corporate organization chart." Friedan argued for the right of a wife and mother to pursue her own identity and career. Many point to this as the beginning of the modern-day feminist (women's liberation) movement.

Birth Control and Abortion

Increasingly attached to the women's movement was the idea of a woman's control of her own body and the issue of birth control and abortion. This issue has since split the United States into pro-life (anti-abortion) and pro-choice (the right to choose an abortion) factions. Americans had debated and discussed this issue since the early twentieth century, but now it exploded onto the American landscape.

Margaret Sanger, pioneer of birth control education and author of *Women and the New Race,* proclaimed, "No woman can call herself free who does not own and control her own body. No woman can call herself free until she can choose conscientiously whether she will or will not be a mother." She is often called the founder of the birth-control movement in the United States. She was a nurse who worked among the impoverished in the poverty-stricken areas of New York City in the early 1900s. Here she saw the results of no birth control methods, dangerous "back-alley" and self-induced abortions, and high rates of infant and maternal deaths. Soon, Sanger came to believe that a woman must plan the size of her family. In 1914, she founded the National Birth Control League. In that same year a grand jury indicted her for sending out copies of the magazine *The Woman Rebel,* which advocated birth control. The government charged her with obscenity under the federal Comstock Law of 1873. The court dismissed her case in 1916. She opened the first birth control clinic in the United States. Police arrested her and she served 20 days in jail in 1917 because her clinic was deemed a public nuisance. Continued government harassment brought public sympathy, and in 1936 Congress amended the Comstock Law. In 1921, she founded the American Birth Control League. In 1942, this organization merged with others and became the Planned Parenthood Federation of America. Sanger later became the first president of the International Planned Parenthood Federation.

As with so many movements in the United States, the pro-choice movement ended up in the courts. Until 1936, states allowed birth control only for the prevention of disease. In 1936, a federal court ruled that birth control was legal for its own sake. Birth control became more and more prevalent, as medical breakthroughs occurred. In 1960, the Food and Drug Administration (FDA) approved birth control pills by prescription. Nevertheless, states passed laws against contraceptive use. In 1965 came the landmark case of *Griswold* v. *Connecticut,* in which the Supreme Court struck down state prohibitions against the prescription, sale, or use of contraceptives. The Court ruled that the use of contraceptives was a privacy issue and the state did not have an important enough interest to prohibit their use. Some judges said that the right to privacy was a right older than the Bill of Rights. In 1972 in *Eisenstadt* v. *Baird,* the Supreme Court declared unconstitutional a Massachusetts law that prohibited unmarried persons from obtaining birth control on the basis that if the "right of privacy means anything," it means that the "individual, married or single, is to be free from unwarranted governmental intrusion into matters so fundamentally affecting a person as the decision whether to bear or beget a child."

The fight surrounding abortion has been fought for the last two centuries. Interestingly, states passed the first abortion laws not as a matter of a woman's choice to bear or not to bear children, but because so many women had died during abortions. In 1821, Connecticut passed the nation's first anti-abortion law because up to one third of all abortions being done ended in the mother's death. Connecticut wanted to control and thereby reduce the dangerous risks of abortion. By 1840, only eight states restricted abortion. Just before the Civil War, Dr. Horatio Storer of the American Medical Association (AMA) began the movement to ban abortions because of medical risks. In 1869, the Catholic Church declared that abortion was the taking of life. Furthermore, the

church warned it might excommunicate anyone who had or performed an abortion. Many Protestant churches opposed abortion not on moral but on sexist grounds: Protestant women should have more babies and thus spread Protestantism. In 1873, Congress passed the Comstock Law, which forbad the use of the mail to send "obscene" or "immoral" materials. It defined "immoral" materials as "every article, instrument, substance, drug, medicine, or thing which is advertised or described in a manner calculated to lead another to use or apply it for preventing conception or producing abortion." By 1900 nearly every state restricted abortion. Women were forced to obtain abortions illegally; this practice often led to the woman's death, especially for the poor who frequently were financially forced to go to "doctors" with little or no medical training.

The right to have an abortion was challenged in the courts. In 1939, Connecticut shut down a birth-control center and seized its contraceptives under an 1879 anti-abortion law. The defendants did not dispute the charges but claimed that the law was unconstitutional because married couples have a natural right that protects their decision regarding procreation. The Connecticut Supreme Court disagreed and found the law constitutional.

In 1967, the National Organization of Women (NOW) added the "Right of Women to Control Their Reproductive Lives" to their Women's Bill of Rights. In the late 1960s and early 1970s, many groups, including Planned Parenthood, the YWCA, and Church Women United came out in support of abortion. In 1970, New York and Hawaii repealed their anti-abortion laws. In response the next year, Dr. John C. Wilke organized the first anti-abortion campaign, which soon became the National Right to Life Movement. The Catholic Church began to organize against legalized abortion.

The watershed year for abortion rights was 1973, marked by the landmark case of *Roe* v. *Wade* and a lesser known companion case, *Doe* v. *Bolton.* In *Roe,* the Supreme Court (voting seven to two) declared that the "right of personal privacy includes the abortion decision, but that this right is not unqualified and must be considered against important state interest in regulation." The Court recognized the right of a woman to obtain an abortion "without undue interference from the State." However, the Court said that this right was not absolute but must be balanced with the states's interest in protecting potential life and a mother's health. To find this balance, the Court divided pregnancy into trimesters. In the first trimester, a woman had an absolute right to abortion. In the second trimester, women's right to privacy still outweighed the state's interest except in cases where the health of the mother was in jeopardy. In the third trimester, the state's interest outweighed the right to privacy and therefore could restrict abortions.

The year following *Roe,* conservative Senators Jesse Helms and James Buckley unsuccessfully sponsored a constitutional amendment to ban abortion. In 1976, the Republican Party Platform and President Gerald Ford called for a constitutional amendment "to restore the protection of the right to life for unborn children." Many cases have followed *Roe;* however, the basic principles have not changed. States have attempted to modify the decision with little result. States have placed parental notifications on abortions with some success. With the changing make-up of the Supreme Court, pro-life forces hope for a change in position of the Court. As this book went to press such a change had not occurred. Polls taken across the United States vary depending on who is doing the polling, but they generally show slightly more than the majority supporting pro-choice positions. Many political observers credit the loss of the Bush-Quayle presidency on a strong pro-choice position by the party in the presidential campaign of 1992. In 1996, much effort was placed on presenting pro-choice views as alternative views held by many Republicans.

Activism

Women's activism increased in the 1960s and 1970s. New deliberations entered into the feminist perspective. Increased and more accurate knowledge of birth control, including the use of contraceptives and abortion, gave women greater control over their own futures. Everywhere, one heard discussion of the women's liberation movement. Television talk shows, news programs, and magazines featured discussions by articulate feminists on the need for deep reforms in American society. Society often became factionalized between those in support of and those opposed to the women's liberation movement. In 1970 a doctoral dissertation by Kate Millett became the best-selling book *Sexual Politics.* Television, magazines, books, newspapers, and commentators waded into the controversy and initiated debates and discussions. Politicians entered the fray. Conservative television commentator Pat Buchanan declared in a syndicated column in 1971, "Rail as they will about 'discrimination,' women are simply not endowed by nature with the same measures of single-minded ambition and the will to succeed in the fiercely competitive world of Western capitalism." Members of the left such as Senator Edward Kennedy

of Massachusetts shot back in 1972 declaring that the right was sexist and attempting to "enslave" women. Rush Limbaugh called and still refers to the extremist members of the women's movement as "femi-nazis."

In 1966 Betty Friedan organized the National Organization for Women (NOW). This organization began fighting for improvements in areas such as child-care centers for professional women who wished to return to work. NOW members lobbied Congress, lectured all across the country, and initiated legal suits against sex discrimination. By 1967, NOW workers had become much more activist and more and more impatient for decisive and bold changes. Young college women and radical activists increasingly took leadership positions within NOW. They also formed a variety of new groups such as SALT (Sisters All Learning Together), WITCH (Women's International Terrorist Conspiracy from Hell), Bread and Roses, and the Women's Liberation Union. Some of these organizations were merely discussion groups. Others were activist and worked for consciousness-raising, more liberal abortion laws, and the passage of an equal rights amendment to the Constitution. Some went so far as to intertwine their movement with Marxist and black revolutionary movements. A minority of women liberationists openly opposed men in general. They viewed men as oppressors of women and denounced them for regarding women as sexual objects. But most groups wanted relationships between men and women that were based on cooperation and mutual respect. They believed that women should be judged as individuals, not by their sex. They felt that advancement and personal rewards should be based on personal achievement. They wanted women to have roles besides those of wife and mother, just as men had separate roles from those of husband and father. For example, many worked for the ordination of women to be priests, pastors, and rabbis, often causing splits within religious faiths.

The "Women's Decade," 1975–1985, began with the International Women's Year observed during 1975. Some 10,000 delegates from 123 nations participated in a women's conference in Mexico City. Many women's groups in the 1980s turned their attention to such economic issues as poverty: Female-headed families accounted for nearly half of all poor families. While gains seemed to be made in the workplace, many

women found that a so-called glass ceiling, another name for discrimination, held them back from attaining promotions. In 1968, activists had established the National Women's Hall of Fame in Seneca Falls, New York; the Women's Rights National Historic Park was set aside there in 1980. However, the largest disappointment of the "women's decade" occurred in 1982. The deadline for ratification of the Equal Rights Amendment expired. It was three states short of adoption.

Affirmative Action

Another area that helped equalize the playing field for women and men was affirmative action. Affirmative action can be defined as (a) a preference for a certain class of persons where all are equally qualified, or (b) a preference for a certain class of persons with lower qualifications. After the passage of Title VII of the Civil Rights Act of 1964, the Courts early ruled that when a promotion is made to a woman over a man where both were equally qualified, to further the goals of a state, there was no denial of equal protection of the law. Women used these rulings to obtain jobs and economic equality. However, a huge public backlash occurred when white males were passed over for minorities or women. Plaintiffs filed so-called reverse discrimination suits, in which they claimed that they were being discriminated against because they were white and male. The

Court agreed in the famous *Bakke* case, and affirmative action programs have decreased up to the present day.

The issue of sexual harassment came to the fore in the early 1990s. In 1991, the televised Anita Hill-Clarence Thomas Senate hearings on allegations of sexual harassment in the workplace helped focus public attention on the issues of power in the workplace. Sexual harassment can take many forms. It can include requests for sexual favors or unwelcome sexual advances. It can be defined as unwelcome verbal, physical, or visual sexual conduct made, either explicitly or implicitly, as a term or condition of any individual's employment or as a basis for employment decisions affecting the individual. It can also be actions of a sexual nature that create an intimidating or offensive working environment. Sexual harassment cases are based on Title VII of the Civil Rights Act of 1964, which forbade discrimination in employment based on sex, race, religion, or national origin. The Equal Employment Opportunity Commission (EEOC) created by the act, issued rules in the 1980s that stated that an employer must provide a workplace free from sexual harassment or intimidation. The U.S. Supreme Court upheld this rule in 1986 when it held that creating a gender hostile or an abusive work environment, even without economic loss for the person being harassed, violated Title VII. Employees who have been subjected to sexual harassment can sue employers in civil court and ask for monetary damages.

In 1981, President Ronald Reagan appointed Clarence Thomas, an African American, to head the civil rights division of the Department of Education; in 1982, President Reagan appointed Thomas to head the EEOC. In 1990, President George Bush appointed him to the U.S. Court of Appeals for District of Columbia Circuit, and in 1991, President Bush appointed him to the Supreme Court to replace Thurgood Marshall. His nomination soon became controversial first because of Thomas's conservative views and additionally because of charges of sexual harassment brought against him by Anita Hill, a former employee at the EEOC.

The road to these accusations had occurred years earlier. When hearings over Thomas's appointment to the U.S. Court of Appeals were approaching, the Federal Bureau of Investigation (FBI) interviewed Anita Hill, then a law professor at the University of Oklahoma. During the interview she stated that Clarence Thomas made unwanted sexual advances toward her while he was her boss at the EEOC. They asked her if she would testify to this and she declined. They again interviewed her before the Supreme Court hearings and again she gave the same statements to the FBI. Once more they asked her if she wanted to testify at the hearings and again she refused. During the hearings, someone leaked these statements to the press. It made headlines across the country. Reporters mobbed her at the law school. Under public and political pressure, she testified to these facts in front of Senate subcommittee. The Senate confirmed Thomas's nomination by the narrow margin of 52 to 48, but not before the media had beamed the hearings into living rooms all across the country. The public soon had a concept of what was sexual discrimination. Surveys showed that most of the supporters of Hill were women and most of the supporters of Thomas were men. A public dialogue began that continues today.

Although women have made remarkable gains in the workplace, the great majority of women are still mired in clerical positions, factory work, retail sales, and service jobs. Secretaries, bookkeepers, and typists account for a large portion of female clerical workers. Women in factories work as machine operators, assemblers, and inspectors. Many women in service jobs work as waitresses, cooks, hospital attendants, cleaning women, and hairdressers. Some women have attained high-level positions, such as chief executive officers of businesses or as superintendents in school districts, but the number of these positions is certainly not equal to women's percentage of the total population (approximately 50 percent).

Women have made gains in the political spectrum as well. In 1971, Patience Sewell Latting was elected mayor of Oklahoma City, then the largest city in the nation with a woman mayor. By 1979, Jane Byrne of Chicago and Dianne Feinstein of San Francisco had become mayors. In 1990, Sharon Pratt Dixon was elected mayor of Washington, D.C.

At the federal and state level, Frances Perkins became the first woman Cabinet member as Secretary of Labor under President Franklin D. Roosevelt. Oveta Culp Hobby became Secretary of Health, Education, and Welfare in the Cabinet of Dwight D. Eisenhower. Carla A. Hills was Secretary of Housing and Urban Development in Gerald R. Ford's Cabinet. Jimmy Carter chose two women for his original Cabinet: Juanita M. Kreps as Secretary of Commerce and Patricia Roberts Harris as Secretary of Housing and Urban Development. Harris was the first African American woman in a presidential Cabinet. After Congress created the Department of Education, President Carter named Shirley Mount Hufstedler to head it. Ronald Reagan's Cabinet included Margaret Heckler, Secretary of Health and Human Services, and Elizabeth Dole, Secretary of Transportation. Under George Bush, Dole became Secretary of Labor. Representative Lynn Martin succeeded her. Bush chose Antonia Novello, an Hispanic, for Surgeon General in 1990. In 1974, Ella Grasso of Connecticut became the first woman Governor elected in her own right. In 1981, Sandra Day O'Connor became the first woman U.S. Supreme Court justice. In 1984, Geraldine Ferraro became the first woman from a major political party to be nominated as vice president. In 1992, more women ran for and were elected to public office than in any other year in United States history.

Throughout the women's movement, the citizenry has not always greeted gains positively. Phyllis Schlafly, a leading opponent of feminist activist politics, denied in *Ms.* magazine in March of 1974 that women had even been treated unfairly. She wrote, "The claim that American women are downtrodden and unfairly treated is the fraud of the century." The movement of women into nontraditional roles has been welcomed by many and decried by many. Women are often told to stay out of men's traditional roles; for example, Hillary Clinton was heavily criticized for her visibility and work in the Clinton administration. The women's movement, much like other human and civil rights movements in the 1990s, might be losing steam. What the future holds, no one knows.

Labor Rights

The United States has had the bloodiest labor history of any industrialized nation on Earth. Labor conditions were horrible at the turn of the twentieth century. The population was skyrocketing. In 1860 the U.S. population was a little over 31 million people. Population grew to over 76 million by 1900 and to over 92 million by 1910. Business growth was high. Railroads, the backbone of U.S. industrialization, had expanded from about 30,000 miles of track before the Civil War to nearly 270,000 miles by the turn of the century. The industrial labor force went from 3 million to 8 million between 1880 and 1910. Large factories, which had existed only in the textile industry before the Civil War, increasingly became more common in a variety of industries. But the high population growth and immigration helped to keep the value of individual workers low.

Working Conditions in General

Sweatshops dominated the cities, where some people worked 70 to 80 hours per week. Conditions were unsanitary. (See the section in this chapter on women's working conditions.) Employers used child labor, especially minority child labor. By 1910, over 70 percent of Jewish girls aged sixteen years and older worked in sweatshops. According to the Commission on Industrial Relations, in 1914, industrial accidents killed 35,000 workers and injured 700,000 more.

On March 25, 1911, a tragedy occurred that brought these terrible working conditions into public view. Fire broke out at Triangle Shirtwaist Company in New York and swept through the eighth, ninth, and tenth floors. These floors were too high for fire ladders that only went up to the seventh floor. Although the law required that doors open outward and be open during business

hours, the company's doors opened inward and often were locked. The *New York Word* reported that "young women were burned to death at their worktables, or jammed against the locked exit door, or leaped to their deaths down the elevator shafts." It went on, reporting further that

> . . . screaming men and women and boys and girls crowded out on the many window ledges and threw themselves into the streets far below. They jumped with their clothing ablaze. The hair of some of the girls streamed up aflame as they leaped. Thud after thud sounded on the pavements. It is a ghastly fact that on both the Greene Street and Washington Place sides of the building there grew mounds of the dead and dying . . .

> From opposite windows spectators saw again and again pitiable companionships formed in the instant of death—girls who placed their arms around each other as they leaped.

One fireman reported at the scene that "They hit the pavement just like hail. . . . We could hear the thuds faster than we could [watch] the bodies fall." Officials found so many bodies that they could not take them all away in ambulances and patrol wagons. Grocers, peddlers, and other citizens volunteered their wagons and handcarts. When the counting was done 146 workers died, most of them Italian or Jewish. This fire galvanized the citizenry and workers. One hundred thousand people marched in a memorial parade down Broadway.

Americans felt conditions were so bad that they considered alternative economic and political systems. Socialism, a system of state ownership of enterprises, rose early in the late nineteenth century and grew quickly in the early twentieth century. Socialism seemed an alternative economic and political system, not the dirty word it has become in the last part of the twentieth century. However, socialism in the Soviet Union tended to discredit the idea for Americans after 1919.

The Progressive Age, or the Age of Reform, began under Theodore Roosevelt and continued through Woodrow Wilson's administration. The muckrakers of the early twentieth century did much to call attention to the inequities and corruption of big business. Upton Sinclair (*The Jungle*) made people look at the excesses of the meatpacking industry. Other muckrakers such as Theodore Dreiser, Frank Norris, the socialist Jack London, Ida Tarbell, and Lincoln Steffens exposed corruption in the cities and in large companies such as Standard Oil (Tarbell). Congress passed

146 workers, most of them Italian or Jewish, died in the Triangle Shirtwaist fire in 1911.

the Meat Inspection Act, the Pure Food and Drug Act, and other laws to control monopolies and some excesses of business. Many individuals considered socialism as an answer because this period provided little help to African Americans, feminists, labor organizers, and socialists. Women moved into the labor movement. In 1900, at 80 years of age, Susan B. Anthony went to hear socialist leader Eugene V. Debs speak. At the end of the speech they clasped hands warmly. Anthony laughed and said, "Give us suffrage and we'll give you socialism." Debs laughed and replied, "Give us socialism and we'll give you suffrage."

Conditions at the turn of the twentieth century were an extension of conditions in the nineteenth century. The first strike for the ten-hour day

came in Boston in 1825. Some strikes occurred during the Civil War. However, labor tensions did not rise dramatically until the latter part of the nineteenth century. Often, tensions arose between police, who usually sided with business, and workers. In 1874, unemployed workers demonstrated in New York's Tompkins Square Park. Police charged into the crowd of men, women, and children, swinging billy clubs indiscriminately. Hundreds were hurt. Abram Duryee, NYC Commissioner of Police, proudly stated, "It was the most glorious sight I ever saw . . ." In the 1870s, railroad workers walked the picket line across the country and the government called out federal troops to put the strike down. In 1884, the Federation of Organized Trades and Labor Unions, soon to be the American Federation of

At the turn of the twentieth century sweatshops dominated the cities, where some people worked 70 to 80 hours per week.

Labor (AFL), passed a resolution demanding that "8 hours shall constitute a legal day's work from and after May 1, 1886."

Beginning on May 1, 1886, thousands of workers picketed and struck demanding the universal adoption of the eight-hour day. In Chicago, 30,000 workers joined 50,000 workers already on strike and brought Chicago manufacturing to a standstill. Fear of violence gripped the city. On Monday, May 3, a huge fight broke out at McCormick Reaper between locked-out unionists and "scabs" (non-unionist workers hired to replace locked-out workers). Chicago police moved quickly with clubs and guns to restore order; they left four unionists dead. A group of angry anarchists, led by August Spies and Albert

Parsons, called on workers to arm themselves and participate in a massive protest demonstration in Haymarket Square on May 4. Only 3,000 showed up and the demonstration appeared to have failed. Then, someone still unknown, threw a bomb that killed seven policemen and injured 67 others. Hysterical city and state government officials rounded up eight anarchists, tried them for murder, and sentenced them to death. On November 11, 1887, the government executed four of them, including Parsons and Spies. All whom they executed were anarchists and advocated armed struggle and violence, but prosecutors found no evidence that any had actually thrown the Haymarket bomb. They died for what they believed, not for the crime that the state convicted them of. A quarter of a million people attended Parson's funeral

On May 1, 1886, thousands of workers began a strike, demanding the universal adoption of the eight-hour work day.

procession to express their outrage at this gross miscarriage of justice. The injustice of Haymarket became a unionist symbol.

Time and again labor called strikes. In the 1880s, strikes occurred in the sugar fields of Louisiana. In the 1890s, garment workers struck the factories of New York and mine workers struck from Pennsylvania to Idaho. Railroad workers again struck. With most of these strikes came violence and government intervention.

With the turn of the new century, strikes were the order of the day. Violence permeated both sides. Business called in strike breakers as well as private and government police. In 1902, scab-herders (those who brought in and controlled strike-breaking workers) killed 14 miners and wounded 22 others at Pana, Illinois. Troops were called out in Cripple Creek, Colorado, to put down a strike. In Dunnville, Colorado, the Colorado Militia attacked striking miners, killing 6 union members, and arrested 15 others. In New York came the "Uprising of the 20,000," an action by female garment workers.

Things were little different on the strikers' side. They beat strike breakers, attacked police, and destroyed company property. In Los Angeles, dynamite destroyed part of Llewellyn Ironworks. In Pennsylvania, workers firebombed a company building. One Chicago union hired a "slugger." They paid him $50 for every scab he "discour-

aged" from working. He merrily described his job, "Oh, there ain't nothin' to it. I gets my fifty, then I goes out and finds the guy they wanna have slugged. I goes up to 'im and I says to 'im, 'My friend, by way of meaning no harm,' and then I gives it to 'im—biff! in the mug. Nothin' to it."

A bomb killed police officers and other workers in a San Francisco parade. Violence begat more violence. Neither side would be outdone by the other.

Workers felt that they were dispensable, but business looked at profit margins, expansion, and stockholders. This view became exaggerated in 1911 with the publication of *The Principles of Scientific Management* by Frederick W. Taylor. This book showed businesses how to divide labor into tasks and how to become more efficient by using this division of labor. It made workers interchangeable. Assembly lines developed. Workers needed little knowledge or few skills to work on assembly lines, because simple tasks were all that this new division of labor required. On these lines, workers felt they had lost their individuality and humanity. They felt more like chattel than workers. It was a system that industry quickly grasped, especially big business and sweatshops. For example, in the fledgling auto industry, Ford sold only 10,607 automobiles in 1909. By 1913, they had sold 168,000. By 1914 they sold 248,000.

Eugene Debs (1855–1926)

The prominent American labor leader founded the American Socialist Party in 1900 and led it for many years in the early part of the twentieth century. Debs ran as Socialist Party candidate for president in 1900, 1904, 1908, 1912, and 1920. As a labor leader he helped form the American Railway Union in 1893, of which he became president. In that capacity he led the great Pullman Strike of 1894. The federal government obtained an injunction against the strike, as President Grover Cleveland sought to suppress the strike through the use of federal troops. Debs was convicted of violating an injunction against the strike and sent to jail for six months. During World War I Debs refused to take part in the government war effort. A leading pacifist, he was sentenced to ten years in jail for his beliefs. He ran for president from prison in 1920, winning almost 920,000 votes. Debs was released from prison in 1921, on the order of President Warren Harding, and he was widely seen as a martyr for his beliefs. His work was a milestone in the development of free speech in America.

Many organizations and unions arose during this period. In 1900, workers founded the International Garment Workers Union. In 1903, women united to form the National Women's Trade Union League, with Mary Morton Kehew as president and Jane Addams as vice president. But the most important union organized was the "one big union," the Industrial Workers of the World (IWW), in 1905. In Chicago, 200 socialists, anarchists, and radical trade unionists met from all over the United States. They included Big Bill Haywood, a leader of the Western Federation of Miners; Eugene Debs, leader of the Socialist party; and Mother Mary Jones, the 75-year-old white-haired matriarch of the United Mine Workers of America. Haywood in his autobiography said that he picked up a piece of lumber that lay on the platform and pounded it as a gavel to begin the convention:

workers . . . This is the Continental Congress of the working-class. We are here to confederate the workers of this country into a working-class

movement that shall have for its purpose the emancipation of the working-class from the slave bondage of capitalism. . . . The aims and objects of this organization shall be to put the working-class in possession of the economic power, the means of life, in control of the machinery of production and distribution, without regard to the capitalist masters.

Haywood became a leader of the IWW. The convention drew up a constitution, whose preamble stated, "The working class and the employing class have nothing in common. There can be no peace so long as hunger and want are found among millions of working people and the few, who make up the employing class, have all the good things of life."

The IWW opposed the idea of individual craft unions. One of its pamphlets explained that "the directory of unions of Chicago shows in 1903 a total of 56 different unions in the packing houses, divided up still more in 14 different national trades unions of the American Federation of Labor." They felt that employers were united in their opposition and so should unions. The IWW took the idea of "one big union" and their inclusiveness philosophy seriously. It included women, foreigners, and minority workers, skilled and unskilled. Conventioneers in Louisiana told Bill Haywood that it was against the law to have interracial meetings in Louisiana. Haywood retorted, "You work in the same mills together. Sometimes a black man and a white man chop down the same tree together. You are meeting in convention now to discuss the conditions under which you labor. . . . Why not be sensible about this and call the Negroes into the Convention? If it is against the law, this is one time when the law should be broken." Haywood invited African Americans into the convention and many accepted.

Followers of the IWW came to be called "Wobblies," first dubbed by their enemies to describe mental instability. They opposed contracts with employers. Wobblies believed such contracts prevented workers from striking on their own or in sympathy with other strikers, and also turned union people into strikebreakers. They began with and improved on the idea that negotiations by leaders should replace continuous struggles by rank and file. They spoke of direct action: "Direct action means industrial action directly by, for, and of the workers themselves, without the treacherous aid of labor misleaders or scheming politicians. A strike that is initiated, controlled, and settled by the workers directly affected is direct action . . . Direct action is industrial democracy." An IWW pamphlet offered this definition: "Shall I tell you what direct action means? The worker on the job shall tell the boss when and where he shall work, how long and for what wages and under what conditions."

Newspapers described the IWW as consisting of people who engaged in violence and militancy. Some of this was true; the research of Patrick Renshaw (*The Wobblies,* 1968) shows that Wobblies were not afraid to engage in violence. However, they usually did not initiate violence but rather responded to company violence with more violence. For example, in McKees Rocks, Pennsylvania, they led a strike of 6,000 workers in 1909 against an affiliate of U.S. Steel. They defied and battled state troopers. They promised a trooper's life for every worker killed. In one gun battle four strikers and three troopers were killed. They also won the strike.

The IWW excelled at developing a rare cooperation and a bond among workers. They had a high level of energy and persisted in their beliefs. They inspired others and mobilized thousands at one place. When companies used police, sheriffs, and the national guard to break strikes and beat, tar, feather, and kill Wobblies, the union seemed to become stronger.

For example, in 1912, in Lawrence, Massachusetts, the IWW struck the American Woolen Company in the middle of January. The average wage was $8.76 a week. Conditions were life-threatening. A female physician in Lawrence, Dr. Elizabeth Shapleigh, wrote, "A considerable number of the boys and girls die within the first two or three years after beginning work . . . thirty-six out of every 100 of all the men and women who work in the mill die before or by the time they are twenty-five years of age."

It was in midwinter, January, when workers received their pay checks. Workers soon realized that their wages, already too low to feed their families, had been cut. They shut down their looms and walked out of the mill. The next day, 5,000 workers at another mill walked off the job. They marched to a third mill, rushed the gates, shut off the power to the looms, and called on the other workers to stop. Soon four mills and 10,000 workers were on strike.

The IWW constitution stated, "There can be no peace as long as hunger and want are found among millions of working people and the few, who make up the employing class, have all the good things of life."

Weeks dragged on and union food for strikers ran low. The strikers needed food and fuel for 50,000 people (the entire population of Lawrence was only 86,000). The IWW set up soup kitchens supported by unions all across the country. Twenty-two companies of militia and two troops of cavalry were called in. Martial law was declared. Police attacked strikers and a riot broke out. Workers' children were hungry and suffering. A call went out across the U.S. for help. The IWW received 400 letters offering to take the children out of Lawrence. The union began organizing the children's departure. On February 10, 100 children left for New York City. The next week another 100 children left to go to New York and 35 children went to Barre, Vermont. The strikers' resolve strengthened. The city cited a statute on child neglect and refused to allow any more children to leave Lawrence. Nevertheless, on February 24, 40 more children prepared to go to Philadelphia. When they arrived at the train station, parents and children found it filled with police. A member of the Women's Committee of Philadelphia described the scene: ". . . the police closed in on us with their clubs, beating right and left, with no thought of children who were in the most desperate danger of being trampled to death. The mothers and children were thus hurled in a mass and bodily dragged to a military truck, and even then clubbed, irrespective of the cries of the panic-stricken women and children." A week later, police beat women with clubs who were returning

Jacob Coxey *(1854–1951)*

Jacob Coxey may be regarded as an American original. He was a businessman whose mode of free expression transformed him into a social reformer. Coxey was a prosperous businessman who was deeply shaken by the financial panic of 1893. He realized that he was compelled to fire more than 40 of his workers because of dire economic conditions beyond their control. Rather than accept these shifts in the tide of affairs, Coxey decided to take the dramatic step of leading a march on Washington, intending to improve the lot of his workers and workers elsewhere. On March 25, 1894, Coxey led a ragtag "Army" of 500 workingmen in that march on Washington. This was one of many such protest marches.

Coxey believed that the march would so shake the consciences of congressmen that they would consider the passage of legislation to create work for the unemployed. Coxey was ridiculed as "General Coxey" for his sincere efforts. When he sought to give a speech explaining his purposes, the demonstrators, including Coxey, were dispersed by the police. Although often regarded as a figure of fun, Coxey continued to promote the cause of unemployed workers and to argue for public works projects to generate new jobs. Coxey returned to the capitol steps in 1944 to deliver the speech he had intended to deliver 50 years before. Coxey's views regarding governmental obligations to provide help for the unemployed were eventually realized after the election in 1932 of President Franklin Delano Roosevelt. Coxey ran and lost as a candidate for the presidency in 1932 and 1936.

members at any one time. People became members for a time and then left. As many as a hundred thousand workers were members at one time or another; that membership made them an influence on the country far beyond their numbers. They traveled everywhere. Businesses greatly feared them. They organized, wrote, spoke, sang, and spread their message and their spirit.

Comradery developed through song. One IWW songwriter and organizer, Joe Hill, wrote dozens of songs. They were satirical, funny, and related to workers' class consciousness. They appeared in *The Industrial Worker,* the official publication of the IWW and its *Little Red Song Book.* He became popular in his time. His song "The Preacher and the Slave" focused on a favorite IWW target, the church:

> Long-haired preachers come out every night,
> Try to tell you what's wrong and what's right;
> But when asked how 'bout something to eat
> They will answer with voices so sweet:
> You will eat, bye and bye,
> In that glorious land above the sky;
> Work and pray, live on hay,
> You'll get pie in the sky when you die.

The Lawrence, Massachusetts, strike inspired his song "Rebel Girl." He dedicated it to one of its leaders, Elizabeth Gurley Flynn:

> There are women of many descriptions
> In this queer world, as everyone knows,
> Some are living in beautiful mansions,
> And are wearing the finest of clothes.
> There are blue-blooded queens and princesses,
> Who have charms made of diamonds and pearl,
> But the only and Thoroughbred Lady
> Is the Rebel Girl.

In November, 1915, prosecutors accused Joe Hill of killing a grocer in Salt Lake City in a robbery. They presented no direct evidence to the court, but they submitted much circumstantial evidence. The jury found him guilty. The court sentenced him to death. The case became known throughout the world. The governor of Utah received 10,000 letters in protest. Nonetheless, a firing squad executed Joe Hill. He wrote Bill Haywood just before he died: "Don't waste any time in mourning. Organize."

While the government killed Joe Hill, political radicals made a martyr of him and his songs and legend lived on. Wobblies sang in the factories and at union meetings. They sang on picket lines. They sang in jails—they especially sang in jails. More than once, jailers called fire depart-

from a meeting. One pregnant woman carried unconscious to hospital gave birth to a stillborn child. The workers resolve then became even stronger. They sang songs. They cried on each other's shoulders. They shared what little food they had. The American Woolen Company soon gave in and settled the strike.

Within ten years, the IWW had become such a threat to business that it was under attack from all segments of the business community. The IWW never had more than ten thousand enrolled

ments to hose down the singing Wobblies to try to stop them from singing. Some jailers tired so of the singing that they allowed Wobblies to escape.

Local authorities passed gag laws to prevent them from speaking (see chapter on First Amendment); the IWW defied these laws. For example, in Missoula, Montana, a lumber and mining area, hundreds of Wobblies illegally arrived by train boxcar after some had been prevented from speaking. Police arrested one after another until they clogged the jails and the courts. The town finally repealed its anti-speech ordinance.

The IWW was not always successful. Many members were killed, beaten, or tarred and feathered. For example, IWW member John Stone told of being released from the jail in San Diego at midnight with another IWW man, Joe Marko, and forced into an automobile:

> We were taken out of the city, about twenty miles, where the machine stopped. . . . [I was struck] with a blackjack several times on the head and shoulders; the other man then struck me on the mouth with his fist. The men in the rear then sprang around and kicked me in the stomach. I then started to run away; and heard a bullet go past me. I stopped. . . . In the morning I examined Joe Marko's condition and found that the back of his head had been split open.

In Everett, Washington, in 1916, over 200 armed vigilantes gathered by the sheriff fired on a boatload of Wobblies. They killed five Wobblies and wounded thirty-one. Wobblies killed two of the vigilantes and wounded nineteen. Vigilantes in Montana seized IWW organizer Frank Little and tortured and hanged him. They left his body dangling from a railroad trestle.

But the vision of One Big Union faded quickly amid bitter divisions following the founding convention. By 1908 the organization had split into two groups, both calling themselves the Industrial Workers of the World. One continued in Chicago, the other in Detroit. But what really destroyed the IWW was World War I.

Many leaders of the IWW opposed World War I. Many members were socialist, and the Socialist Party strongly resisted American intervention in the war. The government used this opposition to destroy the IWW. For example, in September 1917, the Department of Justice made raids on 48 IWW meeting halls. Later that month, they arrested 165 IWW leaders for opposition to the draft. One hundred and one went on trial in

April 1918. All were convicted. And though the IWW still exists today, by the 1920s, the organization had little power.

Still, labor made gains during this period. In 1914, the Clayton Act, which limited the use of injunctions in labor disputes, passed. In the same year, Ford Motor Company raised its basic wage from $2.40 for a nine-hour day to $5 for an eight-hour day. In 1915, Congress passed the LaFollette Seamen's Act, which regulated working conditions of seamen. The next year Congress passed the Eight Hour Day Act, which gave the eight-hour day to railroad workers. In 1917, the U.S. Supreme Court upheld it. In 1918, Congress established the Women in Industry Division of the Department of Labor. In 1920, Congress made it the Women's Bureau. The same year it passed the Transportation Act, which established the Railroad Labor Board. During this period even some conditions in sweatshops and factories improved.

Although some working conditions improved, in general conditions were still horrible. In every year in the decade of the 1920s about 25,000 workers were killed on the job and 100,000 permanently disabled. And in the late teens and early twenties an all-out government attack began upon labor under the guise of the "Red Scare."

A communist economic system with a totalitarian government had just taken over Russia. It spread fear among capitalists in the United States.

The most important union to arise from the labor rights movement was the Industrial Workers of the World (IWW), established in 1905. The IWW excelled at developing a rare cooperation and a bond among workers.

The Great Depression devastated the common working man and his family; little work was available and food was scarce.

An attack against communists and socialists began in the United States. Labor was grouped in with these "subversives." In late 1917, in the name of patriotism, several thousand armed vigilantes rounded up 1,200 striking union members in Bisbee, Arizona, and herded them into boxcars to be shipped off and dumped in the New Mexico desert. In late 1919, the government deported to Russia approximately 250 "anarchists," "Communists," and "labor agitators," christening the beginning of the "Red Scare." Early the next year, the Federal Bureau of Investigation (FBI) began carrying out the nationwide Palmer Raids. Federal agents seized labor literature and labor leaders in the hopes of discouraging labor activity. They turned over arrested citizens to state officials for prosecution under various anti-anarchy statutes.

In the 1920s, the Great Depression hit the farmers. In October 1929 with the Great Crash of the stock market, it was obvious that the depression had hit business. The Great Depression devastated the common working man, but the period saw dramatic growth in the labor movement. One out of three workers looked for work. Little was found. Riots for food occurred. Bread lines were everywhere. Veterans returning from World War I found little or no work. They felt forgotten. They held government bonds that were due in the future, but were worthless now. Yip Harburg wrote a song for the show *Americana* called, "Brother, Can You Spare A Dime." It epitomized veterans' feelings in the words:

Once in khaki suits,
Gee, we looked swell,
Full of that Yankee Doodle-de-dum.
Half a million boots went sloggin' through Hell,
I was the kid with the drum.
Say, don't you remember, they called me Al—
It was Al all the time.
Say, don't you remember I'm your pal—
Brother, can you spare a dime.

The Bonus Army Marches on Washington

The anger of the veteran grew. They gathered together to march on Washington, D.C. They demanded that the government do something about their plight. Called the Bonus Army, veterans massed in Washington in the spring and summer of 1932. They demanded that Congress pay off their government bonus bonds now, when they desperately needed the money.

More than 20,000 veterans came. Under pressure from these people, a bill meeting their demands passed the House but failed in the Senate. Most veterans camped in old government buildings, in Anacostia Flats—a section of Virginia near the Capitol—and across the Potomac. President Hoover sent General Douglas MacArthur and the army to evict them.

Six tanks, four companies of infantry, four troops of cavalry, and a machine gun squadron gathered near the White House. MacArthur led his troops, including aide Major Dwight D. Eisenhower and officer George S. Patton down Pennsylvania Avenue. They used tear gas to clear veterans out of old buildings and set fire to the buildings. Then the army moved across the bridge to Anacostia. Thousands of veterans and their wives and children began to run as the tear gas spread. The soldiers set fire to some of the huts; soon the whole encampment was ablaze. When it was over, the veterans had been dispersed, but two veterans had been shot to death, an eleven-week-old baby had died, gas had partially blinded an eight-year-old boy, two police had fractured skulls, and gas had injured a thousand veterans. Many veterans said it was the trenches of World War I all over.

While strikes were still used, especially sit-down strikes, they fought much of the labor battle in Congress and the courtrooms. In 1930, the Supreme Court upheld the Railway Labor Act's prohibition of employer interference or coercion in the choice of bargaining representative. In

In 1932, veterans rallied in Washington, D.C. to demand that Congress pay off their government bonus bonds. General Douglas MacArthur and the U.S. army were sent to disperse the protestors. Two veterans and an infant were killed, and over a thousand people were injured.

1931, Congress passed the Davis-Bacon Act, which provided for payment of prevailing wages to employees of contractors and subcontractors on public construction. In 1932, the Anti-Injunction Act prohibited federal injunctions in most labor disputes. In 1934, Secretary of Labor Frances Perkins, the first woman named to a Cabinet position, called the first National Labor Legislation Conference to obtain closer federal-state cooperation in working out a sound national labor legislation program. The following year, the Wagner Act, often called the National Labor Relations Act, established the first national labor policy that protected workers' rights to organize and elect representatives for collective bargaining. In the same year, Congress passed the Guffey Act to stabilize the coal industry and improve labor conditions. One of the most important labor laws passed in the history of the United States was the Social Security Act passed in 1935. Later that year, the Committee for Industrial Organization (CIO) formed within the AFL.

The next year, 1936, saw Congress pass the Byrnes Act, commonly called the Anti-Strikebreaker Act. This act declared it illegal to transport or aid strikebreakers in interstate or foreign trade. The Walsh-Healey Act (Public Contracts Act) of 1936 established labor standards, including minimum wages, overtime pay, child and convict labor provisions, and safety standards on all federal contracts. In 1937, the Supreme Court upheld the constitutionality of the Wagner Act. In

Teamsters turned to violence in their 1934 strike in Minneapolis.

1938, Congress passed the Fair Labor Standards Act, which created a twenty-five-cent minimum wage and required time and a half pay for over 40 hours.

While workers suffered through the worst economic times in the United States, labor made its greatest gains. When labor seemed to be making gains, World War II broke out. It crippled labor. Much of America believed a European war was again coming to the United States. Questions arose about how labor would fare in this war. In 1941, the Japanese military bombed the territory of Hawaii and the United States entered World War II.

Labor realized that their opposition to World War I had hurt their cause. They were not about to make the same mistake twice. Despite the initial

opposition of many of its members, soon after the attack at Pearl Harbor, the AFL and the CIO both announced a no-strike pledge for the duration of the war. President Franklin Delano Roosevelt established the National War Labor Board to determine procedures for settling labor disputes; later the Board established a procedure for wartime wage adjustments. In 1942, Congress passed the Stabilization Act, which gave President Roosevelt the authority to "stabilize" wages based on September 15, 1942, levels. Roosevelt soon issued an executive order that created a Committee on Fair Employment Practices to eliminate employment discrimination in war industries based on race, creed, color, or national origin. Simultaneously, Congress passed the Smith-Connally Act, called the War Labor Disputes Act,

Pent up labor troubles came to a head in 1946, with the largest strike wave in history.

which authorized plant seizure if necessary to avoid interference with the war effort.

The country mobilized for war and unions went along with it. For the most part, there were no union troubles. When World War II ended, unions were still intact. However, while unions played their wartime role, much pent-up frustration with wages and conditions grew. Unions wanted to move forward with their demands. The largest strike wave in history as pent up labor troubles spilled forward occurred in 1946. Business called for the government to reduce union powers.

In 1947, Congress passed the Taft-Hartley Act restricting union activities and permitting states to pass "right-to-work" laws. The Supreme Court held that the Norris-La Guardia Act prohibition against injunctions in labor disputes was not applicable to the government. Yet despite setbacks, workers made some gains.

In 1948, General Motors and the United Auto Workers signed the first major contract with an escalator clause. It provided wage increases based on the Consumer Price Index. In 1949, Congress passed an amendment to the Fair Labor Standards Act of 1938 that directly prohibited child labor for the first time. In 1950, the United Auto Workers and General Motors signed a five-year contract that granted pensions, automatic cost of living wage adjustments, and a modified union shop. In 1952, when unions rejected the Wage Stabilization Board's recommendations, President Truman seized the steel industry. An eight-week strike followed during which the Supreme Court found the president's action unconstitutional. In the mid-1950s, the Ford Motor Company and the UAW agreed to a supplementary unemployment compensation plan financed by company contributions.

The 1960s, like the 1950s, were a series of ups and downs. Unions had more political power than ever. They had unionized thousands of shops. Now they had to hold on to them. Critics leveled criticisms of mob corruption at unions. In response, Congress passed the Landrum-Griffen Act, which regulated the internal affairs of unions to lessen corruption. In 1962, President Kennedy issued an executive order that gave federal employee's unions the right to bargain collectively with government agencies. In 1963, Congress passed the Equal Pay Act, and the next year passed the 1964 Civil Rights Act, which prohibited discrimination in employment based on race, color, religion, sex, or national origin. In 1968, Congress passed the Age Discrimination in Employment Act. This act made it illegal to discriminate in hiring or firing persons between ages 40 and 65 based on age.

The 1970s and 1980s saw a decrease in union activity and union membership. By the end of the 1980s, unions began to lose their political power. The year 1970 saw the first mass postal strike in the history of the U.S. Postal Service. That same year, Hawaii became the first state to give its state and local officials the right to strike. Congress passed the Occupational Safety and Health Act (OSHA), which has been under attack by business ever since. In the mid-1970s, the 80,000-member American Federation of State, County, and Municipal Employees began the first legal large-scale strike of public employees. In 1977, Congress raised minimum wage to $2.65.

The 1980s again saw government working with business against unions. In the presidential election of 1980, only one major union supported the candidacy of Ronald Reagan: the air traffic controllers. In 1981, however, they could not agree on their contract and went out on strike. President Reagan fired the nation's striking air traffic controllers and then decertified their union, reasoning that they struck illegally. The latter part of the 1980s and the 1990s saw a political attack on unions by the right wing. They have accused unions of being liberal and not in the best interests of the country.

Excess Government Power

No country can have human rights without controls on government power. Most constitutions, including the Constitution of the United States, limit government power. Bills of rights specifically limit the power of government and give to the individual certain rights, such as the right to privacy or the right to be free from extensive government oversight. The United States has one of the best records concerning limited government intervention. However, even here do we find government excesses from time to time.

For example, during the battle with labor, the government used its power to stop or disrupt union activities. The Justice Department illegally went through the mail to intercept union leaders' correspondence; recently, a letter written in 1917 by Jane Street, Secretary of the Denver IWW Domestic Workers Industrial Union, was found in Washington, D.C. in the National Archives (Department of Justice, Record Group 60, File 18701–28), as a result of a Freedom of Information Act inquiry and search.

Almost universally, during wars, especially unpopular wars, governments tend to step on individual rights. America entered World War I with much civilian opposition, especially from the socialist party. In June 1917, Congress passed the Espionage Act, which had a clause that provided penalties from up to 20 years in prison for "Whoever, when the United States is at war, shall wilfully cause or attempt to cause insubordination, disloyalty, mutiny, or refusal of duty in the military or naval forces of the United States, or shall wilfully obstruct the recruiting or enlistment service of the U.S. . . ." Government used this act to imprison Americans who spoke out or wrote against the war. The government convicted about 900 people and sent them to jail under the Espionage Act. The government did all it could to stop any criticism of the war. Former Secretary of War Elihu Root specifically stated, "We must not have criticism now." He was adamant in this belief when he later said of those speaking against the war, ". . . there are men walking about the streets of this city tonight who ought to be taken out at sunrise tomorrow and shot for treason."

During World War I citizens were encouraged to report to authorities any evidence of seditious behavior. By promoting this type of policing, the government hoped to limit the problem of draft evasion. According to the government, over 330,000 qualified men did not register for the draft during World War I.

The Department of Justice sponsored the American Protective League, whose job among others was to find cases of disloyalty. By June of 1917, it had units in 600 cities and towns and a membership of nearly 100,000. The press reported that their members were "the leading men in their communities . . . bankers . . . railroad men . . . hotel men. . . ." They claimed to have found 3 million cases of disloyalty. Many members acted as vigilantes who broke into people's houses, or checked mail to look for disloyalty. Some states even tested its citizens for disloyalty. The United States Post Office Department began taking away mailing privileges of newspapers and magazines that printed antiwar articles.

In Los Angeles, a film that described British atrocities against the colonists during the Ameri-can Revolution was shown. Its name was *The Spirit of '76*. The government successfully prose-cuted the man who made the film under the Espi-onage Act. The judge in the case said that the film tended "to question the good faith of our ally, Great Britain." The court sentenced him to ten years in prison. Ironically, the case's name was *U.S.* v. *Spirit of '76*.

The media has also supported these restric-tions of rights. In 1917 the *New York Times* ran an editorial saying, "It is the duty of every good citi-zen to communicate to proper authorities any evi-dence of sedition that comes to his notice." The *Literary Digest* suggested that its readers ". . . clip and send to us any editorial utterances they encounter which seem to them seditious or trea-sonable." In 1918, the Attorney General proudly stated: "It is safe to say that never in its history has this country been so thoroughly policed." Why all these efforts? Mainly, many people tried to avoid the draft. By end of World War I, the government classified over 330,000 men as draft evaders.

Sometimes government felt it important to deceive the American public in the name of national security. This has been evident during or just before military actions. Detractors accused President Franklin Delano Roosevelt of knowing beforehand about the sneak attack on Pearl Harbor and used the incident to enter the war against Japan and Germany. There is no evidence to these wild claims. However, it is obvious that he and the government did mislead the public. For example, he specifically misstated the facts in 1941 when he reported the incidents between German submarines and U.S. destroyers. While he expressed surprise, as did the whole country, about the attack on Pearl Harbor, his actions in 1941 obviously angered Japan. When he placed a scrap iron and oil embargo on Japan, White House records show that he was aware that this might provoke a war. In fact, two weeks before the attack, advisers at a White House conference discussed how best to justify the war if Japan did attack. Similar incidents occurred with other presidents; namely, John F. Kennedy's Bay of Pigs Invasion, Lyndon B. Johnson's Gulf of Tonkin incident and the secret bombing of Cambodia, Nixon's secret end to the Vietnam War, and Ronald Reagan's and George Bush's Iran-Contra/El Salvador connections.

World War II has been called the "most popular war in American history" and perhaps it was. Americans were convinced, with heavy government propaganda, that Germany and Japan imperiled their whole way of life. For the most part they accepted the loss of their civil rights. We previously discussed the internment of Japanese and Japanese American citizens. Communities banned books like Erich Maria Remarque's *All Quiet on the Western Front* and Dalton Trumbo's *Johnny Got His Gun*. Government did all it could to repress all talk against the war effort.

The Red Scares of the 1920s and the 1950s probably brought about some of the worst government civil rights atrocities. The use of fear and intimidation to control the citizenry was brought to new heights. Joseph P. McCarthy of Wisconsin served as United States senator from January 1947 until his death on May 2, 1957. In February 1950,

he made a speech to the Republican Women's Club in Wheeling, West Virginia. He claimed to have a list of 57 "known Communists" hidden in the State Department. He withdrew the claim two days later, but in less than two weeks he repeated the claim, this time raising the number to 205 Communists. Soon his charges led to years of Senate and House investigations into subversive activities and the ruination of hundreds of lives.

The term "McCarthyism" will probably long endure in American politics as a synonym for "witch-hunt"—making serious but unsubstantiated charges against people in public life. McCarthy was the chair of the Senate Permanent Subcommittee on Investigations. From here he could investigate alleged communist influence in government. He charged that Presidents Franklin Roosevelt and Harry Truman as well as the American people had been victimized by "20 years of treason." Throughout the investigations, he never produced any evidence of subversion against a single person he accused of disloyalty. Rather than prove innocence or guilt, he used the press and the resulting publicity to humiliate and destroy citizens. The word McCarthyism has come to mean (according to *Webster's New Collegiate Dictionary*) ". . . the use of tactics involving personal attacks on individuals by means of widely publicized indiscriminate allegations esp. on the basis of unsubstantiated charges." Fearful Americans in the cold-war era accepted as fact his charges of people having communist sympathies. If people answered his questions, slick questions and testimony often made them look stupid or worse guilty. The subcommittee did not allow you to cross-examine your accusers. In addition, committee members not only asked questions of what you did but asked who your friends knew and to what associations they had belonged. Many people were not afraid of answering questions about themselves, but they were fearful that their testimony might hurt one of their friends. If you refused to answer on Fifth Amendment grounds, then you received the nickname of a "Fifth Amendment Communist." The public believed that you had to be guilty if you refused to answer questions. To refuse to answer on any other grounds were grounds for "contempt of Congress" and a jail sentence. The subcommittee destroyed authors. People lost their jobs. Hollywood blacklisted directors and actors who refused to answer charges in front of these Congressional committees. Scholars, teachers, and politicians lost their jobs. The subcommittee ruined reputations. In 1953, Arthur Miller wrote "The Crucible," a play about a witch-hunt that many thought was an allegory of these committees on Un-American activities.

Finally, McCarthy was denounced as a demagogue whose campaign hurt democracy. His fall began in 1954, when he conducted 36 days of hearings investigating the Army. The media televised the hearings. The American public soon saw McCarthy for what he was. Many called for his removal, including President Eisenhower, who had appeared on McCarthy's list of "traitors." McCarthy soon lost his chairmanship of the subcommittee. Late in 1954, the Senate voted 67 to 22 to censure him. However, the committees still existed and continued to call citizens before them to explain their un-American activities. The most effective was the House Committee on Un-American Activities (HUAC).

Most historians call this period in the late 1950s the McCarthy Era (even after the Senate removed McCarthy from office). However, it should more correctly be called the J. Edgar Hoover Era. J. Edgar Hoover was the director of the Federal Bureau of Investigation (FBI) from its establishment in 1924 to his death in 1976. Congress established the FBI as the primary agency to investigate violations of federal criminal laws. However, under Hoover leadership for more than 50 years it secretly engaged in practices that violated citizen rights under the Constitution. Individuals under surveillance and those with FBI files included many respected American, such as Dr. Martin Luther King Jr., Albert Einstein, every U.S. president from Truman to Nixon, members of Congress, Librarian of Congress Archibald MacLeish, John Steinbeck, John Kenneth Galbraith, Carl Sandberg, Ernest Hemingway, Sinclair Lewis, and Pearl S. Buck. Organizations under surveillance included the American Friends Service Committee (Quakers), the National Lawyers Guild, the American Civil Liberties Union, the Southern Christian Leadership Conference, labor unions, and religious groups.

From 1924 to 1972, the power of the FBI grew, as did the personal files that Hoover compiled on American citizens. Hoover himself said, "There's something addicting about a secret," and he had many secrets. He also had many informants, including some founders of the American Civil Liberties Union, who often turned information over to him. From 1936 to 1976, the FBI provided the National Conference of Bar Examiners with details of organizational ties and political beliefs of persons applying to practice law. Of 500,000 "subversive" investigations, covering over 1 million Americans from 1960 to 1974, few were ever charged with a criminal offense. In Chicago, at the height of underworld activities from 1966 to 1976, the FBI employed 5,145 informants and created 7.7 million spy files on noncriminal activities of citizens. The FBI went further and began disruptive activities and illegal break-ins. According to Congressional testimony by M. Wesley Swearingen, a veteran of the FBI's elite "bag job squad," the FBI made 25,000 illegal break-ins. The U.S. Senate Select Committee on Government operations reported in 1976 that the FBI had previously established "COINTELPRO" (Counter Intelligence Program). They described "COINTELPRO" as ". . . the FBI's acronym for covert programs directed against domestic groups . . . a sophisticated vigilante operation aimed squarely at preventing the exercise of First Amendment rights of speech and association . . ."

One horrible example of misuse of power occurred to Frank Wilkinson during the 1940s and 1950s. Mr. Wilkinson was the youngest son of a doctor in a conservative Methodist family. He wanted to become a Methodist minister. After a trip to the Holy Land in which he found a desire to help the poor, he met a Catholic priest, Monseigneur Thomas O'Dwyer, who convinced him to help in a slum clearance and public housing program in the Los Angeles area. He and the group protested for the integration of a public housing project in Watts that was going to be built in Chavez Ravine. Winning this fight, O'Dwyer named him to implement the integrated housing project he had fought for. That week, the FBI began a file on him. He soon became the expert on slum clearance and was called to testify before appropriate committees. It was in front of one of these committees, when he was testifying on rat infestation in the slums that his world came tumbling down. Fielding questions of rat infestation, they surprised him with the question, "Mr. Wilkinson, will you now tell us of all the organizations, political or otherwise, with which you have associated?" Mr. Wilkinson had signed every loyalty oath ever given him. He had sworn time and again his allegiance to the country. But, he said later the question was clearly irrelevant and it was an attempt to destroy the program with innuendos. He refused to answer.

His refusal made the headlines of the next day's *Los Angeles Times*. The court disqualified him as an expert witness and struck his testimony from the record. The city council passed a resolution condemning his refusal to answer the question. People called for his firing. Records today show that the FBI was heavily involved in the whole scandal. California's version of HUAC subpoenaed Frank and his wife, Jean, a social studies teacher, to testify. They refused and both were immediately fired from their jobs. The housing program fell apart. Today, instead of a housing project in Chavez Ravine, you will find the Los Angeles Dodgers' ballpark.

No one would hire Frank Wilkinson. Everyone thought he must be a Communist. Finally a Quaker family hired him to clean their department store. He cleaned three floors including 16 toilets for one dollar per hour. The only stipulation was that he could tell no one where he worked and he had to arrive one hour after closing so no one would see where he worked. YMCA leaders told him that his children could not even attend the YMCA summer camp; he broke down in tears, totally crushed. They finally relented under condition that Frank and his wife would not take the children to the departure point nor would they visit the children on the traditional parent-child Sunday chapel service.

Eventually, Mr. Wilkinson began working to abolish the HUAC. He spoke at meetings of his personal experiences. He passed out petitions calling for the dissolution of HUAC. On one trip to Atlanta, calling for signatures to stop HUAC from investigating Martin Luther King Jr. and his organization, he was subpoenaed to testify in front of HUAC. As an ACLU test case, he refused to answer on First Amendment grounds. He knew that the First Amendment stated that "Congress could pass no law . . ." that could stop him from passing out a petition. He believed that HUAC had no authority to pass a law and thus had no authority to question him. Congress cited him for contempt. He was convicted and he appealed his conviction through the court system. His case went to the Supreme Court in 1961 and he lost on a five-to-four decision (*Wilkinson* v. *United States)*. The court ordered him to serve his year in

jail. His First Amendment claims to free speech were rejected.

To make a long story short, he served his time in jail. He and his family went through terrible ordeals. At one time his house was bombed and his daughter barely escaped death. He continued his fight against HUAC. The FBI continued to follow him with up to eight agents per day. They targeted him for disruption through COINTELPRO. They spent millions of taxpayers' dollars to follow a man who broke no criminal law. For 38 years they followed him for his political and social beliefs. Records show that agent after agent wrote to Director Hoover saying he was no threat to the security of the United States. Hoover thanked the agents and told them to continue their surveillance.

One terrible incident came to light nearly 20 years later. A reactionary planned to assassinate Mr. Wilkinson in 1961. The FBI knew of the plot. Instead of warning Mr. Wilkinson, headquarters told them to observe the incident and report back what happened. Fortunately the assassination did not take place. The FBI reported this to Hoover and said they would continue to monitor the situation. If anything happened in the future, they would report it.

Through a series of events, Frank Wilkinson became curious of just what records the government did have on him. Using the Freedom of Information Act, he requested his records. He was not prepared for what he got. He received the materials over years and the first major batch of papers numbered 132,000 pages. If stacked on top of each other, they would be higher than a seven-story building. Again the records show that Mr. Wilkinson never broke a criminal law.

Mr. Wilkinson fought the FBI through the courts and ended up winning a civil law suit. The federal court ordered the FBI to expunge all papers concerning him from their offices. These are now in the National Archives to be opened after all people referenced in them have passed away.

Frank Wilkinson is today the Executive Director Emeritus of the First Amendment Foundation. He is 83 years old and living on social security in Los Angeles. A federal court has given the FBI a restraining order prohibiting them from ever disrupting Mr. Wilkinson again. By federal court order, if they are ever found in the same crowd in which he speaks, he automatically receives a financial settlement with no further adjudication.

During this period, the guidelines that the FBI worked under basically allowed the bureau to do as it wished. There is little record of oversight by either the Justice Department or Congress. After Hoover's death in 1972 and paralleling the Watergate investigations, Congress established a bipartisan Senate Select Committee to Study Government Operations. The late Senator Frank Church (D-ID) and minority leader Barry Goldwater (R-AZ) co-chaired it. The Committee issued a 2,500-page report in 1976 detailing FBI intrusions into the Bill of Rights. The report appalled so many Americans that President Gerald Ford ordered new FBI guidelines set up. His Attorney General, Edward Levi (former dean at the University of Chicago), wrote the first guidelines in 52 years that strictly limited FBI investigation. The guidelines stated, "All investigations undertaken through these guidelines shall be designed and conducted so as not to limit the full exercise of rights protected by the Constitution and laws of the United States." Under President Jimmy Carter, the FBI continued using these guidelines. There has been no evidence of FBI violations of the Bill of Rights during this period.

However, under President Ronald Reagan, the guidelines were changed. The attorney general felt that Ford's guidelines tied the hands of the FBI too strictly. Although we know what was in the Ford guidelines, we do not know what was in the Reagan guidelines. After the Reagan administration wrote them, the guidelines were classified "top secret." If you request the guidelines, you will receive only blank pages with the words "TOP SECRET" on each page. Yet, we can determine if the government is violating citizens' rights by documented actions that it takes.

From 1981 to 1985, the FBI used highly intrusive and disruptive forms of surveillance directed at campus and community groups that peacefully opposed U.S. policy in Central America, especially policy concerning El Salvador and the Contras. Under the "Foreign Counter Intelligence/Terrorist" program, the FBI was allowed to use "special techniques" of surveillance that normally would have been considered illegal when applied to domestic investigations. The Bureau targeted more than 150 church, labor, peace and community organizations—especially those opposed to the Reagan policy in El Salvador. The FBI put under surveillance 56 separate peace demonstrations between 1983 and 1985.

In the 1950s the red-flag word was "communism." In the 1980s and 1990s the red flag word was and still is "terrorism." No longer are people put under surveillance for communist activities, but they can be put under surveillance for terrorist activities. For instance, in the 1980s the FBI began a "Library Awareness Program." FBI agents visited library workers and offered them money to give them lists of books that certain people read. When the American Library Association protested, Director William S. Sessions said that if we know what books people read, we will better know if they have terrorist tendencies. When several librarians signed a petition opposing this practice, they were all placed under a monitoring program in case their opposition would prove to have foreign influence. In 1984, the FBI questioned more than one thousand African American families in west Alabama about voter fraud. They later took a busload of elderly African American voters 165 miles to Mobile to answer questions in front of a grand jury regarding alleged fraud among absentee voters. Civil rights worker claimed that the FBI was trying to intimidate African American voters. Just before the Gulf War, the FBI chose 200 Arab Americans with close ties to local Arab American communities and interviewed them in their homes or workplaces. They asked the individuals about their political views and associations and were also informed that the FBI wanted to help prosecute any hate crimes committed against them. However, the Arab Americans claimed that they were harassing them and accusing them of sedition using McCarthy tactics.

President Bill Clinton called for passage of the bipartisan "Counter-Terrorism" Bill, which he signed into law April 24, 1996. It was introduced 70 days before the Oklahoma City bombing. After the bombing the bill picked up support. Human rights activists call it the most dangerous attack on the Bill of Rights since the J. Edgar Hoover Era. The Counter-Terrorism Bill repealed the current law that prevented the FBI and other federal investigative agencies to base their investigation on First Amendment activities. It authorizes investigations and punishment for legal conduct directly violating First Amendment rights. The law's broad definition of terrorism invites both selective prosecution and intrusions into Bill of Rights protected areas. It criminalizes fund-raising for groups even remotely affiliated with labeled "terrorist" groups.

The greatest threat to any people's human rights is excessive use of power by the government. America's founding fathers drafted the Constitution and the Bill of Rights to limit government power. A sympathetic, benevolent government helps its people. A government caught up in bureaucratic agencies can often lose sight of the people it serves. Only time will tell what path the United States is on. Overall, the record of human rights in the United States is an admirable one. Though the history of the twentieth century is replete with examples of human rights losses, it is also full of examples of the expansion of human rights. However, all citizens must remain vigilant. We must be aware when human rights are threatened. We must be aware when others' rights, not just our own, are threatened. As Pastor Martin Niemoeller of the German Evangelical (Lutheran) Church so poignantly pointed out:

> In Germany, the Nazis first came for the Communists, and I did not speak up, because I was not a Communist. Then they came for the Jews, and I did not speak up, because I was not a Jew. Then they came for the trade unionists, and I did not speak up, because I was not a trade unionist. Then they came for the Catholics, and I did not speak up, because I was not a Catholic. Then they came for me . . . and by that time, there was no one to speak up for anyone.

Bibliography

Alberti, Johannna. *Beyond Freedom: Feminists in War and Peace*. New York: St. Martin's Press, 1989.

Barry, Kathleen. *Susan B. Anthony: A Biography of a Singular Feminist*. New York: New York University Press, 1988.

Beeton, Beverly. *Women Vote in the West: The Woman Suffrage Movement, 1869–1896*. New York: Garland, 1986.

Belknap, Michael. *Urban Race Riots*. New York: Garland, 1991.

Benjamin, Anne M. *A History of the Anti-Suffrage Movement in the United States from 1895 to 1920: Women Against Equality*. Lewiston, N.Y.: Edwin Mellen Press, 1991.

Boswell, T. D., and J. R. Curtis. *The Cuban-American Experience*. New York: Rowman, 1984.

Brooks, John G. *American Syndicalism: The IWW*. New York: Arno Press, 1969.

Chan, S. *Asian Americans: An Interpretive History*. Boston: Twayne, 1991.

De Caux, Len. *The Living Spirit of the Wobblies*. New York: International Publishers, 1978.

Buechler, Steven. *Women's Movements in the United States: Woman Suffrage, Equal Rights, and Beyond*. New Brunswick, N.J.: Rutgers University Press, 1990.

———. *The Transformation of the Woman Suffrage Movement: The Case of Illinois, 1850–1920*. New Brunswick, N.J.: Rutgers University Press, 1986.

Davis, Paulina Wright. *A History of the National Woman's Rights Movement*. 1871. Reprint, New York: Source Book Press, 1970.

DeFrietas, Gregory. *Inequality at Work: Hispanics in the U.S. Labor Force*. New York: Oxford University Press, 1991.

De Laguna, A. R. *Images and Identities: The Puerto Rican in Two World Contexts*. New York: Transition Books, 1985.

Filippelli, Ronald L. *Labor in the USA: A History*. New York: Alfred A. Knopf, 1984.

Finkelman, Paul, ed. *Lynching, Racial Violence and the Law*. New York: Garland, 1992.

Flexner, Eleanor. *Century of Struggle: The Women's Rights Movement in the United States*. Rev. ed. Cambridge, Mass.: Harvard University Press, 1975.

Foner, Philip S. *We the Other People: Alternative Declarations of Independence by Labor Groups, Farmers, Woman's Rights Advocates, Socialists, and Blacks, 1829–1975*. Chicago: University of Illinois Press, 1976.

Friedl, Betty, ed. *On to Victory: Propaganda Plays of the Woman Suffrage Movement*. Boston: Northeastern University Press, 1987.

Garcia, Richard, ed. *The Chicanos in America, 1540–1975*. Dobbs Ferry, N.Y.: Oceana, 1977.

Garner, Les. *Stepping Stones to Women's Liberty: Feminist Ideas in the Women's Suffrage Movement, 1900–1918*. Rutherford, N.J.: Fairleigh Dickinson University Press, 1984.

Garver, Susan, and Paula McGuire. *Coming to North America from Mexico, Cuba, and Puerto Rico*. New York: Delacorte Press, 1981.

Graham, Hugh Davis. *The Civil Rights Era*. New York: Oxford University Press, 1990.

Green, Janet Wells. *From Forge to Fast Food: A History of Child Labor in New York State*. Troy, N.Y.: Council for Citizenship Education, 1995.

Grimes, Alan. *The Puritan Ethic and Woman Suffrage*. New York: Oxford University Press, 1967.

Hing, William O. *Making and Remaking Asian Americans Through Immigration Policy*. Stanford, Calif.: Stanford University Press, 1993.

Kugler, Israel. *From Ladies to Women: The Organized Struggle for Woman's Rights in the Reconstruction Era*. Westport, Conn.: Greenwood Press, 1987.

O'Brien, Edward L., Eleanor Greene, and David McQuoid-Mason. *Human Rights for All.* Minneapolis: West Publishing, 1996.

O'Neill, William. *Everyone Was Brave: A History of Feminism in America.* Chicago: Quadrangle Books, 1971.

Renshaw, Patrick. *The Wooblies.* New York: Doubleday, 1968.

Sinclair, Andrew. *The Emancipation of the American Woman.* New York: Harper and Row, 1966.

Takaki, Ronald. *A Different Mirror: A History of Multicultural America.* Boston: Little, Brown, 1993.

Waggenspack, Beth M. *The Search for Self-Sovereignty: The Oratory of Elizabeth Cady Stanton.* Westport, Conn.: Greenwood Press, 1989.

Ware, Susan. *Beyond Suffrage: Women in the New Deal.* Cambridge, Mass.: Harvard University Press, 1981.

Zinn, Howard. *A People's History of the United States 1492–Present.* New York: Harper's Perennial, 1995.

Civil Rights of Minority Groups

Chapter 3

The Rights of African Americans

Jay A. Sigler and J. Owens Smith

In 1776, when the total population of the United States stood at two and a half million people, there were 570,000 African Americans in the country, only 40,000 of whom were "free persons of color." At the time of American independence slaves accounted for about 25 percent of the population. At the high point of slavery in America, just prior to the Civil War, there were almost two million African Americans in slavery. The conditions of slavery varied from one plantation to another, but nowhere did the slave have civil rights. The only protection provided to slaves was found in Southern slave codes that, in legal terms, at least, banned "unseemly cruelty" and required slave owners to supply the slaves with enough necessities to maintain health. Of course, many slave owners ignored these laws, regarding their slaves as a form of animate personal property.

Under the slave codes there were numerous criminal laws for major and minor offenses committed by slaves, with stiff sentences for misbehavior. Slaves were forbidden to carry firearms, to own horns, whistles, or drums, to hunt, to possess liquor, or to assemble in groups of more than four or five. After 1830, slave preachers were sharply limited in their speech, and all slaves were banned from being instructed in reading and writing.

Outside the South free African American men had many rights, but still fewer than those of white men. African Americans in the North were commonly disenfranchised (denied the right to vote) and were often forbidden from living in neighborhoods of their own choosing. African Americans were sometimes confined by statute to menial labor, even though they were free people. Education for free African Americans was notoriously inferior. Prior to national emancipation state constitutions in the North gave no attention to the rights of African Americans, nor were serious efforts made to stamp out racial segregation.

Even in enlightened regions rights for African Americans were slow to emerge. For example, as late as 1849 the Supreme Judicial Court of Massachu-

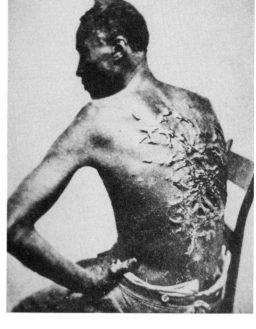

Photo on left; The conditions of slavery varied from one plantation to another, but nowhere did the slave have civil rights. Many slave owners regarded slaves as a form of animate personal property.

Photo on right: Under the slave codes there were numerous criminal laws for major and minor offenses committed by slaves, with stiff sentences for behavior that violated the codes.

setts upheld racial segregation in the public schools *(Roberts* v. *Boston)*. Yet the Massachusetts Constitution specifically stated that "all men, without distinction of color or race, are equal before the law." In 1855 the Massachusetts legislature finally passed a statute legally ending school segregation.

This sad history of slavery is in direct denial of the fundamental precepts that the nation declared in the Declaration of Independence. That document holds the statement, "all men are created equal" to be a self-evident truth. In his original draft of the Declaration of Independence Thomas Jefferson had included a condemnation of King George III for committing a crime against the liberties of men for supporting slavery, although Jefferson was himself a slave owner. This passage was stricken out of the draft at the insistence of Southern representatives in the Continental Congress. Jefferson did succeed in banning slavery in the territories belonging to the new national government in the nation's northwest. The Northwest Ordinance of 1787 clearly reflects Jefferson's views on limiting slavery.

The national Constitution, in its original form, referred to slavery several times without condemning it. Although Article I, Section 9, allowed the prohibition of the importation of slaves after 1808, Article IV, Section 2, required that escaped slaves be returned to their owners. Slaves were worth only three-fifths of the taxing

and voting power of free persons, as a result of an important constitutional compromise on the question of representation. The language of the Fifth Amendment to the Constitution, which was adopted shortly after the First Congress met, did not apply to African American slaves in spite of its language. The language reads: "No person shall be deprived of life, liberty, or property without due process of law . . ." Abraham Lincoln once said of this situation that apparently "all men are created equal except Negroes."

In 1857 the Supreme Court handed down one of its worst blows to civil rights in the notorious case of *Dred Scot* v. *Sanford*. The Court majority declared that slaves were not citizens of the United States and had no rights under the Constitution. The majority opinion was written by Chief Justice Roger Taney, who was prepared to go further than the other justices in declaring African Americans to have no rights. In Taney's view not even free African Americans had rights. This was, he said, the opinion "fixed and universal in the civilized portion of the white race." This meant that African Americans had "no rights which the white man was bound to respect." Not only were African Americans not citizens of the United States, they were hardly persons at all, under the law.

This judicial statement of blatant racism is a low point in the history of the nation and in its development of rights policy. The American Civil War had many causes, but one of the major sources

The Declaration of Independence states that "all men are created equal," and yet American history has seen African Americans bought and sold as property.

was the provocative racism of some of the white extremists. Roger Taney committed the judicial power of the United States to the cause of slavery, with little opposition from his fellow justices. This was one of the few cases in early American history in which judicial power was used to declare a federal law to be unconstitutional. Judicial review, a sword of the Supreme Court against the Congress, was unsheathed in the defense of slavery.

The Civil War and the Rights of African Americans

The forces of slavery were defeated by the Civil War. In 1863, during that war, President Abraham Lincoln issued his Emancipation Proclamation, freeing the slaves in occupied states and territories. All Union personnel—the army of the North—were ordered to assist runaway slaves. The president also announced that he intended to recruit free African Americans into the Union army. Almost 20,000 African American men joined the North, many of them former Southern slaves. African Americans proved themselves the friends of liberty and worthy citizens on the battlefields of the Civil War. This led directly to alleviating the effect of the *Dred Scott* case.

The Thirteenth Amendment to the Constitution (1865) specifically ended slavery and involuntary servitude. The Fourteenth Amendment (ratified on July 9, 1868) declared that all persons born

or naturalized in the United States were citizens of the United States. It also stated, "no state shall make or enforce any law which shall abridge the privileges or immunities of the citizens of the United States." This language specifically reversed the *Dred Scott* decision. The Fourteenth Amendment also forbid any state from denying any person the "equal protection of the laws." This phrase was to be the source of a later expansion of African American rights. The Fifteenth Amendment, the last of the Civil War amendments, was designed to grant African Americans the right to vote.

The effect of these constitutional amendments was to erect a new theory of rights for African Americans. Slavery was ended and a new era had begun. Unfortunately, the victories on the battlefield and in the post-Civil War Congress were short-lived. Legally African American men were given rights they had never had before, but the realization of these rights were the result of a long, protracted struggle. Some say the struggle is not yet over.

With the end of the Civil War in 1865 the Republican Party was firmly in control of the national government. A group of so-called Radical Republicans, with a strong antislavery policy, controlled the party in Congress. The Thirteenth, Fourteenth, and Fifteenth Amendments to the Constitution were the centerpiece of their strategy for changing the scope of rights for African Americans. Southern states were compelled to ratify these amendments as a precondition of reinstate-

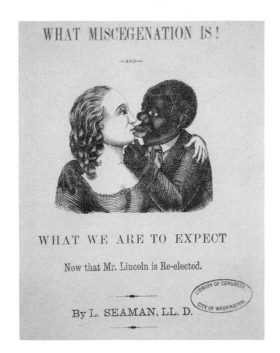

WHAT MISCEGENATION IS!

—AND—

WHAT WE ARE TO EXPECT

Now that Mr. Lincoln is Re-elected.

By L. SEAMAN, LL. D.

Some state courts would not allow intermarriage between whites and African Americans.

ment into the Union. In this atmosphere of compulsion, the campaign for African American rights was resisted, and the cause was tainted.

The first statute to back up the new constitutional rights was the Civil Rights Act of 1866, passed over the veto of President Andrew Johnson. The Act was aimed at enforcing the equal protection of the laws clause of the Fourteenth Amendment by creating criminal punishment for all those who "under color of any law . . . or custom" prevented any person from enjoying his rights for reasons of race or previous condition of involuntary servitude. The Radical Republicans were trying to protect the newly freed slaves from having their rights curtailed by state officials.

Some state judges sought to frustrate this policy of rights for African Americans either by asserting that the Civil Rights Act violated state rights and was unconstitutional, or by narrowly interpreting the meaning of the statute. Some state courts would not allow intermarriage between whites and African Americans; others would not allow African Americans to testify in courts against whites. Throughout the 1870s and 1880s judges in Louisiana, Tennessee, Alabama, Kentucky, and Indiana found ways to evade the spirit of the Civil Rights Act of 1863.

The Radical Republicans passed six other civil rights acts between 1863 and 1875. The last of the civil rights statutes was passed in 1875 as the Second Civil Rights Act. This statute declared

that everyone was entitled to full and equal enjoyment of public accommodations, transportation, theaters, and other public places of amusement. In spite of these statutory achievements, by 1875 the Radical Republicans were out of power in Washington. The pressure for enhancing the rights of African Americans quickly dissipated. No new national civil rights statutes were passed in the United States between 1875 and 1957.

The Supreme Court played an important role in restricting African American rights after the Civil War. In 1876, in *United States* v. *Cruikshank,* the Court held that the Fourteenth Amendment did not reach private acts of racial discrimination, only acts of officials pursuant to state laws. The most significant blow against African American rights was a series of cases in 1883, known as the *Civil Rights Cases,* which invalidated the 1875 Civil Rights Act. The decisions virtually suspended federal activity on behalf of African American rights. The Supreme Court majority held that since African Americans had been sufficiently aided by "beneficent legislation" there was insufficient reason for Congress to use the Fourteenth Amendment to create a positive state program of protecting African American rights by regulating the actions of individuals within states. The Court majority regarded the Tenth Amendment's protection of state's rights as more important than the protection of African American rights. According to Justice Joseph P. Bradley, the Fourteenth Amendment does not authorize enactments on subjects within the domain of the states and cannot regulate "all private rights between man and man in society."

As a result of these and other Supreme Court rulings the rights of African Americans were left to the tender mercies of the state and local governments. Twenty years after the Civil War the nation seemed ready to forget about the Civil War amendments, the civil rights legislation of the Congress, and the cause of African American rights in America. These national civil rights statutes were never repealed, they were simply ignored. The promises of the Civil War amendments seemed empty, as racists in the South and segregationists in the North took political power.

Racial Segregation

The end of slavery in America marked the beginning of an era of racial segregation. Racial

After slavery ended, the former slave states enacted statutes that restricted the rights available to African Americans, including the right to serve on a jury. After these statutes were repealed, segregation emerged in the form of official policies called "Jim Crow laws."

segregation has been a national phenomenon ever since, although unlawful after 1974. Racial segregation began in the North and the West even during slavery, but after Emancipation it became the official policy of Southern state governments that sought a means of preserving white supremacy while providing African Americans with an inferior brand of rights.

After slavery ended the former slave states almost immediately enacted statutes regulating the legal and constitutional status of African Americans. These Black Codes, as they were collectively known, sought to restrict the rights available to African Americans. They were forbidden from entering into most occupations or professions, their movements were regulated, and racial intermarriage was forbidden. Furthermore, African Americans

were excluded from jury duty, were denied freedom of assembly, were deprived of the right to vote, and were forbidden from directing insulting words at whites. A severe criminal code was devised just for African Americans that included the death penalty for rape and other offenses. The Black Codes were so severe that they were offensive to most northerners and were gradually repealed.

In place of the Black Codes a system of racial segregation that was much subtler emerged in the South and elsewhere in America. The term "Jim Crow laws" refers to this official policy of racial segregation that emerged in spite of the Constitution and the civil rights laws of the federal government. Segregation took the form of separate facilities for African Americans and whites. It meant that African Americans could not be a guest at

most hotels and would be forbidden to own homes in some parts of communities. Separate schools, colleges, and universities were built. Separate drinking fountains, toilets, public parks, and swimming pools were maintained. Separate elevators and telephone booths existed in a few cities. All these steps were taken to symbolize a separate and inferior status for African Americans.

At first the Supreme Court blessed this condition. There was a series of Supreme Court rulings in the 1870s and 1880s that narrowly read the constitutional provisions that had been written on behalf of African Americans. Various forms of racial segregation and discrimination were approved. These culminated in the 1896 case of *Plessy* v. *Ferguson* in which the Court found that segregation alone did not violate the Constitution.

The Court concluded that the Fourteenth Amendment's equal protection of the laws guarantee "could not have been intended to abolish distinctions based on color, or to enforce social equality." Such segregation laws that permit and even require "their separation in places where they are liable to be brought into contact do not necessarily imply the inferiority of either race to the other." In effect, the Court fully sanctioned racial segregation by denying that it had any social consequences. For more than a half-century thereafter the separate-but-equal doctrine was accepted as consistent with the Fourteenth Amendment, even though genuine equality of treatment was never really provided.

The foolishness of this policy of racial separation was not obvious to many Americans, but the injustice that it created was evident to a few white statesmen. One of those who deplored the majority view in the *Plessy* case was Justice John Marshall Harlan, the lone dissenter. Harlan was a former slave owner himself, but he saw that the Constitution had been wrongly interpreted. As he said in his dissent to *Plessy* v *Ferguson,* "Our Constitution is color blind, and neither knows nor tolerates classes among citizens." Harlan was ahead of his time, and he predicted that the Court-approved separate-but-equal doctrine would "in time prove to be . . . as pernicious as the decision in the Dred Scott Case."

Most of the important state segregation legislation followed the *Plessy* case. Racial segregation had become an official American policy. These segregation policies not only affected African Americans but other minorities such as Asian Americans and Jews as well. Many minority groups were effectively barred from private and public facilities because of their race or national origin. Opportunities to gain employment or to enter the professions were also tightly rationed by race, religion, gender, and national origins well into the middle of the twentieth century.

Ending Official Segregation

The erosion of racial segregation was slow but steady. It began in 1915 with a Supreme Court decision *(Guinn* v. *United States),* which showed that obvious evasions of the Constitution were intolerable. In this case the grandfather clause, which was aimed at preventing African Americans from voting in the South, was declared unconstitutional. This clumsy device at disenfranchisement was intended to revive the inequitable voting provisions that existed prior to the Civil War; however, the Fifteenth Amendment was clearly being flouted, and the Court struck down the grandfather clause.

A legal campaign against racial segregation was launched in earnest in 1917 with the Supreme Court decision in *Buchanan* v. *Warley.* In that case the Court showed some sense of the unfairness of racial segregation in housing. This was the first major legal victory of the National Association for the Advancement of Colored People (NAACP). The Supreme Court unanimously agreed to strike down a city zoning ordinance that prohibited African Americans from living on so-called white blocks. No government could declare a mandatory policy of housing discrimination. Official acts of government

In 1923, twelve African Americans who were seeking to organize sharecroppers were almost lynched by a violent mob. Instead, after federal troops intervened, the men faced a travesty of a trial. The Supreme Court finally intervened and ordered a fair trial.

that created housing segregation were unconstitutional. This decision did not end housing discrimination, however, which continued as a result of private conduct. It was clear that government could not compel the races to live in particular places.

After World War I the NAACP set a deliberate new course. It aimed at a comprehensive program of reform of segregationist policies through the courts. Correcting racial injustices were also pursued in Congress and the various state legislatures, but the court strategy worked better. A victory for the principle of fair trials for African Americans was won in the 1923 case of *Moore* v. *Dempsey,* in which a dozen African Americans who were seeking to organize sharecroppers were almost lynched by a violent mob. Instead, after the

Zion School for the Colored, 1866.

In 1896, the Supreme Court fully sanctioned racial segregation by denying that it had any social consequences.

intervention of federal troops, five African American defendants were arrested, quickly tried, and declared guilty of murder after a trial lasting one hour and a jury deliberation of five minutes. African Americans were barred from the jury, and African American witnesses were whipped and forced to testify against the defendants. No witnesses were allowed to be called on behalf of the African American defendants. This travesty of a trial required the intervention of the Supreme Court, which set aside the improper conviction

and ordered a fair trial. The Court had become sensitive to the denial of constitutional rights to African Americans in the South.

The NAACP pressed many other claims of racial injustice, but the most famous was the ultimately successful attack on the separate-but-equal doctrine in public education. The campaign began in the 1930s. State professional schools were compelled to admit African Americans to graduate schools on four occasions after Supreme Court

In 1954 the Supreme Court declared school segregation unconstitutional.

rulings. These cases did not overrule the separate-but-equal but rested on the facts showing that the separate African American schools were markedly inferior to the all-white professional schools. However, although invited in these cases to overrule *Plessy* v. *Ferguson,* the Supreme Court persistently refused to do so.

In 1954 the Supreme Court had a chance to change its mind and finally reverse *Plessy.* Instead, the Court declared school segregation unconstitutional, without actually reversing the *Plessy* decision. At the time of the Supreme Court decision in *Brown* v. *Board of Education of Topeka,* segregation of the races in the public schools was required by law in 17 states and the District of Columbia. There were 2,500,000 African American children enrolled in 15,000 separate African American pub-

lic schools. In deciding this case the Supreme Court wiped out this whole system of state-imposed racial segregation. It was accomplished in a remarkable unanimous opinion rendered on behalf of a united Supreme Court by Chief Justice Earl Warren, who had been appointed to the Court in 1953, just a year before the decision. Chief Justice Warren concluded that "separate educational facilities are inherently unequal." This breathtaking accomplishment was the surprising culmination of more than two centuries of litigation and constitutional struggles on behalf of African Americans. It marked the beginning of a new era for the rights of African Americans.

What made the outcome even more surprising was the fact that Earl Warren, while governor and attorney general for the state of California, was a leading proponent of the World War II removal of all persons of Japanese ancestry from their homes on the West Coast to detention centers. Warren changed his racial views and after much careful reconsideration was able to lead the Supreme Court in new directions. None of this was known or anticipated by President Dwight Eisenhower who had appointed Warren to the high court as a political favor.

Ultimately, the Court could see that *Plessy* v. *Ferguson* had to go. No legal justification for any form of official racial segregation could be allowed to stand. In a series of 1955 and 1956 decisions the Supreme Court declared segregation of golf courses, public beaches, and swimming pools to be unconstitutional. Finally, in *Gale* v. *Browder,* a 1956 public transportation case that grew out of the Montgomery, Alabama, bus boycott led by Dr. Martin Luther King Jr., the Supreme Court declared *Plessy* v *Ferguson* to be overruled.

But there was much resistance to the new policy of racial desegregation of the public schools. Governors, state legislatures, and school boards throughout the nation tried to find ways around school desegregation. In 1957, President Dwight Eisenhower, who had been cool to the *Brown* decision, used the powers of his office to enforce a court desegregation ruling. Faced with a threat of violence in Little Rock, Arkansas, and a state governor, Orville Faubus, who aimed to block school desegregation, Eisenhower took strong action. On September 24, 1957, President Eisenhower issued an order authorizing federal troops to enforce court desegregation orders. The soldiers stood on the steps of Central High School in Little Rock while nine African American children entered the school. The Little Rock incident aroused the nation. That same night President Eisenhower addressed the nation to explain and justify his actions. He said that he supported the principle that the Supreme Court ruling on school desegregation was the law of the land, and he was bound to enforce it.

Five years later, in 1962, President John Kennedy found himself in a similar situation. Mississippi Governor Ross Barnett attempted to stop the public desegregation in his state. Barnett tried to prevent the desegregation of the University of Mississippi, but he backed down when confronted with military force and the threat of a judicial contempt citation. In 1963, Alabama Governor George Wallace was forced to back away from a showdown with President Kennedy over the desegregation of the University of Alabama. Faced with massive federal pressure, Governor Wallace stepped aside from the entrance to the university, thus ending racial segregation at the college level in Alabama and projecting Wallace into the national spotlight as a leading symbol of opposition to desegregation.

Outside the South school desegregation was also difficult to achieve. A number of public school boards had arbitrarily drawn district boundaries that had the effect of creating racially segregated schools. One by one the federal courts were used to change these patterns of discrimination. Legal segregation became a dead letter, but *de facto,* or unofficial segregation, remained a problem. Racial segregation that occurs not as a result of deliberate actions of official agencies but because of residential patterns and past economic conditions proved very difficult to change. Whatever the cause, by 1978, 25 years after the *Brown* decision, the Civil Rights Commission reported that 46 percent of American students still attended segregated schools.

Some federal district court judges attempted to order school busing as a remedy for racial segregation. The transportation of public school students from areas where they live to schools in other areas for the purpose of eliminating racially segregated schools became an explosive social issue. Busing led to violence in many northern cities. Although the Supreme Court usually upheld district court busing orders, the remedy became unpopular with many African Americans, who feared violence involving their children. By 1986 the Supreme Court was prepared to allow a school board to terminate 15 years of busing of elementary school students *(Riddick* v. *School Board of City of Norfolk).*

Full compliance with court ordered desegregation has still not been achieved in America. Many school boards are still subject to the supervision of federal court judges who seek to press for more efforts towards desegregation. The Supreme Court has allowed some local school boards to resume control over their educational systems even though racial segregation still is unresolved. In 1995 the Supreme Court allowed the state of Missouri to stop spending money on attempts to attract a multiracial student body through major educational reforms *(Missouri* v. *Jenkins).* Objective evidence shows that although American public schools are much more integrated than they were

A view of the crowd at the 1963 March on Washington.

in 1954, racial segregation still remains in scattered forms all over the nation's public schools.

In many other ways desegregation has succeeded. Racial segregation has been ended in many other aspects of American life. This has been achieved through efforts by the Congress, the state legislatures, the courts, and reforms at the state and local levels. America has been transformed, but to understand how attitudes were changed we must examine the revolution in civil rights thinking that was manifested in the civil rights movement of the 1960s.

The Civil Rights Movement

The school desegregation decision applied only to the public schools. The remaining areas of American society remained segregated in 1954. Some scholars say that desegregation began after the decision in *Brown* v. *Board of Education,* but the truth is that the case had its roots in the long campaign of African American organizations to terminate racial segregation in America. The *Brown* case and its aftermath may have alerted the white majority to racial segregation, but the civil rights movement of direct protest action to end segregation was also critical to dramatic changes in the thinking about patterns of racial segregation in America.

In December 1955, an African American woman named Rosa Parks began a crusade against segregationist laws in Montgomery, Alabama. She was arrested when she refused to surrender her seat in the front of a bus to a white man. Rosa

At the 1963 March on Washington for Jobs and Freedom, nearly a quarter-million Americans heard Martin Luther King Jr. deliver his famous "I Have a Dream" speech.

The school desegregation decision applied only to the public schools. The remaining areas of American society remained segregated in 1954.

Parks was a seamstress, who had been commanded by the bus driver to move to the back of the bus so as to permit white passengers to sit in the seats reserved for them. Three other African Americans complied. Rosa Parks did not, and for this she was arrested and fined $10. No one and no organization planned it, but this arrest started the civil rights movement in America.

Four days after the arrest of Rosa Parks, Dr. Martin Luther King Jr., a 27-year-old Baptist minister in Montgomery, urged a complete bus boycott. Local African American groups, including the Montgomery Improvement Association, helped to orchestrate the boycott. The Montgomery bus boycott began in 1955 as the result of an unplanned act of defiance without national sponsorship. In 1956, the federal district court issued an injunction prohibiting the racial segregation of buses in Montgomery. A small, but significant victory had been won.

Dr. King swiftly emerged as a leader in the boycott campaign. During the Montgomery protest King was arrested and jailed and his house was bombed. After the boycott ended in 1957, the Montgomery Improvement Association was merged into King's newly created organization, the Southern Christian Leadership Conference.

King's leadership was based partly on his magnetic and powerful personality and partly on his philosophy of nonviolent disobedience. An original blend of the teachings of Indian activist Mahatma Gandhi (1869–1948) and the American thinker Henry David Thoreau (1817–1862), non-

Martin Luther King Jr. *(1929–1968)*

Martin Luther King Jr. was the leader of the twentieth-century freedom movement for African Americans. After dramatic events in 1955 he gave a speech in Montgomery, Alabama, that helped bring him to national prominence. He was a leader in the struggle against segregation first in Montgomery, Alabama, and later on a national level. King broadened his attacks on prejudice and exploitation to include most major civil rights issues confronting African Americans and other Americans.

Dr. King was the son of the prominent and influential pastor of the Ebenezer Baptist Church in Atlanta, Georgia. Martin Luther King Jr. was himself ordained as a Baptist minister in 1947, serving as pastor in a church in Montgomery, Alabama, in 1954. This was the site of the boycott by Montgomery blacks against the segregated city bus lines. Dr. King led the boycott (1955–1956). After it succeeded, King organized the Southern Christian Leadership Conference, which gave him his base for further civil rights activities.

Reverend King repeatedly challenged the nation to live up to its egalitarian principles, as set forth in the Constitution, in the Bill of Rights, and in various federal civil rights laws. In his 1964 book, *Why We Can't Wait*, King pointed out that the United States was "a society where the supreme law of the land, the Constitution, is rendered inoperative in vast areas of the nation" because of persistent patterns of racial discrimination. King saw the struggle for civil rights as a resumption "of that noble journey towards the goals reflected in the Preamble to the Constitution, the Constitution itself, the Bill of Rights, and the Thirteenth, Fourteenth, and Fifteenth Amendments."

Protest demonstrations in which Dr. King played a large part fired the imagination of most Americans. After victories in Birmingham and Selma, Alabama, national support grew for changes in the laws. King led the massive 1963 March on Washington, which brought 200,000 Americans together. The passage of the Civil Rights Act of 1964 and the Voting Rights Act of 1965 were made possible by these efforts of King and others in arousing the conscience of Americans about racial discrimination. In 1964 Martin Luther King Jr. was awarded the Nobel Peace Prize.

The tactics adopted by Martin Luther King Jr. were peaceful and nonviolent. An advocate of civil disobedience, King exhorted his followers to avoid violence. This meant that immoral segregation laws could be peacefully violated as a means of showing their injustice. Dr. King wrote one of his most important documents from prison. His 1963 "Letter from Birmingham Jail" is a testimonial to his doctrine of nonviolent change. His doctrine of nonviolence led to his frequent arrests in the 1950s and 1960s. As he explained his basic doctrine in his famous 1963 speech at the Lincoln Memorial: "We must forever conduct our struggle on the high plane of dignity and discipline. We must not allow our creative protest to degenerate into physical violence . . . we must rise to the majestic heights of meeting physical force with soul force."

Martin Luther King Jr. spent only 13 years in the national spotlight before his brutal 1968 assassination by James Earl Ray at a Memphis, Tennessee, motel. Toward the end of his brilliant career he expanded his attacks on segregation to include other issues touching the lives of African Americans. He challenged conditions of poverty and economic injustice, saying that the civil rights movement had to go beyond issues of discrimination to matters of broader human rights. King advocated basic changes in American society, emphasizing equality of treatment and equality of opportunity for all Americans.

violent civil disobedience called for resistance to unjust laws without the use of physical force. Tactics included demonstrations, marches, and public disobedience to law. Followers of King were prepared to march in the streets, sit-in at segregated facilities, or even lay down in front of the police. Passive resistance meant being willing to be dragged or carried to jail rather than to comply with an unjust law. It also meant that no blows were to be struck or shots fired to achieve social justice. The example set by the followers of nonviolent civil disobedience was intended to arouse the mass public out of its indifference to injustice and the deprivation of rights. It was designed to reform and change the laws as well as the conduct of those who enforced the law.

King wrote in *Stride Toward Freedom* (1958), "Our method will be that of persuasion, not coercion. We will say to the people, 'let your conscience decide.'" King saw nonviolent civil disobedience as consistent with his Christian beliefs. He urged his followers that "we must not be bitter and end up hating our white brothers." The spiritual aspect of the civil rights movement cannot be overstated, and King gave it that source of inspiration as part of his religious ministry.

As the civil rights movement spread many other groups organized to promote the rights of African Americans. The NAACP was there before the movement began, and it continued to litigate and pressure Congress to expand African American rights. During the direct action phase of the civil rights movement, the Student Nonviolent Coordinating Committee (SNCC) and the Congress of Racial Equality (CORE) were rivals for publicity and influence with King's Southern Christian Leadership Conference. James Forman, one of the leaders of SNCC, was bolder and more aggressive than most, advocating "reparations," a massive cash repayment to African Americans by white groups, including churches, for years of deprivation and suffering. There were sharp differences in strategy and philosophy during the civil rights movement, but overall realistic and nonviolent deeds gained the most successes.

For over a decade after 1957 African Americans and sympathetic whites engaged in sit-ins, freedom rides, and freedom marches, often risking their lives. The various rights organizations were able to coordinate some of their efforts and set aside their differences. In the beginning, the demonstrations were met with violence and resentment, but eventually the conditions of African Americans was dramatically altered. Public support grew as more whites saw the hardships and prejudice that African Americans confronted. Radio, television, and newspapers magnified the civil rights movement. The world outside of the United States also saw the images of the civil rights demonstrators on television and in the newspapers and was swayed by the sincerity and heroism evident in the civil rights movement.

One graphic episode bears description. In the spring of 1963, during confrontations between African Americans and whites in the streets of Birmingham, Alabama, Police Commissioner Eugene "Bull" O'Connor unleashed police dogs and used cattle prods to suppress peaceful civil rights protesters. These police actions were seen on national television, provoking national indignation and horror. Such scenes only served the cause of advancing African American rights.

Another dramatic image was the massive August 1963 March on Washington for Jobs and Freedom, led by Martin Luther King Jr. Nearly a quarter-million Americans, representing many cultural backgrounds, gathered together on the mall in front of the Washington Monument to hear King deliver his greatest speech, in which he told of his dream for America. In that dream there would be a united nation in which people would "not be judged by the color of their skin but by the content of their character." (For a full transcript of King's "I Have a Dream" speech, see chapter 17.)

There were also martyrs to the movement. Many African American churches were bombed and people killed or maimed during marches and demonstrations. Martin Luther King Jr. and Medgar Evers, leaders in the struggle, paid for their beliefs with their lives. Evers was slain in 1963 and King in 1968.

The Congressional Response: Civil Rights Legislation

There is no doubt that modern civil rights laws were the direct result of the pressures on Congress and the president created by the civil rights movement. Rights groups had proposed various anti-lynching and civil rights bills, but all had languished in Congress, sometimes blocked by the threat of a Senate filibuster. Yet in 1957 the nation's first civil rights law since 1875 finally was enacted into law. This was the first such statute since the post-Civil War era of Reconstruction.

Civil Rights Act of 1957

The Civil Rights Act of 1957 established for the first time a Civil Rights Commission and a new Civil Rights Division within the Justice Department. The nonpartisan Civil Rights Commission was empowered to gather evidence concerning violations of the right to vote and to study and "appraise the laws and policies of the federal government with respect to the equal protection of the laws."

The Civil Rights Division was given more potent authority, including the power to order an injunction or restraining order whenever "any person is about to engage in any act or practice" that would interfere with the right to vote. Criminal punishments for voting offenses were also created.

The 1957 statute also made African Americans eligible to serve on federal juries. This fundamental right had frequently been violated in trials in the South. Any citizen over the age of 21 who was of sound mind and able to write, speak, and understand English was made eligible to serve on juries in federal matters.

The 1957 act required further strengthening, so another statute was passed in 1960 to limit the use of literacy tests as a barrier to voting. Federal officials could be appointed to oversee state and local elections to ensure legal access to the polls, and interracial violence against churches, homes, and schools was made a federal crime.

Civil Rights Act of 1964

The Civil Rights Act of 1964 was even more sweeping. It is the most far-reaching civil rights statute of modern times and forbids discrimination on the basis of race, color, religion, gender, and national origin. Thus, all groups in America were the beneficiaries of strong rights legislation. Women and men, African Americans and whites, and many minorities enjoy greater expended rights as a result of this landmark law.

The 1964 statute was first proposed by President John Kennedy, prompted by Southern resistance to desegregation and violence directed against peaceful civil rights protests. On July 2, President Lyndon Johnson signed the bill into law. The sympathy won by President Kennedy's tragic assassination in 1963 was a factor in gaining passage of the bill through the Congress. The era of ineffective civil rights laws was over.

As a result of the 1964 statute, the Civil Rights Division's authority to challenge segregated public facilities and schools was enhanced, and a Community Relations Service was established to assist communities in resolving discrimination disputes. The attorney general was empowered to intervene in equal discrimination cases. The power of the Civil Rights Commission was increased, and its life extended. These provisions,

which had been deleted by Congress from the 1957 and 1960 civil rights statutes, were critical to enforcement of minority rights.

The Civil Rights law of 1964 created notable new rights as well. It outlawed arbitrary discrimination in voter registration. It barred discrimination in public accommodations, including hotels and restaurants, using the interstate commerce clause of the Constitution as a source of authority. All Americans were entitled to full and equal enjoyment of any place of public accommodation "without discrimination or segregation on the ground of race, color, religion, or national origin."

The 1964 statute also banned employment discrimination, including gender discrimination for the first time. Employment discrimination coverage included state and local governments as well as private sector firms. Finally, the statute created the Equal Employment Opportunity Commission (EEOC) to enforce the laws against discrimination.

Voting Rights Act of 1965

The history of the 1965 Voting Rights Act is largely intertwined with the 1965 campaign for African American voting rights in Alabama. In March 1965 Martin Luther King Jr. and thousands of civil rights supporters made a 54-mile march from Selma to Montgomery, Alabama, the state capital, to dramatize the denial of voting rights to African Americans who had attempted to register in Selma. The march first began on March 7 but was marred by an attack by 200 state troopers and the violent death of James Reeb, a 38-year-old white Unitarian minister from Boston. On March 15 President Lyndon Johnson proposed voting rights legislation to Congress, and the Selma march continued after federal court intervention. On March 25, 1965, Ku Klux Klan members shot and killed Viola Liuzzo, a white civil rights worker from Detroit. On August 6, 1965, President Johnson signed the Voting Rights Act into law.

The nation's shock over the incidences in Alabama in March 1965 led to swift congressional passage of the Voting Rights Act. The Voting Rights Act of 1965 provided for the assignment of federal examiners to conduct registration and observe voting practices in states or counties where discrimination existed. Literacy tests and other discriminatory laws were suspended in the states of Alabama, Alaska, Georgia, Louisiana, Mississippi, South Carolina, and parts of North Carolina. Although the statute was primarily designed to assist African American voters, it was written to include all poor people, regardless of race. Non-English-speaking minorities were included within the Act as well.

Civil Rights Act of 1968

Nine days after Martin Luther King Jr.'s death in April 1968, President Lyndon Johnson signed the Civil Rights Bill of 1968 into law, which provided penalties for those persons attempting to interfere with individual civil rights, including rights workers and demonstrators. The statute also expanded the protections against housing discrimination in home sales and rentals.

Other important federal statutes have been passed since 1968, but none have the magnitude of the 1957, 1964, 1965, and 1968 statutes. The civil rights movement managed to bring about the expansion of rights in America. The statutes that were passed during the height of the movement show a popular, democratic response to the needs of African Americans. Yet, these statutes, important as they are, have not ended racial discrimination in America. There is a sense among most African Americans that more is needed, but there is little agreement about what should be done next and not much political support for further expansion of rights.

Unfinished Business of the Movement

Whatever had been won by the civil rights movement in the Congress, in the courts and in the hearts of many Americans it was still not enough. Following King's assassination, rioting ensued in 100 American cities, including Washington, D.C., with a widespread and devastating loss of life and property. In spite of these events, and as a fitting reminder of the importance of Dr. King, President Johnson signed the Civil Rights Bill of 1968 into law. Yet many whites retreated from their support of the civil rights movement because of the urban violence that had taken place.

In May 1968 Dr. Ralph Abernathy led thousands of Americans, of all cultural backgrounds, on a Poor People's March on Washington. There they established Resurrection City, a settlement of tents and shanties. King had planned the march and demonstration before his death. Fair and equal economic treatment for African Americans was important to King, and there was still unfinished business that the civil rights movement had to accomplish—mainly the unequal economic situation of African Americans. King had intended to lead the way into a promised land of economic opportunity for African Americans. This was a never-launched campaign that reached beyond the ending of racial segregation into a new land of true racial equality. His death left that dream unfulfilled.

Shortly before he died, King gave a speech to African American leaders that is reprinted in Peter Levy's *Let Freedom Ring*. The speech was entitled "Where Do We Go From Here," and in it King revealed his views regarding the progress of African Americans and the distance that they still needed to travel. King underscored the futility of violence and rioting as a means of advancement. He urged his followers to avoid all forms of violence in their quest for rights. Nonetheless, he observed, the movement must address the fact that there were still 40 million poor Americans "raising questions about the economic system, about a broader distribution of wealth." These broader matters of economic justice were on his mind at the time of his death.

King's death left a void in the civil rights movement that no one else was able to fill. Many prominent African Americans including Reverend Jesse Jackson and Dr. Ralph Abernathy tried to keep King's message alive, but none could capture the hearts of all Americans. Both stood at his side at the Lorraine Motel in Memphis, Tennessee, on the day he was killed, and both Abernathy and Jackson tried hard to embody King's message. The vigor and spiritual leadership provided by King proved to be a serious blow to the civil rights movement, and the momentum of the movement slowed. Some more militant African American leaders arose to claim that more violence was needed to press forward the unmet needs of African Americans. Other African American leaders proposed self-segregation from white society.

Cultural assimilation and desegregation was not the chosen path of the Black Power movement. This more militant view took pride in African American culture and sought to maintain its separation from the dominant white culture. Leaders

Ralph D. Abernathy (1926–1990)

Ralph D. Abernathy, one of the major leaders of the civil rights movements of the 1960s, was born March 11, 1926, in Linden, Alabama. Ordained a Baptist minister in 1948, he was usually called by his title of Reverend Ralph D. Abernathy during the years of the civil rights struggles.

Reverend Abernathy met Martin Luther King Jr. while attending Atlanta University in the 1950s. Reverend King was preaching at the Ebenezer Baptist Church in Atlanta at the time. The two met and became close friends.

In 1955 Abernathy and King organized the Montgomery Improvement Association to coordinate a citywide bus boycott in Montgomery, Alabama. This boycott became the springboard for the broader civil rights movement. After the boycott succeeded in ending discrimination on the city's buses, Abernathy helped to form the Southern Negro Leadership Conference. In 1957 this organization finally became known as the Southern Christian Leadership Conference, with Dr. King as its first president.

From the death of Martin Luther King Jr. in 1968 until 1977, Reverend Abernathy served as president of the Southern Christian Leadership Conference, carrying on the legacy of Dr. King and continuing his work as a leader in the civil rights movement until his resignation in 1977. Abernathy died of cardiac arrest in 1990.

such as Stokely Carmichael and Eldridge Cleaver called for revolution. Other militants called for greater power for African Americans, which might require force, regardless of what King may have believed. King opposed the Black Power movement, partly because turning the other cheek in Christian humility was not part of the Black Power program and partly because it was strongly anti-white. In recent years this Black Power approach to African American advancement has faded, but it has not altogether disappeared.

In spite of the failure of the Black Power movement, African American political leaders did emerge. In 1967 Thurgood Marshall was appoint-

ed to the Supreme Court of the United States—its first African American member. In 1969 Shirley Chisholm was elected as the first African American woman in the House of Representatives. African American mayors were elected in Gary, Indiana; Detroit, Michigan; and Newark, New Jersey; and in 1973 Tom Bradley became the first African American elected mayor in a city with a population exceeding one million. In 1977 Patricia Roberts Harris was appointed secretary of the Department of Housing and Urban Development, becoming the first African American woman to serve in a cabinet-level post. In 1989 Army General Colin Powell became the first African American to serve as chairman of the Joint Chiefs of Staff. In 1990 David Dinkins became the first African American mayor of New York City.

In the 1990s the Reverend Louis Farrakhan has attempted to provide African American leadership outside the Christian tradition. As a Black Muslim, Farrakhan has also advocated black self-help and separatism as a means for advancement of African Americans. Farrakhan has been impatient with the pace of African American economic advances and harsh in his criticism of Jews and other whites. His movement, while nonviolent, differs from the classic civil rights movement both as to goals and philosophy. Racial integration is not the target of Farrakhan and other militant African Americans leaders.

Great strides had been made in improving the lives of African Americans. Racial discrimination had been made illegal in most of its forms. Yet many African Americans have been left behind. Many large cities in the United States still have sections consigned to the very poor, many of whom are African American. Crime, drug abuse, and violence are prevalent in these impoverished areas. Public schools are often inadequate, and unemployment is usually very high. The formation of racial "ghettos" had been observed by the famous Kerner Commission Report of 1968 (named after Governor Otto Kerner of Illinois, head of the president's National Advisory Commission on Civil Disorders). In this document, prepared after the rioting that swept American cities following the King assassination, the conclusion was reached that, "our nation is moving towards two societies, one black, one white—separate and unequal." Since 1968 many African Americans have enjoyed greater rights and enhanced economic opportunities, but for those in inner-city "ghettos" life has not improved very much. Perhaps, as the Kerner Commission Report suggested, African Americans in our inner cities have not had the same opportunity as European immigrants have had to raise themselves out of poverty.

Desegregation in America has been the law of the land since the passage of the great civil rights acts of the 1960s. African Americans have been more integrated into the social and economic life of America than ever before. African Americans have made great strides in the fields of sports, the performing arts, business, the military, science, medicine, and others. Yet despite these gains in occupational status the median income of African Americans is still about 59 percent of that for whites. This income disparity has been fairly constant for decades.

The African American Economic Experience

The African American experience in America differed significantly from that of other immigrant groups. African peoples brought here against their will as slaves were kept in bondage for more than 200 years. During this time, they were detribalized and stripped of their cultural heritage, their family structure was destroyed, and they were assigned second-class citizen status for more than 400 years. From the Emancipation Proclamation in 1863 to the passage of the Civil Rights Act in 1964, the national government refused to adopt positive laws to protect civil rights of African Americans as well as their rights to acquire and possess property, although such laws were passed for other groups.

Chapter 9 of this text tells the great story of the ending of segregation in the United States. The first three chapters tell of ending the shame of slavery and of the rise of the civil rights for African Americans. Certainly, the lot of African Americans had improved as a result of Supreme Court rulings and federal and state legislation. Nonetheless, the promise of America to respect the freedom and dignity of all persons is still unfulfilled for African Americans. In particular, fair economic opportunity is still lacking, and many African Americans still remain at the bottom of the economic ladder long after the end of slavery and the civil rights revolution of modern times. In 1962 the famous Swedish sociologist Gunnar Myrdal, whose work was partially the basis for the 1954 *Brown* v. *Board of Education* desegregation decision, stated the problem for African Americans in precise fashion:

> The Negro in America has not yet been given the elemental civil and political rights of formal democracy, including a fair opportunity to earn his living, upon which a general accord was already won when the American creed was first taking form. And this anachronism constitutes the contemporary problem both to Negroes and to whites.

Although much has changed since Myrdal made this profound observation, it remains fundamentally sound. This chapter will outline why African Americans have not yet gained full equality of economic opportunity in America.

The mother lode of society's wealth, the means by which it redistributes its income, is found in trade, commerce, and real estate. For a minority group to flourish in a competitive society, the group needs two forms of support: the means to participate in a culture's economic system, called human capital, and a set of laws to make the participation possible, called bootstraps. If the laws are the bootstraps, think of human capital as the foundation, the "boots" of the minority group: education, on-the-job training, and knowledge of how political and economic systems work. Without this human capital, these "boots" to stand on, a group cannot compete in a competitive, pluralistic society or take advantage of the political and economic opportunities society has to offer. In essence, without education or training, it is harder to get and hold a job. Minority groups generally must look to the government to safeguard their rights to acquire the necessary human capital. The government can take positive steps to create political and economic opportunity, but if a group does not have the necessary human capital, its members will not be able to use such opportunities to their advantage. Likewise, if a group has a sufficient amount of human capital but no bootstraps, its members still will not be able to elevate themselves to the middle class.

From emancipation to the passage of the 1964 Civil Rights Act, the government never issued African Americans a system of protection to safeguard their right to grow and develop, as it did for other groups. African Americans were thus unable to develop a pattern for economic self-

After the Emancipation Proclamation of 1863, African Americans could not be bought and sold as property. Other African American rights, however, like the right to acquire and possess property, were a much longer time coming.

reliance because the U.S. government did not protect their civil rights. Yet, during the same period, the government undertook numerous measures to protect the civil rights of European groups as they gained a foothold in American society. This portion of the chapter, therefore, analyzes the African American experience from the signing of the Emancipation Proclamation until the government started implementing laws to protect African Americans' rights to grow and develop politically and economically.

Emancipation Without a Set of Bootstraps

In studying the cause of inequality among African Americans, social scientists too often attempt to compare the manner in which African Americans were brought over to America with that of the European immigrants. Such a comparison leads sociologists to focus on family structure.

This approach leads social scientists to overlook the failure of the government to issue African Americans a set of bootstraps after emancipation and to provide African Americans with a system of protection that would safeguard their civil right to enter the mainstream of society's income redistribution system.

If the United States government had simply allocated each ex-slave family 40 acres and a mule

after emancipation, this action would have served as a protection against poverty. This measure would have given African Americans economic self-reliance within the first generation of their emancipation. Instead, the limited programs of the Freedmen's Bureau proved inadequate. The second generation of African Americans would have flourished upon the land they inherited from their parents. But the northern industrialists who held the reins of power over the southern economic system after emancipation were not interested in designing a system of protection to ensure African Americans' full enjoyment of the American democratic values—income, safety, and dignity.

The rationale that policymakers gave at the time for not allocating ex-slave families 40 acres and a mule was anchored in the American democratic assumption that anyone who wanted to could "pull himself up by his bootstraps," that is, succeed through his unaided efforts. Parceling out land, they further argued, would add to the huge national debt. But this argument was a contradiction to the existing public policy. At the time that policymakers were arguing against giving African Americans 40 acres and a mule, Congress passed the Homestead Act of 1862, a bootstrap that provided free land for German and Scandinavian immigrants. Instead of offering these groups just 40 acres, the government gave them 160 acres of land. Colleges and universities were granted under the Morrill Act of 1862. These grants had the effect of ensuring that a culture of poverty would not develop among German and Scandinavian immigrants.

Offering ex-slaves a set of bootstraps after emancipation was nothing new. When Russia freed her slaves in 1861, she not only gave them the land on which they had previously worked but provided them with a system of protection that safeguarded their property rights to purchase land. Before the Russian slaves were freed, Alexander II issued several "rescripts" to the nobles in Lebanon province, asking them to consider seriously the possibility of emancipating their serfs on the basis of the following mandatory principles: "(1) the right of the emancipated serf to buy the plot of land on which he lives, (2) the right to buy a parcel of land based upon his needs and ability to pay." To ensure the former slaves' orderly and proper adjustment to their new status, Alexander II established a statute of "temporary obligation," which allowed them to enter into an agreement for a period of 20 years to purchase land from the landowners. The effect of this statute was to allow the slaves to develop a sense of self-determination at their own pace.

The 20-year period in which the Russian slaves could purchase land from their former masters is of political significance here. Almost a generation passed in which the skills for economic self-reliance could be developed among the newly freed slaves. On the contrary, the system of protection that America gave her slaves to purchase land, the Confiscation Act of 1861, lasted fewer than five years. The act allowed the federal government to confiscate the land of Civil War rebels and prevented them from owning land afterward. Consequently, millions and millions of acres of land were suddenly made available for anyone, except the ex-Confederates, to purchase. African Americans took advantage of this opportunity by purchasing a large portion of this land without government assistance under a program sponsored by the Freedmen's Bureau.

The Freedmen's Bureau and the Quest for Economic Self-reliance

It must be understood that the experience of African Americans was vastly different from that of most European immigrants. Many of the immigrants, though impoverished in Europe, saw economic opportunity in America. They expected that they and their children could emerge from poverty into a condition of economic equality through their own efforts. But the fact is that to enter into middle-class status a group must enjoy the fundamental right to seek economic opportunity on an equal basis with others. This right was denied to slaves and to emancipated African Americans after the collapse of slavery. The power of the U.S. government to promote the opportunities of freed African Americans was not used vigorously, and the rights of African Americans were frustrated.

Other American groups did receive economic inducements, subsidies, and protections during various historical periods. However, African American rights to acquire property and to pursue economic opportunity were deliberately limited by laws and by repressive cultural pressures. The U.S. government failed to offer African Americans the same kinds of supports and protections that enabled many other groups to enter into the middle class. Instead, what developed was a culture of poverty among repressed groups, especially African Americans, which made them believe that they were somehow incapable of sharing the American dream of equal economic opportunity.

Although the government refused to issue African Americans a set of bootstraps, as it did for certain white European groups at the time, African Americans still would have achieved economic self-reliance within a generation if their rights to pursue economic opportunities had been placed on a principle of law. Upon the heels of their emancipation, African Americans had an extraordinary craving for land. They perceived owning land as a precondition for real emancipation. With the aid of the Freedmen's Bureau, African Americans moved at a miraculously rapid pace in acquiring land with their own resources. As W. E. B. Du Bois noted, the Freedmen's Bureau was "financed not by taxation but the tolls of ex-slaves; the total amount of rent collected from land in the hands of the bureau, paid mostly by Negroes, amounted to $400,000, and curiously enough it was this rent that supported the bureau during the first years."

Under the Freedmen's Bureau Act of 1865, Congress gave the president the authority to appoint a commissioner of the bureau. This act temporarily gave ex-slaves a system of protection that safeguarded their civil rights to purchase land. The commissioner had the authority to lease unoccupied tracts of land, not exceeding 20 acres, to ex-slaves and white refugees for a period of three years. At the end of this period, the tenants had the right to purchase the land.

Further evidence of the ex-slaves' propensity for self-reliance was their enthusiastic support of the Freedmen's Saving and Trust Company. The bank, chartered by Congress in March of 1865, emanated from the effort of several Union generals to establish banks for the newly freed slaves to put their money. The bank was eventually established by a group of philanthropists. This group took great care to ensure that the bank was established on solid business principles. For example, the group provided that at least two-thirds of the bank's deposits were in government securities. The bank was authorized to use any surplus funds to promote the cause of education among African Americans. Under this charter, the bank was allowed to pay a maximum interest of 7 percent.

The Freedmen's Savings Bank probably was the wealthiest and most financially secure bank in the country at the time. It was reported that in 1874 its total deposits reached approximately $57,000,000. Because two-thirds of these deposits were secured by government bonds, the only way that the bank could have gone under was for the federal government itself to have collapsed, which, at the time, rested within the realm of the impossible. Again, the Freedmen's bank was the only bank in the country chartered by the federal government, and it had a captive clientele of approximately 4 million potential depositors. This factor contributed to its rapid growth in a very short period of time.

Although the bank's headquarters was located in Washington, D.C., it had 34 branches situated throughout the South and in several northern states, including New York and Pennsylvania. Around the 1870s, the board of trustees of the bank changed hands, and the solid foundation on which it rested began to crumble. The new trustees were attracted to the bank's enormous assets. In 1870, they introduced a bill in Congress to amend the bank's charter so that one-half of the deposits already invested in government bonds could be invested in other notes and real estate mortgages. This law opened the bank's vault to predators, and the hard-earned savings of the newly freed men were lost within a period of three years.

Many of the predators were not just the average man on the street. They were young men who later formed the "new nobility of industry" during the latter part of the nineteenth century. Among them was Jay Cooke, banker and financier. The exact amount of money he took from the bank is not known. However, as John Hope Franklin has noted, "At the time when his business was tottering, Jay Cooke borrowed $500,000 at 5 percent interest, and Henry Cooke together with other financiers unloaded bad loans on the bank. After the big financial houses failed in 1873, there was a run on the bank, and many speculating officials resigned, leaving Negroes to take the blame."

The bank charter amendment had a practical political repercussion upon the status of African Americans: It separated their rights to pursue a goal of self-reliance from a principle of law and placed them at the mercy of their competitors and adversaries. This measure helped to foreclose African Americans' freedom to purchase land on their own. Furthermore, many southern state governments opposed the branch banks in their states because they had no control over them; they could not carry out their policy of reinstituting slavery through the guise of the Black Codes unless they could make African Americans totally dependent upon their goodwill.

To further limit African American ability to become self-reliant, President Andrew Johnson issued his Proclamation of Pardon for the ex-Confederates. From this day onward, these individuals were able to reclaim their land. Before the pardon, they could not, as John Hope Franklin noted, legally "reclaim their property until they had been pardoned and had taken the oath." President Johnson had declared before the war that the large plantations would be seized and divided into small farms. But his issuance of the pardon contradicted this promise.

After the pardon, conditions of African Americans began a nosedive from which they have not recovered. African Americans who had bought land with their hard-earned money were pushed off it by the Ku Klux Klan, which was created shortly after the Civil War. The influence of the Freedmen's Bureau began to diminish because Congress significantly curtailed its funds and authority. For example, in 1865, the bureau controlled approximately 800,000 acres of land; in 1868, these acres had been reduced to fewer than 140,000.

President Johnson's Proclamation of Pardon affected African Americans more than economically: It also affected them psychologically. It caused them to lose faith in the federal government to grant them a fair deal. Despite the pardoning of the ex-Confederates, however, many African Americans were able to buy lands throughout the South before the Freedmen's Bank collapsed in 1874. As Du Bois noted, "Virginia Negroes acquired between 80,000 and 100,000 acres of land during the late sixties and early seventies. There were soon a few prosperous Negro farmers with 400 to 1,000 acres of land and some owners of considerable city property. Georgia Negroes had bought, by 1875, 396,658 acres of land, assessed at $1,263,902, and added to this they had town and city property assessed at $1,203,202."

The Black Codes and Their Effect on African Americans

The public policy that had the profoundest effect on African American self-reliance was the Black Codes. The Black Codes were essentially a reenactment of the Slave Codes. They were a set of laws designed to regulate the behavior of the slaves. As Franklin noted, ". . . they covered every aspect of the life of the slaves. There were variations from state to state, but the general point of view expressed in most of them was the same; that is, slaves are not persons but property, and laws should protected the ownership of such property, should protect the whites against any danger that might arise from the presence of large numbers of Negroes. It was also felt that slaves should be maintained in a position of due subordination in order that the optimum of discipline and work could be achieved."

Once the Slave Codes were reenacted as the Black Codes, they had the operative effect of reducing the status of African Americans (i.e., economically, politically, socially, and psychologically) to a subordinate position to whites both in law and in fact. The codes divorced African Americans minds from the land by tying them to the plantation system physically without becoming psychologically a part of it.

The major difference between the conditions of life under the Black Codes and slavery was that under the former system the slave-masters had to pay for their slaves; consequently, the life of the slave carried a monetary value. If a slave was killed, the owner experienced an economic lost.

After slavery, this monetary value was removed and the plantation owner was free to hang or kill an African American at will. More important, these codes institutionalized the white man's word as being the law of the land in defining the legal status of African Americans.

Political Effect

Politically Black Codes shut down African Americans' freedom to enjoy those rights created by the Emancipation Proclamation and the Thirteenth, Fourteenth, and Fifteenth Amendments. These amendments were known as the Civil War Amendments. They were designed to protect the newly freed slaves from hostile legislation by the states.

The Thirteenth Amendment abolished slavery and prohibited involuntary servitude. The Fourteenth Amendment defined citizenship and provided for equal protection of the law. This amendment was important because in the *Dred Scott* decision, the U.S. Supreme Court ruled that the slaves were not citizens and the framers of the Constitution never intended for them to be citizens. The Fifteenth Amendment protected the newly freed slaves' right to political suffrage.

The Black Codes were a sophisticated method of undermining the protection that the Civil War Amendment provided African Americans. The Black Codes were interpreted as laws that came under the purview of the Tenth Amendment on states' rights. Consequently, these codes became political tools by which employers fenced African Americans in on the plantations in such a way that they could not leave the plantation system even if they desired to do so. For example, the codes stipulated that African Americans were free to choose their employers at the end of each year. But this was possible if, and only if, they had cleared their debts with their former employer. However, since the employer kept the books, he had the sole authority to determine whether or not the tenants' debts were cleared. Any discrepancy that the tenant found in the employer's recordkeeping was settled by the employer himself. Under the Black Codes, African Americans could not dispute a white man's word, because such a dispute constituted an act of disobedience and the employer had the authority to fine an African American $1 for every offense.

The codes gave plantation owners the legal right to work African Americans a whole year

The Black Codes were a sophisticated method of undermining the protection that the Civil War Amendments provided African Americans.

without paying them a penny. There was no redress that African Americans could seek for this denial of their basic constitutional rights. The white man's words were the law of the land as far as African Americans were concerned—a practice that lasted until the civil rights movement of the 1950s and 1960s.

Social Effect

The absolute authority that the Black Codes gave whites over the lives of African Americans significantly affected African Americans' social development. The codes relegated the African American male to a caste system, which molded his social and political behavior into a "Sambo" or an "Uncle Tom" personality type. For example,

the Black Codes of the state of Louisiana prescribed that African American males conduct themselves "properly"; that is, they demanded "obedience to all proper orders" that their employer gave them. The social significance of this law was that the term "obedience to all proper orders" was left solely up to the arbitrary and capricious interpretation of the employer. The employer had the discretion to interpret "proper orders"—ranging from leaving home without permission to impudence, swearing, indecent language, or quarreling or fighting among one another. Thus, the authority to levy penalties for disobedience was the tool by which employers could foreclose African Americans' freedom to develop their skills and talents. The Black Codes became the catalyst that prevented African Americans from

After emancipation slaves did not have monetary value to plantation owners, thus they were able to abuse African American workers at will.

developing a sense of self-determination and thereby created the sense of dependency that they currently have.

Without a system of protection to safeguard its freedom to acquire and possess property, a minority group cannot develop a sense of self-determination or self-reliance. Without property, the group cannot grow and develop in a competitive and capitalistic society; it cannot participate in the accumulation of wealth that Western societies value and glorify. The accumulation of property allows individual members within a group to plan for the future with calculation. With property and wealth, individual members will be able to take advantage of the many economic opportunities that society has to offer on a competitive basis. Thus,

over a period of time, it will enable the group to compete on an equal footing in society, thus reducing its need for government assistance.

The lack of a system of protection is one historic cause of the African Americans' failure to develop a sense of self-reliance and self-determination. A group's need for such a system of protection is evidenced by the lack of growth exhibited by the Irish Catholic. They arrived in America between the 1830s and 1850s. Irish Americans remained impoverished for more than four generations; they started escaping the slums in the 1940s and 1950s only when the government intervened and provided them with a system of protection through the various New Deal Programs, namely, the National Labor Relations Act, the National Apprenticeship

Act, and the Federal Housing Act. African Americans, it must be noted, were excluded from participating in these programs because of race.

Economic Effect

Economically, the Black Codes were a discriminatory public policy that kept African Americans legally in slavery without the economic liability that accompanied the institution of slavery. For example, the life of an adult male slave had a value ranging from $500 to $1,400. After slavery, this value was removed and the life of an African American worker became worthless to the plantation owners; they were free to hang African American workers at will, while during slavery such an act would have constituted an economic loss to the slave-master.

In summary, African Americans had a burning desire to purchase land after their emancipation. In order to develop economically, a group must have the right to develop themselves economically to protect their freedom to interact fully in society. The Black Codes not only prevented African Americans from actively participating in such an environment but also foreclosed their freedom to take advantage of a wide range of other economic opportunities in society.

Psychological Effect

In addition to limiting African Americans' opportunity to pursue a wide range of occupations, the Black Codes constrained the full development of their personalities; that is, the codes discouraged the development of a sense of self-determination. These codes denied African Americans the enjoyment of not only America's basic ideals, such as freedom of speech, assembly, petition, and expression, but also other American values such as shared power, income, safety, and dignity.

The American democratic values that the Black Codes denied African Americans were as important to the development of their personalities as air is to fire. The political significance of democratic values in relationship to the development of the personality has been thoroughly analyzed by Harold D. Lasswell, whose writings are dedicated to analyzing the relationship between public policy and society's respect for human dignity.

Lasswell recognizes a close relationship between public policy and the development of individual personalities. He argues that the individual's personality is developed by the degree to which the social environment increases or decreases common values. The personality, he argues, "is an on-going concern which is constantly relating itself as a whole to the environment in which it lives."

The impact that the repressive Black Codes had on African Americans significantly affected the growth and development of their personality; that is, the codes prevented them from developing a personality adequate for growth and development in a competitive society.

The Doctrines of Racism and the Institutionalization of Racial Inferiority

Two doctrines of racism have been adopted by the dominant society to control African Americans: *romantic racism* and *social Darwinism.* Both of these doctrines provided the basis for the policies that fostered racial inequality. The doctrine of romantic racialism was adopted in the 1830s. It explicitly stated that by law African Americans were to occupy a position of subordination to that of whites.

The Black Codes within themselves were not sufficient to place African Americans in a position of inferiority economically, socially, and psychologically. Many southern and northern industrialists felt it necessary to adopt a doctrine of racism to achieve this end. This doctrine is better known as social Darwinism. The social Darwinists extended the interpretation of the biological theory of evolution into a theory of society and civilization. They argued that the status of a race in society was the product of natural evolutionary forces, which consisted of struggle and conflict in which the stronger and more advanced race would naturally triumph over the inferior and weaker race.

The theory of social Darwinism received its maximal expression in the concepts of the "white man's burden" and "manifest destiny," which had the political consequence of conditioning African Americans to become docile and accommodating people. Briefly, these concepts, which were advocated by social scientists and churchmen alike, argued that white Americans were destined either by natural forces or by the will of God to rule North America and possibly the rest of the world.

In addition, all nonwhites were incapable of self-government. This creed, in effect, gave the white race a moral and theological justification for the domination of nonwhite races.

As social Darwinism began to permeate the American thought pattern, the powerful whites had problems keeping African Americans in the South. First, there was Horace Greeley, a journalist, calling, "Go West, young man, go West." Second, economic conditions for African Americans had begun to worsen. With the collapse of the Freedmen Saving Bank, African Americans were unable to secure the capital to purchase land. Unable to elevate themselves economically through the tenancy and sharecropping systems, and cruelly treated by landlords and merchants, African Americans had little incentive to remain in the South. As early as 1879, African Americans began abandoning the South and adhering to Greeley's call to go West. To encourage their migration, Henry Adams of Louisiana and "Pop" Singleton of Tennessee started organizing African Americans for the westward movement. Consequently, thousands of African Americans began migrating from Mississippi, Louisiana, Alabama, Georgia, and Tennessee. Adams claimed to have organized 98,000 African Americans from Tennessee alone.

This westward movement posed a serious threat both to the southerners' and the northern industrialists' plans for economic development of the South. If this migration were left unchecked, they felt that it would rob the South of its irreplaceable cheap labor force, which was necessary for growing cotton. To remedy this problem, whites needed two things: a policy of social control and an African American propagandist whom they could trust and control to impose their policy on African Americans.

The purpose of the social control policy was to convince African Americans not to subscribe to Horace Greeley's urgent plea to go West but instead to stay in the South. To this end, the industrialists recruited Booker T. Washington as the chief spokesman for the African American race.

This effort to keep African Americans in the South is manifested in Washington's famous "Atlanta Compromise" speech, which he gave at the Exposition in 1895. He told African Americans: "To those of my race who depend upon bettering their conditions in foreign land, or who underestimate the importance of cultivating friendly rela-

With little incentive to stay in the South, African Americans began in 1879 to follow journalist Horace Greeley's call to go west.

tions with the Southern white man, who is his next door neighbor, I would say 'cast down your bucket where you are'—cast down in making friends in every manly way of the people of all races by whom we are surrounded." He further sought to condone the South's wholesale violation of the civil rights of African Americans by arguing that "whatever other sins the South may be called to bear, when it comes to business, pure and simple, it is in the South that the Negro is given a man's chance in the commercial world." It is ironic that Washington would make such claims at a time when the practice of reducing African Americans to perpetual indentured servants was a way of life and lynching them for attempting to exercise their basic civil and human rights was a common occurrence.

The philosophy that Washington outlined in his speech was nothing new. It was simply a recapitulation of the American thought pattern of "racial adjustment" that had been brewing since the Civil War. Essentially, Washington argued that the solution to the race problem was for African Americans temporarily to give up three things: political power, insistence on civil rights, and higher education of African American youth. In return for surrendering these basic human and civil rights, Washington proposed to sell African Americans the notion that the solution to the race problem was the "application of the gospel of wealth" and "material prosperity." He also urged African Americans to emphasize self-help and racial solidarity, moral uplift, and economic devel-

opment. It seemingly never occurred to Washington that these goals were unattainable as long as the rights of African Americans to acquire property and to seek employment opportunities rested on the goodwill of their adversaries and competitors and not on a principle of law.

The power elite was successful in elevating Washington to the level of national spokesman for African Americans at the Atlanta Exposition. Washington was practically unknown when he went to the exposition; after he left, he was identified by the white media as the "African Americans leader." The white media, it must be noted, had a tradition of printing news about two types of African Americans: the so-called good nigger, and the bad nigger. When the media wrote about the so-called bad nigger, it was trying to depict the negative image of an African American; when it wrote about the so-called good nigger, it was trying to depict the ideal type of African American. In most cases the ideal was the docile or accommodating "Uncle Tom," after whom African Americans were expected to model their lives.

The political thrust of Washington's philosophy of racial accommodation was to take the basis of civil rights of African Americans off a principle of law and place them upon the goodwill of their adversaries and competitors who, at that time, opposed any expression of economic, political, social, or educational equality.

The most critical step that Washington took to institutionalize the theory of social Darwinian was when he advised African Americans to forget about higher education and to concern themselves with industrial and agricultural education, or "progressive education." The progressive education during that period, at its best, was preparing African Americans, as Frazier noted, for skills that were being outmoded by the progress of the Industrial Revolution, and for lives as small individualistic entrepreneurs at a time when the philosophy of economic individuals was becoming obsolete.

When Washington urged African Americans to forget about higher education, he was not only urging them to forget about thinking altogether, but foreclosing their opportunity to enter into mainstream America. As Du Bois noted, Washington's emphasis upon progressive education coincided with lawmakers' "steady withdrawal of aid from institutions for higher learning." Shortly after the Civil War, the Peabody Fund was established to aid African American education. As a precondition for receiving funds, African Americans were "expected to conform to the racial policy of the foundation" (from the Peabody Fund application form). This policy was designed to shape not only their philosophy of racial adjustment but also their "general social philosophy according to the social philosophy of the northern philanthropic foundation."

While the Peabody Fund was doling out pennies to the African Americans colleges, Congress was doling out to white colleges more than a quarter of a billion dollars in the form of grants and land under the Morrill Act of 1862. The political significance of this act is that it recognized, as Edwin Slosson noted, "the principle that every citizen is entitled to receive educational aid from the government and that the common affairs of life are proper subjects with which to educate or to train men." This principle, however, applied only to whites and European immigrants during the period between 1862 and 1920. Education was made available to prevent the culture of poverty from developing among them. African American schools, for the most part, depended largely on donations from whites who insisted that African American students adopt a philosophy of racial adjustment. This policy was overseen by Booker T. Washington.

After he convinced African Americans temporarily to give up their political rights and to place them on the goodwill of their adversaries and competitors, Washington became the unidirectional political link between African Americans and the American power structure nationally. He had quasidictatorial power to suppress dissent among those African American leaders who overtly criticized his philosophy as one of accommodation. As Gilbert Osofsky noted, although Washington resided in Tuskegee, Alabama, he could use his power to have an African American fired from a civil service job in New York if that African American "published some disparaging remarks about [his] leadership."

Economically, Washington controlled the purse strings—and the decision-making mechanism—for the majority of programs designed to improve the status of African Americans. Any program that did not conform to his ideas of racial adjustment did not receive financial support, because the philanthropists who funded these programs would consult Washington to make sure that the recipients of these programs were

"safe"—that they conformed to the policy of docility—before they would support them.

Devoid of a system of protection to safeguard their civil right to an education, African Americans could not increase the relative size of their middle class; that is, increase the number of African American lawyers, doctors, and businessmen. Any attempt to do so was undermined by the Southern system of injustice and the repressive nature of the plantation system. From the end of the Reconstruction period to the passage of the civil rights laws of the 1960s, the white man's word was the law in the South, severely restricting African American rights. Often, African Americans were forced to take the judgments and the opinions of whites as the law of the land. Southern whites felt it to be their moral obligation to punish, violently, any African Americans who disputed a white man's word.

Hence, the deprivation of these civil rights that Washington forced African Americans to surrender in the 1890s placed them in the culture of poverty until the culture itself began to harden around them. Once developed, it became a self-perpetuating cycle up to the implementation of affirmative action laws in the latter part of the 1960s. Affirmative action took the right of African Americans to seek employment opportunities from under the control of their competitors and adversaries and placed the right instead on a principle of law.

Social-Structure of the American South

Life in the American South continued in a somewhat modified form after the Civil War. The social structure in the South was a classic example of a feudal system in which the aristocracy (landowners) dominated both the economic and political life, whereas the lower-class whites (land tenants) and African Americans (mostly sharecroppers) were left to compete for the meager benefits that were left. The lower-class whites served as a buffer to minimize the conflict between the masses of African Americans and the aristocrats.

The conflict that often emerged between lower-class whites and the African Americans in the South centered around the distribution of tangible and intangible benefits, generally more of the intangible than the tangible. The tangible benefits centered around the ownership of property, and there was very little conflict on that front because it was clear that the aristocrats owned the majority of the land. The real conflict emerged in the struggle for the intangible values, which were manifested in the control of those social and political institutions that were an intimate part of the old caste system of the antebellum South. The whites had come to control these institutions either through their own achievements or, usually, through inheritance. When African Americans were emancipated and the carpetbaggers from the North invaded the South during the Reconstruction Period, African Americans began to pose a threat to intangible values that whites had come to believe to be theirs by birthright—values such as control of the social and political institutions. More important, when African Americans started competing for these values, they began to destroy the false sense of racial superiority that lower-class whites felt toward African Americans. The lower-class whites, for the most part, owned very little land or property. If African Americans had the same social status as whites, whites would not have anyone to feel superior to. Therefore, there was a concerted effort on the part of the whites of the antebellum South to design an environment, both politically and economically, governed by race and class.

The practical consequence of these social divisions was that they prevented African Americans from acquiring the human capital that was indispensable for their competition in the northern industrial society. They were prevented from entering the economic system by law. Race prejudice was not enough to keep them from entering the economic system on a competitive basis. There were also specific laws, such as the Black Codes, that curtailed their opportunity to take advantage of a wide range of economic activities that would have enabled more of them to enter the middle class.

By the time African Americans started migrating North during World War I, they had fully developed a pattern of dependency. This pattern significantly impeded their rapid adjustment to an urban environment.

The African American Migration

The dominant forces that precipitated the African American migration from the American South resembled the forces that uprooted many European peasants. First, both groups were freed from a feudal system that had kept them tied to the land. The European feudal system differed from the plantation system in the American South in that the South continued to hold African Americans in a modified form of slavery on the plantations even after emancipation. In addition, the Industrial Revolution during the seventeenth and eighteenth centuries broke the bonds that held the European peasants to the land. Industrialization did not evolve in America until the nineteenth century. When it did, it surfaced primarily in the North and did not significantly influence the South; the South's economy was restricted primarily to growing cotton and tobacco. At the height of its economy, the South supplied over three-fourths of the world's cotton needs. The South continued to supply the world with cotton up to the turn of the twentieth century, when America began to receive competition from abroad and manufacturers started shifting to synthetic fibers.

The African American labor supply was indispensable to the United States economy. In order for a country to develop economically, a supply of cheap labor must be available. When industrial development began in America, the majority of African Americans were locked into the institution of slavery. If the slaves had been freed in 1830 and had migrated North to fill the labor demand, it would have severely affected the American economy in both the North and the South. Cotton was needed by the North as raw material for manufacturing clothing. The northern clothing factories could not have survived without it. To promote northern industries and the southern economy, manufacturers and southern planters cooperatively adopted a policy of social control. African Americans were confined to the South to support the Southern economy, and whites were recruited from abroad for Northern industries.

When World War I broke out, all of the available manpower in European countries was needed to prosecute the war, thus cutting off the flow of immigrants to America. This curtailment of immigration was further complicated by the Russian Bolshevik Revolution, which precipitated the "red scare" movement in America. To keep out undesirables, Congress passed the 1917 Immigration Act. The act restricted immigration to skilled and educated individuals. This curtailment occurred when American industry was at its peak and when Euro-

If slaves had been freed in 1830 and had migrated North to fill the labor demand, it would have severely affected the American economy in both the North and the South.

pean countries depended on America for food and war materials. Northern industries turned for the first time to the untapped labor force in the South.

Northern industries would not have been so successful in recruiting African Americans if the economic conditions of the South had not begun to free African Americans from the land some 15 years earlier. There were several factors that helped to loosen the bonds that had kept African Americans tied to the plantation since Reconstruction.

Southern crops were suffering from floods and from the effect of an infestation of boll weevils on the cotton crop. The first crop disaster occurred in 1892, when boll weevils from Mexico attacked cotton in Texas. They spread 160 miles a year, until they had invaded all the Southern states

except for the Carolinas and Virginia. The boll weevils significantly lowered the profits of the plantation owners. Before the boll weevil invasion, the South produced approximately 400,000 bales of cotton a year; after the invasion, the production of cotton was cut in half. It was estimated that the South lost $250,000 worth of cotton in the first three years of the boll weevil infestation.

With the reduction in the production of cotton, plantation owners had less money to buy supplies for their tenants. Merchants accustomed to lending money to the plantation owners began to restrict their lines of credit, because the merchants saw no bright future in the Southern staple crop. The agricultural economy was based on borrowing money to plant crops. Any limitation on borrowing operated to depress the economy, thus blocking the wheels of industry for that sector.

The amount of damage the boll weevils could inflict on the cotton depended heavily on the amount of rainfall the crop received. The South experienced its heaviest rainfalls in the summer of 1915, and thousands of African Americans were left destitute. With a decline in cotton production and constraint on credit, many plantation owners were reluctant to continue investing in the cotton industry. As a consequence, many African Americans were left homeless and out of work for the first time since the end of Reconstruction, thus creating a Southern labor surplus.

When northern industries began recruiting the Southern labor surplus, they acquired a labor force with a predominantly agrarian background. They recruited both African Americans and white laborers, but the bulk of the labor supply consisted of African Americans whose ties to the plantation system had been broken by the reduced cotton crop.

The most compelling force expediting the African Americans migration northward was the "Work or Fight" order issued by the War Department during World War I. With this order, the war economy forced the labor unions to suspend their systematic discriminatory policies against hiring African Americans in workshops. For the unions to act to the contrary would have displayed a degree of disloyalty to the war effort. Thus, for the first time labor unions felt external pressure to relax their anti-African Americans policies.

Before the war, African Americans had very little incentive to migrate North, even if by doing so they could escape the restrictions of the Black Codes of the South. The labor unions had systematic discriminatory policies. But with many whites going off to war, as a result of a direct response to the Draft Act requiring all males between the ages of 18 and 45 to register, the large vacuum left in the labor force was filled by African Americans.

As large numbers of African Americans began to abandon the South, the plantation owners became alarmed and tried to curtail the migration by passing strict ordinances designed to constrain the recruiting agents' efforts in facilitating the African American migration. In many cases, these agents offered free passage North. Mississippi, Florida, Georgia, and Alabama were the hardest hit by the African American migration. Some of these states required the recruiting agents to post $1,000 licenses or be subjected to 60 days in jail or a $600 fine. But the state of Georgia had one of the stiffest laws against recruitment. For instance, the city council of Macon passed an ordinance requiring license fees of $25,000 and demanded that the labor agent be recommended by ten local ministers, ten manufacturers, and 25 businessmen. Nevertheless, despite these restrictions, it has been estimated that over one million African Americans left the South in 1918.

Contact with the Northern Cities

When African Americans made contact with Northern cities, there were more jobs available than people to fill them. The war economy had created a greater demands for goods than industries could supply. African Americans did not have to rove around the country from city to city seeking employment. They found work at the end of their journey. However, when the country began to shift from a wartime to a peacetime economy, the situation changed.

During the war, African Americans were fully employed in the economy. However, they did not have a system of protection to safeguard their rights to employment, that is, protection against arbitrary layoffs and dismissals as did the European immigrants. When white soldiers returned home from the war, African Americans were either fired outright or asked to work for lower wages than whites. Thus, the temporary foothold they had gained in the economy was wiped out after the war and during the Great Depression in the 1930s.

At the close of the war, once again, a conflict erupted between African Americans and whites who were competing for the same jobs. The political and social consequences of this conflict were barriers to limit African Americans' freedom to take advantage of a wide range of employment opportunities. These constraints were manifested in a so-called job ceiling that had an effect on African Americans' upward employment mobility, similar to the effect of the Black Codes in the South.

The job ceiling prevented African Americans from elevating themselves to the middle class by their own means. To their dismay, they found that Booker T. Washington's philosophy of "progressive education" led them directly to a stone wall. Under this system of education, African Americans subscribed tenaciously to the Protestant work ethic, working hard and delaying present gratifications for future ones, just to learn that their skin color prevented them from entering the middle class. In the black colleges, for example, African Americans acquired skills as artisans and craftsmen, only to find these occupations closed to them in the North. They were systematically excluded from joining the unions of their chosen trade. As Du Bois noted, those African Americans with "trades either gave them up and hired out as waiters or laborers, or they became job workmen and floating hands, catching a bit of carpentering here or a little brickwork or plastering there at reduced wages."

Through unionization, whites were able to keep African Americans out of job competition with them. Northern whites attempted to derive the same psychological gratification from being better off than African Americans as did the Southern whites. The greatest opposition that African Americans encountered in joining labor unions came from the Irish, who entertained an anti-African American sentiment because African Americans monopolized the service occupations during the 1840s, 1850s, and 1870s, while the Irish were just a level below them. For instance, it was the Irish who launched the race riots against African Americans during the Civil War in cities such as New York, Chicago, Detroit, Cleveland, Buffalo, and Boston.

Unlike the British West Indians, African Americans did not have the protection of a federal government to safeguard their property rights to seek a wide range of employment opportunities. The African American male was deprived of the freedom to express any signs of aggressiveness. Any behavior in the North was met with a system of oppression geared to put him "back in his place," as was the case in the South. In the South, for example, the African American male found that the average white citizen had the legal authority to deprive him of his life, liberty, and property rights without due process of law. In the North, he found this task had been relegated to the police. Regardless of whether they were in the North or the South, African American rights were not protected under the law until the passage of the civil rights laws of the 1960s. These laws were not nearly as effective as the system of protection that foreign subjects received from the

federal government, because foreign relations laws are questions of diplomatic relations with foreign nations. Any tampering with these policies precipitated intervention by officials from Washington.

The Exclusion of African Americans from the New Deal Programs

The cause of the present-day income inequality among African Americans can be attributed not to what happened to them during slavery but to what happened to them from the passage of the National Labor Relations Act (NLRA) in 1935 to the implementation of affirmative action in 1969 (the Philadelphia Plan). The Philadelphia Plan was the first attempt by the federal government to implement affirmative action in the area of craftsmen. The Nixon administration operated on the principle that the problem of inequality among African Americans could be solved by encouraging them to find jobs in the craft category. Prior to the Philadelphia Plan, the government steadfastly refused to offer African Americans a system of protection to enter the economic mainstream. Embedded in this system was an awesome system of government subsidies that enabled many groups to catapult themselves into the middle class.

New Deal labor legislation enabled larger numbers of workers to enjoy economic opportunities previously denied them. The legal recognition of unions and the establishment of a right to collective bargaining transformed the opportunities to improve wages and working conditions in America. Unfortunately, African Americans were not included in these special protections. The unions could discriminate against African Americans without violating the various labor laws. In the original draft of the National Labor Relations Act (NLRA) a clause had been inserted that denied any union the protection of the federal government for collective bargaining if it had a policy of racial discrimination. Senator Robert Wagner, the author of the bill, had included this language. But the American Federation of Labor (AFL), the most powerful of unions, prevailed on Congress to delete this provision. As a result, the unions (often dominated by white ethnics) could deny African Americans most of the newly-won rights. This denial of equal economic opportunity to African Americans was the effective national labor relations policy of the nation until at least the 1970s. African Americans could find work in nonunion shops but usually at a lower wage. Many unions fought for a long time to keep jobs exclusively available to their white members. Even when African Americans could join unions, seniority rules and other techniques were used to keep them from getting better paid jobs.

African Americans experienced a decline in median income between 1950 and 1970. Two basic factors can account for this decline. First, Congress refused to place African Americans' civil rights to acquire property and to pursue employment opportunities on a principle of law, as it had for white ethnic groups. Second, the amount of federally subsidized programs that benefited union and white workers dramatically increased.

Government Refusal to Offer African Americans a System of Protection

The unions' power to limit African American access to a wide range of skilled occupations constituted de facto government action up to 1935. After the passage of the various national labor laws, their power consisted of de jure government action.

Politically, the NLRA gave white ethnic groups the authority to allocate government benefits to their members on the basis of rights and privilege by law. This power included the exclusive right to allocate skilled jobs in those sectors (such as machine operation, welding, and printing) that produced high income, thus giving the unions exclusive control over who could or could not enter the skilled trades. The unions used this power to deny African Americans access to skilled jobs.

One of the most widely used methods by which whites maintained economic and social inequality was the removal of African Americans from the job market. For example, if the economy was flourishing, African Americans could usually find work in nonunion shops. But as soon as there was a recession, the unions were in a position legally to move into non-union shops and use their exclusive bargaining power to force employers to dismiss African Americans and hire whites in their place. Economically, this practice significantly reduced the status of African Americans.

With the cardinal principle of exclusive jurisdiction clothed in the protection of federal law, from 1935 to 1970 the unions precluded a wide range of employment opportunities for African Americans. For instance, the Brotherhood of Electrical Workers of Long Island City, New York, in the 1930s decided to expand its jurisdiction over electrical supply shops that employed several dozen African Americans. With a policy of racial exclusion, the Brotherhood Union moved in and organized these shops. Their first order of business was to force the employers to dismiss all African Americans, particularly those in skilled jobs. This practice was confined not only to New York but was carried out throughout the country. In St. Louis, for instance, employers in 1940 found to their dismay that they could not employ even one skilled African American to build the $2 million Homer Philip Hospital in the heart of the African Americans community. In 1941, when the General Tile Company of St. Louis attempted to hire one highly trained African American worker as a tile setter, all the AFL workers walked off their jobs and held up construction for two months, thus causing the employer to suffer irrevocable economic loss. This strike had a ripple effect upon the employment status of African Americans throughout the country, particularly in the northern cities. It touched the central nervous system of the business world and forced many employers to think twice before they employed African Americans in any capacity. For instance, in 1946 the building committee of the St. Louis Board of Education refused to hire African Americans to perform maintenance work on the 17 schools in the African Americans community in fear of white workers suddenly turning up sick or having to take off from work to take care of personal business. The political significance of these maintenance jobs was that they paid the prevailing union wages, which were covered by the Davis-Bacon Act.

Before the passage of the NLRA, jobs in the building service areas were traditionally filled by African Americans. However, when the Building Service Union was formed in the 1930s, it began to organize hotels, restaurants, and office buildings. Once these businesses were unionized, unions forced employers to discharge all African American waiters, elevator operators, and other service workers to make room for whites. There were a number of instances in which the AFL moved into an open shop, such as in 1948 when the Wehr Steel Foundry of Milwaukee, organized the workers, and made one "blanket demand": fire all your African American employees. The power of the unions to make "blanket demands" on companies to fire African Americans lasted for ten years—from 1937 to 1947. The Taft-Hartley Act of 1947 stripped unions of the power to make "blanket demands" on employers. By this time, the practice had taken its toll in reducing the numbers of skilled African American workers in society. In 1963, Myrna Bain conducted a study of organized labor and African Americans. She found the unions to be extravagant in their use of collective bargaining to push African Americans out of high-paying and skilled jobs. She wrote,

> When the International Brotherhood of Electrical Workers became the collective bargaining agent at the Bauer Electric Company in Hartford, Connecticut, in the late forties, the union demanded and got the removal of all Negro electricians from their jobs. The excuse was advanced that, since their union contract specified "white only," they could not and would not change this policy to provide continued employment for the Negroes who were at the plant before the union was recognized. Similar cases can be found in the Boilermakers' Union and the International Association of Machinists at the Boeing Aircraft Company in Seattle.

From the latter part of the 1940s to the mid-1950s, the competition between the AFL and the Congress of Industrial Organization (CIO) offered African Americans a temporary system of protection to compete freely in skilled occupations. The CIO emerged as a strong competitor for the AFL. The CIO was able to grow fast because it recruited workers, skilled and unskilled alike, who were already on the job, including African Americans; in contrast, the AFL used the cardinal principle of exclusive jurisdiction to recruit only skilled workers.

The AFL soon recognized that the CIO's method of recruitment was building a strong union. If left unchecked, the AFL feared the CIO would eventually drive them out of business. To undermine the CIO's strength, the AFL altered its racial policies from the latter part of the 1940s to the mid-1950s and began recruiting African American workers.

Although the CIO recruited African Americans, its members did not accept them on an equal basis with whites. The CIO confined African Americans to low-paying jobs and prohibited them from participating in the upgrading and seniority systems. In particular, the CIO was able to restrict African Americans' upward mobility by keeping a separate seniority roster. The CIO also attempted to isolate African Americans into segregated locals, both in the South and in the North. Sometimes union workers, rather than the CIO, perpetuated racial domination of good jobs. For example, in the North, white workers walked off their jobs when the CIO attempted to upgrade African Americans and assign them to what had been traditionally considered a "white man's job," i.e., skilled and high-paying jobs. Thus, from the end of World War II until the merger of the AFL and CIO, African Americans' promotion and employment were highly related to competition between these two unions for membership. In the South, for instance, the CIO lost several bargaining units to the AFL largely because of CIO's racial policies. However, the AFL lost several areas to the CIO in the North for the same reason.

The competition between the AFL and CIO in recruiting African American members inadvertently offered African Americans a system of protection for employment. But when these unions merged in 1956, African Americans lost this protection and the unions resumed their policy of limiting African Americans' access to jobs. Consequently, from this date until the implementation of affirmative action, the relative numbers of skilled African American workers declined markedly.

The unions were able to keep the number of skilled African Americans at a significantly low number by their systems of seniority and primordial attachment. Primordial attachment refers to a method of recruitment by which individuals obtained jobs not on the basis of merit and qualifications but through personal connections and friendships. Skilled jobs were also parceled out to individuals on the basis of kinship ties. Since African Americans had previously been excluded from skilled jobs, they were automatically excluded from the recruitment process.

The seniority system also worked to the detriment of the upward mobility and employment of African Americans. For example, during periods of prosperity, this system allowed African Americans to enter the labor market at the lower strata of the economic ladder. Whenever a recession set in, workers were laid off according to seniority; this automatically forced African Americans, the most recently hired employees, to give up their low-

Although many African Americans have become successful in business, it has not been an easy road.

paying jobs. African Americans became the victims of the revolving door.

Hence, with the full blessing of the federal government, the descendants of European immigrants were able to keep African Americans impoverished while they sought government help to lift themselves into the middle class through various federally subsidized programs.

African Americans Lacked a Pattern of Entrepreneurship

Unlike the British West Indian immigrants, after their migration African Americans were not able to develop a class of entrepreneurs; they did not have the necessary human capital, especially managerial know-how, to do so. In the West Indies, the British West Indians acquired the human capital for entrepreneurship; they did not have a white middle- or lower-class population with which to compete on the islands. However, African Americans had these classes of whites to compete with in the South. Therefore, when African American professionals were confronted with racial discrimination, they did not have the human capital with which to start their own businesses, as the West Indians did. Consequently, they were subjected to demotion, arbitrary layoffs, and dismissals. Many African American professionals, lawyers and teachers for example, were forced to seek employment in the post office system.

Because of their lack of managerial experience, African Americans were generally unable to establish businesses in their community. The majority of the businesses in African American communities were owned by West Indian immigrants to the United States. For example, a survey taken of African Americans businesses in Harlem in the late 1950s revealed that a high proportion of the African American owned-and-operated businesses were owned by West Indians. There were some successful African American businessmen in Harlem other than in the service businesses, but their numbers were not commensurate with the numbers of successful West Indians.

It could be argued that African Americans were not able to obtain a foothold in business in Harlem because of the competition from the West Indians and whites. But the West Indians were confined to the East Coast (mostly in New York and Boston), and a poor African American showing in business is endemic throughout the northern cities. If we look at African American migration to Chicago, a city with very few West Indians, we see the same low numbers of African American-owned businesses as in New York.

African Americans who migrated to Chicago were unable to establish competitive businesses with whites as the West Indians did. As St. Clair Drake and Horace Clayton have pointed out, African Americans in Chicago were highly concentrated in the service businesses before the Big

Migration. As far back as 1885, there were over 500 enterprises and 27 fields in which African Americans owned-and-operated businesses. These businesses were in the service fields, with barber shops and moving-and-storage establishments forming the majority of the enterprises.

The number of businesses owned and operated by African Americans increased in Chicago because the Big Migration created a market for them. Although the number of such enterprises increased during this period, the enterprises themselves were similar to those owned by African Americans in Harlem, namely businesses in which African Americans received little or no competition from whites.

The most noticeable large African Americans businesses were the two banks and four insurance companies. They drew the majority of their capital "from within the Negro community to lend money for the purchase of homes." Unfortunately, this information is not captured in the table.

Social scientists have offered many explanations for why African Americans fared so poorly in business during their initial stage of contact in the northern cities. Drake and Clayton, for example, give the following reasons: "(1) difficulty in procuring capital and credit, (2) difficulty in getting adequate training, (3) inability to secure choice locations on the main business street, (4) lack of sufficient patronage to allow them to amass capital and to make improvements, (5) inability to organize for co-operative effect." The difficulty in obtaining capital and credit brings into consideration the broader question of the problems involved in securing initial capital for establishing new businesses.

One major argument that has been advanced to explain African Americans' lack of success in business is that lending institutions have systematically discriminated against African Americans. On the surface, this argument seems to have some validity. But a close examination of lending institutions conducted by Alfred R. Oxenfeldt in *The New Firms and Free Enterprise* reveals that these institutions rarely lend money to small or new enterprises. Oxenfeldt further argues that small and new enterprises are financed primarily by owners, their relatives and friends, and suppliers of materials and equipment; only slight accommodation is extended to small businesses by banking institutions. Therefore, raising capital to start up

new businesses is a problem faced by all groups; they must obtain such funds from other places.

In short, the chief reason African Americans were unable to escape the slums, as did the European immigrants, was because the government consistently refused to provide them with a system of protection that safeguarded their civil rights to enter into the mother lode of America's income redistribution system. The government has limited their civil rights to acquire and possess property. This allowed competing groups to gain economic advantages over African Americans.

African American Progress as a Result of Affirmative Action and Civil Rights

The main argument in this chapter is that in order for a group to enter the middle class collectively, it has to have a "pair of boots"—human capital—and a set of bootstraps—laws that make it possible to use forms of human capital such as education or on-the-job training. One without the other will not enable them to enter the middle class. The Civil Rights Act of 1964, the Voting Rights Act of 1965, and affirmative action policy constituted such a system of protection for African Americans.

The major protection that these measures provided was to create a level playing field by which African Americans could compete on an equal footing in a competitive, multiethnic society. With such protection, their freedom is safeguarded (1) to connect themselves to the mainstream of society's income redistribution system, and (2) to share in the community's material possessions.

Among the civil rights policies adopted in the 1960s, affirmative action, perhaps, has been the most effective. Affirmative action policies represent an attempt by government to correct these historic patterns of racial discrimination that have so damaged the economic opportunities of African Americans. As urged by President Lyndon Johnson, even after the passage of the Civil Rights Act of 1964, affirmative action programs were extended into the public and private spheres as a method of going beyond mere technical equality to compensate for years of economic discrimination. By establishing preferences in hiring, contraction, promotions, and other employment issues, remedial action was provided by various affirmative action programs to bring African Americans into effective equality with others. Given the injustices of the past, preferential treatment was provided in an attempt to give full meaning to African American rights by leveling the economic playing field. This meant that quotas, targets, minority set-asides and other techniques were to be used to give meaning to equality in America.

Affirmative action programs that were implemented by the federal government (and voluntarily by some employers) were pursued for decades, from the Johnson administration until the late 1970s. The election of Ronald Reagan in 1980 was a sign of the majority public reaction against affirmative action. These policies, which Reagan campaigned against, became offensive to many Americans who felt such racial preferences to be unfair and even unconstitutional. The majority tide against affirmative action had crested. Resentment against special opportunities for African Americans was legitimized.

Conferring special opportunities upon whites seemed unfair to many whites who questioned whether the "equal protection of the laws" guaranteed by the Constitution allowed for such differential treatment. The irony, of course, is that the "equal protection" clause was originally intended to elevate the freed slaves to full rights of American citizens. The efforts to complete the process of elevation by giving African Americans job opportunities through affirmative action programs is one of the best ways to ensure that they could fully enjoy economic equality. Affirmative action programs are not designated to operate against whites but to elevate minorities.

In recent years there has been much debate surrounding affirmative action. Since 1978, when the Supreme Court decided the controversial case of Regents of the *University of California* v. *Bakke,* the will to pursue these policies has steadily eroded. Even though many African Americans are still plunged into the deepest forms of poverty there has been a stream of criticism of affirmative action. The Supreme Court, influenced by the widespread criticism, has allowed the further erosion of affirmative action. States and cities around the nation have been aroused by the anti-affirmative action advocates, passing laws and constitutional amendments intended to end the policy.

In 1997 a Republican-dominated Congress refused to confirm President Bill Clinton's nomination of Bill Lann Lee as head of the Justice Department's Civil Rights Division, largely because he has spoken out about the continued need for affirmative action. The U.S. Justice Department, the Office of Economic Opportunity, and President Clinton seemed to believe that there still was a need to provide African Americans with greater economic opportunities through affirmative action programs and preferences. But the issue is still so unpopular among the majority of Americans that the policy seems to be doomed in spite of the outcries of African American leaders.

The income redistribution system, as noted earlier, consists of trade, commerce, and real estate. Among these three, commerce and real estate are the most important in accumulating wealth. From this perspective, African Americans advanced significantly from the position they were in prior to the adoption of the various civil rights measures in the 1960s. As a result, they were able to acquire the necessary entrepreneurial skills to start and successfully operate their own businesses. In the past, the doors to corporate America were closed to them, thus preventing them from acquiring the necessary entrepreneurial skills to compete successfully on a level playing field.

Once the opportunities in business were broadened, many African Americans were able to take advantage of the many economic opportunities that society had to offer. As a result, the number of millionaires among those groups increased substantially. According to a newsletter, *Security Pro,* a large number of African Americans have become millionaires not just in sports and entertainment but in business fields in the open marketplace. The significance of their success cannot be overemphasized. Prior to affirmative action, many jobs such as those for artisans, craftsmen, management, and professionals were closed to them. They were considered to be the "white man's jobs." The civil rights laws removed these artificial barriers; as a result, African Americans began to accumulate wealth as other Americans have.

Many African American business persons have accumulated a significant amount of wealth by taking advantage of the various programs that state and local governments adopted to assist minorities. However, a large number became millionaires without government assistance as a result of the antidiscrimination laws. For example, many young African Americans, both males and females, became millionaires by selling long-distance phone services alone. Others became millionaires by working in public sectors such as the fire department, school system, city government, etc., and invested in real estate part-time and became millionaires.

In the area of voting, the 1965 Voting Rights Act was very instrumental in protecting African Americans' right to political participation and the right to select their own representatives. For example, fewer than 1,500 African Americans were elected in 1970. In 1995, that number had increased to more than 7,000 elected officials.

The importance of a group having the right to elect their own representatives is that they will have someone at the negotiation table to protect their self-interests when decisions are made to authoritatively allocate the community's material possessions, which is a basic democratic principle.

Race and Class in America

The political significance of African Americans having the right to elect their own representatives is tantamount to overcoming racially-biased attitudes. In their article, entitled "Prejudice and Politics: Symbolic Racism Versus Real Threats to the Good Life," Donald R. Kinder and David O. Sears advanced the argument that race prejudice is based on whites' resentment of African Americans more for their lower socioeconomic status than their race.

It follows then that a large percentage of whites' racial bias attitudes against African Americans is intertwined with American sentiment against the lower class. The major reason these attitudes affect African Americans disproportionately is that race and class are mutually inclusive. Society has a tradition of associating all African Americans with the lower class, regardless of their class.

Their entrapment into the lower class can largely be attributed to the racial discrimination that African Americans continue to experience. Historically, they have been denied the right to elect their own representatives to fight for a share of their community's material possessions. However, they have made significant improvements

since they have been granted the right to elect their representatives at local, state, and federal levels. These representatives have been responsible for the passage of numerous policies and programs to benefit their communities.

In the area of social equality, African Americans were severely oppressed prior to the passage of the civil rights measures. Their right to be treated equally socially under the law was more than a matter of attitude; it was a matter of institutional racism. In 1954, for example, racial segregation was widespread and deeply ingrained in the American mind. When the Supreme Court declared it unconstitutional, it signaled an advent of a new day of freedom for African Americans. However, this victory was short-lived because many states resisted the Supreme Court's invasion of states rights. The Supreme Court ruled that the states must desegregate their schools with all deliberate speed. As some commentators have noted, the only thing that the Supreme Court received was a lot of deliberation but no speed.

Since the Supreme Court does not have any enforcement power, very little, if any, progress was made in the area of school desegregation until the passage of the 1964 Civil Rights Act. This act gave the attorney general authority to actively fight white resistance to desegregation by seeking court orders to force districts to desegregate their schools. Whites resisted such efforts by fleeing to the suburbs. Consequently, some inner city public schools are more racially segregated today than they were before the busing program started.

Housing discrimination has been made unlawful. School segregation is unlawful but our suburbs remain effectively separated by race due to housing patterns; some have suggested that this problem can be corrected by providing low income housing for African Americans in the suburbs. This approach does not get at the heart of the problem, that is, the need for quality education.

In order to ensure African Americans a quality education, special measures must be undertaken to ensure that they obtain a quality education regardless of which school they attend. To achieve this goal, emphasis must be placed on standardizing the curriculum. Currently, there is no standardized curriculum; curriculums in the inner cities differ from curriculums in suburban, middle-class schools, yet African American students are

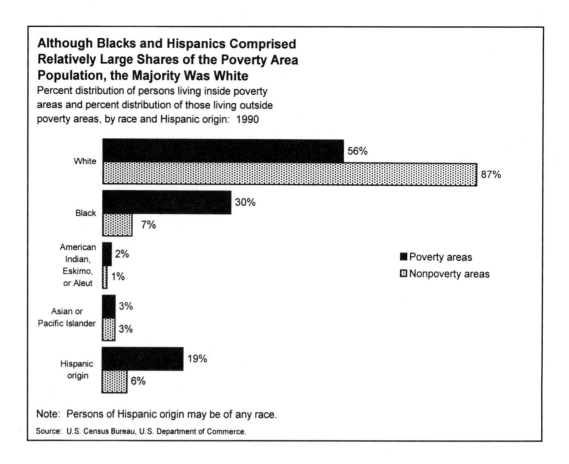

Although Blacks and Hispanics Comprised Relatively Large Shares of the Poverty Area Population, the Majority Was White

Percent distribution of persons living inside poverty areas and percent distribution of those living outside poverty areas, by race and Hispanic origin: 1990

White — 56% (Poverty areas), 87% (Nonpoverty areas)

Black — 30% (Poverty areas), 7% (Nonpoverty areas)

American Indian, Eskimo, or Aleut — 2% (Poverty areas), 1% (Nonpoverty areas)

Asian or Pacific Islander — 3% (Poverty areas), 3% (Nonpoverty areas)

Hispanic origin — 19% (Poverty areas), 6% (Nonpoverty areas)

■ Poverty areas
⊞ Nonpoverty areas

Note: Persons of Hispanic origin may be of any race.

Source: U.S. Census Bureau, U.S. Department of Commerce.

expected to perform as well on the same standardized tests as students in the suburban schools. This practice automatically assumes that the curriculum is irrelevant to a student's performance on a standardized test.

The Continuing Struggle for Civil Rights

The socioeconomic success of African Americans as a result of the protection provided to them by the civil rights laws cannot be denied. They have shown a marked increase in their numbers in the professional, managerial, and craftsmen categories. There still, however, remains the problem of white resistance. In order to understand this resistance better, it should be examined within the framework of various psychological and sociological theories. One theory that is germane to our argument is the theory of relative deprivation. Relative deprivation means that a group in society evaluates its socioeconomic status in relation to the status of another group. If the first group perceives this second group as being well-off socioeconomically compared with their status, the first group will resist any government support for that

second group. Such resistance is at the heart of whites' resistance to civil rights and affirmative action for African Americans.

Whites started evaluating their socioeconomic status relative to that of African Americans' in the early 1970s. They perceived affirmative action as a policy that advanced African Americans' socioeconomic status above theirs. As a result, they began to attack affirmative action programs.

The critics' major argument against affirmative action is that the intent of the 1964 Civil Rights Act was to protect individuals against discrimination, and not groups; therefore, affirmative action constitutes reverse discrimination. These critics have been successful in convincing the U.S. Supreme Court to accept this argument, thus turning affirmative action into a highly emotional and political issue. Currently, politicians are using it in an attempt to advance their political careers.

The problem with the reverse discrimination argument is that the term "racial discrimination" has never been defined within the framework of the equal protection clause. The U.S. Supreme Court has long held that the equal protection clause is a personal right. It protects an individual's property interest in a government benefit. However, as the Supreme Court ruled in the *Board of Regents* v. *Roth* (1972), before the equal protection clause can come into play, there must be a law or a rule of understanding that supports an individual's claim of entitlement to a government benefit. Nevertheless, in the *University of California* v. *Bakke* (1978), the Court attacked the constitutional basis of affirmative action. This doctrine is at the heart of the reverse discrimination controversy. The apparent criterion for determining whether an individual has been discriminated against is his social credentials—his social "merit." However, his social credentials can be used only if he is competing with an affirmative action applicant. In other words, if he is competing with another white applicant, there is no constitutional problem.

Since the *Bakke* decision, the Court has extended this double standard of judicial review to block any agency from adopting an affirmative action policy to advance the cause of African Americans. In *Adarand* v. *Pena* (1995), the Supreme Court ruled that an individual can challenge any agency's affirmative action program by simply alleging that it is using race as a factor. Race can only be invoked if an agency can prove that it has discriminated against African Americans in the past. If such a case can be made, then the courts will permit a public or private employer to adopt an affirmative action program.

The *Bakke* decision provided the framework for the reverse discrimination controversy throughout the 1980s and into the 1990s. In the *Adarand* case, the Supreme Court added fuel to this controversy when it extended non-African Americans an equal protection right to challenge any agency's affirmative action policy to advance the cause of African Americans. This new ruling has given individual non-African Americans a constitutional right to secure a government benefit that they otherwise could not have obtained. For example, since this ruling, Cheryl J. Hopwood, a white female, prevailed in her attempt to enter the University of Texas Law School by alleging that the University's affirmative action program discriminated against her. A Hispanic prevailed in his challenge to the University of Maryland's African American students' scholarship program. The scholarship program was established to recruit twenty poverty-stricken African American stu-

dents from the ghetto in an attempt to break the cycle of welfare dependency among this population. In 1997, California voters passed the so-called civil rights initiative, Proposition 209. This initiative prohibited any government agency from voluntarily adopting an affirmative action program to advance the cause of minorities and women in the areas of college admissions, employment, and contracts.

Prior to the passage of Proposition 209, Governor Pete Wilson, in his attempt to jump-start his failing presidential campaign, ramrodded a proposal through the Regents of the University of California (UC) to rescind the University's affirmative action policy. This policy went into effect for the fall semester of 1997. As a result, the number of African American students dropped significantly. The greatest drop occurred in the professional schools. Take the four UC law schools, for example. The enrollment at UC Berkeley dropped from 20 African American students to 1 African American student. The other three law schools also experienced a drastic drop in African American enrollment. In the medical schools, the picture was even more bleak. At UC San Diego, none of the 196 African American applicants who applied was admitted.

California is now a pace setter for national policy, and one of the major consequences of the state's retrenchment on affirmative action is that whatever happens in California influences the rest of the country. Currently, a group that led the anti-affirmative action movement in California is now attempting to launch a movement to repeal affirmative action programs in other states.

The Need for Civil Rights Protection

African Americans need affirmative action and other civil rights protection not merely to compensate them for past discrimination but to protect them from the tyranny of the ruling majority. Without such protection, society can expect the majority to resist these programs not simply because of racism but because it is not within their self-interests to look out for African Americans. This is the duty and responsibility of the government, according to the philosophy of John Locke.

Civil rights critics have argued that affirmative action should be discontinued because the government has done enough for African Americans. This argument overlooks the fact that America is a multiethnic and pluralistic society in which special interest groups are constantly competing for the scarce resources. Therefore, some form of affirmative action will be needed to safeguard African Americans' right to their fair share of the community's material possessions. How long will such protection be needed? Decidedly, such protection will be needed as long as African Americans are impoverished and continue to represent a disproportionate number of those in prison. Many are in prison because the government has failed to adopt positive measures to help them to escape the negative influences of an impoverished environment, as it had done for earlier immigrant groups.

The strongest evidence that can be marshaled to support the continuous need for affirmative action for African Americans is the experiences of the Irish Catholics, Russians Jews, and Italians. The Irish Catholics came to America in the 1830s and 1840s. They did not begin to escape the slums until the 1940s, almost five generations after they arrived in America. Although the government provided them opportunities in the form of land grants, they were not able to take advantage of these opportunities because they did not have the skills for farming. The Russian Jews, on the other hand, had many skills when they arrived in the 1880s and 1890s; however they were not farmers but artisans and craftsmen. Since the government did not provide workers with the right to collective bargaining, they were not able to escape the slums until the 1940s, approximately two generations after their arrival, as a result of New Deal programs. The Italians' experience was somewhat similar to that of the Russian Jews. They arrived at the same time in the 1880s and 1890s. They were not able to leave the slums until the 1940s, after the New Deal programs were adopted.

African Americans have never received the same level of government support to advance themselves socioeconomically as other groups have. For example, affirmative action was adopted during the Johnson administration in 1965 and implemented during the Nixon administration in 1969. Five years later, critics of civil rights had managed to orchestrate an anti-affirmative action case before the U.S. Supreme Court, *DeFunis* v. *Odegaard* (1974). This case was a prelude to the *Bakke* case and other anti-affirmative action cases.

The importance of these cases is that they provided a framework for critics to launch a protracted anti-civil rights campaign against those measures designed to advance African Americans. Approximately 30 years later, they were successful.

In short, African Americans have benefited markedly from the various civil rights laws passed in the 1960s; however, they have a long way to go before achieving full equality. Their major obstacle is their failure to convince the majority that civil rights and affirmative action are policies that are consistent with liberal democratic theory. Once they accomplish this goal, their quest for equality will be at hand. There is substantial evidence that affirmative action uplifts African Americans to greater equality of opportunity. The retreat from affirmative action is a setback for economic equality of opportunity in America.

Bibliography

Abbott, Martin. *The Freedmen's Bureau in South Carolina*. Chapel Hill, N.C.: University of North Carolina Press, 1967.

Bailey, Thomas A. *The American Pageant: A History of the Republic*. Boston: D. C. Heath, 1956.

Bain, Myrna. "Organized Labor and the Negro Worker." *National Review* (June 1965).

Blaustein, Albert P., and Robert L. Zangrando. *Civil Rights and the American Negro*. New York: Simon and Schuster, 1968.

Dahl, Robert A. *A Preface to Democratic Theory*. Chicago: The University of Chicago Press, 1956.

Davis, Allison, et al. *The Deep South*. Chicago: University of Chicago Press, 1965.

Davis, Arthur P., and Saunders Redding, eds. *Cavalcade: American Writing from 1760 to the Present*. New York: Houghton Mifflin, 1971.

Drake, St. Clair, and Horace R. Clayton. *Black Metropolis*. New York: Harper and Row, 1962.

Du Bois, W. E. B. *Black Reconstruction in America*. New York: Russell and Russell, 1935.

———. *The Souls of Black Folk*. Greenwich, Conn.: Fawcett Publications, 1961.

———. *The Philadelphia Negro*. New York: Benjamin Blom, 1967.

Eagles, Charles, ed. *The Civil Rights Movement in America*. Jackson, Miss.: The University of Mississippi Press, 1986.

Elkins, Stanley. *Slavery*. Chicago: The University of Chicago Press, 1965.

Fleming, Walter L. *Documentary History of Reconstruction*. New York: McGraw-Hill, 1966.

Fogal, Robert, and Stanley Engerman. "The Economics of Slavery." In *The Reinterpretation of American Economic History*. New York: Harper and Row, 1971.

———. *Time on the Cross: The Economics of American Negro Slavery*. 2 vols. Boston: Little, Brown, 1974.

Franklin, John Hope. *Reconstruction*. Chicago: University of Chicago Press, 1961.

———. *From Slavery to Freedom*. New York: Alfred A. Knopf, 1974.

Frazier, E. Franklin. *Black Bourgeoisie*. New York: The Macmillan Company, 1957.

Fredrickson, George M. *The Black Image in the White Mind*. New York: Harper and Row, 1971.

Glazer, Nathan. *Affirmative Discrimination*. New York: Basic Books, 1975.

———. "A New View of Slavery." *Commentary* 58 (August 1974): 68–72.

Gosset, Thomas F. *Race: The History of an Idea in America*. Dallas: SMU Press, 1963.

Gutman, Herbert G. "The World Two Cliometricians Made: A Review-Essay of F + E = T/C." *The Journal of Negro History* 60 (1975): 107.

Handlin, Oscar. *Boston's Immigrants*. Cambridge, Mass.: Harvard University Press, 1959.

Josephson, Matthew. *The Robber Barons*. New York: Harcourt, Brace and World, 1962.

Kinder, Donald R., and David O. Sears. "Prejudice and Politics: Symbolic Racism Versus Real Threats to the Good Life." *Journal of Personality and Social Psychology* 40 (3) (1990): 414–431.

King, Martin Luther, Jr. *Stride Towards Freedom*. New York: Harper and Row, 1958.

Knowles, Louis, and Kenneth Prewitt. *Institutional Racism in America*. Englewood Cliffs, N.J.: Prentice-Hall, 1969.

Lasswell, Harold. *The Analysis of Political Behavior: An Empirical Approach*. New York: Oxford University Press, 1947.

———. *The World Revolution of Our Times*. Stanford, Calif.: Stanford University Press, 1951.

Levy, Peter B. *Let Freedom Ring: A Documentary History of the Civil Rights Movement*. New York: Praeger, 1992.

Lindsay, Arnett G. "The Negro Banking." *Journal of Negro History* 14 (1929): 156–201.

Litwack, Leon F. *North of Slavery*. Chicago: University of Chicago Press, 1961.

Logan, Rayford W. *The Negro in the United States*. Princeton, N.J.: D. Van Nostrand, 1957.

Meier, August. *Negro Thought in America: 1880–1915*. Ann Arbor, Mich.: University of Michigan Press, 1968.

Miliukov, Paul. *History of Russia*. New York: Funk and Wagnalls, 1969.

Myrdal, Gunnar. *An American Dilemma*. New York: Harper and Row, 1962.

Osofsky, Gilbert. *Harlem: The Making of a Ghetto*. New York: Harper and Row, 1963.

Report of the National Advisory Commission on Civil Disorders. Washington, D.C.: U.S. Government Printing Office, 1968.

Slosson, Edwin E. *The America Spirit in Education, a Series of the Chronicles of America*. New Haven, Conn.: Yale University Press, 1921.

Van der Berghe, Pierre. "The United States is a 'Herrenvolk' Democracy." In *Nation of Nations: The Ethnic Experience and the Racial Crisis*. Peter I. Rose, ed. New York: Random House, 1972.

Wood, Forest G. *The Era of Reconstruction*. New York: Thomas Y. Crowell, 1975.

Woodson, Carter G. *A Century of Negro Migration*. New York: Russell and Russell, 1969.

Chapter 4

Asian Americans

Bill Ong Hing

The terms *Asian American, Asian Pacific American,* and *Asian Pacific Islander* are used to describe residents of the United States who themselves are from or their ancestors were from the Asian Pacific region of the world. Although the term Asian American may bring to mind someone of Chinese, Japanese, Vietnamese, Korean, Filipino, or Asian Indian descent, the U.S. Census Bureau actually includes 31 different groups within the Asian Pacific designation. For example, someone of Cambodian, Guamanian, Samoan, Thai, Laotian, Hmong, Hawaiian, or Tongan extraction would also fall within this category. Filipino Americans and Chinese Americans are the largest subgroups.

Although some Asian Americans think of themselves as Asian American, others identify more with their specific ethnic background and regard themselves as Korean American or Vietnamese American, for example. Still others might reject such labels altogether and simply think of themselves as American.

The Asian American population in the United States is not large relative to the entire U.S. population. The approximately nine million Asian Americans represent only 3.3 percent of the U.S. population. Filipinos and Chinese are the two largest groups, followed by Japanese, Asian Indians, Koreans, and Vietnamese.

Immigration has played a key role in the growth and development of Asian America. Except for Japanese Americans, every Asian American group has more foreign-born members than U.S.-born members. But it was not always this way. Prior to 1965, U.S. immigration laws favored immigration from western Europe. These discriminatory immigration laws are a key reason that the number of Asian Americans is relatively small.

Chinese Americans

Chinese were the first Asians to immigrate in significant number. In the 1840s, many were driven to the United States by a rice shortage, war, and the

Chinese laborers employed by the Central Pacific in the Sierra Nevada, 1880.

lure of gold. Early on, the Chinese were welcomed. Chinese were actively recruited to fill needs in railroad construction, laundries, and domestic service. In 1852, the governor of California recommended giving land to Chinese to attract more to immigrate. Ten years later, a report of the California state government proudly reported that the 50,000 Chinese in the state paid almost $14 million a year in taxes and other charges and recognized that their cheap labor aided in the development of new industries in the state. An effort to exclude Chinese in Oregon in 1857 was defeated in recognition that the Chinese were good, dependable workers. Although their ability to handle heavy construction was initially doubted, Chinese were hired by the Central Pacific Railroad. Eventually it was widely acknowledged

that without them, it would have been impossible to complete the western portion of the transcontinental railroad in the time required by the U.S. Congress. By 1882, about 300,000 Chinese had entered and worked on the West Coast.

Despite the official encouragement for importing Chinese labor, the Chinese who arrived soon encountered fierce racial animosity in the 1840s. Irish Roman Catholics in California, replicating the racial prejudice they had suffered on the East Coast, rallied against foreign miners on the West Coast. Racial prejudice and fear of competition from aliens prompted calls for restrictive immigration laws.

In the meantime, control was also asserted over aliens by state and local laws. Latino miners had been forced out of California by a foreign miners' tax in 1850 that they refused to pay. With the expulsion of Latinos, the Chinese stood out as the largest body of foreigners in the state and the rest of the West. The full weight of prejudice fell on them. A new foreign miners' tax, this time directed at the Chinese, was enacted in 1852. "Anticoolie" clubs ("coolie" was a term used to describe low-wage Chinese laborers) surfaced in the early 1850s, and sporadic boycotts of Chinese-made goods soon followed. By 1853 anti-Chinese editorials were common in San Francisco newspapers. Statutes and ordinances like the 1858 Oregon law that required Chinese miners and merchants to obtain monthly four-dollar licenses were not unusual. In 1854, the California Supreme Court decided in the case of *People* v. *Hall* (1854) that Chinese could not testify against whites in court. Hall, a white man, had been convicted of murdering a Chinese man on the basis of testimony by one white and three Chinese witnesses. The state supreme court overthrew Hall's conviction, ruling that the Chinese witnesses should not have testified based on a state law that did not allow African Americans or Native Americans to testify in favor of or against whites in court. The court reasoned that the term "Indian" essentially included Chinese and that Chinese should not be allowed to testify on public policy grounds anyway.

The public school systems of California and other western states were generally segregated. In 1860 California barred Asians, African Americans, and Native Americans from attending its public schools. In 1884 the California Supreme Court held that the 1860 law was unconstitutional. As a result of this decision, the state set up a system of "oriental" (usually Chinese) schools starting in 1885. In a 1902 decision, the U.S. Supreme Court upheld the constitutionality of separate but equal schools for Asian students.

By the late 1860s, the Chinese question became a major issue in California and Oregon politics. Many white workers felt threatened by the competition they perceived from the Chinese, as many employers continued to recruit them as inexpensive laborers and domestic servants. Employment of Chinese by the Central Pacific Railroad was at its peak. Anticoolie clubs increased in number, and mob attacks against Chinese were common. Labor unions demanded laws to prevent Chinese immigration. The sentiment against Chinese combined racism and resentment over their competitiveness over jobs.

The tension between a desire for Chinese labor and nativist (dislike for foreigners) resentment of Chinese immigrants is best captured by the commotion surrounding the 1868 Burlingame Treaty. The treaty between the United States and Chinese governments represents the high-water mark of official acceptance of Chinese. China agreed to end its strict control over allowing its citizens to leave its borders; the United States recognized that the free immigration of Chinese to the American continent was an essential element of trade and commerce.

The treaty was greeted with fanfare and delight in certain quarters of the United States. Many journalists praised the cultural greatness of China and wrote of the special destiny connecting the United States, the youngest nation, with China, the most ancient one.

This celebratory view toward China and its people soon clashed head-on with rising anti-Chinese sentiment in California and the West. Eventually, this sentiment prevailed, and the Burlingame Treaty's provision for free immigration was overrun by a series of laws that first limited and then entirely excluded Chinese from the United States. Only two years after the passage of the treaty, Chinese immigrants were judged unworthy of citizenship or naturalization (the process that enabled other immigrants to become U.S. citizens). Congress in 1870 extended the right to naturalize to aliens of African descent, but Chinese were denied that right because they were thought to have "undesirable qualities."

The trend continued. Five years later, in 1875, Congress passed the Page Law, which prohibited Chinese women from being imported for immoral purposes. The law was enacted in response to claims that Chinese women were being brought into the United States for prostitution. But the enforcement of the statute was so strict that virtually all Chinese women were barred from entering, helping to make the gender ratio among Chinese immigrants quite imbalanced. Within a few years, only 1 in 400 Chinese immigrants was a woman. In 1879, a measure was placed on the California ballot to determine how voters felt about the Chinese: 900 voters favored the Chinese, while 150,000 were opposed.

Despite the discriminatory tendencies of the courts, Chinese residents of San Francisco successfully fought the discriminatory enforcement of San Francisco's Laundry Ordinance, passed in 1880, which governed the sites and manner of laundry operations. Their fight led to the United States Supreme Court landmark decision, *Yick Wo* v. *Hopkins* (1886). In the early 1880s there were about 320 laundries in San Francisco. Of these, about 240 were owned and operated by Chinese residents. About 310 laundries were constructed of wood, as were nine of ten houses in the city. The Laundry Ordinance prohibited wood construction for laundries under the pretext that wood constituted a fire and public safety hazard. In 1885, upon expiration of his business license, Mr. Yick Wo, who had operated a laundry at the same site for 20 years, applied for a renewal of his license but was turned down because his building was of wood construction. Subsequently, he was found guilty of violating the ordinance and jailed. Two hundred other Chinese laundries were denied license renewals. In contrast, all license renewal applications for non-Chinese laundries (even those with wooden buildings) were approved. Mr. Wo challenged the ordinance and the Supreme Court ruled in his favor, reasoning that the discriminatory enforcement of the law violated the equal protection clause of the Fourteenth Amendment.

But in 1881, 25 anti-Chinese petitions were presented to Congress by a number of civic groups, like the Methodist Church and the New York Union League Corps, and from many states, including Alabama, Ohio, West Virginia, and Wisconsin. The California legislature declared a legal holiday to facilitate anti-Chinese public rallies that attracted thousands of demonstrators.

Responding to this national clamor, Congress enacted the Chinese Exclusion Act on May 6, 1882. The law excluded laborers for ten years and effectively slammed the door on all Chinese immigration. It did permit the entry of teachers, students, and merchants, but their quota was quite small. Besides stopping the flow of laborers, the act crippled the development of the Chinese American community because women were defined as laborers. Chinese laborers who had already immigrated therefore had no way to send for wives and families left behind.

Leaders of the anti-Chinese movement, however, were not satisfied. They pressed for exclusion beyond the ten-year period, and by 1904 an indefinite ban on Chinese immigration was in place.

World War II brought about the first cracks in the wall of Asian exclusion. Although liberal congressional forces had for years advocated the repeal of Chinese exclusion on grounds of fairness, not until the United States and China became allies against the Japanese during the war did Congress agree to repeal some aspects of the exclusion laws. Japan had been successfully

Anti-Chinese violence in Rock
Springs, Wyoming, 1885.

exploiting Asian exclusion in its wartime propaganda, and Congress felt compelled to respond to the charges that it was discriminating against the citizens of an ally. Despite stiff opposition from the American Federation of Labor and from some veterans' groups, Congress in 1943 passed the Chinese Repealer. For the first time it allowed Chinese to naturalize and become American citizens; it also struck from the books most of the Chinese exclusion laws. However, the Repealer by no means flung open the door to Chinese immigration: Chinese were allotted a yearly quota of only 105 immigrants under the law.

The loosening of the exclusion laws prompted significant changes in Chinese immigration patterns. Older laborers who had been separated from their families for generations were finally able to petition for their wives, as were merchants and students who had entered previously. Perhaps not surprisingly, women were almost 90 percent of Chinese immigrants from 1946 to 1952.

These reformed immigration patterns substantially remade Chinese communities. Men had outnumbered women 14 to 1 in 1910 and 7 to 1 in 1920. By 1950, however, the margin was under 2 to 1. These changes reflect, in part, the deaths of earlier male immigrants. To a greater degree, however, they are evidence of both the postwar immigration of Chinese women and the birth of children to Chinese American families in the United States.

Although other Asians were allowed to immigrate as part of the Asia-Pacific triangle quota established in 1952, it was not until 1965 that a system was enacted that did not favor certain nationalities. The 1965 amendments to the immigration laws allowed 20,000 immigrant visas for every country not in the Western Hemisphere. The allotment was made regardless of the size of the country, so that mainland China had the same quota as Tunisia. Of the 170,000 visas set aside for the Eastern Hemisphere, 75 percent were for specified "preference" relatives of citizens and lawful permanent resident immigrants, and an unlimited number were available to spouses, children, and parents of U.S. citizens.

The 1965 provisions were not expected to bolster Asian immigration. Since most of the visas were reserved for family reunification, policymakers believed that countries of Asia (and Africa), with low rates of immigration prior to 1965, might in fact be handicapped, since their small numbers presumably meant there were fewer people here who had relatives abroad.

Historically, most Chinese settled on the West Coast. Many settled in rural areas, working in gold mines and on farms and starting up grocery stores, restaurants, laundries, and other small businesses in small towns. Small mining, railroad, and farming communities developed in the late 1800s and continued through the early 1900s, but the number of Chinese Americans working in small businesses in the rural South, Midwest, and Southwest steadily dwindled in the middle of this century. Many children of rural families went to college and later settled in metropolitan areas, abandoning the labor-intensive businesses of their first-generation parents.

Ineligible for citizenship and the target of harsh social attitudes and an array of repressive state and local laws, early Chinese found themselves segregated and excluded. Many laborers were forced to resettle in urban Chinatowns. Some needed jobs when gold mining waned and the transcontinental railroad was completed in 1885, but others had spent their lives working the land and knew little about and even feared urban life. To make matters worse, in 1879, the California legislature passed a law (later declared unconstitutional) requiring towns and cities to remove Chinese from city limits. In Tucson in 1885, a petition was circulated urging that the Chinese be required to live in a Chinatown. Landlords and realtors refused to rent and sell to Chinese outside of Chinatown, and some

whites threatened physical violence to those who ventured beyond certain boundaries.

The first Chinese who came to the vast, undeveloped regions of the western United States provided the manpower to work the mines, drain the ditches, till the soil, harvest the crops, and build the net of railroads that would bind the nation together. By the 1880s, a majority of the agricultural workers in California were Chinese. Chinese immigrants—like the 10,000 who helped build the Central Pacific railroad—also did the heavy manual labor rejected by white settlers in the West.

White workers, feeling threatened by the competition, sought to prevent more Chinese from entering the country and to exclude Chinese Americans already here from all but the lowest-paying jobs. When more Chinese moved to the cities in search of work, organized labor increasingly vilified them and pressured employers and businesses to favor white labor. The impact was soon apparent. In the shoe-making and cigar-rolling industries, hundreds were discharged and replaced by white workers. In many households, white women servants displaced Chinese.

It became more difficult for Chinese immigrants to earn a living. Organized labor's opposition, employment discrimination, anti-Chinese ordinances, and the rabid sentiment that led to the passage of exclusion laws worked together to force them out of the jobs that they had been recruited to fill. Turned away by white employers, they sought self-employment in laundries, where their resourcefulness still mattered, where expenses and rent were low, and where knowledge of English was unnecessary. They were opposed here as well. White-labor laundries were established, and Chinese laundry workers in San Francisco were reduced by one third.

Merchants who entered after 1882 had migrated from southern China and brought with them its centuries-old entrepreneurial tradition. They naturally gravitated toward self-employment in businesses in which they were experienced. Small Chinese-run businesses—laundries, grocery stores, and coffee shops—became common in cities and rural towns where they remained.

Small business was particularly prominent in the development of San Francisco's Chinatown. By the turn of the century, Chinese who made it the nation's largest were mostly male laborers or

self-supporting students. Some ventured outside of Chinatown to find jobs as manual laborers or domestic servants. Most, however, stayed to avoid racial animosity and violence. Their requirements were met, in time, by family-run enterprises that began to appear with the upsurge in merchant immigration before the 1924 Immigration Act. Sequestered by racial and social barriers, the small businesses and residents of Chinatown satisfied one another's needs and helped make Chinatown self-sufficient.

China's alliance with the United States during World War II helped to bring about important changes in Chinese America. When wartime propaganda favorably depicted China as an ally, the stature of Chinese Americans suddenly rose. The mainstream media instructed Americans on the art of distinguishing the Japanese from our "friends" the Chinese. No longer the Yellow Peril, they were immigrants who traced their roots to the land of a close ally. Demand for Chinese men and women in the wartime industries was strong. Shipyards and aircraft factories began to employ engineers, technicians, and assembly-line workers, drawing first from the historically male-dominated Chinese American labor force and then from a pool of women who immigrated after the 1943 Chinese Repealer.

These World War II changes in immigration policies, laws, and official attitudes helped to reconfigure occupational profiles. Chinese America, once almost exclusively merchant and laborer, saw the rise of a new professional class. In 1940, under 3 percent of Chinese Americans held professional and technical jobs; by 1950 more than 7 percent did. The biggest changes in the profile of Chinese Americans, as well as of the rest of Asian America, occurred after the changes in the immigration laws in 1965. The primary evidence of that influence is in the proportion of foreign-born Chinese Americans. From 1940 to 1970, most Chinese Americans were born in the United States, but since 1980, about two thirds of the population has been foreign-born, made up of immigrants and refugees from mainland China (the People's Republic of China), Taiwan (the Republic of China), and Hong Kong (until 1997 a territory of Great Britain). Also, slightly more Chinese

Commodore Matthew Perry.

four U.S. naval ships in Tokyo Bay in 1854. Perry forced the Japanese to sign a treaty in which Japan agreed to open its doors to foreign trade. Commerce helped Japan emerge from centuries of isolation, although the Japanese government continued to regulate the travel of its citizens abroad strictly. Between 1860 and 1880, when almost 200,000 Chinese laborers came to the United States, the Japanese permitted only 335 emigrants.

The first significant numbers of Japanese entered the United States at the height of the Chinese exclusion movement. Agricultural labor demands, particularly in Hawaii and California, led to increased efforts to attract Japanese workers after the exclusion of Chinese. Within a few years of the 1882 Chinese exclusion law, the Japanese government agreed to permit laborers to emigrate to work on Hawaiian sugar plantations.

Like the initial wave of Chinese immigrants, Japanese laborers were at first warmly received by employers. These young and healthy men were needed to perform the strenuous work on Hawaiian sugar plantations. So many of them came that the Japanese became the largest group of foreigners on the islands. Few came to the mainland, so little political pressure was raised to exclude them. Japanese were described as "refined and cultured."

By the turn of the century, unfavorable sentiment toward the Japanese grew as their laborers began to migrate to the western United States. After Hawaii became a possession of the United States in 1898, the Japanese were able to use it as a stepping-stone to the mainland, where the majority engaged in agricultural work. Economic competition with white farm workers soon erupted.

Japanese agricultural workers were more financially independent than the Chinese. They were not fleeing abject poverty as much as deliberately pursuing alternative economic opportunities and higher wages. They had survived a screening process in Japan required of prospective immigrants that was aimed at ensuring that they were healthy and literate. They were determined not to submit to the constraints imposed by agricultural employers. Many intended to eventually become independent farmers, and menial work was regarded simply as a step toward something far better. They considered themselves the competent equals of white workers, with a right to make the most of their opportunities for success.

women than men have immigrated; combined with the death of early immigrants, the community—like the rest of the United States—comprises more women than men.

Although one out of every three Chinese Americans is classified as a professional, a manager or an executive by the U.S. Census, one out of every five is also a service worker. Also, many of those classified as managers are actually small business owners.

News accounts report that the average family income for Chinese Americans is higher than that of the general population. However, Chinese families have more workers per family (1.9) than the general population (1.6) has. In addition, the media tends to ignore the statistic that more Chinese American families (10.5 percent) are considered poor than white American families (7 percent).

Japanese Americans

The early history of Japanese immigration differs considerably from that of the Chinese, mainly because of the strength of its government around the turn of the century. Unlike the weakening Chinese dynasty system, which fell in 1911, the Japanese government was able to negotiate mutually beneficial treaties with the United States over immigration.

The Japanese opening to the West commenced with the arrival of Commodore Matthew Perry and

The determination of the Japanese to secure their place in American society was greatly resented by a rising chorus of white workers. By the 1890s, nativists with the backing of organized labor in California formed the Japanese and Korean Exclusion League (later renamed the Asiatic Exclusion League). The league joined forces with smaller organizations such as the Anti-Jap Laundry League. In those California cities and agricultural communities where competition was the most intense and conspicuous, immigrants encountered violence from whites who claimed that California would be "overrun" by Japanese. Exclusion once again became a major political issue, only this time the Japanese were the target.

After Japan's crushing victories over China in 1895 and Russia in 1905, policymakers viewed exclusion as a means of controlling a potential enemy. Many Americans had regarded Japan as an eager student at the knee of the United States. But when the Japanese Navy defeated its Russian counterpart, American observers realized how much Japan had advanced since Commodore Perry's visit a half-century before and how powerful the "yellow" nation had become, signaling a turning point in relations between the United States and Japan. America was so concerned about these developments that President Theodore Roosevelt helped negotiate a treaty in 1905 that ended the Russian-Japanese war and made a preliminary grant of Korea to Japan. In 1910, Japan would possess Korea outright.

In the wake of the 1906 San Francisco earthquake, fierce anti-Japanese rioting resulted in countless incidents of physical violence. Japanese and Korean students in San Francisco were ordered to segregated schools, an act that incensed Japan and later proved to be a major stumbling block in negotiations over restrictions on Japanese laborers. President Roosevelt eventually persuaded San Francisco to accept Japanese students.

Japanese laborers were eventually restricted but not in conventional legislative fashion. Japan's emergence as a major world power meant that the United States could not restrict Japanese immigration in the heavy-handed, self-serving fashion with which it had curtailed Chinese immigration. To do so would have offended an increasingly assertive Japan when the United States was concerned about keeping a door open to Japanese markets. To minimize potential disharmony

between the two nations while retaining the initiative to control immigration, President Roosevelt negotiated an informal agreement with Japan. Under the terms of the so-called "Gentlemen's Agreement" reached in 1907 and 1908, the Japanese government refrained from issuing travel documents to laborers destined for the United States. In exchange for this severe but voluntary limitation, Japanese wives and children could be reunited with their husbands and fathers in the United States, and the San Francisco school board would be pressured into rescinding its segregation order.

Unlike the Chinese, the Japanese were able to keep their families intact. Since the wives and children of Japanese men in the United States could continue to enter, Japanese immigrants could marry and form families. The Japanese American population steadily increased during the first half of the twentieth century. The community was spared the extreme gender imbalance that had undermined Chinese America. A substantial share of the Japanese women immigrants during this period were "picture brides"—women whose prospective husbands had seen only a picture before the marriage. Given laws that prevented people of color from marrying whites (antimiscegenation laws) and the Japanese custom to arrange marriages, it is not surprising that many men sent back to Japan for brides.

After the Gentlemen's Agreement, exclusionists continued their attack and found alternative means of discouraging newcomers. In addition to continued racial animosity, a sense of economic competition persisted. By the 1910s, Japanese immigrants using intensive farming techniques produced more than 10 percent of California produce while owning only 1 percent of its farmland. So in 1913, the California legislature passed the Alien Land Law, which provided that only aliens who were eligible to citizenship could own land. Since the Naturalization Act of 1870 denied Asians the right to become citizens, the Land Law precluded Japanese from owning property. If they could not halt all immigrants at the border, exclusionists at least hoped to make life so difficult in the United States that none would want to come.

While immigration and landownership restrictions gradually curbed the economic gains that Japanese Americans had made in agriculture, California's Alien Land Law furnished loopholes that allowed creative immigrants to retain land.

Japanese American
field laborers.

The law did not prevent Japanese from leasing, for example, and landownership by corporations was permitted if corporate ownership was chiefly non-alien. As long as they either used corporate forms ostensibly held by whites or transferred title to a citizen child born in the United States, the Japanese could continue to farm their land. These loopholes annoyed white farmers and legislators alike. But active efforts to remove them stalled because the United States did not want to risk offending its World War I ally.

Soon after the war, however, anti-Japanese sentiment on the West Coast quickly regained its prewar intensity. Washington state legislated its own landownership restrictions. Hoping to close the loopholes of its 1913 statute, California enacted the Alien Land Law of 1920, which outlawed

circuitous transfers, including those from alien parents to citizen children. Attempts to avoid this new law through agricultural corporations and cropping contracts failed when the Supreme Court in *Webb* v. *Obrien* (1923) ruled that the discriminatory impact of alien land laws did not violate the constitution. As a result, many Japanese farmers lost control of their land, moved to towns and cities, and began the search for other occupations. For these farmers it was too late when, in 1953, the alien land laws finally were declared unconstitutional because they were racially discriminatory.

Eventually, Japanese were totally excluded in the landmark Immigration Act of 1924. The law is best known for its attack on southern and eastern Europeans, whom the Protestant majority in the United States viewed with disapproval. But the law also provided for the permanent exclusion of any "alien ineligible to citizenship." Since Asians were barred from naturalization under the 1870 statute, the possibility of their entry was cut off indefinitely. The prohibition even included previously privileged merchants, teachers, and students. The primary target were the Japanese, who, while subject to the Gentlemen's Agreement, had never been totally barred by federal immigration law until then.

As a result of the land laws and the 1924 act, in a manner similar to the experience of Chinese Americans after exclusion, many Japanese Americans were forced to move to the cities and find work in small shops and businesses. Many Japanese managed well because of their earlier successes in agriculture. Often pooling resources, they were able to start restaurants, laundries, barber shops, and other service enterprises. Others turned to gardening. Thus, by the 1930s, Japanese Americans who had started as laborers and service workers 20 years earlier had become managers or owners of small businesses. Two thirds of first-generation Japanese Americans in Seattle at the time were self-employed in trades or domestic and personal service businesses such as hotels, groceries, restaurants, laundries, and produce houses.

If domestic land laws and the 1924 Immigration Act seemed unusually tough on Japanese Americans, the beginning of World War II brought about a far more severe regime. After the bombing of Pearl Harbor, the bigotry and fear that had informed earlier anti-Japanese laws became a panic. Japanese Americans suddenly became suspected of acts of sabotage and treason. Though no such acts were ever proved, the civilian government gave in to unprecedented military orders that subjected all West Coast Japanese first to curfews and then to forced evacuation into detention camps under Executive Order 9066. In evacuating the Japanese, the Army generally gave less than seven days' notice, thus forcing families to sell their properties and possessions at a fraction of their true value. Eventually, 120,000 Japanese Americans, most of them citizens by birth, were interned in camps scattered across the country. No similar evacuation was ordered for persons of German or Italian descent in the United States.

One of the most remarkable aspects of the internment was how easily most Americans accepted it. It was wartime and many Americans

challenged the loyalty and commitment of Japanese Americans.

Even the Supreme Court uncritically accepted the premises behind internment. Though the Court purported in *Korematsu* v. *United States* (1944) to apply "strict scrutiny" to the government's order, in reality it accepted at face value the military's fears and accusations that Japanese American citizens were all potential saboteurs. But 40 years later in new court proceedings, Japanese Americans proved that the fears and accusations were made up and baseless. Government intelligence reports did not support the notion that resident Japanese posed a threat to national security.

Redress for the Japanese Americans interned during the war was slow in coming. In 1948 Congress passed the Japanese American Evacuation Claims Act, which appropriated $38 million to reimburse Japanese Americans who had been interned for their losses. This amounted to only 10 cents on the dollar of actual losses. In 1976 President Gerald Ford issued a proclamation that rescinded Executive Order 9066 and apologized to those who had been interned. Finally in 1988, Congress passed the Civil Liberties Act of 1988, authorizing compensation of $20,000 for living survivors of the internment camps.

The war and internment disrupted the economic development for West Coast Japanese who faced difficulties in reestablishing businesses because of dislocation and discrimination. But gradually more and more second-generation Japanese Americans (ironically, many who fought for the United States during the war and qualified for veteran's educational funds) were able to attend college, and many developed greater interests in science and technical fields. They provided the core of a middle class of doctors, dentists, lawyers, and engineers.

Nine years after the Chinese Repealer, Congress enacted the McCarran-Walter (Immigration and Nationality) Act of 1952. The law provided immigration rights for other Asians by removing the prohibition on their naturalization and abolishing the 1917 Asiatic barred zone. Instead, a new restriction zone—the Asia-Pacific triangle—was created that consisted of countries from India to Japan and all Pacific islands north of Australia and New Zealand. A maximum of 2,000 Asians from this new triangle were allowed to immigrate annually.

Japanese American family awaiting internment.

Asian Indian Americans

The advent of the twentieth century witnessed the entry of other Asians, such as Asian Indians, but in even smaller numbers. Even though those seeking trade were among some of the earliest migrants to the United States, Indians had insignificant contacts with this country during the nineteenth century. The poorer workers among them found labor opportunities in British colonies. Furthermore, the voyage to America from India was longer, more complicated, and more expensive. The few thousand who immigrated, most of them men, settled primarily in California, and most of them found agricultural jobs. Their families remained in India while husbands and fathers worked to earn money either to send for family members or to return to India. A small number of more educated Indians also entered, bringing the total number of arrivals from 1881 to 1917 to only about 7,000.

Even small numbers of Asian Indians managed to agitate the Asiatic Exclusion League, which had sprung up in response to Japanese and Korean immigration. Racial and economic nativism was again at the core of the agitation. Asian Indians competed for agricultural jobs and were willing to work for lower wages in other jobs, so nativists used violence to force them out of local jobs. Not satisfied with making life in the United States miserable and even dangerous, exclusionists also persuaded federal immigration authorities to block Asian Indians' entry. Although about 2,000

In 1965 President Lyndon Johnson repealed the McCarran-Walter Act, as part of the Immigration Act of 1965, replacing national origins quotas with an annual allowance of 20,000 immigrants from each country.

Asian Indians immigrated from 1911 to 1917, more than 1,700 were denied entry during the same period, mostly on the grounds that they would need welfare. The California commissioner of state labor statistics concluded that the "Hindu is the most undesirable immigrant in the state. His lack of personal cleanliness, his low morals and his blind adherence to theories and teachings, so entirely repugnant to American principles, make him unfit for association with American people."

Like the Chinese and Japanese before them, Indians sought to have laws discriminating against them overturned by the courts. Lower federal courts had granted them the right to naturalize on the grounds that they were Caucasians and thus eligible "white persons" under the naturalization

laws of 1790 and 1870. But in *United States* v. *Bhagat Singh Thind* (1923), the Court reversed its racial stance, deciding that Indians, like Japanese, would no longer be considered white persons and were therefore ineligible to become naturalized citizens. Naturalization certificates previously granted were canceled, and Indians became subject to the harsh Alien Land Laws.

Strict control of Chinese and Japanese immigration had done little to satisfy the demands of American nativists. They insisted that Asians were racially inferior to whites and should be completely barred. One California legislator called for amending immigration laws so that instead of merely excluding all those ineligible for citizenship, they would exclude "Hindus and all persons of the Mongolian or yellow race, the brown race or the African race." The United States Immigration Commission defined any native of India as Hindu, and the term was often misused to describe all Indians.

Congress responded to this anti-Asian clamor and a renewed xenophobia (fear of foreigners) aroused by the influx of southern and eastern Europeans by passing the Immigration Act of February 5, 1917. The constant flow of Italians, Russians, and Hungarians, which peaked in the first decade of the century, fueled racial nativism and anti-Catholicism, culminating in a controversial requirement that excluded aliens who could not "read and understand some language or dialect." But the act also created the "Asiatic barred zone" by extending the Chinese exclusion laws to all other Asians. Together with the Chinese exclusion laws and the Japanese Gentlemen's Agreement, these provisions declared inadmissible all Asians except teachers, merchants, and students. Only Filipinos and Guamanians, under U.S. jurisdiction at the time, could continue to enter.

Before immigration doors were cracked open again for Asian Indians, 80 percent of the Asian Indian men married women of Mexican descent (as did many Filipino immigrants) and thus were able to enjoy a family life. Many farmers and farm workers were already married in India and intended to send for their wives but were prevented from doing so after 1917. Mexican women offered love, an opportunity for children, domesticity, and housekeeping skills.

Many Indian farming partners in California had known each other in India. The men would settle and work together; when one married, the Mexican wife would move into this joint household, and then the wife would introduce her relatives to her husband's friends or relatives. Many men married sisters of friends' or partners' wives or married sets of related women, reinforcing kinship and economic ties.

The opportunity for Asian Indians to immigrate was not renewed until 1946, when naturalization rights for Indian immigrants and an annual immigration quota for 100 Indian spouses and children of citizens was legislated. Congress took this step in order to strengthen ties with India, which the United States began to regard as a prominent political and military force and as a potentially valuable ally during World War II. Many Indian journalists, propagandists, and politicians came to the United States during and after the war to win American support for their independence movement. After India won independence in 1946 and the two countries grew closer, the relaxation of exclusion became important to their new alliance.

Korean Americans

As with Japan and China, the United States entered into a treaty of friendship and trade with Korea. The agreement with Korea came in 1882, the same year of the Chinese exclusion law. But for 20 years there was no recorded Korean emigration. The earliest Korean immigrants were 7,500 laborers who came to Hawaii between 1902 and 1905; only a few hundred went on to the Pacific coast of the mainland. But in 1905, Japan took over Korea and severely limited Korean emigration.

By and large, the early Koreans who were recruited to the United States were from an unemployed urban class, although many were illiterate farmers from northern Korea, which was suffering from drought and economic difficulties. Many Koreans were used as strikebreakers when Japanese laborers challenged poor working conditions in Hawaii. Because of the very limited nature of their immigration, however, after 1905 Koreans ceased to be perceived as a threat by most laborers on the West Coast.

Especially early on, Korean laborers suffered from the same intense racial animosity that the Chinese and the Japanese experienced. Most white Americans made little distinction among Chinese, Japanese, and Korean. In one highly publicized event in 1913, Korean farm workers were attacked by an angry crowd of white workers and thrown on an outbound train because the crowd had mistaken them for Japanese.

Because Korea was a possession of Japan for most of the first half of the twentieth century, Korean immigration never neared the numbers of Chinese, Japanese, and Filipino immigration. Even after Korea was divided into north and south in 1945, few Koreans were able to immigrate. North Koreans were immediately restrained by their military-dominated government. And South Koreans and other Asians continued to be excluded under the 1924 Act.

The 1952 McCarran-Walter Act opened a small window of opportunity for Korean immigrants. More Koreans were able to enter. The vast

Over 6 million U.S. service men served in Korea during the Korean Conflict (1950–1955).

majority who entered before 1965 were women, many known as war brides because of their marriages to soldiers who fought in the Korean War. More than a third who entered at the time were girls under the age of four, who were adopted by U.S. families sympathetic to the huge number of orphans left after the war.

While early Koreans were mostly agricultural workers, some students and political refugees also entered. The students, mostly men, had to work in low-wage jobs as farm laborers, factory workers, cooks, waiters, chauffeurs, janitors, houseboys, and dishwashers, whereas women worked mainly in sewing sweatshops. A few demonstrated an ability in small business; they started laundries, restaurants, groceries, and shoe-repair shops. Korean-owned hotels could also be found throughout California and Washington.

Changes in the immigration laws in 1965 sparked expansion of the Korean American community. A community that numbered about 45,000 in 1965 totaled about 800,000 by 1990 as a result of immigration. More women than men continue to immigrate from Korea.

Unlike Filipinos and Chinese immigrants, Korean immigrants, and therefore the Korean American community, have not clustered in large residential or inner-city neighborhoods. The economic class of most Korean immigrants provides the explanation. Although some working-class immigrants have begun to reside in Koreatowns, such as in Los Angeles, most Korean immigrants are young and educated and from the urban elite or middle classes of South Korean society. They can afford to live in suburban neighborhoods. Instead of staying in touch by establishing suburban or urban enclaves, they use churches for regular meeting places and often establish a center for social and cultural gatherings.

One in four Korean Americans is employed as a professional, a manager, or an executive, and almost one in five is a service worker. Although the number who fall into the category of managers and professionals is about the same as the general population, the figure includes many small-business owners. Through the mid-1970s many Korean immigrants entered the United States as investors. Other Korean immigrants, confronting strong barriers in the job market, lacking English fluency and knowledge of American customs, facing persistent discrimination, and refused a foothold in white-collar occupations, turned to small business as a practical option.

Newly arriving immigrants, in turn, perceived their predecessors as successful in small business and were encouraged to try their hand. As more opened small businesses—such as fruit and vegetable stores in New York and liquor stores in Los Angeles—they established business and supply networks that made it easier for new arrivals to set up their own shops.

In spite of this seeming success, the average income for full-time Korean American workers is less than that of white Americans.

Filipino Americans

At the turn of the century, the United States was beginning its relationship with the Philippines as it was changing its view toward Japan. After the victory over Spain in 1898 in the Spanish-American War, President McKinley concluded that the people of the Philippines, then a Spanish colony, were "unfit for self-government" and that there was nothing left for the United States to do but to "educate the Filipinos, and uplift and civilize and Christianize them." The takeover met with violent resistance from many Filipinos who had yearned for independence from colonial domination.

If becoming a United States colony had a positive side, it was that Filipinos automatically became noncitizen nationals of the United States. They could travel without regard to immigration laws, they were not subject to exclusion or deportation, and requirements for obtaining full citizenship were relaxed. Yet fewer than 3,000 Filipinos, most of them farm workers in Hawaii, had immigrated by 1910. Not until appreciable numbers came in after World War I (when Chinese and Japanese workers could no longer be recruited) did exclusionary efforts against them begin.

The only Asians not affected by the 1924 law excluding any alien ineligible to citizenship were Filipinos, who remained exempt as nationals and who by then had settled into a familiar pattern of migration. Before 1920, a few resided mostly in Hawaii. They became a source of cheap labor after Japanese immigration was restricted in 1908. Just as the Chinese exclusion law had encouraged employers to look to Japan, so the limitations on Japanese immigrants led to an intense recruitment, especially by Hawaiian sugar plantation owners, of Filipino laborers because of their open travel status as noncitizen nationals.

Growers thought Filipinos (like Mexicans on the mainland) were well-suited to "stoop" labor and were not as aggressive as Japanese workers or as enterprising as Chinese workers. They were praised as especially hardworking, submissive, and reliable. Despite the arduousness of the work in the sugar and pineapple industries, the steady pay lured many Filipino laborers (most of whom were from economically underdeveloped areas of the Philippines populated by poor peasants and farm workers) who could not earn comparable wages in their home country.

By the late 1920s, Filipino laborers began to look beyond Hawaii, where the demand for their labor was shrinking, to the mainland, where the need for cheap labor, especially in agriculture, was growing. Many left Hawaii partly in response to employers' recruitment efforts. Most Filipinos who had come to the mainland previously had been students. But in the late 1920s, laborers came to California predominantly to work on citrus and vegetable farms.

Filipinos differed significantly from travelers from Japan, China, and India. They were Catholics and had been exposed to American culture in their schooling. They entered as wards of the United States and were free to come and go. Because of their special status, they often considered themselves American in important respects. Still, on their arrival familiar cycles of rejection quickly surfaced, much to their consternation. They were met with acceptance by eager employers and then, almost immediately, resentment from white workers, particularly as their numbers increased on the mainland in the late 1920s.

One strain of American thought regarded Filipinos as "savages." The 1904 St. Louis Exposition had featured certain Philippine tribes that practiced head-hunting. Returning American missionaries described "shocking" practices. The paternalistic view was that Filipinos depended on the United States to help them develop socially and culturally; after all, it was said that they had "never produced a great teacher, priest, business man, or statesman." Nevertheless, most white racism directed at Filipino laborers sprang, perhaps paradoxically, not so much from tabloid impressions but more from the immigrants' success at acculturation. They were resented largely for their ability to get jobs and even for their contact with white women. In many respects, they were perceived as a greater threat to white laborers than their Chinese and Japanese predecessors had been.

To white workers in California the privileged immigration status of Filipinos did not change the fact that they were an economic threat who had the physical characteristics of Asiatics. They were just another undesirable Asian race who seemed to be taking over white jobs and lowering standards for their wages and working conditions. As it had toward Chinese and Japanese, white resentment of Filipinos soon boiled over into violence, and numerous anti-Filipino outbursts erupted in California between 1929 and 1934. Their strong concentration in agriculture made them visible and competitive (of the 45,000 reported on the mainland in 1930, about 82 percent were farm laborers), especially during the severe unemployment of the Great Depression. Since Filipinos were often on the bottom of the economic ladder, the Depression struck them particularly hard. Exclusionists suggested that the United States ought to "repatriate" or send back unemployed Filipino workers, for their own benefit as well as for that of the United States.

Calls for the exclusion of Filipino workers were warmly received in Congress, which welcomed any seemingly uncomplicated proposal that promised relief for the Depression's high unemployment. For policymakers, however, dealing with anti-Filipino agitation was not as simple as responding to earlier anti-Chinese, anti-Asian Indian, and even anti-Japanese campaigns. They could travel into the United States legally, so until the Philippines was granted independence, Congress could not exclude Filipinos.

An unlikely coalition of exclusionists, anticolonialists, and Filipino nationalists managed to band together to promote the passage of the Tydings-McDuffie Act in 1934. Many of the exclusionists had initially wished to keep the Philippines, but they soon realized that to exclude Filipino laborers they had to support Filipino nationalists and anticolonialists and grant the nation its freedom. Independence and exclusion became intertwined.

Tydings-McDuffie was everything exclusionists could hope for. When their nation would become independent on July 4, 1946, Filipinos would lose their status as nationals of the United States, regardless of where they lived. Those in the United States would be deported unless they became immigrants. Between 1934 and 1946, however, any Filipino who desired to immigrate became subject to the immigration acts of 1917 and 1924, and the Philippines was considered a separate country with an annual quota of only 50 visas. This was an especially bitter pill for Filipinos to swallow. After being stripped of their noncitizen national status, they now were given half the minimum quota that the 1924 act had established for all other non-Asian nationalities. And the Supreme Court

had made it clear in 1925 that, like Asian Indians and Japanese, Filipinos were not "free white persons" eligible for naturalization.

Like the Chinese and Japanese, Filipinos faced increased racial violence and isolation, which was mainly the product of the same exclusion movement that led to the 1934 Independence Act. In response to rural isolation and antagonism, Filipinos gradually moved to urban areas in California, where Manilatowns or Little Manilas materialized.

As part of the 1946 legislation extending naturalization and immigration rights to Asian Indians, Congress included the Philippines in order to strengthen ties during World War II. The Philippines, like China, became a critical ally in the war against Japan. Almost 10,000 Filipinos took advantage of special citizenship opportunities extended to war veterans and other Filipinos who served in the U.S. Armed Forces, although many more could have benefited had the United States provided naturalization examiners in the Philippines for a longer period of time.

Through the 1920s, most Filipino Americans were farmworkers. In the off-season, they provided service labor for hotels, restaurants, and private homes as busboys, cooks, hotel chauffeurs, dishwashers, domestic help, and gardeners. After 1946, some students and laborers began finding work in factories, retail sales, and certain trades. Gradually, a modestly sized class of professionals started to emerge as well.

Today, about one quarter of Filipino American workers are classified as professionals, managers, or executives, but one in six are service workers. The average family income for Filipino Americans is higher than that of the general population, but as with Chinese Americans there are more workers per family among Filipinos.

Vietnamese Americans

By the year 2000 there will be about 1 million people of Vietnamese descent in the United States. This is a remarkable figure: in 1975 the number of Vietnamese Americans was negligible. But the end of the Vietnam War in April 1975, when the United State withdrew its military forces from Southeast Asia, marked the beginning of an enormous flow of Southeast Asian refugees into the United States. Today, 90 percent of the population of Vietnamese America is foreign-born.

Vietnamese Americans have made themselves noticeable by contributing to the revitalization of several urban centers, and their food enriches the cuisine of many cities. They have also been made conspicuous by the media—sometimes for the educational accomplishments of their children, sometimes for the economic threat they are perceived as posing to white fisherman, and sometimes for their experiences as victims of renewed anti-Asian violence.

After its withdrawal from Southeast Asia, the United States initially wanted to evacuate from Vietnam approximately 17,600 American dependents and government employees. But at the last minute, former employees and others whose lives were threatened were included. These evacuees included approximately 4,000 orphans, 75,000 relatives of American citizens or legal residents, and 50,000 Vietnamese government officials and employees. Mass confusion permitted many who did not fit into these categories to also be evacuated. Between April and December 1975, the United States admitted 130,400 Southeast Asian refugees, 125,000 of whom were Vietnamese.

The exodus did not stop there. Tens of thousands were admitted in the late 1970s (the first wave), and even after the refugee laws were changed in 1980, the United States allowed in hundreds of thousands of Southeast Asian refugees (mostly Vietnamese) in the 1980s in recognition of human rights responsibilities.

The United States has helped many refugees over the years, but Southeast Asians posed a special resettlement problem. They were the largest refugee group ever to so rapidly enter the country, and the challenge they presented began early when they came in entirely unanticipated numbers. U.S. government officials decided to disperse Vietnamese refugees as widely as possible rather than to concentrate them in assigned areas. Officials soon discovered that dispersal was ill-advised and unpopular. Initially, the program produced a settlement pattern approximating that of the rest of the population. Refugees were "neatly" dispersed around the country, with one fifth being placed in California. At least one hundred were relocated in every state except Alaska. Relative isolation, however, quickly proved unacceptable to refugees who began moving from their assigned locations in substantial numbers, a practice commonly referred to as secondary migration.

Although many factors contributed to refugees' decision to resettle, secondary migration principally resulted from poor policy decisions based upon superficial analysis. In a new and often hostile land, forced dispersal deprived Southeast Asians of desperately needed familial, cultural, and ethnic support. Their decision to develop these support systems seemed possible only by forming the kinds of ethnic enclaves that dispersal discouraged. So Vietnamese leaders, particularly the clergy, frequently coordinated ambitious secondary migrations to places like New Orleans, where living together as a community seemed feasible.

By 1980, almost one half of the first wave of Southeast Asian refugees had moved from their assigned locations to a different state, thereby frustrating the dispersal policy's goals of minimizing the impact of refugees on local economies. They became concentrated most heavily in California, Texas, and Louisiana. Urban areas having warm climates and an Asian population were preferred. Thus, by the time the second wave began arriving in 1978, Southeast Asian refugees, particularly the Vietnamese, were no longer as widely dispersed as they had been under the original plan. And the secondary migration of the first wave affected the initial dispersion of the second because newcomers were placed near those with whom they had close ties. Housing shortages, perceived job competition, and high welfare dependency became associated with many of these resettlement areas, only fueling hostility and resentment.

California is the most popular destination for new Southeast Asian refugees and secondary migrants. Although less than 25 percent of the refugee population was placed in California at first, 40 percent now resides there. More than one fourth are located in the South, with about 10 percent in both the Northeast and the Midwest.

The different profiles of early and later entrants influenced the quality of refugee life in the United States. The first wave was relatively well-educated, proficient in English, and experienced in urban living. Though they accepted initial resettlement assistance, these refugees worked aggressively to minimize their subsequent reliance on government benefits. What federal funds they did accept, they used to achieve professional status and create businesses.

The second wave, however, was much poorer and less educated and typically did not possess the skills needed for employment in a technologically complex society. Nor did they have the advantage of government programs designed to assist them with these problems. Many have benefited from the solidarity generated within ethnic enclaves. Some, for example, despite having no established credit and no ability to procure loans from major financial institutions, have managed to start small businesses with money borrowed from friends. Along with first-wave entrants, the newer immigrants helped account for the statistic that Vietnamese-owned businesses had the highest growth rate in the late 1980s—over 400 percent. In general, though, the second wave has remained trapped in low-status service-sector jobs.

Not surprisingly, the Vietnamese have been accused of developing a welfare mentality, and the government has responded to that accusation. Their relatively low rate of labor-force participation has in fact led many Vietnamese refugees to depend on government assistance. Many attribute this dependency to a welfare system that purportedly creates disincentives to work. Policymakers have urged state and local resettlement agencies to expedite job placement for refugees. Under the 1980 Refugee Act, refugees were given 36-month stipends of special refugee cash, medical assistance programs, and other support services. But in 1982 amendments to the act reduced the stipends to 18 months to pressure refugees to become economically independent more quickly. These changes came during the entry of poorer, less-educated, and more devastated second wave. After 1982 most programs stressed employment-enhancing services, such as vocational, English-language, and job-development training. Most refugees are unable to acquire the skills that would qualify them for anything other than minimum-wage jobs in 18 months. They were nonetheless constrained to take these positions in the absence of continued public assistance.

Restrictions on federal assistance thus help to account for increased Vietnamese American concentration in entry-level, minimum-wage jobs requiring little formal education or mastery of English. For many refugees, in fact, these types of jobs and the poverty that results are unavoidable. Indeed, in 1990, a striking one in three Vietnamese families were living below the poverty level. While the average Chinese, Filipino, and Korean American worker earns less than a white American, Vietnamese workers earn even less.

Discrimination and Barriers to Equal Opportunity

Comprehending the history and characteristics of Asian Americans is important to an understanding of the civil rights problems that they confront. Some of the factors that lead to the creation of barriers to equal opportunity for Asian Americans arise out of the tendency for the general public and the media to stereotype Asian Americans.

Model Minority

Asian Americans are often stereotyped as the "model minority." According to this stereotype, which is based partly on uncritical reliance on statistics revealing high average family incomes, educational attainment, and occupational status of Asian Americans, they are hardworking, intelligent, and successful.

As complimentary as it might sound, this stereotype has damaging consequences. First, it leads people to ignore the very real social and economic problems faced by many segments of the Asian American population and may result in the needs of poorer, less successful Asian Americans being overlooked. Second, emphasis on the model minority stereotype may also divert public attention from the existence of discrimination even against the more successful Asian Americans, such as discrimination in job promotion or college admissions. Third, the stereotype may result in undue pressure being put on young Asian Americans to succeed in school and in their careers. This pressure can lead to mental health problems and even teen suicide. Finally, the origin of this stereotype was an effort to discredit other minorities by arguing that if Asian Americans could succeed, so could African Americans and Latinos, and many Asian Americans resented being used in this fashion.

Asian Americans as Foreigners

Because of their facial appearance and usually foreign origin. Asian Americans are often perceived as foreigners by other Americans. Even Asian Americans whose families have been in the United States for generations are frequently the objects of questions and comments such as

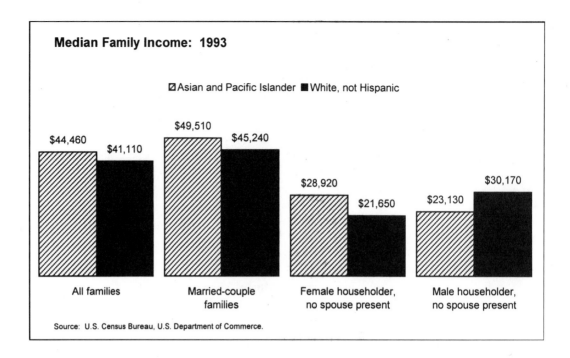

Median Family Income: 1993

☑ Asian and Pacific Islander ■ White, not Hispanic

	Asian and Pacific Islander	White, not Hispanic
All families	$44,460	$41,110
Married-couple families	$49,510	$45,240
Female householder, no spouse present	$28,920	$21,650
Male householder, no spouse present	$23,130	$30,170

Source: U.S. Census Bureau, U.S. Department of Commerce.

"Where did you learn English?" and "You speak such good English."

Asian Americans of all groups tend to suffer when international events cause tensions between the United States and Asian countries. For example, many Americans take out their frustrations about Japan's economic success on Asian Americans of all national origins. The 1982 killing of Vincent Chin, a Chinese American, was prompted by his killers' resentment of the Japanese for their automobile exports to the United States. The perception of Asian Americans as foreigners also impedes their acceptance in important areas of their lives, including employment and education.

Limited English Proficiency

Many Asian Americans, recent immigrants in particular, have limited English proficiency, and some do not speak or understand English at all. Persons with limited English proficiency face a serious barrier to full participation in American society and our economy. A person's ability to learn about and gain access to public services (such as education, police services, and health care), employment, and the larger American society are often hampered by limited English proficiency.

Cultural Differences

Asian Pacific immigrants come from societies that have very different cultures from the mainstream cultures in the United States. Cultural differences often lead to misunderstandings, which in turn can lead to discriminatory treatment or to intergroup tensions, as in the case of Korean American store owners and their customers who are members of other minority groups. These tensions can erupt into full-scale racial conflict.

Religious Diversity

Many Asian Americans belong to religions that are not widely practiced in the United States, such as Buddhism, Hinduism, Islam, and Sikhism. These religions are unfamiliar to most Americans educated in the Judeo-Christian tradition, and these differences generate hostilities against Asian Americans.

Stereotyping Asian Americans as Unaggressive and Lacking in Communication Skills

Asian Americans, while viewed as intelligent and talented at mathematics and science, are considered unaggressive and lacking in good communication skills. This stereotype can blind employers to the qualifications of individual Asian Americans and contribute to failure of Asian Americans to be promoted to managerial levels. It may also lead teachers and counselors to discourage Asian American students from pursuing nontechnical careers.

Southeast Asian refugees at
Fort Indiantown Gap,
Pennsylvania, learn English.

Pre-immigration Trauma

Another factor hampering some Asian Americans' access to equal opportunity arises out of the wartime ordeals they have endured, as well as bad experiences they have had with government officials in their native countries. Many Vietnamese, Cambodians, Hmong, and Laotians refugees have come from war-torn countries and have survived ordeals on their journeys to the United States. Many lost loved ones—parents, children, siblings, cousins—during the war. They often carry scars from psychological trauma that can make it difficult for them to cope with day-to-day life, let alone face the challenge of adjusting to a new society.

Many immigrants and refugees carry a deep distrust of authority arising out of bad experiences

they had with government officials back home. This may deter them from interactions with government agencies in the United States such as police departments, welfare offices, and even schools. As a result, a division may arise between public programs and the community. Because of their hesitation in conveying their needs, many Asian Americans may not receive many basic public services.

Bigotry and Violence Against Asian Americans

Many Asian Americans are forced to endure anti-Asian bigotry, ranging from ignorant and insensitive remarks to stereotypical portrayals of

In the 1870s Chinese immigrants were often harrassed and attacked upon their arrival to San Francisco.

Asians in the media to name-calling, on a regular basis. They are also the frequent victims of hate crimes, including vandalism, assault, and sometimes even murder. Although incidents of bigotry and violence against Asian Americans are reflections of a broader national climate of ethnic, racial, and religious intolerance, they are also reprehensible outgrowths of ingrained anti-Asian feelings that reside among many members of American society.

The racially motivated murder of Vincent Chin in 1982 and the inability of the American judicial system to bring his murderers to justice has become a vivid symbol of hate violence and a source of outrage for many Asian Americans. On the evening of June 19, 1982, Vincent Chin, a 27-year-old Chinese American, met with some

friends in a Detroit bar to celebrate his upcoming wedding. He was confronted by Ronald Ebens and Michael Nitz, two white automobile factory workers who called him a "Jap" and blamed him for the loss of jobs in the automobile industry. Ebens and Nitz chased Chin out of the bar, and when they caught up with him, Nitz held Chin while Ebens beat him on the head, chest, and knee with a baseball bat. Chin died of his injuries four days later.

Ebens and Nitz were initially charged with second-degree murder but subsequently were allowed to plead guilty to manslaughter. Neither was sent to jail by the state court judge; each was sentenced to three years' probation and fined $3,780. After complaints from Asian American communities, the pair was brought to trial again, this time in federal court on the grounds that they had violated Chin's civil rights. But Nitz was found not guilty, and although Ebens was found guilty and sentenced to 25 years in prison, his conviction was thrown out by a higher federal court on technical reasons. Ebens was retried and found not guilty. Neither Ebens nor Nitz ever went to prison for Vincent Chin's murder.

The killing of a 15-year-old Vietnamese boy in Houston illustrates the threat posed to Asian Americans by skinheads. Hung Truong moved to the Houston area from Vietnam with his father in 1980. On August 9, 1990, at 2 A.M., he was walking with three friends when they were approached by two cars that stopped alongside them. Two 18-year-old men, Derek Hilla and Kevin Michael Allison, exited from one car with a club. The two men shouted "White Power!" They chased Truong, who became separated from his friends, and kicked and beat him with their hands and feet. He died later that morning.

Hilla and Allison were charged with Truong's murder. Hilla was known to have racist views and was a violent man. At the trial, Allison denied that he was racist but admitted that the only reason he and Hilla attacked Truong was because he was Vietnamese. The jury convicted Hilla of murder and Allison of involuntary manslaughter. Hilla and Allison were respectively sentenced to 45 and 10 years in prison.

A chilling massacre of school children in Stockton, California, illustrates the tragic consequences of racial hatred. On January 17, 1989, Patrick Edward Purdy dressed in military clothes entered the schoolyard at a local elementary school and repeatedly fired an AK47 assault rifle, killing five Southeast Asian children and wounding 30 others. He then turned the rifle on himself. After an investigation, the attorney general of California concluded that the killings were driven by a hatred of racial and ethnic minorities. Purdy was known to have made resentful comments about Southeast Asians. He apparently chose the particular elementary school as the location for his assault because it was heavily populated by Southeast Asian children.

As many Cambodian refugees moved into New England in the early 1980s, housing-related incidents against them multiplied. In 1981, shortly after he moved into his new house in Portsmouth,

Maine, a Cambodian man was hit on the head by a rock hidden in a snowball thrown by neighbors as he was playing in the snow with his children. When he approached his neighbors, one of them said, "Go back where you came from, gook." Between 1983 and 1987, there were recurrent incidents of violence against Cambodians living in Revere, Massachusetts, and vandalism against their homes, including rocks thrown through windows and several fires that destroyed entire buildings. Similar incidents occurred elsewhere in Massachusetts, such as a fire set by arsonists that left 31 Cambodians homeless in Lynn, Massachusetts, in December 1988.

Similar incidents have occurred elsewhere. In Richmond, California, following numerous incidents of egg throwing and BB-gun shots, eight cars parked outside an apartment complex where several Laotian refugees lived were badly damaged in September 1990. In 1987 in Queens, New York, a Chinese family was the repeated target of a group of young people who threw eggs, drove a car into their front gate, and made statements like "Why don't you move away?" In New Jersey since the 1980s, a group of young men have constantly harassed and assaulted immigrants from India. In apparent reference to the red dot, or "bindi," that some Hindu women place on their forehead to symbolize religious devotion, the group calls themselves the "Dot-busters."

Educational Issues

Asian American students are often portrayed in the media as whiz kids, especially in math, science, and other technical fields. This stereotype is hardly surprising given the types of reports and statistics disseminated by educational commissions, testing services, and some school districts. For example, the Department of Education reports that Asian American high school students get A's more often and fail less than whites or any other racial groups in subjects ranging from English to art. Although Asian Americans comprise only about 3.5 percent of the population, they make up to 25 percent of the entering classes at many prestigious colleges and universities.

These generalized accounts of Asian Americans mask complexities that a closer look reveals. For example, Asian Americans do score the high-

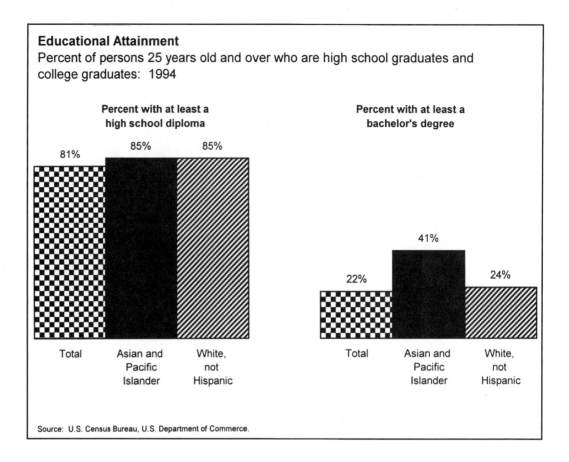

Educational Attainment
Percent of persons 25 years old and over who are high school graduates and college graduates: 1994

Percent with at least a high school diploma

81% — Total
85% — Asian and Pacific Islander
85% — White, not Hispanic

Percent with at least a bachelor's degree

22% — Total
41% — Asian and Pacific Islander
24% — White, not Hispanic

Source: U.S. Census Bureau, U.S. Department of Commerce.

est of all groups on the math section of the Scholastic Aptitude Test. Their verbal scores, however, are lower than those of whites. Consistent with these scores, more Asian American college freshmen have to take remedial English than do other freshmen. Also, the few studies that attempt to break down information group by group reveal substantial differences in the performances of different groups. For example, Filipinos, Hmong, Laotians, Samoans, and Cambodians generally do lower than average, while Chinese, Japanese, and Vietnamese do better. But although many Vietnamese in San Diego and Orange County (in southern California) high schools graduate at the top of their classes, Vietnamese in the same schools have the highest truancy and dropout rates among Asian Americans. In fact in San Diego, the dropout rate among Vietnamese students is higher than that of white students and even higher among Cambodians. Dropout rates among Filipino and Samoan high school students has been reported to be about 50 percent in California, and the same among Laotian students in certain parts of Massachusetts.

Many Asian Pacific immigrant children, particularly those from low-income families, face spe-

cial educational challenges. Their limited English ability and their parents' need to work long hours can affect their educational performance. Southeast Asian refugee children may have even more challenges because they carry scars from the ordeal of surviving the extreme hardships of battlefields and refugee detention camps or arduous boat rides to freedom. Many live in families that have been torn apart by the violence in Southeast Asia. For instance, fewer than half of the Cambodian students in San Diego live in two-parent households (many live with their widowed mothers).

In most Asian American families both parents work, often to support themselves and their children. Many have limited opportunity to learn English. Parents are by and large unable to track progress in school, in part because they do not understand a report card or have time to participate in organizations like the PTA. Children frequently must act for them as interpreters and conduits to the outside world and often become caught up in traditional family responsibilities. They hassle with landlords, arrange for medical care, deal with the legal system, and otherwise assume adult obligations. Some young Southeast Asians who live without their parents really must become adults before their time. This added tension and responsibility can detract from concentration and study time and increase the possibility of dropping out.

The special educational needs of the children of Asian Pacific immigrants soon began to surface after 1965. In the early 1970s, frustrated by the persistent inattention to their needs by school officials, non-English-speaking students of Chinese descent in San Francisco brought a class action lawsuit against officials of the school district. The students argued that they suffered unequal educational opportunities resulting from the officials' failure to establish a program to rectify the students' language problems. Although the lower courts were not sympathetic to the students' claims, the U.S. Supreme Court, in *Lau* v. *Nichols* (1974), unanimously held that the San Francisco school district was in violation of Title VI of the Civil Rights Act of 1964. The school district violated the students' civil rights by not providing them with a meaningful educational opportunity. The school district had an obligation to provide equal educational opportunity for all children, including the responsibility to take affirmative steps "to rectify the language deficiency in order to open" programs for limited English-proficient (LEP) children.

The Supreme Court did not specify what kind of special instruction schools should provide to LEP students. Current guidelines of the Office for Civil Rights in the Department of Education state that school districts may use any method or program that promises to be successful. As a result, some districts use bilingual/bicultural education programs, while others simply supplement regular classes with separate English classes.

At the college level, Asian Americans have faced a different type of civil rights problem. In the 1980s, Asian Americans charged that many prestigious colleges and universities were using discriminatory admissions policies against Asian American applicants. One study of East Coast institutions in 1983 found that in most schools the number of Asian American applicants admitted had barely increased during the 1970s and early 1980s, although the number of Asian American applicants had increased dramatically. For example, at Brown University, although Asian American applicants had among the highest academic records and had increased eight and a half times between 1975 and 1983, the number of those applicants admitted increased from only 74 in

1975 to 140 in 1983. At the University of California at Berkeley, the number of Asian Americans applicants admitted declined by 21 percent between 1983 and 1984, even though their applications increased and academic records remained quite high. Similar patterns appeared at Princeton, Harvard, Stanford, UCLA, and Yale.

Public exposure to the discrepancies and investigations at the various institutions gave rise to changes that have resulted in admissions programs under which more Asian American students have been admitted. For example, although Harvard was cleared of allegations of improper discrimination against Asian American applicants, the university's policy of favoring the children of alumni ("legacies") and recruited athletes was highlighted. As a result, preference for legacies has come under heightened attack. At other schools like U.C. Berkeley, Stanford, and Brown, the admission of Asian American applicants have reached new highs since the discrepancies were exposed.

Employment Discrimination

The perception that there is a "glass ceiling" barring most Asian Americans from attaining management positions (especially upper level management positions) for which they are qualified is a concern frequently voiced by Asian Americans. They feel they are discriminated against and unfairly stereotyped as being unaggressive, having poor communications skills and limited English proficiency, and being too technical to become managers.

Statistical evidence supports the perception. A survey of executives in Fortune 500 companies in 1990 showed that only 0.3 percent of senior executives in the United States were of Asian descent. This represents only one tenth the representation of Asian Americans in the population as a whole, despite their higher-than-average education levels. A study by the U.S. Commission on Civil Rights involving U.S.-born Asian American men (without English language problems) showed that they were less likely to be holding management positions than white men.

Discrimination Based on Accent

The federal courts have held that not giving a person a job or a promotion because of an accent violates Title VII of the Civil Rights Act of 1964 (prohibition of national origin discrimination) except in cases where the accent significantly impairs the individual's ability to perform the particular job. The issue of whether discrimination based on accent was proper was the subject of *Carino* v. *University of Oklahoma Board of Regents* (1984). The case involved a U.S. citizen of Filipino origin who charged that he had been demoted from his supervisory position in a university dental laboratory because of his accent. His employers argued that they were justified in demoting him because his accent hampered his work as a supervisor. The federal courts ruled in Mr. Carino's favor, holding that a foreign accent that does not interfere with one's ability to perform duties of the position is not a legitimate justification for a demotion or failure to hire.

The case of *Fragante* v. *City & County of Honolulu* (1989) provides an example of when a person's foreign accent can be considered an acceptable justification for an adverse employment decision. The federal court found that the Honolulu Division of Motor Vehicles could legitimately deny a Filipino American with a heavy accent a job as a clerk because the position required communication with the public over the telephone and at an information counter. The court cautioned that denying a job because of an accent is legitimate only when the accent would interfere materially with job performance and that the presence of an accent cannot be used as an excuse to deny a job when the real motive is discrimination based on the person's national origin.

English-Only Rules in the Workplace

Employers often seek to impose rules requiring their employees to speak only English while they are on the job. Sometimes these English-only rules are blanket rules banning the use of any language other than English at any time while the employee is at work. Other times the rules are more specific, banning the use of non-English languages when the employee is performing certain duties. English-only rules are a common source of frustration and resentment for many Asian Americans and others whose primary language is not English. They feel that the rules single them out for adverse treatment based on their national ori-

gin, are often adopted for the purpose of discrimination, and repress their ability to express themselves freely.

The Equal Employment Opportunity Commission (EEOC) has held that blanket rules banning the use of non-English languages at all times are almost always illegal, because they will never be justified by business necessity. The EEOC maintains that an individual's primary language is an essential characteristic of national origin; thus, some courts view English-only policies as harassment, a burdensome condition of employment, or discriminatory.

However, EEOC guidelines permit policies that require employees to speak English while they are on duty—provided the employer can show that such a policy is a business necessity compelling enough to override any racial impact. Legitimate business needs that courts have recognized include promoting employee efficiency, productivity, and safety; maintaining order and discipline; and responding to customer preference.

The case of an assistant head nurse in California who filed a discrimination claim against her employer is one example. The hospital had prohibited the nurse and those she supervised from speaking their native Filipino dialect of Tagalog on the maternity unity were they worked. The rule was necessary, hospital administrators asserted, because conversations in Tagalog had resulted in preferential treatment for the nurses who spoke it and adversely affected worker morale and supervision. The court found that the language restriction did not violate the nurses civil rights because it was motivated by a desire to eliminate dissension that could have compromised patient safety. Similarly, officials at New York's Bellevue Hospital, where the vast majority of nurses are Filipino, say an English-only rule was necessary because nurses spoke Tagalog among themselves.

Discrimination Caused by the Immigration Reform and Control Act

In 1986 Congress passed the Immigration Reform and Control Act (IRCA), which made it illegal for employers to knowingly hire undocumented workers. This is often referred to as "employer sanctions." Under IRCA, employers are required to verify the work authorization of all workers, not just those whom employers suspect might not be authorized to work. Unfortunately, studies have shown that IRCA has led employers to discriminate against many foreign-born workers who actually do have permission to work. These employers either intentionally discriminate or unintentionally discriminate out of fear that they might be penalized for hiring an undocumented worker.

The General Accounting Office of the federal government has found a widespread pattern of discrimination against eligible workers as a result of IRCA. Its report found that the proportion of employers adopting discriminatory practices was higher in the western states, New York City, Chicago, and Miami, and especially high in Texas and Los Angeles. These are areas that are heavily populated by Asians and Latinos. The report confirmed that IRCA resulted in widespread discrimination against foreign-looking and foreign-sounding workers.

After the GAO findings were released, the U.S. Commission on Civil Rights called for the repeal of employer sanctions, on the grounds that they have seriously harmed large numbers of Latino and Asian workers who are citizens and legal residents. However, Congress has not repealed employer sanctions. Instead, Congress believes that through employer education programs and enforcement of discrimination laws qualified Asian and Latino workers will not suffer from IRCA's employer sanctions provisions.

Asian Americans are an extremely diverse group. In fact they are many groups who themselves or whose ancestors came from dozens of different countries from the Asia Pacific region of the world. Even within a particular group such as Chinese Americans or Vietnamese Americans, a wide range of occupations, incomes, educational achievement, and needs exists.

The recognition of this broad diversity in Asian America—in fact in all of America—is the key to avoiding civil rights violations. Making generalizations or stereotypes about particular groups leads to actions by individuals and government institutions that are discriminatory or unfair to particular individuals with special needs. Understanding diversity is the best way to address issues involving the workplace, schools, the media, the legal system, and other institutions.

Bibliography

Ancheta, Angelo. *Race, Rights and the Asian American Experience.* New Brunswick, N.J.: Rutgers University Press, 1997.

Chan, S. *Asian Americans: An Interpretive History.* Boston: Twayne, 1991.

Chuman, F. *The Bamboo People: The Law and Japanese-Americans.* Del Mar, Calif.: Publisher's Inc., 1976.

Hing, B. O. *Making and Remaking Asian Americans Through Immigration Policy, 1850–1990.* Stanford, Calif.: Stanford University Press, 1993.

———. *To Be An American: Cultural Pluralism and the Rhetoric of Assimilation.* New York: NYU Press, 1997.

Takaki, R. *Strangers from a Different Shore.* Boston: Little, Brown, 1989.

U.S. Commission on Civil Rights. *Civil Rights Issues Facing Asian Americans in the 1990s.* Washington, D.C: U.S. Government Printing Office, 1992.

Chapter 5

Hispanic Americans

Frank De Varona

Hispanic-speaking Americans, often called "Latinos," are America's fastest growing population group. In 1995 the total population of Hispanics, according to the U.S. Bureau of the Census, was about 27 million. Hispanics are now about ten percent of the American population, and the Census Bureau projects that by the year 2050 the Hispanic population will reach 81 million, about 21 percent of the population. Soon after the year 2000 Latinos will overtake African Americans as the largest American minority group.

The labels "Hispanic" or "Latino" cover a wide number of very different peoples. Most have some ancestors from Spain, but the intermingling of African Americans, Native Americans, Asians, and Spanish immigrants is very complex, and each area of the New World had different patterns of cultural mixtures. Upon their arrival in the Western Hemisphere the Spaniards mixed with conquered Native American nations, such as Toltec, Aztec, Maya, Inca, Taino, and other groups from the various indigenous pre-Columbian civilizations. Enslaved Africans were imported by the Spanish, and these were added to the racial mix. Asian immigrants arrived later to join the medley.

The variety of races and cultures that form the rich Hispanic heritage accounts for the varied appearances of many individuals. Hispanics are hued as black, brown, red, yellow, and white. As one Puerto Rican poet has described Hispanics, they are "all the colors tied."

Latinos have had difficulty finding a term to describe their common characteristics. In 1980 the U.S. Census Bureau applied the term Hispanic to the vastly different groups that have the Spanish language as a common denominator. The term Hispanic is acceptable to some, but insulting to others, who prefer to be called Latinos. Although many Puerto Ricans in New York like to call themselves Latinos, Hispanics is the more widely used term on the American East Coast. In

In 1565, the first permanent European settlement on the United States mainland was established at St. Augustine, Florida, by Pedro Mendenez de Avilés of Spain, 55 years before the Pilgrims arrived from England and landed at Plymouth Rock.

California Latinos is the preferred term. Both terms will be employed in this chapter.

All Latinos prefer to call themselves according to their nations of origin or that of their ancestors. So some are called Spaniards, others Mexican Americans, Nicaraguans, Cubans, Dominicans, and the like. Many Mexican Americans have adopted the term Chicanos (males) or Chicanas (females). This term originated in the Southwest during the civil rights struggles of the 1960s. Militant Mexican Americans, proud of their heritage, like to be called Chicanos as a way of ending their second-class social status.

There are further terms of special meaning to differentiate Hispanics. Puerto Ricans born in New York City often call themselves Nuyorcians, since they were not born in Puerto Rico. *Tejanos* is sometimes used to describe Texans of Spanish origin. New Mexicans may be called *nuevomexicanos,* to give attention to their origins, whereas some would rather be called Hispanos, since that term suggests a connection with the Spanish conquistadors of the seventeenth century. All these subtle shadings are quite significant to these groups because each has had a different historical experience in the United States.

The history of the Hispanics in America is as bound with America's history as much as any other group. Except for Native Americans, Hispanics have been here as long as any other peo-

ples. Spanish settlements in the United States are older than English-speaking settlements. The Spaniards were the first Europeans to arrive in the New World (as they called it), the first to land on these shores, and the first to settle here. In 1513 Juan Ponce de León landed in what is now Florida and became the first European to land on the mainland of what is now the United States. Many previous Spanish explorers had landed on other portions of the New World.

In 1565, the first permanent European settlement on the United States mainland was established at St. Augustine, Florida. The nation's only walled city has the greater distinction of having been founded by Pedro Mendenez de Avilés of Spain 55 years before the Pilgrims arrived from England and landed at Plymouth Rock (1620), and 42 years prior to the brief-lived British colony at Jamestown, Virginia.

The Spanish explorers, missionaries, and settlers brought cattle, horses, new crops, and trees from Europe to the United States. New industries and businesses were established here. Schools, hospitals, and government institutions were created. Spanish law, culture, and religion were all imported to our shores. It is interesting to note that the first integrated public school in America was established by the Spanish at St. Augustine in 1787, and escaped slaves from British America found haven at the free African American city of Fort Mose in *La Florida.*

Spanish rule over what is now the United States included up to 80 percent of what is now the nation. Spain ruled in Florida from 1513 until 1763 and from 1783 until 1821—a total of 288 years, much longer than the era of British colonization. In New Mexico and Arizona the Spanish rule extended from 1598 until 1821, a period of 223 years. Texas was held by Spain from 1691 to 1821, and California flew the Spanish flag from 1769 to 1821. Mexico governed much of the American Southwest after gaining independence in 1821. In the Louisiana territory, an area that encompasses 13 American states, Spanish rule lasted from 1763 until 1803. In Puerto Rico, Spanish rule extended over 405 years, from 1493 until 1898, and ended with the Spanish-American War. A grand total of 211 different Spanish governors administered territories in America that eventually became portions of the United States.

It is impossible to compress the history of Hispanics in the United States into a few paragraphs. However, a few unfamiliar facts about the greatest American land acquisitions will provide a vivid illustration of the conflicts between America's westward expansion and the hopes and dreams of her Hispanic populations. President James K. Polk (1845–1849) had a vision of America shared by many of his fellow countrymen in the middle of the nineteenth century. Believing that Anglo Americans had a historic destiny to rule the area between the Atlantic and the Pacific oceans, Polk was determined to acquire the lands from Texas to the Pacific coast, territory held by Mexico at the time. At first Polk offered Mexico up to $25 million for the purchase of New Mexico and California. When Mexico refused this offer Polk turned to the use of force. On May 11, 1846, President Polk sent to Congress his war message, based on a military incident provoked by the dispatch of General Zachary Taylor (American president from 1849 to 1850) into territory in Texas disputed with Mexico. This military provocation was opposed at the time by Congressman Abraham Lincoln and questioned by General Ulysses S. Grant, later made famous in the American Civil War.

The little-known United States-Mexican War of 1846 to 1848 was brief but productive, from the American point of view. The North American generals defeated the Mexican commanders at almost every battle, including the capture of Vera Cruz and Mexico City. It was a brutal, bloody, ugly war, with atrocities on all sides. At the time Mexico was in complete disarray, having gained independence from Spain in 1823, only 23 years prior to the War.

New Mexico and California were freed from Mexican rule, but the local populations also fought against the oppressive policies of the American occupation forces. The independence of California was engineered by President Polk through the efforts of John Charles Fremont, a captain of the United States Army, repeating a formula for breaking away from foreign rule previously used in Spanish Florida and Mexican Texas. The native population of California revolted against the American occupation forces, but they were defeated.

The war with Mexico was ended by the 1848 Treaty of Guadelupe Hidalgo. Under its provisions the United States received 530,706 square miles, almost one sixth of the current land mass of the nation, excluding Alaska. The states of New Mexico, Arizona, California, Nevada, Utah, and parts of Colorado and Wyoming were carved out of these lands. About 80,000 Mexican citizens living in the ceded territories became U.S. nationals. Some expansionists in the United States Senate advocated the annexation of all Mexico, having swallowed up half. This annexation was not pursued, but other pieces of Mexico were later purchased in 1853.

John F. Kennedy once lamented, "I have always felt that one of the great inadequacies among Americans is their lack of knowledge of the whole Spanish influence, exploration and development in the sixteenth and seventeenth centuries in the southeast and the southwest of the United States, which is a tremendous story." Spanish culture deeply permeated American life. Our American cowboys may be traced to the Spanish *vacqueros*. The English language was enriched by the words rodeo, ranch, corral, adobe, plaza, tornado, hurricane, alligator, and many others. Salsa spices our lives, as does the music, dance, and cuisine of our Hispanic citizens. Hispanics have fought in all of America's wars, including the American Revolution. Thirty-eight brave Hispanics have worn the Congressional Medal of Honor—the nation's highest decoration for valor. Three U.S. Latinos have won the Nobel Prize in medicine, physics, and chemistry.

In 1983 President Ronald Reagan issued a proclamation recognizing the contributions of Hispanic Americans to the American way of life. He noted that "Hispanic Americans have played an important role in the development of our rich cultural heritage and every state has benefitted from their influence." Across the United States there are houses, ranches, plazas, haciendas, missions, and churches that stand as silent and graceful reminders of the rich Latino heritage. The names of many of America's cities, states, and towns bear Hispanic imprints. Florida, Texas, Colorado, Arizona, California, Nevada, Montana, and Oregon are all names derived from Spanish. The long list of Spanish-named cities includes Albuquerque, San Francisco, Los Angeles, Santa Fe, San Diego, and Galveston. The Pacific Ocean, the Gulf of Mexico, the Grand Canyon, Puerto Rico, and the Virgin Islands were originally named (or still are) in Spanish.

Unfortunately, few non-Hispanics are fully aware of the depth of Hispanic culture and history in the United States. Our schools often emphasize the British origins of the nation and neglect the contributions of Hispanics and other groups. The westward migration of English colonists is a familiar story, but the northward movement of people from the Caribbean, Mexico, and South and Central America, as well as from portions of Spanish America, has not been as well described or understood. These northward migration streams still continue, to some extent, but they are very old.

The establishment of the first 13 American colonies is an important story, but it largely tells about the British in North America. At the same time there were two Spanish colonies of greater age in East Florida and West Florida. Hispanics fought and lost the struggle for supremacy in North America. Spain was displaced in North America first by the British and later by the United States. The neglect of the Spanish past of America is partly traceable to the likelihood that the winner of wars writes history from the victor's point of view.

England had been at war with Spain for hundreds of years before American independence. The United States went to war with Spain four times during the nineteenth century. In 1817, General Andrew Jackson invaded Spanish Florida without a declaration of war and captured Pensacola, the capital of West Florida. The United States forced Spain out of Florida entirely in 1821. Later, in 1835, Anglo Americans led a revolt in Texas against Mexican rule there, leading to the loss of one of Mexico's largest states when the United States annexed Texas in 1845. The war against Mexico (1846–48) stripped away more Mexican lands, when defeat led to the surrender of one half of Mexico. For $15 million Mexico relinquished control over vast territories in the Treaty of Guadeloupe Hidalgo. Finally, the United States declared war against Spain in 1898. The defeat of Spain brought Puerto Rico, Guam, and the Philippines under the American flag.

The victors in the various wars against Spain and Mexico portrayed their opponents as violent and cruel. The Spanish were accused of abuse and atrocities against indigenous peoples. Tales of Spanish brutality, murder, and slavery abounded. Stories of Spanish atrocity stoked the fires of American public opinion just prior to the Spanish-American War. Newspapers sometimes invented stories of cruelty by the Spanish against Cuban rebels. Doubtless, the Spanish had earned their reputation for cruelty, but no more so than the British or other colonial powers. All European nations and the Americans themselves did maltreat, kill, and victimize Native Americans. In addition, the Spanish were Catholic, which seemed to be held against them by predominantly Protestant America. The historians of early America were usually Protestant, and they supported the tales of Spanish cruelty.

As late as 1783, when the British finally recognized the independence of the United States by the terms of the Treaty of Paris, the Spanish territories in what is now the United States were twice as large as those of the newly freed Americans. Spain was embroiled in wars and struggles with most of the other nations of Europe. Americans tried long and hard to force the Spanish out of the western and southern lands. American expansionists sometimes also had ambitions to seize parts of Central America, Mexico, and Cuba. Spain and later Mexico were compelled to surrender vast portions of their lands, but the cultural and social influences that they had implanted remained. The most important of these Spanish factors was the Hispanic, or Latino, peoples. The formation of the boundaries of the American nation came at a cost to the governments of Spain and Mexico.

Some Hispanic Firsts in the United States

- The oldest European city in the United States was San Miguel de Gualdape, founded and settled by Spain on the coast of present Georgia in 1526.

- The oldest permanent European city in the United States was San Augustín (St. Augustine), founded by Spain in 1565. The oldest houses, the oldest hospital, and the oldest school were also in this oldest city.

- The oldest state capital in the United States was Santa Fe, founded by the governor of New Mexico, Pedro de Peralta, in 1610; the oldest state building is the Palacio de Gobernadores (Palace of the Governors) erected in Santa Fe.

- The oldest and largest masonry fort in continental United States is the Castillo de San Marcos, whose construction began in 1672.

- The oldest free African settlement in the United States was Gracia Real de Santa Teresa de Mosé, known as Fort Mosé, which was founded in 1738, two miles north of San Agustín.

- The oldest integrated public school in the United States was the Spanish public school of San Agustín founded in 1787.

- The oldest mission, founded by Franciscan Father Junípero Serra, was the mission in San Diego established in 1769.

- The oldest fort in Alaska was founded on Nootka by Spaniards in 1790.

Spanish Colonial Firsts in the United States

- The first clash between Indians and Europeans in what is today a U.S. territory took place on November 14, 1493, on the island of St. Croix. It was here that Columbus's soldiers engaged in combat with Carib Indians. It was also the beginning of the Hispanic presence in the United States.

- With Juan Ponce de León's landfall in Florida in 1513, the Hispanic presence begins on the United States mainland.

- Juan Garrido was the first black Conquistador, known as *El Conquistador Negro*. He served for over 30 years in the Spanish army, fighting alongside Juan Ponce de León in Puerto Rico and Florida and Hernán Cortés in Mexico. In 1538, he was given an estate in Mexico for his valuable services to Spain.

- Alonso Álvarez de Pineda was the first European to see the mouth of the Mississippi River and the first to explore the entire Gulf Coast of Florida, Louisiana, Alabama, Mississippi, and Texas in 1519.

- The first book published about the United States was Álvar Núñez Cabeza de Vaca's *La Relación (The Story)* published in 1542 in Zamora, Spain.

- The first exploration to ten southern states was that of Hernando de Soto and his army from 1539 to 1542. It was the first time that Cuban-born soldiers stepped on U.S. soil and the first time that a European land expedition crossed the Mississippi River. Later, the Spaniards sailed down the river for the first time to the Gulf of Mexico with Luis Moscoso, who assumed command after de Soto's death.

- The first major exploration to various present Southwestern states was that of Francisco Vázquez de Coronado, from 1540 to 1542. One of his lieutenants, García López de Cárdenas, was the first European to see the Grand Canyon in present-day Arizona.

- The first European baby to be born in present United States was Martín Argüelles, who was born shortly after the founding of St. Augustine in 1565.

- The first European city to be put to torch was San Agustín, which was burned by Sir Francis Drake in 1586.

- The first settler and governor of New Mexico was Juan de Oñate, who founded San Gabriel in 1598.

- Gaspar Pérez de Villagrá wrote the first epic poem in the New World, called *Historia de la Nuevo México*, in 1610.

- The first book published in an Indian language in the United States was Father Francisco Pareja's *Grammar and Pronunciation in Timucuan and Castilian Languages* in 1614. The Franciscan missionaries were the first to implement bilingual education in the United States while teaching the Indians in their Florida missions.

- The first successful Indian revolt in North America was that of the Pueblo Indians in New Mexico in 1680. They were conquered by Spaniards 12 years later. The Pueblo Indians were led by Popé, an Indian medicine man.

- The founder of the chain of missions in Arizona was Jesuit priest Eusebio Francisco Kino, who arrived in 1687.

- The first Spanish governor of Texas was Domingo Terán de los Ríos, who was appointed in 1691.

- The first Cuban-born governor of Florida was Laureano Torres de Ayala, named in 1693. During his tenure Torres completed the construction of the Castillo de San Marcos. Three other Havana-born governors served in

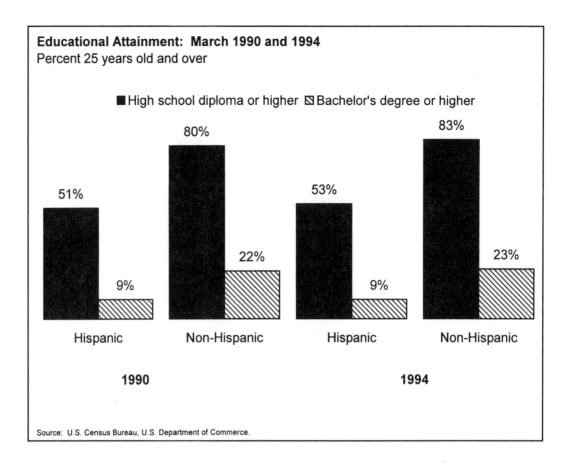

Educational Attainment: March 1990 and 1994
Percent 25 years old and over

■ High school diploma or higher ☒ Bachelor's degree or higher

1990

- Hispanic: 51% / 9%
- Non-Hispanic: 80% / 22%

1994

- Hispanic: 53% / 9%
- Non-Hispanic: 83% / 23%

Source: U.S. Census Bureau, U.S. Department of Commerce.

Florida, and another Havana-born governor served in Louisiana.

- The first successful colonial revolt against a European power was that of the French in Louisiana, who in 1768 refused to accept Spanish rule in the territory. Ten months later, the Spaniards put down the revolt and five French leaders were executed.

- For the first time two land expeditions traveled from Arizona to California in 1774 and 1776, led by Juan Bautista de Anza. On the second one, Anza founded the *presidio* (fort) of San Francisco.

- Two friars, Silvestre Vélez de Escalante and Francisco Atanasio Domínguez, and mapmaker Bernardo Miera were the first Europeans to explore the present state of Utah in 1776.

- The first Spanish diplomatic agent to the 13 colonies was Havana businessman Juan de Miralles, who arrived in Philadelphia in 1778.

- The first time Hispanic soldiers fought for the United States was during the American Revolution; these soldiers were led by General Bernardo de Gálvez from 1779 to 1781.

- The first scientific exploration to Alaska was that conducted by Alejandro Malaspina in 1790.

Mexican American Presence in Post-War United States

Mexican Americans fought bravely during World War II in order to make the world "safer for democracy" as President Franklin D. Roosevelt asked. They mixed with different groups and traveled all over the world. When Mexican Americans returned home, they were unwilling to accept second-class status, segregation, and discrimination. Exclusion of Mexican Americans—from public facilities, such as restaurants, movies, barbershops, swimming pools, and from certain public schools, trade union, and juries—as well as denial of voting rights—was common throughout the Southwest and Midwest during that time.

In December 1945, a regional conference on education was held at the University of Texas in Austin. This conference was organized by Dr. George Sánchez from the University of Texas and Dr. A. L. Campa from the University of New Mexico. The participants at the conference strongly denounced segregation. Veterans of Mexican descent pressured officials at Tempe, Arizona, to accept Mexicans at the city's swimming pool. Mexican Americans began to complain about discrimination and segregation throughout the Southwest and the Midwest.

In 1948, a funeral home in Three Rivers, Texas, refused to conduct reburial services for soldier Félix Longoria. The case drew national attention and in time Longoria was buried with full military honors in Arlington Cemetery in Virginia across from Washington, D.C. At that time, some cemeteries in the Southwest and the South refused to bury Mexicans and African Americans. The Longoria case was a sad reminder that racism and discrimination still impeded the full participation of Mexican Americans in U.S. society. The Mexican American community throughout the United States was outraged over the Longoria incident.

Soon after, a group of Mexican American veterans met at Corpus Christi, Texas, to complain about racism against Latino veterans and the lack of adequate services provided to them by the Veterans Administration Hospital of that city. As a result of this meeting, an organization was formed, the American GI Forum, under the leadership of Dr. Héctor Pérez García. Dr. García had served with distinction as a combat surgeon during World War II. By the end of 1949 over 100 Forum chapters had been organized.

The Forum's initial goal was to inform Mexican Americans and other Latino veterans about their rights under the GI Bill. The organization then expanded its goals to promote political and social reforms, to fight discrimination by filing lawsuits, and to increase political awareness and participation by conducting voter-registration campaigns. A few years later, the organization had over 150 councils in the Southwest, particularly in Texas. During the 1990s the American GI Forum had a membership of more than 20,000 in 30 states, and it remains one of the most important Mexican American organizations today.

The GI Forum was one of many Mexican American organizations founded after World War II in the United States to combat the racism, segregation, and discrimination that kept Latinos in subjugation and oppressed. League of United Latin American Citizens (LULAC), which was founded in 1929, became very active in the post-

war years. LULAC stressed education and English proficiency as a way of upward mobility and fought for equal education opportunities, cultural pluralism, ethnic tolerance, and political, social, and economic inclusion in U.S. society.

LULAC filed a lawsuit against four school districts in Orange County, California, alleging de facto segregation of Mexican American students in 1945. This lawsuit, *Méndez* v. *Westminster School District,* was won by LULAC. Three years later, LULAC initiated another lawsuit, *Delgado* v. *Bastrop Independent School District,* which was also successful. The famous 1954 Supreme Court *Brown* decision that forbade segregation of African Americans did not include Latinos. It was not until 1970 that a federal court ruled that "Mexican Americans constitute an identifiable ethnic minority with a pattern of discrimination . . ."

LULAC expanded from a regional to a national organization with 15,000 members and 200 councils. In 1979, as it celebrated its 50th anniversary, the organization expanded even more by including Puerto Ricans and Cuban Americans. Today, it has more than 100,000 members and continues to fight for civil liberties and for an end to racism and discrimination against Latinos.

In the Greater Chicago area, the Mexican Civic Committee and the Spanish-Speaking People's Council were organized in the 1940s. The latter organization invited Latinos from all groups to join.

Liberals and radicals founded a political organization, Asociación Nacional México-Americana (ANMA), in 1949 under the leadership of Alfredo Montoya. This organization was involved in the 1950 to 1952 copper miners strike at Bayard, New Mexico. ANMA was labeled by the Federal Bureau of Investigation (FBI) as a Communist-front organization and, as result, it lost community support. At one point ANMA had 30 chapters and 4,000 members.

The Civic Unity League was founded by Ignacio López, editor of the Southern California weekly newspaper *El Espectador,* in 1947. Other Unity Leagues were founded to protest incidents of racism and discrimination against Latinos. These organizations were successful in several lawsuits regarding segregation and in the election of Mexican Americans to political offices in the 1940s and 1950s.

Edward Roybal helped found the Mexican American Political Association (MAPA), which supported the election of Mexican American candidates to political office. With MAPA's assistance, he was elected to the U.S. House of Representatives in 1962.

The Community Service Organization (CSO) was started to support the election of Edward Roybal to the Los Angeles City Council in 1947. This organization specialized in organizing the community following the ideas of social activist Saul Alinsky. One of the CSO leaders was Fred Ross Sr., who, with the support of the CSO membership, helped elect Roybal. The CSO fought against police brutality and other civil rights violations. It expanded through California and Arizona. During the 1960s the CSO had 22 chapters and over 50,000 members. Today, the organization has declined although it remains, basically operating in California.

In 1951, leaders of many middle-class Mexican American organizations met at El Paso, Texas, to found the American Council of Spanish-Speaking People. Professor George I. Sánchez was named executive director of the new organization, which had representatives from the Alianza Hispano-Americana (founded in 1894), G.I. Forum, LULAC, and CSO. Tibo J. Chávez, lieutenant governor of New Mexico, was elected president. The American Council of Spanish-Speaking People received funding from foundations to promote civil rights, but it declined when continued funding failed to arrive.

In 1959, Edward Roybal, Eduardo Quevedo, and Bert Corona founded the Mexican American Political Association (MAPA) in Fresno, California. MAPA's goal was to support Mexican Ameri-

can candidates to be elected to political office. In the 1960s a group of tejano leaders organized the Texas MAPA with a similar goal.

With MAPA's assistance Edward Roybal was elected to the U.S. House of Representatives in 1962. Roybal represented his California district until 1993 when at the age of 77 he retired. His daughter, Lucille Roybal-Allard, was elected to California's newly created thirty-third Congressional District. MAPA declined in the 1970s. In 1983, Fernando Chávez, son of César Chávez, was named president of MAPA. Today, it remains basically a California organization.

During the presidential elections of 1960 many Mexican Americans organized Viva Kennedy Clubs throughout the Southwest to support the election of the Democratic Party candidate. After Kennedy's election to president, an effort was made to organize various organizations and create a strong Latino national organization. Delegates from the CSO, LULAC, Viva Kennedy Clubs, and both the California and Texas MAPA met in Phoenix, Arizona, and created the Political Association of Spanish-Speaking Organizations (PASSO). Dr. Héctor García, founder of the American GI Forum, was elected as PASSO's first president. The organization eventually failed and the California MAPA and the CSO left PASSO.

In Phoenix another organization was founded in the 1960s, the American Coordinating Council of Political Education (ACCPE). The new organization had some success in electing Mexican American politicians to school boards and city councils. ACCPE had at its peak 2,500 members in 10 chapters throughout Arizona.

Civil Rights Leaders

The struggle for civil rights in the United States in the 1960s to end discrimination against and segregation of African Americans had a great impact in the Southwest. Four new Chicano leaders emerged to lead the fight for equality in the Southwest: César Chávez, Rodolfo "Corky" González, Reies López Tijerina, and José Ángel Gutiérrez.

César Chávez

César Chávez was the first Chicano leader to attract national and international attention. He has been recognized as a great leader by all Mexican Americans, whether liberal or conservative.

As a child, César Chávez was a migrant farm worker. He grew to feel that his most important mission in life was to organize migrant farm workers. Toward this end, he started the National Farm Workers Association (NFWA), which would grow to become the United Farm Workers, a union with 10,000 members.

Chávez was born in Yuma, Arizona, in 1927, and as a child he worked as a migrant farm worker. His father and Chávez himself had been members of the National Farm Labor Union. In the 1940s, he moved to San Jose, California, and eventually began working for Fred Ross in the Community Service Organization (CSO). Chávez was promoted to the position of general director of the national CSO, but in 1962, he resigned.

Chávez became convinced that his most important mission in life was to organize migrant farm workers, the majority of whom were Mexican Americans. He moved to Delano, California, and began to organize a union that he called National Farm Workers Association (NFWA). Assisted by able union organizers such as Dolores Huerta, Gil Padilla, Fred Ross, and Jim Drake, the

NFWA grew to approximately 1,700 members by 1965. In September of that year, the NFWA joined with 600 Filipinos of the AWOC union led by Larry Itliong in a strike against the grape growers of the San Joaquin Valley.

Chávez charismatic personality turned the *huelga*, or strike, into a national movement known as *La Causa*, or the farm workers' movement. In 1966, Chávez led a 250-mile march from Delano to California's capital of Sacramento to publicize the strike. He attracted national attention by using nonviolent tactics such as boycotting grapes and conducting a 25-day fast. Chávez enlisted support for the Delano Grape Strike from student activists, different civil rights groups, other labor unions, state and national political leaders, and the Catholic Bishops' Committee for the Spanish-

The majority of American migrant farm workers are Mexican American.

Speaking. He used as a symbol the Virgin of Guadalupe. In 1966, Schenley Corporation signed a contract with Chávez's union. Soon after, Almaden, Gallo, and other grape growers signed contracts. However, Di Giorgio Corporation, one of the largest grape growers in the central valley, refused to cave in. Chávez had to merge his NFWA with the Filipino union AWOC. The new union was now called United Farm Workers Organizing Committee (UFWOC). Chávez was able to defeat a challenge by the Teamsters union to represent farm workers in a close vote and, soon after, Di Giorgio and UFWOC signed a contract.

In 1973, most grape growers did not renew contracts with Chávez's union and instead signed up with the rival Teamsters union. However, two years later, the now named United Farm Workers

(UFW; an AFL-CIO affiliate), of Chávez won back most of the contracts. Chávez tried with mixed success to expand his union in Texas and Florida. He led an unsuccessful march in June of 1966 from Río Grande City to Austin, the capital of Texas. The absence of liberal support, lack of organization, the Texas Rangers, the local courts, the right-to-work laws, the abundant supply of cheap undocumented farm labor from Mexico, and internal bickering resulted in an unsuccessful drive to expand his union outside California.

Chávez also led a strike against the lettuce growers in California's Salinas Valley. However, he was unsuccessful and in 1978 the UFW called off the lettuce and grape boycotts. During the 1970s and the 1980s the UFW declined in strength. Chávez began a third grape boycott in

The horrible conditions of migrant housing is a testament to the importance of housing and civil rights advocacy, such as that practiced by Corky Gonzales and Reies López Tijerina.

1984 to complain the excessive use of pesticides by growers. Four years later, he began a 36-day fast to call attention to the four-year-old grape boycott. However, unlike his previous fast, this tactic did not meet with success. During the 1990s the UFW membership was approximately 10,000, and the union had about 100 contracts with vegetables, citrus, and other agriculture product growers. The Chávez's UFW decline was due to the continuous oversupply of undocumented workers, mechanization and automation, changing political and social climate, and the urban setting of the vast majority of Mexican Americans in the United States. Chávez died on April 23, 1993.

César Chávez became a hero and a symbol of social justice and the most important Mexican American civil rights leader recognized both in the United States and abroad.

Rodolfo "Corky" Gonzales

Rodolfo "Corky" Gonzales was born in Denver, Colorado, in 1928. His parents were migrant sugar beet farm workers. He was a professional boxer in the featherweight class from 1947 to 1955. Four years later, he opened an automobile insurance agency and a bail bond business. Gonzalez was very active in the community and in 1963 he founded Los Voluntarios, or the Volunteers. His organization complained about police brutality in Denver.

In 1965, Gonzales was appointed director of the youth programs of the War on Poverty in Denver. A year later, he was fired for participating in the Equal Employment Opportunity Commission (EEOC) walkout in Albuquerque, New Mexico. Gonzalez and other activists complained about the lack of Hispanic representation in that agency. The following year, Gonzales founded the Crusade for Justice, a community-based organization. Later, this organization founded a school, a bookstore, and a social center. He published a newspaper called *El Gallo: La Voz de la Justicia (the Rooster: the Voice of Justice)*.

Gonzales advocated Chicano *nacionalismo* (nationalism), self-determination, ethnic pride, identity, and economic and political autonomy. He also fought against police brutality and in favor of civil rights. Gonzales wrote an epic poem called *I Am Joaquín*. The impact of this poem was enormous; it became the most important work of literature for the *movimiento* in the 1960s. Later, Luis Valdez made this poem into a movie.

Gonzales was one of the many Chicano leaders who boycotted President Lyndon B. Johnson's White House Conference on the Mexican American in October 1967, at El Paso, Texas. The following year, Gonzales participated in the Poor People's March on Washington, D.C., together with Reies López Tijerina. The former boxer issued a document entitled *Demandas de La Raza*, in which he demanded better education, housing, and employment as well as civil rights and land reforms.

In March 1969 in Denver, Gonzales organized the first Chicano Youth Liberation Conference, which was attended by 1,500 people. He developed what he called the *Plan Espiritual de Aztlán* (the Spiritual Plan of Aztlán). The plan had a strong cultural nationalism ideology, breaking with assimilationist and acculturationist attitudes of other middle-class groups such as the GI Forum and LULAC.

Aztec Aztlán refers to the mythical homeland of the Aztec Indians, who lived somewhere in the U.S. Southwest before moving into the central valley of Mexico and founding the city of Tenochtitlán. By using knowledge of Aztlán and the great Indian cultures of Mexico, such as the Aztecs and the Mayas, Gonzales hoped to instill pride among Chicanos in their own origin and culture. During the second annual conference in 1970, Gonzales advocated setting up a separate Chicano political party, which he eventually called La Raza Unida Party (LRUP), in Colorado. That same year, this party ran candidates for state and local offices in Colorado.

In 1972, La Raza Unida Party had its first national convention in El Paso, Texas. José Ángel Gutiérrez, founder of the Texas La Raza Unida Party, and Gonzales fought for control of the party. Gonzales' ideas were defeated at this conference. During the 1970s Gonzales lost power at the national level since the nation, together with many Mexican Americans, became more conservative and rejected the extreme positions of separation advocated by Gonzales. In October 1987, Gonzales was seriously injured in an automobile accident. Today, Gonzales is no longer a national leader, but his contributions to the struggle for equal rights are recognized by most Mexican Americans.

Reies López Tijerina

Reies López Tijerina, known as *El Tigre*, or the Tiger, was a charismatic leader who was born in the fields near Fall City, Texas, in 1926. At the age of 17, he became a preacher of the Assembly of God, a fundamentalist Protestant religious group. Ten years later he quit preaching.

Tijerina moved to Arizona and tried to establish a utopian community, Valle de la Paz (Valley of the Peace), for two years. In 1960 he moved to New Mexico. Tijerina had been studying the land-grant issue and the property rights guaranteed to Hispanics under the Treaty of Guadalupe Hidalgo for some time. He became convinced that most of the problems faced by Hispanics in New Mexico were due to the loss of their lands and the violation of the treaty. The Treaty of Guadalupe Hidalgo guaranteed both individual and communal property rights given to *nuevomexicanos* under Spain and Mexico. Communal property was given to a village or a town *ejido* and could not be sold since the property belonged to all the people in that community. In Mexico *ejido* was a system of communal land ownership by the peasantry. The system was destroyed by the regime of Porfirio Díaz (1830–1915) but was restored by the Mexican Constitution of 1917. Recovering the "stolen" land became Tijerina's new mission in life.

In 1963, Tijerina founded the Alianza Federal de Mercedes, or Federal Alliance of Grants, which later was called Alianza Federal de Pueblos Libres, or Federal Alliance of Free Towns. Tijerina claimed that his organization had 20,000 members.

Tijerina initiated a march on Santa Fe, New Mexico's capital, to draw attention to his perceived injustice of the *nuevomexicanos'* loss of land in the state. On October 15, 1966, Tijerina and 350 Alianza members occupied the Echo Amphitheater campgrounds of the Kit Carson National Forest. Tijerina claimed that this land did not belong to the federal government but to the Pueblo de San Joaquín de Chama under the communal, or *ejido*, rights. Within a week, state police, sheriff's deputies, and park rangers came in. The *aliancistas*—Alianza members—captured two rangers and "tried" and "sentenced" them for trespassing. Later, the *aliancistas* suspended the "sentence."

In June 1967, while Tijerina awaited trial for the Echo Amphitheater incident, *aliancistas* came to the courthouse of the small town of Tierra Amarilla in New Mexico to make a citizen's arrest of the local district attorney. The confrontation turned violent and gunfire was exchanged between local officials and *aliancistas*. Tijerina was arrested again. While awaiting trial, Tijerina visited colleges and universities, giving incendiary and provocative speeches. He also participated in the 1968 Poor People's March to Washington, D.C. Upon arrival in the nation's capital, he tried unsuccessfully to meet with Secretary of State Dean Rusk to discuss the lack of enforcement of the Treaty of Guadalupe Hidalgo.

Tijerina attempted to make other citizen's arrests of prominent officials, such as Supreme Court nominee Warren Burger and New Mexico governor David Cargo. Finally, Tijerina was sentenced to two years in federal prison in January 1970. Tijerina was paroled in July 1971 under the condition that he could not be an officer of the Alianza during the following five years. The Alianza Federal de Pueblos Libres declined during Tijerina's imprisonment and parole. The Alianza had relied on Tijerina's charismatic leadership and his absence hurt the organization. Tijerina faded away as a national leader. During the festivities associated with the twentieth anniversary of the "takeover" of the Tierra Amarilla Courthouse in 1987, there were less than 200 people in attendance. The national media failed to report the celebration.

Tijerina nevertheless publicized the issue of the land-grant and the injustices perpetuated against Mexican Americans regarding the loss of their lands. He also called attention to the sham of the Treaty of Guadalupe Hidalgo and the poverty of Mexican Americans.

José Ángel Gutiérrez

José Ángel Gutiérrez came to national attention at the age of 22. He was born in Texas of an immigrant family from Mexico. His father, a physician, had settled in Crystal City, Texas. Together with other students, Gutiérrez founded the Mexican American Youth Organization (MAYO) at Texas A & I University in Kingsville three years before its official beginning.

MAYO students denounced discrimination in college admissions, segregation in dorms, lack of Latino employees, and a university curriculum that ignored Latinos. MAYO also concentrated in gaining political power. The organization was formally founded at St. Mary's College in San Antonio and soon expanded to colleges and universities as well as high schools. MAYO was not popular with other middle-class Mexican American organizations and Mexican American politicians, such as Congressman Henry González of San Antonio, who disliked the student activists fiery rhetoric. Gutiérrez made the statement "Kill the gringo" at a press conference and used words such as "stampede over him [the gringo]" that

increased anxiety among the Anglo American population.

In 1969, following a school crisis in his hometown of Crystal City that brought about a high school walkout, Gutiérrez decided to organize Mexican Americans politically into La Raza Unida Party (LRUP). In April 1970, Gutiérrez and two other Chicanos were elected to the Crystal City School Board and other LRUP candidates were elected to the city council in Crystal City and other nearby cities as well as school boards. LRUP expanded to Colorado and California.

At the LRUP convention in 1972, Gutiérrez's position of working within the existing two-party system was accepted. Corky Gonzales favored to run a national third party, but his position was not supported by the majority of the participants at the convention. Several LRUP candidates had local success in the next four years. However, as the Democrats and Republicans nominated Mexican Americans as candidates for political offices, the LRUP lost strength and faded away, until finally, internal conflicts and the nation's conservative trend ended the party. Gutiérrez was elected judge in Zavala County, Texas, in 1974, but resigned seven years later and became a college teacher.

These four Mexican American leaders were very important in dramatizing the social, economic, and political injustices as well as racism, discrimination, and segregation endured by Mexican Americans and other Latinos in the 1960s. Each leader concentrated in specific aspects of the Mexican American community, such as the land-grant issue, the plight of the migrant farm workers, ethnic and cultural pride, political power, and so forth. Because of their efforts, the larger American society became aware of and found some solutions to the problems faced by Latinos in U.S. society.

Student Activism

Civil rights leaders—like Corky Gonzales in Denver and activist high school teacher Sal Castro in Los Angeles—as well as Chicano student militants throughout the Southwest engaged in public demonstrations and confrontation tactics across the Southwest during the 1960s. This was the time when students of all backgrounds were demonstrating against the Vietnam War and other perceived injustices in American society throughout the United States.

Chicano students were concerned about poor educational facilities, the Eurocentric curriculum and the quality of teaching, and the lack of Latino teachers and administrators in secondary schools, colleges, and universities. At the high school level, student activists used the tactic called "blowouts" or walkouts or strikes to advance their demands for bilingual and multicultural education, a more relevant curriculum, and more Latino teachers, counselors, and school administrators. At colleges and universities different tactics were used: sit-ins in administrative offices, mass protest demonstrations, and even vandalism against university property. Some faculty members supported the students' demands for incorporating Latino history and culture in the college curriculum, increasing the numbers of Chicano students admitted to universities, and increasing the numbers of Chicano faculty members in the universities.

In the spring of 1968 approximately 10,000 Mexican American students walked out of five Los Angeles high schools. School authorities responded by calling the police, who promptly made mass arrests. Activists in the community complained about police brutality. Chicano students in high schools, colleges, and universities throughout the Southwest also conducted mass protests.

In the 1960s, several students organizations were founded in California. In 1966, the Mexican American Student Association (MASA) was founded at East Los Angeles Community College. That same year, Chicano students founded the United Mexican American Students (UMAS) at Loyola University in Los Angeles. The UMAS, in particular, provided much of the leadership for the 1968 Los Angeles student walkouts.

In Texas, the Mexican American Youth Organization (MAYO), with chapters in many high schools, colleges, and universities, was also very active. In New Mexico, students founded the Chicano Associated Students Organization (CASO), which was influential in adding multicultural courses to the curriculum and getting Dr. Frank Angel appointed to a state university in New Mexico. Dr. Angel became the first Mexican American president of a university in the nation.

An effort was made to bring together all the college and university student groups under one organization. In 1969, a conference was held at the University of California at Santa Barbara and

the Movimiento Estudiantil Chicano de Aztlán (MEChA) was founded. During this period both student and adult activists rejected the name "Mexican American," preferring the use of the term "Chicano."

Not all Mexican American leaders and organizations welcomed the student activism. Political leaders like U.S. representatives Henry González and Eligio "Kika" de la Garza attacked the Chicano militant students as un-American and accused them of engaging in reverse discrimination.

Another militant organization founded during this time was the Brown Berets, which included mostly Chicano high school students as members. The Brown Berets were organized in a paramilitary fashion and stated that their purpose was defending students and the community from police brutality and oppression.

In 1969, the Brown Berets, MEChA, and other organizations formed the National Chicano Moratorium Committee to protest the high percentage of Chicano casualties in the Vietnam War. In August 1970, a national moratorium march was called in Los Angeles to protest against the Vietnam War. The march brought together between 20,000 and 30,000 participants from the nation. Corky Gonzalez had been invited as one of the speakers. At Laguna Park, participants were attacked by 1,200 police officers. In the turmoil 3 people were killed and 400 were arrested, including Corky Gonzales. Rubén Salazar, a popular Los Angeles television reporter, was killed at a bar by high-velocity tear gas projectile fired by a reckless police officer.

By the end of the 1960s, the Chicano movement had made an impact in the Southwest. As a result of student protests and demonstrations, reforms were made in public schools and institutions of higher learning. Courses in ethnic studies were added to the curriculum; more Latinos teachers, counselors, and administrators were hired; facilities were upgraded. In a number of colleges and universities, Chicano studies were offered as a major or a minor field of study. In some colleges Chicano studies were offered as a graduate program. By emphasizing pride in culture and history, the civil rights movement developed a generation of Latino scholars and community-minded professionals. In spite of the progress achieved, Mexican Americans today still lag behind Anglos in educa-

In 1969, the Brown Berets, MEChA, and other organizations formed the National Chicano Moratorium Committee to protest the high percentage of Chicano casualties in the Vietnam War.

tional achievement and have an extraordinarily high dropout rate. There are still many Mexican American students attending inferior schools in barrios across the United States.

Mexican American Organizations Today

Three powerful Mexican American organizations exist today: the National Council of La Raza (NCLR), the Southwest Voter Registration Education Project, and the Mexican American Legal Defense and Education Fund (MALDEF). The NCLR began under the name of Southwest Council of La Raza as a coalition of about 25 Chicano groups in 1968 in Phoenix, Arizona. The organization was supported with a Ford Foundation grant. A year later, under the strong leadership of Raúl Yzaguirre, it changed its name to the National Council of La Raza and expanded its program across the nation. This organization today has ties with more than 100 Latino organizations, runs a variety of programs, and publishes many reports and books emphasizing Hispanic pride, immigrations issues, and problems faced by the Hispanic community in the United States. During the Quincentennial Raúl Yzaguirre organized the National Hispanic Quincentennial Commission and published 10,000 copies of a book called *Hispanic Presence in the United States*. The National Council of La Raza organizes a well-attended annual conference in mid-July.

The Southwest Voter Registration Education Project was founded at San Antonio, Texas, in 1974. Its major goal is Latino voter registration and increased participation during elections. It works with many community groups to encourage Latino citizens in the Southwest to take an active part in political campaigns and elections. This organization has played a very important part in electing Mexican Americans to public office, as thousands of Latinos have registered to vote.

The Mexican American Legal Defense and Education Fund (MALDEF) began with a $2.2 million grant from the Ford Foundation in 1968. MALDEF, under the presidency of Vilma Martínez, a prominent Mexican American lawyer and civil rights leader, has encouraged more Latinos to enter the legal profession and fought to protect the rights of Mexican Americans by filing many lawsuits. In particular, MALDEF fought segregation by filing lawsuits against various Texas school boards. Martínez was succeeded by Joaquín Ávila in the early 1980s, and he was followed by Antonia Hernández. In the 1980s, MALDEF won a lawsuit to end at-large elections, which significantly boosted the election of minority politicians to public office. Today, MALDEF fights discrimination and abuse of immigrants.

Mexican Americans in the Armed Forces

Mexican Americans have fought in the defense of liberty in all U.S. wars from the Ameri-

Henry Barbosa Gonzalez (1916–)

Henry Gonzalez was born in 1916 in San Antonio, Texas. His father was a descendant of early Spanish settlers and a former mayor of Mapimi in the Mexican state of Durango. However, Gonzalez suffered a childhood of poverty and discrimination. He was barred from restaurants and swimming pools by the racist policies in place in Texas. Eventually, he became a leader in the American Congress, one of the most powerful members of the Democratic Party, and one of the most outspoken proponents of minority rights.

Gonzalez earned an engineering degree at the University of Texas, and in 1943 obtained a law degree from St. Mary's University School of Law. Instead of practicing law he entered into business before beginning his political career in 1950.

In 1953 he was elected to the San Antonio City Council, where he sponsored an ordinance that put an end to the city's policies of segregation in recreational facilities.

In 1956 Gonzalez was elected to his first four-year term in the Texas Senate, becoming the first citizen of Mexican descent in 110 years to be seated in that body. As a senator Gonzalez was an outspoken advocate of equal rights for all minorities. He also fought against and filibustered several segregation measures favored by prominent politicians in the state.

In November 1961, Gonzalez won a special election to fill a seat in the United States House of Representatives, and he has held that seat ever since, being reelected in the fall of 1996. Henry Gonzalez has introduced or sponsored legislation on Puerto Rican rights and the Youth Conservation Corps, among many other progressive measures. In 1981 Gonzalez became chairman of the powerful House Banking Committee. From that post he fought the Reagan administration's efforts to cut back federal housing programs. In 1990, under the Bush administration, Gonzalez succeeded in helping the Affordable Housing Act to be enacted.

Since his early days in Congress Henry Gonzalez has been a champion of the rights of various disadvantaged groups. He has fought for better housing, farm worker benefits, and adult basic education, among other causes. He has tried to improve the rights of religious groups and has sought to protect gays and Lesbians against discrimination. He assisted in strengthening the Violence Against Women Act. Although a member of the minority party in the House of Representatives during President Clinton's second term, Gonzalez still fought for individual rights and continued to display an energy that belied his years.

---

can Revolution to the latest conflicts. Many have received the highest award bestowed by the nation—the Congressional Medal of Honor. Richard E. Cavazos became the first Hispanic four-star general in the army. He was Army Attaché at the U.S. Embassy in Mexico and retired in 1984. Carmelita Schmmenti, a nurse, was promoted to the rank of brigadier general in the 1990s. There were many other Mexican Americans promoted to the rank of general in the armed forces in the 1990s.

Mexican Americans in Politics and Government

Three Mexican Americans have served in the United Senate. The first was Octaviano A. Larrazolo, who was born in Mexico and served as governor of New Mexico from 1919 to 1921. He served briefly in the U.S. Senate in 1928. The second was Dennis Chávez, who became the first U.S.-born Hispanic elected to the U.S. Senate. After serving in the New Mexican Legislature, Chávez was elected to the U.S. House of Representatives in 1930. Four years later, he was appointed to the U.S. Senate, and he served in that office until his death in 1982. Joseph M. Montoya became the third Hispanic U.S. Senator. After serving as a state representative and state senator in the New Mexican Legislature, he was elected lieutenant governor of New Mexico. In 1957, he was elected to the U.S. Congress, where he served four terms. In 1964, Montoya was elected to the U.S. Senate and reelected in 1970. Montoya was defeated for reelection in 1976.

Many Mexican Americans have served in the U.S. Congress over the years. Currently, there are many Mexican Americans serving in the U.S. House of Representatives. They are Eligio "Kika" de la Garza, Henry González, Salomón Ortiz, Henry Bonilla, and Frank Tejada, all from Texas; Bill Richardson from New Mexico; and Lucille Roybal-Allard (daughter of former Congressman Edward Roybal), Matthew G. Martínez, Esteban Edward Torres, and Xavier Becerra, from California.

Mexican Americans have been elected as mayors, city council members, governors, state legislators, school board members, and other officers. Among those elected to governor were Raúl Héctor Castro, who served as governor of Arizona from 1975 to 1977; Jerry Apodaca, who served as governor of New Mexico from 1966 to 1974; and Toney Anaya, who was governor of New Mexico from 1983 to 1987.

In 1957, Raymond Telles, a former lieutenant colonel from the U.S. Air Force, was elected mayor of El Paso, Texas. Later, in 1976, Ray Salazar was also elected mayor of El Paso, Texas. In 1981, Henry Cisneros became the first Mexican American mayor of San Antonio in modern times. He served as mayor from 1981 to 1989. In 1992, President Bill Clinton appointed Henry Cisneros Secretary of Housing and Urban Development. In 1983, Federico Peña was elected mayor of Denver, Colorado. President Clinton appointed him Secretary of Transportation in 1992. As of 1993, Cisneros and Peña were the only two Latinos serving in the nation's cabinet.

Eduardo Hidalgo, born in Mexico City, was the first Hispanic appointed Secretary of the Navy by President Jimmy Carter in 1979; he served until 1981. The first Hispanic and Mexican American appointed to the cabinet was Dr. Lauro F. Cavazos Jr., who was at the time president of Texas Tech University. In 1986, President Reagan named him Secretary of Education. Dr. Cavazos was reappointed by President George Bush in 1989 and served until December 1990. Dr. Cavazos's brother is retired four-star General Richard E. Cavazos. President Bush also appointed Mexican American Manuel Luján Jr., a former congressman from New Mexico, as Secretary of the Interior.

In 1949, Edward Roybal was elected to the Los Angeles City Council, becoming the first Mexican American elected to that Council since

Retired four-star General Richard E. Cavazos.

1881. In 1982, Mexican American Gloria Molina became the first Latina elected to the California State Assembly. Five years later, she became the first Latina elected to the Los Angeles City Council, and in 1991, the first elected to the Los Angeles County Board of Supervisors. Other Mexican American women have done well in politics. These women made up approximately 40 percent of the Latinos elected or appointed to municipal offices in towns in the Southwest. Among the Mexican American women elected to city councils were Debbie Ortega in Denver and María Berriozabal in San Antonio.

Several Mexican Americans have served as U.S. ambassadors. The former mayor of El Paso, Texas, Raymond L. Telles, served as U.S. ambassador to Costa Rica from 1961 to 1967. He later served as ambassador to the United States-Mexico Commission of Border Development and Friendship and as commissioner of the Equal Employment Opportunity Commission in Washington, D.C. Benigno C. Hernández served as ambassador to Paraguay from 1967 to 1969. Raúl Castro, who was later elected as governor of Arizona, served as ambassador to three Latin American countries. He served as ambassador to El Salvador from 1964 to 1968 and Bolivia from 1968 to 1969. In 1974, Castro was elected governor of Arizona, and after completing his term as governor, he served as ambassador to Argentina from 1977 to 1981. Philip V. Sánchez, who had served as director of the Office of Economic Opportunity, was named ambassador to Honduras and served from 1973 to 1976, and he later served as ambassador to Colombia from 1976 to 1977. Marí-Luci Jaramillo, a professor from the University of New Mexico, was appointed U.S. ambassador to Honduras in 1977. Dr. Julián Nava was the first Mexican American to be appointed ambassador to Mexico. Later, John Gavin was named U.S. ambassador to Mexico in 1981.

Many Mexican Americans have been named to positions in the federal government. Three Mexican American women have been named treasurers of the United States. President Richard M. Nixon appointed Los Angeles food manufacturer and businesswoman Romana Acosta Bañuelos as treasurer of the United States in 1971. She served for three years in that office. Banker Catherine Dávalos Ortega was appointed treasurer by President Reagan in 1983. At the time the president stated, "You proved that the American dream is alive and well. I can't think of a better name to have on our money than Catherine Ortega" (the U.S. Treasurer's signature is on every dollar bill issued by the government). The third treasurer appointed was Catalina Vázquez Villalpando.

Literature, Drama, and Films

Mexican Americans have written an impressive volume of novels, short stories, essays, plays, and poetry books. The writers have emphasized topics such as cultural adaptation, cultural affirmation, self-awareness and identity, racism, prejudice, discrimination, and economic exploitation. Some Mexican Americans write in English and some in Spanish.

The first important novel, *Pocho* (1959), written by José Antonio Villarreal, was based on a semiautobiographical account of a Mexican American growing up in the Santa Clara Valley of California. Ernesto Galarza's *Barrio Boy* (1971) dealt with the author's family plight as they came from Mexico. Tomás Rivera wrote an award-winning novel, *And the Earth Did Not Devour Him* (1970), dealing with the terrible life of migrant farm workers. Oscar "Zeta" Acosta wrote two autobiographical novels, *The Autobiography of a Brown Buffalo* (1972) and *The Revolt of the Cockroach People* (1973). In his first novel Acosta dealt with the search for machismo through the use of drugs and sex.

Rudolfo A. Anaya has written many plays, screenplays, novels, and anthologies. He wrote *Bless Me, Ultima* (1972), *Tortuga* (1979), and *The Silence of the Llano* (1982). Patricia Preciado Martín has worked on oral and folk histories. She wrote *Images and Conversation: Mexican-Americans Recall a Southwestern Past* (1983). Denise Chávez wrote two novels, *The Last of the Menu Girls* (1986) and *Face of an Angel* (1993). Rolando Hinojosa is a prolific and well-known novelist who writes in English and Spanish. Among his English books are *Dear Rafe* (1985) and *Klail City* (1987). Arturo Islas wrote two autobiographical novels, *The Rain God* (1984) and *Migrant Souls* (1990). Víctor Villaseñor wrote *Rain of Gold* (1990), dealing with his family's move from Mexico to California.

Gary Soto is the most outstanding Latino poet in the United States. Included in his poetry books are *The Elements of San Joaquín* (1977) and *Black Hair* (1985). He also has written novels, among them *Living Up the Street* (1985), *A Summer Life* (1990), *and Pacific Crossing* (1992). Sandra Cisneros, like Gary Soto, is a poet and a novelist. Among her novels are *The House on Mango Street* (1983) and *Woman Hollering Creek and Other Stories* (1991).

One of the most controversial modern writers is San Francisco-born Richard Rodríguez. He wrote *Hunger of Memory: The Education of Richard Rodríguez* (1982), an autobiographical account. Rodríguez's book upset many Latinos for his criticism of bilingual education and affirmative action.

There are many well-known Mexican American playwriters; among them are Carlos Morton, author of *The Many Deaths of Danny Rosales* (1983), and Estela Portillo Trambly, who wrote *Day of the Swallow* (1971). The best known of all is Luis Valdez. As a student leader during "*la huelga*," or the strike, of the farm workers, Valdez prepared *actos* (one-act plays) for his Teatro Campesino (Peasants Theater), showing great sensitivity to the plight of the farm workers.

Luis Valdez has become a symbol and a role model for other Mexican American playwriters. Valdez also became a film producer, bringing some of his plays to the screen. There are many Mexican American theater companies—*compañías de teatro*—in colleges and universities and cities in the Southwest. Some of them are Teatro de Esperanza, or Theater of Hope, in Santa Barbara; Teatro Nuevo Siglo, or New Century Theater, of the University of California at San Diego; Teatro Libertad, or Liberty Theater, in Tucson; and La Compañía de Teatro, or the Company Theater, of Albuquerque.

Luis Valdez and other playwriters organized in 1970 the Teatros Nacionales de Aztlán (TENAZ), or National Theaters of Aztlán, which has sponsored annual Mexican American theater festivals.

Science and Technology

Sidney M. Gutiérrez became an astronaut in 1985 and flew on his first space mission in 1991 aboard the shuttle *Columbia*. He flew again in space aboard the shuttle *Endeavor*. Ellen Ochoa was the first Latina who has flown in space. Dr. Ochoa is also an inventor who has two patents. She became an astronaut in 1991 and two years later flew aboard the shuttle *Discovery*. In 1994, she flew aboard the shuttle *Atlantis*.

Business and Industry

Increasingly, more and more Mexican Americans enter the business world. Two powerful predominantly Mexican American organizations assist thousands of entrepreneurs. Hector Barreto, who moved from Mexico to Kansas City, Missouri, became a successful businessman. At first he opened a Mexican restaurant, then a second one. Later, Barreto went into import and construction businesses. Barreto felt that it was important to organize other Latinos in business to network, share information and concerns, and give back to the community. In 1979, Barreto founded the United States Hispanic Chamber of Commerce (USHCC). During his presidency, Barreto met with President Ronald Reagan to discuss greater Latino representation in the federal government. Barreto was succeeded by Abel Quintela in 1987 and became chairman emeritus or retired honorary chairman of USHCC.

Another powerful business organization is the Texas Association of Mexican American Chambers of Commerce (TAMACC). The organization is based in Austin, Texas, and represents 9,500 Texas Latino businesses. Each year TAMACC holds an annual convention that

Dr. Ellen Ochoa, an inventor and astronaut, was the first Latina to fly in space. In 1991 she flew aboard the shuttle *Discovery*, and in 1994 she was part of the crew on the shuttle *Atlantis*.

attracts leaders of corporations, businesses, and industry. During the conference a free trade show provides participants with contacts, sales leads, and business opportunities. In July 1995, TAMACC held its Twentieth Annual Convention and Business Expo in Dallas, Texas. Some Mexican American businesspersons have done very well. According to *Hispanic Business* magazine's 1994 Rich List, there are 20 Mexican Americans in the United States with a net worth of $25 million or higher. Over half of them live in California and other states in the West. These successful entrepreneurs are the following:

- Antonio R. Sánchez Jr. and his family had a net worth of $55 million in 1994—the largest of any Mexican American in the United States. Antonio R. Sánchez Sr. had a business equipment firm, and in 1966 he founded International Bancshares Corporation in Laredo, Texas. When he died in 1992, his firm was the nation's largest minority-owned bank, with $1.5 billion in assets. Sanchez Sr. had also started the Sanchez-O'Brien Oil and Gas Company in 1973. Currently, his son, Antonio R. Sanchez Jr., is chairperson and CEO of the oil and gas company, which employs 100 people and had $50 million in sales in 1994.

- Daniel D. Villanueva, a former professional football player, owned and operated many Spanish-language television stations. Presently, Villanueva is the chairperson and half

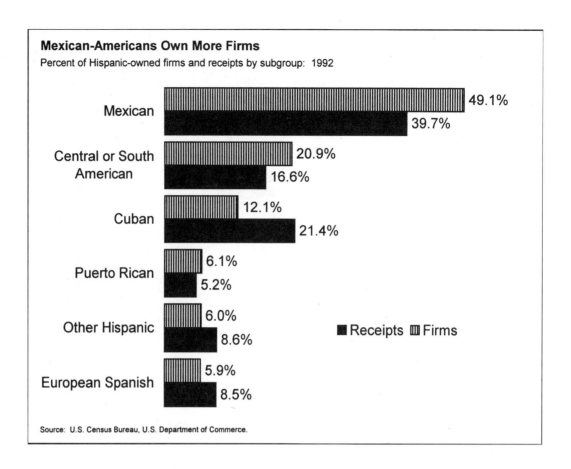

Mexican-Americans Own More Firms

Percent of Hispanic-owned firms and receipts by subgroup: 1992

Mexican — 49.1% / 39.7%

Central or South American — 20.9% / 16.6%

Cuban — 12.1% / 21.4%

Puerto Rican — 6.1% / 5.2%

Other Hispanic — 6.0% / 8.6%

European Spanish — 5.9% / 8.5%

■ Receipts ▥ Firms

Source: U.S. Census Bureau, U.S. Department of Commerce.

owner of an investment firm in Los Angeles. His net worth was $50 million in 1994.

- Carlos Y. Benavides Jr., and his son, Carlos Y. Benavides III, are the owners of 120,000 acres in South Texas. Benavides Jr. served as Webb County judge. Benavides III is building a 22-mile toll road between Mexico and the United States. The family's net worth in 1994 was $45 million.

- Manuel Caldera and his family sold their defense contractor firm in 1984 for $41 million. Today, the Calderas own and operate Amex Financial Services in California. The Caldera family had a fortune of $45 million in 1994.

- Raymond J. Rosendin has an electrical company that operates in 11 western states. The company was founded by Rosendin's father in 1919 and has worked in major defense projects, such as the Trident submarine facilities, and on the space shuttle launch and landing bases. Rosendin Electric, Inc., based in San Jose, California, had 700 employees and $84 million in sales in 1994. The assets of Rosendin and his family were $45 million in 1994.

- Robert R. Alvarez Sr. and his wife Margarita own Coast Citrus Distributors, Inc., one of the largest fresh fruit and vegetable distribution companies in the West. The Alvarez family's fortune was $40 million in 1994.

- Ignacio E. Lozano Jr. published *La Opinión,* the largest daily Spanish newspaper in Los Angeles, until his retirement in 1987. The newspaper was founded by his father in 1926. Today, his son, José Lozano, is the publisher. The Lozano family's net worth was $40 million in 1994.

- Linda and Robert Alvarado are the owners of Alvarado Construction, Inc., of Denver, Colorado, a company that does over $50 million worth of business. Linda Alvarado is a part owner of a major league basketball team, the Colorado Rockies, and sits on the board of Pitney Bowes and Cyprus Amax Minerals Company.

- Roque de la Fuente is the owner of a car distribution company that sells Cadillacs, Pontiacs, Oldsmobiles, General Motor trucks, and Isuzus in San Diego, California. His net worth was $25 million in 1994.

- Enrique "Hank" Hernandez Sr. and family run various companies from Alhambra, California. Hank Hernandez's two sons, Rick and Roland, work in the family businesses, which include a Spanish-language television station in Dallas, Texas. The family's fortune was $35 million in 1994.

- Frank Sepulveda and his wife and daughter are the owners of the largest produce wholesaler in the Southwest, which supports a fleet of over 100 trucks. The Sepulveda family's fortune was $35 million in 1994.

- Rafael E. Vega runs one of the largest vending machine companies in Nevada. His net worth was $35 million in 1994.

- Belia Benavides de Muñoz is a *tejana* who owns a 10,000-acre ranch in south Texas. She is a former Zapata County treasurer with a fortune of $30 million.

- Robert de Lafayette Cox, son of a Mexican mother and an Irish father, played professional football for the Boston Patriots and the Los Angeles Rams. In 1975, he began World Travel and Incentives in Minneapolis and today his company has sales of $48 million a year.

- Daniel S. Peña Sr. and family had a net worth of $30 million in 1994. Peña founded an energy company in Houston, Texas. He owns an estate in California and a castle in Scotland.

- Benjamin and Victor Acevedo are the offspring of Mexican immigrants who founded the Cal State Lumber Sales, Inc., in San Ysidro, California, in 1984. Their net worth was $25 million in 1994.

- Henry J. Aguirre is the largest Latino vendor of Ford Motor Company. Aguirre played professional baseball, serving as a pitcher for the Detroit Tigers. He is 90-percent owner of Mexican Industries in Michigan, an auto supply company with approximately $50 million in annual sales.

- Ernest M. Camacho founded Pacifica Service Corporation, a civil engineering and engraving company with $53.2 million in sales in 1994 and 375 employees. Camacho's fortune was $25 million in 1994.

- Diego Gutierrez and his family own 20,000 acres of land rich in oil and natural gas in South Texas. His family's fortune was $25 million in 1994.

- J. Fernando Niebla owns Infotec Development, Inc., in California. Infotec provides computers to the U.S. Air Force, and QMA Corporation of McLean, Virginia, a software company. His net worth was $25 million in 1991.

Characteristics of the Mexican Americans Today

The population of Mexican origin in the United States is the youngest of all Hispanic groups, according to the U.S. Bureau of the Census. In March 1993, the median age of Mexican Americans was 24.6 years, as compared with Puerto Ricans 26.9 years, Central and South Americans 28.6 years, and Cuban Americans 43.6 years. Mexican Americans still lag in educational attainment. Only 5.9 percent of the Mexican origin population of 25 years and over has completed a Bachelor's degree or higher. This compares with Puerto Ricans, 8.0 percent; Central and South Americans, 15.2; percent; and Cuban Americans, 16.5 percent. Many Mexican Americans are poor, particularly undocumented, unskilled workers who have recently arrived in the United States. According to the U.S. Bureau of the Census, 30.1 percent of Mexican Americans fell below the poverty level in 1992, as compared with 36.5 percent of Puerto Ricans, 26.7 percent of Central and South Americans, and 18.1 percent of Cuban Americans. The percentage of people living below the poverty line in 1992 for the entire nation as a whole was 14.5 and for the non-Hispanic white population was 9.6.

Mexican Americans have enriched U.S. culture with their art, music, theater, dance, cuisine, literature, architecture, and film. Additionally, they have made many contributions in politics, education, business and industry, labor, science, defense, and many other areas of endeavor.

Discrimination against Mexican Americans

Isabel Gonzalez of Denver, Colorado, prepared a study for the Panel on Discrimination of the National Conference for the Protection of the Foreign-Born, which was held in Cleveland, Ohio, in October 1947. Gonzalez explained:

History had made economic exploitation by American interests the lot of the Mexican people both north and south of the border. Powerful interests, like the Great Western Sugar Company, the greatest importer of Mexican labor, the railroads, the mining and lumbering industries, the cotton and fruit growers, and the cattle and sheep industries have succeeded in keeping the Mexican the most underpaid and most oppressed worker so that they will always have a surplus of cheap labor. This is amply demonstrated by the constant demand for importation of Mexican nationals by the sugar industries and the railways, supported by the powerful lobbies maintained by these interests in Washington. . . .

W. Henry Cooke wrote an article on June 5, 1948, in *School and Society* explaining the segregation of Mexican Americans in schools and public facilities. He wrote:

> Schools for "Mexicans" and schools for "Americans" have been the custom in many a Southern California city. It mattered not that the "Mexicans" were born in the United States and that great numbers of them were sons and daughters of United States citizens. It has been the custom that they be segregated at least until they could use English well enough to keep up with English-speaking children. Neither did it matter that many of them had a command of English not that there was a legal basis for their segregation . . .

> We are more conscious of civil rights for all members of society than we once were. What was once winked at in California can now justly be called discrimination. . . .

> That a schoolteacher who took her class to a motion picture theater had to divide them so that the "whites" sat in their proper section and the "Mexicans" in theirs, is evidence of discrimination. When a probation officer finds on his hands a Mexican-American boy who is so brilliant that he gets ahead of his classes and gets into trouble and when this officer tries to place the boy in employment and finds the jobs that are suited to his caliber closed to him because he is a Mexican, there is evidence of discrimination. When a vice-principal of a high school admits that he does not urge Mexican boys to seek varied employment as other boys do because he knows that they cannot do anything more than work in the groves, there is discrimination. When a city council refuses to let Mexican American boys and girls swim in the public pool and when it places at the entrance of the bathhouse a red sign reading FOR WHITE RACE ONLY and when it admits through its city clerk that this is for the purpose of keeping out "Mexican" children, it is both ignorance and discrimination.

> Many instances of this kind could be cited from California. And yet this state is better than some of its neighbors in that it has adequate laws that prohibit these practices. They continue because communities demand them.

Del Río Manifesto

José Ángel Gutiérrez became nationally known at the age of 22. He was a leader in the student protest movement in Texas and one of the founders of the Mexican Americans Youth Organization (MAYO) at Texas A & I University. On March 30, 1969, at San Felipe Del Río, a small town located about 160 miles west of San Antonio, Texas, over 2,000 Mexican Americans gathered to protest the cancellation of a VISTA program by the governor of Texas at the request of local county commissioners. VISTA workers had participated in a protest demonstration against the police beatings of a Mexican worker and his wife.

At Del Río, Gutiérrez and MAYO demanded the reinstatement of the VISTA program and an end to police brutality in Texas. Other-middle class organizations had also participated in the rally, such as the GI Forum and LULAC. Gutiérrez made an inflammatory speech at the rally, saying; "We are fed up. We are going to move to do away with the injustices to the Chicano and if the 'gringo' doesn't get out of our way, we will stampede over him." Earlier Gutiérrez had made the statement "Kill the gringo" at a press conference, creating quite an uproar among Anglos. Participants at the Del Río rally condemned police brutality and racism. They called their statements the Del Río Manifesto. Unfortunately, instances of police brutality still exist today, though many officials in Texas are now more sensitive to Latino issues.

Proclamation of the Delano Grape Workers for International Boycott Day, May 10, 1969

César Chávez founded the National Farm Workers Association in 1963. Later, it became the United Farm Workers Organizing Committee of the AFL-CIO (American Federation of Labor-Congress of Industrial Organization, a national union). In September 1965, the grape workers at Delano, California, under the leadership of César Chávez, went on a *huelga*, or strike, for higher wages and better working conditions. Four years later, the grape workers issued a Boycott Day Proclamation on May 10, 1969:

> We, the striking grape workers of California, join on this International Boycott Day with the consumers across the continent in planning the steps that lie ahead on the road to our liberation. . . . If this road we chart leads to the rights and reforms

we demand, if it leads to just wages, humane working conditions, protection from the misuse of pesticides, and to the fundamental right of collective bargaining, if it changes the social order that relegates us to the bottom reaches of society, then in our wake will follow thousands of American farm workers. Our example will make them free . . .

Grapes must remain an unenjoyed luxury for all as long as the barest human needs and basic human rights are still luxuries for farm workers. The grapes grow sweet and heavy on the vines, but they will have to wait while we reach out first for our freedom. The time is ripe for our liberation.

As a result of the campaign, some improvements in working conditions were obtained.

The Island Commonwealth and the Great Puerto Rican Migration

The island of Puerto Rico is the easternmost and smallest of the Greater Antilles. The 110-by-35-mile island lies between the Atlantic Ocean and the Caribbean Sea. Puerto Rico has year-round warmth, with an average annual temperature of 77° Fahrenheit. More than 3.3 million people live on the island of Puerto Rico with one third of the population concentrated in the San Juan metropolitan area. Puerto Rico is a commonwealth, neither a state nor a territory, an anomalous status invented by American political leaders that is still a source of contention on the island.

On July 22, 1938, Luis Muñoz Marín visited the small town where his father Luis Muñoz Rivera had been born. He announced there the beginning of a new political party called Partido Popular Democrático. Muñoz Marín's father had dedicated his life to the cause of Puerto Rican independence and had later won autonomy for Puerto Rico from Spain. Luis Muñoz Rivera had briefly served as Puerto Rico's prime minister when Puerto Rico was granted self-rule shortly before the Spanish American War in 1898. He later served as the island's representative before the U.S. Congress in Washington, D.C., and worked for the passage of the Jones Act, which granted U.S. citizenship to all Puerto Ricans.

Luis Muñoz Marín grew up and studied in the United States until he returned to his native island in the 1930s to take up his father's cause of bringing autonomy or self-rule to Puerto Rico. The Partido Popular Democrático (PPD), known as the Populares, chose as an emblem the profile of a *jíbaro*, a peasant wearing a straw hat called a *pava*. Under the emblem Muñoz Marín wrote the words "*Pan, Tierra, Libertad*" (Bread, Land, Liberty). These words became the slogan of the Populares.

During the 1940 legislative elections in Puerto Rico, the PPD advocated sweeping economic and social reforms for the island. Muñoz Marín's appeal to the working class proved successful and his party won a slim majority in Puerto Rico's leg-

Luis Muñoz Marín founded the political party Partido Popular Democratico, which advocated sweeping economic and social reforms in Puerto Rico. When his party won a slim majority in 1940 legislative elections, Muñoz Marín began an economic development program that improved the lives of many Puerto Ricans.

islature. Influenced by the New Deal, Muñoz Marín wanted to improve the life of the poor. One of his slogans in this campaign was "*ÁJalda Arriba!* (Up the Hill!)." Luis Muñoz Marín stated, "I speak to the working class, I speak to the agricultural class, I speak, because only with justice done with order and in time will chaos be avoided."

Following his party's victory, Muñoz Marín began an economic development program, known as "Operation Bootstrap," which would eventually improve the standard of living of Puerto Ricans. This program began to develop business and industry on the island, clear slum areas, improve health care and education, provide new housing, and promote agricultural production. After many years, Operation Bootstrap proved to be quite successful in improving the lives of Puerto Ricans.

The PPD won the 1944 election, and later Luis Muñoz Marín was elected governor of Puerto Rico in 1948; he was reelected in 1952, 1956, and 1960. He decided not to seek reelection in 1964. Muñoz Marín's party nominated Roberto Sánchez Vilella and he was elected governor. Luis Muñoz Marín died in 1980. His party continued to be strong and elected Rafael Hernández Colón in the 1970s and again a few years later.

Approximately 65,000 Puerto Ricans fought for our nation during World War II. During this conflict colonial empires around the world began to break up. The United States also began to take measures to end its own colonial rule over Puerto Rico.

In 1946 U.S. President Harry S Truman appointed Jesús T. Piñero as Puerto Rico's first native governor. Two years later, Luis Muñoz Marín became the first elected governor of Puerto Rico, and his party, the Partido Popular Democrático (Popular Democratic Party), known as the Populares, won 392,356 votes to 89,441 for the Republican Statehood group. In 1950, the United States adopted Luis Muñoz Marín's plan for *autonomismo*, or self-rule. On July 4, President Truman signed Public Law 600, known as the Constitution Act. The law stated that it recognized the principle of government by consent and that "the people of Puerto Rico may organize a government pursuant to a constitution of their own adoption."

In August 1951, Puerto Ricans elected 92 delegates to a constitutional convention. Six months later, a constitution, modeled after the U.S. Constitution and giving the island self-government, was drafted. The Puerto Rican Constitution made the island an Estado Libre Asociado, or Free Associated State, which is also known as the Commonwealth of Puerto Rico. Under this arrangement the people of Puerto Rico remain U.S. citizens but they do not pay federal income tax or vote in federal elections unless they live on the U.S. mainland. The Commonwealth of Puerto Rico elects a governor and a legislature and has its own flag. The people of Puerto Rico receive all social services and federal assistance given to the 50 states.

There are three positions regarding the question of Puerto Rican status: commonwealth, statehood, and complete independence. Puerto Ricans in the island and the U.S. Congress have considered the three options for Puerto Rico. In 1964, an election was held and 61 percent of the people on the island voted in favor of the commonwealth status, while 39 percent voted in favor of statehood. In 1989, President George Bush supported a call for a referendum and declared that he was in favor of statehood.

In November 1992, Pedro Roselló, a strong proponent of statehood, was elected governor of Puerto Rico. He called for a referendum to decide the status of Puerto Rico and provided three choices on the ballot, keeping the commonwealth status, statehood, and complete independence. On November 14, 1993, the election was held with large participation. Forty-eight percent of the people of Puerto Rico voted to maintain the commonwealth status, 46 percent voted for statehood, and only 4 percent voted for independence. An opinion poll taken in the United States among Puerto Rican residents showed 68 percent in favor of the Commonwealth, 27 percent for statehood, and 4 percent for independence.

If the island ever voted in favor of statehood and the United States Congress ratified that decision, there would be, of course, two U.S. senators from Puerto Rico and seven U.S. representatives in Congress, who would undoubtedly give more power to Latinos in the United States. Currently there are two Puerto Rican members in the U.S. House of Representatives, one from New York City and one from Chicago. There are no Puerto Rican U.S. senators.

Since 1992 a congressional delegate from Puerto Rico in Congress, has been allowed to vote in the U.S. House of Representatives, as have the delegates from Guam and the Virgin Islands. The current Puerto Rican representative in Congress is Carlos Romero Barceló, who, as a member of the New Progressive Party, favors statehood.

The proponents of commonwealth status fear that Puerto Rico would suffer economically should it become a state. Section 936 of Internal Revenue Code exempts U.S. mainland companies operating on the island from most federal taxation. It is feared that if this exemption is repealed, U.S. multinational companies would move their operations to Mexico or other third-world countries. In 1990, a study conducted by the U.S. Congressional Budget Office stated that statehood could cost Puerto Rico 100,000 jobs in ten years.

A very small number of Puerto Ricans have advocated complete independence from the United States. This small group of individuals founded the Puerto Rican Independence Party (PIP). They are known as the independistas. They believe that independence will free Puerto Rico from the debilitating dependence on the United States that is responsible for holding back Puerto Rico in terms of culture and economic growth. A poll conducted in June 1995 revealed that if elections for governor had been held at that time, the independista candidate, David Noriega, would have received only 7 percent of the votes. The poll also indicated that the current governor Pedro Roselló of the Partido Nuevo Progresista, or New Progressive Party, would have received 38 percent of the votes and Héctor Luis Acevedo of the Partido Popular 27 percent.

On March 1, 1954, Lolita Lebrón and several male companions, who were independistas, attempted to assassinate President Harry S Truman by opening fire at him from the gallery of the U.S. House of Representatives. They missed killing the president but injured five U.S. representatives before being arrested. Lebrón had cried "Free Puerto Rico now!" as the independistas opened fire. Another terrorist group calling themselves Macheteros used violent acts to force independence. (A *machete* is a long knife mostly used by the *jíbaros,* or peasants, to cut sugar cane, and the word *machetero* means a person who carries a *machete*.) In 1983, a group of Macheteros robbed an armored-car company in West Hartford, Connecticut, and took $1.7 million. Very few Puerto Ricans have supported such violent terroristic acts. Certainly, the issue of Puerto Rican status will not go away, and probably a future referendum will consider it again.

The Great Puerto Rican Migration to the U.S. Mainland

After the United States acquired Puerto Rico in 1898, small groups of Puerto Ricans crossed the Atlantic Ocean and arrived in New York City. Most of them were students, merchant marine sailors, garment workers, and cigar makers. By 1910, there were about 1,500 Puerto Ricans living in the United States. With the enactment of the Jones Act that made Puerto Ricans citizens of the United States, Puerto Rican migration increased. After World War I, the poverty and high unemployment on the island as well as the availability of jobs in the United States brought increased numbers of Puerto Ricans to the mainland. By 1930, there were 53,000 Puerto Ricans in the United States, including the more than 45,000 in New York City.

After World War II ended in 1945, the greatest and most important migration to continental United States took place. The continuous problems of overpopulation, unemployment, and high poverty on the island as well as the "pull factors" of high-paying jobs and inexpensive air transportation brought a large influx of Puerto Ricans to the mainland. In 1946, the net migration was 40,000. By 1955, there were approximately 675,000 Puerto Ricans in continental United States, with 500,000 of them living in New York

According to the 1990 census, there are 2.3 million Puerto Ricans in the United States, about 900,000 of them in New York City.

City. By 1960, there were 900,000 Puerto Ricans in the United States. Although the majority of them lived in the state of New York, Puerto Ricans began to settle in New Jersey, Connecticut, Massachusetts, Illinois, Ohio, Pennsylvania, Florida, and California. By the 1960s the Puerto Rican migration began to level off as economic conditions brought about by Operation Bootstrap improved on the island and openings for unskilled jobs diminished in the mainland.

High birth rates of Puerto Ricans residing in the United States have been responsible for the continuous growth of this group. In 1970, there were 1.5 million Puerto Ricans on the mainland, with 818,000 of them living in New York City. Ten years later, the number increased to 2 million on the mainland and 861,000 in New York

City. According to the 1990 census, there are 2.3 million Puerto Ricans in the United States, about 900,000 of them in New York City. The combined population of Puerto Ricans on the island and on the mainland was 6.3 million in 1990. According to the U.S. Bureau of the Census in March 1993, 10.6 percent of the estimated 22.8 million Hispanics in the United States were of Puerto Rican origin. Puerto Ricans today have migrated to other parts of the United States, particularly to the state of Illinois, which has more than 125,000.

Since 1948 the Commonwealth of Puerto Rico has assisted Puerto Ricans who have moved to the United States by opening a migration office in New York City. It later established offices in other U.S. cities with large Puerto Rican populations. The purpose of these migration offices is to assist Puerto Ricans in making a successful transition and adjustment to life in the United States. Officials assist Puerto Ricans with obtaining housing, finding jobs, and protecting them from discrimination and economic exploitation.

Puerto Rican Organizations on the U.S. Mainland

During the 1950s and the 1960s more and more Puerto Ricans began to see themselves as permanent residents of the U.S. mainland. As in World War II, Puerto Ricans fought bravely in the Korean Conflict of 1950 to 1953. Puerto Rico's 65th Infantry Regiment of the U.S. Army obtained fame in the Korean War, as it did in the two previous World Wars. Of the 43,434 Puerto Rican soldiers who fought in the Korean Peninsula, 3,540 casualties (dead, wounded, or missing in action) resulted. Puerto Ricans had one casualty for every 660 people of the Commonwealth, as compared with one casualty for every 1,125 inhabitants of the continental United States. They volunteered in great numbers—to be exact, 91.2 percent of Puerto Rican soldiers in the armed forces had enlisted voluntarily. Several Puerto Ricans attained the rank of general in the U.S. Army. Horacio Rivero became a Rear Admiral in 1955, a Vice Admiral in 1962, and a four-star Admiral in 1964. In 1972, Admiral Rivero retired from the Navy and was then appointed U.S. Ambassador to Spain.

During the mid-1950s, Puerto Ricans in New York organized the National Puerto Rican Forum to promote their interests and fight discrimination. As a result, another organization, the Puerto Rican Community Development Project, was founded and funded by the U.S. Office of Economic Opportunity in 1965 during the War Against Poverty of President Lyndon B. Johnson. This organization promoted a positive self-concept, cultural pride, and political involvement among Puerto Ricans in New York City. The Puerto Rican Family Institute was organized to help Puerto Rican migrants adapt to life in continental United States, and the Puerto Rican Association for Community Affairs was instrumental in the establishment of day-care centers, health clinics, and bilingual programs in schools.

ASPIRA of America was founded during the early 1960s to encourage school-aged Puerto Rican youngsters to finish high school and enter college. In Spanish, the word *aspira* means to strive or to achieve. Puerto Ricans also founded radical organizations such as the Young Lords. The Young Lords were Puerto Rican street gang members in Chicago until 1967. Under the leadership of José (Cha Cha) Jiménez, they organized and as the Young Lords conducted strikes, boycotts, and sit-ins. This organization was also established in 1968 by young Puerto Rican radicals in New York City. Like the Black Panthers, the Young Lords advocated "Power to the People." The two groups called each other *compañeros revolucionarios*, or revolutionary comrades.

The passage of the Voting Rights Act in 1965, which ended the discriminatory practice of making voters pass an English literacy test, helped Puerto Ricans to become more politically involved. Five years later, Puerto Ricans in the Bronx, one of the five boroughs of New York City, elected Hermán Badillo to the U.S. House of Representatives. Badillo, a member of the Democratic Party, became the first Puerto Rican elected to Congress. By 1987, ten Puerto Ricans had been elected as state representatives and state senators as well as city councillors and Bronx borough president.

Many Puerto Ricans have established citizens' groups in New York City, Chicago, Boston, Hartford, Miami, and other cities to fight to end discrimination and obtain better education, housing, and employment. The East Harlem Council for Human Services persuaded New York City officials to tear down some of the El Barrio's (as the Puerto Rican section in East Harlem is called) worst dilapidated housing and replace them with modern public housing projects. A similar Puerto Rican group, the Emergency Tenants Council, had similar successes in Boston. The Puerto Rican Legal Defense and Education Fund was organized in 1972 to provide legal assistance to Puerto Ricans and fight discrimination in housing, education, and employment. In 1977, the National Puerto Rican Coalition was founded with representatives from many national Puerto Rican associations in order to provide Puerto Ricans with a strong voice in national affairs. Another powerful organization is the Puerto Rican Merchants Association, which counts as members the owners of about 5,000 restaurants, bodegas (grocery stores), banks, factories, and other businesses.

ASPIRA, which means in Spanish to strive or to achieve, was created in 1961 under the direction of the Puerto Rican Forum and the Puerto Rican Association for Community Affairs as an action agency to promote educational achievement. Founded by Antonia Pantoja, ASPIRA's motto is "strive to learn." The organization has three goals:

1. Motivation and orientation for capable high school students who wish to enter professional and technical fields.

2. Acquisition by youth of an adequate knowledge of their cultural background to enhance their sense of self-image and identity.

3. Leadership training for young people to increase the desire to face up to community problems.

There are ASPIRA Clubs in New York City, Washington, D.C., Miami, and Puerto Rico. These clubs work with at-risk Latino students to encourage them to go on to colleges or technical institutes. In Miami, ASPIRA also operates an alternative school for at-risk youngsters under a contract with the Dade County Public Schools.

Puerto Ricans in Government, Politics, and Armed Forces

Puerto Ricans on the mainland have made valuable contributions to U.S. life and culture in areas such as government, education, business, literature, entertainment, arts, and sports. As more and more Puerto Ricans have registered to vote and become politically active, they have elected many Puerto Ricans to various political offices. Herman Badillo, who was born in Cagues, Puerto Rico, in 1929, was in 1965 elected as the first Puerto Rican president of Bronx borough and in 1970 became the first to be elected to the U.S. Congress to represent New York City's Twenty First Congressional District, which includes El Barrio. In 1978 Badillo was defeated by Robert García in his reelection bid to the U.S. House of Representatives. García was born in the Bronx borough in 1933 and in 1967 became the first Puerto Rican elected to the New York State Assembly and in the following year the first elected to the state senate. In 1992, three Puerto Ricans were elected to Congress: Luis Gutiérrez from Chicago, Illinois, and José Serrano and Nydia

Velázquez, both from New York City. Velázquez, a former director of the Puerto Rican Affairs Office of the State of New York, became the first Puerto Rican woman elected to Congress. In 1973, Maurice Ferré became the first Puerto Rican mayor of Miami; he served until 1985. In 1992, he was elected to the Metropolitan Dade County (Greater Miami) Commission. His uncle, Luis A. Ferré, was elected governor of Puerto Rico in 1968, serving one term.

Puerto Ricans have been appointed to important federal positions, such as ambassadorships. A Puerto Rican woman, Antonia Novello, was named U.S. surgeon general in 1989 by President George Bush, and she served successfully until she was replaced by President Bill Clinton.

Puerto Ricans have fought bravely in all wars in the defense of freedom and in a greater proportion to their number in the population. Luis R. Esteves was promoted to Adjutant General in 1937, a position he held for 20 years until his retirement. During World War I, he trained officers in Puerto Rico. These officers later led 20,000 Puerto Rican soldiers during World War I. Born in Ponce, Puerto Rico, Horacio Rivero became the first Puerto Rican promoted to four-star admiral in 1964.

Puerto Ricans in Literature, the Arts, and Entertainment

Puerto Rican writers have added a new dimension to U.S. literature and culture. In the 1950s, Celia Vice, a New York City businesswoman, founded Puerto Rican Heritage Publications to publish books that emphasize the Puerto Rican heritage and culture. In 1960, she was honored by the Puerto Rican community for her efforts. Jesús Colón became one of the first to write in English. He wrote *A Puerto Rican in New York and Other Sketches* in 1961. Six years later, Piri Tomas published an autobiography, *Down These Mean Streets,* about growing up poor in New York and being discriminated against. Thomas joined street gangs, used drugs, and committed crimes. He was arrested, convicted, and served time in prison.

Nicholasa Mohr, who was born and grew up in El Barrio, has had a long and successful career as a novelist. She has written many books including *Nilda* (1973), *El Bronx Remembered* (1975), and *Going Home* (1986). Mohr describes Puerto

Rican life in New York with sensitivity and humor. Ed Vega and Edward Rivera have written novels about Puerto Rican life in New York. A more recent novelist is Esmeralda Santiago, who wrote *When I Was Puerto Rican* (1993). Judith Ortiz-Cofer has written two novels, *The Line of the Sun* (1989) and *Silent Dancing: A Partial Remembrance of a Puerto Rican Childhood* (1990), and two books of poetry.

Víctor Hernández Cruz is one of the best known Nuyorican (New York–born Puerto Rican) poets. In the 1960s, a group of Nuyorican poets, who were inspired by the civil rights movement and led by Miguel Algarín, founded the Nuyorican Poets Cafe. In addition to Víctor Hernández Cruz, other Nuyorican poets read their works at the cafe, including Sandra María Esteves, Tato Laviera, and Miguel Piñeiro. In 1976, Laviera wrote his first novel, *La Carreta Made a U-Turn*. René Marqués wrote *La Carreta* (The Oxcart), a play about peasants who moved to cities.

Many Puerto Rican cultural institutions have been organized to promote music, drama, and the arts. There are several theater companies, such as the Puerto Rican Traveling Theater founded in 1967, that have presented the plays of Puerto Rican playwrights, such as Luis Florens Torres and René Marqués. Miriam Colón founded the Puerto Rican Traveling Theater, which has traveled all over the world for more than 25 years.

The Instituto de Cultura Puertorriqueña, or Institute of Puerto Rican Culture, has had a cultural renaissance and uses art to promote self-awareness and identity. The work of artists such as Antonio Martorell, Miguel Pou, and Rosa Ibarra has been displayed. Ibarra's paintings in particular celebrate the strengths and achievements of Latino women and express their warmth and vitality.

Jesús María Sanromá, who was born in Carolina, Puerto Rico, in 1902, became the official pianist of the Boston Symphony from 1926 to 1943. He gave recitals all over the world. Sanromá assisted in organizing the Puerto Rican Conservatory. He died in San Juan in 1984. Another world-famous musician who lived in Puerto Rico for many years was Pablo Casals. Born in Spain, Casals arrived at the island of his mother's birth in 1956. In 1957, he organized the annual Pablo Casals Festival. He was a renown cellist and conductor who helped establish the Puerto Rican Symphony Orchestra. He died in San Juan in 1973 at the age of 96. Popular musi-

Novelist Nicholasa Mohr, who grew up in El Barrio, writes with humor and sensitivity about Puerto Rican life in New York.

cians, like Tito Puente who was born in New York in 1923, have popularized Latin music in the United States. Puente is called *El Rey*, or the King, and plays masterfully the drums, the saxophone, and the clarinet. Puente has played with the bands of Machito, Tito Rodríguez, and Pupi Campo. Later, he organized his own orchestra. He has recorded over 100 albums.

A popular singer and musician is José Feliciano, who was born in Lares, Puerto Rico, in 1945. He has recorded many successful albums and several of his songs, such as "Light My Fire," became hits. Another singer is Tony Orlando, whose mother was Puerto Rican. He became a singer, recording hits such as "Knock Three Times" and "Tie a Yellow Ribbon 'Round the Old Oak Tree." From 1974 to 1976 he had his own television show, "Tony Orlando and Dawn."

Puerto Ricans in Business and Industry

Thousands of Puerto Ricans have established their own small businesses in Puerto Rico and on the mainland. Others have had successful careers working in national or multinational corporations. John Torres, who ran his own bodega (grocery store) with his brother, founded the Metropolitan Spanish Merchants Association in 1963. This organization, which is known as La Metro, represents more than 1,200 small businesses.

The richest Hispanic family in the United States is that of Puerto Rican Joseph A. Unanue. Their net worth was estimated in 1994 to be $340 million. This family founded Goya Foods in 1936. Today, this corporation sells 800 products, from rice, beans, olive oil, and coffee to orange juice and ice cream. With annual sales of almost half a billion dollars, the company projects annual sales in excess of $1 billion by the year 2000.

The second richest Puerto Rican in the United States is Francisco J. Collazo, with a net worth of $40 million. He is the chief executive officer and owner of Colsa Corporation in Alabama, one of the nation's most successful Latino-owned engineering services firms. Mr. Collazo, a former U.S. Army soldier, has obtained the U.S. Armed Forces as one of Colsa's largest customers.

The third richest Puerto Rican in the United States is Richard L. Carrión, with a net worth of $30 million. His grandfather founded the Banco Popular de Puerto Rico, the oldest and largest bank on the island. Mr. Carrión runs this bank today. He also serves on the International Olympic Committee.

The fourth richest Puerto Rican is Stanley Navas, with a net worth of $25 million. Navas served in World War II as a U.S. paratrooper, losing an arm near Anzio, Italy. This handicapped veteran began his concrete pipe manufacturing firm in 1949 with headquarters in Richmond, Virginia. The firm is now a successful company operating in four states. Other wealthy Puerto Ricans are entertainers, such as television producer Geraldo Rivera, who has a fortune of $25 million.

The wealth of these Puerto Rican multimillionaires should not obscure the fact that of all the Latino groups, the Puerto Ricans are the poorest. Thousands are trapped in the cycle of poverty and seem to have no way to escape. Unemployment, drugs, crime, and substandard housing are a stark reality. The mean income for a Puerto Rican household is $25,060—the lowest of all Latino families. In 1992, 36.5 percent of Puerto Ricans lived below the U.S. government poverty level, the highest among Hispanics.

Others Puerto Ricans have successful careers in the corporate world, such as Rita DiMartino, who works for the International Public Affairs Office of AT&T in New York City. In 1982, President Ronald Reagan appointed DiMartino as the U.S. Ambassador to the UNICEF executive board.

Puerto Rican Culture and Language

Puerto Ricans are determined to hand on their heritage and Spanish language. They fully support bilingual education for their children and institutions such as theater companies and the Museum of the Barrio, that display their culture. The 1990 census indicates that a very high percentage of Puerto Ricans on the U.S. mainland speak Spanish at home. It is evident that U.S.-born Puerto Ricans are keeping their Puerto Rican heritage, culture, and language as symbols of their identity and that they view their culture positively.

The Cuban Presence in the United States

The Cuban presence in the United States goes back to the arrival of Cuban-born soldiers in Florida, who came with Hernando de Soto's expedition of 1539. Many Cuban-born individuals lived in Florida during the 286-year rule of Spain in this area. Three of the 52 Spanish governors of Florida were born in Havana, Cuba. Cubans also lived in the Louisiana territory, which was governed by Spain for almost 40 years. One of the governors of Louisiana was also born in Havana.

Over 100,000 Cubans came to the United States during the nineteenth century, during which Cuba fought three wars of independence against Spain. The majority of these Cubans settled in Key West, Tampa, West Tampa, and New York City. After Cuba became independent in 1902, the constant political upheavals and the desire to improve their standard of living brought many Cubans to the United States.

It was, however, the coming to power of Fidel Castro on January 1, 1959, and the subsequent establishment of a Communist regime over the island that brought tens of thousands of Cubans to this nation. The vast majority of the Cuban people had supported the revolution that overthrew dictator Fulgencio Batista. Batista had been in power in Cuba from 1933 to 1944. For the next eight years Cuba had democracy and freely elected two presidents of the Partido Cubano Revolucionario (Auténtico). Fulgencio Batista decided to run for president in 1952. Realizing that he was going to lose the election of March 10, 1952, Batista seized power through a coup d'etat, or *golpe*, with the help of the Cuban army and ruled as a dictator. Cubans of all socioeconomic backgrounds participated in the revolution against Batista. They fought for democracy and the reestablishment of the socially advanced 1940 Constitution, which guaranteed freedom and civil rights to all citizens and strong protection for workers.

The Cuba that Castro took over in 1959 held great promise, since at that time it was one of the most economically developed nations in Latin America. It had the fifth highest per-capita income and the highest percentage of ownership of automobiles, television sets, and radios in Latin America. Although there was poverty in Cuba, the country had a growing middle class of well-educated professionals and a strong, highly motivated entrepreneurial class.

Fidel Castro soon disappointed his numerous followers. Early on the Cuban people saw Castro abandon his promise of free elections and democracy. Instead Castro established a harsh Soviet-style Communist dictatorship. He also crushed the opposition, sending many to the firing wall and to prison. He silenced his opponents by taking over newspapers and magazines as well as radio and television stations. All the freedoms guaranteed by the 1940 Constitution were ignored by his totalitarian government. Foreign and domestic farms, businesses, and industries were confiscated by the government. The upper and middle classes lost their property as bank accounts, homes, furniture, and other assets were taken over.

The Cuban Influx to the United States

The Cuban influx to the United States has had several stages or waves. The initial stage began after the January 1, 1959, takeover of Cuba by Fidel Castro and ended in October 1962. During this period 248,070 Cubans entered the United States and most, as in all subsequent waves, stayed in the Greater Miami area. Other Cubans settled in the states of New York, New Jersey, and California; small numbers of Cubans moved to the rest of the states or to Puerto Rico.

The second stage began when Fidel Castro, concerned about internal problems in Cuba, decided to open an escape valve. He announced that Cubans in the United States could pick up their friends and relatives at the port of Camarioca in September 1965. The so-called Camarioca boatlift brought 4,993 Cubans to the United States. The

José Martí (1853–1895)

José Martí was a Cuban essayist, poet, and patriot. Martí was the leader of the Cuban independence struggle. He was arrested and exiled at the age of 16 years for his political activity but continued to work for independence from Spain. Forced to live a traveling life, Martí spent many years in Mexico, Spain, Guatemala, Venezuela, and the United States. He earned a living as a newspaper writer, working, among other things, as a columnist for the *New York Sun*. Martí was a great admirer of the United States, but he feared the effects of U.S. power and influence. During his stay in the United States (1881–1895), Martí founded the Cuban Revolutionary party and became the leading figure in the independence struggle. He appreciated American aid in the liberation of his country but worried about the future relations of Cuba and the United States after independence was won. José Martí died in Cuba at the battle of Dos Rios in May 1895.

U.S. government then negotiated an orderly immigration agreement with Cuba. Air service between Varadero, Cuba, and Miami, Florida, lasted from September 1965 until April 1973. This air service was called the Cuban Freedom Flights and brought 297,318 Cubans into the United States.

The third stage began with the forced entry of 10,800 Cubans into the Peruvian Embassy in Havana in 1980. Castro angrily announced that all Cubans could leave for the United States from the port of Mariel. The subsequent Mariel boatlift brought 124,779 Cubans to the United States in a three-month period. Castro deliberately released criminals from prisons and patients from psychiatric hospitals to bring havoc to the United States. The U.S. government imprisoned the Mariel felons and has tried for over 15 years to return them to Cuba. The overwhelming majority of the Mariel entrants were law-abiding and have, like the earlier arrivals, adjusted successfully to life in the United States. Both the Camarioca and the Mariel boatlifts brought many working-class individuals and Cubans of African descent to the United States.

The fourth stage can be called the *balseros*, or rafters' influx. As economic and social conditions in Cuba continued to deteriorate, particularly after the end of Soviet aid to Cuba following the disintegration of the Soviet Union in 1989, more and more Cubans have risked their lives trying to cross the Straits of Florida in small boats and rafts. In 1990, 467 *balseros* came to the United States; in 1991 the number increased to 2,203, in 1992 to 2,257, and in 1993 to 3,541. In 1994, the trickle turned into a flood as thousands of people took to the sea, particularly after Castro announced that he would no longer imprison those who left the country illegally. The Bill Clinton administration, reacting to the pleas for action by Florida's governor Lawton Chiles and the anti-immigrant mood of the nation, drastically changed 36 years of policy regarding the acceptance of Cuban refugees to the nation. For years, Cubans had been welcomed and, indeed, encouraged to abandon their Communist island. They were given assistance upon arrival to the United States and welcomed as heroes of the Cold War.

In 1994, President Clinton ordered that Cubans picked up by U.S. Coast Guard ships in the Straits of Florida would not be allowed into the United States and would be sent to the U.S. Guantanamo Naval Base for indefinite detention. Over 30,000 Cubans were housed at Guantanamo, and some for six months in the Panama Canal Zone. The Cubans in Guantanamo lived in deplorable conditions; some rioted when faced with the possibility of an indefinite confinement in tents with poor sanitation, poor food, and no recreational facilities.

On May 2, 1995, President Bill Clinton signed an immigration agreement with Cuba and announced that Cubans at Guantanamo Naval Base would be allowed to enter the United States but that any Cubans picked up in the Straits of Florida would now be repatriated back to Cuba. By July 1, 1995, over 60 Cubans had been repatriated to the Communist island by force. Soon after the president's announcement, the first group of Cuban refugees were picked up at sea and forcibly returned to Cuba. This action produced massive civil disobedience, job strikes, and demonstrations in Greater Miami and to a lesser extent in Union City, New York City, and Washington, D.C. The great majority of Cubans in the United States were horrified at the thought of returning Cubans to the "island prison," particularly when the U.S. government had continually denounced the Castro dictatorship for 36 years and had brought an official condemnation of Cuba at the United Nations for human rights violations. For many Cubans, President Clinton's forced repatriation was equivalent to returning Jews to Nazi Germany or forcing freedom-loving East Germans who had jumped the Berlin Wall back to Communist East Germany. For several days hundreds of Cubans blocked expressways and streets in South Florida to protest the new policy. On May 16, 1995, approximately 10,000 marched in Miami on a day that the leaders of the demonstration called for a general work stoppage.

Thousands of Cuban Americans participated in the half-day general strike and rallied, abandoning their shops, offices, and businesses. The protesters marched on a very hot and humid afternoon from the Bay of Pigs Memorial on Miami's Calle Ocho (Eighth Street) to José Martí Park a few blocks away. Many placards carried by the demonstrators attacked President Clinton, stating: "Clinton—Traitor of Freedom," "Clinton, this will be your Vietnam," and "Klinton loves Kastro." José Miró Torra, president of the Bay of Pigs Veteran association, stated: "Our fight, understand well, is not against the North American people. It is against the Cuban government and all governments that are allied with Cuba."

Five young Cubans went on a hunger strike in front of the Miami Herald newspaper building for five days. On June 8, 1995, over 3,000 Cubans demonstrated against this policy in Lafayette Park in front of the White House. The three Cuban-born U.S. Representatives—Ileana Ros Lehtinen, Lincoln Díaz-Balart, and Bob Menéndez—joined the demonstrators and attacked the new U.S. policy. Earlier, Congressman Díaz-Balart and Metro Dade County Commissioner Pedro Reboredo had been arrested by the police in Washington, D.C.

On June 30, 1995, President and Mrs. Clinton came to Miami to see Mrs. Clinton's brother and sister-in-law's newborn baby. Cubans demonstrated again against the repatriation policy. On July 4, 1995, Cuban Americans demonstrated again in the nation's capital. This demonstration was organized by many Cuban organizations, including the Cuban American Veterans Association (CAVA) presided by retired Colonel Juan Armando Montes. Many Cubans expressed fear in the summer of 1995 that the Clinton administration was moving toward the lifting of the U.S. trade embargo and the reestablishment of diplomatic relations with Cuba. The Clinton administration has consistently denied these accusations and has stated its support for the Cuban Democracy Act, which includes the continuation of the embargo until Cuba restores democracy.

The Cuban Miracle

What makes the Cuban exile experience in the United States unique is how successfully the Cubans adapted to life in a new environment.

Some have called it the Cuban miracle. Over 1.1 million Cubans reside in the United States; in 1995, over 700,000 Cubans lived in the Greater Miami area. The U.S. Bureau of the Census indicated in March 1993 that 4.7 percent of 22.8 million Hispanics in the United States are of Cuban origin. In South Florida, in particular, their impact is noticeable in all areas: politics, education, religion, sports, arts, literature, entertainment, the media, science, business and industry, labor, and so forth. With the growth in number and wealth, Cuban Americans have gained political power at different levels of government. Two Cuban American members of the Republican Party from the Greater Miami area are serving in the U.S. House of Representatives: Ileana Ros Lehtinen and Lincoln Díaz-Balart. In 1982, Ros Lehtinen was the first Hispanic woman elected to the Florida House of Representatives and four years later, the first to the State Senate. In 1989, she became the first Hispanic woman elected to the U.S. Congress. Bob Menéndez, a member of the Democratic Party, was elected to the U.S. Congress in New Jersey.

In 1992, Metropolitan Dade County (the Greater Miami area) elected a Cuban American majority to the County Commission shortly after a judge banned county-wide elections and ordered district elections. Many Cuban Americans are serving as mayors and in the city councils of many municipalities in South Florida and New Jersey. There is a Cuban American mayor in Hamilton, Ohio: Adolf Olivas is the mayor of this city of 70,000 people. Several Cuban Americans serve as representatives and senators in state legislatures as well as school board members and city councilpersons.

Cuban Americans have been making valuable contributions in the field of education. Paul Cejas, a prominent and wealthy businessman and former chairperson of the Dade County School Board, was appointed by Florida Governor Lawton Chiles to the Board of Regents that runs the state university system in 1994. That same year Governor Chiles appointed Cejas to the Governor's Commission on a Free Cuba and he was elected chairperson by the members of the commission. Florida International University in Miami, Florida, is headed by a Cuban American, Dr. Modesto (Mitch) Maidique, as is the Miami Dade Community College Wolfson Campus, which is presided over by Dr. Eduardo Padrón. A Cuban American woman, Dr. Piedad Robertson, became the first

Hispanic president of Boston Community College and later the first appointed to Chief State School Officer of the state of Massachusetts. The superintendent of the Dade County Public Schools—the fourth largest in the nation with an enrollment of over 330,000 students and an annual budget of over $3 billion—is Octavio J. Visiedo. Thousands of Cuban Americans teach and serve as administrators in public and private schools and colleges and universities throughout the nation.

Agustín Román became the first Cuban bishop of the Catholic Church appointed in South Florida. He used his considerable influence to help end the prison riots of Mariel felons a few years ago. There are many Cuban Americans represented in all professions; they are medical doctors, attorneys, engineers, accountants, bankers, teachers, and so forth. The arts have flourished in South Florida, New Jersey, and New York because of the Cuban immigration. Cubans founded institutions that offer outstanding musical and dance performances, plays, and operettas, such as Pro-Arte Grateli and Ballet Concerto. Performers, such as well-renowned and Miami-born Fernando Bujones, have appeared in many ballet productions in the United States and abroad. Every year Natalio Chediak organizes a well-known Miami International Film Festival that attracts U.S. and international movie stars and directors.

Entertainment

Dr. Eduardo Padrón organizes an annual International Book Fair, which brings top national and international writers to Miami. Mario Ernesto Sánchez offers an annual Hispanic Theater Festival with drama productions from the United States, Spain, and Latin America. In June 1995, Sánchez opened the tenth annual festival featuring theater companies from over ten countries. Some plays are in Spanish; others are offered in English, written by Hispanic playwrights who write in that language. Numerous Cuban theater companies, such as Las Máscaras, present plays, particularly comedies.

There are 45 Cuban playwrights living in the United States. Some started their careers in Cuba, such as Leopoldo Hernández, Julio Matas, and Matías Montes Huidobro. Others, like Miguel González-Pando, Dolores Prida, Manuel Pereiras, Héctor Pérez, Luis Santeiro, and Uva Clavijo, wrote plays in the United States. All Cuban playwrights were deeply influenced by the Communist Revolution. Some were imprisoned in Cuba, such as Miguel González-Pando, a Bay of Pigs veteran; and René Ariza, who was sentenced to eight years in prison for "writing short stories and essays whose contents and scope reveal a marked ideological diversion and which are counterrevolutionary propaganda." Reinaldo Arenas, a famous novelist and playwright who committed suicide in 1990, was also sent to prison before arriving in the United States during the Mariel influx in 1980. Cuban painters and sculptures, such as Rafael Consuegra, Carlos Alfonzo, Ramón Carulla, María Brito-Avellana, Demi, and others, sell their work across the United States.

Internationally known Cuban-born entertainers, such as Gloria and Emilio Estefan, Celia Cruz, John Secada, Albita, Olga Guillot, Israel "Cachao" López, and the late Dámaso Pérez Prado, have enriched the musical world. Cuban American actors and actresses, such as César Romero, Desi Arnaz and his children, Andy García, María Conchita Alonso, and Steve Bauer, have become major movie screen entertainers. Famous athletes, such as 1992 Olympics gold medalist swimmer Pablo Morales and 1960s Olympic gold medalist swimmer Donna de Varona, tennis player Mary Joe Fernández, and baseball players Ariel Prieto, Rafael Palmeiro, and José Canseco, are well-known throughout the United States.

Cuban writers have made a mark in literature. Oscar Hijuelos received the 1990 Pulitzer Prize for Fiction for his novel *The Mambo Kings Play Songs of Love,* which was later made into a Hollywood movie. Guillermo Cabrera Infante, Roberto Fernández, Cristina García, and the late Reinaldo Arenas are some of the writers who are widely read in the United States and abroad.

Cuban Americans have served with distinction in the U.S. Armed Forces. Mercedes Cubría retired from the U.S. Army at the age of 70 in 1973 with the rank of lieutenant colonel after a long career that included service in World War II and the Korean War. Erneido Oliva, who was second-in-command of Brigade 2506, became a major general in the U.S. National Guard. Several Bay of Pigs veterans fought in the Dominican Republic and Vietnam, and twelve veterans attained the rank of colonel, including José Raúl (Yayo) de Varona, Johnny de la Cruz, and Nestor Pino.

Cubans in Business and Industry

Cubans have made a major contribution and left a deep imprint in business and industry in the United States, but particularly in South Florida, where the majority of the Cubans reside. In fact, no other immigrant group in the nation's history has done so well in this area in such a short time.

Hispanic Business magazine reported in June 1995 that there are 119 major Hispanic-owned corporations in Florida, most of them Cuban-owned, that earned $3.56 billion in 1994. These Florida corporations' earnings outranked the 123 California-based Hispanic-owned corporations that have earned an income of $2 billion.

The vast majority of the Florida firms are located in South Florida and most of them are owned by Cubans. Hispanics in Greater Miami generate up to $10 billion in business annually, which is about half of the area's gross product. The top-ranked Florida corporation was Carlos M. de la Cruz's companies, which reported revenues of $266.59 million in 1994. Under de la Cruz's companies are: Eagle Brands, Inc. (exclusive South Florida distributor for Anheuser-Busch beers) and three car companies, Miami Honda, Central Hyundai, and Sunshine Ford. The workforce for these companies numbers 550.

The second largest corporation in South Florida was Sedano's Supermarkets of Miami, which reported $253.36 million in revenue in 1994. Its chief executive officer (CEO), Manuel A. Herrán, employs 1,600 workers. Vincam Group in Coral Gables, Florida, deals in employment services and had $193.1 million in revenue in the same year. Sales in 1994 of other large Cuban-owned companies in South Florida were Precision Tracking, $150 million; Mas Tec, Inc., $142 million; Capital Bancorp of Miami, $126.5 million; Avanti/Case-Hoyt, $120 million; Bella Automotive Group, $108.9 million; Gus Machado Enterprises, Inc., $95.6; and Northwestern Meat, $90.4 million.

There are over 65,000 Cuban-owned businesses in the United States, most of them in the Greater Miami area. Many are small family-operated business, such as small grocery stores, restaurants, and gasoline stations. Others are larger corporations, such as construction firms, banks, and factories.

It is astounding how some Cuban Americans who arrived in this country penniless a few years ago are now multimillionaires. In March 1994, *Hispanic Business* magazine reported the 1994 Hispanic Business Rich List Directory. The richest Cuban in the United States was Coca-Cola Chairman of the Board Roberto Goizueta with an estimated net worth of $300 million. In 1991, Goizueta's compensation for his work at Coca-Cola was $80.6 million. The Fanjul brothers do not report their enormous wealth to the media. It is possible that their net worth is greater than Goizueta's.

There were 60 Hispanic individuals in the nation having a net worth in 1994 in excess of $25 million; 23 of these were Cuban Americans and 15 were Cuban Americans from the Greater Miami area. The South Florida Cuban multimillionaires are the following:

Jorge Mas Canosa, who headed the Cuban American National Foundation—the most powerful Cuban organization in the United States—before his death in 1997, was reported to have, together with his family, a net worth of $65 million. Over the years, his firm, Church and Towers of Florida, Inc., made many lucrative contracts by placing underground telephone cables for telephone companies. A merger of this company with Burnup & Sims, which created Mas Tec Company, gave the Mas family $50 million in the new company stock. Mas Tec is one of the few Hispanic publicly traded companies in the United States. This company employed 3,000 individuals in 1995.

Abel Holtz and his sons own Capital Bancorp, the parent company of Capital Bank of Miami, which has $1.2 billion in assets. Their net worth was $50 million. This company employs 800 workers.

José Milton owns J. Milton & Associates, a large property development firm, as well as several large apartment complexes and condominiums. His net worth was $50 million.

Manuel (Manny) D. Medina is the owner of Terremark Investment Services, which builds office buildings, condominiums, and restaurants. In spite of some recent losses in the real estate market, Medina's net worth was reported to be $45 million.

Natan R. Rok is the owner of Rok Enterprises, which controls a large part of the downtown area of Miami and parts of Hialeah and South Miami. His net worth was $45 million.

Amancio Suárez and his family are the owners of approximately 50 percent of Cosmo Communications Corporation, which produces electronic digital radios. They also own Mambisa Broadcasting Corporation and Viva America Media Group, which operate many radio stations, among them WAQI-AM-Radio Mambí and WRTO-FM in Miami. Suárez and his family's net worth was $45 million.

Paul Cejas was the chairman of CareFlorida Health Systems, the largest Hispanic health-care firm in the United States. He merged his company in the fall of 1994 with Foundation Health Corporation of Rancho Cordova, California. After the sale, Mr. Cejas received 5.7 percent of Foundation Health's stock, which has a market value of approximately $90 million. Mr. Cejas has plans to start his own investment firm.

Entertainers Gloria and Emilio Estefan own two hotels in Miami Beach, the Shore Park and the Cardozo, both with acclaimed restaurants. Gloria has sold millions of albums all over the world and Emilio is a songwriter and producer. Their net worth was $40 million.

José Álvarez is the owner of AIB, which represents three insurance companies with $50 million in sales. His net worth was $30 million.

José Arriola owns Avanti Press, which offers services from photography and creative consulting to binding, insertion, and mailing. Avanti also purchased a New York catalog firm. Arriola's net worth was $25 million.

Armando Codina, who came to South Florida as an unaccompanied penniless minor under Operation Peter Pan of the Catholic Church in 1960, later became the first Hispanic to be elected chairperson of the Greater Miami Chamber of Commerce. He is the owner of a large property development company; until recently, his partner in real estate was Jeb Bush, former President George Bush's son and Republican Party candidate for governor of Florida in 1994. Armando Codina is the chairperson of the elite Non-Group, an informal association of Greater Miami's powerful executives and entrepreneurs—such as Wayne Huizenga, owner of the Florida Marlins baseball team; James Batten, chairperson of Knight-Ridder, Inc., which owns many newspapers, including *The Miami Herald;* and the Cuban American Carlos Manuel de la Cruz, CEO of Eagle Brands, Inc. The Non-Group is one of the most powerful groups in Greater Miami and discusses and implements all major projects. Codina's property-development projects include the Beacon Center, Deering Bay, and Cocoplum. His net worth was $25 million.

Carlos de la Cruz Sr. is the CEO of Eagle Brands, Inc., which distributes Anheuser-Busch in Miami. He and his family own three car dealerships. The family's net worth was $25 million.

Antonio M. Sierra is the owner of Business Men's Insurance Corporation, a life and health insurance company. His net worth was $25 million.

Outside South Florida, Cuban Americans have done quite well in the business world. Arturo G. Torres has a chain of restaurants, with headquarters in San Antonio, Texas, and a net worth of $130 million. In Lyndhurst, New Jersey, Gedalio Grinberg & Family distributes prestige watches under the firm North American Watch Corporation. The corporation's net worth is $55 million. Alex Mervelo owns more than 40 La Pizza Loca restaurants. His company is based in Buena Park, California, and Mervelo's fortune is $35 million. The Alarcón family owns radio stations in several states and operates from New York. Their net worth is $30 million. Félix Sabatés of Charlotte, North Carolina, owns Top Sales, two auto race teams, and hockey and basketball teams. His fortune is $30 million. Gilbert L. de Cárdenas owns a cheese factory in California with a net worth of $25 million. Salvador Díaz-Verson Jr., an investor in Columbus, Georgia, has a fortune of $25 million. Nestor Fernández of Ohio manufactures aircraft and auto parts and has a net worth of $25 million.

There are approximately 500 Cubans serving as presidents, vice-presidents, and other high-level bank executive positions who have made Greater Miami an international finance and banking metropolis of the first order in the world. Greater Miami also has 60 domestic banks with 390 branches. Among the best-known banking executives are Luis Botifol, who retired as Chairman of the Board of Republic National Bank and has continued to play an active role in the community, and Carlos Arboleya, who became the first Cuban American bank president in the nation and served for almost 20 years as vice-chairman of the Barnett Banks of Florida. Arboleya, who is now retired, has also served as president of the Greater Miami Chamber of Commerce. A younger Cuban American, Carlos Migoya, is the president of one of the largest banks, First Union Bank.

Many Cuban Americans work in insurance and real estate and in multinational corporations. Enrique Falla and Enrique Sosa work as executive vice-president and senior vice-president/president Dow North America, respectively, of Dow Chemical Company, a multinational corporation with 62,000 employees. Both reside in Miami part of the year.

According to *Hispanic Business,* 5 of the 43 Hispanics who serve on the boards of 57 Fortune 1,000 corporations are Cuban Americans. Armando Codina sits on the board of directors of BellSouth Corporation and Winn-Dixie Stores; Enrique Falla, on Dow Chemical and K-Mart Corporations; and Enrique Sosa, on Dow Chemical. Prominent businesswoman Remedios Díaz-Oliver sits on the boards of Avon Products, Inc., U.S. West Corporation, and Barnett Bank and is president of All American Containers. Roberto C. Goizueta, CEO of Coca-Cola, serves on several boards—Coca-Cola, Eastman Kodak, Ford Motor, and Suntrust Bank.

Cuban American developers and construction firms, both large and small, have made and are making valuable contributions to the economy of South Florida. They have created a powerful and influential organization to represent their interests, the Latin Builders Association. Another powerful institution is the Latin Chamber of Commerce of the United States or Cámara de Comercio Latina (CAMACOL), which is led by Luis Sabines, who also has a Miami street named after him. The CAMACOL, which represents 1,600 small Latino and Cuban businesses, sponsors a yearly meeting in Miami of Chambers of Commerce of different nations in Latin America. In April 1995, the CAMACOL hosted its sixteenth Hemispheric Congress of Latin America's Industrial Corporations and Chambers of Commerce in Miami to help promote trade and investment in the Western Hemisphere. William Alexander was the chair of the congress. Sabines has been a pioneer in bringing Latin Americans to Miami to put them in contact with U.S. Hispanics in business. He feels that CAMACOL has been a bridge to the Americas in strengthening hemispheric ties.

As a counterpart to the Anglo-dominated and very influential Non-Group, Cuban Americans have created another informal group called Mesa Redonda, or Round Table, in Greater Miami. This group is led by educators, government officials, and prominent people in business and the news media. Florida International University President Modesto Maidique is the chairperson of the 24-member agenda-setting group. Among the other members are Miami City Manager César Odio; Dade County Manager Armando Vidal; Publisher of *Diario Las Américas* Horacio Aguirre; General Manager and Vice-President of Channel 51-Telemundo José Cancela; President of Univision Television Group Carlos Barba; Dade County Schools Superintendent Octavio Visiedo; businesspersons Luis Botifoll, Carlos Arboleya, Carlos M. de la Cruz, Armando Codina, and Remedio Díaz-Oliver; CEO of Bacardi Imports and President Juan Grau; Inter-American Transport Equipment Company President Diego Suárez; Executive Vice-President Nation's Bank Adolfo Henriquez; and First Union Bank President Carlos Migoya.

Cuban labor is present in practically all businesses and industries in South Florida. Cuban cheap labor, particularly that of women, was responsible for bringing the major garment industries from New York to South Florida. Cuban craft people and technicians staff many industries, including aircraft, construction, and hospitals. Cubans are represented in all the professions. Approximately 1,000 Cuban lawyers work in Greater Miami. In June 1994, Francisco Angones became the first Cuban American to be elected president of the 74-year-old Dade County Bar Association. Cuban Americans also have their own lawyers' association.

The health-care industry is vital to the economy of Greater Miami. More than 85,000 trained health-care personnel work in the area, many of Cuban background. There are 85 health technology manufacturing firms. Approximately 2,000 Cuban American medical doctors practice in Miami. Some own hospitals, such as the Pan American Hospital with $76 million in sales in 1992, and other clinics or Health Management Organizations (HMO). Vicente Lago, M.D., was elected president to the Dade County Medical Association.

Reasons for the Cuban Economic Success

Cuban Americans are doing better economically than any other Hispanic group in the United

States. According to the U.S. Bureau of the Census in 1992, 18.1 percent of the population of Cuban origin was below the poverty level, as compared with 26.7 percent Central and South Americans, 30.1 percent Mexicans, and 36.5 percent Puerto Ricans. The mean income in 1992 of Cuban households was $35,594, as compared with $29,682 for Central and South Americans, $28,448 for Mexicans, and $25,060 for Puerto Ricans. Although the Cuban household income was higher than any Latino group, it was considerably below the $41,646 of the non-Hispanic white population. Cuban Americans reach higher levels of education than other Latinos owing to the nature of the Cuban influx to the United States. In March 1993, 16.5 percent of the Cuban population 25 years and over had a bachelor's degree or higher, compared with 15.2 percent of Central and South Americans, 8 percent of Puerto Ricans, and 5.9 percent of Mexicans. In the non-Hispanic white (Anglo) population, 23.8 percent has a bachelor's degree or higher. Obviously higher educational attainment translates to higher paying jobs. However, there are many reasons for the success story of the Cuban American community in South Florida. The development of a strong ethnic economy depends on the following factors: level of education, population, density, a large market, business skills, business contacts, a pool of cheap labor, and capital.

Most Cubans who settled in Miami lost all their property in Cuba and came to this country with nothing. The first wave of immigration was as educated as the Anglo American population. These Cubans had been rich or belonged to the professional and technical middle classes. Coming in such large numbers, Cubans resembled Noah's ark: Medical doctors, dentists, bankers, former employees, and fellow business associates also came with their relatives and friends.

The Cubans had an intense desire to succeed, and they had a support group immediately available made up of other Cuban friends, relatives, and associates. The U.S. government, in the middle of the Cold War, welcomed the anti-Communist Cubans and provided considerable assistance through the Cuban Refugee Center. In addition to initial financial and medical support, the government provided retraining for professionals—such as lawyers being trained as teachers. It also provided loans to Cuban students to attend college.

However, the Cuban Refugee Center was unsuccessful in its attempt to relocate Cubans across the United States. Most came back to the "Magic City," as Miami is known.

Hispanic banks, such as the Republic National Bank under the leadership of Luis Botifoll, began to give the so-called character loans in the early 1960s. This was an unheard-of banking practice in large cities in the United States. Cuban businesses were given loans without collateral, based solely on the owner's reputation. Many Cuban businesses started this way. Thus, capital was available for investment and the start-up cost of businesses and industries from both private and public sectors.

There was an enormous pool of highly motivated cheap labor. Cubans were willing to work at any job, regardless how menial or how poorly paid. A high percentage of Cuban women joined the labor force, thus increasing the family income. Cuban women soon dominated entire industries, such as hotel and apparel industries. The apparel industry in Greater Miami employs over 24,000 people and is the third largest in the United States.

Helping in the adjustment process were two factors: Almost all the Cuban newcomers were urban dwellers, and Miami was familiar to most of them owing to years of prior travel as tourists or students. Many spoke English when they came. The semitropical climate of Miami and the sea were similar to those of their island. There was little or no culture shock here.

Cubans had a support group waiting for them, since most of their friends and associates were in South Florida. There was no need to abandon the Cuban culture and the Spanish language and suffer an identity crisis in a forced "melting pot" situation. Cubans strongly advocated cultural pluralism and stated that diversity could be a source of strength. Alejandro Portes and Alex Stepick in their 1993 book *City on the Edge: The Transformation of Miami* explained a most unique phenomenon that has occurred in Miami. They called it acculturation in reverse. The Cubans, instead of losing their culture and language and assimilating into U.S. society, have spread their language, culture, and institutions among the non-Hispanic population in South Florida. Diehard opponents of biculturalism and those unable to tolerate the widespread use of the Spanish language have left

Hunger strikers protesting the forced repartriation of Cuban immigrants stated in an article written in support of their protest: "Just as it would have been monstrious to return Germans who crossed the Berlin Wall back to East Germany or Jews escaping a repressive Soviet Union, it is immoral to return Cubans to Castro's island-prison."

town or have withdrawn into isolated pockets. An important factor in the successful adaptation of Cubans was that Greater Miami was a relatively small southern town with a tourist economy that did not have a powerful establishment like New York and Los Angeles.

Finally, and most importantly, the Cubans brought a high degree of entrepreneurial spirit and business acumen. Many had international contacts, since Havana was a most cosmopolitan city. The Cubans also had a strong personal desire to succeed in business or in their trades or professions: They had just lost their country and wanted to show the Communist Cubans how wrong they had been in choosing a socialist economy and a totalitarian political system. Recent polls have indicated that most Cuban Americans want to remain in South Florida or other parts of the United States after the end of the Communist regime in Cuba. Many, however, still hope that one day they can return to the island of their birth or their grandparents' or parents' birth as successful entrepreneurs and professionals or simply as tourists.

On May 20, 1993, President Bill Clinton commemorated Cuba's Independence Day by inviting about 75 Cuban Americans from New York, New Jersey, and Florida for an afternoon reception on the White House lawn. President Clinton reiterated his support for the embargo-

tightening Torricelli bill, or the Cuban Democracy Act of 1992. He also congratulated the Cuban Americans for their achievements in the United States and for successfully rebuilding their lives and enriching America. In 1992, two surveys were conducted among Cubans in the United States. Professor Juan Clark of Miami Dade Community College did a poll on 4,680 Cuban exiles in the United States and other countries. His survey showed that 34.4 percent would not return to Cuba, 20 percent would, and almost 46 percent were not sure. In the same year, in a similar survey conducted by Sergio Bendixen, 64 percent of Greater Miami Cubans said they would not return to the island and 24 percent said they would.

In 1994, the Washington-based firm of Schroth and Associates conducted another survey that revealed that 80 percent of Cuban Americans would remain in the United States and 16 percent said they would return to Cuba. Another 67 percent said they would go to Cuba to visit only. Pollster Robert Schroth stated "their hearts are on the island, but their money and their families are here." Schroth's poll indicated that 88 percent of the Cuban respondents said the embargo must remain as it is or be toughened. Schroth said, "I have been asking the question for seven years and the answer is always the same."

On May 8, 1995, five young Cubans with no group affiliation began a hunger strike across from

Excerpts from an Article Written by the Five Young Men State the Reasons for Their Hunger Strike

Our appeal is to this great nation's highest and most honorable traditions . . .

Freedom does not exist in Cuba. Indeed, the systematic violation of human rights is a way of life in Cuba. This has been confirmed by Amnesty International, Americas Watch, Freedom House, and other respected human rights organizations. The Cuban government consistently violates all 30 articles of the United Nations Universal Declaration of Human Rights, including freedom of expression, freedom of the press, and freedom of association.

Those many thousands of Cubans who have attempted to express their opposition and dissatisfaction with the Castro dictatorship have faced the barrel of a gun. Many have sacrificed their lives to uphold their ideals. Many others have been brutally tortured and imprisoned under inhumane conditions, denied access to loved ones, and deprived of basic nourishment and medical assistance.

The Cuban government has unleashed a wrath of tragic consequences on many who have tried to flee. Only last July, 70 civilians fleeing in the *13 de Marzo* tugboat were hosed down by Cuban patrol boats. More than 40 defenseless people, including 22 innocent children, drowned while the authorities, according to survivors, "idly watched, shouting insults, and even refusing to toss life jackets to a single child." Unsurprisingly, Castro's regime staged an "investigation," after which those responsible for the merciless murders were routinely excused. Such brutality assaults not only Cubans, but all people of conscience . . .

Under eight presidents, regardless of party affiliation, this nation has rightly characterized the Cuban regime as a "brutal dictatorship." All eight former presidents have concurred on one basic principle: Due to the severe human rights abuses in Castro's Cuba, not a single law-abiding Cuban exile would be repatriated. Last week's policy reversal marks the collusion of the United States with a totalitarian government to prevent those fleeing communism from reaching safe havens by forcibly returning them. This disgracefully violates the spirit of long-standing U.S. laws and international principles to which the United States has long subscribed.

Article 14 of the Universal Declaration of Human Rights says: "Everyone has the right to seek and enjoy in other countries asylum from persecution." Just as it would have been monstrous to return Germans who crossed the Berlin Wall back to East Germany or Jews escaping a repressive Soviet Union, it is immoral to return Cubans to Castro's island-prison.

We urge the Clinton administration to reconsider this shift in U.S.-Cuba policy by exercising essential humanitarian precepts and respecting fundamental principles for the protection of refugees. As has been done in Haiti and South Africa, this country should decisively exercise its influence to lead the international community once and for all in seeking the removal of the root cause of the mass migrations of Cubans. That cause is Fidel Castro's regime.

Our "Fast for Justice" protests the inhumane, new policy of the Clinton administration. Our hunger strike, inspired by the most virtuous American ideals, is a symbol of solidarity with the victims of Castro's oppression.

We peacefully and respectfully seek:

1. The reversal of forced repatriation of Cubans.

2. An immediate and open congressional investigation of the recent secret negotiations and agreement reached by U.S. officials with Cuban diplomats.

3. The resignation of Morton Halperin, the president's national security advisor and the architect of the new policy.

The Miami Herald building in downtown Miami to protest the Clinton administration's reversal of U.S. immigration policy in regard to granting political asylum to Cuban refugees. *The Miami Herald* is Greater Miami's only major English newspaper. The participants were Sebastián Arcos Casabón, human rights activist; Alex Antón, filmmaker; José Cardona, filmmaker; José Dueñas, ex-political prisoner; and Armando Barbarito Hernández, a former opposition member of Cuban government. The five young Cubans hoped that their hunger strike would reverse the forced repatriation of Cubans picked up by the U.S. Coast Guard on the Straits of Florida. After five days, the hunger strike was called off. Although U.S. foreign policy did not change with regard to the repatriation of Cubans, the hunger strike attracted considerable support in the Greater Miami Cuban community and received great attention from national and international news media. Two of the three demands made by the young Cubans were met, partly through their efforts and the massive protests and lobbying efforts of the Cuban community. Morton Halperin was reassigned to other duties not involving Cuba and a congressional investigation of the U.S.-Cuba negotiations was done. However, the strikers main demand—that President Clinton reverse the forced repatriation of Cubans—has not been met.

The Other Hispanics in the United States

There is a growing presence in the United States of a group called the "other Hispanics." This category includes people from the Caribbean islands, Central and South America, and Spain. Also included in this group, according to the U.S. Census Bureau's definition, are people identifying themselves as Hispanic, Spanish, Spanish American but not from any specific country. In March 1993, the Bureau of the Census estimated that of the 22.8 million Hispanics in the United States, 13.4 percent were from Central and South America and 7 percent were from Spain or people that indicated themselves to be Spanish or Spanish American. These two groups represented 20.4 percent of the total Hispanic population of the United States, or 4,652,000 people.

Dominicans in the United States

The largest of this "other Hispanic" group are the Dominicans. It was estimated that in 1993 there were 800,000 people from the Dominican Republic in the New York City Metropolitan area alone. Other Dominicans have settled in New Jersey, Florida, and Puerto Rico. The largest group of Dominicans, however, lives in New York City's Washington Heights. This neighborhood on the island of Manhattan is known as Quisqueya, a name given by the Taíno Indians to the island called today Hispaniola, which is shared by Haiti and the Dominican Republic.

Dominicans began arriving in the United States after the fall of the rule of dictator Rafael Trujillo in 1961. Four years later, the United States and several nations of Latin America under the Organization of Americans States (OAS) sent troops to Santo Domingo to avoid a Communist takeover of that nation. President Lyndon Johnson sent over 20,000 U.S. troops. Poverty and political turmoil have brought both legal and illegal immigration to the United States from that island. Thousands of Dominicans risk their lives crossing the channel known as the Mona Passage, an 80-mile wide strait that separates the Dominican Republic and Puerto Rico. Small boats overloaded with undocumented Dominicans sometimes capsize and many Dominicans drown. Those who survive the trip and make it to Puerto Rico, an estimated 20,000 each year, eventually fly to New York City, since people from Puerto Rico are not required to show passports when they board a plane bound for the U.S. mainland. Currently, 20,000 legal immigrant visas a year are issued to people from the Dominican Republic. The majority of the Dominicans coming to the United States are from the urban middle class. An estimated 33 percent have college degrees or know skilled trades. Because many Dominicans are of African descent, they experience a double discrimination on account of race and ethnic origin.

In New York City two organizations have been formed to assist Dominicans. The Northern Manhattan Coalition for Immigrants Rights assists Dominicans in coping with life in the "Big Apple." The Dominican Small Business Association helps over 9,000 small businesses owned by Dominicans.

Dominicans are making valuable contributions to life in the United States in several fields. A Dominican actress, born in Barahona and known as the "Queen of Technicolor," María Montez, made many Hollywood films in the 1940s. Oscar de la Renta is the wealthiest Dominican in the United States, with an estimated net worth of $35 million in 1994. One of the best known American fashion designers, he now lends his name not only to clothing but also to handbag and perfume manufacturers.

Julia Álvarez is the acclaimed author of two novels, *How the García Girls Lost Their Accents* and *In the Time of the Butterflies*. Her latter novel

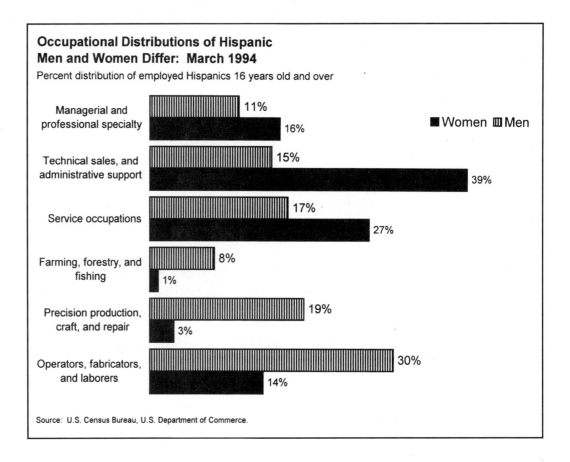

Occupational Distributions of Hispanic Men and Women Differ: March 1994

Percent distribution of employed Hispanics 16 years old and over

■ Women ▥ Men

Occupation	Men	Women
Managerial and professional specialty	11%	16%
Technical sales, and administrative support	15%	39%
Service occupations	17%	27%
Farming, forestry, and fishing	8%	1%
Precision production, craft, and repair	19%	3%
Operators, fabricators, and laborers	30%	14%

Source: U.S. Census Bureau, U.S. Department of Commerce.

was nominated for the National Book Critics' Circle Award. In 1995, Álvarez published *The Other Side/El Otro Lado: Poems,* a collection of poems written with a novelist's sense of narrative and place.

Guillermo Linares has been elected as a city council member, representing the increasing population from the Dominican Republic in New York City.

Dominicans are adapting to life in the United States, and more and more are participating in politics as they become U.S. citizens and develop strong ties in U.S. cities.

The Central American Presence in the United States

The political upheavals and civil wars in Central America have brought ten of thousands of people to the United States. The war against guerrillas in the mountains of Guatemala led 150,000 Maya Indians and other Guatemalans to move to Mexico and the United States during the 1970s and the 1980s. Many Guatemalans moved to California and Florida.

In 1979, the long dictatorship of the Somozas ended in Nicaragua. A Marxist-oriented party called Frente Sandinista de Liberación Nacional (National Liberation Sandinista Front) assumed control of the government in Managua. The word Sandinista came from a guerrilla warfare fighter named Augusto César Sandino, who opposed U.S. intervention and fought against the U.S. marines in Nicaragua during the 1930s. Sandino was killed by the Nicaraguan National Guard led by Anastasio Somoza, who, with the helped of the United States, governed Nicaragua as a dictator. He ruled in Nicaragua until his assassination in 1956. His two sons, Luis and Anastasio Somoza Debayle, ruled after him.

The Sandinistas, led by Daniel Ortega, formed close relations with Cuba and the Soviet Union. They silenced the opposition and established a dictatorship, confiscating the property of the upper and middle classes. President Ronald Reagan, concerned about the establishment of a second Communist county in Latin American, supported the anti-Sandinista guerrillas, known as the Contras (the word comes from *contra revolucionario,* or counter revolutionary), which were operating from Honduras. The war in Nicaragua as well as the totalitarian measures of the Sandinistas brought thousands of Nicaraguans to the United States. In 1990, Violeta Barrios Chamorro was elected president of Nicaragua defeating the Sandinista Daniel Ortega. Chamorro took over a war-ravished country with a ruined economy and galloping inflation. In spite of considerable U.S. financial support, President Chamorro has been unable to improve the standard of living in Nicaragua.

The majority of Nicaraguans settled in California and South Florida. By the 1990s, Greater Miami had the largest population of Nicaraguans in the United States. The Nicaraguan influx overwhelmed social services as well as public schools in South Florida. At one point, so many Nicaraguans refugees were coming that Cuban-born Miami City manager César Odio opened the Bobby Maduro stadium as a temporary shelter for the refugees. Many settled in the small municipality of Sweetwater in South Florida, which became known as Little Managua. Many Nicaraguans have an uncertain legal status in the United States and are facing possible deportation.

Nicaraguans are making valuable contributions to U.S. life. Dr. Horacio Aguirre is the owner and editor of the *Diario Las Américas,* a daily Spanish newspaper in the Greater Miami area that is also shipped to cities such as Washington, D.C., and New York City. Roberto Argüelles is a prominent banker in South Florida. In 1991, Nicaraguan Dennis Martínez became the first Latino pitcher in the major leagues who pitched a perfect game. A Nicaraguan model, Barbara Carrera, made Hollywood movies in the 1970s.

Civil war in El Salvador also brought thousands to the United States. By 1990, there were half a million Salvadorans in Los Angeles alone. With thousands of Salvadorans and Nicaraguans and Guatemalans living in the city, Los Angeles has been called "the Central American capital of the United States."

Contributions of Other Hispanics to the United States

Latin Americans and Spaniards have made and are making valuable contributions to the United States.

Politics and Government

Bob Martínez became the first Hispanic elected as governor of Florida in 1987, after having served as mayor of Tampa from 1979 to 1987. In 1991, President Bush appointed him head of the Drug Enforcement Agency, a position of high rank in the federal government.

Business

Many own small and large businesses throughout the United States. Eight businessmen from Spain, one from Chile, one from the Dominican Republic, and one from Ecuador each had a net worth in 1994 of $25 million or more. Spaniard John Arrillaga has a net worth of $330 million and is the second wealthiest Hispanic in the United States. His company deals in commercial real estate business. Together with his partner they control 5.2 million square feet of office buildings, almost all of it in San Francisco, California.

The Spanish brothers Amigo and Max Soriano have a fortune of $95 million. The brothers founded Western Pioneer, Inc. in the state of Washington to ship supplies to and from Alaska. They also founded Delta Western, which distributed fuel from Alaska. Both companies were sold for $70 million in 1988.

Brothers of Spanish descent born in Latin America, José, Julio, and Elías Liberman deal in the radio station business and in real estate. José was born in Mexico, Julio in Guatemala, and Elías in Costa Rica. The Liberman family's fortune was $35 million in 1994.

Spaniard Lloyd G. Chávez owns the largest car dealership in the state of Colorado, selling more than 30,000 cars a year. Chávez, who fought in War World II, has a net worth of $35 million.

Three other Spaniards are prominent businessmen: Frank L. Fauce from Los Angeles, California, with a net worth of $30 million, owned several television stations that he later sold to Univision Network in 1986; Ed L. Romero from Albuquerque, New Mexico, with a net worth of $25 million, runs a solar energy installation firm that had $66 million in sales in 1992; and Manuel A. Herrán and family from Miami, Florida, with a net worth of $35 million, run the Sedano's supermarkets and pharmacies in South Florida.

Carmelo E. "Tom" Velez from Ecuador founded CTA Incorporated of Rockville, Maryland, in 1979. The company offers engineering services and flight simulators. It has now also entered the satellite launching business. The last

Dr. Severo Ochoa discovered a method for the production of ribonucleic acid (RNA) in a laboratory, for which she received the Nobel Prize in Medicine and Physiology in 1959.

Dominican multimillionaire, Oscar de la Renta, with a net worth of $35 million, has already been mentioned as a world-renowned fashion designer.

Literature, Arts, and Entertainment

Nobel literature winner Chilean Gabriela Mistral lived part of her life in the United States and died here. Another Chilean writer, Isabel Allende, has written several best-selling novels and lives in California. Among her best sellers are *La casa de los espíritus* (1982) (*The House of the Spirits,* 1985), *De amor y de sombras* (1984) (*Of Love and Shadows,* 1987), and *Cuentos de Eva Luna* (1987) (*The Stories of Eva Luna,* 1991).

George Febres, born in Ecuador and related to one of his native country's presidents, fought in the Vietnam War and is a painter. The Smithsonian Institution and the New Orleans Museum of Art display his paintings. Peruvian Alberto Insua paints in bright colors inspired by pre-Columbian myths. Argentine Susana Jaime Mena is a painter and a sculptor. Chilean Jorge Tacla does landscape paintings and recently did a mural for a Bronx courthouse. Venezuelan Marisol Escobar is a sculptor whose works have been displayed at the Museum of Modern Art in New York City and at other museums worldwide.

Venezuelan Julio Bacco won the gold medal in Moscow's International Ballet Competition. He now dances for the American Ballet Theater. Chilean Lupe Serrano is a world-famous ballerina

who also worked from 1953 to the early 1970s in the American Ballet Theater Company.

Spaniard Dr. Severo Ochoa received the Nobel Prize in Medicine and Physiology in 1959 for his discovery of a way to produce ribonucleic acid (RNA) in a laboratory. Dr. Ochoa, a U.S. citizen, worked for over 40 years at New York University.

Another Hispanic, Dr. Luis Walter Álvarez, whose parents were born in Spain, received a Nobel Prize in Physics in 1968 for his discovery of subatomic particles that exist for fractions of a second. Dr. Álvarez, together with his son Walter, a geologist, developed the theory of the destruction of the dinosaurs. An asteroid was named "Alvarez" in their honor.

Dr. Franklin R. Chang-Díaz, who was born in San José, Costa Rica, spoke in Spanish while in outer space aboard the Space Shuttle *Columbia* in 1986. Michael E. López-Alegría, born in Madrid, Spain, is also an astronaut; he completed his training in 1992 and was previously a test pilot.

Argentine César Pelli is one of the best-known U.S. architects. He has designed the United Nations building in Vienna, Austria; the U.S. Embassy in Tokyo, Japan; and is currently designing the Theater of the Performing Arts in Greater Miami. Two other famous architects are José Luis Sert, born in Barcelona, and Peruvian Bernardo Fort-Brescia. Sert has worked on urban design of cities such as Bogotá and Rio de Janeiro and has designed buildings for Harvard and Boston Universities. Fort-Brescia, together with his wife, founded in 1977 the firm Architectonica in Miami. They have designed private homes, apartment buildings, condominiums, and office buildings in Miami, Chicago, San Francisco, and other major cities.

Hispanics from Latin America and Spain, in addition to Mexican Americans, Puerto Ricans, and Cuban Americans, have enriched the cultural life of the United States and are making important contributions in all fields of endeavor.

Issues Affecting Latinos and Their Future Outlook

Hispanics share with African Americans and other minority groups a number of issues: concern about drug abuse, juvenile delinquency, and crime; a desire to end prejudice and discrimination; the need for economic development in low-income

Nicholas Trist, as a representative of the United States, signed the treaty of Guadalupe Hidalgo of 1848, which ended the U.S.-Mexican War and granted much of the present American West and Southwest to the United States.

neighborhoods; desire for increased political participation and redistricting on the basis of race and ethnicity; affirmative action in employment and set asides in the awarding of contracts for minority businesses; and a desire for better education, housing, jobs, health care, and other social services. Since many Hispanics live at or near the poverty level, a safety net of social services is of utmost importance to them. Other issues are more unique to the Hispanic communities, such as immigration, bilingual education, and the imposition of official English. A discussion of crucial issues affecting Latinos today is presented below.

Discrimination and Prejudice

Mexican Americans in the Southwest from 1848 to the 1960s were severely discriminated against in housing, employment, jury selection, public accommodations, and law enforcement and, in essence, became second-class citizens. The rights awarded to them by the Treaty of Guadalupe Hidalgo of 1848, which ended the U.S.-Mexican war, such as ownership of the land and full civil rights, were ignored. Latinos participated actively in the civil rights struggles of the 1960s and 1970s to regain these lost rights.

In the Southwest, Mexican Americans founded numerous organizations in order to fight racism, prejudice, and discrimination and to advance the interest of Mexican Americans.

Some of these organizations were the Alianza Hispano-Americana, the League of United Latin American Citizens (LULAC), the Community Service Organization (CSO), the American GI Forum, the Mexican American Political Organization (MAPO), the Political Association of Spanish Speaking Organizations (PASO), the Mexican American Legal Defense and Education Fund (MALDEF), the National Council of La Raza, and the Southwest Voter Registration Education Project. Puerto Ricans in New York also founded organizations to advance their interest, such as the Museo del Barrio, the Puerto Rican Legal Defense and Education Fund, the Young Lords, ASPIRA, and others. Cuban Americans organized the Spanish League Against Discrimination (SALAD), the Cuban American National Council, the Cámara de Comercio Latino Americana (CAMACOL), and other organizations geared specifically toward bringing freedom and democracy in Cuba, such as the Cuban American National Foundation.

Although discrimination and prejudice against Hispanics have lessened in comparison with the period prior to the 1960s, they still exist today. The current anti-immigrant climate; the initiatives to establish English as the official language (which passed in 18 states); the threat to deny essential social services, such as education and health care, to undocumented immigrants; and the threat to eliminate benefits to immigrants, who are U.S. residents—all have created a negative environment for Hispanics in the United States.

Some Hispanics feel that immigration laws that punish employers with heavy fines for hiring undocumented workers have brought discrimination against U.S.-born Hispanics and legal residents. Robert D. Hershey Jr. wrote an article for *The New York Times* on April 27, 1995, regarding the bias against Hispanic workers who are increasingly finding "intense suspicion, resentment and, in many cases, outright discrimination." Hershey believes that the growing Hispanic labor force is losing ground in the nation because discrimination combined with poor educational background, outmoded skills, and job inexperience is making it difficult for Hispanics to find and keep jobs. California, which is the home of approximately one third of the nation's Latino population, had 11.3 percent Latino unemployment at the beginning of 1995. The Hispanic unemployment rate in California was greater than that of African Americans. Nationwide the Hispanic unemployment rate for the first month of 1995 was 9.1 percent, compared with the Anglo American rate 4.7.

Hershey's article quotes Juan Vargas, the Deputy Major of San Diego, who stated; "There's no doubt that discrimination has increased against Latinos. Proposition 187 has created almost a crisis in the Latino community. It has employers panicked." He also quotes Rodolfo de la Garza, a professor of government at the University of Texas, who said: "When you downsize these labor markets, Hispanics get hit very hard." Often Latinos are the "last hired and the first fired."

Hispanics in government believe that they are vastly underrepresented and are being denied promotions. In 1968, 311 agents brought a lawsuit against their employer, the Federal Bureau of Investigation (FBI), alleging a long history of discrimination. A U.S. district court ruled in favor of the Latino agents and ordered the FBI to address the issue of promotions for Latinos. Two years later, Hispanic agents claimed that the FBI had retaliated against them for bringing the case and filed another lawsuit against their agency. Many Latinos who were born in the United States, or in some cases whose families settled the U.S. Southwest hundreds of years ago, feel that they are treated as if they were illegal aliens.

Of course, Latinos themselves are not immune from racism. Earl Shorris in his book *Latinos: A Biography of the People* (1992) discusses the *racismo* of some Latinos. Some Cuban Americans put down the Mariel entrants who arrived in 1980 and refer to them in a derogatory manner as *los marielitos*. Some Puerto Ricans who lived in Puerto Rico and New York dislike Dominicans. Some Mexican nationals put down "assimilated" Mexican Americans and refer to them as *pochos*. Finally, some Latinos do not like Latinos of a different nationality. Shorris also believes that some U.S.-born or U.S.-legal-resident Hispanics dislike illegal aliens and that discrimination exists against ignorant, poor, and dark-skinned Hispanics by Hispanics who are fair-skinned, educated, and affluent.

Political Participation

The Voting Rights Act of 1965 radically changed U.S. society. This highly effective civil rights law was enacted to end the denial of the right to vote of African Americans in many southern states. Within two years of the passing of this landmark legislation, African American voter registration in Mississippi increased from 6 percent to 60 percent. The number of African American elected officials increased from 100 in 1965 to almost 5,000 by 1989.

Hispanic leaders looked at the success of African American politicians and worked to be included under this law. Organizations such as the Mexican American Legal Defense and Education Fund (MALDEF) worked with congressional leaders to amend the Voting Rights Act so that areas with large number of Hispanic voters would be included under this federal law. By 1975, Hispanics had won the right to be included under the law and the act's jurisdiction was extended to 375 areas outside the South. Latinos also obtained the right to cast ballots written in Spanish.

In 1982, new amendments to the Voting Rights Act required several states to offer minorities a chance at electing representatives. The 1982 amendments to the act required states to redesign districts to allow African Americans and Hispanics to be elected into office. African American and Latino civil rights groups won lawsuits eliminating multimember districts or at-large districts that made it very difficult to elect minority members.

They demonstrated how African Americans and Latinos were severely underrepresented among elected officials. To comply with the courts' rulings and the amended Voting Rights Act, many districts were racially and ethnically gerrymandered by many states. The term "gerrymander" was coined in the early 1800s after Governor Elbridge Gerry of Massachusetts made salamander-shaped districts to favor his political party. Many Hispanics were elected into office at local, state, and national levels as a result of the redesigned districts.

Anglo American citizens and Republican politicians challenged the constitutionality of the new racially and ethnically gerrymandered districts. One of these lawsuits was considered by the U.S. Supreme Court. The court ruled in 1993 that the gerrymandered Twelfth District of North Carolina violated the Constitution's Equal Protection Clause. Justice Sandra Day O'Connor, writing for the majority of the court, stated that such districts violated the principles of compactness and contiguousness. Justice O'Connor questioned all racially inspired gerrymandered districts by declaring that "even for remedial purposes, [it] may Balkanize us into competing racial factions [and] . . . bears an uncomfortable resemblance to political apartheid." O'Connor stated that while race may be a factor in redrawing districts, it could not be the only factor. She remanded the case back to the North Carolina district court to determine if the district should be redrawn.

Nydia Velázquez, the first Puerto Rican woman to serve in Congress, was elected in 1992 to the New York City's Twelfth Congressional District to represent the predominantly Latino neighborhoods of Brooklyn, Manhattan, and Queens. Velázquez was reelected in 1994. Her district is one of the nation's poorest, and now the legitimacy of the borders of this district is also being challenged in a federal lawsuit. The federal lawsuit was initiated by a Republican group.

People who oppose the redrawn districts that guarantee the election of African Americans and Hispanic candidates feel that these gerrymandered districts violate the Constitution's Equal Protection Clause. They argue that voting districts should represent real geographic regions and communities, not special factions or racial or ethnic groups. Opponents state that the amended Voting Rights Act is polarizing the nation, segregating minorities, and creating racial quotas and separatism. They believe that racial redistricting will hurt minorities in the long run.

People in favor of gerrymandered districts point out that minorities are severely underrepresented at all levels of government. Hispanic leaders point out that even though Hispanics comprise ten percent of the nation's population, they make up barely two percent of elected officials. They argue that prejudice and discrimination have been the reasons why minorities have been underrepresented and that the amended Voting Rights Act is a remedy for the past and present discrimination at the ballot box. Proponents also believe that redistricting gives African Americans and Hispanics a fair chance at being elected to political office.

There is no doubt that redistricting and the astounding growth in numbers of Hispanics have brought about an increase in the numbers of Latino elected officials. In 1950 only 20 Latinos were serving as state legislators, and they all came from New Mexico. This state has elected four Hispanic governors and three Hispanic U.S. senators in the past. By 1965, there were 35 Latino legislators in four Southwestern states and three Latinos—Edward Roybal of California and Kika de la Garza and Henry B. Gonzalez from Texas—were serving in Congress. During the last decade, Latinos have been elected at every level of government in many states. According to the National Association of Latino Elected and Appointed Officials (NALEAO), there were 3,147 Latino elected officials in 1985 and by 1994 this number had increased to 4,625, a 47-percent increase. These figures do not include the many Latinos elected to the local school councils of Chicago Public Schools.

At the local level Hispanics have made great progress by challenging the multimember districts or at-large districts. In Chicago, a court-ordered ruling created four Latino wards. In 1985, the U.S. Department of Justice filed a lawsuit forcing the redistricting of the Los Angeles City Council. Gloria Molina was elected the following year to represent a new Hispanic majority district. In 1988, a similar lawsuit was filed by MALDEF against the Los Angeles County—the largest county in the nation with 8.8 million people. The lawsuit was successful and Gloria Molina was elected in 1991 as a member of the Board of Supervisors of Los Angeles County. Another lawsuit resulted in the

Lucille Roybal-Allard, a Democrat from Los Angeles, is one of three Latinas to have served in the U.S. House of Representatives.

no members do not think alike: Some are Democrats and others are Republicans. They have been divided on issues such as the North American Free Trade Agreement (NAFTA), the embargo on Cuba, and the Republican party's Contract with America. Nydia Velázquez feels that the Republican party's Contract with America is attacking working families, immigrants, and the poor people from her district: Even funding for the Hispanic Caucus was eliminated. She believes that the intent of the Republicans is to silence the Hispanics serving in Congress and that the Republicans are attacking bilingual education and education in general as well as specific programs and services that are dear to her. On some issues, such as bilingual education and immigration, Hispanic politicians tend to agree.

Arturo Vargas stated that "when Latino elected officials look to the future, they are optimistic about continued political empowerment, but they are convinced that Latinos must work very had to achieve it." Vargas reported that formidable obstacles still remain. One of the most important is that many Hispanics are not U.S. citizens. That number is estimated to be 7.6 million Latino adults. For this reason, many organizations—such as NALEO, the National Council of La Raza, the Southwest Voters Registration Education Project (SVREP)—are conducting citizenship campaigns in Latino communities. The Southwest Voters Registration Education Project has two offices, one in San Antonio and the other in Los Angeles, and an annual budget of $3 million. Its president, Antonio Gonzalez, claims that SVREP has conducted 1,800 voter registration drives and education campaigns in 200 communities and has trained more than 40,000 leaders on registering Latinos and getting Latinos out to vote. These organizations and others are also encouraging Latinos who are citizens to register to vote. By 1992, there were 4.2 million Latino voters. In spite of these campaigns, Latino registration and voting rates lag behind those of the general population.

election of Simon Salinas as the first Latino to serve on the Monterey County Board of Supervisors in more than a century. In 1993, five Hispanics were elected to the Dade County Metropolitan Commission in South Florida following a successful challenge of at-large elections in the 2-million-strong Dade County. In 1996, the Dade County School Board elected a majority Hispanic board, also as a result of a successful lawsuit.

Arturo Vargas wrote an article, "Ten Years of Latino Political Progress: Bridging the Walls and Pressing Forward," that appeared in *Vista* magazine in September 1995. He explained that redistricting has had a strong impact at the state level. In 1985, there were 119 Latinos elected to state offices; after 1992, this number increased to 163. In Texas, Hispanic state legislators increased to 32 Latinos, and in California, ten Latinos were elected to the State Assembly.

Latinas were also being elected in great numbers, and by 1994 there were 1,104 Latinas elected to political office. Three Latinas have served in the U.S. House of Representatives—Puerto Rican Nydia Velázquez, a Democrat from New York City; Lucille Roybal-Allard, a Democrat from Los Angeles; and Ileana Ros-Lehtinen, a Republican from Greater Miami.

In 1994, 19 Hispanics were serving in Congress and were members of the Congressional Hispanic Caucus. U.S. House of Representatives Lati-

Immigration

Immigration has emerged as one of the most important issues facing the nation during the 1990s. This is a pivotal issue for Hispanics, since many of them are either recent immigrants or have relatives in Latin America and Spain who desire to enter the United States. Linda Chavez estimates that currently one in three Hispanics is an immigrant and one in two Hispanic adults is foreign-born.

In the fall of 1995 there were several immigration bills before the 104th Congress. Responding to a resurgent nativism and an anti-immigration mood across the land, political leaders have drafted several bills that drastically revise the nation's immigration laws, particularly as they relate to law enforcement, border control measures, and reductions in the number of legal immigrants allowed into the country. Some members of Congress are even discussing denying social programs to U.S. legal residents, a move that has prompted many to seek U.S. citizenship. Some of these bills threaten to deny benefits to Hispanic elderly, many of whom have lived and worked in this United States as legal residents for many years.

There have been bills before Congress that would cut financial aid for higher education to legal immigrant students. Over 20,000 U.S. legal residents could lose financial aid in Florida alone. On October 9, 1995, Florida's University Chancellor Charles Reed denounced this kind of thinking and stated, "These people can do everything. They pay taxes. They work in our state. They came here in a legal way." Miami-Dade Community College president Eduardo Padrón also feels this bill is ill-advised. Padrón stated: "It not only deprives the same people we need to incorporate into society, but basically punishes people who followed the rules. . . ."

President Bill Clinton has asked for almost $1 billion in additional funds for the Immigration and Naturalization Service's budget and the hiring of 650 new investigators in 1995. The Immigration and Naturalization Service (INS) has conducted several crackdowns to locate undocumented workers. From June to September 1995, 4,044 illegal workers were found in Alabama, Arkansas, Florida, Georgia, Mississippi, and Tennessee, and 3,400 were sent back to their native countries. Most of the undocumented workers came from Mexico. More than 300 businesses were inspected by the INS during a four-month sweep through the South in what was called Operation SouthPAW (Protecting America's Workers). Ten employers were fined up to $15,000 for employing undocumented workers. The Immigration Reform and Control Act (IRCA) of 1986 for the first time prohibited employers from hiring undocumented workers.

The Clinton administration has begun to deport thousands of Nicaraguans who entered the nation illegally during the Reagan years. At that time President Reagan was supporting the Contra rebels, who were fighting against the Marxist-oriented Sandinista government of Nicaragua. The Reagan administration welcomed the anti-Communist Nicaraguans. It is estimated that there are about 150,000 Nicaraguans in South Florida and several thousands in California.

The Clinton administration claims that Nicaragua now has a democratically elected government. As of October 1995, 10,000 Nicaraguans have been ordered to return home, even though only a couple dozens have been actually deported. Another 50,000 have asylum cases or appeals pending, and if they lose, they will be deported.

Each week hundreds of "bag and baggage" letters are being received by startled Nicaraguans ordering them to report for deportation. Many Nicaraguans have lived in the United States for almost 15 years and do not understand how after all these years they are now facing deportation. Many Nicaraguans have gone underground trying to elude the INS. Some families are afraid to send their children to school or even to a hospital for fear that they would be turned in to the INS. Deportation in Southwestern states such as California, Arizona, New Mexico, and Texas is increasing as the Clinton administration and the INS respond to the national outcry against illegal immigration and the general anti-immigrant nativist sentiment of many Americans. In spite of these measures, the flow of undocumented workers has continued.

A nine-member bipartisan group, the Commission on Immigration Reform headed by former Congresswoman Barbara C. Jordan, issued a report calling for a reduction in the present annual average of 800,000 immigrants to a proposed ceiling of 535,000 immigrants per year. Most of the immigration bills before Congress also call for reducing the numbers of skilled workers sponsored by businesses and political refugees. *The Miami Herald* criticized these measures in an editorial published on October 1, 1995. The editorial stated that the nation needed these skilled workers for its high-tech industry and in academia. It also stated that imposing a 50,000-immigrant ceiling on political refugees was "an arbitrary cap, considering the state of a world plagued by civil strife and despotic government." The author of the editorial felt that the refugee ceiling "violates the spirit of America's traditional, principled commitment to providing a safe haven to those who have a well-grounded fear of persecution."

In 1994, legal immigration to the United States totaled 804,416. It is estimated that at least 200,000 undocumented individuals enter the United States each year. In the 1980s, the nation received 8.7 million new immigrants. The United States is accepting more immigrants than the rest of the world combined. Since the 1960s most of the immigrants came from Asia and Latin America; prior to that they came mostly from Europe. In 1994, 57 percent of the immigrants were close relatives, children, or spouses of U.S. citizens or U.S. residents. Approximately 26 percent of the immigrants had completed college.

Throughout the nation's history newcomers have been blamed for most of the nation's ills, particularly during periods of high unemployment and difficult economic times. Currently, the national mood against immigrants, both legal and undocumented, appears to be very negative. Latino immigrants are particularly feared or disliked in states like Florida, Texas, Arizona, New Mexico, and California—states that have a large percentage of Latinos.

In California, a state that has approximately half of all the undocumented immigrants in the country, approved Proposition 187 by a 59 percent margin on November 8, 1994. This proposition was judged by many observers as one of the most divisive ballot initiatives in California's history. Proposition 187, called "Save Our State" by its proponents, proposed to exclude undocumented aliens from receiving any welfare or social services, including public education and nonemergency medical care. Shortly after its passage, opponents filed many lawsuits alleging that the proposition was illegal and unconstitutional. Ultimately the U.S. Supreme Court will have to decide on the constitutionality of Proposition 187.

Supporters of this proposition felt that California was becoming a third-world nation and that illegal aliens were totally overwhelming the state. State education officials estimated that in 1993 approximately 410,000 undocumented immigrant students were attending schools in California.

Opponents of this proposition, which included nearly all of California's education and social services groups, called the measure mean-spirited and the wrong solution to a complex problem.

California's Governor Pete Wilson strongly supported the initiative, and his popularity increased in the state and across the nation. He declared his candidacy for president in New York City with the Statue of Liberty in the background, and the reduction of the number of immigrants as well as the deportation of undocumented workers became the key issues of his campaign. Many pro-immigrant groups denounced what they perceived as the governor's posturing and pandering to the electorate. In September of 1995, Wilson announced that he was no longer running for president because he had been unable to raise sufficient funds and generate enthusiasm for his campaign. Many Hispanic activists were glad that Wilson had dropped out of the presidential race, since they disliked his support for Proposition 187 and his anti-immigrant campaign rethoric.

Richard D. Lamm, a former governor of Colorado and director of the Center for Public Policy and Contemporary Issues at the University of Denver, testified before the U.S. House of Representatives Judiciary Committee's Subcommittee on Immigration, Refugees, and International Law on March 13, 1990. Lamm recommended that the United States should limit the overall number of immigrants permitted in the nation. His rationale was that increasing the number of immigrants would worsen the nation's problems in education, health care, and the environment. Lamm stated:

> More people do not necessary make for a better society . . . America's growing disenfranchised underclass is not simply going to disappear because we import foreign workers instead of training and retraining our own . . . By artificially reflooding the labor market, this Congress will be denying those people the opportunities they deserve . . . We know, based on experience, that increasing immigration is going to increase the burdens of those school districts that can least afford to absorb them . . .

Palmer Stacy and Wayne Lutton in their book *The Immigration Time Bomb* (1988) argue that the United States should drastically lower the number of new immigrants it allows to enter the country annually. They recommended that the number of new immigrants should be equal to the number of U.S. citizens who emigrate each year, a number of approximately 100,000 per year.

People who feel that immigration should be drastically reduced use the following arguments:

1. The United States is already overcrowded and the nation has air and water pollution, traffic jams, crime, and a multitude of urban problems brought about by too many people living in cities. It is expected that the nation would grow to approximately 383 million by the year 2050.

2. Since approximately one third of the new immigrants are uneducated, the newcomers compete with the nation's poor urban African Americans and Hispanics for jobs and social services. Already unemployment of African American youth is at approximately 40 percent and a high percentage of young Latinos are out of work.

3. The large number of immigrants who are arriving tend to settle among their own national and ethnic groups and keep their languages and cultures. There is a fear that American culture is endangered by too many immigrants.

4. Too much money is being spent to provide social services to new immigrants. These funds should be spent to train the nation's workers and provide services to its poor citizens or give relief to the taxpayers.

Ben J. Wattenberg and Karl Zinsmeister, scholars at the American Enterprise Institute, a conservative think tank in Washington, D.C., recommend that the United States should allow more immigrants in the nation. They argue that in the past newcomers have made valuable contributions to society and that increased immigration would allow the United States to remain a productive and wealthy nation. They stated in an article that appeared in William Dudley's *Immigration: Opposing Viewpoints* (1990):

> Immigration can bring us significant numbers of bold creators and skilled workers. It can diminish whatever labor shortages may be coming our way . . . Immigration can energize whole communities with a new entrepreneurial spirit, keeping us robust and growing as a nation. At a time when the idea of competitiveness has become a national fixation, it can bolster our competitiveness and help us retain our position as the common denominator of the international trade web. And as most Americans continue to believe that we have a mission to foster liberty and the love of liberty throughout the world, immigration can help us fulfill that mission through successful example . . .

Julian L. Simon in his book *The Economic Consequence of Immigration* (1989) recommends that the nation should increase the total immigration quota. As he states:

> Taking in immigrants at a rate equal to, or even far above, the present admission rate improves our average standard of living on the balance . . . Rather than being a matter of charity, we can expect our incomes to be higher rather than lower in future years if we take in more immigrants.

Those who oppose drastic reduction of immigration to the United States use the following arguments:

1. Immigrants help the U.S. economy. The Hudson Institute of America conducted a poll among 38 top economists that included seven Nobel Prize winners. More than 80 percent of the economists stated that immigration in this century has been positive for the economy of the nation; the rest said that it was slightly positive. Two thirds of them believed that increased immigration would bring a higher standard of living in the United States. Moreover, many economists do not believe that newcomers worsen the situation for the nation's poor. George Borjas, an economist at the University of California at San Diego, stated "there is no evidence that illegal immigration has had a significant adverse effect on the earning opportunities of any native group including blacks."

2. Immigrants contribute greatly to the U.S economy. They earned approximately $240 billion in 1995 and pay over $90 billion in taxes each year.

3. Immigrants, including undocumented aliens, work in menial occupations as fruit pickers, domestic help, and dishwashers—work that most Americans would not consider.

4. Since there is a serious shortage of U.S.-born medical doctors, scientists, engineers, and mathematicians, educated immigrants are needed in high-tech industries, at universities, and in the medical field.

5. Immigrants revitalize and invigorate the nation. As a rule most of them are younger, healthier, well-motivated, and determined to succeed in this country. This nation was built by immigrants who brought with them the

The *bracero* program was a plan to bring Mexican agricultural and railroad workers to the United States to counteract the labor shortage brought by World War II. Some believe that a similar guest worker program should be enacted today.

values of discipline, honesty, hard work, and family responsibility.

6. Immigration can keep the nation from aging too fast since most newcomers are young. This young influx of immigrants will protect the nation's pension and health-care systems.

Julian L. Simon, author of *The Economic Consequences of Immigration* (1989) and a professor at the University of Maryland, wrote an article proposing that Congress should consider setting up a guest worker program similar to the *bracero* program of 1942 to 1964. The *bracero* program was a system that permitted the employment of foreign workers. In this case, it referred to the temporary Mexican agricultural and railroad workers first brought into the United States under contract in 1942 as an emergency measure to meet the temporary labor shortage brought by World War II. This article was published by *The New York Times* and *The Miami Herald* on June 23, 1995. Simon believes that Congress, instead of reducing the ceiling on legal immigration and cracking down and deporting illegal immigrants, should set up a guest worker program that would allow foreign workers to come to the United States and be assigned to U.S. companies needing them, with a maximum stay of three to five years. Congress would have to decide which countries would participate, and Simon recommended that most of the workers should come from Mexico, the Caribbean, and Central America. He suggested that illegal

aliens already working in the United States should be given the opportunity to gain guest worker status. Simon also suggested that in order to keep workers from staying in the nation after their term of employment expired, a portion of their pay could be deducted along with income taxes and held in escrow to be returned when they leave for their native countries. Simon believes that his solution to the immigration problem deserves consideration before the entire nation is engaged in a divisive struggle like the one in California in 1994.

During his visit to the United States, Pope John Paul II invoked Emma Lazarus' plea for the nation to embrace the huddle masses of refugees yearning to breath free. Speaking to 80,000 people on October 5, 1995, at Giants Stadium in Newark, New Jersey, just ten miles from the Statue of Liberty, the Pope recited part of the nineteenth-century poem of Emma Lazarus that is inscribed on the Statue of Liberty. He also said, "If America were to turn on itself, would this not be the beginning of the end of what constitutes the very essence of the 'American Experience'?"

The North American Free Trade Agreement (NAFTA)

The North American Free Trade Agreement (NAFTA) divided Latinos as it did many other Americans. This treaty, initiated by President George Bush and Mexican President Carlos Salinas de Gortari, created a regional trading block of three countries, the United States, Mexico, and Canada. The three countries have a population of 370 million people and produce $6 trillion worth of goods and services.

Himilce Novas in her book *Everything You Need to Know About Latino History* (1994) explained that the Hispanic caucus was divided on this issue. Bill Richardson of New Mexico and Henry Bonilla of Texas supported the NAFTA treaty, since they felt it would be beneficial for the three countries involved. Additionally, they felt that NAFTA would bring a closer relationship between Mexico and the United States and that, if the Mexican economy improved as a result of increased trade, a reduction of Mexican undocumented workers entering the United States would result. Other Hispanics in Congress, such as Ed Pastor of Arizona, Matthew Martínez of California, and Ileana Ros-Lehtinen and Lincoln Díaz-Balart of South Florida, opposed this treaty. In general, unions, such as the AFL-CIO, opposed the treaty because they felt that a large amount of U.S. capital investment would flow to Mexico and that many U.S. workers would lose their jobs.

The visit of Mexican President Ernesto Zedillo to the United States in October 1995 renewed the discussion on NAFTA. U.S. Trade Representative Mickey Kantor stated that NAFTA had created 340,000 jobs in less than two years. Critics of NAFTA stated that NAFTA cost the U.S. economy 100,000 jobs lost to Mexico, since wages in that country are low. Ralph Nader's Public Citizen lobby attacked NAFTA, as did union leaders and some Republican presidential candidates. However, the jury is still out on NAFTA. If this treaty favors only a small group and hurts many in the United States, then the NAFTA experiment will be deemed a failure. However, if NAFTA increases trade among the three countries with minimal job losses, and if job creation increases as a result of investment and trade, then NAFTA will be successful and probably expand to include additional countries. Already Chile is anxious to join NAFTA, and other Latin American countries are creating regional free trade agreements.

Bilingual Education

During the nineteenth century there were bilingual schools in different parts of the country.

However, with the wave of patriotism during World War I, these schools changed their curriculum and became monolingual. Obviously, the war against the Kaiser of Germany created the hatred of the enemy's language. The teaching of German was dropped at that time and was not reinstated until 1923, when the U.S. Supreme Court struck down a Nebraska law that forbid the teaching of that language.

In 1962, Coral Way Elementary School in Greater Miami offered bilingual instruction at a time when Cuban refugees were arriving in South Florida in great numbers. The program has since expanded to other schools in South Florida. The Dade County Public Schools became the first U.S. public school district in modern times to offer 50-percent instruction in Spanish and 50 percent in English. Later, bilingual education spread throughout the nation in spite of its critics and vocal opponents.

Bilingual education continues to be a controversial issue, particularly as it relates to whether or not the government should continue funding it. Bilingual education is defined as instruction delivered in English and in another language such as Spanish. Its purpose is to teach the student in his native language while he learns English so that he will not fall behind and get discouraged. Bilingual education for the English-speaking student provides an opportunity to learn another language and acquire sensitivity to, compassion for, and an appreciation of the diversity of cultures and nationalities in an ever increasingly interdependent world.

Opponents of bilingual education argue that it has failed and has been a waste of taxpayers' money. They point out that over $2 billion dollars have been spent by the federal government with minimal results since Congress passed the Bilingual Education Act of 1968. Opponents believe that immigrants would learn English faster if they are immersed in English language classes and not taught in their native languages. Critics of bilingual education, who also favor the melting pot concept (the belief that all citizens should blend together into a homogenized American culture), believe that English holds the nation together. They argue that teaching the native languages of immigrants would divide the nation and assimilation, or "Americanization," would not be achieved. They point out that nations like Canada and Belgium that lack language unity are therefore split culturally and linguistically.

Some Latinos are opposed to bilingual education, among them journalist and novelist Richard Rodriguez, author of *Days of Obligation: An Argument with my Mexican Father* (1991), and Linda Chavez, author of *Out of the Barrio: Toward a New Politics of Hispanic Assimilation* (1991). Both writers argue that Hispanic children are held back in bilingual programs and do not learn English as fast as they should. Chavez in her book cites studies that indicate that bilingual education is not an effective way of learning English.

The vast majority of Hispanics in the United States favor bilingual education and the teaching of the Spanish language and culture to their children. Latinos believe that English is not threatened in the United States and like the idea of cultural pluralism and respect for diversity.

Like African Americans and other immigrants, Hispanics are very proud of their background and seek recognition and respect for their language and culture. They are well aware that Spanish was spoken in North America a century before English and that their ancestors explored and settled most of what is today the United States.

Most Hispanic immigrants realize that learning English is of utmost importance to their economic advancement and adjustment. The great majority of Hispanic immigrants do learn English.

Many Hispanics feel that a multicultural and multilingual population makes the nation more competitive in the global economy and strengthens U.S. security. For that reason, they believe that bilingual education should be federally, state, and locally funded. When properly taught, bilingual education allows students to acquire two languages, improve their self-esteem, acquire a global perspective, and increase academic achievement. Many Hispanics feel that the Spanish that their children speak should be preserved since it is an asset to the nation. They do not want their children to forget Spanish or their grandchildren have to learn it as a foreign language. Educators agree that bilingual education alone will not improve the achievement of Latino students. However, when combined with other measures, it offers Latinos the opportunity to succeed in school.

A great deal of educational research, numerous national reports, and prominent educators support the view that the teaching of foreign languages is very positive. Some of the conclusions of educational research are as follows:

1. The time spent in a foreign language classroom does not cause students to fall behind in the English language; rather, it reinforces English language skills. Foreign language studies tend to increase vocabulary development, reading and grammar skills, memory, and auditory discrimination—all skills that are readily transferable to English. A study conducted at Coral Way Elementary School revealed that national standardized test scores in English were the same or better when compared with the scores of students of similar socioeconomic level who attended monolingual schools.

2. Foreign languages should be taught to students before the age of 10, because the speech patterns in the speech area of the brain have not been permanently established yet, making the learning of a new speech system before this age easier. For this reason, foreign language teaching should begin at the elementary school.

3. Second language learners have been found to be more flexible and creative and to be more effective problem solvers. Learning a foreign language also helps students move toward intercultural competence and achieve an awareness of the global community.

4. Students in schools with a complete bilingual curriculum (one that offers 50 percent of the instruction in English and 50 percent in another language) have been found not to fall behind in English as measured by national standardized testing, because many of the skills learned in the second language are transferable to English. Such has been the experience in school systems like the Dade County Public Schools, the fourth largest in the nation. The Dade County system's magnet bilingual schools, offering French, Spanish, or German and an international curriculum, all have waiting lists. These magnet schools in the Greater Miami area attract students from a wide geographical area, and parents feel their children are receiving an education second to none. In fact, affluent parents have taken their children from exclu-

sive private schools and enrolled them in the public international bilingual magnet schools.

5. Elementary school children who study a foreign language scored higher than children of similar backgrounds on the Torrance Test of Creative Thinking. Foreign language exposure allows students to attain a level of abstraction otherwise not easily reached.

A series of national studies and reports have pointed out the advantages of teaching foreign languages in the nation's schools. In 1979, the report of the President's Commission on Foreign Language and International Studies, called *Strength through Wisdom,* stated, ". . . a nation's welfare depends in large measure on the intellectual and psychological strengths that are derived from perspective visions of the world beyond its own boundaries." The commission recommended that foreign language studies should begin at the elementary school level and continue through the student's entire educational experience. The commission's report also stated that the success of the United States in the international marketplace is related to the ability of its citizens to communicate in a variety of foreign languages and an understanding of the many cultures of the world.

A 1983 report by the National Commission on Excellence in Education, *A Nation at Risk,* stated that the study of foreign languages and cultures was part of a fundamentally sound education along with five other "basics": English, mathematics, natural sciences, computer sciences, and social studies.

In 1985, the Southern Governors Association issued a report stating that "[we] should be able to speak with understanding the language of our clients, our allies, and our trading partners, as well as the languages of our economic and political opponents." Four years later, the National Governors Association issued a report warning "that the economic well-being of the United States was in jeopardy because so many Americans are ignorant of the languages and cultures of other nations. Governor Gerald Baliles of Virginia said "the United States is not well prepared for international trade. . . . we do not know the languages, the cultures or the geographic characteristics of our competitors and opponents. Governor Thomas Kean of New Jersey stated that he would support mandatory foreign language studies for public school students. Ernest Boyer, president

of the Carnegie Foundation for the Advancement of Teaching, endorsed the report of the National Governors and said that "the governors' call for a curriculum with international perspective is both timely and critically important to the civic and economic future of our nation."

Lynne V. Cheney, formerly with the National Endowment for the Humanities, wrote in her book *American Memory: A Report on the Humanities in the Nation's Public Schools* (1987) that, "Studying a second language gives us greater mastery over our own speech, helps us shape our thoughts with greater precision and our expressions with greater eloquence. Studying a foreign language also provides insight into the nature of language itself, into its power to shape ideas and experience."

Former U.S. Secretary of Education Terrel H. Bell stated in his book *The Thirteenth Man: A Reagan Cabinet Memoir* (1988) that:

> Every advanced country in the world except the United States teaches its school children a language or languages other than the native one. This is a standard part of the curriculum because it is recognized that in an interdependent world, communication, competitiveness in world trade, and economic health depend on broad knowledge of other nations and languages are the access to that knowledge. The teaching of foreign languages must become mandatory in our schools.

Currently, the Clinton administration supports bilingual education. In February of 1993, U.S. Secretary of Education Richard Riley stated that bilingualism and multiculturalism were a source of strength in the nation. However, Republicans in Congress have not been supportive of bilingual education and have advocated severe cuts in federal support for these programs. One exception has been Congresswoman Ileana Ros-Lehtinen of Greater Miami, who is a strong supporter of bilingual education and the English Plus movement.

Multicultural Education

Until recently, multicultural education had wide-spread support in the United States. However, the attacks by African American scholars on Eurocentric textbooks and curriculum are met with great concern by many conservative scholars. Thus, a backlash has resulted, and multicultural education has become a battleground in a new cultural war. Whose history and culture should be taught? Do we share a common culture and common values? How much emphasis should be placed on teaching the culture and history of the various ethnic and racial groups of the nation? These are some of the questions being raised by educators at the national, state, and local levels and by the public at large.

Multicultural education is defined as an interdisciplinary, cross-cultural educational process that prepares students to live, learn, and work together to achieve common goals in a culturally diverse world by fostering appreciation, respect, and understanding for persons of a different gender or for persons of different ethnic, racial, religious, or language backgrounds and perspectives. Such an education will enable students to acquire a broader knowledge base while developing appreciation and respect for individual similarities and differences, which will prepare them to function effectively in a culturally and linguistically diverse nation and world. Proponents of multicultural education feel that this kind of curriculum provides students with a positive self-image by helping them to understand their own culture and history and those of others. They also believe that such an education would help combat racism, sexism, prejudice, and discrimination in society.

A major concern of educators who advocate multiethnic education is the reduction of bias in textbooks and other instructional materials. Studies have shown that students who see themselves portrayed with bias and in stereotypical ways tend to internalize these negative ideas and fail to develop their own full potential. Conversely, bias-free materials have a positive effect on their self-concept and attitudes. Bias occur in all kinds of classroom materials, such as nursery rhymes and fairy tales, literature, history textbooks, audiovisual materials, and computer software. The New York Public Schools proposed that all instructional materials to be considered for adoption in the district be evaluated in five areas in which bias appears:

1. Contextual invisibility. All too often textbooks and support materials portray the typical Anglo Saxon American life and exclude other lifestyles and racial and ethnic groups.

2. Stereotyping and characterization. Some instructional materials assigned a traditional and rigid role to groups, thus reinforcing stereotypes and prejudicial attitudes.

3. Historical distortions or omissions. Hispanics have typically been ignored in U.S. history textbooks and most of their contributions to the nation minimized, trivialized, or omitted. Some believe that there has been a "conspiracy of silence" in reporting the Hispanic presence and contributions to the nation. Native Americans, African Americans, and women have similar concerns.

4. Language bias. The use of certain words in instructional materials can reflect bias based on gender, ethnicity, disability, age, or social class.

5. Inaccurate and stereotypic visual images. Pictures can have a powerful impact upon students; as the saying goes, "one picture is worth a thousand words." In many textbooks women and minorities seldom appear in pictures.

Opponents of multicultural education believe that the common experience of the United States is being devalued when multicultural perspectives are overemphasized. Historian Arthur Schlesinger Jr. criticized a New York state multicultural report by saying in 1991 that ". . . we should also be alert to the danger of a society divided into distinct and immutable ethnic and racial groups, each taught to cherish its own apartness from the rest." In the fall of 1995, Senator Bob Dole, the 1996 Republican presidential candidate, irritated many Hispanics of both parties by his comments that only "American" (Anglo American) culture should be taught and emphasized.

Proponents of multicultural education support the view of cultural pluralism. They believe that ethnic groups should retain many of their traditions, such as language and social customs. At the same time, ethnic groups should adopt common values such as due process of law, obedience to laws, participation in politics, and civic responsibility. Those who favor multiculturalism reject the vision of the United States as a melting pot society. This assimiliationist point of view proposes that all the ethnic groups of the nation should give up their original culture and language and mix in the American melting pot.

The cultural pluralists feel that the assimilationist philosophy has a negative impact on the academic performance of minority students and hurts their self-concept. They believe that by failing to include the contributions of all ethnic groups in the curriculum and textbooks, minority

students are alienated from their own education. Some felt that this exclusion amounted to curriculum genocide for minority students.

Former New York Education Commissioner Thomas Sobol stated that a good curriculum should reflect both the common American culture and the multiple perspectives of history. He said, "most people know in their heart that it is not only possible but natural to be a proud American and to be proud of one's family heritage as well."

English Only/Official English

The demands of Hispanics for multicultural education and bilingual education, and for ballots and license examination in Spanish, as well as their rapidly growing numbers in certain parts of the nation, has produced a strong backlash against them. Responding to this anti-Spanish wave, U.S. Senator S. I. Hayakawa, a Republican who served one term representing California, introduced an amendment to the U.S. Constitution in 1981 to make English the official language of the nation. The amendment had two sentences:

> Section 1. The English language shall be the official language of the United States.

> Section 2. The Congress shall have the power to enforce this article by appropriate legislation.

Senator Hayakawa's official English amendment was cosponsored by ten other senators but died in the Ninety-Seventh Congress. The stir it created, however, brought about the founding of a national organization called U.S. English. Hayawaka became honorary chairman of this organization in 1983, and later Linda Chavez served as its president.

Since the founding of U.S. English, 18 states have passed laws stating that English is their official language. In 1986, Proposition 63, which declared English the official language of California, was approved by 73 percent of the voters. In Florida, a similar proposition received 84 percent of the popular vote; in Colorado, 61 percent. Only in Arizona was the election close, and the initiative received 51 percent of the votes.

The battle to pass official-English initiatives in these states polarized Hispanic and non-Hispanic communities in the nation. Two national organizations led the effort to obtain approval for official English in the various states. One organization was English First, which says it has 250,000 members and a budget of $1.5 million. The second and stronger organization is U.S. English, which claims a membership of 400,000 and has an annual budget of $6 million. Many Hispanic leaders have denounced both organizations as racist and anti-Hispanic. Hispanics' worst fears were confirmed when John Tanton, an ophthalmologist from Michigan who had founded U.S. English and the Federation of American Immigration Reform (an organization that wants to restrict rigidly immigration), circulated a memorandum among his supporters. His controversial memorandum was picked up by the press and published in 1988. Tanton questioned the educability of Latinos and what he perceived as negative values that Latino immigrants bring to the nation, such as their lack of involvement in public affairs and corruption (*la mordida*, or Mexican bribe). In more inflammatory text Tanton wrote:

> Can homo contraceptivus complete with homo pregenitiva if borders aren't controlled? Or is advice to limit one family simply advice to move over and let someone else with greater reproductive powers occupy the space? . . . On the demographic point: perhaps this is the first instance in which those with their pants up are going to get caught by those with their pants down!

Tanton's memorandum was denounced as anti-Hispanic racism of the worst kind. It brought about Linda Chavez's resignation as president of U.S. English. Many Hispanic leaders already considered Chavez an "Uncle Tom" Hispanic for her views in favor of official English and her stance against bilingual education and affirmative action. Protesters have picketed her appearances at many colleges and universities. Chavez countered in *Out of the Barrio* that she has been portrayed as a villain of horror movies. Other distinguished board members of U.S. English, such as Walter Cronkite, resigned from the organization. The uproar forced the resignation of John Tanton as well.

Many Hispanics felt that the rancor and divisiveness left after the battles to approve official English in various states intensified prejudice and discrimination against them. Spanish speakers were and still are being rudely told in public places, like restaurants and movie theaters from Miami to Los Angeles, to "speak English, you're in America now!" Samuel C. Kiser, a District Judge in Amarillo, Texas, ruled in September 1995 that a divorced mother who spoke Spanish to her daughter at home would lose her custody since she was "damaging" her by teaching her the "language of maids." The judge awarded the custody to the father, who said he spoke only English to his daughter, even though he was being accused of sexually abusing his daughter. Seventeen Hispanic U.S. Representatives wrote a letter complaining about the judge's decision to the Texas State Commission on Judicial Conduct and requesting that Judge Kiser be fired. Congressman Ed Pastor of Arizona and 1995 Hispanic Congressional Caucus chair stated "it is out-

rageous that someone in such a lofty position would even consider such an ignorant and nonsensical argument." The outcry that followed forced the judge to reverse his ruling. Soon after this incident, *The Miami Herald* published the story of a young Latino couple who were also admonished by a waitress at a South Florida restaurant that they too were "damaging" and "abusing" their children by speaking in Spanish to them.

Linda Chavez stated in *Out of the Barrio* that "despite the ominous warning of opponents and the claims of proponents, official-English laws have had virtually no impact on public policy." She explained that bilingual education continues and ballots in Spanish are still being used in state elections.

Looking Toward the Twenty-First Century

As we look ahead Latinos have achieved leading positions in every profession—in government and politics; in the armed forces; in business and labor; in science and technology; in literature, education, and the arts; in motion pictures and theater; and in sports. Dr. Mario Molina, a professor at Massachusetts Institute of Technology (MIT), received the 1995 Nobel Prize in chemistry, becoming the third U.S. Hispanic to receive such an honor. (The Nobel Prize was shared with two other scientists.) The Royal Swedish Academy of Sciences said that the three scientists had "contributed to our salvation from a global environmental problem that could have catastrophic consequences."

Hispanics have made a permanent mark on the life and culture of the United States and their influence continues to increase through the 1990s. Latinos remain the fastest growing segment of the nation's population and with their growth in numbers they have achieved economic, political, and social clout. In 1995, there were 27,000,000 Hispanics in the nation; one out of every ten Americans was a Latino. According to the U.S. Bureau of the Census the total Hispanic population increased 28 percent from 1991 to 1995, while the U.S. population grew by 6 percent during the same period. The Bureau of the Census estimated that by the year 2000 the Latino population would grow to 31 million; by 2030, to 63 million; and by 2050, to 83 million.

Hispanic Business magazine reported in its October 1995 issue that there were 613,000 Hispanic-owned businesses in the United States. This figure is six times the number of African American companies. Hispanic companies in the United States employed 391,000 people and had annual revenue of $27 billion. Hispanic purchasing power in 1994 was $190 billion. Around the year 2000 Latinos should become the largest minority group in the United States, and it is estimated that they will have a purchasing power of over $300 billion.

The great political change that engulfed the nation in the election of 1994 has concerned many Latino leaders. The 104th Republican-controlled Congress is severely cutting social programs that could hurt many Hispanics and negatively affect the recent gains made by Hispanics in business, education, and employment. Republicans are pushing to eliminate the Minority Business Development Agency, the Small Business Administration, and even the entire U.S. Commerce Department. Speaking before an audience of Latino entrepreneurs attending the U.S. Hispanic Chamber of Commerce annual conference, U.S. Secretary of Commerce Ron Brown stated on October 5, 1995, "All the progressive policies of the last 25 years that the Hispanic chamber has fought so hard for that have helped build a thriving Latino business class are truly under siege today."

Brown, before his tragic death in 1996, defended affirmative action and the value of his own department. He also stated, "sometimes we tend to forget that extraordinary strength that the United States of America has . . . I happen to believe that diversity is the greatest strength we have."

The elimination of affirmative action in college admissions of Hispanics combined with the denial of college assistance loans to Hispanics who are U.S. legal residents could make it harder for Hispanics to make progress in higher education. The intensification of prejudice and discrimination could hurt Hispanics' abilities to obtain and keep jobs.

In spite of these clouds on the horizon most Hispanics are making real progress in the United States. Although many still live in poverty and despair, the vast majority of Hispanics are being integrated into the social and economic mainstream of the nation. This progress can especially be observed in U.S.-born Hispanics who speak English fluently and are more educated than Hispanic newcomers. From Miami to California a new generation of young, affluent, and upwardly mobile Latinos has emerged and they are making a difference in their communities.

The continuous heavy legal and undocumented Latino immigration with poor educational background has resulted in Hispanics continuing to lag behind the general population in income and educational attainment. In 1993, Hispanics had a median income of $23,679 compared with $36,966 for the total U.S. population. In regard to education, 53 percent of Hispanics had earned a high school degree in comparison with 83 percent of the non-Hispanic population in 1994.

The *Vista* magazine issue of September 1995 reported that many Latino elected and community leaders are very positive about the future of Hispanics in the United States. Republican Congressman Henry Bonilla said, "I see a very bright future. You look at small business ownership, it's been growing tremendously. There is also a greater rate of graduation, and of attendance in college. There are tremendous opportunities that lie ahead." Raúl Yzaguirre, President of the National Council of La Raza, stated, "Now I see we're going to be a very significant factor in the future . . . We are becoming more of a force, in politics, in food, in music." Bill Richardson, the Democratic Congressman from Santa Fe, New Mexico, and Chief Deputy Minority Whip of the U.S. House of Representatives, noted, "Hispanics have unlimited political and economic future if they unite as a community."

The impact of the Hispanic presence on the life of the United States will continue to increase, and most Americans will see how they have influenced the United States in every area. Some demographers predict that in the middle of the twenty-first century Hispanics will comprise a third of the population of the nation. Thus, Latinos will become, even more, one of the most important and dynamic segments of the United States. Many Hispanics increasingly believe that their time has now come and that most of them are moving from the fringes to the mainstream of American life.

Bibliography

Acuña, Rodolfo. *Occupied America: A History of Chicanos,* 3d ed. New York: Harper and Row, 1988.

Bannon, John Francis. *The Spanish Borderlands Frontier 1513–1821*. Albuquerque, N. Mex.: University of New Mexico Press, 1974.

Chavez, Linda. *Out of the Barrio: Toward a New Politics of Hispanic Assimilation*. New York: Basic Books, 1991.

De Varona, Frank, ed. *Hispanic Presence in the United States*. Miami, Fla.: Mnemosyne Publishing, 1993.

De Varona, Frank, and Eden Force Eskin. *Hispanics in U.S. History Through 1865*. Vol. 1. Englewood Cliffs, N.J.: Globe Book, 1989.

De Varona, Frank, and Steven Otfinoski. *Hispanics in U.S. History 1865 to the Present*. Vol. 2. Englewood Cliffs, N.J.: Globe Book, 1989.

Fernández-Shaw, Carlos M. *The Hispanic Presence in North America from 1492 to Today*. New York: Facts on File, 1987.

García, Mario T. *Mexican Americans: Leadership, Ideology, and Identity*. New Haven, Conn. and London: Yale University Press, 1989.

Hafen, Leroy R., and Ann W. Hafen. *Old Spanish Trail, Santa Fe to Los Angeles*. Lincoln, Nebr.: University of Nebraska, 1993.

Hauberg, Cliford A. *Puerto Rico and the Puerto Ricans: A Study of Puerto Rican History and Immigration to the United States*. New York: Hippocrene Books, 1974.

Jones, Oscar, and Joy Jones. *Hippocrene U.S.A. Guide to Historic Hispanic America*. New York: Hippocrene Books, 1993.

Kanellos, Nicolás. *The Hispanic Almanac: From Columbus to Corporate America*. Detroit: Visible Ink Press, 1994.

Larsen, Ronald J. *The Puerto Ricans in America*. Minneapolis: Lerner Publications, 1989.

Levadi, Barbara, ed. *Latino Biographies*. Paramus, N.J.: Globe Fearon, 1995.

Lewin, Stephen, ed. *The Latino Experience in U.S. History*. Paramus, N.J.: Globe Fearon, 1994.

Meier, Matt S., and Feliciano Ribera. *Mexican Americans/American Mexicans From Conquistadors to Chicanos*. New York: Hill and Wang, 1972.

Moore, Joan, and Harry Pachon. *Hispanics in the United States*. Englewood Cliffs, N.J.: Prentice-Hall, 1985.

Moquin, Wayne, ed., with Charles Van Doren. *A Documentary History of the Mexican Americans*. New York: Praeger Publishers, 1971.

Novas, Himilce. *Everything You Need to Know About Latino History*. New York: Plume/Penguin Books, 1994.

Pichot, Jane. *The Mexicans in America*. Minneapolis: Lerner Publications, 1989.

Sale, Kirkpatrick. *The Conquest of Paradise: Christopher Columbus and the Columbian Legacy*. New York: Alfred A. Knopf, 1990.

Shorris, Earl. *A Biography of the People*. New York: Avon Books, 1992.

Weber, David J. *The Spanish Frontier in North America*. New Haven, Conn.: Yale University Press, 1992.

Wallace, Katherine. *California Through Five Centuries*. New York: Amsco School Publications, 1974.

Chapter 6

Native American
Civil Rights

Donald A. Grinde Jr.

The term "Civil Rights" implies freedom from governmental caprice. From the advent of European contact, Native Americans have been dispossessed, killed, harassed, and subjugated by colonial, local, state, and federal policies and officials. These oppressive actions were aimed at whole tribes as well as individuals within tribes. Thus, to many American Indians, it often seems paradoxical to examine the subject of American Indian civil rights. However, American Indians have become citizens of the United States and residents of their respective states while maintaining their rights as members of American Indian nations. Like other oppressed groups, American Indians have endured the continued deprivation of their rights by local, state, and federal governments. Often, Native American people seek to exercise religious, treaty, and cultural rights that conflict with state, and federal laws that do not accommodate such practices; when such conflicts occur, American Indians are often denied basic civil rights.

Throughout the history of the United States, Native Americans, like other peoples of color, have encountered private and governmental prejudice. But American Indians' views of their rights under United States law differs from the expectations of most other racial groups. Most Native American rights involve a broad range of preferences, prerogatives, and immunities that are based not on their historical status as a "minority" but on their treaty rights as citizens of tribal governments. Historically, American Indian people have been treated, in the law, as both a "group" with contractual rights (treaties) with the U.S. government and as individuals of color functioning in the broader American society. These two confusing and often contradictory legal statuses have often worked to Native American peoples' disadvantage in the legal system.

Osceola (c. 1804–1838)

This Native American leader led the struggle for the preservation of the Seminole nation of Florida. Born approximately in 1804 in Georgia, he was first known as "Powell," suggesting some English or Scottish ancestry, although Osceola denied that fact.

Osceola moved to Florida with his mother and fought with the Indians against General Andrew Jackson while still in his teens. Osceola was strongly opposed to efforts to move the Seminoles out of Florida. He shared with the Seminole chiefs a refusal to recognize the 1835 Treaty of Payne's Landing. His silent refusal was punctuated by thrusting his knife into a copy of the document. For this gesture he was arrested and imprisoned, escaping after feigning a change of heart regarding the treaty.

After his escape Osceola led a band of young Seminoles who resisted relocation. During this activity the U.S. Indian agent was killed. This event precipitated the Second Seminole War, in which Osceola emerged as a leader of the resistance. Osceola hid the Seminole women and children in the Everglades, while harassing the U.S. troops. He continued this guerrilla campaign for two years. The U.S. officer in command, Thomas S. Jessup, was severely criticized for his ineffectual tactics. Enraged, Jessup tricked Osceola and some his followers into coming out of the Everglades.

In October 1837, when Osceola and his men entered the U.S. compound under a flag of truce, they were arrested and imprisoned. In spite of the public outcry concerning the trickery, Osceola was removed to Fort Moultrie, near Charleston, South Carolina, where he died, possibly from poison, on January 30, 1838. After his death the Second Seminole War continued for several more years, resulting in the extermination of most of the tribe.

Civil Rights and Treaty Rights

To understand the civil rights of American Indian people, it is important to examine the two distinct categories of legal concepts. The first category involves issues associated with civil rights (freedom of religion and speech, due process, voting rights, and freedom from racial discrimination). However, it is important to understand that the rights in this category involve not only constitutional limitations on federal and state governments but also limitations on the prerogatives of tribal governments. The second category involves the rights and disabilities of Native peoples as citizens of tribal entities. As a result of this duality under the law, the United States has instituted immunities, disabilities, and legal preferences that apply to American Indian individuals as well as immunities and rights that are a product of the tribal governmental system. In each of these areas, it is tribal membership that establishes an immunity or a right. All American Indians are given rights in the national constitution, but some rights limitations are created by tribal laws, customs, and regulations.

By the end of the nineteenth century, the federal government was forced to decide how it would conduct its affairs with Native American nations. After the conquest of the tribes was achieved, the remaining American Indian nations were placed on reservations that represented only a small part of their aboriginal territory. As a result, many Native American groups lived on provisions issued by the U.S. government. In order to give the U.S. House of Representatives more say in the conduct of Indian Affairs, the Congress passed on March 3, 1871, the "Indian Appropriations Act," which terminated treaty-making between the tribes and the federal government. After this legislation, Indian affairs would be conducted through ordinary legislation approved in both houses rather than through treaties ratified in the Senate. Moreover, this law also withdrew from noncitizen Indians and from Indian tribes the power to make contracts that involved the payment of money for services relating to Indian lands or claims against the federal government unless these contracts were approved by the Secretary of the Interior and the Commissioner of Indian Affairs. Since many Indian grievances were against the Secretary of the Interior and the Commissioner of Indian Affairs, this statute deprived Native Americans of one of the basic rights in the common law: the right of free choice of counsel for the redress of injuries. These restrictions were further amplified by the Act of May 21, 1872 (see U.S. Statutes At Large, 16:544, 16:566, and 17:136).

Under this legislation, the ability of American Indian nations to stop federal encroachment into the conduct of tribal affairs was eliminated, and the exercise of federal power over American Indian affairs became capricious. Accordingly, tribal-federal relations changed from treaties negotiated between sovereign nations to an oppressive guardianship over a powerless ward. In the early part of the nineteenth century, Chief Justice John Marshall had stated that federal-Indian relations resembled that between a guardian and a ward (*Cherokee Nation* v. *Georgia,* 1831). In the late nineteenth century, the Congress and the courts used these words to ratify this radical transformation in Indian affairs.

Subsequently, the federal government justified its interference in intratribal affairs by asserting that Indian nations were to be protected by the federal government from malevolent local populations. In *United States* v. *Kagama* (1886), the Supreme Court upheld the validity of the 1885 "Indian Major Crimes Act," which imposed certain federal criminal laws on Indians living in federal reservations. The court held:

> [T]hey are spoken of as "wards of the nation," "pupils," as local dependent communities. In this spirit the United States has conducted its relations to them from its organization to this time. . . . These Indian tribes *are* wards of the nation. They are communities *dependent* on the United States. . . . From their very weakness and helplessness, so largely due to the dealing of the Federal Government with them, and its treaties in which it has been promised, there arises the duty of protection, and with it the power. The power of the General Government over these remnants of a race once powerful, now weak and diminished in numbers, is necessary to their protection, as well as the safety of those among whom they dwell.

In other words, federal policy may justify overlooking treaty rights and stipulations.

By focusing on the dependency of American Indian nations and the power flowing from that relationship, the court granted the federal government unlimited power not only to determine what was best in the conduct of Indian affairs but also to act on decisions without consultation with American Indian nations. Thus, the United States government, under the ruse of "protecting" American Indians, instigated a policy that undermined the basic fundamental treaty right of American Indian nations—the ability to sustain themselves as distinct cultural and political entities.

U.S. General George Armstrong Custer (1839–1876) is best known for his ill-fated role in the 1876 Battle of Little Bighorn against the Sioux Indians in South Dakota, where he and his entire regiment was killed.

Forced Citizenship Through Property Rights: Congress's Plenary Powers and the Failure of the General Allotment Act of 1887

The heart of the attack on American Indian rights was the allotment of reservation lands to adult tribal members and then selling the "surplus" lands to non-Indians. On February 8, 1887, the U.S. government passed the "General Allotment Act," which set up a commission to survey and allot reservations in order to distribute lands to individual tribal members (U.S. Statutes at Large, 24:388–91). Basically, federal policy reasoned that traditional Native American lifestyles engendered sloth and dependency. To eliminate these undesired traits, free enterprise was to be introduced in Native American communities so that independence and initiative could be fostered. Although holding property had ceased to be a prerequisite for voting in most states, the allotment act sought to make American Indians voting citizens through individual ownership of land. In theory, individual private property allotments of land would make American Indians taxpaying, churchgoing citizens of the United States.

Although most American Indian nations vigorously resisted allotment policies, the federal government decided to implement the policy over the protest of American Indians. Although the

Sitting Bull (c. 1831–1890)

This Native American leader led the Sioux nation's resistance to the forceful relocation of his people. Born into the Dakota Sioux tribe, Sitting Bull was a warrior from the age of 14 years and about 1856 became head of the Strong Heart warrior society. He was involved with the Minnesota Massacre of 1862, in which a band of Sioux warriors under Little Crow protested white encroachment on Indian lands by slaying 350 white settlers.

In 1866 Sitting Bull became chief of the northern hunting Sioux, with Crazy Horse of the Ogala Sioux as his vice-chief. Two years later Sitting Bull accepted peace with the U.S. government on the basis of promised reservation lands north of the Platt River. But in 1874, after gold was discovered in the Black Hills on some of these reservation lands, miners poured into the Indian territory. Enraged by these treaty violations and the entry into Indian lands many tribes joined forces to resist the incursions. Sitting Bull was made head of the war council for a confederacy of tribes, which included the Sioux, the Arapaho, and the Cheyenne.

The tribes created a force of between 2,500 and 4,000 men. They were ordered by the U.S. forces in the area to return to their reservations by the end of January 1876. Sitting Bull claimed to have had visions of a great battle during a Sun Dance he performed in June 1876. On June 17, 1876, the U.S. forces under the command of General George Crook were defeated by Crazy Horse at the Battle of the Rosebud. On June 25, 1876, the famous battle of the Little Bighorn, in which General George Custer was killed, was won by warriors led by Crazy Horse and Gall, another major Indian leader. Sitting Bull himself "made medicine" during the battle and took no part in the fighting.

In May 1877 Sitting Bull led his people into Canada, but that government would not lend him any assistance. After long suffering and the loss of life to famine and disease, Sitting Bull and 187 tribesmen returned to the United States on a promise of pardon. They surrendered to the U.S. Army in July 1881. Sitting Bull was imprisoned for two years and eventually released in 1883 to the Standing Rock Reservation in South Dakota.

Sitting Bull briefly became a part of Buffalo Bill's Wild West Show, becoming a legend to the American people as a symbol of Indian resistance. Nevertheless, he remained leader of the Sioux and never accepted white rule. In 1889 he led the Ghost Dance uprising of the Sioux. He was ordered arrested, and as Indian warriors attempted to rescue him, Sitting Bull was shot and killed by Indian police. He died at Grand River, South Dakota, on December 15, 1890. A few days later, the U.S. Seventh Calvary massacred the Sioux, at Wounded Knee, South Dakota, ending the Sioux resistance.

Bureau of Indian Affairs and the Allotment Commission conducted alleged "negotiations" with tribal governments, the results were sullied by coercion, fraud, forgery, and duress. Rather than consider the American Indian critique of such policies, the courts took part in the masquerade. Instead of affirming the historical sanctity of vested property rights, the Supreme Court accorded American Indian property rights established through treaties no protection at all. In *Lone Wolf* v. *Hitchcock* (1903), the Kiowa chief, Lone Wolf, sought to negate the validity of the "allotment agreement" that sold Comanche, Kiowa, and Kiowa Apache lands to non-Indians. Under the Treaty of Medicine Lodge (1867), no part of the Kiowa-Comanche Reservation could be sold to the federal government without the approval of three fourths of the adult male Indians. Under the General Allotment Act, Congress allotted the reservation and then sold the "surplus" without obtaining the three-fourths approval stipulated in the 1867 treaty. In upholding the actions of the government, the Supreme Court stated:

> The power exists to abrogate the provisions of an Indian treaty, though presumably such power will be exercised only when circumstances arise which not only justify the government in disregarding the stipulations of the treaty, but may demand, in the interest of the country and the Indians themselves, that it should do so.

> In view of the legislative power possessed by Congress over treaties with the Indians, and Indian tribal property, we may not specially consider [the allegations of fraud], since all these matters, in any event, were solely within the

Although the Pueblo people had endured hundreds of years of Spanish domination, had developed an admirable agricultural system in the desert, and had formulated a spirituality that amazed anthropologists, they were, in the eyes of the court, a "simple" and "superstitious" people and thus governed by the "plenary" powers of Congress.

domain within the legislative authority and its action is conclusive upon the courts.

The judges described this power as "plenary authority over the tribal relations of the Indians," and deemed the exercise of these "plenary" powers as not reviewable by the courts. Theoretically, Congress could use such powers only for the good of the tribes, but the court would not second guess Congress as to what was good for Indian nations. Hence, congressional power under the *Lone Wolf* decision was virtually unlimited.

By 1913, the racist argumentation for this enormous power was expressed in *United States* v. *Sandoval* (1913). In the *Sandoval* case, the Supreme Court upheld Congress's power to impose "Indian" status on the Pueblo Indians of New Mexico even though they had been regarded as citizens since 1877. It reasoned:

> Always living in separate and isolated communities, adhering to primitive modes of life, largely influenced by superstition and fetishism, and chiefly governed according to crude customs inherited through their ancestors, [Pueblo Indians] are essentially a simple, uninformed and inferior people. . . . As a superior and civilized nation [the United States has both] the power and the duty of exercising a fostering care and protection over all dependent Indian communities within its borders.

Although the Pueblo people had endured hundreds of years of Spanish domination, had developed an admirable agricultural system in the desert, and had formulated a spirituality that amazed anthropologists, they were, in the eyes of the court, a "simple" and "superstitious" people

Geronimo (1829–1909) was an Apache brave who partcipated in various forays against white invaders into Apache territory. To the Apaches, he was a hero who embodied the very essence of the Apache values, agressiveness and courage in the face of difficulty.

and thus governed by the "plenary" powers of Congress. As with other people of color, such decisions represent the nadir of Indian-white relations in the early twentieth century. The noted attorney Alvin J. Zionitz states that the plenary power doctrine "in practice means that Congress has the power to do virtually as it pleases with the Indian tribes. It is an extraordinary doctrine for a democracy to espouse. It would justify abolishing the political existence of the tribes." Furthermore Zionitz observes; "Short of that, it justifies the imposition of controls over the lives and property of the tribes and their members. Plenary power thus subjects Indian to national powers outside ordinary constitutional limits." Throughout the twentieth century, the congressional plenary powers in Indian affairs would wreak havoc with American Indian governments, lives, and property in spite of progress made in the realm of civil rights for Native American individuals.

However, the attack on American Indian people in the late nineteenth century was much broader than the subversion of traditional landholding patterns. Federal agents sought to discredit tribal governmental practices and leaders by supplanting them with "American" modes of government. To compound matters, the government actively suppressed tribal religious rituals and beliefs. The government encouraged and subsidized Christian missionaries to proselytize within tribal communities. As a result, zealous missionaries and Indian

agents legally prohibited American Indian religious rituals and dances since they believed in the sanctity of their efforts to convert Indians to Christianity.

Obviously, these actions did not bring to Indians a level of prosperity that white Americans enjoyed. Instead, these policies devastated American Indian individuals and nations. Between 1887 and 1933, over half of the tribal land base was lost to land thieves, tax sales, and governmental sales of "surplus lands." These policies launched a cycle of poverty that extends to this day. As a result, ignorance and ill health became hallmarks of tribal societies. Hence, these racist missionary and civilizing policies did not bring the benefits of American civilization to American Indian people. Instead, Native American people strengthened their resolve to nurture and cleave to their old ways.

This period of "assimilation" was the worst period of American Indian civil rights. In spite of constitutional affirmations, American Indian property rights, free speech, and free exercise of religion were denied. On a more fundamental level, the rights of Native American tribes to continue their distinct tribal status were systematically violated. The resulting damage to American Indian communities and the civil rights of Native Americans has not been mended.

The American Indian Citizenship Act of 1924: A Unilateral Act

By the 1920s, some enlightened individuals decided to reform these "assimilation" policies with new legislation. Although many American Indians had become U.S. citizens through "competency commissions" and treaties, Congress unilaterally granted citizenship to all American Indians in 1924. However, many Indians were wary of being declared citizens through "competency," since it often meant that their federal land allotments were no longer protected and thus subject to sale. A significant amount of the tribal estate was taken from Indians through fraud and state tax sales. In fact, thousands of newly created Native American citizens saw their lands removed from federal protection and sold out from under them.

Many Native American leaders saw the American Indian Citizenship Act of 1924 as a mischief-maker in American Indian policy. They resented the way it was imposed without consultation and consent from American Indian communities. The Tuscarora Chief, Clinton Rickard, summarized the views of many American Indians by stating:

The Citizenship Act did pass in 1924 despite our strong opposition. By its provisions all Indians were automatically made United States citizens whether they wanted to so or not. This was a violation of our sovereignty. Our citizenship was in our own nations. We had a great attachment to our style of government. We wished to remain treaty Indians and reserve our ancient rights. There was no great rush among my people to go out and vote in the white man's elections. Anyone who did so was denied the privilege of becoming a chief or clan mother in our nations.

Although the 1924 American Indian Citizenship Act granted citizenship unilaterally, it did not terminate federal protection of Indian lands and tribal entities. Hence, American Indians acquired a new status as American citizens while maintaining their privileges and rights as members of distinct tribal political units. However, Indian policymakers in 1924 assumed that tribal governments would wither away as American Indians became U.S. citizens. But most tribal governments did not disappear as anticipated and today American Indians enjoy a special dual citizenship.

Poverty, lack of education, and ill health characterized the lives of most Native Americans in the 1920s. When American Indian lands were allotted, the federal government assured communities that they would be supported during the transition from communal ways to the individualistic mores of Euroamerican society. But government promises were not kept, and many American Indians continued to reject American individualism and cling to tribal values. Accordingly, many American Indian communities were devoured by their more greedy and competitive neighbors. By the end of the 1920s, many reformers and Indian leaders understood that instilling private property through allotment and Christianity through missionization had wreaked havoc in Indian country.

The Indian New Deal: An Interlude of Reform

In 1928, the federal government commissioned a study of Indian policy, and the resulting Meriam Report detailed the woeful conditions of American Indians. In health care, Native Americans were found to be without even rudimentary services. Infant mortality rates were twice the national average. American Indians were also seven times more likely to die of tuberculosis than was the general population. Sanitary conditions were bad, and many Indians were disease-ridden. The Meriam report criticized Indian boarding schools as "grossly inadequate." From 1900 to 1926, the Bureau of Indian Affairs separated Indian children from their parents in a cruel attempt to Christianize and "civilize" them. The Meriam Report pointed out the harsh discipline heaped on Indian children. Basically, the boarding schools forbade Native American children to speak their tribal languages, practice their tribal religions, or wear traditional clothes. Violators of these rules were subject to physical abuse. Male American Indian survivors of this period joked that upon arriving at boarding schools a missionary or teacher would point to a picture of Jesus Christ with long flowing hair and state that they were to become like this man—and then order that the boys' long hair be cut. Most boarding schools relied on Native American child labor to keep them going. The Meriam Report characterized boarding schools as overcrowded and staffed with unqualified personnel that provided poor medical care and an unhealthy diet. Under these harsh conditions, Indian literacy rates remained low.

Furthermore, no economic or legal structure appeared to be in place to protect the rights of

From 1900 to 1926, the Bureau of Indian Affairs separated Indian children from their parents in a cruel attempt to Christianize and "civilize" them.

Carlos Montezuma (1867-1923)

Carlos Montezuma was a physician who fought for the abolition of the Bureau of Indian Affairs, the federal agency that still manages Indian affairs on the reservations. He was born among the Yavapai Indians in Arizona but was captured by the Pima Indians, who sold him to a white man, Carlos Gentile. This man named him Carlos Montezuma.

Although he was shifted from one benefactor to another, Montezuma obtained a sound education, graduating from the University of Illinois in 1884 with a bachelor of science degree. In 1889 Montezuma was able to earn a medical degree from the Chicago Medical College. He established his medical career gradually, working with the Indian Service, with the Carlisle Indian School in Pennsylvania, and in private practice in Chicago. Montezuma's experiences with the reservation health systems led him to become an advocate for the abolition of the federal Bureau of Indian Affairs and the reservation system itself. He began to write and speak out on behalf of the exploited Indian peoples.

Montezuma was offered a position as Commissioner of Indian Affairs by both Presidents Theodore Roosevelt and Woodrow Wilson. He refused and continued to advocate abolition of the federal agency. Instead, Montezuma fought for citizenship and equal rights for Native Americans. He stressed the importance of retaining the integrity of Indian cultures. He died in 1923 at the Fort Dowell Reservation where he was born.

Native Americans. The Meriam Report found that only 2 percent of all American Indians earned in excess of $500 per annum and that 96 percent of all Native Americans made less than $200 per year. Almost half of all Native Americans had recently lost their land, since unscrupulous people were manipulating the law to take advantage of Native Americans. Legal authorities were unsure who should hear cases involving Indian and non-Indians as defendants and victims, on reservations or off reservations. Moreover, when such cases were adjudicated justice was not often the result.

Having diagnosed this staggering array of problems, the Meriam Report recommended an infusion of funds to do things correctly. It called for a new office in the Bureau of Indian Affairs to institute new programs and monitor existing ones. The report also stated that the government and especially the Bureau of Indian Affairs had exhibited an extremely hostile attitude toward Indian families and Indian culture. The allotment system that was the cornerstone of Indian policy since 1887 was found to be the major cause of American Indian poverty. In essence, the Meriam Report documented a national scandal, and the deplorable conditions on reservations were a product of governmental policies and neglect. Gradually, Indian policy was taken out of the hands of missionaries and transferred to social scientists in the ensuing decade. American Indian leaders also saw that the persistence of American Indian ways depended on maintaining the land base and tribal identity, and they looked to the Bill of Rights for some of the legal machinery to facilitate this survival process.

The reform community was partly responsible for these excesses, since they had backed the discredited allotment policies. The resulting reforms that emerged in the 1930s were built on the idea that American Indian tribes had a place in twentieth-century America. President Franklin D. Roosevelt's new Commissioner of Indian Affairs, John Collier, instituted a policy to restore the vitality of tribal governments through the Indian Reorganization Act (IRA) of 1934. The IRA encouraged tribes to promulgate their own constitutions and renounced the old allotment policies. In addition, tribal governments were recognized as the fundamental way to implement federal Indian policies. For the first time in over 50 years, the right of Native Americans to sustain distinct tribal entities was upheld. Thus, the idea that tribes would eventually disappear was no longer the underlying assumption behind United States Indian policy.

Paradoxically, federal officials during the 1930s often pursued goals of tribal autonomy with an enthusiasm that limited the Indians' rights of choice. In the zeal for social change, Collier urged the adoption of tribal constitutions that reflected bureaucratic opinions as to how older tribal structures could be converted to contemporary constitutional structures. As a result, IRA constitutions were forced upon many tribes that clearly opposed such measures. During the 1930s, most Native Americans continued to be suspicious of governmental programs to aid them.

Despite these qualms by Indian people, the reforms of the 1930s continued. Tribal governments were revivified and their authority over reservation life was reinforced. Gradually, American Indians started to recover from the devastations of the allotment policy, and health and education programs improved. But these reforms were destined to be short-lived.

Termination Policies: Attempting to End Treaty Rights While Allegedly Boosting Individual Rights in the 1950s

As the Great Depression ended and World War II began, the United States turned to other concerns. The budget for the Bureau of Indian Affairs was cut, and Collier's policies were attacked by politicians whose constituents were dismayed by the bolstering of tribal governmental powers. Racism played an important role in this backlash, as did non-Indian businessmen who had lost their ability to freely plunder the tribal estate. The cost of reforming the administration of Indian affairs was also a source of friction. Oddly enough, a strange ideological attack against American Indians emerged out of the anti-Communist hysteria of the day. This attack painted American Indian ways as un-American and essentially communistic. These ideological salvos paved the way for another attack on American Indian tribalism in the late 1940s and early 1950s.

This new attack on Indian ways was very familiar; it argued that Native Americans should be brought into the mainstream of American life. Right-wing policymakers stated that American Indians should be entitled to the same privileges and rights and subject to the same laws as everyone else. As before, the new policy was said to be in the best interest of Native Americans despite nearly universal opposition among American Indian people. In the late 1940s, the new federal policy was called "liquidation," and for many Native Americans it conjured up images of the Nazi final solution for the Jews during World War II.

Jim Thorpe, whose mother was a Sac Indian, is considered one of the greatest American athletes of all time. After winning several gold medals at the 1912 Olympic games in Stockholm, Sweden, he was forced to give up his awards when it was discovered that he had played semipro baseball. The medals were returned posthumously 70 years later.

In response to these fears, the name for the new U.S. policy was changed to "termination." Because it stressed the abrogation of treaty rights, this policy urged the dismantling of tribal governments, the distribution of the tribal estate to tribal members, and the termination of federal services to individual Indians. Advocates of this disastrous policy stated that they were freeing Native people from federal control. Unfortunately, the wisdom of destroying tribal governments to emancipate American Indians from federal control went unexamined.

"Termination" was both a philosophical and a legislative assault on Native Americans. Philosophically, the termination movement encouraged the assimilation of American Indian individuals into mainstream American life. Hence, the policy espoused an end to the federal government's treaty obligations. In order to establish these goals, termination legislation was implemented in four distinct areas: (1) federal trust responsibilities and treaty relations were to be ended with specified American Indian nations; (2) laws that set Native Americans apart from other citizens were to be repealed; (3) supervisory control over certain individual American Indians and restrictions relating to federal guardianship were to be removed; and (4) services historically rendered by the Bureau of Indian Affairs would be shifted to other local, state, or federal agencies, or to Native American governments.

In 1950, Dillon S. Myer became the new commissioner of Indian Affairs and a principal

Starting in 1953 the Bureau of Indian Affairs (BIA) developed a program to voluntarily relocate, or "assimilate," reservation Indians to urban areas.

tions (concentration camps) a hundred years ago and then the government failed to relocate them and then to integrate them into American society.

In the late 1940s and early 1950s, American Indian policy seemed an arcane backwater to most politicians in Washington. Thus, a few conservatives operating in the House and Senate Interior and Insular Affairs committees as well as in the Senate Public Lands Committee shaped laws and policies for Native Americans. Liberals in Congress, often opposed to these conservative agendas, were persuaded by their conservative comrades that there was impropriety in the Bureau of Indian Affairs and that there was a desperate need to impart civil liberties to another persecuted minority group. These motivations were coupled, in the post-World War II years, with a bipartisan consensus to promote dams, parks, and various development projects that often conflicted with American Indian landholdings and tribal rights. The confluence of these bipartisan interests in the Congress provided the broad-based impetus for many of the termination policies.

In August of 1953, the cornerstone of termination policies, House Concurrent Resolution 108, was passed. It asserted: "[I]t is the policy of Congress, as rapidly as possible, to make the Indians within the territorial limits of the United States subject to the same laws and entitled to the same privileges and responsibilities as are applicable to other citizens of the United States, to end their status as wards of the United States, to grant them all the rights and prerogatives pertaining to American citizenship." In addition, the resolution declared that certain Native Americans "be freed from federal supervision and control and from all disabilities and limitations specifically applicable to Indians."

In 1957, Senator Arthur Watkins, a Republican from Utah, praised virtues of this disastrous policy in this way: "With the aim of 'equality before the law' in mind, our course should rightly be no other. Firm and constant consideration for those of Indian ancestry should lead us all to work diligently and carefully for the full realization of their national citizenship with all other Americans. Following in the footsteps of the Emancipation Proclamation of ninety-four years ago, I see the following words emblazoned in letters of fire above the heads of the Indians—THESE PEOPLE SHALL BE FREE!"

architect of the termination policies. Myer was a career bureaucrat and had headed the War Relocation Authority, which had detained in concentration camps ten of thousands of Japanese Americans as well as of Japanese aliens, from 1942 to 1944. President Harry S Truman's Secretary of the Interior observed that Myer had done "an outstanding job in the maintenance and relocation of the Japanese evacuated from the Pacific Coast region. . . ." Furthermore, it was felt that this "experience well fits him for the position of Commissioner of Indian Affairs." Thus, a man who had created concentration camps for Japanese Americans during World War II was judged worthy and experienced in the affairs of nonwhite people, particularly American Indians. Myer seemed to think that American Indians were herded onto reserva-

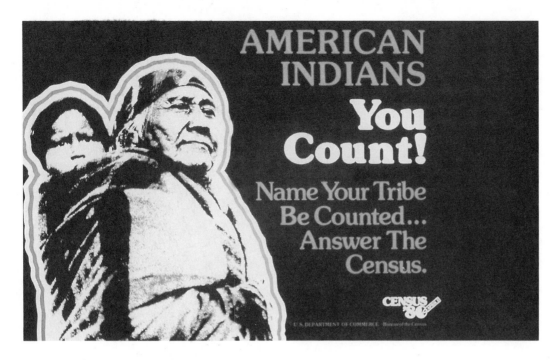

The campaign to destroy American Indian tribal governments also saw a movement in the courts to shore up the rights of American Indians as individual citizens.

This new "assimilationist" policy took on other trappings as well. The Bureau of Indian Affairs (BIA) developed a program to voluntarily relocate reservation Indians to urban areas. The BIA enticed Indian families to move to the city where they were placed in poor housing, given menial jobs, and then forsaken. This policy created poor Indian communities in urban areas like Los Angeles, New York, and Chicago. Senator Watkins characterized the relocation program as "the Indian freedom program." Once again, "assimilation" policies were to be foisted on American Indian people. Even though it was opposed by the overwhelming majority of Native people, policymakers reasoned that termination "would still have to be accepted as a controlling policy." The results of the relocation program are incalculable. Gerald One Feather (Oglala Sioux) observed: "The relocation program had an impact on our . . . government at Pine Ridge. Many people who could have provided [our] leadership were lost because they had motivation to go off the reservation to find employment or obtain an education. Relocation drained off a lot of our potential leadership."

Federal responsibilities and tribal power were further eroded by the passage of Public Law 280, a statute that shifted federal, civil, and criminal jurisdiction in Indian country to certain states. Other states were offered the option of taking jurisdiction over federal Indian reservation when they felt the need. Slowly, education and health programs were shifted to the states through subsequent legislation. In the Truman and Eisenhower administrations, 109 American Indian groups lost their status as federally recognized tribes. In human terms, 13,263 individuals owning 1,365,801 acres of land were denied their treaty rights as Native Americans.

During this era of termination, the doctrine of plenary powers was used to condemn thousands of acres of American Indian lands protected by treaty. With judicial acquiescence, the Congress permitted the Army Corps of Engineers and the Bureau of Reclamation in the Interior Department to seize significant portions of the Colorado River, Chemehuevi Reservation, Fort Mohave, and the Yuma and Gila Bend reservations in Arizona to manage the power and watershed of the Colorado River basin. The Pick-Sloan Plan for the Missouri River basin condemned Chippewa, Mandan, Hidatsa, and Arapaho land in Wyoming; Cree, Crow, Assiniboine, and Blackfoot land in Montana; and 200,000 acres of Sioux land in North and South Dakota. All of this land was flooded when the Oahe, Fort Randal, and Big Bend dams were completed. In western New York, the U.S. government built the Kinzua Dam, which violated the Pickering Treaty of 1794; flooded over 9,000 acres of excellent farm land; ruined the Cold Spring Longhouse, the spiritual center of the Allegany Seneca reservation; and caused the removal of 130 families from the rural area adjacent to the dam and

Ira Hayes was the Pima Indian who is pictured in the famous Iwa Jima flag-raising ceremony. Hayes was a hero of the United States Marine Corps, but after the celebrations at the close of World War II he quickly was forgotten and was unable to find a job or a home. His story became a legend of Indian defeat.

relocation to suburban style-housing several miles away at Steamboat and Jimersontown. In the ensuing legal battles, government attorneys argued that in *Lone Wolf* v. *Hitchcock* (1903) and other cases that "treaty rights do not forbid the taking, by the United States, of lands within the Allegany Reservation." In all of these land confiscations, the federal government exercised its plenary powers over Native Americans by uprooting them from their homelands, disturbing sacred sites, and altering significantly the ecology of the region.

The federal government's flood control projects showed little concern for the treaty and civil rights of American Indians during the 1940s and 1950s. Without a doubt, the federal government was seeking to abrogate its treaty responsibilities during the 1950s with a vengeance, but for reasons other than civil rights.

Paradoxically, the campaign to destroy American Indian tribal governments also saw a movement in the courts to shore up the rights of American Indians as individual citizens. Although the Indian Citizenship Act of 1924 had granted citizenship to all American Indians born in the United States, states with significant Native American populations had developed laws and procedures that severely limited or prohibited American Indians from exercising their right to vote, providing testimony in court, and serving on juries. During the 1950s, these discriminatory practices were struck down by the courts through reinterpreta-

tions of the rights of American Indians under the Fourteenth and Fifteenth Amendments. As the NAACP and other civil rights groups argued test cases that ended the separate but equal doctrine of *Plessy* v. *Ferguson* in the East, civil rights lawyers in the West also whittled away at the discriminatory laws of western states that deprived American Indians of their rights on the basis of race.

American Indians, like African Americans, often had civil rights in theory but not in practice during the first half of the twentieth century. Essentially, racist practices toward Native Americans in the communities where they lived were as flagrant and widespread as the experience of African Americans in the East. Discrimination in public accommodations and racial epithets were an integral part of American Indian life into the 1950s. Consequently, Native Americans were destined to become one of the prime beneficiaries of the 1960s civil rights movement.

The disastrous termination policies were discredited by 1960. All the tribes that had their treaty obligations terminated descended into poverty and ruin; many of the members of the newly terminated tribes were placed on state welfare rolls. The wealth of terminated tribes was raided by non-Indians intent on quick profits. As a result, even sincere supporters of the termination policies became discouraged by their efforts at reform. This was a tragic era for all Native Americans. The Seminole historian Donald Fixico characterized termination as threatening "the very core of American Indian existence—its culture."

American Indians and the 1960s Civil Rights Movement

When the civil rights movement gained momentum in the 1960s, American Indian activists became participants in the struggle. Although the Native American agenda was similar to other minorities in terms of citizenship rights, American Indian people also wanted to protect other rights that were fundamentally different from other groups. American Indians wanted not only to assert their constitutional rights as members of the American political system but also to preserve their special and separate cultural and political communities. In essence, Indians wanted to maintain their right to be different.

Although many Americans failed to understand the diverse aspirations of Native Americans in the 1960s, American Indians did meet with some success in the quest for civil rights and group rights. In the civil rights arena, the legislation and judicial decisions of the 1960s and early 1970s routinely made American Indians a part of the Voting Rights Act, the Fair Housing Act, and the Equal Employment Opportunity Act. For instance, the Voting Rights Act not only bans discrimination against American Indians but also gives them special protection as a people since their primary language may not be English.

Since American Indians have treaty rights that do not apply to other citizens, specific exemptions and stipulations were factored into some of the civil rights legislation. For example, the Equal Employment Act does not bar the granting of Indian employment preferences by employers on or near Indian reservations. This right might be attacked on the grounds of reverse discrimination, but the Supreme Court in *Morton* v. *Mancari* (1974) held that a law granting Indians employment preference in the Indian Health Service and the Bureau of Indian Affairs was constitutional. The decision stated that such a preference was based not on race but on treaty status that Indian Nations had with the United States. Thus, a preference based on a treaty relationship needed to be only "tied rationally" to federal treaty responsibilities to Indians. Hence, it was not governed by the notion of "strict scrutiny" that is applied to racial categories in the Fifteenth Amendment.

Social legislation spawned in the 1960s also acknowledged Indian tribes as unique and distinct political communities. Many Great Society programs (for example, Headstart, Community Action programs, the Comprehensive Older Americans Act, and the Elementary and Secondary Education Act) during this time allowed Indian tribal governments to participate in these programs.

The civil rights movement had an enormous impact on American Indian people and their tribal governments. With newly defined legal rights and economic resources flowing into their communities, there was renewed dignity and determination in the Indian world. As a result of termination policies, Indian leaders had become more cautious. If a tribe enjoyed even moderate economic gains then it could be subjected to the termination process. Under these policies, tribes had stayed impoverished and pliant. However, the civil rights movement swept away these fears and Indians learned that they could press for their rights without fear of losing their treaty status.

Civil Rights Under Federal and State Law: The Dilemma of American Indian Religious Freedom and Other Issues

Oddly enough, one major area of civil rights for American Indians continued to be neglected until the late 1970s. In 1978 Congress passed the American Indian Freedom of Religion Act; it declared that the federal government would seek to preserve and protect the exercise of traditional tribal religions. This was an attempt to give American Indians access to sacred sites on federal lands for religious ritual purposes. In the past, the courts had not been sympathetic to American Indian site-based religious rituals. However, the law proved to be ineffective and did not give the tribes any judicial redress for any federal actions. Moreover, the Supreme Court struck down the heart of the law in *Lyng* v. *Northwest Indian Cemetery Protective Association* (1988) when the Supreme Court ruled that the National Forest Service could construct a road through sacred Indian sites even when such a road clearly destroyed the ability of Native Americans to conduct important rituals that they had practiced in the area from time immemorial. Justice Sandra Day O'Connor, in the majority opinion, admitted that "the government does not dispute, and we have no reason to doubt, that the logging and road-building projects at issue in this case could have devastating effects on traditional Indian religious practices." The majority opinion argued that government activities could not be disrupted by the religious claims of its citizens since there was a wide array of religious beliefs in American society. O'Connor stated that a "sudden revelation" of sacredness to an individual at the Lincoln Memorial ought not to constrain visitation to this federal landmark, as if such a far-fetched possibility were comparable to continuing religious practices of three groups of Indians that extended back thousands of years. Essentially, O'Connor and the majority of the court sought to destroy the notion of American Indian religious freedom with their "sudden revelation" argument so that American Indians could be denied their rights to practice traditional tribal spirituality.

With the federal government excluding itself from enforcing American Indian religious freedom, it was not long before the states were emboldened to pursue a similar course in *Employment Division, Department of Human Resources of Oregon* v. *Smith* (1990). Two Native Americans living in Portland, Oregon (Alfred Smith and Galen Black), were terminated as drug counselors at a private drug rehabilitation program when it was discovered that they had used peyote (a stimulant drug) during a ritual at their Native American church. Subsequently, they applied for unemployment compensation and were denied benefits since the state of Oregon asserted that they were fired for misconduct. When the Supreme Court heard the case, it ruled against Smith and Black and all of Oregon's state courts' decisions in their favor. Thus, this decision not only struck a major blow against Native American religious freedom but also invited state agencies to launch an assault on the Native American Church.

Five justices, led by Antonin Scalia, accepted the idea that the sacramental use of peyote could be prohibited under a state criminal statute even though the state of Oregon did not enforce the law. According to Scalia in the majority opinion, the Oregon statute did not violate the free exercise provisions of the First Amendment or the American Indian Freedom of Religion Act (1978). The court held that no person could hold their religious rights against the state's rights to regulate the use of drugs. Although the use of peyote is a legally sanctioned sacrament in the Native American Church, the court seemed unconcerned and uninformed about the protected legal use of peyote by American Indians in the Native American Church. Incredibly, the court added blatantly discriminatory language to its opinion when it observed that the physical act of drinking wine during Christian communion rituals (even by minors in direct violation of state alcohol statutes) was acceptable.

Essentially, the majority opinion dismissed all previous tests that had delineated the limits of the free exercise clause. Justices on the high court were obviously unhappy with each other since they wrote scathing words in their opinions that accused each other of not knowing what they were doing. For example, the dissenting justices characterized the majority opinion in this way: "The

Court today . . . interprets the [Free Exercise] Clause to permit the government to prohibit, without justification, conduct mandated by an individual's religious beliefs, so long as the prohibition is generally applicable. But a law that prohibits certain conduct—conduct that happens to be an act of worship for someone—manifestly does prohibit that person's free exercise of his religion. A person who is barred from engaging in religiously motivated conduct is barred from freely exercising his religion. Moreover that person is barred from freely exercising his religion regardless of whether the law prohibits the conduct when engaged in for religious reasons, only by members of that religion, or by all persons."

Thus, the high court voided long-held interpretations of the constitutional protections extended over the free exercise of religion, and it voided those protections not just for Native Americans but for everyone else. Essentially, the court threw the issue of American Indian religious freedom into the "community standards" arena that covers pornography and various forms of obscenity. For the first time since the inception of the federal government, the Supreme Court allowed state laws and "community standards" to influence the free exercise of religion. It is too early to determine whether this decision will become the prevailing statement on American Indian religious freedom. In 1994, the Congress passed a second American Indian Freedom of Religion Act but its scope was quite narrow and had little impact. If the *Employment Division, Department of Human Resources of Oregon* v. *Smith* (1990) decision is allowed to stand, there can be no Native American religious freedom in the United States.

During the 1980s, the issue of the reburial of American Indian human remains held by federal agencies was debated. After a thorough investigation in academic circles, it was observed that the federal government "had a firm policy which encouraged the acquisition and retention of these remains." Many American Indians disliked the retention of Native American remains in places like the Smithsonian Institution. Indeed, Native American spiritual leaders argued that American Indian human remains should be placed back in Mother Earth. After a concerted effort by Native American rights organizations, Congress enacted the Native American Graves Protection and Repatriation Act (NAGPRA) of 1990. Essentially, the law enacted four points: First, federal agencies and private museums holding federal grants must inventory their collections of Native American human remains and funerary objects associated with them, and tribal governments must be notified by the agencies that the remains and objects may be returned to them upon request. Second, cultural artifacts and human remains excavated and/or found on federal and tribal lands belong to the respective tribes. Third, the trafficking in Native American cultural objects and human remains acquired in violation of NAGPRA is banned. Fourth, federal agencies and private museums receiving federal monies must prepare an itemized catalogue of other Native American sacred and funerary artifacts and return the objects to a tribe where the right of possession can be established. This law has been characterized by legal scholars as "the single most important piece of human rights legislation for Indian people which has been enacted by the Congress since the passage of the American Indian Freedom of Religion Act of 1978."

Many cases relating to American Indian freedom of religion have also arisen in state prisons, where state prison regulations have prohibited Native American religious practices such as sweat lodges, the wearing of long hair, and pipe ceremonies. Some Native Americans have also had to use the courts to obtain their right to hold public office, to be witnesses in state court, to receive public assistance, to serve as jurors, and to enroll their children in public schools. These legal problems have developed since many states have asserted that because Native Americans are exempt from certain state taxes, they should not be given the rights that other state citizens enjoy.

Many state officials and misinformed members of the public argue that granting American Indians some exemptions from state law is unfair since it denies equal protection to other citizens. This argument has been the basis for contemporary state refusals to acknowledge Native American fishing and hunting rights delineated by treaty. In arguing such cases against Native Americans, state officials often ignore long-standing federal laws that uphold the rights guaranteed in Native American treaties over state laws. In essence, the rights granted in American Indian treaties do not deny equal protection to non-Indians that are not entitled to treaty benefits.

Although it is, theoretically, well established that American Indians have enforceable civil rights like the right to seek and hold public office, to vote, and to be free from discriminatory practices, there is still much conflict in the application of these laws at the federal, state, and local levels. In essence, Native Americans are entitled not only to the entire range of civil rights enumerated in the United States Constitution and the state constitutions but also to their treaty rights. However, the legal enforcement of these rights has always been problematic throughout American history.

Tribalism, Native American Governments, and the Bill of Rights

Today, there are over 750,000 Native Americans residing on almost 300 federal and state Indian reservations. Usually, tribal members share a similar historical and racial background. They identify strongly with the experiences of their kin and the common bonds that unite them. Most Native Americans are keenly aware of federal policies that have sought to rob them of their culture, and they are dedicated to the future survival of their people. The distinctive group values held by Native Americans are often characterized as tribalism. When tribalism clashes with the rights of individuals, stress results between Native American people who believe in the primacy of tribal rights and persons who claim that tribal governments are violating their rights as individuals.

Although almost half of the 300 existing tribal governments have constitutions with some Bill of Rights provisions, the Supreme Court ruled in *Tilton* v. *Mayes* (1896) that the federal Bill of Rights does not apply to American Indian courts or governments. The court reasoned that the Bill of Rights restricts only the powers of state and federal governments. In theory, American Indian tribal governments are not subordinate to either state or federal governments. Since these tribal governments obtain their sovereignty from their indigenous self-governing status, the United States Constitution does not pertain to them.

This legal point seemed of little importance until the advent of the civil rights movement in the 1960s. Beginning in 1961, two special committees (one federal and one private) started to study the issue of civil rights on American Indian reservations. Subsequently, the Special Task Force on Indian Affairs recommended to the Interior Department that tribal governments secure civil liberties on reservations by enacting and enforcing new ordinances. Paradoxically, the Commission on the Rights, Liberties, and Responsibilities of the American Indian (financed by the Fund for the Republic) argued that tribal governments ought to be put under the Bill of Rights since the current system of tribal courts and governments put in jeopardy "the very assumptions on which our free society was established." Hence, the termination-ists reasoned that if they could not abolish Native American governments, they would place them fully within standard constitutional practices. These conflicting viewpoints led to U.S. Senate hearings before Senator Sam Ervin's Subcommittee on Constitutional Rights relating to Native Americans and the Bill of Rights.

Ervin gathered testimony from American Indian and other interested parties for seven years. People related stories about violations of their personal liberties and religious freedoms by tribal governments. Improper court practices by tribal courts were documented. Reservation injustices were caused by poor legal training of tribal lawyers and justices, a lack of resources, and the various states' failure to enforce laws on reservations covered by Public Law 280. In the end, the Subcommittee recorded over a thousand pages of testimony.

The testimony demonstrated that American Indians were deprived of their civil rights through improper state and federal actions. In South Dakota, Native Americans were often treated as virtual slaves, and the police in Gallup, New Mexico, and Pocatello, Idaho, denied medical services to Navajos and Shoshonis—letting them die in jail. Reservation Courts of Indian Offenses cooperated with local police to abduct Native Americans on their reservations and transport them off reservations to expedite arrests. Often, state courts denied rights to counsel, and not-guilty pleas were barred. States with powers under Public Law 280 like California refused to budget enough funds for policing reservations.

Although the civil rights issues in the 1960s brought significant social change for individuals of color, the major difficulty for many Native Americans during this time was to interpret the movement in a manner that supplemented their

unique situation. After much debate, Congress passed the Indian Civil Rights Act in 1968. Essentially, the act mandates that tribal governments give people under its authority the basic civil rights that they enjoy under the U. S. Constitution. However, the legislation was flexible with regards to tribal prerogatives. For instance, the free exercise of religion was included but not the restrictions on the establishment of a state religion. Since some tribal governments are theocracies, the legislation extended protection to them. The act also differed from the Bill of Rights on the right to counsel in criminal cases. The Supreme Court, by 1968, had mandated state and federal governments to pay for counsel in proceedings involving poor criminal defendants. However, tribal governments did not have the funds for such a right so the law asserted that in tribal courts defendants had a right to counsel but only if they paid for it.

Unlike the United States Constitution, the Indian Civil Rights Act of 1968 set limits on punishments issued by tribal courts—the maximum allowed in criminal sentences in tribal courts was $500 and six months in jail. Under the Major Crimes Act of 1883, the federal government had the power to prosecute almost all felonies on Indian reservations. This power has caused many problems. Because federal officials are slow to act on reservation crimes, tribal judges must mete out minimal sentences for serious crimes. The act also failed to address tribal concerns about the possibility of an abundance of federal lawsuits lodged against tribal officials. The act was unclear about which suits might be appropriate, and for over a decade, the federal courts heard a wide array of cases arising from this dilemma. Essentially, federal courts overruled tribal claims of sovereign immunity as well as challenges to jurisdiction of tribal courts. Until 1978, federal courts had unchallenged jurisdiction over suits against tribes.

Limiting Federal Jurisdiction in the Martinez Case

In 1978, the Supreme Court reviewed the right of federal courts to hear cases under the Indian Civil Rights Act in *Santa Clara Pueblo* v. *Martinez* (1978). In a seven-to-one decision, the high court held that since the Act did not surrender the tribal governments' sovereign immunity, Native American nations were immune to suits under the law. Tribal officials were also protected by the Act because the court reasoned that the Act did not grant tribal members the right to file suit. In effect, the court struck down ten years of suits against tribal governments.

The *Martinez* case basically denied federal judicial redress to persons who would sue Native American nations under the Indian Civil Rights Act. The court held out one exception to its ruling; it continued to extend the right of habeas corpus to those persons held in tribal custody. As a result of the *Martinez* case, students of Native American law and civil libertarians expressed concern about the absence of federal judicial review of tribal court decisions. Many asked, Who would defend American Indians from caprice by their own tribal governments? In response, the high court asserted that tribal governments or tribal courts would protect Native American civil rights under the Indian Civil Rights Act. It was a tentative step forward for American Indian self-determination.

The Role of Native American Courts After the *Martinez* Case

In the wake of the *Martinez* decision, tribal courts have played a critical judicial role in the lives of American Indian people. Initially, many people doubted that the tribal courts would safeguard Native American civil rights. However, a survey of the situation after the *Martinez* case indicates that such misapprehensions were unfounded.

Judges in tribal courts formed a national association in 1970 to further judicial education programs for its members. Subsequently, this organization as well as similar entities have offered seminars and training programs around the country for interested tribal judges. As a result, tribal courts have steadily improved their abilities to deal with civil rights issues on their reservations. Some of the larger Native American nations have created courts of appeal, while smaller tribes have established intertribal courts. Increasingly, tribal courts are staffed by judges with law degrees and non-Indian as well as Indian lawyers practice in the courts.

Although the tribal courts have their critics, the Supreme Court continues to uphold the jurisdic-

tion of such courts. In *National Farmers Union Insurance Company* v. *Crow Tribe* (1985) and *Iowa Mutual Insurance Company* v. *LaPlante* (1987), the high court affirmed the right of tribal courts to adjudicate personal injury cases involving non-Indians. Both decisions asserted that federal courts could not take jurisdiction in personal injury cases until the tribal courts had a chance to hear the cases initially and had determined its own jurisdiction in such cases. By the 1990s, tribal courts had become an integral part of tribal government. The Supreme Court asserted in *Oklahoma Tax Commission* v. *Citizen Band Potawatomi Indian Tribe* (1991): "[Native American tribes] exercise inherent sovereign authority over their members and their territory. Suits against Indian tribes are thus barred by sovereign immunity absent a clear waiver by the tribe or congressional abrogation." Since the *Martinez* case, tribal courts have remained virtually the only courts with clear jurisdiction to hear cases against tribal governments and officials involving civil rights violations.

Civil Rights and Treaty Rights Since the 1960s

As the civil rights struggles of the 1960s subsided, Native Americans began a new drive for rights that would take them beyond the gains of the 1960s. With their individual rights as American citizens formally codified in law (although not always affirmed in fact), American Indians started to assert their rights as tribal citizens. These rights were a result of the status of American Indian nations as "domestic" nations. Hundreds of treaties confirmed these rights as well. Treaty rights and self-determination became the focus of Native American efforts when the fervor of the civil rights movement waned.

Native American fishing rights guaranteed through treaties became one of the primary battlegrounds for Native American civil rights. The Native American right to fish on the Nisqually River in Washington state became one of the early focal points of the struggle. The Treaty of Point Elliott, signed by Native American nations and ratified by the United States Senate in the 1850s, provided that American Indians would reserve the right to take "fish at usual and accustomed grounds . . . in common with all citizens of the territory." Native Americans in Washington State

Native American fishing rights guaranteed through treaties became one of the primary battlegrounds for Native American civil rights.

in *United States* v. *Washington* (Phase I) (1974) held that Indians were entitled to almost one half of the salmon harvest in Washington state. Although many non-Indians were enraged, the decision survived judicial review and was reaffirmed by the Supreme Court in *United States* v. *Washington* (1979). American Indians had prevailed in the fight to maintain their century old treaty rights to fish, and they verified that treaty rights do not alter with the passage of time. Moreover, the allocation of fishing resources negotiated in treaties was binding on the descendants of the treaty parties in spite of the different conditions that are now present in non-Indian and American Indian communities.

Eastern American Indians began to assert their rights as well. Tribal attorneys in the eastern part of the United States discovered that many of the treaties that took lands from Native American nations were not ratified by Congress even though the Indian Trade and Intercourse Acts enacted at the end of the eighteenth and beginning of the early nineteenth centuries required it. Hence, the Intercourse Acts voided many old land transactions. These eastern Indian land cases challenged the United States' commitment to the rule of law. With claims almost 200 years old, the ancient rules of law enacted two centuries ago would result in court victories for many eastern American Indian nations. Despite intense pressure from state governments and residents, federal courts ruled favorably on Indian claims cases in the East. Also, many cases were settled out of court (the settlements were subsequently approved by Congress). However, some cases continued in the courts. In 1985, the Supreme Court, in *County of Oneida* v. *Oneida Indian Nation* (1985), upheld Oneida Indian land claims and asserted that abuses perpetrated two centuries ago could be redressed in the courts and the rights of American Indian could be restored.

used this right for over a hundred years before the state of Washington began to infringe on their fishing rights. Although a 1963 federal court decision upheld the fishing rights of Indians, state courts continued to forbid Indians from net fishing. In a series of protests, Native American fishermen were cited, arrested, and jailed for violating state fishing laws. American Indians also lodged complaints of police brutality but to no avail. In spite of their victories in federal court, Native American fishermen were persecuted, threatened, and in one instance, shot by non-Indian vigilantes. In this case, federal authorities in the Nixon administration reacted very slowly.

Undaunted by the odds they were up against, the Indians of Washington state continued their struggle until 1974, when Judge George H. Boldt

Rights to self-government were also regained through congressional acts. Termination policies were formally renounced when the Menominee Tribe of Wisconsin regained its tribal status in 1973. In 1975, the Indian Self-Determination Act granted tribes the right to administer federal assistance programs. Thus, it ended the control of such programs by government administrators who had dominated reservation life for over a century. In 1978, the Indian Child Welfare Act put the welfare of American Indian children firmly in the hands of the tribes and limited the powers of the states in this crucial area. In the past, American Indian children had been taken arbitrarily from their tribal setting and placed in non-Indian environments. The Indian Child Welfare Act sought to curb the power of non-Indians in the affairs of American Indian families. In 1979, the American Indian Freedom of Religion Act sought to honor and nurture traditional Native American religious rituals and practices.

All of these struggles in the 1970s and 1980s grew out of the civil rights struggles of the 1960s. American Indian leaders, lawyers, and activists gained their victories by capitalizing on the gains secured during the 1960s. However, the tribal rights asserted by Native Americans were much different than those claimed by other peoples of color. Clearly, the broader civil rights movement nurtured the rights of American Indians as individuals, but the regaining of tribal rights could be accomplished only by Native Americans. American Indian group rights, however, have remained largely misunderstood by the non-Indian population and present a continuing dilemma for American Indian people and their governments. It also is a challenge to non-Indians and the court system.

The Role of American Indian Militancy in Civil Rights

Although it is difficult to gauge the impact of militant groups like the American Indian Movement (AIM) on the political landscape, the frustrations and aspirations of AIM did reflect much of the anger and despair that many Native Americans had with governmental policies. With the occupation of Alcatraz Island in 1969, the seizure of the Bureau of Indian Affairs headquarters in 1972, and the confrontations at Wounded Knee, South Dakota, in 1973, the injustices in contemporary American Indian life were dramatically portrayed in the media. Young American Indian militants took action in the late 1960s and early 1970s because they believed that system was incapable of reforming itself. AIM was adept at focusing media attention on the deplorable conditions that Native Americans labored under. Often, the agenda of AIM was at odds with tribal governments. Tensions also increased between Indians and non-Indians. AIM's activities on the Pine Ridge Reservation in South Dakota prompted excessive force by federal authorities that engendered a climate of systematic abuse of the civil rights of Native

Vine Deloria Jr. *(1933–)*

Vine Deloria Jr., a lawyer, writer, and professor, was born in 1933 at Martin, South Dakota. He is one of the nations' best known authors on Native American issues. Through his many books and articles he has brought a greater knowledge of Native American life and culture to public awareness than any other single person active on the contemporary scene.

A Standing Rock Sioux, Vine Deloria Jr. comes from a distinguished family. His grandfather was a Yankton chief. His aunt, Ella Deloria, was a noted scholar of Indian ethnology and linguistics. His father, Vine Deloria Sr., was an Episcopal minister, the first American Indian to be named to a national post in the Episcopal Church.

Vine Deloria Jr. has been educated as a lawyer and a scholar. He earned his law degree in 1970 at the University of Colorado School of Law. He has taught at the University of Colorado at Boulder and also at the University of Arizona in Tucson, where he held a post as professor of political science. He is also very active in many public and private organizations concerned with Indian culture and politics.

Vine Deloria Jr. is a leading thinker and a spokesman for Native Americans. He served as the executive director of the National Congress of American Indians from 1964 to 1967. He has advocated Indian people remaining Indian, remaining within their cultures, resisting the decadence that he sees in the larger society. Deloria favors education and ideology—not violence—as a means for achieving dignity and justice for all tribes.

Among his many books, *Custer Died for Your Sins* (1969) and *God Is Red* (1973) are the best known. Some of his other books are *We Talk You Listen* (1970), *Behind the Trail of Broken Treaties* (1974), *The Aggression of Civilization* (1984), and *American Indian Policy in the Twentieth Century* (1985).

American persons both affiliated and not affiliated with AIM. In the final analysis, the impact of AIM was generally positive because it coalesced the determination of Native Americans to advance their rights and demonstrated the lengths that some people were prepared to go if justice was not served. Since the 1970s, the influence and power of AIM have decreased because of federal harassment and systematic campaigns to defame the group.

Backlash and the Renewed Campaign to Eliminate Treaty Rights

The improvements of the rights of American Indians in the 1960s and 1970s nurtured an ominous counterattack by groups determined to eliminate Native American governmental rights and treaty rights. Utilizing the rhetoric of "reverse discrimination," this movement asserts that contemporary Euroamericans should not be held accountable for historical policies that discriminated against and violated the rights of people of color. This ideology also holds that the white majority should not be made to suffer as a result of remedies for past inequities. Although this argument may have some merit in other situations, it completely ignores the context of American Indian treaty rights.

Obviously, the United States government did not grant treaty rights to Native American tribes through any altruistic motives. Treaties were legal agreements for the conveyance of huge amounts of American Indian land. White settlers then entered those lands "legitimately" as a result of these massive land cessions. Despite historical and continued abuse, American Indian nations have not demanded that these lands be reinstated to their original owners. Furthermore, Native Americans have not demanded that non-Indian rights under these treaties be rescinded. Thus, the demands by non-Indians that Native Americans give up their rights is inconsistent with the historical record and difficult to understand. Although the backlash was worrisome throughout the 1980s, it did not achieve any significant legislative victories at the federal level.

Conclusion

Any analysis of the civil rights of Native Americans within the tribal context is fraught with tension and contention between the individualistic values of the dominant society and the more collectivistic virtues of tribalism. Today's Native American communities are spirited, democratic societies. Although tribal courts are relatively new additions, the strides that they have made in nurturing justice are remarkable. There is a growing awareness that tribal courts have emerged as a significant and integral part of tribal governments. There is also a sense that they will safeguard the civil rights of their tribal members. Tensions between Native Americans and their surrounding state governments over treaty rights and religious freedom remain unresolved.

The notion of civil rights is many things to many people, and the Bill of Rights is often regarded as the foundation of freedom and liberty in the United States. History has shown us that individuals and groups may hold basic, fundamental rights to check the caprice of government. Certainly, liberty and freedom involve the balancing of coercive state power against collective and individual rights guaranteed in the Bill of Rights. However, the Bill of Rights does not grant protection for Native Americans from the abuses of tribal, local, state, and federal governments. Often, Native Americans are denied the basic rights that other inhabitants of the United States take for granted. In contemporary legal decisions, American Indian sovereignty has not been deemed compatible with the Bill of Rights. Hence, only the United States Congress can stop the denial of American Indian rights by the non-Indian majority in the courts.

Many American Indian people and nations are better off today than they were in the past, but there are still many civil rights issues that need improvement. In assessing its human rights violations in 1979, the United States government reported that "Native Americans, on average, have the lowest per capita income, the highest unemployment rate, the lowest level of educational achievement, the shortest lives, the worst health and housing conditions, and the highest suicide rate in the United States. The poverty among Indian families is nearly three times greater than the rate for non-Indian families and Native people collectively rank at the bottom of every social and economic statistical indicator." Without a doubt, American Indians continue to suffer injustices that are a product of historically discriminatory poli-

THE MASSACRE OF THE NATIVE AMERICANS

cies toward them as individuals and as members of tribal political entities.

The sensitivity or insensitivity in historical eras to the rights of American Indians marks the ebb and flow of America's faith in democratic principles. Indeed, Felix Cohen once characterized the rights of American Indians in our society as the "miner's canary," implying that if American Indian legal rights suffer then the fundamental freedoms in American democracy are endangered for everyone. Every generation of American Indians wonders if the dominant society will continue to acknowledge the special rights of American Indians granted by previous generations. In the final analysis, the solution to this rights dilemma will demand significant progress in adapting the legal systems of the larger American society so that Native American demands for the recognition and nurturing of their treaty rights and civil rights can be accommodated.

Bibliography

Barsh, Russel Lawrence, and James Youngblood Henderson. *The Road: Indian Tribes and Political Liberty.* Berkeley, Calif.: University of California Press, 1980.

Canby, William C. *American Indian Law.* St. Paul, Minn.: West Publishing, 1981.

Cohen, Felix S. *Felix Cohen's Handbook of Federal Indian Law.* Charlottesville, Va.: Mitchie/Bobbs Merrill, 1982.

Cornell, Stephen. *The Return of the Native: American Indian Political Resurgence.* New York: Oxford University Press, 1988.

Getches, David H., and Charles F. Wilkinson. *Federal Indian Law: Cases and Materials.* St. Paul, Minn.: West Publishing, 1986.

Jaimes, M. Annette. *The State of Native America.* Boston: South End Press, 1992.

Lyons, Oren, et al. *Exiled in the Land of the Free: Democracy, Indian Nations and the U.S. Constitution.* Santa Fe, N. Mex.: Clear Light Publishers, 1992.

Price, Monroe E., and Robert Clinton. *Law and the American Indian.* Charlottesville, Va.: Mitchie/Bobbs Merrill, 1983.

Pevar, Stephen L. *The Rights of Indians and Tribes.* Carbondale and Edwardsville, Ill.: Southern Illinois University Press, 1992.

Shattuck, Petra H., and Jill Norgren. *Partial Justice: Federal Indian Law in a Liberal Constitutional System.* New York: Berg, 1991.

United States Commission on Civil Rights. *American Indian Civil Rights Handbook.* Washington, D.C.: U.S. Government Printing Office, 1980.

West, W. Richard Jr., and Kevin Gover. "The Struggle for Indian Civil Rights." in Frederick E. Hoxie, ed. *Indians in American History.* Arlington Heights, Ill.: Harlan Davidson, 1988.

Wunder, John R. *"Retained by the People": A History of American Indians and the Bill of Rights.* New York: Oxford University Press, 1994.

Zionitz, Alvin J. "After Martinez: Indian Civil Rights Under Tribal Government." *University of California, Davis Law Review* 12 (1979): 1.

Chapter 7

The Immigrant Experience—Irish, Italians, Germans, Poles, Jews, Japanese, and Arabs

Michael Thomas Bedard

When Frederic Loewe, Vienna-born composer of *My Fair Lady,* arrived in the United States during the 1920s, he had a hard time launching his career. Although he was a gifted pianist, he couldn't find a job. One morning while waiting for his piano to be repossessed, he sat down to play. He played with rare inspiration. When he looked up from the piano, he was startled to find that he had an audience of three moving men, who were seated on the floor.

The movers said nothing, and made no movement toward the piano. Instead, they dug into their pockets, pooled enough money to pay the installment due, placed it on the piano and walked out empty-handed.

The above story, illustrates tolerance toward a recently-arrived American immigrant. Unfortunately, not all exchanges between new and native-born citizens have been marked by such understanding. Words of insult such as "Paddy" and "Wop" became part of the American vocabulary. The first, a variation of the Irish word for Patrick, and the second, a bureaucratic term used by immigration officials for Italians "without papers," became slang expressions used by many native-born citizens.

America's love-hate relationship toward immigration parallels its ambivalent attitude toward equal opportunity. Politically, the Declaration of Independence proclaimed "life, liberty and the pursuit of happiness" for all citizens—at a time when only propertied white males could vote. The Thirteenth, Fourteenth, and Fifteenth Amendments to the Constitution, passed in the aftermath of the Civil War, granted civil rights to African American males, yet "Jim Crow" segregationist laws persisted well into the twentieth century.

How can America's ambivalence toward immigrants be explained? Some people were pulled to immigrate by opportunities and others were pushed to immigrate by events in Europe, observes Stanford Professor David M. Kennedy

The Statue of Liberty in New York harbor welcomed millions of new immigrants to the United States throughout the late nineteenth and early twentieth centuries.

shall kill lacked the courage to make such a sacrifice and continued as slaves."

In his own inimitable idiom Patton was invoking what for most Americans was—and still is—the standard explanation of who their immigrant forebears were, why they left their old countries, and what their effect was on American society. In this explanation immigrants were the main-chance-seeking, most energetic, entrepreneurial, freedom-loving members of their Old World societies. They were drawn out of Europe by the irresistible magnet of American opportunity and liberty, and their galvanizing influence on American society made this country the greatest in the world.

And yet not everyone who came to America was pulled here; some were "pushed" by conditions in Europe. Professor Kennedy observes in his article that "a process that eventually put some 35 million people in motion is to be found in two convulsively disruptive developments that lay far beyond the control of individual Europeans." Ultimately 40 percent of this country's population could point to an ancestor who came through Ellis Island.

The first of these forces mentioned by Kennedy needs little elaboration. It was, quite simply, population growth. In the nineteenth century the population of Europe more than doubled, from some 200 million to more than 400 million, even after about 70 million people had left Europe altogether. (Only half of these, it should be noted, went to the United States—one among many clues that the American-as-magnet explanation is inadequate.) That population boom was the indispensable precondition for Europe to export people on the scale that it did. And the boom owed little to American stimulus; rather, it was a product of aspects of European historical evolution, especially improvements in diet, sanitation, and disease control.

The second development was more complex, but we know it by a familiar name: the Industrial Revolution. It includes the closely associated revolution in agricultural productivity. Wherever it occurred, the Industrial Revolution shook people loose from traditional ways of life. It made factory workers out of artisans and, even more dramatically, turned millions of rural farmers into urban wage-laborers. Most of these migrants from countryside to city, from agriculture to industry, remained within their country of origin, or at least within Europe. But in the early stages of industri-

in a November 1996 article published in *The Atlantic Monthly* ("The Price of Immigration: Can We Still Afford to be a Nation of Immigrants?").

One describer of those "pulled" to America by its opportunities was the flamboyant World War II General George S. Patton. Professor Kennedy describes the scene in Tunisia on July 9, 1943:

The occasion was the eve of the invasion of Sicily, and General George S. Patton Jr. was addressing his troops, who were about to embark for the battle. He urged, "When we land, we will meet German and Italian soldiers whom it is our honor and privilege to attack and destroy. Many of you have in your veins German and Italian blood, but remember that these ancestors of yours so loved freedom that they gave up home and country to cross the ocean in search of liberty. The ancestors of the people we

Ultimately 40 percent of this country's population could point to an ancestor who came through Ellis Island.

alization the movement of people, like the investment of capital during the unbridled early days of industrialism, was often more than the market could bear. In time most European societies reached a kind of equilibrium, absorbing their own workers into their own wage markets. But in the typical transitional phase some workers who had left artisanal or agricultural employments could not be reabsorbed domestically in European cities. They thus migrated overseas.

After two centuries, the question remains in America: How does a nation governed by majority rule protect the rights of minorities? A second question also emerges: How do people of diverse backgrounds gain access to the majority culture?

The latter has been posed since the beginning of the republic. The framers of the Constitution considered how the "more perfect union" they envisioned could be enlarged by addressing the immigration issue; Article I, Section 8 of the Constitution grants to Congress, among other duties, the power to "establish a uniform Rule of Naturalization . . . throughout the United States."

When the Federalist and Anti-Federalist political parties were emerging in the 1790s and early 1800s, the issue of who constituted a "real American" dominated the partisan debate of the day. Ironically, the pro-British Federalists and the pro-French Anti-Federalists (that is, the Democratic-Republican party of Thomas Jefferson), argued over which party could better safeguard the American experiment.

During Federalist President John Adams's term, the Alien and Sedition Acts were passed by Congress in 1798. The Alien Acts empowered the president to imprison or exile foreigners who posed a threat to the government. The Naturalization Act mandated that a foreign-born individual live in the United States for 14 years before citizenship could be granted. (The Constitution required that a person must have been for "fourteen Years a Resident within the United States" to be eligible for election to the presidency!)

One hundred and fifty years later, the "true American" question also dominated the political debate of the day. The House of Representatives established a Committee on Un-American Activities (HUAC) and Senator Joseph McCarthy of Wisconsin instituted a one-man witch hunt for alleged enemies of the republic, most of whom were natural born citizens of the United States. Given these situations, it is not surprising that hostility and suspicion have often greeted immigrants to America in search of a better life.

The Irish

"The Irish, the most assimilated Catholic ethnic group in America, were the first to experience the lash of hatred at the hands of native Protestant

Overcrowding and poor sanitary conditions were typical of most immigrant neighborhoods in New York in the late nineteenth century.

Americans," observes Richard Krickus, author of *Pursuing The American Dream: White Ethnics and the New Populism.* He describes how the newly arrived Irish immigrants existed on the bottom rung of America's social ladder:

> In the 1840s Irish immigrants began to enter the United States in large numbers. Unlike those who had previously arrived—the Scotch-Irish Protestants or middle-class Catholics who neatly blended in with the mainstream populace—the newcomers were poor, uneducated Catholics. During the 1840s, 1.7 million Irishmen fled the famine that depleted Ireland's villages and filled its graveyards. Living in dirty, overcrowded hovels along the nation's East Coast cities . . . the Irish who lived in New York City and Boston worked as domestic servants, dug ditches, or labored on the docks toting cargo. Editorialists wrote that they were stupid, lazy, violent, and prone toward drunkenness and criminality. It

was alleged that half of the convicted criminals in the mid-nineteenth century were foreign-born and they were ten times as likely as native Americans to live off the dole; most of these miscreants were Irish.

"Paddy" cartoons filled the publications of the day, with the stereotyped Irishmen wearing top hats and waistcoats, sporting large noses and invariably carrying whiskey bottles. Such portrayals, of course, differed from the way the Irish saw themselves.

One wrote back home: "How often do we see such paragraphs in the paper as an Irishman drowns—an Irishman crushed by a beam—an Irishman suffocated in a pit—an Irishman blown to atoms by a steam engine—ten, twenty Irishmen buried alive by the sinking of a bank."

Immigrant families awaiting processing at Ellis Island.

Anti-Irish hate literature appeared. In 1836 and 1837, "Maria Monk" (an anonymous anti-Catholic writer) wrote two fictitious books about her experiences as an ex-nun in a Montreal convent where priests raped nuns. Over 300,000 copies of the false accounts were sold prior to the Civil War.

A social war raged within America before the military conflict that split the Union. The "domestic Tranquility" mentioned in the Preamble to the Constitution was not evident in events like these:

- A Charleston, Massachusetts, mob burned a convent in 1831.

- In 1844, Irish laborers fought anti-Catholics in the Kensington section of Philadelphia.

- In 1846, a Philadelphia Irish Catholic church was burned. The German Catholic church a few blocks away was left untouched.

Interpreting the Preamble's goal to "provide for the common defense" domestically, native-born citizens formed political organizations to block immigrant assimilation into society. The American, or Know-Nothing, Party constituted one such group. Formed in 1843, its members came from urban lower-middle-class ranks, opposed immigration, hated Catholicism, and sought to ban parochial schools. They saw themselves as defenders of values and traditions held in common only by native-born citizens.

Members of the secret organization replied "I don't know" when asked questions about the party's policies by outsiders, hence its familiar nickname. The Know-Nothing Party carried Massachusetts in 1854 and nominated former President Millard Fillmore for the presidency in 1856. That a former president could be persuaded to carry the party's antitolerance banner speaks to how respectable it was to oppose people based on their national origin and religious preference, a right guaranteed within the Bill of Rights, in the mid-nineteenth century.

But political action against immigrants did not end there. The anti-Catholic, anti-immigrant, and anti-African American Ku Klux Klan was formed in 1866 at Pulaski, Tennessee. Statements against Irish Catholics appeared in mainstream periodicals and were made by a sitting president in the 1870s.

"The unpatriotic conduct of the Romanish population in our chief cities during the late rebellion is well known. They formed a constant menace and terror to loyal citizens; they thronged the peace meetings; they strove to divide the Union; and when the war was over they placed in office their corrupt leaders," observed *Harper's Weekly* in 1872.

Irish immigrants did play a prominent role in the New York City draft riots during the Civil War; however, many Irishmen served in the Union

Irish American clam diggers, Boston, 1882.

Army during the conflict. The "Fighting 69th" regiment, which served with distinction, was composed mainly of Irishmen.

In 1875, President Ulysses S. Grant remarked: "If we are to have another contest in the near future of our national existence, I predict that the dividing line will not be Mason and Dixon's, but between (Protestant) patriotism and intelligence on one side, and (Catholic) superstition, ambition and ignorance on the other. . . ."

As noted by Krickus, Irish power in the cities rested on three pillars: the Catholic Church, the labor unions, and the urban political machines. "Paddy wagons" were originally named for the Irishmen contained within them; they were later named for the Irish policemen who operated them. Ironically, the former members of the "criminal element" eventually dominated the New York City Police Department. The 1960s television series *Batman* was on track when it featured "Chief O'Hara"—obviously an Irishman—as the uniformed head of police in Gotham City, a fictionalized New York City.

In 1928, Democratic presidential candidate and Irish Catholic Al Smith lost his bid for the presidency—in part—owing to his religious affiliation. Thirty-two years later, the Democrats again nominated an Irish Catholic for the presidency—Senator John F. Kennedy of Massachusetts.

His Catholicism had to be addressed head on and it was at two decisive points in the campaign. The first occurred during the West Virginia primary in May of 1960; the second took place before an audience of Protestant clergy in Houston on September 12, 1960.

In 1960, only 5 percent of West Virginians were Roman Catholics. To prove that an Irish Catholic could win the November general election, the state's primary was a "must win" for Kennedy. On May 10, 1960, Catholic Senator Kennedy of Massachusetts defeated Protestant Senator Humphrey of Minnesota in West Virginia's Democratic primary. Humphrey's campaign ended that night.

Four months later, Kennedy made these remarks before the 300-member Greater Houston Ministerial Association, as recounted in *The Making of the President 1960:*

> . . . because I am a Catholic, and no Catholic has ever been elected President, the real issues in this campaign have been obscured. . . . So it is apparently necessary for me to state once again—not what kind of church I believe in, for that should be important only to me, but what kind of America I believe in.
>
> I believe in an America where the separation of church and state is absolute—where no Catholic prelate would tell the President (should he be a Catholic) how to act and no Protestant minister would tell his parishioners for whom to vote. . . .

I am not the Catholic candidate for President. I am the Democratic Party's candidate for President, who happens also to be a Catholic. . . .

But if this election is decided on the basis that 40,000,000 Americans lost their chance of being President on the day they were baptized, then it is the whole nation that will be the loser in the eyes of Catholics and non-Catholics around the world, in the eyes of history, and in the eyes of our own people.

On January 20, 1961, John F. Kennedy was inaugurated as the thirty-fifth president of the United States. The paternal grandson of one Massachusetts state senator and the maternal grandson of another, who had also served as a member of the U.S. House of Representatives and as mayor of Boston for two terms, Kennedy had broken the unwritten rule—the political glass ceiling of its day—that an Irish Catholic couldn't be elected to the nation's highest office.

The Irish came to America during the "Old Immigration" period prior to 1890. From 1820, the year when the federal government began to keep immigration statistics, to around 1890, western and northern Europeans accounted for most of the newcomers. They had the advantage of sharing religious and cultural similarities with those already here.

Yet the Irish experience in America paralleled that of later immigrant groups. All were subjected to the "new kid on the block" syndrome, whereby they were required to "measure up" to "fit in."

New immigrants faced two common practices: a sociological one known as "scapegoating" and an economic one known as "hard times." "Scapegoating" is a means of diverting mass discontent from the people responsible for the conditions breeding unrest. Throughout American history domestic economic stress has periodically given rise to nativist hostility toward foreigners and "outsiders." At the turn of the century, "Catholics and Jews" and "Wops and Polaks" bore the responsibility for the disruption wrought by urbanization and industrialization. Economic hard times have also contributed to the difficulties experienced by the foreign-born at the hands of the native-born. During periods of prosperity, Americans have tended to be more tolerant of alien residents; during periods of hardship, Americans have tended to be less tolerant of immigrant groups.

John Higham, author of *Strangers in the Land: Patterns of American Nativism 1860–1925*, points to the Italian experience in the coal fields of Pennsylvania. "In the seventies and eighties the coal mining country was rapidly becoming the industrial hell of the northeastern United States," he wrote, describing the "grimy company towns," "ravaged landscape," and "class cleavage" that existed in that environment. An economic war between labor and management began in 1865, the year of the Civil War's ending, and strikes, lockouts, and strife pervaded the entire region. Having had enough of native laborers, the mine owners tapped another source: foreign-born workers, from Hungary and Italy. Perceived as creatures of the employers, they experienced hostility and resentment at the hands of Americans who opposed these new strangers.

"Paddy wagons" were originally named for the Irishmen contained within them; they were later named for the Irish policemen who operated them.

The Italians

The Italians constituted one of the largest groups who came to America during the "New Immigration" period. Beginning in the 1890s, more new immigrants came from southern or eastern Europe; 2 million people—47.5 percent of those arriving in the United States from overseas—emigrated from Italy, Poland, and Russia during the decade. Mostly Catholic, they were either unskilled laborers or displaced farmers. Between 1901 and 1910, 6 million immigrants—71 percent of all newcomers—left southern or eastern Europe for the United States.

Between 1901 and 1910, 6 million immigrants—71 percent of all newcomers—left southern or eastern Europe for the United States.

Commenting on stereotypes applied to the new immigrants, Higham observes:

> In the case of the Italians, a rather similar fear of "infuriated foreigners" took a different twist. Anti-foreign sentiment filtered through a specific ethnic stereotype when Italians were involved; for in American eyes they bore the mark of Cain. They suggested the stiletto, the Mafia, the deed of impassioned violence. "The disposition to assassinate in revenge for a fancied wrong," declared the Baltimore *News*, "is a marked trait in the character of this impulsive and inexorable race." Every time a simple Italian laborer resorted to his knife, the newspapers stressed the fact of his nationality; the most trivial fracas in Mulberry Street caused a headline on "Italian Vendetta." The stereotype conditioned every major outburst of anti-Italian sentiment in the 1890's. The distinctive nativism which swarthy *paesani* experienced took the guise of social discipline applied to alleged acts of homicide.

These three actions were taken against Italians in the 1890s:

- In 1891, a New Orleans mob hung eleven Italian suspects following the acquittal of some for the murder of the city's superintendent of police.

- In 1895, Colorado miners and residents killed six Italians involved in a native-born saloonkeeper's death.

- In 1896, a Louisiana town mob broke into a jail and lynched three Italian prisoners.

Hostility toward Italians did not end in nineteenth-century America; it continued into the twentieth century. In 1914, the U.S. Supreme Court upheld a New York statute requiring American citizenship of employees on public projects. Times were hard in the depression year of 1914; the New York City Bricklayers' Union invoked the statute against Italian aliens working on the subway.

Responding to nativist pressures during World War I, Congress passed a deportation law in 1918. It permitted the Secretary of Labor—who presided over the Immigration Bureau—to sign a warrant authorizing the deportation of aliens. Among its grounds for deportation was membership in any organization certified as "subversive" by the secretary.

Ironically, the Immigration Bureau was then headed by the first Italian American ever elected to Congress, Anthony Caminetti of California, while the Secretary of Labor at the time was a naturalized citizen, labor leader William B. Wilson, who was of Scottish origin.

The two clashed on enforcement of the law. Caminetti's bureau attempted to deport 39 alien members of the International Workers of the World (IWW), or "Wobblies," as they were known. But the deportations were largely halted, since Secretary Wilson refused to certify the left-wing labor organization as subversive and required a stringent burden of proof relative to their alleged guilt.

By the dawn of World War II, the Italian presence in America had reached a state of peaceful coexistence with the native born, even though Italy constituted one of three enemy nations. Italian and German Americans were treated as individuals for the purpose of determining their loyalties and allegiances. The same cannot be said for descendants of the third Axis Power—Japan.

The Japanese

Treated as a group, Japanese Americans were "evacuated" from the American West Coast—the area closest to their ancestral homeland—and interned in concentration, or "re-location," camps. They lost most of their possessions, much of their dignity, and all of their honor. Not one case of treason or sabotage was ever prosecuted against a Japanese American during World War II. More information about the Japanese American experience as immigrants are found in chapter 4.

Edison Uno, one of the internees, recounted his wartime experiences in the documentary series *The World At War* (produced by Thames Television in Great Britain, c. 1972):

There was a tremendous change. The change being that we were the same individuals prior to December 7th. December 8th when we went to school, many of our classmates and friends called us dirty Japs, teased us, harassed us and our so-called friends were no longer friends.

The mental anguish that my mother went through—having four of her sons in the service of the United States government—and having her husband labeled a dangerous enemy alien.

We had guards, watchtowers, machine guns. It was a picture of incarceration. We felt that we were prisoners—prisoners in our own country.

Another internee, Isamu Naguchi, drew this comparison later in the program:

In the First World War, as you know, the Germans were hated thoroughly and there was a great deal of discrimination and harassment of the Germans. In the Second World War, we were at war with three different nationalities: the Italians, the Germans and the Japanese.

And I remember that Thomas Mann . . . spoke up for the Germans and said they couldn't be removed because that would be the last despair—having fled Nazi Germany, to be again put into a concentration camp.

And Joe DiMaggio's mother spoke up, you know, and that was a very moving act in San Francisco, I remember.

But the Japanese had really nobody. I think the picking on the Japanese was partly a kind of a logistically rational thing that the Army could handle.

They said no, we can't handle the Germans, but we can handle the Japanese. After all, they couldn't have moved all the Germans and the Italians in this country. They would have had to move half the people out of New York City. It would have been ridiculous.

By the end of World War II more than 100,000 Japanese Americans had been interned mostly on the West Coast. On the other hand, the 600,000 German and Italian Americans were treated individually.

Three lessons emerge. Just as hard economic times have affected immigrant groups, so have hard social and political times. The Japanese Americans, unpopular with many Americans before the war, became even more disliked during it. Planted prior to the Pearl Harbor raid, the bitter seeds of animosity sprouted a hundredfold after it.

Japanese Americans were forced to endure years of animousity following their arrival to the United States, including "evacuation" of their homes and internment in concentration, or "relocation," camps during World War II.

Further, the Japanese American experience during World War II indicates one thing: that the road traveled by "ethnic groups" in America—though an often long and tough one—has not been as rough as that traveled by people of different "racial groups." One former Roosevelt administration official, after describing the jealousy of many Californians for the productive Japanese American farmers, commented that the government acted "hastily and brutally." "Racially" applies as well.

Also evident is the impact of wartime emergency measures on civil rights in America. Executive Order 9066 barred people of Japanese descent from the Pacific coast area. In 1944, the U.S. Supreme Court upheld a 1942 military order enforcing it in *Korematsu* v. *United States*. However, Justice Murphy, one of three dissenters, concluded: "This exclusion [falls] into the ugly abyss of racism . . . The reasons [for the removal] appear . . . to be largely an accumulation of much of the misinformation, half-truths and insinuations that for years have been directed against Japanese Americans by people with racial and economic prejudices."

The Germans

German Americans fared better than their Japanese American counterparts during World War II. However, citizens of German ancestry were hated and discriminated against during the First

Sources of Immigration to the U.S. 1820-1960	
Nations	# Who Came to America
Germany	6,752,000
Italy	4,981,000
Ireland	4,682,000
Austria-Hungary	4,277,000
Great Britain	3,803,000
Canada	3,603,000
Russia	3,345,000
Sweden	1,251,000
Mexico	1,180,000

Source: U.S. Immigration and Naturalization Service

World War. American language changed as German-sounding words were "Americanized": for example, "frankfurters," named for the sausages made in Frankfort, Germany, became "hot dogs." German language and literature courses ceased to be taught in U.S. schools and colleges.

Historically, Germans represented the largest of all the immigrant groups who came to the United States between 1820 and 1960. The table above compares their numbers with those of eight other nationalities.

We The People: An Atlas of America's Ethnic Diversity describes the German contribution this way:

> Germans were the most important white ethnic population other than the English in the period before the American Revolution, making up almost 9 percent of the population in 1790. . . . Their descendants and those of the larger nineteenth- and twentieth-century immigrant groups have made the total German-ancestry population almost equal in size to the English. English and German ancestries were each reported by over 26 percent of those who responded to the ancestry question [in the 1980 census form].

Despite their numbers, German Americans were by no means completely safe from nativism. Richard Krickus observes:

> Once the United States entered the [First World] war . . . the German-Americans came under heavy pressure to "assimilate"; their loyalty was held suspect and as nativist hysteria about a 'German fifth column' spread, businessmen with

German surnames were boycotted and some German language newspapers were forced to close. After American troops set sail for Europe, citizens of German descent were under incessant pressure to demonstrate their loyalty; many responded by relinquishing their membership in German organizations, attending churches which were distinctively 'American,' using English in their meeting halls, and instructing their children not to lapse into German outside the house. Like the Southern Wasps after the Civil War, the German-Americans sought to protect themselves from accusations that they were antipatriotic by wrapping the Stars and Stripes tightly around themselves . . . they first reacted to the war as Old World nationalists but that sentiment was later superseded by New World patriotism.

Germany no longer serves as a major source for immigration to the United States. Today's immigrants, escaping economic hardships or fleeing from politically repressive regimes, tend to come from Third World nations. The table on the following page, based on U.S. Immigration and Nationalization Service figures, indicates the national origin of the 530,639 people admitted to America in 1980.

As shown by the table, only one nation (Great Britain) sends people to America who speak English as their first language; those from the other nine speak in other tongues. Though revisited here, the issue of which language should be spoken in the United States has been raised before, see chapter 4.

"English Only"

Following American entry into the First World War, Iowa's governor mandated by proclamation that English be spoken in all schools—both public *and* private. The sweeping declaration also extended to church services and private telephone conversations, areas normally granted First Amendment "free speech" protection. "English only" directives were not limited to Iowa. By the end of 1919, fifteen states had statutes on the books requiring that English be spoken in *all* schools.

The issue has arisen again. In the 1990s, legislatures across America have debated "English only" bills. The forces allied both for and against such legislation are particularly vocal and polarized in states with large foreign-born populations. As immigrants continue to arrive from lands where English is not the dominant language, this emotionally charged cultural issue will increase in importance.

Major Sources of Immigration to the U.S.

Countries	#Admitted in 1980
Mexico	56,680
Vietnam	43,483
Philippines	42,316
Korea	32,320
China and Taiwan	27,651
India	22,607
Jamaica	18,970
Dominican Republic	17,245
Great Britain	15,485
Cuba	15,054
	530,639

Source: U.S. Immigration and Naturalization Service

The Poles

The Poles brought their Slavic language with them when they began arriving in the 1870s. Their first destination was the coal fields of Pennsylvania. By 1880, Poles had arrived around the Great Lakes in the Midwest; Russo-Polish Jews could also be found in New York City.

Higham recounts one early example of their "welcome": "In the early seventies, at the peak of America's receptiveness to immigrants, native settlers refused to move into the same vicinity with a Polish colony in Illinois, the land nearby long remaining vacant."

Amidst these nativist forces stood one force *for* the alienated Poles: the Roman Catholic Church. Krickus describes the centrality of its place in the everyday life of the Polish:

> The church was a source of security for the immigrants; it was part of the Old World transplanted and a refuge from a frightening environment. In America the church among the Poles took on an importance that was unrivaled even in Poland, where the peasants were among the most devout Catholics on the Continent. Even those who took their religion lightly in the old country were attracted to the church in America because it was the focal point of immigrant life . . .

> The church was the nexus for organizations which proliferated as the immigrant community grew. After World War I the largest Polish parish in the United States, St. Stanislaw Kostka in Chicago, was home for 140 organizations— mutual aid societies, women's organizations, youth groups, cultural associations, and various and sundry other organizations serving the Polish immigrants of the parish. The priest was often the best educated member of the community and he could perform services crucial to the welfare of his parishioners; he found work for the unemployed, served as banker, marriage counselor, judge, and scribe, and intervened with the authorities when one of the faithful broke the law. The church for many years was the only institution to which the immigrant had access which wielded power; even the American authorities respected it.

The church constituted a powerful bastion on which the hopes of Catholic immigrants—the Poles especially—rested. It represented the first stage of access to the majority culture. The Roman Catholic Church served as the intermediary between the larger society and the smaller ethnic community.

Gaining access to local political machines represented the next step in Americanization for immigrants. As a particular community grew and its members became voting citizens, local "pols" would serve its needs and eventually recruit candidates from among its ranks. However, the coming of the New Deal to America eventually diminished both church and machine influence among immigrants, as the federal government provided many services formerly given by those more locally based institutions.

The Jews

Unique in several ways is the Jewish American legacy. Outside the Christian mainstream,

Between 1881 and 1925, 2,650,000 Jews emigrated from Eastern Europe to the United States.

they brought an entirely different religious tradition with them. Their social mobility, built on the foundation of higher education, attained remarkable heights. Their relatively small numbers—currently around 3 percent of the U.S. population—raise special issues of "assimilation" within the larger culture.

The first wave of Jewish emigrants came from Germany before the Civil War. Higham describes how the stereotypes they initially encountered in Europe followed them across the Atlantic:

> Smallest of the prominent immigrant groups, American Jewry was largely a by-product of immigration from Germany. At first, native folk had difficulty in differentiating Jews from Germans, but with the dispersion of Jewish peddlers and shopkeepers throughout the country, the European tradition of the Jew as Shylock came to

life. To a segment of American opinion, the Jews seemed clothed in greed and deceit. It was this conception that had exposed them to the charge of disloyal profiteering during the [Civil] war. Thereafter the persistent Shylock image acquired a significant new dimension. It broadened during the Gilded Age into an indictment of Jewish manners for vulgarity and ostentation. The Jew, it now appeared, was not only mercenary and unscrupulous but also clamorously self-assertive—a tasteless barbarian rudely elbowing into genteel company. In line with this impression, society began to exclude Jews from areas of intimate social intercourse, the most celebrated of the initial proscriptions being at eastern summer resorts.

Jews of Slavic origin constituted the second wave of Jewish immigration. Between 1881 and 1925, 2,650,000 Jews emigrated from Eastern Europe to the United States. They were different from the Western European Jews in many cultural respects. Within the context of the other "New Immigration" peoples, the Jewish immigrants from Eastern Europe experienced serf-like condition within their "ghettos" prior to coming to the United States.

Jewish American families placed a high emphasis on scholarship and entry into the three Learned Professions—theology, law, and medicine. Today, they are well represented in the teaching, legal, and medical fields. In the 1990s, the quiz show *Jeopardy* provided the answer, "This U.S. ethnic group has the highest percentage of college graduates"; the correct question emerged: "Who are the Jews?"

The issue of Jewish "assimilation" has been posed in the popular culture. A 1993 movie, *The Opposite Sex and How to Live with Them,* features the courtship and eventual marriage of a Catholic woman named Carrie Davenport and a Jewish man named David Crown. Carrie introduces David to her WASPish friends at a wine and cheese party.

Following the encounter, David spoke to Carrie about the experience. "Well, what about your friend, Chipper?" David asked. "He was following me from room to room—ah, excuse me David—but what exactly kind of Jew are you? Are you an assimilated Jew or are you a committed Jew?"

Though not assimilated with respect to their religion, the Jews have committed to participating fully in the American mainstream. Politically, they have served in all branches and levels of government. A "Jewish seat" has normally been reserved on the U.S. Supreme Court. One person of Jewish descent—whose family totally assimilated, including conversion to Christianity—was even nominated for the presidency: Barry Goldwater (the original surname was Goldwasser), the arch-conservative Republican candidate in 1964.

The Arabs

What do consumer advocate Ralph Nader, deejay Casey Kasem, heart surgeon Michael De Bakey, Heisman Trophy winner Doug Flutie, and former Senate majority leader George Mitchell have in common? All are Arab Americans.

In the late 1800s, the first Arab immigrants to America, mostly members of the Christian faith, came from Syria and Lebanon. Most became merchants in their adopted country.

Louis Brandeis (1856–1941)

Louis Brandeis was graduated from Harvard Law School in 1877, becoming a successful lawyer in Boston. Brandeis began his governmental career as a vigilant defender of the public interest in the state of Massachusetts. He investigated the insurance industry and fought against the powerful state utilities in that state. Brandeis later became famous for his work as counsel arguing before the Supreme Court in favor of the constitutionality of controversial wages and hours laws in Oregon, Illinois, Ohio, and California. In the 1908 Supreme Court case of *Muller* v. *Oregon,* Brandeis, a highly inventive lawyer, presented a legal brief collecting statistical, economic, sociological, and psychological data to support the need for these protective statutes. This "Brandeis brief" revolutionized the practice of law because it allowed for nonlegal evidence to be considered by American courts.

The fame of Louis Brandeis led to his becoming a major advisor to Woodrow Wilson, formulating many of the political ideas that became Wilson's New Freedom program. In 1916 President Wilson appointed Brandeis to the Supreme Court. Brandeis was the first Jew ever to sit on the Supreme Court. On the Court Brandeis was an advocate of social and economic reform. He was one of few justices who regularly voted to uphold Franklin Delano Roosevelt's New Deal legislation, frequently forcing Brandeis into the role of a dissenter.

Arabs who came to the United States after World War II did so as a result of changing political and economic conditions in their own countries. Displaced Palestinians, dispossessed Egyptians, and escaping Syrians arrived following the founding of the Israeli nation, the confiscations wrought by President Gamal Abdel Nasser's "reforms," and the overthrow of Syria's government by revolution, respectively.

"Immigration from the Middle East picked up dramatically in the 1960s. In fact, more than 75 percent of foreign-born Arab Americans in 1990 had immigrated after 1964. . . . This recent flood is due in large part to the Immigration Act of 1965, which ended a quota system that favored immigrants from Europe," observed Samia El-Badry, author of "The Arab-American Market," an article published in the January 1994 issue of *American Demographics* magazine.

According to the Census Bureau's definition, Arab Americans are people who trace their ancestry to the northern African countries of Morocco, Tunisia, Algeria, Libya, Sudan, and Egypt, and the western Asian countries of Lebanon, occupied Palestine, Syria, Jordan, Iraq, Bahrain, Qatar, Oman, Saudi Arabia, Kuwait, United Arab Emirates, and Yemen.

El-Badry's observations on the Arab American experience give a clear interpretation of census data:

> The 1990 census found 870,000 Americans who list an Arab country among their two top ancestries . . .

> Census data show that 82 percent of Arab Americans are U.S. citizens, and 63 percent were born in the U.S. . . .

> As with many other minorities, Arab Americans are a geographically concentrated group. Over two-thirds live in ten states; one-third live in California, New York, and Michigan. They are also more likely than other Americans to live in metropolitan areas. Thirty-six percent of Arab Americans live in ten metro areas, led by Detroit, New York, and Los Angeles-Long Beach . . .

> Immigrants coming from Arab nations still represent less than 3 percent of all immigrants coming to the United States, but their numbers are growing. In 1992, more than 27,000 people from Arab nations immigrated to the United States—68 percent more than those who came ten years earlier . . .

> The economic and political instability of many Arab countries will spur continued growth in the Arab-American community.

Arab stereotypes include name-calling descriptions such as "A-rabs," "camel jockeys," and "towel heads." Perhaps the most pervasive of stereotypes sees Arabs as "terrorists." The April 19, 1995, bombing of the Oklahoma City federal building was instantly followed by media and public speculation that Arab terrorists were involved. That was not the case.

Even prior to the incident, Arab Americans were subjected to harassment and abuse in the United States. The American-Arab Anti-Discrimination Committee (ADC) tracked 119 "hate crimes" against Arab Americans in 1991—the year of Operation "Desert Storm." The committee defined "hate crimes" as acts of violence "motivat-

ed in whole or in part by bias" that "manifest evidence of prejudice based on race, religion, sexual orientation, or ethnicity"—the U.S. Justice Department's standard for investigating "hate crimes."

Newsweek's February 29, 1988, "My Turn" column featured "The Media's Image of Arabs," by Jack G. Shaheen. He comments:

> America's bogyman is the Arab. Until the nightly news brought us TV pictures of Palestinian boys being punched and beaten, almost all portraits of Arabs seen in America were dangerously threatening. Arabs were either billionaires or bombers—rarely victims. They were hardly ever seen as ordinary people practicing law, driving taxis, singing lullabies or healing the sick . . . A dictionary informed my youngsters that an Arab is a "vagabond, drifter, hobo and vagrant" . . . The Arab remains American culture's favorite whipping boy . . .

> To me, the Arab demon of today is much like the Jewish demon of yesterday. We deplore the false portrait of Jews as a swarthy menace. Yet a similar portrait has been accepted and transferred to another group of Semites—the Arabs. Print and broadcast journalists have started to challenge this stereotype . . .

> It would be a step in the right direction if movie and TV producers developed characters modeled after real-life Arab Americans. We could then see a White House correspondent like Helen Thomas, whose father came from Lebanon, in *The Golden Girls,* a heart surgeon patterned after Dr. Michael DeBakey on *St. Elsewhere,* or a Syrian American playing tournament chess like Yasser Seirawan, the Seattle grandmaster.

The stereotypical Arab American usually portrayed in the mass media presents a false image of this diverse population.

Arab Americans, like other "hyphenated" Americans, have had to endure stereotypes and discrimination. Proving that one's ethnic group can fit into the American "Melting Pot" has served as one of the recurring realities of U.S. history, and not for just the Irish, Italian, German, Polish, Jewish, and Arab Americans among us. The same situation applied equally to the Austrians, Belgians, Czechs, Dutch, French, Greeks, Hungarians, Norwegians, Portuguese, Swiss, Turks, Yugoslavians, and other Europeans who came in search of a better life.

Ethnicity and Civil Rights

The three presidential elections of the 1960s show how attitudes about civil rights changed in America. In 1960, the Republican and Democratic

party platforms both called for moderate change and progress. Once elected, President Kennedy moved prudently to advance the concept of equal employment opportunity for all citizens, but landmark civil rights legislation was not passed during the life of his administration.

That achievement fell to his successor, Lyndon B. Johnson, who enthusiastically signed the Civil Rights Act of 1964. He campaigned for reelection on that and other egalitarian issues and received an amazing 61 percent of the popular vote. Civil rights was a winning issue in 1964.

Four years later, the tide had turned. Civil rights had once again become divisive. Alabama Governor George Wallace seized upon the "white backlash" against it. Appealing to white ethnic voters, he received 9,906,141 votes nationwide—13.5 percent of all those cast—and the 45 electoral votes of Alabama, Arkansas, Georgia, Louisiana, and Mississippi.

In *The Making of the President 1968,* Theodore H. White described Wallace's movement:

> . . . I joined the Wallace campaign in Chicago, four weeks after the Democratic convention. . . . He led his country picnic through the streets of Chicago, and scores of thousands were there to greet him. The signs spoke the emotions he aroused: . . . AMERICA—LOVE IT OR LEAVE IT . . . HAVE OUR SCHOOLS BEEN SOLD TO THE GOVERNMENT? POLISH WANT WALLACE. ITALIAN POWER FOR WAL-LACE. WALLACE—FRIEND OF THE WORKING MAN. VOTERS RING THE BELL OF LIBERTY WITH WALLACE. GIVE AMERICA BACK TO THE PEOPLE, VOTE WALLACE.

White commented that Wallace "was telling the people that their government had sold them out. Alienation is one of the most fashionable words in current American politics. It is the negative of the old words, the old faith that America was a community, and that government served the community. Alienation is disillusion—the sense that government no longer serves the interests of the people."

White ethnic America was questioning the effect on its future that civil rights legislation might bring. And the questions extended beyond the political process into the entertainment industry, including television sitcoms. The fifteenth episode of *The Odd Couple* debated the merits of affirmative action programs.

College quarterback Ernie Wilson, "the greatest Eskimo athlete of all time" and "the greatest quarterback in college football today," retained sports writer Oscar Madison (Jack Klugman) to represent him before pro football talent scouts. But the Eastern Conservatory of Music was also interested in Ernie Wilson and offered him a full scholarship.

Oscar's roommate Felix Unger (portrayed by Tony Randall) heard Ernie playing his cello—badly—and called Effram Goodchild, who had made the scholarship offer. After they listened to his playing, they conferred privately. Felix asked how the conservatory could offer Ernie a scholarship for such awful playing. Mr. Goodchild admitted that they had not heard Ernie's playing before, but that they needed an Eskimo student.

"You offered him a scholarship because he's an Eskimo . . . I think that's terrible," Felix told Goodchild. As if to speak for all angry white ethnics, he exhorted, "A man should have a chance because of his abilities, not because of his ethnic background." Goodchild responded, "We're merely victims of the system," to which Felix retorted, "Well, I think it's a rotten system!"

Felix Unger was not alone in thinking that the affirmative action system was "rotten." Many agreed with him and they didn't exist only on TV sitcoms.

Alexis de Tocqueville, author of *Democracy in America* (1835), observed: "Scarcely any political question arises in the United States which is not resolved, sooner or later, into a judicial question." The political questions raised about civil rights in the 1960s went to the courts during the 1970s. Chief among these cases was *Regents of the University of California* v. *Bakke,* decided by the U.S. Supreme Court in 1978.

In filling the 100 freshman seats available annually, the university's medical school used a two-tier approach. Eighty-four slots were assigned through the regular admissions program without regard to race. The remaining sixteen were reserved for students classified as "economically or educationally disadvantaged."

Alan Bakke, a Caucasian male twice denied admission in the regular program, sued the University of California on the grounds of "reverse discrimination." He claimed that the medical school, by admitting minority candidates with lower scores solely on the basis of race, deprived him of his equal rights under the law.

In a narrow five-to-four decision, the U.S. Supreme Court affirmed the California Supreme Court's order to admit Bakke, found the medical school's particular affirmative action program unacceptable, but upheld the general rule that race may be a factor in admissions.

Politically, affirmative action continued as a "wedge issue." In the presidential election of

1980, the Republican candidate was helped greatly by the defection of "Reagan Democrats," mostly blue-collar workers of Irish, Italian, and Polish background. The Democratic Party's championing of equal opportunity for all hurt it among some of its core groups. Only among women—themselves beneficiaries of affirmative action—did the party of Franklin Delano Roosevelt broaden its appeal in the so-called "gender gap" of the 1980s.

Immigration, aliens both legal and illegal, and affirmative action programs were among the issues in the 1992, 1994, and 1996 elections. The 1992 major party presidential candidates, Republican incumbent George Bush and Democratic challenger Bill Clinton, both favored "free trade" agreements with other nations, but Independent candidate Ross Perot called for an economic policy based on a "Made in the U.S.A." foundation.

In his book *United We Stand: How We Can Take Back Our Country,* Perot wrote: "Take a look at your VCR, or your television, or even your telephone. They weren't manufactured here. They may have American names on them, but they were made overseas. We have allowed entire industries to vanish. Our loss is another nation's gain." His views harken back to the "mercantilist" economic warfare policies of the major European powers in the seventeenth and eighteenth centuries.

An implicit nativist theme was espoused in both Perot campaigns for the presidency. His 1992 criticism of goods made abroad was supplemented by his 1996 stand against the North American Free Trade Agreement (NAFTA); he claimed that Mexico's low-wage labor market would create a "giant sucking sound" of lost American businesses.

In the 1994 election, Proposition 187, which prohibited illegal aliens from receiving social services, passed in California. It sought to deny health, educational, and other taxpayer-supported benefits to unregistered aliens.

Immigration and ending affirmative action programs constituted two emotionally charged issues in the election of 1996. Republican presidential candidate Patrick Buchanan advocated ending all immigration, both legal and illegal.

California's Proposition 209, a measure designed to prohibit "discriminating against or giving preferential treatment to" any person or group in public employment, education, or contracting, passed in 1996 by a 54 percent to 46 percent margin. The words "affirmative action" did not appear on the ballot measure.

CNN political analyst William Schneider provided some interesting interpretations on "Inside Politics Weekend" (November 23, 1996). He cited a *Los Angeles Times* exit poll that revealed that voters supported affirmative action by 54 to 46 percent, the identical margin cast for the ballot measure proposing to end it!

In analyzing the results, Schneider observed that people voted for Proposition 209 to end "preferential treatment" or "quotas" but that they still supported "compensatory measures" designed to assist those hurt by past discrimination. He concluded that the voters agreed with President Clinton's position on affirmative action: "mend it, don't end it."

The results of Proposition 209 indicate that equality of opportunity remains an American ideal but that equality of result or quota programs has been rejected by society at large. The majority of citizens believe that competition for positions and opportunities should be open to all and that the most qualified should prevail.

Affirmative action programs under attack in the 1990s were designed in the 1960s, an era when many sought to "establish justice" for groups discriminated against in the past. The Preamble to the Constitution also contains another stated goal: to "promote the general Welfare."

The debate over affirmative action revolves around these two stated ideals found within the Constitution. Those who see justice in helping groups discriminated against in the past point to the "establish justice" clause; those who see the necessity of maintaining the "melting pot" aspect of American society stress the "general welfare" of the nation at large. Many advocates of the latter view are Americans not covered by affirmative action legislation.

Our national motto, the Latin phrase *E Pluribus Unum*, means "one out of many." Originally meant to convey one union of many states, its meaning today differs from that of the past. In an age of multiculturalism, can many ethnic and racial groups coexist in harmony along values shared in common? In seeking "to secure the blessings of liberty to ourselves and our posterity," Americans of all backgrounds will continue to ponder that question.

Bibliography

Allen, James Paul, and Eugene James Turner. *We The People: An Atlas of America's Ethnic Diversity.* New York: Macmillian Publishing, 1988.

Higham, John. *Strangers in the Land: Patterns of American Nativism.* New Brunswick, N.J.: Rutgers University Press, 1955.

Kessner, Thomas. *The Golden Door.* New York: Oxford University Press, 1977.

Krickus, Richard. *Pursuing The American Dream: White Ethnics and the New Populism.* Garden City, N.Y.: Anchor Books, 1976.

Perot, Ross. *United We Stand: How We Can Take Back Our Country.* New York: Hyperion, 1992.

Chapter 8

Nonethnic Rights

Louis A. Schopfer Jr.

Civil rights are often viewed as those freedoms originally guaranteed in the first ten amendments to the United States Constitution, also known as the "Bill of Rights." Additions to this list of rights flow from other sections of the Constitution and through the process of amending the Constitution. A constitutionally based right is superior to all ordinary laws because the Constitution is the highest source of legal authority in the nation.

These classic constitutional rights include the freedom of speech, press, assembly, and religion; the right to vote; freedom from involuntary servitude; and the right to equality of treatment in public places. Other chapters delve into the meaning of these rights. Rights offenses occur when these individual rights are interfered with or denied. These classic constitutional rights tend to be held by individuals, not because of any group affiliation, but because of the traditional view that rights were held by persons against the intrusion of government.

This chapter considers, in addition to matters touching on religious liberty, another class of rights derived largely from statutes. They are not based on ethnicity or race but are a residual category that has emerged in recent years out of a growing sensitivity to the special needs of other vulnerable members of the population. Some say that these were not rights at all because they are not based in the Constitution. However, whatever they may be called, certain activities are covered by legal protections that apply to individuals in a group or a class of Americans who are given special treatment. For the sake of explanation, we will call these, "special rights." Apart from freedom of religion, the nonethnic rights, treated in this chapter, are a leading set of examples of special rights. Nonethnic rights are liberties that have been recognized by either federal or state government as necessary to protect citizens, without regard to their ethnicity, belonging to a certain group or possessing certain characteristics that, if not recognized, could result in unfair treatment in society.

Equal Rights versus Special Rights?

Are there civil rights that have evolved beyond the vision of the framers of the Constitution? Civil rights have historically included liberties for all citizens regardless of social condition and status, so expansion of the concept of rights to include special rights is controversial. Can some Americans be entitled to rights beyond those afforded generally to the whole of society? If so, is society bound to recognize such claims and enforce those rights? These questions are still unsettled, but they are growing in importance. Religion once was a battleground of rights in America. Now other nonethnic, nonreligious issues have arisen that concern the protection of individuals who are especially vulnerable in American society.

Individual rights are claims to resist the will of popular majorities. People assert their rights against governments and against other individuals who are threatening them. Those who are comfortable with political and economic conditions have little reason to assert their rights. Nonetheless, as Americans we all feel that there may be times when we, too, may express an unpopular opinion or act against current fashions and political views. Nearly all Americans will, at some time, feel their rights invaded, and attempt to assert their own claims. That is why individual and group rights are a vital part of American democracy, while also in opposition to one of its primary aspects: majority rule. Americans always retain the right to be out of step with their fellow Americans.

With the passage of time two classes of rights have appeared in America: "general rights" and "special rights." The rights found in the Bill of Rights and the original version of the American Constitution are the products of centuries of prior historical experience. These are the backbone of rights in America. Broad-based individual rights such as free speech, freedom of assembly, and freedom of religion are available to all. The same general quality applies to the listed criminal procedural protections available in the American Bill of Rights, in the Fourth through the Eighth Amendments, and elsewhere in the Constitution. The right to be safe against an "unreasonable search and seizure" is one that any American can now claim.

Special rights arise because the enjoyment of American rights has not been equal for all Americans. That is why some of the post-Civil War amendments were made to the Constitution: the rights of ex-slaves became a matter of national concern. Each new immigrant group also suffered from some form of discrimination when they came to these shores, and those who were here all along—the Native Americans—were sometimes the objects of cruel extermination or forceful relocation programs. The unequal treatment experienced by various American groups is a blot on the development of American rights. For many group members special rights have been created to balance the scales of justice somewhat. That is why American women, hardly a minority group at all, have been given so many special protections in recent years. That is also why earlier chapters of this book are devoted to some of those groups.

In recent years, certain groups have claimed so called "special rights" for their members. This has been readily apparent in the lobbying efforts of homosexual groups, which have sought legislative relief for endorsement of unpopular causes, such as homosexual marriages. This particular claim has not been recognized and therefore is not a right. However, the United States Supreme Court has not viewed antidiscrimination legislation in the same way, so that laws aimed at protecting homosexuals against discrimination could be valid sources of rights (see the 1996 case of *Romer* v. *Evans,* located among the cases contained in chapter 18). In general, courts have not been willing to recognize special rights arising out of group affiliation, but legislatures have carved out special situations that seem to authorize special regard and special treatment for individuals who happen to belong to particular groups deemed to be in need of legal protection.

Freedom of religion, which is contained in the very First Amendment to the Constitution, is given some attention in this chapter. One of the oldest American rights, it may be regarded as concerned both with individual rights or—as in this chapter—as a leading example of nonethnic rights. America was first settled by religious dissenters, and each American colony took a different view of religious toleration. The early constitutions of the states disenfranchised different religious groups, including Catholics and Jews. In Massachusetts and Maryland, the office of governor had to be held by a Protestant. Today all this has changed, but the issue of religion still retains some salience in political and social life.

Though the rights of women are not guaranteed in the Constitution, thanks in part to women's rights activists such as those pictured here at the March on Washington, there has been steady growth of women's rights in America.

Earlier chapters have dealt with the historical experiences of many Americans who have been victims of discrimination mainly because of their affiliation with particular ethnic or racial groups. Certainly, the sufferings of African Americans, Asian Americans, Hispanic Americans, and Native North Americans deserve attention. Antidiscrimination policies at federal and state levels have improved the condition of many of these Americans, but the treatment of these groups and their members remains a stain on the civil rights history of the nation.

Rights of Women

The idea of the rights of women is based in the belief that women are entitled to live and enjoy life to their fullest human potential in equality with men. Many regard this as a basic human right, stemming from the basic human condition. In fact, women's rights have only slowly arisen in the consciousness of Americans. Women were clearly regarded as inferior to men at the time of Independence, and their subordinate status continued well into the twentieth century. The Bill of Rights and the post-Civil War amendments did not emancipate women. However, the 1920 ratification of the Nineteenth Amendment, which gave women the vote, was a milestone in American history. This story is recounted in chapter 11 on voting rights. Women's employment rights are discussed in chapter 13. This chapter considers other unresolved aspects of women's rights.

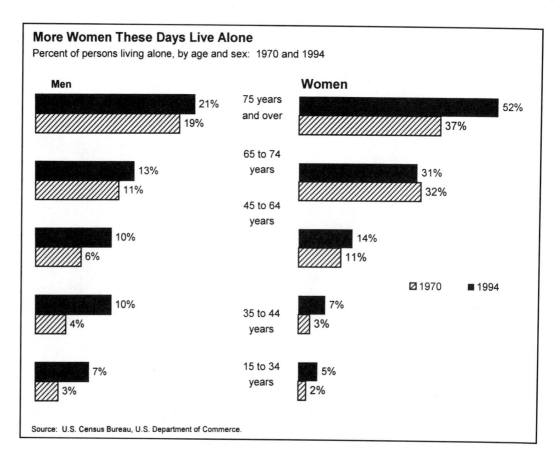

More Women These Days Live Alone

Percent of persons living alone, by age and sex: 1970 and 1994

Men | **Women**

75 years and over — Men: 21% (1994), 19% (1970); Women: 52% (1994), 37% (1970)

65 to 74 years — Men: 13% (1994), 11% (1970); Women: 31% (1994), 32% (1970)

45 to 64 years — Men: 10% (1994), 6% (1970); Women: 14% (1994), 11% (1970)

35 to 44 years — Men: 10% (1994), 4% (1970); Women: 7% (1994), 3% (1970)

15 to 34 years — Men: 7% (1994), 3% (1970); Women: 5% (1994), 2% (1970)

☑ 1970   ■ 1994

Source: U.S. Census Bureau, U.S. Department of Commerce.

The rights of women are not guaranteed in the Constitution; in fact, even the modern campaign for an Equal Rights Amendment failed to gain ratification by the states. The text of the Equal Rights Amendment was approved by Congress in 1972. It reads simply: "Equality of rights under the law shall not be denied by the United States or any state on account of sex." This language was offensive to many other groups in America who feared that radical women's issues could be elevated into public policy matters, protected under the Constitution. Nonetheless, the many victories won in the Congress and in state legislatures have helped women who were victims of discrimination. The slow, steady growth of women's rights has also been supported by judicial interpretations. The result is that while the Equal Rights Amendment is a dead issue, many of the goals of the sponsors of the amendment have been achieved. Indeed, women's rights in America have progressed further than in any other nation. They provide the clearest example of nonethnic rights in the United States.

The Equal Rights Amendment was intended to end finally all forms of sex discrimination. The language was imprecise, but similar to the Nineteenth and Fourteenth Amendments. Two thirds of the states quickly adopted the proposed language, but the amendment never received the three-fourths vote required for ratification. The amendment came close to adoption, but state campaigns by Mormon groups, the National Council of Catholic Women, and other conservative organizations prevented the necessary votes for ratification.

The rights of women also include the rights of girls to grow up and to reach their full human potential. Included within the concept of women's rights is the belief that all women should live free from violence, exploitation, and harassment. Some have expanded the definition of these rights to include the right to marry or not, the right to bear (or not to bear) children, the right to receive adequate food and healthcare, the right to earn a wage in parity to men, the right to own property, and the right to hold public office.

There are some thinkers who believe that women do not constitute a group, since they do not share similar characteristics beyond their gender. Yet, although many women are not ardent advocates of rights, and many abstain from pressing claims of right, there is reason to regard women as sharing in similar social problems because of their gender.

The National Women's Party,
led by leaders Alice Paul and
Lucy Burns, picketing the
White House, January 1917.

Overview

Women in most ancient cultures were traditionally considered chattel, that is, considered largely as property, having no recognition as full members of society. Women in America often were denied the right to make contracts, to own property, to be educated, and certainly, to vote. When they worked, their choice of jobs was severely limited. Although never as fettered as slaves in America, many women felt a deep sympathy with the abolitionist cause, seeing that the freeing of the slaves could lead to greater emancipation of women. After the Civil War the Fourteenth and Fifteenth Amendments gave rights to the newly freed slaves, but many of these were not available to women, especially the vote.

The industrial revolution sparked a need to afford some degree of protection to citizens that society deemed as vulnerable. Consequently, labor laws came into being to protect women in the workplace. Some protective labor laws were passed in a few states to spare women from the worst features of factory life. However, it would be several decades before women would be granted other rights. Most of what may be called women's rights arose only in twentieth century America.

Historical Context

The National Women's Party (1916) under the leadership of their founder Alice Paul, attempted to achieve equal rights for women and in 1916 proposed an Equal Rights Amendment

Alice Paul *(1885–1977)*

Alice Paul was a reformer dedicated to the cause of equal rights for women. Paul was educated at American universities and law schools, yet her education continued abroad. While studying in England from 1907 to 1909 Alice Paul met Emmeline Pankhurst, who introduced Paul to suffrage philosophy and the tactics of militant activism on behalf of women's rights.

On her return to Washington, D.C., Paul began to lobby for the enfranchisement of women. In 1913 she and Lucy Burns organized the first major suffrage parade on the eve of Woodrow Wilson's presidential inauguration. The event led to ridicule and abuse by the onlookers.

From 1913 to 1917 Alice Paul organized the final drive for women's suffrage. Her group, the Congressional Union, succeeded in lobbying Congress and pressuring the president to secure passage of the needed legislation for an amendment to the national Constitution. The ratification of the Nineteenth Amendment in 1920 was due to the work of many women leaders, but the militant strategy of marches, picketing the president, and even hunger strikes were the chief weapons of Alice Paul in alerting the nation to the cause of women's suffrage.

In 1923 Alice Paul turned her attention to equal rights for American women. She wrote an earlier and highly controversial version of the Equal Rights Amendment, sparking splits and debates among various women's groups. Paul spent her last years lobbying for passage of the watered down version of the Equal Rights Amendment, which did pass Congress in 1972 but failed to get the needed state ratifications.

While Alice Paul fought and lost her last battle for the Equal Rights Amendment, she had won her prior campaign to include the language of equal rights in the preamble to the United Nation Charter. Paul also scored notable gains for women's rights as chairman of the Nationality Committee of the Inter-American Commission on Women during the 1930s and 1940s.

(ERA) to the United States Constitution. Paul's group struggled to achieve parity for all women and sought to protect women from abortion and other injustices that they saw as being perpetrated against females as a class of individuals. Others opposed such radical measures out of the fear that a gender neutral amendment would remove certain protections for female workers. This measure failed ratification, as did the 1972 Equal Rights Amendment.

Access of women to the ballot is described more fully in the chapter on voting rights, but it must be noted that the Nineteenth Amendment (1920) guaranteed women the right to vote, establishing a constitutional basis against one form of gender discrimination.

> The right of citizens of the United States to vote shall not be denied or abridged by the United States or by any state on account of sex. Congress shall have power to enforce this article by appropriate legislation.

The Supreme Court has invoked the equal protection clause of the Fourteenth Amendment of the Constitution in an attack on sex discrimination. This process began with the 1971 case of *Reed* v. *Reed,* in which a woman had been denied the right to serve as administrator of her son's estate. Idaho law gave preference to males over females in such appointments. The U.S. Supreme Court overturned the Idaho state law, finding the mandatory preference for males to be arbitrary and in violation of the standards of the equal protection of the laws clause of the Fourteenth Amendment.

The Court has not applied this reasoning to all forms of sex-based classifications but has held that such classification must serve important objectives and must be substantially related to those objectives. If females are more affected by intoxicating beverages than men then it is legitimate for a state to set different standards of intoxication levels for the two genders. The public purpose served is greater highway safety.

Many aspects of women's rights rest in statutes and federal regulations, rather than the Constitution. In 1938, the Fair Labor Standards Act established nationwide standards for minimum wage, overtime pay, and the employment of children. The initial minimum wage was 25 cents per hour. President John F. Kennedy signed an Executive Order (10925) in 1961 that urged feder-

al contractors to hire more minorities. However, the order did not specify enforcement procedures and included the phrase "affirmative action." Two years later, the Equal Pay Act (1963) amended the Fair Labor Standards Act by addressing the issue of equal pay for men and women doing work that requires equal skill, effort, and responsibility. The disappointing aspect of this legislation is that it failed to cover administrative, executive, or professional employees until 1972.

Title IV of the Civil Rights Act of 1964 prohibited discrimination on several factors including sex. The historic legislation signed by President Lyndon B. Johnson expanded the scope of discrimination to encompass hiring, firing, promoting, compensating, and other terms, privileges, and conditions of employment. The act did not require affirmative action unless the court found discrimination. This legislation did not apply to higher education faculty until 1972.

President Johnson signed Executive Order 11246 (1965) requiring federal contractors to adopt "goals and timetables" to achieve proportional representation of racial minorities a responsibility of the United States Department of Labor. Executive Order 11375 (1967) signed by the president expanded the affirmative action definition to include "sex."

The Women's Equity Action League filed a class action suit in 1970 against institutions of higher learning, calling attention to an industry-wide pattern of discrimination against academic women. In 1971, Secretary of Labor J. D. Hodgson issued Revised Order #4, which required federal contractors to devise and implement affirmative hiring and promotion programs for women.

President Richard M. Nixon signed into law Title IX of the Education Amendments Act (1972), which prohibited federally assisted education programs from discriminating on the basis of sex in all education programs and activities, including athletics. Later that year, the Equal Employment Opportunity Act empowered the Equal Employment Opportunity Commission (EEOC) to take legal action in federal court to enforce Title VII of the Civil Rights Act.

The Equal Credit Opportunity Act (1974) prohibited discrimination on the basis of race or gender. Prior to this legislation a woman's income or savings were not counted equally to a man's in determining credit eligibility. In the same year, the Education Equity Act authorized the department of Health, Education, and Welfare to develop non-sexist curricula and nondiscriminatory vocational and career-counseling programs.

The Pregnancy Discrimination Act (1978) extended short-term disability or sick leave to pregnant women and made discrimination as the result of pregnancy illegal. In 1979, the Convention on the Elimination of All Forms of Discrimination against

Women (CEDAW) adopted by the United Nations General Assembly became an international treaty in 1981 when the 20th country ratified it. By the end of 1995, 149 countries had ratified CEDAW. The United States Congress still at this writing has not reached an agreement on the convention. CEDAW affirms a woman's right to nondiscrimination in education, employment, economics and social activities, and reproductive choice.

The Civil Rights Act of 1991 signed by President George Bush made it possible for victims of intentional discrimination based on sex, religion, or disability to recover compensatory and punitive damages. Prior to this act, only race-based discrimination cases could seek financial remedies. Senator Robert Dole introduced the Glass Ceiling Act, Title II of the Civil Rights Act, which established a bipartisan, 21-member Glass Ceiling Commission charged with studying and preparing recommendations on "eliminating artificial barriers to the advancement of women and minorities [to] management and decision making positions in business."

The 1996 Atlanta Olympic Games gave prominence to the important contribution made by American female athletes, but female athletes are rarely supported in most American schools in the same way that male athletes enjoy. Many rights advocates point to the impact Title IX of the Civil Rights Act has had on women and collegiate sports. These same advocates claim that most academic institutions have not gone far enough. They point to the disparity in coach's pay for male and female events and in equipment, even to a lack of support from the school band and cheerleaders. Further attempts to equalize the treatment of male and female athletes may be expected.

In recent years previously all-male bastions of education have had to come to grips with claims of discrimination against women. A woman has a right to an education, but does she have a right to be educated at an all-male institution? In 1996 Shannon Faulkner won a legal challenge as the first woman to be accepted to the all-male Citadel Military Academy in South Carolina. Unfortunately, Ms. Faulkner's legal challenge did not prepare her for the rigors of a military school and she "washed out" after several weeks. However, other women have entered the Citadel since and at this writing were completing their freshman year.

At issue in the Citadel and its Virginia counterpart, Virginia Military Institute (VMI), was whether a state-funded institution could deny access to women. Was this denial a violation of the "Equal Protection Clause" of the United States Constitution? Evidently, some judges have found this or another basis for compelling the entry of female applicants to previously all-male schools.

Similar challenges by women have been waged in other single-gender institutions, but none as fervently as at military academies. What if there is sufficient empirical data to indicate that a same-sex education is more beneficial to women? Should males be prohibited from applying to all-female schools? Some educators argue that teachers have a bias toward males, especially in math and science instruction. This bias, therefore, denies women the opportunity to enter these fields. Would it be appropriate to continue single-sex education for females? Does this single-sex education deny males the same opportunities as claimed in the Citadel experience? These issues will be confronted in the future.

What is Sexual Harassment?

In 1980, a study of federal employees found that 42 percent of women and 15 percent of men claimed that they had been victims of sexual harassment in the workplace. Another study of over 10,000 female federal employees found that these women had suffered sexual remarks (33 percent), leers and suggestive looks (28 percent), touching (25 percent), pressure for dates (15 percent), pressure for sexual favors (9 percent), and approximately 1 percent were victims of rape or sexual assault. Additional studies have indicated that there is a 75 percent chance that sexual harassment will continue or escalate if ignored.

Sexual harassment is defined as unwelcome sexual advances, requests for sexual favors, and other verbal or physical conduct of a sexual nature. The crime of sexual harassment has more to do with power than it does about the sexual desires of the perpetrator. The sexual harassment law is violated when submission to improper conduct is either explicitly or implicitly made a term of employment; submission to or rejection of such conduct is used as the basis for employment decisions, such as the denial of a promotion or a raise; such conduct has the purpose or effect of unreasonably interfering with an individual's work performance or creating an intimidating, hostile, or offensive work environment. Sexual harassment is one of the fastest growing areas of litigation in the country.

An individual need not be a subject of the comments to claim sexual harassment. If someone overhears the comments and finds them offensive, they in turn can claim sexual harassment. Similarly, if an individual stares at the parts of the anato-

Case Problem

At what point does one's freedom from sexually explicit language collide with one's freedom of speech?

Bill works for a company that has a sexual harassment policy. Bill likes to hang up his calendar of the "girls of summer." Even though the pictures are not sexually explicit, they show voluptuous women scantily clad in bathing suits. Bill's coworker, Marge, is offended by the calendar. She finds it demeaning for women to be viewed as sex objects. Should Bill be required to remove the calendar? There may be circumstances when such calendars create a "hostile atmosphere" for women workers.

There are some who argue that attitudes of "political correctness" have choked the individual's right to freedom of expression. But does freedom of expression include dirty jokes or suggestive language? Is sexual teasing permissible conduct in schools or in the workplace? Probably not.

my of another individual, a claim for sexual harassment can also be made. Unwanted advances have been deemed sexual harassment by some public officials. In one extreme interpretation a preschooler's peck on the cheek of a female student was perceived as an unwanted advance—a form of sexual harassment.

Other examples of sexual harassment include constant unwanted invitations for dates; invasion of one's personal space; making obscene gestures; asking questions about one's personal life or sex life; parading explicit drawings or graffiti; kissing or rubbing or touching of the person. The boundaries and strict definition of sexual harassment vary from place to place, but each school and business in the nation is attempting to provide a workable definition.

The federal Equal Employment Opportunity Commission is the major source of most interpretations of sexual harassment. Suits claiming sexual harassment may also be brought in federal or state court. Employers as well as perpetrators may also be liable for permitting sexual harassment.

How Does a Company Protect Itself?

A company can partially protect itself from sexual harassment litigation if it:

1. Distributes a strong sexual harassment policy to all employees and has a written statement of receipt.

2. Establishes a written internal complaint procedure and has an "open door policy" encouraging employees to bring grievances to management.

3. Responds to all complaints in a expeditious, thorough, and confidential fashion.

4. Takes immediate action against employees who have committed sexual harassment, including discipline, reassignment, and counseling.

5. Trains managers, supervisors, and employees on prevention of sexual harassment and documents where and when training takes place and who participated in the training. Documentation can reduce liability by showing an employer's commitment to not tolerating sexual harassment in the workplace.

Other aspects of equal pay and sexual harassment are discussed in chapter 13 on employment rights.

Violence Against Women

Laws that have been designed to protect women and girls from the increasing degree of vio-lence have been promulgated over recent years by many states, with the federal government playing only a limited role in their creation. Most of these laws are passed on the state level, and they are attempts to provide special protections for women, since they are regarded as more vulnerable to crime. Whether these laws amount to the creation of some form of woman's right is questionable, but the physical security of women is a matter of growing concern in public affairs, as various aspects of brutality against women become more evident. All too frequently, women are unwilling to report crimes committed against them, either from fear or from the sense that they will not be believed.

Estimates vary, but according to the most reliable federal figures more than 2.5 million American women are each year the victims of some form of violence. About one third of the violence victims are injured as a result of crime. While the rate of crime against men has dropped since 1973, the rate of crimes against women has remained relatively constant. Still, except for rape, women are much less likely to experience violent crime than men. It should be noted that about one quarter of crimes against women are committed by other women. Taking all the evidence together it is not unreasonable to foresee the emergence of a woman's right to physical security.

Rape

One out of eight adult American women has been the victim of rape, according to the most conservative estimates. Rape is most likely to be committed against a woman by someone she knows, rather than by a stranger. About half of reported rapes led to the arrest of the alleged perpetrator. Over half of all rape prosecutions are dismissed before trial or result in an acquittal. Rape is an important issue for women.

Rape is defined in the criminal law as the use or threat of force against an individual's will with consequent sexual penetration no matter how slight. Plainly, rape is a violent act that is severely punished by law. But sometimes rape seems ambiguous. "Date rape" can be more common than physical acts by strangers. Date rape amounts to a use or threat of force against an individual's will. Rape can occur in a social situation that began as an innocent date. Coercion of any kind may constitute the crime. This interpretation of the crime has redefined the dating relationship between men and women and has raised some interesting issues. When does "no" mean "no," and "yes" really mean "yes"? Women have a right, in any event, to expect to be free from sexual coercion.

Domestic Violence

Domestic violence is probably the most underreported crime in society, domestic violence is defined as the emotional or physical pain or battery committed against an individual in a family or family-like environment. Somewhere between two and four million American women are physically abused each year in such situations. Family violence kills as many women every five years as the total number of American soldiers who died during the Vietnam War. Women may flee from their batterers, but they risk becoming homeless. Domestic violence is an important women's issue.

Some recent state legislation denies the right to own firearms to those persons convicted of domestic violence. That is a step in the right direction. However, as of this writing, there are insufficient legal protections for the victims of domestic violence. Two national organizations provide special help for battered women. The first of these is the National Clearinghouse for the Defense of Battered Women. This group can provide women with critical support, even to the extent of assisting women who have killed or assaulted their abusers in attempting to defend themselves. The National Center for Women and Family Law is less militant, providing legal assistance and information. More significantly, this group is con-

cerned with changing public policy toward domestic violence. The National Center lobbies for more effective laws on behalf of battered women. The Center's National Battered Women's Law Project analyzes state and federal legislative development in this field and produces manuals and other publications.

Stalking

Stalking, as defined in some states and the federal government, is where a person purposely and repeatedly follows another person, and engages in a course of conduct or makes a credible threat with the intent of annoying or placing that person in reasonable fear of death or bodily injury.

A person may be charged with the crime of stalking for such things as purposely and repeatedly following an individual, participating in conduct that alarms or annoys a person, committing threats, or committing an act that places a person in reasonable fear of a bodily injury.

Recent Women's Rights Initiatives

The Family Leave Act provides employees of large companies with newly born or adopted children, seriously ill family members, or a personal disability to take temporary leave from their place of employment and guarantees job security and certain benefits during their absence.

In that vein, the 48-hour hospital stay for new mothers is an attempt by the state and federal government to eliminate the so-called drive-through delivery that was predicted by obstetricians. Legislators and women's groups had complained that the cost-containment provisions of the managed care insurance companies were running contrary to the best interests of new mothers. One insurance industry analyst claimed that this legislation was "the mother of all motherhood issues." The problem with the federal legislation is that it does not compel insurance companies to pay for the extra time, therefore resulting in a "paperless tiger."

The Future of Womens' Rights

What is the future for legislation concerning women's rights? Clearly, more needs to be done about domestic violence and violence against women generally. Women with family responsibilities will also need greater protections to permit them to meet their obligations. Pay discrimination and other employment opportunities will be part of a future agenda. In general, one can expect that the gaps in life opportunities between women and men will gradually be closed.

Some states have even enacted legislation that looks at the inequity in prices for services provided to men and women. Why is a haircut cheaper for a man than for a woman? Why is a man charged less than a third of what a woman is charged at the dry cleaners for the cleaning of equivalent shirts? Some argue that regulation like this creates more red tape and hurts business. Others claim that without this type of regulation women will be treated as second-class citizens. Perhaps this kind of equal treatment can never be legislated.

Rights of Children

In many ways the struggle for civil rights for children has paralleled that of their mothers. If women were considered chattel, that is property, culture has also not been so kind to children.

The rights of children are grounded in the belief that they are entitled to live to their fullest human potential in equality with adult human beings. The rights of children may be regarded as human rights that have been denied just because of youth. The struggle for the rights of children is a complex issue that must balance the rights of adult caregivers (usually parents, but in some cases they could be grandparents or another responsible adult) against those that are dependent upon the caregivers for the protection of these rights.

Children have the right to life. They have a right to live free from violence, exploitation, and harassment. Some have expanded the definition of these rights to include the right to an education, the right to receive adequate food and healthcare, the right to be brought up in a loving and nurturing home environment, and the right to safe and secure housing. These claims have not all been recognized by legal authorities. There also is a great deal of vagueness in these claims of right.

Widespread child poverty may be a problem, but what right is being violated? Statistics from the worldwide relief organization Feed the Children suggest that there are 12 million children living below the poverty line in the United States. These figures are in dispute, because of differing definitions of poverty.

Child Labor

The industrial revolution resulted in the frequent exploitation of children through the use of child labor. Child labor is defined today as work performed by minors that either endangers their health, safety, or welfare. In the nineteenth century however, many parents depended on the income received from the work of their children, and many families felt compelled to allow their children to labor in factories, in mines, and on farms. Today some child labor on family farms is permitted, but since any child labor usually hinders a child from receiving an education and keeps them from play and other developmental activities, most states and the federal government now sharply curtail it.

Prior to the early nineteenth century it was common for children to be treated as property, depriving them of their rights as human beings. In 1912 Congress established the Children's Bureau; however, the Fair Labor Standards Act, which addressed the exploitation of children, was not passed until 1938.

Congress established the Children's Bureau (1912) to help address the child labor issue. Finally, in 1916 Congress passed the Keating-Owen Act, which barred the entry into interstate commerce of articles produced by children, thus putting the federal government in the role of protector of children.

However, the Supreme Court struck down the 1916 law as unconstitutional in *Hammer* v. *Dagenhart* (1918), saying that the federal law infringed on the rights of states and also denied children the "freedom" to make contracts for their work. The campaign against child labor continued, in spite of this critical legal setback.

Congress moved quickly to outlaw this practice by creating a special tax on products made by

child labor with the Revenue Act of 1919. In *Bailey* v. *Drexel* (1922) the Supreme Court again found this action unconstitutional. Congress grappled with a constitutional amendment to protect children. However, such disparate groups as the American Farm Bureau Federation, the National Association of Manufacturers, and the Roman Catholic Church fought to defeat the amendment. The Roman Catholic Church felt such an amendment threatened parental discipline and invaded the privacy of the home.

The Fair Labor Standards Act (1938) attempted to address this exploitation by the establishment of nationwide standards for minimum wage, overtime pay, and the employment of children. The amended Social Security Act (1962) defines an array of child welfare services: first, the pre-

Marion Wright Edelman, founder of the Children's Defense Fund, an advocacy group for poor children, poses with a group of children at the Children's Defense Fund's Children's Day celebration.

vention or resolution of problems of neglect, abuse, exploitation, or delinquency of children; second, protection of and care for homeless, dependent, or neglected children; third, the protection of and the promotion of the welfare of children with working mothers; and fourth, the protection and the promotion of the welfare of all children, including the strengthening of their own homes where possible or needed, and the provision of adequate care for children in foster care or day care or other child care facilities. Later initiatives, especially the Social Security Act, have defined and created precedents for other methods to protect children.

Violence Against Children

The abuse and neglect of children is a quiet problem that plagues many American homes. The issue is, When is abuse, abuse? Paddling children or the infliction of corporal punishment was a common form of parenting for many households in the first part of this century. It is interesting how the nation watched in horror the proposed "caning" of an American juvenile in the country of Singapore in 1996.

Do children have the right to be free of any type of corporal or physical punishment? Most conservatives will argue that the disciplinary problems plaguing the current educational system are the direct result of prohibiting teachers and adult caregivers from physically punishing juvenile offenders. However, social scientists indicate that physical punishment produces only short-term improvement and does not address the inherent problems caused by the discipline problems.

Child Abuse and Neglect

Child abuse and neglect gave credence to the development of the $10 billion foster-care industry, which places children in the homes of adult caregivers while a social worker attempts to correct the deficiencies in the family environment. The foster-care system rewards the "temporary" placement of children and provides no mechanism for the children caught in the system to be broken free, so in fact children who are abused by their parents are subsequently abused by the government, which has neither adequately funded nor staffed the systems. In addition, the system limits the ability of foster families to adopt such chil-

During the Industrial Revolution children were frequently exploited through the use of their labor. Today, labor that endangers the health, safety, or welfare of minors is illegal.

dren, especially those of a different race or ethnicity. Even so, many foster families see foster care as a "back door" adoption service.

It is the opinion of this author that most problems facing abused and neglected children are best resolved through a permanent solution of adoption. Finding new homes for such children may be better than temporary solutions, when abuse and neglect have reached very high levels. In a nation that has so many children in temporary custody, it is absurd that American parents must look either overseas or south of the border to adopt children. It is the responsibility of a judicial system that has failed to provide justice to the most vulnerable of our society that has created this escalating problem.

However, if adoption becomes more prevalent new issues arise. What rights do adoptees have? Some states, concerned with the claims of adopted children, are proposing mutual-consent laws that allow the adoptees the right to get to know their birth parents, if the birth parents agree. Specific statutes in most states provide adoptees some access to information about parentage.

Megan's Law

Megan's Law was passed in the state of New Jersey to give communities the right to know when a convicted sex offender has moved into town. The law was named after seven-year-old Megan Kanka, from Hamilton, New Jersey, who was raped and murdered in 1994 by a convicted sex offender who lived across the street. The murderer was convicted in 1997. The community notification part of the law imposed in New Jersey after 1995 is currently under judicial review. Whose rights are greater, the rights of children to be protected from former sex offenders or the rights of sex offenders for privacy? Notification will most undoubtedly result in harassment from the community at large.

Megan's law has been duplicated in other states, but courts still have not resolved the conflict between the children's need for protection from potential predators and the privacy rights of individuals who have served their terms of punishment for sexual offenses against juveniles. The law could also have a far-reaching impact on laws such as the real-estate disclosure laws, which require agents to inform potential homeowners about any problems on their property.

Megan's Law and its many variations require convicted sex offenders to register with law enforcement authorities. Prosecutors must then classify the offender under a three-tier system according to the apparent risks prosecutors believe they possess of committing another sex offense. Offenders who are classified in Tier Two and Tier Three are subject to notification of individuals, schools or community groups in neighborhoods near their homes or jobs.

The New Jersey Supreme Court has already upheld the constitutionality of the law. The Third Circuit Court handed down a ruling in April 1996 on a related Megan's Law case. The Third Circuit Court ruled that the registration portion of the law was constitutional but refused to rule on the issue of notification since the plaintiff, Alexander Artway, had not been subject to the process. The law raises interesting points. Can a convicted sex offender who has been punished still be punished by registration and community notification and does that constitute "double jeopardy"? These issues move from children's rights to the rights of convicted persons, discussed later in this chapter.

Pornography on the Internet

The Communication Decency Act was signed into law with this thought in mind. The overwhelming argument is that the government has to protect children from indecent communications. The v-chip, a device implantable on televisions, allows parents to exercise some degree of control based on a rating system of what kids watch. The theory behind this chip is that parents could restrict the amount of violence a child can watch. The only difficulty with such a system is the expense the v-chip will place on television manufacturers and on the communications industry to transmit the signal. Some experts have argued that the v-chip could be invoked to prevent the kids from watching news programs.

Privacy Issues

You take your child to Burger King or McDonalds. You fill out a form for the child to become a member or to have a "free" birthday party at the restaurant. Who owns the information? Can Burger King sell the information about your child to a vendor? Does the child have any right to privacy?

A Children's Protection and Parental Empowerment Act is one recent state legislative initiative that would seek to protect the names of children who fill out coupons at fast food restaurants or other retail places. The statute would allow parents the ability to block the child's name from being sold to mail houses or pedophiles.

Curfews

Are curfews for minors an infringement on their rights? One study found that curfews reduced crime by as much as 27 percent in 1994. The Mall of America, the nation's largest shopping com-

THE CUSTODY BATTLE

plex, located in Bloomington, Minnesota, has instituted the first policy aimed at reducing loitering and rowdiness. Children under the age of 16 are barred from the mall after 6:00 P.M. on Fridays and Saturdays. Security officers compel juveniles to prove their age or to go home. Youth who refuse to comply are arrested.

There are other examples of the impact of curfew policies upon young people. In one situation the mall management was concerned about the congregation of more than 2,000 youths inside on a cold Minnesota evening. Some of the violence had resulted in the injuring of uninvolved shoppers. In addition, one customer was shot in February of 1993. Some civil libertarians, however, are concerned that the a curfew policy may be interpreted in a way that discriminates against minority youth.

Many other issues of children's rights are being discussed around the nation. Have children some sort of right to carry pagers or cell phones? Does the state have a valid interest in prohibiting this technology from children, because of its occasional usage by drug dealers? What other rights may be violated to protect children from violence?

The paradigm for parenting has shifted over the years from a model of protection to one of preparation. In past generations parents were presumed to be protecting children from the evils of the world. Some modern models of parenting sug-

gest that children should be prepared for whatever happens to them when outside the home. Since school violence and peer drug usage is quite common there may be a need to better prepare children for coping with these aspects of contemporary life. In the process, we may introduce ideas and discuss behaviors that are frightening and threatening to children. Perhaps children are owed the truth about modern life, and the society must devise laws that protect them against the dangers of adult life.

Other Claims of Rights of Children

On the margins of the topic of children's rights are much more far-reaching claims. Will our courts allow children the ability to voice their preferences on issues of child custody? If children are unhappy with their parents, do they have any recourse against their families? Can children divorce their parents? Can children turn to the law for protection against their own parents? A few cases of this kind have appeared, but no general approach has emerged. Disruption of traditional family arrangements runs against the grain of lawmakers.

If a child in a family situation is injured in an accident or suffers some form of abuse, can the child seek remuneration from their families for these injuries? Can a child sue for physical abuse? Can they sue their parents for claims of unjust treatment when denied some cherished item? Can a child sue for college tuition? Suppose a child is disabled as the result of a narcotic the mother took during pregnancy, can the child sue the parents for this disability? All these questions are being explored by courts around the nation.

Rights of Parents

Civil rights for parents is another emerging claim of right that in many ways is a response to the fears of many parents that the state may be usurping the roles and the responsibilities of parenting. However, parents' rights have often been at issue, especially in the legal arena when parental custody of children was at stake. Courts have often been called upon to decide whether parents were fit to provide the kind of guidance that society expects.

The claim for rights of parents is grounded in the belief that parents are entitled to live to their fullest human potential in the family unit and are to be free of governmental interference in the raising, educating, and disciplining of their offspring. The claim of rights for parents may be one aspect of the right of privacy within the scope of the family. The claim for the rights of parents poses a complex issue that must balance the interests of children against those of the harmony of the family and the household. At some point, still undetermined, society must ensure that it has a need to protect the interests of future generations. Parents as well as the government are responsible for providing children with the knowledge, skills, and abilities to be productive and contributing members of society. The needs of society may create a basis for interference with parents' rights on behalf of the children. For example, compulsory schooling laws in all states require that children receive education, in spite of their parents' wishes regarding the matter.

The claim of rights of parents seems to include the right to raise children in a matter that is consistent with their religious and moral beliefs. Parents have the right to bring up their children in a matter that they believe is appropriate for them, and according to the parents' religious preference, as an aspect of religious liberty. Some have expanded the definition of these rights to include the a claim of a right to educate the children in their own home. Advocates of child welfare have asserted a claim of a right to receive adequate food and healthcare, the right to be nurtured in a loving home, and the right to safe and secure housing.

Overview

Parents were historically viewed as having the absolute authority over their families in the raising, educating, and especially disciplining of their children. Child labor laws restricting such forms of work during the first part of this century were often defeated on the basis that they would have encroached on and eventually destroyed the family unit. Some churches encouraged the defeat of any legislation that could have undermined the parents' absolute authority in the sanctity of the home.

Courts and legislature have frequently had to balance the claimed rights of parents against the rights of children. This balancing act still continues to this day. The Family Leave Act provides parents who work for certain-sized companies the opportunity to take a temporary leave of absence to care for their newly born or adopted children or seriously ill family members. The act guarantees job security and certain benefits during their absence.

In recent years, conservative parents have become increasingly concerned over the educational system's failure to represent their values. This has resulted in two phenomena: home schooling and political action in school districts.

Home schooling is a return to an older tradition of the education of children in the home environment. During the last century, most of this nation's children were educated by a parent or another caregiver. Parents who are fearful of the external influences of schools are permitted, in some states, to provide their children with a curriculum that represents their values. Even then, the state boards of education set limits upon the practice of home schooling to ensure that children are given the skills that they will need later in life. As a result, home schooling is a very rare practice.

Critics claim that home schooling deprives children of the socialization provided by the multi-student environment. In addition, they are concerned that these children will not receive an adequate education. Home schooling advocates argue the benefits of an individualized education that focuses upon the needs of each child. By law parents who provide home schooling need standardized textbooks and other tools of basic education.

Parents sometimes claim rights to determine what their children read, watch, and listen to. Parental censorship over school texts, library books, and other materials available to children has roiled many communities. Parental blacklists are a widespread form of censorship that raises issues affecting the fundamental rights of children. On the whole, this form of censorship may be tolerated by courts because of the immaturity of the children involved.

Should a public library allow children at any age to read and take home a sex education guidebook with explicit pictures of sexual acts? The book *"It's Perfectly Normal"* by Robie H. Harris incorporates all of these features. Should a library or a school censor this book or restrict access to adults? The concern of most parents, is that this particular book does not mention marriage; it merely provides a vague reference to the question with the phrase "there are kids whose mothers and fathers live together." Should government protect families from this sort of communication as it would protect families with the v-chip for television sets or warning labels for offensive rap music? Experts disagree whether such material is injurious to young people.

Another recent trend toward making parents responsible for the misdeeds of their children deserves attention. Parental responsibility laws have been passed in many American cities and a few states, making parents accountable for teenage mischief as well as more serious matters. In Pennsylvania more than four such laws have been passed since 1994. One law allows a person injured by the misdeeds of teenage mischief to sue the parents for damages. Another law allows judges to order parents into treatment, counseling, or "re-education" programs in cases of frequent teenage abuses.

Fines for parents of school truants exist in Pennsylvania and a few other places. A 1997 New Jersey bill proposes possible jail sentences for parents of truant children. Parents are being made responsible in many communities for the cost of removing graffiti on walls of buildings. Some lawmakers propose that parents be held responsible for underage drinking.

The popularity of this kind of legislation suggests that new duties are being placed upon parents. Parental responsibility statutes seek to require parents to take a more active role in the supervision of their children. Whether the state can impose such obligations remains to be seen. If this can be done by legislation, then parents' rights will be diminished and their duties to society increased.

Older Americans

Do individuals have rights on the basis of age? Does a senior citizen preference or special benefit discriminate against nonseniors? How does a person prove age discrimination? Are mandatory retirement ages legal? These questions are all aspects of the growing rights of seniors.

Overview

The Equal Protection Clause of the Fourteenth Amendment (1868) guarantees that all Americans should be protected equally under the law, and this clause restricts, among other issues, discrimination based upon age. Most age discrimination cases involve employment rights, which are also discussed in chapter 13, the employment rights chapter. Other forms of age discrimination are described here. On this topic the major relevant legislation is the Age Discrimination in Employment Act (1968); signed by President Lyndon B. Johnson the act prohibits discrimination in the hiring and the firing of persons 40 years of age or older.

Other problems faced by the elderly include physical abuse, neglect, or maltreatment. Nursing homes and even relatives have sometimes taken advantage of the aged and infirm. Many states have begun to construct a system of laws to protect the elderly against such forms of abuse.

Elder abuse may take a physical form, such as direct beating, unreasonable physical restraint, or prolonged deprivation of food and water. Psychological or emotional abuse is another form of elderly abuse, and may take the form of humiliation, intimidation, or isolation abuse. Failure to protect an elder from health and safety hazards is another. Financial abuse may also occur, including the theft of an elder's money or property by a person in a position of trust.

Rights of Homosexuals

The practice of homosexuality has been widely condemned by cultures throughout Western history, with the exception of the ancient Greeks, who

Fifteen Years From Now, Elderly Population Growth Will Explode

Average annual growth rate (in percent) of the elderly population: 1910-30 to 2030-50

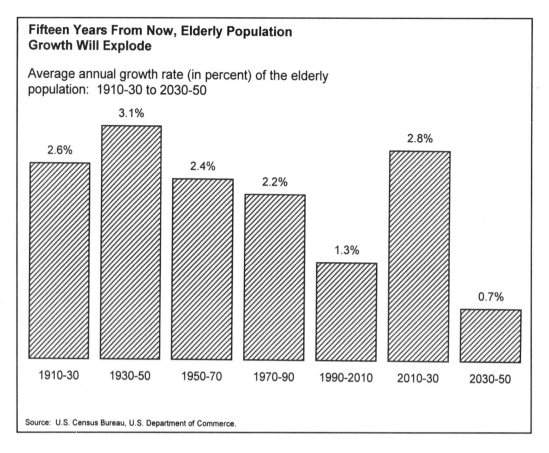

2.6%	3.1%	2.4%	2.2%	1.3%	2.8%	0.7%
1910-30	1930-50	1950-70	1970-90	1990-2010	2010-30	2030-50

Source: U.S. Census Bureau, U.S. Department of Commerce.

During the 1980s, Poverty Was Reduced Among the Elderly

Percent of persons aged 65 and over who were poor, by sex, race, and Hispanic origin: 1979 and 1989

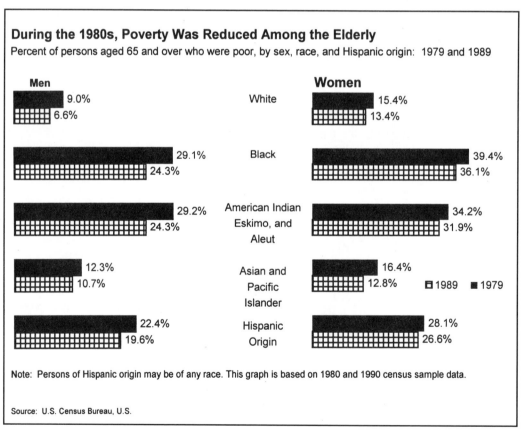

	Men		Women
White	9.0% / 6.6%		15.4% / 13.4%
Black	29.1% / 24.3%		39.4% / 36.1%
American Indian Eskimo, and Aleut	29.2% / 24.3%		34.2% / 31.9%
Asian and Pacific Islander	12.3% / 10.7%		16.4% / 12.8%
Hispanic Origin	22.4% / 19.6%		28.1% / 26.6%

☐ 1989 ■ 1979

Note: Persons of Hispanic origin may be of any race. This graph is based on 1980 and 1990 census sample data.

Source: U.S. Census Bureau, U.S.

Case Problems

Dave is a 48-year-old chief financial officer of a local television station. He serves "at will" of the newly appointed executive director, who is younger than he is. Dave is terminated and his position is filled by a 32-year-old replacement. Is Dave a victim of age discrimination? Maybe or maybe not. What if Dave could prove that other employees at the same age level were terminated? What if Dave could prove that by his termination, his company would save on the expense of providing him retirement benefits?

Dick, who is 36 years old, wants to be a state trooper. In reviewing the requirements, Dick finds he meets or exceeds each of them, with the exception of his age. The academy requires that only those individuals under 35 years of age can apply. Is Dick a victim of age discrimination? If Dick challenges the age requirement, what will he have to do to win his case? Will the state or a potential employer have to show a "compelling interest" in making the age requirement be 35?

Judge Wolpner is an Idaho Superior Court Judge. Idaho has a law that requires members of the judiciary to retire at the mandatory age of 70 years. Is it fair to require a judge to retire at a certain age? Should the requirement be based on ability, instead of age? What about other professions?

Lou is 72 years old and still drives his automobile every day. Does the government have a valid interest in requiring Lou to take another driver's test periodically after reaching a certain age? Should a vision test or a physical test be required periodically?

Ruth is also 72 years old and is in a nursing home. The government provides some assistance for her institutional care under Medicaid and Medicare. Do these government policies create a vested entitlement to medical care for the elderly until their death? Are family members obliged to supply support? Should public or private insurance programs be provided to provide for the needs of the elderly when their finances are exhausted?

What about scams directed at the elderly? Schemes that prey upon the fears or ignorance of elderly homeowners are quite prevalent. Some states vigorously prosecute these frauds. Is this kind of protection something that governments all over the nation should provide to their elderly?

---

accepted the behavior. This does not mean that homosexuals, as a group, have not contributed greatly to civilization; in many cases, they have. The traditional religious Judeo-Christian belief is that sexual intercourse is proper only between a man and a woman and mainly in the context of a marriage relationship. The older Judeo-Christian belief had been that any other relationship is an abomination to a holy and righteous God and subjects the offender to some type of retribution for this sin. In our own time homosexuals have become more tolerated, and prominent public figures have sometimes admitted their status as homosexuals. Even so, considerable social stigma, if not sinfulness, is still attached to homosexual conduct.

Certain homosexual acts are proscribed by the criminal law. In a majority of states, sodomy carries a maximum penalty of 10 to 20 years, and in a few states life imprisonment. Such laws are rarely enforced, but they remain on the books.

Many civil libertarians have argued that private homosexual conduct by adults should be beyond the reach of the law. Gay rights activists have challenged state sodomy laws on the ground that fundamental rights of privacy ought to protect homosexuals. They have looked to the Fourteenth Amendment as a source of those privacy rights. A few state courts have accepted this view and have extended privacy protection to homosexuals. However, the Supreme Court of the United States and most states have rejected this argument.

The leading case to deal with homosexuality is *Bowers* v. *Hardwick* (1986), in which a right of privacy claim for consensual sexual conduct was denied by the Supreme Court. The Court held that previous privacy rulings, which had recognized a broad and fundamental right to decide whether or not to have a child, had no application. As Chief

March on Washington for
Lesbian and Gay Rights, 1993.

Justice Burger saw it, ". . . in constitutional terms there is no such thing as a fundamental right to commit homosexual sodomy." Even so, discrimination against homosexuals has been challenged with success.

In 1996 the Supreme Court decided the significant case of *Romer* v. *Evans,* striking down a controversial antihomosexual provision of the Colorado Constitution. The Colorado provision seemed to the Court majority to place homosexuals in a special class that denied members of the group from enjoying the equal protection of the laws. Amendment 2 of the Colorado Constitution nullified all existing civil rights protections for homosexuals and also barred the passage of new antidiscrimination laws on their behalf. This placed the state's homosexuals "in a solitary class," denying

them protection available to other citizens. This, wrote Justice Anthony Kennedy, "is a classification of person undertaken for its own sake, something the equal protection clause does not permit."

Some see the 1996 decision as a recognition of gay rights. That is probably incorrect. To say that homosexuals may not be the target of hostile laws does not mean that they are entitled to special rights. Homosexuals may not be stripped of their rights because of their conduct or sexual preferences, but the Court has never said that they are entitled to special protections, either. The Court seemed to reject the idea of special rights for homosexuals in favor of the more familiar idea of equal rights.

Even those who oppose homosexuality on religious and moral grounds do not necessarily

feel that those who practice homosexuality in their private lives should be punished on the job. A bill was recently signed into law that seeks to protect homosexuals from workplace discrimination. Laws prohibiting "gay bashing" and other hate crimes against these groups have also been initiated. The subject of discrimination against homosexuals is still developing case by case and statute by statute. Slowly, the emerging principle seems to be that sexual orientation in civilian employment is a denial of fundamental rights. However, violence against homosexuals remains a problem.

Gay Marriage

The Defense of Marriage Act (1996) was signed into law by President William J. Clinton. The statute, initiated by a Republican Congress (some argue as an election-year ploy), states that the federal government will recognize a marriage as constituting a relationship between a man and a woman. The statute foresees the day when one or more states may authorize same-sex partnerships and stipulates that no other state would have to recognize their validity.

The Supreme Court of Hawaii was about to render a decision on a local case involving a same-sex union when the federal law was passed. It is apparent that American society is probably not willing to accept these relationships. The legal issue may be eventually resolved in the United States Supreme Court. Article IV of the United States Constitution requires that "full faith and credit shall be given in each state to the public acts, records and judicial proceedings of every other state." The Constitution, therefore, requires this recognition of one states' laws in another state, so a constitutional issue may arise, if and when a state refuses to give recognition to these unions if they are allowed in another state.

In Mississippi, Governor Kirk Fordice issued an executive order in 1996 banning same-sex marriages. The attempt was designed to strengthen the state's existing sodomy law. The order forbids county clerks from issuing marriage licenses for people of the same sex and to invalidate such licenses from other states. Some critics saw this as an attempt to usurp legislative power to appease the religious right. Some religious moderates would not oppose same-sex unions, if they were called something else instead of "marriage."

Gays in the Military:
Don't Ask, Don't Tell

The United State Supreme Court has rejected a challenge to the Clinton administration's military policy of "don't ask, don't tell." This policy, created by the secretary of defense's "Policy on Homosexual Conduct in the Armed Forces," (July 19, 1993), allows homosexuals in the armed services to refuse to reveal their sexual

**Supreme Court Justice
Stephen Johnson Field
(1831–1899).**

preferences to officials. However, the policy presumes that once announced as homosexuals, these persons are somehow unfit for military service. Many members of the military contend that life is "different" in the military and homosexuality (practicing or celibate) would somehow jeopardize the functioning of the United States armed services. The Clinton administration viewed this as a privacy issue and did not want to compel the identification of one's sexuality. However, if the soldier chooses to reveal this information, it could be cause for dismissal. Prior to the Clinton administration's stance, all branches of the military would remove any soldier as unfit on the belief that the individual was a homosexual.

The Supreme Court left standing a Federal court decision that discharged a highly decorated Navy pilot, Lieutenant Paul G. Thomasson. In March 1994, the day the "don't ask, don't tell" regulations were effective, Lieutenant Thomasson sent letters to four admirals announcing that he was gay. Within weeks, the Navy convened a board of inquiry and eventually gave the officer an honorable discharge. *Thomasson* v. *Perry* was limited to the adverse consequences that flow from a statement of homosexual identity.

Broader challenges to the military policy are making their way through the Federal District Court in New York and the United States Court of Appeals for the Ninth Circuit in San Francisco.

These cases look at sections of the law that state that a service member can be discharged who "has engaged in, attempted to engage in, or solicited another to engage in homosexual act or acts."

Rights of Incarcerated and Convicted Individuals

The framers of the Constitution were concerned about the rights of accused persons, and as such many provisions of the Bill of Rights enunciate these rights. These criminal justice rights are dealt with elsewhere in this book. However, once convicted, individuals may be deemed to have retained certain rights. Even in jail, it seems, the Bill of Rights bestows rights upon convicted persons. A few examples of these rights are given here. Once free, exconvicts also have most but quite not all the rights of ordinary citizens.

Religion in Prison

The question of religious exercise would have been surprising to the reformers who first developed prisons. Prisons were conceived of as places in which inmates would engage in prayerful reflection. The Quakers invented the penitentiary (meaning a place of "penitence") as a tool to rehabilitate offenders. The prison doors were designed smaller, so that the penitent would have to bow and humble himself as he moved around the prison. Religion was involved in the very idea of the penitentiary.

One of the first cases that considered the religious rights of prisoners was *Ho Ah Kow* v. *Nunan* (1879). In that case, a Chinese citizen was held in a San Francisco jail. His jailers cut off the long braid of hair that to him was a symbol of his religious beliefs. The jailers defended their actions as necessary for security, identification of prisoners, and hygiene—grounds that were to become familiar in later years.

Justice Stephen Field, one of the great California Supreme Court justices before he joined the U.S. Supreme Court, when sitting on the circuit court, compared the practice of the California jail with a regulation that would force Orthodox Jewish prisoners to eat pork. He found that it was an offense against the Chinese citizen's religion.

It took 100 years for this issue to surface again. There were two reasons for the long delay.

First, federal courts applied a rigid "hands off" doctrine that prevented them from addressing conditions of confinement—even when those conditions put a prisoner's life and safety at risk. Second, under most state laws during those years, prisoners were considered to be "civilly dead" and to have lost all rights upon imprisonment.

In the 1960s, numerous courts began to address claims by prisoners. In particular, Black Muslims initiated a number of legal challenges when their efforts to practice their religion were ignored or punished by prison officials.

The United States Supreme Court addressed the religious rights of prisoners in *Cooper* v. *Pate* (1964). The Court ruled that a legal challenge by Black Muslim prisoners to restrictions on his religion stated a viable claim for judicial review. Later, a Buddhist prisoner in Texas challenged restrictions that denied the inmate use of the prison chapel, prevented him from corresponding with religious advisors, and restricted him from sharing religious material with other prisoners. In *Cruz* v. *Beto* (1972), the Court found that if the prisoner's allegations were true, "there was palpable discrimination by the state against the Buddhist religion. . . . The First Amendment . . . prohibits government from making a law prohibiting the free exercise of religion." Although this case established that the First Amendment applied to prisoners, the scope of that right was left up in the air. In particular, courts were left to grapple with the standard of review that was to be applied to prisoner cases.

In 1987, the Supreme Court fully addressed the religious rights of prisoners in a case—*O'Lone* v. *Estate of Shabazz* (1987)—involving Muslims who wanted to participate in Friday services. The prisoners maintained that the Muslim Jumu'ah services were an essential rite of their religion and one in which all Muslims were required to participate.

The state did not dispute the sincerity of their beliefs or the importance of the services. Rather, their defense focused on logistic matters: the lack of staff to escort prisoners, the disruption of prison schedule, security concerns, and the fact that other services were available to Muslims.

In a five-to-four vote, the Supreme Court rejected the prisoners claims. The majority held that the religious rights of prisoners were measured under the "rational basis test." A restriction would be upheld if it were rationally related to a legitimate penological interest. Religious freedom exists in prison, but it is limited by essential prison conditions.

Many claims of religious freedom in prison have been litigated in federal and state courts. Judges have had to delve into questions about the nature of a religion in order to determine whether the claim was sincere. In one leading case the judge looked at the individual's state of mind to determine whether he conceived the beliefs as religious in nature. According to this view, the focus of this test is the place of the teachings or belief in mind of the believer. If it is similar to that held by persons who adhere to traditional religions, it is worthy of constitutional protection.

Speech in Prison

The first freedom-of-speech case of prisoners—*Procunier* v. *Martinez* (1974)—considered by the United States Supreme Court challenged California rules that authorized prison officials to censor any mail considered to "unduly complain" or "magnify grievances." In addition, mail could be withheld if it expressed inflammatory political, racial, or religious views or was lewd or defamatory.

The court asserted that the issues in the case concerned the First Amendment rights of prisoners. However, it found that the censorship rules also affected the rights of free citizens. "Whatever the statute of a prisoner's claim to uncensored correspondence with an outsider, it is plain that the latter's interest is grounded in the First Amendment guarantee of freedom of speech." In order to balance these rights with the "legitimate and substantial" interest in the operations of a prison, the court used a two-part test known as the Martinez standard:

1. "The regulation or practice must further an important or substantial governmental interest unrelated to the suppression of expression."

2. "The limitation of First Amendment freedoms must be no greater than is necessary or essential to the protection of the particular governmental interest involved."

Press

In another 1974 case decided by the Supreme Court, four California inmates and three professional journalists challenged these regulations in *Pell* v. *Procunier* (1974), in which prison officials prohibited face-to-face media interviews with specific prisoners. The prison expressed fear that the regulations were necessary to prevent inmates from becoming "Big Wheels," public figures within the prison whose notoriety and influence could create severe disciplinary problems.

The court upheld the claim of the prison officials. Although prisoners had a First Amendment right to communicate with the media, this right could be satisfied through the mail. In addition, the media could interview family, friends, or attorneys who could present a prisoner's point of view. The court also rejected any right based on the power of the media to collect news. It held that the press was not entitled to special treatment beyond that given the general public. The Constitution does not impose on government "the affirmative duty to make available to journalists sources of information not available to the public generally."

Press censorship in prisons has become a major subject of Supreme Court concern. In *Thornburgh* v. *Abbot* (1989), prisoners challenged federal censorship rules that allowed wardens to reject publications that were "detrimental to the security, good order, or discipline of the institution." The court of appeal had struck down these rules under the Martinez standard. The Supreme Court reversed this decision and supported the need for this kind of censorship. In dissent, Justice Stevens criticized the majority as engaging in "a headlong rush to strip inmates of all but a vestige of free communication with the world beyond the prison gate."

Health Care in Prison

Health care is a difficult issue to resolve in the prison environment. How much right does a prisoner have to health care? Is this right equal to that of a free citizen? Does "cruel and unusual punishment" apply to public functions like providing the best medical care for inmates? Are inmates entitled to better care than those afforded to the general public? It was well-established in *Estelle* v. *Gamble* (1976) that "deliberate indifference to serious medical needs of prisoners constitutes 'necessary and wanton infliction of pain' . . . proscribed by the Eighth Amendment." At the minimum, such treatment may cause pain without a penological purpose; in more serious cases, it may amount to torture. Inmates have sued for cases involving the privatization of health care services in the prison or the requirement of a copayment for care.

Probation and Parole

Parole, or early release from incarceration for "good behavior," is usually administered by a board appointed by a governor of the state. The court can also sentence a person to probation, which is an alternative to incarceration and requires periodic visits with a supervisory person appointed by the court. The parole period may last from one year to life, depending on the committed offense. The length of parole is determined by the underlying offense. Because the law regarding parole has changed, the parole period varies greatly.

Visits

The extent of a prisoner's right to visit has been subject to different legal standards. In *Block* v. *Rutherford* (1984) the United States Supreme Court held that contact visits were not a federal constitutional right. The court has also held that visits with any particular person may not be constitutionally protected.

Family visits provide unsupervised overnight visits between a visitor and his or her immediate family. This includes visits with a spouse, children, brothers, sisters, parents, and grandparents. These visits are a privilege and not a right, as defined by the court.

Special visiting restrictions may be placed on exfelons, including parolees and probationers. By statute, former prisoners may not enter an institution without prior approval of the institution head.

Property

After conviction of a crime it is possible for federal authorities to take legal steps to deprive convicted persons of the fruits of crime, through taking those goods or other related property by civil (noncriminal) forfeiture. Federal forfeiture laws have been the subject of recent inmate litigation. On June 24, 1996, the United States Supreme Court upheld civil forfeiture proceedings against a double jeopardy challenge in *United States* v. *Usery.* The federal government had instituted forfeiture proceedings against a defendant who had been indicted and convicted of "manufacturing marijuana."

The federal court of appeal in this, and a companion case, had held that such action violated the constitutional protection against dual punishment. However, the Supreme Court reversed the decision. Forfeiture did not violate the double jeopardy provision of the Fifth Amendment. The Supreme

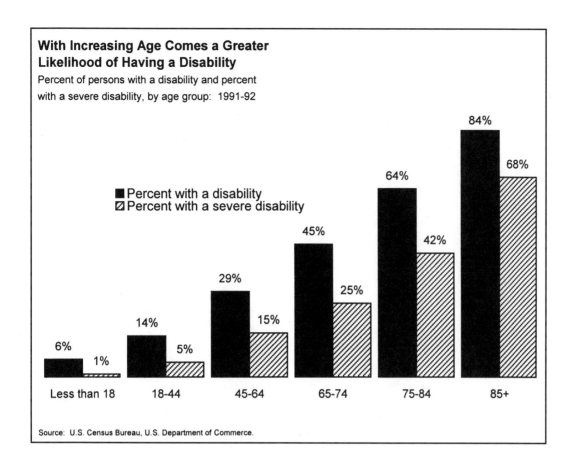

With Increasing Age Comes a Greater Likelihood of Having a Disability

Percent of persons with a disability and percent with a severe disability, by age group: 1991-92

■ Percent with a disability
▨ Percent with a severe disability

Less than 18: 6% / 1%
18-44: 14% / 5%
45-64: 29% / 15%
65-74: 45% / 25%
75-84: 64% / 42%
85+: 84% / 68%

Source: U.S. Census Bureau, U.S. Department of Commerce.

Court stated that civil forfeitures are neither "punishment" nor criminal actions for purposes of the Double Jeopardy Clause. The court cited past cases that viewed forfeiture as civil in nature.

The forfeiture at issue in *Usery* was a civil proceeding under a two-part test that looked at the purpose and effect of the underlying statute.

1. Congress intended the action to be civil, since the procedural enforcement mechanism was distinctly civil in nature.

2. The Court found that there was little evidence, much less the "clearest proof," suggesting that forfeiture proceedings are so punitive in form and effect as to render them criminal.

The Court considered a number of factors in deciding that the forfeiture statutes did not constitute punishment but noted that historically civil forfeiture had not been regarded as a form of punishment. The deterrent effect of the civil forfeiture did not make the statute criminal. Under the court's ruling, forfeiture may still be vulnerable constitutionally if a court finds that it constitutes an excessive fine under the Eighth Amendment or if, under the facts of a particular case, forfeiture could be viewed as punishment.

Privacy for Exconvicts

As pointed out in the section on children's rights, efforts to protect young people from sexual molestation may conflict with the rights of privacy and of protection against double punishment that belong to those who have been released from prison. Yet the federal government is in the process of establishing a computer database to register at least 250,000 sex offenders. The intent of the initiative is to prevent rapists and child molesters from crossing state lines to terrorize unsuspecting victims. Civil libertarians are concerned that the computer registry may violate the constitutional rights of people who have completed their time in incarceration and thus may prevent them from seeking employment or even finding a place to live. This registry also will provide an interesting test case for the use of genetic information and the rights of prisoners to own this information.

Rights of the Physically and Mentally Challenged

The category of the physically and mentally challenged includes any person who is blind, deaf, mentally ill, disabled, retarded, or chronically ill or

Dorothea Dix (1802-1887)

Dorothea Dix was a nurse and a pioneer in the treatment of the insane. She was born in Hampden, Maine, in 1802. Her childhood was difficult, and she often had to take responsibility for her two younger brothers. By the age of 19 her remarkable abilities became evident. She founded a school in her grandparents' house and wrote an elementary-school science textbook as well as a hymnbook.

In 1836 Dix went to England to improve her health. While there she encountered Henry Tuke of York, England, a prison reform advocate who stirred her imagination. On her return to the United States in 1841 she began to teach Sunday school in the House of Corrections in East Cambridge, Massachusetts. At that time Dix became aware of the awful conditions to which imprisoned insane women were subjected. She proceeded to make a study of insane asylums, prisons, and poor houses in the commonwealth of Massachusetts. In 1844 Dix submitted her highly influential report to the legislature.

Dorothea Dix called for the separation of insane persons from the general prison population. She insisted that ropes, chains, and other primitive instruments for the control of the insane be eliminated. She helped found over 32 mental hospitals and provided models for such institutions in other places in America. Her humane policies were enlightened for the period, although the use of institutional care for housing the insane came into disfavor late in the twentieth century. Dix carried her cause of institutionalizing the insane to many European nations, as well as Canada, Russia, and Turkey.

During the Civil War Dorothea Dix was made chief of nurses for the Union Army. In effect, she developed the Army Nursing Corps. Many public buildings were turned into hospitals, and thousands of women entered the nursing profession. Before she died in 1887 Dix's last days were spent at a hospital that she had founded in Trenton, New Jersey.

who has some other sort of handicapping condition. Such disadvantaged persons have not historically enjoyed equal treatment from more fortunate nonhandicapped persons. Recent laws have extended protections to this vulnerable class. Some of these protections resemble rights in their effects.

Overview

Approximately 43 million Americans have one or more physical or mental disabilities, and this number will continue to increase as the population as a whole grows older. Historically, society has tended to isolate and segregate individuals with disabilities, and, despite some improvements, such forms of discrimination against individuals with disabilities continue to be a serious and pervasive social problem.

Discrimination against individuals with disabilities persists in such critical areas as employment, housing, public accommodations, education, transportation, communication, recreation, institutionalization, health services, voting, and access to public services. Congress has found that individuals who have experienced discrimination on the basis of race, color, sex, national origin, religion, or age, have been protected against discrimination, while individuals who have experienced discrimination on the basis of disability have often had no legal recourse to redress such discrimination.

Individuals with disabilities continually encounter various forms of discrimination, including outright intentional exclusion; the discriminatory effects of architectural, transportation, and communication barriers; overprotective rules and policies; failure to make modifications to existing facilities and practices; exclusionary qualification standards and criteria; segregation; and relegation to lesser services, programs, activities, benefits, jobs, or other opportunities.

The federal census data, national polls, and other studies have documented that people with disabilities, as a group, occupy an inferior status in our society and are severely disadvantaged socially, vocationally, economically, and educationally. Individuals with disabilities are a discrete and insular minority who have been faced with restrictions and limitations, subjected to a history of purposeful unequal treatment, and relegated to a position of political powerlessness in our soci-

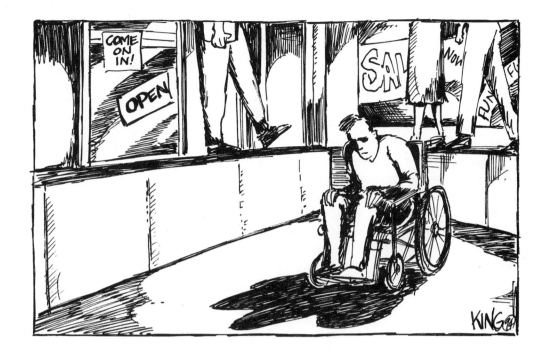

ety, based on characteristics that are beyond the control of such individuals and that result from stereotypic assumptions not truly indicative of the individual ability of such individuals to participate in, and contribute to, society.

The nation's goals regarding individuals with disabilities are to assure greater equality of opportunity, fuller participation, independent living, and economic self-sufficiency for such individuals as can attain it. The continuing existence of unfair and unnecessary discrimination and prejudice not only denies people with disabilities the opportunity to compete on an equal basis and to pursue those opportunities for which our free society is justifiably famous but costs the United States billions of dollars in unnecessary expenses resulting from dependency and nonproductivity.

Significant Legislation

The Architectural Barriers Act (1968) required employers to make buildings accessible to the handicapped. In 1973, Section 504 of the Rehabilitation Act prohibited employment discrimination against people with disabilities. Later that year, the Comprehensive Employment and Training Act (CETA) gave local governments a greater role in implementing training and employment programs for the disadvantaged or for unemployed workers. (This act was superseded by the Job Training Partnership Act in 1982.) The Voca-

tional and Rehabilitation Education Act in 1976 mandated specific administrative measures to enforce affirmative action standards.

Americans with Disabilities Act (ADA)

The Americans with Disabilities Act (1990), landmark legislation signed by President George Bush, required reasonable accommodation by an employer of an employee with a disability and protected employed parents of disabled children against discrimination on this basis. Some features of this legislation are discussed in chapter 13, Employment Rights.

The purpose of the ADA is to provide a comprehensive federal regulatory scheme designed to eliminate both intentional and inadvertent discrimination against Americans who suffer from physical or mental disabilities. The ADA covers every aspect of the public's activity, including employment, government, telecommunications, and public accommodations. However, the ADA legislation is very vague in parts and will require significant interpretation by the courts in future years.

Compliance with the requirements of the ADA is often costly. Ramps must be built, curbs lowered, or elevators installed in buildings when public places are to be made accessible to the handicapped. The Mayor of Indianapolis, Stephen Goldsmith, has lamented that ADA has eroded "the powers not delegated to the United States by

Case Problem

Ryan White was a child hemophiliac who received HIV from a blood transfusion. He became the personification of the innocent victims of this terrible disease. Prior to the Ryan White case, the country was not interested in granting furthering research in the diagnosis and cure for a "homosexual" disease. Ryan White's fellow elementary students rallied to his defense. They felt he should be in school. Ryan White's valiant effort to attend public school was seen by the media and especially many celebrities, like pop singer Elton John, as a means for this child to receive civil rights. Many critics and concerned parents expressed worries that the blood-borne pathogen could infect innocent children, resulting in a "plague" in America's public educational system. Ryan was able to attend school until his early death. This issue is by no means settled.

the Constitution, nor prohibited by it to the States [that] are reserved to the States receptively, or to the People" (Amendment Ten). Mayor Goldsmith claimed that the federal government dictates everything from curb height to other accessibility requirements. He, like many other public officials, feels the statute to be burdensome and costly.

AIDS Rights

Discrimination against individuals infected with acquired immunodeficiency syndrome (AIDS) has recently become a matter for public debate. Some schools have refused to teach AIDS victims, some public health workers have avoided managing AIDS victims, and public attitudes toward those afflicted with this disease have often been highly negative. In effort to combat discrimination against AIDS victims some recent legislation has attempted to provide various forms of protection and assistance for AIDS victims. For example, recent federal legislation provides special housing opportunities for persons with AIDS. (See 42 U.S.C.A., Chapter 131.) Grants, rental assistance, community residences, and other forms of services are made available, to a limited

extent. These new AIDS polices provide an interesting example of how certain illnesses have become issues of rights.

One example of the attempt to decide whether AIDS victims have special rights may be helpful:

Other AIDS victims have demanded a new civil right to know if they may have been contaminated with the AIDS virus by doctors, nurses, or other public health workers. Kimberly Bergalis, a Florida teenager, claimed she had contracted AIDS from her dentist. Kimberly was also the personification of an innocent teenager who had been stricken, supposedly after her HIV-positive dentist performed oral surgery on her. Her testimony before congressional committees forever changed the way dentists and other medical professionals would treat patients. Gloves, face shields, masks, exposure suits, and sterilization changes have become the norm for all health-care providers. Ironically, very few cases have been documented of AIDS transmission from doctor to patient. However, the converse has been more apparent.

The disease of AIDS is a major source of agitation in the public sector. Fear of AIDS is great enough to arouse calls for better protection for AIDS victims. Few diseases have ever created such a sense of urgency, and even fewer have raised civil rights claims. Misunderstanding and fear of the disease has prompted advocates for AIDS victims to seek certain protections from discrimination in employment and housing. Ironically, a child with head lice, a nonfatal disease, can be banned from elementary school until the risk of contagion is removed, but a child who is HIV positive might not be banned.

Freedom of Religion: The Rights of Believers and Nonbelievers

Congress shall make no law respecting an establishment of religion, or prohibiting the free exercise thereof; or abridging the freedom of speech, or of the press; or the right of the people peaceably to assemble, and to petition the government for a redress of grievances.

Overview

Historically, American civil rights have often been closely connected to religious conviction.

Slavery emancipation, women suffrage, and racial equality were the "fruits" of the leadership provided by diverse religious groups who interpreted their religious doctrines to apply to all individuals and also worked for the social changes implied by those doctrines. Martin Luther King Jr. was a minister as well as a civil rights leader. It is because he was able to share his dream in the pulpit that his dream mobilized his congregation and ultimately transformed a reluctant nation into the reality of equality for all citizens, regardless of race or color.

Thomas Jefferson in 1802 penned these words in a letter to the Danbury, Connecticut, Baptist Association: "The First Amendment of the United States has erected a wall of Separation between Church and State, but that wall is a one directional wall. It keeps the government from running the Church, but makes sure that Christian principles will always stay in government." Our founding fathers, therefore, were more concerned with the encroachment of the state into religion, than religion into the state.

The framers designed this amendment to guarantee religious freedom, understanding as do most church officials today, that once government becomes involved with religion and acquires the power to promote religious beliefs, it also acquires the power to suppress them. The framers included a clause prohibiting government support or endorsement of religion out of the conviction that the way to ensure religious freedom was to separate the church from the state so that government could not interfere with religious views and practices.

In addition to the First Amendment, Article VI of the Constitution enforces separation by specifying that members of Congress may be sworn into office with either a religious "Oath" or a nonreligious "Affirmation," and that "no religious test" can be imposed on candidates for public office.

Even though the term does not exist in the constitution, "separation of church and state" has become a mainstay of American democracy, largely sparing citizens from the religious strife that has torn and still tears other societies apart. Consider the blood shed in countries, such as Bosnia and Israel. Separation has worked well, protecting the rights of those whose religious views are not the majority's as well as the rights of those who are not religious. Separation has also protected religious organizations from government interference and influence.

Nevertheless, the principle of separation has been regularly tested. In early America, even after church establishment ended, some state legislators sought to revive the compulsory taxation of citizens to support religious institutions.

Religious freedom is one of our most important traditions and constitutional rights. The courts, Congress, and state and local legislatures stand guard against proposals that would undermine the principle of separation, which protects that freedom.

Background

Religious conflict and persecution pervaded early America, even though most of the settlers had fled England to escape from religious intolerance there. For example, the Puritans established the Massachusetts Bay Colony as a theocratic state in which Catholics, Quakers, and others were regarded as heretics and subject to the death penalty.

In turn, the Catholics who founded Maryland persecuted Protestants and even some Catholics who professed their faith in unconventional ways. On the other hand, the Baptists of Providence, Rhode Island, believed that all religions should be allowed to flourish. Gradually church-state separation came to be seen as the key to ending destructive religious warfare that could have fragmented the new nation and ensuring religious freedom for all citizens.

In this century, public schools were once required to teach the biblical version of the earth's and humanity's creation, while the scientific theory of evolution was prohibited. Throughout our history, sectarian advocates have tried to inject religious exercises such as daily prayer into the public schools. At times, religious minorities, including members of "cults," have been discriminated against because of their beliefs.

Today, most Americans profess a belief in God. A majority of citizens belongs to one or another religious organization. Many do voluntary work for churches, and some give generously to the support of their churches. Many parents have chosen to send their children to religious-affiliated schools rather than use public schools. There is little doubt that religion plays a larger role in the lives of most Americans than in many other nations of the world.

Significant Court Cases

The first significant twentieth-century religious freedom case decided by the Supreme Court was *Cantwell* v. *Connecticut* (1940). Religious freedom cases rarely appeared on the Court's docket in the nineteenth century. The *Cantwell* case involved a state statute that made it a crime for any person to solicit or canvass from home to home for any religious or philanthropic cause without securing the prior approval of the secretary of the county welfare council. This official was empowered to determine whether the cause was a genuine religious one. The case was brought to the Supreme Court by the Jehovah's Witnesses, who argued that the statute was aimed against them. The Court unanimously held that the statute was unconstitutional as a restriction upon religious liberty. The requirement that a public official decide about a religion's character was "a censorship of religion," said Justice Roberts.

It is interesting to note that the Jehovah's Witnesses were involved in many Supreme Court decisions in the 1940s. This unorthodox religious group was subjected to taxation and other forms of discrimination in an effort to discourage their activities. After years of litigation, they were able to convince the Supreme Court that these measures were unconstitutional when applied to discourage the spread of their religious principles.

However, Jehovah's Witnesses could not escape the state criminal law that forbade child labor. According to *Prince* v. *Massachusetts* (1940), the protection of the welfare of children takes precedence over the competing claims of religious freedom. This is the same reasoning that led to one of the few nineteenth-century cases involving religious belief, the 1878 case of *Reynolds* v. *United States*. That decision, amplified by later cases, made it clear that the Mormon practice of polygamy was the kind of criminal act that society was not bound to tolerate. Similarly, the Supreme Court has upheld state statutes that outlaw the use of peyote (a hallucinogen) in Native American ceremonies.

Several other Supreme Court decisions have grown out of problems similar to those faced by Jehovah's Witnesses. In 1963 the Court struck down a South Carolina statute that had the effect of making a member of the Seventh-Day Adventist sect ineligible for unemployment compensa-

tion on the basis of her religious precepts *(Sherbert* v. *Verner)*. Jehovah's Witnesses and Seventh-Day Adventists believe that Saturday is the Sabbath and refuse to work on that day. The state denial of benefits for refusal to work on Saturday amounted to pressure to abandon her religious practices, in violation of the First Amendment right to the free exercise of religion.

The Amish are another American religious group that has sometimes sought the protection of the Constitution to defend their customary practices. Compulsory school attendance laws have been challenged by the Amish. In the leading case, Jonas Yoder, a member of the Old Order Amish religion, refused to send his daughter to school beyond the eighth grade. Mr. Yoder believed that high-school attendance was contrary to the Amish way of life. Many Amish children receive a practical, vocational education from their group that prepares them for life in their community. The Supreme Court agreed with this Amish view of the First Amendment. In the 1967 case of *Wisconsin* v. *Yoder,* the Court held that the compulsory attendance laws were an unconstitutional burden on Yoder and other Amish sharing his views. Strict adherence to the state law would undermine this way of life. Because of the close connection between the conservative Amish lifestyle and religious belief, the Court held that freedom of religion was at stake in this case.

Not all American religious groups have fared so well. Sunday closing laws have been held unconstitutional in spite of the objection of many Jewish businessmen, who regard this as a religiously based public policy. When Orthodox Jewish merchants, whose religious beliefs required them to close on a Saturday, objected to Sunday closing laws, the Supreme Court rejected their argument in the case of *Braunfeld* v. *Brown,* (1961). In 1986 a slim majority of the Supreme Court upheld an Air Force requirement prohibiting the wearing of religious apparel while on duty. When an Air Force clinical psychologist claimed that, as an Orthodox Jew and an ordained rabbi, he wanted to wear his yarmulke (skullcap) while serving as a psychologist, he was court-martialed for this abuse of orders. In *Goldman* v. *Weinberger,* (1986), the Supreme Court rejected this form of religious expression, because of the need to support military rules of discipline.

Freedom of religion requires that government not favor one religion over another. In a landmark 1947 decision, in the New Jersey case of *Everson* v. *Board of Education,* the United States Supreme Court permitted states to bus children to religious day schools just as the state provides police and fire-fighting services. The case is more important for the principles it announced than for its actual result. In *Everson* the United States Supreme Court adopted Thomas Jefferson's view that the Establishment Clause was intended to erect "a wall of separation between church and state" and set forth the following "Everson principles": Neither the state nor the federal government can

1. "Set up a church";

2. Pass laws that aid one religion, all religions, or favor one religion over another;

3. Force a person to attend or stay away from church or believe in any religion;

4. Punish a person for holding or professing religious beliefs;

5. Levy a tax, in any amount, to support any religious activities or institutions;

6. Openly or secretly participate in the affairs of any religious organization or vice versa.

Officially prescribed religious prayer was removed from public schools after *Engel* v. *Vitale,* (1962). The case found that state officials may not compose an official state prayer and require that it be recited in the public schools of the state at the beginning of each school day—even if the prayer is denominationally neutral and pupils who wish to do so may remain silent or be excused from the room while the prayer is being recited.

One year later, in *Abington School District* v. *Schempp* (1963), the Court held that no state law or school board may require that passages from the Bible be read or that the Lord's Prayer be recited in the public schools of a state at the beginning of each school day, even if individual students may be excused from attending or participating in such exercises upon the written request of their parents.

Very few laws specifically discriminate against religious practice. Today, citizens in many communities disagree about whether a model of the infant Jesus in the manger, which officially promotes certain religious beliefs over others, should be displayed on the steps of City Hall. The courts must frequently consider where to draw the line that separates church and state.

Religious Freedom Restoration Act (RFRA)

The Religious Freedom Restoration Act (42 U.S.C. 2000bb–1) was passed in 1993. This statute prevents the state from taking action that substan-

Case Problems

Lemon v. *Kurtzman* (1971) was a case involving public funds for religious schools. Rhode Island's 1969 Salary Supplement Act provided for a 15 percent salary supplement to be paid to teachers in nonpublic schools at which the average per pupil expenditure on secular education is below the average in public schools. Eligible teachers were allowed to teach only courses offered in the public schools, using only materials used in the public schools, and had to agree not to teach courses in religion. The United State Supreme Court found an "excessive entanglement" between government and religion, thus violating the Establishment Clause.

Wallace v. *Jaffree* (1985) examined the issue of a moment of silence in public schools. Alabama Statute authorized a one-minute period of silence in all public schools "for meditation or voluntary prayer." The United States Supreme Court held that this was unconstitutional.

In a recent 1992 case, *Lee* v. *Weisman*, the Supreme Court ruled on school prayer at graduation. Principals of public middle and high schools in Providence, Rhode Island, were permitted to invite members of the clergy to give invocations and benedictions at their schools' graduation ceremonies. The high court found that the practice violated the Establishment Clause of the First Amendment.

tially burdens religious exercise, unless its action furthers a compelling state interest and is the least restrictive means of addressing that interest.

The law is among the most extensive protections of religious activity protected by the United States Congress and has been invoked for a variety of reasons. Following the passage of the Religious Freedom Restoration Act, some churches have sought exemptions from local zoning requirements. In addition, prisoners have requested that they be allowed to wear certain clothing connected to their religious beliefs, and, in one situation, a landlord seeking to avoid fair housing requirements as applied to unmarried couples claimed the protection of the statute.

The 1993 statute was passed to counter a 1990 United States Supreme Court decision (*Employment Division* v. *Smith*) that allowed similar infringements on religious beliefs and practices. It remains to be seen whether courts will apply the statute to satisfy the claims of religious groups or other claimants. *Employment Division* v. *Smith* (1990), involved two members of the Native American Church who lost their jobs because of their ritual use of peyote. State law prohibited employees from using controlled substances in any way. To the Supreme Court, this restriction was neutral. It did not specifically intend to discriminate against Native American religious practice. This Supreme Court decision outraged congressional leaders who subsequently passed the Religious Freedom Restoration Act.

Two examples of the application of the federal law are given here:

- The city of Boerne, Texas, moved to stop a local Catholic church from enlarging its 1923 revival mission-style building in the community's historic district. The archbishop of San Antonio, relying on the Religious Freedom Restoration Act, successfully challenged the zoning ordinance. The church argued that they had outgrown their facility and required a larger one.

- In a Washington, D.C., case, the local zoning board refused to give a particular church permission to run a local soup kitchen. The board was responding to protests from the neighbors. An appeals court overruled the zoning board.

Equal Access Act

The Equal Access Act also provides certain protections for students in the secondary school system. This law seeks to protect students from the intrusion of government against students practicing their religious beliefs.

Recently, abortion advocates objected to an advertisement put up in the Philadelphia Subway System (SEPTA) by a church known as Christ's Bride Ministries. The advertisement warned that "Women who chose abortion suffer more and deadlier breast cancer." SEPTA eventually removed the poster. Dr. Phillip Lee, a federal Health and Human Services executive, warned that the poster was

"unduly alarming" and did not "accurately reflect the weight of the scientific literature." The poster was based on several studies that linked higher cancer rates in women who had abortions.

In June of 1995, the United States Supreme Court ruled in *Rosenberger* v. *The University of Virginia,* that the university had violated the Constitution when it gave funding to 113 student groups, including Muslim, animal-rights, and homosexual activists, but denied funds to a Christian periodical.

Anti-Abortion Ideas

Some very conservative Christians have become politically active in an attempt to prevent abortion, assisted suicide, infanticide, and involuntary euthanasia from becoming acceptable practices in our society. The most extreme of them have even resorted to demonstrations, sit-ins, and acts of violence. These "Pro-life" Christians believe that some medical procedures have become human-rights abuses, and the government not only has the right but the moral obligation to outlaw these terrible "crimes" against the fetus and against humanity. Others contend that "natural law" doctrines make the unborn child a person worthy of protection by the state. However, not all Christians are supportive of these views. Still, many Americans would like to limit access to abortion.

Some critics question whether it is appropriate to commingle morality and politics in religion, believing that it is not a wise idea to mix politics, religion, and medicine in American society. Nevertheless, debate over abortion policy continues. This kind of political debate over conflicting ideas is appropriate to a democracy. However, force applied against physicians or women or clinic workers is illegal. There is no right to apply force against these individuals in the interest of the unborn.

The Supreme Court has supported federal efforts to protect abortion clinics from violent acts committed by zealous anti-abortion advocates. The Court has never recognized any right by religious groups to deny individuals the right to choose access to legal abortion procedures. There is no doubt that anti-abortion advocates may speak out against the evils of abortion as part of their freedom of speech. They may conduct campaigns to change the laws regarding abortion. However, when their speech turns into violent action it will be illegal and run afoul of the rights of others.

Future Problems in Church-State Relations

Mayor of New York City, Rudolph Giuliani, has proposed a plan to use excess capacity at city parochial schools to address the needs of the public schools. The United States Supreme Court may

Some Unresolved Church-State Case Problems

Reverend Don Kimbro is a pastor from Albuquerque, New Mexico. City officials refused to allow pastor Kimbro to exhibit the salvation film "Jesus" and to distribute New Testaments to members of the city-owned Senior Citizens Center. This was despite the fact that the center already offered courses in meditation, yoga, tai chi, computers, and Spanish. The Center even offered a course in the Bible as history.

A street preacher was repeatedly cited and fined by police in Portland, Oregon, for violating a city ordinance prohibiting anyone from speaking to another person more than 10 feet away from the city's historic (and noisy) Pioneer Courthouse Square. No one else was cited under the ordinance, including large tour groups, kids in the playground, and street musicians.

The Phoenix transit officials allowed advertisements promoting homosexual rights, AIDS awareness, and condom use on city buses, but when the Catholic prayer group, Children of the Rosary, asked to post Bible verses, they were denied access. The prayer group was told, "We don't allow advertising on the bus for things like political messages, tobacco or alcohol as a way of keeping the buses from becoming objects of scorn." The 10th District Court of Appeals ruled in favor of each of the religious groups in these three examples.

Groups of Evangelical Christians every year gather at flagpoles before school in September. The event known as "See You At The Flagpole" prompts over a million participants every year. If a teacher participates in this event, does he or she violate the rights of nonreligious students?

A group of Christian Students want to start an Evangelical Bible study group known as "Young Life." The group meets after school every week. Does their presence on school property promote the funding or preferential treatment of one set of religious beliefs over another?

A kindergartner is a member of the Jehovah's Witness; her family does not believe in acknowledging birthdays. Can her family prohibit other recognition of birthdays in school?

A junior high school student is a member of the Mormons; as part of his responsibilities as a Mormon, he must evangelize other students. This evangelism includes the passing out of tracks and other literature. The school has rules that all documents must be reviewed by the principal, prior to distribution. Does this review violate the child's rights?

The ten-day Hindu Navratri festival is a religious celebration in which the members dance all night to honor the goddess Shakti, also known as Kali or Amba in various parts of India. The municipality passes an ordinance that states that no event can go on past midnight. The religious group files suit in federal district court claiming their freedom of religion has been violated. The municipality argues that an outdoor event with 100,000 attendees would disturb the local residents. Who should prevail in this case? The group or the residents? The judge in this Edison, New Jersey, case ruled in favor of the festival organizers.

have to balance the states' need to educate students against religious interests at some point in the future. This may amount to a violation of the First Amendment's separation of church and state, but we shall not know until a proper case arises.

Rights of Immigrants and Resident Aliens

With the exception of Native Americans, the United States of America is a nation of immigrants. During times of economic prosperity and full employment, the public has looked favorably upon immigrants as a means to expand national economic prosperity. However, during times of recession or even economic depression, the public has sought to limit immigration and, at times, discriminated against those individuals not born in this country or belonging to favored immigrant groups. Chapter 7 describes some of the experiences of various immigrant groups.

This historical hostility to new immigrant groups may seem in stark contrast to the symbolism of our Statute of Liberty, the first image for many traveling to the New World, with her

The first image for many new immigrants—the Statue of Liberty—inscribed with the words "Give me your tired, your poor, your huddled masses yearning to be free," starkly contrasts the hostility that new immigrant groups have faced throughout North America's history.

plaque stating, "Give me your tired, your poor, your huddled masses yearning to be free." Immigration laws today have largely removed elements of ethnic or regional prejudice. As it is, most residents enter the United States seeking to become citizens, usually after a five-year waiting period. However, illegal immigrants never seek citizenship, because their entry was never permitted. These individuals may not be protected by the federal Constitution.

The subject of immigrant rights is a new concern, especially after the passage of a series of state and federal laws that seek to limit the public benefits available to legal and illegal immigrants. Some states fear the impact of illegal immigrants on public schools as well as on medical and other social services. Whether those who are not citi-

zens are in some way entitled to services available to citizens has come into question, as community after community has sought to deny some of these services to illegal immigrants because of the enormous costs of providing them.

Recent federal legislation aims at limiting health care, education, and other welfare benefits for many immigrants. The new federal welfare system includes a two-year limit for welfare benefits without work and a five-year lifetime benefit for all citizens. Illegal immigrants would have not even those limited protections. Federal food stamps will also be unavailable to them.

Legal immigrants seeking food stamps and those already receiving federal disability benefits will lose those benefits as part of "welfare reform." It is estimated that more than one million noncitizens will lose the federal benefits. In addition, legal immigrants who have not applied for citizenship will be ineligible for certain other federal assistance programs, including Social Security Insurance (SSI), Medicaid, Aid to Families with Dependent Children (AFDC), and food stamps. Some immigrants will be exempt from the ban, including veterans, refugees seeking political asylum, and people who have lived and worked in the United States for more than ten years.

Some advocates of immigrants' rights contend that this form of treatment amounts to discrimination against immigrants. It seems unlikely that the Supreme Court will view it this way. Probably, Congress and state legislatures can exclude illegal immigrants from benefits under their social programs. Whether legal immigrants can be treated differently from citizens is quite another matter, and this may not meet the Supreme Court's view of the Equal Protection of the Laws clause of the Fourteenth Amendment.

A Final Example: Special Rights of Veterans

Those who have served in the armed forces, especially during times of war or "police action," have been awarded special rights or preference by the government. These "special rights" have been seen as compensation for a soldier's service to his country. In 1944, the Servicemen's Readjustment Act granted every veteran free college education or job training as well as a loan to purchase a home. The federal and state governments enacted laws that give veteran's preference for employment in government service. Federal legislation has ensured that civil rights legislation could not be "construed to repeal or modify any Federal, State, territorial, or local law creating special rights or preference for veterans."

There may be many other groups deserving of legal protection, but the issue of the rights of veterans is a good point of closure. Veterans deserve the gratitude of the nation that they defended. Disabled veterans, in particular, may be owed some special treatment in recognition of their needs. Service-connected disability may give rise to some sort of claim of rights unavailable to those who did not serve in the military. However, for those veterans who were not disabled in the line of duty, the creation of a special preference in hiring or any other kind of special benefit seems a political gesture, not a means of assisting a needy person. Such judgments are made in the state legislatures and the federal Congress.

Some states have given their veteran an absolute preference in all forms of hiring for the civil service. Others have bestowed tax breaks and outright grants of money. These may all be well-deserved, but the question remains whether fully able veterans have special rights or merely a political claim. That issue arises throughout this chapter. The reader must decide whether the rights mentioned here are legitimate or are merely political in nature.

Bibliography

Berry, Mary Francis. *Why ERA Failed.* Bloomington, Ind.: Indiana University Press, 1986.

Flowers, Ronald B. *That Godless Court? Supreme Court Decisions on Church-State Relationships.* Louisville, Ky.: Westminister/John Knox Press, 1994.

Frankel, Marvin E. *Faith and Freedom: Religious Liberty in America.* New York: Hill and Wang, 1994.

Gelb, Joyce. *Feminism and Politics.* Berkeley, Calif.: University of California Press, 1989.

Hidalgo, Hilda. *Lesbians of Color: Social and Human Services.* New York: Haworth Press, 1995.

Zepatos, Thalia. *Women for Change: A Grassroots Guide to Activism and Politics.* New York: Facts on File, 1995.

Section III

Civil Rights and Government: Politics, Policy-making, and the Legal System

Chapter 9

The Politics of Civil Rights: Ending Racial Segregation in America

Howard Ball

To understand the politics of civil rights in America it is necessary to understand the structural characteristics of America's political system. For this, one must begin with the U.S. Constitution, drafted by forty men in the hot Philadelphia summer of 1787, ratified in the fall and winter of 1787–1788, and put into practice in 1789, with the Bill of Rights added a few years later, in 1791.

The American Constitution is, historically, the most enduring of such human creations. For over 200 years, men and women in America have governed under its prescriptions and its grants of power to government. The Constitution's language provides the governing agencies, the Congress, the president, and the federal judiciary (the U.S. Supreme Court and all federal courts created by Congress), with certain grants of power (found in Articles I through III). Powers in the Constitution are divided between the three branches, consistent with the innovative concepts of "separation of powers" and "checks and balances" incorporated into the Constitution by the drafters. The men who met to write the Constitution in 1787 believed that all power in the hands of one governing agency, whether the legislative or the executive, was the definition of tyranny. To minimize the possibility of a tyrannical government, they separated power among the more overtly political agencies of government (the legislative and the executive) and gave each of the governing branches certain powers to check each other's actions. The federal judiciary, with neither the power of the purse (Congress) nor the power of the sword (Executive), was considered the weakest of the agencies of the national government created by the men who wrote the document. However, given the Constitution writers' understanding that courts had the power of judicial review, the federal judiciary, if there was a legitimate case or controversy brought into their courts, could examine whether or not legislative or executive action was "constitutional" (that is, agreeable with a grant of power given to the branch by the Constitution) or was "unconstitutional" (that is, the action taken—

by the president or by the Congress—was beyond the powers granted to that political agency by the Constitution and therefore null and void).

In addition, and critically important for an understanding of the politics of civil rights and liberties in America, the Constitution places limits on the use of the powers granted to the political agencies. These limits are found in the body of the Constitution itself as well as in amendments added to the document, especially the Bill of Rights (Amendments One through Ten) added in 1791, and the Civil War Amendments (Amendments Thirteen through Fifteen), adopted in the years immediately following the end, in 1865, of the American Civil War.

The Constitution as well established a federal pattern of governing; that is, the Constitution created a national government while maintaining, in a somewhat more restrictive fashion, the governments of the states and their local subdivisions, the cities and towns. The concept of federalism means that powers are shared geographically between a national government, with power over citizens and persons in all states and territories, and state governments, with power to enact and enforce legislation over citizens and persons within the state's territorial jurisdiction.

The Preamble to the Constitution lays out the objectives of the new federal structure: "We the People of the United States, in Order to form a more perfect Union, establish Justice, insure domestic Tranquility, provide for the common defence, promote the General Welfare, and secure the Blessings of Liberty to ourselves and our Posterity, do ordain and establish this Constitution for the United States of America." In a way, the history of our nation since these words were written in 1787 is a history of how the responsibilities for moving toward this "more perfect Union" have gradually shifted from the states to the national government.

Clearly, by the time the Great Depression began in 1929 in America, it was obvious that the states, individually, could not successfully respond to the national economic dilemma. The election of the Democratic presidential candidate, New York Governor Franklin D. Roosevelt, in 1932 signaled the creation of a New Deal, which meant the expansion of national governmental responsibilities in a host of social and economic

areas (such as health insurance, social security, old age assistance, minimum wages, unemployment insurance, and regulation of agricultural production) formally associated with state responsibility. Since the 1930s, America has witnessed the growth of the power of the national government in the areas of social and economic regulation and, beginning seriously in the 1960s, the protection of the civil rights of minorities and women owing to unwillingness or incapacity of the states to legislate in these areas. Certainly an examination of the politics of civil rights in America shows how the national government, in order to "establish Justice," especially since the end of the Second World War, has had to pass legislation and enact regulations to protect the civil rights of persons because states and local communities did not act to establish such justice for all persons regardless of race, color, or previous condition of servitude.

American federalism, then, is an extremely important component of the political process. Basically, citizens in America are citizens of the national government as well as of the state in which they reside and, as such, are subject to the laws of both the state and the national governments. In addition, citizens are protected from governmental excess by either government by virtue of constitutional protections found in both national and state constitutions.

Both governments can regulate the behavior of persons living in their respective jurisdictions. And so, for example, the U.S. Congress legislates against organized racketeering that can affect certain persons living in Vermont. The Vermont legislature, in addition, enacts criminal codes that punish certain kinds of behavior considered criminal by the people of that state. If Vermont passes legislation that is in conflict with the legislation created by Congress, the Constitution resolves that conflict with the help of the federal courts, especially the U.S. Supreme Court. Article VI of the U.S. Constitution states that all laws passed by Congress, and all treaties entered into by the United States, "shall be the supreme law of the Land; and the judges in every State shall be bound thereby, any Thing in the Constitution or Laws of any State to the contrary notwithstanding."

All public officials and employees, whether working for the national government or in a state or local government, take an oath to abide by the words of both national and state constitutions. If

American Revolutionary leader Patrick Henry, along with many Americans, opposed the shift from state governments to a central, national government proposed by the Constitution.

they fail to follow the restrictions on the use of their power, or act with excess zeal, they can be held liable, in both civil and criminal courts, for such breaches of their powers and responsibilities.

The argument for the primacy of state action in the American federal system is an old one and goes back to the passage of the Bill of Rights in 1791. Indeed, there was strong opposition to the new Constitution, with its new central, national government and its federalist pattern, during the ratification campaign and elections in 1787–1788. Many Americans agreed with Patrick Henry, an opponent of the new constitutional system, when he said that he "smelled a rat." The argument for states' rights emphasized the primacy of state sovereignty and power and considered the new con-

stitutional proposal, which created a national legislature, an executive branch, and a national judiciary, an usurpation of the preexisting powers of the 13 United States of America.

The Tenth Amendment in the Bill of Rights was an effort to placate these fears. It states that "the powers not delegated to the United States by the Constitution, nor prohibited by it to the States, are reserved to the States respectively, or to the people." State action advocates argue that this amendment provides the states with the substantive right to legislate broadly to protect the health, safety, welfare, and well-being of the people who live in the state. Their view is that all politics is local politics and that the national Congress and the president have few substantive powers regarding the regulation of the people living in the states.

Local majorities in each state, the states rights argument goes, have the power to legislate for the general welfare and happiness of the majority residing in that state. For the national government to interfere with the actions of state legislators and executives is to usurp state power, a violation of the Tenth Amendment. Over the course of American history, the federal courts, especially the U.S. Supreme Court, have been involved in mediating this fundamental federalism conflict. As U.S. Attorney General William Rogers pointed out to his president, Dwight Eisenhower, in May of 1958:

> The essential features of our constitutional form of government—a federal system of Nation and States; with separation of powers between legislative, executive and judicial branches; all acting under the Constitution and the Bill of Rights—have imposed special and heavy responsibilities upon the Supreme Court, whose unique role has been described as "balance wheel" or an "umpire." Since 1803, when Chief Justice Marshall in *Marbury* v. *Madison* upheld its power to invalidate legislation, the Supreme Court has been the center of controversy resulting from its exercise of the delicate and difficult functions thrust upon it by the Constitution. Many of the significant—and what today are regarded as some of the wisest and most profound—decisions of the Court were very unpopular at the time they were made.

As will be seen in an examination of the politics of civil rights in America, the U.S. Supreme Court was the first national policymaker to substantively address questions involving civil rights policy and practice in the states, especially the deep South states of the Old Confederacy. The federal judges, toward the end of the nineteenth century to the present time, were asked either (1) to examine and then to overturn state actions that allegedly denied the minority petitioners due process or equal protection of the laws (found in the Constitution's Fourteenth Amendment), or (2) to declare unconstitutional national legislative actions, challenged by individuals in the states, whose legislative purpose was to end a set of racial discriminatory actions that denied persons the enjoyment of liberty and freedom solely because of their race or color.

Over the generations since the first Congress met in 1789, a general political pattern for policymaking in America has developed. With the exception of the "common defense" goal, a primary responsibility of the national government, especially the Congress (which declares war and raises funds for the support of the armed forces) and the president (who acts as commander-in-chief of the armed forces), the pattern has been that the local community acts to address the particular objective (justice and liberty, domestic tranquility, general welfare) and if that community cannot adequately address—or as in the case of civil rights in America is unwilling to address it—or worse, actively engages in discrimination based on race in violation of both state and national Constitutions, then the next larger political agency has the responsibility for addressing the issue. Finally, if the local or the state political agencies has neither the capacity nor the will to deal with the matter, then the national government has the responsibility for legislating to insure justice and the blessings of liberty, domestic tranquility, and the general welfare.

The examination of civil rights in America clearly shows such a pattern at work, one that led, ultimately, to all three agencies of the national government—the Congress, the president, and the U.S. Supreme Court—acting to redress wrongs suffered by citizens solely due to their race or their color. The national actors acted because the local and state governments, especially those Southern states of the former Confederacy, refused to protect the civil rights of their citizens. Without national governmental actions, the wrongs perpetrated against African Americans would have continued, thereby denying justice and equality to millions of American citizens. Federalism enabled the national government, at an appropriate time, to enter the politics of civil rights to insure justice and the blessings of liberty for minorities in America.

Obviously, it is not an easy matter for a national policy-maker to enter the preexisting local fray. Citizens of the state will cry out in protest that the "feds" are unlawfully interfering in state and local politics and should mind their own business. Therefore, before any formal national action, there are informal suggestions that the state or the local community make changes in the controversial policy before national action, in the form of legislation, executive actions, or federal court orders, occurs.

For years, for example, national leaders tried to persuade Southern officials to address the tragedy of lynchings in their states. For many years, additional efforts were made to persuade Southern politicians that the dilemmas facing the African American citizens living in these Southern states had to be addressed, whether the problem was inferior schooling, or poor housing and health facilities, or menial jobs, or denial of basic political and legal rights.

However, as will be seen, if these efforts to induce change in local and state governmental policymaking fail, if bargaining and negotiation do not produce changes in the way a local community or a state deals with a problem of justice or liberty, then a national agency is called upon to address the alleged wrongs. In the area of civil rights, it will be shown that the first of the national agencies to be involved in this arena were the federal courts, most importantly, the U.S. Supreme Court. Not having political clout in state or national legislative and executive agencies, the oppressed citizens took their grievances against local and state officials and the policies they created into the federal courts in order to find justice.

These civil rights demands, made by men and women who suffered actual injury, began in the early part of the twentieth century. Their law suits were the very first public policy inputs into the national political system. What they were asking for was an end to racial segregation and an end to discrimination based on race or color in America.

The State Actors in the Politics of Civil Rights

"All politics is local" is an observation that has been made by many observers of America's political environment. Who are the major players in the development of public policy at the local and the state levels? Clearly, such an inventory has to include (1) the elected and appointed local and state officials (legislators, executives, and local and state judges); (2) the local and state bureaucrats, that is, those persons responsible for implementing fairly the laws and regulations of the state; (3) the political parties of the state, who are responsible for framing public policy discussions that lead to electoral decisions by the people; (4) the "fourth estate," or the local and state media—that is, the newspapers and radio and television stations—who support certain policy matters and seek to persuade their readers, listeners,

and viewers to support those points of view; and (5) local and state pressure groups, many affiliated with national organizations.

Critically important for an understanding of the politics of civil rights in America, however, are the local and state pressure groups. As Associate Justice William J. Brennan Jr. of the U.S. Supreme Court noted in *NAACP* v. *Button,* a 1963 case heard by the Court: "Under conditions of modern government, litigation may be the sole practicable avenue open to a minority [pressure group] to petition for a redress of grievances."

Although all elected officials have the duty to lead, all elected officials, local and national politicians alike, take their policy cues from their constituents. They win elections because their platform positions mirror the views of a majority of the electorate. The electorate views on public policy issues are developed, to a large extent, by the media and by the pressure groups that the electorate belongs to, from religious and civic groups, to business and economic groups, to social and environmental groups, and to groups such as the Anti Saloon League, the Ku Klux Klan, the White Citizens Councils, and the National Association for the Advancement of Colored People (NAACP). The first two were very important pressure groups that dramatically impacted Southern politics during the first four decades of the twentieth century. The White Citizens Council was an important pressure group in the middle decades of the twentieth century, and the NAACP has been a vital group for the advancement of political, legal, and social equality for African Americans since its formation in 1910.

Pressure groups of all types have existed since the beginning of the Federal Republic in 1789. At first planters, bankers, and shipbuilders formed interest groups seeking favors from government, and later others with similar economic interests followed suit. A wide variety of pressure groups have functioned in America, both at local and state levels and at the national level as well. Some groups are economic—labor or management—while others are social action groups that work for the creation of a public policy that will benefit their constituents. In 1909, in response to a series of violent riots by racist whites against African Americans in Georgia and Illinois, pogroms that left hundreds of African Americans killed and many more hundreds wounded, a hand-

William Lloyd Garrison was one of the social reformers who, in response to a series of violent racist riots against African Americans, wrote "The Call," an edict to create a pressure group to address the evils of racial segregation.

ful of white citizens issued a call to create a pressure group that would address the evils of racial segregation. "The Call," *A Lincoln Emancipation Conference to Discuss Means for Securing Political and Civil Equality for the Negro,* led to the creation of the National Association for the Advancement of Colored People, the NAACP, the first and most powerful of civil rights pressure groups in America.

The Call was announced in the media in February 1909, coincidental with the centennial of the birth of Abraham Lincoln. The Call was a "taking stock of the nation's progress since 1865 [regarding the freedom of the African American men and women]." Initiated by William E. Walling, a white Kentuckian who was alarmed that violence against African Americans was spreading from South to North, the Call was written by social reformers Jane Addams, Henry Moskowitz, Mary W. Ovington, Lincoln Steffens, Oswald Garrison Villard, and William Lloyd Garrison, and signed by dozens of other white and African American fighters for social justice in America. It enumerated the "disheartening" segregationist activities that had dramatically reduced the civil and political rights of African Americans since the end of the Civil War, a war that saw "over one hundred thousand soldiers give their lives" on behalf of freedom for the slaves.

Concluding with the argument that "silence under these conditions means tacit approval. . . .

Hence, we call upon all the believers in democracy to join in a national conference for the discussion of the present evils, the voicing of protests, and the renewal of the struggle for civil and political liberty." Within the year, the NAACP was created and, since 1910, the organization has been an active participant (definitely the most active—and successful—civil rights pressure group) in national and state politics, especially in the courts.

Like so many other pressure groups, the NAACP tried to engage in lobbying for civil rights in state and the national legislatures as well as in the state and national executive branches of government. Furthermore, like so many other pressure groups, the NAACP provided campaign support for candidates and judicial nominees who supported their goals and it campaigned against persons who disagreed with their goals.

In addition, and critically important to an understanding of the politics of civil rights in America, the NAACP initiated a new strategy that was to be employed by many other pressure groups: litigation as a legal form of pressure-group activity. Because the NAACP was not successful in achieving their goals through legislative and executive lobbying, they sought to achieve their goal, the end of racial segregation and discrimination based on race and color, in state and federal courts. As will be seen, this proved to be a very successful strategy, one that was to open up, in subsequent decades, the halls of the Congress and the doors of the White House to representatives of the NAACP and other minority groups seeking freedom and justice for their members.

The National Authorities in Public Policymaking: Congress, President, and the Federal Courts

In making their case for changing the civil rights policy in America, the NAACP, early in its history, developed three strategies: (1) lobbying Congress for antilynching legislation, (2) educating the public about the evils of racial discrimination, and (3) beginning in 1915, presenting legal suits in state courts, with ultimate appeals to the U.S. Supreme Court, that challenged existing patterns and practices of racial segregation and discrimination based on race and color. For the

NAACP, it was clear that they could not effect changes in local and state policy regarding racial discrimination and segregation. The states, especially the 11 states of the Old Confederacy, were categorically committed to a social, economic, and political pattern of white supremacy, of Jim Crow apartheid, and any effort to try to persuade state legislators and executives was doomed.

Therefore, as will be seen, the NAACP's lobbying efforts were almost exclusively aimed at convincing national political actors, the Congress and the president, of the need to address the reality of apartheid in America and to hope that the national legislature and the president would take actions that would provide the NAACP's constituents with a modicum of freedom and liberty. It was to prove to be a very difficult task for, at the time of the birth of the NAACP in 1910, America had a history of 300 long years of cruel and unequal treatment of African Americans and other minorities—and women.

The Politics of Civil Rights: Ending the Public Policy of Racial Segregation in America

Slavery was a legitimate concept in American history from its very beginnings. In August 1619, the first shipment of approximately 20 African American slaves arrived at Point Comfort, near Jamestown, Virginia. From this early seventeenth-century date through the end of the Civil War, in 1865, slavery was legally recognized in law and politics and African Americans were seen as mere objects of chattel property, much like oxen and wagons were, to be bought and sold at the whim of the slave owner; the slaves had absolutely no legal and civil rights. From the very beginning of the British colonialization of America, African American slaves had no legal personality and were firmly classed as *things*. By the time of the Constitution, almost a century after slavery had come to America, Southern state constitutions contained clauses that perpetuated slavery by forbidding the state legislature to emancipate them.

The 1787 Constitution referred to them as chattel property and spoke about them only in property and electoral enumeration terms, for the document protected the business of slavery and counted the African American as three-fifths of a person for state representational purposes. They were not citizens, did not have the right to vote, and were left to the tender mercies of their slave owners.

The U.S. Supreme Court, in the *Dred Scott* v. *Sandford* decision of 1856 validated this view of slaves as property with no right to sue in a court of law because the slave, not being a citizen or even a person under the law, had no standing to sue.

The Civil War and the Civil War Amendments: Public Policy Change by National Policymakers and Adverse Responses by the States

The lengthy, bloody Civil War was an effort to end the pattern and practice of slavery that existed at the time. After the war's end, a radical Republican Reconstruction Congress succeeded in introducing and getting ratified in the states what are known as the Civil War Amendments (Thirteen through Fifteen) to the Constitution. These amendments ended slavery (the Thirteenth Amendment), announced citizenship for all persons born or naturalized in the United States, and restricted states from abridging the privileges or immunities of citizens of the United States, from depriving any person of life, liberty, or property without due process of law, nor shall any state deny any person the equal protection of the laws (the Fourteenth Amendment). In the Fifteenth Amendment, the Congress insured that the right of citizens to vote would not be abridged or denied by the United States or by any state on account of race, color, or previous condition of servitude.

Furthermore, each of these amendments had a concluding section that stated: "Congress shall have power to enforce this article by appropriate legislation." The national Congress, concerned about the plight of the recently freed slaves in the South, and aware of terrorist groups such as the Ku Klux Klan that had sprung up to terrorize the new African American citizens, in the 1860s and 1870s, passed a series of civil rights acts to protect these new citizens, to punish those who acted to deprive African Americans of their new political and legal freedoms, and to prohibit any discrimination against African Americans in places of public accommodations, that is, in theaters, restaurants, hotels, and so forth. The Congress, through the late 1870s, was committed to a national public policy that would in the end remove all the "badges of slavery" that African Americans, after the Civil War, still wore. (The phrase "badge of slavery" was a metaphor used to describe the legal restrictions that had been imposed on slaves by state governments.)

However, the pendulum swung against this public policy and, by the early 1880s, due to changes in national politics and the conservativism of the U.S. Supreme Court, the policies of the radical Reconstruction Congress had been eviscerated. There was a return to the badges of slavery, and the plight of the African American became extremely dire in the Old Confederacy and throughout America.

Reversing the Public Policy: The U.S. Supreme Court Strikes Down Civil Rights Legislation, 1883–1896

This reversal of public policy toward the African American community was seen most clearly in U.S. Supreme Court opinions that invalidated most of the legislation passed by the radical Reconstruction Congress. The Supreme Court, using its power of judicial review, concluded that the Congress had acted unconstitutionally in trying to protect the newly freed slaves from racial segregation and discrimination.

The Court concluded that Congress did not have the power to tell private individuals how to behave toward African Americans. The Civil War Amendments prohibited certain forms of *state* action, not private actions, and therefore the Congress had overstepped its authoritative use of power when it attempted to redress purely private behavior, however intolerant and discriminatory, against African Americans.

The *Plessy* Decision and a New Public Policy: The Era of Separate But Equal, 1896–1954

The 1896 case of *Plessy* v. *Ferguson* was the watershed litigation in which the U.S. Supreme Court drew the segregation curtain down on the African American community in America, especially those African Americans living in the South. With the decision in *Plessy,* by a seven-to-one vote, the Supreme Court ushered in—and legiti-

matized—the era of formal racial segregation, also known as Jim Crowism. In the case, one from Louisiana that challenged that state's segregation of the two races into separate railroad cars, the majority held that the Equal Protection clause of the Fourteenth Amendment did not prohibit Louisiana from providing facilities for its citizens that were equal but separate.

With this opinion, the Court legitimatized the formal state-ordered policy of segregation of the African American and Caucasian races. As a consequence, the legal and political status of the African American plummeted to pre-Civil War levels.

By the turn of the twentieth century, conditions had dramatically worsened for African Americans. They quickly faced a myriad of state-enforced racial segregation, or Jim Crow, practices that affected their lives from birth to death. There emerged as a consequence of state political actions, a policy of racially segregating hospitals, cemeteries, churches, schools, playgrounds. By the turn of the twentieth century, *every* social activity engaged in by humans was segregated by race—without any regard for the "equality" suggested by the Court in *Plessy.* All social relations became "separate," but they were never "equal."

Furthermore, violence and intimidation had increased in the South, and lynchings of African Americans by *entire communities* of whites became all too common. Violent riots by whites against black communities—in Atlanta, Georgia, in 1906; in Louisville, Kentucky, in 1907; and in Springfield, Illinois (the birthplace of Abraham Lincoln), in 1908—became the norm throughout the South, and African Americans feared for their lives.

In response to these terroristic attacks on them, African Americans had few alternatives. Many sought solace in the African American Church, with its message of a better afterlife. Many turned to the accommodationist views of Booker T. Washington, who maintained that African Americans must find their vocational niche in the Southern community and not seek the political and legal equality announced in the Civil War Amendments.

Still other African Americans heard the words of W. E. B. Du Bois, who spoke, in his classic book published in 1905, *The Souls of Black People,* of the struggle African Americans had living in two

Booker T. Washington (1856–1915)

Booker Taliaferro Washington was born a slave on a plantation in Franklin County, Virginia. The exact location is uncertain, although Washington thought that "it was near a crossroads post office called Hale's Ford." His birthdate was April 5, 1856; his father, a white man, was unknown to him.

After the Civil War, Booker T. Washington worked in salt furnaces and coal mines in West Virginia, attending school part-time until he was able to enter the Hampton Institute in Virginia. His tuition there was paid by a friend of the principal, and Washington worked as a janitor to earn his room and board.

After three years at Hampton (1872–1875) Washington taught at a school for African American children in Malden, West Virginia. After further study he was appointed as an instructor at Hampton Institute, where he was given charge of the education of 75 Native American students. Later, Washington developed a night school at Hampton Institute.

Booker T. Washington became a national figure after organizing a school for African Americans at Tuskegee, Alabama, in 1881. The Tuskegee Institute, concentrating in industrial training as a means for the economic independence of African Americans, became a leading educational institution in the nation. As presi-

dent of Tuskegee Institute, which he and his associates built from a little shanty and a church into a major educational institution, Booker T. Washington was regarded as a leader on the national and international scene.

Unfortunately, Washington's moderate views were sometimes seen as too accommodating to white fears concerning African Americans. In 1895 he made a speech in Atlanta, Georgia, on the place of the African American man in American life. In this so-called Atlanta Compromise, Washington seemed to advocate a policy that pursued social equality for African Americans only after they had attained economic equality. This speech brought him many white financial supporters, but it may have discouraged other African American leaders.

Washington's tactics may have been questioned, but his devotion towards the improvement of the cause of African Americans cannot be denied. The habits of hard work, thrift, and economy that he championed were just one means for the advancement of his people. Booker T. Washington was so prominent during his lifetime that presidents and wealthy businessmen admired him and lent assistance to his causes. President Theodore Roosevelt consulted Booker T. Washington frequently, especially regarding federal appointments to judgeships.

worlds. Some joined the movement he created in 1905, called the Niagara Movement. His organization demanded freedoms for African Americans, including free speech, manhood suffrage, the abolition of all distinctions based solely on race and color, and demanded that African Americans receive the best education possible rather than solely vocational education at places like Washington's Tuskegee Institute, an African American technical and vocational college in Alabama.

Many African Americans, close to one million all told, fled the South to northern cities such as Chicago and New York, whereas others were captivated by the magical words of Marcus Garvey and his back-to-Africa movement. Marcus Garvey was a leading proponent of black nationalism, who sought to foster worldwide unity among all black people by emphasizing the greatness of

their African heritage. In 1916 he moved to New York City and urged a "back to Africa" movement, because he believed that African Americans could not secure their rights in any nation where they are a minority race. Over a half million African Americans joined his Universal Negro Improvement Association and contributed $10 million to that organization's coffers.

However, for many other millions of African Americans out-migration from the South, whether to New York or to Liberia, was not the practical answer. The question for them became a harsh choice: Either live with separate-but-equal Jim Crow racism or, in some manner, organize to fight against this de jure racial segregation. With the creation of the NAACP in 1910, which saw Du Bois's very-small-in-numbers Niagara Movement folded into it, the African American community in

America had still another alternative. They could join this national organization, consisting of local chapters across America, in its efforts to seek equality and justice—political, social, and economic—for African Americans.

The NAACP was the first and the largest of America's national civil rights pressure groups. A decade after its creation, in 1919, there were over 300 chapters across America, with over 100,000 members, half of them living in the South. By 1939, over 1,600 chapters had over 300,000 members. By 1993, there were over 2,200 local chapters across America, with over 500,000 members.

Attacking the Public Policy of Racial Segregation: Inroads by the NAACP, 1910–1936

The NAACP was formed to try to end America's continual discriminatory practices against African Americans. These practices and policies were both local and national in nature, for the U.S. Supreme Court had clearly spoken out on the legitimacy of racial segregation—so long as there were separate but equal facilities for both African Americans and whites. Nevertheless, the national guideline was in place: Separation of the races was legitimate. States, especially Southern states, quickly adapted Jim Crow codes and followed with restrictions on African American voting rights. By the time of the NAACP's birth, African Americans were victimized by terror, denied political rights and, socially, were segregated in every human activity imaginable, from birth to death.

The African American, even growing up in the North, lived in a dual world. According to Martin Duberman in *Paul Robeson: A Biography,* he followed the established protective tactic of African American life in America:

> to "act right," to exhibit maximum affability and minimum arrogance. . . . Any overt challenge to the 'natural supremacy' of whites had to be avoided. Above all, do nothing to give them cause to fear you, for then the oppressing hand which might at times ease up a little, will surely become a fist to knock you down again.

Given this harsh political and social reality, the NAACP's main focus at its creation in 1910 was a radical one: to achieve absolute political and social equality for African Americans. Initial proposals involved orchestrating some sort of attack on the practice of peonage in the South, try-

ing to get Congressmen to introduce antilynching legislation, and trying to end the disenfranchisement of African Americans in the South.

In 1915, the NAACP began to view litigation as a form of social process for achieving these goals. The judgment to use the Courts to seek the NAACP's goals of racial and political equality proved a mandatory one, for no other political avenue was open to the organization. The NAACP had failed to persuade Congress to legislate against lynching in Southern states, and it had utterly failed to dent Southern state politics with respect to political and social equality of African Americans.

Under President Arthur Spingarn's leadership, the NAACP began to challenge the constitutional validity of Jim Crow segregation as well as the de jure denial of equal justice and due process for African Americans. Between 1915 and 1936, in the absence of any strategic plan for using the courts to change racist and discriminatory policies, the NAACP brought ten cases to the U.S. Supreme Court in four general areas: suffrage, residential racial-zoning ordinances, restrictive housing covenants, and due process and equal protection for African Americans accused of crimes. It won nine of the ten. These early NAACP cases were:

- Primaries in State Elections:
  Nixon v. *Herndon,* 1927
  Grovey v. *Townsend,* 1932 (NAACP loses case)

- Voting Procedures:
  Guinn v. *U.S.,* 1915 (amicus curiae)

- State Enforced Racial Segregation:
  Buchanan v. *Warley,* 1917
  Harmon v. *Tyler,* 1927
  City of Richmond v. *Deans,* 1930

- Private Restrictive Housing Covenants:
  Corrigan v. *Buckley,* 1926

- Procedual Rights in Criminal Cases:
  Moore v. *Dempsey,* 1923
  Hollins v. *Oklahoma,* 1935
  Brown v. *Mississippi,* 1936

While successful in nine of ten cases, the NAACP had not addressed the major concern of African Americans about Jim Crowism: the separate and desperately unequal public school system that had existed in the South as well as the segregated graduate and professional educational system that existed in America at this time. As Thurgood Marshall, a major African American legal advocate for social justice and the main legal advocate for the NAACP between 1938 and 1961, said: "The only solution to our problem is that of breaking down segregation in the public schools."

About six years before Thurgood Marshall joined the NAACP, the organization received a grant of money from the Garland Fund and brought onboard a person to develop a long-term litigation strategy for the African American civil rights pressure group. The name of the lawyer was Nathan Margold, one of a number of Harvard Law School-trained Jewish lawyers, whose mentor was Harvard Law School Professor Felix Frankfurter, soon to become an Associate Justice of the U.S. Supreme Court. For almost two years, Margold worked to develop a legal strategy for the NAACP to use in fighting racial segregation and discrimination.

For Margold, eradicating inferior public education for African Americans was a major concern but not the only task for the NAACP. The essential characteristic of the plan as formulated by Margold was to target segregated facilities as they were provided for and administered by the states. The goal was to force the Southern states, through victories in court, to come up with millions of dollars to be used to make African American facilities, that is, schools, hospitals, playgrounds, parks, and so forth, the equal of the white facilities. The belief was that such financial pressures on the white community would lead the community to abandon *Plessy's* dual system of separate but [un]equal facilities. Ultimately, however, for Margold and for the NAACP legal advocates led by Thurgood Marshall, the primary objective was the overturning of the separate-but-equal doctrine announced in the 1896 *Plessy* opinion of an earlier Court.

Charles Houston and Thurgood Marshall: Leading the NAACP in the Battles Against Jim Crow, 1936–1950

In 1932, the South, at the time Margold was developing the NAACP's legal strategy to combat racial segregation, consisted of 30 million people in the 11 states of the former Confederacy. It was according to Edward L. Ayers in *The Promise of the New South: Life After Reconstruction* a "feudal land, an Americanized version of a European society in the Middle Ages." There were the ruling nobles, lords of the plantation, and the African

Thurgood Marshall *(1908–1993)*

Born in Baltimore, Maryland, on July 2, 1908, Thurgood Marshall had an illustrious career in the law, capped by his 1967 appointment by President Lyndon Johnson to the Supreme Court—the first African American to hold that high office. Marshall served on the Court for 24 years. From 1961 to 1965 he sat as a federal circuit judge for the second circuit. Marshall was Solicitor General of the United States from 1965 to 1967.

Thurgood Marshall was the son of a sleeping-car porter and a primary school teacher, and the great-grandson of a slave. Marshall was named after his paternal grandfather, Thoroughgood Marshall, a freeman of Maryland who enlisted in the Union Army during the Civil War. Later Marshall shortened his name to Thurgood. Marshall was a brilliant student, graduating from Howard University's law school in 1933 at the top of his class. His application to the University of Maryland Law School was rejected because he was not white.

After a brief career in private legal practice, Marshall began working for the National Association for the Advancement of Colored People (NAACP) eventually becoming the director-counsel of the NAACP's Legal Defense and Educational Fund. While national special counsel, Marshall was a major figure in the major antidiscrimination cases of the time. He was part of the team that argued the NAACP's view of the *Brown v. Board of Education* case in 1954. He also argued NAACP cases involving voting rights and other challenges to segregation in the nation. Of the 32 cases he argued before the Supreme Court, Marshall won 29.

Marshall died in 1993 at the age of 84, only two years after retiring from the Supreme Court in 1991. After his death, Marshall was laid in state in the Great Hall of the Supreme Court of the United States, on the same bier where President Lincoln had been placed after his assassination.

Americans, its peasants, its vassals. Its "values were rooted in the land, in stability and permanence, in hierarchy and status, in caste and class and race. The highest virtues were honor and duty, loyalty and obedience."

Charles Hamilton Houston (1895–1950)

This lawyer and educator was the only child of William and Mary Houston. Like his father before him, Charles Hamilton Houston combined teaching at Howard University with an active legal practice. However, Charles Houston earned his first law degree at the Harvard Law School. In 1923 Houston earned another honor, becoming the first African American to earn the Doctor of Juridical Science degree at Harvard.

In 1931 Houston was appointed vice-dean at Howard Law School. However, he took a leave of absence from Howard in 1935 to work for the NAACP. From 1935 until 1940 Houston was the NAACP's first full-time paid special counsel. Thurgood Marshall, his former student at Howard, served as assistant special counsel and, after 1938, as special counsel.

Houston argued in whole or in part many of the major desegregation cases before the Supreme Court of the United States during the late 1930s and 1940s. He was a severe critic of segregation in the United States military. Houston spearheaded the campaign to desegregate the schools of the District of Columbia. A man of strong principles, he resigned from the Fair Employment Practices Commission in 1945 because he could not persuade President Truman to act decisively against discrimination by the Washington Capitol Transit Company. When he died in 1950 Houston was widely recognized as one of the chief architects of the desegregation campaign in America.

Everyone living in the South, male and female, African American and white, knew their place in the society. The NAACP was the interloper, the outside agitator who threatened the established order. It was a very dangerous role for the organization and for all those African Americans who supported it, joined it, and became plaintiffs in lawsuits against the South's "virtues."

Margold left the NAACP in 1933, and the task of implementing the strategy was left to the two men who would come to be recognized as the giants of African American legal advocacy,

Charles Hamilton Houston and Thurgood Marshall. Houston, a graduate of Amherst and the Harvard Law School, at the young age of 34 years became the Assistant Dean of Howard Law School in 1929 and remained the dean until he went to the NAACP as its initial Special Counsel in 1934. He created a first-rate law school, accredited by the legal association within a few years of his taking over the law school. (He could not be named Dean of the Law School, for Howard, funded by Congress, had to have white persons in such positions.)

The key belief of Houston was that lawyers were "social engineers," men who had to be trained to use the law to achieve desired social and political goals. He advocated the principle that became the basic NAACP strategy for a quarter of a century: Changing and invalidating the laws will change society; avoid violent confrontations with the white power structure while the legal social engineers challenge racial segregation and discrimination in local, state, and federal courts. Houston created a rigorous law school curriculum at Howard Law School and placed great demands on the African American students who came to study at what was to become the major bastion of civil rights legal training.

Thurgood Marshall, who had grown up in segregated Baltimore, had gone to Lincoln University, a predominantly African American undergraduate institution. Because he was African American, he was not admitted to the University of Maryland's law school and instead attended Howard University's Law School. Thurgood was Houston's star pupil and, in 1935, two years after graduating first in his class at Howard, Marshall was invited to join with Houston as the legal arm of the NAACP.

In 1936, he was brought into the NAACP as Assistant Special Counsel and, in 1938, when Houston left the NAACP because of health problems, Thurgood Marshall became Special Counsel, a position he held for over 24 years. (In 1950, Marshall was appointed Director-Counsel of the newly created corporation that would act as the legal arm of the NAACP. It was called the Legal Defense and Educational Fund, Inc., or simply "the Inc. Fund.") The Inc. Fund's task, its central purpose as written in its charter of incorporation (New York), was to provide free legal aid to African Americans who suffered legal injustice and who could not afford an attorney to argue their case in court. Thurgood Marshall's prime focus was on the obvious reality that had escaped many Northern "liberals": Racial segregation, Jim Crowism, was a tool for maintaining the social, political, legal, and basic human subordination of African Americans by whites.

Houston and Marshall were the mainstays of the legal office of the NAACP. Indeed, there would always be a small legal staff working in the Inc. Fund's New York office. In 1954, the year the Supreme Court struck down the *Plessy* precedent, there were only five full-time legal staffers in the office. In 1936, there were the two men, the mentor Houston and his star law school student Marshall, to implement a litigation strategy that would end racial segregation and discrimination in America. It was a herculean task and it took men like Houston and Marshall to accomplish it.

For these two men, the NAACP had to force the South to equalize expenditures by petitioning the courts, ultimately the U.S. Supreme Court, to review litigation that challenged racial segregation in a variety of areas, including education, voting discrimination, housing, transportation, and criminal justice. The hope, and their ultimate goal; was to convince the U.S. Supreme Court, in education litigation, to overturn the 1896 precedent that legitimatized Jim Crowism, *Plessy* v. *Ferguson.*

Short of that, their tactical strategy was to convince the courts that Jim Crow separation of the public schools as practiced was unconstitutional because there was no equality of facilities and faculty salaries: Either order equalization of expenditures and teacher salaries or desegregate the schools themselves. Since the local and state political and educational leaders were categorically unwilling to move in these directions, the task was to convince courts, through legal argumentation, to order such action to occur in these segregationist communities in the South.

For Marshall there was a great deal of satisfaction when Maryland courts ordered the University of Maryland, in 1936, to allow African Americans to be admitted to the University. Five years after the University rejected Marshall, it was attorney Marshall who forced the University, through litigation, to open its door to African Americans. That 1936 case, *Donald Murray* v. *University of Maryland,* began the battle in which the NAACP directly challenged, and ended, the practice of segregation.

The Houston-Marshall duo worked together through 1938, when Houston stepped aside and Marshall took over the leadership responsibilities, to bring litigation that challenged separate but equal as practiced. At the same time, they began preparing for the time when the NAACP would challenge the constitutionality of the separate-but-equal policy itself. Changing such a national public policy, validated by the U.S. Supreme Court by a seven-to-one vote, was a daunting challenge, for the NAACP had to develop a line of legal argumentation that would persuade the U.S. Supreme Court to overturn a precedent that had been policy for over 50 years. Their hope was that they could convince the justices sitting on the Court that *Plessy* "stigmatically" injured African Americans, physically as well as psychologically, by denying them the equal protection of the laws and should be overturned in favor of the concept of racial equality.

Developing and implementing this legal strategy for African Americans was not an easy task, both outside the NAACP and internally as well. There were members of the NAACP who criticized the pressure group's commitment to the litigation strategy to achieve its goals of justice and equality. W. E. B. Du Bois, a major African American leader, left the NAACP in 1934 because of the conflict he had with the legal strategists. He argued that, with all the litigation, African Americans in 1934 were worse off, economically, politically, and socially, than they were in 1915. After Du Bois left the organization (he was the editor of its monthly journal, *Crisis,* from the inception of the organization to 1934), others in the NAACP continued to criticize the emerging legal strategy outlined by Margold and tactically implemented by Houston and then by Marshall. For them, it was better to work within the existing Jim Crow system, with all its faults, than to risk legal actions that would just stir up hatred and fear on the part of whites, responses that inevitably, and tragically, led to hooded terrorism, lynchings, beatings, and loss of jobs and homes.

Local and state public policy with respect to the treatment of African Americans was so firmly rooted in the soil and psyche of the white South that most African Americans did not believe that litigation could change these segregationist policies very easily, if at all; better to live with the recognized evil than act and trigger even more terror and violence against African Americans. Houston and Marshall, however, believed that the only way to change this entrenched public policy of racial segregation and discrimination was to go to court. For the NAACP, it was sue in court or live with the brutality of Jim Crowism and second-class citizenship.

Beyond the internal carping about the legal strategy, yet another major problem the two men faced was a practical one. They had to work with local cooperating attorneys in these Southern states when filing law suits that challenged racial segregation policy, and that proved to be an immense problem, because there were few competent African American lawyers in these Southern states (for example, two in Mississippi, three in Louisiana, twelve in Georgia). Moreover, many of these African American lawyers were not interested in associating themselves with a radical civil rights pressure group such as the NAACP. They wanted to maintain their local practice, and cooperating with New York lawyers trying to overturn Jim Crow was not the way to increase their legal business in, say, Jackson, Mississippi!

Finally, after (1) quelling internal criticism, (2) finding a handful of local attorneys that they could work with to initiate lawsuits, and, crucially (3) finding African Americans willing to become plaintiffs in these highly visible, very controversial lawsuits, Houston and Marshall then faced the daunting task of convincing a bevy of state and federal white judges, including the nine justices of the U.S. Supreme Court, to accept the legal arguments of this African American pressure group.

The two men were steely tough and single-minded in their efforts to attack the evils of racial segregation and discrimination. The broadly defined evils they attacked, again and again, and after 1938, with Thurgood Marshall leading the charge, were lynch mobs, Jim Crowism, economic and political suppression, housing discrimination, cruel, unabating poverty. Although the pressure group could try to influence Congress and the public, the NAACP could succeed in wiping out these evils only through the courts. African American attorneys, the "social engineers" trained by Houston, were the men and, later on, the women who would wipe out these racial policies.

The concept of Rule of Law was for Houston, Marshall, and dozens of other African American lawyers who worked for the NAACP the only way

to topple the policy of racial segregation and discrimination in America. Ironically, these African American lawyers, men who had suffered indignity after indignity in courts of law throughout the South, were the hardy advocates for change through the Rule of Law.

Convincing the Court that an earlier precedent of the Court was incorrect is the most difficult challenge that any lawyer faces, regardless of race or color. Judges had to be persuaded that the earlier precedent, followed nationally for over 50 years, was erroneous and thus subject to overturn. Sitting on the Court during this period of NAACP legal activity were dozens of justices, some from the South (Justice Hugo Black of Alabama, who was a member of the Alabama chapter of the Ku Klux Klan before becoming a member of the Court; Justice Stanley Reed of Kentucky; Chief Justice Fred Vinson of Kentucky; and Justice Tom C. Clark of Texas, among others), who held very different views about overturning precedent, the value of *Plessy,* and the very constitutionality of Jim Crowism.

Some justices adamantly supported the continuation of the *Plessy* doctrine and would not consider overturn as a valid judicial action, while others were considered friends of the NAACP and would favorably respond to the legal appeals of the African American pressure group. Indeed, one of the justices sitting on the Court was Felix Frankfurter, who had been a member of the NAACP's legal counsel advisory staff and who had, in 1930, recommended Nathan Margold for the task of developing a legal strategy for the NAACP. The NAACP thought that Frankfurter was an ally they could count on in the upcoming litigation effort to attack racial segregation. As events unfolded, the organization's faith in Frankfurter's help was somewhat misplaced.

After 1939, Marshall and his small legal staff began to implement the first of the Margold strategies: calling on the courts to order equalization of educational and other segregated facilities in the hope that this huge financial headache would force local and state political leaders to eschew Jim Crowism for integration. Marshall and his small staff of lawyers, mostly Howard Law School graduates, began the work of implementing the equalization of facilities strategy outlined by Margold. His discussions with his legal staff were more like open forums where various tactics were knocked about and different arguments were discussed and debated. Selecting cases very carefully, that is, selecting education cases where the likelihood of success in the courts was the greatest, Marshall and his lawyers continued to hammer away, indirectly, at the *Plessy* precedent, hoping that local and state segregationist leaders would change the policy because of the financial costs associated with providing equal facilities for African American school children and for those African Americans attending graduate and professional schools.

In this time, from 1938 to 1945, Marshall was also arguing and frequently winning court cases that focused on police brutality against African Americans. A critically important victory for Marshall and the NAACP, and for the entire society, came in *Chambers* v. *Florida,* a 1940 case involving four African Americans who confessed to murdering an elderly white man—but only after eight days and nights of continual police questioning without the benefit of attorneys present on their behalf. In a moving opinion, Justice Hugo Black, the former Klansman from the state of Alabama, speaking for a unanimous Supreme Court, overturned their convictions:

> Under our constitutional system, courts stand against any winds that blow as havens of refuge for those who otherwise might suffer because they are helpless, weak, outnumbered, or because they are non-conforming victims of prejudice and public excitement. Due process of law commands that no such practice as that disclosed by this record shall send any accused to his death. No higher duty, no more solemn responsibility, rests upon this Court, than that of translating into living law and maintaining this constitutional shield.

This was one of Thurgood Marshall's 29 successes in bringing litigation into the U.S. Supreme Court. However, while it established a precedent regarding police interrogations, it was a tragic victory. Isaac Chambers, one of the four young African Americans falsely accused and convicted of murder was so profoundly affected by the trauma of the trial and conviction and sentence of death that he suffered a mental breakdown and was hospitalized in a mental institution, languishing there for the remainder of his life.

Thurgood Marshall quickly became known across the South as "Mr. Civil Rights." He traveled extensively, from one Southern state court to another, working with local African American

Hugo Black *(1886–1971)*

Hugo Black was associate justice of the Supreme Court from 1937 until 1971. During those vital years of his judicial career Black emerged as a major figure in the development of a liberal philosophy of government. Black had been an Alabama lawyer and a senator from that state from 1927 to 1937. As a senator he was a proponent of many of the more progressive New Deal measures, most notably the Wages and Hours Law of which he was a sponsor.

When President Franklin Delano Roosevelt appointed Hugo Black to the Court in 1937 there was bitter opposition from the public and the Senate because of Black's earlier membership in the Ku Klux Klan. However, Black became one of the Court's staunchest defenders of civil liberties, especially against perceived violations of freedom of speech, freedom of religion, and due process of law.

attorneys to bring suit against racial segregation or to defend African Americans accused of serious criminal behavior. Soon the words of hope for African Americans in the rural South were: "Thurgood is coming."

Annually, he would travel tens of thousands of miles across the South, in dilapidated cars and buses and in Jim Crow railroad cars. Because of the Jim Crow reality in the South, there were no hotels for Marshall to stay in while he appeared in court, so local African Americans, at great risk to themselves (for housing "that radical New York Nigger lawyer"), would provide a place for Marshall to stay. There were few places for him to eat his meals in these Southern segregated towns, so Marshall either ate and drank pop from vending machines or had sandwiches made by local African Americans. It was a harsh existence and yet Marshall, Mr. Civil Rights, did it without thinking twice. Literally, if he did not get into that local court in some Godforsaken hamlet in Georgia, there would be no one else to defend African Americans.

His reputation was so great that when he arrived in a small town in Kentucky or Alabama or Georgia to argue a case on behalf of the NAACP, local white high schools and local white small businesses would close for the day to see this "New York Nigger" do his thing in the courtroom. This was not without danger, and many times Thurgood Marshall was told to be out of town before the sun set, and on a few occasions, including an incident in Kentucky in 1946, he was almost lynched by angry whites who would follow him out of town, stop his car, force him out, and threaten death.

By 1938, the NAACP and the Inc. Fund, led by Marshall, instituted three different types of school segregation and discrimination suits: desegregation of professional and graduate schools, equalization of the salaries of African American and Caucasian school teachers and administrators, and suits challenging the inequities in the physical facilities of African American public schools in the segregated separate-but-equal *Plessy* context. (In 1946, in Mississippi, African American teachers received a $426 annual salary, whereas white school teachers received $1,211.)

All told, by the time of the 1954 *Brown* litigation, Marshall had brought 34 such cases to the Supreme Court, winning all but four of them and thereby changing the local and state policies regarding racial segregation and discrimination. For Marshall and the NAACP Inc. Fund, it was an attrition strategy that set the stage for the overturn of *Plessy*.

Through 1947, although winning cases that called for better facilities, admission of African Americans to graduate school, equalization of salaries, and freedom in interstate travel, Marshall seldom mentioned the second strand of the Margold plan: a direct legal assault on the constitutionality of segregated education, which meant a frontal attack on the continued constitutional viability of *Plessy*. Marshall clearly knew that this attack had to happen; it was just a question of when and where it would occur. *Plessy* had to be overturned to resolve the problems African Americans faced in the society.

The Second World War ushered in the modern age of racial conflict in America. It turned out to be a great leveler with regard to relations between white Americans and African Americans. African American soldiers came back from the war with a different attitude toward Jim Crowism.

Racial tensions heightened after the war because of African Americans' new demands for rights and the subsequent increase in terror and intimidation by whites in response to these new demands by local African Americans. And it was focused primarily in the old traditional South, where, in 1945, 75 percent of the 13 million African Americans still lived.

It took African American leadership to marshall these new feelings that stirred in the minds and souls of the veterans. These new leaders, beginning with Martin Luther King Jr., would come in 1955 and the years that followed. For the moment, after 1945, the NAACP benefited from this new, aware African American constituency, and many of the veterans, men such as Aaron Henry and Medgar Evers, both of Mississippi, became local and state NAACP leaders.

In 1947, Marshall saw that the time had come to attack *Plessy* directly:

> You cannot accomplish [equality] by giving lip service to opposition to Jim Crow education and then continuing to build monuments to this segregation in the form of Jim Crow schools in order to establish "Jim Crow DeLuxe" [schools]. The only sane approach is a direct attack on segregation [*Plessy*] per se.

In an article in the Baltimore *Afro-American,* Thurgood Marshall told the NAACP and the South that the Inc. Fund was ready and that it would:

> attack the separate but equal doctrine by establishing in court—by a preponderance of evidence (scientific, social, biological)—that there was no rational basis for race based distinctions. [To this time] NAACP lawyers in order to get the campaign under way accepted the doctrine that the state could segregate . . . provided equal accommodations were afforded. . . . Now the NAACP is making a direct, open, all-out fight against segregation. There is no such thing as 'separate but equal.' Segregation itself imports inequality.

All in all, from 1947 through its victory over separate but equal in 1954, Marshall and the NAACP Inc. Fund brought class action suits in eight cases. These suits involved, between 1947 and 1950, three suits involving graduate and professional educational discrimination in Texas and Oklahoma.

Marshall brought these suits to persuade the Supreme Court to end a Southern state policy of not allowing African Americans to enter white-only graduate and professional schools. The state policy was very segregationist: African Americans had to go to their school; if none existed in the state, then the state could send the African American to a neighboring state that admitted African Americans to its professional or graduate schools or else had an existing separate African American graduate or professional school.

Texas had established an African American law school with three faculty members and 10,000 books in the law library. The school was located in three basement rooms in a state building in Austin, Texas, to avoid admitting African Americans to the all-white University of Texas Law School.

Marshall, on behalf of Mr. Sweatt, an African American who wanted to attend the University of Texas Law School, sued the state of Texas, arguing that the law school established exclusively for African Americans could not provide them with a legal education equal to that offered to whites. In an Oklahoma case, Marshall, on behalf of a 68-year-old African American educator, Mr. McLaurin, who had been admitted to the formerly all-white University of Oklahoma Graduate School of Education but once admitted, found himself totally segregated from the other students, all white, in class, in the library, and in the cafeteria.

Marshall's legal strategy was to show the justices of the U.S. Supreme Court, for both cases had wound their way from state court to the Supreme Court, that a good education in a professional school or a graduate school, called for a mix of students and faculty and that a segregated education was scientifically unjustifiable, socially destructive, and legally unconstitutional. As part of his strategy, he used the expert testimony of scholars and deans.

The Court, however, was very reluctant to do any overruling of *Plessy*. Frankfurter, the one-time legal counsel to the NAACP, wrote the Chief Justice, Fred Vinson, of Kentucky, and said bluntly:

> It seems to me desirable now not to go a jot or tittle beyond [where the Court has been on this issue. We cannot overturn *Plessy*]. The shorter the opinion, the more there is an appearance of unexcitement and inevitability about it, the better.

Writing for a unanimous Court, Vinson ordered Texas to admit Sweatt to the University of Texas Law School because the Court "found no substantial equality in the educational opportunities

While the *Brown* decisions began the end of racial segregation, the acts of protesters and activists nationwide have contributed much to the desegregation process.

afforded white and Negro law school students by the state." However, Vinson added that the Court did not feel the need "to reach [Sweatt's and Marshall's] contention that *Plessy* v. *Ferguson* should be re-examined in light of contemporary knowledge respecting the purposes of the Fourteenth Amendment and the effects of racial segregation."

In the McLaurin case, Vinson wrote, also for a unanimous Court, that the segregation experienced by the African American educator was unconstitutional because it restricted "his ability to study, to engage in discussions, and exchange views with other students and, in general, to learn his profession." Sweatt went on to complete his legal studies at the University of Texas and became the first African American graduate of the law school. Unfortunately, McLaurin's stressful experiences while the case was moving in the courts led to his withdrawing from the University of Oklahoma.

Thurgood Marshall and his small staff of five lawyers in the Inc. Fund were gloomy after these decisions. Marshall had hoped that the Court would address the constitutionality of separate but equal facilities itself, that is, the continued constitutionality of *Plessy*. But, as was the case throughout his life as a legal advocate for the NAACP, Marshall did not spend much time brooding over these cases. Just as these higher education cases were being announced, the NAACP moved to challenge separate-but-equal educational facilities in public schools across the South and Southwest.

The *Brown* Decisions, 1954–1955, Cautiously Begin the End of the Policy of Racial Segregation

By 1950, 17 southern and border states and the District of Columbia had a system of de jure segregated public school facilities. Four other states, including Kansas, permitted school districts to choose to use separate-but-equal schooling in the public schools.

By 1950, Thurgood Marshall and the NAACP Inc. Fund had prepared the ground for challenging separate-but-equal public school segregation in four states (South Carolina, Virginia, Delaware, and Kansas) and the District of Columbia. The decision to frontally attack *Plessy* closed one era in the NAACP's attack on segregation but opened wide another era.

In all five cases, African American plaintiffs had tried, unsuccessfully, to obtain admission to public schools on a nonsegregated basis. Given the existence of *Plessy,* in each case the petitioners lost in the local courts, and Thurgood Marshall took direct appeal from the district courts to the U.S. Supreme Court. For him the major question was whether "the Court was now ready to meet the NAACP's direct challenge of segregation per se as unconstitutional."

In June 1952, the Court announced that it would hear the cases, brought together under the name of *Brown* v. *Board of Education of Topeka, Kansas,* in December 1952. Clearly, the stage was set for the direct challenge to *Plessy,* the 1896 precedent that had been used for half a century in the South to establish separate and unequal facili-

ties for African Americans. The cases were consolidated, as Justice Tom C. Clark, an Associate Justice from Texas, noted, "so that the whole question [of the validity of *Plessy*] would not smack of being a purely Southern one."

At the trial level, in all five cases, Marshall and his NAACP legal staff, working with local African American attorneys in these trial courts, presented expert witnesses in order to develop the argument that segregated young African Americans were adversely affected psychologically by the segregation and that they suffered "stigmatic injury." For the NAACP lawyers, equality of school expenditures, and other such measures, without integration would not resolve the problem of African American identity, a problem that had become the major one for African Americans living in a segregated society.

Although (Justices Hugo Black and William O. Douglas) would have tackled the *Plessy* matter head on and voted to overturn the 1896 precedent, most of the other justices were very concerned about the impact of an overturn of *Plessy*. Justices Frankfurter and Jackson believed that the Court "was nowhere near ready to take on the issue" and that most of the justices were willing to procrastinate on hearing the matter. As Philip Elman, then with the Solicitor General's Office and a former law clerk to Frankfurter, said: "The Court's strategy . . . was to delay, delay—putting off the issue as long as possible." For Frankfurter, the concern about using one's own private feelings to decide the issue of segregation was great. He said to his brethren:

> However passionately any of us may feel, however fiercely any one of us may believe that such a policy of segregation as undoubtedly expresses the tenacious conviction of Southern states is both unjust and shortsighted, he travels outside his judicial authority if on the basis of his private feelings he declares unconstitutional the policy of segregation.

Furthermore, he, along with Jackson and one or two other justices, was concerned about the impact on the nation if the Court overturned the policy of racial segregation that had existed, legitimately, since the end of the nineteenth century, and ordered immediate integration of the public schools. The key problem was, for them, the practical impact of such a judgment. Would the Court order be obeyed? Would it be disobeyed by the local governments? If so, what could be done about such willful disobedience to an order of the Court? Could an order ending segregated educational facilities and replacing separate-but-equal schools with integrated schools be carried out without chaos, rioting, bloodshed, and anarchy?

The Chief Justice, Fred Vinson, of Kentucky, was not as uncertain as Frankfurter and Jackson. He was unwilling to accept the argument, put forward by Thurgood Marshall, that *Plessy* was no longer a viable precedent for the nation. It was precedent for over 50 years and Vinson was not ready to change it. Fellow Southerners on the Court, Tom C. Clark (Texas) and Stanley Reed (Kentucky), agreed with their chief about the continued validity of the *Plessy* doctrine.

With all these views expressed by the justices, it was not surprising that the Court did indeed procrastinate. It was a divided, deeply split Court that discussed the cases after the oral argument ended in December 1952. The NAACP argument presented by Marshall, in which the civil rights organization had, radically, refused to concede equality without an end to separate but equal, was the most militant position the NAACP had ever taken in its 42-year history. But, as Marshall had concluded barely five years earlier, it was time to attack *Plessy* frontally.

In May 1953, the Court issued an order that concealed its deep-seated division on the question of overturning *Plessy.* It scheduled reargument for the upcoming Term of the Court for all five cases and developed five questions for both sets of lawyers to address. These were the procrastination questions, and the rescheduling until the following October 1953 gave the Court additional time to ponder the fundamental question that Thurgood Marshall had raised for the NAACP. The Court asked the lawyers for answers to the following questions: What was the congressional intent of the legislators who drafted the Civil War Amendments? What was their understanding of public school education when they drafted the Amendments? Does the federal judiciary have the authority to end public school segregation? What kinds of remedies could the Court fashion if it had authority to end segregated schooling? Was *Plessy* consistent with the Fourteenth Amendment?

The Court also asked the U.S. government to file a brief with the Court on these questions and on the general question of the constitutionality of

Earl Warren *(1891–1974)*

Earl Warren was born on March 19, 1891, in Los Angeles, California, into a Scandinavian immigrant family. As fourteenth chief justice of the United States (1953–69) he led the Supreme Court toward a number of its landmark civil rights decisions. Among these was the 1954 unanimous decision of the Supreme Court, which ended school segregation in America: the vital *Brown* v. *Board of Education* case. Warren also paved the way toward the Court's voting rights decisions, the reapportionment decisions, and a number of cases that expanded the rights of accused persons in ways that changed the nature of criminal justice administration in the United States. Indeed, it has been said that Earl Warren helped create a "revolution" of rights in America.

None of this vast liberal shift in rights policy was foreseen when President Eisenhower appointed Warren as chief justice in 1953 to succeed Fred M. Vinson in that post. Warren had supplied Eisenhower with important political support in the presidential campaign of 1952 and became Eisenhower's first appointment to the Supreme Court. Warren's career before coming to the Supreme Court was essentially legal and political. At first he was a city attorney in Oakland, California, and rose to become Alameda County district attorney. Warren served as state of California attorney general from 1939–43 (including a period during World War II when Japanese Americans from California were interned in "relocation centers"). From 1943 to 1953 Warren was governor of California. In 1948 Warren ran as vice-presidential candidate with Thomas Dewey in an unsuccessful Republican party campaign.

While chief justice, Earl Warren headed the commission that investigated the assassination of President John Kennedy. He retired from the Supreme Court in 1969 and died five years later in 1974. In his *Memoirs* (1977) Warren wrote that he was not "an inspired student." He explained, "I did well in the subjects I liked, . . . but was lackadaisical in the others, to my lasting regret." The *Memoirs* also describe Warren's important role in shaping American rights policies.

segregated education. The Solicitor General's Office worked on the brief and, for the first time since *Plessy,* the national government called for an overturn of the precedent. However, the Solicitor General's office asked the Court for a delay from October to December (1953) in order for the government to prepare the *amicus curiae* brief. It was granted and the rearguments were postponed until December 7, 1953. Then fate intervened, for on September 8, 1953, Chief Justice Vinson suffered a massive heart attack and died. Hearing of the Chief's passing, Frankfurter remarked to his law clerks: "This is the first indication that I have ever had that there is a God."

Within a short time, President Eisenhower appointed California Governor Earl Warren to the center seat on the Court. Warren, a very popular Republican governor, had been the Party's vice-presidential candidate in 1948, and during the recent 1952 Republican convention, had strongly supported candidate Eisenhower and brought his California delegation over to Ike's side. As a reward, Eisenhower promised Warren the first available seat on the Court. Less than seven months later, Warren was nominated to fill the first available seat, that of the Chief Justice of the United States.

The appointment was a dramatic one with regard to the school segregation litigation that faced the Court. Warren, in less than six months, turned the Court from a five-to-four split tribunal to a unanimous nine-to-zero Court in favor of overturning *Plessy.* Moving skillfully among the justices, after hearing the oral arguments in December 1953, Warren was ultimately able to bring all of them around to his position that segregation was inherently unequal and violative of the Constitution.

In the conference session after the December 1953 oral arguments, he told his colleagues, fairly bluntly: "I don't see how in this day and age we can set any group apart from the rest and say that they are not entitled to exactly the same treatment as all others. [The Civil War Amendments] were intended to make the slaves equal with all others. Personally, I can't see how today we can justify segregation based solely on race." He argued that *Plessy* was premised on the concept of the inherent inferiority of the colored race and "if we are to sustain segregation, we must do it on that basis." If any of his colleagues wanted to defend the continued vitality of *Plessy,* they had to argue that the African American is racially inferior to the white

person. None rose to the challenge in the conference, although Stanley Reed remained opposed to overturn *Plessy* until the last moment, and Warren set about the task of writing an opinion for the Court that all nine justices could agree on. Warren's message was a clear one and would have overjoyed Thurgood Marshall. *Plessy* was morally wrong, it violated fundamental standards of decency, and it classified people as inferior simply because of the color of their skin.

Throughout the winter and early spring of 1954, Warren spoke to all the brethren, and finally convinced Reed that, for the sake of unanimity on such an important issue, he should join the Court majority—which he did. On Monday, May 17, 1954, Warren read the opinion for a unanimous Court.

> In approaching this problem, we cannot turn the clock back to 1868 when the [14th] Amendment was adopted, or even to 1896 when *Plessy* v. *Ferguson* was written. We must consider public education in the light of its full development and its present day place in American life throughout the nation. Only in this way can it be determined if segregation in public schools deprives these plaintiffs of the equal protection of the laws. . . . To separate them [African American children] from others of similar age and qualifications solely because of their race generates a feeling of inferiority as to their status in the community that may affect their hearts and minds in a way unlikely ever to be undone. . . . Therefore, we conclude—unanimously—that in the field of public education the doctrine of "separate but equal" has no place. Separate educational facilities are inherently unequal.

For white segregationists in the South and elsewhere, May 17 became known, instantly, as "Black Monday." Almost immediately after the Court's opinion was announced, segregationist whites in the South, and Southern U.S. senators and congressmen in Washington, D.C., began to plot a strategy that would evade, avoid, and delay the implementation of *Brown.* The congressional delegations introduced a "Southern Manifesto," written by Strom Thurmond of South Carolina and Harry Byrd of Virginia, and signed by all 19 Southerners in the Senate except for Tennessee Senators Albert Gore and Estes Kefauver and the Senate Majority Leader, Lyndon B. Johnson, from Texas. Another 84 Southern members of the U.S. House of Representatives signed it as well, although another 24 members did not.

The Manifesto was, simply put, a document of defiance and hatred of the *Brown* decision of the unanimous U.S. Supreme Court. Its foundation was the Tenth Amendment of the Constitution, and it maintained that the Supreme Court clearly abused their judicial power in their "unwarranted" decision of May 17, 1954. Since neither the Constitution itself nor the Fourteenth Amendment mentioned education, the Court had usurped power by forcing the South to end racial segregation in its educational facilities. The Manifesto ended with the pledge by the signers that they would "use all lawful means to bring about a reversal of this decision . . . and to prevent the use of force in its implementation."

The NAACP, on the other hand, while pleased with the Court's decision to overturn *Plessy,* was disappointed because the Court did not order an immediate end to school segregation. As Richard Kluger noted, "there was no dancing on the tables in Harlem," because the Court ordered both sides to direct their attention, in written briefs and oral argument during the following term of the court, to the question of how best to implement *Brown.*

For Thurgood Marshall and his staff, their work was just beginning. However, for all African Americans, May 17, 1954, was a day of rejoicing, for the overthrowal of *Plessy* was a watershed event in American history. As an African American reporter wrote: "'Black Monday' was the day we won; the day we took the white man's law and won our case before an all-white Supreme Court with a Negro lawyer. . . . And we were proud."

Brown moved African Americans from apathy to demands for equality and led, as will be seen shortly, to the birth of the modern civil rights movement in America. In many ways, *Brown* meant the beginning of work for the Court, for the NAACP, and for the local communities in the South whose constitutional foundation for state-enforced racial segregation had just been smashed.

The Court in 1954 dealt with the substantive question—the validity of *Plessy*—and had not examined how to go about fashioning a remedy that would enable the adversely affected white segregationist communities to obey the order of the Court. For the Court, as Frankfurter wrote in a note to the chief justice, "the most important problem [was] to fashion appropriate provisions against evasion [by the South]."

Thurgood Marshall's response to the Court the following April 1955 was direct: The Court

must order an immediate end to segregated schools within a year, two at the most. Justice Hugo Black was the only member of the Court to support Marshall's position. Black argued, in the Court's conference session after the oral arguments, that the Court should issue a decree on the matter, one that called for immediate school integration, "and quit. The less we say the better off we are. . . . Nothing could injure the Court more than to issue orders that cannot be enforced."

However, Justice Frankfurter was able to persuade the rest of the Court, including a reluctant Black, that (1) the U.S. District Court judges in the Southern states should have the responsibility for approving public school integration plans, and that (2) the standard for implementing the plans was to be a flexible one, taking into account a variety of local conditions, but that there should be school integration "with all deliberate speed."

The May 1955, *Brown, II* opinion of a unanimous Supreme Court, created a gigantic workload for the NAACP. The order of the Court meant that, in every school district, in every state that had segregated public education—thus in many thousands of school districts across the South and Southwest—local school board officials, under heavy and constant pressure by the white power structure in each town and city, had to draw up integration plans that met with the approval of the NAACP officials in that city or town and that finally passed muster when presented to the U.S. District Court judge sitting in a federal court in that part of the state.

That was the complexity that faced these persons if the town or city *obeyed* the order of the Supreme Court. There were many thousands of school districts, in the deep South (Mississippi, Alabama, Louisiana, Georgia, South Carolina, Florida, and Texas), whose leadership simply evaded or avoided or dramatically delayed following the order of the Court. And that meant that the NAACP had to go into federal district courts to have the federal district court judge intervene in order to begin to plan for an end to segregated public education.

The burden of enforcing the *Brown* decision of the Court fell on "58 lonely men," as one author referred to the U.S. District Court judges in the Southern and border states who had been given the enforcement responsibilities for school desegregation by the justices of the U.S. Supreme

Rosa Parks *(1913–)*

Rosa Parks has been called "the mother of the movement" for her bravery in Montgomery, Alabama, in a 1955 bus incident in that city. On December 1, 1955, as Rosa Parks was riding home from work, the bus driver ordered her to surrender her seat to a white man. She refused. For this offense against segregation Parks was arrested and fined the sum of $14. This was the spark that led to the bus boycott that began the civil rights movement.

Parks was born and raised in Alabama, attending racially segregated schools in that state. She studied at all-black Alabama State College. Later she joined the local NAACP chapter, eventually becoming the local NAACP secretary.

The bus boycott was organized by little-known African Americans who became involved in the protracted campaign to force the city of Montgomery, Alabama, to desegregate public transportation. In particular, Dr. Martin Luther King Jr. took the lead in the struggle to end the southern practice of racial segregation. The treatment given Rosa Parks was a symbol of all that was wrong with segregation. The long bus boycott ended on December 21, 1956, when the U.S. Supreme Court held that racial segregation on city buses was unconstitutional. Rosa Parks and Dr. King were heroes of a movement that eventually changed the laws of the nation to end racial discrimination.

For her efforts Rosa Parks was subjected to hostile acts and threats. She and her family moved from Alabama to Detroit, Michigan, in 1957. Rosa Parks continued to play an important role in the civil rights movement. She marched on Washington in 1963 and into Montgomery, Alabama, in 1965. Rosa Parks received the Martin Luther King Jr. Nonviolent Peace Prize in 1980 in recognition of her many years of dedication to the cause of ending racial discrimination. In 1987 she and her husband formed the Raymond and Rosa Parks Institute of Self-Development in Detroit, Michigan.

Court. Although there were some federal judges who were committed to a "good faith" effort to implement *Brown,* such as Frank Johnson of Alabama and S. Skelly Wright of Louisiana, there were many more "segregationists" sitting on these federal district court benches, men like Judge Wilson Warlick of North Carolina, who said that he was a "states' rights individual"; Judge Gordon West of Louisiana, who believed that the Fourteenth Amendment was "unconstitutional and a great tragedy"; and Judge William Atwell, of Texas, who continued to act as if, in his words, "the real law of the land is the same today as it was on May 16, 1954."

Simply, the politics of racial segregation took on a much different hue after 1955. As Thurgood wanly observed, after the *Brown, II* implementation order of the Court, the Inc. Fund had to become involved in "trench warfare" with the local white political and social power wielders in these thousands of districts across the South. "We have to go case by case, county by county, state by state" to battle segregation. By the early 1960s, the NAACP's Inc. Fund attorneys had filed over 300 school segregation cases in federal courts across the South. (In 1981, in Mississippi, for example, there were still school districts in the southeastern part of the state, Soucier, Mississippi, for one example, that had not yet integrated. A quarter of a century after *Brown* there were still Jim Crow public schools in the state.) It was not an easy task, and the NAACP's Inc. Fund attorneys remained bogged down in the courts with many hundreds of school segregation cases from 1956 onward. Even after the Supreme Court, concluded in 1968 that the time for "all deliberate speed" was over and that school districts had to "integrate now," the Inc. Fund continued to bring lawsuits into federal courts because local school boards were not acting to integrate immediately.

Interestingly, in the late 1950s, the U.S. Supreme Court used the *Brown* precedent to strike down many local statutes and ordinances that had segregated other public facilities such as parks, playgrounds, and golf courses. They would not even hold oral argument in these suits; they would summarily rule against the segregated facility in a short per curiam order, citing *Brown* as precedent for their order.

Through 1955, the American civil rights movement had only one cutting edge, and that was the NAACP lawyers implementing their litigation strategy. Coincidental with the *Brown* victory of 1954 and the weak implementation order in *Brown, II,* 1955, which created a very complex legal agenda for Thurgood Marshall and his small staff of NAACP lawyers, there emerged—suddenly and dramatically—in the South a modern civil rights movement that, for over a decade, between 1955 and 1965, was instrumental in changing both state and national policy in the areas of racial segregation and race discrimination.

In response to continued terror and violence, including lynchings of African Americans, African Americans began to marshall their forces in the effort to end the terror and to enlarge opportunities for them and for their children to participate in the good life in America. The civil rights movement took on a new look not only because the NAACP had, after 40 years in the legal wilderness of litigation in the state and federal courts, successfully challenged the *Plessy* doctrine, but because of a new African American civil rights protest strategy that was introduced for the first time in 1955: a form of Gandhian nonviolent direct action by organized groups of African Americans protesting racial segregation and discrimination.

While NAACP lawsuits, both before and especially after *Brown,* successfully struck down segregation in one area of public life after another, massive white Southern resistance, including terror and violence, mounted. It seemed to many African Americans and other civil rights supporters that more had to be done than suing in court to end segregation. Civil disobedience became the new strategy employed by protesting African Americans, complementing the NAACP's legal efforts to end racism and discrimination based on racism.

The year-long Montgomery, Alabama, bus boycott began in December 1955 when Rosa Parks, an African American, was arrested for refusing to give up her seat on a segregated bus to a white passenger. The boycott was led by a young, 25-year-old brand-new Christian minister, Dr. Martin Luther King Jr., and it involved about 50,000 African Americans living in Montgomery, Alabama, in the first nonviolent direct action against Jim Crowism. Initially called the Montgomery (Alabama) Improvement Association, MIA, it was shortly transformed into the first region-wide nonviolent direct-action civil rights

group, the Southern Christian Leadership Conference, SCLC, and King became its head.

Within a few years other groups were formed or were restrengthened for carrying out this new African American nonviolent direct-action protest strategy, including the Student Nonviolent Coordinating Committee, SNCC, and the Council on Racial Equality, CORE. In early 1960, SNCC college students in North Carolina began to use the sit-in to overcome racial segregation in places of public accommodation and, in 1961 through the passage of the 1965 Voting Rights Act, began voter registration drives in the deep South states of Georgia, Alabama, and Mississippi, the latter state referred to by SNCC workers as the "middle of the iceberg." Meanwhile, CORE workers took dangerous, bloody "freedom rides" from Washington, D.C., to the deep South (Alabama and Mississippi) to integrate interstate travel and public accommodations.

All these had the dramatic effect of involving the other two branches of the national government in the effort to redirect civil rights policy in America. As a consequence of NAACP legal victories, accompanied by massive nonviolent direct action, the Congress and the presidency became directly involved in the passage of legislation, the issuance of executive orders, and the use of federal marshalls and other federal employees to oversee registration and voting practices in the South. In addition, for the first time since the Civil War almost a century earlier, Presidents Eisenhower (R) and Kennedy (D) used federal troops in Mississippi, Alabama, and Arkansas, with accompanying violence and bloodshed, to enforce orders of the federal courts that were being turned aside by the white Southern segregationists in these states.

Conclusion: The Politics of Civil Rights in a Federal System

The first effort to address national and regional policies of racial segregation and race discrimination began in 1910 with the establishment of the NAACP. Since presidents, governors, Congress, and state legislators were all totally unresponsive to the demands of the African American pressure group's quest for equality of treatment, equal employment opportunity, and an end to terror and lynchings, the NAACP focused, beginning in 1915, on litigation as a strategy to achieve social change.

Case by case, placing themselves and their clients at great risk, Charles Hamilton Houston, Thurgood Marshall, and a very small band of other brave African Americans obtained victories in the form of court orders declaring various types of racial segregation unconstitutional. Finally, in *Brown*, in 1954, nine white men sitting on the Supreme Court overturned the foundation of Jim Crowism in the South, the fictitious separate-but-equal *Plessy* doctrine.

However, by 1955, it was clear that additional strategies for overturning the centuries-old commitment to white racial superiority were needed. Alone, the Supreme Court, even working closely with the NAACP, could not succeed in changing public policy. Legislators and executives, at national, state, and local levels, had to be prodded to action by a strategy other than the litigious one. The strategy, used successfully for a decade, was nonviolent direct action that forced national policymakers to respond to the cruelty and bigotry of the South in the form of civil rights legislation, voting rights legislation, aggressive Justice Department actions to protect civil rights workers and punish violators of their civil rights, and strongly worded executive orders that moved to a policy of affirmative action.

Thurgood Marshall was reluctant to endorse the radically new approach of the mass MIA-type boycott. But, in the end, he was compelled to use his Inc. Fund staff to defend the protesters when the cases were heard in court. The small staff of NAACP Inc. Fund lawyers defended MIA, SCLC, SNCC, and CORE protesters through all their nonviolent protest actions and subsequent arrests and imprisonment. For the legal staffers, it was a relief to do this type of advocacy, because it took them away from the onerous, chronic trench warfare of the never-ending school segregation litigation battles in the South.

However, Thurgood Marshall, who believed so strongly in the power and the authority of the Rule of Law, was continuously chagrined by the actions of the African American nonviolent direct action protesters and cried out: "All that walking was for nothing! They could just as well have waited while the bus case went up through the courts, without all the work and worry of the boy-

cott." However, one of the Montgomery, Alabama, African American participants, spoke for the thousands of marchers when he said this of Marshall's wry observations: "He wasn't there—he didn't know what it did *for us*, how proud we were that we walked all the way."

After the King boycott ended successfully, the NAACP ran into serious troubles in Alabama and other southern states. State attorneys general brought suit against the NAACP in state courts trying to close down the organization by trying to acquire the membership lists of the state NAACP affiliates. This lawsuit led to a decade of litigation and a number of Supreme Court decisions on behalf of the NAACP. However, the constant threat to the African American organization led to a dramatic loss of membership in these states. For NAACP leaders like Roy Wilkins, the executive director of the organization, it was the MIA boycott that put the NAACP out of business in Alabama and threatened the organization in other states.

In the late 1950s, the NAACP, the first major African American civil rights pressure group, an organization of lawyers and middle-class "black bourgeoisie," as SNCC literature pictured the group, whose primary strategy was to change society through changes in the law, was being overtaken by the more dynamic, action-oriented nonviolent direct-action civil rights groups. It was criticized by these new African American action groups (SCLC, SNCC, CORE) as too conservative and too cautious and too unwilling to organize the poor, uneducated African Americans living in the rural South and in Northern urban ghettos.

However, if it were not for the NAACP and especially the untiring work of Thurgood Marshall, the modern (1955–1965) civil rights movement would not have happened. *Brown* climaxed, for Marshall, his lawyer colleagues, and the NAACP, decades of injustice. He had led a legal revolution and, by 1955, other organized groups with younger leaders in the African American community were continuing the battles the NAACP Inc. Fund had waged and had won under Marshall's leadership.

Thurgood Marshall was to move on from the NAACP to government work. In 1961, he was appointed by President John F. Kennedy to serve as a federal judge on the Second Circuit U.S. Court of Appeals. He was only the second African American in American history to be appointed to the U.S. Court of Appeals. (Thurgood's friend, William Hastie, was the first African American ever appointed to the U.S. Court of Appeals.)

In 1965, Marshall became the U.S. Solicitor General, and, in 1967, President Lyndon B. Johnson, a Texas Democrat, named him to be the first African American Associate Justice of the U.S. Supreme Court. He served as an associate justice until his retirement in 1991. In January 1993, Thurgood Marshall passed away. He did more than any African American in the twentieth century to change the landscape of America and will always be remembered as Mr. Civil Rights.

Bibliography

Ayers, Edward L. *The Promise of the New South: Life After Reconstruction.* New York: Oxford University Press, 1992.

Baker, Liva. *The Second Battle of New Orleans: The Hundred Year Struggle to Integrate the Schools.* New York: HarperCollins, 1996.

Ball, Howard, and Philip Cooper. *Of Power and Right.* New York: Oxford University Press, 1992.

Belknap, Michael. *Federal Law and Southern Order.* Athens, Ga.: University of Georgia Press, 1987.

Duberman, Martin B. *Paul Robeson: A Biography.* New York: Ballantine, 1989.

Greenberg, Jack. *Crusaders in the Courts.* New York: Basic Books, 1994.

Kluger, Richard. *Simple Justice.* New York: Random House, 1975.

Peltason, Jack. *Fifty Eight Lonely Men.* Urbana, Ill.: University of Illinois Press, 1962.

Rowan, Carl T. *Dream Makers, Dream Breakers: The World of Justice Thurgood Marshall.* Boston: Little, Brown, 1993.

Woodward, C. Vann. *The Strange Career of Jim Crow.* New York: Oxford University Press, 1955, 1974.

Chapter **10**

Civil Rights
and Government

Michael Reggie and Steve Jenkins

How often have you heard someone say, or have you personally thought, "Excuse me, I have a right to my opinion!"? People often relay such thoughts and comments during heated discourse and debate. Believing in freedom of conscience and freedom of expression seems as integral to American identity as the declaration of the right to life, liberty, and the pursuit of happiness. Though some may accuse our citizens of constitutional illiteracy, the First Amendment seems personally profound and fundamental to most. Poll Americans on the street to identify their most important freedoms and they invariably note those embodied in the First Amendment. Americans see "We, the people" as sovereign. Embedded in the evolution of the United States, and in the respective state constitutions with their varied Declaration of Rights, is the struggle to secure these freedoms in times of tyranny. As we shall see, the struggle continues.

The Constitution Convention adopted the one and only Constitution of the United States in September of 1787. By September 1789, enough states had ratified the Constitution to make it the "supreme law of the land" (see body of Constitution, Article VI). What rights did the Constitution guarantee "We, the people"? The Preamble and text of the Constitution contain no expressed rights (see Preamble for wording). The only time the term "right" appears in the body of the Constitution is in Article III, Section 8. It gives power to Congress "to promote the progress of science and useful arts, by securing for limited times to authors and inventors the exclusive right to their respective writings and discoveries." So what did Congress have the power to promote? Did it only promote the right of an individual, acting as an author, artist, or inventor, to protect his or her inventions and intellectual property by means of congressionally enacted copyright and patent laws? Were the people living in the newly formed United States without any rights, except those guaranteed by Article III? What about rights in other Articles? It would be an intellectual challenge to examine and identify any

A strict reading of Amendment One reveals only 45 words: "Congress shall make no law respecting an establishment of religion, or prohibiting the free exercise thereof; or abridging the freedom of speech, or of the press, or the right of the people peaceably to assemble, and to petition the Government for a redress of grievances."

inalienable rights in the body of the Constitution, although most state constitutions included some form of a Bill or Declaration of Rights.

You might ask, if the supreme law of the land does not protect my fundamental rights, what does? Does might make right? Does the government and all who are "We, the people" have unlimited rights, since many often describe the Constitution as developing a "limited form of government"? What about your freedom of expression? What about protecting your right to practice or not practice religious beliefs? What about petitioning the government with grievances, as our colonists did with the Declaration of Independence? Even before the states adopted and ratified the Constitution, they could not answer these

questions without serious discussion, debate, and dynamic conflict. Again, many colonies, as newly formed states, had declarations of rights. However, many residents of the new states and nation were concerned that without a clear statement of rights accompanying the new Constitution, government tyranny or anarchy would confront the people. Many influential supporters of Constitutional ratification conditioned their support with a sacred promise to include a "Bill of Rights" to the Constitution.

The Bill of Rights

By 1791, and after much debate regarding what rights to include in the new Bill of Rights, "We, the people" had our first ten amendments, the "Bill of Rights." Since surveys 200 years later have suggested a lack of awareness and support for these fundamental rights, some might argue that "We, the people" no longer have a claim to these rights. Nevertheless, dare the government try to take one of our fundamental freedoms, and we might have fighting words and revolutionary war. And how are these rights ordered?

A strict reading of Amendment One reveals only 45 words: "Congress shall make no law respecting an establishment of religion, or prohibiting the free exercise thereof; or abridging the freedom of speech, or of the press, or the right of the people peaceably to assemble, and to petition the Government for a redress of grievances." Why did the framers of the Bill of Rights choose these precise words? Scholars have written and debated much about the wording and linguistic layout, but what do they mean? Most textbooks in civics and government classes might paraphrase these rights as:

- "the establishment clause"—government cannot establish an official religion nor can it favor any religion or nonreligion over another.

- "the free exercise clause"—a person has a right to his or her own religious beliefs without government interference with those beliefs.

- "freedom of speech"—the government cannot interfere with a person's freedom of expression.

- "freedom of the press"—the government cannot censor, interfere with, or control the press (i.e., newspapers, electronic media, all means of communication).

- "the right to peaceably assemble"—the government cannot prohibit the freedom to gather and associate.

- "the right to petition"—the people have the right to petition government to express grievances and to seek changes.

Does the Bill of Rights grant powers to the government, or does the wording of the First Amendment clearly limit government intrusion into our lives, our freedoms, our inalienable rights? The latter seems to be the intent, and through the doctrine of incorporation, the First Amendment protects persons from government interference and potential tyranny. Originally the Bill of Rights

applied only to the national government. Indeed, the first five words of the Fifth Amendment stated, "Congress shall pass no law. . . ." However, relying on the equal protection clause of the Fourteenth Amendment, the Supreme Court has taken some rights in the Bill of Rights and made these guarantees apply to state and local governments as well. This application is known as incorporation.

Much of the Bill of Rights including the rights under the First Amendment has been incorporated. Compared with the constitutions of states and other nation-states, the Constitution of the United States has few words, and limits the power of the federal government. Yet these few words have led to volumes of interpretation by judges (i.e., the judicial branch), by lawmakers (i.e., the legislative branch), by administrators (i.e., the executive branch), as well as in daily discourse and dispute by "We, the people."

If these freedoms are fundamental, why do we see and hear headlines that seem to contradict these sovereign, almost sacred, rights? In any given week, the headlines might blurt

"Ku Klux Klan Displays Cross at the Statehouse Plaza"

"Native Americans Fired and Denied Unemployment Benefits for Using Peyote in Religious Ceremonies."

"University Adopts Strict Speech Code to Curb Racism and Sexism"

"President Signs Communications Decency Act to Grant Greater Government Control Over Exploding Electronic Media"

"Supreme Court Upholds Injunction Restricting Picketing at Clinics Performing Abortions"

"Election Commission Rejects Petitions and Denies Candidate a Place on the Ballot"

Whatever our personal opinions regarding each of these headlines, Americans might sense a "wake-up" call developing over government intrusion into our daily lives. Furthermore, many Americans are concerned about the erosion of our First Amendment freedoms as they apply these headlines to everyday experiences. To better understand these conflicts, this chapter examines each freedom in historical and contemporary context.

The First Amendment's separation of church and state has led to bitter public policy debates and legal disputes, ranging from arguments over religious displays on public lands to prayers in public schools and legislative forums.

The Establishment Clause

Constitutional historian Leonard Levy has noted that from the first initiative of James Madison to keep the promise of a Bill of Rights that included religious, speech, press, and conscience freedoms, the wording and interpretations have been varied and volatile (see Levy's *The Establishment Clause* and *The Annals of Congress*). Many new states gave aid or support for religions, often calling the aid contributions instead of taxes. Legal historian Mark De Wolfe Howe characterized the government's response to the "establishment clause" as supporting "de facto Protestant establishment" until the twentieth century. Even today, government leaders express deeply divided convictions regarding the establishment of or support for religion. Recently, members of Congress are again introducing a proposed constitutional amendment to authorize public prayer in public schools. Chief Justice William Rehnquist wrote in an address before the Christian Legal Society, "The Establishment Clause did not require government neutrality between religion and irreligion nor did it prohibit the federal government from providing non-discriminatory aid to religion." (See *Wallace* v. *Jaffree.*) While serving as the Attorney General of the United States, Edwin Meese III declared, "the First Amendment forbad the establishment of a particular religion or a particular church. It also precluded the federal government from favoring one church, or one church group

over another. That's what the First Amendment did, but it did not go further. For example, it did not preclude federal aid to religious groups so long as that assistance furthered a public purpose and so long as it did not discriminate in favor of one religious group against another."

Prayer

These disagreements often lead to bitter public policy debates and legal disputes, ranging from arguments over religious displays on public lands to arguments over prayers in public schools and legislative forums. For example, is prayer that begins each day in public schools different from the prayer offered by a chaplain before each day's legislative session? Does such conduct in schools or in capitols suggest government support or favoritism toward religion?

The dispute regarding prayer in public schools is examined in the chapter on education (chapter 12). Conflicts confronting the "establishment clause" continue beyond the schoolhouse grounds. In 1983, plaintiffs asked the highest court of the land, the Supreme Court of the United States, to resolve a conflict regarding chaplains. The government often paid these chaplains at taxpayers' expense as they offered prayer before the beginning of each legislative session. This practice of clergy-initiated verbal prayer has had a long history in many local legislative bodies, state capitols, and even Congress. Ever since Nebraska became a state, the legislators have opened each session with vocal prayer. From 1965 to the 1983 case, *Marsh* v. *Chambers,* the same Presbyterian minister served as the chaplain of the Nebraska legislature, leading the lawmakers in prayer each morning. Taxpayers filed a formal complaint in the courts claiming that this practice clearly violated the establishment clause. The case finally worked its way to the Supreme Court. Writing for the majority, Chief Justice Warren Burger declared the practice so much a part of our historical custom (see legal historian Howe's aforementioned reference to "de facto establishment") that chaplain-led prayers before legislatures were "part of the fabric of society." (See *Marsh* v. *Chambers.*) To this day, many legislative bodies, including Congress, begin each day with a tax-paid chaplain leading the members in prayer. Justice William O. Douglas wrote a scathing dissent. Douglas claimed that the "establishment clause" embraced fundamental values protecting personal religious beliefs from government interference or support. Douglas argued that the establishment clause protected personal privacy in matters of religion, government neutrality towards religion, freedom of conscience, the prevention of government trivialization of religion (e.g., legislative-led prayers might seem as hollow as the passing phrase, "have a nice day"), and the withdrawal of religion from the legislative and political arenas. Burger, Rehnquist, and other justices insisted that several traditions historically hold our society together without necessarily establishing government favoritism towards religion. For example, our coins and bills contain the long-accepted phrase "In God We Trust." Article III of the Constitution grants expressed power to Congress to regulate the printing and coinage of money. Every time we pull out United States currency we continue this tradition.

Public Religious Displays

So chaplains praying before legislative and other government bodies day in and day out has become part of our historical tradition, much like the phrases "In God We Trust," and "God Save the United States and this Court," the traditional opening of the United States Supreme Court. If these traditions do not violate the establishment clause, then can government allow the use of public lands for potentially perceived religious prac-

tices (e.g., decorating Christmas trees and singing Christmas carols in city hall or in the courthouse square)? In fact, the president of the United States annually lights a Christmas tree in Washington, D.C. The city of Pawtucket, Rhode Island, like many other towns and cities across the nation, owned and annually erected a Christmas display in its downtown shopping district. The display in Pawtucket included, among other things, a Santa's house, a Christmas tree, cut-out animal figures at a manger, colored lights, and a life-sized nativity scene. Some residents of Pawtucket lodged a formal complaint in court, alleging that the nativity scene and general Christmas display proved city (i.e., government) support for Christianity. They claimed that government showed favoritism for one religion and violated the establishment clause. The case came before the U.S. Supreme Court, and like the Marsh case, Chief Justice Burger wrote the majority decision for the Court, with a concurring vote by Justice Sandra Day O'Connor providing the swing vote in a five-to-four decision. Like Marsh, Burger emphasized the historical tradition of conveying "Seasons Greetings" in a public way during the Christmas holidays. Justice Burger carefully reviewed each item found in the downtown shopping district. While admitting that the city paid for seasonal items with taxpayer's funds, Justice Burger maintained that the costs were minimal and the tradition of acknowledging religious influences in governmental settings had historical roots dating to the nation's founders. For example, he noted that the chambers of the U.S. Supreme Court were decorated "with a notable and permanent—not seasonal—symbol of religion: Moses with the Ten Commandments." (See *Lynch* v. *Donnely.*) Justice O'Connor's concurring opinion suggested that the Court consider not so much the strict standards of government "establishing" religious support but whether government action endorsed religion: "Applying that formulation (i.e., endorsement test) to this case, I would find that Pawtucket did not intend to convey any message of endorsement of Christianity or disapproval of non-Christian religions. . . . Celebration of public holidays, which have cultural significance even if they also have religious aspects, is a legitimate secular purpose. . . ." (See *Lynch.*) In another strongly worded dissent by Justice William Brennan, along with Justices Thurgood Marshall, Harry Blackmun, and John Paul Stevens, Brennan declared, "Under our constitutional scheme, the role of safeguarding our 'religious heritage' and of promoting religious beliefs is reserved as the exclusive prerogative of our Nation's churches, religious institutions, and spiritual leaders. Because the Framers of the Establishment Clause understood that "religion is too personal, too sacred, too holy to permit its 'unhallowed perversion' by civil (authorities), . . . the Clause demands that government play no role in this effort . . . the city's action should be recognized for what it is: a coercive, though perhaps small, step toward establishing the sectarian preferences of the majority at the expense of the minority, accomplished by placing public facilities and funds in support of the religious symbolism and theological tidings that the creche conveys." (See *Lynch*.)

Just five years after the *Lynch* case, the Supreme Court found itself again visiting the issue surrounding traditional religious displays on public land. In 1989, the Court considered the case of *Allegheny County* v. *American Civil Liberties Union, Greater Pittsburgh Chapter*. For many years, the Holy Name Society, a Roman Catholic group, had donated a creche to the Allegheny County Courthouse. They displayed it at the bottom of the Grand Staircase in the courthouse. The manger scene had an angel with a banner proclaiming, "Gloria in Excelsis Deo" (i.e., in Latin "Glory to God in the Highest"). Several residents of Pittsburgh, along with the Greater Pittsburgh Chapter of the American Civil Liberties Union, sued in federal court to halt this display on grounds that the display violated the establishment clause. This group of dissenting citizens also demanded that the federal court prohibit the city from displaying an 18-foot Chanukah menorah and 45-foot decorated Christmas tree outside the City-County Building. Again, the justices of the Court were divided in their opinions regarding these two challenges. Again, Justice O'Connor provided the swing vote. She wrote a concurring opinion. She concluded that the public display in front of the City-County Building did not violate the establishment clause, because it included a collection of seasonal symbols (e.g., the menorah, Christmas tree, and a sign saluting liberty). The collective symbols "conveyed a message of pluralism and freedom of belief during the holiday season." However, regarding the manger scene at the bottom of the Grand Staircase, O'Connor joined Justices Blackmun, Brennan, Marshall, and

Stevens in declaring that the manger scene violated the establishment clause. The controlling opinion, written by Justice Blackmun, concluded that the "crèche's angel's words endorse a patently Christian message: 'Glory to God for the birth of Jesus Christ.'" For these justices, along with O'Connor, the manger scene is clearly an endorsement of Christianity and therefore a violation of the establishment clause. Four justices dissented from this exception. Some legal scholars have suggested that Allegheny's dual decision will create confusion for many government officials as they decide what is permissible and what is not permissible in holiday displays. Others suggest that this decision encouraged the cluttering of public places with religious symbols to create a distinctly plural approach to religion without endorsing any one faith.

To confuse the matter more, in 1995, the Court had to revisit the establishment clause in a case examining whether the Ku Klux Klan (KKK) could raise a cross in the statehouse plaza in Columbus, Ohio. The KKK claimed that this religious symbol, alongside other religious symbols, did not violate the establishment clause. In this case, *Capitol Square Review & Advisory Board* v. *Pinette*, Ohio law granted the Review and Advisory Board the power to regulate public access to the statehouse plaza. Under state law, the square was available "for use by the public . . . for free discussion of public questions, or for activities of a broad public purpose." Generally, any group could use the square by simply completing an official application. The application primarily addresses issues of safety, sanitation, and noninterference with other uses of the square. The application was neutral in addressing the speech content of any proposed event.

In December 1993, the Advisory Board authorized the state to erect its annual Christmas tree, along with granting an application to place a menorah in the square near the Christmas tree. The Board also received an application from an officer of the Ohio Ku Klux Klan, requesting permission to erect a cross on the square during the same holiday season. Although the Board granted the application from the Jewish rabbi for displaying a menorah in the square, the Board denied the KKK application. The KKK appealed this decision in the United States District Court for the Southern District of Ohio. The Board argued that the presence

Ku Klux Klan march, 1925.

of the cross on the statehouse plaza would imply government endorsement of religion, specifically Christianity. The KKK argued that the raising of the cross was an entirely private expression entitled to First Amendment protection. Furthermore, because the Board had permitted the display of a traditional Christmas tree and menorah without expressing concern for the Board or state's endorsement of religion, then the Board's action clearly intended to discriminate against the Ku Klux Klan. This would deny them access to this well-established public forum. The Ohio Southern District federal court agreed with the Klan's arguments and ordered the Board to grant the permit to the KKK to erect the cross. The Board granted this permit, along with several subsequent requests from the KKK to continue to erect crosses on the statehouse square. However, the Board appealed the federal court's order to the Sixth Circuit, and ultimately, to the Supreme Court.

Justice Antonin Scalia wrote the leading opinion upholding the lower federal court orders and supporting the right of the KKK to erect the cross on statehouse grounds. Justice Antonin Scalia concluded that the city had made the public square available for private expression and that the mere presence of the cross would not, and should not, imply state endorsement or establishment of religion. Scalia relied on recent precedents (see *Lamb's Chapel* and *Widmar*) to conclude that observers should not take "perceived" endorsement as actual state endorsement. While acknowledging that such perception was likely, he

stated that the city could not deny the KKK's request solely because of "erroneous conclusions" by some of the public.

Justice Stevens wrote a scathing dissent, claiming that the controlling opinion completely ignored the power of public perception. If the city allowed the cross at the very seat of government, the capitol square, then most, or at least many people, would see some connection between the presence of the cross and the state's support for its public display. Furthermore, Justice Stevens pointed out that many other churches applied for permits to erect crosses that would surround the KKK cross and in effect demonstrate other Christian sects' opposition to the KKK cross. The very presence of so many crosses would imply government endorsement of the Christian religion. In addition, Justice Stevens asked what image the casual observer might take away if he or she saw a hooded Klansman holding, or standing next to, the very same cross. Stevens drew a political analogy. He noted that "neutral" third parties that permitted use of their property to display political campaign signs still appeared to carry with them the approval of the property owner in permitting the display of the campaign message. So it is with the state permitting the placement of various messages, including religious symbols, on government property. Such placement will imply support for the message, much like a yard sign implying endorsement of a candidate or a cause.

Stevens emphasized that the Court must examine this case, like all conflicts, in context. Here, the facts seemed clear that the KKK applied for a permit to erect a cross in direct defiance of the Board's approval of the rabbi's permit to erect a menorah as a symbol of celebrating the Jewish Chanukah. Instead of emphasizing pluralism and tolerance, the competing symbols seemed to promote intolerance.

Although the First Amendment wording seems clear about no government establishment of religion, the aforementioned conflicts and cases show that individual and group interpretation of what constitutes establishment varies immensely, even among members of the same Supreme Court. These precedents have led some to suggest that the Court should attach a list of exceptions after each clause of the First Amendment. For example, no establishment of religion, except

- Public prayers before legislative and other government bodies.

- Public displays, official symbols, and other public proclamations based on the historical origins and practices of religions as part of the nation's tradition, if there is no direct endorsement by government.

- Public places, such as town or courthouse squares, traditionally used for purposes of promoting a variety of opinions, either secular or religious.

The list is much longer. One might shorten or lengthen it depending on decisions of appeals courts, especially the U.S. Supreme Court. Judicial interpretation can touch all of our lives as we personally confront conflicts that engage our First Amendment freedoms.

Free Exercise Clause

Recall the language of the First Amendment, as incorporated by the Fourteenth Amendment: "Congress [i.e., government] shall make no law . . . prohibiting the free exercise [of religion]." Therefore, we might ask, may we practice any religious beliefs? Can we participate in a religion that accepts, or even, promotes polygamy, that is, marrying more than one wife or husband? (See *Reynolds* v. *United States,* 1878.) What if our religious beliefs include the sacrifice of animals *(Church of Lukumi Babalu Aye, Inc.* v. *City of Hialeah, 1993).* Would the Court protect human sacrifice under the free exercise clause? May a person refuse lifesaving medical treatment because his or her religious beliefs do not approve of human medical practices? What if medical treatment may improve the quality of someone's life, but religious beliefs prohibit the treatment? Does a parent have the right to refuse medical treatment for a child based on religious beliefs? May a person refuse to serve in the military if his or her religious beliefs oppose war?

When such conflicts rise to the threshold of being contested in court, then appeals court judges or the U.S. Supreme Court decide answers to these kinds of cases. For example, members of the Mormon church had believed in and practiced a form of polygamy for many years. The Mormon church believed that plural marriage was part of their religious practice that supported strong family values and spiritual growth. This belief, along with other beliefs that seemed to be out of the mainstream, led many people to persecute the Mormons. They burned out Mormon communities, tarred and feathered leaders, and forced them to move westward across the new, expanding United States. Many Mormons settled in what is now the state of Utah. During the Grant presidency (1869–1876), President Grant appointed James McKean as Chief Justice of the Utah Territorial Supreme Court and General J. Wilson Shaffer as territorial governor of this region. President Grant charged these two judicial and executive leaders

with the task of ending the Mormon practice of polygamy. Shaffer had hundreds of Mormons arrested and charged with violating a federal antibigamy statute. The Mormons chose one of their church leaders, George Reynolds, to test this federal law and attempt to have it declared unconstitutional on grounds it violated the Mormon's "free exercise" right guaranteed by the First Amendment. The government convicted Reynolds in territorial district court of practicing polygamy. The Utah Territorial Supreme Court upheld the conviction on appeal from Reynolds. Reynolds then appealed his case to the U.S. Supreme Court.

In 1879, the U.S. Supreme Court heard Reynolds's appeal and handed down a unanimous decision upholding the antibigamy statute and the conviction. It ruled that the practice of polygamy lay outside First Amendment protections. In writing the unanimous decision, Justice Waite acknowledged that the belief and practice of polygamy expressed a sincere religious belief of the Mormons. However, he said the practice of polygamy did not outweigh the greater public interest of protecting the social fabric of society from the destructive practice of having multiple wives. Furthermore, Justice Waite relied on the influence of Thomas Jefferson in concluding that "a wall of separation between church and state" existed, and if the state permitted polygamy as religious practice, this would tear the fabric of the wall into shreds. *Reynolds* v. *United States* has continued to spark public debate as controversies arise over state prohibitions of certain practices that might offend "public interest" (e.g., same-sex marriages, or opposition to the use of certain substances, like peyote, in Native American religious ceremonies). Some scholars believed that the Reynolds decision drew a distinct line separating belief from conduct—that is, you are entitled to hold any religious belief without government interference, but if the practice of your beliefs creates a greater harm to society, then government would have a compelling interest in restricting the practice.

"Strict Scrutiny"

Since Reynolds, the Court has had to decide many additional conflicts in this area. The Court has generally used a "strict scrutiny" test to decide the constitutionality of government action that in any way interferes with an individual or group's "free exercise" protection. Strict scrutiny means that the government must demonstrate a compelling interest before infringing on any person's "free exercise" claim.

For example, the Court has decided several cases involving the practices of the Jehovah's Witnesses. In 1940, Court ruled eight-to-one to uphold a requirement that Jehovah's Witness students stand and salute and pledge allegiance to the flag of the United States over objections by their parents on religious grounds. (See chapter 12, Education Rights, *Minersville School District* v. *Gobitis*.) In response, Americans attacked Jehovah Witnesses all across the country as unpatriotic. The U.S. Justice Department recorded over 300 attacks on Jehovah's Witnesses. The attackers burned their meeting halls to the ground and beat, tarred, and feathered Witnesses. In Litchfield, Illinois, "patriots" beat one Witness until he bent down and kissed the flag. In Richmond, West Virginia, a mob forced nine Witnesses to drink huge amounts of castor oil, causing severe stomach cramps and internal bleeding. Then the mob, led by the local sheriff, dragged them before a flagpole where the Sheriff preached, "For God and country we associate ourselves together for the following purposes: To uphold and defend the Constitution of the United States of America, to maintain law and order; . . . to safeguard and transmit to posterity the principles of justice, freedom and democracy." More than a hundred newspapers across the country decried this treatment of Jehovah's Witnesses. Even First Lady Eleanor Roosevelt spoke against the attacks. Political science and legal journals attacked the Supreme Court decision as turning away from the historic role of protecting minorities.

In 1943, the Court revisited the flag-salute case in *West Virginia State Board of Education* v. *Barnette*. Owing to a change of mind of some justices and the replacement of other justices by President Franklin Roosevelt, a new majority of the Court upheld the right of Jehovah's Witness students to refuse to pledge allegiance to an authority other than their religion and their higher appeal to Jehovah, their God. In the majority decision Justice Robert Jackson wrote one of the most powerful defenses of personal freedom in the history of the Court. He said

> The very purpose of the Bill of Rights was to withdraw certain subjects from the vicissitudes of political controversy, to place them beyond the reach of majorities and officials and to establish them as legal principles to be applied by the courts. One's right to life, liberty, and property, to free speech, a free press, freedom of worship and assembly, and other fundamental rights may not be submitted to vote; they depend on the outcome of no elections. . . . If there is any fixed star in our constitutional constellation, it is that no official, high or petty, can prescribe what shall be orthodox in politics, nationalism, religion, or other matters of opinion or force citizens to confess by word or act their faith therein.

Jackson's "fixed star" was the First Amendment. The Court went on to strike down local ordinances that lawmakers had passed specifically to prohibit Jehovah's Witnesses from distributing literature. Usually, the government could not demonstrate a compelling interest to infringe on the practices of Jehovah's Witnesses, except for medical treatment.

Medical Treatment of Minors

Several lower courts and courts of appeals have weighed whether the parents of minor children could refuse medical treatment based on their parents' religious beliefs. Generally many of these conflicts involved providing blood transfusions to minor children in lifesaving situations. For example, a car has struck a six-year-old child crossing a street. An emergency ambulance takes the child to the nearest public hospital for treatment. The doctors treating the child and other hospital authorities contact the parents for permission to treat the severely injured child. The parents refuse permission, claiming that a blood transfusion would violate their religious belief. This scenario has been common among practicing Jehovah's Witnesses. According to these beliefs, a blood transfusion would condemn their child to an eternity in hell, because in their biblical interpretation God did not mean for any person to mix their blood with the blood of others. The question becomes, Does the public hospital have a compelling interest to perform the emergency blood transfusion despite the parents' religious objection?

Most lower courts have sided with doctors and hospitals. They have normally granted temporary custody of the minor child to a government agency (e.g., Department of Child Services) that in turn would grant permission for the necessary medical treatment. Upon recovery from the lifesaving procedure, and with assurance that the child was not in deadly danger, the court would again give parents custody. In 1968, in the case

J.W. v. *King County Hospital,* the Supreme Court upheld the government's interest in providing life-saving medical procedures for minor children even when the parents opposed such treatment because of their "free exercise" beliefs. The Court has yet to render a decision on cases involving the government seeking treatment for nonlifesaving procedures, although some courts, using abuse and neglect statutes, have declared parents temporarily incompetent and granted guardianship to a child-service state agency to grant authority to the appropriate medical experts to perform remedial surgery. One instance was to improve the looks of a minor child. Judge Hugh Elwyn's made a decision under the Family Court Act of New York. In this case Judge Elwyn declared Kevin Sampson, age 15, a "neglected child" and ordered Kevin to undergo a series of operations by duly qualified surgeons to correct a facial condition called neurofibromatosis, because in Judge Elwyn's words the condition was "grotesque and repulsive" and could "exert a most negative effect upon his personality development, his opportunity for education and later employment and upon every phase of his relationship with his peers and others," [65 Misc. 2D 658 (N.Y. Fam. Ct. 1970), affirmed, 377 App. Div. 2D 668 (1971), affirmed, 278 N.E. 2D 918 (N.Y. 1972)]. Throughout this case, Kevin's mother opposed the medical procedure and the accompanying blood transfusions on religious grounds, but Judge Elwyn felt the state had a compelling interest to improve Kevin's looks and potential for success.

Religious Expression, or Illegal Drug Use?

If the "free exercise" clause protects religious beliefs, but not always religious conduct, what might be the outcome if you claimed that part of your religious sacraments include the smoking of a substance normally classified as illegal (e.g., smoking peyote, a hallucinogen derived from the plant *Lophophora williamsii Lemaire)*? Again the Supreme Court had to decide whether the Constitution protected this conduct under the "free exercise" clause.

Alfred Smith and Galen Black worked for a private drug rehabilitation organization. Their employers fired them from their jobs once they discovered that they had participated in a religious ritual of the Native American Church that included the sacrament of smoking peyote. Smith and Black,

once fired, sought unemployment benefits from Employment Division of the Oregon Department of Human Resources. Smith and Black contended that their firing was unjust and therefore they were entitled to unemployment compensation. The Employment Division contended that their employers fired them for work-related "misconduct." Smith and Black appealed the Employment Division's decision through the courts. The U.S. Supreme Court decided this case, *Employment Division, Department of Human Resources* v. *Smith,* in 1990. The justices divided in their opinions regarding Smith and Black's belief that the "free exercise" clause protected their right to receive their unemployment benefits. Justice Scalia wrote the majority opinion upholding the Employment Division's decision to deny the benefits to Smith and Black. Among other reasons, Justice Scalia provided a brief synopsis of the two distinctly different paths that "free exercise" cases have taken. In upholding "free exercise" over government intrusion, Justice Scalia reviewed the Court's findings in several recent cases:

- In 1940, the Court invalidated a licensing system for religious and charitable solicitations under which the licensing administrator had the power to deny a license to any cause he deemed nonreligious (see *Cantwell* v. *Connecticut).*

- In 1943, the Court invalidated a flat tax on solicitation as applied to the dissemination of religious ideas (see *Murdock* v. *Pennsylvania).*

- In 1925 (see *Pierce* v. *Society of Sisters)* and in 1972 (see *Wisconsin* v. *Yoder),* the Court upheld the right of parents to choose the appropriate education of their children, whether it be private schooling in Pierce, or not requiring high-school education in Yoder, when such government compliance (i.e., attending public schools or complying with the compulsory attendance laws) offended religious beliefs.

- In 1963 (see *Sherbert* v. *Verner),* 1981 (see *Thomas* v. *Review Board, Indiana Employment Division),* and 1987 (see *Hobbie* v. *Unemployment Appeals Commission of Florida),* the Court invalidated state unemployment compensation rules that conditioned the availability of benefits upon an applicant's willingness to work under conditions forbidden by his or her religious beliefs.

Although he acknowledged the Court's support of the "free exercise" in these cases, Justice Scalia made it clear that no case had ever upheld the right to receive government compensation while admitting to committing criminal acts such as smoking peyote, even though the peyote was used as part of a religious sacrament. In addition, Justice Scalia reviewed recent cases in which the Court had supported government action over "free exercise" where government established a compelling interest. For example:

- In 1986, in *Bowen* v. *Roy,* the Court upheld a requirement that to receive government benefits, the recipients must provide Social Security numbers, even if the Native American recipients' religious beliefs opposed the use of any numbering of individuals.

- In 1988 (see *Lyng* v. *Northwest Indian Cemetery Protective Association),* the Court upheld the government's power to grant logging and road construction on lands previously used for religious purposes, even though the Court recognized that the government construction "could have devastating effects on traditional Indian religious practices."

- In 1986 (see *Goldman* v. *Weinberger),* the Court upheld military dress regulations forbidding the wearing of yarmulkes, although wearing the yarmulke was a symbol of Captain Goldman's religious beliefs.

- In 1987 (see *O'Lone* v. *Estate of Shabazz),* the Court upheld a prison's power to refuse to excuse inmates from work requirements to attend their particular worship services.

In so many cases, justices prefer to weigh precedents in reaching decisions, because their decision will likely establish a new precedent. In the peyote case, Justice Scalia concluded that the government has a compelling interest to prohibit harmful conduct, such as ingesting peyote. He strongly emphasized that Smith and Black had remedies other than having the Court sanction the smoking of peyote. For Justice Scalia, state legislatures should resolve conflicts in which religious beliefs collided with government interests. Scalia specifically identified some states that had made an exception to their drug laws to accommodate the sacramental use of peyote as a religious belief and practice (see Arizona revised statutes, 1989; Colorado revised statutes, 1985; and New Mexico

Annotated Statute, as Supplemented, 1989). Absent such government exemption, Justice Scalia and the controlling majority upheld the government's power to deny the unemployment benefits.

Justice Blackmun, joined by Justices Brennan and Marshall, issued a strongly worded dissenting opinion. First, Blackmun repeated the importance of the strict scrutiny test (i.e., government must demonstrate a compelling interest before infringing on a fundamental freedom such as the "free exercise" clause). Furthermore, Blackmun emphasized the extent to which government had gone to exempt the sacramental use of peyote from criminal drug conduct. Pointing to expert testimony from previous cases, Blackmun said about this state policy that, "the State failed to prove that the quantities of peyote used in the sacraments of the Native American Church—same church as Black and Smith—are sufficiently harmful to the health and welfare of the participants so as to permit a legitimate intrusion under the State's police power" (see *State* v. *Whittingham,* 1973, Arizona) and "as the Attorney General . . . admits, the opinion of scientists and other experts is 'that peyote . . . Works no permanent deleterious injury to the Indian'" (see *People* v. *Woody,* California). Also, Blackmun noted that Federal Regulations of the Drug Enforcement Administration had included the following exemption as of 1989: "The listing of peyote as a controlled substance in Schedule I does not apply to the nondrug use of peyote in bona fide religious ceremonies of the Native American Church, and members of the Native American Church so using peyote are exempt from registration." In addition, Blackmun noted that 23 states, many with significant Native American populations, have statutory or judicially crafted exemptions in their drug laws for religious use of peyote. Drawing a parallel with the exemption granted the Roman Catholic Church for use of wine in giving sacraments during Prohibition, Justice Blackmun concluded that the peyote use was limited to the Native American Church religious sacrament. Similarly, as with the wine exemption for Catholics, government should recognize the free exercise clause and prohibit government from punishing this limited, religious usage. In a strongly worded conclusion, Blackmun claimed "Oregon's attitude toward respondents' [Smith and Black] religious peyote use harkens back to the repressive policies pursued a century ago: 'In the government's view, traditional practices were not morally degrading, but unhealthy.

Indians are fond of gatherings of every description, a 1913 public health study complained, advocating the restriction of dances and 'sings' to stem contagious diseases. In 1921, the Commissioner of Indian Affairs, Charles Burke, reminded his staff to punish any Indian engaged in any dance which involves . . . The reckless giving away of property . . . Frequent or prolonged periods of celebration . . . In fact, any disorderly or plainly excessive performance that promotes superstitious cruelty, licentiousness, idleness, danger to health, and shiftless indifference to family welfare.'"

Justice Scalia's decision commanded the majority opinion, but his suggestion, combined with much of Justice Blackmun's dissenting analysis, led to a legislative review and a possible remedy for conflicts like this involving sacraments of the Native American Church. In October 1992, Congress passed the Religious Freedom Restoration Act. This act prohibits any agency, department, or official of the United States or any State (the government) from burdening a person's exercise of religion, even if the burden results from a rule of general applicability, with the exception that the government may burden a person's exercise of religion only if it showed that application of the burden to the person is (1) essential to further a compelling governmental interest and (2) the least restrictive means of furthering that compelling governmental interest.

Many legal scholars believe that Smith and Black's "free exercise" claim would have resulted in a different opinion by the Oregon Employment Division had they modified the regulations to accommodate this religious exemption. Others, like Justice Scalia, may continue to claim that the government had a compelling interest to make a clear statement prohibiting the use of any illegal controlled substance.

Years before the Oregon case at the height of the "Love Generation" in 1968, an interesting case came before the federal courts. The hippie movement with its philosophy of "tripping out" on drugs had started a new religion, the New-American Church. The public knew them as the "Boo-hoos." Their church sacrament was marijuana, their seal was a three-eyed toad, and their song was "Puff the Magic Dragon." The federal district court denied an exemption to drug laws, noting that their religion was only a sham and a way to get around drug laws (*U.S.* v. *Kuch*).

Legislatures will continue to fight over conflicts regarding religious freedom. They will often spill over to people seeking remedies from the courts. With the increase in and recognition of diversity, representatives will fight more battles over religious and political correctness. Because of the increasing interdependency of the global village and broadened religious contacts, "We, the people" must be active if the spirit of the religious freedom is to be kept alive.

Freedom of Speech

This is the third protected freedom of the First Amendment, often called "free speech" or "freedom of expression." Many people believe that this is the most important freedom in the Bill of Rights. Justice Hugo Black said:

> Freedom to speak and write about public questions is as important to the life of government as is the heart of the human body. In fact, this privilege is the heart of our government! If that heart is weakened, the result is debilitation; if it be stilled, the result is death.

Again, a seemingly simple phrase that has produced prolific opinions and lively discussion and debate, sometimes resulting in dangerous and deadly consequences.

Although adopted as part of the Bill of Rights in 1791, it did not take long for controversy to arise over what the founders meant by "freedom of speech." In 1798, a faction of the Federalist Party controlled Congress, and because of concern and alarm about criticism of foreign and domestic policy, and especially for repelling the revolutionary fervor and violence of the French Revolution of 1789, the new Congress passed the Sedition Act of 1798. This Act made it a crime to "write, print, utter or publish . . . Any false, scandalous, and malicious" expression against the government, Congress, or the president. Persons found guilty of violating the Sedition Act were subject to fines up to $2,000 and up to two years in jail. Police arrested several prominent political opponents of the Federalists. Prosecutors tried them and the courts found them guilty under the law. History has suggested that Thomas Jefferson and other anti-Federalists helped some of those convicted pay their fines. When Jefferson became president and assumed office in 1801, the Act had expired and Jefferson pardoned any persons remaining imprisoned for violating the Act. As an aside and yet a significant reflection of historical periods of intolerance, we note that the court records of these convictions are replete with references to the "Irish and Scot Irish rabble" involved in this odious and offensive speech. Some group is even chosen as a constant target for labeling in our struggles over majoritarian tyranny and protection of fundamental freedoms. The constitutional historian, Leonard Levy, has made the case that even the Jefferson administration attempted to suppress speech or expression that criticized them. The Jefferson administration filed several seditious libel suits against critics in the early 1800s. By 1812, the Supreme Court rejected the federal common law of seditious libel. Slowly, libel law shifted from being a matter of criminal law to being a matter of civil law. However, the courts never overturned the Sedition Act of 1798, though Justice Brennan mentioned the law in *New York Times* v. *Sullivan*. He said that "although the Sedition Act was never tested in this Court, the attack upon its validity has carried the day in the court of history." This case will be examined further on in the "free press" discussion.

Limitations on Freedom of Speech

Our nation's history is strewn with examples of government attempting to limit speech, press, and expression. For much of our history, local, state, and sometimes federal governments succeeded in suppressing freedom of expression, speech both pure and symbolic. For example, by the beginning of the twentieth century, many states had enacted laws making flag desecration, or inappropriate use of the flag, a crime. In 1907, the Supreme Court upheld a Nebraska law that made it a crime to use the flag for commercial purposes *(Halter* v. *Nebraska)*. This 1907 case involved a brewery attempting to add to the Fourth of July celebration by affixing United States flags to their beer bottle labels. Halter and his partner were found guilty of violating the Nebraska law, making it a crime to display the flag in a commercial way (i.e., the 1903 Nebraska statute made it a crime for "any person who . . . [s]hall place or cause to be placed . . . [a]ny advertisement of any nature, upon any flag, standard, color, or ensign of the United States of America"). Government officials arrested Halter and his brewery partner, Haywood, and convicted them of violating this 1903 statute. Government prosecutors claimed that Halter and Haywood "unlawfully exposed to public view, sold, exposed for sale, and had in their possession for

sale, a bottle of beer upon which, for purposes of advertisement, was printed and painted a representation of the flag of the United States."

Often, legal history depends on the theory of the case—that is, what theory, or rationale, will you apply to protect your conduct or actions? Here, the brewery owners and their legal counsel chose to apply the personal liberty clause of the Fourteenth Amendment of the Constitution in their defense. An examination of Court briefs and arguments show a complete disregard of First Amendment application. Applying First Amendment theory to protect expression and speech seemed absent from most legal debate at the time. The context of time and events often reshape our theory.

War may be the greatest threat to individual liberties. Many argue that the Bill of Rights only apply in peacetime. No rights will be saved if the country is defeated. Therefore, all resources must be used to ensure the survival of the republic, and this survival often requires the temporary loss of individual rights. The loss of rights during the Civil War is a good example of this philosophy. The government arrested thousands of people who spoke out against the war. Lincoln and others in the North argued that this was necessary to save the Union. The courts upheld the government in most cases during the war.

The Espionage Act

The United States entry into World War I provoked lively debate, disagreements, and explosive expression. In the context of the time, workers in many areas of the world united collectively for a plethora of purposes; humane working hours, a living wage, a fair distribution of wealth, a value for their labor, and a prohibition on child labor. In the 1890s and in the early 1900s, workers had rebelled against governments in many areas of the world, including the United States. At the turn of the century, many Americans began questioning the United States political and economic system. Socialism began to grow. The government stepped in and attempted to quash dissent. In 1909, for example, one radical speaker was arrested for reading the Declaration of Independence to a crowd. Russia was in the midst of the Bolshevik revolution; Germany and other European countries had experienced widespread strikes. Workers' parties and socialist, communist, and anarchist movements provided a real or perceived

During the Vietnam War, anti-war protesters, exercising their right to free speech, became commonplace.

scare. In 1917, Congress passed the Espionage Act, which made it a crime to engage in expression or conduct that might jeopardize the security of the United States during their war efforts.

Two months after the passage of the Espionage Act, government officials arrested Charles Schenck for violating the act by printing and distributing 15,000 leaflets denouncing the new draft law and the war. The court convicted him and sentenced him to six months in jail. His case went to the U.S. Supreme Court, where the Court ruled unanimously against him and established the "clear and present danger" precedent. Justice Oliver Wendell Holmes (the Court's famous liberal justice) said: "The most stringent protection of free speech would not protect a man in falsely shouting fire in a theater and causing a panic. . . . The question in every case is whether the words used are used in such circumstances and are of such a nature as to create a clear and present danger that they will bring about the substantive evils that Congress has a right to prevent." Thus the Supreme Court limited free speech and endorsed the Espionage Act. Although Schenck lost his case, the Supreme Court incorporated First Amendment protections (*Schenck* v. *United States*). The Court acknowledged that the First Amendment freedom of expression extended to all persons. Federal, state or local governments could not prohibit it unless the expression created a "clear and present danger" to the security of the United States. The Court upheld Schenk's conviction for violating the

1917 Espionage Act because Schenck's advocacy of pacifism and draft resistance created a "clear and present danger" to the nation's war effort. This "clear and present danger" exception to the free speech clause has remained with us throughout the twentieth century.

About 900 people were sent to jail under the Espionage Act. German Americans were attacked and beaten with the tacit consent of Americans. For example, after a mob nearly killed some radicals opposed to World War I, the next day's headlines read, "Near Lynchings Give Pro-Germans Needed Lesson." The government arrested, convicted, and imprisoned several notable persons, including socialist leader and presidential candidate Eugene Debs. Debs was arrested and imprisoned for verbally advocating resistance to the wartime draft (*Debs* v. *United States*). The courts convicted Debs in 1918 for speaking out against the war and draft in a two-hour speech. The Supreme Court upheld his conviction, with Justice Holmes saying that it was the "natural and intended effect" of Deb's speech to obstruct recruiting.

Many examples of the "average" person fighting for freedom of speech occurred during this time. In South Dakota, farmer and self-declared socialist Fred Fairchild got into an argument about the legitimacy of participating in World War I. He said, "If I were of conscription age and had no dependents and were drafted, I would refuse to serve. They could shoot me, but they could not

Oliver Wendell Holmes (1841–1935)

Oliver Wendell Holmes is one of the best known of the members of the Supreme Court of the United States. Holmes served as associate justice from 1902 to 1932, during a period when few civil rights stands were taken by the Court majority. Nonetheless, Holmes, often in dissent, managed to carve out a position that later became important in the history of American rights.

Holmes was the son of a famous author and physician of the same name. He served with distinction in the Civil War and took a law degree in Harvard in 1866 after the war. Holmes was so highly regarded as a legal thinker that he taught constitutional law at Harvard while editing the *American Law Review* and other important legal works. As a legal philosopher Holmes attacked the prevailing views of the place of law in society, contending that law could best be understood as a response to the needs of society, not merely as an abstract body of rules.

As a result of his prominence, Holmes was appointed to the Massachusetts supreme judicial court in 1882, where he served for twenty years. Holmes became chief justice of that court in 1899. He was appointed to the United States Supreme Court in 1902 by President Theodore Roosevelt. Holmes served on the Supreme Court of the United States for 30 years.

Oliver Wendell Holmes had a number of strict beliefs about the role of judges in a democracy. He preached "judicial restraint," believing that popular majorities not unelected judges, should dominate public policies. During his years on the Supreme Court the majority frequently struck down social legislation in the name of the Constitution. Minimum wage and hour laws, passed by state legislatures, were frequently nullified by judicial decisions. Holmes protested, becoming known as the "great dissenter" for his pains. Later courts tended to adopt the views of Holmes, vindicating him in the 1930s and 1940s.

In free speech cases Holmes took a different approach. In defense of the First Amendment, he often opposed popular measures that repressed speech. He developed a "clear and present danger" test to validate such legislation. Restrictions on speech, he felt, were justified only when the public interest is faced with some immediate threat, not merely abstract speech. He set forth these views in dissents in two 1919 cases: *Abrams* v. *United States* and *Schenck* v. *United States* cases. In 1925 Holmes applied the "clear and present danger" test again against the conviction of an early leader of the American Communist Party in his classic dissent in *Gitlow* v. *New York*. The Holmes doctrine of "clear and present danger" is the view of the Supreme Court majority today.

Oliver Wendell Holmes gradually emerged as an American folk hero. Sometimes called the "Magnificent Yankee," many books and films have been made about him. He retired from the Supreme Court in 1932, at the age of 91, and died in 1935, three years later. His long and active life was filled with glorious and funny stories, including an occasion during the Civil War when, while defending the city of Washington, he saw a tall civilian in a stovepipe hat standing on a wall watching the firing of snipers. As a captain Holmes told the civilian to get down before the fool got shot. The civilian was his commander-in-chief, Abraham Lincoln, who reacted with amusement but obeyed the young officer.

make me fight." Government officials arrested him and tried and convicted him under the Espionage Act. The court sentenced him to a year and a day at Leavenworth Penitentiary.

The "Fighting Words" Doctrine

Earlier in the twentieth century, support for free speech came from an unlikely source. The I.W.W. (Industrial Workers of the World, called Wobblies) fought for free speech and the right to give speeches when they wished. In the early 1900s hundreds of Wobblies illegally hitched rides on boxcars to congregate in Missoula, Montana. Here city leaders prevented some I.W.W. members from speaking there by the town's passage of an antispeech ordinance. Police arrested them by the hundreds until they clogged the jails and the courts so completely that the town repealed its antispeech ordinance. In 1909 Spokane, Washington, passed a law to stop street meetings and arrested a Wobbly who tried to speak there. In response thousands of Wobblies marched into the town to speak. Police arrested each one as he began to speak. Soon the jail held 600 Wobblies. Jail conditions were oppressive. Many men died in their cells. However, the city gave in and the I.W.W. won the right to speak. The same situation happened in Fresno, California, and in Aberdeen, Washington, in 1911. The next year in San Diego, Jack White, another Wobbly, was sentenced to six months on bread and water in the county jail in a free speech fight. When asked to speak to the court, he said:

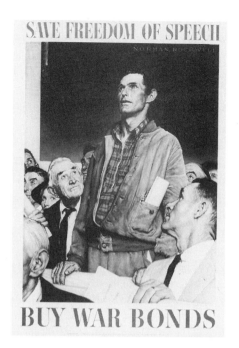

> The prosecuting attorney, in his plea to the jury, accused me of saying on a public platform at a public meeting, "To hell with the courts, we know what justice is." He told a great truth when he lied, for if he had searched the innermost recesses of my mind he could have found that thought, never expressed by me before, but which I express now, "To hell with your courts, I know what justice is," for I have sat in your court room day after day and have seen members of my class pass before this, the so-called bar of justice. I have seen you, Judge Sloane, and others of your kind, send them to prison because they dared to infringe upon the sacred rights of property. You have become blind and deaf to the rights of man to pursue life and happiness, and you have crushed those rights so that the sacred right of property shall be preserved. Then you tell me to respect the law. I do not. I did violate the law, as I will violate every one of your laws and still come before you and say "To hell with the courts." . . .
>
> The prosecutor lied, but I will accept his lie as a truth and say again so that you, Judge Sloane, may not be mistaken as to my attitude, "To hell with your courts, I know what justice is."

The social unrest of the twentieth century led the Court to expand the "clear and present danger" standard to include a "fighting words" exception to First Amendment protection. This exception more often happened in turbulent times such as the labor unrest and deep depression of the 1930s, World War II during the 1940s, and post-war Cold War tensions between the United States and the Soviet Union during the 1950s and 1960s. Other eras would include spin-off conflicts during wars of national liberation, such as the revolutions in Cuba and Southeast Asia, and also the violence accompanying the civil rights movement in our nation. During these periods the courts allowed prosecution of persons for using expression that would be highly likely to incite violence. Many legal scholars argued that such prosecution amounted to persecution for having strongly held political positions that seemed to go beyond the

traditional boundaries of Democratic and Republican Party dissent. Some historians and legal scholars have even suggested that the Republican Party hierarchy under the Nixon administration considered the views of the "Stop the War Now" McGovern movement of the Democratic Party to be beyond normal mainstream dissent and therefore subject to government scrutiny, investigation, spying, and any other means to stop this effort to end the war in Southeast Asia. The Nixon probes into the antiwar movement, Pentagon Papers' leaks, the left wing of the Democratic Party, and other concerns over political protests led to a series of Court cases, including some involving executive privilege *(United States* v. *Nixon)*, publishing secret leaks from Pentagon war studies *(U.S.* v. *New York Times Publishing Company)*, and some federal court cases involving symbolic protests over the flag *(Street* v. *New York, Smith* v. *Goguen, Spence* v. *State of Washington, Texas* v. *Johnson,* and *United States* v. *Eichman),* and even a Supreme Court case examining if burning your draft card could be considered protected expression under the First Amendment *(U.S.* v. *O'Brien).*

Although some scholars have promoted a path of tolerance for strong advocacy of opinion, others have suggested that such tolerance has provoked words and actions that wound emotionally, psychologically, and physically. Those advocating a tolerance for pluralistic expression have suggested that the "marketplace of ideas" will prevail and the more

Those advocating a tolerance for pluralistic expression have suggested that the "marketplace of ideas" will prevail and the more just, humane ideas will govern our daily dignity and respect for one another.

just, humane ideas will govern our daily dignity and respect for one another. These advocates stress that the framers of the First Amendment intended us to protect even the speech we hate. They even ask, why would we need First Amendment protections if we had consensus and agreed with one another's expressions and actions? Clearly, the founding fathers formed the nation in rebellion, and expression challenging authority and tyranny is imperative if freedom is to prevail. Some of today's legal scholars, known as critical legal scholars or critical race and feminist theorists, have suggested that pure tolerance for strong speech promotes emotional and psychological violence. In addition, they believe that such speech promotes destructive and deadly actions. Some scholars of the school of critical theorists have suggested codes of conduct to prohibit expression that provokes harassment and damaging discrimination. These codes became common on some college campuses as college administrators attempted to minimize verbal and violent confrontation and the resulting legal conflicts, both civil and criminal. Since most scholars view institutions of higher learning as citadels of free expression, creativity, and inventiveness, it is appropriate to examine "free speech" issues as they emerge in campus discourse and debate.

Chaplinsky v. New Hampshire

To understand further the historical context of the "fighting words" doctrine, consider another important case involving First Amendment expression for a practicing Jehovah's Witness. Counsel argued this case on free speech grounds, not "free exercise." In the early 1940s, a Jehovah's Witness named Chaplinsky was busy preaching and proselytizing about his strongly held religious beliefs to people passing on a public street. Some passersby complained to local law enforcement officials and a Rochester, New York, city marshal approached Chaplinsky with the admonition to "go slow" (in today's parlance, "chill" or "cool down"). Chaplinsky responded by calling the marshal "a God-damned racketeer" and "a damned fascist." While yelling this face to face, Chaplinsky continued by charging publicly that "damned fascists" made up the whole government of Rochester. Government officials arrested, tried, and convicted Chaplinsky under a statute that prohibited addressing "any offensive, derisive or annoying word to any other person . . . or calling that person by any offensive or derisive name." The language of the statute

appeared very broad, leading some to suggest this was the "no-name calling" law. Chaplinsky appealed his conviction, arguing that the statute violated his free speech protection, especially the right to criticize politicians—an arguably inalienable right older than the Constitution and the nation itself. Despite Chaplinsky's claim, the majority of the Supreme Court upheld the conviction and the statute. The majority opinion concluded, "There are certain well-defined and narrowly limited classes of speech, the prevention and punishment of which have never been thought to raise any Constitutional problem. These include the lewd and the obscene, the profane, the libelous, and the insulting or "fighting" words—those by which their very utterance inflict injury or tend to incite an immediate breach of the peace. . . . Such utterances are no essential part of any exposition of ideas, and are of such slight social value as a step to truth that any benefit that may be derived from them is clearly outweighed by the social interest in order and morality."

Campus Conduct Codes

The U.S. Supreme Court in 1942 decided *Chaplinsky* v. *New Hampshire*. This decision might seem to be the appropriate precedent to use in establishing campus conduct codes designed to reduce and eliminate hate speech, harassment, and discrimination. Several universities that are part of state schools of higher education adopted such conduct codes in the 1980s. The wording of the state university codes often modeled those of the University of Michigan and the University of Wisconsin. The University of Michigan rule stated that they could discipline students if the following conduct occurred in an academic or educational area (e.g., a library or a computer center):

Any behavior, verbal, or physical, that stigmatizes or victimizes an individual based on race, ethnicity, religion, sex, sexual orientation, creed, national origin, ancestry, age, marital status, handicap or Vietnam-era veteran status, and that

a. Involves an express or implied threat to an individual's academic efforts, employment, participation in University sponsored extra-curricular activities or personal safety; or

b. Has the purpose or foreseeable effect of interfering with an individual's academic efforts, employment, participation in University sponsored extra-curricular activities or personal safety; or

c. Creates an intimidating, hostile, or demeaning environment for educational pursuits, employment or participation in University sponsored extra-curricular activities.

The University of Michigan, Ann Arbor campus, had taken the lead in adopting this code after a series of incidents creating conflict and tension among various students and groups of students on the campus. Prior to the adoption of this code in 1987, the campus confronted "unknown persons" distributing fliers declaring "open season" on African American students. The fliers called African American students "saucer lips, porch monkeys, and jigaboos." During that same year, a campus disk jockey broadcast racist jokes from the campus radio station, and more than once, unknown persons had displayed Ku Klux Klan robes, fliers, and other paraphernalia of the KKK. Clearly the school designed the code to discourage the type of conduct found in the *Chaplinsky* "name-calling" prosecution. Nevertheless, like *Chaplinsky*, many students, staff, and legal scholars argued that the code violated fundamental First Amendment "free speech protections."

As a response to several incidents of discrimination and harassment on the various campuses of the University of Wisconsin, their Board of Regents adopted a comparable code in 1989. Prior to the adoption of the code, the campuses had been through tensions and turmoil as fraternities mocked minority students in the form of large caricatures displayed at fraternity parties. Fraternities even held "slave auctions" where fraternity pledges performed skits in blackface, imitating African American performers. Beyond the fraternity confrontations, many minority and women students had reported incidents of hate speech and harassment. The Wisconsin code provided stern discipline for students if they engaged in the following forms of conduct in nonacademic matters:

Making racist or discriminatory comments, epithets or other expressive behavior directed at an individual or at different individuals, or for physical conduct, if such comments, epithets or other expressive behavior or physical conduct intentionally:

1. Demean the race, sex, religion, color, creed, disability, sexual orientation, national origin, ancestry or age of the individual or individuals; and

2. Create an intimidating, hostile or demeaning environment for education, university-related work, or other university-authorized activity.

A third state university, the University of Connecticut, enacted a conduct code that was also eventually challenged in court as violating "free speech" protections of the First Amendment. Again, responding to campus unrest among varying groups and individual complaints alleging harassment, racism, and damaging discrimination, the university adopted a new conduct code. The University's Department of Student Affairs produced what was considered a comprehensive regulation to "Protect Campus Pluralism." The Connecticut regulations stated that "every member of the University is obligated to refrain from actions that intimidate, humiliate, or demean persons or groups or that undermine their security or self-esteem." The regulations prohibited the "use of derogatory names, inappropriately directed laughter, inconsiderate jokes, anonymous notes or phone calls, and conspicuous exclusion from conversations and/or classroom discussions." The Student Affairs office provided a list of the "signs" of proscribed "Harassment, Discrimination and Intolerance." The "signs" included:

- stereotyping the experiences, background, and skills of individuals.

- treating people differently solely because they are in some way different from the majority.

- responding to behaviors or situations negatively because of the background of the participants.

- imitating stereotypes in speech or mannerisms.

- attributing objections to any of the above actions to "hypersensitivity" of the targeted individual or group.

This last sign seems to echo in everyday experiences (e.g., a person shares a treasured joke that the recipient takes as trashy, and when the recipient objects, the joke teller responds, "Lighten up," "Don't have a cow," or "Come on, it's just a joke"). At the University of Connecticut, such a response could lead to disciplinary actions. The regulations required students to immediately inform the Discrimination and Intolerance Response Network if "any student experienced or witnessed any of the signs" and to be aware that "the University will not tolerate such behavior." The foundation of the regulations can be summarized by the following phrase from the regulations: "All members of the University community are responsible for the maintenance of a positive environment in which everyone feels comfortable working and learning."

A fourth university to experience a court challenge to its discrimination and harassment policy was Central Michigan University. Central Michigan, like the aforementioned campuses, had experienced typical turmoil and tension and had in response adopted a policy designed to discourage "any intentional, unintentional, physical, verbal, or nonverbal behavior that subjects an individual to an intimidating, hostile or offensive educational, employment or living environment by demeaning or slurring individuals through . . . [w]ritten literature because of their racial or ethnic affiliation; or by using symbols, epitaphs or slogans that infer negative connotations about an individual's racial or ethnic affiliation." The University's introduction to this policy stated; "Regardless of whether the courts and statutes have declared these actions unlawful, the University has declared them to be a violation of University policy: . . . Discriminatory harassment, whether or not it rises to the level of legally forbidden discrimination, will not be tolerated." Again, many students, staff, and legal scholars argued that this policy was too broad and unenforceable—how can you forbid "unintentional" speech or conduct?

Of course, conduct codes applied to public colleges and universities involved direct government action. Therefore, some could argue that direct government action triggers a violation of the First Amendment (the First Amendment language which states that government shall make no law abridging the freedom of speech, or of the press). As a remedy to such a violation, persons could seek redress by changing government policy through changing regulations or regulators, changing legislation or legislators, or challenging the government policy in court. The question is, can private colleges and universities enact conduct codes of any manner since their action does not involve direct government action?

In 1990, Stanford University, a private school, adopted a conduct code, "Fundamental Standard Interpretation: Free Expression and Discriminatory Harassment," that, among other regulations:

- Prohibits harassment, including discriminatory intimidation by threats of violence, and also includes personal vilification of students based on their sex, race, color, handicap, religion, sexual orientation, or national and ethnic origin.

- Speech or other expression will constitute harassment by personal vilification if it (a) was intended to insult or stigmatize an individual or individuals based on sex, race, color, handicap, religion, sexual orientation, or national and ethnic origin; (b) was addressed directly to the individual or individuals whom it insults or stigmatizes; and © used insulting or "fighting" words or nonverbal symbols.

Some students disciplined for violating this code challenged it as violating the California Education Code, the U.S. Constitution, and the California Constitution.

Ask yourself, wouldn't you prefer to attend classes and share campus collegiality in an atmosphere free of hate speech, harassing actions, and cruel and crude conduct, where all celebrate your self-esteem and heritage? Wouldn't you prefer a positive environment that encourages working and learning in a comfortable, compassionate world? These conduct codes have become contagious beyond our borders. Our northern neighbors in Canada have considered and encouraged campuses to adopt similar codes. The Ontario Ministry of Education recently provided financial incentives to campuses to adopt a goal of "zero tolerance" towards harassment and discrimination. The campuses were encouraged to develop and apply conduct codes that incorporated the following ideas:

- Each campus member will be responsible for helping to create an environment that is free of harassment and discrimination.

- Students can best accomplish work and learning in an environment of understanding and mutual respect.

- The campus will strictly prohibit any attacks on any person or group based on "race, ancestry, place of origin, color, ethnic origin (including language, dialect, or accent), citizenship, creed, sex, sexual orientation, disability, age, marital status, family status, receipt of public assistance, and/or record of provincial offenses or pardoned federal offenses."

University campuses were required to publicly post notices of the code, which applied to university contractors and visitors as well as to students and staff. The campuses were also urged to provide due process for any person accused of violating the code, and after proper due process students, staff, visitors, and contractors could still face severe consequences for violating this code—suspension, expulsion, firing, discharge, or other sanctions.

Beauharnais v. Illinois

While most legal scholars would argue that our First Amendment rights and other constitutional protections end at our nation's borders, those residing within our borders can claim protection of fundamental freedoms from government intervention and the tyranny of authority, whether the authority is legislators or campus regulators. Or can they make such a claim? Are there other Supreme Court precedents later than *Chaplinsky* that might give guidance to a constitutional challenge to most of these campus speech and conduct codes?

In 1952, a citizen of Chicago, Mr. Beauharnais, distributed a leaflet and petition that demanded the mayor and city council of Chicago "to halt the further encroachment, harassment and invasion of white people, their property, neighborhoods, and persons by the Negro." Beauharnais's leaflet added, "if persuasion and the need to prevent the white race from becoming mongrelized by the Negro will not unite us, then the aggressions, rapes, robberies, knives, guns and marijuana of the Negro, surely will." The state of Illinois prosecuted and convicted Beauharnais under a state law that stated:

> It shall be unlawful for any person, firm or corporation to manufacture, sell, or offer for sale, advertise or publish, present or exhibit in any public place in this state any lithograph, moving picture, play, drama or sketch, which publication or exhibition portrays depravity, criminality, unchastity, or lack of virtue of a class of citizens, of any race, color, creed or religion to contempt, derision, or obloquy or which is productive of breach of the peace or riots . . .

Beauharnais challenged his conviction on First Amendment "free speech" grounds. In 1952, in *Beauharnais* v. *Illinois,* the U.S. Supreme Court upheld the conviction. The Court sustained the Illinois courts' decision not to allow "truth" as a defense. The Court stated that state legislatures had the right to require "good motives" and "justi-

fiable ends" besides truth as elements in enacting laws. The Court suggested that the published leaflet distributed by Beauharnais might provoke "race riots" and that such a threat is sufficient of meet the "justifiable ends" element of the law. Some legal scholars, especially those of the "critical legal/race/feminist" studies schools, point out that the U.S. Supreme Court has never explicitly overturned the *Beauharnais* precedent. This precedent, along with *Chaplinsky* and certain other legal arguments, have led some scholars to support campus conduct codes. Beyond the above precedents, the proponents of the codes have argued that

- Punishing hate speech teaches people that racism is intolerable and unacceptable.

- Hate speech is harmful to all members of society but especially to members of minority groups who are victims of virulent, verbal abuse.

- Tolerance of hate speech on campuses is especially harmful, because campuses should be citadels of civil discourse and debate.

- Hate speech may be limited, as libel and child pornography have been limited: in other words, there is no pure, absolute protection of all expression under the First Amendment.

- Hate speech has little or no First Amendment value, and like the tests for pornography, the government can demonstrate a compelling interest to restrict hate speech.

- Certain precedents of the U.S. Supreme Court have placed prohibitions of hate speech, such as *Chaplinsky* and *Beauharnais* (and in chapter 12, please note the case of Matthew Fraser, in which the Supreme Court upheld disciplinary action against Fraser for giving an auditorium speech during student council elections. School officials punished him for his uncivil speech and for using implicit sexual innuendos in the speech).

- The Fourteenth Amendment's equal protection clause outweighs the First Amendment's "free speech" clause, especially when such hate speech vilifies and stigmatizes an entire class of people (e.g., African Americans, Hispanic Americans, homosexuals, feminists) as being "inherently unequal"—a label and stigma struck down by the Court in *Brown* v. *Board of Education.*

- Enactment of campus speech and conduct codes send a clear message by the university administration that they will not tolerate biased, belligerent "fighting words."

- When introduced effectively with appropriate notification and education, campus speech and conduct codes can help promote tolerance and sensitivity to all and a respect for individual differences and group diversity.

- Incidents of intolerance and violence have become so widespread that campuses must take a lead in stopping such conduct and the speech advocating and endorsing such action.

If these are compelling arguments for supporting speech and conduct codes, then who would oppose them except racists, bigots, bullies, and others labeled as intolerant of minorities or persons who have historically been victims of harassment and discrimination? Of course, would support for such codes suggest that the supporters are also intolerant of certain speech—speech that offends their point of view? This then is the difficult dilemma and paradox. This chapter examines arguments against many campus speech and conduct codes and examines the court's responses to challenges to some of the aforementioned university codes.

Many modern precedents support the right to exercise First Amendment free speech in a manner that many would construe as hateful speech and even deplorable conduct, such as the 1992 *R.A.V.* v. *St. Paul* case striking down the law making cross-burning—the symbolic expression and act—a crime. This case is reviewed in greater depth further on, but Justice Scalia, writing for the majority, made an emphatic declaration that government—at any level—cannot penalize the use of selected symbols or content-directed speech. The general arguments opposing speech and conduct codes follow these premises:

- Hate-speech codes only address the outward, more blatant forms or signs of bias and bigotry (e.g., it would probably be a clear violation of most speech and conduct codes if a student said, "Hey, nigger, get out of my face," but would it violate such codes if a faculty member expounded on one of the contemporary treatises on race and eugenics to

discuss why certain groups of students should not be given opportunities through affirmative action policies?).

- Hate-speech codes may harm the very minority groups they are designed to protect (e.g., could some students oppose a speech by a militant member of the Nation of Islam on the basis that such speech is likely to be anti-Semitic and offensive, or could a student lodge a discipline complaint against an affirmative action beneficiary who had stated that most "rich, yuppie white students" were just jealous of someone else receiving an opportunity they had been born with and gained from the sweat and labor of the other student's hard, working servants and slaves?).

- Hate-speech codes are actually designed to protect administrators from being embarrassed by acts of racism, sexism, and other forms bigotry (e.g., a police department mandates sensitivity training to teach street officers in civilian interactions how to respond to incidents of police harassment and excessive force; therefore, if any charges of abuse are made, the department chief can respond that the department does not tolerate improper police conduct.

- Hate-speech and conduct codes go against the very concept of the university (i.e., universities are designed to promote the marketplace of ideas, not to suppress the discussion and debate of controversial and complex ideas and problems).

- Hate-speech codes stifle student discussion and debate, chilling freedom of expression. University officials have sometimes applied these codes in questionable circumstances (e.g., administrative officials punished an Anglo student for labeling Justice Clarence Thomas a "racist," while they did not punish an African American student for calling Thomas an "Uncle Tom").

- Some might argue that speech and conduct codes prove impotence by minorities (i.e., buzz words, such as "feminazi" or "nigger" so perplex and cause paranoia among minorities that they cannot rationally combat such speech through discourse and debate, but must rely instead on protection from a more powerful authority—e.g., government—thus minorities are rendered more powerless).

- Speech and conduct codes add rules in a weak effort to address serious problems without promoting the serious educational and prevention efforts necessary to improve relations and teach respect for diversity and differences of opinions.

- In addressing these conflicts, universities should devote their valuable resources through lively discussion and debate rather than by passing simple rules and spending time and money enforcing and litigating the problems arising from the codes.

And what has happened when students have challenged the codes in court? If an administrator disciplined a student or a staff member for violating one of these codes, such as the Michigan and Wisconsin codes, could that student or staff member challenge the code as a violation of the member's First Amendment free speech rights? Under such a challenge to the code, would the courts give greater weight to the *Chaplinsky* and *Beauharnais* precedents, or to cases like *Brandenburg* v. *Ohio* and *R.A.V.* v. *St. Paul,* or even the varying decisions regarding flag and draft card desecration. Keep *Chaplinsky* and *Beauharnais* in mind during the following review of the precedents that more than likely would support striking down these public university codes as violations of the First Amendment.

In the 1969 *Brandenburg* case, the Supreme Court had to consider a challenge to an Ohio law that led to the conviction of Brandenburg for making the following public speech at a Ku Klux Klan rally, "If our President, our Congress, our Supreme Court, continues to suppress the white, Caucasian race, it's possible that there might have to be some revengence taken. . . . Personally, I believe the nigger should be returned to Africa, the Jew returned to Israel." If Brandenburg had given such a speech on a campus with speech and conduct codes, it appears that Brandenburg's speech would be subject to disciplinary action. Officials charged, convicted, and punished Brandenburg in Ohio for violating Ohio's criminal syndicalism law that made it a crime to "advocate . . . [t]he duty, necessity, or propriety of crime, sabotage, violence, or unlawful methods of terrorism as a means of accomplishing industrial or political

reform . . . [a]nd for voluntarily assembling with any society, group, or assemblage of persons formed to teach or advocate the doctrines of criminal syndicalism." A majority of the Court voted to overturn Brandenburg's conviction. In addressing the "free speech" challenge to this law, the Court concluded that a state may not "forbid or proscribe advocacy of the use of force or of law violation except where such advocacy is directed to inciting or producing imminent lawless action and is likely to produce such action." This "imminent" test of immediate or near immediate lawless action has been used in subsequent precedents. Using the Brandenburg "imminent test," the Court struck down the conviction of a protestor in Indiana in 1973, though the protestor had angrily remarked to his fellow protestors in public to "take the street later." In this case, *Hess* v. *Indiana,* the Court concluded that while Hess's speech implied illegal action later, there existed no evidence to link his speech to provoking "imminent disorder."

R.A.V. v. St. Paul

In one of the more recent "free speech" cases involving hate speech and destructive conduct, *R.A.V.* v. *St. Paul,* the Court considered a symbolic attack on the Jones family, living in St. Paul, Minnesota. In an early June morning of 1990, the Jones family, of African American heritage, awoke to find a cross burning in their yard. The Jones family had recently moved into this predominantly white neighborhood. The state, as law enforcers, arrested, tried, and convicted Robert Viktora for violating a St. Paul city ordinance that made it a crime:

> Whoever places on public or private property a symbol, object, appellation, characterization or graffiti, including, but not limited to a burning cross or Nazi swastika, which one knows or has reasonable grounds to know arouses anger, alarm or resentment in others on the basis of race, color, creed, religion or gender commits disorderly conduct and shall be guilty of a misdemeanor.

Viktora, the perpetrator of the cross burning, claimed that he was sending a strong message to the Jones' family from the Ku Klux Klan. A juvenile at the time, the court called him R.A.V. throughout the record to protect his true identity as a juvenile, thus the case citation *R.A.V.* v. *St. Paul.* Viktora claimed that the St. Paul ordinance that he was found guilty of violating was unconstitutional because it specifically punished expression toward some groups while not protecting expression for all groups.

Writing for a five-person majority, Justice Scalia agreed with Viktora's objection to the ordinance as violating the "free speech" clause of the First Amendment. Scalia concluded that the ordinance was unconstitutional because:

> The ordinance applies only to "fighting words" that insult, or provoke violence, "on the basis of race, color, creed, religion, or gender." Expressions containing abusive invective, no matter how vicious and severe, are permissible unless they are addressed to one of the specified disfavored topics. Those who wish to use "fighting words" in connection with other ideas—to express hostility, for example, on the basis of political affiliation, union membership, or homosexuality—are not covered. The First Amendment does not permit St. Paul to impose special prohibitions on those speakers who express views on disfavored subjects. In its practical operation, moreover, the ordinance goes even beyond mere content discrimination, to actual viewpoint discrimination. Expressions containing some words—odious racial epithets, for example—would be prohibited to proponents of all views. Still, "fighting words" that do not themselves invoke race, color, creed, religion, or gender—aspersions upon a person's mother, for example—would seemingly be usable ad libitum in the placards of those arguing in favor of racial, color, etc. Tolerance and equality, but could not be used by that speaker's opponents. . . . St. Paul has no such authority to license one side of a debate to fight freestyle, while requiring the other to follow Marquis of Queensbury rules.

In one stroke of his pen, Justice Scalia's five-member majority seemed to have provided the powerful precedent needed to strike down most speech and conduct codes. Some challenges to campus codes reveal the court's view of Scalia's conclusion that such codes are too exclusive, protecting some groups from offensive speech while leaving the nonprotected groups to mean-spirited verbal assaults protected by First Amendment "free speech." To Scalia, detractors could attack a student or a staff member professing to belong to a political party for example, as a "rotten Republican" or a "Dumb Democrat." No matter how emotionally damaging such comments might be to the receiver of the message, the attack is permissible under the First Amendment. On the other hand, a comment such as "jungle bunny" made to an African American or "greasy wetback" to a Hispanic American would be punishable under ordinances, laws, or rules like the St. Paul ordinance.

This precedent strikes down any rules and regulations that attempt to punish speech that is content or viewpoint directed.

Because many legal scholars have suggested that the *R.A.V.* precedent is so powerful that it probably will invalidate any like-minded campus codes, it should be noted that while the decision was unanimous in outcome, the legal rationale supporting the outcome varied among the justices. The other four justices, not joining Scalia's opinion and reasoning, concluded that the specific St. Paul ordinance was too broad and vague, but they did not agree with Scalia's sweeping analysis for invalidating the rule-making effort of the ordinance. In one concurring opinion, Justice Blackmun stated that there were no First Amendment protections for cross-burning, especially when the intent of the cross-burning conduct was "driving minorities out of their homes by burning crosses on their lawns." In another concurring opinion, Justice Stevens claimed that a well-worded ordinance "would have been legitimate had the law not been too sweeping." In other words, four of the justices suggested that there might be other remedies for punishing conduct that is racially motivated.

Wisconsin v. *Mitchell*

The Court made such penalty-enhancement remedies a reality when it upheld, unanimously, a Wisconsin law that increased the severity of punishment (e.g., lengthening the duration of sentencing) for crimes committed against victims who were intentionally chosen because of the race, religion, disability, or sexual orientation of the victim. In this precedent setting case following *R.A.V.* the Court in 1993, in *Wisconsin* v. *Mitchell,* concluded, "Whereas the ordinance struck down in the St. Paul case was explicitly directed at expression. . . . The Wisconsin statute in this case is aimed at conduct unprotected by the First Amendment." State prosecutors believed that the unprotected conduct in this aggravated assault case was provoked by the phrase, "Do you all feel hyped up to move on some white people?" Todd Mitchell, a young African American, said this after discussing a scene from the movie *Mississippi Burning,* which showed a young African American praying on his knees while being beat to death by Klan members. When they saw a young white male walking on the opposite side of the street, Mitchell said to the assembled teens,

"There goes a white boy. Go get him." Although the evidence in the trial court did not link Mitchell with the actual aggravated assault, prosecutors tried and convicted Mitchell for inciting the aggravated assault. As an accomplice, the court gave Mitchell the maximum two-year sentence for the assault, along with two more years under the penalty-enhancement law. Mitchell challenged the penalty-enhancement phase as punishing his "free speech" rights because the law was content-based and not neutral; in other words, conduct aimed at specific groups triggered the penalty enhancement. Although the justices had varying opinions in reaching their decision, the Court overwhelmingly upheld the authority of Wisconsin to pass a law with a penalty-enhancement clause. One might ask, if penalty enhancements are permissible to deter certain street language and fighting words, could such penalties apply to campus conduct? Keep in mind the competing precedents of the highest Court in response to challenges of the type of campus code: which precedent should take precedent in these cases?

Doe v. Michigan

The University of Michigan's campus code was developed to reduce racial and sexual harassment on campus. Consider the case of the graduate student in the field of biopsychology who feared discussing certain theories regarding genetic differences based on race and sex that might influence behavior (e.g., some contemporary writings of the now deceased scientist Richard Hernstein). As discussion and debate emerged from Charles Murray and Hernstein's work *The Bell Curve* regarding the genetic influence of race on aptitude and intelligent testing, some campuses experienced fierce protest, boycotts, and threatened disruption of speakers, like Murray, who had been invited to address their theses. The graduate student requested identification as John Doe for fear of reprisal if his true identity were revealed. He feared that others would punish him for discussing or seeking to do research in this field of genetics and behavior, for fear of violating the campus code. He believed that some might interpret his research and theories as "stigmatizing or victimizing" certain groups of people. Doe felt the campus code stifled research and the purpose of pursuing truth, or at the very least, testing out hypotheses. Thus, Doe argued that the campus code violated his First Amendment right to "free speech" as well as his academic freedom. Doe challenged the code in court. A federal district court agreed with Doe and struck down the core elements of the campus code that restricted speech. The Court concluded, "However laudable or appropriate an effort this may have been, the Court found that the Policy swept within its scope a significant amount of verbal conduct or verbal behavior which is unquestionably protected speech under the First Amendment." Among the incidents the court cited as being included in this code were the following: (1) A graduate student in the School of Social Work was cited for violating the code because in a research class the student expressed his belief that homosexuality was a disease and that he intended to develop a counseling plan for changing gay clients to straight; (2) another student was disciplined for reading an allegedly homophobic limerick; and (3) during orientation for a preclinical dentistry class, a student stated that he had heard that minorities had a hard time in this particular course and were not treated fairly. According to the federal court, these disciplinary incidents should have constituted protected expression under the First Amendment and should not have been punished.

Following the precedent set in *Doe* v. *Michigan* in 1989, several other federal courts have struck down campus codes as being too broad and vague. Courts have struck down even those school codes that appeared to narrow the coverage to focus on the conduct between the perpetrator of the hate speech and his or her intended victim, arguing that restricting speech was not a proper remedy to racist, sexist, intolerant behavior. Consistently courts noted that there were existing remedies if the verbal behavior went beyond mere words to physical assault. If an actual assault, with or without battery, had occurred, the campus authorities could respond with prosecution of the behavior and not persecution of the speech. Some courts noted the Supreme Court precedent in *Gooding* v. *Wilson,* decided in 1972, in which a suspect verbally exploded at police officers stating, ". . . I'll kill you . . . I'll choke you to death. . . . if you ever put your hands on me again, I'll cut you all in pieces." Could these words be construed as "fighting words" under *Chaplinsky* and considered to be a clear breach of peace? The Supreme Court said no. Such an interpretation would go beyond *Chaplinsky* and that the prosecution and conviction should be overturned as an overbroad application

of *Chaplinsky*. If such a direct verbal assault is protected speech, how can any of the campus codes stand up to constitutional scrutiny?

Beyond the "free speech" protections of the First Amendment, 38 states have affirmative "free speech" clauses in their state constitutions, and students and staff may use state court remedies in challenging restrictive campus speech and conduct codes. This has happened in several cases and has led the California Superior Court to strike down the Stanford University code as having a "chilling effect" on students' and staff members' speech.

So is all speech protected under the First Amendment? As already noted, the Supreme Court has written volumes of opinions that in some way uphold limitations or restrictions on free speech (e.g., the First Amendment clearly does not protect obscenity, breaches of national security, and libel). And about 'fighting words' prohibitions, the Court has never officially overturned *Chaplinsky* and *Beauharnais*. Cases like *R.A.V.* seem to suggest that the Court believes it almost impossible to draft a law that is all inclusive. In other words, if you were attempting to reduce any "ism" (attacks on race, sex, sexual orientation, religion, ethnicity, dialects, accents, weight, size, etc.), where would such a list end? Although the Ontario guidelines as well as certain campus codes seem to be very long in the list of protected groups, I am sure someone can claim

not to be protected and therefore be offended by someone else's speech (e.g., "those blue-eyed people are just too insensitive, while brown-eyed people are so passionate"). We may agree that this speech might offend someone, but should we create a rule or category prohibiting such comments? Any rule, specifying protection for a particular group or groups, will by its very derivation exclude other groups and therefore be discriminatory towards someone or some group. A few institutions have attempted to respond to the court's striking down of the Michigan and Wisconsin codes by revising their campus codes to be more generic. For example, the State University of New York at Albany, which had a code similar to the codes cited here, recently modified its code to define "fighting words" as "Engaging in verbal or physical behavior that is directed at an individual and according to a person of reasonable sensibilities is likely to provoke an immediate violent response." These revised codes have yet to be effectively challenged in court.

Intervention and Education Initiatives

Maybe the response to offensive, harassing speech and conduct is not the traditional, knee-jerk reaction of rule-making. As some scholars have noted, our society seems to respond to many problems by making a rule prohibiting the conduct provoking the problem, instead of focusing on changing the behavior and relations that led to the problem. Even the penalty enhancement laws that now exist in more than half the states do not seem to be a deterrent to conduct or criminal behavior motivated by racism, sexism, and so on. In fact, most social scientists examining incidents of hate crimes will readily acknowledge that hate crimes and harassment incidents and litigation is on the rise. So what response should we have to remain vigilant toward our First Amendment "free speech" protection while creating a more tolerant, less hateful world?

Some university officials, and also scholars and leaders from the legal and social science communities, have suggested planning and carrying out preventive education and intervention initiatives. In other words, they have tried to integrate "freedom of expression" into daily discourse with dignity and respect. Some universities have adopted formal policies to encourage such initiatives. For example, Texas Tech University adopted the following "Human Dignity Statement":

> Any expression of hatred or prejudice is inconsistent with the purpose of higher education in a free society. While bigotry exists in any form in the larger society, it will be an issue on the college campus. There must be a commitment by the institution to create conditions where bigotry is forthrightly confronted.

Among the initiatives set up on campuses are the development of task forces consisting of students with multiethnic, multicultural, and as Cornel West has suggested, multicontextual backgrounds. The purpose of these task forces would be to plan programs to address effectively the problems of hatred and bigotry. Such programs might include educational sessions designed to teach tolerance of diversity or to conduct workshops promoting prosocial human relations and effective communication. Other programs might be designed to increase the recruitment of students and staff with these diverse backgrounds and developing service projects that bring individuals and groups together in cooperative and collaborative learning experiences. Other programs could create workshops and sessions that focus on developing empathy for any groups who have suffered the pains and wounds of prejudice, bigotry, and harassment. Other programs might provide alternative means of dispute resolution, such as mediation to help persons come together and improve respect and relations among students and staff with a "win-win" outcome for all.

Sexual Harassment

Day to day, free speech creates controversies as it clashes with attempts to curb speech or expression that creates an uncomfortable response from others. One contemporary controversy emerges from attempts to reduce sexual harassment—a controversy some believe engages "free speech" protection. One of the more provocative responses to sexual harassment and humiliation has been the attempt by some feminist legal scholars, such as Catherine MacKinnon and Andrea Dworkin, to persuade legislators, especially at the local level, to enact ordinances that would prosecute perpetrators of this form of harassment and humiliation. Dworkin and MacKinnon managed to mobilize disparate groups, including strong pro-family associations, and helped draft a local antidiscrimination ordinance in Indianapolis. The ordinance called for civil remedies to victims of "sexually explicit works in which women are presented as sexual objects who enjoy pain or humiliation. . . . or are presented in scenarios of degradation, injury, [or] abasement . . . or are presented as sexual objects for domination, conquest, violation, exploitation, possession, or use." Please note that this ordinance, much like the campus codes, was directed toward reducing or providing remedies to persons victimized by certain forms of expression. Furthermore, the ordinance did not address only "obscene" expression because this would require applying the 1973 *Miller* v. *California* decision where the Supreme Court established the precedent that examines the prurient interest, patent offensiveness, on redeeming literary, artistic, political or scientific value of the expression. While many supported the goal of reducing harassment and humiliation towards others based on gender and sexual orientation, some of the strongest supporters of the goal opposed the means—the ordinance—as a way to achieve the goal. Specifically, groups like the American Civil Liberties Union (ACLU) and the American Booksellers Association (ABA) decided to challenge the ordinance as violating the "free speech" protections of the First Amendment. A federal judge, and a majority of the Seventh Circuit Court of Appeals, agreed with the challengers and struck down the Indianapolis ordinance. The case, *American Booksellers Association* v. *Hudnut,* decided by the Seventh Circuit in 1985 and affirmed by the U.S. Supreme Court in 1986, ended some of these more unusual local ordinances. Yet, much needs to be done to reduce the clearly identified harassment and humiliation.

Instead of challenging many incidents with constitutional connections, the legislatures of states and the United States responded with laws to deal with sexual-harassment. Through Title VII of the Civil Rights Act of 1964, and the Civil Rights Act of 1991, persons had civil remedies if they were victims of harassment based on sex, race, religion, or national origin. Most legal scholars, and specialists in sexual-harassment awareness training, agree that sexual harassment often takes two distinct forms of challenge. One is the quid pro quo harassment that is usually characterized by a supervisor or an employer approaching a subordinate or an employee and soliciting sexual favors. For example, a boss says to one of his female employees, "If you want to keep your job, you must go out with me." The courts have consistently supported the employees in such blatant extortion for sexual favors. The second area involving potential claims of sexual harassment fall under the "hostile environment" umbrella—that is, "whether the environment would reasonably be perceived, and is perceived, as hostile or abusive." The Court used this wording in one of the more recent Supreme Court cases, *Harris* v. *Forklift Systems, Inc.* Justice Ruth Bader Ginsburg, in a concurring opinion, suggested that the "inquiry (that is, did sexual harassment occur?) should center, dominantly, on whether the discriminatory conduct has unreasonably interfered with the plaintiff's work performance." So what is the difference between upholding laws prohibiting "hostile environments" in the workplace and the campus codes that attempted to reduce and eliminate "hostile environments"? Blatant acts (such as displaying obscene or grossly offensive photos or illustrations, or telling odious jokes directly to an individual to "get a rise" or "to rile them up") that intend to harass and harm will not be tolerated under these civil rights provisions. Yet what is conduct that is "reasonably perceived . . . as hostile or abusive"? Nearly all of our readers would probably perceive the aforementioned conduct as hostile and abusive, but what if someone makes a statement that he or she does not perceive or intend to be offensive? For example, a veteran oil field worker, who happens to be female and

accepted as "one of the boys," tells a young male worker, before you pick up a woman "you better get yourself some condoms because there are too many deadly diseases going on out there." Is the veteran female oil worker's speech protected, or has she created a hostile environment? What if she goes one step further in her expression and says, "Heck, any of the guys around here will give you some condoms, you can even buy them over at the truck stop." Again, is this protected expression or a violation of the young man's right to be free from a "hostile environment"? This short exchange illustrates where we may witness more clashes between the First Amendment and sexual harassment laws. Even more recently, the media has reported several incidents of six- and seven-year-old students punished (e.g., suspended from school) for kissing girls in their classrooms or on school playgrounds. Assessing intent, and determining what is a hostile environment, will continue to clash with First Amendment claims.

Freedom of the Press

Most scholars perceive our next clause as an integral element of the "free speech" clause. Examine the First Amendment carefully: a comma or a colon does not even separate press and speech. "Congress shall make no law . . . abridging the freedom of speech or of the press." As we observed in the passage regarding the Sedition Act of 1798, Congress shortly after adopting the Bill of Rights attempted to restrict speech and press. As some legal scholars and judges have asked, what is the difference between the provocative passages of a pamphleteer and the oratory of the soap box campaigner? Currently, the electronic explosion and new media frontier will give us a vastly new arena to consider constitutional questions and controversies.

Challenges to the right of "free press" have fallen into the following areas:

- Prior restraint: Should government have the power to stop publication and communication of a message prior to its publication?

- National security: Will the communication of information in some way endanger the security of the nation?

- Obscenity: Is the message being communicated obscene and therefore not protected speech, and does the medium of communica-

tion make a difference; for example, would production and distribution of films and videotapes be considered differently than providing these films over cable or traditional television airwaves?

- Libel: May persons offended by speech, especially speech expressed through print or electronic media, seek relief by suing the parties involved in the communication (e.g., publishers, authors, producers)?

- Gag orders and competing rights: May courts impose gag orders to reduce the likelihood of endangering a person's right to a fair trial? Do Fifth and Sixth Amendment due process rights in criminal prosecution outweigh the presses' efforts to pursue a story and the public's right to know about the prosecution, especially in high-profile cases, like the Oklahoma City bombing case or the O.J. Simpson case?

- Governing electronic communication through regulation and licensing: Does the government have the power to restrict communication over radio, television, or the information highway (the Internet)?

- Commercial speech: Does commercial speech, whether it is buying and broadcasting advertising for toys or legal services, have the same "free speech and press" protections as traditional political speech, and if the same

protections do apply, then do all persons have a right to communicate and receive information. Is a "fairness doctrine" constitutional, or can those with the greater capital control communication absolutely?

Restriction of the Press

There is a long tradition of attempting to restrain publications even before others have a chance to hear, see, or receive the message. Old English tradition required printers and pamphleteers to seek government licenses or stamps of approval prior to printing and distributing publications. This licensing requirement was often used for censoring any messages that the government agent might wish to suppress or prevent from distribution.

Like many other guaranteed freedoms of the First Amendment, efforts to apply and incorporate these freedoms into everyday life from a national perspective did not become widespread until the twentieth century. Why did it take so long for Americans to see the Bill of Rights as protecting individuals from government excesses and intrusion? There are many historical treatises and theories investigating the incorporation efforts, and the area should continue to peak curiosity. With the acknowledgment of the twentieth century application and a view toward the twenty-first century, we should note that the Supreme Court addressed the problem of licensing and restriction of press in

Lovell v. *City of Griffin* in 1938. This case is also important in examining the Court's application of constitutional principles to First Amendment challenges. Alma Lovell, a practicing Jehovah's Witness, refused to seek written permission from the appropriate officials of the city of Griffin to permit her or any other person to distribute or sell circulars, magazines, pamphlets, or handbooks. Alma contended she had direct permission from Jehovah and therefore it would be an act of disobedience to go to another source of authority to perform the duties expected of her as a follower of Jehovah. After her arrest and conviction for violating the city's ordinance by not receiving prior approval from the city manager, Alma appealed her conviction as violating her First Amendment rights of freedom of religion, freedom of speech, and freedom of the press. In a unanimous decision, the Supreme Court focused on the speech and press issues raised by the case, especially the requirement for prior approval from the government to distribute published materials. The Court overturned Lovell's conviction. Chief Justice Hughes, writing for the eight-to-zero decision, declared, "Whatever the motive which induced this city's ordinance adoption, its character is such that it strikes at the very foundation of freedom of the press by subjecting it to license and censorship." By 1938, the Court had affirmed the "free press" right even in local communities.

Near v. Minnesota

Prior to the Lovell decision, a highly divided Supreme Court, in a five-to-four vote had examined a now famous "free press" case, *Near* v. *Minnesota*. Again the turbulent times of the twenties and thirties gave context for this decision. Unlike the media mergers and massive communication monopolies of today, the early part of the twentieth century experienced an explosion of small independent publishers, especially of magazines and newspapers. Many people, especially government officials who were often the targets of investigations and commentaries in these independent publications, sought ways to reduce, inhibit, or prohibit these scurrilous attacks in the press. In 1925, the Minnesota legislature passed a statute, the Public Nuisance Abatement Law, that became characterized as the Minnesota Gag Law. The law permitted persons offended by press stories to seek injunctive relief from judges to prohibit publication of stories, and entire issues, prior to distribution. A

judge, acting without a jury, had the power to issue temporary, on-going, and permanent injunctions against any publisher who published magazines or newspapers that contained "obscene, lewd, lascivious, malicious, scandalous, and defamatory" messages. One local attorney, Floyd Olson, sought relief from a judge to shut down a flamboyant weekly newspaper, the Saturday Press, published by J. M. Near in Minnesota. The local judge agreed with Olson that certain speech published in this newspaper violated the Minnesota Gag Law, and the judge issued an injunction closing down the newspaper's publication. Individuals and groups with often conflicting viewpoints came together in common ground to oppose the judge's ruling. The American Civil Liberties Union and the conservative Chicago publisher, Colonel McCormick, used their extensive legal resources to help Near challenge this injunction. These national forces wanted to see the Supreme Court strike down such gag laws as violating the free press protection of the First Amendment. As mentioned, a highly divided Court ruled for Near and presented a strongly worded precedent restricting government power to restrain publication prior to its distribution. Writing for the five-person majority, Chief Justice Hughes declared "the injunctive scheme [i.e., prior restraint] was the essence of censorship. . . . The fact that the liberty of the press may be abused by miscreant purveyors of scandal does not make any the less necessary the immunity of the press from previous restraint in dealing with official misconduct. Subsequent punishment for such abuses as may exist is the appropriate remedy, consistent with constitutional privilege." In Near, the Court struck down the government's power to engage in prior restraint in all but national security emergencies, but the Court left in place the right to civil remedies to an individual wronged by "miscreant purveyors of scandal." Civil libel is one such remedy.

Libel

Libel is the right to sue if one believes his or her reputation has been defamed and damaged. Laws governing it are very old. Until the mid- to late-twentieth century, courts continued to follow common law tradition concerning libel. As late as 1933, the following definition dominated the application of common law libel: "Common law libel covers all written communications that tend to expose one to public hatred, shame, obloquy, contumely, odium, contempt, ridicule, aversion, ostracism, degradation, or disgrace, or to induce an evil opinion of one in the minds of right-thinking persons, and to deprive one of their confidence and friendly intercourse in society" *(Kimmerle* v. *New York, N.Y.).*

Imagine that you wrote a letter to an editor of a local newspaper, criticizing the elected sheriff and calling the sheriff a bigoted bully, and the newspaper published your letter. Under the *Kimmerle* definition of civil libel, the sheriff could sue you for damages to his or her reputation, for defamation of character. Under the traditional common law practice, "truth" might be your only defense to this characterization, and if the matter went before a civil jury, you would have to prove the truthfulness of your allegation of the sheriff being a "bigoted bully." Surely, this libel doctrine might produce a "chilling effect" on printed and published communications. In 1964, the U.S. Supreme Court considered the conflicts emerging over criticism of public figures and First Amendment protections of free speech and press. The 1964 case, *New York Times* v. *Sullivan,* provided the court with an opportunity to reverse this "chilling effect." In previous discussion, in *Beauharnais* v. *Illinois* (1952), the Supreme Court had upheld group libel law, claiming that libelous utterances are not "within the area of constitutionally protected speech." Remember the *Beauharnais* and *Chaplinsky* precedents had been used to support the hate-speech campus conduct codes.

The *Sullivan* Case

In the *Sullivan* case, L. B. Sullivan, the Montgomery, Alabama, police commissioner, had sued the *New York Times* newspaper, along with naming four African American clergymen, for libel. Sullivan claimed that the newspaper and clergymen had definitely defamed his character and ruined his reputation by placing an advertisement in the *Times* criticizing the conduct of the Montgomery police in handling civil rights and student demonstrators. The ad was a full-page fund-raising advertisement appealing for funds to fight back against the racist, reactionary conduct of the Montgomery Police Department. While the ad was provocative, it never mentioned Police Commissioner Sullivan by name. During the lower court trial phase of the case, evidence showed that some information contained in the ad was inaccu-

William Joseph Brennan Jr.
(1906–1997)

William J. Brennan Jr. played a powerful role in the constitutional expansion of civil rights in America during the years of his service on the Supreme Court of the United States. Brennan was associate justice from 1956 until his retirement in 1990. During the late 1950s and 1960s, when Earl Warren was chief justice, Brennan was the chief architect of many of the Court's most liberal landmark decisions.

Brennan, of Irish Catholic descent, was appointed to the Supreme Court in 1956 by Republican President Dwight D. Eisenhower. In later years Eisenhower referred to the appointment as one of his worst mistakes. Brennan proved to be much more liberal and much more a defender of the poor than Eisenhower had expected.

William J. Brennan authored the crucial *Cooper* v. *Aaron* case in 1958, which forged the Supreme Court's response to the massive southern resistance to racial desegregation. Brennan's decision in *Baker* v. *Carr* (1962) opened the door to the reapportionment of state legislatures. This decision drastically changed the nature of political representation in America. In *New York Times* v. *Sullivan* (1964), Brennan led the Supreme Court in extending the protection of the First and Fourteenth Amendments to the criticism of public officials by the press. In other decisions Brennan restricted loyalty oaths, government regulation of pornography, and public school prayer.

A leading exponent of individual rights, Brennan urged others to move further to expand those rights. He also fervently believed that it was the proper role of federal judges to actively promoted individual rights. When he retired in 1990 the Supreme Court had changed greatly in its composition, with a much less activist group of judges. In his later years on the Court Brennan was forced into becoming a spokesman for a minority viewpoint on rights. Nevertheless, most of the major decisions of Brennan remain untouched by changes in judicial attitudes, forming a permanent legacy of American rights. Brennan died in 1997.

rate. Under the common libel law instructions, the jury rendered a verdict on behalf of Sullivan. It then awarded Sullivan $500,000 in damages. The Alabama Supreme Court also upheld this jury verdict. The *New York Times* and clergymen appealed the case to the Supreme Court, claiming that the libel law violated their free speech and press protections. Justice William Brennan, writing the controlling opinion for the Court, claimed that the Court must examine this case in the context of the times, "against the background of a profound national commitment to the principle that debate on public issues should be uninhibited, robust, and wide-open, and that it may well include vehement, caustic and sometimes unpleasantly sharp attacks on government and public officials."

This contextual analysis is exceptionally exciting in the sense that many critical legal theorists and those exploring new frontiers in conflicts involving law and everyday life have spun off of these same turbulent times, often citing *Brown* v. *Board of Education* as the springboard for a new revolution of inclusion for all persons, and the ongoing civil rights movement of the sixties. This inclusion seems to have again become an issue in the nineties and probably into the twenty-first century. William Brennan, William Douglas, and Thurgood Marshall gave special impetus to this revolution in civil rights of which the *Sullivan* case set an important precedent.

Justice Brennan went on to talk about history and the need for protest overturning the Sedition Act of 1798. He noted that this case reflected "a national awareness of the central meaning of the First Amendment . . . that legal restraints on citizen criticism of government and public officials are inconsistent with the First Amendment." Brennan claimed that the potential for civil libel lawsuits created an even greater threat to the fundamental freedoms of speech and press than did criminal prosecution. According to Brennan's controlling opinion, concern over public persecution by means of lawsuits for civil damages cast "the pall of fear and timidity imposed upon those who would give voice to public criticism [creating] an atmosphere in which the First Amendment freedoms cannot survive." Brennan did not eliminate the remedy of libel suits if one wished to seek damages for defamation, but his opinion did establish a new standard of proof for cases involving published criticisms of public officials. The

public official suing under libel protection must prove by clear and convincing evidence "that the statement was made with 'actual malice'—that is, with knowledge that it was false or with reckless disregard of whether it was false or not." While Brennan acknowledged that there might be cases and circumstances where actual malice was intended in publications, he went on to declare, "Erroneous statement is inevitable in free debate, and it must be protected if the freedoms of expression are to have the 'breathing space' that they 'need to survive.'"

Brennan voiced a serious concern for any law like the Alabama statute, because concerned citizens and "would-be critics of official conduct may be deterred from voicing their criticism, even though it is believed to be true and even though it is in fact true, because of doubt whether it can be proved in court or fear of the expense of having to do so." Libel laws like this would "dampen the vigor and limit the variety of public debate." As examined further on in a discussion of SLAPPs (Strategic Lawsuits Against Public Participation), Brennan's concern for the fear of financial ruin in defending one's statements could have the greatest chilling effect on free speech and press.

What "public officials" does the *Sullivan* precedent include? Although *Sullivan* appeared to apply to nonelected officials, the Supreme Court expanded this definition to mean "those among the hierarchy of government employees who have, or appear to have, substantial responsibility for or control over the conduct of public affairs" *(Rosenblatt* v. *Baer)*. The definition was expanded further to candidates for public office in the case, *Monitor Patriot Co.* v. *Roy*.

Public Figures

Some readers may wonder where persons like movie stars, professional athletes, and others whose faces often appear in the supermarket tabloids fall within this area of libel law. Shortly after the *Sullivan* case, the Supreme Court, while highly divided in opinion, expanded the domain of public officials to include public figures in two 1967 cases, *Curtis Publishing Co.* v. *Butts* and *Associated Press* v. *Walker*. Essentially, some would suggest that by making it more difficult for public officials and public figures to sue the print and electronic media for libel, the press would have greater freedom to engage in public debate.

Of course, others have suggested that these rulings gave the press a special license for sensationalism.

Gertz v. *Robert Welch, Inc.*

In 1974 with *Gertz* v. *Robert Welch, Inc.,* Gertz, a prominent civil rights attorney, successfully sued the publisher of *American Opinion,* the prominent publication of the John Birch Society. Like the Rodney King case minus the media madness, Gertz filed a police brutality suit for his client, an African American male. Gertz maintained that Welch's publication had defamed his character by claiming that Gertz had "communist connections" and by accusing Gertz of framing the police officer in the original police brutality case. In writing the controlling opinion for a five-to-four majority, Justice Lewis Powell expanded the free press protection against libelous lawsuits. Justice Powell claimed, "public officials and public figures usually enjoy significantly greater access to the channels of effective communication and hence have a more realistic opportunity to counteract false statements than private individuals normally enjoy." Furthermore, Powell claimed that public figures invite the "risk of closer public scrutiny" since these individuals have chosen to be in the public spotlight. We know that we may identify public officials as elected or appointed government officials, but what distinguishes a public figure? How do we know who is a public figure and who is a "private person" without the closer public scrutiny? Justice Powell identified the following characteristics in identifying public figures: "In some instances an individual may achieve such pervasive fame or notoriety that he becomes a public figure for all purposes and in all contexts. More commonly, an individual voluntarily injects himself or is drawn into a particular public controversy and by that becomes a public figure for a limited range of issues. In either case, such persons assume special prominence in the resolution of public questions." Here, a lower court jury had awarded Gertz a substantial sum to recover from the defamation damages incurred from the *American Opinion* article. However, the lower court judge overturned the jury award and granted the verdict in favor of the defendant, Welch. The lower court judge, using the aforementioned libel precedents, contended that they must prove "actual malice" here since the case dealt with a matter of significant public issue. In reversing the lower court judge's decision to over-turn the jury verdict, Justice Powell went to great lengths to try to clarify concepts such as "public officials," "public figures," and "public issues." Justice Powell claimed that Gertz deserved the same privacy rights as a private individual, not a public figure. Although the case had received some attention because of the public issue of police misconduct, this issue could not hold Gertz to the higher standard of being in the public spotlight. Powell concluded his controlling reasoning by saying, "Private individuals are not only more vulnerable to injury than public officials and public figures, they are also more deserving of recovery." Gertz, as a private figure, deserved what the trial jury had awarded him in recovery.

So what protections do you have if you engage in public participation (e.g., organizing protests, speaking out at rallies, coordinating petition drives, etc.)? Can the press and other persons engage in a feeding frenzy, attacking your every move, examining and revealing your private life as you increase your public participation? Many remember the shocking treatment given by the media to celebrities such as Princess Diana and O. J. Simpson, but anyone could become a "public figure." And what recourse or remedy do you have if you are targeted for your public actions? The Supreme Court, while often divided in reasoning, has generally agreed that an individual should be able to pursue a participatory public life without fear of the press or others ruining the person's reputation. Specifically, the Court has ruled, "A lawsuit no doubt may be used . . . [a]s a powerful instrument of coercion or retaliation . . . [r]egardless of how unmeritorious the . . . [s]uit is, the target will most likely have to retain counsel and incur substantial legal expenses to defend against it. Furthermore, the chilling effect upon a target's willingness to engage in constitutionally protected activity is multiplied where the complaint seeks damages in addition to injunctive relief" *(Bill Johnson's Restaurants* v. *NLRB).* Furthermore, this case suggested that the First Amendment will not protect some nuisance actions. The Court concluded, "Such suits are not within the scope of First Amendment protection: 'The First Amendment interests involved in private litigation—compensation for violated rights and interests, the psychological benefits of vindication, public airing of the disputed facts—are not advanced when the litigation is based on intentional falsehoods or on knowingly frivolous claims. Furthermore, since sham litigation by definition does not involve a bona fide grievance, it does not come within the first amendment right to petition.'. . . Baseless litigation is not immunized by the First Amendment right to petition."

Citizens will continue to contest the law of libel. It will evolve as legislatures and courts establish different statutes and precedents. In protecting the right to petition, the Supreme Court is moving to a greater recognition of that protection.

Electronic Media

What about the protection of communication through the electronic media? Do you have all First Amendment protections on the information superhighway, the Internet, on cable television, on cellular phones, on whatever wizardly wonders are on the horizon? If the government regulates and licenses some electronic media (e.g., radio, television, utilities like telephonics), then how do our religious clauses enter into the picture, sound, or message? What about the right to free speech, press, assembly, and petition by way of these mediums? What about privacy rights? Are they also part of the First Amendment umbrella? There is nothing absolute about our fundamental freedoms.

First, who controls the airwaves and television times? Are the airwaves provided the same protection of free speech and press as the print media? Recall that the First Amendment does not protect certain forms of expression in the print media, such as obscenity, threats to national security, fighting words, and libel. In practice, someone can challenge governmental attempts to prohibit or restrict any expression that might be construed as unprotected speech. However, the government has the greater burden of proving a compelling interest in prohibiting the questioned expression. Therefore, what might be considered obscene and unprotected speech on radio or television? One could argue, as in the print media, that in the absence of the traditional test of obscenity, then the reader, viewer, or hearer of the expression voluntarily participates in selecting to receive the message. In other words, you have every right to turn off the radio or television, you may tune to another station, you are not a captive audience. Therefore, if the message is offensive to you, you chose your own poison.

In one of the more notorious tests of offensive speech on the airwaves, a parent objected to a monologue being played on public radio, specifically Pacifica Radio. This was the famous comedy monologue called "Filthy Words" by George Carlin. A New York radio station broadcast this monologue in the mid-afternoon in which Carlin goes through a litany of obscene words not considered proper for public broadcast by the FCC (Federal Communications Commission). The radio station broadcast a warning to listeners prior to playing the monologue, informing the listeners that the following monologue by George Carlin included "sensitive language which might be regarded as offensive to some listeners." The FCC received a complaint from a man who said he had heard the broadcast while driving with his young son. In *FCC (Federal Communications Commission)* v. *Pacifica Foundation,* the Supreme Court upheld the power of the FCC to regulate the timing of this type of expression (i.e., not permitting offensive language during morning or afternoon listening time when young children are more likely to hear it). In recognizing the FCC's power in regulating radio and television, Justice Stevens observed, "Of all forms of communication, it is broadcasting that has received the most limited First Amendment protection." While the Court did not deem the Pacifica situation obscene using the Miller test, the majority of the Court subscribed to the regulatory power of the FCC in proscribing a time and a place for such expression. The Court majority concluded that words did not need to be obscene to be prohibited. The FCC has the authority to consider audience, medium, time of day, and method of transmission as relevant factors in determining whether to invoke sanctions. The Pacifica decision, combined with the 1969 decision in *Red Lion Broadcasting Co.* v. *FCC* and along with statutory action by Congress, has led some legal scholars and public policy analysts to suggest that the government may exercise greater power in controlling the electronic airwaves, for the effective "public interest" of all.

The Communications Decency Act (CDA) and the Internet

As our electronic frontier expands and nearly explodes, we see and hear more controversial cases. Who will control what cable and satellite television broadcast? What about the information highway, that is, the Internet? Who will have the power to regulate such media and messages, particularly in the light of knowing some transmissions come from far beyond the borders of the United States? The first major effort to control the Internet medium was by Congress. In 1996, Congress passed and President Clinton signed the Communications Decency Act (CDA). This act was part of a larger statute called the Telecommunications Act of 1996. Even prior to the passage of this act, a broad coalition of organizations and individuals warned that the passage would inhibit expression, and most of those protesting the new act claimed that parts of the act were clearly unconstitutional.

As soon as the president signed this act into law, these organized groups challenged the constitutionality of several of the provisions of the act. The American Civil Liberties Union, later joined by the American Library Association and another twelve groups, including Apple Computer, Inc., sued the chief law enforcement officer, Attorney General Janet Reno. Specifically, these groups challenged the following provisions of this new law:

- The provision that any person in interstate or foreign communications, who, "by means of a telecommunications devise, knowingly makes, creates, or solicits, and initiates the transmission of any comment, request, suggestion, proposal, image or other communication which is obscene or indecent, knowing that the recipient of the communication is under 18 years of age, shall be criminally fined or imprisoned."

- The patently offensive provision, because it makes it a crime to use an "interactive computer service" to send or display in a manner available to a person under age 18, "any comment, request, suggestion, proposal, image, or other communication that, in context, depicts or describes, in terms patently offensive as measured by contemporary community standards, sexual or excretory activities or organs, regardless of whether the user placed the call or initiated the communication."

- The provisions that make it a crime for anyone to "knowingly permit any telecommunications facility under his or her control to be used for any activity prohibited in this Act."

- The provision that criminalizes speech over the Internet that transmits information about abortions or abortifacient drugs and devices, prohibiting the sending and receiving of information over the Internet by means regarding "where, how, or of whom, or by what means any drug, medicine, article, or thing designed, adapted, or intended for producing abortion may be obtained or made."

The organizations who combined as plaintiffs challenging the Communications Decency Act noted in the stipulated facts that even the discussion of the *FCC* v. *Pacifica Foundation* case would transmit George Carlin's seven-dirty-words monologue to anyone who enters the Internet transmission.

Also, all parties acknowledged in the stipulated facts that "there is no effective way to determine the identity or the age of a user who is accessing material through e-mail, mail exploders, news groups or chat rooms." The government offered no evidence that there is a reliable way to ensure that they could screen recipients and participants in such a forum for age.

Despite elaborate wizardry interwoven to try to block certain transmissions, most experts concluded that such blocking efforts could be broken, codes decoded, and the expense prohibitive for many casual users of the Internet. Besides attempting to block transmissions of domestic communications, this case also showed that nearly 40 percent of the content of the Internet originates from transmission sites outside the United States. In other words, current technology cannot stop most transmissions once someone is online. Thus, the court was left to examine how the First Amendment would apply to this twenty-first century technology.

So how would the medium of the Internet differ from other forms of transmitting information (e.g., by radio, television, or telephone)? We have already noted those areas of speech not protected by the First Amendment (e.g., obscenity, libel, national security). What about those gray areas? For example, several of the plaintiffs were noncommercial and not-for-profit organizations, educational consortia, and public interest groups. Some information transmitted by way of the Internet may contain messages deemed "indecent" or "offensive" by some persons, while providing valuable information. Many Internet messages transmitted contained life-saving information on protection from AIDS, birth-control information, and even warnings and preventive information regarding prison rape.

While acknowledging that some of this information might be offensive, all parties agreed that the plaintiffs were not purveyors of pornography.

Since much of the governing provisions of the CDA relied on interpretations of "indecent" and "patently offensive." Since the Internet is an international medium, with speech transmitted beyond our shores, and with an acknowledgment that the technology to block transmissions is currently limited, the appellate court struck down several key provisions of the CDA as vague and unfair.

In acknowledging the unconstitutional aspects of CDA, the federal appeals court granted the preliminary injunction to halt the carrying out of CDA. The court upheld the prohibition regarding transmitting pornography to children, but the court also concluded that there are times when mature minors may benefit from the freedom to receive information others might find offensive. For example, the court noted that material routinely acceptable according to the standards of New York City, such as the Broadway play *Angels in America*, might be far less acceptable in smaller communities in the United States since the play involves homosexuality and AIDS portrayed in graphic language. The court noted that this play, like other classics, may invite revulsion from some. Yet it may receive accolades from others, as this play did by receiving two Tony Awards and a Pulitzer prize for its author. In fact, some educators would deem such artistic expression appropriate educational material for some eleventh- and twelfth-grade students. Such material might be readily available on the Internet, and the court felt this transmission should fall within the scope of protected speech. Quoting an earlier Supreme Court decision, the appeals court concluded, "minors are entitled to a significant measure of First Amendment protection, and only in relatively narrow and well-defined circumstances may government bar public dissemination of protected materials to them" (*Erznoznik* v. *City of Jacksonville*).

Furthermore, the appeals court noted the unique interactive and potential participatory nature of the Internet in creating a true "marketplace of ideas." This court quoted Justice Holmes from his famous Abrams dissent, "When men have realized that time has upset many fighting faiths, they may come to believe even more than they believe the very foundations of their own conduct that the ultimate good desired is better reached by free trade in ideas—that the best test of truth is the power of the thought to get itself accepted in the competition of the market. . . . (*Abrams* v. *United States*).

This court noted that the "marketplace of ideas" debate has been greatly criticized owing to political and economic realities. Who has the power and wealth to control the medium for the message? As the Supreme Court noted in *Miami Herald Publishing Co.* v. *Tornillo,* a few wealthy voices dominate most marketplaces of mass speech. So what about the Internet? This decision concluded, "As the most participatory form of mass speech yet developed, the Internet deserves the highest protection from governmental intrusion. . . . The absence of governmental regulation of Internet content has unquestionably produced a kind of chaos, but as one of plaintiffs' experts put it with such resonance at the hearing [on CDA]: *What achieved success was the very chaos that the Internet is. The strength of the Internet is that chaos.* Just as the strength of the Internet is chaos, so the strength of our liberty depends upon the chaos and cacophony of the unfettered speech the First Amendment protects. For these reasons, I without hesitation hold the CDA unconstitutional on its face."

As this text goes to press, the cases and controversy over attempts to censor the Internet continue. In July 1996, shortly following the Philadelphia Federal Court three-judge panel ruling discussed above, Janet Reno, acting for the Justice Department, appealed this CDA decision. Some critics of the CDA ruling have suggested that politics and ideology played an important role in the federal court case. Cathy Cleaver, Director of Legal Studies for the Family Research Council, claimed that federal judge Dolores Sloviter, Chief Judge of the Third Circuit Court of Appeals and an appointee of President Carter, made "an arrogant decision which flies in the face of the Supreme Court and our society. . . . Cyberspace is a work in progress. We should not squander the opportunity to examine and appreciate a world where pornography knows no bounds. Failure to enact strong laws is a concession that the information superhighway should belong to pornographers. It would be like leaving a loaded gun in a playground."

This conflict will continue in public debate, and also in the courts. Will truth and justice prevail in the marketplace? Will the wealthy and politically powerful continue to dominate the marketplace?

Access to the Marketplace and the Media

At the time of passage and adoption of the First Amendment, the most complex medium might have been the printing press and the proliferation of pamphlets, newspapers, and occasional news magazines. Clearly the framers of the First Amendment had not considered the impact of radio, traditional television, cablevision, satellite transmissions, the Internet, or even the telephone. Not until 1927, with the Radio Act, and the 1934 Communications Act, did Congress attempt to regulate the airwaves. Why did the airwaves need regulation, while the print media did not? For one obvious reason, the airwaves are limited. There are only so many frequencies on the radio, and the same is true of television. Therefore, the early Congressional action required those stations licensed to serve the "public interest, convenience, or necessity." So what is this "public interest"? For example, should all candidates for public office have equal access to the airwaves? Should radio and television air all viewpoints and controversies? Is there a right to send and receive information and persuasive arguments using our electronic media?

The "Fairness Doctrine"

To provide some semblance of fairness, Congress empowered the Federal Communications Commission to regulate access to the electronic mass media. The FCC initially promulgated the "fairness doctrine," requiring broadcasters to "afford reasonable opportunity for the discussion of conflicting views on issues of public importance." Therefore, if a candidate for public office attacks another candidate's views on any issue, especially those likely to inflame public opinion (e.g., abortion, death penalty, legalization of marijuana, immigration, etc.), should the media give the candidate's opponent or opponents equal time?

Specifically, the FCC has rejected a quid pro quo equal time provision, but the earlier fairness doctrine was soon tested in *Red Lion Broadcasting Co., Inc.* v. *Federal Communications Commission* in 1969. In *Red Lion,* an eight-to-zero majority, with Justice Douglas not participating, concluded that the fairness doctrine is of the utmost importance to the listening and viewing public. The Supreme Court concluded that the public has a right to have broadcasters "function consistently with the ends and purposes of the First Amendment. . . . It is the right of the viewers and listeners, not the right of broadcasters, which is paramount." The Court did not conclude that all electronic broadcast became a marketplace of ideas; instead, the Court made clear that the domain of the "fairness doctrine" remains with the regulatory policy of the FCC.

Some First Amendment advocates claimed that the FCC was infringing on free speech and free press by requiring broadcasters to provide time to respond to other viewpoints. In a concurring opinion in *CBS (Columbia Broadcasting Systems)* v. *DNC (Democratic National Committee),* Justice William O. Douglas proclaimed, "the fairness doctrine has no place in our first amendment regime. It puts the head of the camel inside the tent and allows administration after administration to toy with TV or radio." Douglas seems to have identified the serious problem of politicizing the doctrine from one administration to another.

By the middle of the Reagan presidency, it had become apparent that Reagan appointees to the FCC, especially chairman Dennis Patrick, would weaken the fairness doctrine. Among the cases showing this change, was a complaint filed by the Syracuse Peace Council demanding a fair response to the Meredith Corporation's WTVH-TV station airing of commercials endorsing the construction of a nuclear power plant in the area.

In response to the Syracuse Peace Council's complaint, the FCC did conclude that WTVH had violated the fairness rules in airing pronuclear commercials while not providing air time for antinuclear responses. The Meredith Corporation challenged the FCC's conclusion in the D.C. Court of Appeals. The Court of Appeals upheld the FCC's decision, and most importantly, affirmed the FCC's administrative jurisdiction in determining if the station had not satisfied fairness doctrine requirements. They sent the case back to the FCC to assess satisfaction of the fairness doctrine requirement. As Justice Douglas had warned, upon reconsideration and under the leadership of chairman Patrick, the FCC concluded that the fairness doctrine violated the intent of the First

Amendment and "contravened the public interest." On August 4, 1987, the FCC formally eliminated the fairness doctrine, and President Reagan proceeded to veto any legislative attempts to reimpose the doctrine.

The D.C. Court of Appeals shed light on the diminishing role of the fairness doctrine in the *Meredith* case. The Court wrote, "The explosive growth of information sources—in both traditional broadcasting sources (radio and television) and new substitutes for broadcasting such as cable TV, SMATV, VCRs and LPTV—made the Fairness Doctrine no longer necessary to assure that the public has access to a variety of viewpoints." Shortly after that, the FCC repealed the fairness doctrine.

Some critics of the repeal point out that many lower-income families simply cannot spare the extra cash for regular cable payments and cannot afford computers let alone on-line services or other multimedia. Some syndicated talk show hosts, like Ellen Ratner of Talk Radio News Network, have suggested, "The fairness doctrine is simply saying that you must somehow reach the needs of the community, and it puts on paper what should be happening anyway. I truly believe that, to have an honest discussion and be entertaining, you must have both points of view."

Fairness and Accuracy In Reporting (FAIR) like many other critics and organized activists concerned with an oligarchic control of the multimedia, went further and called for a multitude of viewpoints and voices to be heard. The Media Access Project, a not-for-profit telecommunications law firm, began advocating reinstatement of the fairness doctrine after its death in 1987. Yet most public policy analysts acknowledge that public officials will focus on winning elections and pushing special interests. Of course, those interests do not always coincide with several viewpoints being presented on the public airwaves. In addition, the multimedia magnates, combined with merger mania, are focused on profit-making, not necessarily promoting the public interest.

So in the famous Jeffersonian admonition calling for an enlightened citizenry to firmly preserve democracy, Americans must ask, how are we to enlighten, inform and energize citizens to make informed judgments if the citizens have a limited marketplace of ideas from which to shop and invest? What responsibility, if any, does government have in giving the people a right to receive information and a right to free speech and press?

Campaign Contributions

Even former Judge Robert Bork agreed that the framers intended political speech and public policy debate to be "highly protected" speech, while suggesting commercial and other forms of speech to be "low protected" speech. While giving lip service to this higher degree of protected speech, the strict constructionists, like Bork, Rehnquist, and Scalia, support the Court opinions that have given the wealthiest the greater voice in the political arena. The landmark 1976 case, *Buckley* v. *Valeo,* set forth a force for money and influence peddling that has continued in a series of political speech cases through the 1995–1996 term.

The *Buckley* case challenged the Federal Election Campaign Act (FECA) and the regulations of the Federal Election Commission (FEC). The Federal Election Campaign Act of 1971, as amended in 1974, attempted to place limits on campaign contributions and expenditures. It also attempted to create greater accountability for recording the funding sources. Much of this reform emerged from the congressional and legal investigations of the financial improprieties connected with the Watergate scandal. Individuals contributed sacks and grocery bags full of money, with only a handful of individuals knowing the source of the contributions. No one knows what promises were made in the negotiations for contributions. The series of financial fiascos and subsequent obstruction of justice led to the eventual conviction of several White House officials and officials with the Committee to Re-Elect the President (CREEP), and also the resignation of President Nixon in 1974. Congress passed an amendment to the Federal Election Campaign Act with an intent to reduce or prevent such campaign excesses.

Opponents challenged the amended FECA as violating free speech rights of the First Amendment, and the right of contributors to remain anonymous. The challengers claimed FECA deprived them of raising whatever funds necessary to access the modern and expensive media. The limitations would severely limit individuals and groups from spreading their message and promoting their candidates and causes. In the 1976 *Buckley* case, the Court struck down provisions in the Federal Election Campaign Act that restricted campaign contributions and expenditures. The opinions of the justices varied greatly, reflecting much of the current debate on campaign finance on the eve of the 1996 presidential election.

As for limiting the amount an individual could give to a candidate's campaign for the presidency or Congress, the Court upheld a $1,000 maximum per individual. In addition, it upheld the reporting of larger contributions in presidential and congressional campaigns. Yet beyond the contribution limitations on outside individuals, the plethora of opinions making up a controlling opinion pretty much gutted the remainder of the FECA. For example, government could not prohibit individuals from spending an infinite amount on his or her campaign. Thus, multimillionaires may spend millions of their own money to buy television, radio, and any other advertising time to promote themselves and their election. In addition, the Court declared that "independent" efforts that might help promote a candidate or a cause could not be limited in either contributions or expenditures. Therefore, if the Democratic or Republican National Committees wished to spend millions from contributions given directly to the DNC or RNC to promote a presidential or congressional candidate, the FEC could not place limits on these contributions and expenditures. The FEC could generally impose reporting on larger amounts, but it could place no limits on contributions or expenditures. The ruling is universal to all campaigning interests independent of the candidate. Therefore, large conservative (e.g., the Christian Coalition or business associations) or liberal organizations (e.g., labor unions and teacher associations) could spend millions promoting their candidates and causes, with the same end in view—to elect their person to the presidency or Congress.

The Supreme Court has upheld this free-wheeling, money-driven dynamic in several subsequent cases. In *Buckley*, a majority of the Court did accept the Congressional provision and power to place a ceiling on how much a presidential candidate can spend, if the candidate accepts public financing of his or her campaign. However, like Ross Perot's 1992 election bid, in which he received 19 percent of the vote from those participating, he did not have to abide by the spending limits since he accepted no federal matching funds. Furthermore, candidates have found a variety of ways to promote their message without worrying about spending limits, especially when they rely on other forums to raise money for them that are technically independent of their campaigns.

In 1985, in *Federal Election Commission* v. *National Conservative Political Action Committee,* the Supreme Court ruled laws could not apply spending ceilings to those individuals or groups spending independently to help a publicly funded candidate. Here, the Court struck down portions of the Presidential Election Campaign Fund Act that made it a criminal offense for an independent political action committee (PAC) to expend more than $1,000 for presidential candidates who accepted matching public financing. Writing for the majority, Chief Justice Rehnquist claimed, "To say that their collective action in pooling their resources is not entitled to full First Amendment protection would subordinate the voices of those of modest means as opposed to those sufficiently wealthy to be able to buy expensive media ads with their own resources." In the majority opinion, this legislation was too broad and the government could not convey a compelling interest in regulating "independent" group expenditures.

In *First National Bank* v. *Bellotti,* the Court applied the same rationale in striking down a Massachusetts statute. This law had made it a crime for corporations to make contributions and expenditures to influence ballot initiatives or referenda unless the proposed ballot issue materially affected the corporation. In striking down this law on First Amendment grounds, Justice Powell wrote, "The inherent worth of the speech in terms of its capacity for informing the public does not depend on the identity of its source, whether corporation, association, union or individual."

A pattern appears concerning campaign financing and protected speech. In 1986, in the *Federal Election Commission* v. *Massachusetts Citizens for Life (MCFL),* the Court upheld the right of a nonprofit voluntary association, Massachusetts Citizens for Life, to make expenditures for candidates and causes. Most recently, at the end of the 1996 term, the Supreme Court again struck down any attempts to regulate political speech broadly in the case *Colorado Republican Federal Campaign Committee* v. *Federal Election Commission.*

The one exception to this series of cases was in 1990 with *Austin* v. *Michigan Chamber of*

Commerce, where the Michigan legislature had enacted a law prohibiting corporations from using corporate treasury funds for independent expenditures in elections for public office. The Michigan statute permitted corporations to make expenditures from segregated funds, such as political action committees, but not from their general treasury. Here, a majority of the justices distinguished between smaller nonprofit organizations, such as Massachusetts Citizens for Life, and larger organizations, such as the Chamber of Commerce. The majority opinion claimed that smaller organizations would have an undue burden in segregating their funds from campaign to general expenses, while large organizations, like the Chamber, could easily establish a separate, voluntary political action committee within its structure.

Writing for the majority, Justice Thurgood Marshall, claimed, "The State's decision to regulate only corporations is precisely tailored to serve the compelling state interest of eliminating from the political process the corrosive effect of political 'war chests' amassed with the aid of the legal advantages given to corporations." This opinion seemed to contradict *Buckley* and *Bellotti,* and several justices dissented. Writing in dissent, Justice Scalia argued that Marshall's opinion endorsed an antispeech principle, in essence, "too much speech is an evil that the democratic majority can proscribe." Also in dissent, Justice Kennedy stated that Marshall's majority opinion meant "the Court upholds a direct restriction on the independent expenditure of funds for political speech for the first time in history." Although some might argue with Kennedy's historical recollections, the Scalia and Kennedy positions now clearly dominate the Court's majority thinking in matters of campaign finance.

With the 1996 decision granting the Colorado Republican Campaign Committee limitless spending in campaigns, scholars generally agree that the current Court is not going to uphold most government initiatives to limit political speech. Therefore, campaign finance reform may become a moot issue in the judicial arena. Clearly, with the revelations and outcry for action to control campaign spending, after the more than $2 billion spent in the 1996 election with alleged irregularities and with contributions from sources outside the United States, Congress will probably take some action for finance reform. Simultaneously,

one can imagine a member of Congress opposed to campaign finance reform contacting a constitutional scholar and, asking, "If I vote for restrictions or stronger regulations on campaign contributions and expenditures, are the federal courts likely to strike down the legislation?" Looking at the precedents, the scholar might very well respond yes. Therefore, this legislator can claim he or she supported campaign finance reform, but those darn federal judges killed it. So will it take a constitutional amendment to reform the corrupting influence of money in political campaigns? And if Congress passed such an amendment, and public sentiment seems to favor some drastic action to curb the excesses, would the new amendment clash with the First Amendment? Then one must ask, which amendment will prevail in the opinions of the current Court?

Commercial Speech

Before leaving the area of speech in modern times and with multimedia, consider the protections of commercial speech. The analogy with political speech might be closer than you imagine. Some have compared the current campaign of money madness with commercial campaigns investing millions to make Joe Camel a cultural icon worthy of customer brand loyalty. In the current climate, commentators often argue that if you can spend millions to persuade consumers to purchase a particular brand of toilet tissue, then what is the difference with the selling of Mr. or Ms. Smith to go to Washington to govern from the nation's capitol? So is commercial speech afforded the same protections as political speech? Are paid advertisements much different from political ads?

As discussed earlier, *New York Times* v. *Sullivan* involved a paid advertisement, and Justice Brennan strongly afforded it the same First Amendment protections as speech in a public forum. The first major Supreme Court decision granting greater protection of commercial speech occurred in 1976, in *Virginia State Board of Pharmacy* v. *Virginia Citizens Consumer Council, Inc.* A Virginia state law prohibited pharmacists from advertising the price of prescription drugs. The Virginia Citizens Consumer Council, along with some behind the scene support from large drugstore chains, challenged the Virginia law as violating the commercial speech rights of pharmacies to advertise prices, and the rights of consumers to receive information. The Supreme Court struck down the Virginia law as infringing on the free speech rights of the pharmacists and the rights of consumers. According to Justice Blackmun's majority opinion, the consumer's interest in

the free flow of information may be as keen, if not keener by far, than his interest in the day's most urgent political debate. . . . When drug prices vary as strikingly as they do, information as to who is charging what becomes more than convenience. It could mean the alleviation of physical pain or the enjoyment of basic necessities. . . . Advertising, however tasteless and excessive it sometimes may seem, is nonetheless dissemination of information as to who is producing and selling what product, for what reason, and at what price. So long as we preserve a predominantly free enterprise economy, the allocation of our resources largely will be made through many private economic decisions. It is a matter of public interest that those decisions, in the aggregate, be intelligent and well informed. To this end, the free flow of commercial information is indispensable.

The next major case, *Central Hudson Gas & Electric Corp.* v. *Public Service Commission of New York,* found justices developing a test to determine when the First Amendment protected certain commercial speech. The majority of justices contended that it could under the following circumstances, when

- The message is misleading or involves illegal activity.

- The government regulation advances a substantial government interest.

- The regulation must directly advance the asserted government interest.

- The regulation must not be more extensive than is necessary to serve the governmental interest at stake.

Applying this test to *Central Hudson* illustrates the reasoning. In *Central Hudson,* the electric utility claimed that a government regulation banning the promotional advertising by an utility violated the utility's First Amendment speech protection. The Public Service Commission claimed that such self-promoting advertising was contrary to the overall national energy conservation policy.

In response to the first criteria, the justices agreed that the utilities pro-electric use message was not misleading or illegal. The justices also agreed that the second criteria had been satisfied, that is, the government has a substantial interest in conserving energy and preserving a fair rate structure. Regarding the third criteria, the majority of justices did not believe this regulation directly advanced the stated government interest. The majority said the relationship between the regulation and a fair rate formula was too tenuous and speculative.

The government could not show a correlation between rate increases or decreases and utility advertisement. Therefore, the Court claimed the regulation was "silencing the utility's promotional advertising." And according to Justice Powell's controlling opinion, the Commission's regulation could not satisfy the fourth criteria. The government did not tailor the regulation narrowly enough to satisfy the government interest. The regulation banned all advertising whether or not it had an impact on energy conservation or utility rates. Therefore, the Court struck down the broad ban on this commercial speech, and in so doing, created an intermediate test that went beyond rational basis but not as stringent as the strict scrutiny test.

In 1993, in *Cincinnati* v. *Discovery Network, Inc.,* the Court struck down a local ordinance that banned news racks distributing "commercial publications" but not news racks distributing newspapers. Using the fourth part of the Central Hudson test, Justice Stevens wrote for the majority, "It was the city's burden to establish a 'reasonable fit' between its legitimate interests in safety and esthetics and its choice of a limited and selective prohibition of news racks as the means chosen to serve those interests."

Most recently, at the end of the 1995–1996 term, the Court ruled, in *44 Liquormart* v. *Rhode Island,* that the state law forbidding the advertising of liquor prices violated the free speech rights of liquor stores and liquor corporations. Again, this time by unanimous vote, the justices claimed that the state had failed to meet its "heavy burden" of regulating, and in this case, prohibiting liquor price advertisements.

This decision seems to relegate an earlier Court decision to a different era. Ten years earlier, in *Posadas de Puerto Rico Assoc.* v. *Tourism Co. of Puerto Rico,* Justice Rehnquist had written a controlling opinion upholding a local Puerto Rican ordinance prohibiting advertising about casino gambling to the native population of Puerto Rico. Simultaneously, people in the United States, and in many other areas outside Puerto Rico,

Since Congress repealed the Eighteenth Amendment in 1933, federal laws governing the sale of liquor have eased. However, until 1996 the advertising of liquor prices was still forbidden in some states.

could read, hear, and see advertising promoting casino gambling in Puerto Rico. Using the *Central Hudson* test, Justice Rehnquist believed the local ordinance satisfied all parts of the test and was therefore a valid prohibition. Interestingly, the opponents of the ban did not argue against government involvement. Many opponents suggested expanding speech by having commercials discouraging gambling. Justice Rehnquist suggested that such "counter-speech" proposals are better left to the legislative branch to decide.

Most scholars believe the *Posadas* decision to be an anomaly. Most cases, like the recent *44 Liquormart* case, uphold the First Amendment claim of commercial advertisers. In *Carey* v. *Population Services International,* the Court struck down a ban on the advertisement of contraceptives, much like the bans on abortion advertising they have struck down.

Many question where the *44 Liquormart* case may take public policy. Already, the Supreme Court has ordered the U.S. Court of Appeals for the Fourth Circuit to review its upholding of a Baltimore city ordinance banning cigarette billboards. If you cannot ban advertisements promoting liquor sales, how can you ban advertisements for cigarettes? An even more intriguing hypothetical may now be played out in California, where a majority of those voting in the November election enacted an initiative permitting doctors to prescribe the use of marijuana as treatment for some

physical and emotional maladies. Imagine some counterculture magazines, or for that matter, Internet transmissions, that promote the personal cultivation of marijuana for medicinal purposes. Will this be protected commercial speech?

Freedom of Assembly and Petition

The last two clauses of the First Amendment prohibit government from interfering with "the right of the people peaceably to assemble, and to petition the Government for redress of grievances." The right of peaceful assembly has taken many twists and turns. Sometimes the question has been as basic as deciding if it is legal for a crowd of people gathered on a street corner to engage in lively discussion and debate. Are those engaging in rap and hip-hop rhythm and blues exercising their assembly right, or are they obstructing the public flow of traffic, causing safety problems? Or are they just being annoying to those passing by? Would the age of the street-corner crowd make a difference? Would the time of the gathering make a difference? Would the affiliation of the corner crowd make a difference? What if some belonged to a social club or a gang? What if some were members of a militia, or religious zealots promoting a particular cause, or members of competing advocacy groups promoting specific causes or candidates?

The conflicts involving speech and assembly are more difficult than in traditional pure speech cases. Assembly is speech and conduct. By the late-twentieth century, the Court had carved out some basic guidelines regarding speech and assembly. Most of the boundaries involve time, place, and manner of public expression. Expression in public places remains a fundamental right, yet the Court has upheld a variety of rules, regulations, and laws governing the time, place, and manner of such expression.

Antiabortion Protest

One of the more recent and controversial cases involved assembly in and around medical clinics performing abortions. The case also involved peaceful picketing in front of the residencies of workers from those medical clinics, including the doctors and the nurses involved in reproductive counseling and termination of pregnancies. In 1994, in *Madsen* v. *Women's Health Center, Inc.,* the Court examined if an injunction restricting assembly and picketing around an abortion clinic and the residencies of clinic workers violated the assembly rights of those picketing, sitting-in, and talking and confronting those entering the clinics and residencies.

Examining the range of opinions in *Madsen* is tantamount to a tour of the evolution of regulations governing the time, place, and manner of peaceful assembly. Many medical clinic protesters opposing abortions claimed that their expression is following in the grand tradition of civil rights protesters. They pointed out that these protestors engaged in sit-ins, picketing, marches, boycotts, and other conduct to achieve rights for those excluded from fundamental freedoms and economic and educational opportunities. Examples of these groups would be racial or ethnic or other minorities—especially people of color, feminists, people with disabilities, and people choosing alternative lifestyles, such as the gay community. The antiabortion protesters launched daily campaigns at clinics throughout the United States, claiming to seek the fundamental right to life for unborn fetuses.

In this campaign and specifically in the *Madsen* case, the protestors would engage in a variety of tactics to try to stop abortions, such as:

- Impeding access to the clinic by congregating on the paved portion of the street outside the clinic and clinic parking area.

- Marching in front of the clinic's driveway.

- Confronting cars and individuals in and out of the cars who might be coming to the clinic and engaging them in "sidewalk counseling" to dissuade them from seeking or supporting others entering the clinic to terminate a pregnancy.

- Shoving antiabortion literature through the windows of the approaching cars, and sticking such literature into the faces and hands of those attempting to enter the clinics.

- Singing, chanting, and sometimes using loudspeakers and bullhorns to broadcast their anti-abortion messages.

- Sitting-in at the front entrances of the clinics to attempt to block entrance for patients and staff.

- Picketing in front of clinic employees' residences.

- Performing other self-described nonviolent civil disobedience (e.g., blocking doorways, lying down and letting their bodies go limp as law enforcement officers tried to remove them from the clinic doorways).

In *Madsen*, the Women's Health Center sought an injunction to stop the protesters from interfering with staff and patients trying to use the clinic for legitimate medical purposes. A state court granted the injunction and essentially created a 36-foot buffer zone around the clinic entrances and driveway. It established a 300-foot buffer zone around the clinic that prohibited protesters from approaching patients and potential patients unless these patients consented to talk and counseling. It then extended this 300-foot buffer zone to prohibit picketing any closer to the residences of clinic staff. Finally, it restricted excessive noisemaking within the earshot of the clinic.

Despite the injunction, the protesters continued to carry out their tactics to stop the abortions from being performed. The state court had made clear in the injunction that government interests included (1) protecting a pregnant woman's freedom to seek lawful medical or counseling services, (2) ensuring public safety and order, (3) promoting the free flow of traffic on public streets and sidewalks, (4) protecting citizens' property rights, and (5) assuring residential privacy. The protesters claimed that the injunction infringed on their First Amendment rights of speech and assembly. Furthermore, the protesters claimed that all of their actions had been nonviolent on behalf of the voiceless, the unborn.

The Court's varied opinions revisited many precedents addressing assembly. The majority opinion noted that the 1993 Florida Supreme Court in *Operation Rescue* v. *Women's Health Center, Inc.,* had already upheld the state court's injunction. The majority, concurring, and dissenting opinions each agreed that the public streets, sidewalks, and rights-of-way in and around the clinic constituted a traditional public forum, in the tradition of *Frisby* v. *Schultz*. In *Frisby* (1988), the Court considered a local ordinance prohibiting picketing "before or about" any residence. Lawmakers clearly enacted this ordinance to protect doctors' residences from being targeted with focused picketing by antiabortionists. Justice

In 1983 the Supreme Court struck down the broad ban against leafleting and picketing on sidewalks adjoining the Supreme Court, but it did uphold restrictions regarding the time, place, and manner of the picketing and leafleting.

O'Connor, in the Court's controlling opinion, stated, "A public street does not lose its status as a traditional public forum simply because it runs through a residential neighborhood." Although the Court acknowledged the public forum, the majority still voted to uphold the ordinance because the picketing was not directed toward a public flow of information but instead focused on harassing specific doctors and their families in their homes because they were a captive audience.

Peaceable Assembly

Justices also noted that right existed also in the shadows of the Supreme Court and the White House where conflicts had arisen over peaceable assembly. In 1983, in *United States* v. *Grace,* the Court considered whether leafleting and picketing on sidewalks adjoining the Supreme Court was protected speech. There had been a government ban on such conduct. The majority of the Court recognized that such conduct might interfere with the public flow of traffic and possibly safety on the sidewalks and stairs leading to the Court, but the Court also acknowledged the First Amendment freedom of speech and assembly. Therefore, the Court struck down the broad ban but upheld restrictions regarding the time, place, and manner of the picketing and leafleting. In other words, government could impose some boundaries on the protesters. In 1988, *Boos* v. *Barry,* the Court struck down a District of

Columbia ordinance that prohibited the display of signs critical of foreign governments displayed within 500 feet of that government's embassy. The ordinance also permitted police to disperse demonstrators who gathered within 500 feet of the embassies if the police reasonably believed that the demonstrators posed a threat to the peace and security of the embassy. Interestingly, the majority opinion of the Court upheld the dispersal portion of the ordinance but ruled unconstitutional the sign prohibition. The Court reasoned that the sign prohibition was content-based: not permitting signs critical of the specific government embassy being targeted. On the other hand, the authority of law enforcement officials to order the dispersal of a potentially unruly crowd was content-neutral, and solely focused on the conduct, or forecasted conduct, of the demonstrators.

How about peaceful assembly around polling places? Years ago, politicians and political workers approached voters at polling places with campaign materials and stuck literature in their faces and hands. They often advocated, often vociferously, for the approaching voter to support their candidate or cause. Are such speech and conduct protected? In *Burson* v. *Freeman,* the Court considered this question in examining a Tennessee law that prohibited the solicitation of votes and the dissemination of campaign materials within 100 feet of a polling place. Justice Blackmun, in a controlling plurality opinion, noted that the conduct conveyed fundamental free speech protecting political expression. Blackmun also noted that the polling place constituted a public forum and clearly poll workers were distributing materials and advocating for a particular point of view, and therefore, the prohibiting law in effect banned content-based speech. After applying a strict scrutiny test, the plurality of the Court concluded that the state has a compelling interest in enforcing the law—the interest of protecting people's "right to cast a ballot in an election free from intimidation and fraud." The controlling opinion noted that the 100-foot zone free of campaigners was not "an unconstitutional compromise."

In deciding *Madsen*, both the majority and dissenting opinions invoked *NAACP* v. *Claiborne Hardware*. In the Court's controlling opinion, the NAACP could not be held liable for economic damages or hardships incurred by white business owners despite a strongly sponsored boycott of these businesses by the NAACP. The businesses, like the hardware store, argued that leaders of the boycott, backed by the NAACP, had intimidated and outright threatened people with reprisals if they patronized the businesses. The Court acknowledged that one of the civil rights leaders, Charles Evers, had warned an audience of mainly African Americans, "If we catch any of you going in any of them racist stores, we're going to break your damn neck." A majority of the Court concluded that advocacy of force and violence alone would not justify prohibiting the speech or requiring damages for making the speech. The Court further stated, a speaker must be free "to stimulate his audience with spontaneous and emotional appeals for unity and action in a common cause."

In his strongly worded dissent in *Madsen*, Justice Scalia revisited the *Claiborne* case, claiming that the boycott leaders had even posted watchers outside stores to take photos and names of any persons frequenting the boycotted businesses. Scalia asked how this form of conduct was any different from antiabortion protesters who held vigils in front of clinics and near the residences of those working in the clinics, especially doctors who performed abortions. The Court has upheld the conduct of members of the NAACP and their boycott supporters, while states have restricted most conduct of antiabortion protesters imposed injunction.

In the *Madsen* case, the majority and concurring opinions upheld the state court injunction, with a few exceptions. Among the exceptions were the following First Amendment guidelines:

- The injunction prohibiting "images observable" (e.g., graphic protest signs) sweeps more broadly than necessary to achieve the government interest of assuring privacy for patients and clinic staff.

- The Court noted that the curtains covering the windows could be closed so clinic workers might not see protest signs.

- The 300-foot ban around the clinic and around staff residences is too broad absent any evidence that the protesters' speech would incite violence or constitute "fighting words."

- The Court did suggest that reasonable measures may be taken, by injunction if necessary, to prevent intimidation and ensure access to the clinic. Concerning the areas around clinic workers' residences, the Court suggested other limited remedies (e.g., a reasonable boundary to protect the privacy and tranquility of the home; limits on the time, duration of picketing, and number of picketers; and turning down the volume on any sound amplification if the protests seem to overwhelm a neighborhood.

The Court's controlling opinion represents a delicate balance in protecting the rights of those wishing to engage in peaceable assembly and the rights of others affected by the assembly. *Madsen* presents a line of late-twentieth century cases that describe the results of tailoring the often competing interests to reach a reasonable balance. Justices, like Scalia, accused the majority in *Madsen* of hypocrisy. Much like his criticism involving "hate speech" and the "abortion" conflicts, Scalia suggests the Court has recognized one set of principles for some groups (e.g., civil rights protesters) while failing to recognize the rights of others (e.g., antiabortion protesters).

So where are we left with our fundamental freedom to assemble? As conflicts arise, the Court will continue to visit this freedom, and most likely, it will maintain a delicate balance that will probably include some regulation regarding the time, place, and manner for expressing this right.

With the evolution and dominance of two major political parties in the twentieth century—Democrats and Republicans—access to the ballot has become more restrictive.

Freedom to Petition

The right to petition the government for redress of grievances seems as fundamental as "Hey, I have a right to my opinion." It also appears fundamental in whatever form, whether direct petitioning to lawmakers, to executive branch leaders, or to school board members, or petitioning for access to the ballot in order to have your voice and vote expressed.

Access to the Ballot

This chapter will focus on the right to petition the government for access to the ballot. Traditionally, individual states have determined most election laws (other than the Constitutional requirements for federal office holding). Therefore, there is a complex maze of state laws and regulations governing access to the ballot. That is why some state ballots had more than 50 persons listed as presidential candidates. Some states included the Green Party candidate, the New Labor Party candidate, the Natural Law Party, the Taxpayers' Party, the Socialist Workers Party, and on and on. Other states had far fewer—as few as four candidates listed—candidates from the Democratic, Republican, Reform, and Libertarian Parties. How would a citizen even know who he or she could vote for if all candidates do not appear on the ballot? What if I had worked hard for the Green Party presidential candidate, Ralph Nader, and then moved to a state where the Green Party's petitions for ballot access did not meet the state's requirement? Must I choose from candidates I have not supported as the "lesser of evils?"

Answers to these questions have not been found in the body of our U.S. Constitution. Everyone planning to seek to have a voice and a vote as a candidate or in promoting a cause needs to check each state's requirements for access to the ballot. Deciding ballot-access requirements and the right to petition to become a candidate or to have an issue (e.g., an initiative or referendum) on the ballot has presented itself in cases of controversy before the Supreme Court, especially in the late-twentieth century. Be mindful that in our early history during times of limited franchise and many political factions, access was probably much easier and far less restrictive. With the evolution and dominance of two major parties in the twentieth century, those in party power often moved to enact laws that restricted ballot access so that the main parties could monopolize the political process and limit the parameters of debate.

Every local, state, and federal election found these conflicts to be alive and highly debatable. As a general public, we are more likely to be aware of these conflicts in the field of selecting presidential candidates. With media focus on those with power, funds, and influence, we have particularly noted the conflicts when a well-known figure breaks off from the traditional parties to form an independent candidacy or a new party. The twentieth century is full of examples: Teddy Roosevelt's Bull Moose Party, Eugene Debs's Socialist Party, Henry Wallace's Progressive Party.

In more recent history, Congressman John Anderson broke from the Republican Party to run as an independent candidate. His inability to gain access on some state ballots led him to file a complaint in federal court that the Supreme Court eventually decided by a five-to-four vote. In 1983, in *Anderson* v. *Celebrezze,* Justice Stevens writing for the majority concluded that Ohio's petitioning requirements for ballot access placed too great a burden on potential candidates. Ohio required independent candidates to file their nominating petitions in March in order to appear on the November election. Think about that—many political candidates, even among the major political parties, are still waging a battle for the party's nomination until late spring or early summer. The nominees for president from the Democratic and Republican Parties are not even chosen, officially, until delegates cast votes for them at their party's nominating conventions, which are usually held in late July or August of the election year. What if you had been a candidate, coming in a close second and standing for some far different positions than your party competitors? Could you have time to break away, form an independent candidacy, and still have access to the ballot in all 50 states and the District of Columbia? This is the type of conflict and question the court decided in the *Anderson* case. The Court struck down the Ohio requirement for March filing petitions because it infringed on the rights of voters and candidates. Justice Stevens warned that states must focus on the right of voters to have choices and not "with the tendency to have ballot access restrictions to limit the field of candidates from which voters might choose." So what would be a reasonable deadline, a requirement that would not necessarily violate your petition rights? The Court has left the specifics unanswered: There is no universal right to access anytime and on any ballot.

In two more recent cases, *Munro* v. *Socialist Workers Party* (1986) and *Norman* v. *Reed,* (1992) the Court's majority seemed highly divided about ballot access and petition requirements. In the *Munro* case, the Court rejected the Socialist Workers Party's claim that the petition and electoral requirements were violating their First Amendment right to a petition for a redress of grievances. The state of Washington required all minor party candidates for office to receive at least 1 percent of all votes cast for that office in the state's primary election in order to have the candidate's name placed on the general election ballot for November. The majority of the Court concluded, "Because Washington affords a minor party candidate easy access to the primary election ballot and the opportunity for the candidate to wage a ballot connected campaign, we conclude that the magnitude of the Washington law's 1% requirement has slight effect on constitutional rights."

In the *Norman* case, the Court's majority ruled the other way. Writing for the majority, Justice David Souter, struck down an Illinois law for imposing a more stringent burden on access to the county ballot. The Illinois law required citizens wishing to establish a new party to obtain 25,000 signatures of registered voters on petitions from

After being denied the Republican nomination in 1912, Theodore Roosevelt ran on his own third-party ticket, the Bull Moose (or U.S. Progressive) Party.

each district where the party wished to run a candidate. Therefore, someone running for a Cook County board of directors would need 25,000 verified petition signatures from each district where they would run a candidate. The effect of this law was to prevent the Harold Washington Party, which had already qualified for the ballot in the city of Chicago, from qualifying on the ballot in the county encompassing Chicago, Cook County. Souter claimed the law was unnecessarily broad to achieve the state interest in preventing misrepresentation and electoral confusion by new parties.

At this point, most legal scholars acknowledge that the Court has not developed any clear guidelines to establish the meaning of the right to petition. Generally, the Court has placed a much greater burden on state government to show a compelling interest for petition restrictions if the limits place severe burdens on your rights of political association (e.g, as demonstrated in the *Anderson* and *Norman* cases). Simultaneously, the Court has looked upon more minor requirements as requiring a lesser burden of state interest (e.g., the *Socialist Workers Party* case).

The Supreme Court issued its loudest, clearest pronouncement regarding petition protection in a Hawaii petition and ballot access case, *Burdick* v. *Takushi*. In the *Burdick* case, which upheld a Hawaii state law restricting write-in candidacies, the majority quoted the *Anderson* case to illustrate the Court's careful case-by-case consideration. The majority concluded, "A court considering a challenge to a state election law must weigh 'the character and magnitude of the asserted injury to the rights protected by the First and Fourteenth Amendments that the plaintiffs seeks to vindicate' against 'the precise interests put forward by the State as justifications for the burden imposed by its rule,' taking into consideration the extent to which those interests make it necessary to burden the plaintiff's rights."

As with all other ingrained First Amendment rights, our judicial branch attempts to weigh our claims of conflict. With the right to petition, the Court seems to be searching for a Holy Grail that represents a delicate balance.

In the headline grabbers earlier in this chapter, you may have noted that none of our First Amendment rights are absolute. Their protection is at the mercy of the judges and justices, who we Americans hope apply a reasonable test and use reasonable precedents as a guide to uphold our fundamental freedoms. Often we can find precedents to support almost any side of a conflict. Therefore,

we need to be ever more vigilant to scrutinize the selection, nominations, and election of judges who have the power to determine the extent to which we may claim our First Amendment rights. We must devote as much time and energy to court watching and campaigning as we do to other governmental action, and at least as much energy than we spend in work and recreation, for the court's actions will reach out to us in our communities, homes, and workplaces. As the founders of the American Civil Liberties Union often proclaim, "The price of liberty is eternal vigilance."

Bibliography

Abernathy, Glen. *The Right of Assembly and Association*. New York: Columbia University Press, 1981.

Alley, Robert S. *The Supreme Court on Church and State*. New York: Oxford University Press, 1988.

Easton, Susan M. *The Problem of Pornography: Regulation and the Right to Free Speech*. New York: Routledge, 1994.

Eldridge, Larry D. *A Distant Heritage: The Growth of Free Speech in Early America*. New York: New York University Press, 1994.

Fish, Stanley. *There Is No Such Thing as Free Speech and It's a Good Thing, Too*. New York: Oxford University Press, 1994.

Frankel, Marvin. *Faith and Freedom: Religious Liberty in America*. New York: Hill and Wang, 1994.

Gamwell, Franklin I. *The Meaning of Religious Freedom: Modern Politics and the Democratic Resolution*. Albany, N.Y.: State University of New York Press, 1995.

Levy, Leonard. *The Establishment Clause: Religion and the First Amendment*. New York: Macmillan, 1986.

Smolla, Rodney. *Free Speech in an Open Society*. New York: Vintage Books, 1992.

U.S. Department of Justice. *Address of Attorney General Meese Before the Christian Legal Society*. Transcript of September 29, 1985.

Chapter 11

The Right to Vote

Roger Barbour

The right to vote, also known as the right of suffrage, or the right of elective franchise, is perhaps the most important of all of our fundamental rights. Without the right to vote, a citizen could not realistically enjoy the freedoms, safeguards, and powers provided under the Constitution. If the people could not vote, we would not have a democracy but instead a monarchy, an oligarchy of the powerful few, or a dictatorial government.

The Right to Vote: The Basis of a Representative Democracy

The right to vote is the most critical and central component of any democracy. In a democratic society, the sovereign power resides in and is exercised by the whole body of free citizens. This means that the power to govern belongs collectively to all the citizens. In this regard, the right of each citizen to exercise the right to vote becomes the basis of the democratic model. In a society consisting of any sizable population whatsoever, this individual authority to govern must be delegated to a representative of the people. However, the right to choose the leaders of the nation is an essential feature of any regime which calls itself "democratic."

To carry out the day-to-day functioning of the local, state, and federal governments, the citizens elect representatives of the people. These representatives in turn form the respective governments and theoretically implement the will of the people. Thus, through the guaranteed right to vote, the people in effect govern themselves. By casting their ballot for the representatives of their choice, the citizen can choose the candidate who most closely resembles the voter, in terms of the her or his views on how the government should be run.

The right to vote is therefore the central component of a representative democracy. The courts of this nation have held the right to vote in extremely high

regard; it has been elevated among most sacred of principles and institutions. For example, the Supreme Court of New Jersey has termed this fundamental right as "the basic right of suffrage, a civil and political franchise—of the very essence of our democratic process—that is to be liberally and not strictly construed . . ." (The New Jersey Supreme Court, opinion of Justice Heher in *Gangemi* v. *Berry,* 25 N.J. 1, 12, 1957).

With this setting in mind, it can easily be understood why the right to vote is such an important aspect of our daily enjoyment of freedom. However, the right to vote is also associated with a long and troublesome evolution that continues to this day.

Historical Background

Voting in America, during the early history of the nation, was restricted to white, male property owners whose holdings were worth a specified dollar figure. Gradually, property restrictions were removed in most states. However, prior to the civil rights movement and the women's suffrage movement, women and people of color were precluded from exercising their fundamental right to vote. The right to vote was essentially guaranteed only to white males. The right to vote was, in effect, dominated by the more affluent and restricted to men. Political democracy was not at all a reality to many Americans during the early days of the Republic.

One interpretation of the early origins of suffrage explains:

> The right to vote did not share in the glorious history of other democratic values. At the time of the American Revolution it was not among the inalienable blessings of man. So, our Constitution of 1776 limited the right to vote for representatives in the council and assembly to inhabitants "worth fifty pounds" (Art. IV), and required that a member of the legislative council be a "freeholder . . . and worth at least one thousand pounds, proclamation money, or real and personal estate" within his county, and that a member of the assembly worth half that much (Art. III). Universal suffrage was a long way off. (*Gangemi* v. *Rosengard,* 44 N.J. 166, 169, 1965).

As our nation matured, so too evolved the morality and civic conscience of our society and its citizens. These former legal limitations and these outright denials of the right to vote were eliminated. However, at first they tended to be merely transformed into more subtle forms of hoarding the right to vote. For example, instead of statutorily or constitutionally monopolizing the right to vote and securing it only to wealthy white males, the use of poll taxes, literacy tests, and other special qualifications were employed to similarly deny the right to vote to women and people of color.

Other groups that struggled for or continue to fight for the meaningful right to vote include young Americans between the ages of 18 and 21 years, the elderly, the disabled, and language minorities. The young Americans found their redress in the Twenty-sixth Amendment to the United States Constitution. The elderly, disabled, and language minorities are fighting their battle through federal and state legislative enactments. These struggles will be described later.

Constitutional Provisions

Although there is no safeguard mentioned directly within the original text of the United States Constitution specifically enumerating the right to vote as a fundamental franchise guaranteed to all citizens, the right is the subject of several constitutional amendments. These constitutional amendments are designed to secure the vote to all citizens, regardless of their race, color, gender, or religion.

A constitutional amendment carries with it the same authority as the body or actual text of the Constitution itself. The amendments are as powerful as if they were originally drafted with the Constitution in 1787, and as ratified by the States in 1788. In fact, some of our most fundamental rights and freedoms are found in the "Bill of Rights," or the first ten Amendments to the Constitution. As such, the right to vote is embedded in the document and given effect just like any other provision or safeguard found within the Constitution.

In addition, Article I, Section 2, clause I of the United States Constitution expressly provides for the election of United States congressmen by a vote of the people. The section mandates: "The House of Representatives shall be composed of members chosen every second year by the people of the several States, and the electors in each State shall have the qualifications requisite for electors of the most numerous branch of the State legislature." Here the original text of the Constitution dictates the process and qualifications that are applied to the congressional electorate.

The election of United States senators, however, was originally allocated to the legislatures of each state and not to the citizens at large (Article I, Section 3). However, both of these constitutional sections on voting were included within the very first article of the Constitution, just after the Preamble itself. As such, the importance of the issue of voting becomes apparent. It is the central feature of a representative democracy such as that of

the United States. This notion is supported by the placement of voting concerns directly after the Preamble. The right to vote was therefore of paramount importance to the drafters of the Constitution and was addressed in a limited fashion in the first portion of the Constitution.

The Constitutional Amendments

The right to vote was considered to be so important that it has been the subject of four different constitutional amendments. These constitutional amendments span a period from 1870 to 1971. The Fifteenth, Nineteenth, Twenty-fourth, and Twenty-sixth Amendments all have a dramatic impact on the right to vote. The Fifteenth Amendment, adopted after the Union victory in the Civil War, prohibits laws or conduct that deny or abridge the right to vote because of race, color, or previous condition of servitude (ratified 1870). The Nineteenth Amendment was the result of victory in the Women's Suffrage Movement. The movement and the amendment secured the right to vote to all women (ratified 1920). The Twenty-fourth Amendment prohibits the use of poll taxes in an attempt to prevent or limit one from exercising their fundamental right to vote (ratified 1964). The Twenty-sixth Amendment reduced the lawful age limit from 21 to 18 years, thus allowing a large number of college-age adults to exercise their right to vote for the first time (ratified 1971).

The Fifteenth Amendment

Amendment XV (ratified 1870)

Section 1. The right of citizens of the United States to vote shall not be denied or abridged by the United States or by any State on account of race, color, or previous condition of servitude.

Section 2. The Congress shall have power to enforce this article by appropriate legislation.

During the period after the Civil War, the right to vote was evolving. The Fifteenth Amendment was an effort to secure the right equally to all citizens of the United States, regardless of the color of their skin. For African Americans, particularly, who had recently attained "citizen status" as a result of the Union Army's victory in the Civil War, the right to vote was a critical aspect of securing and maintaining not only their freedom but the fundamental right to participate in our democratic form of government. Voting is a fundamental aspect of a representative democracy that is to be enjoyed equally by all members of society.

In 1870, the Civil War had just concluded and the right to vote was not a reality for many Americans simply by virtue of the color of their skin. This unjust situation needed attention with the utmost urgency, and immediate safeguards had to be implemented addressing this inequality. Without question, these safeguards demanded to be of the Constitutional kind.

The Fifteenth Amendment was ratified in 1870 and was intended to secure the right to vote to all "male" citizens, regardless of race or color. However, the enforcement of the amendment was rather sporadic, and in many instances, nonexistent, especially in the former confederate southern states. As portrayed through *Quiet Revolution in the South:*

> [B]y the turn of the century white conservative officials had effectively nullified the black vote as a political force in the eleven states of the former Confederacy. The elimination of black suffrage was made possible by northern indifference to the plight of southern blacks, . . . southern intimidation of potential black voters, corruption and fraud at the ballot box, Supreme Court decisions striking down various provisions of the Enforcement Act of 1870 and the Force Act of 1871, and subsequent court decisions permitting southern states to rewrite their constitutions to exclude blacks by devices such as literacy and good character tests and the poll tax. The Fifteenth Amendment, ignored by racist southern officials and racist courts, was a dead letter.

However, even though perhaps ineffective in its early days, the Fifteenth Amendment paved the way for federal legislation that would remedy the gravest of inequalities. The amendment explicitly provided that "Congress shall have power to enforce this article by appropriate legislation." By virtue of the amendment itself, the federal government was authorized to take action and eliminate the injustices suffered by African Americans throughout the first half of the twentieth century. Through the enactment of federal legislation, southern African Americans were able to put an end to most of the tactics used by southern officials to obstruct the African American voter.

The Nineteenth Amendment

Amendment XIX (1920)

Section 1. The right of citizens of the United States to vote shall not be denied or abridged by the United States or any State on account of sex.

Section 2. Congress shall have power to enforce this article by appropriate legislation.

Women experienced struggles similar to those endured by African American citizens in attempting to exercise their fundamental right to vote. Equally important, this denial of the right to vote also demanded redress at the constitutional level. For decades women became politically organized, fighting to obtain an equal platform upon which to exercise their elective franchise.

Combining forces with the Anti-Slavery Society, the women's movement of the mid-nineteenth century became known as the Equal Rights Association. Prior to 1869, the existing women's rights coalition was associated and allied with the abolitionist movement, battling for the passage of the Thirteenth Amendment banning slavery and the Fifteenth Amendment guaranteeing the right to vote. However, as the 1860s came to an end, a division emerged concerning the two groups. With the realization that the Fourteenth Amendment specified "male" citizens in the apportionment clause of Section 2, and that the Fifteenth Amendment would benefit primarily males of color only, activists such as Susan B. Anthony needed a new direction. Anthony began to believe that the women's movement had to focus solely on the woman's right to vote. Without the right to vote, all other rights were immaterial, and perhaps, unattainable.

Realizing that under the Fifteenth Amendment, a woman's right to vote would not be properly guaranteed, a new movement began to emerge. This movement was headed by Susan B.

Election Day!

In 1920, with the ratification of the Nineteenth Amendment to the U.S. Constitution, women gained the right to vote.

Anthony and became known as the National Woman Suffrage Association. The new movement would now be concerned directly with obtaining the right to vote for women.

In 1920 the long-fought battle of the Women's Suffrage Movement culminated with the ratification of the Nineteenth Amendment to the United States Constitution. By virtue of the most preeminent and empowering source of law in the hierarchy of this government's legitimacy, physical characteristics such as gender, race, or skin color would heretofore no longer be tolerated as barriers to the right to vote.

A Heroine in the Battle for Women's Suffrage

One of the many heroines of the women's suffrage movement deserves attention because of

her militant approach to the cause and her ultimate success.

Upon joining the newly organized National American Woman Suffrage Association (NAWSA) in 1890, Carrie Chapman Catt (1859–1947) quickly rose in the ranks of the suffrage movement. In 1895 she began work on securing a constitutional amendment for women's suffrage by winning the vote in individual states. By 1900, she had succeeded Susan B. Anthony as president of NAWSA. Despite an organizational split in 1915, Carrie Chapman Catt would continue to push for a constitutional amendment. Her efforts succeeded when both houses of Congress passed the amendment by 1919. Ratification would take place the following year. During the long process toward ratification by the required 36 states, Catt would command her

Susan B. Anthony *(1820–1906)*

Susan Brownell Anthony was a social reformer and a leader of the women's suffrage movement. The daughter of a Quaker abolitionist, Anthony was born in 1820 in Adams, Massachusetts. She began her career as a teacher in New York State, where she agitated for causes such as equal pay for women teachers, coeducation, and college education for women. She also was active in the antislavery movement and attended the 1848 Seneca Falls, New York, convention—the first women's rights convention.

Anthony was also active in the movement to ban alcohol but was forbidden to speak at a temperance rally because of her sex. Anthony subsequently formed the Daughters of Temperance, since a male organization refused to accept women members. At a 1851 meeting of the Daughters of Temperance she met Elizabeth Cady Stanton, who became her close ally in the later struggle for women's suffrage. She and Stanton organized the Women's Suffrage Association in 1869. In addition to seeking the vote for women, both Anthony and Stanton sought to obtain improvements in the property rights of women and in the cause of equal pay for women teachers.

After the Civil War Susan B. Anthony concentrated her efforts on the women's suffrage struggle, giving speeches and lectures on the subject. She led campaigns for the women's vote in states all over the nation. From 1868 to 1870 she edited the crusading journal *Revolution,* which called for suffrage for women, equal education for women, and greater employment opportunities, and even encouraged women to join labor unions.

Anthony was successful in Wyoming in 1870, the first state to give women the vote. She kept up the campaigns in California, Michigan, Pennsylvania, and Colorado. From 1881 to 1886 she collaborated with Elizabeth Cady Stanton and Matilda Gage to prepare the *History of Woman Suffrage.* In 1890 the two major women's suffrage groups united. In 1904 Susan B. Anthony became the formal head of the single largest group fighting for women's suffrage. Many mass demonstrations and setbacks were to lie ahead for the advocates of the vote for women. Although she died in 1906 before final victory was attained, the passage of the Nineteenth Amendment in 1920 is a final tribute to the memory of Susan B. Anthony.

workers as a general commands troops. "There should be a mobilization of at least 36 state armies," she said, "and these armies should go prepared to give their lives and fortunes for success, and any coward among us who dares to call retreat, should be court-martialled."

The Twenty-Fourth Amendment

Amendment XXIV (1964)

Section 1. The right of citizens of the United States to vote in any primary or other election for President or Vice President, for electors for President or Vice President, or for Senator or Representative in Congress, shall not be denied or abridged by the United States by reason of failure to pay any poll tax or other tax.

Section 2. The Congress shall have power to enforce this article by appropriate legislation.

The third constitutional amendment addressing the right to vote was adopted in 1964. At the height of the civil rights movement, and at a time

when access to the polling place was extremely crucial, the Twenty-fourth Amendment to the United States Constitution was ratified. This constitutional safeguard prevented the use of poll taxes as a pretext and a veiled attempt to hoard the vote and monopolize the political process for those who had traditionally exercised political control. (This aspect of the right to vote is discussed further under the heading, "Denial of the Vote.")

Twenty-sixth Amendment

Amendment XXVI (1971)

Section 1. The right of citizens of the United States, who are eighteen years of age or older, to vote shall not be denied or abridged by the United States or any State on account of age.

Section 2. The Congress shall have power to enforce this article by appropriate legislation.

A final citizen group that achieved redress at the constitutional level was that of young adults, between the ages of 18 and 21 years of age. These

high school seniors, politically active college students, concerned taxpayers, and other politically interested citizens who had attained the age of 18 could now exercise their fundamental right to vote. The right to vote was expanded, which in turn broadened the views and philosophies of the voter base. Citizens who had otherwise reached the age of majority, and who were therefore subject to the consequential realities of adulthood, were now also given the political tools to help shape the society within which they must live.

The average adult between the ages of 18 and 21 is active in work, college, or politics. For the citizens who had achieved the age of 18, yet were denied the right to vote and shape the government by which they are to be governed, a fundamental unfairness results. The Twenty-sixth Amendment to the United States Constitution helped to remedy this condition; it prohibited the federal or state governments from abridging the right of young Americans to vote.

Strict Scrutiny Standard of Judicial Review

When a law, a regulation, or a governmental practice has an impact on a fundamental right such as the right to vote, courts of this country use what is known as "strict scrutiny" to interpret and evaluate the law, the regulation, or the practice. Strict scrutiny mandates that the governmental

authority must justify the law or the practice before the reviewing court. In order for the law or the practice to withstand challenge, the government must satisfactorily prove to the court that the challenged law, regulation, or practice has been developed and is implemented in its least burdensome and least restrictive form.

The United States Supreme Court has mandated that any law, regulation, or governmental practice that restricts a fundamental right or classifies certain groups of people differently concerning a fundamental right must be "necessary" to achieve a "compelling or overriding" government purpose. Specifically, when considering a case involving the Equal Protection Clause and a suspect classification, the Supreme Court declared that "any classification which serves to penalize the exercise of [a fundamental] right, unless shown to be necessary to promote a compelling governmental interest, is unconstitutional" (*Shapiro* v. *Thompson*, 1968, citing *Skinner* v. *Oklahoma*, 1942).

An example of this strict-scrutiny standard of review as it concerns the right to vote can be seen in a Supreme Court case that arose out of the state of Tennessee in 1972. Tennessee had voting laws that required newly arrived citizens to reside in the state for one year, and when voting at the local level, in that county for three months, prior to being permitted to register to vote. When these durational residency requirements were challenged in court, the United States Supreme Court ultimately ruled that the voting regulations were unconstitutional. Again, the Court held that "Durational residence laws must be measured by a strict equal protection test: they are unconstitutional unless the State can demonstrate that such laws are '*necessary* to promote a *compelling* governmental interest'" *(Dunn* v. *Blumstein,* 1971; quoting *Shapiro* v. *Thompson,* 1968).

When related to exercising the right to vote, it is very clear that any governmental purpose behind a law or a practice that impacts on the right to vote must be legitimate. In other words, the law or the practice cannot merely be a pretext for otherwise monopolizing, controlling, or influencing in any way the right to vote. Therefore, any restrictions placed on the right to vote must be absolutely necessary toward the achievement of some extremely important and absolutely legitimate governmental interest or purpose. This is what the Supreme Court has advanced when interpreting and applying the two key words from the strict scrutiny standard of judicial review: "necessary" and "compelling."

Statutory Provisions

Voting rights are not only safeguarded through the United States Constitution but are also secured by various provisions of the United States Code ("The Code"). Specifically, "Title 42 of the United States Code Chapter 20—Elective Franchise," codifies numerous statutory provisions that impact on many aspects of the right to vote.

In 1965, Congress enacted the Voting Rights Act. This legislation was enacted to help ensure that all citizens are freely able to exercise their fundamental right to vote. (The Voting Rights Act will be discussed specifically further on in terms of enforcement of the act).

Similarly, the right to vote is the subject of numerous legislative enactments instituted by state governments. Each state has codified legislation that governs the elective franchise. However, the statutes enacted on the federal level overrule any laws passed by the states or localities that are inconsistent with the federal legislation. For example, the code, which comprises statutes enacted by the United States Congress, supersedes or preempts any laws enacted by states or localities that are contradictory to the federally enacted legislation; that is, the federal legislation is paramount in the hierarchical chain of command. Any state or local law or practice that conflicts with a federal law on the same subject must yield to the federal legislation.

Where the United States Congress sees fit to enact legislation on a given subject, then that subject is presumed to be of such importance to all Americans, that the federal legislation must control it. Any inconsistent state or local law or ordinance must yield in order to promote uniformity and equality. Yet within the parameters of federal legislation, states and localities are free to implement their own statutes and administrative regulations that will have an impact on the voting franchise.

The United States Code

The statutory provisions codified under "Chapter 20—Elective Franchise" have a dramatic impact on the right to vote. Various sections of this statutory enactment assure to all citizens, regardless of race, national origin, gender, status, age, or any other discretionary or discriminative trait, that they will have equal access and opportunity to exercise their individual right to vote. (All that is required in order to exercise the right to vote, is bona fide U.S., state, and/or local citizenship, and attainment of the age of 18 years.)

In order to protect various citizens from discriminatory, discretionary, or arbitrary conditions or qualifications associated with the fundamental right to vote, Congress has enacted prohibitive legislation. For example, under the code, Congress has declared that the right to vote shall not be affected by a citizen's race, color, or previous condition of servitude. The statute reads in pertinent part:

> All citizens of the United States who are otherwise qualified by law to vote at any election by the people in any State, Territory, district county, city, parish, township, school district, municipality, or other territorial subdivision, shall be entitled and allowed to vote at all such elections, without distinction of race, color, or previous condition of servitude; any constitution, law, custom, usage, or regulation of any State or Territory, or by or under its authority, to the contrary notwithstanding. (42 U.S.C.A. Section 1971(a)(1))

Specifically, this legislation acts in conjunction with the aforementioned Fifteenth Amendment. The legislation was enacted to help combat

By providing free transportation to registration headquarters, African Americans made their hard-won right to vote more accessible to all.

any of the remnants of slavery that acted to preclude African Americans from exercising their fundamental right to vote. As an additional safeguard, it can be employed to preempt any state or local law, practice, custom or the like, that was used in the past, or could be used in the future, to deny various citizens the right to vote. (Various examples of denying the right to vote, and the governmental responses thereto, will be discussed under the heading, "Denial of the Vote.")

Voting Fraud Violates the Right to Vote

Although the right to vote is considered to be among the most important of all our fundamental rights, the freedom to exercise the right must be applied in a fair and equitable manner. In order for the right to be legitimate, and for it to apply equally to all citizens, there can be no association whatsoever of fraud with the right to vote. The United States Code deals with various aspects of fraud as it pertains to voting. Concepts such as giving false information and falsifying records in connection with registration are addressed under the code, as are issues such as voting more than once.

To assure the integrity of the vote, the code demands that voters meet simple administrative requirements, such as registering to vote within the relative political subdivision of residence. This ensures that only those citizens who are governed by a given locality be authorized to vote for that locality's governmental representative of the people. For example, only the residents of State A can vote for the representatives of State A. Furthermore, only those residents who are registered in State A can so vote.

These uncomplicated administrative requirements are designed to prevent fraud and to insure integrity. The code declared that the falsification of records, or the giving of false information when registering to vote, is an unlawful practice. For example, the code declares:

> Whoever knowingly or willingly gives false information as to his name, address, or period of residence in the voting district for the purpose of establishing his eligibility to register to vote, or conspires with another individual for the purpose of encouraging his false registration to vote or illegal voting, or pays or offers to pay or accepts payment either for registration or for voting shall be fined not more than $10,000 or imprisoned not more than five years, or both[.] (42 U.S.C.A. Section 1973i(c))

With the breadth of this statutory provision, practically any form of fraudulent voting, of conspiring to vote fraudulently, or of paying someone else to so vote is made unlawful and subject to penalty.

Another statutory provision addressing fraud deals with the idea of "one citizen, one vote." Under section 1973i(e), it is unlawful to vote more than once in the same election. There the code provides: "Whoever votes more than once in an election [for President, Vice President, Member of the United States Senate, or Member of the United States House of Representatives] shall be fined not more than $10,000 or imprisoned not more than five years, or both" (42 U.S.C.A. Section 1973i(e)). With both of these code sections, the penalties involved are quite severe. As such, they present the importance of the right to vote and, especially, the importance of conducting an election that is associated in no way with the aforementioned concepts of fraud.

If the vote is not conducted and kept absolutely free of fraud, or of the mere appearance of fraud for that matter, the legitimacy of the democratic state is immediately threatened. In order for the people to consent to a representative form of government, the selection of the representatives must be open equally to all citizens who are to be so governed. If citizens vote who are not entitled to vote, or if citizens vote more than once, the right to vote is not equally apportioned as

mandated by the concepts of a republican form of government. As a result, serious legislation needed enacting, and an aggressive enforcement of the legislation is demanded, in order to maintain the legitimacy of any democratic state.

Denial of the Vote

Denying the right to vote, or hindering the right in any manner, is a direct attack on one of this country's most sacred institutions. As a democratic republic, the right to vote is a fundamental franchise that enjoys the utmost protection from the United States Constitution, our individual state constitutions, and federal and state statutes alike. In order for a representative democracy to be functionally legitimate, the right to vote must not be denied, except in limited circumstances that are considered acceptable by the ordinary citizen, such as restricting the voting rights of prisoners and children.

When the government, or an agent of the government, acts to hinder or deny the right to vote, such restrictive practices must be closely examined. As mentioned previously in Section I, any governmental laws, regulations, practices, or restrictions that have an impact on the fundamental right to vote are strictly scrutinized by the courts of this country. If not directly necessary towards the advancement of a compelling and therefore legitimate government interest, the restriction will be invalidated as being unconstitutional.

It must be noted, however, that this idea of strict scrutiny and the *constitutional* protection of fundamental rights applies only to actions taken by the federal government, a state government, or some local governmental entity or political subdivision. Any actions that are taken by purely private citizens against another private citizen, resulting in a denial of the right to vote, are addressable in a private civil court action. In such a wholly private matter, civil rights legislation provides the aggrieved voter with a means for relief.

The United States Code

So sacred was the notion of a freely accessible right of suffrage, that any attempt to deny or hinder the right to vote through threats, intimidation, coercion, or the like, was strictly prohibited under the United States Code. For instance, the code declares:

> No person, whether acting under color of law or otherwise, shall intimidate, threaten, coerce, or

Society has chosen to withhold certain rights and privileges from prisoners that are secured to law-abiding citizens. By virtue of their criminal acts, prisoners have chosen to relinquish certain fundamental rights—among these, the right to vote.

attempt to intimidate, threaten, or coerce any other person for the purpose of interfering with the right of such other person to vote or to vote as he may choose, or of causing of such other person to vote for, or not to vote for, any candidate . . . at any general, special or primary election held solely or in part for the purpose of selecting or electing any such candidate. (42 U.S.C.A. Section 1971(b))

As can be seen by the expansive language used in this statutory provision, many kinds of activities are covered. The statute prohibits all acts that interfere with freely exercised voting, and it also covers any attempted act of denying or interfering with the complete and unabridged freedom of the voter.

Aside from lawfully conducted campaigning and free speech guarantees, the statutory protections of section 1971(b) are quite encompassing.

The statute protects the voter from threats or intimidation directed at preventing him or her from voting in the first place. It also protects the voter from threats or intimidation designed to cause the voter to vote in a certain way, for a particular candidate, or for a particular party.

Denying the Right is Legitimate in Certain Cases

In a few limited contexts, society has not only tolerated but has demanded that certain citizens not be permitted to vote. For example, society accepts withholding the right to vote from those individuals who are convicted of felonies and incarcerated in the prisons of this country. As defined by *Black's Law Dictionary,* a felony is a "crime of a graver or more serious nature than those designated as misdemeanors; . . . Under many state statutes, any offense punishable by death or imprisonment for a term exceeding one year" is a felony.

Since prisoners have chosen to commit crimes that demonstrate a lack of concern for their citizenship rights, they have by virtue of their criminal acts chosen to relinquish certain fundamental rights. Thus they are legitimately denied rights and privileges otherwise secured to law-abiding citizens. The right to vote is just one of the many fundamental rights that a person relinquishes when choosing not to live by the rules of this society.

This reasoning can be explained as being a social contract between the individual citizen and the citizenry at large. In exchange for the guarantee of certain fundamental rights and freedoms, including the right to vote, a citizen agrees to live and abide by the rules and regulations that apply equally to all members of the contract. When felons choose to violate societal laws, they break the social contract that guarantees their fundamental rights and freedoms. In turn, and as a result, they are no longer protected as are law-abiding people.

Another situation that involves an acceptable denial of the right to vote pertains to competency. Competency involves both mentally incompetent individuals and underaged citizens. Those who are adjudged as mentally incompetent, and those who have not yet attained the age of 18 years, can be, and are, denied the right to vote. Again, the provisions of social policy that deny the right to vote to mental incompetents and juveniles are largely accepted by a majority of the citizenry.

No Discretionary or Discriminatory Denials or Abridgment

The fundamental right to vote demands a guarantee that extends to all citizens, regardless of race, national origin, gender, status, age, or any other discretionary or discriminatory character. Not only is this concept embedded in such founding documents of this country as the Declaration of Independence and the United States Constitution, but it is also entrenched in the congressionally enacted laws of the United States. The United States Code contains several references to the pro-hibition of denying the right to vote because of an immutable characteristic. For example, the code mandates

(a) No voting qualification or prerequisite to voting or standard, practice, or procedure shall be imposed or applied by any State or political subdivision in a manner which results in a denial or abridgment of the right of any citizen of the United States to vote on account of race or color. . . .

(b) A violation of subsection (a) of this section is established if, based upon the totality of the circumstances, it is shown that the political processes leading to nomination or election in the State or political subdivision are not equally open to participation by members of a class of citizens protected by subsection (a) of this section in that its members have less opportunity than other members of the electorate to participate in the political process and to elect representatives of their choice. (42 U.S.C.A. Section 1973(a),(b))

The prohibition against discriminatory denials of the right to vote are afforded to all citizens through other sections of the code. For example, under section 1973j of Title 42, the code provides for civil and criminal sanctions against those who deprive, attempt to deprive, or conspire to deprive citizens of secured rights concerning their right to vote. This statutory section also provides penalties for destroying, defacing, mutilating, or altering ballots or official voting records when an examiner has been appointed following an election in a political subdivision:

Specifically, the broad protections of section 1973j provide in pertinent part:

(a) Whoever shall deprive or attempt to deprive any person of any right secured by section [1973 Denial or abridgment of right to vote on account of race or color; 1973a Proceedings to enforce the right to vote; 1973b Suspension of tests or devices to determine eligibility; 1973c Alteration of voting qualifications and procedures; 1973e Examination of applicants for registration; 1973h No poll taxes; 1973i(a) Prohibited Acts: Failure or refusal to permit casting or tabulation of vote] shall be fined not more than $5,000, or imprisoned not more than five years, or both.

(b) Whoever, . . . destroys, defaces, mutilates, or otherwise alters the marking of a paper ballot which has been cast in such election, or alters any official record of voting in such election tabulated from a voting machine or otherwise, shall be fined not more than $5,000, or imprisoned not more than five years, or both.

(c) Whoever conspires to violate the provisions of subsection (a) or (b) of this section . . . shall be fined not more than $5,000, or imprisoned not more than five years, or both. (42 U.S.C.A. Sections 1973j(a), (b), (c))

Under these statutory provisions, not only is discriminatory conduct against women or people of color prohibited, but any attempt to deny any citizen's right to vote is prohibited.

The sweep of these statutory protections is rather encompassing. The penalties provided are quite severe. These statutes show that the right to vote is highly valued in America.

Qualifications, Limitations, and Denying the Vote

Although the right to vote is fundamental, and is to be afforded equally to all, there are certain qualifications that are associated with exercising the right. For administrative purposes, and to prevent fraud, states and localities are permitted to place certain qualifications on the right to vote. However, any qualifications that a state or a political subdivision can impose on the voting franchise are rather limited. The qualifications must fall within the boundaries of the federal and state constitution and within the mandates of federal voting rights legislation. In short, there are very limited qualifications that can be placed on the voting franchise, concerning the ordinary citizen and his or her individual right to vote.

Qualifications of Voters

The majority of these voter qualifications are necessary for administrative reasons and for the prevention of voting fraud. For example, in order to qualify for the right to vote, the governing political subdivision can legitimately require the voter to register with the local election board prior to being permitted to cast a ballot.

Constitutional Provisions

In *Constitutional Law: Principles and Policy,* Jerome A. Barron et al. points out that in *Mobile* v. *Bolden* (1980), the United States Supreme Court noted that

Almost a hundred years ago th[is] Court unanimously held that "the Constitution of the United States does not confer the right of suffrage upon any one." It is for the states "to determine the conditions under which the right of suffrage may

be exercised, absent of course the discrimination which the Constitution condemns." It is true that the Equal Protection Clause confers a substantive right to participate in elections on an equal basis with other qualified voters.

However, even though the explicit right to vote may not be addressed, it has been given the status of a fundamental right. For example, Barron et al. also note that "'Other rights, even the most basic are illusory if the right to vote is undermined.'. . . The 'right to exercise the franchise in a free and unimpaired manner is preservative of other basic civil and political rights.' It has been suggested that voting has a special relation to first amendment rights" (quoting *Wesberry* v. *Sanders,* 1964, and *Reynolds* v. *Sims,* 1964).

The United States Constitution does in fact have several provisions that briefly detail qualifications associated with the right to vote. The first requirement affecting the right to vote is found almost immediately in Article I, Section 2, clause 1. This constitutional section provides: "The House of Representatives shall be composed of Members chosen every second Year by the People of the several States, and the Electors in each State shall have the Qualifications requisite for Electors of the most numerous Branch of the State Legislature." Here we see that the House of Representatives was explicitly intended to be a true representation of the people. The people of the various states are to elect their representatives, and the electors are to be merely qualified as if voting for their own state or local representatives.

Similarly, clause 1 of Section 2, Article I, providing for the election of United States senators and the qualification of state electors, declares: "The Senate of the United States shall be composed of two Senators from each State, [chosen by the Legislature] thereof, for six Years; and each senator shall have one Vote." This section was amended in 1913 by the Seventeenth Amendment to the United States Constitution, making the election of senators the same as that of congressmen. The constitutional provisions for federal senators now demands: "The Senate of the United States shall be composed of two Senators from each State, elected by the people thereof, for six years; and each Senator shall have one vote. The electors in each State shall have the qualifications requisite for electors of the most numerous branch of the State legislatures."

Statutory Provisions

The general rule is that the legislature (federal, state, or local) cannot add to or take away from the qualifications as outlined in the relevant constitution. The mode and manner of the exercise of the right of suffrage is usually left to the discretion of the state legislature, but the constitutional qualifications on electors cannot be enlarged by the lawmaking authority. However, not only are the state legislatures and local lawmaking authorities confined within their respective constitutions, they are also greatly subjected to the demands and mandates of federal legislation.

Registration Provisions

In order to register, the voter must merely satisfy minimal residency and age requirements. The United States Congress has permitted the implementation of various minimal requirements by the states and local political subdivisions concerning citizens who desire to exercise their fundamental right to vote. Among these minimal qualifications is the demand for registration. Before voting, the citizen must first register with the state or the locality within which she or he chooses to vote. Section 1973e of Title 42 to the United States Code provides in pertinent part:

(a) The examiners for each political subdivision shall, . . . examine applicants concerning their qualifications for voting. An application to an examiner shall be in such form as the Director may require and shall contain allegations that the applicant is not otherwise registered to vote.

(b) Any person whom the examiner finds . . . to have the qualifications prescribed by State law not inconsistent with the Constitution and laws of the United States shall promptly be placed on a list of eligible voters.

(c) The examiner shall issue to each person whose name appears on such list a certificate evidencing his eligibility to vote. (42 U.S.C.A. 1973e(a)-(c))

As noted previously, these statutory provisions are primarily authorized for preventing voter fraud and for administrative and ministerial purposes. In order to prevent citizens from exercising their vote randomly, from county to county, precinct to precinct, or even state to state, political subdivisions are authorized to require that citizens be registered within their respective jurisdiction in order to vote.

Residency Provisions

Another voter qualification that has been seriously restricted by the United States Code concerns the requirement of residency. Particularly, there is a prohibition against durational or lengthy residency requirements for presidential and vice presidential elections. For example, the Code explains

The Congress hereby finds that the imposition and application of the durational residency requirement as a precondition to voting for the offices of President and Vice President, and the lack of sufficient opportunities for absentee registration and absentee balloting in presidential elections—

(1) denies or abridges the inherent constitutional right of citizens to vote for their President and Vice President;

(2) denies or abridges the inherent constitutional right of citizens to enjoy their free movement across State lines; . . .

(4) in some instances has the impermissible purpose or effect of denying citizens the right to vote for such officers because of the way they vote; . . . (42 U.S.C.A. Section 1973aa-1(a))

Through judicial action, this prohibition against durational residence requirements has been applied to the states and municipalities. (See "No Durational Residency Requirements" further on).

A Limit to Voter Qualifications

Although states and political subdivisions are authorized to place certain qualifications on the right to vote, these regulations are by no means unchecked. In fact, they are quite limited in order to prevent discriminatory abuses. Essentially, qualifications such as voter registration and residency requirements are imposed solely for administrative reasons, the prevention of voter fraud, and the like. In any regard, any qualifications for voting are not permitted to result in a denial or an abridgment of the right to vote. They must be reasonable in their design and fair in their application.

No Durational Residency Requirements

As stated before, durational residency requirements have been severely limited by the United States Supreme Court in terms of their ability to deny the right to vote. In 1971, the Court declared in *Dunn* v. *Blumstein* that

durational residence laws must be measured by a strict equal protection test: They are unconstitutional unless the State can demonstrate that such

laws are 'necessary to promote a compelling governmental interest.' . . . A heavy burden of justification is on the State, and [any] statute will be closely scrutinized in light of its asserted purposes.

It is not sufficient for the State to show that durational residence requirements further a very substantial state interest. In pursuing that important interest, the State cannot choose means that unnecessarily burden or restrict constitutionally protected activity. *(Dunn* v. *Blumstein,* 1971)*

In ruling that the residency laws of Tennessee were unconstitutional, the United States Supreme Court severely restricted any durational residency period that a state or a locality could impose on a voter as a prerequisite to registration.

Under the voter registration laws of Tennessee prior to 1971, a citizen had to be a resident of the state for one year, and a resident of the county for three months, before being permitted to register to vote therein. Basing its reasoning on the previously cited portion of the Federal Voting Rights Act (42 U.S.C.A. Section 1971aa-1), the *Dunn* Court declared that such lengthy residency requirements would be too burdensome on the voter. Similarly, by referring to section 202 of the Voting Rights Act of 1965, the Supreme Court "found 'no explanation why the 30-day period between the closing of new registrations and the date of election would not provide, in light of modern communications, adequate time to insure against . . . frauds'" (*Dunn,* 405 U.S. at 349, n.19).

Thirty days would now be the maximum limit within which states could require residency before a voter qualifies to vote. States or localities are permitted to close the voter registration books 30 days before the relevant election in which a voter wishes to vote.

No Poll Taxes or Voting Fees

The Twenty-fourth Amendment to the United States Constitution provides that a citizen's right to vote for president, vice president, senator, or representative, "shall not be denied or abridged by the United States by reason of failure to pay any poll tax or other tax." The Twenty-fourth Amendment's prohibition against poll taxes is an attempt to prevent a denial of the vote that is based on status or financial affluence. It is in turn also designed to help put an end to pretextual methods of discriminating against citizens based on their race, color, or any other immutable characteristic or status at birth.

Throughout history, the poll tax has been a means of depriving financially burdened and other disadvantaged citizens equal access to the voting franchise. Some citizens could not afford to pay the poll tax, whereas others chose to forgo voting in favor of the immediate necessities of their daily life required by their families. The poll tax acted as a barrier that obstructed access to the polling place.

The United States Code also prohibits the imposition of any form of poll tax in order for citizens to be able to exercise their right to vote. Section 1973h provides

> The Congress finds that the requirement of the payment of a poll tax as a precondition to voting (i) precludes persons of limited means from voting or imposes unreasonable financial hardship upon such persons as a precondition to their exercise of the franchise, (ii) does not bear a reasonable relationship to any legitimate State interest in the conduct of elections, and (iii) in some areas has the purpose or effect of denying persons the right to vote because of race or color. Upon the basis of these findings, Congress declares that the constitutional right of citizens to vote is denied or abridged in some areas by the requirement of payment of a poll tax as precondition to voting. (42 U.S.C.A. Section 1973h)

Whatever the interpretation, it is clear that Congress has declared that any form of poll tax necessarily tends to deny or abridge the right to vote.

Similarly, the United States Supreme Court has addressed the issue of the poll tax as a prerequisite to voting. In *Harper* v. *Virginia State Board of Elections* (1966), the Court declared:

> We conclude that a State violates the Equal Protection Clause of the Fourteenth Amendment whenever it makes the affluence of the voter or payment of any fee an electoral standard. Voter qualifications have no relation to wealth nor to paying or not paying this or any other tax. Our cases demonstrate that the Equal Protection Clause of the Fourteenth Amendment restrains the States from fixing voter qualifications which invidiously discriminate. (383 U.S. 663 (1966)

Whether it causes an outright prevention, strongly discourages, or merely dissuades one from voting, the outcome is the same: The fundamental right to vote has been thwarted. As such, the imposition of poll taxes as a prerequisite to voting has been abolished in this country as a violation of the voter's constitutional and statutory civil rights.

Tests and Similar Devices Prohibited

Another skeptical voting qualification that has been viewed with suspicion, and hence done away with, is the use of pretextual voter qualification tests to establish the right to vote. The United States Code declares such tests to be a threat to the right to vote and a possible means of denying or abridging the right to vote. As such, the code has declared

> No citizen shall be denied, because of his failure to comply with any test or device, the right to vote in any Federal, State, or local election conducted in any State or political subdivision of a State.
>
> As used in this section, the term "test or device" means any requirement that a person as a prerequisite for voting or registration for voting (1) demonstrate the ability to read, write, understand, or interpret any matter, (2) demonstrate any educational achievement or his knowledge of any particular subject, (3) possess good moral character, or (4) prove his qualifications by the voucher of registered voters or members of any other class. (42 U.S.C.A. Section 1973aa(a) and (b))

Again, the right to vote was being denied as a result of being conditioned on such unreasonable qualifications. The use of "tests or devices" as a preconditioned qualification for the fundamental right to vote was viewed as a means of disenfranchising various groups of citizens. As with the use of poll taxes, this voting qualification was declared to be a potential means of hoarding the vote, and denying representation to less privileged classes of citizens.

Age Requirements

As introduced before the Twenty-sixth Amendment to the United States Constitution secured the right to vote for citizens who have attained the age of 18 years, as of 1971. However, through the 1970 version of the extended and amended Voting Rights Act of 1965, the United States Congress had attempted, via federal legislation alone, to lower the voting age for state elections from 21 to 18 years old. The constitutionality of this congressional enactment was challenged, and the United States Supreme Court ruled that this portion of the Act violated traditional, and constitutionally secured concepts of states' rights. As noted by Barron et al.:

> The Court struck down the provisions of the Act lowering the voting age to 18 in state elections. Justice Black, announcing the judgment of the Court in *[Oregon* v. *Mitchell]*, argued that Article I [section] 2 was 'a clear indication that the Framers intended the States to determine the qualifications of their own voters for state offices[.]' . . . The Constitution he contended was intended to preserve the independence of the states and '[n]o function is more essential to the separate and independent existence of the States and their governments than the power to determine within the limits of the Constitution the qualifications of their own voters for state, county, and municipal offices and the nature of their own machinery for filling local public offices.'

Somewhat delayed but not discouraged, this failed first attempt at securing the right to vote to all citizens who had attained the age of 18 years, signaled a realization that constitutional demands were necessary. The Twenty-sixth Amendment to the United States Constitution was declared ratified on July 1, 1971, and the amendment provided the constitutional authority on which the federal congress could act. The congress wasted no time in passing legislation designed to secure the rights of young adults to vote not only in federal elections but in state and local elections as well.

In attempting to enforce the newly mandated provisions of the Twenty-sixth Amendment, the United States Congress enacted federal legislation that helped to secure the vote for 18-year-old citizens. Section 1973bb of the Title 41 of the United States Code provides

(a)(1) The Attorney General is directed to institute, in the name of the United States, such actions against States or political subdivisions, including actions for injunctive relief, as he may determine to be necessary to implement the twenty-sixth article of amendment to the Constitution of the United States.

(2) The district courts of the United States shall have jurisdiction of proceedings instituted under this subchapter, . . . and any appeal shall lie to the Supreme Court. . . .

(b) Whoever shall deny or attempt to deny any person of any right secured by the twenty-sixth article or amendment to the Constitution of the United States shall be fined not more than $5,000 or imprisoned not more than five years, or both. (42 U.S.C.A. Section 1973bb)

Expressly authorized through the enabling provisions of the Twenty-sixth Amendment itself, this piece of federal legislation was able to withstand any states' rights challenges and thus became particularly important in the arena of voters' rights.

The statutory section provides rather severe penalties for anyone attempting to deny the right to vote to teenagers who are at least 18 years old. A $5,000 fine and the potential for five years of imprisonment is a rather potent deterrent. As a result, various high school seniors, politically active college students, concerned taxpayers, and any other interested citizens who have attained the age of 18 can freely cast their votes for the candidates of their choice.

Voting Accessibility

In addition to initially concentrating on the protection of voting rights for women and for people of color, the federal voting legislation now expressly addresses the voting rights of elderly, handicapped, and language-minority citizens as well. Through federal legislation, the elderly, the handicapped and disabled, and citizens of language minorities are provided with accessible voting registration and polling places.

The Elderly and Handicapped

The Americans with Disabilities Act of 1990 and the 1984 supplement to the Federal Voting Rights Act probably have the most impact directly on the access to the polls. Title 42, section 1973ee of the United States Code was adopted on September 28, 1984, and directly addresses the issues of accessibility to registration and polling place as these issues affect the elderly and handicapped citizens of our nation. For example, that statutory section begins

It is the intention of Congress in enacting this subchapter to promote the fundamental right to vote by improving access for handicapped and elderly individuals to registration facilities and polling places for Federal elections. (42 U.S.C.A. Section 1973ee)

Within each State, . . . each political subdivision responsible for conducting elections shall assure that all polling places for Federal elections are accessible to handicapped and elderly voters. (42 U.S.C.A. Section 1973ee-1(a))

This federal legislation mandates that each political subdivision be responsible for ensuring that the registration facilities and procedures and the polling places for the casting of ballots are both freely accessible to handicapped and elderly citizens.

In addition, the code mandates that the election officer for each state must report to the Federal Election Commission concerning the number of accessible and inaccessible polling places. The report must also detail the reasons surrounding the existence of any inaccessible voting places.

Registration Requirements and Accessibility of Polling Places

The code also specifically addresses the registration requirements that are to be implemented and satisfied by each state and political subdivision. For example, section 1973ee-2 mandates that each "state or political subdivision responsible for registration for Federal elections shall provide a reasonable number of accessible permanent registration facilities." In addition, section 1973ee-3(a) provides that

Each state shall make available registration and voting aids for Federal elections for handicapped and elderly individuals, including—(1) instructions, printed in large type, conspicuously displayed at each permanent registration facility and each polling place; and (2) information by telecommunications devices for the deaf. (42 U.S.C.A. Section 1973ee-3(a))

The code is not limited to providing enhanced accessibility for the deaf. Section 1973aa-6 addresses a broad spectrum of handicapped individuals by declaring: "Any voter who requires assistance to vote by reason of blindness, disability, or inability to read or write may be given assistance by a person of the voter's choice, other than the voter's employer or agent of that employer or officer or agent of the voter's union" (42 U.S.C.A. Section 1973aa-6). This classification of people enables a given voter to prevent being denied the right to vote simply because he or she would need assistance in exercising a fundamental right to vote.

In addition, section 1973ee-3 further provides that handicapped persons shall not be required to present notarizations or medical certificates in order to vote by absentee ballot. Also, the section mandates that notice of the availability of the aids provided through this section is to be published by the chief election officer of each state to the citizens. Such notice must be publicized in a manner calculated to reach the elderly and handicapped citizens of the electorate.

Prohibition Against English Only Obstacles

Another recent amendment to the federal legislation that protects the right to vote against arbitrary, discriminatory, or inadvertent denials, is one provision of the basic law: specifically, section 1973b(f) of the Federal Voting Rights Act, which declares in a pertinent part:

(1) The Congress finds that voting discrimination against citizens of language minorities is pervasive and national in scope. . . . [W]here State and local officials conduct elections only in English, language minority citizens are excluded from participating in the electoral process. . . . The Congress declares that, in order to enforce the guarantees of the fourteenth and fifteenth amendments to the United States Constitution, it is necessary to eliminate such discrimination by prohibiting English-only elections, and by prescribing other remedial devices.

(2) No voting qualification or prerequisite to voting, or standard, practice, or procedure shall be imposed or applied by any State or political subdivision to deny or abridge the right of any citizen of the United States to vote because he is a member of a language minority. (42 U.S.C.A. 1973b(f)(1) and (2))

In an attempt to rectify some of the same obstructions that were faced by African Americans when the Voting Rights Act was enacted in 1965, the 1975 amendments attempted to address the barriers to voting that were preventing language minorities from freely exercising their right to vote.

Registration Requirements and Accessibility of Polling Places

Other provisions of the federal Voting Right Act also mandate the remedial provisions that are to be observed in order to promote freer access to registration and the polling place. For example, section 1973aa-1a of title 42 provides that before "August 6, 2007, no covered State or political subdivision shall provide voting materials only in the English language." The section defines a covered state or municipality as one where 5 percent of the citizens of voting age are members of a language minority, or where more than 10,000 of the citizens of voting age are members of a language minority.

The federal legislation further declares that whenever any state or political subdivision covered by the section "provides any registration or voting notices, forms, instructions, assistance, or other materials or information relating to the electoral process, including ballots, it shall provide them in the language of the applicable minority group as well as the English language"[.] (42 U.S.C.A. Section 1973aa-1a(c)). This provision attempts to place the language-minority citizen on an equal level with his or her fellow citizens.

As such, access to voter registration and to the polling places cannot be denied to the citizen who is not literate in the English language. Voting may not be denied to citizens based upon their race, color, gender, status, or any other immutable or discriminatory and arbitrary ground. Although there are certain individuals who can be legitimately denied the right to vote (the insane, the imprisoned, infants), the right to vote is a fundamental franchise that is to be afforded equally to all citizens. Though there are various qualifications and restrictions that can be placed as perquisites to the right to vote, the institution is rather liberally available to those who are citizens and at least 18 years of age.

The Right to be a Candidate

The right to vote is directly affected by the right to be a candidate. Not only is the selection of candidates important to those who vote but, obviously, the selection process is also critical to those who wish to become a candidate and subsequently an office holder and a representative of the people. As such, the right to be a candidate becomes rather significant when discussing the right to vote. Without the ability to help shape the process that chooses the candidates for elective office, the right to vote can become hollow.

However, unlike the right to vote itself, the right to be a candidate has not yet been classified as a fundamental right. As such, the degree of scrutiny that reviewing courts will impose on laws or restrictions that affect the right to be a candidate is generally less than that imposed on outright denials of the right to vote. With the fundamental right to vote, "strict scrutiny" is always required (i.e., the law or regulation must be necessary to a compelling government interest). However, with the right to be a candidate, the United States Supreme Court has declared that "intermediate scrutiny" can be appropriate. Under intermediate scrutiny, the government is saddled with a lesser burden of justification.

The guiding language under "intermediate scrutiny" asks whether the law or the restriction is substantially related to an important, and thus legitimate, government objective. Unlike strict scrutiny, the law or the regulation need not be absolutely necessary to a compelling government interest. Basically, the law must be needed to support an important government interest, as opposed to a necessary government interest.

For example, and as explained in *Matthews* v. *Atlantic City* (1980), the Supreme Court of New Jersey declared:

> [T]he right to be a candidate for office has never been held by either the United States Supreme Court or this Court to enjoy "fundamental" status. . . . There is no fundamental right to run for office. . . . [W]e recognize the importance of legislative interests in maintaining the integrity of the electoral process. To permit the furtherance of these interests without unduly restricting the electorate's freedom of choice, we hold that a requirement or restriction for candidates for elective office must be reasonably and suitably tailored to further legitimate governmental objectives. (*Matthews* v. *Atlantic City,* 84 N.J. 153, 161, 168, 169, 1980)

The critical analysis of a reviewing court, however, emphasizes the overall impact on the right to vote that any restrictions on candidacy may entail. The restrictions cannot be so burdensome as to ultimately deny the right to vote by monopolizing or controlling the candidacy pool. While examining two authoritative United States Supreme Court cases that analyzed state restrictions placed on the right to be a candidate, Barron et al. explain in their book:

[T]he Court noted that "[o]ur primary concern is with the tendency of ballot access restrictions 'to limit the field of candidates from which voters might choose.'" It reasoned that "[t]he right to vote is 'heavily burdened' if that vote may be cast only for majority-party candidates at a time when . . . other candidates are 'clamoring for a place on the ballot[.]'" [A]n election campaign is an effective platform for the expression of views on the issues of the day, and a candidate serves as a rallying point for like-minded citizens."

While recognizing that the state's "important regulatory interests are generally sufficient to justify reasonable, nondiscriminatory restriction," the Court [emphasized that the critical] "inquiry" . . . "is whether the challenged restriction unfairly or unnecessarily burdens the 'availability of political opportunity.'" (Quoting *Andersen* v. *Celebrezze*, 1983, and *Bullock* v. *Carter*, 1972)

Though the United States Supreme Court has not yet granted fundamental-rights status to the claimed right to be a candidate, if that right when restricted subsequently impairs the fundamental right to vote, constitutional "strict scrutiny" will be applied to judge the validity of the governmental restriction.

This section of the chapter will explore the eligibility requirements concerning candidates for election. An investigation of both the constitutional and the legislative provisions that affect the right to be a candidate will be made, based largely on the experience in one state (New Jersey), because each state has slight differences in candidacy laws. This section also examines the laws surrounding the electoral process, including the nomination of candidates and the primary elections and general elections that follow.

Eligibility Requirements for Candidates

Although limited by the Constitution of the United States and by state constitutions alike, there are certain legitimate, and as the courts have termed them, "reasonable requirements," that a state legislature can place on the right to be a candidate. As mentioned before, the right to be a candidate is not as protected as the right to vote, yet any qualifications that infringe directly or indirectly on the right to vote are presumptively unreasonable.

Constitutional Requirements

The Constitution establishes the minimum requirements for members of the United States House of Representatives and the United States Senate. As recent failures of the congressional term-limit activists demonstrates, the Constitution also essentially establishes the maximum requirements that can be placed on candidates and officeholders.

Article I, Section 2, clause 2 of the United States Constitution details the qualifications for congressional representatives. That section provides "No person shall be a Representative who shall not have attained the Age of twenty-five Years, and been seven Years a Citizen of the United States, and who shall not, when elected, be an Inhabitant of that State in which he shall be chosen." Thus the Constitution expressly legitimizes the restrictive qualifications of age, citizenship, and residency. Any citizen who wishes to be considered as a candidate must therefore satisfy these criteria in order to throw a hat into the campaign.

Similarly, the Constitution provides the requisite qualifications that must be satisfied by those desiring to be considered as a candidate for the United States Senate: "No person shall be a Senator who shall not have attained the Age of thirty Years, and been nine Years a Citizen of the United States, and who shall not, when elected, be an inhabitant of that State for which he shall be chosen."

As with the requirements for representatives, age, citizenship, and residency of the state that the candidate is to represent are the constitutional requisites that need be satisfied. In drafting the first Article of the United States Constitution, the founding fathers viewed these three qualifications as the legitimate limitations that can be used to qualify a candidate for office.

In addition, the Constitution provides for the procedural requirements that accompany the election processes involved with representatives and senators. Clause 1 of the fourth section of Article I provides the where, when, and how of conducting elections and voting. The Article proclaims,

> The Times, Places and Manner of holding Elections for Senators and Representatives, shall be prescribed in each State by the Legislature thereof; but the Congress may at any time by Law make or alter such Regulations, except as to Places of choosing Senators. (Article I, Section 4, clause 1).

Therefore, each state is responsible for determining and implementing the procedural aspects of their elections. However, by the second provision in this clause (in addition to the Supremacy

Clause and the Necessary and Proper Clause), it is also clear that Congress has reserved the right to enact federal legislation such as the Voting Rights Act, which will both preempt and shape state election laws.

Legislative Requirements

With the protection of the right to vote predominantly in mind, the legitimate qualifications that the lawmakers of a governmental division can place on a candidate are rather limited. For example, as explained by the New Jersey Supreme Court:

> The right to vote freely for the candidate of one's choice is of the essence of a democratic society, and any restrictions on that right strike at the heart of the representative government.
>
> The power to prescribe qualifications for [elective offices is] expressly limited by reasonableness: the exclusion from office must not be "arbitrary."
>
> Far from being unrestricted, the power to prescribe qualifications for elective office is sharply limited by the constitutional guaranty of a right to vote. A prescribed qualification for office must relate to the needs of officeholding as such or the special needs of the particular office involved, with the voters free to judge the personal or individual fitness of the candidates who have those basic qualifications. *(Gangemi* v. *Rosengard,* 44 N.J. 166, 170-171, 1965)

For the most part, statutory limitations are reflective of the limitations and qualifications as outlined in federal and state constitutions. Among these legitimate qualifications that a governmental subdivision can place on a candidate are the requirements of age, citizenship, and some length of durational residency in the jurisdiction for which the candidate seeks an elective office. Usually a period of six months' to two years' residency is required. The legislatures have therefore taken the three aforementioned constitutional qualifications and added to the third category of residency a durational requirement. These qualifications are permitted in order to prevent ensure fraud and to ensure that each candidate has the required community ties necessary to adequately represent the people and their surrounding needs.

While analyzing a challenge to a New Jersey durational residency provision that required candidates to be residents of the community for two years, the New Jersey Supreme Court illustrated the legitimacy of candidacy qualifications as follows:

> Like age, residence, or citizenship restrictions on public office holding, a durational residency requirement is directed at maintaining the integrity of the ballot by preventing fraudulent and frivolous candidacies. It ensures that candidates have some knowledge of local affairs and, conversely, that local voters have an opportunity to learn about a candidate to intelligently assess his fitness for office. Properly drawn, a durational residency requirement is directed at providing a sufficient period of time for these two "educational" functions to take place. *(Matthews* v. *Atlantic City,* 84 N.J. at 170)

This aspect of permitting a durational residency requirement, though a legitimate qualification for candidates, is unreasonable for the voter.

The Nominating and Electoral Process

In order to exercise the right to vote meaningfully, a citizen must also be able to participate in the selection process for those who will ultimately appear on the ballot list. So too must the "would-be" candidate be allowed to participate in the nomination processes. The nomination process must be freely open to all candidates who meet the district's eligibility requirements. In addition, the primary election, the preliminary run-off where competitors from a single party battle to see who will win the right to represent their party, must be accessible to all. The nomination of candidates and voting in primary elections are both critical aspects of the right to vote. They can be subject only to the legitimate eligibility qualifications that are applicable equally to all citizens.

Nominations of Candidates

As with the general eligibility conditions that all candidates must meet, there are also procedural requirements that must be followed and satisfied in order for a candidate to be successfully nominated as a candidate for elective office. Determined by the United States Supreme Court and through the Constitution, states are freely able to implement the election laws that govern the nomination process. As discussed earlier, this state authority is subject only to the parameters of the federal Constitution, the state constitution, and any preemptive federal legislation.

Here justifiable qualifications designed to prevent fraud and ensure the credibility of the election deal primarily with the procedural requirements that a citizen must satisfy in order to

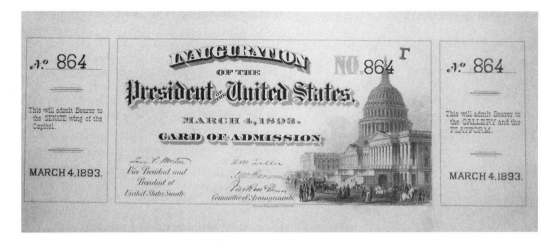

The winner of the general election achieves the ultimate goal of representing the people while serving in the elective office; in the case of these inauguration tickets, the winner was Grover Cleveland, who was elected president of the United States in 1885 and again in 1893.

successfully be nominated as a candidate. For example, there are statutory provisions that detail the requirements for obtaining the requisite signatures on nomination petitions.

State controls on the petition process include the number of signatures needed to qualify a citizen for nomination as a potential party representative. Also legitimate are regulations governing the manner in which the nomination signatures are obtained and verified. The number of witnesses necessary for the verification of each signature, the deadlines for obtaining the minimum number of signatures, and the filing requirements behind the nomination petitions are all the subject of legitimate government regulation.

Primary Elections

The primary election is the preliminary election in which competing candidates of a single party campaign against one another in order to secure their own party's nomination. The nomination entails the right to represent that party in the general election. As defined by *Black's Law Dictionary,* a "primary election [is] for the nomination of candidates for office or of delegates to a party convention, designed as a substitute for party conventions."

The primary election is usually held some months before the general election. The winner of the primary election goes on to run in the general election. In the general election, the nominated candidate of one party competes against the nominated candidates from other parties. In turn, the "at-large" winner of the general election achieves the ultimate goal of representing the people through election to the particular elective office.

The right to participate in primary elections, from the voters' standpoint, is a statutory, and not a constitutional right in many states. There is no federal constitutional, right to participate in any primary election. As illustrated in the state of New Jersey, where the Supreme Court has declared:

> The right to vote, as guaranteed by the plain language of our State Constitution, does not subsume an unfettered right to be involved in a party's internal decision-making process, which is all that a primary election is. In this state, the right to participate in a political party's primary election is a statutory one. (*Smith,* supra, 81 N.J. at 73-73).

As such, each state has election laws that govern the conduct of primary elections and the eligibility of a particular voter to vote in a particular party's primary election.

Among the legitimate restrictions placed on the conduct of primary elections is the time frame prior to the primary election within which a voter must declare his party affiliation and a candidate must announce her candidacy. Similarly, the preparation of the ballot for both primary and general elections has been the subject of state regulation. Provisions of New Jersey's statutory election laws address these procedural provisions, and they have been addressed by the New Jersey Supreme Court as well.

For example, mandatory voter registration and candidate affiliation requirements designed to prevent "party raiding" were analyzed by the New Jersey Court in *Smith* v. *Penta*. In this case a challenge was lodged against two statutory provisions; one required a voter to declare party affiliation 50 days prior to the primary election, and another required nominating petitions for candidates to be filed 40 days before the primary election. The challengers asserted that the inconsistency in time frames between voter and candidate registration (50 and 40 days prior to election day respectively) impaired a citizen's right to vote.

The challengers claimed that the right to vote was being denied because the prospective voter was required to register with a particular party before knowing who and with what party all the potential candidates would be affiliated. Relying on a ruling of the United States Supreme Court, the New Jersey Court explained:

> In *Rosario* v. *Rockefeller,* the [United States] Supreme Court sustained a New York statute that conditioned the right to vote in a particular party's primary on his having declared an affiliation with that party eight to eleven months before the date of the primary election. The Court found the state interest in preventing [party] raiding sufficient to justify the exclusion. Raiding occurs when members of one party vote in the primary election of the other party with the intention of nominating a weak candidate who could probably be defeated by the candidate of their true party in the general election. Obviously, raiding will tend to weaken the political party attacked and if successful will result in a fraudulent candidacy. *(Smith* v. *Penta,* 81 N.J. at 70-71)

The state interest of protecting the credibility of elections, and preventing fraud, were considered as sufficiently reasonable to justify the legislative action and restrictions. In order to protect the right to vote, it can therefore become necessary to restrict or qualify an unlimited right to vote in certain circumstances.

Another area of the electoral process that has been the subject of litigation is the preparation of the ballot. For example, challenges have been made regarding the placement and positioning of candidates on the ballot. Concerning such issues, the "Legislature [may] adopt reasonable regula-

tions for the conduct of primary and general elections. Such regulations, of course, may control the manner of preparation of the ballot, so long as they do not prevent a qualified elector from exercising his constitutional right to vote for any person he chooses" *(Quaremba* v. *Allan,* 67 N.J. 1, 11, 1975).

The ability of the voter to freely exercise her right to vote, subject to limited and legitimate state controls, is the ultimate concern of the courts. Generally, the prevention of fraud is a state administrative concern and designed to ensure not only the legitimacy of the election but also the perception of legitimacy in the eyes of the public.

Apportionment and Reapportionment

The idea behind apportionment relates directly to the basic concept of a representative democracy and the right of the citizens to vote. The right to vote is in fact greatly affected by such concepts as apportionment and reapportionment. In order for the right to vote to be meaningful, there must be a parallel right to equal representation. Without a fair basis for apportioning representatives among the people, the concept of a representative democracy would be diminished, if not rendered pointless.

Apportionment is the concept that governs the disbursement of elected representatives evenly amongst the people. According to *Black's Law Dictionary* reapportionment pertains to a "realignment or change in the legislative districts brought about by changes in population and mandated by the constitutional requirement of equality of representation." The idea is that the people are to be represented on an even basis, in order to ensure that all people have equal access to government representation.

As explained through *Black's Law Dictionary,* apportionment is defined as the

> process by which legislative seats are distributed among units entitled to representation. It is a determination of the number of representatives which a State, county, or other subdivision may send to a legislative body. The U.S. Constitution provides for a census every ten years, on the basis of which Congress apportions representatives according to population; but each State must have at least one representative.

Equal apportionment is central to any notion of equal representation. If the elected offices are not evenly apportioned among the people, then certain groups of citizens will have more input and thus more of an impact on the policies that evolve through our governmental representatives. Conversely, other groups of citizens who are denied equal representation will have less of an opportunity and an ability to shape the policies by which they are governed.

Constitutional Requirements and Mandates

The language of the United States Constitution, and its interpretation by the United States Supreme Court, determines the validity of any state or local laws, regulations, or practices that affect the apportionment of elective representatives. Through the Constitution and specifically the amendments thereto, equal representation for equal numbers of people is a concept that is to be enjoyed by all citizens.

Article I, Section 2 Provisions

The concept of equally apportioned representation, continually reassessed over a fixed period of years, is directly embedded in the United States Constitution. The concept has also been addressed in several constitutional amendments, in order to effect a nondiscriminatory application. Apportionment was initially addressed in the third clause of Section 2, Article I of the Constitution. The section clause 3, which appears in brackets, has subsequently been repealed and amended by section 2 of the Fourteenth Amendment (ratified 1868). However, the clause as originally drafted and ratified, provided

> [Representatives and direct Taxes shall be apportioned among the several States which may be included within this Union, according to their respective Numbers, which shall be determined by adding to the whole Number of free Persons, including those bound to Service for a Term of Years, and excluding Indians not taxed, three fifths of all other Persons.]. The actual Enumeration shall be made within three Years after the first Meeting of the Congress of the United States, and within every subsequent Term of ten years, in such Manner as they shall by Law direct. The Number of Representatives shall not exceed one for every thirty Thousand, but each State shall have at Least one Representative[.] (Article I, section 2, clause 3)

This original draft of the apportionment clause provided the fundamentals, and the basis for equal representation was established. Through the ratification of subsequent amendments, the protections of equal representation were applied to all citizens, replacing the original emphasis on white males.

The Fourteenth Amendment

After the defeat of the southern states in the Civil War, the newly won freedoms of many Americans had to be addressed at the constitutional level, in order to help secure essential freedoms. Through the Fourteenth Amendment to the United States Constitution, not only did the amendment introduce such concepts as the privileges and immunities clause (safeguarding United States citizens in general from discriminatory and arbitrary state laws), the due process clause (protecting life, liberty, and property against arbitrary government depravations), and the equal protection clause (guaranteeing that all individuals are viewed and treated as equal in the eyes of the law) but it also addressed the idea of equal apportionment of elected representatives.

Specifically eliminating the references to "free Persons" and "three fifths of all other Persons," the Fourteenth Amendment provides

> Representatives shall be apportioned among the several States according to their respective numbers, counting the whole number of persons in each State, excluding Indians not taxed. But when the right to vote at any election for the choice of electors for President and Vice-President of the United States, Representatives in Congress, the Executive and Judicial officers of a State, or the members of the Legislature thereof, is denied to any of the male inhabitants of such State, being twenty-one years of age, and citizens of the United States, or in any way abridged, except for participation in rebellion, or other crime, the basis of representation therein shall be reduced in the proportion which the number of such male citizens shall bear to the whole number of male citizens twenty-one years of age in such State.

As written, the amendment mandated that all male citizens be counted when determining the apportionment of representatives to elective office. Unfortunately for women, young adults, and the native Americans, this concept of equal representation was not yet realized.

As discussed previously under the heading, "Denial of the Right to Vote," the inequities that were still faced after the ratification of the Four-

The first African Americans elected to the House and the Senate included (front row) Senator H. R. Revels of Mississippi, and Representatives Benjamin S. Turner (Alabama), Josiah T. Walls (Florida), Joseph H. Rainy (South Carolina), R. Brown Elliot (South Carolina), (second row) Robert C. DeLarge (South Carolina), and Jefferson H. Lonc (Georgia).

teenth Amendment by women, young adults, and African Americans were specifically addressed by the Fifteenth Amendment (1870), the Nineteenth Amendment (1920), and the Twenty-sixth Amendment (1971), respectively.

Reapportionment

Reapportionment is the concept of redistributing the representatives of the people. Reapportionment is based on a legitimate determination that the representatives are no longer, or perhaps were never, apportioned equally. As mentioned previously, reapportionment entails realigning the representatives according to shifts or changes in the population of voting districts.

In order to ensure that shifting populations and demographic trends do not skew the basis of equal representation, the representatives are reapportioned on a regular basis. As mandated by the United States Constitution, representatives are reapportioned after each ten-year census according to any changes in demographics that have occurred.

The Supreme Court and Legislative Districts

Legislative districting is the process of dividing up and defining the voting districts within a particular jurisdiction. According to *Black's Law Dictionary* it is defined as the "establishment of the precise geographical boundaries of each such unit or constituency."

Up until the 1960s, the United States Supreme Court had consistently ruled that the concepts of state reapportionment and state legislative districts were to be left solely to the discretion of the individual states. The Court abstained from getting involved in controversies involving state districting plans by invoking the "political question" doctrine. This doctrine holds that if the issue in controversy before the court is one that is either (1) committed by the Constitution to another branch of government, (e.g., the legislative or executive branches) or (2) incapable of being resolved or enforced by the judicial process, then the Courts of this country will not decide the issue. As such, the issue is termed as being "nonjusticiable."

State Districting and Reapportionment Come Before the Court

Reflected in such concepts as the separation of powers and federalism, the Court had traditionally left the issue of state reapportionment to the control of the individual states. For example, in *Colgrove* v. *Green* (1946), the United States Supreme Court held that it "is hostile to a democratic system to involve the judiciary in the politics of the people." The notion was that the apportioning of state representatives was beyond the jurisdiction of the courts. The Court had traditionally determined:

The short of it is that the Constitution has conferred upon Congress exclusive authority to secure fair representation by the States in the popular House and left to that House determination whether States have fulfilled their responsibility. If Congress failed in exercising its powers, whereby standards of fairness are offended, the remedy ultimately lies with the people. Whether Congress faithfully discharges its duty or not, the subject has been committed to the exclusive control of Congress. An aspect of government from which the judiciary, in view of what is involved, has been excluded by the clear intention of the Constitution cannot be entered by the federal courts because Congress may have been in default in exacting from States obedience to its mandate.

This line of reasoning, though perhaps theoretically desirable, was nonetheless realistically improbable. Instead, the outcome of historic Congressional inaction concerning equal apportionment of representatives was the clear underrepresentation of certain groups—white as well as minority citizens. As a result, the Court abandoned this line of reasoning which had previously precluded federal courts from entertaining any issues pertaining to apportionment and legislative districting. The jurisdiction of the courts was to be opened to the concept of political representation.

With the Supreme Court's decision in the landmark case of *Baker* v. *Carr* (1962), this previous judicial indifference yielded to the political pressures that were growing. In *Baker,* the Court held for the first time that federal courts did in fact have jurisdiction over state legislative districting plans. Through the use of the Fourteenth Amendment, the federal courts could now adjudicate issues involving state apportionment and state legislative voting districts.

At the core of the *Baker* decision was the judicial pronouncement that districting based on equal population was to be the fundamental force behind the drawing of legislative districts, their boundaries, and the reapportioning thereof. The equal protection clause of the Fourteenth Amendment became the foundation from which the Supreme Court was to launch the judges of the federal District Courts into a new activity. Those judges at the lowest levels of the federal judicial ladder would hear claims of discrimination based on unequal representation.

The Court decided that standards would be established for state legislative districts from that time forward, and the assurance of equal representation was the ultimate goal of any redistricting plan. In overruling the trial court's determination

that cases such as *Colgrove* v. *Green* had precluded federal courts from addressing issues involving reapportionment and redistricting plans, the United States Supreme Court explained: "We understand the District Court to have read the cited cases as compelling the conclusion that since the [citizens] sought to have a legislative apportionment held unconstitutional, their suit presented a 'political question' and was therefore nonjusticiable. We hold that this challenge to an apportionment presents no nonjusticiable 'political question.'" Since the citizen challenge was based upon claims that the apportionment of representatives amounted to "discriminatory treatment of a racial minority violating the Fifteenth Amendment[,]" the Court declared that the issue was appropriate for judicial resolution (*Baker,* at 230). Ultimately, the Court held that the "allegations of a denial of equal protection present[ed] a justiciable constitutional cause of action upon which [the challengers were] entitled to a trial and a decision. The right asserted is within the reach of judicial protection under the Fourteenth Amendment" (*Baker,* at 237).

The availability for judicial review and hence judicial protection was established in the 1962 case of *Baker* v. *Carr.* The precise parameters of this newly created equal protection standard were later entrenched in the case of *Wesberry* v. *Sanders* (1964).

In *Wesberry,* the United States Supreme Court declared that among the plain and direct objectives of the Constitution was the idea of equal representation for equal numbers of people. As a result, the paradigm of "one-man, one-vote" became the focus of legislative districts and reapportionment. Specifically, the *Wesberry* Court declared that

> . . . the command of Art. I, [Section] 2, that Representatives be chosen "by the People of the several States" means that as nearly as is practicable one man's vote in a congressional election is to be worth as much as another's. . . . We do not believe that the Framers of the Constitution intended to permit the same vote-diluting discrimination to be accomplished through the device of districts containing widely varied numbers of inhabitants. (*Wesberry* at 7-8)

As such, governing standard has evolved that mandates that any "state statute which denies the rule of one-man, one-vote is violative of equal protection laws" (citing *Baker* v. *Carr,* 1962). Accordingly, since the Landmark decision of *Baker* v. *Carr,* and the implementing decision of

Wesberry v. *Sanders,* the principle of "one-man, one-vote" has been applied to the individual states by the United States Supreme Court. Therefore, state districting plans that dilute the vote of minority groups are not only unconstitutional but are also a violation of, and therefore preempted by, the federal Voting Rights Act.

In another United States Supreme Court decision, the idea of equal representation was once again in the spotlight. In interpreting *Reynolds* v. *Sims* (1964), Terry B. O'Rourke explains in *Reapportionment: Law, Politics, Computers:*

> the fundamental principle of representation in this country is one of equal representation for equal numbers of people[.] [T]he equal protection clause [of the Fourteenth Amendment] requires that seats in both houses of bicameral state legislatures must be apportioned on the basis of population. The majority's "fundamental principle" of representation was derived from the right to vote. . . . "[T]he right of suffrage can be denied by a debasement or dilution of the weight of a citizen's vote just as effectively as by wholly prohibiting the free exercise of the franchise." Observing that the discrimination resulting from legislative districting plans which gave the same number of representatives to unequal numbers of people was "easily demonstrable mathematically," he concluded that the weight of votes of citizens Amerely because of where they happen to reside, hardly seems justifiable.

Gerrymandering

Aside from express or outright denials of the right to vote, modern political times have experienced more subtle measures designed to dilute the right to vote. Though not as direct, these practices nevertheless result in a denial of the right to vote. An example of this can be seen through the concept of "gerrymandering." Gerrymandering is the practice of drawing voting districts geographically in a discriminatory manner in order to influence the right to vote. According to *Black's Law Dictionary* this practice is usually directed at securing "a majority for a given political party in districts where the result would be otherwise if they were divided according to obvious natural lines."

Under the Voting Rights Act of 1965, there was no mandate that the states adopt or define any particular form of congressional voting districts. However, the Act does prohibit districting plans that have the purpose or intent of diluting or weakening the vote of certain groups of minority citizens *(Shaw* v. *Hunt,* 1994). Similarly, in *Shaw*

v. *Reno,* the United States Supreme Court held that "a State's drawing of congressional districts, [that] explicitly distinguish between individuals on racial grounds falls within the core of the Equal Protection Clause's prohibition against race-based decisionmaking[.]" *(Miller* v. *Johnson,* 1995; citing *Shaw* v. *Reno,* 1993).

In *Miller* v. *Johnson,* the United States Supreme Court built on this reasoning, and held that the equal protection clause of the Fourteenth Amendment prohibited state redistricting plans that had "no rational explanation save as an effort to separate voters on the basis of race."

In *Miller* v. *Johnson,* the Georgia legislature had proposed three legislative districts that had a majority population composed of African American voters. These districts were the result of irregular geographical borders specifically designed to create "majority-black" voting districts. This was done in an attempt to obtain the necessary preclearance from the Department of Justice as mandated under the terms of the Voting Rights Act for any change in "standard practice or procedure with respect to voting" (Voting Rights Act of 1965, Section 5, amended 42 U.S.C.A. Section 1973c). In striking down Georgia's congressional redistricting plan the Supreme Court affirmed the decision of the District Court and determined that "it was a racial gerrymander in violation of the Equal Protection Clause [because] the State Legislature's purpose, as well as the District's irregular borders, showed that race was the overriding and predominant force in the districting determination. The [District C]ourt [correctly] assumed that compliance with the [Voting Rights] Act would be a compelling [state] interest, but found that the plan was not narrowly tailored to meet that interest[.]" *(Miller,* (syllabus), at 2480).

With *Miller,* the modern stage was now set. Any legislative changes in voting districts that were based solely or primarily on racial considerations must be able to withstand strict scrutiny analysis by the federal courts. If governmental actions that affect the right to vote are not necessary to a compelling government interest and are not also "narrowly tailored" to meet that interest only, the government action will not be permitted to withstand citizen challenge.

In 1996 the Supreme Court dismissed as moot a Louisiana redistricting case involving the

Fourth Congressional District. Other defeats to minority representation occurred in Texas, Florida, Georgia, and North Carolina. In all these decisions the Supreme Court indicated that race had been given excessive consideration in drawing district lines. This kind of racial gerrymandering had produced a significant number of African Americans and Hispanics in Congress, but the Court stood firm in its opposition, on grounds of the "equal protection of the laws."

Supermajorities

The concept of requiring more than a mere 51 percent majority in order to implement certain referendum actions has been addressed and approved by the United States Supreme Court. For example, in *Gordon* v. *Lance* (1971), the Court validated a governmental requirement that referendum votes be approved by 60 percent of the voting electorate. Thus the concept of the extraordinary or supermajority was legitimized.

In contrast, the Supreme Court in *Town of Lockport* (1977) upheld the defeat of a county referendum where the government had demanded a majority vote from different classes of voters, even though these voters were all members of the overall county electorate. Under New York's Municipal Home Rule Law, changes involving the powers of local governments are to be approved via referendum votes of the local citizens.

In Niagara County, for example, "a county board of supervisors may submit a proposed charter to the voters for approval. If a majority of the voting city dwellers and a majority of the voting noncity dwellers both approve, the charter is adopted." Therefore, there is the potential for the majority of one class to approve and the majority of another class to disapprove, with the overall electorate's majority approving and the referendum still failing owing to the one class disapproving. As a result, there is the possibility of a minority of the voters controlling the outcome of governmental referendums.

In *Town of Lockport,* this very scenario played itself out. The proposed "charter created the new offices of County Executive and County Comptroller and continued the county's existing power to establish tax rates, equalize assessments, issue bonds, maintain roads, and administer health and public welfare services" (*Lockport,* at 262).

The city voters approved the charter, while the noncity voters disapproved the charter. However, a "majority of those voting in the entire county [had] favored the charter" (*Lockport,* at 260-62). Nevertheless, due to the referendum requirements that a majority of both city and noncity voters be achieved, the referendum did not pass and the proposed charter was rejected.

Upon review by the United States Supreme Court, the issue was presented as "whether there is a genuine difference in the relevant interests of the groups that the state electoral classification has created; and, if so, whether any resulting enhancement of minority voting strength nonetheless amounts to invidious discrimination in violation of the Equal Protection Clause" (*Lockport,* at 268).

The citizen action group that had challenged the referendum provisions asserted that all the voters within the county had identical interests concerning the adoption or the rejection of a new county charter. In striking this premise as unacceptable, the Supreme Court upheld the governmental majority vote requirements, determining that no violation of the Equal Protection Clause occurred. Specifically, the Court held:

> The provisions of New York law here in question no more than recognize the realities of . . . substantially differing electoral interests. Granting to these provisions the presumption of constitutionality to which every duly enacted state and federal law is entitled, we are unable to conclude that they violate the Equal Protection Clause of the Fourteenth Amendment.

As such, the extraordinary majority provisions were held as constitutional: They did not amount to a denial of the right to vote and were therefore permitted to stand.

The Voting Rights Act of 1965: Impact and Enforcement

As a democratic republic, the right to vote is a fundamental franchise that enjoys the utmost protection from the United States Constitution, our individual state constitutions, and federal and state statutes alike. In order for a representative democracy to be functionally legitimate, the protections and guarantees that are expressed in and advanced through the Voting Rights Act must be effectively enforced.

The Voting Rights Act of 1965 is perhaps one of the most important pieces of legislation ever to be enacted in the area of voter rights. Through this federal legislation, the fundamental right to vote is protected and strengthened. The act parallels and advances fundamental principles comprising the right to vote, principles that are expressed in our federal and state constitutions. For example, the act has been interpreted and analyzed as providing Congress "with authority to control national elections and, to a limited extent, state elections." Its control of the latter is confined to the enactment of legislation enforcing provisions of the United States Constitution, notably the Thirteenth, Fourteenth, Nineteenth, and Twenty-fourth Amendments. This section will focus primarily on the impact that the act has had on voting rights and on the subsequent enforcement of the act by the United States Department of Justice.

Historical Background of the Voting Rights Act

Upon the defeat of the Confederate States by the Union Army, the nation faced many new struggles. By guaranteeing freedom to African Americans, the end of the Civil War presented certain dilemmas for the victorious forces of the Union. One such area concerned the right to vote. While the Congress was attempting to secure these newly found freedoms by passing the Thirteenth, Fourteenth, and Fifteenth Amendments, reluctant forces in the southern states of the former Confederacy were figuring out ways to attempt to defeat or discourage the rights of African Americans concerning the right to vote.

As explained by the authors in *Quiet Revolution in the South,* federal action was indeed necessary in order to help secure the fundamental right to vote:

> After the Civil War, southern states were required by the *Military Reconstruction Acts of 1867* to adopt new constitutions granting universal male suffrage regardless of race as a precondition for readmission to the Union. The Fifteenth Amendment, ratified in 1870, seemed to guarantee blacks the franchise by prohibiting vote discrimination on the basis of "race, color, or previous condition of servitude." Nonetheless, by the turn of the century white conservative officials had effectively nullified the black vote as a political force in the eleven states of the former Confederacy. The elimination of black suffrage was made possible by northern

> indifference[,] . . . southern intimidation of potential black voters, corruption and fraud at the ballot box, Supreme Court decisions striking down various provisions of the Enforcement Act of 1870 and the Force Act of 1871, and subsequent court decisions permitting southern states to rewrite their constitutions to exclude blacks by devices such as literacy and good character tests and the poll tax.

With the struggles faced by African Americans at the ballot box, the United States Congress could hardly ignore their plight. Along with other citizens and minority groups, access to the polling place, or lack thereof, was a major area of concern that demanded redress. However, it was not until passage of the Voting Rights Act of 1965 that the last major barriers to voting were breached.

The Voting Rights Act was originally passed by the United States Congress on August 6, 1965 (Public Law 89-110, 89th Congress, S. 1564). The Act was subsequently amended and reauthorized for additional five-year and seven-year periods on June 22, 1970, and August 6, 1975 (Public Law 91-285, 91st Congress, H.R. 4249 and Public Law 94-73, 94th Congress, H.R. 6219). Thereafter, on August 5, 1982, the Voting Rights Act was reauthorized by Congress for the next 25 years, taking guarantees provided through the act well into the next century.

Impact on Voting Rights

Undoubtedly, the Voting Rights Act of 1965, as originally enacted, and as amended, has enhanced access to the polling place for a large number of citizens. It has done so by prohibiting blatant and outright denials of the right to vote that are based on discriminatory or discretionary practices. The act has also eliminated many pretextual laws, regulations, customs, and practices that operated to deny access to the vote.

For example, as illustrated by the author in *Federal Review of Voting Changes,* the impact of the Voting Rights Act has been quite enormous:

> Since it was enacted in 1965, the Voting Rights Act has proved to be one of the milestones on the path toward full civil rights for minorities in the United States. Under its original provisions, . . . thousands of blacks have registered and voted, some for the first time in their lives. This, in turn, has led to an increase in the number of blacks who have run for and won public offices throughout the South[.] Before 1965, about 72 black elected officials were serving in the 11 states of the South, including the seven covered

It was not until the passage of the Voting Rights Act of 1965 that the last major barriers to voting were breached. The Voting Rights Act prohibits blatant and outright denials of the right to vote that are based on discriminatory or discretionary practices.

by the Voting Rights Act of 1965. As of May 1975, there were more than 1,100 black officials in just the seven southern states covered by the Act. Now the protections of the Act have been extended to . . . Spanish-speaking persons, American Indians, Asian-Americans, and similar language minorities [who] have not been able to participate fully in the electoral process.

With its continued Congressional reauthorization, and the expansive nature of the amendments, the act has experienced perhaps an even larger-than-expected impact on the fundamental right to vote.

In addition, the Voting Rights Act has had not only a significant impact with respect to federal voting patterns and elections but a profound impact on state and local voting rights. "Section 5 . . . has prevented many discriminatory practices from being instituted because of legislatures, county councils and other governing bodies realize that they would not be cleared under [Justice Department preclearance requirements]" (*Hunter,* at 11).

Enforcement by the U.S. Department of Justice

The Voting Rights Act provides the American citizen with a powerful means of seeking redress for violations concerning the right to vote. The Act also provides the means and the ability of enforcement for the federal government, enabling the democratic idea of equality at the ballot box to become attainable.

The provisions of the Voting Rights Act demand that any covered jurisdiction clear proposed changes in voting laws, regulations, or procedures with the U.S. Department of Justice as a prerequisite to their enactment. This mandate helps to secure the right to vote by eliminating the ability of state or local subdivisions to enact voting requirements that, although neutral on their surface, actually have a tendency to burden certain groups of citizens and top blunt their voting rights. Not only are blatant discriminatory policies prohibited but so too are policies that are either less obvious in nature or have a discriminatory impact. As explained by one commentator while discussing the preclearance provisions of the Act,

> . . . the wisdom of Section 5 has become evident. The most frequent use of Section 5 in recent years has been to combat practices which were barely realized to be discriminatory when the Voting Rights Act was passed in 1965. These practices include such techniques as racial gerrymandering of legislative districts, annexations, and the use of majority requirements for election. Because of Section 5, both staff lawyers of the Department of Justice and members of civil rights organizations have become expert in detecting practices which tend to be discriminatory (*Hunter,* at 11).

Perhaps the most important aspects of the Voting Rights Act, and the best safeguards for the right to vote in general, are the reporting and authorization provisions of section 5. By requiring that states and localities obtain authorization prior to implementing changes, the Justice Department can best monitor the right to vote and its accessibility to all citizens.

Accessibility to government to correct abuses is quite available, as either the United States Attorney General or a private citizen can employ the provisions of the Voting Rights Act to combat denials of the right to vote. Generally, when the citizen chooses to access the protections, the Justice Department has acted to enforce the citizen's rights. As noted by the authors of *Section Five, U.S. Voting Rights Act of 1965: Voting Changes That Require Federal Approval,* and the Institute of Government at the University of Georgia, "the courts have given an increasingly liberal construction to section five and, doubtless, will continue doing so in the future. In light of this, officials in covered jurisdictions [must] be keenly aware of this act and how it is interpreted to avoid having voting-related changes enjoined or invalidated."

Not only are the preclearance provisions of section 5 important but also the enforcement of other protective provisions by the Department of Justice is critical toward ensuring the guarantees of a right to vote. A large increase in African American registration in the South resulted from this reform.

As a tool for securing the fundamental right to vote, and the equal exercise of that right, the Voting Rights Act of 1965 has proved indispensable. For example, in 1995 the Civil Rights Division created a Minority Language Task Force to ensure that minority language citizens were able to fully participate in the electoral process. The Division even has monitored elections to ensure that officials are complying with the minority-language provisions of the law regarding Native Americans, Hispanic Americans, and Chinese Americans. Residents in many parts of the nation can receive ballots in languages other than English.

The Civil Rights Division of the U.S. Justice Department also has authority, under the Voting Rights Act, to initiate lawsuits to object to discriminatory election plans and may informally complain about such plans at any time. The division has reviewed about 10,000 voting election plans and objected to about 150 plans. The division enforces the National Voter Registration Act, which is intended to simplify voter registration. In spite of challenges by a handful of states, the division has won every such case, including those brought against Illinois, California, and Pennsylvania.

In order for voting rights to be enforced effectively in the regions of the country that were, and are, ultimately covered by the Voting Rights Act, federal legislation was inevitable. Citizens who believe that their state or local government has unreasonably restricted their right to vote should contact responsible officials at the state level, and if still unsatisfied, resort to the U.S. Justice Department for assistance.

Bibliography

Barron, Jerome A., et al. *Constitutional Law: Principles and Policy.* 4th ed. Charlottesville, Va.: The Michie Company, 1992.

Black, Henry Campbell. *Black's Law Dictionary.* 6th ed. St. Paul, Minn.: West Publishing, 1990.

Catt, Carrie Chapman, and Nettie Rogers Shuler. *Woman Suffrage And Politics: The Inner Story of the Suffrage Movement.* Seattle, Wa.: University of Washington Press, 1969.

Claude, Richard. *The Supreme Court and the Electoral Process.* Baltimore: The Johns Hopkins Press, 1970.

Coolidge, Olivia. *Women's Rights: The Suffrage Movement in America, 1848–1920*. New York: E. P. Dutton, 1966.

Davidson, Chandler, and Bernard Grofman, eds. *Quiet Revolution in the South*. Princeton, N.J.: Princeton Paperbacks, 1995.

Hunter, David H. *Federal Review of Voting Changes: How to Use Section 5 of the Voting Rights Act*. Washington, D.C.: Joint Center for Political Studies, 1975.

McKay, Robert B. *Reapportionment: The Law and Politics of Equal Representation*. New York: The Twentieth Century Fund, 1965.

Naar, M. D. *The Law of Suffrage and Elections*. Trenton, N.J.: Naar, Day and Naar, Printers, 1985.

O'Rourke, Terry B. *Reapportionment: Law, Politics, Computers*. Washington, D.C.: American Enterprise Institute for Public Policy Research, 1972.

Severn, Bill. *Free But Not Equal: How Women Won the Right to Vote*. New York: Julian Messner, 1967.

Weeks, J. Devereux, and Norman J. Slawsky. *Section Five, U.S. Voting Rights Act of 1965: Voting Changes that Require Federal Approval*. Athens, Ga.: Institute of Government, University of Georgia, 1981.

Chapter **12**

Education Rights

Steve Jenkins

The efforts to open public schooling to all constitute a formidable experience that models the civil rights struggles of all groups. What happens once a group enters the open schoolhouse doors? In some cases, when the schoolhouse doors have been opened for a previously excluded group, an included group with powerful backers has tried to establish their own separate schools that would allow them to continue to exclude those who have won the right to public schooling. Although some might argue that *Brown* v. *Board of Education* and subsequent civil rights cases have opened the schoolhouse doors to excluded groups, (e.g., most recently, female students obtained the right to attend previously all-male institutions receiving state funding), we are now witnessing efforts to privatize schooling through vouchers, charter schools, and other means. This effort may very well lead to de jure segregation as well as exclusiveness. One of the greatest public policy debates as we enter the twenty-first century will be our discussion and debate regarding the future of public education. Will we continue to develop public schools to bring our increasingly diverse population together, or will we remove or reduce the role of government and permit parents to determine all aspects of their children's schooling by giving parents direct vouchers or tuition reimbursements? This debate is being played out at every level of government—local, state, and federal—and by every branch of governments, legislative, executive, and judicial.

Listen to any news story or read any daily newspaper about schools, or just bring up the subject of today's youth and schooling. What's the consequence of these hot topics? Talking or reading about teaching and schools today is likely to stir strong emotional responses. Consider the following headlines:

"Principal Censors Students' Articles From High School Newspaper"

"School Installs Metal Detectors and Conducts Random Searches"

"Legislators Call for School Choice with Parent Vouchers"

"Students Suspended for Refusing to Salute the Flag"

"Students Suspended for Wearing Alleged Gang Colors"

"Desegregation Still the Law While Segregated Schools Grow"

"Moment of Silence and School Prayer Leads to Shouting Match"

"Governor and Key Legislators Call for English-Only Requirements"

"Wheelchair Student Denied Opportunity in Cheerleader Tryouts"

"Teen Pregnancy on the Rise, Child Care Centers Opened in Local Schools"

"Sex and AIDS Education Curriculum Meets Strong Opposition"

The historical context of these headlines may change, but the basic conflicts have existed since the early European settlers to this land first arrived.

The nature of the conflicts can be found in some fundamental questions:

• Who needs schooling? Is it a right or a privilege?

• Who will provide funding and support for the schooling, government or private associations?

• Who will teach and what will be taught?

• How are learning, education, and schooling related?

The history behind and contemporary conflicts over answers to these questions have led to an ongoing struggle over inclusion. Although inclusion may seem to be the buzzword in the Special Education community as we end the twentieth century, the real question has been, who will be included in our nation's formal network of schooling? Many groups have been excluded from our formal process, and the history of civil rights in the United States cannot be understood without examining the struggle to provide equal educational and economical opportunities for all.

The Origins of Public Education in America

The early Anglo settlers often arrived at the shores of this New World escaping persecution and prosecution for unconventional beliefs and lifestyles, often based on religious conflicts with state-supported religion in Europe. So in different settlements, colonists sometimes established schools to promote their religion and lifestyles, and these schools varied from community to community in what was taught and how.

An extensive learning system existed among the Native American tribes. Many tribes had developed complex governing confederations; hunting, gathering, and farming were among the skills learned by these Native Americans from early age. Since hunting, gathering, and farming as well as the political economy of trade were so important to the new settlers, why didn't they emulate the educational system of the Native American tribes?

The answer perhaps has much to do with dominance and submission. Whose ways will dominate, and who will submit to this domination? This chapter will examine the clashes over power and influence that have shaped our social and legal framework of schooling. The concept of assimilation to "whiteness" has effected many immigrant groups, even leading one social historian, Noel Ignatiev, to write a scholarly treatise, *How the Irish Became White* (Routledge Press, 1995), based on this concept.

The emphasis on education, or at least lip service to its importance, rang forth from the nation's beginning. From the founding of the United States, the discussion, debate, and decisions regarding the role of schooling for the young have seen a continual conflict between the states and federal government.

If you examine the United States Constitution, you will find no reference to education or schooling, unless you interpret the elastic clause of Article I, Section 8, clause 18 as granting Congress additional powers, including possibly the education of the young. Some have also referred to the "general welfare" clause of the Preamble and to Article I as supporting a role for the federal government. The nation's first Congress did address this very concern.

Early Education Ordinances

In the Land Ordinance of 1785, the Continental Congress required the settlers and the governors of each new state to reserve the sixteenth section of every township "for the maintenance of public schools within the township." In other

words, 640 acres of every new township had to be set aside for public schools.

In July of 1787, the Continental Congress enacted the Northwest Ordinance to reinforce the expansion and development of new states and to support westward expansion, including schools for the young in the new states and territories. The ordinance included the following admonition: "religion, morality, and knowledge being necessary to good government and the happiness of mankind, *schools and the means of education shall be forever encouraged*," [emphasis added]. What religion, morality, and knowledge should be taught is part of the ongoing struggle over education rights as we enter the twenty-first century.

When Congress made this pledge, most of those populating the new lands were still excluded from the process (e.g., women, slaves, Native Americans, often children of indentured servants, believers in the wrong faith). So should the new states have led the initiative to include all in the schooling of our nation's young—schooling for anyone in our expanding borders?

Within this context, recall Horace Mann, who is often cited in high school and college American history books as the "father of public education." As Massachusetts commissioner of education and as a leader in advocating public education, in 1848 Mann wrote, "For the creation of wealth, then— for the existence of a wealthy people and a wealthy nation—intelligence is the grand condition . . . The greatest of all arts of political economy is to change a consumer into a producer; and the next greatest is to increase the producing power—an end to be directly attained, by increasing his intelligence." Keep this emphasis in mind throughout this chapter's examination of the purpose of schooling. Do schools exist to feed the political economy—to create producers and increase the quantity and quality of production?

Although the U.S. Constitution makes no mention of the right to an education, most state constitutions by the late nineteenth century provided for expressed power to establish free public schools. States absorbed the schooling power under the traditional interpretation of the Tenth Amendment. Specifically, the Tenth Amendment, last but certainly not least among the ten amendments called the Bill of Rights, reserved many powers for and to the individual states with the following language: "The powers not delegated to the United States by the Constitution, nor prohibited by it to the States, are reserved to the States respectively, or to the people." In addition, this constitutional power is supported by the supremacy clause of the body of the Constitution—that is, the Constitution is the supreme law of the land (see Article VI). Some legal scholars have referred to these reserved powers as "police powers." In terms of the forced assimilation of those determined to be included in schooling, it is noteworthy that the phrase police powers is associated with a state's power to educate the young.

Most state constitutions, as originally adopted upon each state's entry into the United States, provided some explicit article calling for free public education. The language may vary as the following provisions illustrate:

- That free government rests, as does all progress, upon the broadest possible diffusion of knowledge, and that the Commonwealth should avail itself of those talents which nature has sown so liberally among its people by assuring the opportunity for their fullest development by an effective system of education throughout the Commonwealth. (Commonwealth of Virginia's Constitution)

- The legislature shall provide for a system of common schools by which a free school shall be established. (Arizona Constitution)

- The general assembly shall provide for the establishment and maintenance of a thorough and uniform system of free public schools. (Colorado Constitution)

- It shall be the duty of the General Assembly to provide, by law, for a general and uniform system of Common Schools, wherein tuition shall be without charge, and equally open to all. (Indiana Constitution)

- Education in public schools through the secondary level shall be free. (Illinois Constitution)

- A general diffusion of knowledge being essential to the preservation of the liberties and rights of the people, it shall be the duty of the legislature of the State to establish and make suitable provision for the support and maintenance of an efficient system of free public schools. (Texas Constitution)

- Schools and the means of education shall forever be encouraged in this state. The legislature was required to establish schools as soon as practicable and necessary, where the poor shall be taught gratis. (Missouri Constitution of statehood, 1820, and amended in 1875 as follows: A general diffusion of knowledge and intelligence being essential to the preservation of the rights and liberties of the people, the general assembly shall establish and maintain free public schools for the gratuitous instruction of all persons in this state

within ages not in excess of twenty-one years as prescribed by law.)

Clearly every state, under the Tenth Amendment and the expressed provisions of their respective state constitutions, has provided for some system of legislative action to establish and maintain free public schools. In most states, the state lawmakers have established and recognized the incorporation of individual schools districts to carry out the state's constitutional mandates. Although the local districts exercise enormous discretionary power, they still must operate under the color of state and federal law, and certainly in consonance with the other provisions of the state and United States Constitution.

With such an overlapping of constitutional and legal layers, it is easy to understand why the judicial branch has taken on a special role in responding to complaints over the complexities and controversies emerging from fulfillment of the state's constitutional provisions for a free public school system. Remember our judicial system often breaths life into law through interpretation, and volumes exist on the rights to and the responsibilities of public schooling.

The reason the courts played a significant role, especially in the late twentieth century, is that more and more individuals and groups have complained of not being included, of being denied fundamental freedoms, and are demanding a greater role in answering those critical questions posed previously. The question has not been, Why are those courts and judges sticking their nose into our school business? The question has been, Who is knocking on the schoolhouse door, and if the visitors are permitted in, who will help them become school participants endowed with their fundamental constitutional protections? When the schoolhouse doors have remained closed or the welcome limited and restrictive, the complainants have gone knocking on the courthouse doors. The courts have often received the formal complaints and have often sought remedies that ensured inclusion and secured freedoms for all participating in the schooling process.

Crossing the Compulsory Attendance Border

Many of the students entering the class of 2000 are enrolled as a matter of habit, as a requirement of the state's compulsory attendance law. So how do the compulsory attendance laws work: At what age do you have to enter school and how long must you remain in school until you can withdraw with or without parent permission? Must you attend a public school?

Every state has a compulsory attendance law. In addition to the governmental powers requiring school attendance, the state has also been able to call on the common law tradition known as *parens patriae*, meaning that the state may serve as parents to all persons to provide for the commonwealth and individual welfare. A Kentucky court recognized this common law compulsory attendance power in 1922 in *Strangeway* v. *Allen*. An Illinois court enunciated this doctrine as early as 1882. In *County of McLean* v. *Humphreys,* the Illinois state court concluded, "It is the unquestioned right and imperative duty of every enlightened government, in its character of *parens patriae,* to protect and provide for the comfort and well-being of such for its citizens. . . . The performance of these duties is justly regarded as one of the most important of governmental functions, and all constitutional limitations must be so understood as not to interfere with its proper and legitimate exercise."

Most states require young people to be in school between the ages of 6 and 16 years, although some states extend the age to 17 or 18 years. Students may also remain in school, tuition free, until 21 years of age. Must students attend public schools during these ages, or may they attend a private school, or can a parent choose to school a child at home? Is attendance in schools a fundamental civil right or is it a privilege extended to youth by state government?

By the early twentieth century, with the increasing waves of immigrants and burgeoning urban populations, with some first efforts at juvenile reform and rehabilitation, most states passed compulsory attendance laws. It is clear from the historic record that some states decided that public schools would be the best place to "homogenize," or "Americanize," to achieve "the melting and whiting" of the population. Requiring all students to attend public schools would assure that students would receive similar teachings and thus avoid the indoctrination that many believe would come from parochial (church-affiliated) schools.

One such state requiring attendance in public schools was Oregon. The Oregon legislature passed a law in the 1920s requiring all "normal" children between the ages of 8 and 16 to attend public schools, at least until the completion of eighth grade. Two glaring observations about this law stand out: one, schooling did not begin until age eight—kindergarten, preschool, and formal early childhood development was not an imperative or a right; and two, schooling was provided through the eighth grade: Then what?

Many private and parochial schools challenged this law as violating their Fourteenth Amendment rights protecting their life, liberty, and property from improper state action. Some might also argue, as is demonstrated in future cases in this chapter, that this violates the First Amendment freedom of association.

The First Challenge

This first major challenge to compulsory attendance laws occurred in the case, *Pierce* v. *Society of the Sisters of the Holy Names of Jesus and Mary,* heard by the U.S. Supreme Court in 1925. In the tradition of the Supreme Court's deference to property and money interests, as exemplified in *Scott* v. *Sandford,* where Dred Scott was essentially considered property and therefore powerless to decide as an inalienable right to "pursue happiness," constitutional scholars characterized similar cases as "property-conscious jurisprudence." The Pierce case was decided primarily on property interests of parochial and private schools.

The attorneys for the Sisters of the Holy Names school argued that the Fourteenth Amendment prohibited states from "denying individuals life, liberty, and property without due process of law." In this case, the parochial schools argued that Oregon's Compulsory Education Act deprived their schools of valuable property interests. The private and parochial schools had a long-established history of constructing schools and engaging in long-term contracts with teachers and parents. Compelling all Oregon "normal" students to attend public schools would shut down the parochial and private schools, and in so doing, deprive these incorporated entities (i.e., church and private schools) of property interests, economically destroying the schools, those affected by the schooling, and deny the right of parents to choose where to school their children.

While the justices of the Court acknowledged Oregon's constitutional commitment to provide schooling for all "normal children," the justices also sided with the interests of the private and parochial schools. In other words, the state has a power to establish a process (e.g., age and academic requirements) to offer, and even compel, parents and their children to comply with schooling their children between ages 8 and 16, but parents are under no obligation to fulfill this requirement by sending their children to only public schools. The state's interest in schooling youngsters could still be met through attendance of private and parochial schools. The Court acknowledged that none of the appellees (e.g., parochial and private schools) questioned the state's right to "regulate all schools, to inspect, supervise and examine them, their teachers and pupils; to require that all children of proper age attend some school, that teachers shall be of good moral character and patriotic disposition, that certain studies plainly essential to good citizenship must be taught, and that nothing be taught which is manifestly inimical to the public welfare." This recognition of state power will be ever so powerful in the examination of future cases involving who will be taught, who may teach, what may be taught, and so on.

So the state's power to require compulsory school attendance was clearly recognized by the mid-1920s, yet the Court concluded that parochial and private schools can meet the compulsory attendance requirement without losing their property interests. The Court concluded that the appellees are protected against arbitrary, unreasonable, and unlawful interference with their patrons and the consequent destruction of their business and property. Therefore, the injunctions against enforcing Oregon's public school only law were upheld.

Our more recent challenges to compulsory education laws have occurred in the areas of "religious freedom" and "parental power" to determine the education of their children through such means as home schooling. The "religious exception" and "religious exemption" to compulsory attendance laws received the highest Court's attention in 1972.

The Amish Exception

In 1972, the Court heard the case of the *State of Wisconsin* v. *Yoder,* where Amish families led

by the Yoder family challenged that state's compulsory attendance requirement beyond eighth grade. Amish families opposed Wisconsin's attendance age because it would require most children from Amish religious families to attend high school. High school attendance clashed with the traditional goals of Amish families.

The Amish parents argued that schooling beyond the basics taught in elementary school clashed with their religious values and often made their children turn against their basic religious beliefs. The Amish religion rejects the competitiveness of traditional society, deemphasizes material success, and tries to shelter the young from the temptations and sinful ways found in contemporary society, especially the modern high school. The Amish emphasized the importance of their religious teachings and family values. The Amish pointed to a long history of Christian teachings towards a self-sustaining community. The young people received the necessary skill training to be self-sufficient, contributing members of the Amish community. Since the Amish lived a rather isolated existence cloistered from contemporary society, the Amish argued that to send their children on to high school through age 16 could in effect damage or even destroy the fundamental fabric of the Amish community.

In a highly divided and lively debated decision, a majority of the justices of the Supreme Court sided with the Amish and granted an exception to the compulsory school attendance law to age 16. In other words, children from families who practiced the Amish faith did not have to attend high school in Wisconsin. Any skill development beyond the eighth grade could be, and history demonstrated would be, taught at home.

Since the Amish based their opposition on freedom of religion, the Court used a strict scrutiny test to examine if the state had a compelling interest to require children from Amish parents to attend school to age 16. In this specific case, involving this particular Christian sect, the Court could not determine a compelling state interest to require schooling beyond the elementary level, and therefore, a majority of the justices granted an exemption for Amish children. A majority of the justices applied a three-part test in balancing religious freedom with the compelling state interest. This majority said the Court must determine the following:

- Whether the individual's beliefs are legitimately religious and if they are sincerely held.

- Whether the state regulation unduly restricts the religious practices of a particular religious society or religious community.

- Whether the state has a compelling interest justifying the regulation and whether the compelling interest is of such importance as to overcome the right to free exercise of religion.

As reported, in applying this test, a majority granted the Amish a limited exemption from the compulsory attendance law. In a noted dissent, Justice William O. Douglas asked a classic question regarding the rights of young people to determine their destiny. Douglas suggested that some children from Amish families may choose to pursue education beyond elementary school, and high school would be the next logical sequence. Shouldn't children, as they are reaching the age of a mature minor, have a right to attend school, even if their parents refused on religious grounds? In dramatic fashion, Douglas's dissent presented several of the arguments on behalf of students' rights that would be the battleground into the twenty-first century. Douglas reminded this very Supreme Court that it had already given precedent to recognizing the rights of young people protected under the same Constitution as adults.

Douglas reviewed a series of cases in which the Court had specifically ruled that children, especially nearing the teenage years, are "persons" within the meaning of the Bill of Rights and the Fourteenth Amendment (e.g., see *Haley* v. *Ohio, In re Gault,* and *In re Winship—Gault and Winship* have been prominent cases emerging from the 1960s). Furthermore, Douglas quoted from the *Tinker* case in his dissent in *Yoder,* stating, "Students, in school as well as out of school, are 'persons' under our Constitution. They are possessed of fundamental rights which the State must respect, just as they themselves must respect their obligations to the State," *(Tinker* v. *Des Moines Independent Community School District,* 1969).

As in the ongoing debates between student-centered educational environments and administrative-driven authoritative institutions, Douglas clearly stakes out ground for students to have the right to say yes to additional schooling.

Several lower state and federal courts have been asked to provide religious exemptions for other youngsters based on the *Yoder* precedent, but in most instances, the courts have ruled against the exemption, contending that the state has a compelling interest in maintaining compulsory attendance laws. Some states even revised their compulsory attendance statutes, and provided for an exemption section, often called the "Amish exception." Under such exceptions, some religious groups have sought the same relief or exemption from state regulation as the Amish achieved beyond the elementary educational requirements.

For example, the state of Iowa modified its compulsory attendance law and provided the following wording for the so-called Amish exception: "When members or representatives of a local congregation of a recognized church . . . established for ten years or more within the State of Iowa prior to July 1, 1967, which professes principles or tenets that differ substantially from the objectives, goals, and philosophy of education embodied in the standards set forth in section 257.25 (i.e., the educational standards for public schools in Iowa), and rules adopted in implementation thereof . . .", then such religious societies or communities can apply to the state superintendent of schools for this exemption. The state superintendent, subject to the approval of the state board of public instruction, may, but is not required to, grant the exemption.

Challenges to the Amish Exception

Soon after adopting this exception to Iowa's compulsory attendance law, a religious-based school sought exemption. The Calvary Baptist Christian Academy, identified in court records as supported by a fundamentalist Baptist church in Charles City, Iowa, sought a declaratory judgment action (an order by which a court can compel an action by declaring a legal victory for the claimant) challenging Iowa's compulsory attendance statute and other reporting requirements of the law. In addition to seeking court-directed declaratory judgment, the church academy applied to the state board of public instruction for relief and exemption under the Amish exception. The sought action was finally decided by the Supreme Court of Iowa in *Johnson* v. *Charles City Community Schools Board of Education,* 1985.

The Iowa Supreme Court applied the three-pronged test from the Yoder case and ruled against the church academy's exemption request. First and foremost, the Court made it clear that the state has a fundamental responsibility to provide for the schooling of its youth:

> The state has a clear right to set minimum educational standards for all its children and a corresponding responsibility to see to it that those standards are honored. When such standards are set in place, compliance with them falls within the ambit of the fundamental contract between the citizen and society. It need scarcely be said that each of us, in order to enjoy membership in an organized social order, is pledged to adhere to a number of minimum norms. Of these, one of the most central is society's duty to educate its children. . . . The nature and extent of education remain largely a matter of personal choice. But there are basic minimums and, this being true, it is up to the people as a whole to set them. One way they have done this is to enact compulsory education statutes. A citizen must submit to them, persuade society to change them, or join a society without them . . .

The Court concluded that it was not persuaded to change these minimum educational requirements. So next the Court examined the Amish exception. Did the Calvary Baptist Christian Academy and its supporting church fall under the exemption clause of the compulsory attendance law? Again, the Court made it clear that the Iowa legislature, and the U.S. Supreme Court, did not intend this exception to apply to all religions. If this were the case, all church-affiliated and parochial schools could apply for the exemption. The Court acknowledged that the church members in this case had sincerely held religious beliefs. But as to the other prongs of the three-tier test, the Court concluded that the Iowa compulsory attendance law did not unduly restrict the religious practices of the church members and their children, nor did the religious beliefs and practices outweigh the state's compelling interest in enforcing the regulations.

In plain, public policy analysis, the Iowa Supreme Court claimed that the fundamental Baptist practices were not nearly as distinct as the Amish. In the Court's opinion, "Plaintiff's children, for all the distinctive religious convictions they will be given, will live, compete for jobs, work, and move about in a diverse and complex society. . . . The plaintiffs have not established that their children's educational needs are significantly different from those of other children." This

emphasis on the purpose of schooling (i.e., preparation for success in the larger society) will be noted time and again as we examine other conflicts and cases.

The Amish exception rule has been tested by many denominations in many states who have revised their compulsory attendance laws to include this religious exemption. As noted above, most church communities have not been successful. For example, the Commonwealth of Virginia adopted a broadly worded exemption, "a school board . . . shall excuse from attendance at school any pupil who, together with his parents, by reason of *bona fide* religious training or belief, is conscientiously opposed to attendance at school. . . . The term *bona fide* religious training or belief does not include essentially political, sociological, or philosophical views or merely a personal moral code."

When a group of fundamentalist parents opposed the compulsory attendance law and requested a religious exemption, the Virginia Supreme Court ruled against the parents, reasoning that a school board did not need to state the reasons for denying a religious exemption (see *Johnson* v. *Prince William County School Board*, 1991).

Homeschooling

Where have parents pursued relief from the power of the state and the compulsory attendance laws when the religious exemption has not worked? Many parents, primarily through strong legislative lobbying backed by fundamental Christian communities, have persuaded state legislatures to adopt homeschooling statutes that in many instances grant greater power and autonomy to the individual family in deciding the schooling of their children.

The state statutes governing homeschooling vary widely in regulation and enforcement, almost leading an observer to suggest that parents may seek and find a homeschooling law to meet their individual needs. In 1982, only two states, Nevada and Utah, had laws permitting homeschooling. By the mid-1990s, nearly 35 states had such statutes. Two such statutes each with dramatic differences in their homeschooling laws, will be examined here. Curiously, the differences are separated only by a political border, since each state buttresses up against the other.

For example, in *Murphy* v. *State of Arkansas* (1988), the U.S. Eighth Circuit Court of Appeals rejected the religious claims of evangelical Christians, who had been violating the Arkansas compulsory attendance laws by not complying with the Attendance Act or the Arkansas Home School Act. The Murphy family claimed that they had been following their religious teachings, much like the families of the Amish children. The Arkansas compulsory attendance act requires parents to provide schooling for their children through the age of 16 years in a public, private, or parochial school or by educating their children at home in compliance with the regulations of the Arkansas Home School Act. The Home School Act requires parents to notify in writing the superintendent of their nearest school district of their intent to homeschool, the name and age and grade of each child who is to be homeschooled, a copy of the core curriculum to be offered, the schedule of instruction (e.g., time of day, number of hours) and the qualifications of the person providing the homeschool instruction. The Act also requires parents to have their home-schooled children take standardized tests annually, and at the age of 14, submit to a minimum performance test. The administration and analysis of the tests would be the sole responsibility of the Arkansas Department of Education.

The Murphy family claimed that according to their firmly held religious beliefs the "Christian Scriptures require parents to take personal responsibility for every aspect of their children's training and education." The Murphys were educating six children at home, ages 4 through 18, providing them with an "education that is pervasively religious in nature and which does not conflict with the religious beliefs they hold, based upon their understanding of the scriptures." Furthermore, the Murphys claimed that their moral testing and instruction was sufficient to meet the state standardized test requirements.

The judges of the Eighth Circuit rejected the Murphys' claims and affirmed the lower court finding requiring the Murphys to submit to the minimum Arkansas regulations for homeschooling. The judges suggested that Arkansas had already gone a long way to empower parents in schooling decisions. The opinion stated,

> By providing the option of home schooling, Arkansas allows parents vast responsibility and accountability in terms of their children's education—control far in excess of limitations on reli-

gious rights that have been previously upheld. . . . Arkansas requires neither that the parent instructing the home-schooled student be a certified teacher nor that the parent follow a mandated curriculum. The state's only safeguard to ensure adequate training of the home-schooled student is the standardized achievement test. Even regarding this test, the state allows wide latitude to the parents. The parent may choose a test administered from a list of nationally recognized standard achievement tests and may be present while the test is administered. . . . Finally, the Murphys make no showing, as made by the Amish in Yoder, that the state can be assured its interest will be attained if appellants' religious beliefs are accommodated. We reject the Murphys' argument that parental "testing" of children provides a sufficient safeguard to assure the state's interest in education is protected. Likewise, parental affidavits concerning the children's progress would also be insufficient. In the end, we believe that the state has no means less restrictive than its administration of achievement tests to ensure that its citizens are being properly educated.

So are the Murphys stuck with the Arkansas regulations? Actually, the Murphys could travel a few miles south, relocate in Texas, and find quite different results. For example, lobbying by strong religious groups led the Texas legislature to enact the following exemptions based on religious beliefs:

• Parents have the right to request an exemption from classroom and other school activities that conflict with a parent's religious or moral beliefs, provided the parents present a written request assuring that the request is not being made to avoid a test or prevent a child from taking a subject for an entire semester.

• Parents also have the right to request that their children be excused from school for religious observances, and the request may include travel time to and from the observance.

• Parents may also have children exempted from immunization requirements for students if the parent presents an affidavit stating "the immunization conflicts with the tenets and practice of a recognized church or religious denomination of which the student is an adherent or member, except that this exemption does not apply in times of emergency or epidemic declared by the commissioner of health."

In addition to these exemptions for parents who may choose homeschooling, the Texas compulsory education statute failed to define the term "school." This led to an interesting precedent, with a state district court judge deciding that homeschooling falls within the compulsory attendance law, with very little requirement for state regulation. The state court judge did suggest that homeschoolers meet certain minimal requirements, such as:

- That the children be taught by parents or those standing in parental authority (no certification requirements).

- That the homeschoolers have a curriculum consisting of books and other written materials (now modified to include computer software and the Internet).

- That the curriculum be designed to meet basic educational goals of reading, spelling, grammar, mathematics, and a study of good citizenship.

Furthermore, the state court judge held that the Texas Education Agency (TEA) and the Texas State Board of Education lacked the authority to enforce a more restrictive interpretation of the compulsory education law. This decision was affirmed by the Texas Supreme Court in *Texas Education Agency* v. *Leeper,* 1994. The Supreme Court acknowledged that TEA has the authority to establish some minimum guidelines that might include requesting test results to determine if students are being taught "in a bona fide manner." But the Court added that administration of such tests could not be a prerequisite to exemption from the compulsory attendance law.

To date, TEA and the State Board of Education has not promulgated any enforcement rules, some suggest because they fear the political and judicial repercussions of invading family rights to homeschool. Since the Leeper case was a class-action lawsuit, the Supreme Court holding applies in all Texas public school districts. In addition, the Court held that attendance officers (often called truant officers in some jurisdictions) are prohibited from initiating charges against parents simply because they are instructing their children at home. In other words, the only way a family could be investigated for truancy or educational neglect would be to react to a complaint that schooling is not taking place.

Interestingly, the one exception to all state homeschooling initiatives is the role of special education. If a child is receiving or has received special education services, then the nearest school district's special education department is required by federal law (i.e., by the Individuals with Disabilities Education Act—IDEA) to provide services to the homeschooled child if requested by the parents. (The special education aspect will be explored further on in an examination of expanding inclusion of all in schooling.)

The *Yoder* case and subsequent challenges, as well as the strong movement toward homeschooling, leads to several questions:

- Are parents withdrawing their children from public schools because they are not satisfied with what is being taught? Who is teaching, or how they are teaching?

- Are parents withdrawing from public schools because parents do not want their children mixing with "them"?

As discussed earlier, the history of schooling in the United States has been strewn with efforts of "out groups" trying to get "in," since a good education has been equated with the pursuit of the American dream of success, especially economic and social status improvement. The struggle toward inclusion has presented primary problems for policymakers and the courts.

In the language of critical pedagogists, our society is made up of many communities, or subcultures, surrounded by borders: There are racial and ethnic borders, religious borders, class borders, gender borders, language borders, ideological or political borders, directional borders (left, right, center), age borders, ability borders, and so on. Schooling has often been a barrier to border crossing or a bridge to border crossing. Several cases have led to critical court decisions that built bridges or constructed barriers.

Crossing the Color Border: The Black/White Line

In 1903, the renowned scholar and founder of the Niagara movement and the National Association for the Advancement of Colored People (NAACP), W. E. B. Du Bois wrote in *The Souls of Black Folk,* "the problem of the twentieth century is the problem of the color line." As we will examine, the Du Bois prediction has been prophetic, and as we near the twentieth century many may claim that the challenge of the twenty-first century will be crossing color and class borders.

Paramount in crossing the color border are the culminating cases, referred to as *Brown* v. *Board of Education of Topeka, Kansas* I (1954) and *Brown* II (1955). Both of these cases involved several community efforts by African American students and parents to cross the racial border and integrate the public schools of their respective communities. Prior to 1954, public schools were characterized by de jure segregation. De jure segregation meant that the law required students to be segregated by race, and as practiced in most of these cases, this required separate school systems for black and white students. As in South Africa, the apartheid practiced along racial lines in the United States was more widespread than black and white. Essentially, the borders and barriers erected one school system for "whites" and another for "nonwhites" (e.g., African Americans, Native Americans, Hispanic Americans, Asian Americans).

The *Plessy* and *Roberts* Cases

Under the doctrine of "separate but equal" established by the U.S. Supreme Court in *Plessy* v. *Ferguson* (1896), every public school district with black and white student populations and legal segregation had to provide equal educational opportunities for all children. This meant separate but equal facilities. Therefore, if each state's compulsory school attendance law required school attendance from ages 6 or 7 years to 16 or 17, then all young people residing in these states were entitled to a free public education. Yet if the law prohibited school integration of the races, then separate but equal schools had to be provided for all students covered by the state attendance law.

The *Plessy* case dealt with efforts to desegregate interstate railroad travel, in other words, to end the practice of having separate travel cars for "colored" passengers and "white" passengers. This case validated and nationalized the doctrine of separate but equal, but the conflict of segregated schools by color had a much longer history.

One of the first major battlegrounds for ending school desegregation was the case of Sarah Roberts in Boston, Massachusetts, culminating in the Massachusetts Supreme Court case, *Roberts* v. *City of Boston* (1849). Massachusetts appeared to be ripe for ending school segregation. Remember, this was the home of the father of public education, Horace Mann. Furthermore, the Massachu-

William Edward Burghardt (W. E. B.) Du Bois *(1868–1963)*

W. E. B. Du Bois became one of the most outstanding intellectuals and civil rights activists of the twentieth century. Born February 23, 1868, Du Bois was educated at Fisk University and at Harvard, where he earned his Ph.D. degree. Du Bois was, for a time, professor of Latin and Greek at Wilberforce University and at the University of Pennsylvania. W. E. B. Du Bois was a professor of economics and history at Atlanta University from 1932 to 1944.

Du Bois was one of the founders of the National Association for the Advancement of Colored People (NAACP) in 1909. The formation of this organization was based on the belief that Negroes should achieve civil and political equality as soon as possible. He was the NAACP's director of publications from 1910 until 1932, editing *Crisis* magazine, an important journal of civil rights. In 1944 he returned to Atlanta University to become head of the NAACP's special research department. Du Bois held that position until 1948.

Du Bois was unhappy with developments in the United States, turning his attention to broader issues of international concern. He emigrated to Africa in 1961, hoping to assist in the liberation of black people all over the world. In Ghana Du Bois edited the *Encyclopedia Africana,* with the support of Kwame Nkrumah, the former president of Ghana. Du Bois died in Ghana at the age of 95.

W. E. B. Du Bois was a prolific scholar, thinker, and writer. His books covered topics in history, economics, and political theory. Among the better-known books are *The Suppression of the Slave Trade* (1896); *The Philadelphia Negro* (1899); *The Souls of Black Folks* (1903); *John Brown* (1909); *The Negro* (1915); *The Gift of Black Folk* (1924); *Dusk of Dawn* (1940); *Color and Democracy* (1945), and a trilogy entitled *Black Flame* (1957–1961).

setts state constitution provided for "equality under the law for all persons," a precursor of the U.S. Constitution's Fourteenth Amendment. Under this constitutional provision and by legislative action, the state had repealed laws forbidding interracial marriages in 1843. The state had also ended segregation in public transportation, including railroad travel, and most of the state, except Boston, had already desegregated their school systems. Boston also had a fervent abolitionist and antislavery movement.

Benjamin Roberts, one of the leaders of Boston's Anti-Slavery Society, sued the Boston public school system on behalf of his nine-year-old daughter, Sarah. Sarah attended a visibly inferior public school established for "colored" children. Sarah walked passed several "white only" public schools to attend the only school she was legally allowed to attend. Much like Linda Brown, more than 100 years later, the Roberts' decided that the equal protection clause of the Massachusetts Constitution should provide the right for Sarah and all other children, regardless of color, to attend public schools nearest their neighborhood.

The Roberts family hired well-known antislavery, abolitionist, and civil rights leader Charles Sumner to argue this case. Sumner appealed the case to the Massachusetts Supreme Court. Sumner used the form of evidence that would later be referred to as the "Brandeis brief" (social science information based on research) to argue that the segregated school system of Boston effectively "branded a whole race with the stigma of inferiority and degradation." Furthermore, Sumner suggested that the segregated schools "exclusively devoted to one class must differ essentially, in its spirit and character, from that public school known to the law, where all classes meet together in equality."

Sumner's arguments were prophetic and prolific. Sumner argued that Sarah had been excluded from the school nearest to her home "on the sole ground of color." Sumner likened such blatant apartheid and discrimination to the caste system of India and to the exclusion of Jews in Europe to ghettos and Jewish quarters. In attacking "separate but supposedly equal," Sumner claimed that even if those excluded chose to attend the "colored" schools, the "compulsory segregation from the mass of citizens is of itself an inequality which we condemn."

Sumner's next passage is worth emphasizing:

. . . It is said that these separate schools are for the benefit of both colors, and of the Public Schools. In similar spirit Slavery is sometimes said to be for the benefit of master and slave, and of the country where it exists. There is a mistake in the one case as great as in the other. This is clear. Nothing unjust, nothing ungenerous, can be for the benefit of any person or any thing. . . . The whites themselves are injured by the separation. Who can doubt this? With the Law as their monitor, they are taught to regard a portion of the human family, children of God, created in his image, coequals in his love, as a separate and degraded class; they are taught practically to deny that grand revelation of Christianity, the Brotherhood of Man. Hearts, while yet tender with childhood, are hardened, and ever afterward testify to this legalized uncharitableness. Nursed in the sentiments of Caste, receiving it with the earliest food of knowledge, they are unable to eradicate it from their natures. . . . Their characters are debased, and they become less fit for the duties of citizenship. . . . The school is the little world where the child is trained for the larger world of life. It is the microcosm preparatory to the macrocosm, and therefore it must cherish and develop the virtues and the sympathies needed in the larger world. And since, according to our institutions, all classes, without distinction of color, meet in the performance of civil duties, so should they all, without distinction of color, meet in the school, beginning there those relations of Equality which the Constitution and Laws promise to all. . . . Nothing is more clear than that the welfare of classes, as well as of individuals, is promoted by mutual acquaintance. Prejudice is the child of ignorance. It is sure to prevail, where people do not know each other. Society and intercourse are means established by Providence for human improvement. They remove antipathies, promote mutual adaptation and conciliation, and establish relations of reciprocal regard. Whoso sets up barriers to these thwarts the ways of Providence, crosses the tendencies of human nature, and directly interferes with the laws of God.

Regardless of your belief in divine Providence, in Sumner's words, using the schools as a mirror of society, we must prepare our children to live with mutual respect and equal rights for all. Anything short of full economic and educational equality for all will lead to injustice for all. If you want peace, you must work for justice. The struggle for inclusion in schools is the pursuit of justice, and the *Roberts* decision foreshadowed dangerous days and decades ahead.

Justice Shaw of the Massachusetts Supreme Court laid a further foundation for "separate but equal." Justice Shaw agreed with Sumner in theory "that all persons out to stand equal before the law." Yet in Justice Shaw's opinion, the equal rights must be adapted to people's "respective relations and conditions." Justice Shaw suggested that racial classification falls within the adapted conditions people often lived by at the time in Boston. Therefore, school segregation by race was a legitimate school board action to maintain appropriate social conditions. This rationale of maintaining "respective relations and conditions" would be powerful as case by case, conflict by conflict, so many made efforts to open school house doors to all. While Justice Shaw's opinion was cited in the nationalized *Plessy* case, historically segregated schools were short lived in Boston following the *Roberts* decision. By 1855, the Massachusetts legislature outlawed the practice of segregated schools throughout the state, including Boston.

Between 1850 and 1900, the nation experienced the *Dred Scott* case, John Brown's antislavery raids; the civil war; Radical Reconstructionists in Congress (including U.S. Senator Charles Sumner); the passage and adoption of the Thirteenth (prohibition of slavery), Fourteenth, and Fifteenth (prohibiting states from denying adult males the right to vote regardless of color) Amendments; the rise of the Ku Klux Klan and extreme reaction to Reconstruction; the adoption of "Black Codes" and Jim Crow laws; and ultimately, U.S. Supreme Court cases affirming the practice of separate but equal.

Two very important precedents emerged from the *Plessy* case of 1896. Homer Plessy, the plaintiff and appellee in the case, had been legally classified as an octoroon (seven-eighths Caucasian and one-eighth African). Under the "color of Louisiana" law, the presence of any "African blood" made one nonwhite, or colored. The plaintiff's attorneys, including the well-known civil rights lawyer Albion Tourgee, argued that the Louisiana law requiring separate but equal public accommodations, such as rail transportation, violated the spirit and specific language of the Fourteenth Amendment, that is, denied the fundamental rights of citizenship and equal protection of the laws. Tourgee railed against laws based on the color of one's skin, saying, "A law assorting the citizens of a State in the enjoyment of a public franchise on the basis of race, is obnoxious to the spirit of republican government." Like Charles Sumner 50 years earlier, and much like Thurgood Marshall a half century later, Tourgee compared the segregation with slavery and the permanent establishment of a caste system. Tourgee suggested that the effect (i.e., the meaning and result) of the Fourteenth Amendment was to place all social classes on the same level of right, as citizens, and entitled to equal protection of the laws.

John Brown (1800–1859)

This American abolitionist was unable to succeed in business, but he became famous for his work on behalf of the slaves in America. His ardent abolitionist activities sometimes broke out into acts of violence, as when he and his sons killed five proslavery men in Kansas during the struggle between proslavery and antislavery forces there. In that action John Brown claimed that he was an instrument in the hand of God.

Late in 1857 Brown enlisted men in an ambitious project to free the slaves in the West Virginia border region. Brown aimed to set up a place to which slaves could flee and to use it to stir up further antislavery activity. On October 16, 1859, Brown and 21 followers led a raid against the U.S. arsenal at Harper's Ferry Virginia. He succeeded briefly in taking possession of the town, until a federal force led by Colonel Robert E. Lee defeated Brown's men. John Brown was captured. On December 2, 1859, he was hanged for his deeds. Because of his dignified demeanor at his trial and his antislavery motivation John Brown was regarded by abolitionists as a martyr to the cause; however, slaveholders saw Brown as a menace and a fanatic.

With the exception of Justice John M. Harlan's dissent, based on his firmly held belief of a color-blind Constitution, the majority of Supreme Court justices, led by Justice Henry B. Brown, once and for a very long time made legalized separation of the races a "reasonable" form of regulation that government could exercise under the Constitution. Justice Brown concluded that government could enact regulations consistent with "the established usages, customs, and traditions of the people." The one significant example of the "most common instance" of this recognized power was the presence of segregated schools in many states and in the District of Columbia. Brown even cited the *Roberts* case, claiming that even under the equal protection clause of the Massachusetts Constitution, the Supreme Court of Massachusetts upheld "the establishment of separate schools for white and colored children."

With *Plessy* v. *Ferguson* (1896), the Supreme Court once and for a very long time made legalized separation of the races a "reasonable" form of regulation that government could exercise under the Constitution.

It is worth quoting Justice Brown's majority decision because it rings with the racist venom spouted throughout the resistance to civil and equal rights struggles, and sadly, echoes some of the contemporary commentaries blaming those excluded for their own condition and their feelings regarding their social status, position, and opportunity. Justice Brown rejected the argument that the enforced separation of the races continued to stamp "the colored race with a badge of inferiority . . . If this be so . . . it is because the colored race chooses to put that construction upon it. . . . If the two races are to meet upon terms of social equality, it must be the result of natural affinities, a mutual appreciation of each other's merits and a voluntary consent of individuals. . . . Legislation is powerless to eradicate racial instincts or to abolish distinctions based upon physical differences, and the attempt to do so can only result in accentuating the difficulties of the present situation."

It should also be noted that Justice Harlan's dissent acknowledged that "the white race deems itself to be the dominant race in this country. . . . And so it is, in prestige, in achievements, in education, in wealth, and in power. . . . But in view of the Constitution, in the eye of the law, there is in this country no superior, dominant, ruling class of citizens. There is no caste here. Our Constitution is color-blind, and neither knows nor tolerates classes among citizens." Who believed this in 1896? Who acts on this belief today?

As noted, two powerful precedents emerged that served as arguments for nearly a century, until the present. Certainly, the argument that legislation and government assertiveness cannot eliminate prejudice has continued in the opposition to every major civil rights initiative, regardless of what group is seeking basic civil and equal rights.

The sentiments of 1964 are prominent in today's public policy debate regarding equal opportunities for all. Keep in mind that while *Plessy* established separate but equal, the thrust of the decision was to make government impotent in eradicating racial prejudice for many decades. The *Plessy* case should stand as a lesson in ignorance and bigotry.

In regard to race, it is shameful and shattering to read Justice Brown's comments regarding "racial instincts" and "physical differences," when the plaintiff, Homer Plessy, might have very well passed as white under most instances. Justice Brown's ignorance about "race" might be explained, although not excused, by late nineteenth-century "common knowledge" and pseudo-science, but sadly, many of the same stereotypes and assumptions remain to this day.

Plessy's legitimation of race as a "natural, physical condition and instinctly acknowledged" did much to shape and reinforce decades of dangerous and deadly conduct. And *Plessy's* failure to buttress the power of government to fight for equal rights left many people from many identity groups (e.g., immigrants, Native Americans, Asian Americans, Hispanic Americans, and African Americans) adrift in murky misery instead of pursuing the American dream of equal rights and equal opportunity in public accommodations, in the labor market, and in the schools. Because schools have often been viewed as a great equalizer or, at least, as providing opportunities for pursuing the American dream, it is so important to observe how *Plessy* quickly shaped segregated schooling late into the twentieth century.

Challenges to the Doctrine of Separate But Equal

Within three years of *Plessy*, the Supreme Court rendered a decision greatly limiting the meaning of separate but equal in public schools. In *Cummings* v. *County Board of Education* (1899), the Court ruled that a county school district was under no obligation to provide a separate but equal high school for "colored" children. Furthermore, rejecting the relief sought by the attorneys for the "colored" families that all high schools be shut down, the Court strongly deferred to the power of states to control schools: "The education of the people in schools maintained by state taxation is a matter belonging to the respective states, and any interference on the part of Federal authority with the management of such schools cannot be justified except in the case of a clear and unmistakable disregard of rights secured by the supreme law of the land. We have no such case to be determined."

Two other cases directly assaulted any efforts to integrate schools. In *Berea College* v. *Kentucky* (1908), a majority of the U.S. Supreme Court upheld the power of Kentucky's state government to regulate a private corporation, like Berea College, since the state also incorporated this private school. Specifically, the Kentucky law was passed to prohibit integration in any school, public or private. The Kentucky law prohibited any school from providing instruction to both races at the same time unless the classes were conducted at least 25 miles apart. The effect of the decision was to discourage even private schools from seeking to open their doors to all.

In *Gong Lum* v. *Rice* (1927), a majority of the U.S. Supreme Court held that states could segregate "Mongolian" children (or other Asian Ameri-

Fred Vinson (1890–1953)

Fred Vinson was the thirteenth chief justice of the United States Supreme Court. Appointed in 1946 by his friend, President Harry S Truman, Vinson led the Supreme Court to reconsider its views regarding racial segregation. Although unwilling to overrule *Plessy* v. *Ferguson*, the major precedent to endorse segregation, Vinson helped pave the way for the historic 1954 *Brown* v. *Board of Education* desegregation opinion. Prior to joining the Supreme Court, Vinson had a distinguished career as a judge, a legislator, and a federal administrator. Earl Warren replaced Vinson as chief justice after Vinson's death.

cans) from the "Caucasian" (white) schools and compel any nonwhite students to attend schools provided for African American children. To some extent, this decision sealed the fate of efforts of any minority peoples from receiving an equal education in public schools.

Following these two defeats for school inclusion and integration, civil rights advocates, led by legal defense teams, especially those of the National Association for the Advancement of Colored People (NAACP) developed an all-out strategy that revisited some of the arguments in the original *Roberts* case. Specifically, this legal strategy used the doctrine of separate but equal to place the emphasis on equal. The legal question became, if the schools are separate, are they in fact equal for all children attending regardless of color?

Three cases of the NAACP's equal facilities focus reached the U.S. Supreme Court. Strategically, all three cases focused on separate but equal applications as effecting legal education in state-supported law schools. The first case reaching the high court, *Missouri ex rel. Gaines* v. *Canada* (1938), required the University of Missouri system either to admit Lloyd Gaines or to provide him with a separate and equal law school education. The Missouri legislature immediately moved to establish a separate state-supported law school at Lincoln University, an all-black college, in the state's capitol. The next two cases, *Sweatt* v.

Painter and *McLaurin* v. *Oklahoma State Regents for Higher Education* (1950), effectively served to end the doctrine of "separate but equal" in the state supported law schools.

The NAACP's legal defense strategy in the 1950 cases had persuaded the majority of the justices of the U.S. Supreme Court that no law school, however equal or accommodating, can serve to prepare law students as graduates to serve in the larger society where they will in effect be intermingling and interacting with people of all colors. Writing for the majority in the *Sweatt* case, Chief Justice Frederick M. Vinson concluded, ". . . The law school to which Texas is willing to admit Sweatt excludes from its student body members of the racial groups which number 85 percent of the population of the State and include most of the lawyers, witnesses, jurors, judges, and other officials with whom he will inevitably be dealing when he becomes a member of the Texas Bar. With such a substantial and significant segment of society excluded, we cannot conclude that the education offered Sweatt is substantially equal to that which he would receive if admitted to the University of Texas Law School."

Vinson's rationale of schooling to prepare law students for effective and inevitable interaction in the larger society looms large in the examination of the attempts to desegregate and integrate all public schools.

The *Brown* Cases

The next milestone in the effort to provide equal educational opportunity is the case commonly known as *Brown I. Brown* v. *Board of Education of Topeka, Kansas* (1954), actually combined four separate public school desegregation cases before the Court. The cases, involving students and parents from Kansas, South Carolina, Virginia, and Delaware, were recognized as a class-action suit. The outcome of such a suit would extend beyond the parties in each of these four cases, and in effect, could apply to all children of school age throughout the United States.

The stipulated facts in each of these cases clearly demonstrated that the public school districts in each of these respective communities did not provide a separate but equal facility, staff, expenditure, and so on, for all children regardless of color. Simply stated, each community, for example, spent far more for white children, created smaller class sizes in white schools, and improved physical plants in facilities for white children than that community offered to "colored" children. The districts, as defendants, conceded that much more needed to be done to try to equalize the public schools for all students, but none of the defendants suggested breaking down the wall of segregation between the schools.

Case analysis must take place within a historical context, and the *Brown* I case certainly exemplifies this requirement. Several significant events had taken place to prepare the nation for the Brown decision. Many African Americans and other people of color living in the United States had served honorably and, in many instances, heroically in World War II. The same soldiers who fought to end the extreme prejudice against so many designated groups (e.g., Jews, gypsies, union leaders, leftists, people with physical and mental disabilities, anti-Nazi activists) in Europe were coming home to face extreme prejudice and persecution in their own communities. Recognizing this blatant hypocrisy, President Truman established a Committee on Civil Rights, and by the end of 1947, Truman's Civil Rights' Committee issued a searing report, *To Secure These Rights.* Among other recommendations, the report called for an end to legally enforced segregation in all public life in the United States. Truman quickly moved to implement some of these recommendations where he had the greatest power. As commander in chief, Truman began to desegregate and integrate the Armed Services.

In addition to the presidential report and initiatives, many Americans, especially policy leaders, were quite moved by Gunnar Myrdal's comprehensive examination of race relations in the United States. Myrdal's report was published as *An American Dilemma* (1944). Myrdal's research had been funded by the Carnegie Corporation of New York, with the objective to complete a "comprehensive study of the Negro in the United States." Myrdal made clear to all Americans what African Americans had known and lived for decades. According to Myrdal's findings, "social segregation and discrimination is a system of deprivations forced upon the Negro group by the white group. This is equally true in the North and in the South, though in this respect, as in all others, there is more segregation and discrimination in the South, and thus the phenomenon is easier to observe."

Lieutenant Lee Rayford, a member of the Tusskegee Airmen, an all African American unit of fighter pilots active during World War II.

Myrdal's findings, along with the recommendations of the Civil Rights Committee, helped the NAACP legal defense team adopt a strategy to attack segregated schooling head on and to produce evidence of the devastating mental and emotional damage of segregation, especially upon impressionable young people.

In the tradition of the famous "Brandeis brief," the NAACP team decided to bring in expert testimony from social scientists to demonstrate why the doctrine of separate but equal could no longer be tolerated.

Among the noted social scientists testifying was Professor Kenneth Clark of the City College of New York. As an experiential psychologist, Clark had conducted several experiments, especially some involving children's selection and affinity toward "colored" and "white" dolls. So many children, especially the African American children, ascribed negative characteristics to the "colored" dolls and expressed a desire to want to identify with the "white" dolls. This led Clark to conclude, in his expert opinion, "My opinion is that a fundamental effect of segregation is basic confusion in the individuals and their concepts about themselves conflicting in their self images. . . . The conclusion which I was forced to reach was that these children [that is, the African American children in at least one of the *Brown* cases], like other human beings who are subjected to an obviously inferior status in the society in which they live, have been definitely

harmed in the development of their personalities; that the signs of instability in their personalities are clear, and I think that every psychologist would accept and interpret these signs as such."

The social scientific conclusion presented in these school desegregation cases seemed clear: If you keep children segregated by color, and one color has been bombarded with negative impressions and images, then the bombarded children are bound to feel inferior, and such feelings of inferiority can significantly effect their academic and social well-being. These findings are still being argued today. Yet at the time, the expert testimony of Clark and others, combined with Myrdal's findings, appeared to prepare justices of the U.S. Supreme Court to make a sweeping decision regarding maintaining segregated public schools.

After oral arguments and rearguments, and after reviewing various "friend of the court" briefs, and following extensive conferencing among the Justices to attempt to formulate a unanimous decision, Chief Justice Earl Warren delivered the opinion for a unanimous court in May of 1954 in *Brown* v. *Board of Education*. Warren's opinion was not very long, but the message is alive and well as we discuss, deliberate, and debate the future of public schooling in the United States.

Since the Brown decision became a watershed in public schooling, it is worth quoting extensively from Justice Warren's opinion. Writing in 1954, Warren stated,

> Today, education is perhaps the most important function of state and local governments. Compulsory school attendance laws and the great expenditures for education both demonstrate our recognition of the importance of education to our democratic society. . . . It is the very foundation of good citizenship. . . . It is a principal instrument in awakening the child to cultural values, in preparing him for later professional training, and in helping him to adjust normally to his environment. In these days, it is doubtful that any child may reasonably be expected to succeed in life if he is denied the opportunity of an education. Such an opportunity, where the state has undertaken to provide it, is a right which must be made available to all on equal terms. . . . We conclude that in the field of public education the doctrine of "separate but equal" has no place. Separate educational facilities are inherently unequal. . . . We have now announced that such segregation is a denial of the equal protection of the laws.

The message of *Brown* seems clear. If we as a society place such value on schooling, and we obviously do from the compulsory attendance laws to the extensive taxing to support the schools, then our schools must be inclusive, offering equal educational opportunity to all. The Court further noted that segregated schooling cannot provide such equal opportunity to all. With this clear statement from our highest court, did all the states, local communities, and school boards move expediently to implement this extensive class action remedy?

The *Brown* decision sent social shockwaves throughout the land, especially in the South. The decision was met with so much derision and divisiveness that many predicted a second civil war, with echoes of "states' rights" heard across the South. In many respects, *Brown's* use of the Fourteenth Amendment did create a revolution. The revolution created varied rippling effects and ramifications that would touch almost everyone's life in some way.

At the federal level, many members of Congress, especially those from the South, issued a Southern Manifesto that reinforced states' rights and power under the Tenth Amendment and sought to limit the power of the federal judiciary—a cry that continues today. At the state and local level, a variety of reactions were noted. In some states, the state legislatures attempted to amend their state constitutional requirement for free public schools, in effect permitting the state to stop funding public schools that had to be desegregated and redirect state funding to private all-white academies. In other states, governors threatened pre-Civil War actions such as secession and nullification. Some governors (e.g., in Alabama, Mississippi, and Arkansas) even used the military arm of the state (i.e., law enforcement and the state national guard) to surround previously all-white public schools and block the entrance of any "nonwhites" into these schools.

Some of the Supreme Court Justices recognized that a wave of revulsion and reaction might sweep areas of the nation with resistance to the *Brown* decision, and within a year of *Brown* I, the Court handed down a second *Brown* decision to give greater clarity to the original desegregation decision. In order to minimize refusal and resistance to implement *Brown* I, Chief Justice Warren in *Brown* II (1955), ordered state and local governing units to "effectuate a transition to a racially nondiscriminatory school system . . . with all deliberate speed."

Even with this judicial admonition to desegregate with all deliberate speed, many of the aforementioned tactics continued to be used, and with each act of resistance came another judicial or presidential executive order to remedy the wrongful act. Unfortunately, the judicial process works slowly, and presidents often respond more to public opinion pressure or to power and influence than to decisions of the Supreme Court.

School Desegregation Cases

The following section lists the cases and the remedies each sought to continue efforts toward effective school desegregation; some of the judicial responses in many ways are being reargued in the court of public opinion and expert analysis today.

Cooper v. *Aaron* (1958)

The Little Rock Board of Education adopted a plan to gradually integrate the previously all-white public high school, Central High. The plan included admitting nine African American students to Central High. The majority in the Arkansas legislature opposed any efforts to comply with the Court's decision. The legislature moved swiftly to nullify the local school board plan, and the governor dispatched the state national guard to prevent the nine students of color from attending Central High. With the national guard's presence, the nine children confronted not only military might blocking their entrance to Central High but also violent, angry mobs of white citizens intimidating those who dared to walk the walk toward equal educational opportunity. With political pressure and public opinion mounting nationwide, especially from the television scenes of mob violence, President Eisenhower sent in the 101st Airborne, nationalized the state national guard, and ordered that the nine students be admitted to Central High. Under federal military protection, Central High was finally, although minimally, desegregated. In the *Cooper* case, the Little Rock Board of Education brought suit requesting more time to prepare for school desegregation in light of the hostile reaction. The Court's response was a unanimous and firm ruling: "In short, the constitutional rights of children not to be discriminated against in school admission on grounds of race or color declared by this Court in the *Brown* case can neither be nullified openly and directly by state legislators or state executive or judicial officers, nor nullified indirectly by them through evasive schemes for segregation whether attempted 'ingeniously or ingenuously.'"

Did this lead to an immediate desegregation, and subsequent integration, of all public schools in Arkansas? Of course not, but it did take another stride in the direction of ending legally enforced school segregation.

Goss v. Board of Education (1963)

Two Tennessee school boards proposed desegregation plans that provided for voluntary transfers for a student to move from a school where he or she would be in the racial minority back to the student's former segregated school. This also led to a quick resegregation of the schools, even though the Board gave a "freedom of choice" rationale to the voluntary transfer program. The Supreme Court was not fooled by this guise, and again, a unanimous Court struck down this plan. The Court ruled that any plan that has the effect, even absent intent, of producing racially segregated schools is unconstitutional. The Court made clear that the Fourteenth Amendment prohibits state action that denies equal protection of the law, and this plan clearly violated the spirit and letter of the Fourteenth Amendment.

Griffin v. County School Board of Prince Edward County (1964)

The Virginia legislature wheeled and dealed, and ranted, and resisted desegregation in some creative ways. First, the state legislature voted to cut off funds to any public schools that permitted white and nonwhite children to attend together. The lawmakers also offered to pay tuition grants to children in private "nonsectarian schools" and to extend public retirement benefits to teachers transferring over to the newly created private "nonsectarian" schools. The Supreme Court of Appeals of Virginia ruled that this drastic action of cutting off state funds violated the Virginia State Constitution.

Thwarted in this direction, the Virginia legislature went even further and repealed the state's compulsory attendance laws and made local attendance a matter of local option. The state would provide any family who planned to take the local option with a tuition grant. The plan was touted as Virginia's "freedom of choice" plan. Once again, astute scholars and jurists saw through this rouse.

The United States Supreme Court, in a seven-to-two decision, voted to strike down this so-called freedom of choice plan. According to the majority decision, this plan did not provide equal educational opportunity for two reasons. First and foremost, it appeared that the intent of the state was to avoid having to desegregate the public schools with all deliberate speed. Ending the compulsory attendance law certainly appeared to be a way to get around the *Brown* I and *Brown* II decisions. Secondly, the voucher or tuition grant plan would have the effect of benefiting white students more than African American students because there were far more well established private academies for wealthy white students than private schools for African American children. Voucher plans (discussed further on) are still the center of controversy in many communities.

Green v. County School Board of New Kent County and Raney v. Board of Education (1968)

Again, two more schools attempted to circumvent the *Brown* decisions by introducing another so-called freedom of choice plan. Each of these districts had already established two high schools: one for white students and one for African American students. Under the new planned desegregation, students were given a choice of which of the two schools to attend.

To some extent, Kenneth Clark and other social scientists' assessment of public perception of school quality directed the decisions young people and parents made regarding which school to attend. Under this choice plan, no white students applied to transfer to the African American school, and due to the increased number of African American students seeking admission to the previously all-white school, the districts, in each case, denied the transfer requests of many African American students. In both districts, the all-African American schools remained segregated. Although this is a reality under de facto segregation in many urban areas today, the U.S. Supreme Court made its ruling in these two cases based on the historical context of setting up the transfer plan. In these two 1968 cases, a unanimous Court ruled against the voluntary transfer plan. The unanimous decisions first noted that the districts had a long history of permitting and in some instances supporting segregation and noted secondly that the planned remedies were inadequate in adopting a "unitary, nonracial school system."

These cases are also important because the Supreme Court gave greater monitoring power to the federal courts to assure compliance in meeting the unitary school plans (plans within a single school district). Specifically, the Supreme Court concluded that federal district courts should retain jurisdiction over such desegregation plans to ensure the following: (1) Each school district develops, adopts, and implements a constitutionally acceptable plan (i.e., one meeting the requirements of equal protection and equal opportunity as interpreted from the Fourteenth Amendment), and (2) the adopted plan is operated in a constitutionally permissible fashion until the goal of a desegregated, nonracially operated school system is finally achieved.

Desegregation Plans

What type of plan could public school districts adopt to achieve the goal of a unitary, nonracially operated school system? One major incentive in developing desegregation plans is to keep the flow of federal funds to these districts. Failure to comply with the desegregation orders could lead to cutting off the federal funds, especially the targeted funds designated by the civil rights legislation of the 1960s. So what could public school systems do to achieve effective desegregation and ensure the flow of federal funds?

In remedying this problem, school systems and federal district judges relied on the expertise and recommendations of social scientists and educators specifically trained to address efforts of desegregation and integration. The two most common resolutions offered and implemented were comprehensive busing proposals and the development of magnet schools that also required busing or other means of transportation. Now, how would this work? Imagine for a moment an average-sized city and school district with approximately 25,000 students. Prior to any desegregation order, students attended schools closer to the proximity of their neighborhoods. This neighborhood school concept resulted in some schools being overwhelmingly attended by students classified from only one race. Therefore, you might have, as mentioned in some of the preceding cases, one high school with 95 percent or more white students and another school with 95 percent or more of students of color. Often attendance patterns reflect neighborhood compositions.

Most of the court-appointed experts suggested that some sort of redistribution of the student population would have to be initiated. For example, some plans recommended massive busing of African American students to predominantly white schools, while sending some white students to predominantly African American schools. What percentage would remedy, or qualify, the segregation problem? At what point would the school become desegregated? At what point would the school be integrated? If the school district had a school-aged population of 30 percent African American, 20 percent Hispanic, 47 percent Anglo or white, and 3 percent other, should each school's student population be a mirror reflection of this mix?

Did the *Brown* case and subsequent desegregation cases require reapportionment based on "race"—a concept that we earlier acknowledged is a construction of public policy and socialized perception? Or did the *Brown* case simply require some mixing of students, and an end to any legal efforts to keep schools segregated? The key in answering this question is in understanding the Court's discussion of developing a "unitary" school system.

Two U.S. Supreme Court cases helped to give meaning to the goal of "unitary." In *Alexander* v. *Holmes County Board of Education* (1969), the Court defined a unitary system as one "within which no person is to be effectively excluded from any school because of race or color." Ten years later, in *Columbus Board of Education* v. *Penick* (1979), the Court stated the term "unitary" has been defined as the status a school system achieves "when it no longer discriminates between school children on the basis of race." The Court suggested that unitary achievement is attained when the school system affirmatively removes all vestiges of race discrimination of the formerly dual system. Keep in mind that the dual system is the system in which law and practice resulted in separate schools based on the color of one's skin.

Suppose the following situation exists: A school system has several racially isolated schools. There are no laws, board policies, or any direct governmental effort to segregate the schools by race. So how would we get so many racially isolated schools if there was not a strict government prohibition on school integration? Do "birds of a feather just flock together," or what causes schools to remain dominated by one race? According to many scholars and investigative reporters, the following factors contribute to school segregation: discriminatory practices by real estate companies; the failure by the state legislature to take any action to end residential segregation by race, and complicity by the school system in not moving affirmatively to desegregate (e.g., instead of redrawing attendance boundaries to disperse or reassign an increasing minority population, the school district just moves in some portable buildings to deal with overcrowding and still maintaining the racially isolated school; allowance by the district of a voluntary transfer program that, in effect, allows white children to transfer to schools where they are not the small minority); and often economic circumstances, along with redlining practices, contribute to "white flight" (e.g., families moving out of the particular school district to a more affluent, predominantly white school but still living in the area where their jobs are located). The results of such practices may include segregated schools that reflect neighborhood patterns of segregation. In these circumstances, often determined to be de facto segregation, does the government have an affirmative duty to desegregate, or even more bluntly, integrate the schools?

The federal courts have examined answers to these questions on a case-by-case basis when there have been actual challenges and conflicts regarding the current status of school desegregation. Remember, the courts are not looking for additional complaints and cases. Courts react; they are not proactive. So if the courts are not proactive and vigilant toward achieving the *Brown* decisions directives, who is responsible for making sure that our nation's schools do not once again become segregated by race or by other means?

Monitoring School Desegregation

Technically, especially in light of the civil rights legislation of the 1960s, the U.S. Department of Justice and the U.S. Department of Health, Education, and Welfare (now two separate cabinet level departments: the Department of Education and the Department of Health and Human Services) each had civil rights divisions with specific responsibilities to monitor school desegregation. Unfortunately, the efforts by the federal government to enforce school desegregation and promote integration were short-lived. Although the reversal of the *Brown* precedent has been gradual, owing to many social circumstances, *Brown* has become less important while new efforts at segregation and resegregation loom large in our nation's schools.

This is not to suggest that the official federal government response was a return to resegregation. The official policy has been, and still is, compliance with the Court's decisions and the policies promulgated to support desegregation. The U.S. Department of Education and Justice Department Office for Civil Rights (OCR) still monitors schools and certainly investigates citizens complaints for any of the following: practices of discrimination within the school; failure to provide equal education opportunities for students with limited English skills; ability grouping or tracking that results in segregation on the basis of race, national origin, or gender; racial harassment in the schools; failure to provide equal education opportunities for pregnant students; failure to appropriately identify the need for special education and related services for certain student populations, including the homeless; and discrimination on the basis of sex in athletic programs. These areas are still being monitored by the OCR today. Without the initiative and enforcement power, the OCR is helpless to make a difference in desegregation.

The attack on desegregation and the *Brown* decision never really ended. By 1968, with

By 1968, with Richard Nixon's election as president based on tactics Republican strategists would later call the "Southern strategy," strong signs of reversing desegregation efforts began to emerge.

Richard Nixon's election as president based on tactics Republican strategists would later call the "Southern strategy," strong signs of reversing desegregation efforts began to emerge. Nixon fired Leon Panetta (who resigned his position as President Clinton's White House chief of staff in 1996), who was at that time the director of the Department of Health, Education, and Welfare's civil rights office. Nixon had claimed that Panetta was too aggressive in pursuing desegregation remedies. H. R. Haldeman's, President Nixon's chief of staff, recently published diaries reveal the following:

> Feb. 4 . . . He (Nixon) plans to take on the integration problem directly. Is really concerned about situation in Southern schools and feels we have to take some leadership to try to reverse Court decisions that have forced integration too far, too fast. Has told Mitchell (then Nixon's attorney general) to file another case, and keep filing until we get a reversal.

So before desegregation had made much of an impact, policymakers were already trying to reverse the *Brown* decision, even from our nation's highest offices. This policy also applied to the Supreme Court. In 1971 President Nixon appointed William H. Rehnquist, a Justice Department attorney, to a vacancy on the Supreme Court. Although Rehnquist was confirmed by the Senate, it was noted by constitutional scholars and court watchers that Rehnquist, while serving as a Supreme Court clerk to Justice Jackson, had written a strongly worded memo opposing the *Brown* decision. Rehnquist's memo had stated, "I realize

that it is an unpopular and unhumanitarian position, for which I have been excoriated by 'liberal' colleagues, but I think *Plessy* v. *Ferguson* was right and should be reaffirmed." Later, in Rehnquist's 1986 confirmation hearings to be elevated to chief justice, he said the earlier memo was not his opinion but that of Justice Jackson, who he was clerking for at the time. Most analysts of Supreme Court cases on school desegregation have concluded that Rehnquist's opinions have not embraced a strong affirmative role, especially supporting busing, in ending segregated schools.

With those in higher offices doing little to end school segregation, and certainly not taking a strong stance for integration, what would happen to desegregation efforts as they effected local school districts? This question continues to be answered on a case-by-case basis, and different federal circuit courts seemed to have rendered different standards to determine if a school system has met the "unitary, nondiscriminatory" status. For example, the First and Fifth Circuit Courts of Appeals seem to have created a less stringent standard than other circuits. In a Fifth Circuit case, *Ross* v. *Houston Independent School District* (1983), the majority of the Fifth Circuit ruled "that a school system can achieve unitary status incrementally and that, when it does so, the court will abdicate its supervisory role as to the particular aspect of the desegregation plan when proclaimed unitary."

Whereas certain circuits applied the aforementioned definition, other federal circuits tended to return to the factor test emerging from the earlier U.S. Supreme Court decision in *Green* v. *County School Board of New Kent County* (1968). In a case that eventually worked its way to the U.S. Supreme Court, *Pitts by Pitts* v. *Freeman* (1989), the Eleventh Circuit Court of Appeals expanded the Green test and suggested that a school district should not be declared unitary until the "totality of deficiencies" are addressed with "good faith" attempts to remedy the wrongs. The deficiencies to examine should include (1) student assignment, (2) faculty composition, (3) other staff assignments, (4) transportation, (5) extracurricular activities, (6) facilities, and (7) quality of education. The Eleventh Circuit, in applying the six Green case factors and then adding the seventh subjective consideration of "quality of education," concluded with the following determination for unitary status: "If the school system fulfills all . . . factors at the same time for several years, the court should declare that the school system has achieved unitary status. If the school system fails to fulfill all these factors at the same time for several years, the district could should retain jurisdiction."

Local Control of School Desegregation

By the early 1990s, most federal courts appeared ready to let local control determine the future of school desegregation and integration. Keep in mind that the Reagan and Bush administrations appointed more than two thirds of all current federal judges between 1980 and 1992. Furthermore, the Clinton appointments have tended to be moderate and uncontroversial, since President Clinton has been quick to accept withdrawals from any candidates who appeared to be heading for a tough Senate confirmation challenge. Some have suggested that since Republicans gained control of the Senate, scrutiny of judicial appointments would be their revenge for the rejection of Judge Robert Bork to the Supreme Court.

Many desegregation scholars, including Gary Orfield, who directs the Harvard Project on School Desegregation, and some of the attorneys of the NAACP's Legal Defense Fund, have concluded that the three watershed cases of the 1990s have significantly reduced affirmative government efforts to desegregate public schools. In 1991 in *Board of Education of Oklahoma* v. *Dowell,* Chief Justice Rehnquist wrote a majority opinion that reflects and foreshadows many of the school law cases today; that is, let the local school district, the state legislature, and if necessary, the local federal district court decide these matters. In the *Dowell* case, Rehnquist referred to the original federal district's decision to terminate federal jurisdiction over the Oklahoma public school system's desegregation plan.

In the original case, the district court noted that the Oklahoma public schools had made a good faith effort to comply with the 1972 court-ordered desegregation decree. Rehnquist even quoted from the 1977 case to terminate federal jurisdiction:

> The Court has concluded that the (desegregation) plan worked and that substantial compliance with the constitutional requirements has been achieved. The School Board, under the oversight of the Court, has operated the (desegregation) plan properly, and the Court does not foresee that the termination of its jurisdiction will result in the dismantlement of the plan or any affirmative action by the defendant to

undermine the unitary system so slowly and painfully accomplished over the 16 years during which the cause has been pending before this court. . . . The School Board, as now constituted, has manifested the desire and intent to follow the law. The court believes that the present members and their successors on the Board will now and in the future continue to follow the constitutional desegregation requirements.

With that pronouncement, the district court terminated its jurisdiction.

So how did the case become a controversy that once again had to be adjudicated? Would the local school board and larger community fulfill the constitutional requirements and the dream of equal educational opportunity? How did the 1977 case become a 1991 Supreme Court case?

The faith in local leadership was not born out by some supporters of school integration who felt the local district was slowly returning to a pattern of segregated schools. Parents from the original suit, along with others effected by school district decisions regarding desegregation, complained and succeeded in reopening the case. After much consideration, Chief Justice Rehnquist made some foreshadowing findings. According to Rehnquist, even upon rehearing the case, "The District Court found that present residential segregation was the result of private decisionmaking and economics, and that it was too attenuated to be a vestige of former school segregation . . . and that the neighborhood assignment plan (a new district policy) was not designed with discriminatory intent." With this, Rehnquist sent the case back to the lower district court to once again resolve. To no one's surprise, the lower court pretty much maintained their earlier decision for local control, still terminating the court's oversight role, but with a suggestion that the local school district continue to maintain an advisory committee to continue to review the district's confirmed compliance as a unitary system.

Furthermore, what did Rehnquist's majority opinion foreshadow? Two major findings: (1) absent overt intent and practice of government-imposed segregation, the court will probably conclude that segregation is emerging from "private decisionmaking and economics," and (2) absent this finding of discriminatory intent, the courts should not impose or take jurisdiction over local districts. In other words, if neighborhoods become resegregated by private choice and the ability to

afford to move to certain neighborhoods is governed by personal economic success, the government has no role to mandate massive desegregation plans, even if the effect leaves local schools segregated.

The highest court was to decide two more cases by 1996, and each has continued to affect our efforts to have public schools with inclusive populations of all young people with a rainbow of colors and hues representing students and staff. In *Briggs* v. *Elliott,* one of the original cases joined with *Brown* in decisions I and II, upon reargument and decision of the lower district court, federal Judge John Parker forecast a distinction that has remained since. In Judge Parker's 1955 decision in *Briggs,* he noted, ". . . It is important that we point out exactly what the Supreme Court has decided and what it has not decided in this case. . . . It has not decided that the states must mix persons of different races in the schools or must require them to attend schools or must deprive them of the right of choosing the schools they attend. What it [i.e., the U.S. Supreme Court] has decided, and all that it has decided, is that a state may not deny to any person on account of race the right to attend any school that it maintains . . . The Constitution, in other words, does not require integration. It merely forbids discrimination."

If full integration was never our goal as a matter of public policy, then we should not be sur-

prised to find ourselves today asking why Linda Brown's grandchildren attend segregated schools, and why so many other children and grandchildren of those who spent years and much of their lives struggling to end segregated schooling attend single race schools, often dominated by a minority population.

Let me provide a personal story to illustrate the complexities of desegregation. I can recall sitting in a federal judge's chambers discussing a comprehensive interdistrict voluntary desegregation consent decree involving city and suburban school districts in St. Louis city and county. The judge was going to have to revisit whether the decree should be extended, especially in light of a lawsuit from the state of Missouri asking to be absolved of any further cost remedy that had been part of the original decree in which the state was found at fault in hindering desegregation efforts in the 1960s and 1970s. The state has borne much of the burden of the costs of transporting students from city to county school districts, to special magnet school programs, and for a variety of enrichment programs to those schools remaining racially isolated in the city of St. Louis. The federal judge, who had inherited the case from another senior federal district judge, was not looking forward to wading into these volatile waters. The original case in this jurisdiction had begun in 1972 and it was now 1990. The case seemed to be passed along to every newcomer to the bench, and

A school desegregation protest in St. Louis, 1933.

this newcomer's school desegregation baptism had landed in his court. I sensed the case had placed a heavy burden on the judge, especially when the district docket had so many other demands. I tried to show empathy for the demands he faced, and asked how he might fashion a "win-win" remedy for all, especially at a time when even leaders of the African American community were divided as to whether government should invest more in the segregated schools to improve the quality of education, or whether so many African American youth should continue to be bused to predominately white suburban districts that received a premium of state funding for every minority student accepted.

Yet this particular judge, like others I have spoken with, asked, "What business does a federal judge have trying to make decisions about the daily operations of public schools?" He reminded me that the decisions in this case affect tens of thousands of students, staff, and parents. He asked, "Wouldn't this matter better be settled among professional educators and public policy-makers? As a sitting judge, I rely heavily on the recommendations of court-appointed experts and advisory committees, whose agenda may be personal gain or political power, or whatever." The judge has little opportunity to truly immerse him or herself in the daily operations of schools, and unfortunately, rarely hears directly from those most affected by the court's decisions.

The current precedents the courts will review besides the *Dewell* decision will be *Freeman* v. *Pitts*, 1992, and *Missouri* v. *Jenkins II*, 1995. The *Pitts* case had the Supreme Court reviewing an earlier decision regarding declaring a district unitary, even if it had not met all seven factors identified in the earlier *Green* case and the subsequent *Pitts* decision in the Eleventh Circuit Court of Appeals. Not surprisingly, in a split decision, a majority of the Supreme Court decided in favor of the district being relieved of court jurisdiction. The majority of the Court concluded that it was "inevitable" that "demographic makeup of school districts . . . may undergo rapid change" and "racially stable neighborhoods are not likely to emerge" when so many factors of private choice and economic ability contribute to changing residential patterns. The majority ruled that as long as the district had made a good faith effort and had not intentionally contributed to resegregation or continued segregation, then the district could not be found to be at fault and the district could regain governing control as a unitary system.

The *Jenkins* case dealt an even greater blow to efforts to desegregate large urban areas. Remember, busing—massive cross-district busing, or even busing from one end of a district to another where residential patterns seem to cut along racial or ethnic lines—and the development of attractive magnet schools—schools attracting students and staff from many races from traditionally white majority schools to minority, predominantly African American have been the two most dominant means of desegregating schools. After a series of protracted court cases (including an earlier visit in a 1990 Supreme Court decision with a slight majority upholding much of the desegregation plan while striking down a head-tax or surcharge on earnings tax), the Court revisited the Kansas City, Missouri, plan after the state's political leaders sued to end the state's funding burden in the case. Fatefully, Chief Justice Rehnquist wrote the majority opinion for a closely divided court, a five-to-four decision that some have suggested will be the watershed case to resegregate schools throughout the nation. Specifically, the state of Missouri, led by legislative Republicans, an ambitious attorney general, and a less-than-enthusiastic governor, had asked the court to relieve the state from having to continue to pay in this 18-year-old case with the federal district court serving oversight. The state's complaint included requests not to have to fund substantial salary increases for instructional and non-instructional staff, and not to have to continue to pay for the elaborate magnet school program designed to attract white students from surrounding school districts but that failed to demonstrate any significant academic achievement for those minority students who had been behind grade level performance. The Eighth Circuit Court of Appeals had rejected most of the state's requests, pointing out that the district had attracted quite qualified staff and many out-of-district white students to their magnet programs. Although the Court of Appeals did not direct the court to retain jurisdiction forever, and the court strongly suggested trying to review and declare the district unitary as soon as possible, and when the district had been determined to have met the ongoing *Green* case factors.

Justice Rehnquist, with a strongly worded concurring opinion from Justice Clarence Thomas, sunk the decision of the Court of Appeals. Rehnquist warned the federal judiciary not to confuse their mission. In Rehnquist's controlling opinion, it is not the duty of federal courts to achieve racial balance in our public schools. Circumstances, beyond government's control, had led to patterns of resegregation, and the duty of the federal court, now and forever, should be "to restore state and local authorities to control" the school system. Justice Thomas's strongly worded concurring opinion went further. Thomas

declared, "The Constitution does not prevent individuals from choosing to live together, to work together, or to send their children to school together, so long as the State does not interfere with their choices of the basis of race." So if neighborhoods, churches, workplaces, and other places of gathering happen to be racially segregated, that is a free choice issue as long as the government is not affirmatively promoting discrimination or segregation. And what about the benefits of overcoming the vestiges of slavery and decades of brutally enforced Jim-Crow segregation laws, the rationale for ending the doctrine of separate but equal, the social scientific evidence demonstrating the benefits of integration instead of the detriments of segregation? Justice Thomas's opinion was strongly worded and certainly could be construed as reaching the opposite conclusion from the dynamic testimony of sociologist Kenneth Clark. Thomas stated, "It never ceases to amaze me that the courts are so willing to assume that anything that is predominately black must be inferior." Thomas went on to attack Clark's assumption that segregation harms children's "mental and educational development" and that such assumptions rest on "an assumption of black inferiority." Thomas then concluded by noting that "black schools can function as the center and symbol of black communities, and provide examples of independent black leadership, success, and achievement."

One hundred years following *Plessy,* and less than probably two decades of sincere attempts to make schools truly integrated and inclusive, the highest court appears to have placed a stamp of approval on separate but equal, although little evidence has ever demonstrated that one school district, or for that matter, one school to another, has provided equal educational opportunity.

In the battleground of segregation, Justice Rehnquist has made it clear that those who continue to seek school integration should find another avenue to remedy this situation and should preferably begin with local control. The federal courts, and certainly the Supreme Court, is not likely to stand up for school integration anytime soon, a very sad commentary on the centennial anniversary of the *Plessy* decision. If the courts are not going to use the Fourteenth Amendment to promote integrated, inclusive schools, will the courts ensure that our segregated school-aged populations receive at least an equal educational opportunity?

Before examining efforts to equalize public school funding, readers need to be beware of other means of excluding unwanted children from our public school classrooms. First, some schools that desegregated found themselves segregating students within the individual school buildings. The cloak of the segregation came out of an educational policy termed "tracking." Tracking seemed to indicate that students learn better if they are with like-learners, and determination for a student's track was often dependent on teacher subjectivity and some standardized tests that clearly did not take into account cultural differences among students.

Crossing the Economic Borders

Drive around any public school district. If it is a district of any significant size (i.e., in a town or a city of 25,000 or more, or in a residential area of a larger city with a population of 25,000 or more), you may see many different schools, ranging from old physical plants with leaking roofs and worn-out wiring and water pipes to brand new buildings with state-of-the-art technology. If you drive in a district with a homogeneous socioeconomic status, then observe the surrounding districts, some are going to be poorer and able to afford less in quality and quantity, while others will be much richer. So imagine that you move into a residency on Second Street in Middleville, USA. The south side of the street, where your new residency is located, is in the attendance zone of for Middleville Public Schools. Young people living on the north side of the street are in the attendance zone of University City school system, a state-of-the-art district. Because of elaborate state and local funding sources, Middleville is able to spend about $6,000 a year for high school students, whereas University City spends about $10,000 per student at the high school level. Which district would you rather have your children attend?

Public Education and the United States Constitution

The U.S. Supreme Court considered this controversy not long after grappling with the first series of school desegregation cases based on children's color. In 1973, in the case *San Antonio Independent School District* v. *Rodriguez,* the Court rendered a decision that still reverberates among lawmakers and policymakers at all levels of government. As with the 1995 *Jenkins* case, the Rodriguez case was decided by the narrowest of margins, five to four.

Writing for the majority, Justice Lewis F. Powell first determined that "education," or public-supported school, is not a fundamental constitutional right under the Fourteenth Amendment. In setting the tone for the opinion to follow, Justice Powell said, "Education, perhaps even more than welfare assistance, presents a myriad of 'intractable economic, social, and even philosophical problems.' The very complexity of the problems of financing and managing a statewide public school system suggests that 'there will be more than one constitutionally permissible method of solving them,' and that, within limits of rationality, 'the legislature's efforts to tackle the problems' should be entitled to respect."

Leading to Justice Powell's declaration of public education as a privilege and a prerogative of states, and not a fundamental constitutional right, had been two earlier federal court opinions that were affirmed by the U.S. Supreme Court although not directly decided by the Court. These two cases seemed to set the tone for the narrow majority opinion in the *Rodriguez* case.

In 1968, in *McInnis* v. *Shapiro,* some Illinois parents had also challenged the question, What role should government play in providing equal educational opportunity for all? What responsibilities do state and local governments have to ensure the Fourteenth Amendment's equal protection of the laws to all students attending public schools? The northern Illinois district federal judge made his decision with deference to state and local school funding mechanisms, concluding: "unequal expenditures per student, based upon the variable property values and tax rates of local school districts, do not amount to an invidious discrimination. Moreover, the statutes which permit these unequal expenditures on a district to district basis are neither arbitrary nor unreasonable." So according to this federal judge, even if each district provided significantly different expenditures per student, such expenditures are not unreasonable.

Shortly after the U.S. Supreme Court affirmed this decision, another federal court rendered a similar decision in the Commonwealth of

Virginia. In 1969, in *Burress* v. *Wilkerson,* another group of parents had complained about the Virginia state formula that provided distributive funding to local districts. The complainants, the plaintiff parents, claimed that the state formula denied equal protection by not considering the variety of educational needs present in the local districts. As in the preceding *McInnis* case, the federal district court in the *Burress* case took a hands-off position when looking at the possibility of the judiciary in becoming enmeshed in the financing of public schools. In the western district of Virginia federal court, the district judge decided, "The courts have neither the knowledge, nor the means, nor the power to tailor the public moneys to fit the varying needs of these students throughout the state. We can only see to it that the outlays on one group are not invidiously greater or less than that of another. No such arbitrariness is manifest here."

A prudently reasonable person might ask, If the courts cannot try to tailor funding formulas to meet individual school district formulas, then how could the court determine if a current funding formula was invidious or not? No criteria was established for being invidious. Once again, the federal courts had seemed to state that local districts were on their own in trying to establish equal educational opportunity.

Although some scholars and court watchers supporting a constitutional protection for equal educational opportunity were discouraged about the federal court's decisions in these cases, a ray of hope emerged from two well-publicized cases. In *Serrano* v. *Priest,* the California Supreme Court concluded that public schooling is a "fundamental interest" of the state, and in applying the equal protection clause of the California constitution in assessing this case, the highest court of the state decided that property wealth was a "suspect class." As the works in this comprehensive book of readings has demonstrated, anytime a class is considered suspect, the courts must apply a strict scrutiny test to determine if the discrimination can be considered permissible and constitutional.

According to the California Supreme Court, state and local governments, including the state assembly and local public school boards, do not have a compelling interest to treat one property class different from another, and absent the compelling interest, the state assembly and local school boards needed to develop a formula to eradicate the great disparities in school revenues. The *Serrano* case was initially decided in 1971. At about the same time, the Rodriguez family, living in the westside barrio of San Antonio, and whose children attended the very poor Edgewood Public School system, challenged the gross inequality their children experienced by living on the wrong side of the street. Demetrio Rodriguez, the father, prayed for relief for his children so they could receive a better education than he received. Rodriguez's attorneys presented evidence that his children attended Edgewood Elementary School, where the building was crumbling, classrooms lacked basic supplies, and almost half the teachers were not certified and worked on emergency permits. Rodriguez worked hard, had served in the Navy and the Air Force, and wanted his children to have an equal educational opportunity and to have greater educational and economic success than he had had. Rodriguez and five other families from Edgewood, at the advice of their attorney, filed suit in federal court complaining that the Texas public school finance plan denied the poor children the equal protection of the laws granted by the Fourteenth Amendment.

Remember, the *Serrano* case was decided by the California Supreme Court and the claim of unequal treatment was based on the California Constitution. The *Rodriguez* case, like the *McInnis* and *Burress* case precedents, was filed in federal court. In regards to the theory and the strategy of a case, no federal court had ever applied the equal protection clause to a guarantee of educational economic equality. Furthermore, no federal court had ever found social class status (e.g., one's income or poverty level) to be a suspect class. Without strict scrutiny, the federal court needed only to find a rational basis to explain the disparities in funding. A three-judge panel of the federal court in San Antonio ruled on behalf of the Rodriguezes and the other families in this original lawsuit. The rationale of the federal panel was focused on the state's obligation to remedy the inequalities arising from the local tax inequities.

The facts of the *Rodriguez* case are worth repeating in this chapter because in a microcosm this evidence illustrates so many of the problems confronting our public school system. The attorneys for the Rodriguez family used two districts within almost visual sight of one another to demonstrate the gross inequalities in school funding. The Alamo Heights section of San Antonio, a predominantly Anglo district overlooking Edgewood and other poorer areas of San Antonio, is populated by many lawyers, doctors, bankers, and other professionals with higher socioeconomic status than most of the inhabitants of the other area of San Antonio. Alamo Heights, after figuring local property values and state and federal funding, spent an average of $45,095 per student. The Edgewood District, while taxing themselves at the highest property value rate in the city, was only averaging $5,429 per pupil. Most of the disparity emerged from immense differences in property value. The parents in Edgewood, paying the highest possible percentage of property tax managed to raise only $26 in property tax for each student. Alamo Heights taxed themselves at the lowest city rate and still managed to raise $333 for each student, eight times more than Edgewood. With such measurable differences in funding, Alamo Heights could certainly do much more for their residents and students than Edgewood.

The lower federal court judges declared that state funding of public schools had to assure "fiscal neutrality," which was interpreted to mean that the quality of a child's education should not be a function of the district where the child resides but should be determined by the wealth of the state as a whole. In this court's opinion, the state had not adequately met the fiscal neutrality standard. Rodriguez's initial victory was short-lived because the federal court allowed the legislature reasonable time to remedy the inequities but mandated that such remedies should be addressed within two years. Recognizing that the remedy might call for greater state expenditures, the Texas attorney general's office and the political powers in Austin balked at this possibility. The state filed an appeal of this decision to the U.S. Supreme Court.

Knowing the right advocates can also have an impact. In this Supreme Court appeal, the state of Texas retained renowned constitutional rights lawyer, Charles Alan Wright, to argue on behalf of the state. Wright quickly persuaded 25 other state attorney general's offices to file "friend of the court" briefs on behalf of Texas's reasoning. Ironically, by this time, the San Antonio Independent School District had sided with Rodriguez, since the remedy, and the additional funding, would likely have to come from the state, not the local school district.

Wright's arguments managed to persuade five justices. Wright began by acknowledging the gross inequities. He even decried the consequences of such unequal funding, but he added, if the Supreme Court upheld the lower courts ruling, then the Court "would impose a constitutional straight jacket on the public schools of fifty states." Furthermore, Wright suggested that if the Court upheld the lower court decision that "very little is to be left of local government." A fact of our society is that "the poorest people live in the poorest districts and the richest people live in the richest districts." The economic inequities in school spending is merely a consequence of this cold fact. Wright did not advocate inequities, he just reemphasized that daily adage, "Well, life's sometimes unfair." The majority of the Supreme Court Justices accepted Wright's appeal.

In addition to the aforementioned comments from Justice Powell's majority opinion, Justice Powell voiced some additional concerns that continue to plague equal educational opportunity. Justice Powell admitted that there were many poor school districts in Texas because there were many poor people who belonged to "a large, diverse, and amorphous class, unified only by the common factor of residence in districts that happen to have less taxable wealth than other districts." Poverty is just a fact of life. Powell went on to point to the obvious, that education "is not among the rights afforded explicit protection under our Federal Constitution." Powell then went further to suggest granting education a constitutional status of a guaranteed right might lead to a slippery slope of government being responsible for other needs that some might construe as fundamental rights. Powell asked, "How for instance is education to be distinguished from the significant personal interests in the basics of decent food and shelter? Empirical examination might well buttress an assumption that the ill-fed, ill-clothed, and ill-housed are among the most ineffective participants in the political process." Does the government have a responsibility to feed, cloth, and house persons? Powell found no such protection in this majority's interpretation of the Constitution.

Who brought us this five-person majority opinion that seemed to stand Chief Justice Earl Warren's admonition of education as a fundamental right in his *Brown* I and II decisions, less than 20 years earlier? Four of the five majority justices in *Rodriguez*, including Justice Powell, had been appointed by President Nixon. A strongly worded dissent by Justice Thurgood Marshall called the majority opinion "a retreat from our historic commitment to equality of educational opportunity." And responding to Justice Powell's suggestion that Texas legislators can remedy this inequality, Justice Marshall said sarcastically, Powell's remarks "will doubtless be of great comfort to the schoolchildren of Texas' disadvantaged districts, but considering the vested interests of the wealthy school districts in the preservation of the status quo, they are worth little more."

When Rodriguez was informed of Powell's decision overturning the lower federal court opinion, he uttered in frustration, "The poor have lost again." The good news, for students in many states, is the spirit and energy that Rodriguez and others brought to the pursuit for equal educational opportunity. He has never given up. Some 12 years later, Rodriguez joined more parents in a suit filed by the Mexican American Legal Defense and Education Fund, using a suggestion Justice Brennan had often advocated and a successful strategy used in the earlier *Serrano* case: Go to the state constitution and use its explicit reference of education as a fundamental right and insist on its equal application. Several state lawsuits were filed with this strategy in mind.

Rodriguez revisited became *Edgewood* v. *Kirby,* with state court opinions rendered in 1987, 1989, 1991, and 1995. All the judges, to the Texas Supreme Court, agreed with the original Travis County, Texas, court judge Harley Clark in declaring the existing system of financing public schools in Texas unconstitutional. The Texas Supreme Court ruled, "There must be a direct and close correlation between a district's tax effort and the education resources available to it; in other words, districts must have substantially equal access to similar revenues per pupil at similar levels of tax effort. . . . Certainly, this much is required if the state is to educate its populace efficiently and provide for a general diffusion of knowledge statewide."

The Texas decision calling for the legislature to remedy the gross inequities followed the lead of some other states, including Kentucky, New Jersey, and Missouri. Responding to citizen suits calling for implementation of the constitutional requirement to provide for free public schooling, courts in

each of these respective states ruled on behalf of the parents from the poorer school districts.

State Constitutions and the Issue of Educational Financing

Americans continue to pursue inclusion regardless of race and economic status, and soon we will see others pursue schooling regardless of gender, ability, special needs, or status as children of aliens. For example, in seeking compliance with the New Jersey state constitution's "thorough and efficient" clause providing for universal public schooling, the New Jersey Supreme Court ruled in *Robinson* v. *Cahill* (1973) that the "thorough and efficient" standard required that "The Constitution's [i.e., New Jersey's] guarantee must be understood to embrace that educational opportunity which is needed in the contemporary setting to equip a child for his role as a citizen and as a competitor in the labor market." The state or local school board was thus required to equip each child for equal opportunity for success.

On the other hand, parents in other states who have sought to use their state constitutions to demand equal educational opportunity have not been as successful. In Louisiana, Illinois, Kansas, Montana, Oregon, New York, Georgia, and Michigan, the state courts have followed the U.S. Supreme Court's *Rodriguez* decision in concluding that economic inequality, educational disparity, and poverty is a fact of life, and if there are to be remedies, the complaining parties must seek policy changes through the respective legislative decisions. The history of this pursuit demonstrates that legislative bodies have not been proactive in addressing this problem.

Two recent state court cases regarding equal inclusion in public schooling regardless of one's socioeconomic background have recently been handed down in Connecticut and Maryland. Both cases could have far-reaching effects on equal educational opportunity if the opinions become guideposts to future funding proposals. The Connecticut case, *Milo Scheff, et al.* v. *William A. O'Neill, et al.,* was brought on behalf of 18 schoolchildren living in Hartford and two surrounding suburban communities. The parents of these children brought suit against the governor, the state board of education, and various other state officials, seeking remedy for the educational inequities in

the Hartford public schools that had resulted primarily from racial, ethnic, and socioeconomic isolation (i.e., class borders). In July 1996, the Connecticut Supreme Court handed down a dynamic decision on behalf of equal education opportunity.

Writing for a unanimous court, Connecticut Chief Justice Peters opinion stated, "The public elementary and high school students in Hartford suffer daily from the devastating effects that racial and ethnic isolations, as well as poverty, have had on their education. Federal constitutional law provides no remedy for their plight. The principal issue in this appeal is whether, under the unique provisions of our state constitution, the state, which already plays an active role in managing public schools, must take further measures to relieve the severe handicaps that burden these children's education. The issue is as controversial as the stakes are high. We hold today that the needy schoolchildren of Hartford have waited long enough." The chief justice, in upholding the constitutional separation of powers, left the specifics of the remedy to be worked out, legislated and implemented by the legislative and executive branches of government.

Even more recently (December 1996), two state judges in Maryland ruled favorably on a settlement agreement reached in the case of *Bradford* v. *Maryland State Board of Education*. The Baltimore City Circuit judges Kaplan and Garbis ruled

that: (1) all public schoolchildren in Maryland have a right to an adequate education, as measured by contemporary educational standards and (2) the children in Baltimore City are not receiving a constitutionally adequate education. Without going to trial, the parties agreed to a comprehensive revision of state funding and support for the public schools in Baltimore that would include the following initiatives:

> I. A substantial commitment of financial resources earmarked for school improvement to the Baltimore City Public Schools; II. A new management team committed to school improvement; III. Planning, reporting and evaluation—all tied to student achievement, and including measurable outcomes, timelines, curriculum reform and associated staff development; and IV. Increased opportunities for parental involvement.

Will Hartford and Baltimore become beacons of fully inclusive, integrated schools that provide the equal educational opportunity for equal employment opportunities? The decisions in these cases give direction to public policy debate.

The Alien Border Crossing

Currently the public schoolhouse doors are open to all youngsters regardless of color and socioeconomic status. Other attempts to keep other groups out of the public schools fail as bridges are built and borders crossed. However, much of young people's educational opportunities and subsequent economic success rests greatly on where they live, the color of their skin, and their socioeconomic status. The doors are open, but the lights and learning may dim if we do not keep our eye on the prize of providing equal education for each child entering the public schools.

The next question is, Does the state have to provide free public education for children of aliens, and can the state require instruction in the "official language" of the state or nation?

History has demonstrated strong rushes of anti-immigration sentiment among policymakers at many times in our nation's short history. Although Texas had once been part of northern Mexico, once it became dominated by Anglo powerbrokers, the state of Texas took many steps to discriminate against persons of Mexican ancestry. As legal and illegal immigration to the United States increased from south of the border, many border states, especially Texas, Arizona, and California, adopted state policies to try to limit services and entitlements to illegal aliens, including the children of illegal immigrants. In 1975, the Texas legislature revised their public schooling statutes, adding a special provision stating that the state must withhold funding to any local school districts for the education of children who were not "legally admitted" into the United States.

Parents of children who were in Texas illegally sued the state of Texas, claiming that the state's restrictive policy of funding denied these children Fourteenth Amendment rights of due process and of equal protection of the laws to all persons, not just citizens. The parents' legal complaint worked its way to the U.S. Supreme Court in the case, *Plyler* v. *Doe* (1982). In a closely held opinion of five to four, Justice William J. Brennan rendered a decision that amounted to inclusion of these children in the Texas public schools. Although the decision amounted to a victory for these children, the decision did not grant sweeping entitlements to illegal aliens.

Justice Brennan agreed with the parents' interpretation of the Fourteenth Amendment. The Fourteenth Amendment protection of persons means all persons, including aliens. However, with such constitutional protection, Brennan applied a strict scrutiny test for the illegal aliens. Brennan acknowledged that states could demonstrate a compelling interest in prohibiting the flow of illegal immigrants, but he drew a strong distinc-

tion between the language of the law and how it targeted children specifically and was not directed toward parental responsibility. Brennan was adamant that the state should not be punishing minor children who may be in the United States solely because of the conduct of their parents. Furthermore, if children are residing within the Texas borders, they should be granted the same educational opportunities of the children of legal aliens and citizens.

Brennan could not, in the light of the earlier *Rodriguez* case, recognize education as a fundamental federal right protected by the U.S. Constitution, but he did conclude that education has a greater impact than other government benefits. In Brennan's majority opinion, he stated, "Public education is not a 'right' granted to individuals by the Constitution. But neither is it merely some governmental 'benefit' indistinguishable from other forms of social welfare legislation. Both the importance of education in maintaining our basic institutions, and the lasting impact of its deprivation on the life of the child, mark the distinction. . . . In sum, education has a fundamental role in maintaining the fabric of our society. We cannot ignore the significant social costs borne by our Nation when select groups are denied the means to absorb the values and skills upon which our social order rests. . . ."

Another border has been crossed, another class or group will be permitted to seek a free public education without fear of being excluded as an "alien," an outsider. Although states cannot deny access to public education for children of illegal immigrants, efforts to restrict immigration are currently very hot topics.

Crossing the Language Border

As in earlier periods of antiforeign sentiment, some of the states bordering the United States have recently attempted to pass legislation mandating that if an immigrant comes to the United States the government will only communicate with them using the "official" language of the state. Following this rationale, some states have passed official English-only laws. The United Sates Supreme Court, in its 1996–1997 term, is hearing a case involving Arizona's official English statute, *Arizonans for Official English* v. *Arizona*.

Such statutes have a significant bearing, if not in force, then by strong public opinion expressed by those who wish to exclude some from the mainstream culture. Nearly 20 states have already passed English-only laws. Also, how does this effect public schooling? If these laws (e.g., the Arizona initiative) were to be enforced, then any person speaking languages other than English could be prohibited from receiving a public education. This would not only affect predominantly Spanish-speaking families, especially of the southwest United States, but could affect children from other parts of the globe as well. If "English only" is the rule, are we going to punish children in school who speak in another language? Are parents of children not going to be properly informed about their children's progress if they do not speak English? Will these same parents, who are taxpayers, be denied access to the ballot box because they cannot read or understand English?

Although there is some historical evidence that John Adams advocated an official academy to "purify, develop, and dictate usage of" English, most evidence seems to suggest that necessity and other factors contributed to North America, including the United States, being moderately tolerant of multilingualism. However, with the influx of Chinese immigrants, especially in the West to work on completing the intercontinental railroad, more pressure emerged from nativist groups who advocated English-only laws at the end of the nineteenth and into the twentieth century.

The term "nativist" may seem arrogant since archaeological evidence seems to indicate that Native Americans, commonly called Indians, were present long before any English-speaking persons arrived. Furthermore, the real Native Americans spoke many dialects from tribe to tribe. Later, in justifying sending Native American children to English-only boarding schools, federal officials claimed that even Native Americans had Asian roots since they probably migrated to the United States by migration. Such antiforeign sentiment was strongly expressed following World War I when states considered adopting English-only laws to reduce the German immigration influence.

In 1919, the Nebraska state legislature passed a law stating "No person, individually or as a teacher, shall, in any private, denominational, parochial or public school, teach any subject to any person in any language other than the English lan-

There is some historical evidence that President John Adams advocated an offical academy to "purify, develop, and dictate usage of" English, yet most evidence seems to suggest that necessity and other factors contributed to North America, including the United States, being moderately tolerant of multilingualism.

guage." The instructor at Zion Parochial School in Hamilton County, was charged and convicted under this law. He was accused of teaching the German language to ten-year-old children. This conviction was upheld by the Nebraska Supreme Court, and the U.S. Supreme Court acknowledged the state supreme court's reasoning in upholding the conviction as an exercise of police power, stating,

> The statutory purpose of the statute is clear. The legislature had seen the baneful effects of permitting foreigners, who had taken residence in this country, to rear and educate their children in the language of their native land. The result of that condition was found to be inimical to our own safety. To allow the children of foreigners, who had emigrated here, to be taught from early childhood the language of the country of their parents was to rear them with that language as their mother tongue. It was to educate them so that they must always think in that language, and, as a consequence, naturally inculcate in them the ideas and sentiments foreign to the best interests of the country. . . . The obvious purpose of this statute was that the English language should be and become the mother tongue of all children reared in this state. The enactment of such a statute comes reasonably within the police power of the state. . . . (*Meyer* v. *Nebraska,* 1923).

The U.S. Supreme Court recognized the state's power, but at the same time, the Court suggested that this power had to be balanced with a person's Fourteenth Amendment rights of "life, liberty and property." The Court's opinion in *Meyer* tilted the balance to Meyer's liberty and property interest as well as to the liberty interests of parents to hire a language instructor for their children. The Court concluded, "Practically, education of the young is only possible in schools conducted by especially qualified persons who devote themselves thereto. The calling always had been regarded as useful and honorable, essential, indeed, to the public welfare. Mere knowledge of the German language cannot reasonably be regarded as harmful. Heretofore it has been commonly looked upon as helpful and desirable. Plaintiff in error taught this language in school as part of his occupation. His right thus to teach and the right of parents to engage him so to instruct their children, we think, are within the liberty of the amendment. . . ."

The *Meyer* case situation may have stemmed the anti-German tide expressed in legislation, but the ruling did not end discrimination or prejudice toward others who spoke languages other than English. More recently, the parents of Chinese-speaking students sued the San Francisco Unified School District for failing to provide appropriate English instruction to students who did not use English as a primary language. More recently, in December 1996, the U.S. Supreme Court heard oral arguments regarding making English the official language, and the public sentiment is very much like that expressed in the rationale of the Nebraska Supreme Court.

The San Francisco Unified School District lawsuit brought by the parents of Chinese-speaking students in 1974, *Lau* v. *Nichols,* became a landmark case testing both the constitutional freedom of multilingual education and the supportive civil rights legislation. The majority of the Court did not believe this case rose to the constitutional question of equal protection, but certainly the majority expressed that the state of California and the San Francisco public school system violated the Civil Rights Act of 1964.

The majority of the Court made clear that Congress intended for all persons to have an equal educational opportunity under the civil rights legislation of the 1960s. Not having an opportunity to acquire English was certainly a setback to equal opportunity. Specifically, the Court stated,

> Basic English skills are at the very core of what these public schools teach. Imposition of a requirement that, before a child can effectively participate in an educational program, he must already have acquired those skills is to make a mockery of public education. We know that

those who do not understand English are certain to find their classroom experiences wholly incomprehensible and in no way meaningful. . . . There is no equality of treatment merely by providing students the same facilities; textbooks, teachers, and curriculum; for students who do not understand English are effectively foreclosed from any meaningful education.

The Court then went on to cite the federal regulations providing for adequate language instruction, regulations that would later fall under the umbrella of bilingual education. In 1970, as the Court noted, the federal Department of Health, Education and Welfare had promulgated regulations stating, "Where inability to speak and understand the English language excludes national origin-minority group children from effective participation in the educational program offered by a school district, the district must take affirmative steps to rectify the language deficiency in order to open its instructional program to these students. . . . Any ability grouping or tracking system employed by the school system to deal with the special language skill needs of national origin-minority group children must be designed to meet such language skill needs as soon as possible and must not operate as an educational deadend or permanent track."

Accordingly, the Court found that the San Francisco public school system had not taken affirmative steps to meet the skill needs of the Chinese-speaking students, and therefore the case was sent back to the local federal court, to assure that the language skills are provided. From the *Lau* case, several actions have been taken by the executive, legislative, and judicial branches to provide for appropriate language instruction to assure equal educational opportunity.

In 1974, the same year as *Lau*, the U.S. Congress passed the Equal Educational Opportunities Act (EEOA), which laid the foundation for bilingual education. The EEOA states "no state shall deny educational opportunity to an individual on account of his or her race, color, sex, or national origin, by . . . the failure by an educational agency to take appropriate action to overcome language barriers that impede equal participation by its students in its instructional programs." Following this principle, and in a long series of federal cases, the circuit courts basically said school districts must satisfactorily answer three questions regarding appropriate language instruction:

- Is the school district's program based upon recognized, sound educational theory or principles?

- Is the school district's program or practice designed to implement the adopted theory?

- Has the program produced satisfactory results?

School districts still have a great deal of latitude in implementing bilingual programs, and to date, the U.S. Supreme Court has not ruled on the English-only laws, with the exception of the pending case from Arizona. The truly frightening reality is to observe the heated discussion and debate that arises among Anglos who clearly speak a different native tongue than that found in England, when they expound upon the need for "those" people to learn "our" language in order to survive in "our" culture. Such diatribes are directed mostly to Spanish-speaking persons in certain areas, Asian-speaking people in other areas, and most recently toward African Americans. In the case of African Americans, some well-intentioned scholars have suggested that history and circumstances have produced a unique language variation, sometimes called Ebonics, that should be acknowledged as a minority dialect and therefore that bilingual or English as a Second Language (ESL) education should be provided for these students.

Crossing the Special Needs Border

What about equal educational opportunity for children who have been designated as having physical, learning, emotional, and behavioral disabilities? The history of treating persons with such disabilities has been depressingly dismal until the mid- to late twentieth century. This is not to say that the entire history is marked with tragedy; there have been rays of sunlight primarily emerging from the advocacy on behalf of those with specific disabilities. For example, as early as 1817, the Connecticut legislature appropriated funding for the American Asylum for the Education of the Deaf and Dumb (still in existence as the American School for the Deaf). However, the term "dumb" was used for decades simultaneously to indicate if one could not hear, then one must also remain dumb. Even this early open door to the hearing impaired resulted from strong lobbying from the parents of those suffering from the hearing disabilities, as well as the leadership of Thomas Gal-

Thomas Gallaudet, nineteenth-century pioneer educator of the hearing impaired.

laudet, who had been trained in the French method of manual communication for the deaf.

Such openings still occurred with a general public perception to treat these persons as different, as disabled, and to some extent deviant—labeled deaf and dumb—from normal. Such students were excluded from general education, and only exceptionally could such persons effectively function in the hearing community.

The treatment of children with other disabilities was even more abdominal, bordering on the bizarre, and in some cases, even treating those with disabilities as "freaks" and "sideshows" of the abnormal. Many of those with disabilities were thrown into larger institutions, away from their families, a sort of warehousing in what was called "hospitals for lunatics." Locked away, the disabled were out of sight and all too often out of the mind of public debate and certainly were denied a chance for equal educational opportunity. Of course, there were strong advocates on behalf of those with disabilities, and in many cases, advances in treatment and services were made.

As a matter of public policy, it appears that educational leaders could not agree about what differences should be treated as disabilities and then deciding the appropriate treatment once a disability had been identified. For instance, children with learning disabilities were often labeled "imbeciles" or "morons," and the segregated treatment of such persons was grossly different from inclusion in regular classrooms. In 1893, in the case of *Watson* v. *City of Cambridge,* a Massachusetts state court decided that if a student was labeled an imbecile, the characteristic of imbecility was grounds for expulsion from the public schools. Some two decades later, in the case *State ex rel. Beattie* v. *Board of Education* (1919), a Wisconsin state court decided that a student with disabilities, although capable, could be excluded from regular public school classes because his disability had "a depressing and nauseating effect on the teachers and school children."

Such decisions set up terrible, segregated conditions for children with a variety of disabilities. Even children suffering from cerebral palsy or struck with poliomyelitis were prohibited from attending regular public schools. In many cases, the fate and educational opportunity of these children became dependent on the wealth of a family or the charity of organizations or churches. The parents of the children had to find placement and treatment for their children, often in residential schools or with private tutors. In all too many cases, if the parents did not have the means, the children never received any formal education.

Two landmark cases changed the equal rights and civil rights of parents and children with disabilities forever, at least to date. In *Pennsylvania Association for Retarded Children* v. *Commonwealth* (1971), a federal court ruled that children who had been designated "retarded" were entitled to a free public education. This ruling further ordered the "retarded" children to be educated in regular classrooms rather than segregated from the normal school population. This case, often referred to as the PARC case, created the following precedent: "free, public program of education and training appropriate to the child's capacity, within the context of a presumption that, among the alternative programs of education and training required by statute available, placement in a regular public school class is preferable to placement in a special public school class (e.g., a class for 'handicapped' children) and placement in a special public school class is preferable to placement in any other type of program of education and training."

The second critical case occurred right in the shadows of the nation's highest governing institutions, *Mills* v. *Board of Education of the District of Columbia* (1972). In this case, the federal court concluded that in the nation's capitol there were approximately "22,000 retarded, emotionally disturbed, blind, deaf, and speech, or learning disabled children, and perhaps as many as 18,000 of these children [were] not being furnished with programs of specialized education."

In this case the district court made a thorough examination of the failure of the D.C. Public schools to adequately educate "exceptional children," including those diagnosed as mentally retarded, emotionally disturbed, physically handicapped, hyperactive, or with behavioral problems. The court found the problem of failing to educate these children, numbering in the tens of thousands, to be an abomination. Not only were the exceptional children being denied an education, but often when they were admitted to school, these children and their parents found the students summarily suspended or expelled from regular public schooling.

The defendants in this case, the District of Columbia Board of Education, claimed that the district had insufficient funding to provide for normal children and so many exceptional children. The district court did not look favorably upon the defendant's cost effectiveness rationale. In a strongly worded opinion, which could serve as a basis of supporting all sorts of necessary and sufficient public school programs, the district court ruled,

> The defendants (the D.C. Public school system) are required by the Constitution of the United States, the District of Columbia Code, and their own regulations to provide a publicly supported education for 'exceptional' children. Their failure to fulfill this clear duty to include and retain these children in the public school system, or otherwise provide them with publicly supported education, and their failure to afford them due process hearing and periodic review, cannot be excused by the claim that there are insufficient funds.... The District of Columbia's interest in educating the excluded children clearly must outweigh its interest in preserving its financial resources. If sufficient funds are not available to finance all of the services and programs that are needed and desirable in the system then the available funds must be expended equitably in such a manner that no child is entirely excluded from a publicly supported education consistent with his needs and ability to benefit therefrom. The inadequacies of the District of Columbia School System, whether occasioned by insufficient funding or administrative inefficiency, certainly cannot be permitted to bear more heavily on the 'exceptional' or handicapped child than on the normal child ...

With this summary, the district court affirmed a proposed "order and decree," and in this consent agreement, the school system pledged to provide (1) a free appropriate education, (2) an Individualized Education Plan (IEP) for each exceptional child, and (3) appropriate due process procedures. The consent decree went on for several pages, and many believe it served as the foundation for upcoming federal legislation to address the needs of children with disabilities.

The *PARC* and *Mills* cases, along with some investigative reporting exposing the squalid conditions under which children with disabilities were often kept seemed to awaken public consciousness to take action to remedy these problems, to find effective ways to include, instead of exclude, so many capable children. By the mid-1970s, Congress enacted the first Education for All Handicapped Children Act, often referred to as Public Law 94B142. This act has been amended several times to meet changing needs and desires, often of the advocates of the children effected by this legislation. In 1990, the name of the act even changed to reflect the sensitivity against labeling young people as handicapped. The new act is called Individuals with Disabilities Education Act (IDEA), and it is up for renewal in the spring of 1997.

IDEA has spurned an extensive, expansive, and expensive course of conduct regarding children with disabilities. Some law firms that have represented school districts are now specializing in special education law. There are a host of newsletters and periodicals devoted to instructional programs and policies as well as to legal responses.

Through litigation and state and federal regulations school districts have developed programs and procedures that direct several specific areas of concern under IDEA, specifically as the act applies to

• Free Appropriate Public Education (FAPE)

• Procedural safeguards (due process for students classified as special)

• Individualized Education Program (IEP)

• Least Restrictive Environment (LRE)

• Separate school placement

• Related services

• Discipline and "Stay Put" policies

• Attorney's fees

• Tuition reimbursement

Each of these areas have been refined by litigation and subsequent court decisions. Some of these rulings bear directly on the future of special education and public policy.

So what does free appropriate public education mean? The original EAHCA, now IDEA, was defined by statute, that is, "special education and related services which (a) have been provided at public expense, under public supervision and direction, and without charge, (b) meet the standards of the state education agency, (c) include an appropriate preschool, elementary, or secondary education in the state involved, and (d) are provided in conformity with the individualized education program required under this title."

Although the courts, as well as the federal government, expect the state education agencies and local school districts to carry out the tenets of IDEA's FAPE, the actions of the state and local districts are subject to compliance review. The courts have concluded that this act is designed "to benefit" the child. Furthermore, federal district courts have made it clear that the children do not have to demonstrate that they will benefit or are benefiting from the prescribed education plan, it still must be designed to attempt "to benefit" the child (see for example, *Timothy W.* v. *Rochester, New Hampshire, School District,* 1989).

As noted, IDEA provides for childrens' educational needs in preschool through what is normally considered adulthood, age 21, unless otherwise ordered by the courts. Such long-range schooling is quite different from the mainstream compulsory schooling provisions, which, in general, cover ages 6–16. In the case of children diagnosed as special needs learners, the schooling (education and intervention) may take place, at government expense, from 1 day old to 21 years of age. In addition, unlike most mainstream schooling, students with special needs who may regress in physical, emotional, academic, or psychological development owing to being out of a schooling setting for too long, are entitled to extended year or year-round education and related services. In the precedent setting case for extended year schooling, *Battle* v. *Commonwealth of Pennsylvania* (1980), the federal circuit court claimed that the IEP must be designed to "meet the unique needs" of each student, and in their words, traditional 180 school days a year may not meet these unique needs. The court stated: "Rather than ascertaining the reasonable educational needs of each child in light of reasonable education goals and establishing a reasonable program to attain those goals, the 180 day rule imposes with rigid certainty a program restriction which may be wholly inappropriate to the child's educational objectives." This doctrine, to develop IEPs for each student with special needs, has been reaffirmed by many federal courts.

Given such strong statutory language, are there any limits a school district may impose for students with special needs, or do parents have unlimited resources that they may call upon to meet the needs of their children? May parents demand maximum services for their children with special needs, and if the answer to this question is yes, will such demands lead to inequalities for regular, mainstreamed children? Once again, the federal courts have been asked to address several of these questions and concerns.

In 1982, in one of the watershed cases following the *PARC* and *Mills* decisions, the Supreme Court laid down a fundamental foundation to answer the question, how much schooling and services may be considered enough? In *Board of Education of Hendrick Hudson Central School District* v. *Rowley*, the Court basically concluded that a state and local public school district were not required to maximize the potential of each student serviced by the district's special education department.

In this case, which became known as the *Rowley* decision, the Court concluded that each district had to be responsible for being in compliance with IDEA, in 1982 known as EAHCA. The Court suggested that each district comply with two legal threshold standards: "First, has the state complied with procedures set forth in the Act. And, second, is the individualized educational program developed pursuant to the Act's procedures reasonably calculated to enable the child to receive educational benefits?" The Court also addressed the question, Are there any limits to what the state or local district should provide? The Court answered, "We therefore conclude that the basic floor of opportunity" provided by the Act consists of access to specialized instruction and related services which are individually designed to provide educational benefit to the handicapped child."

The specific result in the *Rowley* case, as the Court's two-prong standard was applied, was that the parents of Rowley did not have the right to dictate the educational provisions for their children. In this case, the Rowleys wanted a full-time interpreter for their child who suffered from a hearing loss. The local school district had provided the child with an FM hearing aid, specialized tutoring for one hour each day, and speech therapy for three hours each week. The school district had also provided an interpreter for this student for a two-week period to determine if a full-time interpreter might be in the best interest of this child's IEP. The interpreter reported after the two weeks that his services were not needed. The parents still pursued their demands for a full-time interpreter, a decision that was eventually decided by an independent examiner. The independent examiner agreed with the local school district that their services had been sufficient and a full-time interpreter was not needed. This case, eventually decided by the Supreme Court, also affirmed the independent examiner's ruling that the school district had met its required compliance standard.

It should be noted that the number of children receiving special services has increased dramatically since the first federal legislation. Today, school districts must provide special services (1) for students covered under IDEA, the Americans with Disabilities Act (previously referred to as the Rehabilitation Act); (2) for students covered by Section 504 of the Vocational Rehabilitation Act (these might be students covered under the DSM, the Diagnostic Statistical Manual—provided to psychologists, psychiatrists, therapists, and so on); the bilingual federal legislation and English as a Second Language (ESL) laws mentioned earlier. These categories are often covered in a single school district with specialized departments for special education, for compensatory education, and for bilingual education. Some districts employ directors of special populations to administer local programs to be in compliance with the federal standards. What drives these departments, and how are students chosen for participation in such programs?

Like so much of our history of public education, money has been a driving force. The federal government expenditures to local districts to meet the needs of these special populations has increased. Some worry that with the call for greater state and local control, the educational civil rights of those who had been excluded or provided for inadequately for so many years will also suffer as policymakers decide how to divide up the money pie to schools. Many professional educators, devoted to inclusion and critical pedagogy, are dismayed and torn by the direction of educational policy. Although they might be in the forefront to argue for the civil rights of those with disabilities, they also recognize that everyone has both abilities and disabilities. Why should some be labeled special instead of all?

To qualify for special education services, a parent must permit his or her son or daughter to be diagnosed as having a specific learning, emotional, or physical disability, or even a combination of the above. Of course, the diagnosis is often accompanied with a label, sometimes generic like learning or emotional disability, sometimes more specific such as mentally retarded or severally emotionally disturbed (S.E.D.). At one point, such labels led school districts to establish separate, segregated programs for the labeled children. The districts and some experts contend this was in the best interest of the specific child as well as the interests of other children. To these experts and districts, the students with special needs had at least got their foot in the schoolhouse door. But for many parents this was not enough.

Even those who were admitted in the front door of the schoolhouse had to be concerned about being segregated in "special places" for the "special ed" kids. Often it was like a leper colony inside the regular school, or sometimes separate public schools were set up specifically for certain "special education" children. Many parents argued that least restrictive environment meant that all children, especially those labeled as having disabilities, deserved to be included in the regular educational mainstream with specific modifications to be made to meet the students' IEP.

Ironically, inclusion efforts found some support in the Reagan era, during which the federal government looked for ways to reduce federal funding, whereas the most expensive programs were the separate placement programs. The separate placement programs often called for creating separate physical plants with all their concomitant needs—additional staffing, maintenance, custodial services, and so on. The less expensive programs have included the special education children in with regular classrooms, possibly with a teacher's aid or other professional providing some service in the regular classroom.

While inclusion has created debates among experts in special education, it has also created a larger public policy debate in the area of civil rights. To some extent, one could argue that special education inclusion programs are comparable to affirmative action programs; that is, those children who have been excluded or denied adequate education in the past are being compensated for by both placement in a regular school environment as well as provision of additional instructional and support services. Of course, such policies lead others to say, what about our normal children? Why aren't they treated special? Why do they receive fewer support services?

Eventually, Congress may place limits and demand greater categorical protections so as to limit the numbers receiving special education funding, but consensus seems to be that this will not take place even if state and local school districts are encouraged to privatize, adopt voucher proposals, and establish quasiprivate charter schools. Most agree that children receiving special education support and services will still be compensated under any alternative schooling system.

So how should a public school respond to a student whose misconduct emerges from his or her disability? According to IDEA's current "stay put" provision, and the various court rulings, a student with a related disability may be suspended for up to ten days. By the end of ten days an additional due process hearing to consider a change in placement and a modification to the students IEP must be held. If the district feels that the student may continue to be a threat and the district has not had reasonable time to develop an acceptable and appropriate plan of action for the student, the district may ask the courts to issue a temporary injunction to allow additional time for the district to respond to the student's needs while protecting the general welfare of the school community. During this additional time, the district may provide home instruction for the student or make arrangements for a temporary alternative educational placement. And of course, due process permits the parents to appeal this additional time out of the student's previous placement, and the courts will have the final determination, if all parties cannot

All persons regardless of race, religion, dialect and language differences, different abilities and disabilities now have a right to a free public education from at least age 6 to 21, with extended coverage for some classifications.

reach agreement. In all cases to date, the courts have issued an injunction where one has been sought because of the potential danger to the student with the disability and the regular school staff and students. Such injunctions have occurred in many federal jurisdictions throughout the United States. As with so many other issues involving schooling, the courts rarely take a position to grant license to any student to behave in any way in school. Judges often rely upon the expertise of educators in making such decisions, upholding school action, and even issuing injunctions where necessary, particularly to keep schools safe.

We have now included children under almost every classification that the law has recognized: All persons regardless of race, religion, dialect and language differences, different abilities and disabilities now have a right to a free public education from at least age 6 to 21, with extended coverage for some classifications. The one classification we have not singled out is gender. Efforts by females to receive equal educational opportunity include the recent foray into previously established all-male, military academies.

Crossing the Gender Barrier

If the *Brown* cases, I and II, remain our watershed for educational civil rights, then shouldn't any school supported with government funds be required to open their doors to all? Although this

may seem logical, it has hardly been accompanied by easy access for those previously excluded. One of the more recent barriers to be breached was the all-male military academies. The two cases receiving the most media ink and attention in the 1990s were Shannon Faulkner's attempt to enter The Citadel in Charleston, South Carolina, in 1993, and more recently, the efforts of female students to enter the Virginia Military Institute.

Why would a woman want to enter these types of military schools, where intimidation and harassment seem to be part of "long-honored" tradition? The same question has in essence been asked of every excluded group. In other words, why would young African American children want to attend a school where others have demonstrated they are not wanted? Why should Jehovah's Witness students want to remain in a school where they are singled out and ostracized because of the exercise of their religious beliefs? Why would gay students want to establish school-sponsored gay rights clubs at schools where students taunt and tease about fags or queers? These important questions are probably better addressed by what we need to do in schools to promote tolerance, sensitivity, and respect for diversity. This next discussion, however, will solely examine the right of females to attend these previously all-male military institutes.

In 1993, a federal judge ruled that Shannon Faulkner, a female student, could attend day classes at The Citadel, while reserving for future hearings her right to join the military corps. The 100 percent male Citadel had been a bastion of southern tradition and of military tradition. Shannon Faulkner was about to break these long-standing traditions. Upon hearing the full case after The Citadel lost appeals in the Fourth Circuit, the original federal district judge ordered Shannon to become a member of the corps. The Citadel appealed this decision, and this time the Fourth Circuit upheld the enrollment unless South Carolina could establish a comparable educational leadership program for women cadets. Hurriedly, South Carolina agreed to create an alternative school at Converse College in Spartanburg. Until this school was ready, the federal district court insisted that Faulkner be allowed to enter as a cadet and a member of The Citadel corps. Faulkner entered the program, became seriously ill, and left the school. Many believed that this was just

In 1995 the Supreme Court refused to overturn a ruling that allowed Shannon Faulkner the opportunity to enter The Citidal, a formerly all-male military school in Charleston, South Carolina. Though she eventually left the school, the ruling has sparked much controversy.

rewards: "See, we told you—females cannot make it in this place! This is what happens when you try to go somewhere where you are not wanted or capable!"

While this incident and issue made the rounds of the talk show pundits and inspired media debate, others were seeking to end the all-male military school tradition once and for all. They wanted to break down the barriers and build more bridges of equal educational opportunity.

In the next case, the United States government entered into the debate with the Justice Department supporting a suit brought by a group of females who were attempting to gain entrance into Virginia Military Institute (VMI) an all-male military institute. The Justice Department claimed that VMI received state and federal funding and must therefore provide equal educational opportunity regardless of gender. The state of Virginia argued that it provided an alternative girl's academy, the Mary Baldwin School, that offered comparable programs to those of VMI. Again, the Justice Department refused to accept separate but equal treatment, arguing that such segregation officially ended with the *Brown* decisions. Furthermore, the Justice Department contended that females had already proven themselves in the United States armed services, and therefore, Virginia and VMI had no rational basis to deny women equal access to VMI. This case became

one of the last rulings of the U.S. Supreme Court in the 1995–1996 term. A majority of the Court claimed VMI had no rational basis or compelling or substantial government interest in maintaining same gender schools, excluding persons on account of sex.

Justice Ruth Bader Ginsburg wrote a strongly worded opinion on behalf of the majority and upholding the Justice Department's argument. Ginsburg wrote, "Women seeking and fit for a VMI-quality education cannot be offered anything less under the state's obligation to afford them genuinely equal protection . . ." *(United States* v. *Virginia, VMI, et al.,* 1996). Justice Thomas, who often sides with Justice Scalia, did not participate in this opinion, claiming a conflict of interest since his son attends VMI. Even without the help of Justice Thomas, Justice Scalia managed a scathing dissent. Scalia claimed that Ginsburg and the controlling majority had gone too far in judicial activism and arrogance. Scalia wrote, "Change is forced upon Virginia, and reversion to single-sex education is prohibited nationwide, not by democratic processes but by order of this court." He went on to characterize Ginsburg's decision as not the interpretation of a Constitution, but the creation of one. To date, the female students who won the right to attend VMI are adapting as well, and in some cases better, than other students, despite the continual criticism of some conservative columnists and talk show pundits.

Brown and subsequent Court victories paved the way for nearly universal public education for persons, roughly between 6 and 16 years of age, residing in the United States. Thousands of youngsters continue to fall through the cracks, who are not receiving something comparable to public schooling. Some of these youngsters are being homeschooled, some are chronic truants, and some are homeless; some have had so many problems, in and out of school, that they drop out.

By maximizing our commitment to making public schools citadels of democracy where all participants have a voice, protected by the declaration and Bills of Rights of our state and United States constitutions, a welcome learning-centered, community-centered public school system will be created. In order to accomplish this, first and foremost, there must be assurances that all who enter the schoolhouse receive constitutional protections. This can be done by practicing the rights and responsibilities that are inalienable to all.

Inside the Public Schools: Rights and Responsibilities

Thanks to application of the incorporation theory that has been discussed in other sections of the book, students and staff have received the protections of the Bill of Rights in our public schools. Some major constitutional conflicts have erupted on our public schoolhouse grounds. Public schools are emphasized because our state and federal constitutions protect us from coercive and repressive government action. We are not protected by private actors by our constitutions. In other words, if we agree to attend a private or parochial school, we are in effect consenting to follow the rules of that school. We always have the choice of not attending the school if we do not like the rules. We can enter the public schools and at least be under the umbrella of the rights protected under our Bill of Rights.

Conflicts and First Amendment Freedoms

The first clause of the First Amendment prohibits government from establishing or favoring one religion, or any religion, over other religions or no religions. It also prohibits government from interfering with an individual's free exercise of his or her religious beliefs. The next clause protects us from government interference with freedom of speech and of the press. And the last clause protects the right of the people peaceably to assemble and to petition the government for redress of grievances. We will examine each clause as we study a case in conflict.

When can the Public School (i.e., the Government) Interfere with Religious Practices?

What if your religious beliefs required that you start adulthood and work in your community prior to the age of 16? If you practiced this belief, your parents and you would defy the state's compulsory school law. This was the case in *Wisconsin* v. *Yoder,* 1972. As discussed earlier in this chapter, by a slim majority the Court did not believe that the state had proven a compelling interest to interfere with the Old Order Amish religious tradition of leaving school by the end of eighth grade. In addition, the Court and lower courts have not upheld other attempts by parents to withhold their children from schooling on religious grounds.

Can the Public School Require Children to Recite the Pledge of Allegiance to the United States Even if This Pledge Violates Sacred Religious Teachings?

As discussed in the chapter on First Amendment freedoms, religious persecution has often invoked complaints of government interference with the free exercise of religion. The Jehovah's Witness faith has been in the forefront of many such conflicts and cases. In the first of two powerful cases decided in the historical context of World War II, the Gobitis family, practicing Jehovah's Witnesses, refused to have their children participate in the school ceremony saluting the flag and saying the pledge of allegiance to the United States. According to the Jehovah's Witness teachings, if their children participated in such a ceremony, they would be placing other gods before God, pledging loyalty and allegiance to an authority that is subservient to God. For the Gobitises such practices would be so contrary to their religious teachings that they in fact would compromise their beliefs. The Gobitises presented extensive religious testimony supporting their beliefs, especially chapter 20 of the Book of Exodus, and the verses, "Thou shalt have no other gods before me"; "Thou shalt not make unto them any graven image, or any likeness of any thing that is in heaven above, or that is in the earth beneath, or that is in the water under the earth"; and "Thou shalt not bow down thyself to them, nor serve them. . . ." In this case, *Minersville School District* v. *Gobitis* (1940), the United States Supreme Court heard arguments for attorneys representing each party. In response to the Gobitises' complaint that the patriotic pledge violated their free exercise of religion, the Minersville public schools claimed that the patriotic practice promotes good citizenship and support for our country. Surely, public schools have the right to assure good citizenship and loyalty to the country. Such a compelling government interest outweighs this individual family's complaint about violation of the free exercise clause.

And how did the Court rule? Remember to place this decision in the context of the time. The United States had not yet declared war on Germany or Japan, but war fever was certainly stirring among much of the populace. Many believed patriotism would be paramount to the survival of the West, certainly to the United States. With only one dissenting opinion, Justice Felix Frankfurter wrote the opinion for the Court. Justice Frankfurter poured fuel on the patriotic fervor. The Court not only yielded a ruling giving discretion to the legislative body to make and enforce such rules or laws with the support of the executive branch, it also reinforced the importance of a sort of "patriotic indoctrination." Justice Frankfurter claimed, "The ultimate foundation of a free society is the binding tie of cohesive sentiment. Such a sentiment is fostered by all those agencies of the mind and spirit which may serve to gather up the traditions of a people, transmit them from generation to generation, and thereby create the continuity of a treasured common life which constitutes a civilization." Quoting from another decision cited in this book regarding flag desecration, *Halter* v. *Nebraska* (1907), Justice Frankfurter wrote, "We live by symbols. . . . The flag is the symbol of the Nation's power, the emblem of freedom in its truest, best sense. . . . It signifies government resting on the consent of the governed; liberty regulated by law; the protection of the weak against the strong; security against the exercise of arbitrary power, and absolute safety for free institutions against foreign aggression."

Frankfurter then turned to the power of legislative bodies to help mold the traditions that secure our freedom, including the pledge and flag salute:

Justice Felix Frankfurter.

The case before us must be viewed as though the legislature of Pennsylvania had itself formally directed the flag salute for the children of Minersville; had made no exemption for children whose parents were possessed of conscientious scruples like those of the Gobitis family; and had indicated its belief in the desirable ends to be secured by having its public school children share a common experience at those periods of development when their minds are supposedly receptive to its assimilation, by an exercise appropriate in time and place and setting, and one designed to evoke in them appreciation of the nation's hopes and dreams, its sufferings and sacrifices. The precise issue, then, for us to decide is whether the legislatures of the various states and the authorities in a thousand counties and school districts of this country are barred from determining the appropriateness of various means to evoke that unifying sentiment without which there can ultimately be no liberties, civil or religious.

Frankfurter then echoed a sentiment that has been heard by those complaining of judicial activism throughout the latter part of the twentieth century. Continuing with his strongly worded patriotic appeal, Frankfurter wrote, ". . . The courtroom is not the arena for debating issues of educational policy. It is not our province to choose among competing considerations in the subtle process of securing effective loyalty to the traditional ideals of democracy, while respecting at the same time individual idiosyncracies among a people so diversified in racial origins and religious allegiances. So to hold would, in effect, make us the school board for the country. That authority has not been given to this Court, nor should we assume it." Frankfurter concluded with an acknowledgment that parents have an important role in imparting values, and if the parents desired an exemption from this patriotic ceremony, then the parents and any other objectors needed to seek relief from the legislature, not from the courts. With this final lesson in civics via Frankfurter, he reversed the lower court decision on behalf of the Gobitis family and ruled in favor of the Minersville School District.

During the next three years, the nation experienced many changes—changes that would reshape the world's history into the twenty-first century. The United States entered World War II after the Japanese attack on the U.S. naval fleet in Hawaii. Soldiers from the United States were fighting in the Pacific and in Europe. Jehovah's Witness groups were increasingly persecuted and in some cases prosecuted. The state of West Virginia, a neighbor to Pennsylvania, followed Justice Frankfurter's suggestion and passed a law mandating flag salute and pledges in every public school throughout the state of West Virginia.

The policy adopted by the West Virginia legislature is important because it touches on the public educational debate today regarding the promotion of the values of western civilization, or an American canon, as opposed to the balkanization that some claim would result from adopting a multicultural curriculum. The West Virginia legislature seemed to have few reservations about promoting patriotism or what some believed was indoctrination and blind obedience to authority. The new law required "all schools to conduct courses of instruction in history, civics, and in the Constitutions of the United States and of the State for the purpose of teaching, fostering and perpetuating the ideals, principles and spirit of Americanism, and increasing the knowledge of the organization and machinery of the government." The act also required all private, parochial, and denominational schools to prescribe courses of study "similar to those required for the public schools."

At the direction of the State Superintendent of Schools, the West Virginia Board of Education adopted a resolution containing recitals taken largely from the Court's *Gobitis* opinion. The Board of Education required all teachers and pupils to participate in the salute and pledge honoring the nation. Failure to participate would be considered an act of insubordination and dealt with accordingly. The specific salute and pledge included the following instructions: The saluter was to make a "stiff-arm salute," right hand raised with palm turned up while the following words were repeated:

> "I pledge allegiance to the Flag of the United States of America and to the Republic for which it stands; one Nation, indivisible, with liberty and justice for all." Note: No reference to "under God."

For students, failure to comply meant a charge of insubordination followed by the consequence of expulsion. Readmission would be denied until the student complied with the salute and pledge ceremony. While the student was out of school contemplating compliance, the district would report the student "unlawfully absent" and file against the student and parents delinquent proceedings. Such prosecution could subject the parents to a fine of $50 and a jail term of 30 days. The children were threatened with reformatories maintained for criminally inclined juveniles. One might ask, what civic lesson was being learned from the enforcement of this policy?

A group of parents practicing the Jehovah's Witness faith strongly opposed this new statewide policy. The parents sued in federal district court complaining that the new state policy violated their First Amendment free exercise of religion protection. Like the parents in Minersville, these parents noted in their complaint that compliance with the new state law promoting daily pledges and salutes would violate their religious law. Once again, the Jehovah's Witness parents informed the court that the flag is considered an image and pledging loyalty to this graven image would be sacrilegious. The Jehovah's Witness's pointed to the importance of verses 4 and 5 in Exodus, Chapter 20. Why should the Jehovah's Witness parents have to face eternal damnation for complying with a law that clearly violated their religious teachings? A three-judge panel of the federal district court restrained the Board of Education from enforcing the law on the plaintiffs. The Board immediately appealed this case to the United States Supreme Court.

The year was 1943 when the Court rendered a decision in this case, *West Virginia State Board of Education* v. *Barnette*. Justice Robert H. Jackson wrote the controlling opinion for a deeply divided court. Essentially, three justices concurred with

Justice Jackson's opinion but wrote separate concurring opinions, thus making six justices supporting Jackson's opinion, and three justices, including Justice Frankfurter, dissenting. Justice Jackson claimed that Frankfurter's opinion regarding the need to strengthen national unity was misdirected. For Jackson, the strength lies in protecting fundamental freedoms like those enunciated in the Bill of Rights, not in the recitation of a meaningless pledge. Justice Jackson wrote, "Government of limited power need not be anemic government. Assurance that rights are secure tends to diminish fear and jealousy of strong government, and, by making us feel safe to live under it, makes for its better support. Without promise of a limiting Bill of Rights, it is doubtful if our Constitution could have mustered enough strength to enable its ratification. To enforce those rights today is not to choose weak government over strong government. It is only to adhere as a means of strength to individual freedom of mind in preference to officially disciplined uniformity for which history indicates a disappointing and disastrous end."

Justice Jackson then drew a different portrait of education and public schools. According to Jackson's opinion, "Free public education, if faithful to the ideal of secular instruction and political neutrality, will not be partisan or enemy of any class, creed, party, or faction. If it is to impose any ideological discipline, however, each party or denomination must seek to control, or, failing that, to weaken, the influence of the educational system." In respect to Justice Frankfurter's concern that the Court could not serve as "the school board for the country," Justice Jackson wrote, "The Fourteenth Amendment, as now applied to the States, protects the citizen against the State itself and all of its creatures—Boards of Education not excepted. . . . That they are educating the young people for citizenship is reason for scrupulous protection of Constitutional freedoms of the individual, if we are not to strangle the free mind at its source and teach youth to discount important principles of our government as mere platitudes."

Jackson concluded with a call for national unity in upholding the Bill of Rights, not in coercing individuals through indoctrination and prosecution. Jackson stated,

National unity, as an end which officials may foster by persuasion and example, is not in question. The problem is whether, under our Constitution, compulsion as here employed is a permissible means for its achievement. . . . Struggles to coerce uniformity of sentiment in support of some end thought essential to their time and country have been waged by many good, as well as by evil, men. Nationalism is a relatively recent phenomenon, but, at other times and places, the ends have been racial or territorial security, support of a dynasty or regime, and particular plans for saving souls. . . . Those who begin coercive elimination of dissent soon find themselves exterminating dissenters. Compulsory unification of opinion achieves only the unanimity of the graveyard. . . . It seems trite but necessary to say that the First Amendment to our Constitution was designed to avoid these ends by avoiding these beginnings. . . . We set up government by consent of the governed, and the Bill of Rights denies those in power any legal opportunity to coerce that consent. Authority here is to be controlled by public opinion, not public opinion by authority.

Jackson then ended with this oft-quoted passage: "If there is any fixed star in our constitutional constellation, it is that no official, high or petty, can prescribe what shall be orthodox in politics, nationalism, religion, or other matters of opinion, or force citizens to confess by word or act their faith therein." Jackson then ruled that the Minersville decision and the holdings of any per curiam decisions that had proceeded and foreshadowed it were overruled. The Jehovah's Witness children could now attend school without fear of coercion, prosecution, and punishment.

Why did the Court change its mind in a short three years? As mentioned several times in this chapter and others, we must analyze conflicts within the contexts of the circumstances. Many significant events had occurred between the *Gobitis* ruling and the *Barnett* opinions, including the declaration of war in 1941, our intelligence sources and some reportage of Nazi atrocities, persecution of the Jehovah's Witnesses, and probably most important, the retirement and subsequent appointment of new justices to the Supreme Court by President Franklin D. Roosevelt (judges more sympathetic to minority rights).

Clubs in School

Students exercising their religious freedoms in public schools involve clubs that often meet during or after school, use of school facilities, and released time for students to exercise their religious freedom and education.

While we know that many religious practices in schools, prayer and bible reading for example, have been deemed unconstitutional under the establishment clause, in some situations students have won the right to engage in religious practice in the public schools. The real test of such practice occurred in 1990, *Board of Education of the Westside Community Schools* v. *Mergens.* This case applied the Equal Access Act to gain an opening inside the public schoolhouse door. The Equal Access Act was passed during the Reagan administration and was intended to allow church groups to have equal access to public school facilities. The Equal Access Act, passed by Congress, provided that schools receiving federal funding and permitting noncurricular activities and club (e.g., chess club, photography club) meetings had to allow students to equal access to school facilities even for religious activities.

The *Mergens* case became a free exercise and Equal Access case because Bridget Mergens, a student with strong religious convictions, and other students and parents sued in federal court claiming that the Westside Community School prohibited their free exercise of religious beliefs. In filing the complaint, Mergens and other Christian students argued that the school singled their group out and denied them access to the school. The Mergens group admitted that they wanted to establish a Bible club. The club would not need a faculty sponsor, but they did wish to use school facilities for their meetings. The purpose of the meetings would be to allow students an opportunity to read and study the Bible, to have Christian fellowship, and to pray together. Membership in this club would be voluntary and open to all students regardless of their religious affiliation. Mergens also argued that the exclusion of their Bible study group amounted to a denial of the students' freedom of speech, association, and free exercise of religion, in addition to violating the 1984 Equal Access Act.

The School Board responded that the Equal Access Act did not apply to Westside, and even if it did, the Board argued that this act itself violated the establishment clause of the First Amendment. In addition, the School Board argued that Westside did not establish a limited public forum for any club, only clubs that had curriculum-related goals. Westside claimed that all 30 student clubs are curriculum related because they support the intent of the school's curriculum to "further the school's overall goal of developing effective citizens by requiring student members to contribute to their fellow students."

The justices of the Supreme Court considered the language of the Equal Access Act, "It shall be unlawful for any public secondary school which receives Federal financial assistance and which has a limited open forum to deny equal access or a fair opportunity to, or discriminate against, any students who wish to conduct a meeting within that limited open forum on the basis of the religious, political, philosophical, or other content of the speech at such meetings." The justices defined a "limited open forum" as one existing whenever a public secondary school "grants an offering to or opportunity for one or more noncurriculum-related student groups to meet on school premises during noninstructional time." The majority of justices suggested that a limited public forum is triggered, or exists, anytime a public school permits one or more "noncurriculum-related student groups" to meet on campus before or after classes. One major consideration was a determination that Westside was not providing a "limited public forum." Ten student clubs were challenged by Mergens and others as being noncurriculum related. The clubs they identified included Interact (a service club related to Rotary International), Zonta (the female counterpart to Interact), Chess club, Subsurfers (a club for students interested in scuba diving), the National Honor Society, the Photography club, Future Business Leaders of America, and the Student Advisory Board and Student Forum (two clubs focusing on student government). The School Board contended that all these clubs were curriculum-related.

The majority of justices saw the Board's claim as invalid; they rejected this argument and claimed that Westside had indeed established limited public forums. The majority opinion stated, "Allowing such a broad interpretation of 'curriculum-related' would make the Equal Access Act meaningless. . . . A public secondary school cannot simply declare that it maintains a closed forum and then discriminate against a particular student group on the basis of the content of the speech of the group."

Since the Court concluded that Westside had established a limited public forum, the Court ruled that Westside could not deny Mergens and her friends an opportunity to have their Bible study club. The majority of justices claimed that they were able to decide this class on failure to comply with the Equal Access Act and did not need to consider any First Amendment constitutional violations.

By 1993, the Supreme Court applied the First Amendment in another conflict involving the right of groups to use public schools for specific religious purposes. In *Lamb's Chapel* v. *Center Moriches Union Free School District,* ruled that public school boards in New York could not open their schools for some groups yet exclude others. Such exclusion amounted to a violation of the free speech clause of the First Amendment.

In *Lamb's Chapel*, an evangelical church sought permission to use public school facilities to show a film series on traditional Christian family values. The public school acknowledged that the facilities had been used by social and civic groups but noted that the school board regulations specifically prohibited use of the school for religious purposes. Although the federal district court and the Court of Appeals agreed with the school district and upheld their right to exclude certain types of programs, like the proposed religious series, as long as the exclusion was "reasonable and viewpoint neutral," a significant majority of the United States Supreme Court disagreed with this finding, and concluded that denial of the facilities violated the church's First Amendment protections.

It should be noted that the Equal Access Act has now opened many schools to other clubs and club meetings and activities. The myriad of clubs included gay and lesbian youth alliance clubs, "skinhead clubs," and other groups that some from the religious community have found offensive. The gay and lesbian clubs have particularly come under assault, with states like Utah trying to forbid the use of school facilities for any non-school-related group. This issue will likely be the focus of litigation and legislation for years to come.

The establishment clause of the First Amendment had been triggered far more often than the free exercise provision until the 1990s. Some previous religion cases of the 1990s have been examined in other parts of this book. The conflicts over public schools in any way supporting religious expression will probably continue as public policy issues, as powerful constituencies continue to debate school prayer, funding of vouchers that may be used for religious schooling, and other

such issues with the group known as the "Christian Right."

There have been many establishment clause cases that have caused our current Congress to consider religious liberty and religious equality laws as well as constitutional amendments that will permit greater religious practice in our public schools. Although some of these matters were touched upon in chapter 9, as an aspect of the rights of religious groups, some issues deserve closer attention for their impact upon the public schools.

In 1947, in *Everson* v. *Board of Education,* the Supreme Court considered the issue of parents being reimbursed by the government for transportation costs to schools, public, private, or parochial. A New Jersey law provided for this reimbursement. Some parents filed a suit complaining that such reimbursements to parents of children who attended parochial school or other sectarian schools amounted to support for religion, a clear violation of the establishment clause. A highly divided Supreme Court ruled on behalf of the state law and thus permitted parents to continue to be reimbursed. The majority opinion emphasized that the reimbursement really went to the parents and thus focused solely on safe transportation for children, and was neutral in regards to religion. This issue of neutrality has hit high marks in recent years, beginning with a case examining tax deductions to parents to pay for certain school-related costs, *Mueller* v. *Allen,* 1983.

In the *Mueller* case, the state of Minnesota had a law permitting state taxpayers to claim a deduction on their state income tax for certain school-related items. Parents were permitted a $500 deduction per child for parents with children in kindergarten through sixth grade, and a $700 deduction per dependent for children in grades 7 through 12. The complainants in this case were parents who argued that the granting of such deductions amounted to state support for religious instruction. A critical argument from these parents seemed to be an economic analysis of school costs. These parents pointed out to the court that few parents, if any, of public school students could justify $500 to $700 in deductions. Therefore, those who took full tax deductions clearly used these deductions to offset the tuition costs for their children in parochial, sectarian schools. The justices in this case applied what was considered the basic test for establishment case, the Lemon test, based on the case *Lemon* v. *Kurtzman,* 1971. The Lemon test is a three-prong test, and any affirmative answer to any of the following questions would trigger the establishment clause and cause the government action to be unconstitutional. To apply the Lemon test, think of the letters:

- P = PURPOSE OF THE GOVERNMENT ACTION

- E = EFFECT OF THE ACTION

- E = EXCESSIVE ENTANGLEMENT

In other words, does the government action have a stated purpose of supporting or endorsing religion? Does the action have the effect of favoring religion? And lastly, does the action create an excessive entanglement with government and religion?

In applying this test to the Minnesota statute, five justices believed that the answer to all three questions was no, and therefore, the establishment clause was not being violated in this case. According to the majority of justices, the tax deduction was taken by the parents and open to all parents regardless of where the children attended school. For these justices, there was no direct aid to parochial, private, sectarian schools. According to the majority opinion, "A state's decision to defray the cost of educational expenses incurred by parents, regardless of the type of schools their children attend, evidences a purpose that is both secular and understandable." The five-member majority then concluded their opinion with an ominous forecast of where such cases might be going. Justice Rehnquist, writing for the majority, praised the role of private educational institutions in our nation, writing, "Finally, private educational institutions, and parents paying for their children to attend these schools, make special contributions to the areas in which they operate." Quoting from an earlier opinion, *Wolman* v. *Walter* (1977), Rehnquist recalled, "Parochial schools, quite apart from their sectarian purpose, have provided an educational alternative for millions of young Americans; they often afford wholesome competition with our public schools; and in some States they relieve substantially the tax burden incident to the operation of public schools." Rehnquist then concluded with a summation of why this statute does not violate the three-prong Lemon test. In conclusion, Rehnquist wrote, "Thus, we hold that the Minneso-

ta tax deduction for educational expenses satisfies the primary effect inquiry of our Establishment Clause cases. . . . Turning to the third part of the Lemon inquiry, we have no difficulty in concluding that the Minnesota statute does not 'excessively entangle' the state in religion."

Where will this slippery slope end? If legislators can give tax deductions, can they also give tax refunds, or even more directly, may state legislatures pass a law that permits parents to receive an educational voucher directly from the state that they may use to send their children to a school of their choice? The U.S. Supreme Court will likely be called upon to answer these questions before the end of the twentieth century.

Public School Vouchers

The issue of vouchers, free choice, and the future of public schooling will continue to be the focus of major public policy debates at the state and federal level. Much is being written about school choice. Some states have granted permission for parent reimbursement for school transportation and school textbooks. Some have suggested that such differences will rise up once again as different state legislatures attempt to expand choice and voucher programs. Again, check out the state constitutional provisions.

Establishment clause confrontations in schools occurred throughout the late twentieth century, involving both student and school cocurricular activities as well as the content of what is taught in the classroom.

School Prayer

Many of the Bible reading and official prayer cases have been reviewed in an earlier chapter. A recent case deals with public schools setting aside specific time for moments of silence, prayerful thought, or silent voluntary prayer. Efforts at enacting some comparable practice have been tried throughout U.S. schools, especially after the *Engel* and *Schempp* decisions. The Court addressed the issue in 1985 in the case *Wallace* v. *Jaffree.* In this case, an African American lawyer living in Mobile, Alabama, filed suit in federal court challenging three different Alabama statutes that in one way or another, according to Jaffree, promoted religion in the Mobile public schools.

Jaffree filed the suit on behalf of his young children. He claimed that they faced harassment and intolerance because they did not participate in daily prayer or moments of silence.

The three Alabama laws allowed for a one-minute period of silence in all public schools for meditation (1978 statute), a period of silence for meditation or voluntary prayer (1981 statute), or "teachers to lead willing students in a prescribed prayer to Almighty God . . . The Creator and Supreme Judge of the world" (1982 statute). By time the case reached the Supreme Court, lower federal courts, especially the Court of Appeals, had dealt with two of the three laws in question. Jaffree even dropped his opposition to the "moment of silence for meditation," but he wanted the other statutes declared unconstitutional. The Court of Appeals actually declared the other two practices unconstitutional, as violating the establishment clause. The lower court federal judge, Brevard Hand, had upheld all of the statutes, although he acknowledged that the latter two clearly respected an establishment of religion. Hand had reasoned that the state of Alabama has the power to establish a state religion if it so chooses. The Court of Appeals reacted strongly to such an interpretation and the Supreme Court, in a majority opinion written by Justice Stevens, gave Judge Hand a lecture about the importance of the Fourteenth Amendment, the incorporation doctrine, and the individual freedoms of the First

Amendment being protected from any government action, local, state, or federal. When the case reached the Supreme Court, the opinion focused on only one of the remaining laws: the period of silence for meditation or voluntary prayer. The other two statutes had been addressed and decided, the moment for meditation was permissible; the prayer was out.

Faced with determining if a moment of silence for meditation or voluntary prayer violated the establishment clause, the majority of justices looked to the intent of the Alabama legislature in passing this law. In the *Jaffree* case, the Court had reviewed testimony in the lower federal court trial. At trial, the prime sponsor of the law in controversy had testified. The sponsor, State Senator Donald G. Holmes, had testified that his bill was an "effort to return voluntary prayer to our schools. . . . It is a beginning and a step in the right direction." With this testimony as part of the record, Justice Stevens's opinion was clear and concise. Stevens wrote, "The Legislature enacted (this law) . . . for the sole purpose of expressing the State's endorsement of prayer activities for one minute at the beginning of each school day. . . . Such an endorsement is not consistent with the established principle that the Government must pursue a course of complete neutrality toward religion."

Proponents of specific prayer provisions in the public schools did not end their quest with the

Jaffree decision. Some school authorities continued to permit and even initiate prayer for school related events such as graduation ceremonies and honors awards. Finally, in 1992, the Court addressed the issue of invocations and benedictions led by clergy at official school activities like graduation. In *Lee* v. *Weisman,* a narrow majority of the Court ruled against permitting school sponsored prayers.

Some proponents of officially sanctioned prayer in public schools saw *Weisman* as a partial victory because the majority of justices abandoned the traditional three-prong Lemon test. In the *Weisman* case, the majority of the Court applied a coercion test. In other words, was there anything in the practice that amounted to government coercing participation in or sanctioning of the religious activity? In this case, the Court pointed out that the school produced a graduation ceremony pamphlet that included information about a religious ceremony, like the invocation and benediction, to be used during graduation ceremony. Although the guidelines called for the prayer to be universal and given by clergy and no public school official involved in saying the prayer, the Court noted that the mere mentioning of the ceremony in the school produced pamphlet indicated an intent on the part of the school (i.e., government) to control the religious ceremony. The second factor the Court considered was the coercion involved in making attendees hear, see, and observe the religious ceremony during graduation, even if the ceremony offended their religious or nonreligious beliefs. The Court concluded that psychological and social pressure did exist for all of those attending. Lastly, the Court addressed the school's argument that graduation is a voluntary school activity. While acknowledging that the graduation ceremony was voluntary and not related to actually receiving one's diploma, the majority of the Court concluded that most high school seniors expected to participate in graduation as a culmination of their high school experience, and therefore, the graduation and the religious ceremony were not really voluntary but, in this case, were part of actual high school activities.

Did the *Weisman* case put an end to school-sponsored or -sanctioned ceremonies? Hardly. In the last few years, lower federal courts and the different Courts of Appeals have issued conflicting rulings depending on the facts of the religious incidents. For example, if some students spontaneously speak a prayer at a school function, is this government-sanctioned prayer? In some cases, courts have suggested if the facts support that the student prayer was purely spontaneous and occurred at a voluntary school event (e.g., a football team kneeling in the locker room before a game and a student giving a prayer), then the Court has not viewed this as the school coercing students to participate in this event. Other courts have suggested that if the school expects or can forecast a likelihood that students will attempt to inject a religious practice at a school-sponsored function, then the school must take steps to keep the school neutral and not supportive of the planned religious activity. Since the Supreme Court sometimes attempts to resolve conflicting rulings from the lower federal courts, the Court may take one of these cases in the near future.

In the interim, the Republican-led Congress, combined with some conservative Democrats, have proposed a "Prayer Amendment" as well as some federal statutes that the proponents believe would sustain constitutional challenge. The two prayer amendments awaiting action from the 105th Congress have the following wording: "Nothing in this constitution shall prohibit the inclusion of voluntary prayer in any public school program or activity. No person shall be coerced by the United States or by any State to participate in such prayer. Neither the United States nor any State shall prescribe the content of any such prayer" (House Joint Resolution 20); and "Nothing in this Constitution shall be construed to prohibit individual or group prayer in public schools or other public institutions. No person shall be required by the United States or by any State to participate in prayer. Neither the United States nor any State shall prescribe the content of any such prayer" (House Joint Resolution 12). In addition to these amendments, Republican Representative Henry Hyde introduced the "Religious Equality Amendment" in the 104th Congress. This amendment stated, "Neither the United States nor any state shall deny benefits to or otherwise discriminate against any private person or group on account of religious expression, belief, or identity; nor shall the prohibition on laws respecting an establishment of religion be construed to require such discrimination." Like the other proposed amendments, this amendment is intended to allow the government at all levels to be more accommodating to religious practices. Of course these amendments would not go in to effect until passed by Congress and ratified by three fourths of the states.

The other area of establishment clause cases have involved the conduct within the classroom: Who is taught, where are they taught, and what is taught?

The who and where questions have primarily arose when states or local schools have attempted to meet the needs of parochial or private school students. Using the Lemon test, the Court considered two cases addressing these questions in 1985, *Grand Rapids School District* v. *Ball* and *Aguilar* v. *Felton.* In the *Grand Rapids* case, the school district had adopted two programs, "shared time" and "community education," that provided classes, at government expense, to nonpublic students in classrooms located in and leased from the nonpublic schools. The shared time program offered students in parochial and nonpublic schools supplementary instruction, including remedial and enrichment math, reading, art, music, and physical education classes that these students would not otherwise receive. These supplemental courses helped these students to fulfill the state of Michigan's core curriculum. Most of the classes were taught to elementary students, whereas the math remedial was available to high school students. Anyone, children and adults, could participate in the community education programs that commenced at the close of the normal school day. Many of the programs were offered in nonpublic school buildings, with teachers paid at public expense. The courses offered Wee Arts and Crafts, Home Economics, Spanish, Gymnastics, Yearbook Production, Drama, Humanities, Chess, Model Building, Nature Appreciation, and Christman Arts and Crafts.

A group of concerned parents brought suit in the *Grand Rapids* case, claiming that the school system was in effect establishing religious practice since the government paid the salaries of the staff and conducted the classes in nonpublic and parochial schools. In a narrow majority, Justice William J. Brennan wrote the opinion for the majority. Brennan applied the Lemon test (purpose, effect, and excessive entanglement). As to the purpose of the government action, Brennan and his majority agreed with the lower federal court and the Court of Appeals that the purpose of these two programs was secular and did not intend to advance any religion directly. Next Brennan considered the effect of the action. Brennan concluded that the shared time and community education program promoted religion in three ways: "1) the teachers participating in the programs may become involved in intentionally or inadvertently inculcating particular religious tenets or beliefs; 2) the program may provide a crucial symbolic link between government and religion, thereby enlisting—at least in the eyes of impressionable youngsters—the powers of government to the support of the religious denomination operating the school; and 3) the programs may have the effect of directly promoting religion by impermissibly providing a subsidy to the primary religious mission of the institutions affected." With this effect and entanglement, Brennan ruled that these programs violated the establishment clause of the First Amendment.

In the second case, *Aguilar* v. *Felton,* the Court considered a program funded with federal dollars to pay public school employees to teach "Title 1" programs in parochial schools in New York City. The Title 1 programs provided federal compensatory funding for remedial classes, reading skills, remedial mathematics, English as a second language, and guidance services. Regular public school staff (e.g., teachers, guidance counselors, psychologists, psychiatrists, and social workers) volunteered to teach in the parochial schools. The amount of time that each professional spent in the parochial schools was determined by the number of students in the particular program and the needs of these students. The complaining parents argued that once again government funds were being used to promote religion. The school district responded that this case was not like the *Grand Rapids* case for two reasons: first, the staff volunteered for the assignment, and second, the New York City public schools had established an elaborate supervisory structure to ensure that the federally paid staff did not engage in aiding or favoring religion in any way—in other words, to ensure that they conducted only secular programs.

Justice Brennan wrote the majority opinion for another close decision. Brennan claimed "the aid is provided in a pervasively sectarian environment" (the staff conducted the Title 1 programs in parochial schools) and "because assistance is provided in the form of teachers, ongoing inspection is required to ensure the absence of a religious

message." With these two factors, Brennan concluded, ". . . the scope and duration of New York's Title 1 program would require a permanent and pervasive State presence in the sectarian schools receiving aid. . . . This pervasive monitoring by public authorities in the sectarian schools infringes precisely those Establishment Clause values at the root of the prohibition of excessive entanglement." Once again, under the Lemon test, the government was found to have violate the establishment clause.

Ironically, the Clinton administration has asked the Supreme Court to review and overrule its 1985 decision in *Aguilar*. This presidential initiative was delivered by Solicitor General Walter Dellinger. Dellinger cited a dormant rule in federal rules of civil procedure that authorizes courts to release parties from earlier judgments on the basis of mistakes, inadvertence, excusable neglect, newly discovered evidence, fraud, or a variety of other grounds (see Rule 60 (b) under the Federal Rules of Civil Procedure). In this call to revisit the case, Dellinger revealed "newly discovered evidence" that the New York City Board of Education had paid for the cost of complying with the *Aguilar* ruling, which meant paying hundreds of millions of dollars for transporting parochial school students to public schools for instruction or teaching those students in mobile vans near the parochial schools. The irony is that most Court watchers believe that if the Court reexamines this

case, the result might be quite different because the composition of the Court has changed dramatically since *Aguilar* and *Grand Rapids*. The test to be applied might even be the coercion test and not the Lemon test.

Another content-oriented question is that, what if what is taught has some religious basis? Does such instruction and accompanying curriculum violate the establishment clause? One of the contemporary cases that was a present-day version of the Scopes trial was *Edwards* v. *Aguillard,* a case decided by the Supreme Court in 1987. In the 1970s and 1980s, many critics of teaching evolution re-emerged with what was presented as a scientific alternative, creation science, to the traditional evolution theory. Several states, especially in the South, adopted laws that required a balance treatment of creation science and evolution in the public schools. One of the first states to adopt such a law was Arkansas, the same state that had suffered defeat before the Supreme Court in *Epperson* v. *State of Arkansas* (1968). In the *Epperson* case, the Supreme Court claimed that the Arkansas law that made it a crime for a public school teacher to teach the theory of evolution was clearly unconstitutional. Writing for a nearly unanimous majority opinion, Justice Fortas concluded, "In the present case, there can be no doubt that Arkansas has sought to prevent its teachers from discussing the theory of evolution because it is contrary to the belief of some that the Book of Genesis must be the exclusive source of doctrine as to the origin of man." Therefore, Fortas summarized that such a practice was intended to favor "the fundamentalist sectarian conviction" to explain the reason for humankind's existence. Responding to this defeat, the state of Arkansas legislature enacted a balanced treatment of evolution theory in 1981. The legislative history made clear that this law challenged evolution not only as merely an alternative. The proponents of the creation science theory suggested that teaching evolution was a religious teaching: It amounted to secular humanism, and therefore, any teacher teaching evolution was in fact favoring the religion of atheism. The law was quickly challenged and by 1982, a federal court struck down this new law as violating the establishment clause (see *McLean* v. *Arkansas Board of Education*). On appeal, the Supreme Court let stand the lower court ruling.

Following this defeat, the Supreme Court agreed to consider a similar case emerging from Louisiana. In 1987, in *Edwards* v. *Aguillard,* the Supreme Court, in a majority opinion delivered by Justice Brennan, declared a Louisiana Creationism Act as unconstitutional. The Louisiana law required the state's public schools to offer "Balanced Treatment for Creation-Science and Evolution-Science in Public School Instruction." In striking down the law, Justice Brennan noted, "The Court has been particularly vigilant in monitoring compliance with the Establishment Clause in elementary and secondary schools. Families entrust public schools with the education of their children, but condition their trust on the understanding that the classroom will not purposely be used to advance religious views that may conflict with the private beliefs of the student and his or her family. Students in such institutions are impressionable and their attendance is involuntary."As in the *Epperson* decision, Justice Brennan noted that the underlying purpose of the Louisiana statute was an intent to advance a religious interpretation over an alternative, scientific theory clearly recognized by the larger scientific community. Brennan even acknowledged that the Creationism Act was a "product of the upsurge of 'fundamentalist' religious fervor." And then Brennan concluded, "In this case, the purpose of the Creationism Act was to restructure the science curriculum to conform with a particular religious viewpoint. Out of many possible science subjects taught in the public schools, the legislature chose to affect the teaching

of the one scientific theory that historically has been opposed by certain religious sects. As in Epperson, the legislature passed the Act to give preference to those religious groups which have as one of their tenets the creation of humankind by a divine creator . . . Because the primary purpose of the Creationism Act is to advance a particular religious belief, the Act endorses religion in violation of the First Amendment."

Although these creationism laws have been declared unconstitutional, their effect may have been achieved among many in the public schools. Science teachers often try to avoid discussing any theories regarding evolution or creation for fear of complaints from parents, reprimands from administrators, ostracism from fellow fundamentalist church members, or just the avoidance of controversy. In addition to this "chilling" effect, some proponents of creationism have developed a new tactic to introduce creation science in the public schools. This new approach, the Uniform Origins Policy act, calls for "disclosure of relevant scientific information that makes classroom presentations more objective by including both the strengths and weaknesses of concepts on origins presented by the public school teacher or textbook" (see "Creationism Is Not Dead" by Frederick Edwards, National Center for Science Education, Berkeley, California).

The cases involving creationism are linked to the larger struggle over what should be taught in the classroom. For some time, conservative fundamentalist groups have challenged curriculum and methods of teaching. One of the common attacks has already been mentioned, the suggestion that the public schools are promoting secular humanism and therefore violating the establishment clause because secular humanism favors atheism.

Soon Congress will be faced with the Parental Rights and Responsibilities Act, which will allow parents a greater voice in determining how their children will be educated. This act may easily be interpreted to mean that parents may opt out of programs that in some way offend their religious teachings. Opponents of this act point out that the bill will not only interfere with academic freedom in school, it will also make it more difficult to prosecute child abuse and neglect cases.

In terms of free speech and press in the schools, three cases stand out clearly. In *Tinker* v.

Des Moines Independent Community School District (1969), a majority of justices recognized the importance of the First Amendment in protecting the expression of students and staff, and the Court provided some parameters for deciding cases involving speech and expression in schools. Writing for the majority in *Tinker*, Justice Abe Fortas gave a ringing note of approval for symbolic speech that did not cause a disruption of the normal school process. The case has some unique facts, but essentially, three students were suspended by public school authorities for wearing black armbands as a symbolic protest of the Vietnam War. Justice Fortas concluded that public school officials had initiated an antiarmband policy to specifically suppress a certain viewpoint. Also, Judge Fortas noted that even with media and public attention to the protest, the schools had no reported disruptive incidents. The schools seemed to function without any record of disruption. Among the well-quoted phrases of *Tinker* was Fortas's declaration, "It can hardly be argued that either students or teachers shed their constitutional rights to freedom of speech or expression at the schoolhouse gate." Then Fortas concluded, "In the absence of a specific showing of constitutionally valid reasons to regulate their speech, students are entitled to freedom of expression of their views."

The *Tinker* decision has been tempered by two other free expression cases, although *Tinker* remains vital and vivid because students continue to rely on their constitutional protections to enforce certain speech and expression in schools. The two other cases, *Bethel School District* v. *Fraser* (1986), and *Hazelwood School District* v. *Kuhlmeier* (1988), are products of the post-Warren Court. They had the imprint of Chief Justices Burger and Rehnquist. In *Bethel*, the Court considered a case involving a student's nomination speech before a student assembly. The speech contained some passages that some felt were offensive, with possible sexual innuendo, although the speech was never considered to fall within the traditional categories of unprotected speech (e.g., it was not "fighting words" and not "obscene"). The student giving the speech with offensive passages was Matthew Fraser. The day following the speech the principal suspended Fraser and removed his name from possible consideration as the recognized honor student to give the commencement speech at the school graduation. The student sought relief in federal court to have the suspension removed from his record and to restore his academic standing by restating his name to the list of possible graduation speakers. Writing for the majority, Chief Justice Burger gave a lesson on civics and civility and suggested that Fraser had gone beyond tolerable boundaries of permissible speech. Burger quoted two noted historians, Charles and Mary Beard, in his majority opinion, saying,

> The role and purpose of the American public school system was well described by two historians, saying, 'public education must prepare pupils for citizenship in the Republic. . . . It must inculcate the habits and manners of civility as values in themselves conducive to happiness and as indispensable to the practice of self-government in the community and the nation' [quote from the Beards' book, *New Basic History of the United States*] . . . We hold that petitioner School District acted entirely within its permissible authority in imposing sanctions upon Fraser in response to his offensively lewd and indecent speech. . . . The First Amendment does not prevent the school officials from determining that to permit a vulgar and lewd speech such as respondent's would undermine the school's basic educational mission. A high school assembly or classroom is no place for a sexually explicit monologue directed towards an unsuspecting audience of teenage students. Accordingly, it was perfectly appropriate for the school to disassociate itself to make the point to the pupils that vulgar speech and lewd conduct is wholly inconsistent with the 'fundamental values' of public school education.

Tinker and *Bethel* both dealt with student expression, and everyday students are confronted with expression issues. Sometimes the conflict emerges from interpretations of dress codes (Are someone's colors truly gang related and likely to disrupt school, or is the student making a fashion statement? Is pierced jewelry in the nose or other body parts likely to cause disruption in the classroom, or is this a cultural or an individual statement?), to the wearing of sweatshirts with messages, to the reading of individual poetry that portrays "ghetto" and "barrio" life in the words of those living, even if such language is offensive to some?

These constitutional protections lead into another free speech and press case, and some other cases involving our Fourth, Fifth, and Eighth Amendment protections. All of these cases have been decided by the Supreme Court, so public school officials should have some guidelines to follow in applying the Constitution and those rights that are not shed when you enter school grounds.

The case of *Hazelwood School District* v. *Kuhlmeier* (1988), has set a standard for determining what is permissible regarding the content of any school function. In *Kuhlmeier,* a high school principal ordered the sponsor of the school newspaper to remove several articles from a monthly edition. The articles that were deleted involved student investigative reports on teen pregnancy, teen suicide, and the effect of divorce on teens. The students were never notified of the decision to delete the articles. Their first knowledge of the missing articles occurred on the day the newspapers were delivered to be distributed to the student body. Up until that moment, the students had seen page proofs, had received praise from their newspaper sponsor, and were anxious to see their work committed to the printed page.

Recently three students sought to restrain school authorities from deleting their articles in a student newspaper. The lower court federal judge ruled on behalf of the school authorities, noting that the articles may have provoked some disruption even though the students had followed all of the appropriate journalistic standards. The lower court judge claimed that the school principal served as a better judge of what will fall within given academic principles. The school principal claimed that the school newspaper was really a lab for the journalism class and as such the content of the paper had to follow the given school curriculum guidelines, and these particular articles went beyond those standards. For a variety of reasons, the Eighth Circuit Court of Appeals reversed the lower judge's ruling and clearly stated that the principal's actions had violated the students' First Amendment rights. The school district then appealed the case to the Supreme Court.

Writing for the majority, Justice Byron R. White reminded the readers of the opinion of the rollercoaster application of First Amendment protections in schools. White acknowledged that students do not shed their constitutional rights at the schoolhouse door, but then he proceeded to revisit the precedent established in the *Bethel* decision. White wrote, ". . . The First Amendment rights of students in the public schools 'are not automatically coextensive with the rights of adults in other settings,' [quoting from *Bethel*] . . . and (these rights) must be 'applied in light of the special circumstances of the school environment.' . . . A school need not tolerate student speech that is inconsistent with its basic educational mission." White went on to uphold the school official's authority to determine what is appropriate for any school-sponsored situation, including school newspapers, theatrical productions, and any other expressive activities that students, parents, and members of the public might reasonably perceive to bear the imprimatur of the school. Such a far-reaching decision has led to much discussion and debate about what is appropriate and has been at the core of some academic freedom claims raised by teachers (see for example, Cissy *Lacks*, English teacher, v. *Ferguson-Florissant School District,* as reported in the *St. Louis Post-Dispatch,*1996).

In regard to searches of students in public schools, read *New Jersey* v. *T.L.O.* (1985), and for drug testing of student athletes, see *Vernonia School District* v. *Wayne Acton* (1995). In each of these cases a majority of the Supreme Court applied the Fourth Amendment and concluded that the searches and the drug test were reasonable.

Students also have due process protections. In *Goss* v. *Lopez* (1975), the Court ruled that school officials must provide for a fair hearing anytime a student is denied schooling for more than ten days. As mentioned earlier this standard is even more stringent when it applies to special needs learners.

The Court has even considered corporal punishment under a case where parents claimed that the paddling of their sons violated the Eighth Amendment's protection from "cruel punishment," (see *Ingraham* v. *Wright,* 1977). Although the Court concluded that this particular paddling did not constitute "cruel and unusual punishment," the Court did suggest that some paddling might be excessive and violative of the Eighth Amendment. The majority opinion also offered parents several other remedies if they opposed the corporal punishment policy. Parents could work to change the policy; parents and other citizens could lobby state legislators to pass a state law prohibiting corporal punishment in all public schools; and parents could always file civil and criminal charges against a school official if he or she actually assaulted a student.

Each day students and staff are confronted with conflicts that often involve fundamental freedoms (e.g., expression, privacy, due process, and an equal voice and vote). Plainly, education rights

READING, WRITING AND REINFORCEMENTS

exist even if there is no federal guarantee of a right to education. Although students, faculty, parents, and school administrators cannot know all the nuances of their various rights and obligations, this chapter should serve as an introduction to a topic of great and growing importance for all Americans.

Bibliography

Alexander, Kern, and M. David Alexander. *The Law of Schools, Students and Teachers.* 2d ed. St. Paul, Minn.: West Publishing, 1995.

Ascher, Carol, Norman Fruchter, and Robert Berne. *Hard Lessons: Public Schools and Privatization.* New York: Twentieth Century Fund, 1996.

Bauman, Paul C. *Governing Education: Public Sector Reform or Privatization.* Needham Heights, Mass.: Allyn & Bacon, 1996.

Edwards, Frederick. *Creationism is Not Dead.* Berkeley, Calif.: National Center for Science Education, 1995.

Fraser, James W. *Reading, Writing and Justice: School Reform as If Democracy Mattered.* Albany, N.Y.: State University of New York Press, 1997.

Gaddy, Barbera B., T. William Hall, and Robert J. Marzano. *School Wars: Resolving our Conflicts over Religion and Values.* San Francisco, Calif.: Jossey-Bass, 1996.

Orfield, Gary. *Dismantling Desegregation.* New York: W. W. Norton, 1996.

Richards, Craig, Rima Shore, and Max Sawicky. *Risky Business: Private Management of Public Schools.* Washington, D.C.: Economic Policy Institute, 1996.

Rose, Mike. *Possible Lives: The Promise of Public Education in America.* Boston: Houghton Mifflin Co., 1995.

Stainback, William, and Susan Stainback, eds. *Controversial Issues Confronting Special Education: Divergent Perspectives.* 2d ed. New York: Allyn and Bacon, 1966.

Vinovskis, Maris A. *Education, Society, and Economic Opportunity.* New Haven, Conn.: Yale University Press, 1995.

Williams, John. *Race Discrimination in Public Higher Education.* Westport, Conn.: Praeger Books, 1997.

Chapter 13

Employment Rights

Jay A. Sigler

There is no constitutional guarantee of a right to work in America. Although there have been as many as 80 separate federal job training and vocational education programs, such as the Job Corps for disadvantaged youth, there is no language in the Constitution to support, nor is there any strong political support for, the proposition that every American has the right to earn a living at a private or publicly supported job. Those Americans who have jobs or are seeking employment, however, are provided with a number of legal protections against discrimination and unfair treatment. Some of these protections are granted by federal or state statutes; others are rooted in the Constitution itself. Moreover, as will be shown, the development of civil rights for all Americans began with the elimination of the worst form of labor ever used in our nation: slavery.

Nationwide, the American Civil Liberties Union (the ACLU—the nation's most prominent general civil rights organization) receives more complaints about abuses by employers than about abuses by the government. Examples of abuses reported to the ACLU include the following:

- In California, a job applicant was denied a job because he refused to answer questions about his sex life on a "psychological test." At least a million job applicants are required to take similar tests every year.

- In Pennsylvania, an employee was fired because he pointed out serious safety defects in his employer's products. At least 200,000 Americans are fired every year, many of them because of "disloyalty" to the organization.

- In Indiana, an employee was fired because she smoked cigarettes in her own home. Approximately 6,000 American companies now attempt to regulate off-duty smoking and other private behavior.

There are approximately 100 million workers, part and full-time, public and private. All of those employed in the private sector are governed by a doctrine

called "employment-at-will." This doctrine, a product of nineteenth-century antilabor laws, gives employers the unfettered right to fire workers at any time, for any reason, or for no reason at all. The employment-at-will doctrine empowers employers to impose urine tests and intrusive "personality" and "integrity" tests on their employees. The power to fire-at-will permits employers even to suppress their employees' right to free speech somewhat. There are federal and state laws that prohibit discrimination against individuals on the bases of race, religion, sex, national origin, age, and disability, but these laws require only that employees be treated equally. Private employers are, therefore, generally free to do whatever they wish to their employees as long as they do so in a nondiscriminatory manner.

There are several categories of employees who are not governed by employment-at-will:

• Federal, state, and local government workers are broadly protected by the Fifth and Fourteenth Amendments, which prohibit the government from depriving any person of "life, liberty or property" without due process of law. These employees are considered to have a legally protected property interest in their jobs, and the right to due process places significant restrictions on arbitrary dismissals by government officials for reasons unrelated to job performance. Some additional protection is provided by federal, state, and local civil service laws.

• Virtually all collective bargaining agreements between labor unions and employers almost always stipulate that unionized employees can be fired only for just cause and only after a hearing before a neutral arbitrator. However, less than 20 percent of American workers belong to unions today, since union membership has been declining for years. Plainly, one of the benefits of union membership is avoidance of the employment-at-will doctrine. On the other hand, unions are often the reason why some employers seek to locate their facilities in areas of the nation where unions are weak.

• Senior executives, performers, athletes, and some other well-situated employees, whose numbers are very small, work under individual employment contracts that provide protection against unjust dismissal. Talented and fortunately well-placed individuals need not fear being fired. That is why baseball and football players cannot be dismissed for poor performances without violating their contracts. Obviously, music performers and theatrical performers are other examples of people who cannot be fired at will. Of course, contracts can be broken, but payment must be made under the written terms of the contract.

Employees do have some legal rights, including the right to speak freely, the right to a hearing, the right to privacy, and the right not to be victims of discrimination. Women and men have the right to be paid equally for the same work. Both have the right not be subjected to sexual harassment. Handicapped and disabled persons have rights of more limited kind. However, these legal rights are not as clear and well-defined as other civil liberties, especially since most of them are given by statute, whereas others, such as rights of minorities, are deriven from the Constitution. The civil rights of employees may change as statutes are amended or court interpretations change. Employee rights lack the fundamental character of rights found in the Constitution or civil rights legislation.

Employers have legal rights that arise out of labor agreements and from other types of law concerning private property. Their rights are inferior to civil rights and yield to them when public policy so provides. Employers still have the power to choose the nature and the terms of employment and to discharge employees when necessary or when they fail to perform their duties. Even these powers, though, may be restricted by government policy and by the terms of labor union contracts.

Some employee rights are less fundamental and more political than those mentioned in other chapters; that is the source of the controversy sur-

rounding the affirmative action issue. On the one hand, the Fourteenth Amendment guarantees the "equal protection of the laws." On the other hand, some employers have set up arrangements of preferential hiring for members of certain groups because the groups have been historic victims of discrimination. At stake is a clash of fundamental principles, raising the political issue of whether historical wrongs can be corrected by establishing a preference system.

Employee rights may also be somewhat different from state to state in the American federal system. No one should take the observations made in this chapter as true for all parts of the nation, since this area of legal rights is highly variable. Careful readers will need to examine the situation in their state to see whether it differs from the general conditions described in this chapter. State civil rights statutes differ in their coverage, usually depending on the number of employees in the private organization.

Described here are the general principles that have emerged governing the civil rights of employees. What is omitted are the principles of labor-management relations and the laws governing how contracts for labor are made. These matters are important but are not part of a worker's basic rights. Similarly, problems of unemployment compensation or payments for worker injury on the job are not discussed here.

Samuel Gompers (1850–1924)

This famous American labor leader was born in London in 1850. He immigrated to the United States in 1863, working as a cigar maker. An ardent labor unionist, he founded the Organized Trades and Labor Union, which was reorganized in 1886 to become the nation's largest labor union—the American Federation of Labor. As a labor leader Gompers opposed socialistic ideas and avoided most radical positions. Instead he favored a position advocating higher wages, shorter hours, and greater job freedom. By avoiding direct political activities he sought to gain respectability for the labor movement in America. Consequently, there never was an important labor union political movement in America.

Free Speech Rights of Employees

Employees sometimes criticize or complain about management. The boss is an object of gossip and fun in some workplaces. As long as harmless chatter about work doesn't interfere with productivity on the job, this kind of idle talk is acceptable and normal. However, the free speech that Americans expect to be an obvious right is subject to restrictions. The First Amendment does allow employees to speak out on "matters of public concern" but does not guarantee the same scope as would exist in the home, in a public place, or at a political meeting.

One public employee was fired for her remarks made after listening to a radio report of the attempted assassination of President Ronald Reagan. On March 30, 1981, after hearing the announcement of the attempt on Reagan's life, she turned to a fellow employee and said, "If they go for him again, I hope they get him." For this remark, which was overheard by a superior, she was fired on the spot. The Supreme Court ordered the reinstatement of the fired clerk, on the ground that her statement, although unpleasant, was a comment "on a matter of public concern," and it did not impair the discipline of her office. Offhand remarks to fellow government workers on political matters cannot be pun-

ished in this way, unless it is shown that morale is lowered or in some other way the function and the mission of the office is undermined.

Criticism of the organization may result in severe punishment by the employer. Certainly, a private company can fire an employee simply for being disloyal or for interfering with the work of the organization. Even in government civil service positions, which are usually protected by some form of job tenure, employee criticism can result in harsh penalties.

The First Amendment safeguards political speech, not simply employee gripes or complaints. Matters that are purely of personal interest are not protected by the First Amendment. Employees who complain about low pay or poor working conditions may be disciplined for these remarks. Unhappy workers cannot hide behind the Constitution and may suffer for their acts and speech so long as only private matters are at stake.

Courts have ruled that employees can be fired or otherwise disciplined for acts that "interfere with harmony among co-workers" or "interfered with a close working relationship between the employee and the supervisor in a situation that called for personal loyalty and confidence."

Whistleblowers

Government employees have the right to speak out and to communicate what they regard as illegal actions or mismanagement. The federal whistleblower statute protects federal workers from retaliation for revealing misdeeds of other public employees. Whistleblowers who are fired or otherwise punished for revealing embarrassing information to the public may have their rights vindicated in a later hearing. However, whistleblowers may be regarded as disruptive individuals, and they may lose their claims at a hearing if they cannot show that they attempted to correct the problems they revealed prior to going to the press or the public.

Many states also have whistleblower statutes, designed to protect public employees from being punished for honest attempts to reveal wrongdoing. In some states managers who retaliate against whistleblowers may be severely punished. Of course, the employee must prove that actions taken against him or her were directly related to the whistleblowing activity.

Teachers

In 1968 the Supreme Court held, for the first time, that a government employer cannot fire or severely discipline an individual simply because they did not like something the individual said or wrote. In *Pickering* v. *Board of Education of Township High* (1968), the Court protected a teacher's constitutional right to free speech. This case involved a teacher who was fired for sending a letter to the local newspaper in which the school board was criticized. The Supreme Court asserted that a government employer cannot fire a public employee simply for exercising free speech, especially not a teacher, since "teachers are, as a class, the members of the community most likely to have informed and definite opinions as to how funds allotted to the operation of the school should be spent."

Teachers have free speech rights to discuss political issues, and they may show their support for political issues in restrained fashion, but they may not incite students to violence. During the Vietnam War some teachers and students in Des Moines, Iowa, expressed their objections to the war by wearing black armbands at school. The Supreme Court ruled that teachers and students have the right to make peaceful political statements in school, so long as their conduct did not "materially and substantially interfere with the requirements of appropriate discipline in the oper-

ation of the school" *(Tinker* v. *Des Moines School District,* 1969).

In another case, a teacher was fired after making a speech at an annual dinner of the teachers' association. During the speech she attacked and insulted many other teachers. The judge refused to order that the fired teacher be rehired. Teachers may not make false charges against principals or other school officials.

Employee criticism of higher officials is rarely protected by First Amendment considerations. The Supreme Court has also indicated that the right to free speech is not unlimited. There is a balance that must be made between the right of public employees to speak out on "matters of public concern" and the good order of the organization for which they work. There is always a risk that public employees will run to the newspapers with stories about their employers. Unless these were legitimate "matters of public concern," the courts will not allow the First Amendment to be used to complain about private issues that make individuals unhappy.

Employee Religious Practices

Religious discrimination in employment can be as pervasive a problem as racial or sexual discrimination. Title VII of the Civil Rights Act of

John L. Lewis (1880–1969)

John L. Lewis, the son of an immigrant Welsh coal miner, was himself a miner, and he became a major American labor leader. He rose through the union ranks to become president of the United Mine Workers of America, a group that won and retained the fierce loyalty of miners. The militant union was opposed to low wages and the harsh and dangerous working conditions imposed by mine owners. Lewis fought vigorously to build up the union and to increase its power. He was, at one time, among the most important officials in the American Federation of Labor, but he split from that national union in 1935 to form the rival Committee for Industrial Organization (CIO). For political reasons, however, John L. Lewis pulled the United Mine Workers out of the CIO in 1942. Lewis was an aggressive leader, often alienating other union officials and national politicians. Even so, he did succeed in improving the health, safety, wages, and working conditions of American coal miners.

1964 prohibits employers from discriminating on the basis of religion and seems to require employers to adjust their practices to accommodate an employee's religious observances. This federal law applies to nearly all businesses in the nation that hire more than 15 employees.

Religious discrimination in hiring may be more common than is generally believed. However, it is very difficult for a job applicant to prove that his or her religious preferences were the main basis for not being hired. There are a growing numbers of religious discrimination complaints before federal and state agencies but very few victories for complainants. Employers cannot ask an applicant or an employee questions that pertain to his or her religious preferences. Such questions would raise possible legal violations.

Perhaps one of the most unusual claims of religious discrimination was made by a Native American against a New Mexico trucking company. The Native American was a member of a church that used the substance "peyote" in its religious ceremonies. The prospective employee insisted that his religious use of peyote would not impair his ability to drive a truck. The company contended that its decision not to hire the applicant was based upon the significant health and safety risks that were posed by a driver who ingests peyote. In this case a federal court of appeals eventually held that the employer should make greater efforts to accommodate the religious practices of the applicant by making some arrangement that would ensure that he would not ingest peyote any time close to his working hours.

In spite of this unusual ruling, very few decisions of courts require employers to accommodate their business practices to the religious needs of their employees, let alone to those of job applicants. Employers are usually hesitant to hire employees of minority religions, but there is little they can do to inquire into the religious beliefs of applicants.

Once hired additional issues arise about what steps an employer must take to accommodate the religious practices of an employee. In a 1977 case, an airline employee (Mr. Hardison) of Trans World Airlines was a member of the Worldwide Church of God, a religion that prohibits its adherents from performing any work from sunset on Friday until sunset on Saturday. When Hardison was asked to work on Saturday he explained that his religion forbid him from doing so. However, his union was not willing to make adjustments that would violate the seniority rights of other workers. The only other means suggested by the employee was a four-day work week, excluding Saturdays.

When Hardison's religious rights were tested in the Supreme Court, the decision supported the employer. The Court was unwilling to impose on the Trans World Airlines any requirement to violate the union contract that established seniority rights or to set up a special four-day schedule for Hardison. In angry dissents three justices responded that the majority decision meant that an employer "need not grant even the most minor special privilege to religious observers to enable them to follow their faith," a conclusion that may present "adherents of minority religions with the cruel choice of surrendering their religions or their job" (*TransWorld Airlines Inc.* v. *Hardison*, 1977). However, the majority view is still the law.

In general, employees may be allowed by their employers to take unpaid leaves to accommodate their religious beliefs. Religious holidays or days prescribed for prayer or rest can be met by the sacrifice of an employee's pay, since pay can be reduced by the employer for unworked days. Employers can—and many do—allow for paid religious holidays as a matter of contract. School boards frequently allow teachers to take off for religious holidays, but each teacher contract arrangement is unique. Employees may use "personal time" under contracts for their religious practices. However, it is would be unreasonable for an employee to insist on payment for days missed for religious practices that were not agreed to or recognized by employers.

Seventh Day Adventists and Orthodox Jews have made claims against their employers about their religious needs regarding the Saturday Sabbath, but courts have usually not supported them. A Tampa, Florida, police officer who was a Seventh Day Adventist was not upheld in his claim that he needed his Saturday Sabbath for religious reasons. He was required to rotate shifts just like other Tampa police, which would mean that he would have to work on some Saturdays.

Your employer has a responsibility to make reasonable accommodations for your religious practices. However, this does not mean that the employer must suffer an undue burden. If your religion prohibits you from working on Saturday, the employer might decide not to hire you because the job requires some Saturday work. Large employers may be more able to make such an accommodation, because other workers could be enlisted to work on Saturdays. If your religious practices require you to wear particular garments, this can usually be accommodated. What is reasonable depends on the particular circumstances. It would be unreasonable for a worker to conceal his religious needs or to choose a Sabbath day arbitrarily.

The Fourth Amendment and Privacy Rights

The Fourth Amendment, which protects the privacy of citizens from "unreasonable searches and seizures," gives substantial protection to public sector employees against their employers' intrusions into their private affairs. In general, a government employer cannot order a search of an employee or his belongings in the absence of any suspicion that the particular employee has done something illegal.

Private sector employees, on the other hand, have virtually no legal right to question even the most intrusive practices of their employers. Employees can be subjected to "sniff" searches by dogs and searches of their lockers, desks, purses, and even their cars if they choose to park in the company parking lot. Both job applicants and current employees can be required to answer extremely intrusive questions about their private lives and personal beliefs on "psychological," "personality," and "integrity" tests.

Modern computer technology and new technological surveillance devices have made possible even more sophisticated forms of employer spying in the workplace. More and more employees are being subjected to electronic surveillance through video display terminals, observation by hidden cameras installed in work areas and locker rooms, and monitored telephone calls. With few exceptions, these increasingly widespread practices are legal. The privacy of private employees is not protected to any great extent by either federal or state constitutions, although there are some state statutes that have begun to recognize privacy rights in the workplace.

Lockers and desks at work may be subjected to searches under certain circumstances described by courts in various rulings. In one Texas case a private employer provided the employee with a lockable locker and a key to keep things inside private. Later the employer searched the locker without the permission of the employee. The employee sued. The jury found in favor of the employee's privacy rights, awarding $100,000 in punitive damages to the victim. The employee had a legitimate right to believe that her locker contents were private and personal.

However, an employer may warn employees that lockers and desks are subject to periodic searches; such a warning removes the employee's expectations of privacy. An unannounced and unpermitted search would probably be legal in such a situation. Even government employees will lose their Fourth Amendment rights when told in advance about the employer's plans to inspect desks and lockers.

The security guards at one U.S. Mint were subject to periodic searches. A bag of freshly minted quarters was found in one employee's locker. The regulations specifically states that "no mint lockers in mint institutions shall be considered to be private lockers." The search that produced the bag of money was legal and therefore no invasion of property. The lesson here is that employer rules may specify that desks and lockers are not private and personal spaces. The employee who hides things in these spaces can expect to be subject to searches. Otherwise, the only time that employee desks and lockers may be searched is when the employer has "reasonable suspicion" that something illegal will be found.

There is a greater right of privacy in your own clothing, pockets, wallets, and purses. People have a legitimate expectation that the things that they carry on their person are private. Employers, public or private, must have a very good reason for probing into the clothing, wallets, or purses of employees. A search would be improper unless a strong reason to suspect the employee of possessing stolen property, or something similar, existed.

In one case, a customs officer searched the jacket of an employee, looking for some emeralds that had disappeared. The jacket was hanging on a coat rack in plain view. The customs officer searched several persons but only those employees of whom he was suspicious. The search was upheld by a federal court as reasonable because the customs officer had good reasons to suspect the employee, who had handled the package of gems at some point.

In certain sensitive jobs, because of the high risk of dishonesty or national security, the employee's privacy rights may be curtailed. Employees who work in top-secret defense activity will be subjected to stricter searches than will normal employees, and courts will support those searches. Employees at gambling casinos are routinely searched for cash or chips as part of their employment. However distasteful these searches, there is strong reason for these sensitive or high-risk employees to know that they have less vigorous privacy rights than most other workers. That policy goes with the job.

Drug Testing

Drug testing poses special problems. Employers may not want to employ drug addicts and may screen them out at time of employment. Drug use on the job is bad for business and will make customers or clients want to go elsewhere. However, some drug users may restrict their practice to their own homes and not use them on the job. Even so, in jobs that require physical or mental sharpness a real risk to the public may be created by private drug use. As a result, many private and public employers are turning to pre-employment testing of applicants and random testing of employees for possible drug use.

With respect to urine testing for drugs, however, the U.S. Supreme Court has ruled that government employees can be required to take such tests, even if the employer does not suspect drug use, if the person's job is "safety sensitive," or if the job involves carrying a weapon or having access to classified information. Some federal courts have ruled that random strip searches and drug tests of prison guards are lawful, because of the nature of their work. However, other state and federal courts have ruled against random drug tests of other employees, including police.

The exact limits of the power to require drug tests are not yet known because the federal Supreme Court hasn't clearly drawn the limits on drug testing. A few states have begun to write policies for private and public employers. These statutes differ a great deal and should be examined with care by those interested in the issue.

In all but a handful of states, an employee can be required to submit to a urine test or can be terminated without legal recourse even where nothing about the employee's job performance or history suggests illegal drug use. If the employee refuses, he or she can be terminated without legal recourse. Private sector employees have virtually no rights regarding drug testing, unless legislation provides them.

Background Checks and Lie Detectors

When applying for a job, you should be aware that an extensive background check may be used to examine your past life. Background reports can range from a verification of an applicant's Social Security number to a detailed account of the potential employee's history and past conduct. Lots of pieces of information might be included in a background check. Driving records, vehicle registration, credit records, education records from school, criminal records, prior bankruptcy, medical records, military service records, records of licensing boards are just some sources that can be used, although access may be limited by some federal or state laws. In addition, statements by prior employers, teachers, and neighbors might be collected. Sometimes these background checks are made by companies in that business, such as Employer's Information Service, Interfact, Avert, and Pinkerton Security, and Investigation Services. Employers may also create a "clearinghouse" of information about potential employees.

Fourth Amendment privacy rights can be expanded by statute. Lie detectors had been used extensively by employers in the 1980s, especially for job applicants. In 1988, Congress passed the Employee Polygraph Protection Act, which bars the use of polygraphs (lie detectors), voice stress analyzers, and other similar mechanical job-screening devices by private employers. This statute does not apply to the pharmaceutical industry, to security-guard companies, or to governmental employees. Employees who are suspected of specific incidents of theft may be subjected to these devices, in any case. Mere rumors of undesirable conduct by an employee is not a ground to use these intrusive techniques.

Due Process of Law and Public Employees

The Fifth and Fourteenth Amendments to the Constitution say that governments cannot deprive people of "life, liberty, or property without due process of law." This is one of the oldest ideas embedded in the Bill of Rights, and it has a complex, special, technical meaning that lawyers and law professors can best understand. However, public employees have obtained certain rights as a result of court interpretations of the historic phrase "due process of law," and these rights can be simply explained.

In general, due process in this context means that a public employee has a property interest in his employment after he has passed a period of probation. Civil service workers get lifetime tenure once they have satisfactorily performed their jobs during a trial, probationary period. Teachers may get tenure in the same way. Governments do not have to grant tenure to their employees, but if they do the employees obtain a form of property that is protected by the idea of "due process of law."

People who have a property interest in their employment cannot be dismissed from their position without an opportunity to examine the charges against them. They must be notified of those charges, be given an explanation of the evidence against them, and be given an opportunity to present their side of the story before they can be dismissed. Some sort of trial-like process must be used to consider the charges against a public employee. A fair and impartial officer must preside at that hearing. The accused has a right to a lawyer and a right to cross-examine witnesses. Failure to provide these elements of fair procedure amount to a denial of "due process of law" and should result in a reversal of the adverse decision against the employee.

Due process also means that the procedures spelled out in an employee handbook must be followed. Other rights may be provided to public employees by state and local authorities under contracts. All these rights make it very difficult to fire a tenured public employee, because courts have held that a vital property right is at stake. In many cases, the dismissed employee not only may be rehired by decision of a judge or jury but may receive additional monetary damages as an award as compensation for the violation of the right to due process of law.

Private employees do not usually have such rights. They may be fired or disciplined without any hearing, or without any reasons given, unless union contracts create such rights. Usually, private employees may rely on the employee handbooks that state whatever rights the employer chooses to permit the employee to have. Courts usually require employers to honor the terms of their employee manuals. Of course, no one can be fired or punished on the job because of their race, religion, national origin, gender, age, or disability because of national policies against discrimination.

The Thirteenth Amendment and Its Enforcement

When the American Constitution was first written, one form of labor was implicitly preserved: slavery. Slavery was part of the American labor system in some states down to the Civil War (1861–1865). Slaves were regarded in slaveholding states as a form of property, subject to the complete control of their owners. Although not mentioned by name, slavery was an important issue at the Constitutional Convention in 1787. At

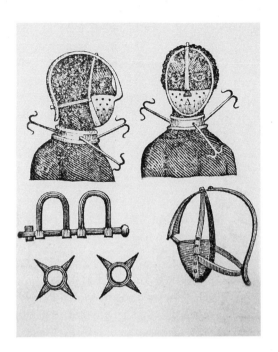

Pictured here are apparatus designed for the purpose of capturing slaves. Just before the Civil War, antislavery forces attempted to protect the status of slaves who escaped to free states by passing laws that prevented the slave masters from reclaiming the escaped slaves. In 1867 the Supreme Court struck down these antislavery fugitive slave statutes and declared them unconstitutional.

that time slavery was on the wane in the North, but the southern states looked upon it as a major source of wealth and production. Even though many northern states had abolished slavery (Pennsylvania, Massachusetts, Connecticut, Rhode Island, New York, and New Jersey, in that order), the delegates to the Convention made important concessions to proslavery sentiments.

The first concessions concerned the slave trade. Article II, Section 9 of the Constitution states: "The migration or importation of such persons as any of the states now shall think proper to admit, shall not be prohibited by Congress prior to the year one thousand eight hundred and eight." Any reference to slaves or slavery was avoided because of the taint of shame associated with the institution in the minds of many Americans. The word "slave" never appears in the American Constitution. Instead "such persons" or "other persons" was used when referring to slaves. Slavery clearly violated the claims of the equality of all Americans, but it took the Civil War to terminate the institution, long after most European nations had abolished it.

Just before the Civil War, antislavery forces attempted to protect the status of slaves who escaped to free states by passing laws that prevented the slave masters from reclaiming the escaped slaves. In 1867 Chief Justice Roger Taney, writing for a Supreme Court majority, struck down these antislavery fugitive slave

statutes and declared them unconstitutional. In the process, Taney declared that the Constitution did not protect the exslaves because they were not citizens. Congress, he said, had no power to forbid slavery. He reached this conclusion by lumping together slaves and freed Negroes as one group who "had been subjugated by the dominant race, and, whether emancipated or not, yet remained subject to their authority." This shocking racist view was not accepted by several other members of the Supreme Court, but it remained the law of the land until the termination of the Civil War.

The Thirteenth Amendment to the Constitution reversed the *Dred Scott* decision. The Amendment, when it was ratified in 1865, was the first change in the language of the Constitution since the Bill of Rights, 61 years earlier. Its language is simple:

> Neither slavery nor involuntary servitude, except as punishment for a crime whereof the party shall have been duly convicted, shall exist within the United States, or any place subject to their jurisdiction.

The institution of slavery was forever abolished in the United States. Involuntary servitude still exists in various forms, however. A more important effect and a lasting effect of the Thirteenth Amendment is that Congress was given for the first time specific power to enforce the civil rights of Americans against the states and private individuals. Section II of the Thirteenth Amendment declares, "Congress shall have power to enforce this article by appropriate legislation." Under this language Congress may enact penalties against private persons and corporations, whether or not the states have done so.

The historical importance of the Thirteenth Amendment reaches all Americans of all races. As the Supreme Court explained in 1906, the amendment is not "a declaration in favor of a particular people. It reaches every race and every individual, and if in any respect it commits one race to the nation, it commits every race and every individual thereof. Slavery or involuntary servitude of the Chinese, of the Italian, of the Anglo-Saxon are as much within its compass as slavery or involuntary servitude of the African."

The history of the 1866 Civil Rights Act demonstrates how hard it was to change the discriminatory policies of some of the states. In 1866, just after the Civil War, the Congress, in an attempt to protect the newly freed slaves against discrimination, passed the first of many civil rights acts. The Civil Rights Act provides that "all persons . . . shall have the same right . . . to make and enforce contracts . . . as is enjoyed by white citizens."

In 1865 and 1866 the former slave states had enacted statutes that regulated the legal and constitutional status of African Americans. Known as the "Black Codes," these state laws attempted to reimpose the controls imposed by slavery, even though slavery had been made unconstitutional by the passage of the Thirteenth Amendment.

The Black Codes covered many topics, but their provisions regarding employment—in various guises—permitted compulsory African American labor, even if according to the Constitution slavery was officially dead. Elaborate labor contract laws were put in place to allow continued oppression. Farm labor laws and apprenticeship laws were artfully constructed to preserve the elements of compulsory labor. Further, vagrancy and pauper laws were passed to punish those who were unwilling to work under these restrictions or were unable to work because of physical handicaps.

The Civil Rights Act of 1866 was the first act of national civil rights legislation. This first American national civil rights act was insufficient, by itself, to change the patterns of prior history, but it was a bold first step in that direction. The Civil Rights Act of 1866 was designed to benefit all Americans (not including American Indians), although its primary purpose was to overturn the *Dred Scott* decision by asserting that African Americans had the same right to enjoy the equal protection of the laws as was held by other citizens. In all jurisdictions citizens were to have equal rights to sue and to make contracts as well as to hold, purchase, sell, and inherit all forms of private property. These rights were accompanied by criminal provisions against violators. Anyone who, "under color of any law . . . or custom" prevented a citizen from enjoying those rights was subject to criminal penalties. The denial of civil rights was made a federal crime, enforceable, if needed, in federal courts. Federal judges were empowered to enforce judgments under the act, as they saw fit.

President Andrew Johnson, an ardent supporter of state's rights, vetoed the bill, but Congress voted to override the president. At first, the new statute was effective to protect the freed slaves, but as state courts resisted the statute, it

President Andrew Johnson, an ardent supporter of state's rights, vetoed the Civil Rights Act of 1866, but Congress voted to override him.

began to fall into disuse. Congress revived it several times to overcome the objections of the states and to reinvigorate the policy of protecting African Americans against discrimination. Sections of the statute survive today and form the basis of suits against public officials who interfered with the enjoyment of constitutionally protected rights. The reach of the statute has gone beyond the issue of employment, although it also still applies to discrimination in that area.

Involuntary Servitude and Peonage

Involuntary servitude remains a problem in America. The Civil Rights Act of 1866 and its several later companion acts were insufficient to manage a hidden problem: compulsory labor. Although slavery is gone, various labor practices remain that amount to forced labor.

From time to time you hear about a prominent entertainer who refuses to perform, although he or she is under contract to perform. No judge can force entertainers to perform, to sing, dance, or act against their will. To force them to perform would be a violation of their constitutional rights. It would amount to involuntary servitude. However, a judge could issue an order for an entertainer not to perform for another, in violation of a contract. Even then, a judge can do that only if the employee has talents that are "unique or extraordinary."

Athletes formerly were subject to monopolistic labor practices that prevented them from leaving one team to perform for another. No athletes can be compelled to play baseball or football against their will, even if they have a contract to play. However, courts are reluctant to hold that being prevented by contract from playing with another team amounts to involuntary servitude. Such exclusive contracts may violate other federal or state laws, but they do not amount to involuntary servitude.

More serious problems of this kind affect the poor and the vulnerable much more than they affect famous athletes and entertainers. The working conditions of some individuals so closely resemble slavery, whether or not a wage is paid, that shocking abuses of individual rights take place. One type of abuse is known as "peonage." This is a system of debt bondage in which a worker is held to provide services until he or she has paid off a financial obligation. At first, peonage was widespread in southern states, but now peonage problems may arise anywhere. Migrant farm workers and immigrant laborers of all sorts are at risk. Domestic workers, providing services in the home, can be reduced to peonage. Factory workers turning out cheap clothing are subject to this kind of exploitation.

In 1867 Congress passed the Peonage Abolition Act. The Act declared unlawful "the holding of any person to service or labor under the system known as peonage." When it was interpreted by the Supreme Court for the first time, peonage was restricted to forced servitude to repay debts. By 1911 the Supreme Court was prepared to apply the Thirteenth Amendment more broadly. The Court struck down the use of criminal penalties to enforce labor contracts. Slowly the laws of southern states, which kept African Americans and migrant workers in various forms of servitude, were peeled away, creating freedom for workers to leave exploitative employment.

Basic Text of Peonage Statute

UNITED STATES CODE
TITLE 42
CHAPTER 21
SUBCHAPTER I

§ 1994. Peonage abolished

The holding of any person to service or labor under the system known as peonage is abolished and forever prohibited in any Territory or State of the United States; and all acts, laws, resolutions, orders, regulations, or usages of any Terri-

tory or State, which have heretofore established, maintained, or enforced, or by virtue of which any attempt shall hereafter be made to establish, maintain, or enforce, directly or indirectly, the voluntary or involuntary service or labor of any persons as peons, in liquidation of any debt or obligation, or otherwise, are declared null and void.

Peonage has been defined by one federal court as "the exercise of domination over their persons and liberties by their master, or employer, or creditors, to compel the discharge, by service or labor, against the will of the person performing the service." There is direct federal power over peonage by virtue of Article II, the enforcement clause, of the Thirteenth Amendment.

The threat of deportation or of reporting illegal aliens has been used to extract labor from some workers. So far, courts have been divided in finding whether these situations amount to peonage, although it seems a close question.

In 1996 the Justice Department uncovered a coerced labor situation involving Thai immigrants (some of them illegal aliens) in California who were kept in virtual servitude to their "employers." The workers were confined to dormitories surrounded by barbed wire when not in the factory. The garment workers were released from their dormitories on rare holidays, such as Christmas, but were otherwise kept in close confinement while working at assigned tasks. This was an obvious case of illegal peonage.

Anyone, white or African American, Hispanic or Native American, could be subject to peonage. Slavery has not disappeared altogether in America.

The Fourteenth and Fifteenth Amendments

In labor matters these two post-Civil War amendments had little impact prior to the twentieth century. When the Congress passed a series of civil rights acts in 1866 it believed that the rights of all Americans would be secure against state action. Congress kept passing other versions of civil rights acts, which were met by some of the objections of advocates of state's rights. In particular the language of one section of the Civil Rights Act of 1871 seemed to clearly protect the rights all. Section 1983 of that Act protected "rights privileges or immunities" secured by the Constitution. Until

1873 many believed that this phrase covered all fundamental constitutional rights, but the Supreme Court read the language differently. The effect of the Supreme Court's narrow view held back enforcement of civil rights for decades. Gradually, the Supreme Court shifted its views, permitting many forms of federal actions to be taken against officials acting "under color of state law."

Now the Fourteenth Amendment extends many of the rights of the Bill of Rights to actions of state and local governments. For labor relations, another part of the Civil Rights Act has taken on great significance, because it uses the Fourteenth Amendment in a manner that reaches certain discriminatory practices of private individuals, too.

Section 1981 says that "all persons" have the same right to "make and enforce contracts" as "white citizens." Since an employment contract falls under this section, Congress can and does intend to prohibit private job discrimination; *so, private employers must provide the same opportunity to make employment contracts to blacks or other minorities as they extend to whites.* In fact, this section makes employment discrimination against Arabs, Asians, and Hispanics unlawful. Job discrimination against whites is also a violation of the law. However, because rights regarding private employment discrimination flow from a statute and not directly

from the Bill of Rights, Congress can change this policy for political reasons and choose to permit private job discrimination.

Discrimination and the Civil Rights Act of 1964

Title VII of the Civil Rights Act of 1964 is the basic federal antidiscrimination statute dealing with employment. Passed in 1964—a fitting memorial to slain President John Kennedy—this was the nation's first civil rights act passed in the twentieth century. The act consists of eleven titles, each concerned with a different aspect of discrimination. Title VII covers businesses that have 15 employees during at least 20 weeks of the year, and to government workers, federal, state, and local. Religious and educational organizations are covered by the act. However, Title VII allows religious organizations to discriminate on the basis of religion. Labor unions, state bar associations, and medical boards are subject to the provisions of the act.

The main section of Title VII says:

It shall be an unlawful employment practice for an employer:

(1) to fail or refuse to hire or to discharge any individual, or otherwise to discriminate against any individual with respect to his compensation, terms, conditions, or privileges of employment, because of such individual's race, color, religion, sex or national origin, or

Title VII of the Civil Rights Act of 1964 stipulates, among other things, that it is unlawful for an employer to discriminate on the basis of race, color, religion, sex, or national origin.

(2) to limit, segregate, or classify his employees or applicants for employment in any way which would deprive[rive or tend to deprive any individual of employment opportunities or otherwise adversely affect his status as an employee, because of such individual's race, color, religion, sex or national origin. (42 U.S.C.. sec. 2000e–2)

The Civil Rights Act of 1964 has been amended several times in the past few decades. The first amendment took place in 1972, expanding the powers of the Equal Employment Opportunity Commission (EEOC). It was changed again in 1978 to include protection for pregnant women and childbirth. In 1991 the act was amended again to adjust and alter certain Supreme Court interpretations. Changes in the basic act so far do not show any desire on the part of the Court to change the basic policies, but the changes do affect the outcome of certain claims and change the obligations of public and private employers somewhat.

Title VII violations repeatedly reach the Supreme Court for interpretation. This section is the most litigated part of the Civil Rights Act of 1964. Racial discrimination cases abound, but sex discrimination cases are also numerous, since the acts bans discrimination by gender. Although the main purpose of the act is to "open employment opportunities for Negroes in occupations which have been traditionally closed to them," the Supreme Court has read the statute to protect everyone, including women, Hispanics, American Indians, and whites (in affirmative action cases). The act specifically bans discrimination based on "the country where the person was born" or "the country from which his or her ancestors came."

The Civil Rights Act of 1964 created the Equal Employment Opportunity Commission (EEOC) the frontline federal agency responsible for the enforcement of the statute. The EEOC writes regulations under the act; investigates possible discrimination; attempts to settle complaints by negotiations prior to filing suits; and, if all else fails, files lawsuits on behalf of victims against businesses, governments, and other organizations. Obviously, EEOC action is dependent on how vigorously the agency pursues its work. Leadership and staffing of EEOC has become subject to political influence.

Title VII antidiscrimination suits are complex and take a long time to decide. First the victim of alleged discrimination must follow certain state and federal procedures before a suit is filed. Then the EEOC may file suit or conduct further investigations. The victim must make a formal charge in writing under oath, naming the individual or group that allegedly discriminated. The nature of the discrimination must be described, whether it be in the hiring, firing, promoting, or paying actions. These charges must be filed with the regional office of the EEOC, but if similar state or local antidiscrimination laws exist, the charge must first be filed with the state or local agency.

Intentional and unintentional discrimination is barred by the Civil Rights Act of 1964. If the employer's rules or practices have an adverse impact on minority groups or women, it may be illegal discrimination, even if it appears to be unintended or neutral. For example, one employer had a rule that forbade employees to transfer from one job to another. Since in the past only members of one race had been permitted to apply for certain jobs, the impact of the rule was illegal. Past discrimination was being maintained by this innocent-seeming policy.

In one landmark Supreme Court case, all job applicants had to have a high school diploma and also pass a Wonderlich Intelligence Test and the Bennett Mechanical Comprehension Test before they could be considered for employment. The firm, Duke Power Company, had no obvious intention to use these tests for the purpose of discrimination, yet the Supreme Court held them to be "discriminatory in operation" and illegal under the Civil Rights Act of 1964. The Court found that these particular tests prior to employment had an adverse impact upon a protected group, because they kept many more African Americans than whites from getting jobs at Duke Power.

Employers may require applicants to take tests, but the tests may not be "designed or used" to discriminate. Now the employer must prove that such pre-employment tests accurately predict later job performance. The test must "measure the person for the job, not the person in the abstract." A legal pre-employment test may measure a skill required for the job. A person who wants to be a mail carrier can be tested in the skills required for the job. A test for prison guards must not be biased against women, if the skills entailed are not gender based.

Height and weight questions may be proper only if the job involves strength and agility. Applicants to become police officers or fire fighters can be required to demonstrate stamina, skill, and a basic level of running ability. Teachers can be required to take a test to demonstrate that they know the subject matter to be taught. Height and weight requirements have been ruled to be discriminatory unless they bear a reasonable relationship to job requirements.

Job applicants may be required to be able to communicate in English. Basic fluency is usually a "business necessity" in dealing with customers, clients, and coworkers. These language requirements are not regarded as discrimination against those who cannot speak or understand English, since that skill can be learned and is needed on most jobs. However, it would be discriminatory to turn down an applicant who merely has a foreign accent. Only a radio announcer can be required to speak English with special clarity. A teacher or a librarian would be expected to speak better English than a factory worker, because of the greater need to communicate effectively.

Peculiar requirements of employment may make sense to the courts. Safeway stores had a requirement that employees have no beards. This was upheld as a legal effort to uphold the public image of the firm. On the same ground, the New York City Transit Authority was allowed to reject applicants who were on methadone maintenance. This rule was held to be a proper means to reassure the public about the safety of the city subways.

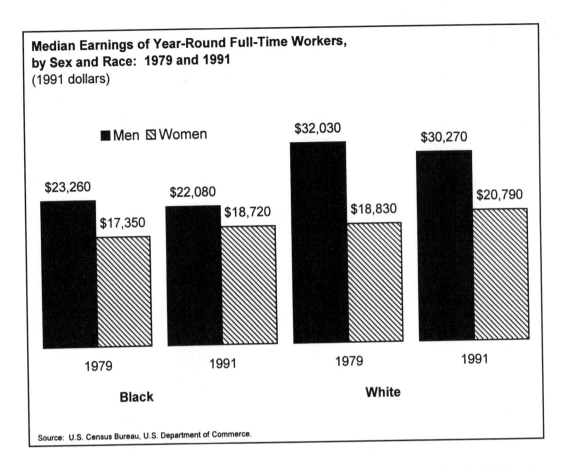

Median Earnings of Year-Round Full-Time Workers, by Sex and Race: 1979 and 1991
(1991 dollars)

■ Men ⊠ Women

$23,260 — $17,350 — 1979 — Black
$22,080 — $18,720 — 1991 — Black
$32,030 — $18,830 — 1979 — White
$30,270 — $20,790 — 1991 — White

Source: U.S. Census Bureau, U.S. Department of Commerce.

An employer can refuse to hire persons previously convicted of a crime only when the specific position being filled requires trust or integrity. But if the job involves merely maintaining the ground around a factory, such a requirement is illegal and discriminatory. Whether convicted criminals can work on the ground of public schools is not altogether clear, because a potential risk to young children may be involved.

In general, there are certain questions that may not legally be asked of job applicants. Employers cannot ask about age, race, sex, or religion. They cannot inquire about what church a person attends or what nationality his or her name may be. Women cannot be asked questions about their marital status, their children, or their plans for having children. All such questions are regarded by the EEOC as automatically objectionable, as they may be the basis of acts of discrimination.

The Equal Pay Act and Sex Discrimination

Governments cannot discriminate against people because of their gender. The Fourteenth Amendment guarantees "any person" the "equal protection of the laws." That is why the Supreme Court in 1971 struck down an Oregon statute that said "males must be preferred to females" in the selection of the administrator of the estate of a dead person. Two years later the Supreme Court declared unconstitutional the rule of the armed forces that treated female military personnel differently than male personnel in receiving dependency payments. Widowers and widows must receive the same kind of Social Security benefits for the same reason.

Most complaints of discrimination against women are filed as alleged violations of Title VII of the Civil Rights Act of 1964, as amended by the Equal Employment Opportunity Act of 1972. This statute prohibits discrimination by employers, employment agencies, and labor organizations on the basis of race, color, religion, sex, or national origin. It extends to employers with 15 or more fulltime employees and applies to hiring, discharge, compensation, promotion, classification, training, apprenticeship, referrals for employment, union membership, and "terms, conditions [and/or] privileges of employment. . . ."

Most sex discrimination cases under Title VII are brought under a "disparate treatment" theory,

Participation Rates: Percent in Labor Force		
	MALE	*FEMALE*
Total	75.5	61.0
Ages		
25-34	92.6	74.0
35-44	92.8	77.1
45-54	89.1	74.6
55-64	65.5	48.9
65 plus	16.8	9.2
Marital Status		
Single	73.7	66.7
Married	77.5	60.7
Education		
H.S. only	89.3	68.6
College	94.2	81.8
Women with Children	Single	Married
6-17	67.5	76.0
Under 6	52.2	61.7

Source: *Statistical Abstract of the United States 1996*, pp. 399-400.

that is, under a claim by the plaintiff that she was treated differently as an individual because of her gender. However, the Supreme Court has recently allowed an employer to use gender as a factor for affirmative action purposes. In response to certain other Supreme Court's decisions, Congress passed the Pregnancy Disability Act of 1978, which prohibits sex discrimination based on health and maternity benefits, maternity leaves, job safety, and fetal protection policies as well as on height, weight, agility, and strength requirements.

Pre-employment physical qualifications, such as minimum height and weight requirements, tend to disqualify female job applicants. Consequently, both the EEOC and the courts generally consider such requirements to be sexually discriminatory when an applicant's height and weight are not indicative of an ability to perform.

The major area of unequal gender treatment is in the workplace. Women make less money in their jobs than men do. To remedy this apparent labor inequity, Congress passed the Equal Pay Act in 1963, as an amendment to another statute. The Equal Pay Act is much narrower than the Civil Rights Act of 1964, although it protects the employment interests of the largest single population group in America—women. Because it deals with all forms of gender inequality, the act also protects men if they are paid less than women for the same kind of work, something that doesn't happen often.

Essentially, the Equal Pay Act requires equal pay for equal work. Plaintiffs must prove that their work was equal to the work of an employee of the opposite sex. Pay discrimination based upon race, religion, or national origin is not covered by this statute but may be prohibited by the Civil Rights Act of 1964.

When jobs are "substantially equal" in nature, pay must be provided equally. Courts can decide whether jobs are substantially equal. Equal work does not mean identical work, only that the basic job duties and functions are the same. Sometimes it is hard to determine whether jobs are truly equal, but that task depends on the specific facts in each working situation.

Male barbers and female beauticians must be paid equally because their jobs are much the same in skill, effort, and working conditions. On the other hand, people who work in banks do not necessarily have the same level of responsibilities. Bank tellers can be paid less than bank managers or other bank employees who have responsibility for important decisions.

Unequal treatment of women (or men) comes in many forms. Fringe benefits may be higher for one gender than another. Vacations or health benefits or commissions may be made more generous for one sex than another. All these arrangements would violate the Equal Pay Act. In one case, a female manger of the women's section of a health club was given a lower commission rate than her male counterpart, but because there were more females who joined the club than males the owner maintained that the total pay for the male and female employees was almost the same. The federal court disagreed, holding that the 5 percent commission paid the female was illegal because it was lower than the 7.5 percent paid the male employee.

The Equal Pay Act allows employers to attempt to justify different wage rates for males and females. The most common defense permitted is that the unequal pay is for "factors other than sex." The employer must prove that sex was not a factor in the unequal pay situation. One example is the different payment of workers according to shifts. Premium higher payments may be made for less desirable evening and weekend work. Even so, women must be given the same opportunity to work the undesirable shifts as men, or else unequal pay rates have been set. Temporary or part-time work may be a justification for a differing wage scale. Again, women and men must be treated equally when doing this kind of hiring.

Pay rates may differ because of the effects of seniority—number of years of service to the employer. If a man is paid at a higher rate than a women solely because he has worked more years for the employer, the statute permits unequal payment. Although it is true that seniority may disadvantage some women employees, a fair and rational seniority system is legal. In many private firms senior male workers are much better paid than female workers. Seniority unintentionally creates a lower paid group of women workers, but this legal loophole for seniority does help explain certain differences in male and female wage rates. Many women workers lose their seniority status when they leave work to raise families.

The statute provides that an employer who is in violation of its provisions may not "reduce the wage rate paid of any employee." If an employer is shown to have violated the Equal Pay Act, he must raise the wage rate of the lower paid employee to match that of the higher paid employee. In addition, he must pay the complaining party the difference between what he or she should have been paid and what they were actually paid. A court may also order additional damages to the complaining party, including attorneys' fees if any were incurred. A court order may also be obtained forcing the employer not to pay future employees unequally.

An employee will normally go to the federal Equal Employment Opportunity Commission office at one of its branches to initiate a complaint under the Equal Pay Act. However, a state or local government agency may also handle such matters under its laws. The complaining party could go to any of these public agencies to seek relief or he or she can directly file a federal lawsuit.

Sexual discrimination takes many other forms besides unequal pay. There definitely is a "glass ceiling" for women. This glass ceiling is an invisible barrier that hampers women from being promoted into the top echelons of public and private employment. Study after study reveals the persistence of this glass ceiling, but it is very difficult to prove in individual cases. A wide assortment of laws address sex discrimination. The Equal Pay Act was passed in 1963. Title VII of the Civil Rights Act of 1964 prohibits sex discrimination in the terms, conditions, and privileges of employment (hiring, firing, and promoting). The Pregnancy Discrimination Act of 1978 prohibits discrimination based on pregnancy, childbirth, or related medical conditions. The Supreme Court of the United States has decided that sex discrimination in pension plans also violates Title VII of the Civil Rights Act of 1964.

Sex discrimination issues may involve violations of the due process clause of the Fifth or the Fourteenth Amendments to the Constitution. The equal protection clause of the Fourteenth Amendment has been used in other sex discrimination suits. Public employees may sue state and local governments for sex discrimination under the Civil Rights Act of 1871, in what are called "Section 1983 cases." Obviously, sex discrimination matters can be quite complex, so victims may need legal help. Some of this legal help may be provided for free or at low cost by various women's advocacy groups.

The Family and Medical Leave Act

One of the most significant developments in relation to how the law views family responsibilities is the Family and Medical Leave Act of 1993 (FMLA). Passed, in part, in response to the outcry to support "family values," the FMLA applies to employers of 50 or more employees, all public sector employers that are subject to federal minimum wage laws, and the federal government.

Employees are eligible for family or medical leave after working for 12 months or at least 1,250 hours. Part-time employees are eligible for such leaves, as these numbers average 24 hours a week. There is an exception for highly paid employees. Under certain circumstances, highly paid employees are eligible for leave but are not guaranteed re-employment.

The statute permits eligible employees to take up to 12 weeks of unpaid leave for:

1. The birth, adoption, or foster-care placement of a child if the leave is taken within 12 months of the birth, adoption, or placement.

2. The serious medical condition of a parent, spouse, or child (parents need not be the biological parents of the employee).

3. The worker's own serious medical condition that prevents the worker from performing the essential functions of his or her job.

With the exception of highly paid individuals, employees, upon returning from leave, must be given back their former position or one with fully equivalent benefits, pay, and "terms and conditions of employment" 29 U.S.C. S2614(a)(1).

Failure to abide by the FMLA can subject the employer to a complaint filed with the Department of Labor or a private lawsuit for lost wages plus interest, attorney's fees, expert witness fees, and punitive damages. The Department of Labor has now issued extensive regulations interpreting the statute, but compliance with the statute has been spotty, since enforcement is costly.

Sexual Harassment

The topic of sexual harassment is of special interest to women, although a few males have been victims of this discriminatory practice. As women are a growing part of the workforce, a genuine need exists for employers to develop enlightened policies to avoid situations that may amount to sexual harassment. In a 1988 study of federal workers, 42 percent of women reported being sexually harassed within a two-year period of time. Later studies show that more than half of women can expect to be sexually harassed during their working careers. In 1992–1993, sexual harassment cases amounted to 5.4 percent of all cases filed before the federal Equal Employment Opportunity Commission. The investigation of these complaints has been slow, and many of those filing complaints report that they have become victims of reprisals because of their complaints.

Title VII of the Civil Rights Act of 1964 has been the cornerstone of federal policy in sex harassment issues, and many state laws also deal with the issue to some extent. In 1980 the EEOC issued guidelines declaring sexual harassment to be a form of sex discrimination. Not until 1986— 22 years after the passage of the 1964 Civil Right Act—did the Supreme Court rule that sexual harassment violated the laws concerning sex discrimination. Now sex harassment is regarded as just one type of sexual discrimination.

There have been several highly publicized allegations of sexual harassment. In 1991, Anita Hill, a law professor, claimed that Clarence Thomas, while head of the Equal Opportunities Employment Opportunity Commission, had sexually harassed her. This claim led to Senate hearings, and Clarence Thomas was confirmed as a member of the United States Supreme Court, in spite of Professor Hill's stories.

In 1991 several officers of the U.S. Navy were charged with flagrant acts of sexual harassment at a convention held in Las Vegas, Nevada. The so-called Tailhook convention led to the dismissal of certain officers and reprimands for others. In 1994 President Clinton was sued for alleged sexual harassment while governor of Arkansas. In 1995 Senator Robert Packwood of Oregon resigned his seat largely because of his conduct before a Senate Ethics Committee investigating multiple charges of sexual harassment. Clearly, sexual harassment is one of the major employment issues of our times, for ordinary employers as well as those in high office.

The law concerning sexual harassment is still somewhat unsettled, but the major elements are clear enough. A coordinated policy is emerging as a result of judicial decisions and rulings of the Equal

In the United States men and women have a right to work free of sexual harassment.

Employment Opportunity Commission. Although greater protections are afforded public employees, all employees enjoy some protections not available before 1980. Congress and the state legislatures are still attempting to refine the nature of sexual harassment, but the most significant features can be understood now because of the definitions that the EEOC and the courts have established.

Sex harassment is present when employees are asked for sexual favors in exchange for job advantages or the employee is threatened with the withdrawal of job benefits. The alleged victim must attempt to prove that the harasser has denied job benefits, such as a promotion or a salary increase, because requests for sexual favors were not granted or because a discharge or a demotion was a consequence of a denial of sexual favors. This form of sexual extortion is a clear violation of the laws, but it must be proved. In one 1994 case it was claimed that "supervisors demanded sex from their female subordinates, made threats against employees who refused their advances, and retaliated against employees who complained (*Neal* v. *Ridley,* 1994).

The EEOC Guidelines on Discrimination Because of Sex define sexual harassment of this kind as "unwelcome sexual advances, requests for sexual favors." Sexual harassment also exists when "submission to such conduct is made either explicitly or implicitly a term or condition of an individual's employment." Explicit conditions are plain enough, but "implicit" conditions require extensive proof on the part of the complaining person. These guidelines are strongly endorsed by the Supreme Court.

The EEOC Guidelines also condemn conduct "which has the purpose or effect of unreasonably interfering with an individual's work performance or creating an intimidating, hostile, or offensive working environment." Hostile environment sexual harassment has a much more subtle nature and is much less easy to detect and report. For this reason, according to the leading court decision, the complainant must prove (1) that she was subject to unwelcome sexual harassment; (2) the harassment was based on sex; (3) the harassment affected a term, condition, or privilege of employment; and (4) the employer knew or should have known of the harassment and failed to take remedial actions." Obviously, this "hostile environment" form of harassment can cost employers a lot of money. They must take steps to find out whether an atmosphere that accepts sexual harassment is present in their workplace, and they must also take steps to change the environment, or else they risk being sued for large sums by alleged victims of harassment.

Crude remarks, sexual jokes, and sexual taunts and remarks may, if tolerated, create a hostile environment for workers. Slapping parts of the anatomy or touching in unwanted ways may create a hostile environment, but even words, whistles, catcalls, sex stories, lewd photographs, and the like may violate the policy against sexual harassment. The facts of each case will be different, but employers must be on guard not to allow conduct that could later bring such charges against the firm. In order to establish the existence of a hostile environment, the plaintiff must show that the behavior lasted over time and pervaded the work setting. One or two incidents, however unpleasant, will not be sufficient for the purpose of showing a "hostile environment."

The 1993 Supreme Court decision in *Harris* v. *Forklift Systems, Inc.,* was a milestone for sexual harassment law. In that case a female employee was expected to obtain coins from her supervisor's front pant's pockets. She was told, in the presence of other employees, "You're a woman, what do you know?" She was called a "dumb ass woman." These remarks, although not sexual in nature, were regarded as part of a hostile environment. In fact, EEOC policies indicate that just creating an antifemale environment is enough, without showing any sexual acts or threats. The Supreme Court decision was also important because it did not require the victim to prove psychological or other injury, only that a hostile environment existed for a long period of time.

Some courts have set a "reasonable person" measurement for judging sexual harassment situations. This means that the feelings of the particular female (or male) victim of harassment are not the measuring stick, but, instead, the question is how a reasonable woman might have felt about the working environment. Some people are hypersensitive to sexual and antifemale situations. Their feelings are not sufficient to win a case. They must show that most people would have felt as they did about the hostile environment. But what seems reasonable to a man may not be reasonable to a woman, so the standard in many states is what a "reasonable woman" might believe or feel.

Some courts do not accept the "reasonable woman" standard, insisting that each circumstance be judged by the current prevailing social standards at work. This might mean that a woman police officer or a woman construction worker might be expected to endure more in the way of sexist behavior than in an office setting.

Employers must all have a procedure by which employees can complain of harassment. The complaint must be taken seriously, and if it proves accurate, steps must be taken to correct improper conduct. The employer must also try to prevent the recurrence of harassment. Merely having the coworker or the supervisor who did the harassing undergo psychological counseling may be insufficient, as one 1992 case decided.

Employers must have an explicit sexual harassment policy that is communicated to all employees. The policy must say what will be done to those who commit such acts of harassment. Ignorance of the law is no excuse. Employers and all employees are expected to comply with statutes and EEOC rulings.

Further action is likely. Congress may eventually define sexual harassment more precisely. The rights and duties of employers and employees will be more clearly described. In this very delicate area of workplace tension, it is probably best for every person to know what he or she can do

and say. Men and women have a right to work free of sexual harassment.

Affirmative Action

Affirmative action, the conferring of special benefits upon certain individuals by virtue of their membership in a group, is a policy that is pursued in only a few nations of the world and has been applied to members of diverse racial, religious, gender, and ethnic groups. Affirmative action programs have often been bitterly attacked by members of majority groups, who feel that they are injured in some way by them. Many Americans also believe that equal treatment under the law is violated by an approach that offers preferences to certain individuals that place them in an unequal and advantaged position. However, such a view neglects to note that members of certain groups have not been able to compete for economic opportunity because the practices of the past often favored the majority.

Presidential orders of President Lyndon Johnson imposed affirmative action in education and employment. It was Lyndon Johnson's goal to go beyond mere equality of opportunity in order to bring about increased minority (later, women were included) employment opportunities and greater access to education. Affirmative action obligations were later placed on employers with construction contracts, which were financed by funds provided by the federal government. In 1977 Congress passed the Public Works Employment Act, which authorized setting aside $4 billion in construction grants to states and local governments, with the condition that "at least 10 per centum of the amount of each grant shall be for minority business enterprises." The constitutionality of many minority "set-aside" programs is now in doubt. Recent Supreme Court rulings have indicated that the equal protection of the laws guaranteed by the Fourteenth Amendment prevents explicit minority preferences.

At the national level, Presidents Nixon, Ford, and Carter led the way in developing affirmative action policies. First, by executive order, moneys were set aside to assure that certain portions of federal expenditures were used to benefit members of minority groups. Second, detailed regulations and procedures were established for nonfederal entities, such as universities, public school systems, and large private employers, obliging them to make hiring and promotion decisions in a race- or gender-conscious way. President Carter pressed hard to obtain more "underrepresented minorities" in the federal civil service, a campaign renewed under President Clinton. The federal Office of Equal Economic Opportunity, created by statute in 1968, led the way in defining the meaning of affirmative action.

Recipients of federal grants today are usually required to adhere to affirmative action policies. Other private employers are not required to apply affirmative action. Even so, many employers have, for a variety of reasons, imposed affirmative action on themselves voluntarily. Affirmative action can be imposed by a court order only in extreme cases of serious past discriminatory conduct, not merely to remedy imbalances in the work force.

One goal of affirmative action policies— sometimes called "positive discrimination"—is to repay past indignities and injustices, but a larger purpose is to improve economic opportunities. In the case of economically disadvantaged persons, which includes women, greater earning power for group members is a major goal of affirmative action. Access to the professions and the skilled trades has been limited for certain groups. Consequently, affirmative action policies have attempted to compensate for historic disadvantages by enhanced opportunities for higher education and apprenticeships for skilled trades. Another goal of affirmative action is to provide representation in public employment to a cross-section of the population. In recent years the U.S. State Department and many other federal agencies have deliberately sought to locate, hire, and promote minority and female applicants in order to provide a democratically representative profile to other nations and to our own citizens.

In the United States African Americans, women, Hispanic Americans, and Native Americans have been greatly aided by affirmative action policies. Not all minorities have been included in the privileged groups. Asian Americans, for example, are generally not included, although some programs exist to aid them. Women are not actually a minority, but they have historically been less well paid than men and often limited in employment and promotion opportunities.

At times, new groups have been added to the list of affirmative action beneficiaries. For example, disabled veterans were added to federal benefits in 1976. In that year the federal Department of Labor established affirmative-action obligations for government contractors and subcontractors, requiring them to make special efforts to recruit, employ, and promote disabled veterans and veterans of the Vietnam War. In fact, many states have long given veterans preferences in hiring. Oddly, veteran's preferences may conflict with efforts of women to gain employment, since women are not benefited as much as men by prior military service.

Critics contend that preferential hiring that favors women and African Americans represents an unjust form of discrimination against white males. In the hiring of urban police officers and fire fighters, special opportunities have been provided in recent years so that those sectors of employment opportunity would be more open to groups that had been historically underrepresented or excluded altogether.

President Ronald Reagan reached the White House in 1980, standing on a Republican Party platform that opposed "quotas, ratios, and numerical requirements." Not surprisingly, he took steps to dismantle much of the bureaucratic machinery that supports federal efforts toward affirmative action. Although he created no flat ban against affirmative action, pressure on private businesses, on government contractors, and even on the employment practices of federal and state governments diminished. President Reagan appointed Clarence Thomas as head of the Equal Economic Opportunity Commission, knowing that Thomas was rather unsympathetic to affirmative action. Clarence Thomas is now a member of the Supreme Court. President Bush, while not as vehement about the subject, did little to advance affirmative action programs, whereas President Clinton, aware of widespread public resentment, retreated on the issue in advance of the 1996 elections. Nonetheless, there is an entrenched civil rights bureaucracy at the federal level devoted to protecting affirmative action. Only a dedicated opponent of the policy can cut back further than President Reagan managed to do during his two terms in office.

For its part the Supreme Court has been suspicious of affirmative action programs, but not overtly hostile. In 1974 the Court avoided the issue *(De Funis* v. *Odegaard),* but Justice William O. Douglas argued against affirmative action, warning that "the equal protection clause commands the elimination of racial barriers, not their creation in order to satisfy our theory as to how society ought to be organized." In 1978 the Court showed itself to be badly divided on the issue *(Regents of the University of California* v. *Bakke),* which held racial quotas for university admission to be unconstitutional while permitting race to be used as a "plus" along with other admissions factors. Since then the Supreme Court has often frowned on affirmative action programs that set up double standards by race or gender for job applicants for public and private sector positions. Scholarships cannot be created only for minority applicants.

The Court has stated (by a narrow five-to-four vote) that "race-conscious class relief" was appropriate where an employer or a union "has engaged in persistent or egregious discrimination, or where necessary to dissipate the lingering effects of pervasive discrimination"—*Local 28 Sheet Metal Workers* v. *Equal Employment Opportunity Commission* (1986), p. 445. In 1987, again by a five-to-four vote, the Court upheld a 50 percent promotion quota for minority candidates for positions in a state police department, because of prior serious discrimination.

The Supreme Court appeared to have protected affirmative action against the Reagan administration's antiquota policies. However, newer appointees to the Supreme Court have placed more limits upon affirmative action. The Court now requires strong proof of prior discriminatory action before it will uphold any sort of race, sex, or gender quota. In 1989 the Court declared a 30 percent quota for minority contractors as an unconstitutional violation of the rights of white contractors, because there was insufficient proof of past discrimination in public contracting *(Richmond* v. *J. A. Corson Company).* This policy approach to affirmative action was the creation of "set asides" in public contracts. Thus, women or minority firms were guaranteed a portion of all public contracts, regardless of competitive bids from nonminorities. The United States Supreme Court has sharply limited the availability of "set asides" as contrary to the equal protection of the laws guaranteed by the Constitution since 1980 *(Fullilove* v. *Klutznick).* Some small loopholes may still exist, but most public agencies, even in predominantly minority-populated cities, have reluctantly turned away from such practices.

The Supreme Court has never stricken down special classes or supplementary training for economically disadvantaged persons, regardless of costs. The Court has never insisted that only "merit" competitive considerations be applied in employment or education. The Court has consistently upheld federal and state antidiscriminatory legislation, intended to benefit women and minorities.

Affirmative action policies are quite different from antidiscrimination policies. Antidiscrimination policies usually make it unlawful to discriminate against an individual on grounds of race, religion, ethnicity, gender, age, or physical disability. So it is illegal to refuse to hire an older person because of his age or a disabled person because of his disability. It is illegal to refuse to rent a hotel room to someone because of his religion.

Affirmative action became an issue in the presidential campaign of 1996. The issue was foreshadowed by popular referenda in California and elsewhere and became a central point of contention between the Democratic and Republican parties. Defenders of affirmative action programs pointed to the many opportunities that had been opened up for minorities and women in the three decades since such programs began. Nonetheless, affirmative action was on the defensive. State, local, and national government civil rights agencies had become less vigilant, in the face of majority opposition. Perhaps three decades of social experimentation were drawing to a close.

Plainly, women and minorities had made great economic and social strides, partly as a result of affirmative action, but preferential treatment ran against the grain of American values. The protected categories were expanded to include disabled veterans and the handicapped, but affirmative action lost its forward movement. The political tide eventually shifted against the policy, but affirmative action lived on. Thirty years of affirmative action opened the doors of opportunity to women and minorities, but the goals of affirmative action have been only reluctantly pursued in many of America's workplaces. More teachers, fire fighters, and police have been hired from the ranks of women and minorities than ever before, but the greatest successes came in the military, where minorities and women have reached the highest ranks.

Employment Rights of the Disabled

The employment provisions of the Americans with Disabilities Act (ADA) are enforced under the same procedures now applicable to race, color, sex, national origin, and religious discrimination under Title VII of the Civil Rights Act of 1964, as amended, and the Civil Rights Act of 1991. Complaints regarding actions that occurred on or after July 26, 1992, may be filed with the Equal Employment Opportunity Commission or designated state human rights agencies. Available remedies include hiring, reinstatement, promotion, back pay, front pay, restored benefits, reasonable accommodation, attorneys' fees, expert witness fees, and court costs. Compensatory and punitive damages also may be available in cases of intentional discrimination or where an employer fails to make a good faith effort to provide a reasonable accommodation.

Discrimination against individuals with physical or mental disabilities is also prohibited by another federal statute: the Rehabilitation Act. The Rehabilitation Act applies only to government employees, recipients of federal financial assistance, and federal governmental contractors. The ADA reaches most forms of employment, public services, public accommodations, and telecommunications.

Employment discrimination is prohibited against "qualified individuals with disabilities." This includes applicants for employment and employees. An individual is considered to have a "disability" if he or she has a physical or mental impairment that substantially limits one or more major life activities, has a record of such an impairment, or is regarded as having such an impairment. Persons discriminated against because they have a known association or relationship with an individual with a disability also are protected.

The first part of the definition makes clear that the ADA applies to persons who have impairments and that these must substantially limit major life activities such as seeing, hearing, speaking, walking, breathing, performing manual tasks, learning, caring for oneself, and working. An individual with epilepsy, paralysis, HIV infection, AIDS, a substantial hearing or visual impairment, mental retardation, or a specific learning disability is covered, but an individual with a minor, nonchronic condition of short duration, such as a sprain, a broken limb, or the flu, generally would not be covered.

The ADA requires that employers post a notice describing the provisions of the ADA. It must be made accessible, as needed, to individuals with disabilities. A poster is available from the EEOC summarizing the requirements of the ADA and other federal legal requirements for nondiscrimination for which the EEOC has enforcement responsibility. The EEOC also provides guidance on making this information available in accessible formats for people with disabilities.

EEOC guidelines indicate that there are many special circumstances that are exceptions to the general protections available to handicapped persons. The basic statute does not protect current users of illegal drugs. Alcoholics may be held to the same employment standards as other workers. Employers can refuse to hire individuals who have communicable diseases for jobs involving food handling.

For purposes of the ADA, drug users are not considered to be disabled persons, although alcoholics may be. Although a current user of illegal drugs is not protected by the ADA if an employer acts on the basis of such use, a person who currently uses alcohol is not automatically denied protection. An alcoholic is a person with a disability and is protected by the ADA if he or she is qualified to perform the essential functions of the job. An employer may be required to provide an accommodation to an alcoholic. However, an employer can discipline, discharge, or deny employment to an alcoholic whose use of alcohol adversely affects job performance or conduct. An employer also may prohibit the use of alcohol in the workplace and can require that employees not be under the influence of alcohol.

Age Discrimination

The Age Discrimination in Employment Act (ADEA) was passed in 1967 to protect the rights of older workers. This statute makes age discrimination against workers over the age of 40 unlawful. Congress passed amendments to the ADEA in 1974 to extend coverage to government employees. Later amendments have also increased coverage.

Under the ADEA an employer may not discharge, refuse to hire, or otherwise discriminate on the basis of age in compensation, terms, conditions, or privileges of employment. The plaintiff in an age-discrimination case bears the burden of proving that the discriminatory action was taken on the basis of age. The plaintiff need not prove that age was the sole factor motivating the employer's decision but only that age was a "determining" factor: The plaintiff would not have been fired or treated adversely but for the employer's motive to discriminate. The plaintiff may meet this burden by direct evidence that age was a determining factor in the discharge or by proving

The Age Discrimination in Employment Act (ADEA) was passed in 1967 to protect the rights of older workers. This statute makes age discrimination against workers over the age of 40 unlawful.

the case through an indirect proof method developed by various court rulings.

The purpose of the basic statute was stated by Congress:

> It is therefore the purpose of this chapter to promote employment of older persons based on their ability rather than age; to prohibit arbitrary age discrimination in employment; to help employers and workers find ways of meeting problems arising from the impact of age on employment (Title 29, Chapter 14, Section 621, U.S.C.).

Under the ADEA employers cannot indicate an age preference in job ads, although minimum ages may be stated. Once hired, the older worker cannot be paid less or denied promotions because of his age. Employers may let older workers go if their position has been eliminated, but the employer must prove that age was not a consideration in that decision.

An employer may require a medical examination to determine whether an older worker is still qualified for his job. However, a medical exam is appropriate only for jobs demanding physical capabilities. The ADEA requires the employee or his spouse to be offered group health insurance under the same conditions as for any covered employee who is under age 65.

Two means by which plaintiffs can establish a violation have emerged from the case law; plaintiffs can show that a specific policy had a disparate impact on the aged as a protected class or that they were subjected to disparate treatment because of their age. Under a disparate-impact theory, the plaintiff attacks an apparently neutral rule or policy. Once disparate impact is demonstrated, the burden of production (not the burden of persuasion) shifts to the employer, who must simply prove a business necessity for the rule or the policy under challenge.

Most age cases are brought under a "disparate treatment" theory. In 1973, the U.S. Supreme Court in *McDonnell Douglas Corp.* v. *Green* established the burden of shifting proof method most commonly used in disparate-treatment cases, because few age-discrimination cases turn on direct or "smoking gun" evidence. McDonnell Douglas requires the plaintiff to establish simply that he or she (1) is a member of the protected age group, (2) was doing the job well enough to meet the employer's legitimate expectations, (3) was discharged or demoted in spite of performance, and that (4) the employer sought a replacement for him or her.

Once the plaintiff establishes a prima facie case, the burden of going forward with the evidence passes to the employer and the employer must spell out a legitimate, nondiscriminatory reason for the plaintiff's discharge or demotion. However, because the burden of persuasion never really "shifts" from the plaintiff, if the defendant articulates a legitimate nondiscriminatory reason for its actions, the presumption of discrimination dissolves and the plaintiff must prove that the defendant's proffered reasons are a pretext or a "cover-up" for age discriminations. To overcome the employer's justification, the plaintiff must prove "pretext" by demonstrating that the employer's actions were "motivated" by age based prejudice or "animus."

The Supreme Court may reverse lower court interpretations of the Age Discrimination in Employment Act.

Alien Workers

Noncitizens have some of the rights of Americans, but very few rights in the employment field. The Immigration and Naturalization Act provides that it is unlawful for an employer to hire an alien knowing that he or she is not authorized to work. Every employee hired after November 6, 1986, must be verified by the employer as eligible to work in this country. If an employer has engaged in a "pattern or practice" of knowing violations, the Immigration and Naturalization Service (INS) can fine an employer up to $3,000 for each unauthorized alien and even impose a criminal sentence of up to six months in extreme cases. Criminal sanctions are rarely used, though. The INS usually seeks civil monetary damages.

In practice, there is a rather widespread practice of hiring illegal aliens for work in certain low-wage industries. The illegal alien and the employer are both subject to detection and punishment, but the resources and staff of the INS are too limited to catch every violator. As a result, illegal workers run the risk of deportation and employers the risk of being fined when they flout the immigration laws. Under these circumstances it is hard for illegal immigrant workers to assert the violations of their rights, since they would then expose themselves to possible deportation proceedings.

Congress has become inclined toward stricter requirements for employers who hire foreign workers. Elaborate employment verification forms must be filled out by employers. Every new employee must complete the Employment Verification Form on the first day of employment (Form I-9). By the third day of employment each new hire must provide the employer with acceptable documentation showing identity and employment eligibility. Employers should not accept mere statements of employees that they are eligible for employment but insist that positive proof must be produced. The U.S. Department of Labor and the INS conduct about 60,000 inspections each year to ensure that proof of eligibility has been provided.

Plainly, the problems of alien workers are severe. They enjoy few rights and protections under American law. The fear of being exposed and possibly deported may make alien workers vulnerable to labor exploitation. Agricultural workers are especially subject to severe working conditions. Many farmers depend on migratory farm workers to provide low-cost labor at times of harvest. Many state agencies have attempted to ameliorate the worst conditions of migratory laborers, but there is little doubt that many migrant workers are exploited.

Approximately 85 percent of all migrant farm workers are minorities, predominately of Hispanic origins. Mexican Americans and Puerto Ricans work side by side with Mexican nationals and other foreigners who are allowed to enter the United States legally for temporary work. Many undocumented illegal aliens are among the migrant workers, in spite of tightened federal laws on immigration control. Illegal immigrants are not eligible for most forms of public assistance. Some states have sought to deny public education to the children of these illegal immigrants.

Other Subjects

A century ago the law in all states strongly favored employers over employees. That situation has been corrected by major political victories won for workers in America. The relative power of labor and management has fluctuated in the twentieth century, but certain features of the legal landscape have become permanent. Labor management relationships are usually subject to state and federal laws. Collective bargaining is protected by federal and state law. There is some form of a worker's right to strike in every state. Similarly, there are other forms of state and federal legislation on topics such as minimum wages, wages and hours, and worker health and safety. Laws governing the labor of women and children are also important in every state.

Bibliography

Decker, Kent. H. *Privacy in the Workplace: Rights.* Horsham, Pa.: LRP Publications, 1994.

Edwards, Richard. *Rights at Work: Employment Relations in the Post-Union Era.* Washington, D.C.: Brookings Institution, 1993.

O'Neil, Robert M. *The Rights of Public Employees.* Carbondale, Ill.: Southern Illinois University Press, 1993.

Outten, Wayne N. *The Rights of Employees and Union Members.* Carbondale, Ill.: Southern Illinois University Press, 1994.

Chapter 14

Housing Rights

Jay A. Sigler

Nothing in the American Constitution guarantees a right to decent housing for citizens. The Supreme Court has never held adequate housing to be an aspect of the liberties of an American. However, although there is no right to public housing, not even for the homeless, there are restrictions on how housing is provided in the private and public sectors. Many of these restrictions derive from federal and state statutes; others, from the federal Constitution itself. Moreover, government agencies that provide public housing have been held, on occasion, to be effectively discriminating against minorities. The U.S. Justice Department has begun to act more vigorously against private and public housing discrimination in recent years. The federal Department of Housing and Urban Development (HUD) has also been deeply involved.

There may be a right to "fair housing." The former head of the federal Department of Housing and Urban Development Henry Cisneros has stated:

> Every American has a right to fair housing. The right to live where you choose, to raise a family, to own a home—in dignity and without fear of discrimination—is a fundamental right guaranteed to all. It cannot be denied to anyone because of race, color, national origin, religion, sex, familial status, or handicap.
>
> The Department of Housing and Urban Development enforces the Fair Housing Act, which protects you against violations of your housing rights. We want you to know how you are protected and what to do if you believe you have been discriminated against.
>
> I pledge to you that the Department will act quickly and efficiently on all complaints of discrimination brought to our attention, and that every American will receive the full protection of the law.

Some states have come to recognize the need to provide adequate housing for all income groups. There may be an emergent right of housing at the state level, usually based on an interpretation of both the federal and state constitutions. A few state and local agencies have also taken steps to provide fair housing opportunities for minority group members, the poor, the disabled and the mentally handicapped. These states are the current leading actors on the frontiers of housing rights in America.

A Historical Overview

The origins of the American housing problem can be traced to the first few decades of the mid-nineteenth century. The immigrant flood into the United States after 1830 deposited a large number of unskilled people in New York City and several other Eastern cities. The availability of jobs determined where the immigrants settled, either in the large industrial centers or in the smaller mining and mill towns of Massachusetts, Connecticut, New Jersey, New York, Pennsylvania, Ohio, and Illinois. Each ethnic group tended to settle in a different area. For example, the Poles settled in the textile towns of New England and the stock-yard area of Chicago.

Wherever they came from, the immigrants needed both work and shelter. In New York City many natives vacated their houses and moved to more distant points in Manhattan, partly to enjoy the charms of nature and also to escape the developing commercial area. Many of the new owners saw a chance to make money on the new immigrants, who were in no position to haggle over the quality of their housing. The older homes were often cut up into tenements, changing large old family houses into crowded small apartments. Soon the New York tenements were bulging with people.

Some new housing was constructed to meet the demands of the poor new immigrants. Flimsy three- and four-story buildings sprang up in the downtown area, filled with workingmen and their families. Some bedrooms were the size of closets, and many homes had few windows. Even former stables and cellars were pressed into service, reconverted to be rented to the new immigrants.

In 1834 the New York City health officer reported that bad health conditions were caused by "the crowded and filthy state in which a great portion of our population live." In 1843 a private crusade was launched by the New York Association for Improving the Condition of the Poor (AICP). Led by wealthy merchants and businessmen, the group aimed to alleviate the crime, disease, and vice so typical of the urban slums. The association reflected the views of many members of the mid-

Some new, though often inadequate, housing was constructed to meet the demands of the new immigrants who flooded the housing market in the mid-nineteenth century.

dle class that the poor were lazy and improvident. Their wretched condition was usually attributed to their defects of character and a lack of concern for their own future. However, some members also saw that many of the woes of the poor could be traced to their miserable and overcrowded housing conditions.

The state of New York and the city of New York did little to correct the housing conditions of the poor immigrants, in spite of pressure from the AICP. In 1856 the state shed its indifference by appointing a select committee of the assembly to "examine the condition of tenant houses in New York and Brooklyn." The shocked investigators condemned the capitalist "avarice" and the public "lethargy" that had contributed to the clearly evident housing evils. They called for "wise and sim-

ple laws" that would create "more general social comfort and prosperity, and less, far less expenditure for the support of pauperism and crime." But the committee also exhibited a hostility to the immigrants themselves, saying, "We must as a people act upon this foreign element, or it will act upon us." They warned that "we must decompose and cleanse the impurities which rush into our midst, or . . . we shall receive their poison into our whole national system." Early housing reformers had little sympathy for the plight of the poor immigrants. Rather, they feared the possible results of their poverty and poor housing.

In 1867 the state of New York introduced very minimal tenement regulations with the passage of the Tenement House Law. The statute was designed for the city of New York to relieve the urban hous-

By 1890 there were 35,000 tenements in New York City, housing over one million of the city's total population of 1,500,000.

ing conditions of immigrants and poor people there who were often housed in terrible cramped and unsanitary buildings. These laws were the beginnings of all tenement and housing codes.

The standards of the Tenement House Law of 1867 were very low. The city Board of Health was given broad powers of discretion to implement the law. For example, with regard to fire protection the law required that all tenements have a fire escape "or some other means of egress." Sometime local officials accepted an inconveniently located wooden ladder. As for sanitation, landlords could satisfy the law by providing merely one privy for every 20 inhabitants, and this could be located in the yard.

The conditions of tenement life appalled and shocked some urban reformers. By 1890 there

were 35,000 tenements in New York City, housing over one million of the city's total population of 1.5 million. The conditions of life for tenement dwellers in New York and other large urban centers were plainly horrendous. As reformers pointed out, in many cases young boys grew up in conditions that encouraged them to live on the streets, join gangs, and roam the city seeking for thrills. The children of immigrants were described by one observer as "the dangerous classes of New York," considered ignorant and insensitive and "far more brutal than the peasantry from whom they descend."

On the eve of the First World War most of the nation's major cities were filled with large numbers of foreign-born people. In 1910 more than 72 percent of foreign-born Americans lived in urban

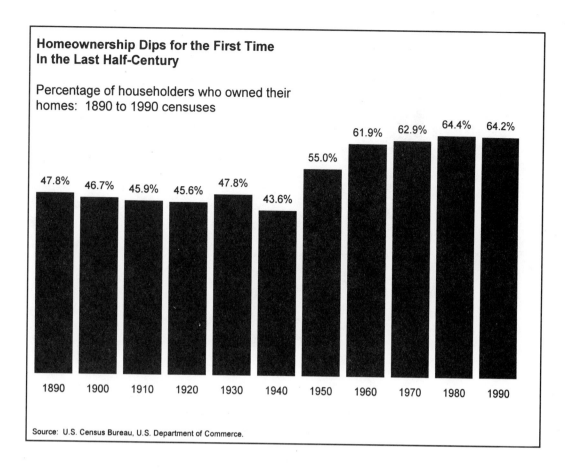

Homeownership Dips for the First Time In the Last Half-Century

Percentage of householders who owned their homes: 1890 to 1990 censuses

47.8% — 1890
46.7% — 1900
45.9% — 1910
45.6% — 1920
47.8% — 1930
43.6% — 1940
55.0% — 1950
61.9% — 1960
62.9% — 1970
64.4% — 1980
64.2% — 1990

Source: U.S. Census Bureau, U.S. Department of Commerce.

areas—twice the number of native-born Americans. For Italians and Jews the number of urban dwellers was closer to 90 percent. The foreigners could move from city to city, but wherever they went the housing conditions tended to be deplorable. Crowded tenements were the norm, with several families crammed into a single cold-water flat.

There was little mixing between the middle classes of the big cities and the urban immigrants who were crowded into the tenements. Still, some members of the middle class did try to improve the housing conditions of the less fortunate. Housing reformer Jacob A. Riis, a journalist, aroused a mass public to the condition of the urban poor. Riis's book, *How the Other Half Lives: Studies Among the Tenements of New York,* stirred the conscience of most readers when it was published in 1890. In that book Riis described the daily lives of the tenement dwellers, some of whom were driven to desperation and even suicide. Riis actually experienced these conditions firsthand when he once found himself in a police lodging house, for lack of a home. He was ejected from the shelter when he complained that his watch had been stolen, only to be called a thief himself for even owning a valuable watch.

Jacob Riis advocated major improvements in the environment of the poor, calling for broad neighborhood reconstruction. Unfortunately, few political leaders followed his suggestions for improving the lives of the tenement slum dwellers. Instead, tougher tenement laws were passed to eliminate some of the worst features of the conditions he described so well. Other reformers felt that urban planning and model housing developments were a better answer than reconstructing the urban environment.

Some idealists called for decentralized housing development, away from the urban centers. These cleaner, safer houses would not breed the crime and viciousness of the urban slums. Of course, the tenement dwellers could not afford to rent houses in distant developments, so their plight was essentially untouched by such proposals. Anyway, few builders were willing to spend their money on low rent housing.

Another approach to the urban housing problem was to limit the numbers of new immigrants. If immigration were choked off, the tenements would not be teeming with poor people. This approach was favored by people who did not

A 1930 housing protest, New York.

believe that immigrants were really as good as native Americans. Class and ethnic hostility added to the widespread belief that these immigrants were somehow inferior to native Americans. Opponents of immigration used the same racist language applied to unpopular minorities today. The "dirty Italian," the "lazy Irishman," and the "greedy Jew" became racial stereotypes of the inferior immigrants. Many of the politically dominant white, Anglo-Saxon native Americans feared and insulted the different-looking foreigners.

For many political leaders the solution to the miserable housing conditions spreading to many American cities was to reduce the flow of immigration sharply, rather than to improve housing conditions. Immigration reached its highest point in 1900. Immigration restriction was a trend that began in the 1880s and reached its culmination after World War I. Business and union leaders alike feared the foreign-born Americans, and in 1924 a new, very restrictive immigration policy was signed into law. Immigration was reduced to a mere trickle.

By 1920 many experts were convinced that some sort of federal action was needed to meet housing needs in the nation. During the First World War some public housing had been built to assist workers, although these were sold immediately after the war to private owners. Direct government intervention to house the poor and to set basic housing

standards finally became acceptable. The United States Housing Corporation was created in 1920.

Federally subsidized housing began under President Herbert Hoover, in the early days of the Great Depression. The Reconstruction Finance Corporation was authorized to make loans to private corporations in order to provide some housing for low-income families. The Reconstruction Finance Agency regulated rents and the rate of return to private investors.

Even before the election of Franklin Roosevelt in 1932 the nation had begun to recognize the need of the poor for decent housing. Under President Roosevelt subsidized housing was given over to a new federal Public Works Administration (PWA), as part of their activities. However, this promising program was terminated in 1934, because the rents charged were higher than most low-income families could afford.

After the cancellation of the PWA housing program, another approach was embraced by the Roosevelt administration. Roosevelt was most concerned with job creation to help deal with the Depression. He turned the Reconstruction Finance Agency into a builder and a landowner. In 1934 the National Housing Act was passed, creating the Federal Housing Administration. This agency was designed to provide mortgage credit on terms that borrowers could afford. Cheaper mortgages would result in more houses. Mortgage insurance, which was underwritten by the federal government, would also make more housing available to Americans of modest means. The truly poor might not obtain much help from these programs, but a large number of middle- and lower-middle-class Americans were enabled to own their own houses once the Federal Housing Administration made long-term, low-cost mortgages available.

The very poor would need housing subsidies. The U.S. Chamber of Commerce and the savings and loan institutions opposed this form of help to the poor. However, in 1937 Congress approved the U.S. Housing Act, which encouraged the construction of new apartments for low-income families. Occupants would pay for operating costs and utilities, while local housing authorities would operate the houses.

The conditions described by Jacob Riis were common in many large eastern American cities until stiffer housing codes and sanitary laws were gradually instituted in the 1930s and later. Gradually the older immigrant groups were replaced in the cities by new urban migrants—African Americans, Puerto Ricans, and other Hispanics. They rarely were housed in tenement conditions, but for many of these modern-day American urban poor, housing conditions, although not as bad as in 1900, were still well below the urban housing standards of other industrial nations.

Given the serious shortage of decent housing in American cities, more and more efforts have been organized to find new ways to replenish the housing stock adequately and also to find ways to help the urban poor. But housing rights remain political issues, to be resolved by the voters and their representatives, and are not yet general rights. In actuality, many of our states are segregated by race and income because of the differences between communities in the housing field. Some communities have large, sumptuous homes with large lots and plantings, while nearby towns consist of rundown and even abandoned houses. These disparities are evident to all Americans, but they are accepted as part of our free market system. Those who can afford to purchase modern housing should be free to do so, without discrimination. There is some evidence that some minorities do not have equal opportunity to obtain mortgage loans or insurance. There is some evidence that minority renters and buyers may be subjected to discriminatory conditions. Where such circum-

stances exist, rights are being violated. There is evidence, in spite of the many laws on the subject, that realtors, banks, insurance companies, and other financial institutions have attempted to maintain segregated housing patterns. Only continued vigilance by federal and state authorities can keep violations from happening.

Zoning and Land Use Laws

Land use and zoning laws can be used by communities to keep their neighborhoods segregated or even to keep unwanted groups out. In 1917 the Supreme Court decided in *Buchanan* v. *Warley* that municipal zoning laws could not specify where persons of one racial group or another might live. Blatant use of zoning laws for racial exclusion are clearly unconstitutional and a denial of the equal protection of the laws. However, zoning may still be used by local governments as a means of providing for the public health, safety, and welfare. There is a strong judicial tendency to uphold municipal zoning laws as long as some rational basis for these determinations exists. State courts may overturn local zoning laws from time to time, but federal courts tend to be reluctant to question the purposes and motives of the zoning authorities.

Until 1948 private restrictive covenants were the primary device for maintaining racial segregation in America. A restrictive covenant is a contract among landowners to limit the way in which their land may be used. Even now, landowners may collectively agree that all houses shall be on three-acre lots and be built back 50 feet from the curb. But a racially restrictive covenant is illegal. Landowners may not agree among themselves never to sell their property to African Americans, Native Americans, Asian Americans, or Hispanic Americans. Neither may they refuse to sell land to Jews or Moslems, for that would be religious discrimination.

The effect of these racially restrictive covenants was to contribute to the myth of African American inferiority. The practice supported a policy that denied some citizens their dignity, as well as access to better housing. The 1948 Supreme Court decision of *Shelley* v. *Kraemer* was a blow that toppled this systematic segregation. The case was pursued by the National Association for the Advancement of Colored People (NAACP) and was the first important legal victory in their decades-long struggle to desegregate American life.

Five years after the *Shelley* decision the Supreme Court ruled in *Barrows* v. *Jackson* (1953) that a state court could not enforce a racially restrictive covenant in any way. People who sold their houses to African Americans could not be sued by segregationist landowners for the breach of restrictive covenant. In effect, segregationists could not go to courts to uphold their illegal agreements. Courts may not use their formidable powers on behalf of segregation.

As late as 1968 real estate brokers could legally "steer" minority group members to special sections of town where minorities were supposed to reside. They could even advertise the fact of racial segregation in the newspapers. Federal statutes changed all that—at least officially. The official textbook of most appraisers, *The Appraisal of Real Estate,* still refered to a decline in property values caused by people of a "lower economic status and different social and economic background"—a coded manner of describing minority customers. This kind of language was gradually softened, but the attitude remains ingrained in many realtors. As late as 1977 certain training materials used by appraisers used the term 100-percent "Caucasian" to describe a neighborhood not adversely affected by minorities.

Substantial changes in national policy towards minority housing issues began to occur in 1968, largely as a result of the civil rights movement, and also the tragic assassination of Dr. Martin Luther King Jr., its leader. The Fair Housing Act of 1968 made it illegal to discriminate on the basis of race, color, religion, or national origin. Sex discrimination was added as a feature in 1974. The passage of the Fair Housing Act was a milestone in American history. For the first time some version of housing rights had come into being.

After the 1948 *Shelley* v. *Kramer* decision and the Fair Housing Act of 1968 communities that wished to perpetuate segregation had to resort to various disguises. Zoning and building restrictions could be used, in effect, to discourage minorities or working-class people. The label "exclusionary zoning" could be used for this practice. Not until the 1950s did a few federal courts question this use of zoning laws. By the 1970s some federal courts were prepared to find that communities had used their zoning powers to discriminate against low-income members of the population.

In 1971 the federal Supreme Court upheld a state law requiring voters to approve public housing projects before they could be constructed. In 1976, the Court also upheld a similar suburban charter provision, which submitted all approvals of zoning changes to a popular referendum. Thus, a majority of residents could protect the community against undesired types of construction by blocking such changes. Although race or class could not constitutionally be the overt basis of such a zoning determination, it required little municipal effort to avoid reference to those topics.

The Supreme Court has been unwilling in recent years to expand housing rights in America by closely examining local zoning laws. The justices have held (*Arlington Heights* v. *Metropolitan Housing Development Corp.*, 1977) that statistical disparities in racial representation in a locality do not amount to a discriminatory racial classification. If a community, through its zoning laws, decides that there shall be no multifamily housing, that is not, by itself, a discriminatory policy, in the view of the Court. Of course, the absence of multifamily housing may have the effect of denying affordable housing to the less affluent, including minority group members, but the Court requires much stronger proof of a deliberate effort to purposely exclude racial minorities. Absent convincing proof of an intention of a community to discriminate, the Court will not intervene to protect minority group members, and it is almost impossible to locate such proof in the official records of any town or municipality.

In 1983 the Supreme Court did unanimously invalidate a city zoning ordinance in the case of *City of Cleburne* v. *Cleburne Living Center.* That case did not involve race, social class, or ethnicity but the needs of the mentally retarded. The municipality banned the operation of a group home for the mentally retarded. The Court held, on narrow grounds, that unrelated people could live together in a common home elsewhere in the same community, so the zoning ordinance was unreasonable. Mentally retarded persons were being treated differently from others in the same community, for no valid reason other than a dislike or fear of the mentally retarded. This decision was not intended to recognize some general right of the mentally retarded.

Zoning decisions are presumed to be valid unless there is no rational basis to support the

I HAVE A DREAM... – MARTIN LUTHER KING

rules. Courts will rarely question the wisdom or the intentions of legislators or zoning officials. Zoning that amounts to a taking of private property will be questioned, but that issue is treated in chapter 16. There is a property rights movement that opposes zoning, viewing it as an inappropriate use of government power.

Zoning restrictions are still commonly used by most American communities. Unless designed to discriminate, most will be accepted by courts as valid use of municipal authority. The following kinds of zoning restrictions are to be found:

1. Limits upon the number of bedrooms.

2. Regulations that discourage the construction of apartment buildings.

3. Bans on apartment construction.

4. Requirements that houses be of a minimum size or be built on lots of a minimum size.

5. Detailed construction standards that may drive up the cost of construction.

6. Requirements of extensive infrastructure (roads, services) imposed on developers.

7. Outright prohibition of certain types of construction.

Exclusionary zoning is illegal, but use of these various tactics is not presumed to be improper. The burden of proving that a community's zoning ordinances are a disguised manner of keeping out poorer people rests upon those who challenge zoning.

Mount Laurel, New Jersey: Toward Housing Rights

Integration of American suburbs is one of the major potential methods of alleviating economic and racial discrimination. Zoning laws in the suburbs tend to perpetuate segregation and to preserve the sharp contrasts between central cities and their suburbs. Racial and economic exclusion is unlawful, but breaking through the barriers that keep the poor and minorities in central cities is very difficult. America is becoming more and more suburbanized, but this development only hardens the lines between the more affluent and the poor.

Exclusionary zoning practices by suburban communities has not diminished very much over the past few decades. By zoning for low densities a suburb can exclude renters and poor people generally. Low-income people cannot afford expensive large lots for single houses. Most are effectively barred from the schools, the services, and the growing economies of the suburbs.

A few states made a more direct attack upon exclusionary zoning. New Jersey took the lead with its 1975 decision in the *Mount Laurel* case (*Southern Burlington County NAACP* v. *Mount Laurel*). This first of many such decisions in New Jersey was important because the Supreme Court of the state of New Jersey was prepared to rule that in carrying out their powers to provide for the

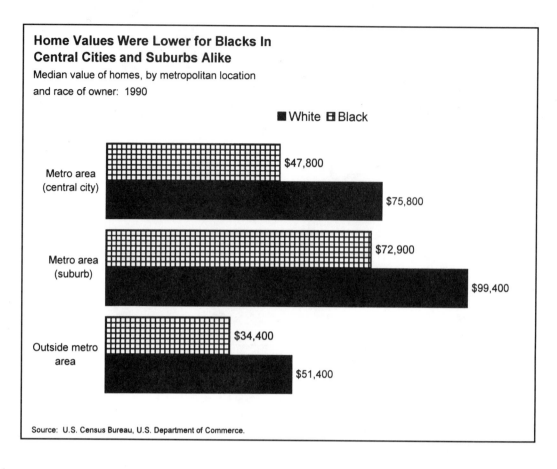

Home Values Were Lower for Blacks In Central Cities and Suburbs Alike

Median value of homes, by metropolitan location and race of owner: 1990

■ White ⊞ Black

Metro area (central city)
⊞ $47,800
■ $75,800

Metro area (suburb)
⊞ $72,900
■ $99,400

Outside metro area
⊞ $34,400
■ $51,400

Source: U.S. Census Bureau, U.S. Department of Commerce.

general welfare, local municipalities had a constitutional obligation to consider regional, not just local, welfare in making zoning decisions. Specifically, the New Jersey Court held that every "developing" community had an obligation to use its zoning powers in a positive manner, affording the opportunity for the construction of low- and moderate-income housing. The Court held that the state constitution's equal protection of the laws clause had been violated by Mount Laurel's zoning laws, which allowed only single-family detached houses on sizable lots.

The New Jersey court recognized that many developing municipalities surrounded stagnant (and poor) central cities. Zoning had been used to prevent poor inner-city workers from taking advantage of the job and dwelling conditions of developing suburban communities. The *Mount Laurel* decision influenced other state courts and went much further than the Supreme Court of the United States has been willing to go in recognizing the existence of a right to affordable housing.

The later events of the *Mount Laurel* case in New Jersey suggest that powerful forces are resistant to the changes it proposes. For nearly ten years municipalities in New Jersey failed to comply with the ruling of the New Jersey Supreme Court. In 1983 the Court issued a second decision that provided more stringent guidelines and more specific remedies designed to compel municipal compliance with the policy. Many of the loopholes and evasions that had followed the first decision were closed or altered.

The New Jersey state legislature was forced by the second *Mount Laurel* decision to enact a statute that encouraged the construction of low- and moderate-cost housing. Government subsidies and tax abatements were encouraged by the New Jersey Supreme Court, and many of these were enacted into law. The Fair Housing Act of 1985 created a Council on Affordable Housing that would assist and encourage communities to comply with the court ruling.

The Fair Housing Act created an administrative agency that had a nine-person governing body, composed of private citizens, developers, and public officials. This Council on Affordable Housing (COAH) separated the state into four regions and prepared projections for the low- and moderate-income housing needs of each. COAH

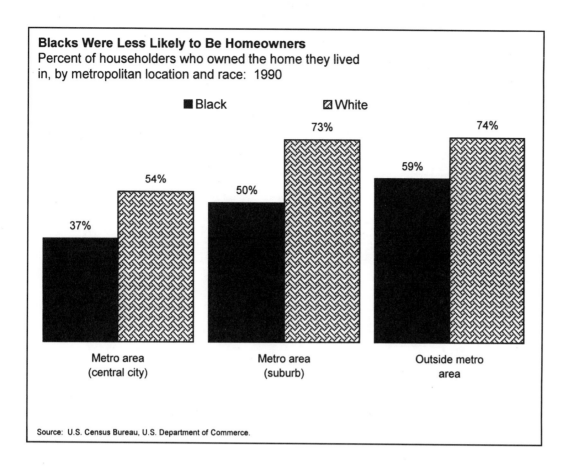

Blacks Were Less Likely to Be Homeowners
Percent of householders who owned the home they lived
in, by metropolitan location and race: 1990

■ Black   ▨ White

Metro area (central city): Black 37%, White 54%
Metro area (suburb): Black 50%, White 73%
Outside metro area: Black 59%, White 74%

Source: U.S. Census Bureau, U.S. Department of Commerce.

determined the housing needs, set time limits on compliance, and had limited power to enforce its regulations. After exhausting a very elaborate set of procedures, COAH can grant or deny certification to a municipal plan for meeting fair share housing obligations.

In December 1990 the New Jersey Supreme Court directed COAH to determine criteria for development fee ordinances and then to review and approve the ordinances for municipalities.

COAH is an administrative and regulatory organization. It does not produce, fund, or compel municipalities to expend local funds to build affordable housing. Funding is usually provided by the New Jersey Department of Community Affairs (DCA) through its various housing programs or by the New Jersey Housing Mortgage Finance Agency (HMFA) using its bonding capabilities or its federal tax credit allocations. Some municipalities also expend their own funds or use bonding resources.

Often municipalities can meet a portion of their fair share obligation through rehabilitation of existing units. To provide a realistic opportunity for the construction of new units, municipalities may

zone specific sites for residential developments by the private sector. Developers must agree to build a fixed percentage of affordable units—usually 20 percent—of the total constructed on the site, to market to low- and moderate-income households and to maintain affordability for 30 years.

Other methods for meeting the obligation include municipally sponsored construction using for-profit or nonprofit builders, the purchase of existing units for sale or rent to eligible householders, regional contribution agreements (RCAs), the creation of accessory apartments within existing structures, a buy-down program, and the provision of alternative or congregate living arrangements.

From 1987 through 1994, COAH granted substantive certification to 161 municipalities, of which 42 had fair share obligations of zero. The remaining 119 municipalities have ongoing obligations totaling just over 21,000 units. Through August 1995 over 2,950 of these units have been transferred through RCAs to the state's urban areas. An additional 1,214 units were transferred by court-settled towns.

The New Jersey Fair Housing Act permits certified or court-ordered municipalities to trans-

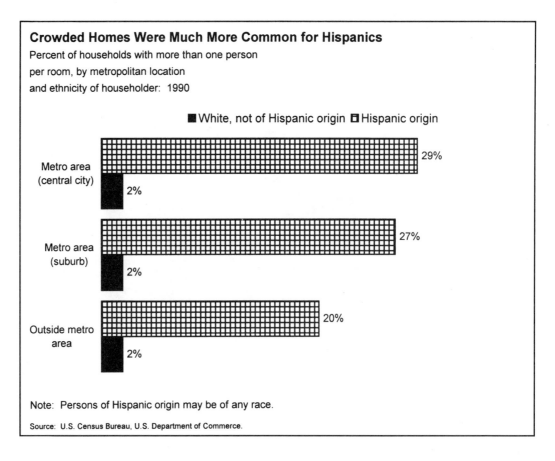

Crowded Homes Were Much More Common for Hispanics

Percent of households with more than one person
per room, by metropolitan location
and ethnicity of householder: 1990

■ White, not of Hispanic origin ☐ Hispanic origin

Metro area
(central city)
29%
2%

Metro area
(suburb)
27%
2%

Outside metro
area
20%
2%

Note: Persons of Hispanic origin may be of any race.

Source: U.S. Census Bureau, U.S. Department of Commerce.

fer up to 50 percent of their fair share obligations to one or more municipalities within the applicable housing region. The sending municipality must transfer a negotiated payment now established at $20,000 per unit as the minimum. Funds may be used to subsidize new construction or to rehabilitate existing units for occupancy by low- or moderate-income households.

By the end of 1994, 39 RCAs had been signed, involving 19 receiving and 33 sending municipalities. At an average of more than $19,000 per unit, 4,172 units have been or will be built or restored to standard condition at a total cost of approximately $81 million.

In April 1995 Governor Christine Todd Whitman signed into law an amendment to the Fair Housing Act, increasing the COAH membership to 11, including the Department of Community Affairs Commissioner, who also serves as chairperson.

The New Jersey programs for affordable housing have produced only modest results. Few homes have actually been constructed for poor and middle-income persons. Nonetheless, the modest scale of the New Jersey example is a model for the nation. Suburban segregation is being combated. New housing opportunities for the poor and minorities are being created. In the process a new form of right—a right to affordable housing—is emerging.

Federal Fair Housing Act

Title VIII of the Civil Rights Act of 1968 (Fair Housing Act) prohibits discrimination in the sale, rental, and financing of dwellings based on race, color, religion, sex, or national origin. Title VIII was amended in 1988 (effective March 12, 1989) by the Fair Housing Amendments Act, which:

- Expanded the coverage of the Fair Housing Act to prohibit discrimination based on disability or on familial status (presence of child under age of 18, and pregnant women).

- Established new administrative enforcement mechanisms with HUD attorneys bringing actions before administrative law judges on behalf of victims of housing discrimination.

- Revised and expanded Justice Department jurisdiction to bring suit on behalf of victims in Federal district courts.

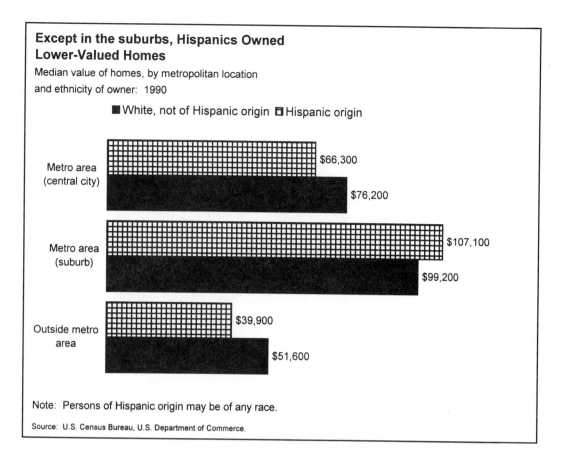

Except in the suburbs, Hispanics Owned Lower-Valued Homes

Median value of homes, by metropolitan location and ethnicity of owner: 1990

■ White, not of Hispanic origin ☐ Hispanic origin

Metro area (central city)
☐ $66,300
■ $76,200

Metro area (suburb)
☐ $107,100
■ $99,200

Outside metro area
☐ $39,900
■ $51,600

Note: Persons of Hispanic origin may be of any race.

Source: U.S. Census Bureau, U.S. Department of Commerce.

In connection with the act's prohibitions on discrimination against the disabled, design and construction requirements ("accessibility guidelines") have been established for certain new multifamily dwellings developed for first occupancy on or after March 13, 1991.

The federal Department of Housing and Urban Development (HUD) has had a lead role in the enforcement of the Fair Housing Act since its adoption in 1968. The 1988 amendments, however, have greatly increased the department's enforcement role. First, the newly protected classes have proved significant sources of new complaints. Second, HUD's expanded enforcement role has taken the department beyond investigation and conciliation into the mandatory enforcement area for the first time.

Complaints filed with HUD and not successfully conciliated are reviewed by HUD's Office of Fair Housing and Equal Opportunity, which determines whether or not reasonable cause exists to believe that a discriminatory housing practice has occurred. Where reasonable cause is found, the parties to the complaint are so notified by HUD's issuance of a Determination, as well as a Charge of Discrimina-

tion, and a hearing is scheduled before a HUD administrative law judge. Either party—complainant or respondent—may cause the HUD-scheduled administrative proceeding to be terminated by electing instead to have the matter litigated in federal court. Whenever a case has been so elected, the Department of Justice takes over HUD's role as counsel seeking resolution of the charge on behalf of aggrieved persons, and the matter proceeds as a civil action. Either form of action—the Administrative Law Judge (ALJ) proceeding or the civil action in Federal district court—is subject to review in the U.S. Court of Appeals.

The U.S. Justice Department's Civil Rights Division has taken the lead in enforcing actions under the federal Fair Housing laws. In fiscal year 1994, the Civil Rights Division of the U.S. Department of Justice filed a record 176 cases under the amended Fair Housing Act. That exceeded the previous record (set in the prior fiscal year) by nearly 40 percent. Already in fiscal year 1995, the Division is on another record setting pace.

As a result of its fair housing testing program, the first of its kind in any federal agency, the Division has filed 20 federal suits, resulting in settlements totaling about $1.5 million, to compensate victims of discrimination.

The Division filed five lending discrimination cases in 1995—more than in any previous administration—resulting in compensation for hundreds of victims and court orders to ensure the discriminatory practices end. The division is working closely with the industry to encourage voluntary compliance.

The division recently settled its first case against a major insurance company that allegedly violated the Fair Housing Act. The division alleged that employees of American Family Insurance Company in Wisconsin instructed agents not to write homeowner policies to African Americans. It also alleged that the company had failed to offer homeowners' insurance in the predominantly African American community in Milwaukee on the same terms that it offered such insurance in the majority white areas.

Although the volume of housing discrimination complaints is falling, the complaints that are filed represent only the smallest fraction of likely violations. Race remains the most common basis for FHAA violations. The major issues being tracked give a much clearer picture of filed and potential discrimination as they relate to methods of discrimination and analysis of the current trends.

Overt housing discrimination still means refusing to sell or to rent housing to someone on the basis of race, color, religion, sex, or national origin. Such allegations were particularly common with regard to rental housing, ranging from 37 percent in fiscal year 1992 to 33 percent in fiscal year 1994. Allegations of attempts to use coercion, threats, or intimidation to interfere with one's opportunity account for less than 19 percent of complaints. Taken together, these two major issues represent over 50 percent of the cases filed.

Most victims of housing discrimination are unaware of their rights. Consequently, the volume of discrimination complaints has been surprisingly low. Added to this lack of knowledge has been the attitude of some past HUD administrators who were little interested in vigorously enforcing housing rights. This attitude seems to have changed during the Clinton administration. Recently, the federal department of Housing and Urban Development has sought to educate citizens about their housing rights.

HUD Information

The following information is presented from HUD materials.

What Housing Is Covered?

The Fair Housing Act covers most housing. In some circumstances, the Act exempts owner-occupied buildings with no more than four units, single-family operated by organizations and private clubs that limit occupancy to members.

What Is Prohibited?

In the Sale and Rental of Housing: No one may take any of the following actions based on race, color, national origin, religion, sex, familial status, or handicap:

- Refuse to rent or sell housing
- Refuse to negotiate for housing
- Make housing unavailable
- Deny a dwelling
- Set different terms, conditions, or privileges for sale or rental of a dwelling
- Provide different housing services or facilities
- Falsely deny that housing is available for inspection, sale, or rental
- For profit, persuade owners to sell or rent (block busting) or
- Deny anyone access to or membership in a facility or service (such as a multiple listing service) related to the sale or rental of housing.

In mortgage lending no one may take any of the following actions based on race, color, national origin, religion, sex, familial status, or handicap:

- Refuse to make a mortgage loan
- Refuse to provide information regarding loans
- Impose different terms or conditions on a loan
- Discriminate in appraising property
- Refuse to purchase a loan or
- Set different terms or conditions for purchasing a loan.

In addition, it is illegal for anyone to:

- Threaten, coerce, intimidate or interfere with anyone exercising a fair housing right or assisting others who exercise that right.

- Advertise or make any statement that indicates a limitation or preference based on race, color, national origin, religion, sex, familial status, or handicap. This prohibition against discriminatory advertising applies to single-family and owner-occupied housing that is otherwise exempt from the Fair Housing Act.

Housing Opportunities for Families

Unless a building or community qualifies as housing for older persons, it may not discriminate based on familial status. That is, it may not discriminate against families in which one or more children under 18 live with:

- A parent
- A person who has legal custody of the child or children or
- The designee of the parent or legal custodian, with the parent's or custodian's written permission.

Familial status protection also applies to pregnant women and anyone securing legal custody of a child under 18.

Exemption: Housing for older persons is exempt from the prohibition against familial status discrimination if the HUD Secretary has determined that it is specifically designed for and occupied by elderly persons under a federal, state, or local government program or it is occupied solely by persons who are 62 or older or it houses at least one person who is 55 or older in at least 80 percent of the occupied units; has significant services and facilities for older persons; and adheres to a published policy statement that demonstrates an intent to house persons who are 55 or older. There are minor exemptions from this HUD rule.

If You Think Your Rights Have Been Violated

If you think your rights have been violated, you may fill out a Housing Discrimination Complaint form. Write HUD a letter, or telephone the HUD Hotline. You have one year after an alleged violation to file a complaint with HUD, but you should file it as soon as possible.

What to Tell HUD

- Your name and address.
- The name and address of the person your complaint is against.
- The address or other identification of the housing involved.
- A short description of the alleged violation (the event that caused you to believe your rights were violated).
- The date(s) of the alleged violation.

Where to Write

Send the Housing Discrimination Complaint Form or a letter to the HUD office nearest you or to:

Office of Fair Housing and Equal Opportunity
U. S. Department of Housing and Urban Development
Room 5204
Washington, D.C. 20410-2000

Where to Call

If you wish, you may use the toll-free Hotline number: 1-800-669-9777. (In Washington, D.C., call 708-0836.)

HUD also provides:

- A toll-free TDD phone for the hearing impaired: 1-800-927-9275. (In Washington, D.C., call 708-0836.)
- Interpreters
- Tapes and Braille materials and
- Assistance in reading and completing forms.

What Happens When You File A Complaint?

HUD will notify you when it receives your complaint. Normally, HUD also will:

- Notify the alleged violator of your complaint and permit that person to submit an answer
- Investigate your complaint and determine whether there is reasonable cause to believe the Fair Housing Act has been violated and
- Notify you if it cannot complete an investigation within 100 days of receiving your complaint.

Mortgage Lending

In September of 1992 the U.S. Department of Justice reached a settlement in its first "pattern or practice" suit against a mortgage lender. Under the consent agreement, the Decatur Federal Savings and Loan Association agreed to pay damages to individuals claiming discrimination as well as to implement special programs and remedial actions to meet credit needs of African American home buyers. The case was particularly significant for its reliance on aggregate Home Mortgage Disclosure Act (HMDA) data, putting lenders on notice that the federal government will use this data source to support more aggressive fair housing enforcement actions.

In the Financial Institutions Reform, Recovery, and Enforcement Act of 1989, Congress expanded the range of data collected and published under HMDA. More than 9,300 commercial banks, savings banks, thrift institutions, credit unions, and mortgage companies were required to report the race, gender, and income of all applicants for mortgage loans. This data become vitally important in public and private efforts to identify patterns of mortgage lending discrimination, especially the aforementioned case. HMDA data for 1992 showed again that African American and Hispanic mortgage loan applicants were more likely to be denied credit than whites or other minorities. The review of 7.7 million home purchase and refinancing loan applications by the Federal Reserve Board revealed that African American loan applicants were twice as likely to be turned down as whites, while Hispanics were more than 50 percent more likely to be rejected regardless of the type of loan sought.

The mortgage lending industry, despite these figures, and in light of the above settlement, claimed that the data did not prove systemic discrimination because it failed to account for loan-to-value ratios, debt loads, credit history, and other underwriting factors that they felt could explain the disparities. This attitude provided somewhat of an impasse until the October 1992 publication of the landmark study by the Federal Reserve Bank of Boston.

This study provided the most compelling evidence yet that white home buyers are significantly more likely to receive mortgage loans than similarly qualified African Americans. This study refutes for the first time the argument that publicly available data showing racial disparities in application rejection rates reflect differences in creditworthiness rather than a pattern of discrimination.

The Clinton administration has vigorously enforced tough fair lending laws and regulations. In 1994 there was a sharp increase in the number of mortgage loans to minorities. Federal community investment rules now require public disclosure of every mortgage lender's loans by race and income. As a result, there has been a recent rise in lending in inner cities as well as in rural areas. In many cities, according to officials of the Federal Reserve Board, minorities can now find mortgage credit on terms at least as good as those available to affluent whites.

In February 1996, the *Wall Street Journal* made a computer analysis of millions of mortgages taken from the latest data available. This analysis showed that home loan approvals to African Americans soared by 38 percent from 1993 to 1994. Loan approvals for Hispanics rose by 31 percent, while approvals for Asians went up 17 percent. Some dramatic changes in bank lending policies have been reported, such as Wells-Fargo's 1996 promise of $45 billion for lower income and small business loans over 10 years.

Long-time bank critic, John Taylor, the head of the National Community Reinvestment Coalition, remarked that "five years ago, most banks didn't take the community lending laws seriously," but now "there's more lending in low income urban and rural communities than ever before." The Community Reinvestment Act, which requires banks to lend in every community where they take deposits, is having a definite impact. Tough fair lending enforcement actions were taken by President Clinton's Justice Department. Several banks were sued for violations of the basic act.

However, some members of Congress are seeking to weaken the act, exempting many banks and savings and loans from its provisions. If this effort to cut back on minority lending succeeds, the gains of recent years will be reversed. Moreover, a less active and vigorous enforcement of the act by a new national administration would be a setback for minority group members.

The goal of federal regulators must be a society in which all people are treated equally when it comes to applying for bank loans and credit. Lenders still reject a much higher percentage of African American applicants than whites. Many African American applicants are rejected because of poor credit records. Poor applicants pose higher

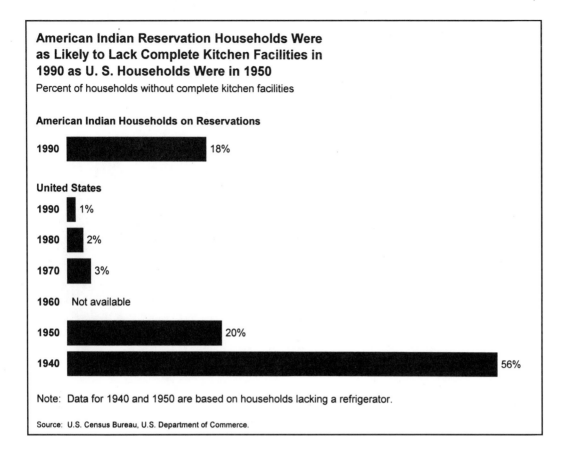

American Indian Reservation Households Were as Likely to Lack Complete Kitchen Facilities in 1990 as U. S. Households Were in 1950

Percent of households without complete kitchen facilities

American Indian Households on Reservations

1990 ████████████████ 18%

United States

1990 █ 1%

1980 █ 2%

1970 █ 3%

1960 Not available

1950 ████████████████ 20%

1940 ██ 56%

Note: Data for 1940 and 1950 are based on households lacking a refrigerator.

Source: U.S. Census Bureau, U.S. Department of Commerce.

risks to lenders. If an applicant has a spotty credit record or has a high level of debt to income, he will probably be rejected for a loan. If he is unable to afford the down payment, he surely will be rejected. Whatever laws may be enforced, there is no way to compel a bank to give a loan to a poor credit risk. Equal treatment of all loan applicants does not mean equal success in getting the loan.

The final major issue of discrimination under emphasis for reforms in the regulation of lending practices is redlining (to withhold home-loan funds or insurance from neighborhoods considered poor economic risks) and property insurance. HUD has asserted that the protection of the FHAA extends to victims of insurance redlining, arguing that property insurance is so important to obtaining mortgage credit that redlining clearly violates the Fair Housing Act's prohibition against activities that "make unavailable or deny" housing on a discriminatory basis.

Native American Housing

Perhaps Native American housing conditions are the most deplorable in the nation. Nearly one in five (18 percent of) Native American house-

holds on reservations were severely crowded (more than 1.5 persons per room) in 1990. The comparable figure for the nation as a whole was 2 percent. This information was released in an official statistical brief, entitled "Housing of American Indians on Reservations," from the Commerce Department's Census Bureau. In this section of the chapter the phrase "American Indian" is often used rather than the more acceptable term, "Native American," because that is the terminology employed by federal agencies.

Among the nation's 48 largest reservations (500 or more American Indian households), median household size was as low as 2.49 people for the Osage Reservation and as high as 4.47 for the Zuni Pueblo. Median home size varied from just 3.1 rooms for the Navajo to 5.3 rooms for the Mescalero Apache and Nez Perce.

Less than half of American Indians' housing on reservations was connected to public sewers and many lacked complete plumbing or kitchens, according to three statistical briefs released by the Commerce Department's Census Bureau focusing on the state of American Indian housing in 1990. The Census Bureau briefs

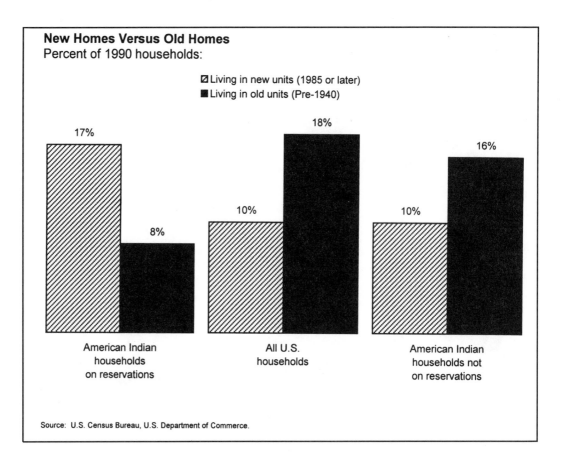

New Homes Versus Old Homes
Percent of 1990 households:

☑ Living in new units (1985 or later)
■ Living in old units (Pre-1940)

17%

8%

18%

10%

10%

16%

American Indian
households
on reservations

All U.S.
households

American Indian
households not
on reservations

Source: U.S. Census Bureau, U.S. Department of Commerce.

examine housing data for U.S. reservations and trust lands collected in the 1990 Census of Population and Housing. They also examine plumbing equipment, fuels, and structural characteristics for the 48 reservations with 500 or more American Indian households. Just under half the households were connected to a public sewer, one of the Census Bureau briefs said. The comparable figure for all U.S. households was 76 percent. This is due in part to the rural nature of most reservations. About one in five American Indian reservation households disposed of sewage by means other than public sewer, septic tank, or cesspool (e.g., outhouses, chemical toilets, and facilities in another structure). Nationally, 1 percent of all households used these methods of sewage disposal.

About one in five American Indian households on reservations lacked complete plumbing facilities in their homes—hot and cold piped water, a flush toilet, and a bathtub or a shower. This compared with fewer than 1 percent of all households nationally. About 6 out of every 10 American Indian homeowners on the Navajo Reservation did not have complete plumbing. About 18 percent of American Indian households

on reservations in 1990 did not have complete kitchens (i.e., a sink with piped water, a range or a cook stove, and a refrigerator). In 1950, about 20 percent of all U.S. households lacked complete kitchens. By 1990, only 1 percent of households nationally was without one or more of these amenities. The majority of American Indian homes on reservations (53 percent) did not have a telephone. This was true for only 5 percent of all households nationally.

Although rarely used nationally, wood was used to heat one out of every three American Indian homes on reservations in 1990. Bottled, tank, or LP (liquified petroleum) gas and electricity, at 22 percent and 19 percent, respectively, were the next most commonly used fuels. In 1940, 23 percent of U.S. households used wood as fuel, but since 1950 wood has been a fuel used very little at the national level.

The analyses also found that American Indian households on reservations were only about half as likely as all households nationally to live in an "old" home, that is, one built before 1940. They were likelier to live in mobile homes (14 percent against 7 percent nationally), and only 5 percent (compared with 27 percent for all households nationally) lived in multiunit structures.

HUD Indian Housing Programs: Assisted Housing

The Public and Indian Housing program is administered by the Office of Public and Indian Housing. Under the Public and Indian Housing program, HUD gives grants to public housing agencies (PHAs, including Indian housing authorities—IHAs), to finance the capital cost of the construction, rehabilitation, or acquisition of public housing developed by PHAs. Eligible families and individuals must qualify as "low-income families," which are those with incomes no higher than 80 percent of the median income for the area. To cover the shortfall between tenant rents and operating expenses, HUD pays operating subsidies to many PHAs. To cover modernization of existing public housing, HUD makes modernization grants to PHAs.

To develop Public and Indian Housing, a PHA generally hires a contractor to proceed with a program approved by HUD, or a private builder constructs units on agreed terms, in response to an invitation by the PHA, and then sells the project to the PHA. Alternatively, a PHA may acquire existing housing, if that is more efficient than constructing new units. IHAs may build rental or home ownership units.

The 1992 Act provides that up to 20 percent of development funds may be used for major reconstruction of obsolete public housing projects. For fiscal year 1995, grant funding was available for approximately 7,000 units of regular public housing and 2,900 units of Indian public housing. Clearly, much more must be done nationally to raise the level of housing available to Native Americans.

The Disabled

In 1988 the Fair Housing Act was amended to attack the problem of housing discrimination for the handicapped. The act now prohibits discrimination based upon handicap in the sale or renting of housing. New dwelling units with four or more apartments must have handicapped-accessible features. However, tenants may be made to bear some of the costs of restoring the premises to its original conditions after leaving. Included among the handicapped are those persons who have a disease, so that those with AIDS or with HIV infection are covered by the statute.

The Department of Housing and Urban Development has issued rules and regulations to implement the Fair Housing Act.

Housing for the mentally retarded poses additional problems. Many communities resist special houses for such handicapped people because they are an unpopular group. So-called group homes for developmentally disabled persons will resemble surrounding private homes, but the residents are, in some ways, different from the rest of the community.

However, state agencies have scattered small housing units for the mentally retarded in different communities. For example, the Michigan State Housing Development Authority has financed the construction of some housing units especially for the mentally retarded. In addition, a few older houses have been rehabilitated for these handicapped people, and rental arrangements have also been made. Michigan is regarded as having one of the better programs of this kind, but each state goes about it in a different way.

Housing and the Elderly

The American population is growing older, as the percentage of people over the age of 65 continues to rise. From 1900 to 1990 the older population of the United States increased tenfold, from 3 million persons to 31.5 million. From 1990 to 2050 the number of people over the age of 65 will rise to a projected 68 million persons, about 22.9 percent of the total population. The aging of the population will give rise to claims of the elderly to some sort of housing rights.

The graying of America is a social issue, but it has not yet become a political issue in the housing field. However, people who are old, poor, and of minority status may be at special risk and may need special consideration. The elderly are by no means always poor. Some are relatively affluent and need little economic help. Others are less lucky and may live close to the poverty line. Housing arrangements for people who are frail, old, and poor may require the intervention and help of the federal or state governments.

In 1956, for the first time, the federal government explicitly sought to help poor older persons by

Additional Protection If You Have a Disability (Excerpts from HUD Documents)

If you or someone associated with you:

Have a physical or mental disability (including hearing, mobility and visual impairments, chronic alcoholism, chronic mental illness, AIDS, AIDS Related Complex and mental retardation) that substantially limits one or more major life activities, have a record of such a disability or are regarded as having such a disability your landlord may not:

1. Refuse to let you make reasonable modifications to your dwelling or common use areas, at your expense, if necessary for the handicapped person to use the housing. (Where reasonable, the landlord may permit changes only if you agree to restore the property to its original condition when you move.)

2. Refuse to make reasonable accommodations in rules, policies, practices or services if necessary for the handicapped person to use the housing.

Example: A building with a "no pets" policy must allow a visually impaired tenant to keep a guide dog.

Example: An apartment complex that offers tenants ample, unassigned parking must honor a request from a mobility-impaired tenant for a reserved space near her apartment if necessary to assure that she can have access to her apartment.

However, housing need not be made available to a person who is a direct threat to the health or safety of others or who currently uses illegal drugs.

All new buildings with four or more units, must, by HUD regulations, have an elevator with the following features:

- Public and common areas must be accessible to persons with disabilities.

- Doors and hallways must be wide enough for wheelchairs

All units must have:

- An accessible route into and through the unit

- Accessible light switches, electrical outlets, thermostats and other environmental controls

- Reinforced bathroom walls to allow later installation of grab bars and

- Kitchens and bathrooms that can be used by people in wheelchairs.

New buildings with four or more units which have no elevator must be ground floor units. They still must have the features described above. These requirements for new buildings do not replace any more stringent standards in state or local law.

---

amending the Housing Act to make older people eligible for low-rent public housing. By 1981, under the Reagan administration, such federal programs were targeted for termination because, it was felt, the private sector could provide for the needs of the elderly poor. In fact, the private market has done little to provide low-cost housing for the elderly.

In 1990 the National Affordable Housing Act was passed; the act included substantial provisions for elderly housing. It was planned to add many new housing units through programs for the elderly and the handicapped. Unfortunately, the budget reductions of recent years has cut into these plans. Few new publicly assisted houses and apartments have actually been built for the elderly poor population.

Rental assistance for the elderly was essentially dormant during the Reagan and the Bush administrations, and the Clinton administration attempted to revive this program, but the budget-reduction mood swept the Congress in the 1990s, reducing support for such programs to minimal levels. As a result, there is a national shortage of affordable apartments for the elderly poor.

It appears that the housing needs of the elderly poor in the next century will be met by state programs or by private sector initiatives, if at all. The most that can be expected is federal or state regulation of such entities as private nursing homes, boarding houses, life-care facilities, retirement hotels, and continuing care retirement communities springing up all over the nation. Few states have done more than attempt to regulate nursing homes, so as to protect the interests of the elderly. The risk that elderly poor persons will be abused or ill-treated in private facilities is substantial. The rights of the elderly against such exploitation are largely the result of the enforce-

ment efforts of the various agencies that inspect and police the conditions of these establishments.

Homelessness

In the richest nation on earth, a large and growing number of people have no homes of their own. Some have lost their homes because they cannot afford to pay for housing; their poverty has made them homeless. Others cannot manage a home because of mental disorders, substance abuse, alcoholism, or severe physical disabilities. Some Americans are forced by their circumstances to live on the streets, in the subways, in bus terminals, or in temporary shelters. For most homelessness is a temporary condition. For some, it is nearly permanent.

According to estimates of the Urban Institute, there are between 500,000 to 600,000 American homeless people. Official government estimates are much lower. The Census Bureau claims that the 1990 census revealed only 228,821 homeless. The Census Bureau has been sued by advocates of the homeless who contend that this figure was a deliberate short count. In 1995 the Clinton administration budgeted nearly $1.7 billion to help an estimated 131,000 homeless, but the person in charge of the Clinton policy, HUD Assistant Secretary Andrew M. Cuomo, said, "I don't think we'll ever know how many homeless there are."

The literally homeless are those who are defined by government as living in shelters or other transient lodging. Another, larger category of people are at risk because they are experiencing the kind of poverty that leads to homelessness. Battered wives who spend time in a shelter may be temporarily homeless. A runaway teenager is homeless. Based on this broader view, a 1990 Columbia University study estimated that seven million people had experienced homelessness between 1985 and 1990. Hard-core permanent homelessness is probably much smaller. Some experts estimate the figure as around 400,000.

Homeless people tend to be homeless for substantial periods, with ten months the median in one national survey. Most of the homeless are male, and only between 20 percent and 30 percent of the homeless are families with children, although this figure has been rising recently. Some analysts claim that about one-third of the homeless consist of single parents with young children, usually women and their children. Studies of homelessness are notoriously unreliable, but it does seem that nearly half the homeless have not graduated from high school. Over half are non-white. Mental illness accounts for about one fifth the cases, if you count those who report a history of mental hospitalization.

Economic factors strongly influence homelessness. Unemployment and low paid employment are major causes of homelessness. The price

of rental housing and of other housing is another factor. The lack of low-cost housing in an area may drive some people into the streets, but no one knows how prevalent that may be.

One political explanation for homelessness was the sharp reduction of federal housing subsidies, which began in the 1980s under President Reagan. This reduction in housing subsidies continues at present. Inexpensive housing stock is shrinking in America. However, that doesn't mean that simply building more public housing or sharply increasing subsidies to the poor will completely solve the problem of homelessness. For those among the homeless who are drug addicts or have severe mental disturbance, simply building more low-cost housing will not meet their needs.

There is no right to a home, or even to decent shelter, although statutes or policies of local governments may establish some limited protections against discrimination. American rights theory does not recognize a claim to a right to decent shelter. Many other nations have similar problems, but no industrialized, advanced society has so large a number of people living on the streets and in other public places. Americans have not even established the principle that a family should have a residence in which all close family members can reside together. The most that can be said about the emerging American approach to homelessness is that the federal government and many commu-

nities regard it as a duty to provide some sort of temporary shelter for the truly destitute.

National recognition of the issue of homelessness came in 1987 with the passage of the McKinley Homeless Assistance Act. The federal statute defines a homeless individual as one "who lacks a fixed, regular and adequate nighttime residence." Probably there is even a larger group of people, not covered by the statute, who are not literally homeless because they can "double up" in other people's homes. This much larger group may share the housing of their relatives and friends.

People who are forced by economic circumstances to go back to their parent's homes are not literally homeless. They have a roof over their heads, but they own or rent no home of their own. Squatters, illegal occupants of homes that they have no right to occupy, are still another group that could be considered homeless. Then there are those who can afford only a cheap hotel room from time to time. They may be considered the "part-time homeless." None of these groups are covered by federal law.

Title II of the McKinney Act established the Interagency Council on the Homeless as an independent agency in the executive branch. In November 1993, after receiving no appropriation for fiscal year 1994, the tasks of the Interagency Council were assumed by a Working Group of the White House Domestic Policy Council. The council consists of 17 agencies and is chaired by the secretary of HUD.

The McKinney Act established a block grant program for services to the mentally ill and for demonstration projects for community services to the homeless. Significant federal funding is provided under the McKinney Act to communities that are making efforts to help the homeless. The National Affordable Housing Act of 1990 revised the McKinney Act to help states and communities bring together resources to build lower-cost, affordable housing, but this policy has been very sharply curtailed by reductions in HUD's budget.

The Council/Working Group has various duties, including (1) planning and coordinating all federal activities and programs to assist the homeless, (2) monitoring and evaluating assistance to homeless persons provided by other levels of government and the private sector, (3) ensuring that technical assistance is provided to help communities and organizations assist the homeless, and (4) disseminating information on federal resources available to assist the homeless.

Several states have attempted to deal with homelessness in a systematic way. Usually this means that various state services are coordinated to some extent. Departments of mental health, welfare agencies, and alcohol and drug officials may be brought together to discuss the issues of homelessness. One or another public agency may be put in charge of some kind of emergency shelter program, coupled with some efforts at providing food. Sometimes private charities are enlisted to assist with the task, or the government may support charitable efforts such as soup kitchens or emergency shelters in church halls and basements.

In spite of the sporadic efforts made to assist the homeless in some states and communities, no single national approach to the problem has emerged. Most difficult of all is the problem of finding long-term housing for the homeless; in only a few instances has this been done. The state of Connecticut has a number of programs that help homeless people find and afford permanent housing. A few other states have followed their lead. The focus in most states remains on emergency shelters. Temporary shelter is obviously not permanent housing.

Most homeless programs are aimed at the immediate emergency needs of individuals and

Sometimes the Homeless Win Discrimination Suits

An Easthampton, Massachusetts, landlord and rental agency have agreed to pay a formerly homeless family and the Housing Discrimination Project (HDP) a total of $16,500 to settle a housing discrimination complaint filed against them in Federal Court.

The complainants, a young couple, alleged that they were denied housing by local landlords Bernard and Julia Gawle as well as by their rental agents, the Taylor Agency, solely because they had infant twins. The couple was given a $5,000 settlement and allowed immediate occupancy in one of the Gawles' apartments. HDP received compensation for its testing work as well as its legal fees, which brought the total settlement amount to $16,500.

The young couple were separated by homelessness. The mother had given birth to twins in January 1995 and was living in a local shelter because she and her partner had not been able to find suitable housing. He was forced to live in a rooming house while they continued their housing search.

The couple found what they thought was a suitable apartment in Easthampton owned by the Gawles. They applied for the apartment and believed that the landlords seemed eager to rent to them. However, the Gawles delayed action on their application for over a week and the couple began to suspect that they were experiencing housing discrimination.

The couple complained to the HDP, which conducted fair housing tests to determine if discrimination was keeping the couple from securing the apartment. Upon calling the Taylor Agency, a tester was informed that the Gawles would not rent an apartment in the building to people with small children. With this corroborating evidence, the couple filed a complaint against the Gawles and the Taylor Agency in Federal Court in Springfield. The defendants agreed to settle the case shortly thereafter.

families for food and shelter. Long-term approaches to homelessness are virtually nonexistent in most communities. In effect, most homeless programs are a form of first aid, not an attempt at a cure. Little has been done to provide the poor with services to prevent homelessness. The elimination or even the reduction of homelessness is not possible until the causes are understood and treated. The recognition that there may be some sort of right for people who are not mentally ill, drug-addicted, or otherwise severely impaired to have a home of their own would be a first step toward a new national policy on homelessness.

Continuing Problems with Housing Discrimination

There is strong evidence that residential segregation in America is a continuing problem. Despite nearly 20 years of statutes and official actions supposedly aimed at the reduction of segregated housing, racial and ethnic minorities still confront obstacles in obtaining access to decent housing. In 1991 *USA Today* (November 11, 1991) reported that Hispanics were highly concentrated in two metropolitan areas—New York and Los Angeles. The same survey of the 1990 census data claimed that African Americans were highly segregated in two thirds of the metropolitan areas, where they made up at least 20 percent of the population. Some critics contend that housing segregation in America is as prevalent today as when the civil rights movement began in the 1960s.

Within metro areas at the time of the 1990 Census of Population and Housing, the Census Bureau said, the median value of homes Asians or Pacific Islanders owned was $184,000, double that of white-owned homes ($91,700). Contributing to this wide variation at the national level was the large concentration of Asian-Pacific Islander homeowners in California and Hawaii, two states where median home values were well above the U.S. median. The median value of homes owned by Hispanic householders in metro areas was $84,600 and that of homes owned by African Americans was $55,500. Because of geographic differences in median home values, disproportionate concentrations of some population groups, and the incomparability of race groups with Hispanics,

who may be of any race, valid comparisons are not possible.

Nationally, the Census Bureau said, home ownership in the nation's 335 metropolitan areas eluded most African American and Hispanic householders. Only about four in ten of each group were owners, much lower than the two in three metro white householders who owned their homes. Just over half of Asian or Pacific Islander householders owned their homes. In 16 of the 25 metro areas with the highest Asian or Pacific Islander populations, home values were higher.

New York City had the highest number of African American households (762,309) among metro areas in 1990, but Jackson, Mississippi, had the highest percentage of African American householders (37 percent). Among the top 50 African American metro areas, the most expensive African American-owned homes were in San Francisco, California, where the median value was $223,200; the gap was largest in the Philadelphia, Pennsylvania-New Jersey metro area, where the African American median home value was 68 percent lower than that of whites. Los Angeles and Long Beach, California, had the highest number of Hispanic households (784,171), and 39 of the 50 metro areas with the highest number of Hispanic households were located in either the West or the South. California and Texas were home to half of them.

In December 1995 an investigation of the U.S. Department of Housing and Urban Development found that employees of the Boston Housing Authority (BHA) had been setting aside choice public housing development townhouses exclusively for white tenants. The townhouse units, known to be the most desirable apartments, were 99.3 percent white at the time of the investigation. Despite a 1988 compliance agreement to move minorities into historically white projects in a cluster of the Mary Ellen McCormack Development in Boston, the brick two-story units remained white only until an Asian family moved in during the month of April of 1995.

The HUD investigation showed that BHA employees made the townhouses an oasis for white applicants. There was a citywide waiting list for public housing, but about 85 percent of the families on that list were minorities. The draft report of the HUD investigators uncovered evidence of "intentional discrimination as well as discriminatory intent." The tenant selection process used by the Boston Housing Authority employees "departed completely" from the usual tenant selection process, according to the HUD investigative report; the selection system was manipulated to exclude minorities from the most desirable townhouse units. The draft report was obtained by the *Boston Globe* newspaper and featured as a page-one story on Wednesday, December 13, 1995.

In another important 1995 case involving public housing, a sweeping order was issued by HUD Administrative Law Judge Constance T. O'Bryant. The Housing Authority of Las Vegas, Nevada (HALV), was ordered to pay $163,590 for racial discrimination and racial steering of African Americans to segregated African American housing. Her November order came after three days of hearings on a complaint by Marie Campbell, a 42-year-old African American, and her 12-year-old daughter, Michelle Kirkland. In 1993, Ms. Campbell complained to HUD that the authority steered her and her daughter to a predominantly African American complex and later refused to transfer them to another complex because of their race. The order is seen as significant because it involves strong federal governmental action against discriminatory local governmental practices that have long continued in many cities.

Public housing policies remain a sore point. According to some housing advocates, there is an inequality in the actual housing provided to low-income African American families under federal programs. Not only is the public housing substandard, but, say some critics, the services provided are also inferior to those available to poor whites. These claims may be inaccurate, but more vigorous enforcement of the antidiscrimination laws would restore some faith in the fairness of public housing policies.

No one knows exactly how extensive housing discrimination may be in America. There are many rumors and stories, but unless there is dramatic proof, as in the cases just mentioned, violations of housing rights are open to speculation. Nonetheless, the American Civil Liberties Union (ACLU), a leading civil rights organization, contends that HUD has failed to act vigorously enough to enforce the Fair Housing Law and other federal statutes intended to correct housing

inequities. Certainly, from 1989 to 1992 there were very few race discrimination cases brought to trial by the federal agency.

The civil rights movement of the 1960s succeeded in getting the fair housing laws passed. In fact, the passage of the Fair Housing Act may have been the high-water mark of the movement. Enforcement of these laws has been sporadic and weak, until recently. Racial and class segregation still are widespread in America. The continued suburbanization of the nation has only compounded the problem, as more and more former urban residents move out of central cities—an option usually not available to less affluent persons.

Housing discrimination can affect the living conditions, education, and employment of African American and Hispanic Americans. Deprived of residential mobility and discouraged from owning their own homes, many minority families are unable to flee stagnant or unsafe neighborhoods. Two thirds of African American and Hispanic children are concentrated in high-poverty schools in which educational achievement is low and dropout rates are high. The employment possibilities for minority jobseekers are diminished by the ongoing movement of jobs from the cities to the suburbs, where housing discrimination is particularly severe. Altogether, these effects of housing discrimination create a vicious cycle: Discrimination imposes social and economic barriers on African Americans and Hispanics, and the resulting hardships fuel the prejudice that leads whites to associate minorities with neighborhood deterioration.

New Strategies toward Housing Discrimination

Ending racial and economic segregation will be a difficult task. At the very least, minority communities must be made more aware of what their rights to open housing may be. Far fewer complaints are made each year to HUD than are justified by the real housing conditions. Educational efforts by federal and state officials would help alert people to their rights.

Some discriminatory practices are very hard to detect. If realtors are steering minority people away from particular areas or if landlords are avoiding renting to minorities, there will be little hard evidence of those practices. Various forms of "testing" can be used to show that such discriminatory practices exist. Until the use of testing is expanded, there will be no concrete information on the scope and extent of housing discrimination.

Testing is a procedure that has individuals (auditors or testers) apply for housing and negotiate a transaction even though they are not actually seeking to buy or rent. The testers are paired, and the minority member of the pair is matched by race, ethnicity, or gender and then sent in to act as though he or she were a serious customer. Presumably, the tester would expect to receive the same treatment as that received by members of that group that is the basis of the test. In most tests a white person is sent in to attempt the same transaction as a minority individual. If the white person receives preferential treatment, the test reveals discrimination. What is being tested is the attitude and conduct of the bank or the realtor when confronted with a mock client.

Testers must be carefully selected and trained. They must know how to make good, reliable notes on their experiences. Information gathered by testers must be carefully assembled and reliably collected. Even if these factors are controlled, comparability is always a problem because people may dress or talk differently. The different treatment that testers may receive cannot rest upon their personal differences.

This technique of testing or auditing for housing discrimination has been used from time to time. It is an effective means of measuring the extent of discrimination, but it poses some problems. Opponents of testing claim that considerable deception is involved in testing. Further, a certain bias may be introduced by the process, since it is designed to find evidence of discrimination. Nevertheless, testing is the best tool available for detecting discrimination in a community, and when it is used it may disclose patterns of discrimination that would be otherwise impossible to locate.

Some reformers have suggested that testing be made more available under the Fair Housing law. Testing is costly, though, and enjoys little political support. Evidence produced by testing may be used in court, but those who rely on testing must show that the testing research was fair and carefully designed according to the best methods used in the social sciences.

Testing can result in changed attitudes towards housing discrimination. Consider the following situation:

> A racial housing discrimination case in South St. Louis County (Missouri) filed by the U.S. Department of Justice (DOJ) was settled in January 1996. This settlement will further fair housing throughout the region in several ways. Forder Road Apartments has agreed to institute a number of practices in their management systems that will ensure fair treatment for all apartment seekers, including fair housing education for their employees and detailed record-keeping. In addition, the Consent Order includes a provision that the Metropolitan St. Louis Equal Housing Opportunity Council (EHOC) will receive most of the $30,000 monetary settlement to be used to continue their programs in the greater St. Louis area. These programs are designed to combat illegal discrimination in the sale and rental of housing and to educate the public concerning fair housing.

> The DOJ filed a complaint against Forder Road Apartments in April 1994, alleging racially discriminatory housing practices based on fair housing testing conducted in 1993. The testers used in the DOJ investigation were recruited by EHOC. Without admitting the allegations made in this case, Marjorie A. and Vince F. Stanec and Andy Thielemier, owners and employees of Forder Road Apartments, have entered into this settlement agreement with the DOJ.

Some states have taken a fresh look at the need to help the homeless and the very poor to find affordable housing. In Florida in 1994 the legislature declared that the crisis that this state faces in providing affordable housing for very-low-income, low-income, and moderate-income persons is intensified by the rising cost of land and construction. The legislature found that there were publicly owned lands and buildings that could be suitable to be marketed, sold, leased, or exchanged for the development of affordable housing. The Florida Department of Community Affairs was ordered to contract with an appropriate person, association, corporation, or other entity, public or private, to conduct an inventory of publicly owned lands and publicly owned buildings suitable for the development of affordable housing for very-low-income, low-income, and moderate-income persons. Since the state owns many properties and holds title to considerable amounts of land, it could turn some of this to the use of assisting the poorest members of the population to obtain affordable housing. This approach is just one of many new strategies to deal with the real need to find adequate, permanent housing for the poor and the near-poor.

Further development of housing rights at the federal level will largely depend on the forceful leadership of the White House. If the president wants to push the boundaries of housing rights, most of the legal tools are already available. HUD's Office of Fair Housing and Equal Development has primary responsibility for the development of policy, guidance, procedures, and regulations for FHEO programs and initiatives. The negotiations and settlements of several major civil rights cases are powerful tools of the department. HUD can continue to shift the department's resources from costly litigation to addressing long-standing problems of segregation programs funded by the department.

In addition to the Fair Housing Act (Title VI of the Civil Rights Act of 1964), the Department of Housing and Urban Development can more vigorously enforce Section 504 of the Americans with Disabilities Act and the Age Discrimination Act of 1975. The Justice Department and other federal agencies can also play a more active part in the future of housing rights.

Bibliography

Folts, W. Edward, and Dale E. Yeatts. *Housing and the Aging Population.* New York: Garland, 1994.

Momeni, Jamshid A., ed. *Race, Ethnicity and Minority Housing in the United States.* Westport, Conn.: Greenwood Press, 1986.

Sternlieb, George, James Hughes, and Robert Burchall. *America's Housing, Prospects and Problems.* New Brunswick, N.J.: Center for Urban Policy Research, 1980.

Zarembka, Arlene. *The Urban Housing Crisis.* Westport, Conn.: Greenwood Press, 1990.

Chapter 15

Criminal Justice

Jay A. Sigler

How would you feel if you were seized by a policeman while walking in your neighborhood and taken without any explanation to the police headquarters and held in jail for a week without any reasons given by officials? If you were also denied any chance to contact your friends and family or a lawyer, you probably would feel like a helpless victim of the police. As an American, this terrible situation, so common in dictatorships, is a fundamental violation of your rights.

In England, before the rights described in this chapter were given to accused persons, it was possible to punish and convict a man without a regular trial and subject him to cruel punishment for refusal to admit his "crimes." In 1637 John Lilburne, an English Puritan dissenter, was brought to a special court of Star Chamber, which dealt harshly with unpopular political figures. Lilburne was accused in Star Chamber of sending "factitious and scandalous books" from Holland to England. He was given no chance to have a hearing, a trial, or even representation by counsel. When he refused to answer questions about his conduct, he was immediately ordered to be punished.

For his refusal to testify against himself Lilburne was fined, tied to a cart, and whipped on his bare body through the streets of London. After that, he was placed in a pillory with his neck in a hole for several hours. When he made speeches from the pillory, he was gagged until his mouth bled. Then he was removed from the pillory and thrown into solitary confinement with irons on his hands and legs for ten days. Lilburne was also denied food during his confinement. He was released a few days later, having been convicted of nothing.

The horrible treatment received by Lilburne was so shocking that the Parliament abolished the Star Chamber, decided Lilburne's sentence was illegal, and ordered reparations (money) be paid to him. In England, after centuries of abuse of individual rights, including torture of suspects, it was gradually understood that

Without individual rights, accused persons can be subjected to cruel punishment in order to elicit a confession. This sort of punishment is part of England's history.

criminal defendants were entitled to some protections that restricted the powers of government. By the time of the American Revolution, many of these rights had been won, even for colonists.

Today, American citizens are surrounded by a wall of constitutional rights to protect them against the arbitrary acts of the police and other government agents. On rare occasions this protective wall is not sufficient to protect individuals against the power of the government, but a greater knowledge of individual rights can restrain government officials while the slow process of the criminal law is set in motion. If it comes to a trial to determine the guilt or innocence of an accused person, numerous constitutional protections are available to the accused. But most people have little risk of a criminal trial. They encounter policemen almost every day, and most policeman are highly trained to know their constitutional rights and respect them. For the few who violate those rights, severe punishments are available.

Criminal Rights in Action

Consider the actual claim of a college student in New Hampshire. This student, named Adam Crook, was riding to his chemistry class one day in 1995. He was ordered to stop by a policeman, who thought he saw that Crook was riding his bicycle the wrong way on a one-way street. After being detained by the policeman, Crook began to write down the number of the police car's license. He began to copy into his notebook the arresting officer's name and number from his badge. Then, according to Crook's version of the story, the arresting officer ripped the notebook out of his hands. Crook says that the policeman then began to shout, "This is my office. You won't go into someone's office and treat them this way. You don't put on a big show on my street." Crook was arrested and put in handcuffs. Much later, Crook filed suit against the officer, charging him with assault and battery, as well as false arrest, asserting he had been maltreated physically. This kind of encounter occurs from time to time. Policemen must enforce the law, but they don't have unlimited authority to do so. This makes police work difficult, because policemen are open to such suits when they exceed their authority. If police use excessive force or otherwise abuse their authority, they may be sued.

Justice Robert Jackson of the Supreme Court of the United States once wrote that constitutional protections are "not just for the benefit of the accused . . . (but) are the best insurance for the government itself against those blunders which leave lasting stains on a system of justice." It often appears as though persons accused of crime are sometimes given exceptional protection in the United States, subjecting the police and prosecutors to severe restrictions. This is done in the name of the rule of law.

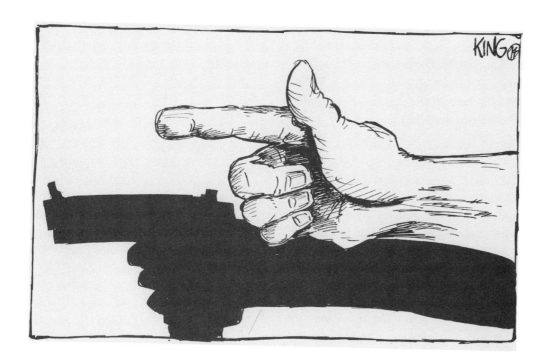

Procedural rights of accused persons have been given great importance in our criminal justice system, especially in the past 40 years. In general, the rights of the accused seem to be expanding, in spite of periodic public excitement about so-called, crime waves. But this tendency can be seen in many nations, even those with a lower crime rate than that of the United States.

It should be no surprise, then, that dealing with issues of criminal procedure has become the main business of the Supreme Court during the past four decades. In addition, during that period, juveniles below the age capable of committing crimes have also been extended many, but not all, of the protections provided by the Constitution.

As it was originally written, the Constitution of the United States had only a few provisions regarding criminal justice. A close look at the Constitution does show that the drafters were aware of at least three rights that the history of the American colonies had demonstrated were very significant. These three situations are specified in the original text:

> "The privilege of the writ of *habeas corpus* shall not be suspended, unless when in cases of rebellion or invasion the public safety may require it." (Article 1, Section 9)

> "No bill of attainder or *ex post facto* law shall be passed." (Article 1, Section 9)

> "No state shall . . . pass any bill of attainder, *ex post facto* law, or law impairing the obligation of contracts." (Article 1, Section 10)

So from the beginning of the current American system of government, as a free nation under the Constitution, three rights were spelled out to restrict national and state powers over the criminal law. Few Americans are aware of the meaning of habeas corpus, ex post facto, or bill of attainder, but to the Founding Fathers these rights were at the cornerstone of American liberty.

Habeas Corpus

An American cannot be sent to prison without a trial. This may seem obvious, but in many nations this precious right does not exist. Without it, individual freedom is impossible, because otherwise at any time a person could be confined indefinitely against his will for any reason or for no reason at all. Around the world prisons are filled with men and women who have not been convicted of any crime. In America, that is impossible.

The writ of habeas corpus is the most important safeguard to personal liberty in America. The writ can be traced back to seventeenth-century England. Habeas corpus means that anyone who is held by the police or other government officials can regain his personal freedom by applying to a judge. After the individual makes his habeas corpus application, the judge must find out whether the individual is being held by the police for just cause. People who are held in jail must be let go pending trial if a court issues a writ of habeas corpus. Only in cases of first-degree murder or another extremely serious criminal charge can a person be held in jail before a trial. Even then, he or she can seek legal help to prepare for the trial.

The Constitution says that the writ of habeas corpus may be suspended "when in cases of rebellion or invasion the public safety may require it." During the Civil War President Abraham Lincoln temporarily suspended this great right because of what he believed to be wartime emergencies. For this suspension Lincoln was denounced by Supreme Court Chief Justice Roger Taney, who claimed that the president of the United States cannot suspend the writ unless Congress or the courts gives him that power. Congress eventually did so, allowing the president to suspend the writ "whenever, in his judgment, the public safety may require it." Congress has also extended the writ of habeas corpus to apply to the actions of state officials, so the writ is available in virtually any arrest situation in America, except in a presidentially declared wartime emergency situation.

Bill of Attainder

In English history a "bill of attainder" was an act of Parliament that charged someone with treason and at the same time pronounced a death penalty upon him. In effect, it was a legislative decree that declared a person a criminal without the need of any trial. In fifteenth- and sixteenth-century England bills of attainder were commonly used to punish political enemies of the king or Parliament. They were also used by colonial legislatures before the American Revolution. In modern times, victims of Hitler and Stalin were subjected to similar treatment, either by executive order or by act of a legislature. Punishment of an individual by legislative decree is unconstitutional in America.

The people who drafted this part of our Constitution wanted to make such arbitrary, unjust actions impossible. To a very large extent, they succeeded. The Supreme Court of the United States has several times struck down certain federal statutes that seemed to declare individuals criminals without giving them the opportunity to stand trial. However, the legislatures of America have rarely indulged in this kind of punishment during our nation's history.

After the Civil War some doctors and lawyers were made to swear that they had not aided the Confederate cause. Any such punishment of former rebels and ex-Confederates without a trial was deemed by the Supreme Court to be an unconstitutional bill of attainder. During the anti-Communist hysteria of the 1950s, Congress actually named three federal employees who were not to receive their salaries because of alleged subversion. This assumption of guilt without a trial was another illegal bill of attainder. In a similar case in 1965, the Court declared that a statute that made it a crime for a member of the Communist Party to serve as an officer of a labor union was a bill of attainder and unconstitutional.

Ex Post Facto

The English Parliament in the seventeenth and eighteenth century, while America was a colony, also found other ways to create criminal penalties unfairly. In England it was possible for Parliament to make an action illegal that was perfectly innocent at the time it was committed. Retroactively, these statutes labeled a past action criminal. By this trick, anyone could be made a criminal long after he did something.

The Constitution drafters, familiar with this English device, wanted to prevent it from being used in our new nation. Both state and national governments are forbidden from making ex post facto criminal laws. All retroactive criminal laws are unconstitutional.

This does not mean that Congress may not increase a punishment for an existing crime. Adding additional years to a penalty for a past crime for which a person has been tried and convicted is not unconstitutional. Nor is it improper for Congress to terminate old-age benefits or to increase taxes on money earned in the past. Such statutes are not criminal in nature and do not come under the ban of the Constitution. Congress or a state legislature may pass retroactive noncriminal legislation, although it is usually politically unpopular to change the laws in this way.

The Bill of Rights and Criminal Justice

When it was ratified in the summer of 1788, the American Constitution contained only a few individual rights. Many state legislators insisted that they would vote against ratification because the Constitution did not contain guarantees of basic rights. Popular demand for a Bill of Rights was based on the fear of an all-powerful government that could oppress the people. Memories of colonial abuses of power were still fresh. However, the idea of a Bill of Rights was rooted in English history. The English people had suffered from royal tyranny and had built up legal protections against persecution of individuals. In fact there was an English Bill of Rights of 1689, well before the American Revolution.

As in the English Bill of Rights, the American rights, first drafted by James Madison, were largely concerned with the rights of persons accused of crime. Many other rights, found in other chapters of this book, were also added by James Madison and the first Congress in 1789. The first eight amendments, as they were eventually ratified by the state legislatures in 1791, form the American Bill of Rights, and have remained unchanged from that time to this.

Beyond the rights mentioned in the original Constitution, additional constitutional limitations were placed on the criminal law powers of government by later amendments to the Constitution. Twenty-three new rights were created by the first ten amendments to the Constitution, added in 1791. The first eight amendments contained twelve additional rights concerning criminal procedure. It was clearly understood by the public that none of these new rights applied to the states, which had their own constitutions. Until 1868 no portion of the Bill of Rights applied to the states. The Civil War changed all of that, because Congress amended the Constitution after the war was won to restrict certain powers of the states, especially those who had fought against the North.

After the Civil War Congress was concerned with the rights of the newly freed slaves and proposed some constitutional changes to end slavery and also to safeguard the rights of the freed African Americans. The states ratified the Fourteenth Amendment to the Constitution in 1868. This amendment reads, in part, "nor shall any state deprive any person of life, liberty or property without due process of law." The persons whom Congress had in mind at the time were the ex-slaves, who might otherwise have been abused by the Southern states that had lost the

Civil War. Yet, in time, the rights of ex-slaves against the states were held to include all Americans. The Fourteenth Amendment has long been a source of individual rights against state and local governments.

By means of judicial interpretation the Bill of Rights has been extended to the states through the Fourteenth Amendment. At the beginning of the twentieth century states were not required to provide jury trials in criminal cases; now they are. Freedom from unreasonable searches and seizures, the privilege against self-incrimination, the guarantee against double jeopardy, and the rights to counsel and to a speedy trial were once available only in federal courts. Now these rights are required in all courts. This extension of the Bill of Rights was accomplished by the Supreme Court by a slow judicial incorporation of the requirements of the federal Bill of Rights into a national approach to criminal justice. Without this judicial standardization of criminal justice there would have been 51 different ways in which accused persons were treated—one for each state, and another for the national government.

Even so, not all of the federal Bill of Rights applies to the states, as with grand jury indictments, a procedure used federally to make a formal criminal accusation: Not all states use grand juries. Verdicts in state criminal trials need not be unanimous, although they must be in federal cases. To a minor degree, protections available to criminal defendants are sometimes slightly lower than in federal trials.

The Bill of Rights was ratified in 1791 and the Fourteenth Amendment in 1868, but the rights of accused persons are not frozen in time. The Supreme Court has sometimes held that rights not available in 1791 or 1868 may still operate to restrict the powers of government. After all, modern police forces did not exist in those times. The Supreme Court often takes a more generous view of our rights, expanding them beyond the historical conditions that existed when the Bill of Rights was first ratified or extended to the states. After all, when the Bill of Rights was ratified, the defendant in a criminal case was barred from testifying in his own behalf in many states. Most people would agree that fairness today would permit such testimony. History matters, but it does not bind the Supreme Court in applying the Bill of Rights.

Arrests and Entrapment

The language of the Fourth Amendment to the Constitution states, "The right of the people to be secure in their persons, houses, papers, and effects, against unreasonable searches and seizures, shall not be violated, and no warrant shall issue, but upon probable cause, supported by oath or affirmation, and particularly describing the place to be searched, and the persons or things to be seized." This language, while clear enough, is strange to most people who are unfamiliar with the criminal process.

A police officer does not need a warrant to arrest a suspect if a felony is committed in his presence. An arrest without warrant is possible if the person detained may reasonably be suspected of having recently committed a crime. This means that if a minor offense is committed outside of his immediate presence, a warrant must be obtained. Several states permit arrest without a warrant on "reasonable grounds" for all offenses, even if the policeman did not see the crime committed. In all other cases a warrant must be issued before an arrest can be made. A warrant is a written order of a judge or a court clerk when authorized. There are two types of warrants: arrest warrants and search warrants.

What is an arrest? The Boston Police were accused by the American Civil Liberties Union (ACLU) of Massachusetts of illegally detaining and photographing people on the street, in violation of their constitutional rights. The ACLU pointed to many incidents as examples of this police practice. In one, 20 police officers rounded up 16 youths in a housing development, lined them up against a wall, ordered them to disclose their names and social security numbers, and then snapped their photographs. After that, according to an eyewitness, they were released. Not one of the youths was charged with anything. The ACLU asked Boston Police Commissioner Paul Evans to turn over the photographs and to cease the practice of sweeping the streets and photographing young people. The complaint was referred to the police department's Internal Affairs Division for investigation. Whatever happened in Boston, it was not a proper arrest.

An illegal arrest or any other unreasonable seizure of an individual is a violation of the Constitution's Fourth Amendment. To be lawful an arrest must be made with "probable cause." Probable cause is a practical notion that is intended to bar an arbitrary arrest, an arrest made with no reasonable justification. A policeman must make a judgment to arrest a suspect swiftly, but he cannot do so carelessly. As the Supreme Court has indicated, a judge, looking at the conduct of a policeman at the time of arrest, must be convinced that the policeman acted reasonably under all the circumstances. Simple good faith or good intentions on the part of the officer is not enough.

Arrest merely on suspicion of having committed a crime will not do either. Long after the arrest judges may find that an arrest had been improper, if they believe that "probable cause" was lacking. On the whole judges do not frequently throw out a criminal charge because of an improper arrest, but they will defend the Fourth Amendment when it has been clearly ignored or violated. As a rule of thumb in arrests, it can be said that to be justifiable, it must be more probable than not that a crime has been permitted and that the detained person has done the deed.

The use of deadly force in making an arrest is unreasonable "unless the suspect threatens the officer with a weapon or there is probable cause to believe that he has committed a crime involving the infliction or threatened infliction of serious physical harm." This use of force is part of the scandal that arose in the City of Los Angeles over the police beating of Rodney King on March 3, 1991. King claimed that excessive force was used in making his arrest and after he was taken into custody. The whole incident was captured on videotape by George Holliday, an eyewitness who offered his videotape of the beating of Rodney King to the Los Angeles police, who, at the time, refused the offer.

The legal rules governing the use of force require that the suspect must pose an immediate threat to the safety of officers or others. In the case of Mr. King the videotape taken during his arrest showed that he had been effectively subdued by the police and restrained on the ground by them while certain police continued to beat him physically. It was also clear that for much of the time he was not able to resist the arrest. Excessive police force of this kind is subject to civil and criminal punishment. In 1993 two Los Angeles policemen were tried and convicted of the crime of depriving Mr. King of his constitutional rights. Most police departments have specific policies governing the

use of force by officers. After the King incident, and several trials of police held in its wake, these procedures have been made clearer and stronger.

To understand arrest better, consider a common urban problem. In most large American cities there are numbers of homeless people who are, for various reasons, forced to live on the streets. Some of them irritate residents just because they are laying on the streets and alleys. This is not, by itself, a crime. They cannot be arrested merely for vagrancy or for engaging in conduct that is "annoying" to a passerby. Some of these individuals resort to street begging. This is not a crime, although it may be a nuisance. At some point the behavior of a homeless person may amount to a crime, if the city government can describe in sufficient detail an act with some definite criminal component. Stealing, violence, or even threatening violence will be sufficient to constitute a crime. Under these circumstances an arrest may be possible. Otherwise, city police cannot arrest homeless people and put them in jail. The homeless may be compelled to move from a particular location, but there is a risk that too much force might be applied. If that is done, policemen can be disciplined. The best and most lawful tactic is to talk to the homeless and persuade them to leave the streets, not to arrest them. Even the homeless have rights as Americans.

Sometimes secret agents and undercover policemen are used to obtain sufficient evidence for an arrest. Private citizens, working as agents of the police, may also be employed to get evidence on a criminal suspect. These tactics are typically used in crimes involving prostitution, liquor and narcotic sales, and gambling. Undercover agents are often able to gather evidence of secretive conduct by working from the inside and by becoming acquainted with the suspects. These secretive crimes are difficult to detect otherwise. However, there is a risk of "entrapment," which arises when the police agent actively encourages the commission of a crime.

The presence of entrapment is a defense to a suspect's otherwise criminal act, but it does not always succeed. Any situation in which "the criminal design originates with the police agents and they implant in the mind of an innocent person the disposition to commit the offense" is an entrapment. The defense may claim that the crime would not have been committed but for the invitation of the police agent; then the prosecution must prove that the defendant was disposed to commit such a crime even without the inducement of the police agent. Unfortunately, the Supreme Court has never held that entrapment is forbidden by the Constitution. It is up to a judge to decide whether to recognize this defense in a particular case, and judges differ on the question. The Constitution does not bar conviction of a defendant for the sale of narcotics supplied to him by a government agent.

Searches and Seizures

As part of their work police sometimes stop suspicious persons in order to question them or to investigate doubtful conduct. As part of the procedure there may be a search for dangerous or illegal weapons. This police technique of "stop and frisk," the most common form of police search, is used when there are insufficient grounds for an arrest. Restraining a person on the street is a "seizure" and exploring the surfaces of a suspect's clothing is a "search," for the purposes of the Fourth Amendment. A frisk of subjects can be used as a police tool, even without a search warrant, subject to the tests of reasonable conduct required by the Constitution.

The Fourth Amendment, together with the self-incrimination clause of the Fourteenth Amendment, forbids the federal government from convicting a person of a crime by using testimony or evidence that was obtained by an "unreasonable search and seizure." This kind of evidence is inadmissible in a federal court, whether it was taken by state, local, or federal officers. The same rule of inadmissibility applies in state courts.

The Supreme Court has attempted to set limits to police conduct during these temporary seizures of suspects. According to the Court, the standard is that "the detaining officer must have a particularized and objective basis for suspecting that particular person stopped of criminal activity." This is a lower standard than that required for an arrest. A stop-and-frisk search will be upheld if the arresting officer had a reasonable suspicion that a crime has been, or is about to be, committed and if the suspect is the person who committed or plans to commit the act; therefore, a suspect may be stopped and searched near the scene of a recent robbery merely because he met a victim's general description of the offender. Similarly, a suspect may be stopped because of information given by a usually reliable informant, although an anonymous tip is insufficient.

Stopping a vehicle is a "search," but stopping a pedestrian is not. The Fourth Amendment, in this context, means that a brief stop of a pedestrian for questioning is permissible, as long as the individual knows that he or she can leave. Police are permitted to make inquiries without a warrant. If the individual who is stopped reasonably believes that he is not free to leave, then the standards of probable cause required for an arrest apply. It does not matter what the policeman believes, only that the detained person reasonably believes that he is being held. As long as the detained person feels free to terminate the encounter, no arrest has taken place.

If the suspect appears armed and dangerous, a "protective search" may be made by the police official. This requires a substantial possibility, not a certainty, that the suspect may be armed and potentially dangerous. Even then, courts require a two-step procedure for a search. First the officer must pat down the surface of the suspect's clothing. Then, only if she feels something that may be a weapon, she may intrude below the surface, and into a pocket. This search without a warrant is limited to looking for guns, knives, clubs, or "other instruments for the assault of the police officer." The search is limited to the purpose of protecting the officer from harm and is not permitted as a means of finding other evidence of a crime.

The passenger part of an automobile may be examined as part of a protective search. If the police officer has a reasonable suspicion that the suspect is armed and dangerous, he may look at places where a weapon might be placed or hidden, without first having to obtain a search warrant. A protective search is especially required if a risk exists that the suspect can gain immediate access to the weapon.

On the other hand, fingerprinting at the station is considered differently. The detention of a suspect at a police station poses no great risk to the police officer, so the standards to support such a search could be as high as in any arrest and search. Normally, a warrant would be required for fingerprinting; however, statutes have been passed authorizing station-house detention and fingerprinting of suspects, which suggests that in many places involuntary fingerprinting may be legal as part of the police investigative process. To the courts, fingerprinting seems much less an obtrusive form of search than most others.

In general, the Fourth Amendment requires that "no warrant shall issue, except upon probable cause." A valid arrest warrant or a search warrant may be issued only after a statement or complaint that sets forth the facts establishing probable cause. Although many circumstances exist in which arrests and searches may be made without

CLANCY, GET THE BOYS AND SURROUND THE LOCKER!

probable cause, courts strongly prefer arrest or search warrants, on the ground that a neutral and detached judge will make a better decision than a policeman who is hot on the trail of crime. The warrant process also has the advantage of creating a written record of the circumstances in advance of an arrest or search. Otherwise, courts must rely upon the testimony of the officers about their reasons and intentions.

To obtain a search warrant the police must show that the items sought are connected to criminal activity and that the items will be found in the place to be searched. Sufficient information must be presented to the judge to allow him to determine probable cause. The magistrate will not merely issue a blank check for a search. The magistrate who issues the warrant must be "neutral and detached" and may not have any personal interest in the matter.

If evidence beyond the scope of the warrant is seized, the evidence removed will be "suppressed," meaning that it cannot be used at a criminal trial. Minor errors will not defeat a search. If the search is of an automobile, the warrant must direct the officer to one automobile, either by license number or by make of the vehicle. A mistake of color or year of manufacture is regarded as a minor error.

A valid warrant for the search of a person must provide his or her name. If the individual's name is unknown, then an otherwise complete description of his or her appearance, approximate age, height, and weight, or any aliases will be sufficient.

A search of property for special items must list the material sought, at least in a general way. A statement that "cases of whiskey" are sought will be sufficient. However, where a search warrant is aimed at books, papers, and documents, greater detail is needed. Courts are very sensitive about privacy issues with such items. First Amendment free speech issues may also be involved. As a result, warrants for documents or books clearly and definitely describe the items to be seized.

Invalid warrants may sometimes be used to gather evidence for a criminal trial, as a so-called good faith exception to the general rules about warrants. If the warrant was issued by an impartial judge, and if the officer was honest and not reckless in preparing his warrant request, the evidence taken may be used. However, the officer using the warrant must have "an objectively reasonable belief" that the warrant was valid.

Federal laws and most state laws also limit the amount of force that may be used to bring about a search. An officer may not break into a home or business until notice of authority is given and entrance refused. The major exception to this rule is if risk exists that notice might result in the destruction of the evidence being sought. In those situations entry without notice is proper.

An Ohio Case Example
Widener v. *Frye*, 809 F. Supp. 35 (S.D. Ohio, 1992)

During a class test an Ohio high school teacher thought she noticed a strong odor of marijuana in the room, coming from one student in particular. The teacher called a security guard, who took the student to the principal's office. The guard and the principal both detected the odor of marijuana, and observed that the boy appeared to be sluggish.

Another security guard was summoned. Then, with the boy's permission, his bag and jacket were searched for marijuana. The guards then proceeded to pat down the student under his arms while he was dressed. The boy then emptied his pockets, on request of the guards. No evidence of drugs or drug use was uncovered by this search.

Then the female principal left the room so that the two male security guards could search further. The guards requested the boy to remove his shoes and socks, lift his shirt and lower his pants so they could search further. An intimate search of his body took place, but no evidence of drugs was found.

When these searches were challenged in federal court they were found by the judge to be reasonable. The odor of marijuana and the boy's lethargic appearance were deemed sufficient to justify the search. The strip search itself was said to have been carried out in a reasonable manner. The fact that the boy was embarrassed to some degree did not make the search unreasonable.

While making a search, an officer may discover other incriminating evidence not described in the warrant. If the search is lawful and the police stumble upon such evidence, it may be used in later trial. However, the items can be seized only if there is probable cause that they are "fruits, instrumentalities or evidence of crime." A warrant is not a hunting license for anything on the searched premises. If the item to be seized is not listed in the warrant and is not in plain view the officer may need to go back to the judge to get another warrant.

The law of search and seizure is highly technical, and the degree to which a court will uphold a policeman's judgment differs from place to place, so it is best for amateurs not to delve too deeply into this issue. If a complex problem of this sort arises, a lawyer should be consulted as quickly as possible.

The average citizen should know that if the police observe a traffic violation, they are empowered to stop the vehicle and request to see the driver's license and the vehicle registration. A similar authority is present if there is reasonable suspicion that a driver is unlicensed or a vehicle is stolen or unregistered. Spot checks at roadblocks are also permissible. Checkpoints to seek out intoxicated drivers are usually acceptable procedure.

The other point every one should know is that your person or property can be searched whenever you consent to it. If you do not want to be searched, you can say so; otherwise, you may lose your rights under the Fourth Amendment. A consent must be voluntary and knowing. Ignorant, mentally ill, or intoxicated persons may be unable to give their consent, and evidence taken from them may be invalidated later because of their condition. It is best to be polite and pleasant if you choose to withhold your consent; otherwise, you may be considered to be resisting arrest, especially if you behave violently or abusively. Besides, you should be aware that police have the authority to search individuals in the course of a lawful arrest for the commission of a crime.

Students should be aware that although they are protected by the Fourth Amendment against unreasonable searches and seizures, school authorities are authorized to conduct limited searches without a warrant or even probable cause. In some schools police dogs are used to chase the scent of marijuana, cocaine, hashish, and heroin. School lockers, books, and personal belongings may be sniffed, as a form of search. Such searches have been held to be lawful by courts around the country.

Courts deem a search lawful if there are "reasonable grounds for suspecting" that the search will uncover a violation of law or a proper school regulation. There is some right to privacy for school desks and lockers, but it is not an unlimited right. Because public school lockers are on public property, student privacy rights are few. Courts have been attempting to draw lines between student privacy rights and the authority of school officials. The circumstances of the age of the students and the seriousness of the suspected problem will be weighed by courts when searches are challenged by students. If police are involved or there is a risk of a criminal charge, a higher standard of protection of individual rights may apply.

Wiretapping and Eavesdropping

Wiretapping and eavesdropping are just special forms of searches, but in our high technology era they are of increasing importance. Most citizens have little to fear in this area, as agents of the government are unlikely to be eavesdropping on private conversations.

Wiretapping is subject to the same controls as other government searches. The Federal Communications Act of 1934 makes it illegal to wiretap telephone conversations without the consent of one of the parties. However, there is a broader federal statute, the Crime Control and Safe Streets Act of 1968, which permits the attorney general or other officials in the U.S. Justice Department to apply to a federal judge for an order permitting wiretapping or other electronic eavesdropping. Most states allow prosecutors to use wiretaps to provide evidence of murder, kidnapping, or other serious crimes. Some of these statutes allow wiretapping in cases of narcotic drugs and marijuana.

A judge will not issue an order permitting electronic surveillance unless facts are shown that there is probable cause that an individual is committing, has committed, or is about to commit a particular offense. No judicial order may exceed 30 days, and the judge may set a shorter limit. In an emergency situation involving immediate danger of death or serious physical injury, in conspiratorial activities that threaten the national security, or in organized crime conspiratorial activities, an interception of communications may be made by authorities. However, in such emergencies a court order must be obtained within 48 hours after the interception.

Sometimes police will use secret agents to obtain incriminating statements. Informants may be electronically wired up in such a way as to record incriminating statements made in the presence of the government agent. Technically, this kind of secretive recording is not "tapping" and is not governed by the same statutes. No invasion of the premises of a suspect has taken place. In fact,

courts have held that the Fourth Amendment does not cover this kind of situation.

However, courts try to discourage deceptive practices and fraudulent practices by police informants. In one case, the secret agent engaged the defendant in conversations in a restaurant, in his car, and in his home. The informer did not testify at the trial, but the narcotics agents who were listening to the conversations did testify. Because of the trusted relationship between the wired informant and the suspect, the Supreme Court threw out this transmitted and recorded evidence. But this case was unusual because of the extensive trust that the defendant had placed in the wired agent. In general, police and government agents may record conversations secretly by wiring their agents, and this is a common procedure. Several Mafia leaders have been convicted on this kind of secret-recording evidence.

Recording devices may even be placed in advance in rooms (or prison cells) where meetings are held to plan criminal acts. Of course, wired police agents may not actively encourage the commission of crimes in order to get evidence. This form of "entrapment" may invalidate later criminal charges, because the defendant may claim (with mixed success, in court) that he would not have considered a criminal act unless he had been enticed into it by the police agent.

Interrogation and Confessions

The questioning of suspects by the police has come under close scrutiny of the Supreme Court of the United States. As a result of judicial suspicions, a number of legal boundaries to police conduct have been set. These judicial reactions represent an effort to ensure the reliability of confessions made by suspects and to discourage police brutality to suspects.

In 1964 The Supreme Court declared that some sort of right to counsel arose when a policy inquiry had narrowed to a particular suspect. If a suspect has been taken into custody and requests the help of a lawyer, the Sixth Amendment to the Constitution guarantees him the right to "have the assistance of counsel for his defense." Furthermore, the police have a duty to warn a suspect of his absolute right to remain silent after an arrest.

The Basic Federal Wiretapping Statute

626A.06 Procedure for Interception of Wire or Oral Communications

Subdivision 1. The applications. Each application for a warrant authorizing or approving the interception of a wire, electronic, or oral communication shall be made in writing upon oath or affirmation to a judge of the district court, of the court of appeals, or of the supreme court and shall state the applicant's authority to make such application. Each application shall include the following information:

(a) the identity of the investigative or law enforcement officer making the application, and the officer authorizing the application;

(b) a full and complete statement of the facts and circumstances relied upon by the applicant, to justify the applicant's belief that an order should be issued, including (I) details as to the particular offense that has been, is being, or is about to be committed, (ii) except as provided in subdivision 11, a particular description of the nature and location of the facilities from which or the place where the communication is to be intercepted, (iii) a particular description of the type of communications sought to be intercepted, (iv) the identity of the person, if known, committing the offense and whose communications are to be intercepted;

(c) a full and complete statement as to whether or not other investigative procedures have been tried and failed or why they reasonably appear to be unlikely to succeed if tried or to be too dangerous;

(d) a statement of the period of time for which the interception is required to be maintained. If the nature of the investigation is such that the authorization for interception should not automatically terminate when the described type of communication has been first obtained, a particular description of facts establishing probable cause to believe that additional communications of the same type will occur thereafter;

(e) a full and complete statement of the facts concerning all previous applications known to the individual authorizing and making the application, made to any judge for authorization to intercept, or for approval of interceptions of, wire, electronic, or oral communications involving any of the same persons, facilities, or places specified in the application, and the action taken by the judge on each such application;

(f) where statements in the application are solely upon the information or belief of the applicant, the grounds for the belief must be given; and

(g) the names of persons submitting affidavits in support of the application.

Subd. 2. Additional showing of probable cause. The court to whom any such application is made, before issuing any warrant thereon, may examine on oath the person seeking the warrant and any witnesses the person may produce, and must take the person's affidavit or other affidavits in writing, and cause them to be subscribed by the party or parties making the same. The court may also require the applicant to furnish additional documentary evidence or additional oral testimony to satisfy itself of the existence of probable cause for issuance of the warrant. . . .

Subd. 5. Duration of warrant. No warrant entered under this section may authorize or approve the interception of any wire, electronic, or oral communication for any period longer than is necessary to achieve the objective of the authorization, nor in any event longer than 30 days. . . .

Subd. 9. Secrecy of warrant proceedings. A warrant for intercepting communications and the application, affidavits, and return prepared in connection therewith, and also any information concerning the application for, the granting of, or the denial of a warrant for intercepting communications shall remain secret and subject to all the penalties of this chapter for unauthorized disclosure to persons not lawfully engaged in preparing and executing such a warrant, unless and until the same shall have been disclosed in a criminal trial or proceeding or shall have been furnished to a defendant pursuant to this chapter.

To show how this works in practice, consider the facts in a 1977 case, *Brewer* v. *Williams*. Williams was being transported from Davenport, Iowa, to Des Moines, Iowa, on a murder charge. The police had assured Williams's lawyer that he would not be questioned during the trip; yet, when a police detective mentioned that the murder victim's body hadn't been found and that a decent Christian burial for the body would be denied him, Williams led the police to the body. The Supreme Court declared in this case that Williams deserved to have the advice of counsel. The evidence that Williams provided of his knowledge of the place of the victim's body had to be excluded from his murder trial. In effect, Williams was being questioned during the trip to Des Moines and he could not protect himself adequately without a lawyer.

The right to counsel begins when the suspect has been arrested and the government has committed itself to prosecuting him for a crime. However, the privilege against self-incrimination arises at an even earlier stage. This privilege "is fully applicable during a period of custodial interrogation," that is, while the suspect is being held and questioned.

The privilege against self-incrimination arises under the Fifth Amendment to the Constitution. The Fifth Amendment asserts that no person "shall be compelled in any criminal case to be a witness against himself." This means, at least, that in any federal proceeding, civil or criminal, a witness cannot be forced to give evidence that might subject him or her to a later criminal prosecution. In general, the same is true in state courts.

In a famous 1966 decision called the *Miranda* case, the Supreme Court sharply defined a "constitutional code of rules for confessions" (as it was described by dissenting judges). When "the individual is first subjected to police interrogation while in custody at the station or otherwise deprived of his freedom of action in a significant way," the rules come into effect. These rules do not apply to general questioning on or around the scene of a crime.

The person in custody "must first be informed that he has the right to remain silent," so as to reduce the pressure to injure his own interests. This warning "must be accompanied by the explanation that anything said can and will be used against the individual in court." He must also "be clearly informed that he has the right to consult with a lawyer and to have the lawyer with him

WARNING

The constitution requires that I inform you of your rights:

You have a right to remain silent. If you talk to any police officer, anything you say can and will be used against you in court.

You have a right to consult with a lawyer before you are questioned, and may have him with you during questioning.

If you cannot afford a lawyer, one will be appointed for you, if you wish, before any questioning.

If you wish to answer questions, you have the right to stop answering at any time.

You may stop answering questions at any time if you wish to talk to a lawyer, and may have him with you during any further questioning.

Rev. 9-79

This poster is used to remind police officers that they are required to make suspects aware of their rights prior to an interrogation. Any statement that is made by a suspect in circumstances that violate this requirement may not be admitted into evidence.

during interrogation." If he cannot afford a lawyer one "will be appointed to represent him."

A suspect must be told of these rights by the police, even if he or she is aware of them. The individual may then exercise those rights as he or she chooses. If, after receiving these warnings, the suspect "indicates in any manner, at any time prior to or during questioning, that he wishes to remain silent, the interrogation must cease." And if the suspect requests a lawyer, the questioning must cease until one is present. Statements made by a suspect without the presence of a lawyer are not easy to use in court. The government must "demonstrate that the defendant knowingly and intelligently waived his privilege against self-incrimination and his right to retained or appointed counsel."

Any statement made by a suspect in circumstances that violate these rules may not be admitted into evidence. Moreover, the Supreme Court has said that the prosecution may not "use at trial the fact that the defendant stood mute or claimed his privilege in the face of accusation." Guilt must be proven beyond a reasonable doubt, based on other evidence produced by the prosecution at the time of trial.

No nation places as severe a burden on police procedures as the United States. A high regard for individual rights seems to be coupled with a judicial suspicion of the quality of police concern for those rights. Even so, police have learned to accept the *Miranda* rules, and many suspects continue to confess voluntarily to crimes anyway. Probably, nearly as many confessions are given now as there were before these warnings were required.

Efforts made in Congress to "repeal" the *Miranda* rules are probably unconstitutional. Rights received under the Constitution cannot be taken away by mere legislation. The Constitution must be amended or the Supreme Court must revise its views concerning these rights if *Miranda* requirements are to be changed.

The *Miranda* rules apply to "questioning initiated by law enforcement officers." They do not apply to questions asked by private citizens. They do not apply to interrogation by school principals or other school officials. Any statements made to these individuals need not be preceded by a warning, and statements given can be used as evidence in criminal trials. It is not clear whether the *Miranda* rules apply to parole or probation officers.

Many other tactics of the police and prosecutor are not protected by the privilege against self-incrimination. For example, speeding motorists may be required to give blood or breath samples to arresting officers. Although this may seem to be a violation of the privilege against self-incrimination, courts have held otherwise. As one judge put it, the privilege protects a suspect only from being compelled to express the "contents of his mind."

Your body can give testimony, without any violation of the Fifth Amendment occurring. Police can take fingerprints and photographs or ask suspects to put on a coat or a hat, to repeat words that are written down, or to listen to what a witness says. A suspect can refuse to answer questions posed to him by invoking the privilege against self-incrimination, but only if he is a suspect. Witnesses do not have the privilege.

Police may require suspects to provide fingerprints, blood and hair samples, photographs, and measurements. Victims may also examine photographs taken of the defendant as a means of verifying identity. These identification techniques are not prohibited by the self-incrimination privilege. Failure to cooperate with the police in these matters may result in a court order compelling the suspect to undergo the police procedure.

Police lineups are another tool familiar from the TV screen. This technique can be used only after the accused has been formally indicted for the crime. Even then, the suspect must be notified about the planned lineup, and it cannot be held unless the suspect has his lawyer present. This requirement is imposed by federal courts because of two constitutional rights of the defendant: the right to confrontation and the right to counsel. If this required lineup procedure is not followed, the testimony taken at the lineup is inadmissible at trial.

Right to Counsel

The right to counsel is found in the Sixth Amendment to the Constitution. It states that an accused is "to be informed of the nature and cause of the accusation; to be confronted with the witnesses against him; to have compulsory process for obtaining witnesses in his favor, and to have the assistance of counsel for his defense."

In England, at the time of the adoption of the American Constitution, a person accused of a felony had no right to a lawyer. In fact, even if the person was willing to pay for counsel, the English courts denied him such a right. Because of the English common law practice the right to counsel was included in the American Bill of Rights. However, the right to counsel was not broadened to its current scope until well into the twentieth century. By 1932 the Supreme Court was prepared to insist that the due process cause of the Fourteenth Amendment made right to counsel a fundamental right in death penalty cases.

Then, in 1963, in the famous case of *Gideon v. Wainright,* the Court extended the right to counsel to all criminal cases involving poor people. In that case, by a nine-to-zero vote, the Court held that all indigent people are entitled to lawyers at criminal trials. The facts were these: Clarence Gideon had been convicted of a crime in a case in which the trial judge denied him the right to have court-appointed lawyer. From his jail cell, Gideon wrote a letter to the Supreme Court, asking to have his conviction reviewed and a new trial held. The Supreme Court agreed with Gideon and appointed lawyer Abe Fortas to represent him. Fortas, who was appointed two years later to the Supreme Court himself, argued the case for Gideon. The result was a victory, with a new trial ordered for Gideon, this time with the help of another court-appointed lawyer. Gideon's lawyer was able to cross-examine the state's witnesses, which Gideon had been unable to do for himself at his trial. Finally, Clarence Gideon was found innocent of the crime for which he had been previously convicted several years before.

After this decision many legal experts argued that the right to counsel should begin before a criminal trial takes place. That expansion took place in just two years. By 1964 the Supreme Court agreed that to deny a suspect in a criminal case the right to counsel violated the Sixth Amendment. The right to counsel began at the point where "the investigation is no longer a general inquiry into an unsolved crime but has begun to focus on a particular suspect." By taking this view, the American right to counsel became as broad as in any nation in the world, especially since it included the right to have free lawyers for people who could not afford to pay for one.

The right to counsel in the United States applies to criminal proceedings, including some misdemeanors (minor criminal offenses), but the right to court-appointed counsel does not apply to cases in which imprisonment is not at stake. The right to counsel does not extend to legislative investigations or administrative hearings. In informal juvenile proceedings there is no right to counsel. A probation revocation proceeding is not a part of the original criminal case, so there is no right of counsel then. If the defendant appeals from his conviction in a criminal case, he has no right to court-appointed counsel, although some courts may grant one.

The Supreme Court has been deeply concerned with protecting the rights of poor people in criminal cases. Even though there is no right of counsel in very minor offenses, where only the risk of fines is at stake, the Court has granted poor defendants other special rights. Indigent defendants have, at least, a right to get a free record of all the testimony taken at criminal trials or hearings preliminary to trials. In one such case a poor person was fined $500 for disorderly conduct and interference with a police officer. When he sought to appeal from a judgment in which he was held not entitled to court-appointed counsel, the higher courts agreed to order a free transcript (trial record) for him so that he could challenge his conviction. Providing a free transcript is not as effective a help to a poor person as a free attorney would be, but the costs of providing free legal

help in all kinds of criminal trials is more than the Supreme Court is willing to order.

To be indigent for the purposes of court-appointed counsel it is not necessary that a defendant be absolutely broke. It is sufficient if the accused lacks the financial resources to retain a competent attorney to defend him. Some authorities hold that the resources of members of his family may be considered. If the accused's spouse has adequate income or property, the court may not agree to appoint counsel on his behalf. The question of whether an accused person is indigent enough to be entitled to the assignment of counsel must be determined according to the facts of each individual case.

The American Bar Association Standards for the Administration of Criminal Justice suggest that the constitutional right to counsel should be provided in all types of criminal proceedings, whenever the offense is punishable by loss of liberty. For other offenses, appointed counsel are not required. However, the issue of right to counsel should not depend on whether the crimes is called a felony, a misdemeanor, or something else.

Bail and Speedy Trial

The Eighth Amendment provides, in part: "Excessive bail shall not be required."

Bail is the security (money or property, usually) required of a person accused of a crime to ensure that he will be present at trial. Bail allows accused persons to be free pending trial. Pretrial release permits the accused to continue with his life intact until the trial is held. Bail allows families to remain together and lets the accused stay employed. Bail also permits the accused to work with his attorney in preparing his defense.

In noncapital crimes (those that do not involve the possibility of a death sentence) bail is usually available as a right. Most American states grant an absolute constitutional right to bail in noncapital cases. However, Congress or the some state legislatures can define other classes of crime that are nonbailable. The national Constitution bans only "excessive bail"; it does not provide an absolute right to be free on bail prior to trial. For example, Congress has decided that bail should not be provided to defendants who present a threat of harm to witnesses.

All individuals are presumed innocent of crime until convicted at a trial. So, individuals may not be punished in advance of trial on the ground that they may be violent persons. Still, if an accused person is considered by the prosecution to pose, while awaiting trial, a genuine "danger to the community," pretrial detention may be possible under federal statute. Even then, a "prompt detention hearing" must be held before a neutral judge at which the prosecution must prove not the guilt of the accused but that "no conditions of release can reasonably assure the safety of the community." In practice, this kind of protective pretrial detention is very rarely used in the United States.

Bail, in many states, is almost always posted by a bond provided to a defendant in noncapital offenses. Judges have usually insisted on money bail paid by the defendant or a bond posted on his behalf by a hired bondsman. However, the conditions of bail sometimes cannot be met by very poor people, who must then stay in jail awaiting trial. For those who can afford bail a bond may be posted, which costs money, or property may be deposited with the court instead of money. If a judge agrees, some other condition of release, such as third-party supervision, may be set. Unless a judge agrees to place an accused person in the custody of a designated person or organization, money or property is required to gain freedom pending trial. Sadly, many of these poor detainees are released much later, and a few of them are ultimately sentenced to prison.

Bail reform in some states has made it much easier for poor people to remain free, awaiting trial. Until recently, bail bonds were supplied by private bondsmen who collected a fee amounting to ten percent of the amount set by the court. The bondsmen had extraordinary powers to pursue and capture those who failed to appear in court (jumped bail). Now many state courts run the bail system directly and tend to set low bail for those defendants who have a job and strong community ties. In many states the bail bondsman has disappeared, as judges took over the function directly. Wherever possible, judges release defendants on their own promise to appear on the due date for trial. Sometimes a signature bond allows for release of an accused person. Cash is only owed after the defendant fails to appear. Sometimes a small down payment to the court is required in advance.

The amount of bail is usually determined by the seriousness of the offense charged. For violent crimes the bail amount will be high. Murder charges may result in very high bail or no bail at all. The character and mental condition of the defendant are taken into account as well as the potential danger to the community posed by the defendant's release.

Individuals placed on bail are subject to a number of restrictions placed upon them by a judge. Travel is usually restricted. A prohibition may be placed against the possession of any dangerous weapon. Another requirement, restraint from indulgence in intoxicating liquor or drugs, may be imposed. If needed, a judge may also insist on a restriction that a defendant not associate with certain individuals. While on bail the individual must report regularly to an officer of the court or other designated person.

Bail is one of those constitutional rights that benefit most those who can afford to exercise it. Judges may post high bail with little fear of reversal by other higher courts. They set the amount of bail without fully knowing whether the accused person can afford the costs. On the other hand, many movements in the nation seek to make bail more available to the poor and to detain fewer people prior to trial. One other solution to this problem may be to provide, at least, humane detention centers apart from jails to hold those who are awaiting trial and cannot post bail.

No one really knows for sure how much bail is "excessive." The judge sets bail in order to discourage the accused from "jumping bail," that is, from avoiding trial by slipping away from the area. If the defendant does not show up for trial, he or she loses the money or property posted for bail.

Speedy trial would also greatly reduce the pain for an accused person by reducing the time period before the trial begins. The Sixth Amendment to the Constitution states, "the accused shall enjoy the right to a speedy trial." This right applies to all federal and state trials.

Criminal trial court dockets are crowded in most states. Backlogs in criminal trials are the major source of delay. There is no clear rule about how long a delay will be acceptable to the Supreme Court, under the Sixth Amendment. The Court balances the length of the delay and the reasons for the delay against the defendant's claim of rights. Pres-

In 1975 the Supreme Court decision in *Taylor* v. *Louisiana* denied states the right to prevent women from serving on juries. However, that does not mean that women must be proportionally represented.

sure has been placed upon trial courts to handle more criminal cases to reduce delay, but it is possible for a delay of several years to take place anyway.

If the defense demands a speedy trial, the government must attempt to provide one. The government may not deliberately slow down the process so as to gain advantages over a defendant. Frequent government delays and postponements could amount to a denial of a defendant's constitutional rights. Once formal charges are made against an individual, following an arrest, the government must make reasonable efforts to get the trial started. More commonly, court backlogs caused by the great number of criminal cases waiting to be tried delay the beginning of criminal trials. These are not the fault of the prosecution, but judges must work hard to prevent undue delay, remembering the ancient judicial observation that "justice delayed is justice denied." After all, as long as an accused person is awaiting trial he is under a great deal of uncertainty and tension. In the worst situation, an accused may simply be sitting in jail because bail could not be posted.

The Supreme Court has urged legislatures to take steps to speed up criminal trials. Backlogs still remain in spite of pressure from state courts and legislatures. Probably more judges and more courtrooms are necessary to cope with the swelling numbers of criminal cases on the court dockets, but these cost money, and the Supreme Court has been unwilling to order states to spend their money in that fashion.

Jury Trial

The Sixth Amendment also provides that in all criminal prosecutions the accused shall enjoy the right to a speedy trial, "by an impartial jury of the state and district wherein the crime shall have been committed." This provision applies in state and federal courts for serious criminal offenses. For minor offenses, including traffic violations, there is no right to a trial by jury. Any offense that carries a potential sentence of more than six months must be tried by a jury, if one is requested. In cases heard before justices of the peace, magistrates, traffic courts, or police courts, Americans have no right to trial by jury because these tribunals have jurisdiction only over minor offenses.

The number of jurors in a federal trial is set at 12 by statute. States may have as few as six jurors. The Constitution requires a unanimous jury verdict only in federal courts. Most states require unanimous jury verdicts, but some do not. For example, in Louisiana, a nine-to-three verdict is sufficient for a conviction. The U.S. Supreme Court has insisted on a unanimous verdict only when a state trial jury is as small as six.

The Sixth Amendment requires an "impartial jury." This means that the jury must be drawn from a "fair cross section of the community." A defendant is deprived of his right to a fair trial if any identifiable segment with a role in the community is systematically excluded from the trial or the grand jury. A systematic exclusion of African Americans from juries has been held to be a denial of a fair trial and of the equal protection of the laws. The same is true for Mexican-born citizens and women. However, that does not mean that all such groups must be proportionally represented on juries. Race may not be considered a factor for exclusion or inclusion on a jury.

If a defendant is convicted in a state that systematically excludes community groups, an unfair trial takes place. The defendant need not prove that the verdict was effected by the exclusion. The verdict of an unfair jury will be reversed simply because the defendant has been deprived of his or her constitutional right to a fair jury. The defendant need not be a member of the group that has been systematically excluded.

In a jury trial the accused has the right to confront witnesses against him face to face. This right guarantees the defendant an opportunity to cross-examine those witnesses; it also gives the jury an opportunity to observe the demeanor of the state's witnesses. A trial judge may not ordinarily conceal the identity of a government witness. A trial judge may not exclude a defendant from the courtroom when a witness is testifying, although special circumstances may make that necessary.

The right to an impartial jury means that jurors must not have a fixed, preconceived idea of the guilt or innocence of an accused person. The jurors must be able to lay aside any notions of guilt or innocence that they brought to the trial. In addition, defendants must be protected against unfair, excessive pretrial publicity. Inflammatory stories may create an unfair trial when jurors are effected by it. The judge has a duty to protect the jury against news media accounts that could inflame the jury. Of course, if jurors are subjected to possible influence or prejudice during the trial an unfair trial may result.

The prosecution in all criminal cases bears the burden of proof. This burden must be proven "beyond a reasonable doubt"—a high standard that ensures that every fact necessary to constitute a crime has been proven to the satisfaction of the jury. The "reasonable doubt" standard applies to juvenile proceedings in which the defendant is charged with a violation of criminal law. The issue of "juvenile delinquency" must also be proved beyond a reasonable doubt. Noncriminal conduct by juveniles is subject to a lower standard of proof.

The defendant has a right not to testify at his or her criminal trial. That right arises from the privilege against self-incrimination. No judge or prosecutor may comment adversely on the defendant's refusal to take the stand. The judge may give instruction to the jury that the defendant's silence should play no role in their deliberations.

The right to trial by jury can be waived (surrendered) by a defendant, with the consent of the prosecution and the judge. The waiver must be "knowing and intelligent." The effect of the waiver is that the judge alone presides over the case, without a jury.

Although defendants rarely waive their right to a jury trial, they very commonly avoid trial altogether simply by pleading guilty. In 80 to 90 percent of all criminal cases, a defendant is likely to plead guilty rather than stand trial; the prosecution frequently offers to drop a criminal charge or to charge the defendant for a crime at a lesser offense as a way of saving the government the cost of a full criminal trial. "Plea bargaining," as it is called, is at the heart of the American system of criminal justice. Without it there would be many more criminal trials and many delays as courts attempted to cope with a huge new number of criminal cases. Plea bargaining also has a major impact on sentencing, because the defendant usually expects a lower sentence or parole as the government's part of the bargain.

A guilty plea must be voluntary, just as a confession must be. The voluntary nature of a guilty plea is not changed by the defendant's plea bargain with the prosecution. If the bargain is broken and the defendant is charged with a different, higher offense, or if the prosecution otherwise makes a major change in the terms of the deal that led to the guilty plea, the defendant can change his plea. In this situation, courts will say that the guilty plea is improper and can be changed to a not-guilty plea. The judge decides whether or not the guilty plea promises had been broken.

Sentencing and Retrials

After the conclusion of trial the convicted individual no longer enjoys the same degree of constitutional protection of his rights. When he makes his sentencing decision a judge may look at all the factors that are relevant to the appropriate sentence of a particular individual. His record of past crimes, his attitude toward the victims of the crime, and facts about the life and circumstances of the convicted person may all be considered. But the defendant has no right to cross-examine the people who supply information to the sentencing judge. When adding up the evidence about the proper sentence for a particular person the judge has considerable discretion. Even if a sentencing hearing is provided, the standard is no longer the "beyond a reasonable doubt" measure of guilt or innocence—just a lower standard that the facts surrounding the sentencing decision are more probably true than not.

Most sentences are based upon the recommendations of a presentence report. This report is a document prepared by a probation officer who has studied the defendant and is familiar with his conduct. Not all judges use these presentence reports, and they can ignore them at will. However, if the defendant is to remain on probation, the report assumes greater importance. Even if the offender is sent to prison, the report follows him and may be used by prison authorities in determining how the individual will be treated. It is almost impossible for the offender to challenge the recommendations of the report.

The Fifth Amendment to the federal Constitution states that no person "shall be twice put in jeopardy" for the "same offense." Double jeopardy means that if a defendant is acquitted he may not be tried again for that offense, barring the prosecution from appealing an acquittal. Even if some error was made at the trial court level, the prosecution may not appeal. The prosecution is not allowed to wear down a defendant with repeated trials or threats of trials. When O.J. Simpson was found "not guilty" by the trial court in 1995, the prosecution could not appeal that determination, although Simpson could have appealed if he had lost the case.

If there is a mistrial, then a retrial can be held without violating the double jeopardy rule. A mistrial means that a jury is dismissed before a verdict is reached. Using the *Simpson* case, again, if the errors made in that trial had aborted the trial before the jury rendered its verdict, Simpson could have been tried again. However, most appellate courts would frown on retrials unless the defendant requested one. If a mistrial is ordered over the objections of the defense, the retrial will be barred unless the "declaration of a mistrial was dictated by 'manifest necessity' or the 'ends of public justice.'"

When jurors fail to agree on a verdict, a so-called hung jury results. A retrial will be permitted in this circumstance or when a juror is ill or incapacitated during the trial because of the occurrence of an uncontrollable event. Double jeopardy is not violated in these circumstances.

In general, appellate courts are unwilling to subject defendants to repeated criminal trials because of the "harrowing experiences of a criminal trial." Trial court judges will rarely grant mistrials because the defendant has a right "to continue with the chosen jury." When a trial judge orders a mistrial, an appellate court must determine whether the trial court could have used some means of permitting the trial to continue to reach a verdict by the jury. If so, the mistrial will be held improper and a retrial banned by the double jeopardy clause.

However, the double jeopardy clause does not apply to two separate trials before federal and state criminal courts. If a defendant is tried for robbery in a federal court but is acquitted at the trial, he or she could be prosecuted again for a violation of state law. According to the U.S. Supreme Court, the same facts and witnesses may be produced in the two trials, but double jeopardy is not violated because there are two separate legal authorities— state and federal—each with its own system of criminal law. The federal principle of separate powers over crimes triumphs over the principle of double jeopardy. Fortunately, these sorts of double trials almost never occur, because they are avoided by most prosecutors as a matter of policy.

A double jeopardy plea is available only in a criminal case, not in a civil proceeding arising out of the same facts. Even if an individual is acquitted in a criminal case, he or she can be tried again in a private civil action brought by relatives of his victim. Such a suit is called a "wrongful death" case. In civil cases, because there is no risk of criminal punishment, the rules of proof are much more relaxed than in a criminal case. Most constitutional rights and privileges do not apply to private civil cases. A defendant would have to appear and give testimony in a civil case, whereas he or she cannot be compelled to do so in a criminal case. The standard of proof in a civil case is "preponderance of the evidence," meaning a probability that the facts alleged are more true than not. There is no right to a trial by jury in a civil case, although juries are often used. For all these reasons, it is possible for a person acquitted in a criminal trial to lose at a subsequent civil trial. However, the losing party in a civil trial can only be compelled to pay damages, usually money, to the winning parties.

Juvenile Justice

In most states offenders under the age of 18 years are treated as juveniles. If they commit acts that injure others, their property, or themselves, they are regarded as children under the law and provided with special tribunals to handle juvenile offenses. Traffic offenses may be heard in traffic court, just as with adult offenders. Sixteen and 17-year-old drivers do not need special consideration. However, serious traffic violations committed by individuals below the age of 18, such as reckless homicide, may be sent to juvenile courts.

There are certain offenses peculiar to young people, known as "status offenses," that cannot apply to adults. States differ on the definition of these status offenses, but conduct such as being habitually truant, being "wayward," or being "habitually disobedient" to parents, teachers, or guardians may each amount to a status offense. Unruly children or "children in need of supervision" fill the dockets of the juvenile courts. These vague offenses could not be crimes if committed by adults, and juvenile courts have broad discretion in managing them.

An act of "delinquency" is really a violation of a state or federal law that would be a crime if committed by an adult. Delinquency offenses, although heard in juvenile courts, are subject to some of the same constitutional rules that apply to criminal trials. Juvenile offenders have many of the same rights as adults in criminal trials. Some acts of delinquency are special to children. Violations such as "running away," possessing an air gun, and drinking alcohol fall under this type of delinquency. Some states regard violations of curfew as delinquency violations.

Serious criminal offenses cannot be heard in juvenile courts if state law places them under criminal jurisdiction. In Louisiana murder, rape, burglary, and kidnapping are heard in regular criminal courts. In North Carolina all cases that could receive the death penalty are heard in criminal courts, if the offender is age 14 or older. Typically, states exclude offenses punishable by death or life imprisonment from the jurisdiction of juvenile courts. Some states have turned even misdemeanors (traffic offenses, trespass, fish and game violations) committed by children into adult crimes. Since the state laws vary so much and are still changing, it is best to examine the current law of your own state with the most recent material available, if you are interested in this topic. Whatever your state criminal law now says is a reflection of the current public concern with deterring crime committed by young people.

Prior to 1967 the constitutional rights afforded adults were not extended to children and youths in juvenile proceedings. In theory, young people had been given whatever protections a juvenile court judge thought were necessary to protect the interest of the young. It had been believed that individualized treatment of young people required none of the formal protections afforded adults in criminal trials. This paternalistic view of juvenile justice was swept away in the case of *In re Garlt* (1967) by the Supreme Court, which established the principle that a child—and where appropriate, his parents—has a constitutional right to be informed promptly and directly of all criminal charges against him. The 1967 case also held that if a child is faced with a possible loss of liberty, he or she is automatically entitled to counsel; otherwise, the child has a right to legal assistance. If indigent (legally poor), the child is entitled to an assigned free counsel.

In subsequent rulings the Supreme Court expanded the rights of young people who break the law. Children and youths are presumed innocent until proven guilty of juvenile offenses. Guilt must be proven beyond a reasonable doubt. The rights to a speedy trial, to cross-examine witnesses, and to privilege against self-incrimination were all made applicable to juvenile proceedings.

The right to a jury trial does not apply to juvenile matters, which are usually heard by a single judge. Juvenile proceedings are still conducted in a more parental manner than in an adult criminal trial. Judges, probation officers, and social workers play a much more active role than lawyers in most juvenile proceedings. Also, the

Sample New York State Juvenile Case
In the Matter of Neftalid. (Anonymous), Appellant.

Decided May 2, 1995

A juvenile delinquency petition was filed against appellant charging that on February 6, 1993, he committed acts, which if committed by an adult, would constitute the crimes of assault in the second degree (Penal Law § 120.05[3]), assault in the third degree (Penal Law § 120.00[1]) and resisting arrest (Penal Law § 205.30). The police report annexed to the petition relates that the juvenile verbally assaulted two police officers as they were exiting the building in which they had just responded to a report of a burglary. Although the officers proceeded past the juvenile, he continued to taunt them, prompting the officers to order him to cease such behavior. The juvenile responded by challenging the officers to a fight, flailing his arms at them. A scuffle ensued, resulting in the juvenile's arrest. Both officers were treated for injuries sustained while attempting to subdue the juvenile.

After entering his denials at the initial appearance on February 10, 1993, the juvenile was released into the custody of his mother, pending a fact-finding hearing. Prior to the hearing but 34 days after the initial filing of the petition, the juvenile moved to dismiss alleging that the petition was jurisdictionally defective because it did not contain any non hearsay supporting depositions as required by the Family Court Act and was erroneously dated the previous year, before the alleged incident even occurred. The relevant supporting document annexed to the petition was the police report that contained the signature of the reporting officer and the signature of another individual, apparently a police sergeant, who signed in a box marked "certified by."

Family Court denied the motion, finding the supporting deposition, i.e. the police report, sufficient and in compliance with CPL 100.30(1)(b). The court indicated it looked to CPL 100.30(1)(b) for interpretive assistance in construing Family Court Act §§ 311.2 and 311.3, even though no specific direction is contained in these provisions (see Family Court Act § 303.1[1]). Family Court further held that the incorrect date recited on the face of the petition was an insignificant, non-prejudicial error capable of correction by amendment, which it directed to reflect the proper date, and that the juvenile waived any objection to this defect by failing to timely file his motion.

Subsequent to a fact-finding hearing at which the two police officers testified, Family Court adjudged the juvenile a delinquent and placed him with the Division for Youth for 18 months. Family Court stated that the juvenile exhibited "an escalating pattern of dangerous delinquent behavior, marked by multiple arrests for a variety of crimes which, if committed by an adult, would constitute these crimes together with a [drug] problem."

setting is much more informal and the proceedings are not open to the public and the press. The names of parties and witnesses are not made public. Every effort is made to avoid branding the young person as a criminal and reform, not punishment, is the goal. More serious offenders are being sent, with greater frequency, to the regular criminal courts. Very minor offenders may not even be handled in a juvenile hearing, but more casually, in other kinds of meetings.

Perhaps the most serious problems confronting juvenile violators is the nationwide shortage of court-assigned defense counsel. Those who can afford lawyers are able to gain some measure of fair treatment, but substantial numbers of poor juveniles are forced by circumstances to appear before a juvenile court without a lawyer. The constitutional right to counsel is weakened by the unavailability of defense lawyers for juveniles, many of whom are minority group members.

The American Bar Association (ABA), the main professional organization of American lawyers, released a report in 1995 entitled, "A Call for Justice." This report documents that the juvenile justice system is severely overstrained by the absence of sufficient numbers of qualified defense lawyers to assist poor clients. The result of this condition is the prospect of longer sentences and more time spent in prison. The report shows that many public defenders in juvenile courts are inexperienced and overworked. Caseloads of 500 clients in a year are common. The ABA report called for more funds for juvenile defense lawyers and much smaller caseloads.

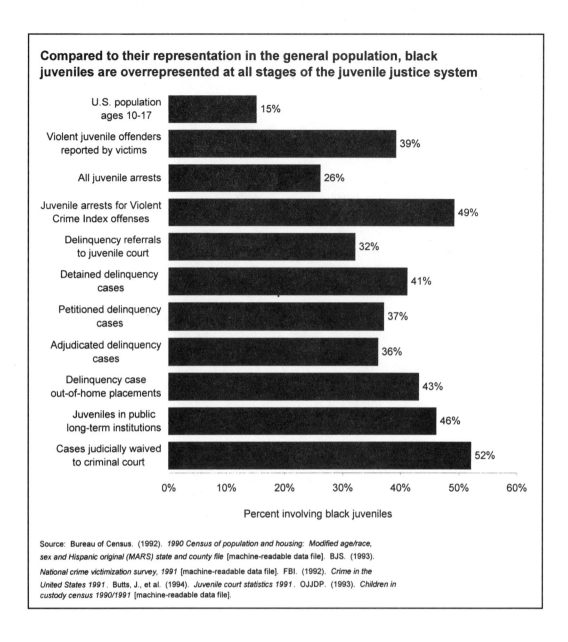

Compared to their representation in the general population, black juveniles are overrepresented at all stages of the juvenile justice system

Category	Percent
U.S. population ages 10-17	15%
Violent juvenile offenders reported by victims	39%
All juvenile arrests	26%
Juvenile arrests for Violent Crime Index offenses	49%
Delinquency referrals to juvenile court	32%
Detained delinquency cases	41%
Petitioned delinquency cases	37%
Adjudicated delinquency cases	36%
Delinquency case out-of-home placements	43%
Juveniles in public long-term institutions	46%
Cases judicially waived to criminal court	52%

Percent involving black juveniles

Source: Bureau of Census. (1992). *1990 Census of population and housing: Modified age/race, sex and Hispanic original (MARS) state and county file* [machine-readable data file]. BJS. (1993). *National crime victimization survey, 1991* [machine-readable data file]. FBI. (1992). *Crime in the United States 1991*. Butts, J., et al. (1994). *Juvenile court statistics 1991*. OJJDP. (1993). *Children in custody census 1990/1991* [machine-readable data file].

Punishment

The Eighth Amendment bans both "excessive fines" and "cruel and unusual punishment." Little has been said by the Supreme Court about the meaning of "excessive fines," but a lot has been written about "cruel and unusual punishment." Both clauses bind the federal and state courts.

In 1867, the Supreme Court observed that it was "safe to affirm that punishment of—torture . . . and all others in the same line of cruelty, are forbidden by the Amendment." On the other hand, the Court found that the death penalty inflicted by shooting was not "cruel and unusual." In 1890 the Court suggested that a state could not punish by "torture or a lingering death, such as burning at the stake, crucifixion, breaking at the wheel, and

the like." Clearly, such cruelties are forbidden in America, and in any civilized society. The same could be said for whipping, branding, mutilation of parts of the body, or any other similar excessive use of force by public authorities.

A punishment that is disproportionate to the crime will be held to be unconstitutionally cruel. A court must determine the issue, based on history, precedent, and the attitudes of the public and elected officials. Twelve years in irons at hard labor for commission of a minor offense was deemed "excessive" in 1910, and it would be today. In another decision, an excessive sentence was also held to be unconstitutional when a judge ordered a life sentence for a convicted felon, without possibility of parole, for the commission of a seventh nonviolent felony. Probably, if parole had been available, the Supreme Court would have upheld the sentence.

Neither the state or national government may incriminate behavior that is essentially an illness. The acts of sale, possession, and use of prohibited drugs can be made a crime, but addiction to drugs is an illness and cannot be made a crime because, courts have held, the individual is powerless to control his conduct. In the same sense, being mentally ill cannot be made a crime, nor can habitual drunkenness or having a venereal disease. Conditions of health cannot be incriminated without violating the Eighth Amendment prohibition of "cruel and unusual punishments." Casual readers must be aware that other acts involving this undesired behavior may be incriminated, so public drunkenness is a minor crime, although being addicted to alcohol is not. These special applications of the "cruel and unusual punishments" clause may change from time to time because of judicial perceptions about particular uncontrollable behavior. Consequently, read the latest court rulings in your jurisdiction with care when investigating this topic.

If there is a strong public feeling that a particular punishment is "barbaric," the Supreme Court will deny the legislature the power to impose such a punishment. On these grounds, the Supreme Court held that an army deserter could not be denied his American citizenship for that offense. The Court felt that making the accused a "stateless person, deprived of the right to have rights" is too cruel a punishment for any crime. For similar reasons a state may not impose the death penalty on a prisoner who is insane at the time of the punishment. Juvenile offenders cannot be considered fully responsible for murder at some tender age, but there is no national agreement on what that age may be, so the death penalty is, at least, constitutional for very serious crimes committed at the age of 16 years or above.

Capital punishment, the use of the death penalty as a sentence in a criminal case, is not, by itself, cruel and unusual punishment. When the judge or jury responsible for the death sentence have adequate guidance, and there is a review process to guard against arbitrary or discriminatory application of the punishment, the death penalty will be upheld as constitutional. The Supreme Court has wavered on this issue, but it is clear that

At the time of this picture, "cruel and unusual punishment" was forbidden by the Eighth Amendment. Does this picture depict "cruel and unusual punishment"? The answer to this question has changed as the definition of "cruel and unusual punishment" continues to evolve.

the selective and capricious application of death penalty violates the Eighth and Fourteenth Amendments. Since the topic of the death penalty is emotionally charged, it is not surprising that legislatures have experimented considerably with its use as a punishment. The Supreme Court has been sympathetic to some of these experiments, but the Court is cautious in weighing the constitutional issues surrounding the death penalty.

If the sentencer has limited discretion concerning the imposition of the death penalty, the Supreme Court will be satisfied. There must be some aggravating and mitigating factors considered by the sentencer. This means that the sentencer must consider, for example, the especially violent nature of the murderous deed and the possible mitigating effects of the prior life and conduct of the felon before imposing the death penalty. A mandatory capital punishment for a broad category of homicides would be unconstitutional, unless accompanied by the opportunity of the sentencer to consider some mitigating or aggravating factors about the crime or the defendant. The sentencing jury may consider such factors as the harm caused to the victim's family, and the probable future dangerousness of the defendant's behavior.

Victim's Rights

Crime victims have, in the past, been virtually ignored by the criminal justice system. Many victims suffer renewed pain when they participate as witnesses in the criminal trial, but they are usually denied any larger role in the criminal process. Victim's fears and feelings of helplessness are often aroused by being brought into criminal trials. Some crime victims regard the criminal process as a form of repeated victimization.

Victims can be compelled to testify in criminal trials, even though they may prefer not to confront the people who have harmed them. At trial, victims will be subjected to demanding cross-examination, reopening issues that many would rather forget. Sometimes the personal lives and habits of victims are exposed at criminal trials by lawyers for the accused. It is not surprising that many victims choose to not report crimes rather than to endure the criminal process.

Criminal victims typically receive no compensation for their personal injuries from the person who harmed them, nor do families of victims. Murderers, drunk drivers, and others who cause injuries and death are not forced to pay money to their victims for their wrongs as part of the criminal process. It is possible for victims to try to recover damages at a separate civil trial, but they must bring such private claims at their own expense, bearing all the risks and costs.

In 1982 the President's Task Force on Victims of Crime recommended that the United States Constitution be amended to guarantee that "the victim, in every criminal prosecution, have the right to be present and hear at all critical stages of judicial proceedings." Although the federal Constitution has not been modified in this way, several states have recognized victim's rights. California was the first state to do so in 1982. Rhode Island followed in 1986. In 1988 Florida and Michigan

joined the parade. Now Texas, Washington, Arizona, New Jersey, Colorado, Illinois, Kansas, and Missouri recognize victim's rights as well. In another approach, there is a Victim's Constitutional Amendment Network in Fort Worth, Texas, which is tracking the development of victim's rights nationwide. Most states have attempted to provide crime victims with rights, but few have taken victim's rights into their constitutions.

The basic nature of victim's rights differ in each state constitution, but New Jersey has some of the most far-reaching provisions. The New Jersey Constitution states that "a victim of a crime shall be treated with fairness, compassion and respect by the criminal justice system." A crime victim has the right to be present at a criminal trial, and in addition, a victim has other rights "as may be provided by the legislature."

In 1985 the New Jersey Legislature passed a Crime Victim's Bill of Rights. The most important features are the right to be notified of any changes in the status of criminal charges against the alleged wrongdoer; the right to advance notice of the defendant's appearance before a judge or any plea bargain that might have been submitted to a court; assistance in meeting the burden of making court appearances; and a right "to make a statement about the impact of the crime for inclusion in the pre-sentence report or at time of parole consideration." The victim may also issue a written statement about the impact of the crime "prior to the prosecutor's final decision whether formal charges will be filed."

All these rights are designed to reduce the pain and suffering of crime victims. In addition, the state of New Jersey may award sums of money up to $25,000 to compensate victims for injuries. Many states have established funds to repay money damages to victims out of state moneys, usually in rather small sums. To collect from the perpetrator of a crime the victim must still sue him in a private civil suit.

Civil Rights Crimes

One of the most controversial aspects of federal criminal law is the enforcement of federal criminal civil rights. Victims of discrimination had been physically beaten and battered by individuals and mobs. The Ku Klux Klan and other white supremacy groups long terrorized African Americans who sought to improve their lives and to use their constitutionally guaranteed civil rights. Voters were physically intimidated; those who spoke out about their rights were even lynched, at times. People who peacefully exercised their civil rights often found themselves targets of vicious attacks.

After the civil rights movement of the 1960s began to gain widespread support, violence soon broke out. In 1963 in Birmingham, Alabama, during the height of Reverend Martin Luther King Jr.'s desegregation efforts, demonstrators were treated brutally by state and local law enforcement officials, some of them using billy clubs and savage dogs. The Ku Klux Klan rode again in those years, as dozens of black churches were bombed or burned. Three "freedom riders" working for civil rights in Mississippi (two African Americans and one white) were brutally murdered. Subsequent investigations by the Federal Bureau of Investigation implicated the sheriff, his deputies, and 16 private individuals.

Technically, it is a federal crime to "deprive, either directly or indirectly, any person or class of persons of the equal protection of the laws." Unfortunately, until the past few decades, this aspect of federal criminal law was enforced only infrequently. There are several federal laws that can be applied to those who are deprived of their civil rights. Criminals who terrorize others can be brought to justice, if the federal government is vigilant.

Under the Clinton administration, a re-energized Civil Rights Division has been actively enforcing the nation's civil rights laws. The following examples are just a few of its substantial accomplishments in enforcement of criminal rights statutes during one year:

• In fiscal year 1994 (July, 1, 1994–June 30, 1994), the Division filed a record 76 criminal cases in which it charged 139 defendants—also a record. That year the Criminal Section was successful in 90.2 percent of its prosecutions—its second highest rate ever.

• Among its many cases, the Division obtained several convictions against law enforcement officers for physical and sexual assaults against suspects and prison inmates.

• The Division doubled the number of defendants charged in cases of racially motivated violence (73) over the previous year, including the convictions of:

(a) two L.A. police officers involved in the 1991 beating of Rodney King. After earlier acquittals on state charges, both defendants received prison terms of 30 months. An appeals court affirmed the verdicts and asked the lower court to resentence the two to no less than 70 months.

(b) a Nashville man who went on a racially motivated arson spree—including throwing Molotov cocktails at the home of an African American family while they were sleeping. The man, who was sentenced in May 1995 to 8 years in prison, was a member of the Aryan Faction, a white supremacist organization dedicated to driving African Americans out of the Clarksville, Tennessee, area.

(c) two defendants who pleaded guilty in February 1995 to civil rights violations for engaging in a racially motivated shooting of four Latinos in rural Maine.

(d) one of two white men in Cicero, Illinois, who brutally beat two African Americans with a bat. Although the state prosecution resulted in the conviction of only one defendant, the Division successfully convicted the second defendant, who received a six-year sentence.

Civil rights criminal laws have been used extensively against police misconduct. However, individual police officers have considerable immunity from suit unless it can be shown that their conduct violated "clearly established" constitutional standards. Federal criminal civil rights statutes enable the Justice Department to bring criminal charges against law enforcement officials who "willfully" deprive people of their constitutional rights, as in the four policemen accused of the Rodney King beating. In such shocking situations police abuse can be dealt with, but police brutality is usually very difficult to prove.

A victim of police brutality cannot sue a whole police force unless it can be shown that the injury that was suffered was part of a municipal "policy" or "custom." It is very unlikely that a police force will be ordered by a court injunction to cease particular police practices. In a 1983 case involving the use of choke holds to restrain sus-

Poverty and lack of work opportunities have resulted in criminal justice supervision of a disproportionate number of African Americans and Hispanics.

departments could be more widely permitted. Law enforcement officials could be made more liable for their criminal conduct. Furthermore, Congress could appropriate more money to the Civil Rights Division to allow it to investigate and prosecute all forms of deprivation of individual civil rights. However, many citizens, fearing the prevalence of crime in America, may not want to weaken the resolve of policemen to discharge their dangerous work. Excessive attention to civil rights issues can discourage police work, but that creates a choice that the voters ultimately have to make.

Impact of the Criminal Justice System

It is a fact that a large percentage of persons in prison are African Americans and Hispanics. In 1990 a national report indicated that one in four young African American men were either in prison, on probation, or on parole. By 1995 the figures worsened. By that year, according to a report of the Sentencing Project, a nonprofit organization interested in sentencing reforms, about one in every three African American males between the ages of 20 and 29 were under some form of criminal justice supervision. Some members of minority groups believe that their rights are less carefully regarded by police and prosecutors than are the rights of the rest of the population; yet, there are other explanations to account for the large proportion of minority group members who are subject to the criminal justice system.

Get-tough sentencing laws passed in most states in the past two decades have had a disproportionate impact on African Americans and Hispanics. Judges have been mandated by legislatures in many states to lay heavy sentences on offenders. In the effort to stamp out crime, using and selling drugs and drug-related offenses have been much more heavily punished. Since the drug business is booming in poor urban areas, many young men have turned to the drug trade to make money. These are the men who are filling up the jails with greater frequency, and many of them are poor African Americans and Hispanic Americans. To some extent, then, the disproportionate impact of the criminal justice system on certain groups is a function of their poverty and the lack of opportunity for honest work.

Crime control is a problem for people of all races and ethnic groups. The constitutional rights

pects, the Supreme Court refused to uphold a lower court injunction against the Los Angeles Police Department, even though more than a dozen people had died as a result of choke holds. Former justice Thurgood Marshall pointed out in his dissent to this ruling *(Lyons* v. *City of Los Angeles)* that the majority view would make it impossible for a court to enjoin (judicially stop) a shoot-to-kill order by a police department. However, such an official policy probably would be enjoined by the Supreme Court today because it would be an illegal municipal policy.

Federal criminal civil rights laws can be strengthened. If Congress desires, the Justice Department could be even more active in protecting individual civil rights. Suits against police

The U.S. Department of Justice, Bureau of Justice Statistics report on Incarceration:

The nation's state and federal prisons had to find room for 83,294 more inmates last year—the second largest annual increase in history and just 1,470 fewer than the 84,764 increase recorded in 1989. The total number of men and women in prison last December 31 was 1,053,738—a new record.

Overall, almost 1.5 million people were incarcerated in the United States in 1994. State and federal prisons, which primarily hold convicted felons serving longer sentences, contained about two-thirds of the total. Locally operated jails, which primarily hold people awaiting trial or serving sentences of a year or less, held the other third.

At the end of 1994 state prisons held 958,704 men and women and federal prisons held 95,034 inmates. California (125,605) and Texas (118,195) together held more than one in every five inmates in the nation. Seventeen states, each holding fewer than 5,000 inmates, accounted for 4 percent of all prisoners.

Prison populations increased by at least 10 percent in 16 states last year. Texas reported the largest growth (28 percent), followed by Georgia (20 percent). Alaska and Connecticut reported fewer prisoners who had been sentenced to more than a year.

The average sentence length and time served for state prisoners has remained stable in recent years. Between 1985 and 1992, the years for which comparable data are available, half of the state prisoners served at least 48 months.

In the federal system, however, the "truth in sentencing" provisions of the Sentencing Reform Act of 1984 have contributed to increasing the median time served in prison from 15 months in 1986 to 24 months in 1992.

The incarceration rate for prisoners sentenced to more than a year reached a record 387 per 100,000 U.S. residents last December 31. States with the highest incarceration rates were Texas (636 inmates per 100,000 residents), Louisiana (530), and Oklahoma (508). North Dakota (78) had the lowest, followed by Minnesota (100) and West Virginia (106).

Since 1980 per capita incarceration rates rose the most in the South (from 188 to 451) and West (from 105 to 333). The rate in the Northeast rose from 87 to 285, and the rate in the Midwest from 109 to 297.

In absolute numbers, violent offenders were the greatest contributors to state prison inmate growth. Between 1980 and 1993, the number of violent offenders grew by an estimated 221,300, the Bureau of Justice Statistics (BJS) estimated using 1993 data.

More than a quarter of the state and federal inmates were in prison for drug offenses (234,600 prisoners) in 1993. Prisoners serving a drug sentence increased from 8 percent of the state and federal prison population in 1980 to 26 percent in 1993. In federal prisons, inmates sentenced for drug law violations were the single largest group—60 percent in 1993, up from 25 percent in 1980.

At the end of the year, states reported they were operating between 17 percent and 29 percent over capacity, while the federal system was operating at 25 percent over capacity.

Because of prison construction and the creation of new prison beds, the ratio of the inmate population to the capacity of state prisons has remained almost the same since 1990.

The average growth in the number of state and federal prisoners sentenced to at least a year's incarceration was equal to the need for 1,542 more beds per week in 1994.

During 1994 almost 5 percent of all state prisoners—48,949 inmates in 21 jurisdictions—were held in local jails or other facilities because of prison crowding.

The number of female inmates grew 10.6 percent last year, compared to an 8.5 percent increase among male inmates. On December 31, 1994, there were 64,403 women in state and federal prisons—6.1 percent of all prisoners. The rate of incarceration for inmates serving a sentence of more than a year is 746 males per 100,000 U.S. male residents, vs. 45 females per 100,000 female population.

Between 1980 and 1993, the number of white and black female inmates grew at a faster pace than the number of male inmates in either racial group. During this period the number of white males grew 163 percent, the number of black males grew 217 percent, the number of white females 327 percent, and the number of black females 343 percent. An estimated 1,471 blacks per 100,000 black residents and 207 whites per 100,000 white residents were incarcerated in the nation's prisons on December 31, 1993.

provided for all are insufficient to guarantee that crime can be reduced. That is part of a larger social problem.

Civil Disabilities: The Rights of Ex-Offenders

A convicted person loses many important civil and constitutional rights as a result of his conviction. Many of the privileges usually associated with citizenship are also lost, at least temporarily. For years, most states have curtailed the right of ex-offenders to vote, to hold political office, to obtain certain occupational licenses, or to serve on a jury. Even after the convict has been released from prison, and completed probation or parole he may, in many states, be disqualified from some or all of these rights that most American citizens hold. The consequences of conviction of a crime may even last a lifetime. This process of losing civil rights has been called "civil disabilities," and the scope and extent of these disabilities varies widely from state to state, although there are fewer such disabilities at the federal level.

The loss of these rights tends to be automatic. While imprisoned a convict loses most of his or her rights under so-called state civil death statutes. Convicts may make legal contracts, own property, and execute wills and most other legal documents while in prison, but they may lose many others of the privileges of American citizenship.

Every state in the union has some form of civil disability law. Some are embodied in statutes, others in state constitutions. No one knows exactly how many civil disability statutes there are or how extensive they may be, because the sources for this information are scattered over the statute books.

For many ex-convicts the most significant civil disability may be the loss of occupational licenses. In effect, this means that many ex-convicts cannot pursue certain kinds of economic activities. Certainly, such statutes may make sense when the tasks involve sensitive work requiring great trust, but these disability statutes are usually quite broad and vague. The applicant for most licenses must have a "good moral character," and this language has restricted many ex-convicts who seek to become lawyers or brokers. Usually, the determination of "good moral character" is left to the discretion of the licensing board. Professions such as medicine, dentistry, the law, and teaching are most closely licensed. However, licenses for barbers, taxi drivers, peddlers, and chauffeurs may also be denied to ex-convicts in some states.

Conviction of a crime may prevent a person from being permitted to enter the United States. Under federal immigration law a criminal conviction may be sufficient ground for denial of an application for entry. Conviction of one nonpolitical crime "involving moral turpitude" will have that effect, although this prohibition will not apply to persons below the age of 18 years. Conviction of two or more nonpolitical crimes will debar an application, even if "moral turpitude" is not involved. Conviction for trafficking in narcotics will defeat an entry application. Even conviction for possession may have the same result.

A criminal conviction has serious consequences for a person who is seeking to become an American citizen. Federal law requires that a person seeking naturalization be of "good moral character." A person may be found to lack "good moral character" if he is convicted of a crime that could have prohibited entry into the country. A conviction for murder, for two or more gambling offenses, or for a range of other serious crimes that result in imprisonment for more than 180 days will also defeat a citizenship application.

Many states bar ex-convicts from holding public office. According to federal law a person convicted of falsifying, removing, or destroying public records may not hold public office. Those convicted of taking bribes are forbidden to hold federal offices, and the same is true in most states. Furthermore, many federal and state statutes require an officeholder to give up his or her office once convicted for a serious offense.

About half the states deny the privilege of voting in elections to ex-convicts. Some contend that this denial of the right to vote is designed to protect the integrity of the electoral process, although this defense of the denial of voting rights seems far-fetched. Federal law permits states to disenfranchise ex-convicts. Each state has very different lists of criminal offenses that cause the loss or the suspension of the right to vote.

Lost civil rights can be restored by a pardon. Any ex-convict may apply for a pardon, although there is no right to be considered for a pardon. Pardons are usually issued by an executive, such as the president or a state governor. Some states have special administrative boards that have the power to grant pardons. No court may compel a pardoning authority to issue a pardon.

In some states civil rights are automatically restored even without a pardon when statutory conditions are satisfied. This makes the restoration of rights automatic and nondiscretionary. Completion of parole, the expiration of a fixed period of time, or in some generous states, mere release from prison will automatically restore lost civil rights. Plainly, those states that have adopted automatic restoration of rights believe that a convict has paid his debt to society in full when he has met the conditions prescribed. Automatic restoration of rights permits the ex-convict to have the same rights as other American citizens.

Bibliography

Fletcher, George P. *With Justice for Some: Victim's Rights in Criminal Trials.* Reading, Mass.: Addison-Wesley, 1995.

Grano, Joseph D. *Confessions, the Truth and the Law.* Ann Arbor, Mich.: University of Michigan Press, 1993.

Kottler, John C. *Legal Guide for Police: Constitutional Issues.* Cincinnati, Ohio: Anderson Publishing, 1992.

La France, Arthur B., and Arnold H. Loewy. *Criminal Procedure.* Cincinnati, Ohio: Anderson Publishing, 1994.

Landynski, Jacob. *Search and Seizure and the Supreme Court.* Baltimore, Md.: John Hopkins University Press, 1966.

Sigler, Jay A. *Double Jeopardy.* Ithaca, N.Y.: Cornell University Press, 1969.

Chapter 16

The Future of Civil Rights

Jay A. Sigler

Predicting the future of American rights is just as difficult as predicting tomorrow's politics. The issues of the twenty-first century are barely evident in the headlines of our day. No crystal ball is necessary to discern the dim outlines of problems of our time that may expand into the next century, but specific predictions can go wrong. Books written in the 1950s failed to anticipate the fullness of the civil rights revolution that began in the 1960s. This chapter focuses on the most likely course of the future of American rights. The future of American rights will be as surprising as the past has been; this chapter represents an attempt to anticipate these surprises.

Over one hundred years ago, on March 11, 1861, the Congress of the Confederate States adopted a constitution that created a "right of property in Negro slaves." If they had won the Civil War the Confederate constitution would have expanded slavery into all the conquered territories. The loss of the Civil War and the subsequent passage of the Thirteenth, Fourteenth, and Fifteenth Amendments fundamentally changed the path of civil rights in America.

It took 100 years of rights development after the Civil War to create our modern notions of civil rights. The process was not swift, smooth, or easy. Resistance to the rights of African Americans, Native Americans, and other American minorities delayed the growth of American rights. Nevertheless, the general direction of American rights policies has been progressive. More and more Americans enjoy rights with each passing generation. There is every reason to believe that this trend will continue into the future, in spite of the changing moods of the Supreme Court, the Congress, president, or state governments.

On May 16, 1865, Massachusetts enacted the first modern civil rights law in the nation. This statute introduced the then radical idea that the government had the duty to assure to every person, without regard to his race, color, or equality, to

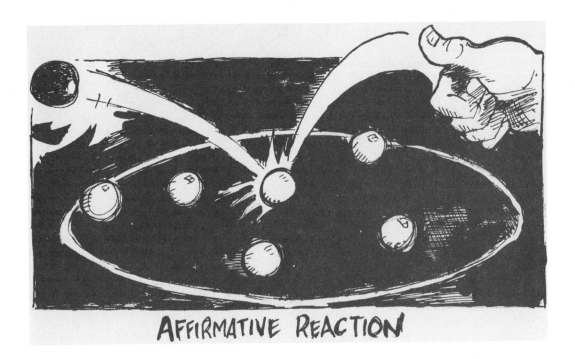

AFFIRMATIVE REACTION

equality of treatment in places of public accommodation. The simple idea that people should not be victims of discrimination in hotels, motels, transportation, or other public places took a century to fully unfold. The same slow but certain progress is true of most American rights.

There have been setbacks to American rights in the past century. The lynching of African Americans and Hispanics without trials continued well into the twentieth century. Minorities did suffer murder and brutal treatment in some places in America during the past century. The suppression of free speech and of radical political ideas also sprung up from time to time. The internment of Japanese Americans during World War II shows how fragile the rights of Americans are during wartime. However, these deficiencies in American rights practices have been corrected to some extent with the passage of time. The broad movement of American rights is toward expansion of those rights. Each setback became a milestone towards new rights development.

Some observers say that most Americans today are tired of talking of rights. The majority population may be impatient with new rights demands from minorities, gays, and women (although women are a majority themselves). Few contemporary political leaders are willing to press forward with new rights policies. However, seen from the viewpoint of the history of rights, the present period is probably only a pause in the

onward movement of American rights. American rights and democracy are now so closely linked that each new right seems to forward the cause of greater democracy.

The controversy over affirmative action should be over in the next century, if minority access to economic opportunities expand. Preferences for individuals because of their group affiliation may run against the grain of American thinking. However, if group friction in America heightens because of economic discontent, and mass demonstrations emerge, the long-simmering tensions between various groups may result in major rights concessions. Demographic tendencies suggest that in the future America's minority populations will increase, especially Spanish speakers. The white majority will shrink, and many minority group members will expect to be able to enter the American middle class.

The line between liberties and entitlements has become blurred. The basic needs of Americans has led many to claim social benefits as an aspect of American citizenship. Thomas Jefferson's language in the Declaration of Independence was of "life, liberty and the pursuit of happiness." Many Americans have interpreted this to mean some sort of right to be taken care of by the state. This view is simply incorrect; Jefferson's language is not part of the Bill of Rights. Instead, the Constitution speaks of "life, liberty and property." In the next century the struggle between these two views of citizen's rights will probably be resolved. In our time, the American economic system regards private property as an essential feature of our democracy. Today, there is no right to a pension, to a job, to food or housing, or not to be poor. Tomorrow is another matter.

Vast technological and economic changes are about to occur in America. The dawn of the electronic age will usher in whole new ways of thinking and conducting public and private business. New technologies will give rise to new rights problems. Shifting demographic patterns, a communications revolution, and a rising set of expectations will inevitably cause new demands for social change. Among these demands new rights will loom large.

The Right to Life

For many Americans the right to life is closely linked to the abortion issue. Many women prefer to speak of their "reproductive rights." The controversy that currently divides the public over the abortion issue has its roots in a 1973 decision of the United States Supreme Court. In that year the Court decided the *Roe* v. *Wade* case and determined that the right to "liberty" found in the Fourteenth Amendment encompassed important rights to privacy. These included the right of a woman to make personal, private decisions about reproduction. At the center of the decision was the newly discovered right of a woman to choose to have an abortion. By this decision the Supreme Court struck down over 30 state laws that had made the administration of an abortion criminal, except where the life or the health of the mother was at stake. These abortion statutes had allowed for the punishment of both the woman involved and the physician who had performed the operation.

Roe v. *Wade* became one of the most controversial decisions of the twentieth century. Religious groups and others offended by the decision rallied their forces and mounted a major campaign to reverse the case. Violent incidents took place at many abortion clinics, including the murders of a few physicians. Mass demonstrations were adopted as a tactic to discourage women's use of such clinic facilities. Federal statutes were passed to limit such demonstrations.

By 1980 anti- and proabortion political groups were mobilized for action. The *Roe* v.

Wade case became involved in political platforms, campaigns, and lobbying efforts. Judges appointed to the federal courts were closely questioned on their views of the case as a factor in judicial confirmation. Presidents Reagan and Bush both attempted to find prospective judges who opposed *Roe* v. *Wade.*

Women's groups also took up the cause, attempting to protect and defend the decision and to preserve the newly won right to choose abortion. In 1987 they mobilized their friends in Congress to defeat the nomination of Judge Robert Bork to the Supreme Court. Judge Bork was highly qualified, but his views on abortion and privacy rights were rejected by a majority of the Senate Judiciary Committee. After this victory by the women's coalition groups, later Supreme Court appointments also hinged on their views regarding *Roe* v. *Wade,* although two women justices were appointed, Sandra Day O'Conner and Ruth Bader Ginsburg, who were not opposed to that decision.

The political and social struggle over *Roe* v. *Wade* should not distract you, the reader, from considering the genuine conflict of values that are involved. Whatever you may think or believe about the decision, the courts have reluctantly entered the realm of the abortion controversy but have avoided theological questions. The rights of an unborn child or fetus are a matter of some concern to many Americans, but courts have not ruled on the matter.

As a practical matter the fetus is not independent of the support provided by its mother's body for a period of time, but at some point in time the fetus can be said to have a form of viable life of its own, even though it has not been technically "born." The possible technological uses of fetal tissue give urgency to the issue, although an injury to an unborn child had long been a matter of legal concern, even before *Roe* v. *Wade.* The "right to life" issue is far broader than abortion policy. It may be the most fundamental right of all, since there is the possibility that life can be artificially generated (cloned) or that a fetus can be carried and delivered by someone other than its biological mother. Modern technology also makes possible the identification of specific flaws in a person's genes. Genetic engineering is a frontier of the right to life. Current law is not in pace with technology and has avoided theology.

Operation Rescue founder Randall Terry.

Roe v. *Wade* established a trimester system for state laws concerning abortion. During the first three months of pregnancy a woman has an almost absolute right to have an abortion performed. Only if a state could show a "compelling" reason in that period could it take steps to curtail the right. As the Court said, the "physician in consultation with his [or her] patient, is free to determine, without regulation by the state, that . . . the patient's pregnancy should be terminated."

Under *Roe,* after the first trimester and before the viability of the fetus, the state "may regulate the abortion procedure to the extent the regulation reasonably relates to the preservation and protection of maternal health." Accordingly, a state may establish the medical qualifications for the person performing the operation, insuring that all persons involved follow proper medical procedures. The facility where the abortion is performed could be regulated, too. However, the Supreme Court found that the right to perform an abortion could be prohibited entirely during the third trimester, since at that point the state could decide to protect the potential for life of a viable fetus.

It is important to have an accurate view of *Roe* v. *Wade* because of the delicate balance it created. The right to personal privacy afforded the woman in the first trimester disappears in favor of the fetus in the third trimester. This careful balance of rights is often missed in the emotional debate that surrounds the right to life. There are

two versions of the right to life found in *Roe* v. *Wade:* The woman's right to choose and the state's right to regulate abortions. In 1992 both were changed. The right of the fetus to be born alive was not declared to be at issue.

By 1992, because of appointment politics, the judicial support for *Roe* v. *Wade* had weakened. In that year the Supreme Court upheld some features of Pennsylvania's stringent laws restricting abortion in that state. Only two justices, Harry A. Blackmun and John Paul Stevens, were firm supporters of the woman's right to an abortion. Several justices were firmly opposed to *Roe* v. *Wade.* Justice O'Conner, although a woman, did not give unqualified support to the decision. As a result, the lines drawn in *Roe* v. *Wade* were substantially changed, but the decision was not overruled.

The pivotal 1992 case was *Planned Parenthood of Southeastern Pennsylvania* v. *Casey.* The decision struck down part of a Pennsylvania law that would have required a spouse to be notified before a woman could have an abortion. More significantly, the Court upheld certain other provisions of the same statute, including parental consent for underage women, a 24-hour waiting period, elaborate provisions to ensure informed consent, and a number of other reporting and recordkeeping requirements imposed by state law.

Women's so-called reproductive freedom was sharply curtailed by the Pennsylvania statute.

Three justices—Sandra Day O'Conner, Anthony M. Kennedy, and David H. Souter—joined in a very unusual joint opinion, which represented the majority view. The opinion still accepted the basic proposition that the right to an abortion is protected by the Constitution, as part of the "liberty" right found in the due process clause of the Fourteenth Amendment. But the joint opinion rejected the trimester test applied in *Roe* v. *Wade*. The justices felt that the state of Pennsylvania could place limits on women's rights even in the first trimester; however, state restrictions could not impose an "undue burden" or place a "substantial obstacle" in the way of a woman's right to choose.

Spousal notification was deemed an "undue burden." Women might have "very good reasons for not wishing to inform their husbands of their decision to obtain an abortion." Some women had been psychologically and physically abused by their husbands. A spousal notification requirement would make abortions more difficult and expensive and would otherwise "impose a substantial obstacle" to a woman's right to choose. However, the state could attempt to persuade a woman not to have an abortion. The state could provide a woman with information about the risks of abortion and the nature of the procedure involved. A 24-hour waiting period was not an "undue" burden," even though some costs might be incurred by the delay. The "informed consent policy" of the state of Pennsylvania was not regarded as an "undue" intrusion upon women's rights, nor was it unreasonable for a state to impose parental consent upon women who were under the age of 18.

Four members of the Supreme Court in 1992 stated their belief that *Roe* v. *Wade* should be overruled. They believed that the 1973 decision was wrong. It is quite possible that *Roe* v. *Wade* will eventually be overruled, although women's groups are still hopeful that future Supreme Court appointments will protect the right to choose. It is also possible that new versions of the right to life philosophy may strain the existing legal standards. Fetal rights may be seen by some people as important as a woman's right to choose. Political forces may be overtaken by new developments in medical technology.

The vague standard of an "undue burden" may or may not survive changes on the membership of the Supreme Court. In any event, woman's right to choose may be determined in the state legislatures

Statement of Purpose: Presbyterians Pro-Life

Presbyterians Pro-Life seeks to be a prophetic witness to the Presbyterian Church (USA) upholding the sacred value of human life and the family. We believe the Scriptures teach that God, who made us in His own image, has forbidden us to shed innocent blood.

Therefore, Presbyterians Pro-Life is committed to protecting the right to life of every human being from the moment of conception to the moment of natural death. In decisions about life and death, the sanctity of life of both mother and child must be respected, and every effort to preserve their lives should be made. This leads us to stand against abortion, infanticide, euthanasia, and any other practice which would devalue human life.

Presbyterians Pro-Life is convinced that a return to the Biblical teaching concerning the sacred value of the family is essential to recovering respect for the sacred value of individual human lives. God has ordained the family, the basic social unit of all human institutions, to propagate, protect and nurture human life.

Presbyterians Pro-Life is committed to strengthening the bonds of family love and nurture, and to protecting innocent life.

more than in the Supreme Court. American voters will have to decide whether they agree with the stiff standards of Pennsylvania restricting women's rights. Public opinion in America still favors many aspects of women's rights. Ultimately, public opinion, not the Supreme Court, will determine the scope and the extent of women's right to choose.

Fetal Rights

Most "right to life advocates" contend that the right of the fetus begins at the moment of conception. This has never been the view of the Supreme Court. The 1992 *Casey* decision does not recognize that a fetus is a person. The Court has never held that a developing organism has rights such as those of a live person. Instead, the Supreme Court has looked to the interests of the state in regulation of abortion as the central issue.

Common law in the United States does not generally recognize rights of a fetus from the moment of conception. Generally, until the child is born alive, rights are not an issue. Neither criminal nor civil law grants rights to the fetus. This approach is embedded in American law even deeper than the *Roe* v. *Wade* decision. Therefore, it will be very difficult to convince most American courts to accept the essentially theological issue about the fetus as a person. Children are born at just a few months of age or even sooner. When they are born our law attaches legal rights to them.

Fetal rights deserve some fresh attention in the light of new knowledge about environmental hazards confronted by the unborn. A mother's treatment of her own body may do severe damage to the fetus and could reduce the quality of his or her life. A pregnant mother who heavily uses drugs, contracts AIDS, or consumes large amounts of alcohol will damage her child's brain and physical development. Stunted development, mental retardation, and drug addiction can result from the bad habits of a mother. Bad eating practices, smoking, and reckless physical activities can do severe harm to the fetus. The right to life movement has not addressed these issues, but they may be more important to society than the right to choose abortion. A careless mother could be considered to have committed a form of abuse on her own fetus.

We now know that the most critical period for structural development in human gestation occurs between the third and twelfth week. We also know, thanks to medical research, that brain cell proliferation does not cease until six to eight months after birth. Exposure to dangerous substances any time during these periods will prevent full development of the child. Birth defects of various kinds may be produced by events and habits during pregnancy. If the interests of society in a properly developed fetus are to be protected, much more than antiabortion laws will have to be considered. More research will probably reveal other improper practices of pregnant women.

Do pregnant women have the right to abuse their own bodies in ways that injure the development of their child? Is the woman's right to choose to have an abortion sometimes a way of preventing the birth of a deformed, diseased, or sickly child? On the other hand, now that it is possible to detect in advance possible genetic damage to a fetus due to no fault of the pregnant mother, can the state impose a duty to bear a deformed child? Does a deformed fetus have the right to be born? All these questions will be part of our future rights developments. They will have to be resolved, simply because the state of our knowledge of the risks to the unborn child increases day by day.

Children continue to be born in America with severe birth defects. Some of these are caused by the behavior of the mother. Other defects are due to known and predictable genetic flaws. Nutrition and educational programs for pregnant women will provide a small solution. Larger solutions await a reconsideration of the modern meaning of the right to life. While the battle over abortion rights still rages newer issues will arise that have more far-reaching significance for the quality of life of future generations.

There is growing scientific evidence that workplace hazards may cause injury to a fetus. A pregnant mother, working in a hazardous workplace, may jeopardize the status of her unborn child. Pregnant workers in chemical plants, pesticide firms, and the oil industry may be subjected to unusually hazardous conditions. Toxins in other lines of work will be revealed by future medical research. Smoking in the workplace is probably as injurious to the fetus as most other toxins. We shall have to consider new types of state and federal legislation to protect the rights of unborn children. As it is, lawsuits have been instituted based on such potential fetal injuries.

Human Fetal Tissue

Another aspect of the right to life is the future use of human fetal tissue. The problem began in the mid-1980s with the experimental transplantation of human tissue, following spontaneous or elective abortions, to human patients with Parkinson's disease. By 1987 the University of Wisconsin was studying the transplantation of human fetal pancreatic cells into patients with diabetes. All states have adopted the Uniform Anatomical Gift Act, which permits either parent, subject to the objection of the other, to donate fetal tissue, following a spontaneous or a deliberate abortion, for the purposes of research, education, or transplantation. Some states have begun to restrict the use of fetal tissue in response to pressure from those who believe that something is morally wrong with the use of this material.

The moral issue seems to be whether the fetus should be viewed as mere potential human life or a living being. This is similar to the abortion controversy, except that the issue of the right of a woman to choose an abortion is not involved. The use of fetal tissue for research and transplantation raises the possibility that because of the scarcity of the material, pregnant women would be pressured to consent to an abortion. But even in the case of spontaneous abortion, many would contend that whatever the research benefits, the practice of using fetal tissue is offensive. Modern medical research and even cures may depend upon the availability of fetal tissue, so the issue could have great significance for the future of medicine.

Courts and legislatures will have to consider the fetal tissue problem in the near future. Certainly, financial gain should not be a ground for tissue donation. The law could assure, at the least, that the parents would receive no money for their actions. Similarly, family planning agencies should not profit from the sales of these materials. Federal funding of medical research that employs fetal tissue is currently under attack. Whether the society should permit the practice at all is for the people to decide through their elected representatives. The balance between the needs of medical research and the common conceptions of morality must be decided upon after due public deliberation.

At the other end of life, serving the needs of the very old, medical science has made considerable strides in raising health standards. The life span of Americans has steadily grown. It is possible that medical research will allow for the extension of life to 120 years or beyond. Longevity has always been considered a good thing, but it may come at a very high financial cost. For the first time Americans may have to consider whether there may be limits to the use of health care. We may decide that the extension of life span should not be a high priority of medical research. Somehow the society may be forced to choose to answer the question of how much is owed to the very old. The aging of our society continues onward. Who shall decide what is the limit of a person's life?

The Right to Die

Death is an uncomfortable topic. Many people would rather not think or talk about it. But for a variety of reasons courts and legislatures have begun to deal with the question of choosing to die. The issue of the right to die first reached national attention in 1976, when the state of New Jersey's Supreme Court decided a case involving a young person named Karen Ann Quinlan who had been severely injured in an auto accident. Ms. Quinlan was hospitalized for many years and was regarded by her physicians as irreversibly comatose. Her life was thought to be sustained only by a respirator. The New Jersey Court recognized the right of Ms. Quinlan's parents to disconnect the respirator and outlined a series of steps and procedures that could be taken in future cases, without judicial intervention. Since 1967 other states have faced similar issues, with different results.

Some federal courts have recognized a constitutional "right to die," giving patients a new right to decide the time and the terms of their own deaths. Some judges contend that the "right to die" is part of personal liberties and personal privacy, which are fundamental. One federal court used the equal protection of the laws clause of the Fourteenth Amendment to strike down state laws restricting the choice of death. The federal Supreme Court has never ruled clearly on the issue, so it cannot be said that there is yet a clearly established constitutional right to die. Legislatures around the country have begun to address the issue, setting up elaborate conditions and circumstances under which life-sustaining medical treatment could be withheld.

Most Americans are disturbed about the claim that there is some kind of right to die. The idea of voluntary suicide—of choosing to die— offends the moral sensibilities of many people. Many church leaders regard the idea of suicide with horror, regarding it theologically as sacrilege or denial of God's plan for man. Even so, there is a growing demand among a minority of Americans to select the time, place, and manner of their death. This demand is especially strong among those who are subject to an incurable disease and in acute daily pain. In most states the laws still regard "mercy killing" by physicians at the request of patients to be illegal, but these laws are being tested and may gradually be changed.

Euthanasia

Some regard the claimed right to die as merely a modern form of euthanasia. The Webster New

Collegiate Dictionary definition of euthanasia is "the act or practice of killing or permitting the death of hopelessly sick or injured individuals . . . in a relatively painless way for reasons of mercy." Actually, there are those who believe in euthanasia for other reasons than mercy, such as improving the quality of human stock. Euthanasia can be a dangerous idea, used to support highly offensive social practices.

Euthanasia has been called "mercy killing" by its supporters, but it is a form of medical killing. Euthanasia is not a new issue. The phrase, drawn from the Greek, means a "good death." The ancient Greek philosopher Plato wrote that "if a man has a sickly constitution and intemperate habits, his life was worth nothing to himself or to anyone else." Plato justified the withholding of medical treatment for such people, believing "they should not be treated though they be rich as Midas." However, Plato did not advocate the deliberate use of medical skills to terminate the lives of the sickly.

Other defenders of euthanasia have proposed the elimination of the sickly, the deformed, and the "unfit" by deliberate use of medical skills. In the hands of Nazi fanatics euthanasia was used to justify the extermination of orphans, deformed people, the mentally ill, and retarded individuals. This was part of the Nazi effort to "purify the Aryan race." Genocide against Jews was another part of their killing program.

Who decides that a person is unfit to live? Those who believe in the use of medicine to preserve the health of a favored race or a particular class, while ending the lives of those less favored or less fortunate, are committing a form of murder.

The question of ending life cannot be avoided. Voluntary euthanasia, done with the patient's knowing consent, or based upon the patient's fundamental beliefs and choice as to his method of dying, is a different issue than involuntary euthanasia, committed by a government or a group that imposes its will on its victims. Active involuntary use of medical techniques to end a life is illegal in all societies. Involuntary euthanasia should stay illegal because it is always a form of murder.

There may be circumstances, however, when euthanasia could be both moral and legal. Religious believers may not want to adopt euthanasia for themselves. They may believe it to be immoral

and irreligious. Still, nonbelievers may desire some form of a right to choose their method and time of death. At the moment the whole subject of voluntary euthanasia is shrouded in doubt and arouses a great deal of speculation and confusion.

Advance Directives

Even if the "right to die" is offensive to most Americans as an abstract matter, when confronted with certain personal issues Americans demonstrate a growing sympathy for some form of that right. Many Americans consider that by providing their family and their doctors with some written form of preference about acute medical care they may avoid some of the turmoil and uncertainty that can surround them when they are very seriously injured or are very old and weak. Many Americans have prepared these instructions, called "advance directives" for the use of their family or their physicians as a way of expressing their preferences ahead of the emergency situation.

Approximately 90 percent of the American public, when polls have been taken, seem to want advance directives. Both the young and the healthy express at least as much interest in planning as those older than age 65 and those in fair-to-poor health. The population clearly seeks more control over both their future medical care and also the method, timing, and place of their death. How disheartening for a patient to fear that his or her doctor cannot be trusted in a matter of such importance. It appears that many doctors have no respect for patients' wishes. Ironically, maintaining trust in the medical profession is one of the four traditional reasons, cited in any number of court decisions, for restraining patient control over ending their life.

An advance directive is a general term that refers to any instruction or statement regarding future medical care. The advance directive is a relatively new device that allows an active role for the patient in future decisions about life-sustaining treatments. These directives are intended to serve as instructions to medical care providers and to the family members. The goal of such directives is to specify in advance the types of medical procedures people would or would not want to undergo if they become mentally incompetent or otherwise unable to communicate their wishes.

The two basic types of advance directives are the living will and the durable power of attorney.

The living will is a legal document that allows a competent adult to state the kind of health care he or she wants and under what circumstances, in the event of incapacity. The durable power of attorney, sometimes called a "health care proxy" is a legal document that allows a competent adult to appoint someone he or she trusts to decide about medical treatment, including life-sustaining measures, in the event of decision-making incapacity.

The more controversial and illegal physician-assisted suicide and euthanasia currently is even less popular among physicians. Few doctors want to assist patients to carry out their desire to die. Medicine is a healing profession. It runs against the grain to expect physicians to use their skills to end a patient's life rather than prolong it. Killing patients cannot be made a duty of physicians, whatever we may believe about honoring the wishes of a terminally ill person.

When a physician applies the latest medical technology to keep a terminally ill patient alive for a few more days or weeks, however, he or she may be doing no favor to the patient. The cost of the medical technology may also place a financial burden on the survivors. In this event the physician may withhold care, which will have the effect of shortening a patient's life. On the other hand withholding care is not killing in any moral sense. It is simply letting nature takes its final course. In a theological sense, it may be accepting God's will.

Some medical experts contend that medical care for elderly people at the end of their natural life span should consist largely of pain relief rather than extension of life. Daniel Callahan, Director of the Hastings Medical Center, has written in a professional journal that "in its long-standing ambition to forestall death, medicine in the care of the aged has reached its last frontier," but he feels that "medicine should now restrain its ambition at that frontier" because the costs of that effort are prohibitive. The money spent in age-extending medicine could be better spent to help the young. Money cannot abolish death, but it can assist the younger portion of the population live longer, healthier lives. As the American population contains larger proportions of elderly people, this issue of spending money on more life-extending medicine will become more pressing.

Tremendous advances in medical technology may make the almost indefinite prolongation of life a real possibility. Ventilators, artificial organs, and cloning of organs and tissues are becoming increasingly available techniques. Artificial hearts are available now but kidneys and livers are possible future developments. Artificial support systems for prolonging life are already found in our hospitals. Tubes, pumps, and machines are hooked up to keep patients barely alive. But death may not be a purely private question. Other social issues may become more important than preserving the life of a very old or very sick person.

The issue of right to life is becoming pressed upon the courts. The usual context of the judicial inquiry is the decision to give or to withhold medical care. A number of state statutes have created a right to allow individuals to express their preferences concerning acceptable and nonacceptable treatment if they ever reach the point at which artificial life support systems are being considered. This form of voluntary euthanasia is tolerated in those states. Of course, it is possible that a very ill person could change his mind when in the hospital.

In February 1996 the U.S. Supreme Court was asked to decide whether a Michigan man should live or die, a decision that could determine the fate of thousands of sick and injured people across the country. Mary Martin, wife of a west Michigan man gravely injured in a 1987 automobile-and-train crash, asked the Court to overturn a Michigan Supreme Court decision and allow doctors to remove the feeding tube that has kept her husband alive for more than nine years. Mr. Martin is unable to walk, talk, eat, or roll over; he wears diapers, and has a colostomy bag. He is confined to a nursing home, where he requires around-the-clock care.

Michael Martin's mother and sister disagree and have asked the Supreme Court to stay out of the case. They contend that Martin's life is not all that bad and want him to remain hooked up to his feeding tube until the "good Lord takes him." Martin, now 45, suffered grave and irreversible brain injuries in the car-train accident that killed his daughter.

Mrs. Martin testified in court that before the accident her husband repeatedly told her that "if I ever get sick, don't put me on any machines to keep me going if there is no hope of getting better." She claimed that in asking the hospital to remove the feeding tube that kept him alive she was merely following his express desires.

But Martin's mother contended that Martin is conscious, not in pain, and has indicated a desire to go on living. Whether Martin's current wishes are known is unclear. That is an issue that the Supreme Court may have to decide.

In a 1990 right-to-die case from Missouri, the U.S. Supreme Court refused to allow doctors to remove a feeding tube from Nancy Cruzan, who was comatose. The justices said the Missouri court acted properly when it ruled there was no "clear and convincing" proof that Cruzan wanted to be taken off life-sustaining equipment.

The University of Michigan Medical Center, William Beaumont Hospital, and Henry Ford Health System, all in Michigan, urged the Supreme Court to take the case. They claimed that the medical profession would be thrown into "a state of turmoil" if Michael Martin's wishes were rejected.

But Michigan's Protection and Advocacy Service Inc., filed a brief supporting Martin's right to live. An attorney for the group said allowing Martin to die could "result in the deaths of thousands of incompetent people who cannot speak for themselves." To decide otherwise would mean that courts would allow people to make life-and-death decisions for their own financial or personal benefit.

Euthanasia is much harder to justify when a patient has not voluntarily given his consent in advance. Then there is a strong possibility that other relatives may try to frame the decision of life or death in a way that favors them. Some physicians withhold life-support systems from comatose patients when they believe that the patient would want it that way. The physician's assumption that the patient would have chosen death rather than the alternative of life support systems may be much less selfish than the judgment of interested parties, but it is still an involuntary form of euthanasia, done against the patient's will or, at least, without the patient's knowledge and agreement.

Involuntary euthanasia by physicians raises the gravest issues in this field. A strong risk exists that cost considerations or private views of physicians may be imposed on helpless patients, yet it is believed that this practice, which is rarely spoken about in medical circles, is very common. Given the increasing potential to use technological devices to extend life artificially, this issue will arise with greater frequency in the future.

Competency

One of the major issues in recognition of the right to die is a determination of competency. Has the patient the capacity to reason? Does the patient understand and appreciate the nature and the consequences of their health care decisions?

Patients who are demented or in acute pain may lack this capacity. People may have the right to make health care decisions for themselves, but their judgment may be impaired. If that is so, perhaps their judgment must be disregarded.

Only someone with advanced training in psychology or psychiatry could determine whether a health care decision was fully rational. Depression, a widespread mental illness, may cause people to desire their own death, even if they are not terminally ill. Deeply disturbed individual cannot be trusted to make wise decisions for themselves.

Because the difficulty of making a determination that a person has made a reasoned health care choice for himself, many hospitals insist that physicians consult with special professional committees when in doubt. A hospital board may assist in making the difficult decision to honor a patient's request to die. In many states judicial intervention may be required, as well. The decision to die may seem the most personal of rights, but the choice of death has an impact on family, friends, and the whole society, so safeguards against unwise decisions must be created.

Assisted Suicide

Assisted suicide, which is even more complex than the withholding of life-sustaining medical treatment, seems to require even more safeguards. The right to end one's life when not terminally ill in the hospital creates a severe test of law and ethics. Suicide is a crime in every state. Physician-assisted suicide poses special problems, which the career of Dr. Jack Kevorkian illustrates.

Dr. Jack Kevorkian is the leading advocate of assisted suicide. A pathologist, Dr. Kevorkian has been engaged in providing information and clinical assistance to individuals who wish to consider the possibility of suicide because of very acute illness and pain. In a series of cases decided in 1996, Dr. Kevorkian was found not guilty of a violation of state laws against assisted suicide. The doctor insisted that assisted suicide was a right, not a crime.

In two 1996 Michigan cases Dr. Jack Kevorkian was found not guilty of causing the deaths of two chronically ill patients. Carbon monoxide poisoning had been the cause of both deaths, and the doctor had instructed the patients on the means of self-administration of the deadly gas. Both victims had signed consent forms for "medically assisted suicide." Under examination at his criminal trial, Dr. Kevorkian insisted that he did not want to cause the death of the patients; his only wish was to help them to fulfill their own wish to end their suffering. The patients controlled the dosage by pulling a lever. The patients determined the amount of the dosage, knowing how much carbon monoxide was needed to cause death. One victim suffered from bone cancer, another from Lou Gehrig's disease.

Advances in medical technology have allowed many fragile newborns to survive the trauma of birth. During the past two decades the survival rates of low-birth-weight babies has dramatically increased. Among infants weighing 1,000 to 2,500 grams, the survival rate has improved from less than 50 percent in 1961 to over 90 percent in 1991. Medical science will make it possible for more and more very low birth weight children to survive. Nearly all of these children are born prematurely, before the "normal" term of nine months. Many of them are born with congenital abnormalities. What are the rights of the prematurely born? Should seriously ill newborns be aggressively treated? Highly sophisticated and very expensive medical equipment will make this situation a very common public issue. Does the right to life include the possibility of a severely handicapped life, bought at great expense to the parents and society? Brought to extremes, families may be forced to lose their homes or savings in order to protect the right to life of these fragile young people. Who shall decide such issues, state legislatures, courts, theologians, or philosophers?

Physicians are generally opposed to assisted suicide. According to one recent poll, only 40 percent would actually assist a patient in dying. Contrast these numbers with a 1993 Harris Poll that showed that 70 percent of the U.S. population favors physician-assisted suicide for terminal patients. Researchers found that hematologists and cancer specialists were the strongest opponents of euthanasia and assisted suicide, while psychiatrists were the strongest proponents of the two practices. Moreover, female doctors were significantly more likely to support assisted suicide than male doctors, whereas both sexes had similar attitudes toward euthanasia. The researchers concluded that "the polarized attitudes of physicians will make it difficult to formulate and implement laws and policies concerning assisted suicide and euthanasia."

In an April 1994 editorial in its official newspaper, the American Medical Association (AMA) reiterated its firm opposition to physician-assisted suicide. In an editorial headed "No To Physician Assisted Suicide," the AMA reaffirmed its 1993 declaration that assistance in a suicide is "fundamentally inconsistent with the physician's professional role." The editorial says it is "illogical" to argue that the practice is "a natural extension" of a physician's task. Assisted suicide is not about healing. Nor is intentionally causing death an ethical approach to helping a patient in pain." The editorial urges doctors to improve pain control and other ways in which "medicine helps patients live as best they can until the end."

In spite of the current policy of the AMA, patients may demand that their wishes concerning the termination of life be honored. If the treatment preferences of patients are to be honored, doctors may face the difficult prospect of relinquishing, at least in part, this central element of their professional role. That is what the right to die finally requires.

The Rights of Children and Youth

The treatment of children and young people has gone through a historic set of changes. Americans have long struggled to relate the adult's world to the separate experiences of childhood and adolescence. From the beginning of American history attempts have been made to spell out the legal rights and duties of children and young people. The earliest American rights document, the Massachusetts Bay Colony *Body of Liberties* (1641), declared that rebellious children were subject to capital punishment. It also allowed children to defend themselves against abuse. This conflict between the family rights of parents and child protection by the state has marked the entire history of children's rights in America.

Rights for children is a complex subject. The very notion of a right implies the capacity to reasonably use it. But children are regarded as immature and not fully able to reason for themselves. That is why the parents have been the principal source of authority over children, not the state. Yet some parents inflict harm upon children, and this situation has caused the government to intervene on many historic occasions. As early as 1646 Virginia passed a statute allowing local authorities to remove children from homes without the consent of their parents. In 1747 the selectmen of Watertown, Massachusetts, after hearing complaints about families "under very needy and suffering circumstances," warned some parents that because the parents were raising their children "in idleness, ignorance, and irreligion," the selectmen were prepared to "take effectual care that such children be

Before child labor laws became effective, many parents regarded their children's labor as an honorable source of family income.

forthwith put into such families where they may have good care taken of them." In the absence of the family, orphan children have been protected by the state throughout American history.

The education of children by the state is a practice established by law in the nineteenth century. Previously, parents alone chose whether and how their children should be educated. In 1852 Massachusetts became the first state to mandate compulsory school education for all children. This meant that parents could no longer choose to leave their children in ignorance. Other states promptly followed suit. This state intervention on behalf of children was not provided because children asked for it, but because public authorities believed that children required it to become responsible, effective adults.

The Health and Welfare of Children

When child labor was abolished, another aspect of parental authority was lost with it. Many parents had regarded the labor of their children as an honorable source of income to the family. However, to protect children against the abuses of factory owners and other employers, state laws were passed on behalf of children to protect them against the hard work that had been demanded of adults. In 1882 New York passed the Factory Act, which prohibited child labor by children under the age of 13. After a very long struggle, child labor

under the age of 16 was prohibited by federal law in 1933, and the first permanent national child labor law became effective in 1938.

The campaign for child labor laws and for other forms of child protective statutes were usually led by various groups of children's advocates. The New York Children's Aid Society was the first of these. The Society was able to convince the city of New York to pass a truancy law, which specified that families could not receive relief payments unless their children were in school. The New York Children's Aid Society also helped the many vagrant street children of the poor, many of whom had turned to crime by inventing a system of "placing out" such children to other people who could care for them better than their own families.

In 1875 the national Society for the Prevention of Cruelty to Children was founded. This group took up the cause of abused and neglected children. They led a crusade against family violence. Finally, in 1912 the Children's Bureau was created as a child advocacy group within the federal government.

In the 1920s the federal government began efforts to promote children's health. Through the passage of the Sheppard-Towner Act, preventive health care was encouraged. This act funded public health nurses who would teach parents how to care for children. It also established clinics where children could receive medical examinations and mothers could learn about nutrition and sanitation. Prenatal care was another goal of the federal program, and health education was provided to pregnant women. After intensive campaigning by the American Medical Association (AMA), however, Congress repealed the Sheppard-Towner Act in 1929. The AMA was deeply concerned with improving the health of infants in America.

During the early New Deal of Franklin Roosevelt (1932–1938), the basis for the current national welfare system was laid. Few new programs were started on behalf of children until the passage of the Social Security Act. In that statute Aid to Families with Dependent Children became a feature of the federal approach to helping children. It should be noted that the federal funds provided were channeled through the family. Dependent children received no direct assistance.

The problem of violence within the family and the need to protect children from physical harm has been recognized for over a century, yet the scope and extent of child abuse has become more and more obvious with the passage of time. Few cases of child abuse were reported or detected before improved reporting techniques were required. In 1962 the Children's Bureau sponsored a national conference on child abuse. The conference led directly to stronger laws requiring the reporting of such incidents. In 1973 Congress passed the Child Abuse Prevention and Treatment Act, which requires states to meet federal standards on custody matters. One of the provisions of the act grants state welfare agencies the power to remove a child from a family for three days if the agency feels the child is in danger. The statute also created the National Center on Child Abuse and Neglect as a clearinghouse for reports and information.

Advocacy of Children's Rights

The children's rights movement was never fully formed or coherent in the United States. The notion that children might have rights aside from those of their parents was born in the wake of a 1967 Supreme Court decision, *In re Gault*. That case involved a 15-year-old boy who was caught making obscene telephone calls. Because of his age, a hearing was provided for the criminal offense before a juvenile court judge. The boy was found guilty by the judge and sent to the state

industrial school to be held there until he would reach the age of 21. His parents sued on the ground that their son's rights to due process of law had been violated. They pointed out that had he been treated as an adult the sentence would have been much less severe.

Justice Hugo Black, writing for the Supreme Court majority, overruled the state courts and found that "the Constitution requires that he be tried in accordance with the guarantees of all the provisions of the Bill of Rights made applicable to the states by the Fourteenth Amendment." The state could not have unchecked authority to deal with juveniles as they sought fit.

Some observers saw this decision as an opportunity for a platform that could broaden the rights available to young people. Later court decisions found that children are entitled to lawyers in juvenile hearings and to some limited form of due process of law in the schools. The legal rights of children were broadened in many other ways, including the right to sue government agencies to challenge the appropriateness of their treatment by state agencies. Children had gained legal rights within the welfare system.

There was a surge of litigation in the 1970s on behalf of the needs of handicapped children. Nearly 2 million such children had been excluded from public schools. An additional 3 or 4 million received inadequate education. In 1972, retarded children received a major legal victory in Pennsylvania with the state Supreme Court's decision that declared that denying handicapped children an education was unconstitutional. Handicapped children have been especially at risk in the adult world. In 1975 Congress passed the Education for All Handicapped Children Act. This statute, originally the idea of children's advocacy groups, required schools to make provisions for the special needs of handicapped young people.

Radical child rights advocates wished to press the children's agenda still further. Outspoken leaders of a new child liberation movement wished to endow children with a full slate of rights of their own. Richard Farson, in his book *Birthrights* (1974), argued that the best way to create a better world for children begins with the realization that "our world is not a good place for children . . . because every institution in society discriminates against them." The civil rights movement on behalf of disadvantaged adults alerted Americans to "the dawning recognition that children must have the same right to full participation in society, that they must be valued by themselves, not just as potential adults."

John Holt, another child liberationist, wrote his book *Escape from Childhood* (1974) in the same year. Both authors regard children as being excessively dependent upon and subservient to adults. John Holt proposed granting many "adult" rights to children. Children should have the right to vote, the right to privacy, the right to travel, the right to make money, the right to live away from home, and "the right to do, in general, what any adult may legally do." This would amount to a radical reconstruction of the American family.

More moderate advocates of expanded children's rights want to improve conditions for children in society, in the schools, in the home, and in the juvenile justice system. Full autonomy or a full list of adult rights for children is not the goal of these reformers. Instead, the claim is that children still need the protection of adults. Adult advocates of children's rights could improve the conditions of the juvenile justice system and the treatment of children in shelters and correctional centers. As Marian Wright Edelman, the creator of the Children's Defense Fund, has said, if children "are to receive fair treatment and recognition in this country, children require the same planned, systematic advocacy, legal and otherwise that the NAACP Legal Defense and Education Fund, for example, instigated for blacks three decades ago."

Ms. Edelman was an attorney for the Jackson, Mississippi, office of the NAACP Legal Defense and Education Fund during the struggle for rights for African Americans in the South. She was also the author of the Comprehensive Child Care Act of 1971. The Children's Defense Fund, which she heads, has several areas of policy emphasis. The Fund works to protect handicapped and retarded children within the schools. Special needs children are given special advocacy. The Children's Defense Fund resists the use of children in medical research and experimentation. Reform of the juvenile justice system, child development, day care, and children's rights to privacy are also on the agenda for action.

The political agenda of the child advocates is opposed by a more conservative group of thinkers who believe that children's primary psychological

"HOW ABOUT ME?"

This poster parallels children's rights abuses with the civil rights abuses committed against African Americans prior to emancipation.

need is for stronger, more authoritative parents. This group advocates expanded parents' rights and decreased state intervention on behalf of children. They point to Supreme Court opinions such as *Wisconsin* v. *Yoder* (1972), in which the Court held that parents could remove their children from public school at the age of 14. They favor strengthening the family, rather than the state, as a means for assisting children.

Parents' Rights

Prevalent legal theory still holds that parental authority should be honored, except when limits are placed by law. Parents have the right to name a child, to custody of a child, and to choose the child's religion and education. Parents decide what a child shall eat, how children shall dress,

Platform of the Libertarian Party: Children's Rights

Children are human beings and, as such, have all the rights of human beings.

We recognize that children who have not reached maturity need guardians to secure their rights and to aid in the exercise of those rights. We hold that guardianship belongs to those who most love and value the child and his or her development, normally the parents and never the state.

We oppose all laws that empower government officials to seize children and make them "wards of the state" or, by means of child labor laws and compulsory education, to infringe on their freedom to work or learn as they choose. We oppose all legally created or sanctioned discrimination against (or in favor of) children, just as we oppose government discrimination directed at any other artificially defined sub-category of human beings. Specifically we oppose ordinances that outlaw adults-only apartment housing.

We also support the repeal of all laws establishing any category of crimes applicable to children for which adults would not be similarly vulnerable, such as curfew, smoking, and alcoholic beverage laws, and other status offenses. Similarly, we favor the repeal of

"stubborn child" laws and laws establishing the category of "persons in need of supervision." We call for an end to the practice in many states of jailing children not accused of any crime. We seek the repeal of all "children's codes" or statutes which abridge due process protections for young people. We further favor the abolition of the juvenile court system, so that juveniles will be held fully responsible for their crimes.

Whenever parents or other guardians are unable or unwilling to care for their children, those guardians have the right to seek other persons who are willing to assume guardianship, and children have the right to seek other guardians who place a higher value on their lives. Accordingly, we oppose all laws that impede these processes, notably those restricting private adoption services or those forcing children to remain in the custody of their parents against their will.

Children should always have the right to establish their maturity by assuming administration and protection of their own rights, ending dependency upon their parents or other guardians and assuming all the responsibilities of adulthood.

and even what they shall read or what movies and television shows they should watch. Within the privacy of the home parents have considerable authority over children, if they are able to assert it.

When children run away from home or engage in chronic disobedience state intervention is limited, and unless there is evidence that their home is unsafe, the children will be returned to parental custody. However, deeper intervention by the state may take place when parents do not discharge their duties to their children. Children are entitled to parental support and nurturance. The state has the power to intervene and assume guardianship or temporary custody when neglect, abuse, or parental incompetence is present. Then children can be taken away from parents and put in more suitable homes. Of course, in all these decisions the child has some voice but very little power.

In recent years it has become obvious that the rights of children and young people need to be

clearly stated. Because of their age and presumed immaturity, children are generally subject to the care of their parents, who make decisions for them on their behalf. Young people, when they go to school, soon learn that they do not have the same rights as adults. Changing social conditions, including the decline of the numbers of two-parent families, have called some of these issues into question. To the horror of their parents, some children have even gone so far as to institute suits against their parents, claiming a right of divorce from "unfit parents" or a right to be able to choose to live with their natural rather than their adoptive families.

Carried to extremes these claims of the right of children and young people can disrupt the traditional family system. Fuller attention to the rights of young people can drastically limit the conditions under which schools may conduct the education process.

But these issues and claims will not disappear. Children and young people should be informed of the limits of their rights, even if that means that questions that have not been extensively aired are finally considered.

But there are problems that children in America still confront. As the Children's Defense Fund has pointed out, every day in America, one mother dies in childbirth, three children and youths under age 25 die from HIV infection, 15 children under age 20 are killed by guns, and 255 children and youth under age 18 are arrested for drug offenses. In America each day 95 babies die before their first birthday and 564 babies are born to mothers who had late or no prenatal care. Statistics show that over 3,000 young people are subject to corporal punishment in school each day, and over 13,000 public school students are suspended from school each day. These are social problems and not just children's problems, and some sort of action is necessary to make childhood in America more secure.

Most political parties have avoided addressing children's issues. One of the more provocative statements of children's rights is to be found in the platform of the Libertarian Party. That document does not state the current condition of children's rights, but it does concisely pose one set of political claims for future generations of children and youths. A better, more responsible approach to children's rights must be constructed.

Animal Rights

Concern for the treatment of animals in America has a long history. The American Society for the Prevention of Cruelty to Animals, the oldest national group to take up the cause of animal maltreatment, was organized in 1866. The American Humane Association, with similar goals, was founded in 1877. Both organizations were formed to prevent cruel treatment of animals. In the 1970s and 1980s more radical groups emerged. These organizations tended to take up other neglected aspects of the treatment of animals, including the use of animals in research, product testing, and teaching.

People for the Ethical Treatment of Animals (PETA) was founded in 1980 and is the largest organization focused on these new issues. PETA is active and aggressive. It conducts rallies and demonstrations intended to draw public attention to the use of animals in experimentation, the slaughter of animals to be consumed as human food, and the manufacture of fur apparel. PETA has also at times endorsed the actions of the Animal Liberation Front, an international organization that is willing to use illegal means to promote their views of animal rights.

The Animal Liberation Front has claimed responsibility for raids and break-ins on laboratories around the world, attempting to disclose and disrupt scientific experimentation on animals. It has also "liberated" animals used as food, for clothing, or entertainment. "Liberation" seems to mean the release of animals held by researchers and others. The cause of radical animal rights has also been promoted by other, more violent means, such as arson, theft of research, bomb threats, and the defacement of property.

Many groups have sprung up in reaction to the radical tactics of some "animal rights" groups. Scientists have defended their use of animals for research purposes, claiming that advances in human health are made possible by the use of nonhuman subjects in laboratories. Animals research, they contend, can be both life-saving and life-enhancing for human beings. Medical progress, they claim, depends upon continued use of animals in research. As one group, Saving Lives Coalition, expressed in June 1992: "Should animal research be lost to the scientific community, the victims would not be the scientists. The victims would be all people; ourselves, our families, our neighbors, our fellow humans. Human life is at stake; human suffering is at issue."

Animal activists fly the banner of "animal rights." They generally regard animals as having rights as important, in their way, as those of some human beings. Ingrid Newkirk, one of the founders of PETA, expressed this view in its most extreme form in the famous statement that "there is no rational basis for saying that a human being has special rights . . . (since) a rat is a pig is a dog is a boy." A slightly different view comes from Alex Pacheco, another PETA founder, who said that "we feel that animals have the same rights as a retarded human child." Animal suffering cannot be justified, according to the animal rights movement, in the name of the supposed benefits to humans. According to their views, animal rights are virtually on a par with human rights.

However, most of the medical establishment and the scientific community do not accept the notion of animal rights, believing that the consequence of such rights would be lost opportunities to help human beings. Perhaps some research conducted on animals could have been conducted in some other way that was less harmful to animal welfare, but, even so, few doctors accept that elimination of animals from medical tests is a realistic possibility. Former U.S. Surgeon General C. Everett Koop has claimed that "virtually every major medical advance for both humans and animals has been achieved through biomedical research using animal models to study and find a cure for a disease and through animal testing to prove the safety and efficacy of a new treatment." The animal rights advocates are not willing to concede that their policies would set back the cause of medical research.

Animal Rights versus Animal Welfare

A distinction must be drawn between the animal rights movements and the advocates of those concerned with better animal welfare, generally. Animal welfare advocates acknowledge the suffering of nonhumans and attempt to reduce that suffering through "humane" treatment, but they do not have as a goal elimination of the use and exploitation of animals. The animal rights movement goes significantly further by rejecting the exploitation of animals and according them rights in that regard. A person committed to animal welfare might be concerned that cows get enough space and proper food, but would not necessarily have any qualms about killing and eating cows, so long as the rearing and slaughter were "humane." The Animal Welfare movement is represented by such organizations as the Society for the Prevention of Cruelty to Animals and the Humane Society.

Animal liberation is, for many people, a synonym for animal rights. Some people prefer the term "liberation" because it brings to mind images of other successful liberation movements, such as the movements for the liberation of slaves and the liberation of women, whereas the term "rights" often encounters resistance when an attempt is made to apply it to nonhumans. The phrase "Animal Liberation" became popular with the publication of Peter Singer's classic book of the same name. An animal liberationist is not necessarily one who engages in forceful civil disobedience or unlawful actions.

The fundamental principle of the animal rights movement is that nonhuman animals deserve to live according to their own natures, free from harm, abuse, and exploitation. This goes further than just saying that we should treat animals well while we exploit them or before we kill and eat them. The principle says that animals have the right to be free from human cruelty and exploitation, just as humans possess this right. The withholding of this right from nonhuman animals based on their species membership is referred to as "speciesism."

The logical problem of animals as holders of rights should be obvious. Animals do not know they have rights. Since they are not conscious of having rights, it is impossible for them to claim or assert those rights. Animals are not rational enough to understand they have rights, so they cannot choose to use a right or to surrender it. These obstacles do not deter the advocates of animal rights, no more than those who champion the right to life of a fetus. After all, an unborn child also lacks any capacity to reason and is incapable of claiming a right.

Animal rights are outside the mainstream of American thinking at present, but it is worthwhile to consider whether or not those claims deserve serious consideration. There is no doubt that society uses animals as food, as clothing, and as objects of testing. There is no question that cruel techniques have sometimes been used to gain the benefits provided by animals. If, in the future, more and more Americans are persuaded that animal rights deserve serious attention, more humane treatment of animals will result. How many Americans will be willing to forgo animal food or agree to suspend animal testing? That depends on the success of the argument for animal rights.

In 1975, Peter Singer's influential book, *Animal Liberation: A New Ethics for Our Treatment of Animals,* laid the foundation for thinking about animal rights. Another essential book was written by Thomas Regan and published in 1983. This book, *The Case for Animal Rights,* builds upon Singer's work. Both authors try to build a logical, nontheological argument.

Peter Singer argues that all beings that have feelings seek to avoid pain. Human beings, he says, have ruthlessly and cruelly inflicted unnecessary pain on animals exploited for human purposes. This kind of animal suffering should be stopped because all forms of life that have feeling have essentially the same rights because all are equals with respect to the infliction of pain. According to Singer, the difference among the species is no more meaningful than the differences that exist among human beings, such as race and gender. Since animals cannot speak for themselves, it is the duty of humans to speak for them and to lessen their suffering. Singer quotes the English nineteenth-century philosopher Jeremy Bentham, who said that the question about animals is not "Can they talk or reason?" but "Can they suffer?"

Both Singer and Regan agree that animals are not equal to human beings in all respects. Both assert that a normal adult human being has more value than any animal. Beyond this, they disagree about the justifications for different forms of animal suffering. However, both say that animals are being coerced against their will to be the subjects of medical research. Pain is inflicted upon animals by humans without regard to the moral worth of animals. Their rights may not be the same as humans, but they have some rights, especially since they lack the capacity of reason that humans have. Humans are bound to treat them humanely, not because animals know they have rights but because of their inability to assert their claims to be free from cruelty and pain inflicted by humans.

Animal research does raise issues that makes people uncomfortable. Activists want an immediate end to animal research. Although they have not been able to gain widespread support, a few major gains have been made. Cruelty to animals has become a more pressing concern of federal and state agencies.

The animal rights movement has had some successes, in spite of its radical tactics. In 1976 the federal Animal Welfare Act of 1970 was amended to include many more persons and organizations under its coverage. More humane conditions for animal transport were enacted into law. In 1985 the Food Security Act amended the Animal Welfare Act again to state that no animal may be used in more than one major operative experiment, from which it is allowed to recover, except in case of scientific necessity or other special circumstances, as determined by the Secretary of Agriculture. The 1985 statute is also called the "Federal Laboratory Animal Welfare Act," and it requires annual reports on the humane treatment of laboratory animals. In the 1985 statute Congress did express a "public concern for laboratory animals" but accepted the need for the use of animals in "certain kinds of research." The statute placed some procedural safeguards upon animal experimentation. In 1992 The U.S. Animal Enterprise Protection Act placed additional limitations upon the trade in animals.

Courts have never recognized the legitimacy of animal rights. The Constitution of the United States appears to have no place for animal rights. Courts have sometimes questioned the procedures used by animal experimenters, but they have not been willing to view any animal as a holder of any form of right. Federal courts have recognized the legal standing to sue of an animal rights organization. In *Animal Legal Defense Fund* v. *Youtter* (1991), the district court judge held that an animal rights group could argue on behalf of birds, rats, and mice within the meaning of the federal Laboratory Animal Welfare Act. Another federal judge agreed that the failure of the Secretary of Agriculture to issue regulations to include birds, rats, and mice was "arbitrary and capricious" *(Animal Legal Defense Fund* v. *Madigan,* 1992).

Mahatma Gandhi, the Indian statesman and philosopher, once said that "the greatness of a nation and its moral progress can be judged by the way its animals are treated." By widening the circle of compassion to deserving nonhumans, we ennoble humans. However, the notion of rights has never before been connected with nonhumans. To recognize animal rights would greatly extend the scope of rights discourse in America to an extent that may render human rights less meaningful. Sympathy with the pain of animals may lead to major reforms in the treatment of animals. Substitute measures for animal experimentation may eventually be required. All these reforms lie ahead, but the language of rights may only obscure these issues and inflame passions in the ongoing controversy over better treatment for animals. Vegetarians may believe it cruel and inhumane to eat animal flesh, but until the majority of the population agrees, the terminology of animal rights is just a means of moral persuasion, not a valid legal claim to a right.

Environmental Rights against Property Rights

Only in the twentieth century have Americans been concerned with environmental pollution and

the depletion of our natural resources. In the previous century outdoorsmen were concerned with the threat of loss of the vanishing wilderness. In the mid-twentieth century, the danger of environmental pollution was an even greater threat. Both the conservationists and the environmentalists were alarmed at the by-products of industrial America. The loss of natural resources, the cutting of ancient forests, and the preservation of threatened species of wildlife seemed to require government intervention. Later, the waste products of America's farms and factories poisoned the land, the streams, the lakes, the oceans, and the very air of the nation. However, in the process of expanding their policies, conservationists and environmentalists challenged traditional American views of private property. The collision between the

goals of the conservationists and the environmentalists with the property rights of Americans was a feature of twentieth-century politics. However, the issues were not resolved to the satisfaction of most Americans. What was required was a new definition of property rights consistent with the competing claims of environmentalists and conservationists.

The American Conservation Movement

The American conservation movement began in the late nineteenth century, partly in response to the shrinking of the wilderness, which had seemed inexhaustible until pressured by the settlement and industrialization of the nation. Conservationists like Gifford Pinchot, John Muir, and Theodore Roosevelt were motivated by a desire to preserve America's natural resources for the enjoyment of the public. The protection of and prudent use of natural resources and the planned use of public lands, forests, wildlife, water, and minerals were goals of Roosevelt's Conservation Program. During the administration of Presidents Theodore Roosevelt (1901–1909) and Franklin D. Roosevelt (1933–1945), large amounts of land were acquired and set aside for public use and enjoyment.

A system of national parks was created on many of the public lands. Later, portions of the public lands were set aside as permanent wilderness areas. Many western states contain vast amounts of these public lands within their borders. Some degree of private exploitation of public lands has been authorized by the Forest Service and the National Parks. The limits of private uses of public lands have not been established during the twentieth century and are likely to be a major issue of the next century. Although there is no "right" of private companies to use public lands, the pressure on limited American resources and the quest for corporate profits has caused a review of the very notion of "public lands" within a system of private property.

The National Park Service was established in 1916 within the Department of Interior. The management, sale, and leasing of federal lands is largely the responsibility of the federal Bureau of Land Management (established in 1946), which is also a part of the Department of Interior. The Bureau of Land Management controls huge amounts of timber, minerals, oil, and gas. Some of the land itself is suitable for grazing. Private interests have obtained rights to the use of portions of these federal land and properties.

Conservationists complain that commercial development and creeping urban sprawl ominously encroach on park boundaries. Permitted mining operations and oil and gas drilling continue to threaten our most popular national parks, such as Glacier, Yellowstone, Glen Canyon, and Denali. Conservationists say that off-road vehicles are destroying the beaches at Assateague, Cape Cod, Fire Island, and Cape Lookout. Acid rain is degrading air and water quality and ravaging the forests of Acadia in Maine, the Great Smokies in Tennessee and North Carolina, and Shenandoah National Park in Virginia. Pollution from power plants and motor vehicle traffic fouls the air and is so severe that the National Park Service has found that it affects 90 percent of the natural scenic vistas in parks from coast to coast. Friends of wildlife assert that poachers armed with high-powered automatic rifles, silencers, scanners, and other deadly hunting gear are slaughtering the wildlife in our national parks and forests. The year 1997 was a frightening one for parks.

Not since the 1940s, when Congress tried to open the national parks to logging and mineral extraction, have these national treasures been viewed as both exploitable and expendable. For example, larger parts of the Arctic National Wildlife Refuge have been opened to oil and gas drilling. During a recent session of Congress, legislative initiatives threatened parks with reduction or removal from the park system or would have impaired the Park Service's ability to manage and preserve these areas. Congress has also threatened to weaken the Endangered Species Act (1973) to allow more timber sales in old-growth forests.

The Expansion of Environmentalism

The protection of wildlife was one goal of the conservation movement, but environmentalism expanded as conservationism continued. A new stage of environmental concern was triggered by Rachel Carson's 1962 book, *Silent Spring*. In this book Carson pointed out the perils of pesticide use. Public concern was organized into a new environmental movement questioning the quality of the nation's air, land, and water. The public health was more at risk than ever before, environmentalists claimed, because of new technologies, advances in chemicals, and the massive increase in use of energy sources such as coal and oil. Pollution had existed in past societies, but never, said the environmentalists, on a scale with modern America. Industrialization had produced a peril to the population requiring new national legislation.

In 1969 the National Environmental Policy Act was passed in response to the environmental movement, which had captured the popular imagination. In 1970 the Clean Air Act became law, and in the same year the Occupational Safety and Health Act was signed into law. In the 1970s a flood of environmental legislation streamed out of Washington, supported by both major political parties. Clean water, new insecticide laws, solid waste, toxic substances, hazardous material, surface mining, and a host of other previously unregulated areas became part of the agenda for action. In 1972 the Noise Control Act was passed to regulate "noise pollution."

Safer drinking water and cleaner rivers and streams did result from this flurry of legislation, but the relationships between government and business were permanently altered. The rights of private property became redefined, on a piecemeal basis. Businesses were required to monitor their toxic and other wastes. Private premises were inspected by government officials to ensure compliance with the environmental laws, and a host of paper reporting requirements were imposed on American business. Strict government regulation meant that industries had to raise the standards of their operations for the safety of their workers and the protection of the general public, regardless of the impact of these laws on profits.

Environmental Justice

Until recently, environmentalism was the province of well-educated and more affluent Americans. Conservation and environmental groups are led by largely middle-class whites. Twenty large environmental organizations have claimed to speak for all Americans. The various laws and regulations of federal and state agencies have been heavily influenced by the views of these groups. More and more of the less affluent have joined the ranks of the conservation and environmental movements, but many of these poorer Americans may have been the unintended victims of some of the policies of environmentalism.

There is evidence that current environmental laws have a disproportionate effect on the poor, including ethnic and racial minorities. One of the nation's largest environmental groups, the Environmental Defense Fund, has admitted that inequities exist. The Executive Director of that group has noted that three out of four toxic waste dumps "are sited in predominately African American or Latino communities." Two million tons of radioactive uranium residue have been dumped on the tribal lands of Native Americans. Polluters have displaced some pollution to the areas occupied by some of the least powerful American groups.

In 1987 the Commission for Racial Justice of the United Church of Christ in Cleveland issued a report that set the tone for a new environmental justice movement. The report, *Toxic Wastes and Race in the United States,* concluded that toxic waste sites were most likely to be placed in minority communities. Apparently, poor people and people of color bear a disproportionate share of exposure to hazardous waste materials.

Since then, a number of other groups and individuals have raised the banner of environmental justice. Native American rights organizations, the National Association for the Advancement of Colored People (NAACP), and poverty lawyers all over the nation have begun to fight for better treatment of minorities and the poor. The Sierra Club and the Environmental Defense Fund have both lent legal assistance to the cause of environmental justice. Indeed, white working-class families have also joined in the struggle, as they have resisted the siting of toxic waste incinerators in their neighborhoods.

The Clinton administration has recognized the validity of some of the complaints of environmental justice activists. The appointment of Carol Browner as head of the Environmental Protection Agency (EPA) brought national attention and respectability to the movement. Environmental justice is said to have a high place on EPA's agenda.

In 1994 President Clinton signed Executive Order 12898, requiring that each federal agency "make achieving environmental justice part of its mission by identifying and addressing, as appropriate, disproportionately high and adverse human health or environmental effects of its programs, policies and activities on minority and low-income populations." The Clinton administration also agreed to investigate complaints against the states of Louisiana and Mississippi for alleged violations of the Civil Rights Acts of 1964 because of the way hazardous waste facilities had been sited.

A few environmental justice claims have been upheld in the federal courts. Most claimants must establish that there was a discriminatory intent, say, in the siting of a waste-handling facility. However, some victories have been won under sections of the civil rights laws that require a lower standard of proof. Whether intended or not, if it can be shown that the location of a waste site facility actually has had discriminatory effects on minorities and the poor, courts will find a violation of law.

The Environmental Agency has begun to be more vigilant. In addition to the complaints against Mississippi and Louisiana, the EPA Office of Civil Rights has investigated wrong doing by other governments. In all these environmental justice complaints the alleged wrongdoer is a state or local government. In the past, EPA had been less likely to bring enforcement actions on behalf of poor and minority communities.

Some environmental justice suits have been won in state courts. In one California case minority groups protested the location of an incinerator on the outskirts of Kettleman City, California. Ninety percent of the community are Latino. Lawyers argued that the county's environmental review process improperly excluded community members from full participation because the environmental impact report and the hearings were not translated into Spanish. Forty percent of the town's residents speak only Spanish. The case was won, and the siting decision was reconsidered.

Most environmental rights issues are fought on a case-by-case basis. Until Congress or state legislatures pass more general siting policies that take into account the impact of these decisions on minorities and the poor, the only available resource are scattered civil rights statutes. Eventually, as new statutes are passed, a clearer statement of the contours of environmental justice will probably develop. These statutes will give status to the hard-fought environmental justice cause. Some have proposed that an Environmental Equal Rights Act be passed that would identify certain communities as "environmentally disadvantaged," giving some greater protection to those areas.

Childhood Lead Poisoning

Another major issue on which environmental justice advocates have focused is childhood lead poisoning. Lead has been removed from paint and gasoline, as result of federal legislation in 1978. Lead poisoning has serious medical effects, including possible loss of intelligence. However, many older buildings contain pre-1978 lead paint. Peeling and flaking lead paint has been the source of lead exposure. Since many older building have been occupied by poorer children, it is claimed that they are especially at risk. Poor and minority children in urban areas are at the greatest risk of exposure for lead poisoning.

Environmental justice lawyers have turned to the courts for relief. In New York City, a jury recently awarded substantial damages to a young child after experts had testified that her mental retardation was due to lead exposure. Other awards have been won in suits in California, Massachusetts, and the District of Columbia.

In 1986 California passed Proposition 65, which goes beyond the issue of lead poisoning to provide stiff penalties for businesses that fail to warn employees about the presence of toxic chemicals. Landlords also must warn tenants about these conditions, just as manufacturers must warn consumers. Proposition 65 also creates a private right of action for suits based on failure to warn about exposure to chemicals "known to the state of California" to cause cancer or reproductive toxicity. This law can be used by advocates of the poor, but it is available to all. It seems to create a new, broad right of protection against hazardous materials listed by government. At the same time, it creates individual legal rights to sue businesses that fail to warn the public.

Private Property Rights

In the American legal system one of the most fundamental of all legal principles is the protection of private property. The rights of private property are derived from the common law of England and reach back to the thirteenth century. The English philosopher John Locke contended that property was one of man's most fundamental rights, a right that government was bound to protect and defend. The American Constitution was prepared by individuals steeped in Lockean thought. They believed that property rights were an essential part of the agreement that had formed the new nation. The Founders of America believed that the main purpose of having a government is to protect rights, particularly property rights.

The Constitution contains many features designed to protect private property. The Fifth Amendment, which binds the national government, mentions property twice. It states that no person can be deprived of "life, liberty or property without due process of law." It also says "nor shall private property be taken for public use, without just compensation." The due process of law phrase is repeated in the Fourteenth Amendment (ratified in 1868) as a means of limiting the powers of state government. The listing of "life, liberty and property" appears in two places in the American Constitution, strongly suggesting that these three rights lie at the heart of the American system of government. The framers of the Constitution thought that freedom depended on the sanctity of private property.

Under the common law, which was adopted by Americans, an owner of land had the right to use his or her property as he or she thought fit, unless that use interfered with another's "use and enjoyment." Landowners could use all of the natural resources—land, minerals, water, air—to which their property gave them access. Until recently, property rights included an unquestioned right to pollute their own property. Modern legislation has placed limits on this view of private property. The common law had recognized that pollution that effected a neighbor could be unlawful. Modern environmental law protects all Americans, including strangers far away.

Before the 1960s only landowners had environmental rights. Some form of access to air and water went with the ownership of land. The emergence of environmental regulation in the public interest changes the contours of rights. Environmental law deprives landowners of the full use of their property. The protection of the environment in the public interest does not destroy property rights: It modifies and limits them. Property owners no longer have an unrestricted authority to pollute their own property or the streams, rivers, lakes, air, or oceans. Regulation has imposed new responsibilities on the owners of land. However, to the degree that it is allowed by regulation or by local laws of zoning, landowners may use their property for their own private purposes. However, some landowners contend that their right to use their property have been so restricted by government as to reduce the value of their property.

Private Property and Government "Takings"

Zoning laws impose community controls on the use of private property. They designate sections of the territory of a community for designated uses. Taken together, zoning law and environmental regulation have changed the old common law view of private property. The justification for these changes in the rights of property is the greater community need to protect all residents or the general public.

How much of a burden is it fair to place on an individual property owner in order to protect community interests? The Fifth Amendment of the U.S. Constitution establishes one basic rule for this decision: When private property is taken for public use, the owner must be fairly paid for the property. The Fifth Amendment requires that private property not be "taken" for public use without just compensation. This is a deceptively simple requirement. When the government actually takes possession of private property, such as taking a person's land to build a new jail or highway, the owner clearly is entitled to be paid the fair market value of the land taken. But with zoning the government does not take the title to land, so how does this constitutional issue of "takings" even arise? It arises because the U.S. Supreme Court ruled in 1922 that a government regulation that severely restricts property use—one that goes "too far"—can be so onerous that it has the same practical effect as a seizure of property. Trying to determine how far is "too far" has proved to be one of the most hotly contested and legally confusing areas of land-use law.

The Fifth Amendment's Takings Clause reads, "nor shall private property be taken for public use without just compensation." As currently interpreted by the Supreme Court, that clause enables owners to receive compensation when all their property is taken by a government agency and title actually transfers to the government. A taking also takes place whenever their property is physically invaded by government order, either permanently or temporarily, or when a regulation for other than health or safety reasons takes all or nearly all of the value of the property.

With over a dozen U.S. Supreme Court decisions on this topic in the past 20 years, two clear rules have emerged. First, a zoning restriction that requires a physical invasion of a person's property is automatically a "taking" that requires compensation. For example, a regulation requiring that the public be allowed to use vacant land for a park is a taking. Second, a landowner is entitled to compensation if a regulation renders the owner's property completely worthless. It is very important to note, however, that a reduction in value, such as might occur when a property is rezoned from a valuable commercial use to a less valuable residential use, is not in itself unconstitutional. Evidently, such a reduction in value is a misfortune the landowner must suffer as a member of society. For there to be an automatic right to compensation under the constitution, the regulation must remove all practical use of the property so that it has no reasonable value left.

If a case does not fit into one of these two rather narrow categories, the courts will conduct an individual review of the case to determine if a regulation has gone "too far." The courts consider both the economic impact on the person affected and the character of the governmental action. In these case by case reviews, the government usually wins in court unless there has been clearly improper conduct, such as using zoning to lower the price of a parcel the city is trying to buy. Since most land use restrictions, even stringent ones, leave the property owner some form of remaining use of the property, even if it is not the most profitable use, this is not considered a taking under the Constitution.

In response to the nature of the law in this area and the lack of a constitutional requirement to reimburse owners for reductions in land values, many landowners have pushed for legislative action. North Carolina has considered legislation that would require government to analyze the taking issue prior to enactment of land use regulations. Other legislative proposals go beyond this consideration to require compensation for reductions in property values even in cases in which the constitution does not mandate compensation.

The U.S. House of Representatives passed a bill in March 1996 to require the federal government to pay compensation to landowners if wetland or endangered species regulations reduce property values by more than 20 percent. Other proposals have been floated in Congress as a result of campaigns by backers of the so-called property rights movement. This movement seeks a clearer definition of "property." Turning to the chief author of the Bill of Rights, James Madison, property rights advocates note that Madison believed that "as a man is said to have a right to his property, he may be equally said to have a property in his rights."

Only a few cases have emerged about the federal Endangered Species Act (ESA). Some property owners complain that federal and state protections for animals, plants, fish, and insects pose a threat to their rights. Certainly, federal regulations restrict the modification of endangered species habitats. Land developments all over the country have the potential to have drastic effects on private property uses. However, the political backlash against this approach would be too strong. Few federal regulators are willing to press the protection of animals and plants to such an extent.

Many opponents of the ESA are advocates of "takings" legislation that would require taxpayer pay-offs to individuals and corporations whenever environmental protection laws, including the ESA, somehow reduce the value or profit-making potential for their property. In its most radical form, takings legislation would force taxpayers to pay individuals and corporations not to pollute the air, not to foul the water, and not to destroy endangered species habitat, ignoring the costs to taxpayers and property owners downwind, downstream, and throughout the community.

The revived and expanded views of property rights have derived some strength from recent court rulings. The Supreme Court's most recent pronouncements on these matters have set three controlling factors on the nature of government restrictions on private property: (1) The restriction must be related to a valid public purpose; (2) the impact of the regulation must require compensation when property owners are deprived of "all economically feasible use"; and (3) compensation will not be required for a taking when the government restricts a use that has been limited under prior "background principles of common law."

The leading decision is *Lucas* v. *South Carolina Coastal Council* (1992). In this case the Court held that a state coastal setback ordinance had deprived a property owner of all economically feasible use of his land. The ordinance had been designed to limit the use of land for development in sensitive coastal areas. The state claimed that it had merely applied to the property the existing common law rules regarding a "nuisance," which gave them this power, without requiring payment to the landowner.

The Supreme Court set some boundaries on the powers of state governments by indicating that the harm that the regulation or taking addressed must be a major harm and a long-established harm. The Court gave the example of a landfill that would flood another's land or a nuclear plant that had to be removed from an earthquake fault.

Government actions in such cases would not be a "taking" under the Fifth Amendment. No payment to the property owner would be required. Government restrictions on property need not be compensated when they were not "previously permissible under relevant property law and nuisance law principles." In this case the property owner had to be paid because the prior common law had not prohibited his development activities.

The Supreme Court's reference to the common law is interesting because it shows that common law principles still govern private property to some extent. Even so, the Supreme Court decisions have drawn vague boundaries around the right to private property. More litigation is expected. Until then we can only know that some forms of government regulation or zoning will be unconstitutional "takings." The future of the law of "takings" is somewhat unpredictable.

The Development of Constitutional Environmental Rights

Zealous environmentalists would like to believe that environmental rights are as significant as the Bill of Rights. No court has accepted this approach. Even in the state of Pennsylvania where the Constitution guarantees every state citizen the right to a clean and healthful environment, the state Supreme Court has ruled this provision unenforceable. If there are to be environmental rights, they must go well beyond mere regulation. Environmental rights may be recognized in the next century only if citizens feel as strongly about them as they do the more traditional rights found in the federal Constitution. As it stands, the environmental rights movement has only just begun to specify the elements of the kind of rights they believe will be needed.

It is premature to say that clean air, clean water, and the nation's wealth of species are part of our rights as Americans. Government regulations and land use laws merely restrict the rights of property, they do not create new rights for all the people. The so-called environmental bills of rights that various environmental organizations have proposed are essentially political. They are aimed at preserving the gains in environmental laws and regulations of the last few decades.

The question of where the exact boundaries of the rights of property should be are still unresolved. We really don't know how far is "too far" for a restriction to go before compensation should be paid to the owner. At what point do we shift the burden and costs of living in a civilized society from the individual landowner to all taxpayers? Some say that this is a strictly legal question for the courts, but it is more often a public policy choice for us as citizens. The resolution of this question warrants informed public debate and a careful balancing of competing legitimate concerns—and no doubt some tough choices for our federal, state, and local elected officials.

The advantage of having a true environmental bill of rights is that the tension between the rights of property and the rights of the general public would be settled for a long period of time. The pressure of land development on the space still left in America may force us to seriously recognize environmental rights. Americans may yet decide that the quality of the air they breathe and the water they drink is in grave peril. Our fragile seashores and disappearing fisheries may disturb us enough to rethink the rights of property. Pollution from our industries may prove to be an overwhelming problem, in spite of government regulations. The ozone layer, global warming, or other worse, looming natural catastrophes may alarm us enough to change the basic structure of our rights. Until then, the rights of private property will still

be taken seriously. Elevating environmental rights to a constitutional plane would change the rights of property, one of the oldest aspects of rights in America.

A system of government regulation has been grafted on to the common law to modify the rights of property. As owners of property in sensitive wetlands fully realize, the use of their property requires numerous permits from federal, state, and local authorities. Property owners cannot use their property as they see fit. Polluters must adopt measures to reduce pollution. Economic growth in our capitalist system must include a calculation of the costs of compliance with government regulation.

The Right to Employment

In modern America few people are able to provide for their own subsistence needs by farming or other forms of home production. In an urbanized and heavily populated society, a large proportion of the people are working as employees of private firms or of the government. Most Americans are able to rely on employment opportunities provided by corporations, small businesses, nonprofit organizations, or government agencies. Some Americans are able to form their own business enterprises, and are, as a result, self-employed. In our society, however, a large and growing number of people are not employed by others, are not self-employed, and are unable to provide for their own food and shelter by their own efforts.

In America, as in many industrialized societies, a certain amount of unemployment is regarded as acceptable by government policymakers. Four or five percent unemployment is considered tolerable. Most American economists believe that a certain amount of unemployment is desirable, in order to lower inflationary price pressures. True full employment would require a reexamination of economic principles.

Unemployment compensation is provided to workers who are temporarily unemployed. However, there may be many more people who have not held a job for long periods of time. The skills and education required in many jobs today may consign more and more individuals to the ranks of the permanently unemployed. Unemployment compensation is merely a cushion against short-term unemployment, not a solution to protracted unemployment.

Minority groups have been hit harder by unemployment in America than most others. At times unemployment levels for African Americans, Native Americans, and Hispanic Americans have reached 15 percent. Young people, seeking to enter the workforce for the first time, have also been subjected to high rates of unemployment. The introduction of new technologies has also eliminated many jobs, usually in the name of so-called corporate downsizing. Indeed, few jobs in America are as secure today as they have been in past generations.

There is a legitimate case for a new American right to employment. Many twentieth-century declarations of rights in other nations include a right to employment, which means a right to be provided with the opportunity to work. Such a right does not exist under American law, even though there are federal statutes that speak of "full employment." Still, a right to employment would cause enormous economic change in America, and it would come at a high price.

Article 23 of the Universal Declaration of Rights states that "everyone has the right to work, to free choice of employment, to just and favorable conditions of work and to protection against unemployment." The United States and other members of the United Nations are signatories to the Universal Declaration of Rights. Nonetheless, the document has no force in American courts and does not obligate our government to create a new constitutional right. No American legislature is bound to enforce a right to work.

At present, American policy sometimes calls for economic stimulation in the form of lower taxes or lower interest rates, expecting that these efforts may generate new jobs. But full employment has never been attained in America, and it cannot be said that any national administration has pursued full employment as a goal.

Welfare Policies

American welfare policies have been used to assist those on the bottom rungs of the economic ladder. Those who are frequently or permanently unemployed in America find themselves forced to take state welfare payments as a means of meeting their needs for food and shelter. Standard American welfare programs have not been sources of employment. Instead, they have been attempts to assist those who are unable to provide for their own economic needs.

American welfare policy reforms sometimes call for beneficiaries to work, or to attempt to work, after a period of time on the welfare rolls. Instead of welfare recipients remaining as dependents of the state for indefinite periods, new "workfare" programs deliver the message that welfare payments will come to an end. Welfare recipients in reform states must eventually get off welfare and get a job. Converting welfare to workfare sounds like a good idea, but moving welfare recipients into jobs is more difficult than it may seem. There may not be enough jobs to employ all the people on welfare, even if they are well-trained. Those former welfare recipients who are employed may not be able to earn enough money to meet their needs. Many jobs do not pay subsistence wages.

Twenty-five American states place time limits on welfare payments, creating a "sink or swim" approach to helping people. Those who cannot or will not obtain jobs may be cut off from public assistance. Exceptions can be made for mothers with very small children. States often provide welfare recipients with education (usually up to high school equivalency), career counseling, resume writing, or even with actual job searches. However, states have not created or invented jobs for welfare recipients. Child care is not usually provided, and post-secondary education is never pro-

vided to welfare recipients. Specific job training is rarely offered.

It is unlikely that welfare reform will actually generate new jobs. It may be that our economy cannot create enough jobs in the private sector to absorb all those who may want employment. A very few American politicians have called for government to be an "employer of last resort," meaning that if jobs could not be created in the private sector that the government would create them. Such a policy would be extremely expensive and would mean higher taxes to support that right.

A right to employment would mean paid employment, at a "decent wage." Unpaid employment would be little more than forced labor. Paid employment is essential if people are to provide for their basic needs. As it is, many former welfare recipients work at low-wage jobs that may pay less than welfare. For example, an employee at a fast-food hamburger place may put in long hours and still not reach levels of income to provide minimal needs. Some of these workers fall below the official federal government poverty line even though they are employed full-time.

In the future, advances in technology may replace many workers with machines. On the other hand, technology should reduce many of the most tedious, dangerous, and arduous aspects of labor. At the very least, advances in technology will mean enhanced productivity for each Ameri-

can worker. Enhanced productivity may also mean fewer jobs for people. Shorter work weeks and fewer full-time jobs may also be in store for future generations. The opportunity to work for decent pay may become a significant future right for all Americans. Work may not be just a means of removing people from the welfare roles but a needed part of the individual dignity for all adult Americans. Work provides one of the major satisfactions in many people's lives. The opportunity to have meaningful and adequately paid work could become a valued right, especially as routine labor is replaced by mechanical devices.

Labor Rights

A right to employment is not the same as the right of workers to organize into trade unions. That right already exists in America as an aspect of free speech. Workers have the right under the First Amendment to organize themselves and to promote their collective interests. This constitutional right is extended in the federal statutes that protect the labor negotiations process. But the right of workers to act collectively is far less controversial than the right to employment, which means a right never to be unemployed. No American union has ever won such a right for its members.

The so-called American "right to work" statutes found in some states have nothing to do with guaranteed employment. On the contrary,

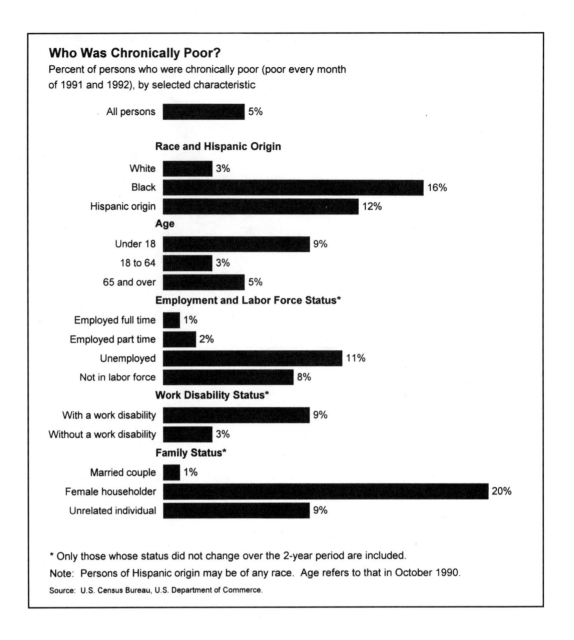

Who Was Chronically Poor?

Percent of persons who were chronically poor (poor every month of 1991 and 1992), by selected characteristic

All persons — 5%

Race and Hispanic Origin

White — 3%
Black — 16%
Hispanic origin — 12%

Age

Under 18 — 9%
18 to 64 — 3%
65 and over — 5%

Employment and Labor Force Status*

Employed full time — 1%
Employed part time — 2%
Unemployed — 11%
Not in labor force — 8%

Work Disability Status*

With a work disability — 9%
Without a work disability — 3%

Family Status*

Married couple — 1%
Female householder — 20%
Unrelated individual — 9%

* Only those whose status did not change over the 2-year period are included.

Note: Persons of Hispanic origin may be of any race. Age refers to that in October 1990.

Source: U.S. Census Bureau, U.S. Department of Commerce.

they are aimed at resisting the spread of exclusive union bargaining arrangements, allowing workers to hold a job without being members of unions. The right involved is the right of a worker not to join a union as a condition of employment. Obviously, such statutes are favored by employers who wish to discourage union activities.

To further confuse careless readers, there are other labor rights mentioned from time to time, such as a right to strike, or so-called rights to a paid vacation, sick leave, bonuses, minimum wages, maximum hours, and a number of other specific labor-management issues. These matters are important but not as fundamental as a right of employment. Such "rights" exist only by virtue of labor-management agreements or specific statutes.

A new American right of employment could borrow the language found in the Constitution of Japan. Article 27 of the Japanese Constitution states that "All people shall have the right and the obligation of work." Article 28 of the Japanese Constitution guarantees the right of workers to organize and to bargain collectively. Neither right is found in the American Constitution. Of course, just listing a right in a constitution does not ensure that everyone who wants a job can have one. In fact, although Japanese unemployment has been lower than that in America, there are always a number of Japanese who cannot find work.

The implementation of a right-to-employment policy would be very expensive and controversial. One approach might be to provide private employers with subsidies to hire people on the unemployment rolls. This has been tried in Europe with limited success. Another approach, used in America during the Great Depression of the 1930s, was to create massive public works projects, with federal hiring of large numbers of workers to help build bridges, post offices, highways, dams, and other public works. Massive amounts of federal funds had to be poured into these programs, but jobs were created.

Conservative critics contend that only by large tax reductions can new jobs be created in the private sector. However, with reduced tax revenues the federal government would have much more limited capacity to promote or generate new jobs. At the close of the twentieth century those who believe that the forces of free competition can be trusted to produce the jobs of the future are politically powerful. The will to create a meaningful right to employment is lacking. However, if the future shows a long-term sharp shrinkage of job opportunities for Americans, a popular demand for a right to employment may develop.

Many legal experts have spoken of the need for a right to welfare. There are Supreme Court cases that have extended to welfare recipients the right to due process of law on questions involving welfare payments. A right to welfare has been established in many European nations, but a right to employment would seem more suitable for those able-bodied people who are able to work. For others who are physically handicapped or otherwise unable to enter the workforce some forms of protection may be needed, but it questionable whether a right to welfare would change very much in their lives.

Other Possible Future Rights

The future development of American rights is largely dependent on trends in American politics.

The Right to Bear Arms

Some powerful groups in our society believe that there is a fundamental American right to bear arms, although such a right is unknown to most civilized societies. Some groups claim that the Second Amendment "right to bear arms" bans federal or state statutes designed to restrict and control the use of handguns and assault weapons, although

this view of rights is not grounded in current law. The issue will probably not be decided in the courts but in the Congress and the legislatures. The Supreme Court has never read the Second Amendment in the manner preferred by the National Rifle Association and the many other anti-gun control lobbyists. It is unlikely that the Supreme Court will ever read the Constitution to create an unrestricted private right to own and use weapons. However, it is possible that legislatures will be persuaded to roll back restrictions on gun controls, in order to placate powerful lobbyists or a public aroused by those forces. If that happens, there will be an informal recognition of some of the claims of the various gun lobbyists, regardless of the prevailing court interpretation of the Second Amendment.

It is quite possible that some form of limited right to bear arms may be pushed through state legislatures and incorporated in state constitutional law. The state of Florida is a leading example of such a limited "right to bear arms." Florida recognizes a right to bear arms, but like many states, sets strict regulations on possession and purchase. Concealed weapons usually require special licenses.

Smoking

It is also politically possible for smokers, an American minority, to become politically active to resist further limitations upon their nicotine habit. The facts about smoking increasingly point to the severe public health risks created by smokers. Smoking is now forbidden in most schools and in some restaurants. Many firms have created smoke-free areas, and it is likely that smoking will be driven entirely from the workplace and from other public areas. Federal regulations restricting smoking are almost certainly going to increase, with the possibility that advertising for cigarettes, cigars, pipes, and other smoking gear will be forbidden altogether. As the zone of places wherein smokers may indulge their habit shrinks, the possibility of a serious smokers' rights political campaign increases. The public assault on smoking is likely to create a political reaction.

It may be that smokers and others who have addictive habits will receive some kinds of protections for the private indulgence of their habits. What form this will take will depend on future public attitudes to addiction. Since use of many other addictive substances has been criminalized, it is possible

that tobacco addiction will be treated in the same way. On the other hand, attitudes toward addiction may change if the public accepts addiction as a form of illness rather than a moral flaw. Some form of limited right to tobacco for private consumption seems a possible political compromise. Extending that approach to alcohol and other addictive substances is another possible development. Toleration of the use of addictive substances does not signal approval of these practices; toleration is merely a different approach to dealing with the problems of addiction, attempting to confine the further spread of addiction without penalizing the addict.

There may be other candidates for future American rights development, but it is hard to discern them on the horizon at the current time. The shifting tides of politics will swirl in different directions in the next century. New generations of Americans will take over the reigns of government. New members of the Supreme Court will be seated. The Constitution is a growing organism and is seen afresh by each new generation of Americans. The tides of American rights will ebb and flow, but new rights will perpetually be deposited upon the rich American shore.

International and Comparative Rights

The United States has always been in the vanguard of civil liberties. When the Bill of

Rights was ratified in 1791 the new nation took the lead in the advancement of human rights. Many other nations borrowed heavily from the American example when they also chose to provide their citizens with greater liberties. Portions of the American Bill of Rights have found their way into the constitutions of many other nations. Although it is fair to say that Americans pioneered in the development of civil liberties, our nation's record in race relations and its treatment of minorities has dimmed somewhat our reputation for rights development. It is true that America is still far ahead of most other countries in its protection of citizen's rights, but some nations have expanded the boundaries of civil liberties well beyond the original American notions. In addition, various international organizations have invented new rights that have not taken root in the United States. It is worth considering these alternative versions of civil liberties, because some of them may be pathways of our own future.

The Japanese Constitution

The 1947 Constitution of Japan, following military defeat and foreign occupation, was designed to eliminate the authoritarian structure of its past and to pave the way towards political democracy. As part of the process, Japanese citizens received new rights. Article 1 of the Japanese Constitution of 1947 reduced the position of the

Emperor of Japan by stating that he derives "his position from the will of the people, with whom resides sovereign power." The document was also used to reject Japan's nationalistic past, as the Constitution of Japan specifically renounced the use of warfare.

The Japanese Constitution was prepared with the help of the staff of the occupying American forces. There is some American influence on the ideas contained in the Constitution, but most of the Constitution is distinctive and more modern views of rights are described. Article 13 of the Japanese Constitution guarantees the people's "right to life, liberty and the pursuit of happiness," borrowing the language of Thomas Jefferson, and not the American Bill of Rights language, which includes "life, liberty and property."

Article 14 states that "all of the people are equal under the law and there shall be no discrimination in political, economic or social relations because of race, creed, sex, social status or family origin." This language is much broader and more specific than the equivalent American Fourteenth Amendment.

Article 16 declares that "every person shall have the right of peaceful petition for the redress of damage, for the removal of public officials, for the enactment, repeal or amendment of laws." This kind of direct democracy is unknown to the American Constitution.

Freedom of religion is guaranteed by the Japanese Constitution, but all religious organizations are forbidden to "receive any privileges from the state." Academic freedom is guaranteed in addition to free speech. This seems to suggest that teachers have rights to freely pursue their research and teaching.

In Japan, all citizens are guaranteed the "right to an equal education correspondent to their ability." The American Constitution has no such guarantee. Some American state constitutions do recognize some form of a right to education.

In the social sector, the Japanese Constitution states that "all people shall have the right to maintain the minimum standards of wholesome and cultured living." Toward this end, Article 25 says that "the state shall use its endeavors for the promotion and extension of social welfare and security, and of public health." Some American statutes extend to our citizens some forms of social assis-

tance, but there is no constitutional right to welfare nor to health.

The Japanese Constitution was the first of the post-World War II Constitutions. The rights contained in that document exceed previous concepts of citizen rights. The Japanese Supreme Court has attempted to apply these new rights in cases that it has considered. The new rights conferred on Japanese citizens have expanded the traditional versions of rights that had been based largely on American ideas and experiences.

The Portuguese Constitution

One of the longest of modern constitutions is Portugal's Constitution of 1976. This constitution goes further than any other in promoting active state participation in expanding citizen rights. For example, Article 39 of the Portuguese Constitution gives political parties, trade unions, and professional organizations the right to broadcasting time on radio and television. During elections competing political parties "shall have the right to regular broadcasting time fairly apportioned." Since the Constitution declares that "television shall not be privately owned," this means that the national government will provide free airtime for political speech.

In addition, citizens, under Article 48, have "the right to objective information about acts of state and other public bodies and to be informed by the government and other authorities about the management of public affairs." The concept of freedom of information is embodied in statutes in the United States, but official secrecy is still used for some information.

The Portuguese Constitution gives the clearest expression of environmental rights. Article 66 states that "everyone shall have the right to a healthy and ecologically balanced human environment and the duty to defend it." The same article also mentions the prevention and control of pollution as a duty of the government. In addition, the government is obliged to "promote the rational use of natural resources, safeguarding their capacity for renewal and ecological stability." Whether or not these goals can be realized remains to be seen.

The Spanish Constitution

The 1978 Spanish Constitution also deserves attention. Many of the new rights that are not found in the American Constitution appear in that document. The Spanish Constitution is notable for its expression of the "right to health protection." According to Article 43 of the Spanish Constitution, public authorities must "watch over public health and hygiene through preventive measures and through necessary care and services." The Constitution also gives "everyone the right to enjoy an environment suitable for the development of the person."

A unique feature of the Spanish Constitution requires the government to "guarantee the defense of consumers and users, protecting their safety, health and legitimate economic interests." Consumers have some legal protections in the United States but not on a scale with those envisioned for Spanish citizens. In fact, the Spanish Constitution's Article 51 calls upon the government to "promote the information and education of consumers and users."

The Canadian Constitution

The Canadian Constitution has also expanded the boundaries of civil liberties. The Constitution of 1982 recognizes the rights of various minority peoples. The aboriginal peoples of Canada (Indians, Inuits, and Metis) received special treatment in the Constitution. As a bilingual country, the language rights of both French and English language populations are given protection, too.

The Canadian Constitution built upon the American experiment with affirmative action. In the United States the Supreme Court has been suspicious of affirmative action programs because of the Fourteenth Amendment's language about the equal protection of the laws. Equal protection of the laws is guaranteed in Article 15 to all Canadians "without discrimination based on race, national or ethnic origin, colour, religion, sex, age or mental or physical disability." However, a section of the same article allows any program "that has as its object the amelioration of conditions of disadvantaged individuals or groups including those that are disadvantaged because of race, national or ethnic origin, colour, religion, sex, age or mental or physical disability." As a result, the Canadian Supreme Court is invited to uphold programs that provide for special advantages for individuals or groups that are mentioned. Affirmative action programs are constitutionally permitted in Canada.

Other Constitutions

Some nations have given individuals access to the courts as a means of direct enforcement of their rights. The German Constitution's Article 93 says that a "complaint of unconstitutionality . . . may be entered by any person who believes that one of his basic rights . . . has been violated by public authorities." The 1982 Nigerian Constitution declares that "any person who alleges that any of (his rights) . . . may apply to a High Court in that state for redress." The Spanish Constitution and the Irish Constitution also seem to provide direct access to the courts. By contrast, the American Constitution does not guarantee that a court will review all citizen claims of a deprivation of rights. Whether these other nations actually enforce the right of access to the courts in unclear, but at least the right to a hearing seems to exist. In effect, an American citizen has no assurance that a claim of a denial of his rights will be heard in a court.

No one can be certain that these constitutional rights assigned to the citizens of other nations are fully honored. Doubtless, some of these rights are intended to make promises that these nations are not yet prepared to fulfill. Even so, our Bill of Rights took a century to develop into a fundamental source of American rights. The slow process of judicial interpretation and of statutory enforcement took a long time. Political and social developments took place that gave rich meaning to our Bill of Rights, and these, too, took long to emerge. The same may be said of these new rights abroad. The mere fact that they are listed in among a nation's fundamental rights means that they will eventually take on some genuine meaning. The question for Americans is whether or not lessons can be learned from the rights experiences of other nations.

The Universal Declaration of Human Rights

The United States is also a signatory to many international rights documents. Among them, the most visionary is the Universal Declaration of Human Rights. This 1948 document is not binding law in American courts, but it does express some of the highest ideals in the international community.

Work on the Universal Declaration of Human Rights began at the very beginnings of the United Nations Organization. The Declaration contains many of the traditional rights and freedoms found in the American Constitution. However, it also contains many of the newer rights that appeared after World War II, such as the right to social security, the right to work, the right to adequate health care, the right to education, the right to rest and leisure, and the "right to security in the event of unemployment, sickness, disability, widowhood, old age or other lack of livelihood in circumstances beyond his control." To see the United Nations' Universal Declaration of Human Rights in its entirety, see Chapter 17.

Bibliography

Blank, Robert H. *Biomedical Policy*. Chicago: Nelson-Hall Publishers, 1995.

Carson, Rachel. *Silent Spring*. Boston: Houghton Mifflin, 1962.

Cohen, Howard. *Equal Rights for Children*. Totowa, N.J.: Littlefield-Adams, 1980.

Hanna, Kathi, ed. *Biomedical Politics*. Washington, D.C.: National Academy Press, 1991.

Hawes, Joseph M. *The Children's Rights Movement*. Boston: Twayne Publishers, 1991.

Konvitz, Milton. *A Century of Civil Rights*. New York: Columbia University Press, 1961.

Lauterpacht, Hersh. *International Law and Human Rights*. New York: F. A. Praeger, 1950.

Regan, Thomas. *The Case for Animal Rights*. Berkeley, Calif.: University of California Press, 1983.

Section IV

Significant Documents and Major Civil Rights Cases

Chapter 17

Historical Documents

Jay A. Sigler

This chapter furnishes a collection of basic documents in the development of civil rights in America and assembles them in a simple format that can be used in several ways. For those who wish to obtain an overview of the history of American rights, this chapter serves as an indispensable starting point. Tracing the history of rights developments from their sources in history through to contemporary times should be an easy task if the reader follows the chronological arrangement of documents. A fuller appreciation of rights history requires the study of chapter 18, in which key decisions of the United States Supreme Court may be found. Taken together, chapters 17 and 18 supply an accurate description of the evolution of American rights. These chapters are a kind of road map of American rights, but like all maps, they can only point the way.

For those who are more concerned with the status of their rights today some of the material is still very useful. The Constitution and the Bill of Rights are essential reading. This chapter highlights sections of the Constitution that are most relevant for American rights, rather than merely reproducing the whole document. Similarly, in the last part of this chapter the editor presents portions of the United States Code indicating some of the current rights policies. The best and most accurate source for national law is always the Statutes of The United States, as collated in the United States Code.

In preparing the documents presented here a number of choices had to be made. For the sake of easier comprehension many selections are abridged, but wherever texts are brief, the whole is presented. The original language of each rights document is used throughout, except for Magna Carta, where the text is written in Latin.

These documents speak for themselves. They are not filtered through the interpretation of a so-called "expert" or a judge's views. Some introductory explanations provide a historic context, but the reader may adopt his or her own interpretation of the texts. For rights to be meaningful each individual must first be aware of their foundation, and then fashion his or her own rights priorities.

The material presented here is accurate and true to the historic period in which it arose. Those who find, after reading these documents, that they may have been deprived of their rights in some way should not rely solely on their own personal interpretations. They should seek legal help, whether through a public agency, a rights organization, or a private attorney. The subtle shades of meaning that surround American rights cannot be learned in a single reading, but require years of practical experience.

Magna Carta (1215)

Magna Carta, issued in 1215 by King John at Runneymede, is the most famous document of British constitutional history. The charter was issued under the threat of force by powerful barons and church officials, and reissued at various times. Magna Carta is usually regarded as the starting point in the development of individual rights because of the concessions made by the English king. In reality, this brief document is related to the rise of the guarantee of jury trial and the writ of habeas corpus *(which requires person held unlawfully in custody to be released), and only incidentally related to the history of most other rights. However, it is a very significant statement of rights because it later became a symbol of the monarchy's dwindling powers and a foundation for the development of individual rights during the seventeenth century in England and America.*

A careful reading of the text, which was translated from the Latin original, reveals medieval thinking concerning rights; while the privileges of the church and the nobility are given close attention, only limited rights for women are provided. The treatment of Jews in Magna Carta is also very revealing of medieval attitudes and prejudices. The "ancient liberties and free customs" of free cities do not exist today, like many of the other thirteenth century rights mentioned. Article 39 is still the most important contribution to modern rights.

Other English documents must be consulted elsewhere for those who want a deeper appreciation of fundamental rights in England before the

American Revolution. The English parliament passed several pieces of legislation in the seventeenth century that influenced subsequent American thinking. The Petition of Right *of 1689 declared the rights of Parliament to act against the monarch. The* Habeas Corpus Act *of 1679, and the* Bill of Rights *of 1689 contain some phrases that later appear in American documents. However, in spite of their names, these English statutes were quite different from the American rights developed from them.*

THE MAGNA CARTA (The Great Charter):

Preamble:

John, by the grace of God, king of England, lord of Ireland, duke of Normandy and Aquitaine, and count of Anjou, to the archbishop, bishops, abbots, earls, barons, justiciaries, foresters, sheriffs, stewards, servants, and to all his bailiffs and liege subjects, greetings. Know that, having regard to God and for the salvation of our soul, and those of all our ancestors and heirs, and unto the honor of God and the advancement of his holy Church and for the rectifying of our realm, we have granted as underwritten by advice of our venerable fathers, Stephen, archbishop of Canterbury, primate of all England and cardinal of the holy Roman Church, Henry, archbishop of Dublin, William of London, Peter of Winchester, Jocelyn of Bath and Glastonbury, Hugh of Lincoln, Walter of Worcester, William of Coventry, Benedict of Rochester, bishops; of Master Pandulf, subdeacon and member of the household of our lord the Pope, of brother Aymeric (master of the Knights of the Temple in England), and of the illustrious men William Marshal, earl of Pembroke, William, earl of Salisbury, William, earl of Warenne, William, earl of Arundel, Alan of Galloway (constable of Scotland), Waren Fitz Gerold, Peter Fitz Herbert, Hubert De Burgh (seneschal of Poitou), Hugh de Neville, Matthew Fitz Herbert, Thomas Basset, Alan Basset, Philip d'Aubigny, Robert of Roppesley, John Marshal, John Fitz Hugh, and others, our liegemen.

1. In the first place we have granted to God, and by this our present charter confirmed for us and our heirs forever that the English Church shall be free, and shall have her rights entire, and her liberties inviolate; and we will that it

be thus observed; which is apparent from this that the freedom of elections, which is reckoned most important and very essential to the English Church, we, of our pure and unconstrained will, did grant, and did by our charter confirm and did obtain the ratification of the same from our lord, Pope Innocent III, before the quarrel arose between us and our barons: and this we will observe, and our will is that it be observed in good faith by our heirs forever. We have also granted to all freemen of our kingdom, for us and our heirs forever, all the underwritten liberties, to be had and held by them and their heirs, of us and our heirs forever.

2. If any of our earls or barons, or others holding of us in chief by military service shall have died, and at the time of his death his heir shall be full of age and owe "relief", he shall have his inheritance by the old relief, to wit, the heir or heirs of an earl, for the whole barony of an earl by £100; the heir or heirs of a baron, £100 for a whole barony; the heir or heirs of a knight, 100s, at most, and whoever owes less let him give less, according to the ancient custom of fees.

3. If, however, the heir of any one of the aforesaid has been under age and in wardship, let him have his inheritance without relief and without fine when he comes of age.

4. The guardian of the land of an heir who is thus under age, shall take from the land of the heir nothing but reasonable produce, reasonable customs, and reasonable services, and that without destruction or waste of men or goods; and if we have committed the wardship of the lands of any such minor to the sheriff, or to any other who is responsible to us for its issues, and he has made destruction or waste of what he holds in wardship, we will take of him amends, and the land shall be committed to two lawful and discreet men of that fee, who shall be responsible for the issues to us or to him to whom we shall assign them; and if we have given or sold the wardship of any such land to anyone and he has therein made destruction or waste, he shall lose that wardship, and it shall be transferred to two lawful and discreet men of that fief, who shall be responsible to us in like manner as aforesaid.

5. The guardian, moreover, so long as he has the wardship of the land, shall keep up the houses, parks, fishponds, stanks, mills, and other things pertaining to the land, out of the issues of the same land; and he shall restore to the heir, when he has come to full age, all his land, stocked with ploughs and wainage, according as the season of husbandry shall require, and the issues of the land can reasonable bear.

6. Heirs shall be married without disparagement, yet so that before the marriage takes place the nearest in blood to that heir shall have notice.

7. A widow, after the death of her husband, shall forthwith and without difficulty have her marriage portion and inheritance; nor shall she give anything for her dower, or for her marriage portion, or for the inheritance which her husband and she held on the day of the death of that husband; and she may remain in the house of her husband for forty days after his death, within which time her dower shall be assigned to her.

8. No widow shall be compelled to marry, so long as she prefers to live without a husband; provided always that she gives security not to marry without our consent, if she holds of us, or without the consent of the lord of whom she holds, if she holds of another.

9. Neither we nor our bailiffs will seize any land or rent for any debt, as long as the chattels of the debtor are sufficient to repay the debt; nor shall the sureties of the debtor be distrained so long as the principal debtor is able to satisfy the debt; and if the principal debtor shall fail to pay the debt, having nothing wherewith to pay it, then the sureties shall answer for the debt; and let them have the lands and rents of the debtor, if they desire them, until they are indemnified for the debt which they have paid for him, unless the principal debtor can show proof that he is discharged thereof as against the said sureties.

10. If one who has borrowed from the Jews any sum, great or small, die before that loan be repaid, the debt shall not bear interest while the heir is under age, of whomsoever he may hold; and if the debt fall into our hands, we will not take anything except the principal sum contained in the bond.

11. And if anyone die indebted to the Jews, his wife shall have her dower and pay nothing of that debt; and if any children of the deceased are left under age, necessaries shall be provided for them in keeping with the holding of the deceased; and out of the residue the debt shall be paid, reserving, however, service due to feudal lords; in like manner let it be done touching debts due to others than Jews.

12. No scutage nor aid shall be imposed on our kingdom, unless by common counsel of our kingdom, except for ransoming our person, for making our eldest son a knight, and for once marrying our eldest daughter; and for these there shall not be levied more than a reasonable aid. In like manner it shall be done concerning aids from the city of London.

13. And the city of London shall have all its ancient liberties and free customs, as well by land as by water; furthermore, we decree and grant that all other cities, boroughs, towns, and ports shall have all their liberties and free customs.

14. And for obtaining the common counsel of the kingdom anent the assessing of an aid (except in the three cases aforesaid) or of a scutage, we will cause to be summoned the archbishops, bishops, abbots, earls, and greater barons, severally by our letters; and we will moreover cause to be summoned generally, through our sheriffs and bailiffs, and others who hold of us in chief, for a fixed date, namely, after the expiry of at least forty days, and at a fixed place; and in all letters of such summons we will specify the reason of the summons. And when the summons has thus been made, the business shall proceed on the day appointed, according to the counsel of such as are present, although not all who were summoned have come.

15. We will not for the future grant to anyone license to take an aid from his own free tenants, except to ransom his person, to make his eldest son a knight, and once to marry his eldest daughter; and on each of these occasions there shall be levied only a reasonable aid.

16. No one shall be distrained for performance of greater service for a knight's fee, or for any other free tenement, than is due therefrom.

17. Common pleas shall not follow our court, but shall be held in some fixed place.

18. Inquests of novel disseisin, of mort d'ancestor, and of darrein presentment shall not be held elsewhere than in their own county courts, and that in manner following; We, or, if we should be out of the realm, our chief justiciar, will send two justiciaries through every county four times a year, who shall alone with four knights of the county chosen by the place of meeting of that court.

19. And if any of the said assizes cannot be taken on the day of the county court, let there remain of the knights and freeholders, who were present at the county court on that day, as many as may be required for the efficient making of judgments, according as the business be more or less.

20. A freeman shall not be amerced for a slight offense, except in accordance with the degree of the offense; and for a grave offense he shall be amerced in accordance with the gravity of the offense, yet saving always his "contentment"; and a merchant in the same way, saving his "merchandise"; and a villein shall be amerced in the same way, saving his "wainage" if they have fallen into our mercy: and none of the aforesaid amercements shall be imposed except by the oath of honest men of the neighborhood.

21. Earls and barons shall not be amerced except through their peers, and only in accordance with the degree of the offense.

22. A clerk shall not be amerced in respect of his lay holding except after the manner of the others aforesaid; further, he shall not be amerced in accordance with the extent of his ecclesiastical benefice.

23. No village or individual shall be compelled to make bridges at river banks, except those who from of old were legally bound to do so.

24. No sheriff, constable, coroners, or others of our bailiffs, shall hold pleas of our Crown.

25. All counties, hundred, wapentakes, and trithings (except our demesne manors) shall remain at the old rents, and without any additional payment.

26. If anyone holding of us a lay fief shall die, and our sheriff or bailiff shall exhibit our letters patent of summons for a debt which the deceased owed us, it shall be lawful for our

sheriff or bailiff to attach and enroll the chattels of the deceased, found upon the lay fief, to the value of that debt, at the sight of law worthy men, provided always that nothing whatever be thence removed until the debt which is evident shall be fully paid to us; and the residue shall be left to the executors to fulfill the will of the deceased; and if there be nothing due from him to us, all the chattels shall go to the deceased, saving to his wife and children their reasonable shares.

27. If any freeman shall die intestate, his chattels shall be distributed by the hands of his nearest kinsfolk and friends, under supervision of the Church, saving to every one the debts which the deceased owed to him.

28. No constable or other bailiff of ours shall take corn or other provisions from anyone without immediately tendering money therefor, unless he can have postponement thereof by permission of the seller.

29. No constable shall compel any knight to give money in lieu of castle-guard, when he is willing to perform it in his own person, or (if he himself cannot do it from any reasonable cause) then by another responsible man. Further, if we have led or sent him upon military service, he shall be relieved from guard in proportion to the time during which he has been on service because of us.

30. No sheriff or bailiff of ours, or other person, shall take the horses or carts of any freeman for transport duty, against the will of the said freeman.

31. Neither we nor our bailiffs shall take, for our castles or for any other work of ours, wood which is not ours, against the will of the owner of that wood.

32. We will not retain beyond one year and one day, the lands those who have been convicted of felony, and the lands shall thereafter be handed over to the lords of the fiefs.

33. All kydells for the future shall be removed altogether from Thames and Medway, and throughout all England, except upon the seashore.

34. The writ which is called praecipe shall not for the future be issued to anyone, regarding any tenement whereby a freeman may lose his court.

35. Let there be one measure of wine throughout our whole realm; and one measure of ale; and one measure of corn, to wit, "the London quarter"; and one width of cloth (whether dyed, or russet, or "halberget"), to wit, two ells within the selvedges; of weights also let it be as of measures.

36. Nothing in future shall be given or taken for a writ of inquisition of life or limbs, but freely it shall be granted, and never denied.

37. If anyone holds of us by fee-farm, either by socage or by burage, or of any other land by knight's service, we will not (by reason of that fee-farm, socage, or burgage), have the wardship of the heir, or of such land of his as if of the fief of that other; nor shall we have wardship of that fee-farm, socage, or burgage, unless such fee-farm owes knight's service. We will not by reason of any small serjeancy which anyone may hold of us by the service of rendering to us knives, arrows, or the like, have wardship of his heir or of the land which he holds of another lord by knight's service.

38. No bailiff for the future shall, upon his own unsupported complaint, put anyone to his "law", without credible witnesses brought for this purposes.

39. No freemen shall be taken or imprisoned or disseised or exiled or in any way destroyed, nor will we go upon him nor end upon him, except by the lawful judgment of his peers or by the law of the land.

40. To no one will we sell, to no one will we refuse or delay, right or justice.

41. All merchants shall have safe and secure exit from England, and entry to England, with the right to tarry there and to move about as well by land as by water, for buying and selling by the ancient and right customs, quit from all evil tolls, except (in time of war) such merchants as are of the land at war with us. And if such are found in our land at the beginning of the war, they shall be detained, without injury to their bodies or goods, until information be received by us, or by our chief justiciar, how the merchants of our land found in

the land at war with us are treated; and if our men are safe there, the others shall be safe in our land.

42. It shall be lawful in future for anyone (excepting always those imprisoned or outlawed in accordance with the law of the kingdom, and natives of any country at war with us, and merchants, who shall be treated as if above provided) to leave our kingdom and to return, safe and secure by land and water, except for a short period in time of war, on grounds of public policy-reserving always the allegiance due to us.

43. If anyone holding of some escheat (such as the honor of Wallingford, Nottingham, Boulogne, Lancaster, or of other escheats which are in our hands and are baronies) shall die, his heir shall give no other relief, and perform no other service to us than he would have done to the baron if that barony had been in the baron's hand; and we shall hold it in the same manner in which the baron held it.

44. Men who dwell without the forest need not henceforth come before our justiciaries of the forest upon a general summons, unless they are in plea, or sureties of one or more, who are attached for the forest.

45. We will appoint as justices, constables, sheriffs, or bailiffs only such as know the law of the realm and mean to observe it well.

46. All barons who have founded abbeys, concerning which they hold charters from the kings of England, or of which they have long continued possession, shall have the wardship of them, when vacant, as they ought to have.

47. All forests that have been made such in our time shall forthwith be disafforested; and a similar course shall be followed with regard to river banks that have been placed "in defense" by us in our time.

48. All evil customs connected with forests and warrens, foresters and warreners, sheriffs and their officers, river banks and their wardens, shall immediately by inquired into in each county by twelve sworn knights of the same county chosen by the honest men of the same county, and shall, within forty days of the said inquest, be utterly abolished, so as never

to be restored, provided always that we previously have intimation thereof, or our justiciar, if we should not be in England.

49. We will immediately restore all hostages and charters delivered to us by Englishmen, as sureties of the peace of faithful service.

50. We will entirely remove from their bailiwicks, the relations of Gerard of Athee (so that in future they shall have no bailiwick in England); namely, Engelard of Cigogne, Peter, Guy, and Andrew of Chanceaux, Guy of Cigogne, Geoffrey of Martigny with his brothers, Philip Mark with his brothers and his nephew Geoffrey, and the whole brood of the same.

51. As soon as peace is restored, we will banish from the kingdom all foreign born knights, crossbowmen, serjeants, and mercenary soldiers who have come with horses and arms to the kingdom's hurt.

52. If anyone has been dispossessed or removed by us, without the legal judgment of his peers, from his lands, castles, franchises, or from his right, we will immediately restore them to him; and if a dispute arise over this, then let it be decided by the five and twenty barons of whom mention is made below in the clause for securing the peace. Moreover, for all those possessions, from which anyone has, without the lawful judgment of his peers, been disseised or removed, by our father, King Henry, or by our brother, King Richard, and which we retain in our hand (or which as possessed by others, to whom we are bound to warrant them) we shall have respite until the usual term of crusaders; excepting those things about which a plea has been raised, or an inquest made by our order, before our taking of the cross; but as soon as we return from the expedition, we will immediately grant full justice therein.

53. We shall have, moreover, the same respite and in the same manner in rendering justice concerning the disafforestation or retention of those forests which Henry our father and Richard our brother afforested, and concerning the wardship of lands which are of the fief of another (namely, such wardships as we have hitherto had by reason of a fief which anyone held of us by knight's service), and

concerning abbeys founded on other fiefs than our own, in which the lord of the fee claims to have right; and when we have returned, or if we desist from our expedition, we will immediately grant full justice to all who complain of such things.

54. No one shall be arrested or imprisoned upon the appeal of a woman, for the death of any other than her husband.

55. All fines made with us unjustly and against the law of the land, and all amercements, imposed unjustly and against the law of the land, shall be entirely remitted, or else it shall be done concerning them according to the decision of the five and twenty barons whom mention is made below in the clause for securing the peace, or according to the judgment of the majority of the same, along with the aforesaid Stephen, archbishop of Canterbury, if he can be present, and such others as he may wish to bring with him for this purpose, and if he cannot be present the business shall nevertheless proceed without him, provided always that if any one or more of the aforesaid five and twenty barons are in a similar suit, they shall be removed as far as concerns this particular judgment, others being substituted in their places after having been selected by the rest of the same five and twenty for this purpose only, and after having been sworn.

56. If we have disseised or removed Welshmen from lands or liberties, or other things, without the legal judgment of their peers in England or in Wales, they shall be immediately restored to them; and if a dispute arise over this, then let it be decided in the marches by the judgment of their peers; for the tenements in England according to the law of England, for tenements in Wales according to the law of Wales, and for tenements in the marches according to the law of the marches. Welshmen shall do the same to us and ours.

57. Further, for all those possessions from which any Welshman has, without the lawful judgment of his peers, been disseised or removed by King Henry our father, or King Richard our brother, and which we retain in our hand (or which are possessed by others, and which we ought to warrant), we will have respite until the usual term of crusaders; excepting those things about which a plea has been raised or an inquest made by our order before we took the cross; but as soon as we return (or if perchance we desist from our expedition), we will immediately grant full justice in accordance with the laws of the Welsh and in relation to the foresaid regions.

58. We will immediately give up the son of Llywelyn and all the hostages of Wales, and the charters delivered to us as security for the peace.

59. We will do towards Alexander, king of Scots, concerning the return of his sisters and his hostages, and concerning his franchises, and his right, in the same manner as we shall do towards our own barons of England, unless it ought to be otherwise according to the charters which we hold from William his father, formerly king of Scots; and this shall be according to the judgment of his peers in our court.

60. Moreover, all these aforesaid customs and liberties, the observances of which we have granted in our kingdom as far as pertains to us towards our men, shall be observed by all of our kingdom, as well clergy as laymen, as far as pertains to them towards their men.

61. Since, moreover, for God and the amendment of our kingdom and for the better allaying of the quarrel that has arisen between us and our barons, we have granted all these concessions, desirous that they should enjoy them in complete and firm endurance forever, we give and grant to them the underwritten security, namely, that the barons choose five and twenty barons of the kingdom, whomsoever they will, who shall be bound with all their might, to observe and hold, and cause to be observed, the peace and liberties we have granted and confirmed to them by this our present Charter, so that if we, or our justiciar, or our bailiffs or any one of our officers, shall in anything be at fault towards anyone, or shall have broken any one of the articles of this peace or of this security, and the offense be notified to four barons of the foresaid five and twenty, the said four barons shall repair to us (or our justiciar, if we are out of the realm) and, laying the transgression before

us, petition to have that transgression redressed without delay. And if we shall not have corrected the transgression (or, in the event of our being out of the realm, if our justiciar shall not have corrected it) within forty days, reckoning from the time it has been intimated to us (or to our justiciar, if we should be out of the realm), the four barons aforesaid shall refer that matter to the rest of the five and twenty barons, and those five and twenty barons shall, together with the community of the whole realm, distrain and distress us in all possible ways, namely, by seizing our castles, lands, possessions, and in any other way they can, until redress has been obtained as they deem fit, saving harmless our own person, and the persons of our queen and children; and when redress has been obtained, they shall resume their old relations towards us. And let whoever in the country desires it, swear to obey the orders of the said five and twenty barons for the execution of all the aforesaid matters, and along with them, to molest us to the utmost of his power; and we publicly and freely grant leave to everyone who wishes to swear, and we shall never forbid anyone to swear. All those, moreover, in the land who of themselves and of their own accord are unwilling to swear to the twenty five to help them in constraining and molesting us, we shall by our command compel the same to swear to the effect foresaid. And if any one of the five and twenty barons shall have died or departed from the land, or be incapacitated in any other manner which would prevent the foresaid provisions being carried out, those of the said twenty five barons who are left shall choose another in his place according to their own judgment, and he shall be sworn in the same way as the others. Further, in all matters, the execution of which is entrusted to these twenty five barons, if perchance these twenty five are present and disagree about anything, or if some of them, after being summoned, are unwilling or unable to be present, that which the majority of those present ordain or command shall be held as fixed and established, exactly as if the whole twenty five had concurred in this; and the said twenty five shall swear that they will faithfully observe all that is aforesaid, and cause it to be observed with

all their might. And we shall procure nothing from anyone, directly or indirectly, whereby any part of these concessions and liberties might be revoked or diminished; and if any such things has been procured, let it be void and null, and we shall never use it personally or by another.

62. And all the will, hatreds, and bitterness that have arisen between us and our men, clergy and lay, from the date of the quarrel, we have completely remitted and pardoned to everyone. Moreover, all trespasses occasioned by the said quarrel, from Easter in the sixteenth year of our reign till the restoration of peace, we have fully remitted to all, both clergy and laymen, and completely forgiven, as far as pertains to us. And on this head, we have caused to be made for them letters testimonial patent of the lord Stephen, archbishop of Canterbury, of the lord Henry, archbishop of Dublin, of the bishops aforesaid, and of Master Pandulf as touching this security and the concessions aforesaid.

63. Wherefore we will and firmly order that the English Church be free, and that the men in our kingdom have and hold all the aforesaid liberties, rights, and concessions, well and peaceably, freely and quietly, fully and wholly, for themselves and their heirs, of us and our heirs, in all respects and in all places forever, as is aforesaid. An oath, moreover, has been conditions aforesaid shall be kept in good faith and without evil intent.

Given under our hand—the above named and many others being witnesses—in the meadow which is called Runnymede, between Windsor and Staines, on the fifteenth day of June, in the seventeenth year of our reign.

Excerpts From the Massachusetts Body of Liberties (1641)

These excerpts are drawn from the Massachusetts Body of Liberties of 1641, the first code of laws enacted in New England. Although they hardly deserve to be called a statement of rights, they do show the state of mind of the early settlers and their leaders in Massachusetts. For their time, the Body of Liberties was more generous than most laws in England, especially in the rights extended to accused persons and the limitations placed upon the use of torture and punishment. The document also reveals concern with wife-beating, although the treatment of "witches" described is itself extremely brutal and cruel. American rights had a long way to go from this humble beginning.

The original spelling is retained here.

No man shall be beaten with above 40 stripes, nor shall any true gentleman, nor any man equall to a gentleman be punished with whipping, unles his crime be very shamefull, and his course of life vitious and profligate.

No man shall be forced by Torture to confesse any Crime against himselfe nor any other unlesse it be in some Capitall case, where he is first fullie convicted by cleare and suffitient evidence to be guilty, After which if the cause be of that nature, That it is very apparent there be other conspiratours or confederates with him, Then he may be tortured, yet not with such Tortures as be Barbarous and inhumane.

Civill Authoritie hath power and libertie to see the peace, ordinances and Rules of Christ observed in every church according to his word, so it be done in a Civill and not in an Ecclesiastical way.

If any man at his death shall not leave his wife a competent portion of his estaite, upon just complaint made to the Generall Court she shall be relieved.

Everie married woeman shall be free from bodilie correction or stripes by her husband, unlesse it be in his owne defence upon her assalt. If there be any just cause of correction, complaint shall be made to Authoritie assembled in some Court, from which onely shall she receive it.

If any man after legall conviction shall have or worship any other god, but the lord god, he shall be put to death.

If any man or woeman be a witch, (that is hath or consulteth with a familiar spirit,) they shall be put to death.

If any person shall Blaspheme the name of god, the father, Sonne or Holie Ghost, with direct, expresse, presumptuous or high handed blasphemie, or shall curse god in the like manner, he shall be put to death.

If any person slayeth an other suddaienly in his anger or Crueltie of passion, he shall be put to death.

If any man or woeman shall lye with any beaste or bruite creature by Carnall Copulation, They shall surely be put to death. And the beast shall be slaine, and buried and not eaten.

If any man lyeth with mankinde as he lyeth with a woeman, both of them have committed abhomination, they both shall surely be put to death.

If any person committeth Adultery with a maried or espoused wife, the Adulterer and Adulteress shall surely be put to death.

The Virginia Declaration of Rights (1776)

The Virginia Declaration of Rights was written by George Mason and adopted by the Virginia Constitutional Convention on June 12, 1776. Drawn upon by Thomas Jefferson for the opening paragraphs of the Declaration of Independence, it was widely copied by the other colonies and became the basis of the federal Bill of Rights. Although it contains different provisions from those found in the Bill of Rights, some identical phrases are found in this document.

A DECLARATION OF RIGHTS made by the representatives of the good people of Virginia, assembled in full and free convention which rights do pertain to them and their posterity, as the basis and foundation of government.

Section 1. That all men are by nature equally free and independent and have certain inherent rights, of which, when they enter into a state of society, they cannot, by any compact, deprive or divest their posterity; namely, the enjoyment of life and liberty, with the means of acquiring and possessing property, and pursuing and obtaining happiness and safety.

Section 2. That all power is vested in, and consequently derived from, the people; that magistrates are their trustees and servants and at all time amenable to them.

Section 3. That government is, or ought to be, instituted for the common benefit, protection, and security of the people, nation, or community; of all the various modes and forms of government, that is best which is capable of producing the greatest degree of happiness and safety and is most effectually secured against the danger of maladministration. And that, when any government shall be found inadequate or contrary to these purposes, a majority of the community has an indubitable, inalienable, and indefeasible right to reform, alter, or abolish it, in such manner as shall be judged most conducive to the public weal.

Section 4. That no man, or set of men, is entitled to exclusive or separate emoluments or privileges from the community, but in consideration of public services; which, nor being descendible, neither ought the offices of magistrate, legislator, or judge to be hereditary.

Section 5. That the legislative and executive powers of the state should be separate and distinct from the judiciary; and that the members of the two first may be restrained from oppression, by feeling and participating the burdens of the people, they should, at fixed periods, be reduced to a private station, return into that body from which they were originally taken, and the vacancies be supplied by frequent, certain, and regular elections, in which all, or any part, of the former members, to be again eligible, or ineligible, as the laws shall direct.

Section 6. That elections of members to serve as representatives of the people, in assembly ought to be free; and that all men, having sufficient evidence of permanent common interest with, and attachment to, the community, have the right of suffrage and cannot be taxed or deprived of their property for public uses without their own consent or that of their representatives so elected, nor bound by any law to which they have not, in like manner, assembled for the public good.

Section 7. That all power of suspending laws, or the execution of laws, by any authority, without consent of the representatives of the people, is injurious to their rights and ought not to be exercised.

Section 8. That in all capital or criminal prosecutions a man has a right to demand the cause and nature of his accusation, to be confronted with the accusers and witnesses, to call for evidence in his favor, and to a speedy trial by an impartial jury of twelve men of his vicinage, without whose unani-

mous consent he cannot be found guilty; nor can he be compelled to give evidence against himself; that no man be deprived of his liberty except by the law of the land or the judgment of his peers.

Section 9. That excessive bail ought not to be required, nor excessive fines imposed, nor cruel and unusual punishments inflicted.

Section 10. That general warrants, whereby an officer or messenger may be commanded to search suspected places without evidence of a fact committed, or to seize any person or persons not named, or whose offense is not particularly described and supported by evidence, are grievous and oppressive and ought not to be granted.

Section 11. That in controversies respecting property, and in suits between man and man, the ancient trial by jury is preferable to any other and ought to be held sacred.

Section 12. That the freedom of the press is one of the great bulwarks of liberty, and can never be restrained but by despotic governments.

Section 13. That a well-regulated militia, composed of the body of the people, trained to arms, is the proper, natural, and safe defense of a free state; that standing armies, in time of peace, should be avoided as dangerous to liberty; and that in all cases the military should be under strict subordination to, and governed by, the civil power.

Section 14. That the people have a right to uniform government; and, therefore, that no government separate from or independent of the government of Virginia ought to be erected or established within the limits thereof.

Section 15. That no free government, or the blessings of liberty, can be preserved to any people but by a firm adherence to justice, moderation, temperance, frugality, and virtue and by frequent recurrence to fundamental principles.

Section 16. That religion, or the duty which we owe to our Creator, and the manner of discharging it, can be directed only by reason and conviction, not by force or violence; and therefore all men are equally entitled to the free exercise of religion, according to the dictates of conscience; and that it is the mutual duty of all to practice Christian forbearance, love, and charity toward each other.

The Declaration of Independence (1776)

The Declaration of Independence of the Thirteen Colonies of North America is the first national independence document in world history. Adopted by the Second Continental Congress on July 4, 1776, the Declaration announced the separation of those colonies from Great Britain and established the United States. Drafted by Thomas Jefferson between June 11 and June 28, 1776, the Declaration of Independence is at once the nation's most cherished symbol of liberty and Jefferson's most enduring monument.

Jefferson's draft was revised by Jefferson, John Adams, and Benjamin Franklin, sent to Congress, and revised again into its current language. Here, in exalted and unforgettable phrases, the Declaration of Independence expressed the convictions and articulated the ideals held by most Americans. The political philosophy of the Declaration was not new; its ideals of individual liberty had already been expressed by John Locke and by other European philosophers. What Jefferson did was summarize this philosophy in "self-evident truths" and set forth a list of grievances against the king in order to justify before the world the breaking of ties between the colonies and the mother country. The principles stated in the Declaration of Independence that "all men are created equal" and that they possess the inalienable rights to "life, liberty, and the pursuit of happiness" remain the foundation of all American rights.

Action of Second Continental Congress, July 4, 1776

The unanimous Declaration of the thirteen United States of America

WHEN in the Course of human Events, it becomes necessary for one People to dissolve the Political Bands which have connected them with another, and to assume among the Powers of the Earth, the separate and equal Station to which the Laws of Nature and of Nature's God entitle them, a decent Respect to the Opinions of Mankind requires that they should declare the causes which impel them to the Separation.

WE hold these Truths to be self-evident, that all Men are created equal, that they are endowed by their Creator with certain unalienable Rights, that among these are Life, Liberty and the Pursuit of Happiness—That to secure these Rights, Governments are instituted among Men, deriving their just Powers from the Consent of the Governed, that whenever any Form of Government becomes destructive of these Ends, it is the Right of the People to alter or to abolish it, and to institute new Government, laying its Foundation on such Principles, and organizing its Powers in such Form, as to them shall seem most likely to effect their Safety and Happiness. Prudence, indeed, will dictate that Governments long established should not be changed for light and transient Causes; and accordingly all Experience hath shewn, that Mankind are more disposed to suffer, while Evils are sufferable, than to right themselves by abolishing the Forms to which they are accustomed. But when a long Train of Abuses and Usurpations, pursuing invariably the same Object, evinces a Design to reduce them under absolute Despotism, it is their Right, it is their Duty, to throw off such Government, and to provide new Guards for their future Security. Such has been the patient Sufferance of these Colonies; and such is now the Necessity which constrains them to alter their former Systems of Government. The History of the present King of Great Britain is a History of repeated Injuries and Usurpations, all having in direct Object the Establishment of an absolute Tyranny over these States. To prove this, let Facts be submitted to a candid World.

HE has refused his Assent to Laws, the most wholesome and necessary for the public Good.

HE has forbidden his Governors to pass Laws of immediate and pressing Importance, unless suspended in their Operation till his Assent should be obtained; and when so suspended, he has utterly neglected to attend to them.

HE has refused to pass other Laws for the Accommodation of large Districts of People, unless those People would relinquish the Right of Representation in the Legislature, a Right inestimable to them, and formidable to Tyrants only.

HE has called together Legislative Bodies at Places unusual, uncomfortable, and distant from the Depository of their public Records, for the sole Purpose of fatiguing them into Compliance with his Measures.

HE has dissolved Representative Houses repeatedly, for opposing with manly Firmness his Invasions on the Rights of the People.

HE has refused for a long Time, after such Dissolutions, to cause others to be elected; whereby the Legislative Powers, incapable of the Annihilation, have returned to the People at large for their exercise; the State remaining in the mean time exposed to all the Dangers of Invasion from without, and the Convulsions within.

HE has endeavoured to prevent the Population of these States; for that Purpose obstructing the Laws for Naturalization of Foreigners; refusing to pass others to encourage their Migrations hither, and raising the Conditions of new Appropriations of Lands.

HE has obstructed the Administration of Justice, by refusing his Assent to Laws for establishing Judiciary Powers.

HE has made Judges dependent on his Will alone, for the Tenure of their Offices, and the Amount and Payment of their Salaries.

HE has erected a Multitude of new Offices, and sent hither Swarms of Officers to harrass our People, and eat out their Substance.

HE has kept among us, in Times of Peace, Standing Armies, without the consent of our Legislatures.

HE has affected to render the Military independent of and superior to the Civil Power.

HE has combined with others to subject us to a Jurisdiction foreign to our Constitution, and unacknowledged by our Laws; giving his Assent to their Acts of pretended Legislation:

FOR quartering large Bodies of Armed Troops among us:

FOR protecting them, by a mock Trial, from Punishment for any Murders which they should commit on the Inhabitants of these States:

FOR cutting off our Trade with all Parts of the World:

FOR imposing Taxes on us without our Consent:

FOR depriving us, in many Cases, of the Benefits of Trial by Jury:

FOR transporting us beyond Seas to be tried for pretended Offences:

FOR abolishing the free System of English Laws in a neighbouring Province, establishing therein an arbitrary Government, and enlarging its Boundaries, so as to render it at once an Example

and fit Instrument for introducing the same absolute Rules into these Colonies:

FOR taking away our Charters, abolishing our most valuable Laws, and altering fundamentally the Forms of our Governments:

FOR suspending our own Legislatures, and declaring themselves invested with Power to legislate for us in all Cases whatsoever.

HE has abdicated Government here, by declaring us out of his Protection and waging War against us.

HE has plundered our Seas, ravaged our Coasts, burnt our Towns, and destroyed the Lives of our People.

HE is, at this Time, transporting large Armies of foreign Mercenaries to compleat the Works of Death, Desolation, and Tyranny, already begun with circumstances of Cruelty and Perfidy, scarcely parallelled in the most barbarous Ages, and totally unworthy the Head of a civilized Nation.

HE has constrained our fellow Citizens taken Captive on the high Seas to bear Arms against their Country, to become the Executioners of their Friends and Brethren, or to fall themselves by their Hands.

HE has excited domestic Insurrections amongst us, and has endeavoured to bring on the Inhabitants of our Frontiers, the merciless Indian Savages, whose known Rule of Warfare, is an undistinguished Destruction, of all Ages, Sexes and Conditions.

IN every stage of these Oppressions we have Petitioned for Redress in the most humble Terms: Our repeated Petitions have been answered only by acts which may define a Tyrant, is unfit to be the Ruler of a free People.

NOR have we been wanting in Attentions to our British Brethren. We have warned them from Time to Time of Attempts by their Legislature to extend an unwarrantable Jurisdiction over us. We have reminded them of the Circumstances of our Emigration and Settlement here. We have appealed to their native Justice and Magnanimity, and we have conjured them by the Ties of our common Kindred to disavow these Usurpations, which, would inevitably interrupt our Connections and Correspondence. They too have been deaf to the Voice of Justice and of Consanguinity. We must, therefore, acquiesce in the Necessity, which denounces our Separation, and hold them, as we hold the rest of Mankind, Enemies in War, in Peace, Friends.

WE, therefore, the Representatives of the UNITED STATES OF AMERICA, in GENERAL CONGRESS, Assembled, appealing to the Supreme Judge of the World for the Rectitude of our Intentions, do, in the Name, and by Authority of the good People of these Colonies, solemnly Publish and Declare, That these United Colonies are, and of Right ought to be, FREE AND INDEPENDENT STATES; that they are absolved from all Allegiance to the British Crown, and that all political Connection between them and the State of Great-Britain, is and ought to be totally dissolved; and that as FREE AND INDEPENDENT STATES, they have full Power to levy War, conclude Peace, contract Alliances, establish Commerce, and to do all other Acts and Things which INDEPENDENT STATES may of right do. And for the support of this Declaration, with a firm Reliance on the Protection of divine Providence, we mutually pledge to each other our Lives, our Fortunes, and our sacred Honor.

Excerpts From the Constitution of the United States (1789)

America was the first nation to consciously create a single written constitution as a framework for government. The idea of a written constitution was not that different from the written charters that some of the colonies had. After the American Revolution each new state prepared its own constitution, each of which had a bill of rights.

The first national government of the United States was not established until 1781. The Articles of Confederation were based upon a written constitution, and it lasted until 1789. It was replaced by a new constitution, the document of 1789, which has lasted longer than any other constitution in the world. When it was written, the United States Constitution contained a few rights but omitted most rights found in state bills of rights. Many of the framers of the Constitution believed that a bill of rights was unnecessary since each state had its own.

The excerpts here are printed to reveal some basic rights in the original Constitution of 1789,

and also to show that some rights were denied to slaves and Native Americans. The word "slavery" is never mentioned in the Constitution because of the delicate feelings of many delegates, who sought to deny that slavery was firmly a part of the constitutional system. One of the more shameful features of the Constitution, the so-called "three-fifths compromise," is reproduced here. This compromise counted a slave as three-fifths of a white free person for the purposes of representation and taxation. The importation of slaves was prohibited after 1808, but slavery was otherwise untouched by the Constitution.

Constitution of the United States

Article I

Section 2. Representatives and direct Taxes shall be apportioned among the several States which may be included within this Union, according to their respective Numbers, which shall be determined by adding to the whole Number of free Persons, including those bound to Service for a Term of Years, and excluding Indians not taxed, three fifths of all other Persons. [Eliminated by Amendment XIV.]

Section 9. The Migration or Importation of such Persons as any of the States now existing shall think proper to admit, shall not be prohibited by the Congress prior to the Year one thousand eight hundred and eight, but a Tax or duty may be imposed on such Importation, not exceeding ten dollars for each Person.

The Privilege of the Writ of Habeas Corpus shall not be suspended, unless when in Cases of Rebellion or Invasion the public Safety may require it.

No Bill of Attainder or ex post facto Law shall be passed.

Section 10. No State shall enter into any Treaty, Alliance, or Confederation; grant Letters of Marque and Reprisal; coin Money; emit Bills of Credit; make any Thing but gold and silver Coin a Tender in Payment of Debts; pass any Bill of Attainder, ex post facto Law, or Law impairing the Obligation of Contracts, or grant any Title of Nobility.

Article III

Section 2. The trial of all crimes, except in cases of impeachment, shall be by jury, and such trial shall be held in the state where the said crimes shall have been committed.

Section 3. Treason against the United States shall consist only in levying War against them, or in Adhering to their Enemies, giving them Aid and Comfort. No Person shall be convicted of Treason unless on the Testimony of two Witnesses to the same overt Act, or on Confession in open Court.

The Congress shall have Power to declare the Punishment of Treason, but no Attainder of Treason shall work Corruption of Blood, or Forfeiture except during the Life of the Person attainted.

Article IV

Section 1. Full Faith and Credit shall be given in each State to the public Acts, Records, and judicial Proceedings of every other State. And the Congress may by general Laws prescribe the Manner in which such Acts, Records and Proceedings shall be proved, and the Effect thereof.

Section 2. The Citizens of each State shall be entitled to all Privileges and Immunities of Citizens in the several States.

A Person charged in any State with Treason, Felony, or other Crime, who shall flee from Justice, and be found in another State, shall on Demand of the executive Authority of the State from which he fled, be delivered up, to be removed to the State having Jurisdiction of the Crime.

No Person held to Service or Labour in one State, under the Laws thereof, escaping into another, shall, in Consequence of any Law or Regulation therein, be discharged from such Service or Labour, but shall be delivered up on Claim of the Party to whom such Service or Labour may be due. [Rendered meaningless by Amendment XIII.]

Section 4. The United States shall guarantee to every state in the Union a republican form of government.

Article VI

No religious test shall ever be required as a qualification to any office or public trust under the United States.

The Bill of Rights (1791)

The original 1789 Constitution contained no bill of rights. When the delegates gathered at the Pennsylvania State House in May 1787 to "revise"

the Articles of Confederation, Virginia delegate George Mason wrote, "The Eyes of the United States are turned upon this Assembly and their Expectations raised to a very anxious Degree." Mason had earlier written the Virginia Declaration of Rights that strongly influenced Thomas Jefferson in writing the first part of the Declaration of Independence. He left the convention bitterly disappointed, however, and became one of the Constitution's most vocal opponents. "It has no declaration of rights," he was to state. Ultimately, George Mason's views prevailed. When James Madison drafted the amendments to the Constitution that were to become the Bill of Rights, he drew heavily upon the ideas put forth in the Virginia Declaration of Rights, but added some ideas of his own. Madison is usually regarded as the prime author of the Bill of Rights.

During the debates on the adoption of the Constitution, its opponents repeatedly charged that the Constitution as drafted would open the way to tyranny by the central government. Fresh in their minds was the memory of the British violation of civil rights before and during the Revolution. They demanded a bill of rights that would spell out the immunities of individual citizens. Several state conventions in their formal ratification of the Constitution asked for such amendments; others ratified the Constitution with the understanding that the amendments would be offered.

On September 25, 1789, the First Congress of the United States therefore proposed to the state legislatures 12 amendments to the Constitution. The first two of these met arguments that concerned the number of constituents for each representative and the compensation of congressmen and were not ratified. Articles 3 to 12, however, ratified by three-fourths of the state legislatures in 1791, constitute the first 10 amendments of the Constitution, known as the Bill of Rights. The first and second articles printed here are the two unratified amendments and are not part of the Bill of Rights. The sections of the Bill of Rights (originally Articles 3 to 12) are now referred to by the numbers of the respective amendments, given here in parenthesis.

The Bill of Rights is the fundamental source of American rights, but the significance of its language has changed. For example, even the simple words of the Eighth Amendment have shifted in meaning over time, due largely to judicial inter-pretation. As the Supreme Court explained in a 1910 decision (Weems v. United States), "What constitutes a cruel and unusual punishment has not been exactly decided . . . the Eighth Amend-ment should not be controlled by what the framers of the Bill of Rights had experienced." As a later court stated, (Trop v. Dulles, 1958) "the meaning of the Eighth Amendment must be drawn from the evolving standards of decency that mark the progress of a maturing society." Other provisions of the Bill of Rights are subject to a similar process of growth and alteration.

Congress OF THE United States begun and held at the City of New-York, on Wednesday the Fourth of March, one thousand seven hundred and eighty nine.

THE Conventions of a number of the States having at the time of their adopting the Constitu-tion, expressed a desire, in order to prevent mis-construction or abuse of its powers, that further declaratory and restrictive clauses should be added, extending the ground of public confidence in the Government, as will best insure the benefi-cent ends of its institution

RESOLVED by the Senate and House of Representatives of the United States of America, in Congress assembled, two thirds of both Houses concurring, that the following Articles be pro-posed to the Legislatures of the several States, as Amendments to the Constitution of the United States, all or any of which Articles, when ratified by three fourths of the said Legislatures, to be valid to all intents and purposes, as part of the said Constitution;

ARTICLES in addition to, and Amendment of the Constitution of the United States of Ameri-ca, proposed by Congress, and ratified by the Leg-islatures of the several States, pursuant to the fifth Article of the original Constitution.

Article the first [Not Ratified]

After the first enumeration required by the first Article of the Constitution, there shall be one Representative for every thirty thousand, until the number shall amount to one hundred, after which the proportion shall be so regulated by Congress, that there shall be not less than one hundred Rep-resentatives, nor less than one Representative for every forty thousand persons, until the number of Representatives shall amount to two hundred; after which the proportion shall be so regulated by Congress, that there shall not be less than two hundred Representatives, nor more than one Rep-resentative for every fifty thousand persons.

Article the second [Amendment XXVII—ratified in 1992]

No law, varying the compensation for the ser-vices of the Senators and Representatives, shall take effect, until an election of Representatives shall have intervened.

Article the third [Amendment I]

Congress shall make no law respecting an establishment of religion, or prohibiting the free exercise thereof; or abridging the freedom of speech, or of the press; or the right of the people peaceably to assemble, and to petition the Govern-ment for a redress of grievances.

Article the fourth [Amendment II]

A well regulated Militia, being necessary to the security of a free State, the right of the people to keep and bear Arms, shall not be infringed.

Article the fifth [Amendment III]

No Soldier shall, in time of peace be quar-tered in any house, without the consent of the Owner, nor in time of war, but in a manner to be prescribed by law.

Article the sixth [Amendment IV]

The right of the people to be secure in their persons, houses, papers, and effects, against unreasonable searches and seizures, shall not be violated, and no Warrants shall issue, but upon probable cause, supported by Oath or affirmation, and particularly describing the place to be searched, and the persons or things to be seized.

Article the seventh [Amendment V]

No person shall be held to answer for a capi-tal, or otherwise infamous crime, unless on a pre-sentment or indictment of a Grand Jury, except in cases arising in the land or naval forces, or in the Militia, when in actual service in time of War or public danger; nor shall any person be subject for the same offence to be twice put in jeopardy of life or limb; nor shall be compelled in any crimi-nal case to be a witness against himself, nor be deprived of life, liberty, or property, without due process of law; nor shall private property be taken for public use, without just compensation.

Article the eighth [Amendment VI]

In all criminal prosecutions, the accused shall enjoy the right to a speedy and public trial, by an impartial jury of the State and district wherein the crime shall have been committed, which district shall have been previously ascertained by law, and to be informed of the nature and cause of the accusation; to be confronted with the witnesses against him; to have compulsory process for obtaining witnesses in his favor, and to have the Assistance of Counsel for his defence.

Article the ninth [Amendment VII]

In Suits at common law, where the value in controversy shall exceed twenty dollars, the right of trial by jury shall be preserved, and no fact tried by a jury, shall be otherwise re-examined in any Court of the United States, than according to the rules of the common law.

Article the tenth [Amendment VIII]

Excessive bail shall not be required, nor excessive fines imposed, nor cruel and unusual punishments inflicted.

Article the eleventh [Amendment IX]

The enumeration in the Constitution, of certain rights, shall not be construed to deny or disparage others retained by the people.

Article the twelfth [Amendment X]

The powers not delegated to the United States by the Constitution, nor prohibited by it to the States, are reserved to the States respectively, or to the people.

Jefferson's First Inaugural Address (1801)

Thomas Jefferson regarded his electoral victory of 1800 as a "revolution" comparable to the American Revolution of 1776. Although this was an exaggeration of the facts—there was no mass uprising on behalf of Jefferson—the election did represent a shift to a new vision of America. The election was a triumph for budding American democracy, and a victory for the "forgotten common man." More than in any previous American election entrenched aristocrats suffered a setback at the polls.

Thomas Jefferson was inaugurated president on March 4, 1801, in the swampy village of Washington, which had become the new national capital. Spurning the pomp that had been associated with prior presidential inaugurations, Jefferson walked from his boardinghouse on foot to the capitol to deliver his address. The address itself is a classic statement of democratic ideals, including Jefferson's strong view of American rights. Embedded within this address are many of the major themes of American rights, including a concern for minority rights against popular majorities. The address was delivered in an age when few Americans could vote and slavery was still acceptable, but it foreshadowed the future of American rights. The principles enunciated in this speech were gradually fulfilled in American experience, although "equal and exact justice for all men" still eludes us.

President Jefferson served as the nation's leader from 1801 until 1809. As president he doubled the size of America through the Louisiana Purchase of 1803, acquiring from France a vast area of 828,000 square miles that had been formerly held by the Spanish. Thomas Jefferson died on July 4, 1826, on the fiftieth anniversary of the Declaration of Independence. Although he was proud of his work as America's third president, Jefferson is better remembered for writing the Declaration of Independence.

Thomas Jefferson's First Inaugural Address, Delivered in Washington, District of Columbia

Called upon to undertake the duties of the first executive office of our country, I avail myself of the presence of that portion of my fellow citizens which is here assembled to express my grateful thanks for the favor with which they have been pleased to look toward me, to declare a sincere consciousness that the task is above my talents, and that I approach it with those anxious and awful presentiments which the greatness of the charge and the weakness of my powers so justly inspire. A rising nation, spread over a wide and fruitful land, traversing all the seas with the rich productions of their industry, engaged in commerce with nations who feel power and forget right, advancing rapidly to destinies beyond the reach of mortal eye, when I contemplate these transcendent objects, and see the honor, the happiness, and the hopes of this beloved country committed to the issue, and the auspices of this day, I shrink from the contemplation, and humble myself before the magnitude of the undertaking. Utterly, indeed, should I despair did not the presence of many whom I see here remind me that in the other high authorities provided by our Constitution I shall find resources of wisdom, of virtue, and of zeal on which to rely under all difficulties. To you, then, gentlemen, who are charged with the sovereign functions of legislation, and to those associated with you, I look with encouragement for that guidance and support which may enable us to steer with safety the vessel in which we are all embarked amidst the conflicting elements of a troubled world.

During the contest of opinion through which we have passed the animation of discussions and of exertions has sometimes worn an aspect which might impose on strangers unused to think freely and to speak and to write what they think; but this being now decided by the voice of the nation, announced according to the rules of the Constitution, all will of course arrange themselves under the will of the law, and unite in common efforts for the common good.

All, too, will bear in mind this sacred principle, that though the will of the majority is in all cases to prevail, that will to be rightful must be reasonable; that the minority possesses their equal rights, which equal law must protect, and to violate would be oppression.

Let us, then, fellow citizens, unite with one heart and one mind. Let us restore to social intercourse that harmony and affection without which liberty and even life itself are but dreary things. And let us reflect that, having banished from our land that religious intolerance under which mankind so long bled and suffered, we have yet gained little if we countenance a political intolerance as despotic, as wicked, and capable of as bitter and bloody persecutions.

During the throes and convulsions of the ancient world, during the agonizing spasms of infuriated man, seeking through blood and slaughter his long lost liberty, it was not wonderful that the agitation of the billows should reach even this distant and peaceful shore; that this should be more felt and feared by some and less by others,

and should divide opinions as to measures of safety. But every difference of opinion is not a difference of principle. We have called by different names brethren of the same principle. We are all republicans, we are all federalists. If there be any among us who would wish to dissolve the Union or to change its republican form, let them stand undisturbed as monuments of the safety with which error of opinion may be tolerated where reason is left free to combat it. I know, indeed, that some honest men fear that a republican government can not be strong, that this Government is not strong enough; but would the honest patriot, in the full tide of successful experiment, abandon a government which has so far kept us free and firm on the theoretic and visionary fear that this Government, the world's best hope, may by possibility want energy to preserve itself? I trust not. I believe this, on the contrary, the strongest Government on earth. I believe it the only one where every man, at the call of the law, would fly to the standard of the law, and would meet invasions of the public order as his own personal concern. Sometimes it is said that man cannot be trusted with the government of himself. Can he, then, be trusted with the government of others? Or have we found angels in the forms of kings to govern him? Let history answer this question.

Let us, then, with courage and confidence pursue our own Federal and Republican principles, our attachment to union and representative government. Kindly separated by nature and a wide ocean from the exterminating havoc of one quarter of the globe; too high-minded to endure the degradations of the others; possessing a chosen country, with room enough for our descendants to the thousandth and thousandth generation; entertaining a due sense of our equal right to the use of our own faculties, to the acquisitions of our own industry, to honor and confidence from our fellow citizens, resulting not from birth, but from our actions and their sense of them; enlightened by a benign religion, professed, indeed, and practiced in various forms, yet all of them inculcating honesty, truth, temperance, gratitude, and the love of man; acknowledging and adoring an overruling Providence, which by all its dispensations proves that it delights in the happiness of man here and his greater happiness hereafter, with all these blessings, what more is necessary to make us a happy and a prosperous people? Still one thing more, fellow citizens, a wise and frugal

Government, which shall restrain men from injuring one another, shall leave them otherwise free to regulate their own pursuits of industry and improvement, and shall not take from the mouth of labor the bread it has earned. This is the sum of good government, and this is necessary to close the circle of our felicities.

About to enter, fellow citizens, on the exercise of duties which comprehend everything dear and valuable to you, it is proper you should understand what I deem the essential principles of our Government, and consequently those which ought to shape its Administration. I will compress them within the narrowest compass they will bear, stating the general principle, but not all its limitations.

- Equal and exact justice to all men, of whatever state or persuasion, religious or political;

- peace, commerce, and honest friendship with all nations, entangling alliances with none;

- the support of the State governments in all their rights, as the most competent administrations for our domestic concerns and the surest bulwarks against anti-republican tendencies;

- the preservation of the General Government in its whole constitutional vigor, as the sheet anchor of our peace at home and safety abroad;

- a jealous care of the right of election by the people, a mild and safe corrective of abuses which are lopped by the sword of revolution where peaceable remedies are unprovided;

- absolute acquiescence in the decisions of the majority, the vital principle of republics, from which is no appeal but to force, the vital principle and immediate parent of despotism;

- a well disciplined militia, our best reliance in peace and for the first moments of war, till regulars may relieve them;

- the supremacy of the civil over the military authority;

- economy in the public expense, that labor may be lightly burthened;

- the honest payment of our debts and sacred preservation of the public faith;

- encouragement of agriculture, and of commerce as its handmaid;

- the diffusion of information and arraignment of all abuses at the bar of the public reason;

- freedom of religion;

- freedom of the press, and

- freedom of person under the protection of the habeas corpus, and trial by juries impartially selected.

These principles form the bright constellation which has gone before us and guided our steps through an age of revolution and reformation. The wisdom of our sages and blood of our heroes have been devoted to their attainment. They should be the creed of our political faith, the text of civic instruction, the touchstone by which to try the services of those we trust; and should we wander from them in moments of error or of alarm, let us hasten to retrace our steps and to regain the road which alone leads to peace, liberty, and safety.

I repair, then, fellow citizens, to the post you have assigned me. With experience enough in subordinate offices to have seen the difficulties of this the greatest of all, I have learnt to expect that it will rarely fall to the lot of imperfect man to retire from this station with the reputation and the favor which bring him into it. Without pretensions to that high confidence you reposed in our first and greatest revolutionary character, whose preeminent services had entitled him to the first place in his country's love and destined for him the fairest page in the volume of faithful history, I ask so much confidence only as may give firmness and effect to the legal administration of your affairs. I shall often go wrong through defect of judgment. When right, I shall often be thought wrong by those whose positions will not command a view of the whole ground. I ask your indulgence for my own errors, which will never be intentional, and your support against the errors of others, who may condemn what they would not if seen in all its parts. The approbation implied by your suffrage is a great consolation to me for the past, and my future solicitude will be to retain the good opinion of those who have bestowed it in advance, to conciliate that of others by doing them all the good in my power, and to be instrumental to the happiness and freedom of all.

Relying, then, on the patronage of your good will, I advance with obedience to the work, ready to retire from it whenever you become sensible how much better choice it is in your power to make. And may that Infinite Power which rules the destinies of the universe lead our councils to what is best, and give them a favorable issue for your peace and prosperity.

Excerpts From John Stuart Mill's *On Liberty* (1859)

John Stuart Mill published his book, On Liberty, *in 1859. The book contains a classic defense of the individual's right to think and act for himself. Mill poses the possibility of human happiness in a good society. In such a society, where each person "thinks and acts for yourself," much more is meant than "think and act as you please." According to Mill government groups and institutions that try to tell people what to think and do are repressive and wrong. The challenge is to draw the line between individual liberty and the good of the whole society. This Mill attempts to do in a way that still stands as the classic statement of free speech and freedom of action. Mill's views have had particular influence on the development of rights in America because of Americans' devotion to the ideal of the free individual.*

Mill's statement of individual liberty is extreme and strong. It clearly calls for respect for each individual, but it also applies only to mature persons, not to children or "young persons below the age which the law may fix as that of manhood or womanhood." Those who are in need of the care of others cannot exercise full freedom because they are not able to make sound judgments.

In his lifetime Mill attacked such interferences with freedom as American prohibition laws and Sunday closing laws. He championed complete religious toleration and the rights of women, feared the "tyranny of the majority," and advocated a massive extension of voting privileges. He believed that America had the most democratic of all societies, but warned about what he called the "moral police."

There is a sphere of action in which society, as distinguished from the individual, has, if any, only an indirect interest; comprehending all that portion of a person's life and conduct which affects only himself, or if it affects others, only with their free, voluntary, and undeceived consent and participation. When I say only himself, I mean directly, and in the first instance: for whatever affects himself, may affect others through himself . . . This, then is the appropriate region of human liberty. It comprises, first, the inward domain of consciousness; demanding liberty of conscience, in the most comprehensive sense; liberty of thought and feeling; absolute freedom of opinion and sentiment on all subjects, practical or speculative, scientific, moral or theological. The freedom of expressing and publishing opinions may seem to fall under a different principle, since it belongs to that part of the conduct of an individual which concerns other people; but being almost of as much importance as the liberty of thought itself, and resting in great part on the same reasons, is practically inseparable from it. Secondly, the principle requires liberty of tastes and pursuits; of framing the plan of our life to suit our own character; of doing as we like, subject to such consequences as may follow; without impediment from our fellow creatures, so long as what we do does not harm them, even though they should think our conduct foolish, perverse, or wrong. Thirdly, from this liberty of each individual, follows our liberty, within the same limits, of combination among individuals; freedom to unite, for any purpose not involving harm to others: the persons combining assumed to be of full age, and not forced or deceived.

No society in which these liberties are not, on the whole, respected, is free, whatever may be its form of government; and none is completely free in which they do not exist absolute and unqualified. The only freedom which deserves the name, is that of pursuing our own good in our own way, so long as we do not attempt to deprive others of theirs, or impeded their efforts to obtain it. Each is the proper guardian of his own health, whether bodily, mental and spiritual. Mankind are greater gainers by suffering each to live as seems good to themselves, than by compelling each to live as seems good to the rest . . .

Apart from the peculiar tenets of individual thinkers, there is also in the world at large an increasing inclination to stretch unduly the powers of society over the individual, both by the force of opinion and even that of legislation; and as the tendency of all the changes taking place in the world is to strengthen society, and diminish the power of the individual, this encroachment is not one of the evils which tend spontaneously to disappear, but on the contrary, to grow more and more formidable. The disposition of mankind, whether as rulers or fellow citizens, to impose their opinions and inclinations as a rule of conduct for others, is so energetically supported by some of the best and the worst feelings of human nature, that it is hardly ever kept under restraint by anything but a want of power; and as the power is not declining, but growing, unless a stronger barrier of moral conviction can be raised against the mischief, we must expect, in the present circumstances of the world, to see it increase . . .

If all mankind, minus one, were of one opinion, and only one person were of the contrary opinion, mankind would no more be justified in silencing that one person, than he, if he had the power, would be justified in silencing mankind. Were an opinion a personal possession of no value except to the owner; if to be obstructed in the enjoyment of it were simply a private injury, it would make some difference whether the injury was inflicted on a few persons or on many. But the peculiar evil of silencing the expression of an opinion is, that it is robbing the human race; posterity as well as the existing generation; those who dissent from the opinion, still more than from those who hold it. If the opinion is right, they are deprived of the opportunity of exchanging error for truth: if wrong, they lose, what is almost as great a benefit, the clearer perception and livelier impression of truth, produced by its collision with error.

The Emancipation Proclamation (1863)

President Abraham Lincoln issued the Emancipation Proclamation on September 22, 1863, utilizing his wartime powers of office. On January 1, 1863, President Lincoln formally freed all slaves residing in territory in rebellion against the federal government. This Emancipation Proclamation actually freed few people. It did not apply to slaves in border states fighting on the Union side; nor did it affect slaves in southern areas already under Union control. Naturally, the states in rebellion did not act on Lincoln's order. But the Proclamation did show Americans—and the world—that the Civil War was now being fought to end slavery. What began as an expedient move during wartime ended as a moral commitment to end all forms of slavery.

When Lincoln announced the Proclamation to be in effect on January 1, 1863, he added an

announcement that he would recruit African Americans for service in the armies of the North. This encouraged many African Americans to leave the South, gain their freedom, and join in the war to end slavery. Almost 200,000 former southern slaves chose to fight for the North.

Slavery was finally put to an end with the passage of the Thirteenth Amendment to the Constitution on December 18, 1865.

A Proclamation:

Whereas on the 22nd day of September, A.D. 1862, a proclamation was issued by the President of the United States, containing, among other things, the following, to wit:

That on the 1st day of January, A.D. 1863, all persons held as slaves within any State or designated part of a State the people whereof shall then be in rebellion against the United States shall be then, thenceforward, and forever free; and the executive government of the United States, including the military and naval authority thereof, will recognize and maintain the freedom of such persons and will do no act or acts to repress such persons, or any of them, in any efforts they may make for their actual freedom.

That the executive will on the 1st day of January aforesaid, by proclamation, designate the States and parts of States, if any, in which the people thereof, respectively, shall then be in rebellion against the United States; and the fact that any State or the people thereof shall on that day be in good faith represented in the Congress of the United States by members chosen thereto at elections wherein a majority of the qualified voters of such States shall have participated shall, in the absence of strong countervailing testimony, be deemed conclusive evidence that such State and the people thereof are not then in rebellion against the United States.

Now, therefore, I, Abraham Lincoln, President of the United States, by virtue of the power in me vested as Commander-In-Chief of the Army and Navy of the United States in time of actual armed rebellion against the authority and government of the United States, and as a fit and necessary war measure for suppressing said rebellion, do, on this 1st day of January, A.D. 1863, and in accordance with my purpose so to do, publicly proclaimed for the full period of one hundred days from the first day above mentioned, order and designate as the States and parts of States wherein the people thereof, respectively, are this day in rebellion against the United States the following, to wit:

Arkansas, Texas, Louisiana (except the parishes of St. Bernard, Palquemines, Jefferson, St. John, St. Charles, St. James, Ascension, Assumption, Terrebone, Lafourche, St. Mary, St. Martin, and Orleans, including the city of New Orleans), Mississippi, Alabama, Florida, Georgia, South Carolina, North Carolina, and Virginia (except the forty-eight counties designated as West Virginia, and also the counties of Berkeley, Accomac, Northhampton, Elizabeth City, York, Princess Anne, and Norfolk, including the cities of Norfolk and Portsmouth), and which excepted parts are for the present left precisely as if this proclamation were not issued.

And by virtue of the power and for the purpose aforesaid, I do order and declare that all persons held as slaves within said designated States and parts of States are, and henceforward shall be, free; and that the Executive Government of the United States, including the military and naval authorities thereof, will recognize and maintain the freedom of said persons.

And I hereby enjoin upon the people so declared to be free to abstain from all violence, unless in necessary self-defence; and I recommend to them that, in all case when allowed, they labor faithfully for reasonable wages.

And I further declare and make known that such persons of suitable condition will be received into the armed service of the United States to garrison forts, positions, stations, and other places, and to man vessels of all sorts in said service.

And upon this act, sincerely believed to be an act of justice, warranted by the Constitution upon military necessity, I invoke the considerate judgment of mankind and the gracious favor of Almighty God.

Post Civil War Amendments (1865–70)

One of the major purposes of the North in fighting the Civil War (1861–65) was to end slavery and all of its features. A constitutional amend-ment was chosen as the best means to alter the original constitutional text and create permanent protections for the newly-freed slaves. In the process, a number of new rights were added to the list of American rights. Some of these rights had immediate impact, while others took generations to unfold.

The Thirteenth Amendment immediately stamped out slavery in America. The Fourteenth Amendment reversed one of the Supreme Court's most controversial pro-slavery decisions, the 1857 Dred Scott decision. The Fifteenth Amendment guaranteed the right to vote, although it took many years and considerable turmoil until that right was truly available to African Americans. Racial segregation continued to be lawful until 1954, in spite of these provisions of the Constitution.

The Civil Rights Act of 1866 was the world's first genuine civil rights statute. It was passed by an activist Congress to enforce the Thirteenth Amendment. In all jurisdictions citizens were to enjoy the equal protection of the laws, including the right to sue, the right to enter contracts, and the right to own property. Some portions of the statute are still in force and are reprinted later in this chapter. Other sections of the statute, which provided for criminal punishments for those who "under color of any law . . . or custom" deprived any person from enjoying those rights because of race or previous condition of servitude, were resisted by powerful forces. President Andrew Johnson vetoed the Civil Rights Bill and was over-ridden by Congress. Congress had to reenact the provisions of this bill several times in later years before the Supreme Court or the executive branch would take it seriously.

Most important of these new rights was the following language of the Fourteenth Amendment: "nor shall any State deprive any person of life, liberty, or property, without due process of law; nor deny to any person within its jurisdiction the equal protection of the laws." In time, this provision became a means of imposing constitutional constraints upon the states on behalf of the rights of individuals. Thus, the post-Civil War amendments not only ended slavery, but they simultaneously created broader rights for every citizen.

Leaders of the nineteenth century women's movement contended that the right to vote in a federal election was a privilege of national citi-

zenship conferred by the first section of the Four-teenth Amendment. The Supreme Court rejected this view in Minor *v.* Happersett *(1875).*

In 1869 African American men still could not vote in many states, including most northern states outside New England. The Republican Party, barely victorious in the presidential elections of 1868, decided to advocate African American male enfran-chisement in every state. When it was found that the Fourteenth Amendment voting provisions were being deliberately evaded, the Fifteenth Amendment was ratified in 1870 and was intended to protect the right of newly freed slaves. Sadly, the Supreme Court's subsequent interpretation of the Fifteenth Amendment did not assist in the practical enforce-ment of the new voting rights legislation, and many African Americans continued to be denied the right to vote well into the twentieth century.

Amendment XIII

Passed by Congress January 31, 1865. Rati-fied December 6, 1865.

Note: A portion of Article IV, Section 2, of the Constitution was superseded by the Thirteenth Amendment.

Section 1. Neither slavery nor involuntary servitude, except as a punishment for crime whereof the party shall have been duly convicted, shall exist within the United States, or any place subject to their jurisdiction.

Section 2. Congress shall have power to enforce this article by appropriate legislation.

Amendment XIV

Passed by Congress June 13, 1866. Ratified July 9, 1868.

Note: Article I, Section 2, of the Constitution was modified by Section 2 of the Fourteenth Amendment.

Section 1. All persons born or naturalized in the United States, and subject to the jurisdiction thereof, are citizens of the United States and of the State wherein they reside. No State shall make or enforce any law which shall abridge the privileges or immunities of citizens of the United States; nor shall any State deprive any person of life, liberty, or property, without due process of law; nor deny to any person within its jurisdiction the equal pro-tection of the laws.

Section 2. Representatives shall be appor-tioned among the several States according to their respective numbers, counting the whole number of persons in each State, excluding Indians not taxed. But when the right to vote at any election for the choice of electors for President and Vice-President of the United States, Representatives in Congress, the Executive and Judicial officers of a State, or the members of the Legislature thereof, is denied to any of the male inhabitants of such State, being twenty-one years of age* and citizens of the Unit-ed States, or in any way abridged, except for par-ticipation in rebellion, or other crime, the basis of representation therein shall be reduced in the pro-portion which the number of such male citizens shall bear to the whole number of male citizens twenty-one years of age in such State.

Section 3. No person shall be a Senator or Representative in Congress, or elector of Presi-dent and Vice-President, or hold any office, civil or military, under the United States, or under any State, who, having previously taken an oath, as a member of Congress, or as an officer of the Unit-ed States, or as a member of any State legislature, or as an executive or judicial officer of any State, to support the Constitution of the United States, shall have engaged in insurrection or rebellion against the same, or given aid or comfort to the enemies thereof. But Congress may by a vote of two-thirds of each House, remove such disability.

Section 4. The validity of the public debt of the United States, authorized by law, including debts incurred for payment of pensions and bounties for services in suppressing insurrection or rebellion, shall not be questioned. But neither the United States nor any State shall assume or pay any debt or obligation incurred in aid of insurrection or rebel-lion against the United States, or any claim for the loss or emancipation of any slave; but all such debts, obligations and claims shall be held illegal and void.

Section 5. The Congress shall have the power to enforce, by appropriate legislation, the provi-sions of this article.

* Changed by Section 1 of the Twenty-Sixth Amendment.

Amendment XV

Passed by Congress February 26, 1869. Rati-fied February 3, 1870.

Section 1. The right of citizens of the United States to vote shall not be denied or abridged by the United States or by any State on account of race, color, or previous condition of servitude.

Section 2. The Congress shall have the power to enforce this article by appropriate legislation.

Woman's Suffrage Amendment (1920)

The simple language of the Nineteenth Amendment disguises the importance of the changes in American values that it represents. An attempt had been made by women's advocates to include women within the provisions of the Fifteenth Amendment, but it failed ingloriously and was rejected by the Supreme Court. Thus, the extension of voting rights to African American males did not open the same doors to women. The state of Wyoming gave women the right to vote in 1890, after a long women's rights crusade. Many western states followed the lead of Wyoming. The remaining states were forced into line by the passage of the Nineteenth Amendment.

The growth of the women's suffrage movement was promoted by the endorsement of Theodore Roosevelt's 1912 Progressive Party. World War I also contributed to the cause by prompting President Woodrow Wilson to give the proposed amendment his support, seeing this concession as "a vitally necessary war measure." Thus, in the 1920 elections one of the voters was Charlotte Woodward Pierce who, as a 19-year-old girl, had attended the 1848 Seneca Falls Convention that started the movement for female suffrage.

The campaign for women's suffrage was as protracted and militant (but much less violent) as the later struggle of the 1960s to end racial segregation. It all began in 1848 with a meeting of 300 persons at a church in Seneca Falls, New York. Elizabeth Cady Stanton and Lucretia Mott led the way, preparing the ground for the later efforts of Susan B. Anthony.

The suffragists campaign cry was "Equal Rights for Men and Women," an extension of the promise of the Declaration of Independence. For many years the champions of women suffrage were few, and the heroines who received so much abuse are now revered for their courage and persistence.

In addition to the Nineteenth Amendment, the proposed Equal Rights Amendment is also printed here. Despite the efforts of many women's rights groups, the needed number of state ratifications was never obtained. Opponents of this proposal contended that it carried the concept of women's rights too far and could create unforeseen changes in the laws.

Amendment XIX

Passed by Congress June 4, 1919. Ratified August 18, 1920.

The right of citizens of the United States to vote shall not be denied or abridged by the United States or by any State on account of sex.

Congress shall have power to enforce this article by appropriate legislation.

Inoperative Article

(Proposed 1972; Expired Unratified 1982)

Article—

Section. 1. Equality of rights under the law shall not be denied or abridged by the United States or by any State on account of sex.

Section. 2. The Congress shall have the power to enforce, by appropriate legislation, the provisions of this article.

Section. 3. This amendment shall take effect two years after the date of ratification.

Desegregation of the Armed Forces (1948)

On July 26, 1948, President Harry S Truman signed Executive Order 9981, ending racial segregation in the armed forces of the United States. Clearly, this was an essential first step in promoting equal treatment for all Americans. Six years later the desegregation of the nation's public schools was ordered in 1954 by the Supreme Court.

Executive Order 9981, which applies "to race, color, religion or national origin," was supported by stringent enforcement machinery.

Executive Order No. 9981 (1948)

Whereas it is essential that there be maintained in the armed service of the United States the highest standards of democracy, with equality of treatment and opportunity for all those who serve in our country's defense:

Now, therefore, by virtue of the authority vested in me as President of the United States, by the Constitution and statutes of the United States, and as Commander-in-Chief of the armed services, it is hereby ordered as follows:

1. It is hereby declared to be the policy of the President that there shall be equality of treatment for all persons in the armed services without regard to race, color, religion or national origin. This policy shall be put into effect as rapidly as possible, having due regard to the time required to effectuate any changes without impairing efficiency or morals.

2. There shall be created in the national military establishment an advisory committee known as the President's Committee on Equality of Treatment and Opportunity in the Armed Services, which shall be composed of seven members, to be designated by the President.

3. The Committee is authorized on behalf of the President to examine into the rules, procedures and practices of the armed services in order to determine in what respect such rules, procedure and practices may be altered or improved with a view to carrying out the policy of this order. This Committee shall confer and advise with the Secretary of the Army, the Secretary of the Air Force, and shall make such recommendations to the President and to said Secretaries as in the judgment of the Committee will effectuate the policy hereof.

4. All executive departments and agencies of the Federal Government are authorized and directed to cooperate with the Committee and its work, and to furnish the Committee with such information or the services of such persons as the Committee may require in the performance of its duties.

5. When requested by the Committee to do so, persons in the armed forces or in any of the executive departments and agencies of the Federal Government shall testify before the Committee and shall make available for the use of the Committee such documents and other information as the Committee may require.

6. The Committee shall continue to exist, until such time as the President shall terminate its existence by Executive order.

Library Bill of Rights (1948)

The American Library Association is the largest organization of professional librarians in the United States and most librarians are members. Because libraries are on the front lines of First Amendment censorship issues, a need for clearer guidelines and statement of rights was perceived. The statement was originally adopted June 18, 1948, and amended February 2, 1961, and January 23, 1980, by the ALA Council.

In interpreting this Library Bill of Rights the American Library Association has stated that it is "unswerving in its commitment to human rights and intellectual freedom; the two are inseparably linked and inextricably entwined." The Association has also asserted its belief that "freedom of opinion and expression is not derived from or dependent on any form of government or political power" and that "this right is inherent in every individual."

Library Bill of Rights

The American Library Association affirms that all libraries are forums for information and ideas, and that the following basic policies should guide their services.

1. Books and other library resources should be provided for the interest, information, and enlightenment of all people of the community the library serves. Materials should not be excluded because of the origin, background, or views of those contributing to their creation.

2. Libraries should provide materials and information presenting all points of view on current and historical issues. Materials should not be proscribed or removed because of partisan or doctrinal disapproval.

3. Libraries should challenge censorship in the fulfillment of their responsibility to provide information and enlightenment.

4. Libraries should cooperate with all persons and groups concerned with resisting abridgment of free expression and free access to ideas.

5. A person's right to use a library should not be denied or abridged because of origin, age, background, or views.

6. Libraries which make exhibit spaces and meeting rooms available to the public they serve should make such facilities available on an equitable basis, regardless of the beliefs or affiliations of individuals or groups requesting their use.

District of Columbia Voting Amendment (1961)

Residents of the District of Columbia were granted voting rights in presidential elections by the Twenty-third Amendment. Opposition to the Amendment came almost entirely from the Southern states, which at the time of the proposal (1960) did not want to enfranchise African Americans, who constitute a majority in the District. The District still has no congressional representation and very little control over its own internal affairs.

Also printed here is an inoperative part of the Constitution. Although passed by Congress in 1978, this proposed amendment failed to gain ratification by the states in a timely fashion. This amendment would have given the District of Columbia representation in Congress but would not have created statehood for the District of Columbia.

Amendment XXIII

Passed by Congress June 16, 1960. Ratified March 29, 1961.

Section 1.

The District constituting the seat of Government of the United States shall appoint in such manner as Congress may direct:

A number of electors of President and Vice President equal to the whole number of Senators and Representatives in Congress to which the District would be entitled if it were a State, but in no event more than the least populous State; they shall be in addition to those appointed by the States, but they shall be considered, for the purposes of the election of President and Vice President, to be electors appointed by a State; and they shall meet in the District and perform such duties as provided by the twelfth article of amendment.

Section 2. The Congress shall have power to enforce this article by appropriate legislation.

Inoperative Article

(Proposed 1978; Expired Unratified 1985)

Article—

Section. 1. For purposes of representation in the Congress, election of the President and Vice President, and article V of this Constitution, the District constituting the seat of government of the United States shall be treated as though it were a State.

Section. 2. The exercise of the rights and powers conferred under this article shall be by the people of the District constituting the seat of government, and as shall be provided by the Congress.

Section. 3. The twenty-third article of amendment to the Constitution of the United States is hereby repealed.

Section. 4. This article shall be inoperative, unless it shall have been ratified as an amendment to the Constitution by the legislatures of three-fourths of the several States within seven years from the date of its submission.

Excerpt From Dr. Martin Luther King's Speech at the Lincoln Memorial, Washington, DC (1963)

On August 28, 1963, over 250,000 people gathered together at the Lincoln Memorial in Washington, D.C., in order to raise the nation's awareness and concern on behalf of pending civil rights legislation being considered in Congress. During this demonstration Dr. Martin Luther King Jr. delivered his famous "I Have a Dream" speech that stated his vision of civil rights. This speech is a compelling modern reconstruction of the views of our early leaders, as expressed in the Bill of Rights and the Declaration of Independence. It also articulates the anguish and frustration of the long wait for racial justice in America.

I Have a Dream

In a sense we have come to our nation's capitol to cash a check. When the architects of our republic wrote the magnificent words of the Constitution and the Declaration of Independence, they were signing a promissory note to which every American was to fall heir. This note was a promise, yes black men as well as white men, would be guaranteed the inalienable rights of life, liberty, and the pursuit of happiness. It is obvious that America has defaulted on this promissory note insofar as her citizens of color are concerned. Instead of honoring this sacred obligation, America has given the Negro a bad check: a check which has come back marked "insufficient funds." But we refuse to believe that the bank of justice is bankrupt. We refuse to believe that there are insufficient funds in the great vaults of opportunity in this nation. So we have come to cash this check— a check that will give us upon demand the security of justice.

We have also come to this hallowed spot to remind America of the fierce urgency of now. This is not the time to engage in the luxury of cooling off or to take the tranquilizing drug of gradualism. Now is the time. To make real the promises of democracy. To rise from the dark and desolate valley of segregation to the sunlit path of racial justice, now is the time. To lift our nation from the quicksands of racial injustice to the solid rock of brotherhood, now is the time. To make justice a reality for all of God's children.

It would be fatal for the nation to overlook the urgency of the moment and to underestimate the determination of the Negro. The weltering summer of the Negro's legitimate discontent will not pass until there is an invigorating autumn of freedom and equality. Nineteen-hundred and sixty-three is not an end, but a beginning. Those who hope that the Negro needed to blow off steam and will now be content will have a rude awakening if the nation returns to business as usual. There will neither be rest nor tranquillity in America until the Negro is granted his citizenship rights. The whirlwinds of revolt will continue to shake the foundations of our nation until the bright day of justice emerges.

But there is something that I must say to my people who stand on the warm threshold which leads to the palace of justice. In the process of gaining our rightful place we must not be guilty of wrongful deeds. Let us not seek to satisfy our thirst for freedom by drinking from the cup of bitterness and hatred.

We must forever conduct our struggle on the high plane of dignity and discipline. We must not allow our creative protest to degenerate into physical violence. Again and again we must rise to the majestic heights of meeting physical force with soul force. The marvelous new militancy which has engulfed the Negro community must not lead us to a distrust of all white people, for many of our white brothers, as evidenced by their presence here today, have come to realize that their destiny is tied up with our destiny and their freedom is inextricably bound to our freedom. We cannot walk alone.

And as we walk, we must always make the pledge that we shall always march ahead. We cannot turn back. There will be those who will ask the devotees of civil rights, "when will you be satisfied?" We can never be satisfied as long as the Negro is the victim of unspeakable horrors of police brutality. We can never be satisfied as long as our bodies, heavy with the fatigue of travel, cannot gain lodging in the motels of the highways or the hotels of the cities. We cannot be satisfied as long as the Negro's basic mobility is from a smaller ghetto to a larger one. We can never be satisfied as long as our children are stripped of their selfhood and robbed of their dignity by signs reading, "For Whites Only." We can never be satisfied as long as a Negro in Mississippi cannot vote and a Negro in New York believes that he has nothing for which to vote. No. No we are not satisfied, and we will not be satisfied until justice rolls like water and righteousness like a mighty stream.

I am not unmindful that some of you have come here out of great trials and tribulations. Some of you have come fresh from narrow jail cells. Some of you have come from areas where your quest for freedom left you battered by the storms of persecution and staggered by the winds of police brutality. You have been victims of creative suffering. Continue to work with the faith that unearned suffering is redemptive.

Go back to Mississippi, go back to Alabama, go back to Georgia, go back to Louisiana, go back to the slums and ghettos of our northern cities, knowing that the situation can and will be changed. Let us not wallow in the valley of despair.

I say to you, my friends, that in spite of the difficulties and frustrations of the moment, I still have a dream. I have a dream deeply rooted in the American dream. I have a dream that one day this nation will rise up and live out the true meaning of its creed: "We hold these truths to be self-evident—that all men are created equal."

I have a dream that one day on the red hills of Georgia the sons of former slaves will be able to sit together at the table of brotherhood. I have a dream that even in the state of Mississippi, a desert state sweltering with the heat of injustice and oppression, will be transformed into an oasis of freedom and justice.

I have a dream that my four children will one day live in a nation where they will not be judged by the color of their skin but by the content of their character.

I have a dream today.

I have a dream that one day the state of Alabama, whose governor's lips are presently dripping with the words of interposition and nullification, will be transformed into a situation where little black boys and black girls will be able to join hands with little white boys and little white girls and walk together as sisters and brothers.

I have a dream today.

I have a dream that one day every valley shall be exalted, every hill and mountain shall be made low, the rough places will be made plain, and the crooked places will be made straight, and the glory of the Lord shall be revealed, and all flesh shall see it together.

This is our hope. This is the faith with which I return to the South. With this faith we will be able to transform the jangling discords of our nation into a beautiful symphony of brotherhood. With this faith we will be able to work together, to pray together, to struggle together, to go to jail together, to stand up for freedom together, knowing that we will be free one day.

This will be the day when all of God's children will be able to sing with a new meaning "My country 'tis of thee, sweet land of liberty, of thee I sing. Land where my fathers died, land of the pilgrim's pride, from every mountainside, let freedom ring."

And if America is to be a great nation this must become true. So let freedom ring from the prodigious hilltops of New Hampshire! Let freedom ring from the mighty mountains of New York! Let freedom ring from the heightening Alleghenies of Pennsylvania!

Let freedom ring from the curvaceous peaks of California!

But not only that; let freedom ring from Stone Mountain of Georgia!

Let freedom ring from every hill and every mole hill of Mississippi. From every mountainside, let freedom ring.

When we let freedom ring, when we let it ring from every village and every hamlet, from every state and every city, we will all be able to speed up that day when all God's children, black men and white men, Jews and Gentiles, Protestants and Catholics, will be able to join hands and sing in the words of that old Negro spiritual, "Free at last! Free at last! Thank God almighty, we are free at last!"

The Universal Declaration of Human Rights

The Universal Declaration of Human Rights was adopted by the General Assembly of the United Nations on November 10, 1948, by a vote of 48 nations to none with 8 abstentions. The adoption of the Declaration without dessent shows that the governments of the world were ready in 1948 to consider expanding the concepts of rights to its broadest limits. No nation has embodied these rights ideals fully in its internal laws, yet the preamble claims that the member states are pledged to these ideals. As a statement of future goals there is no better place to turn than the Universal Declaration of Human Rights, one of the most important rights documents ever written.

Preamble

Whereas recognition of the inherent dignity and of the equal and inalienable rights of all members of the human family is the foundation of freedom, justice and peace in the world,

Whereas disregard and contempt for human rights have resulted in barbarous acts which have outraged the conscience of mankind, and the advent of a world in which human beings shall enjoy freedom of speech and belief and freedom from fear and want has been proclaimed as the highest aspiration of the common people,

Whereas it is essential, if man is not to be compelled to have recourse, as a last resort, to rebellion against tyranny and oppression, that human rights should be protected by the rule of law,

Whereas it is essential to promote the development of friendly relations between nations,

Whereas the peoples of the United Nations have in the Charter reaffirmed their faith in fundamental human rights, in the dignity and worth of the human person and in the equal rights of men and women and have determined to promote social progress and better standards of life in larger freedom,

Whereas Member States have pledged themselves to achieve, in co-operation with the United Nations, the promotion of universal respect for and observance of human rights and fundamental freedoms,

Whereas a common understanding of these rights and freedoms is of the greatest importance for the full realization of this pledge,

Now, therefore,

The General Assembly

Proclaims this Universal Declaration of Human Rights as a common standard of achievement for all peoples and all nations, to the end that every individual and every organ of society, keeping this Declaration constantly in mind, shall strive by teaching and education to promote respect for these rights and freedoms and by progressive measures, national and international, to secure their universal and effective recognition and observance, both among the peoples of Member States themselves and among the peoples of territories under their jurisdiction.

Article 1

All human beings are born free and equal in dignity and rights. They are endowed with reason and conscience and should act towards one another in a spirit of brotherhood.

Article 2

Everyone is entitled to all the rights and freedoms set forth in this Declaration, without distinction of any kind, such as race, colour, sex, language, religion, political or other opinion, national or social origin, property, birth or other status.

Furthermore, no distinction shall be made on the basis of the political, jurisdictional or international status of the country or territory to which a person belongs, whether it be independent, trust, non-self-governing or under any other limitation of sovereignty.

Article 3

Everyone has the right to life, liberty and the security of person.

Article 4

No one shall be held in slavery or servitude; slavery and the slave trade shall be prohibited in all their forms.

Article 5

No one shall be subjected to torture or to cruel, inhuman or degrading treatment or punishment.

Article 6

Everyone has the right to recognition everywhere as a person before the law.

Article 7

All are equal before the law and are entitled without any discrimination to equal protection against any discrimination in violation of this Declaration and against any incitement to such discrimination.

Article 8

Everyone has the right to an effective remedy by the competent national tribunals for acts violating the fundamental rights granted him by the constitution or by law.

Article 9

No one shall be subjected to arbitrary arrest, detention or exile.

Article 10

Everyone is entitled in full equality to a fair and public hearing by an independent and impartial tribunal, in the determination of his rights and obligations and of any criminal charge against him.

Article 11

1. Everyone charged with a penal offense has the right to be presumed innocent until proven guilty according to law in a public

trial at which he has had all the guarantees necessary for his defense.

2. No one shall be held guilty of any penal offense on account of any act or omission which did not constitute a penal offense, under national or international law, at the time when it was committed. Nor shall a heavier penalty be imposed than the one that was applicable at the time the penal offense was committed.

Article 12

No one shall be subjected to arbitrary interference with his privacy, family, home or correspondence, nor to attacks upon his honour and reputation. Everyone has the right to the protection of the law against such interference or attacks.

Article 13

1. Everyone has the right to freedom of movement and residence within the borders of each State.

2. Everyone has the right to leave any country, including his own, and to return to his country.

Article 14

1. Everyone has the right to seek and to enjoy in other countries asylum from persecution.

2. This right may not be invoked in the case of prosecutions genuinely arising from non-political crimes or from acts contrary to the purposes and principles of the United Nations.

Article 15

1. Everyone has the right to a nationality.

2. No one shall be arbitrarily deprived of his nationality nor denied the right to change his nationality.

Article 16

1. Men and women of full age, without any limitation due to race, nationality or religion, have the right to marry and to found a family. They are entitled to equal rights as to marriage, during marriage and at its dissolution.

2. Marriage shall be entered into only with the free and full consent of the intending spouses.

3. The family is the natural and fundamental group unit of society and is entitled to protection by society and the State.

Article 17

1. Everyone has the right to own property alone as well as in association with others.

2. No one shall be arbitrarily deprived of his property.

Article 18

Everyone has the right to freedom of thought, conscience and religion; this right includes freedom to change his religion or belief, and freedom, either alone or in community with others and in public or private, to manifest his religion or belief in teaching, practice, worship and observance.

Article 19

Everyone has the right to freedom of opinion and expression; this right receive and impart information and ideas through any media and regardless of frontiers.

Article 20

1. Everyone has the right to freedom of peaceful assembly and association.

2. No one may be compelled to belong to an association.

Article 21

1. Everyone has the right to take part in the government of his country, directly or through freely chosen representatives.

2. Everyone has the right of equal access to public service in his country.

3. The will of the people shall be the basis of the authority of government; this shall be expressed in periodic and genuine elections which shall be by universal and equal suffrage and shall be held by secret vote or by equivalent free voting procedures.

Article 22

Everyone, as a member of society, has the right to social security and is entitled to realization, through national effort and international cooperation and in accordance with the organization and resources of each State, of the economic, social and cultural rights indispensable for his dignity and the free development of his personality.

Article 23

1. Everyone has the right to work, to free choice of employment, to just and favourable condi-

tions of work and to protection against unemployment.

2. Everyone, without any discrimination, has the right to equal pay for equal work.

3. Everyone who works has the right to just and favourable remuneration ensuring for himself and his family an existence worthy of human dignity, and supplemented, if necessary, by other means of social protection.

4. Everyone has the right to form and to join trade unions for the protection of his interests.

Article 24

Everyone has the right to rest and leisure, including reasonable limitation of working hours and periodic holidays with pay.

Article 25

1. Everyone has the right to a standard of living adequate for the health and well-being of himself and of his family, including food, clothing, housing and medical care and necessary social services, and the right to security in the event of unemployment, sickness, disability, widowhood, old age or other lack of livelihood in circumstances beyond his control.

2. Motherhood and childhood are entitled to special care and assistance. All children, whether born in or out of wedlock, shall enjoy the same social protection.

Article 26

1. Everyone has the right to education. Education shall be free, at least in the elementary and fundamental stages. Elementary education shall be compulsory. Technical and professional education shall be made generally available and higher education shall be equally accessible to all on the basis of merit.

2. Education shall be directed to the full development of the human personality and to the strengthening of respect for human rights and fundamental freedoms. It shall promote understanding, tolerance and friendship among all nations, racial or religious groups, and shall further the activities of the United Nations for the maintenance of peace.

3. Parents have a prior right to choose the kind of education that shall be given to their children.

Article 27

1. Everyone has the right freely to participate in the cultural life of the community, to enjoy the arts and to share in scientific advancement and its benefits.

2. Everyone has the right to the protection of the moral and material interests resulting from any scientific, literary or artistic production of which he is the author.

Article 28

Everyone is entitled to a social and international order in which the rights and freedoms set forth in this Declaration can be fully realized.

Article 29

1. Everyone has duties to the community in which alone the free and full development of his personality is possible.

2. In the exercise of his rights and freedoms, everyone shall be subject only to such limitations as are determined by law solely for the purpose of securing due recognition and respect for the rights and freedoms of others and of meeting the just requirements of morality, public order and the general welfare in a democratic society.

3. These rights and freedoms may in no case be exercised contrary to the purposes and principles of the United Nations.

Article 30

Nothing in this Declaration may be interpreted as implying for any State, group or person any right to engage in any activity or to perform any act aimed at the destruction of any of the rights and freedoms set forth herein.

The Poll Tax Amendment (1964)

During the 1890s a number of southern states turned to the poll tax as a way of maintaining white supremacy. As a precondition for voting, this tax at first had impact upon the voting rights of poor whites as well as poor African Americans. Later, some voting registrars learned to use the tax mostly against African Americans, by requiring them to produce receipts of poll tax payment—an obligation not imposed on white voters.

Many attempts to abolish the poll tax in federal elections failed in Congress. When the Twenty-fourth Amendment was finally submitted to the states in 1962 it forbade the use of the poll tax only in federal elections, being worded in a manner that did not refer to state elections. Two years later the Supreme Court, in Harper *v.* Virginia Board of Elections *(1966), held that requiring the payment of a poll tax as a precondition for voting in state elections violated the equal protection of the laws guarantee of the Fourteenth Amendment. Since then the poll tax has virtually disappeared.*

Amendment XXIV

Passed by Congress August 27, 1962. Ratified January 23, 1964.

Section 1. The right of citizens of the United States to vote in any primary or other election for President or Vice President, for electors for President or Vice President, or for Senator or Representative in Congress, shall not be denied or abridged by the United States or any State by reason of failure to pay poll tax or other tax.

Section 2. The Congress shall have power to enforce this article by appropriate legislation.

Youth Voting Rights (1971)

The most recent constitutional rights development was the ratification of the Twenty-sixth Amendment in 1971. The lowering of the voting age to 18 improves upon the rights bestowed in the Fourteenth Amendment, which made 21 the age of voting and representation. Advocates of the Twenty-sixth Amendment contended that it was unjust to require young people to serve their nation in the military, while denying them the vote. Opponents of the Amendment feared that young people were too immature and too subject to the influence of their teachers to cast an intelligent vote. These fears were swept aside in this important step to broaden the rights of young people.

The very rapid ratification of the Twenty-sixth Amendment shows that it was widely supported throughout the nation. It is interesting to note that unlike the poll tax amendment of 1964 and the District of Columbia voting amendment of 1961, the Twenty-sixth Amendment applies to all elections.

Amendment XXVI

Passed by Congress March 23, 1971. Ratified July 1, 1971.

Note: Amendment 14, Section 2, of the Constitution was modified by Section 1 of the Twenty-sixth Amendment.

Section 1. The right of citizens of the United States, who are eighteen years of age or older, to vote shall not be denied or abridged by the United States or by any State on account of age.

Section 2. The Congress shall have power to enforce this article by appropriate legislation.

United States Code, Civil Rights Provisions (1871–present)

Virtually all the various statutes enacted over the course of American history by the national government are collated into the United States Code. The United States Code is a convenient means provided by Congress of gathering together various statutory provisions and organizing this material into coherent public policies. Since civil rights policies are frequently based in statutes, and these statutes are often amended, it is one task of the U.S. Code to give an accurate statement of the latest version of those policies, incorporating all changes. Readers can consult this title in any large public library to find updated changes in the statutes surrounding civil rights.

Title 42, chapter 21 is the civil rights section of the statutes of the United States, which contains the most basic civil rights policies in force. The first three sections excerpted here are the most important, in terms of the civil rights of Americans. The passages printed are used by the lawyers for the U.S. Justice Department to give specific implementation to the various national civil rights statutes, and by individuals to sue for their rights before federal courts.

Each of these sections is the result of civil rights statutes passed at different times in American history and are a vital part of the machinery of justice in America. Section 1981 states the general principles of equal rights are derived from the amended Constitution and bestow equal rights to African Americans "as enjoyed by white citizens." Sections 1983 and 1985 give a victim of rights deprivation a right to sue the perpetrator for damages for the injuries caused.

One of the oldest provisions is Section 1983, the second excerpt. As originally enacted in 1871, this section was intended to protect the rights of the newly freed slaves. It has been interpreted in various ways over the years but currently serves as the major weapon to uphold individual rights against the actions of states, municipalities, or other individuals. This section is vital to an understanding of rights in America.

Section 1985 is even broader than 1983 and was originally passed just after the Civil War. It was aimed at criminal conspiracies and all other efforts to interfere with voting, arrests, and fair trials. The statute forbids intimidation of parties, officials, or witnesses. Actions for damages by those deprived of their rights is made possible by this section.

§ 1981. Equal rights under the law

(a) Statement of equal rights

All persons within the jurisdiction of the United States shall have the same right in every State and Territory to make and enforce contracts, to sue, be parties, give evidence, and to the full and equal benefit of all laws and proceedings for the security of persons and property as is enjoyed by white citizens, and shall be subject to like punishment, pains, penalties, taxes, licenses, and exactions of every kind, and to no other.

(b) "Make and enforce contracts" defined

For purposes of this section, the term "make and enforce contracts" includes the making, performance, modification, and termination of contracts, and the enjoyment of all benefits, privileges, terms, and conditions of the contractual relationship.

(c) Protection against impairment

The rights protected by this section are protected against impairment by nongovernmental discrimination and impairment under color of State law.

§ 1983. Civil action for deprivation of rights

Every person who, under color of any statute, ordinance, regulation, custom, or usage, of any State or Territory or the District of Columbia, subjects, or causes to be subjected, any citizen of the United States or other person within the jurisdiction thereof to the deprivation of any rights, privileges, or immunities secured by the Constitution and laws, shall be liable to the party injured in an action at law, suit in equity, or other proper proceeding for redress. For the purposes of this section, any Act of Congress applicable exclusively to the District of Columbia shall be considered to be a statute of the District of Columbia.

§ 1985. Conspiracy to interfere with civil rights

(1) Preventing officer from performing duties

If two or more persons in any State or Territory conspire to prevent, by force, intimidation, or threat, any person from accepting or holding any office, trust, or place of confidence under the United States, or from discharging any duties thereof; or to induce by like means any officer of the United States to leave any State, district, or place, where his duties as an officer are required to be performed, or to injure him in his person or property on account of his lawful discharge of the duties of his office, or while engaged in the lawful discharge thereof, or to injure his property so as to molest, interrupt, hinder, or impede him in the discharge of his official duties;

(2) Obstructing justice; intimidating party, witness, or juror

If two or more persons in any State or Territory conspire to deter, by force, intimidation, or threat, any party or witness in any court of the United States from attending such court, or from testifying to any matter pending therein, freely, fully, and truthfully, or to injure such party or witness in his person or property on account of his having so attended or testified, or to influence the verdict, presentment, or indictment of any grand or petit juror in any such court, or to injure such juror in his person or property on account of any verdict, presentment, or indictment lawfully assented to by him, or of his being or having been such juror; or if two or more persons conspire for the purpose of impeding, hindering, obstructing, or defeating, in any manner, the due course of justice in any State or Territory, with intent to deny to any citizen the equal protection of the laws, or to injure him or his property for lawfully enforcing, or attempting to enforce, the right of any person, or class of persons, to the equal protection of the laws;

(3) Depriving persons of rights or privileges

If two or more persons in any State or Territory conspire or go in disguise on the highway or on the premises of another, for the purpose of depriving, either directly or indirectly, any person or class of persons of the equal protection of the laws, or of equal privileges and immunities under the laws; or for the purpose of preventing or hindering the constituted authorities of any State or Territory from giving or securing to all persons within such State or Territory the equal protection of the laws; or if two or more persons conspire to prevent by force, intimidation, or threat, any citizen who is lawfully entitled to vote, from giving his support or advocacy in a legal manner, toward or in favor of the election of any lawfully qualified person as an elector for President or Vice President, or as a Member of Congress of the United States; or to injure any citizen in person or property on account of such support or advocacy; in any case of conspiracy set forth in this section, if one or more persons engaged therein do, or cause to be done, any act in furtherance of the object of such conspiracy, whereby another is injured in his person or property, or deprived of having and exercising any right or privilege of a citizen of the United States, the party so injured or deprived may have an action for the recovery of damages occasioned by such injury or deprivation, against any one or more of the conspirators.

Peonage

Slavery was abolished by the ratification of the Thirteenth Amendment in 1865. However, other forms of forced labor or debt peonage still persist. Most cases of peonage occur with domestic servants who are compelled to work without pay, or for food and shelter only. Other recent cases involve sweatshop garment laborers and others doing unpaid factory work. Actual physical restraint applied against workers to compel them to work is also clearly unlawful under this statute.

§ 1994. Peonage abolished

The holding of any person to service or labor under the system known as peonage is abolished and forever prohibited in any Territory or State of the United States; and all acts, laws, resolutions, orders, regulations, or usages of any Territory or State, which have heretofore established, maintained, or enforced, or by virtue of which any attempt shall hereafter be made to establish, maintain, or enforce, directly or indirectly, the voluntary or involuntary service or labor of any persons as peons, in liquidation of any debt or obligation, or otherwise, are declared null and void.

Voting Rights Legislation

Voting rights are essential in a democracy. The Voting Rights Act of 1965 *is the basic rights document for an understanding of this important right. However, the statute has been amended many times since 1965. What appears here are extracts from the current operative provisions of the* Voting Rights Act.

§ 1971. Voting rights

(a) Race, color, or previous condition not to affect right to vote; uniform standards for voting qualifications; errors or omissions from papers; literacy tests; agreements between Attorney General and State or local authorities; definitions

(1) All citizens of the United States who are otherwise qualified by law to vote at any election by the people in any State, Territory, district, county, city, parish, township, school district, municipality, or other territorial subdivision, shall be entitled and allowed to vote at all such elections, without distinction of race, color, or previous condition of servitude; any constitution, law, custom, usage, or regulation of any State or Territory, or by or under its authority, to the contrary notwithstanding.

(2) No person acting under color of law shall—

(A) in determining whether any individual is qualified under State law or laws to vote in any election, apply any standard, practice, or procedure different from the standards, practices, or procedures applied under such law or laws to other individuals within the same county, parish, or similar political subdivision who have been found by State officials to be qualified to vote;

(B) deny the right of any individual to vote in any election because of an error or omission on any record or paper relating to any application, registration, or other act requisite to voting, if such error or omission is not material in determining whether such individual is qualified under State law to vote in such election; or

(C) employ any literacy test as a qualification for voting in any election unless (i) such test is administered to each individual and is conducted wholly in writing, and (ii) a certified copy of the test and of the answers given by the individual is furnished to him within twenty-five days of the submission of his request made within the period of time during which records and papers are required to be retained and preserved pursuant to title III of the Civil Rights Act of 1960 (42 U.S.C. 1974 et seq.): Provided, however, That the Attorney General may enter into agreements with appropriate State or local authorities that preparation, conduct, and maintenance of such tests in accordance with the provisions of applicable State or local law, including such special provisions as are necessary in the preparation, conduct, and maintenance of such tests for persons who are blind or otherwise physically handicapped, meet the purposes of this subparagraph and constitute compliance therewith.

(3) For purposes of this subsection -

(A) the term "vote" shall have the same meaning as in subsection (e) of this section;

(B) the phrase "literacy test" includes any test of the ability to read, write, understand, or interpret any matter.

(b) Intimidation, threats, or coercion

No person, whether acting under color of law or otherwise, shall intimidate, threaten, coerce, or attempt to intimidate, threaten, or coerce any other person for the purpose of interfering with the right of such other person to vote or to vote as he may choose, or of causing such other person to vote for, or not to vote for, any candidate for the office of President, Vice President, presidential elector, Member of the Senate, or Member of the House of Representatives, Delegates or Commissioners from the Territories or possessions, at any general, special, or primary election held solely or in part for the purpose of selecting or electing any such candidate.

(c) Preventive relief; injunction; rebuttable literacy presumption liability of United States for costs; State as party defendant

Whenever any person has engaged or there are reasonable grounds to believe that any person is about to engage in any act or practice which would deprive any other person of any right or privilege secured by subsection (a) or (b) of this section, the Attorney General may institute for the United States, or in the name of the United States, a civil action or other proper proceeding for preventive relief, including an application for a permanent or temporary injunction, restraining order, or other order. If in any such proceeding literacy is a relevant fact there shall be a rebuttable presumption that any person who has not been adjudged an incompetent and who has completed the sixth grade in a public school in, or a private school accredited by, any State or territory, the District of Columbia, or the Commonwealth of Puerto Rico where instruction is carried on predominantly in the English language, possesses sufficient literacy, comprehension, and intelligence to vote in any election. In any proceeding hereunder the United States shall be liable for costs the same as a private person. Whenever, in a proceeding instituted under this subsection any official of a State or subdivision thereof is alleged to have committed any act or practice constituting a deprivation of any right or privilege secured by subsection (a) of this section, the act or practice shall also be deemed that of the State and the State may be joined as a party defendant and, if, prior to the institution of such proceeding, such official has resigned or has been relieved of his office and no successor has assumed such office, the proceeding may be instituted against the State.

(d) Jurisdiction; exhaustion of other remedies

The district courts of the United States shall have jurisdiction of proceedings instituted pursuant to this section and shall exercise the same without regard to whether the party aggrieved shall have exhausted any administrative or other remedies that may be provided by law.

(e) Order qualifying person to vote; application; hearing; voting referees; transmittal of report and order; certificate of qualification; definitions

In any proceeding instituted pursuant to subsection (c) of this section in the event the court finds that any person has been deprived on account of race or color of any right or privilege secured by subsection (a) of this section, the court shall upon request of the Attorney General and after each party has been given notice and the opportunity to be heard make a finding whether such deprivation was or is pursuant to a pattern or practice. If the court finds such pattern or practice, any person of such race or color resident within the affected area shall, for one year and thereafter until the court subsequently finds that such pattern or practice has ceased, be entitled, upon his application therefor, to an order declaring him qualified to vote, upon proof that at any election or elections (1) he is qualified under State law to vote, and (2) he has since such finding by the court been (a) deprived of or denied under color of law the opportunity to register to vote or otherwise to qualify to vote, or (b) found not qualified to vote by any person acting under color of law. Such order shall be effective as to any election held within the longest period for which such applicant could have been registered or otherwise qualified under State law at which the applicant's qualifications would under State law entitle him to vote.

Native American Religious Rights

Native American religious rights have been recognized by statute only in the past few decades. This section of the U.S. Code expresses those rights. One of the many controversies that have arisen surrounding religious rights concerns the many Native American materials found in museum collections around the country.

§ 1996. Protection and preservation of traditional religions of Native Americans

On and after August 11, 1978, it shall be the policy of the United States to protect and preserve for American Indians their inherent right of freedom to believe, express, and exercise the traditional religions of the American Indian, Eskimo, Aleut, and Native Hawaiians, including but not limited to access to sites, use and possession of sacred objects, and the freedom to worship through ceremonials and traditional rites.

Civil Rights Act of 1964

The most prominent federal civil rights legislation since the Civil War is the Civil Rights Act of 1964. *Decisions of the Supreme Court, decided after the Fourteenth Amendment was ratified, limited the Congressional power to enforce the Fourteenth Amendment to the prohibition of state action. (Since 1964 the Supreme Court has changed its position and expanded the reach of the Fourteenth Amendment to include some acts of private discrimination.) In order to include the*

actions of individuals who were violating the civil rights of other Americans, Congress enacted the Civil Rights Act of 1964 *under its power to regulate interstate commerce. Discrimination based on "race, color, religion, or national origin" in public establishments that had a connection to interstate commerce or was supported by the state is prohibited. (See 42 U.S.C. § 2000a.) Public establishments include places of public accommodation (e.g., hotels, motels, trailer parks), restaurants, gas stations, bars, taverns, and places of entertainment in general. This legislation was passed in response to the civil rights movement of the early 1960s.*

§ 2000a. Prohibition against discrimination or segregation in places of public accommodation

(a) Equal access

All persons shall be entitled to the full and equal enjoyment of the goods, services, facilities, privileges, advantages, and accommodations of any place of public accommodation, as defined in this section, without discrimination or segregation on the ground of race, color, religion, or national origin.

(b) Establishments affecting interstate commerce or supported in their activities by State action as places of public accommodation; lodgings; facilities principally engaged in selling food for consumption on the premises; gasoline stations; places of exhibition or entertainment; other covered establishments

Each of the following establishments which serves the public is a place of public accommodation within the meaning of this subchapter if its operations affect commerce, or if discrimination or segregation by it is supported by State action:

(1) any inn, hotel, motel, or other establishment which provides lodging to transient guests, other than an establishment located within a building which contains not more than five rooms for rent or hire and which is actually occupied by the proprietor of such establishment as his residence;

(2) any restaurant, cafeteria, lunchroom, lunch counter, soda fountain, or other facility principally engaged in selling food for consumption on the premises, including, but not limited to, any such facility located on the premises of any retail establishment; or any gasoline station;

(3) any motion picture house, theater, concert hall, sports arena, stadium or other place of exhibition or entertainment; and

(4) any establishment (A)(i) which is physically located within the premises of any establishment otherwise covered by this subsection, or (ii) within the premises of which is physically located any such covered establishment, and (B) which holds itself out as serving patrons of such covered establishment.

Equal Pay Act of 1963

Title 29 (Labor), chapter 8 of the United States Code contains the relevant provisions of the Equal Pay Act of 1963. *This section is most used to protect women against wage discrimination by employers. This section of the Code is merged with Fair Labor Standard and minimum wage provisions. Women have other employment rights scattered throughout the U.S. Code, but these are the most basic. (Below is an excerpt from section 206(d) of 29 U.S.C.A.)*

(d) Prohibition of sex discrimination

(1) No employer having employees subject to any provisions of this section shall discriminate, within any establishment in which such employees are employed, between employees on the basis of sex by paying wages to employees in such establishment at a rate less than the rate at which he pays wages to employees of the opposite sex in such establishment for equal work on jobs the performance of which requires equal skill, effort, and responsibility, and which are performed under similar working conditions, except where such payment is made pursuant to (i) a seniority system; (ii) a merit system; (iii) a system which measures earnings by quantity or quality of production; or (iv) a differential based on any other factor other than sex: Provided, That an employer who is paying a wage rate differential in violation of this subsection shall not, in order to comply with the provisions of this subsection, reduce the wage rate of any employee.

(2) No labor organization, or its agents, representing employees of an employer having employees subject to any provisions of this section shall cause or attempt to cause such an employer to discriminate against an employee in violation of paragraph (1) of this subsection.

(3) For purposes of administration and enforcement, any amounts owing to any employee which have been withheld in violation of this subsection shall be deemed to be unpaid minimum wages or unpaid overtime compensation under this chapter.

(4) As used in this subsection, the term "labor organization" means any organization of any kind, or any agency or employee representation committee or plan, in which employees participate and which exists for the purpose, in whole or in part, of dealing with employers concerning grievances, labor disputes, wages, rates of pay, hours of employment, or conditions of work.

Age Discrimination Act of 1967

Title 29 (Labor), chapter 14 of the U.S. Code provides a precise statement of federal age discrimination policy, derived from the Age Discrimination Act of 1967. *Section 623 provides an overview of that policy.*

§ 623. Prohibition of age discrimination

(a) Employer practices

It shall be unlawful for an employer -

(1) to fail or refuse to hire or to discharge any individual or otherwise discriminate against any individual with respect to his compensation, terms, conditions, or privileges of employment, because of such individual's age;

(2) to limit, segregate, or classify his employees in any way which would deprive or tend to deprive any individual of employment opportunities or otherwise adversely affect his status as an employee, because of such individual's age; or

(3) to reduce the wage rate of any employee in order to comply with this chapter.

(b) Employment agency practices

It shall be unlawful for an employment agency to fail or refuse to refer for employment, or otherwise to discriminate against, any individual because of such individual's age, or to classify or refer for employment any individual on the basis of such individual's age.

(c) Labor organization practices

It shall be unlawful for a labor organization -

(1) to exclude or to expel from its membership, or otherwise to discriminate against, any individual because of his age;

(2) to limit, segregate, or classify its membership, or to classify or fail or refuse to refer for employment any individual, in any way which would deprive or tend to deprive any individual of employment opportunities, or would limit such employment opportunities or otherwise adversely affect his status as an employee or as an applicant for employment, because of such individual's age;

(3) to cause or attempt to cause an employer to discriminate against an individual in violation of this section.

(d) Opposition to unlawful practices; participation in investigations, proceedings, or litigation

It shall be unlawful for an employer to discriminate against any of his employees or applicants for employment, for an employment agency to discriminate against any individual, or for a labor organization to discriminate against any member thereof or applicant for membership, because such individual, member or applicant for membership has opposed any practice made unlawful by this section, or because such individual, member or applicant for membership has made a charge, testified, assisted, or participated in any manner in an investigation, proceeding, or litigation under this chapter.

(e) Printing or publication of notice or advertisement indicating preference, limitation, etc.

It shall be unlawful for an employer, labor organization, or employment agency to print or publish, or cause to be printed or published, any notice or advertisement relating to employment by such an employer or membership in or any classification or referral for employment by such a labor organization, or relating to any classification or referral for employment by such an employment agency, indicating any preference, limitation, specification, or discrimination, based on age.

(f) Lawful practices; age an occupational qualification; other reasonable factors; laws of foreign workplace; seniority system; employee benefit plans; discharge or discipline for good cause

It shall not be unlawful for an employer, employment agency, or labor organization -

(1) to take any action otherwise prohibited under subsections (a), (b), (c), or (e) of this section where age is a bona fide occupational qualification reasonably necessary to the normal operation of the particular business, or where the differentiation is based on reasonable factors other than age, or where such practices involve an employee in a workplace in a foreign country, and compliance with such subsections would cause such employer, or a corporation controlled by such employer, to violate the laws of the country in which such workplace is located;

(2) to take any action otherwise prohibited under subsection (a), (b), (c), or (e) of this section-

(A) to observe the terms of a bona fide seniority system that is not intended to evade the purposes of this chapter, except that no such seniority system shall require or permit the involuntary retirement of any individual specified by section 631(a) of this title because of the age of such individual; or

(B) to observe the terms of a bona fide employee benefit plan -

(I) where, for each benefit or benefit package, the actual amount of payment made or cost incurred on behalf of an older worker is no less than that made or incurred on behalf of a younger worker, as permissible under section 1625.10, title 29, Code of Federal Regulation (as in effect on June 22, 1989); or

(ii) that is a voluntary early retirement incentive plan consistent with the relevant purpose or purposes of this chapter . . .

(3) to discharge or otherwise discipline an individual for good cause.

Disabilities Act of 1990

The essential elements of the Disabilities Act of 1990 *are found in the U.S. Code. The opening sections of those provisions are extracted here. The official title of this anti-discrimination section is Title 42—The Public Health And Welfare—Chapter 126—Equal Opportunity For Individuals With Disabilities, Subchapter I—Employment. The full statute, and the many administrative interpretations of it are, as with all public policies, far more complicated than this extract can show.*

§ 12112. Discrimination

(a) General rule

No covered entity shall discriminate against a qualified individual with a disability because of the disability of such individual in regard to job application procedures, the hiring, advancement, or discharge of employees, employee compensation, job training, and other terms, conditions, and privileges of employment.

(b) Construction

As used in subsection (a) of this section, the term "discriminate" includes -

(1) limiting, segregating, or classifying a job applicant or employee in a way that adversely affects the opportunities or status of such applicant or employee because of the disability of such applicant or employee;

(2) participating in a contractual or other arrangement or relationship that has the effect of subjecting a covered entity's qualified applicant or employee with a disability to the discrimination prohibited by this subchapter (such relationship includes a relationship with an employment or referral agency, labor union, an organization providing fringe benefits to an employee of the covered entity, or an organization providing training and apprenticeship programs);

(3) utilizing standards, criteria, or methods of administration -

(A) that have the effect of discrimination on the basis of disability; or

(B) that perpetuate the discrimination of others who are subject to common administrative control;

(4) excluding or otherwise denying equal jobs or benefits to a qualified individual because of the known disability of an individual with whom the qualified individual is known to have a relationship or association;

(5) (A) not making reasonable accommodations to the known physical or mental limitations of an otherwise qualified individual with a disability who is an applicant or employee, unless such covered entity can demonstrate that the accommodation would impose an undue hardship on the operation of the business of such covered entity; or

(B) denying employment opportunities to a job applicant or employee who is an otherwise qualified individual with a disability, if such denial is based on the need of such covered entity to make reasonable accommodation to the physical or mental impairments of the employee or applicant;

(6) using qualification standards, employment tests or other selection criteria that screen out or tend to screen out an individual with a disability or a class of individuals with disabilities unless the standard, test or other selection criteria, as used by the covered entity, is shown to be job-related for the position in question and is consistent with business necessity; and

(7) failing to select and administer tests concerning employment in the most effective manner to ensure that, when such test is administered to a job applicant or employee who has a disability that impairs sensory, manual, or speaking skills, such test results accurately reflect the skills, aptitude, or whatever other factor of such applicant or employee that such test purports to measure, rather than reflecting the impaired sensory, manual, or speaking skills of such employee or applicant (except where such skills are the factors that the test purports to measure).

Chapter 18

The Major Civil Rights
Case Decisions

Jay A. Sigler

The words and phrases of the Constitution, the Bill of Rights, the Civil War
Amendments, and civil rights legislation do not describe the full meaning of
American rights. The national Supreme Court has become a leading source of
interpretation of the rights of Americans. To obtain a more precise understanding
of those rights a few of the most important Supreme Court decisions are presented here. These cases should be read with care, but even if every phrase is not
quickly grasped, taken together they reveal the slow, gradual expansion of American rights.

This collection of cases reveals the modern development of civil rights.
Most of these cases arose late in the twentieth century. Few civil rights decisions
of any serious significance were made prior to World War I, apart from some
post-Civil War decisions that limited the scope of the Fourteenth and Fifteenth
Amendments.

Prior to emancipation in the nineteenth century, the Supreme Court endorsed
slavery and largely ignored minority rights issues. In the eyes of the Court the
Bill of Rights did not seem to apply to such matters. In fact, in 1833 the Supreme
Court held that the federal Constitution's Bill of Rights did not even apply to the
states—a position that it altered only in 1925. Since then most of the Bill of
Rights has been extended to cover state actions.

The Supreme Court became a major source of fundamental rights during the
twentieth century. No one can say what the next century will hold, yet the cases
printed here reveal a strong trend towards a broader and more generous view of
American rights. If the past is any guide, we may expect more and more new
rights to emerge from judicial interpretations of the Constitution and of major
civil rights statutes.

Dred Scott v. Sandford
60 U.S. 393 (1856)

Dred Scott was a Missouri slave owned by an army officer, John Emerson. Emerson took Scott to military posts in Illinois and on federal territory north of the line drawn by the Missouri Compromise (the controversial Fugitive Slave Law of 1850), where slavery had been prohibited by an act of Congress. Scott claimed that he had been emancipated by virtue of his residence on free soil, and sued in Missouri courts for his freedom.

When the suit began Dred Scott was a resident of New York State. Scott returned to Missouri in 1852 to begin another suit for his freedom. The Missouri trial court ruled against Dred Scott on the ground that the state law did not accept the validity of New York laws or of unconstitutional federal laws, and under Missouri law Scott was never a free person or even a citizen of the United States. At first, the Missouri courts had decided in favor of Dred Scott because of his residence in a free state, but by 1852 they had decided against him in a close two-to-one vote. The slim court majority asserted that Missouri would not impose the law of other jurisdictions—including federal law—against state citizens of Missouri. The Court held that Scott's residence in a free state did not change his status as a slave in Missouri.

When the Supreme Court of the United States finally agreed to hear this case in 1857 there was a wide split in the judicial opinions. Seven justices agreed that Dred Scott was still a slave, although each gave different reasons. Chief Justice Roger Taney wrote a strong pro-slavery opinion to support his view. Among other things, Taney found the Missouri Compromise itself to be unconstitutional.

OPINION of Chief Justice Roger B. Taney, for the Supreme Court.

1. The facts upon which the plaintiff relies did not give him his freedom and make him a citizen of Missouri.

2. The clause in the Constitution authorizing Congress to make all needful rules and regulations for the government of the territory and other property of the United States applies only to territory within the chartered limits of some of the States when they were colonies of Great Britain, and which was surrendered by the British Government to the old Confederation of the States in the treaty of peace. It does not apply to territory acquired by the present Federal Government by treaty or conquest from a foreign nation.

3. The United States, under the present Constitution, cannot acquire territory to be held as a colony, to be governed at its will and pleasure. But it may acquire territory which, at the time, has not a population that fits it to become a State, and may govern it as a Territory until it has a population which, in the judgment of Congress, entitles it to be admitted as a State of the Union.

4. During the time it remains a Territory, Congress may legislate over it within the scope of its constitutional powers in relation to citizens of the United States, and may establish a Territorial Government, and the form of the local Government must be regulated by the discretion of Congress, but with powers not exceeding those which Congress itself, by the Constitution, is authorized to exercise over citizens of the United States in respect to the rights of persons or rights of property.

IV

1. The territory thus acquired is acquired by the people of the United States for their common and equal benefit through their agent and trustee, the Federal Government. Congress can exercise no power over the rights of persons or property of a citizen in the Territory which is prohibited by the Constitution. The Government and the citizen, whenever the Territory is open to settlement, both enter it with their respective rights defined and limited by the Constitution.

2. Congress has no right to prohibit the citizens of any particular State or States from taking up their home there while it permits citizens of other States to do so. Nor has it a right to give privileges to one class of citizens which it refuses to another. The territory is acquired for their equal and common benefit, and if open to any, it must be open to all upon equal and the same terms.

3. Every citizen has a right to take with him into the Territory any article of property which the

Constitution of the United States recognizes as property.

4. The Constitution of the United States recognizes slaves as property, and pledges the Federal Government to protect it. And Congress cannot exercise any more authority over property of that description than it may constitutionally exercise over property of any other kind.

5. The act of Congress, therefore, prohibiting a citizen of the United States from taking with him his slaves when he removes to the Territory in question to reside is an exercise of authority over private property which is not warranted by the Constitution, and the removal of the plaintiff by his owner to that Territory gave him no title to freedom.

V

1. The plaintiff himself acquired no title to freedom by being taken by his owner to Rock Island, in Illinois, and brought back to Missouri. This court has heretofore decided that the status or condition of a person of African descent depended on the laws of the State in which he resided.

2. It has been settled by the decisions of the highest court in Missouri that, by the laws of that State, a slave does not become entitled to his freedom where the owner takes him to reside in a State where slavery is not permitted and afterwards brings him back to Missouri.

Conclusion. It follows that it is apparent upon the record that the court below erred in its judgment on the plea in abatement, and also erred in giving judgment for the defendant, when the exception shows that the plaintiff was not a citizen of the United States. And the Circuit Court had no jurisdiction, either in the cases stated in the plea in abatement or in the one stated in the exception, its judgment in favor of the defendant is erroneous, and must be reversed.

Plessy v. Ferguson
163 U.S. 537 (1886)

Plessy was a citizen of the United States and a resident of Louisiana, of mixed descent, "in the proportion of seven-eighths Caucasian and one-eighth African blood" (as he was described in Louisiana law). On June 7, 1892, he engaged and paid for a first-class passage on the East Louisiana Railway from New Orleans to Covington, in the same state. He entered a passenger train and took possession of a vacant seat in a coach where passengers of the white race were accommodated. Plessy was required by the conductor, under penalty of ejection from said train and imprisonment, to vacate the railroad coach and occupy another seat in a coach assigned for persons not of the white race, and for no other reason than that the petitioner was of "the colored race." Upon Plessy's refusal to comply with that order, he was, with the aid of a police officer, forcibly ejected from the coach and imprisoned in the parish jail of New Orleans. Plessy was held to answer a charge made by the arresting officer to the effect that he was guilty of having criminally violated an act of the General Assembly of the State.

The Louisiana Supreme Court was of the opinion that the law under which the prosecution was made was constitutional and denied the relief requested by the petitioner. Plessy then obtained a writ of error (a form of appeal from state decisions) from the United States Supreme Court, which was allowed by the Chief Justice of the Supreme Court of Louisiana.

This decision is important because it reveals the racial attitudes in a once highly segregated society. The dissent of Justice Harlan appears here because it was prophetic and in many ways anticipated the future course of race relations in America.

MR. JUSTICE BROWN delivered the opinion of the court.

This case turns upon the constitutionality of an act of the General Assembly of the State of Louisiana, passed in 1890, providing for separate railway carriages for the white and colored races. Acts 1890, No. 111, p. 152. . . .

The first section of the statute enacts that all railway companies carrying passengers in their coaches in this State shall provide equal but separate accommodations for the white and colored races by providing two or more passenger coaches for each passenger train, or by dividing the passenger coaches by a partition so as to secure separate accommodations: Provided, that this section shall not be construed to apply to street railroads.

No person or persons, shall be admitted to occupy seats in coaches other than the ones assigned to them on account of the race they belong to.

By the second section, it was enacted that the officers of such passenger trains shall have power and are hereby required to assign each passenger to the coach or compartment used for the race to which such passenger belongs; any passenger insisting on going into a coach or compartment to which by race he does not belong shall be liable to a fine of twenty-five dollars, or in lieu thereof to imprisonment for a period of not more than twenty days in the parish prison, and any officer of any railroad insisting on assigning a passenger to a coach or compartment other than the one set aside for the race to which said passenger belongs shall be liable to a fine of twenty-five dollars, or in lieu thereof to imprisonment for a period of not more than twenty days in the parish prison; and should any passenger refuse to occupy the coach or compartment to which he or she is assigned by the officer of such railway, said officer shall have power to refuse to carry such passenger on his train, and for such refusal neither he nor the railway company which he represents shall be liable for damages in any of the courts of this State.

The third section provides penalties for the refusal or neglect of the officers, directors, conductors, and employees of railway companies to comply with the act, with a proviso that "nothing in this act shall be construed as applying to nurses attending children of the other race. . . ."

The information filed in the criminal District Court charged in substance that Plessy, being a passenger between two stations within the State of Louisiana, was assigned by officers of the company to the coach used for the race to which he belonged, but he insisted upon going into a coach used by the race to which he did not belong. Neither in the information nor plea was his particular race or color averred. The petition for the writ of prohibition averred that petitioner was seven-eighths Caucasian and one-eighth African blood; that the mixture of colored blood was not discernible in him, and that he was entitled to every right, privilege and immunity secured to citizens of the United States of the white race; and that, upon such theory, he took possession of a vacant seat in a coach where passengers of the white race were accommodated, and was ordered by the conductor to vacate said coach and take a seat in

another assigned to persons of the colored race, and, having refused to comply with such demand, he was forcibly ejected with the aid of a police officer, and imprisoned in the parish jail to answer a charge of having violated the above act.

The constitutionality of this act is attacked upon the ground that it conflicts with the Thirteenth Amendment of the Constitution, abolishing slavery, and the Fourteenth Amendment, which prohibits certain restrictive legislation on the part of the states.

It does not conflict with the Thirteenth Amendment, which abolished slavery and involuntary servitude, except as a punishment for crime is too clear for argument. Slavery implies involuntary servitude—a state of bondage. . . .

A statute which implies merely a legal distinction between the white and colored races, and which must always exist so long as white men are distinguished from the other race by color—has no tendency to destroy the legal equality of the two races, or reestablish a state of involuntary servitude. Indeed, we do not understand that the Thirteenth Amendment is strenuously relied upon by the plaintiff in error in this connection. . . .

We think that the enforced separation of the races, as applied to the internal commerce of the state, neither abridges the privileges or immunities of the colored man, deprives him of his property without due process of law, nor denies him the equal protection of the laws, within the meaning of the Fourteenth Amendment. . . .

HARLAN, Dissenting Opinion.

It is said in argument that the statute of Louisiana does not discriminate against either race, but prescribes a rule applicable alike to white and colored citizens. But this argument does not meet the difficulty. Everyone knows that the statute in question had its origin in the purpose not so much to exclude white persons from railroad cars occupied by blacks as to exclude colored people from coaches occupied by or assigned to white persons. Railroad corporations of Louisiana did not make discrimination among whites in the matter of accommodation for travelers. The thing to accomplish was, under the guise of giving equal accommodation for whites and blacks, to compel the latter to keep to themselves while traveling in railroad passenger coaches. No one would be so wanting in candor as to assert the contrary. The fundamental objection, therefore, to the statute is that it interferes with the personal freedom of citizens. "Personal liberty," it has been well said, consists in the power of locomotion, of changing situation, or removing one's person to whatsoever places one's own inclination may direct, without imprisonment or restraint unless by due course of law.

If a white man and a black man choose to occupy the same public conveyance on a public highway, it is their right to do so, and no government, proceeding alone on grounds of race, can prevent it without infringing the personal liberty of each.

It is one thing for railroad carriers to furnish, or to be required by law to furnish, equal accommodations for all whom they are under a legal duty to carry. It is quite another thing for government to forbid citizens of the white and black races from traveling in the same public conveyance, and to punish officers of railroad companies for permitting persons of the two races to occupy the same passenger coach. If a State can prescribe, as a rule of civil conduct, that whites and blacks shall not travel as passengers in the same railroad coach, why may it not so regulate the use of the streets of its cities and towns as to compel white citizens to keep on one side of a street and black citizens to keep on the other? Why may it not, upon like grounds, punish whites and blacks who ride together in streetcars or in open vehicles on a public road or street? Why may it not require sheriffs to assign whites to one side of a courtroom and blacks to the other? And why may it not also prohibit the commingling of the two races in the galleries of legislative halls or in public assemblages convened for the consideration of the political questions of the day? Further, if this statute of Louisiana is consistent with the personal liberty of citizens, why may not the State require the separation in railroad coaches of native and naturalized citizens of the United States, or of Protestants and Roman Catholics?

The answer given at the argument to these questions was that regulations of the kind they suggest would be unreasonable, and could not, therefore, stand before the law. . . .

The white race deems itself to be the dominant race in this country. And so it is in prestige, in achievements, in education, in wealth and in power. So, I doubt not, it will continue to be for all time if it remains true to its great heritage and holds fast to the principles of constitutional liberty. But in view of the Constitution, in the eye of the law, there is in this country no superior, dominant, ruling class of citizens. There is no caste here. Our Constitution is color-blind, and neither knows nor tolerates classes among citizens. In respect of civil rights, all citizens are equal before the law. The humblest is the peer of the most powerful. The law regards man as man, and takes no account of his surroundings or of his color when his civil rights as guaranteed by the supreme law of the land are involved. It is therefore to be regretted that this high tribunal, the final expositor of the fundamental law of the land, has reached the conclusion that it is competent for a State to regulate the enjoyment by citizens of their civil rights solely upon the basis of race.

In my opinion, the judgment this day rendered will, in time, prove to be quite as pernicious as the decision made by this tribunal in the Dred Scott Case. It was adjudged in that case that the descendants of Africans who were imported into this country and sold as slaves were not included nor intended to be included under the word "citizens" in the Constitution, and could not claim any of the rights and privileges which that instrument provided for and secured to citizens of the United States; that, at the time of the adoption of the Constitution, they were considered as a subordinate and inferior class of beings, who had been subjugated by the dominant race, and, whether emancipated or not, yet remained subject to their authority, and had no rights or privileges but such as those who held the power and the government might choose to grant them.

The recent amendments of the Constitution, it was supposed, had eradicated these principles from our institutions. But it seems that we have yet, in some of the States, a dominant race—a superior class of citizens, which assumes to regulate the enjoyment of civil rights, common to all citizens, upon the basis of race. The present decision, it may well be apprehended, will not only stimulate aggressions, more or less brutal and irritating, upon the admitted rights of colored citizens, but will encourage the belief that it is possible, by means of state enactments, to defeat the beneficent purposes which the people of the United States had in view when they adopted the recent amendments of the Constitution, by one of which the blacks of this country were made citizens of the United States and of the States in which they respectively reside, and whose privileges and immunities, as citizens, the States are forbidden to abridge. Sixty millions of whites are in no danger from the presence here of eight millions of blacks. The destinies of the two races in this country are indissolubly linked together, and the interests of both require that the common government of all shall not permit the seeds of race hate to be planted under the sanction of law. What can more certainly arouse race hate, what more certainly create and perpetuate a feeling of distrust between these races, than state enactments which, in fact, proceed on the ground that colored citizens are so inferior and degraded that they cannot be allowed to sit in public coaches occupied by white citizens. That, as all will admit, is the real meaning of such legislation as was enacted in Louisiana.

The sure guarantee of the peace and security of each race is the clear, distinct, unconditional recognition by our governments, National and State, of every right that inheres in civil freedom, and of the equality before the law of all citizens of the United States, without regard to race. State enactments regulating the enjoyment of civil rights upon the basis of race, and cunningly devised to defeat legitimate results of the war under the pretence of recognizing equality of rights, can have no other result than to render permanent peace impossible and to keep alive a conflict of races the continuance of which must do harm to all concerned. This question is not met by the suggestion that social equality cannot exist between the white and black races in this country. That argument, if it can be properly regarded as one, is scarcely worthy of consideration, for social equality no more exists between two races when traveling in a passenger coach or a public highway than when members of the same races sit by each other in a street car or in the jury box, or stand or sit with each other in a political assembly, or when they use in common the street of a city or town, or when they are in the same room for the purpose of having their names placed on the registry of voters, or when they approach the ballot box in order to exercise the high privilege of voting.

There is a race so different from our own that we do not permit those belonging to it to become citizens of the United States. Persons belonging to it are, with few exceptions, absolutely excluded from our country. I allude to the Chinese race. But, by the statute in question, a Chinaman can ride in the same passenger coach with white citizens of the United States, while citizens of the black race in Louisiana, many of whom, perhaps, risked their lives for the preservation of the Union, who are entitled, by law, to participate in the political control of the State and nation, who are not excluded, by law or by reason of their race, from public stations of any kind, and who have all the legal rights that belong to white citizens, are yet declared to be criminals, liable to imprisonment, if they ride in a public coach occupied by citizens of the white race. It is scarcely just to say that a colored citizen should not object to occupying a public coach assigned to his own race. He does not object, nor, perhaps, would he object to separate coaches for his race if his rights under the law were recognized. But he objecting, and ought never to cease objecting, to the proposition that citizens of the white and black race can be adjudged criminals because they sit, or claim the right to sit, in the same public coach on a public highway.

The arbitrary separation of citizens on the basis of race while they are on a public highway is a badge of servitude wholly inconsistent with the civil freedom and the equality before the law established by the Constitution. It cannot be justified upon any legal grounds. . . .

Brown v. Board of Education 347 U.S. 483 (1954)

This decision is probably the most important Supreme Court ruling of the twentieth century. In four consolidated cases the Court held that racial segregation of public school children was unconstitutional, in violation of the Fourteenth Amendment's guarantee of the equal protection of the laws.

These four cases were the culmination of a 20-year campaign led by the National Association for the Advancement of Colored People (NAACP). It took that length of time for the Supreme Court to consider the admission of African American applicants to state university law schools and to publicly supported graduate schools and universities. Public elementary and secondary school segregation was at stake in the Brown *case.*

When it was argued, NAACP lawyer Thurgood Marshall led the preparation. Marshall had been an NAACP lawyer and coordinator of litigation for many years, providing overall strategy for the campaign against segregation. In 1961, President John F. Kennedy appointed Marshall to a position on the United States Court of Appeals for the Second Circuit, over the strong opposition of southern senators. In 1967, Thurgood Marshall was appointed by President Lyndon Johnson to succeed Justice Tom C. Clark on the Supreme Court.

Chief Justice Earl Warren announced the Supreme Court's decision in Brown v. Board of Education *on May 17, 1954. It was a unanimous opinion, displaying the Court's solidarity on a major public issue. The key 1896 segregation decision,* Plessy v. Ferguson, *was undermined, to be specifically overruled in a later case.*

MR. CHIEF JUSTICE WARREN delivered the opinion of the Court.

These cases come to us from the States of Kansas, South Carolina, Virginia, and Delaware. They are premised on different facts and different local conditions, but a common legal question justifies their consideration together in this consolidated opinion.

In each of the cases, minors of the Negro race, through their legal representatives, seek the aid of the courts in obtaining admission to the public schools of their community on a nonsegregated basis. In each instance, they had been denied admission to schools attended by white children under laws requiring or permitting segregation according to race. This segregation was alleged to deprive the plaintiffs of the equal protection of the laws under the Fourteenth Amendment. In each of the cases other than the Delaware case, a three-judge federal district court denied relief to the plaintiffs on the so-called "separate but equal" doctrine announced by this Court in Plessy v. Ferguson, 163 U.S. 537. Under that doctrine, equality of treatment is accorded when the races are provided substantially equal facilities, even though these facilities be separate. In the Delaware case, the Supreme Court of Delaware adhered to that doctrine, but ordered that the plaintiffs be admitted to the white schools because of their superiority to the Negro schools.

The plaintiffs contend that segregated public schools are not "equal" and cannot be made

"equal," and that hence they are deprived of the equal protection of the laws. Because of the obvious importance of the question presented, the Court took jurisdiction. Argument was heard in the 1952 Term, and reargument was heard this Term on certain questions propounded by the Court.

Reargument was largely devoted to the circumstances surrounding the adoption of the Fourteenth Amendment in 1868. It covered exhaustively consideration of the Amendment in Congress, ratification by the states, then-existing practices in racial segregation, and the views of proponents and opponents of the Amendment. This discussion and our own investigation convince us that, although these sources cast some light, it is not enough to resolve the problem with which we are faced. At best, they are inconclusive. The most avid proponents of the post-War Amendments undoubtedly intended them to remove all legal distinctions among "all persons born or naturalized in the United States." Their opponents, just as certainly, were antagonistic to both the letter and the spirit of the Amendments and wished them to have the most limited effect. What others in Congress and the state legislatures had in mind cannot be determined with any degree of certainty.

An additional reason for the inconclusive nature of the Amendment's history with respect to segregated schools is the status of public education at that time. In the South, the movement toward free common schools, supported by general taxation, had not yet taken hold. Education of white children was largely in the hands of private groups. Education of Negroes was almost nonexistent, and practically all of the race were illiterate. In fact, any education of Negroes was forbidden by law in some states. Today, in contrast, many Negroes have achieved outstanding success in the arts and sciences, as well as in the business and professional world. It is true that public school education at the time of the Amendment had advanced further in the North, but the effect of the Amendment on Northern States was generally ignored in the congressional debates. Even in the North, the conditions of public education did not approximate those existing today. The curriculum was usually rudimentary; ungraded schools were common in rural areas; the school term was but three months a year in many states, and compulsory school attendance was virtually unknown. As a consequence, it is not surprising that there should be so little in the history of the Fourteenth Amendment relating to its intended effect on public education.

In the first cases in this Court construing the Fourteenth Amendment, decided shortly after its adoption, the Court interpreted it as proscribing all state-imposed discriminations against the Negro race. The doctrine of "separate but equal" did not make its appearance in this Court until 1896 in the case of Plessy v. Ferguson, supra, involving not education but transportation. American courts have since labored with the doctrine for over half a century. In this Court, there have been six cases involving the "separate but equal" doctrine in the field of public education. . . . In more recent cases, all on the graduate school level, inequality was found in that specific benefits enjoyed by white students were denied to Negro students of the same educational qualifications. Missouri ex rel. Gaines v. Canada, 305 U.S. 337; Sipuel v. Oklahoma, 332 U.S. 631; Sweatt v. Painter, 339 U.S. 629; McLaurin v. Oklahoma State Regents, 339 U.S. 637. In none of these cases was it necessary to reexamine the doctrine to grant relief to the Negro plaintiff. And in Sweatt v. Painter, supra, the Court expressly reserved decision on the question whether Plessy v. Ferguson should be held inapplicable to public education.

In the instant cases, that question is directly presented. Here, unlike Sweatt v. Painter, there are findings below that the Negro and white schools involved have been equalized, or are being equalized, with respect to buildings, curricula, qualifications and salaries of teachers, and other "tangible" factors. Our decision, therefore, cannot turn on merely a comparison of these tangible factors in the Negro and white schools involved in each of the cases. We must look instead to the effect of segregation itself on public education.

In approaching this problem, we cannot turn the clock back to 1868, when the Amendment was adopted, or even to 1896, when Plessy v. Ferguson was written. We must consider public education in the light of its full development and its present place in American life throughout the Nation. Only in this way can it be determined if segregation in public schools deprives these plaintiffs of the equal protection of the laws.

Today, education is perhaps the most important function of state and local governments. Compulsory school attendance laws and the great expenditures for education both demonstrate our recognition of the importance of education to our democratic society. It is required in the performance of our most basic public responsibilities, even service in the armed forces. It is the very foundation of good citizenship. Today it is a principal instrument in awakening the child to cultural values, in preparing him for later professional training, and in helping him to adjust normally to his environment. In these days, it is doubtful that any child may reasonably be expected to succeed in life if he is denied the opportunity of an education. Such an opportunity, where the state has undertaken to provide it, is a right which must be made available to all on equal terms.

We come then to the question presented: Does segregation of children in public schools solely on the basis of race, even though the physical facilities and other "tangible" factors may be equal, deprive the children of the minority group of equal educational opportunities? We believe that it does.

In Sweatt v. Painter, supra, in finding that a segregated law school for Negroes could not provide them equal educational opportunities, this Court relied in large part on "those qualities which are incapable of objective measurement but which make for greatness in a law school." In McLaurin v. Oklahoma State Regents, supra, the Court, in requiring that a Negro admitted to a white graduate school be treated like all other students, again resorted to intangible considerations: ". . . his ability to study, to engage in discussions and exchange views with other students, and, in general, to learn his profession." Such considerations apply with added force to children in grade and high schools. To separate them from others of similar age and qualifications solely because of their race generates a feeling of inferiority as to their status in the community that may affect their hearts and minds in a way unlikely ever to be undone. . . .

Segregation of white and colored children in public schools has a detrimental effect upon the colored children. The impact is greater when it has the sanction of the law, for the policy of separating the races is usually interpreted as denoting the inferiority of the negro group. A sense of inferiority affects the motivation of a child to learn. Segregation with the sanction of law, therefore, has a tendency to [retard] the educational and mental development of negro children and to deprive them of some of the benefits they would receive in a racia[lly] integrated school system.

Whatever may have been the extent of psychological knowledge at the time of Plessy v. Ferguson, this finding is amply supported by modern authority. Any language in Plessy v. Ferguson contrary to this finding is rejected.

We conclude that, in the field of public education, the doctrine of "separate but equal" has no place. Separate educational facilities are inherently unequal. Therefore, we hold that the plaintiffs and others similarly situated for whom the actions have been brought are, by reason of the segregation complained of, deprived of the equal protection of the laws guaranteed by the Fourteenth Amendment. This disposition makes unnecessary any discussion whether such segregation also violates the Due Process Clause of the Fourteenth Amendment.

Because these are class actions, because of the wide applicability of this decision, and because of the great variety of local conditions, the formulation of decrees in these cases presents problems of considerable complexity. On reargument, the consideration of appropriate relief was necessarily subordinated to the primary question—the constitutionality of segregation in public education. We have now announced that such segregation is a denial of the equal protection of the laws. In order that we may have the full assistance of the parties in formulating decrees, the cases will be restored to the docket, and the parties are requested to present further argument on Questions 4 and 5 previously propounded by the Court for the reargument this Term The Attorney General of the United States is again invited to participate. The Attorneys General of the states requiring or permitting segregation in public education will also be permitted to appear as amici curiae upon request to do so by September 15, 1954, and submission of briefs by October 1, 1954.

It is so ordered.

Mapp v. Ohio
367 U.S. 643 (1961)

In 1957, seven police officers broke into the home of Dolly Mapp in Cleveland, Ohio, looking for a bombing suspect and some hidden gambling materials. The police claimed that they had a warrant for the search, but they failed to produce one at the time. Instead of finding what they sought the police found several allegedly obscene books and photographs.

Dolly Mapp was arrested, tried, and convicted for possession of obscene matter. Her appeal to the Ohio Supreme Court was rejected on the ground that although the police search had been unlawful, the then current interpretation of the Bill of Rights allowed for the use of this kind of tainted evidence in a criminal trial.

The Supreme Court reversed this Ohio decision. In doing so, the federal Supreme Court held that the national Constitution extended the protection of the due process clause of the Fourteenth Amendment in such a way as to apply the standards of the Fourth Amendment regarding searches and seizures. Not only was the national Bill of Rights applied to state police practices, but the federal rule against the use of illegal evidence in criminal trials was also applied to state courts.

MR. JUSTICE CLARK delivered the opinion of the Court.

Appellant stands convicted of knowingly having had in her possession and under her control certain lewd and lascivious books, pictures, and photographs in violation of 2905.34 of Ohio's Revised Code. As officially stated in the syllabus to its opinion, the Supreme Court of Ohio found that her conviction was valid though "based primarily upon the introduction in evidence of lewd and lascivious books and pictures unlawfully seized during an unlawful search of defendant's home. . . ." 170 Ohio St. 427B428, 166 N.E.2d 387, 388.

On May 23, 1957, three Cleveland police officers arrived at appellant's residence in that city pursuant to information that a person [was] hiding out in the home, who was wanted for questioning in connection with a recent bombing, and that there was a large amount of policy paraphernalia being hidden in the home.

Miss Mapp and her daughter by a former marriage lived on the top floor of the two-family dwelling. Upon their arrival at that house, the officers knocked on the door and demanded entrance, but appellant, after telephoning her attorney, refused to admit them without a search warrant.

They advised their headquarters of the situation and undertook a surveillance of the house.

The officers again sought entrance some three hours later when four or more additional officers arrived on the scene. When Miss Mapp did not come to the door immediately, at least one of the several doors to the house was forcibly opened and the policemen gained admittance. Meanwhile Miss Mapp's attorney arrived, but the officers, having secured their own entry, and continuing in their defiance of the law, would permit him neither to see Miss Mapp nor to enter the house. It appears that Miss Mapp was halfway down the stairs from the upper floor to the front door when the officers, in this highhanded manner, broke into the hall. She demanded to see the search warrant. A paper, claimed to be a warrant, was held up by one of the officers. She grabbed the "warrant" and placed it in her bosom. A struggle ensued in which the officers recovered the piece of paper and as a result of which they handcuffed appellant because she had been "belligerent" in resisting their official rescue of the "warrant" from her person. Running roughshod over appellant, a policeman "grabbed" her, "twisted [her] hand," and she "yelled [and] pleaded with him" because "it was hurting." Appellant, in handcuffs, was then forcibly taken upstairs to her bedroom where the officers searched a dresser, a chest of drawers, a closet and some suitcases. They also looked into a photo album and through personal papers belonging to the appellant. The search spread to the rest of the second floor including the child's bedroom, the living room, the kitchen and a dinette. The basement of the building and a trunk found therein were also searched. The obscene materials for possession of which she was ultimately convicted were discovered in the course of that widespread search.

At the trial, no search warrant was produced by the prosecution, nor was the failure to produce one explained or accounted for. At best, "There is, in the record, considerable doubt as to whether there ever was any warrant for the search of defendant's home." 170 Ohio St. at 430, 166 N.E.2d at 389. The Ohio Supreme Court believed a "reasonable argument" could be made that the conviction should be reversed "because the 'methods' employed to obtain the [evidence] . . . were such as to offend 'a sense of justice,'" but the court found determinative the fact that the evi-

dence had not been taken "from defendant's person by the use of brutal or offensive physical force against defendant." 170 Ohio St. at 431, 166 N.E.2d at 389–390.

The State says that, even if the search were made without authority, or otherwise unreasonably, it is not prevented from using the unconstitutionally seized evidence at trial, citing Wolf v. Colorado, 338 U.S. 25 (1949), in which this Court did indeed hold that, in a prosecution in a State court for a State crime, the Fourteenth Amendment does not forbid the admission of evidence obtained by an unreasonable search and seizure. . . .

I

Seventy-five years ago, in Boyd v. United States, 116 U.S. 616, 630 (1886), considering the Fourth and Fifth Amendments as running "almost into each other" on the facts before it, this Court held that the doctrines of those Amendments apply to all invasions on the part of the government and its employees of the sanctity of a man's home and the privacies of life. It is not the breaking of his doors, and the rummaging of his drawers, [p*647] that constitutes the essence of the offense; but it is the invasion of his indefeasible right of personal security, personal liberty and private property. . . . Breaking into a house and opening boxes and drawers are circumstances of aggravation; but any forcible and compulsory extortion of a man's own testimony or of his private papers to be used as evidence to convict him of crime or to forfeit his goods, is within the condemnation . . . [of those Amendments]. . . .

The right to privacy, no less important than any other right carefully and particularly reserved to the people, would stand in marked contrast to all other rights declared as "basic to a free society." Wolf v. Colorado, supra, at 27. This Court has not hesitated to enforce as strictly against the States as it does against the Federal Government the rights of free speech and of a free press, the rights to notice and to a fair, public trial, including, as it does, the right not to be convicted by use of a coerced confession, however logically relevant it be, and without regard to its reliability. Rogers v. Richmond, 365 U.S. 534 (1961). And nothing could be more certain than that, when a coerced confession is involved, "the relevant rules of evidence" are overridden without regard to "the incidence of such conduct by the police," slight or frequent. Why should not the same rule apply to what is tantamount to coerced testimony by way of unconstitutional seizure of goods, papers, effects, documents, etc.? We find that, as to the Federal Government, the Fourth and Fifth Amendments and, as to the States, the freedom from unconscionable invasions of privacy and the freedom from convictions based upon coerced confessions do enjoy an "intimate relation" [n8] in their perpetuation of "principles of humanity and civil liberty [secured] . . . only after years of struggle. . . ." Bram v. United States, 168 U.S. 532, 543–544 (1897).

V

Moreover, our holding that the exclusionary rule is an essential part of both the Fourth and Fourteenth Amendments is not only the logical dictate of prior cases, but it also makes very good sense. There is no war between the Constitution and common sense. Presently, a federal prosecutor may make no use of evidence illegally seized, but a State's attorney across the street may, although he supposedly is operating under the enforceable prohibitions of the same Amendment. Thus, the State, by admitting evidence unlawfully seized, serves to encourage disobedience to the Federal Constitution which it is bound to uphold. Moreover, as was said in Elkins, "[t]he very essence of a healthy federalism depends upon the avoidance of needless conflict between state and federal courts." 364 U.S. at 221. . . . Yet the double standard recognized until today hardly put such a thesis into practice. In nonexclusionary States, federal officers, being human, were by it invited to, and did, as our cases indicate, step across the street to the State's attorney with their unconstitutionally seized evidence. Prosecution on the basis of that evidence was then had in a state court in utter disregard of the enforceable Fourth Amendment. If the fruits of an unconstitutional search had been inadmissible in both state and federal courts, this inducement to evasion would have been sooner eliminated. . . . Federal-state cooperation in the solution of crime under constitutional standards will be promoted, if only by recognition of their now mutual obligation to respect the same fundamental criteria in their approaches.

However much in a particular case insistence upon such rules may appear as a technicality that inures to the benefit of a guilty person, the history of the criminal law proves that tolerance of short-cut methods in law enforcement impairs its enduring effectiveness. . . .

. . . The criminal goes free, if he must, but it is the law that sets him free. Nothing can destroy a government more quickly than its failure to observe its own laws, or worse, its disregard of the charter of its own existence. . . . The federal courts themselves have operated under the exclusionary rule of Weeks for almost half a century; yet it has not been suggested either that the Federal Bureau of Investigation [n10] has thereby been rendered ineffective, or that the administration of criminal justice in the federal courts has thereby been disrupted. Moreover, the experience of the states is impressive. . . . The movement towards the rule of exclusion has been halting, but seemingly inexorable.

The ignoble shortcut to conviction left open to the State tends to destroy the entire system of constitutional restraints on which the liberties of the people rest. Having once recognized that the right to privacy embodied in the Fourth Amendment is enforceable against the States, and that the right to be secure against rude invasions of privacy by state officers is, therefore, constitutional in origin, we can no longer permit that right to remain an empty promise. Because it is enforceable in the same manner and to like effect as other basic rights secured by the Due Process Clause, we can no longer permit it to be revocable at the whim of any police officer who, in the name of law enforcement itself, chooses to suspend its enjoyment. Our decision, founded on reason and truth, gives to the individual no more than that which the Constitution guarantees him, to the police officer no less than that to which honest law enforcement is entitled, and, to the courts, that judicial integrity so necessary in the true administration of justice.

The judgment of the Supreme Court of Ohio is reversed, and the cause remanded for further proceedings not inconsistent with this opinion.

Reversed and remanded.

Engel et al. v. Vitale et al. 370 U.S. 421 (1962)

This was one of the Supreme Court's most controversial decisions. Official state prayers were banned from the public school classrooms as a result. Later cases made it clear that Bible read-

ing in public schools was equally offensive to the Constitution. Many religious groups have sharply criticized this interpretation of the First Amendment, but the logic of the decision is clear.

MR. JUSTICE BLACK delivered the opinion of the Court.

The respondent Board of Education of Union Free School District No. 9, New Hyde Park, New York, acting in its official capacity under state law, directed the School District's principal to cause the following prayer to be said aloud by each class in the presence of a teacher at the beginning of each school day:

"Almighty God, we acknowledge our dependence upon Thee, and we beg Thy blessings upon us, our parents, our teachers and our Country."

This daily procedure was adopted on the recommendation of the State Board of Regents, a governmental agency created by the State Constitution to which the New York Legislature has granted broad supervisory, executive, and legislative powers over the State's public school system. These state officials composed the prayer which they recommended and published as a part of their "Statement on Moral and Spiritual Training in the Schools," saying: "We believe that this Statement will be subscribed to by all men and women of good will, and we call upon all of them to aid in giving life to our program."

Shortly after the practice of reciting the Regents' prayer was adopted by the School District, the parents of ten pupils brought this action in a New York State Court insisting that use of this official prayer in the public schools was contrary to the beliefs, religions, or religious practices of both themselves and their children. Among other things, these parents challenged the constitutionality of both the state law authorizing the School District to direct the use of prayer in public schools and the School District's regulation ordering the recitation of this particular prayer on the ground that these actions of official governmental agencies violate that part of the First Amendment of the Federal Constitution which commands that "Congress shall make no law respecting an establishment of religion"—a command which was "made applicable to the State of New York by the Fourteenth Amendment of the said Constitution." The New York Court of Appeals, over the dissents of Judges Dye and Fuld, sustained an order of the

lower state courts which had upheld the power of New York to use the Regents' prayer as a part of the daily procedures of its public schools so long as the schools did not compel any pupil to join in the prayer over his or her parents' objection.

We granted certiorari to review this important decision involving rights protected by the First and Fourteenth Amendments. We think that by using its public school system to encourage recitation of the Regents' prayer, the State of New York has adopted a practice wholly inconsistent with the Establishment Clause. There can, of course, be no doubt that New York's program of daily classroom invocation of God's blessings as prescribed in the Regents' prayer is a religious activity. It is a solemn avowal of divine faith and supplication for the blessings of the Almighty. The nature of such a prayer has always been religious, none of the respondents has denied this and the trial court expressly so found:

> The religious nature of prayer was recognized by Jefferson and has been concurred in by theological writers, the United States Supreme Court and State courts and administrative officials, including New York's Commissioner of Education. A committee of the New York Legislature has agreed.

> The Board of Regents as amicus curiae, the respondents and intervenors all concede the religious nature of prayer, but seek to distinguish this prayer because it is based on our spiritual heritage. . . .

The petitioners contend among other things that the state laws requiring or permitting use of the Regents' prayer must be struck down as a violation of the Establishment Clause because that prayer was composed by governmental officials as a part of a governmental program to further religious beliefs. For this reason, petitioners argue, the State's use of the Regents' prayer in its public school system breaches the constitutional wall of separation between Church and State. We agree with that contention since we think that the constitutional prohibition against laws respecting an establishment of religion must at least mean that in this country it is no part of the business of government to compose official prayers for any group of the American people to recite as a part of a religious program carried on by government. . . .

By the time of the adoption of the Constitution, our history shows that there was a widespread awareness among many Americans of the dangers of a union of Church and State. These people knew, some of them from bitter personal experience, that one of the greatest dangers to the freedom of the individual to worship in his own way lay in the Government's placing its official stamp of approval upon one particular kind of prayer or one particular form of religious services. They knew the anguish, hardship and bitter strife that could come when zealous religious groups struggled with one another to obtain the Government's stamp of approval from each King, Queen, or Protector that came to temporary power. The Constitution was intended to avert a part of this danger by leaving the government of this country in the hands of the people rather than in the hands of any monarch. But this safeguard was not enough. Our Founders were no more willing to let the content of their prayers and their privilege of praying whenever they pleased be influenced by the ballot box than they were to let these vital matters of personal conscience depend upon the succession of monarchs. The First Amendment was added to the Constitution to stand as a guarantee that neither the power nor the prestige of the Federal Government would be used to control, support or influence the kinds of prayer the American people can say—that the people's religions must not be subjected to the pressures of government for change each time a new political administration is elected to office. Under that Amendment's prohibition against governmental establishment of religion, as reinforced by the provisions of the Fourteenth Amendment, government in this country, be it state or federal, is without power to prescribe by law any particular form of prayer which is to be used as an official prayer in carrying on any program of governmentally sponsored religious activity.

There can be no doubt that New York's state prayer program officially establishes the religious beliefs embodied in the Regents' prayer. The respondents' argument to the contrary, which is largely based upon the contention that the Regents' prayer is "nondenominational" and the fact that the program, as modified and approved by state courts, does not require all pupils to recite the prayer but permits those who wish to do so to remain silent or be excused from the room, ignores the essential nature of the program's constitutional defects. Neither the fact that the prayer may be denominationally neutral nor the fact that its observance on the part of the students is voluntary can serve to free it from the limitations of the Establishment Clause, as it might from the Free Exercise Clause, of the First

Amendment, both of which are operative against the States by virtue of the Fourteenth Amendment. Although these two clauses may in certain instances overlap, they forbid two quite different kinds of governmental encroachment upon religious freedom. The Establishment Clause, unlike the Free Exercise Clause, does not depend upon any showing of direct governmental compulsion and is violated by the enactment of laws which establish an official religion whether those laws operate directly to coerce nonobserving individuals or not. This is not to say, of course, that laws officially prescribing a particular form of religious worship do not involve coercion of such individuals. When the power, prestige and financial support of government is placed behind a particular religious belief, the indirect coercive pressure upon religious minorities to conform to the prevailing officially approved religion is plain. But the purposes underlying the Establishment Clause go much further than that. Its first and most immediate purpose rested on the belief that a union of government and religion tends to destroy government and to degrade religion. The history of governmentally established religion, both in England and in this country, showed that whenever government had allied itself with one particular form of religion, the inevitable result had been that it had incurred the hatred, disrespect and even contempt of those who held contrary beliefs. That same history showed that many people had lost their respect for any religion that had relied upon the support of government to spread its faith. The Establishment Clause thus stands as an expression of principle on the part of the Founders of our Constitution that religion is too personal, too sacred, too holy, to permit its "unhallowed perversion" by a civil magistrate. Another purpose of the Establishment Clause rested upon an awareness of the historical fact that governmentally established religions and religious persecutions go hand in hand.

The Founders knew that only a few years after the Book of Common Prayer became the only accepted form of religious services in the established Church of England, an Act of Uniformity was passed to compel all Englishmen to attend those services and to make it a criminal offense to conduct or attend religious gatherings of any other kind—a law which was consistently flouted by dissenting religious groups in England and which contributed to widespread persecutions of people like John Bunyan who persisted in holding "unlawful [religious] meetings . . . to the great disturbance and distraction of the good subjects of this kingdom. . . ." And they knew that similar persecutions had received the sanction of law in several of the colonies in this country soon after the establishment of official religions in those colonies.

It was in large part to get completely away from this sort of systematic religious persecution that the Founders brought into being our Nation, our Constitution, and our Bill of Rights with its prohibition against any governmental establishment of religion. The New York laws officially prescribing the Regents' prayer are inconsistent both with the purposes of the Establishment Clause and with the Establishment Clause itself. . . .

There is of course nothing in the decision reached here that is inconsistent with the fact that school children and others are officially encouraged to express love for our country by reciting historical documents such as the Declaration of Independence, which contain references to the Deity or by singing officially espoused anthems, which include the composer's professions of faith in a Supreme Being, or with the fact that there are many manifestations in our public life of belief in God. Such patriotic or ceremonial occasions bear no true resemblance to the unquestioned religious exercise that the State of New York has sponsored in this instance. . . .

It has been argued that to apply the Constitution in such a way as to prohibit state laws respecting an establishment of religious services in public schools is to indicate a hostility toward religion or toward prayer. Nothing, of course, could be more wrong. The history of man is inseparable from the history of religion. . . . It is neither sacrilegious nor antireligious to say that each separate government in this country should stay out of the business of writing or sanctioning official prayers and leave that purely religious function to the people themselves and to those the people choose to look to for religious guidance.

The Judgment of the Court of Appeals of New York is reversed and the cause remanded for further proceedings not inconsistent with this opinion.

Reversed and remanded.

Gideon v. Wainwright 372 U.S. 335 (1963)

Clarence Gideon was a poor man who was convicted and tried of a minor felony before a Florida state court. Gideon had asked the Florida trial court for the appointment of a lawyer to defend him, but the court denied his request because Florida law gave the right to court-appointed counsel only to those accused of very serious crimes. Gideon was forced to defend himself in trial court, but he lost and was convicted and sent to prison. While in prison Gideon sought a writ of habeas corpus from the Supreme Court of the United States on the ground that the federal Bill of Rights gave him the right to a court-appointed lawyer because of his poverty. The right to court-appointed counsel was deemed so important that 24 other groups supported Clarence Gideon's claim in briefs submitted to the Supreme Court. The results of this intervention were a victory for Gideon in the Supreme Court of the States and an expansion of the Bill of Rights.

MR. JUSTICE BLACK delivered the opinion of the Court.

Petitioner was charged in a Florida state court with having broken and entered a poolroom with intent to commit a misdemeanor. This offense is a felony under Florida law. Appearing in court without funds and, without a lawyer, petitioner asked the court to appoint counsel for him, whereupon the following colloquy took place:

The Court: Mr. Gideon, I am sorry, but I cannot appoint Counsel to represent you in this case. Under the laws of the State of Florida, the only time the Court can appoint Counsel to represent a Defendant is when that person is charged with a capital offense. I am sorry, but I will have to deny your request to appoint Counsel to defend you in this case.

The Defendant: The United States Supreme Court says I am entitled to be represented by Counsel.

Put to trial before a jury, Gideon conducted his defense about as well as could be expected from a layman. He made an opening statement to the jury, cross-examined the State's witnesses, presented witnesses in his own defense, declined to testify himself, and made a short argument "emphasizing his innocence to the charge contained in the Information filed in this case." The jury returned a verdict of guilty, and petitioner was sentenced to serve five years in the state prison. Later, petitioner filed in the Florida Supreme Court this habeas corpus petition attacking his conviction and sentence on the ground that the trial court's refusal to appoint counsel for him denied him rights "guaranteed by the Constitution and the Bill of Rights by the United States Government." Treating the petition for habeas corpus as properly before it, the State Supreme Court, "upon consideration thereof" but without an opinion, denied all relief.

Since 1942, when Betts v. Brady, 316 U.S. 455, was decided by a divided Court, the problem of a defendant's federal constitutional right to counsel in a state court has been a continuing source of controversy and litigation in both state and federal courts. To give this problem another review here, we granted certiorari. 370 U.S. 908. Since Gideon was proceeding in *forma pauperis,* we appointed counsel to represent him and requested both sides to discuss in their briefs and oral arguments the following: "Should this Court's holding in Betts v. Brady, 316 U.S. 455, be reconsidered?"

I

The facts upon which Betts claimed that he had been unconstitutionally denied the right to have counsel appointed to assist him are strikingly like the facts upon which Gideon here bases his federal constitutional claim. Betts was indicted for robbery in a Maryland state court. On arraignment, he told the trial judge of his lack of funds to hire a lawyer and asked the court to appoint one for him. Betts was advised that it was not the practice in that county to appoint counsel for indigent defendants except in murder and rape cases. He then pleaded not guilty, had witnesses summoned, cross-examined the State's witnesses, examined his own, and chose not to testify himself. He was found guilty by the judge, sitting without a jury, and sentenced to eight years in prison.

Like Gideon, Betts sought release by *habeas corpus,* alleging that he had been denied the right to assistance of counsel in violation of the Fourteenth Amendment. Betts was denied any relief, and, on review, this Court affirmed. It was held that a refusal to appoint counsel for an indigent defendant charged with a felony did not necessarily violate the Due Process Clause of the Fourteenth Amendment, which, for reasons given, the Court deemed to be the only applicable federal constitutional provision.

The Court said: Asserted denial [of due process] is to be tested by an appraisal of the totality of facts in a given case. That which may, in one setting, constitute a denial of fundamental fairness, shocking to the universal sense of justice, may, in other circumstances, and in the light of other considerations, fall short of such denial. 316 U.S. at 462. Treating due process as "a concept less rigid and more fluid than those envisaged in other specific and particular provisions of the Bill of Rights," the Court held that refusal to appoint counsel under the particular facts and circumstances in the Betts case was not so "offensive to the common and fundamental ideas of fairness" as to amount to a denial of due process. Since the facts and circumstances of the two cases are so nearly indistinguishable, we think the Betts v. Brady holding, if left standing, would require us to reject Gideon's claim that the Constitution guarantees him the assistance of counsel. Upon full reconsideration, we conclude that Betts v. Brady should be overruled.

II

The Sixth Amendment provides, "In all criminal prosecutions, the accused shall enjoy the right . . . to have the Assistance of Counsel for his defense." We have construed this to mean that, in federal courts, counsel must be provided for defendants unable to employ counsel unless the right is competently and intelligently waived. Betts argued that this right is extended to indigent defendants in state courts by the Fourteenth Amendment. In response, the Court stated that, while the Sixth Amendment laid down no rule for the conduct of the States, the question recurs whether the constraint laid by the Amendment upon the national courts expresses a rule so fundamental and essential to a fair trial, and so, to due process of law, that it is made obligatory upon the States by the Fourteenth Amendment. 316 U.S. at 465.

We think the Court in Betts had ample precedent for acknowledging that those guarantees of the Bill of Rights which are fundamental safeguards of liberty immune from federal abridgment are equally protected against state invasion by the Due Process Clause of the Fourteenth Amendment. This same principle was recognized, explained, and applied in Powell v. Alabama, 287 U.S. 45 (1932), a case upholding the right of counsel, where the Court held that, despite sweeping language to the contrary in Hurtado v. California, 110 U.S. 516 (1884), the Fourteenth Amendment "embraced" those "fundamental principles of liberty and justice which lie at the base of all our civil and political institutions," even though they had been "specifically dealt with in another part of the federal Constitution." 287 U.S. at 67. In many cases other than Powell and Betts, this Court has looked to the fundamental nature of original Bill of Rights guarantees to decide whether the Fourteenth Amendment makes them obligatory on the States. Explicitly recognized to be of this "fundamental nature," and therefore made immune from state invasion by the Fourteenth Amendment, or some part of it, are the First Amendment's freedoms of speech, press, religion, assembly, association, and petition for redress of grievances.

For the same reason, though not always in precisely the same terminology, the Court has made obligatory on the States the Fifth Amendment's command that private property shall not be taken for public use without just compensation, the Fourth Amendment's prohibition of unreasonable searches and seizures, and the Eighth's ban on cruel and unusual punishment. . . .

We accept Betts v. Brady's assumption, based as it was on our prior cases, that a provision of the Bill of Rights which is "fundamental and essential to a fair trial" is made obligatory upon the States by the Fourteenth Amendment. We think the Court in Betts was wrong, however, in concluding that the Sixth Amendment's guarantee of counsel is not one of these fundamental rights. . . .

We concluded that certain fundamental rights, safeguarded by the first eight amendments against federal action, were also safeguarded against state action by the due process of law clause of the Fourteenth Amendment, and among them the fundamental right of the accused to the aid of counsel in a criminal prosecution. . . .

The right of one charged with a crime to counsel may not be deemed fundamental and essential to fair trials in some countries, but it is in ours. From the very beginning, our state and national constitutions and laws have laid great emphasis on procedural and substantive safeguards designed to assure fair trials before impartial tribunals in which every defendant stands equal before the law. This noble ideal cannot be realized if the poor man charged with crime has to face his accusers without a lawyer to assist him. . . .

The right to be heard would be, in many cases, of little avail if it did not comprehend the right to be heard by counsel. Even the intelligent and educated layman has small and sometimes no skill in the science of law. If charged with crime, he is incapable, generally, of determining for himself whether the indictment is good or bad. He is unfamiliar with the rules of evidence. Left without the aid of counsel, he may be put on trial without a proper charge, and convicted upon incompetent evidence, or evidence irrelevant to the issue or otherwise inadmissible. He lacks both the skill and knowledge to adequately prepare his defense, even though he has a perfect one. He requires the guiding hand of counsel at every step in the proceedings against him. Without it, though he be not guilty, he faces the danger of conviction because he does not know how to establish his innocence.

The Court in Betts v. Brady departed from the sound wisdom upon which the Court's holding in Powell v. Alabama rested. Florida, supported by two other States, has asked that Betts v. Brady be left intact. Twenty-two States, as friends of the Court, argue that Betts was "an anachronism when handed down," and that it should now be overruled. We agree.

The judgment is reversed, and the cause is remanded to the Supreme Court of Florida for further action not inconsistent with this opinion.

Reversed.

Miranda v. Arizona 384 U.S. 436 (1966)

Criminal suspect Ernesto Miranda was taken into police custody in Phoenix, Arizona, on suspicion of kidnapping and rape. Miranda was a poor 23-year-old youth who had not completed the ninth grade. The Phoenix police placed him in a lineup, where he was viewed by the witness complaining against him. After that, Miranda was interrogated for two hours by police officers, and he confessed to the crimes during that time.

In his typed and signed confession Miranda acknowledged his guilt. Miranda had been told that his confession might be used against him, yet he gave it, according to the police, voluntarily.

The police admitted that neither before nor during the questioning had Miranda been advised of his right to consult with a lawyer before answering any questions. Subsequently, Miranda was tried and convicted of kidnapping and rape by an Arizona jury that had relied on his confession, which was produced in evidence at his trial. After his conviction, Miranda sought to appeal to the Supreme Court to free him because of the improper means used to extract his confession.

The Supreme Court considered this case as one of a group of four cases that tested the meaning of the self-incrimination clause of the Fourth Amendment to the Constitution. In each of the cases the defendant had been held in custody and kept by police in a room to prevent contact with a lawyer or the outside world. No warning was given to these suspects at the time the interrogation began. Because of these police practices the Supreme Court felt impelled to specify the exact rights of suspects in criminal detention cases.

MR. CHIEF JUSTICE WARREN delivered the opinion of the Court.

The cases before us raise questions which go to the roots of our concepts of American criminal jurisprudence: the restraints society must observe consistent with the Federal Constitution in prosecuting individuals for crime. More specifically, we deal with the admissibility of statements obtained from an individual who is subjected to custodial police interrogation and the necessity for procedures which assure that the individual is accorded his privilege under the Fifth Amendment to the Constitution not to be compelled to incriminate himself. . . .

III

Today, then, there can be no doubt that the Fifth Amendment privilege is available outside of criminal court proceedings, and serves to protect persons in all settings in which their freedom of action is curtailed in any significant way from being compelled to incriminate themselves. We have concluded that, without proper safeguards, the process of in-custody interrogation of persons suspected or accused of crime contains inherently compelling pressures which work to undermine the individual's will to resist and to compel him to speak where he would not otherwise do so freely. In order to combat these pressures and to permit a

full opportunity to exercise the privilege against self-incrimination, the accused must be adequately and effectively apprised of his rights, and the exercise of those rights must be fully honored.

It is impossible for us to foresee the potential alternatives for protecting the privilege which might be devised by Congress or the States in the exercise of their creative rulemaking capacities. Therefore, we cannot say that the Constitution necessarily requires adherence to any particular solution for the inherent compulsions of the interrogation process as it is presently conducted. Our decision in no way creates a constitutional straitjacket which will handicap sound efforts at reform, nor is it intended to have this effect. We encourage Congress and the States to continue their laudable search for increasingly effective ways of protecting the rights of the individual while promoting efficient enforcement of our criminal laws. However, unless we are shown other procedures which are at least as effective in apprising accused persons of their right of silence and in assuring a continuous opportunity to exercise it, the following safeguards must be observed.

At the outset, if a person in custody is to be subjected to interrogation, he must first be informed in clear and unequivocal terms that he has the right to remain silent. For those unaware of the privilege, the warning is needed simply to make them aware of it—the threshold requirement for an intelligent decision as to its exercise. More important, such a warning is an absolute prerequisite in overcoming the inherent pressures of the interrogation atmosphere. It is not just the subnormal or woefully ignorant who succumb to an interrogator's imprecations, whether implied or expressly stated, that the interrogation will continue until a confession is obtained or that silence in the face of accusation is itself damning, and will bode ill when presented to a jury. Further, the warning will show the individual that his interrogators are prepared to recognize his privilege should he choose to exercise it.

The Fifth Amendment privilege is so fundamental to our system of constitutional rule, and the expedient of giving an adequate warning as to the availability of the privilege so simple, we will not pause to inquire in individual cases whether the defendant was aware of his rights without a warning being given. Assessments of the knowledge the defendant possessed, based on information as to his age, education, intelligence, or prior contact with authorities, can never be more than speculation; a warning is a clear-cut fact. More important, whatever the background of the person interrogated, a warning at the time of the interrogation is indispensable to overcome its pressures and to insure that the individual knows he is free to exercise the privilege at that point in time.

The warning of the right to remain silent must be accompanied by the explanation that anything said can and will be used against the individual in court. This warning is needed in order to make him aware not only of the privilege, but also of the consequences of forgoing it. It is only through an awareness of these consequences that there can be any assurance of real understanding and intelligent exercise of the privilege. Moreover, this warning may serve to make the individual more acutely aware that he is faced with a phase of the adversary system— that he is not in the presence of persons acting solely in his interest.

The circumstances surrounding in-custody interrogation can operate very quickly to overbear the will of one merely made aware of his privilege by his interrogators. Therefore, the right to have counsel present at the interrogation is indispensable to the protection of the Fifth Amendment privilege under the system we delineate today. Our aim is to assure that the individual's right to choose between silence and speech remains unfettered throughout the interrogation process. A once-stated warning, delivered by those who will conduct the interrogation, cannot itself suffice to that end among those who most require knowledge of their rights. A mere warning given by the interrogators is not alone sufficient to accomplish that end. Prosecutors themselves claim that the admonishment of the right to remain silent, without more, "will benefit only the recidivist and the professional." Brief for the National District Attorneys Association as *amicus curiae*, p. 14. Even preliminary advice given to the accused by his own attorney can be swiftly overcome by the secret interrogation process. Cf. Escobedo v. Illinois, 378 U.S. 478 , 485, n. 5. Thus, the need for counsel to protect the Fifth Amendment privilege comprehends not merely a right to consult with counsel prior to questioning, but also to have counsel present during any questioning if the defendant so desires.

The presence of counsel at the interrogation may serve several significant subsidiary functions, as well. If the accused decides to talk to his interrogators, the assistance of counsel can mitigate the dangers of untrustworthiness. With a lawyer present, the likelihood that the police will practice coercion is reduced, and, if coercion is nevertheless exercised, the lawyer can testify to it in court. The presence of a lawyer can also help to guarantee that the accused gives a fully accurate statement to the police, and that the statement is rightly reported by the prosecution at trial.

An individual need not make a pre-interrogation request for a lawyer. While such a request affirmatively secures his right to have one, his failure to ask for a lawyer does not constitute a waiver. No effective waiver of the right to counsel during interrogation can be recognized unless specifically made after the warnings we here delineate have been given. The accused who does not know his rights and therefore does not make a request may be the person who most needs counsel. . . .

Finally, we must recognize that the imposition of the requirement for the request would discriminate against the defendant who does not know his rights. The defendant who does not ask for counsel is the very defendant who most needs counsel. We cannot penalize a defendant who, not understanding his constitutional rights, does not make the formal request, and, by such failure, demonstrates his helplessness. To require the request would be to favor the defendant whose sophistication or status had fortuitously prompted him to make it. . . .

It is settled that, where the assistance of counsel is a constitutional requisite, the right to be furnished counsel does not depend on a request.

This proposition applies with equal force in the context of providing counsel to protect an accused's Fifth Amendment privilege in the face of interrogation. Although the role of counsel at trial differs from the role during interrogation, the differences are not relevant to the question whether a request is a prerequisite.

Accordingly, we hold that an individual held for interrogation must be clearly informed that he has the right to consult with a lawyer and to have the lawyer with him during interrogation under the system for protecting the privilege we delineate today. As with the warnings of the right to remain silent and that anything stated can be used in evidence against him, this warning is an absolute prerequisite to interrogation. No amount of circumstantial evidence that the person may have been aware of this right will suffice to stand in its stead. Only through such a warning is there ascertainable assurance that the accused was aware of this right.

If an individual indicates that he wishes the assistance of counsel before any interrogation occurs, the authorities cannot rationally ignore or deny his request on the basis that the individual does not have or cannot afford a retained attorney. The financial ability of the individual has no relationship to the scope of the rights involved here. The privilege against self-incrimination secured by the Constitution applies to all individuals. The need for counsel in order to protect the privilege exists for the indigent as well as the affluent. In fact, were we to limit these constitutional rights to those who can retain an attorney, our decisions today would be of little significance. The cases before us, as well as the vast majority of confession cases with which we have dealt in the past, involve those unable to retain counsel. While authorities are not required to relieve the accused of his poverty, they have the obligation not to take advantage of indigence in the administration of justice. Denial of counsel to the indigent at the time of interrogation while allowing an attorney to those who can afford one would be no more supportable by reason or logic than the similar situation at trial and on appeal struck down in Gideon v. Wainwright, 372 U.S. 335 (1963), and Douglas v. California, 372 U.S. 353 (1963).

In order fully to apprise a person interrogated of the extent of his rights under this system, then, it is necessary to warn him not only that he has the right to consult with an attorney, but also that, if he is indigent, a lawyer will be appointed to represent him. Without this additional warning, the admonition of the right to consult with counsel would often be understood as meaning only that he can consult with a lawyer if he has one or has the funds to obtain one. The warning of a right to counsel would be hollow if not couched in terms that would convey to the indigent—the person most often subjected to interrogation—the knowledge that he too has a right to have counsel present. As with the warnings of the right to remain silent and of the general right to counsel, only by effective and express explanation to the indigent of this right can there be assurance that he was truly in a position to exercise it.

Once warnings have been given, the subsequent procedure is clear. If the individual indicates in any manner, at any time prior to or during questioning, that he wishes to remain silent, the interrogation must cease. At this point, he has shown that he intends to exercise his Fifth Amendment privilege; any statement taken after the person invokes his privilege cannot be other than the product of compulsion, subtle or otherwise. Without the right to cut off questioning, the setting of in-custody interrogation operates on the individual to overcome free choice in producing a statement after the privilege has been once invoked. If the individual states that he wants an attorney, the interrogation must cease until an attorney is present. At that time, the individual must have an opportunity to confer with the attorney and to have him present during any subsequent questioning. If the individual cannot obtain an attorney and he indicates that he wants one before speaking to police, they must respect his decision to remain silent.

This does not mean, as some have suggested, that each police station must have a "station house lawyer" present at all times to advise prisoners. It does mean, however, that, if police propose to interrogate a person, they must make known to him that he is entitled to a lawyer and that, if he cannot afford one, a lawyer will be provided for him prior to any interrogation. If authorities conclude that they will not provide counsel during a reasonable period of time in which investigation in the field is carried out, they may refrain from doing so without violating the person's Fifth Amendment privilege so long as they do not question him during that time.

If the interrogation continues without the presence of an attorney and a statement is taken, a heavy burden rests on the government to demonstrate that the defendant knowingly and intelligently waived his privilege against self-incrimination and his right to retained or appointed counsel. Escobedo v. Illinois, 378 U.S. 478, 490, n. 14. This Court has always set high standards of proof for the waiver of constitutional rights, Johnson v. Zerbst, 304 U.S. 458 (1938), and we reassert these standards as applied to in-custody interrogation. Since the State is responsible for establishing the isolated circumstances under which the interrogation takes place, and has the only means of making available corroborated evidence of warnings given during incommunicado interrogation, the burden is rightly on its shoulders. . . .

In Re Gault
387 U.S. 1 (1967)

Fifteen-year-old Gerald Gault was committed to Arizona's State Industrial School until he was 21-years-old for a juvenile offense under the Arizona Juvenile Code. Gault had been adjudicated as a "delinquent child" for making an obscene telephone call to a neighbor while on probation for another juvenile offense. If Gault had been tried as an adult his maximum punishment under the criminal law would have been a $50 fine and two months in jail.

The Arizona Juvenile Code provided severe punishment for young people, but few rights or protections for them. Gault had no preliminary notice of his juvenile hearing. His case was decided a few days after he was told to appear. Gault was given no opportunity to cross-examine the witnesses against him. He was offered no right to plead self-incrimination. The severe punishment given to Gault was based largely upon his own admissions about the telephone call, and he had been given no warning of the impact of his statements.

The case was ultimately appealed to the Supreme Court where it set new principles for juvenile justice.

MR. JUSTICE FORTAS delivered the opinion of the Court.

This is an appeal under 28 U.S.C. ' 1257(2) from a judgment of the Supreme Court of Arizona affirming the dismissal of a petition for a writ of habeas corpus. 99 Ariz. 181, 407 P.2d 760 (1965). The petition sought the release of Gerald Francis Gault, appellants' 15-year-old son, who had been committed as a juvenile delinquent to the State Industrial School by the Juvenile Court of Gila County, Arizona. The Supreme Court of Arizona affirmed dismissal of the writ against various arguments which included an attack upon the constitutionality of the Arizona Juvenile Code because of its alleged denial of procedural due process rights to juveniles charged with being "delinquents." The court agreed that the constitutional guarantee of

due process of law is applicable in such proceedings. It held that Arizona's Juvenile Code is to be read as "impliedly" implementing the "due process concept." It then proceeded to identify and describe "the particular elements which constitute due process in a juvenile hearing." It concluded that the proceedings ending in commitment of Gerald Gault did not offend those requirements. We do not agree, and we reverse. We begin with a statement of the facts. . . .

We do not in this opinion consider the impact of these constitutional provisions upon the totality of the relationship of the juvenile and the state. We do not even consider the entire process relating to juvenile "delinquents." For example, we are not here concerned with the procedures or constitutional rights applicable to the pre-judicial stages of the juvenile process, nor do we direct our attention to the post-adjudicative or dispositional process. . . . We consider only the problems presented to us by this case. These relate to the proceedings by which a determination is made as to whether a juvenile is a "delinquent" as a result of alleged misconduct on his part, with the consequence that he may be committed to a state institution. As to these proceedings, there appears to be little current dissent from the proposition that the Due Process Clause has a role to play. . . The problem is to ascertain the precise impact of the due process requirement upon such proceedings.

From the inception of the juvenile court system, wide differences have been tolerated—indeed insisted upon—between the procedural rights accorded to adults and those of juveniles. In practically all jurisdictions, there are rights granted to adults which are withheld from juveniles. In addition to the specific problems involved in the present case, for example, it has been held that the juvenile is not entitled to bail, to indictment by grand jury, to a public trial or to trial by jury. It is frequent practice that rules governing the arrest and interrogation of adults by the police are not observed in the case of juveniles. . . .

Unfortunately, loose procedures, high-handed methods and crowded court calendars, either singly or in combination, all too often, have resulted in depriving some juveniles of fundamental rights that have resulted in a denial of due process.

Failure to observe the fundamental requirements of due process has resulted in instances, which might have been avoided, of unfairness to individuals and inadequate or inaccurate findings of fact and unfortunate prescriptions of remedy. Due process of law is the primary and indispensable foundation of individual freedom. It is the basic and essential term in the social compact which defines the rights of the individual and delimits the powers which the state may exercise.

The Supreme Court of Arizona rejected appellants' claim that due process was denied because of inadequate notice. It stated that "Mrs. Gault knew the exact nature of the charge against Gerald from the day he was taken to the detention home." The court also pointed out that the Gaults appeared at the two hearings "without objection." The court held that, because "the policy of the juvenile law is to hide youthful errors from the full gaze of the public and bury them in the grave-yard of the forgotten past," advance notice of the specific charges or basis for taking the juvenile into custody and for the hearing is not necessary. It held that the appropriate rule is that the infant and his parent or guardian will receive a petition only reciting a conclusion of delinquency. But, no later than the initial hearing by the judge, they must be advised of the facts involved in the case. If the charges are denied, they must be given a reasonable period of time to prepare.

We cannot agree with the court's conclusion that adequate notice was given, in this case. Notice, to comply with due process requirements, must be given sufficiently in advance of scheduled court proceedings so that reasonable opportunity to prepare will be afforded, and it must "set forth the alleged misconduct with particularity." It is obvious, as we have discussed above, that no purpose of shielding the child from the public stigma of knowledge of his having been taken into custody and scheduled for hearing is served by the procedure approved by the court below. The "initial hearing" in the present case was a hearing on the merits. Notice at that time is not timely, and even if there were a conceivable purpose served by the deferral proposed by the court below, it would have to yield to the requirements that the child and his parents or guardian be notified, in writing, of the specific charge or factual allegations to be considered at the hearing, and that such written notice be given at the earliest practicable time, and, in any event, sufficiently in advance of the hearing to permit preparation. Due process of

law requires notice of the sort we have described—that is, notice which would be deemed constitutionally adequate in a civil or criminal proceeding. It does not allow a hearing to be held in which a youth's freedom and his parents' right to his custody are at stake without giving them timely notice, in advance of the hearing, of the specific issues that they must meet. Nor, in the circumstances of this case, can it reasonably be said that the requirement of notice was waived.

IV

Right to Counsel

Appellants charge that the Juvenile Court proceedings were fatally defective because the court did not advise Gerald or his parents of their right to counsel, and proceeded with the hearing, the adjudication of delinquency, and the order of commitment in the absence of counsel for the child and his parents or an express waiver of the right thereto. The Supreme Court of Arizona pointed out that "[t]here is disagreement [among the various jurisdictions] as to whether the court must advise the infant [p*35] that he has a right to counsel." It noted its own decision in Arizona State Dept. of Public Welfare v. Barlow, 80 Ariz. 249, 296 P.2d 28 (1956), to the effect "that the parents of an infant in a juvenile proceeding cannot be denied representation by counsel of their choosing." It referred to a provision of the Juvenile Code which it characterized as requiring "that the probation officer shall look after the interests of neglected, delinquent and dependent children," including representing their interests in court. The court argued that "the parent and the probation officer may be relied upon to protect the infant's interests." Accordingly, it rejected the proposition that "due process requires that an infant have a right to counsel." It said that juvenile courts have the discretion, but not the duty, to allow such representation; it referred specifically to the situation in which the Juvenile Court discerns conflict between the child and his parents as an instance in which this discretion might be exercised. We do not agree. Probation officers, in the Arizona scheme, are also arresting officers. They initiate proceedings and file petitions which they verify, as here, alleging the delinquency of the child, and they testify, as here, against the child. And here the probation officer was also superintendent of the Detention Home. The probation officer cannot act as counsel for the child. His role in the adjudicatory hearing, by statute and, in fact, is as arresting officer and witness against the child. Nor can the judge represent the child. There is no material difference in this respect between adult and juvenile proceedings of the sort here involved. In adult proceedings, this contention has been foreclosed by decisions of this Court. A proceeding where the issue is whether the child will be found to be "delinquent" and subjected to the loss of his liberty for years is comparable in seriousness to a felony prosecution. The juvenile needs the assistance of counsel to cope with problems of law, to make skilled inquiry into the facts, to insist upon regularity of the proceedings, and to ascertain whether he has a defense and to prepare and submit it. The child "requires the guiding hand of counsel at every step in the proceedings against him." Just as in Kent v. United States, supra, at 561–562, we indicated our agreement with the United States Court of Appeals for the District of Columbia Circuit that the assistance of counsel is essential for purposes of waiver proceedings, so we hold now that it is equally essential for the determination of delinquency, carrying with it the awesome prospect of incarceration in a state institution until the juvenile reaches the age of 21. . . .

We conclude that the Due Process Clause of the Fourteenth Amendment requires that, in respect of proceedings to determine delinquency which may result in commitment to an institution in which the juvenile's freedom is curtailed, the child and his parents must be notified of the child's right to be represented by counsel retained by them, or, if they are unable to afford counsel, that counsel will be appointed to represent the child.

V

Confrontation, Self-Incrimination, Cross-Examination

Our first question, then, is whether Gerald's admission was improperly obtained and relied on as the basis of decision, in conflict with the Federal Constitution. For this purpose, it is necessary briefly to recall the relevant facts. . . .

The constitutional privilege against self-incrimination is applicable in such proceedings: an admission by the juvenile may [not] be used against him in the absence of clear and unequivocal evidence that the admission was made with knowledge that he was not obliged to speak, and would not be penalized for remaining silent. . . .

[T]he availability of the privilege does not turn upon the type of proceeding in which its protection is invoked, but upon the nature of the statement or admission and the exposure which it invites. . . . [J]uvenile proceedings to determine "delinquency," which may lead to commitment to a state institution, must be regarded as "criminal" for purposes of the privilege against self-incrimination. . . .

Furthermore, experience has shown that "admissions and confessions by juveniles require special caution" as to their reliability and voluntariness, and "[i]t would indeed be surprising if the privilege against self-incrimination were available to hardened criminals, but not to children."

[S]pecial problems may arise with respect to waiver of the privilege by or on behalf of children, and . . . there may well be some differences in technique—but not in principle—depending upon the age of the child and the presence and competence of parents. . . . If counsel was not present for some permissible reason when an admission was obtained, the greatest care must be taken to assure that the admission was voluntary. . . .

Gerald's admissions did not measure up to these standards, and could not properly be used as a basis for the judgment against him.

Absent a valid confession, a juvenile in such proceedings must be afforded the rights of confrontation and sworn testimony of witnesses available for cross-examination.

Tinker v. Des Moines Independent Community School District 393 U.S. 503 (1969)

This decision established certain boundaries for student free speech and expression rights in America. The impact of this decision does not amount to full, adult protection under the Bill of Rights. On the other hand, it does provide a guidepost for school officials in dealing with similar assertions of student rights.

MR. JUSTICE FORTAS delivered the opinion of the Court.

Petitioner John F. Tinker, 15 years old, and petitioner Christopher Eckhardt, 16 years old, attended high schools in Des Moines, Iowa. Petitioner Mary Beth Tinker, John's sister, was a 13-year-old student in junior high school.

In December, 1965, a group of adults and students in Des Moines held a meeting at the Eckhardt home. The group determined to publicize their objections to the hostilities in Vietnam and their support for a truce by wearing black armbands during the holiday season and by fasting on December 16 and New Year's Eve. Petitioners and their parents had previously engaged in similar activities, and they decided to participate in the program.

The principals of the Des Moines schools became aware of the plan to wear armbands. On December 14, 1965, they met and adopted a policy that any student wearing an armband to school would be asked to remove it, and, if he refused, he would be suspended until he returned without the armband. Petitioners were aware of the regulation that the school authorities adopted.

On December 16, Mary Beth and Christopher wore black armbands to their schools. John Tinker wore his armband the next day. They were all sent home and suspended from school until they would come back without their armbands. They did not return to school until after the planned period for wearing armbands had expired—that is, until after New Year's Day.

This complaint was filed in the United States District Court by petitioners, through their fathers, under ' 1983 of Title 42 of the United States Code. It prayed for an injunction restraining the respondent school officials and the respondent members of the board of directors of the school district from disciplining the petitioners, and it sought nominal damages. After an evidentiary hearing, the District Court dismissed the complaint. It upheld the constitutionality of the school authorities' action on the ground that it was reasonable in order to prevent disturbance of school discipline. 258 F.Supp. 971 (1966). The court referred to, but expressly declined to follow, the Fifth Circuit's holding in a similar case that the wearing of symbols like the armbands cannot be prohibited unless it "materially and substantially interfere[s] with the requirements of appropriate discipline in the operation of the school." Burnside v. Byars, 363 F.2d 744, 749 (1966).

I

First Amendment rights, applied in light of the special characteristics of the school environment, are available to teachers and students. It can hardly be argued that either students or teachers shed their constitutional rights to freedom of speech or expression at the schoolhouse gate. This has been the unmistakable holding of this Court for almost 50 years. In Meyer v. Nebraska, 262 U.S. 390 (1923), and Bartels v. Iowa, 262 U.S. 404 (1923), this Court, in opinions by Mr. Justice McReynolds, held that the Due Process Clause of the Fourteenth Amendment prevents States from forbidding the teaching of a foreign language to young students. Statutes to this effect, the Court held, unconstitutionally interfere with the liberty of teacher, student, and parent . . .

II

The problem posed by the present case does not relate to regulation of the length of skirts or the type of clothing, to hair style, or deportment. Cf. Ferrell v. Dallas Independent School District, 392 F.2d 697 (1968); Pugsley v. Sellmeyer, 158 Ark. 247, 250 S.W. 538 (1923). It does not concern aggressive, disruptive action or even group demonstrations. Our problem involves direct, primary First Amendment rights akin to "pure speech."

The school officials banned and sought to punish petitioners for a silent, passive expression of opinion, unaccompanied by any disorder or disturbance on the part of petitioners. There is here no evidence whatever of petitioners' interference, actual or nascent, with the schools' work or of collision with the rights of other students to be secure and to be let alone. Accordingly, this case does not concern speech or action that intrudes upon the work of the schools or the rights of other students.

Only a few of the 18,000 students in the school system wore the black armbands. Only five students were suspended for wearing them. There is no indication that the work of the schools or any class was disrupted. Outside the classrooms, a few students made hostile remarks to the children wearing armbands, but there were no threats or acts of violence on school premises.

The District Court concluded that the action of the school authorities was reasonable because it was based upon their fear of a disturbance from the wearing of the armbands. But, in our system, undifferentiated fear or apprehension of disturbance is not enough to overcome the right to freedom of expression. Any departure from absolute regimentation may cause trouble. Any variation from the majority's opinion may inspire fear. Any word spoken, in class, in the lunchroom, or on the campus, that deviates from the views of another person may start an argument or cause a disturbance. But our Constitution says we must take this risk, Terminiello v. Chicago, 337 U.S. 1 (1949); and our history says that it is this sort of hazardous freedom—this kind of openness—that is the basis of our national strength and of the independence and vigor of Americans who grow up and live in this relatively permissive, often disputatious, society.

In order for the State in the person of school officials to justify prohibition of a particular expression of opinion, it must be able to show that its action was caused by something more than a mere desire to avoid the discomfort and unpleasantness that always accompany an unpopular viewpoint. Certainly where there is no finding and no showing that engaging in the forbidden conduct would "materially and substantially interfere with the requirements of appropriate discipline in the operation of the school," the prohibition cannot be sustained. Burnside v. Byars, supra, at 749.

In the present case, the District Court made no such finding, and our independent examination of the record fails to yield evidence that the school authorities had reason to anticipate that the wearing of the armbands would substantially interfere with the work of the school or impinge upon the rights of other students. Even an official memorandum prepared after the suspension that listed the reasons for the ban on wearing the armbands made no reference to the anticipation of such disruption.

On the contrary, the action of the school authorities appears to have been based upon an urgent wish to avoid the controversy which might result from the expression, even by the silent symbol of armbands, of opposition to this Nation's part in the conflagration in Vietnam. It is revealing, in this respect, that the meeting at which the school principals decided to issue the contested regulation was called in response to a student's statement to the journalism teacher in one of the schools that he wanted to write an article on Vietnam and have it published in the school paper.

It is also relevant that the school authorities did not purport to prohibit the wearing of all symbols of political or controversial significance. The record shows that students in some of the schools wore buttons relating to national political campaigns, and some even wore the Iron Cross, traditionally a symbol of Nazism. The order prohibiting the wearing of armbands did not extend to these. Instead, a particular symbol—black armbands worn to exhibit opposition to this Nation's involvement in Vietnam—was singled out for prohibition. Clearly, the prohibition of expression of one particular opinion, at least without evidence that it is necessary to avoid material and substantial interference with schoolwork or discipline, is not constitutionally permissible.

In our system, state-operated schools may not be enclaves of totalitarianism. School officials do not possess absolute authority over their students. Students in school, as well as out of school, are "persons" under our Constitution. They are possessed of fundamental rights which the State must respect, just as they themselves must respect their obligations to the State. In our system, students may not be regarded as closed-circuit recipients of only that which the State chooses to communicate. They may not be confined to the expression of those sentiments that are officially approved. In the absence of a specific showing of constitutionally valid reasons to regulate their speech, students are entitled to freedom of expression of their views. As Judge Gewin, speaking for the Fifth Circuit, said, school officials cannot suppress "expressions of feelings with which they do not wish to contend." Burnside v. Byars, supra, at 749.

As we have discussed, the record does not demonstrate any facts which might reasonably have led school authorities to forecast substantial disruption of or material interference with school activities, and no disturbances or disorders on the school premises in fact occurred. These petitioners merely went about their ordained rounds in school. Their deviation consisted only in wearing on their sleeve a band of black cloth, not more than two inches wide. They wore it to exhibit their disapproval of the Vietnam hostilities and their advocacy of a truce, to make their views known, and, by their example, to influence others to adopt them. They neither interrupted school activities nor sought to intrude in the school affairs or the lives of others. They caused discussion outside of the classrooms, but no interference with work and no disorder. In the circumstances, our Constitution does not permit officials of the State to deny their form of expression.

We express no opinion as to the form of relief which should be granted, this being a matter for the lower courts to determine. We reverse and remand for further proceedings consistent with this opinion.

Reversed and remanded.

MR. JUSTICE STEWART, concurring.

Although I agree with much of what is said in the Court's opinion, and with its judgment in this case, I cannot share the Court's uncritical assumption that, school discipline aside, the First Amendment rights of children are coextensive with those of adults. Indeed, I had thought the Court decided otherwise just last Term in Ginsberg v. New York, 390 U.S. 629. I continue to hold the view I expressed in that case:

[A] State may permissibly determine that, at least in some precisely delineated areas, a child—like someone in a captive audience—is not possessed of that full capacity for individual choice which is the presupposition of First Amendment guarantees.

Roe v. Wade
410 U.S. 113 (1973)

Roe v. Wade *has become one of the most controversial Supreme Court decisions in recent history. The 1973 decision represents a high water mark in the struggle of many women's groups against restrictive state law concerning abortion.*

The facts of the case are simple. A single pregnant woman (called Jane Roe, but actually revealed later to be Norma McCorvey) joined in a suit to challenge the constitutionality of the Texas criminal abortion law. That law, as well as similar laws in other states, limited abortion to circumstances in which medical advice determined that the woman's life would be at stake if an abortion were denied. Some other state laws were less restrictive, but by 1972 the Supreme Court was ready to address the issue of abortion laws in general, and this case provided an opportunity to do so.

This 1973 decision seemed to establish an unrestricted right of a woman to choose an abor-

tion during the first three months of her pregnancy. In the second three months some sort of state restrictions on a woman's right to choose might be justified by concern for the health of the woman. Only in the last three months of pregnancy could the state intervene on behalf of the unborn child, asserting a public policy superior to the right of the pregnant woman.

In later decisions the Supreme Court has retreated. The Court has stricken down some requirements of parental and spousal consent as a part of the abortion decision, but upheld other restrictions on a woman's right to choose an abortion. Nevertheless, Roe *v.* Wade *has not been overturned, in spite of severe political pressure placed on the Court. Some members of Congress believe that no Supreme Court justice should be confirmed unless they agree to reverse the case.*

MR. JUSTICE BLACKMUN, delivered the opinion of the Court.

The District Court held that the appellee failed to meet his burden of demonstrating that the Texas statute's infringement upon Roe's rights was necessary to support a compelling state interest, and that, although the appellee presented "several compelling justifications for state presence in the area of abortions," the statutes outstripped these justifications and swept "far beyond any areas of compelling state interest." 314 F.Supp. at 1222B1223. Appellant and appellee both contest that holding. Appellant, as has been indicated, claims an absolute right that bars any state imposition of criminal penalties in the area. Appellee argues that the State's determination to recognize and protect prenatal life from and after conception constitutes a compelling state interest. As noted above, we do not agree fully with either formulation.

The appellee and certain amici argue that the fetus is a "person" within the language and meaning of the Fourteenth Amendment. In support of this, they outline at length and in detail the well known facts of fetal development. If this suggestion of personhood is established, the appellant's case, of course, collapses, for the fetus' right to life would then be guaranteed specifically by the Amendment. The appellant conceded as much on reargument. On the other hand, the appellee conceded on reargument that no case could be cited that holds that a fetus is a person within the meaning of the Fourteenth Amendment. . . .

Texas urges that, apart from the Fourteenth Amendment, life begins at conception and is present throughout pregnancy, and that, therefore, the State has a compelling interest in protecting that life from and after conception. We need not resolve the difficult question of when life begins. When those trained in the respective disciplines of medicine, philosophy, and theology are unable to arrive at any consensus, the judiciary, at this point in the development of man's knowledge, is not in a position to speculate as to the answer. . . .

In areas other than criminal abortion, the law has been reluctant to endorse any theory that life, as we recognize it, begins before live birth, or to accord legal rights to the unborn except in narrowly defined situations and except when the rights are contingent upon live birth. For example, the traditional rule of tort law denied recovery for prenatal injuries even though the child was born alive.

That rule has been changed in almost every jurisdiction. In most States, recovery is said to be permitted only if the fetus was viable, or at least quick, when the injuries were sustained, though few courts have squarely so held. In a recent development, generally opposed by the commentators, some States permit the parents of a stillborn child to maintain an action for wrongful death because of prenatal injuries. Such an action, however, would appear to be one to vindicate the parents' interest and is thus consistent with the view that the fetus, at most, represents only the potentiality of life. Similarly, unborn children have been recognized as acquiring rights or interests by way of inheritance or other devolution of property, and have been represented by guardians *ad litem*. Protection of the interests involved, again, has generally been contingent upon live birth. In short, the unborn have never been recognized in the law as persons in the whole sense.

X

In view of all this, we do not agree that, by adopting one theory of life, Texas may override the rights of the pregnant woman that are at stake. We repeat, however, that the State does have an important and legitimate interest in preserving and protecting the health of the pregnant woman, whether she be a resident of the State or a nonresident who seeks medical consultation and treatment there, and that it has still another important

and legitimate interest in protecting the potentiality of human life. These interests are separate and distinct. Each grows in substantiality as the woman approaches term and, at a point during pregnancy, each becomes "compelling."

With respect to the State's important and legitimate interest in the health of the mother, the "compelling" point, in the light of present medical knowledge, is at approximately the end of the first trimester. This is so because of the now-established medical fact, referred to above . . . that, until the end of the first trimester mortality in abortion may be less than mortality in normal childbirth. It follows that, from and after this point, a State may regulate the abortion procedure to the extent that the regulation reasonably relates to the preservation and protection of maternal health. Examples of permissible state regulation in this area are requirements as to the qualifications of the person who is to perform the abortion; as to the licensure of that person; as to the facility in which the procedure is to be performed, that is, whether it must be a hospital or may be a clinic or some other place of less-than-hospital status; as to the licensing of the facility; and the like.

This means, on the other hand, that, for the period of pregnancy prior to this "compelling" point, the attending physician, in consultation with his patient, is free to determine, without regulation by the State, that, in his medical judgment, the patient's pregnancy should be terminated. If that decision is reached, the judgment may be effectuated by an abortion free of interference by the State.

With respect to the State's important and legitimate interest in potential life, the "compelling" point is at viability. This is so because the fetus then presumably has the capability of meaningful life outside the mother's womb. State regulation protective of fetal life after viability thus has both logical and biological justifications. If the State is interested in protecting fetal life after viability, it may go so far as to proscribe abortion during that period, except when it is necessary to preserve the life or health of the mother.

Measured against these standards, Art. 1196 of the Texas Penal Code, in restricting legal abortions to those "procured or attempted by medical advice for the purpose of saving the life of the mother," sweeps too broadly. The statute makes no distinction between abortions performed early in pregnancy and those performed later, and it limits to a single reason, "saving" the mother's life, the legal justification for the procedure. The statute, therefore, cannot survive the constitutional attack made upon it here.

XI

To summarize and to repeat:

1. A state criminal abortion statute of the current Texas type, that excepts from criminality only a lifesaving procedure on behalf of the mother, without regard to pregnancy stage and without recognition of the other interests involved, is violative of the Due Process Clause of the Fourteenth Amendment.

(a) For the stage prior to approximately the end of the first trimester, the abortion decision and its effectuation must be left to the medical judgment of the pregnant woman's attending physician.

(b) For the stage subsequent to approximately the end of the first trimester, the State, in promoting its interest in the health of the mother, may, if it chooses, regulate the abortion procedure in ways that are reasonably related to maternal health.

(c) For the stage subsequent to viability, the State in promoting its interest in the potentiality of human life [p*165] may, if it chooses, regulate, and even proscribe, abortion except where it is necessary, in appropriate medical judgment, for the preservation of the life or health of the mother.

2. The State may define the term "physician," as it has been employed in the preceding paragraphs of this Part XI of this opinion, to mean only a physician currently licensed by the State, and may proscribe any abortion by a person who is not a physician as so defined.

In Doe v. Bolton, post, p. 179, procedural requirements contained in one of the modern abortion statutes are considered. That opinion and this one, of course, are to be read together.

This holding, we feel, is consistent with the relative weights of the respective interests involved, with the lessons and examples of medical and legal history, with the lenity of the common law, and with the demands of the profound problems of the present day. The decision leaves the State free to place increasing restrictions on abortion as the period of pregnancy lengthens, so long as those restrictions are tailored to the recognized state interests. The decision vindicates the right of the physician to administer medical treatment according to his professional judgment up to the points where important state interests provide compelling justifications for intervention. Up to those points, the abortion decision in all its aspects is inherently, and primarily, a medical decision, and basic responsibility for it must rest with the physician. If an individual practitioner abuses the privilege of exercising proper medical judgment, the usual remedies, judicial and intra-professional, are available.

XII

Our conclusion that Art. 1196 is unconstitutional means, of course, that the Texas abortion statutes, as a unit, must fall. The exception of Art. 1196 cannot be struck down separately, for then the State would be left with a statute proscribing all abortion procedures no matter how medically urgent the case. . . .

We find it unnecessary to decide whether the District Court erred in withholding injunctive relief, for we assume the Texas prosecutorial authorities will give full credence to this decision that the present criminal abortion statutes of that State are unconstitutional. . . .

It is so ordered.

Regents of the Univ. of California v. Bakke 438 U.S. 265 (1978)

Allan Bakke was one of 2,664 applicants for 100 available admissions openings to the University of California at Davis Medical School. Eighty-four of the one hundred slots were filled by the normal admissions process. However, 16 of the slots were filled by a special admissions program established in 1970. This special admissions program was produced in response to a faculty concern about the low representation at the medical school of African American, Latino, Asian, and Native American students.

The special admissions program allowed applicants to have a lower grade point average or a lower standard test score than usual applicants. There was a separate admissions committee for applicants of minority groups.

Bakke was a white male applicant who was rejected twice for admission. In both years that Bakke was rejected some special applicants were admitted with lower scores. He filed suit against the special admissions program at University of California-Davis, claiming that the program violated Title VI of the federal Civil Rights Act of 1964, which forbade racial or ethnic preferences in programs supported by federal funds. On constitutional grounds, Bakke also contended that the setting aside of special positions for minorities denied him the "equal protection of the laws" guaranteed by the Fourteenth Amendment. In effect, Bakke accused the University of California of reverse discrimination against him in favor of minority group applicants.

The University of California-Davis cross-claimed for a declaration that its special admissions program was lawful. The case was ultimately appealed to the Supreme Court. The Supreme Court held that the university's special admissions program violated the Equal Protection Clause. Since the university could not satisfy its burden of demonstrating that Bakke would not have been admitted had it not been for the special admissions program, the court ordered his admission to Davis.

The Bakke *decision invalidated this particular special admissions program but permitted universities to take race into account as a factor in admissions decisions. Since this case, the Supreme Court has been suspicious of affirmative action programs.*

MR. JUSTICE POWELL announced the judgment of the Court.

The state certainly has a legitimate and substantial interest in ameliorating, or eliminating where feasible, the disabling effects of identified discrimination. The line of school desegregation cases, commencing with Brown, attests to the importance of this state goal and the commitment of the judiciary to affirm all lawful means towards its attainment. In the schools cases, the states were required by the courts to redress the wrongs worked by specific instances of racial discrimination. That goal was far more focused than the remedying of "societal discrimination," an amorphous

concept of injury that may be ageless in its reach into the past.

Hence, the purpose of helping certain groups whom the faculty of the Davis Medical School perceived as victims of "societal discrimination" does not justify a classification that imposes disadvantages on persons like respondent, who bear no responsibility for whatever harm the beneficiaries of the special admissions program are thought to have suffered. To hold otherwise would be to convert a remedy heretofore reserved for violations of legal rights into a privilege that all institutions throughout the nation could grant at their pleasure to whatever groups are perceived as victims of societal discrimination. That is a step we have never approved.

MR. JUSTICE POWELL concluded.

In summary, it is evident that the Davis special admission program involves the use of an explicit racial classification never before countenanced by this Court. It tells applicants who are not Negro, Asian, or "Chicano" that they are totally excluded from a specific percentage of the seats in an entering class. No matter how strong their qualifications, quantitative and extracurricular, including their own potential for contribution to ethnic diversity, they are never afforded the chance to compete with applicants from the preferred groups for the special admissions seats. At the same time, the preferred applicants have the opportunity to compete for every seat in the class.

The fatal flaw in petitioner's preferential program is its disregard for individual rights as guaranteed by the Fourteenth Amendment. Such rights are not absolute. But when a state's distribution of benefits or imposition of burdens hinges on the color of a person's skin or ancestry, that individual is entitled to a demonstration that the challenged classification is necessary to promote a substantial state interest. Petitioner has failed to carry this burden. For this reason, that portion of the California court's judgment holding petitioner's special admissions program invalid under the Fourteenth Amendment must be affirmed.

In enjoining petitioner from ever considering the race of an applicant, however, the courts below failed to recognize that the state has a substantial interest that legitimately may be served by a properly devised admissions program involving the competitive consideration of race and ethnic origin. For this reason, so much of the California court's judgment as enjoins the petitioner from any consideration of race must be reversed.

R.A.V., Petitioner v. City of St. Paul, Minnesota
505 U.S. 377 (1992)

This case tested the limits of the toleration of speech in America. It involved a St. Paul, Minnesota, ordinance aimed at penalizing those who commit bias-motivated crimes. In the process of weighing the protections provided by the First Amendment against the offense of cross-burning on the lawn of an African American family, the Court attempted to spell out that the First Amendment cannot be stretched as far as some advocates of racial harmony would like. On the other hand, footnote number one in this opinion points out that other laws may have been violated by this particular conduct, including the strict statutes aimed at criminal damages to property or at terroristic acts. The specific municipal ordinance involved here was not the only weapon available against race-based acts of violence.

MR. JUSTICE SCALIA delivered the opinion of the Court.

In the predawn hours of June 21, 1990, petitioner and several other teenagers allegedly assembled a crudely-made cross by taping together broken chair legs. They then allegedly burned the cross inside the fenced yard of a black family that lived across the street from the house where petitioner was staying. Although this conduct could have been punished under any of a number of laws, one of the two provisions under which respondent city of St. Paul chose to charge petitioner (then a juvenile) was the St. Paul Bias-Motivated Crime Ordinance, St. Paul, Minn. Legis. Code 292.02 (1990), which provides: "Whoever places on public or private property a symbol, object, appellation, characterization or graffiti, including, but not limited to, a burning cross or Nazi swastika, which one knows or has reasonable grounds to know arouses anger, alarm or resentment in others on the basis of race, color, creed, religion or gender commits disorderly conduct and shall be guilty of a misdemeanor."

Petitioner moved to dismiss this count on the ground that the St. Paul ordinance was substan-

tially overbroad and impermissibly content-based and therefore facially invalid under the First Amendment. The trial court granted this motion, but the Minnesota Supreme Court reversed. That court rejected petitioner's overbreadth claim because, as construed in prior Minnesota cases, see, e.g., In re Welfare of S. L. J., 263 N. W. 2d 412 (Minn. 1978), the modifying phrase "arouses anger, alarm or resentment in others" limited the reach of the ordinance to conduct that amounts to "fighting words," i.e., "conduct that itself inflicts injury or tends to incite immediate violence . . ." In re Welfare of R. A. V., 464 N. W. 2d 507, 510 (Minn. 1991) (citing Chaplinsky v. New Hampshire, 315 U. S. 568, 572 (1942)), and therefore the ordinance reached only expression "that the First Amendment does not protect." 464 N. W. 2d, at 511.

The court also concluded that the ordinance was not impermissibly content-based because, in its view, the ordinance is a narrowly tailored means toward accomplishing the compelling governmental interest in protecting the community against bias-motivated threats to public safety and order . . . We granted *certiorari*, 501 U. S. 708 (1991).

I

In construing the St. Paul ordinance, we are bound by the construction given to it by the Minnesota court . . . Accordingly, we accept the Minnesota Supreme Court's authoritative statement that the ordinance reaches only those expressions that constitute "fighting words" within the meaning of Chaplinsky. 464 N. W. 2d, at 510–511. Petitioner and his amici urge us to modify the scope of the Chaplinsky formulation, thereby invalidating the ordinance as "substantially overbroad," Broadrick v. Oklahoma, 413 U. S. 601, 610 (1973). We find it unnecessary to consider this issue. Assuming, arguendo, that all of the expression reached by the ordinance is prescribable under the "fighting words" doctrine, we nonetheless conclude that the ordinance is facially unconstitutional in that it prohibits otherwise permitted speech solely on the basis of the subjects the speech addresses.

The First Amendment generally prevents government from proscribing speech, see, e.g., Cantwell v. Connecticut, 310 U. S. 296, 309–311 (1940), or even expressive conduct . . . because of disapproval of the ideas expressed. Content-based regulations are presumptively invalid . . . From 1791 to the present, however, our society, like other free but civilized societies, has permitted restrictions upon the content of speech in a few limited areas, which "are of such slight social value as a step to truth that any benefit that may be derived from them is clearly outweighed by the social interest in order and morality." Chaplinsky, supra, at 572.

We have recognized that the "freedom of speech" referred to by the First Amendment does not include a freedom to disregard these traditional limitations . . . but a limited categorical approach has remained an important part of our First Amendment jurisprudence.

We have sometimes said that these categories of expression are "not within the area of constitutionally protected speech," Roth, supra, at 483; Beauharnais, supra, at 266; Chaplinsky, supra, at 571–572, or that the "protection of the First Amendment does not extend" to them, . . . Such statements must be taken in context, however, and are no more literally true than is the occasionally repeated shorthand characterizing obscenity "as not being speech at all, . . ."

What they mean is that these areas of speech can, consistently with the First Amendment, be regulated because of their constitutionally prescribable content (obscenity, defamation, etc.)—not that they are categories of speech entirely invisible to the Constitution, so that they may be made the vehicles for content discrimination unrelated to their distinctively prescribable content. Thus, the government may proscribe libel; but it may not make the further content discrimination of proscribing only libel critical of the government. We recently acknowledged this distinction in Ferber, 458 U. S., at 763, where, in upholding New York's child pornography law, we expressly recognized that there was no "question here of censoring a particular literary theme. . . ."

Our cases surely do not establish the proposition that the First Amendment imposes no obstacle whatsoever to regulation of particular instances of such prescribable expression, so that the government "may regulate [them] freely," post, at 764 (White, J., concurring in judgment). That would mean that a city council could enact an ordinance prohibiting only those legally obscene works that contain criticism of the city government or, indeed, that do not include endorsement of the city government. Such a simplistic, all-or-nothing-at-all approach to First Amendment protection is at odds with common sense and with our jurisprudence as well. It is not true that "fighting words" have at most a "de minimis" expressive content, ibid., or that their content is in all respects "worthless and undeserving of constitutional protection," sometimes they are quite expressive indeed. We have not said that they constitute "no part of the expression of ideas," but only that they constitute "no essential part of any exposition of ideas." Chaplinsky, 315 U. S., at 572 (emphasis added).

The proposition that a particular instance of speech can be prescribable on the basis of one feature (e.g., obscenity) but not on the basis of another (e.g., opposition to the city government) is commonplace, and has found application in many contexts. We have long held, for example, that nonverbal expressive activity can be banned because of the action it entails, but not because of the ideas it expresses—so that burning a flag in violation of an ordinance against outdoor fires could be punishable, whereas burning a flag in violation of an ordinance against dishonoring the flag is not. See Johnson, 491 U. S., at 406–407. . . . Similarly, we have upheld reasonable "time, place, or manner" restrictions, but only if they are justified without reference to the content of the regulated speech. . . . And just as the power to proscribe particular speech on the basis of a noncontent element (e.g., noise) does not entail the power to proscribe the same speech on the basis of a content element; so also, the power to proscribe it on the basis of one content element (e.g., obscenity) does not entail the power to proscribe it on the basis of other content elements.

In other words, the exclusion of "fighting words" from the scope of the First Amendment simply means that, for purposes of that Amendment, the unprotected features of the words are, despite their verbal character, essentially a non-speech element of communication. Fighting words are thus analogous to a noisy sound truck: Each is, as Justice Frankfurter recognized, a "mode of speech," Niemotko v. Maryland, 340 U. S. 268, 282 (1951) (Frankfurter, J., concurring in result); both can be used to convey an idea; but neither has, in and of itself, a claim upon the First Amendment. As with the sound truck, however, so also with fighting words: The government may not regulate use based on hostility—or favoritism—towards the underlying message expressed. . . .

In our view, the First Amendment imposes not an "underinclusiveness" limitation but a "content discrimination" limitation upon a State's prohibition of prescribable speech. There is no problem whatever, for example, with a State's prohibiting obscenity (and other forms of prescribable expression) only in certain media or markets, for although that prohibition would be "underinclusive," it would not discriminate on the basis of content. See, e.g., Sable Communications, 492 U. S., at 124–126 (upholding 47 U. S. C. 223(b)(1) which prohibits obscene telephone communications). Even the prohibition against content discrimination that we assert the First Amendment requires is not absolute. It applies differently in the context of prescribable speech than in the area of fully protected speech. The rationale of the general prohibition, after all, is that content discrimination "rais[es] the specter that the Government may effectively drive certain ideas or viewpoints from the marketplace. . . . " But content discrimination among various instances of a class of prescribable speech often does not pose this threat.

When the basis for the content discrimination consists entirely of the very reason the entire class of speech at issue is prescribable, no significant danger of idea or viewpoint discrimination exists. Such a reason, having been adjudged neutral enough to support exclusion of the entire class of speech from First Amendment protection, is also neutral enough to form the basis of distinction within the class. To illustrate: A State might choose to prohibit only that obscenity which is the most patently offensive in its prurience—i.e., that which involves the most lascivious displays of sexual activity. But it may not prohibit, for example, only that obscenity which includes offensive political messages. . . .

II

Applying these principles to the St. Paul ordinance, we conclude that, even as narrowly construed by the Minnesota Supreme Court, the ordinance is facially unconstitutional. Although the phrase in the ordinance, "arouses anger, alarm or resentment in others" has been limited by the Minnesota Supreme Court's construction to reach only those symbols or displays that amount to "fighting words" the remaining, unmodified terms make clear that the ordinance applies only to "fighting words" that insult, or provoke violence, "on the basis of race, color, creed, religion or gender." Displays containing abusive invective, no matter how vicious or severe, are permissible unless they are addressed to one of the specified disfavored topics. Those who wish to use "fighting words" in connection with other ideas—to express hostility, for example, on the basis of political affiliation, union membership, or homosexuality—are not covered. The First Amendment does not permit St. Paul to impose special prohibitions on those speakers who express views on disfavored subjects. . . .

In its practical operation, moreover, the ordinance goes even beyond mere content discrimination, to actual viewpoint discrimination. Displays containing some words—odious racial epithets, for example—would be prohibited to proponents of all views. But "fighting words" that do not themselves invoke race, color, creed, religion, or gender—aspersions upon a person's mother, for example—would seemingly be usable *ad libitum* in the placards of those arguing in favor of racial, color, etc. tolerance and equality, but could not be used by those speaker's opponents. One could hold up a sign saying, for example, that all "anti-Catholic bigots" are misbegotten; but not that all "papists" are, for that would insult and provoke violence on the basis of religion. . . ." What we have here, it must be emphasized, is not a prohibition of fighting words that are directed at certain persons or groups (which would be facially valid if it met the requirements of the Equal Protection Clause); but rather, a prohibition of fighting words that contain (as the Minnesota Supreme Court repeatedly emphasized) messages of "bias-motivated" hatred and in particular, as applied to this case, messages "based on virulent notions of racial supremacy." 464 N. W. 2d, at 508, 511. One must wholeheartedly agree with the Minnesota Supreme Court that "[i]t is the responsibility, even the obligation, of diverse communities to confront such notions in whatever form they appear," ibid., but the manner of that confrontation cannot consist of selective limitations upon speech.

St. Paul's brief asserts that a general "fighting words" law would not meet the city's needs because only a content-specific measure can communicate to minority groups that the "group hatred" aspect of such speech "is not condoned by the majority . . . The point of the First Amendment is that majority preferences must be expressed in some fashion other than silencing speech on the basis of its content.

Despite the fact that the Minnesota Supreme Court and St. Paul acknowledge that the ordinance is directed at expression of group hatred, Justice Stevens suggests that this "fundamentally misreads" the ordinance. Post, at 18–19. It is directed, he claims, not to speech of a particular content, but to particular "injur[ies]" that are "qualitatively different" from other injuries. Post, at 9. This is word-play. What makes the anger, fear, sense of dishonor, etc. produced by violation of this ordinance distinct from the anger, fear, sense of dishonor, etc. produced by other fighting words is nothing other than the fact that it is caused by a distinctive idea, conveyed by a distinctive message. The First Amendment cannot be evaded that easily. It is obvious that the symbols which will arouse "anger, alarm or resentment in others on the basis of race, color, creed, religion or gender" are those symbols that communicate a message of hostility based on one of these characteristics. St. Paul concedes in its brief that the ordinance applies only to "racial, religious, or gender-specific symbols" such as "a burning cross, Nazi swastika or other instrumentality of like import." Brief for Respondent 8. Indeed, St. Paul argued in the Juvenile Court that [t]he burning of a cross does express a message and it is, in fact, the content of that message which the St. Paul Ordinance attempts to legislate . . .

The content-based discrimination reflected in the St. Paul ordinance comes within neither any of the specific exceptions to the First Amendment prohibition we discussed earlier, nor within a more general exception for content discrimination that does not threaten censorship of ideas. It assuredly does not fall within the exception for content discrimination based on the very reasons why the particular class of speech at issue (here, fighting words) is prescribable. As explained earlier, see supra, at 8, the reason why fighting words are categorically excluded from the protection of the First Amendment is not that their content communicates any particular idea, but that their content embodies a particularly intolerable (and

socially unnecessary) mode of expressing whatever idea the speaker wishes to convey.

St. Paul has not singled out an especially offensive mode of expression—it has not, for example, selected for prohibition only those fighting words that communicate ideas in a threatening (as opposed to a merely obnoxious) manner. Rather, it has proscribed fighting words of whatever manner that communicate messages of racial, gender, or religious intolerance. Selectivity of this sort creates the possibility that the city is seeking to handicap the expression of particular ideas. That possibility would alone be enough to render the ordinance presumptively invalid, but St. Paul's comments and concessions in this case elevate the possibility to a certainty. St. Paul argues that the ordinance comes within another of the specific exceptions we mentioned, the one that allows content discrimination aimed only at the "secondary effects" of the speech, see Renton v. Playtime Theatres, Inc., 475 U. S. 41 (1986). According to St. Paul, the ordinance is intended, "not to impact on [sic] the right of free expression of the accused," but rather to "protect against the victimization of a person or persons who are particularly vulnerable because of their membership in a group that historically has been discriminated against." Brief for Respondent 28.

Even assuming that an ordinance that completely proscribes, rather than merely regulates, a specified category of speech can ever be considered to be directed only to the secondary effects of such speech, it is clear that the St. Paul ordinance is not directed to secondary effects within the meaning of Renton . . . It hardly needs discussion that the ordinance does not fall within some more general exception permitting all selectivity that for any reason is beyond the suspicion of official suppression of ideas. The statements of St. Paul in this very case afford ample basis for, if not full confirmation of, that suspicion. . . . The dispositive question in this case, therefore, is whether content discrimination is reasonably necessary to achieve St. Paul's compelling interests; it plainly is not. An ordinance not limited to the favored topics, for example, would have precisely the same beneficial effect. In fact the only interest distinctively served by the content limitation is that of displaying the city council's special hostility towards the particular biases thus singled out. That is precisely what the First Amendment forbids.

The politicians of St. Paul are entitled to express that hostility but not through the means of imposing unique limitations upon speakers who (however benightedly) disagree. Let there be no mistake about our belief that burning a cross in someone's front yard is reprehensible. But St. Paul has sufficient means at its disposal to prevent such behavior without adding the First Amendment to the fire. The judgment of the Minnesota Supreme Court is reversed, and the case is remanded for proceedings not inconsistent with this opinion.

It is so ordered.

Roy Romer, Governor of Colorado v. Richard G. Evans et al.
116 S. Ct. 1620 (1996)

In 1992 the citizens of Colorado, by popular referendum, amended the state constitution in such a way as to eliminate most state and local laws intended to protect gays, lesbians, and bisexuals against discrimination in housing, employment, education, public services, and in many other areas of life. Although the state governor, Roy Romer, was opposed to the passage of this constitutional amendment, he was bound to enforce it, as were all other officers of the state of Colorado.

The case does not establish gay, lesbian, and bisexual rights as a matter of federal civil rights. Instead, it strongly indicates that no group can be singled out for a denial of protection against discrimination, even by means of a popular vote. Though gays, lesbians, and bisexuals may face disapproval, they may not be stripped of their protection against discrimination. If local governments wish to specifically protect members of a particular group they may do so. The case is interesting for its use of prominent historical civil rights decisions which have marked rights victories achieved by other groups.

MR. JUSTICE KENNEDY delivered the opinion of the Court.

One century ago, the first Justice Harlan admonished this Court that the Constitution "neither knows nor tolerates classes among citizens." Plessy v. Ferguson, 163 U. S. 537, 559 (1896)

(dissenting opinion). Unheeded then, those words now are understood to state a commitment to the law's neutrality where the rights of persons are at stake. The Equal Protection Clause enforces this principle and today requires us to hold invalid a provision of Colorado's Constitution.

I

The enactment challenged in this case is an amendment to the Constitution of the State of Colorado, adopted in a 1992 statewide referendum. The parties and the state courts refer to it as "Amendment 2," its designation when submitted to the voters. The impetus for the amendment and the contentious campaign that preceded its adoption came in large part from ordinances that had been passed in various Colorado municipalities. For example, the cities of Aspen and Boulder and the City and County of Denver each had enacted ordinances which banned discrimination in many transactions and activities, including housing, employment, education, public accommodations, and health and welfare services. Denver Rev. Municipal Code, Art. IV 28–91 to 28–116 (1991); Aspen Municipal Code 13–98 (1977); Boulder Rev. Code 12-1-1 to 12-1-11 (1987). What gave rise to the statewide controversy was the protection the ordinances afforded to persons discriminated against by reason of their sexual orientation. See Boulder Rev. Code 12-1-1 (defining "sexual orientation" as "the choice of sexual partners, i.e., bisexual, homosexual or heterosexual"); Denver Rev. Municipal Code, Art. IV 28–92 (defining "sexual orientation" as "[t]he status of an individual as to his or her heterosexuality, homosexuality or bisexuality").

Amendment 2 repeals these ordinances to the extent they prohibit discrimination on the basis of "homosexual, lesbian or bisexual orientation, conduct, practices or relationships." Colo. Const., Art. II, 30b. Yet Amendment 2, in explicit terms, does more than repeal or rescind these provisions. It prohibits all legislative, executive or judicial action at any level of state or local government designed to protect the named class, a class we shall refer to as homosexual persons or gays and lesbians. The amendment reads:

> No Protected Status Based on Homosexual, Lesbian, or Bisexual Orientation. Neither the State of Colorado, through any of its branches or departments, nor any of its agencies, political

subdivisions, municipalities or school districts, shall enact, adopt or enforce any statute, regulation, ordinance or policy whereby homosexual, lesbian or bisexual orientation, conduct, practices or relationships shall constitute or otherwise be the basis of or entitle any person or class of persons to have or claim any minority status, quota preferences, protected status or claim of discrimination. This Section of the Constitution shall be in all respects self-executing . . .

Soon after Amendment 2 was adopted, this litigation to declare its invalidity and enjoin its enforcement was commenced in the District Court for the City and County of Denver. Among the plaintiffs (respondents here) were homosexual persons, some of them government employees. They alleged that enforcement of Amendment 2 would subject them to immediate and substantial risk of discrimination on the basis of their sexual orientation. Other plaintiffs (also respondents here) included the three municipalities whose ordinances we have cited and certain other governmental entities which had acted earlier to protect homosexuals from discrimination but would be prevented by Amendment 2 from continuing to do so. Although Governor Romer had been on record opposing the adoption of Amendment 2, he was named in his official capacity as a defendant, together with the Colorado Attorney General and the State of Colorado.

The trial court granted a preliminary injunction to stay enforcement of Amendment 2, and an appeal was taken to the Supreme Court of Colorado. Sustaining the interim injunction and remanding the case for further proceedings, the State Supreme Court held that Amendment 2 was subject to strict scrutiny under the Fourteenth Amendment because it infringed the fundamental right of gays and lesbians to participate in the political process. Evans v. Romer, 854 P. 2d 1270 (Colo. 1993)(Evans I).

To reach this conclusion, the state court relied on our voting rights cases, e.g., Reynolds v. Sims, 377 U. S. 533 (1964); Carrington v. Rash, 380 U. S. 89 (1965); Harper v. Virginia Bd. of Elections, 383 U. S. 663 (1966); Williams v. Rhodes, 393 U. S. 23 (1968), and on our precedents involving discriminatory restructuring of governmental decisionmaking, see, e.g., Hunter v. Erickson, 393 U. S. 385 (1969); Reitman v. Mulkey, 387 U. S. 369 (1967); Washington v. Seattle School Dist. No. 1, 458 U. S. 457 (1982); Gordon v. Lance, 403 U. S. 1 (1971).

On remand, the State advanced various arguments in an effort to show that Amendment 2 was narrowly tailored to serve compelling interests, but the trial court found none sufficient. It enjoined enforcement of Amendment 2, and the Supreme Court of Colorado, in a second opinion, affirmed the ruling. Evans v. Romer, 882 P. 2d 1335 (Colo. 1994) (Evans II). We granted *certiorari* and now affirm the judgment, but on a rationale different from that adopted by the State Supreme Court.

II

The State's principal argument in defense of Amendment 2 is that it puts gays and lesbians in the same position as all other persons. So, the State says, the measure does no more than deny homosexuals special rights. This reading of the amendment's language is implausible. We rely not upon our own interpretation of the amendment but upon the authoritative construction of Colorado's Supreme Court. The state court, deeming it unnecessary to determine the full extent of the amendment's reach, found it invalid even on a modest reading of its implications. The critical discussion of the amendment, set out in Evans I, is as follows:

The immediate objective of Amendment 2 is, at a minimum, to repeal existing statutes, regulations, ordinances, and policies of state and local entities that barred discrimination based on sexual orientation. See Aspen, Colo., Mun. Code 13–98 (1977) (prohibiting discrimination in employment, housing and public accommodations on the basis of sexual orientation); Boulder, Colo., Rev. Code 12-1-2 to 4 (1987) (same); Denver, Colo., Rev. Mun. Code art. IV, 28B91 to -116 (1991) (same); Executive Order No. D0035 (December 10, 1990) (prohibiting employment discrimination for "all state employees, classified and exempt' on the basis of sexual orientation); Colorado Insurance Code, 10-3-1104, 4A C. R. S. (1992 Supp.) (forbidding health insurance providers from determining insurability and premiums based on an applicant's, a beneficiary's, or an insured's sexual orientation); and various provisions prohibiting discrimination based on sexual orientation at state colleges. . . .

The 'ultimate effect' of Amendment 2 is to prohibit any governmental entity from adopting similar, or more protective statutes, regulations, ordinances, or policies in the future unless the state constitution is first amended to permit such measures." 854 P. 2d, at 1284–1285, and n. 26.

Sweeping and comprehensive is the change in legal status effected by this law. So much is evident from the ordinances that the Colorado Supreme Court declared would be void by operation of Amendment 2. Homosexuals, by state decree, are put in a solitary class with respect to transactions and relations in both the private and governmental spheres. The amendment withdraws from homosexuals, but no others, specific legal protection from the injuries caused by discrimination, and it forbids reinstatement of these laws and policies.

The change that Amendment 2 works in the legal status of gays and lesbians in the private sphere is far-reaching, both on its own terms and when considered in light of the structure and operation of modern anti-discrimination laws. That structure is well illustrated by contemporary statutes and ordinances prohibiting discrimination by providers of public accommodations. "At common law, innkeepers, smiths, and others who 'made profession of a public employment,' were prohibited from refusing, without good reason, to serve a customer." Hurley v. Irish-American Gay, Lesbian and Bisexual Group of Boston, Inc., 515 U. S. ___, ___ (1995) (slip op., at 13). The duty was a general one and did not specify protection for particular groups. The common law rules, however, proved insufficient in many instances, and it was settled early that the Fourteenth Amendment did not give Congress a general power to prohibit discrimination in public accommodations, Civil Rights Cases, 109 U. S. 3, 25 (1883). In consequence, most States have chosen to counter discrimination by enacting detailed statutory schemes. See, e.g., S. D. Codified Laws 20-13-10, 20-13-22, 20-13-23 (1995); Iowa Code 216.6-216.8 (1994); Okla. Stat., Tit. 25, 1302, 1402 (1987); 43 Pa. Cons. Stat. 953, 955 (Supp. 1995); N. J. Stat. Ann. 10:5-3, 10:5-4 (West Supp. 1995); N. H. Rev. Stat. Ann. 354-A:7, 354-A:10, 354-A:17 (1995); Minn. Stat. 363.03 (1991 and Supp.1995).

Colorado's state and municipal laws typify this emerging tradition of statutory protection and follow a consistent pattern. The laws first enumerate the persons or entities subject to a duty not to discriminate. The list goes well beyond the entities covered by the common law. The Boulder ordinance, for example, has a comprehensive definition of entities deemed places of "public accommodation." They include "any place of business engaged in any sales to the general public and any place that offers services, facilities, privileges, or advantages to the general public or that receives financial support through solicitation of the general public or through governmental subsidy of any

kind." Boulder Rev. Code 12-1-1(j) (1987). The Denver ordinance is of similar breadth, applying, for example, to hotels, restaurants, hospitals, dental clinics, theaters, banks, common carriers, travel and insurance agencies, and "shops and stores dealing with goods or services of any kind," Denver Rev. Municipal Code, Art. IV, 28–92.

These statutes and ordinances also depart from the common law by enumerating the groups or persons within their ambit of protection. Enumeration is the essential device used to make the duty not to discriminate concrete and to provide guidance for those who must comply. In following this approach, Colorado's state and local governments have not limited antidiscrimination laws to groups that have so far been given the protection of heightened equal protection scrutiny under our cases. See, e.g., J. E. B. v. Alabama ex rel. T. B., 511 U. S. __, __ (1994) (slip op., at 8) (sex); Lalli v. Lalli, 439 U. S. 259, 265 (1978) (illegitimacy); McLaughlin v. Florida, 379 U. S. 184, 191–192 (1964) (race); Oyama v. California, 332 U. S. 633 (1948) . . . Rather, they set forth an extensive catalogue of traits which cannot be the basis for discrimination, including age, military status, marital status, pregnancy, parenthood, custody of a minor child, political affiliation, physical or mental disability of an individual or of his or her associates—and, in recent times, sexual orientation. Aspen Municipal Code 13B98(a)(1) (1977); Boulder Rev. Code 12-1-1 to 12-1-4 (1987); Denver Rev. Municipal Code, Art. IV, 28B92 to 28B119 (1991); Colo. Rev. Stat. 24-34-401 to 24-34-707 (1988 and Supp. 1995).

Amendment 2 bars homosexuals from securing protection against the injuries that these public-accommodations laws address. That in itself is a severe consequence, but there is more. Amendment 2, in addition, nullifies specific legal protections for this targeted class in all transactions in housing, sale of real estate, insurance, health and welfare services, private education, and employment. See, e.g., Aspen Municipal Code 13–98(b), (c) (1977); Boulder Rev. Code 12-1-2,12-1-3 (1987); Denver Rev. Municipal Code, Art. IV 28B93 to 28–95, 28–97 (1991). Not confined to the private sphere, Amendment 2 also operates to repeal and forbid all laws or policies providing specific protection for gays or lesbians from discrimination by every level of Colorado government. The State Supreme Court cited two examples of protections in the governmental sphere that are now rescinded and may not be reintroduced. The first is Colorado Executive Order D0035 (1990), which "forbids employment discrimination against 'all state employees, classified and exempt' on the basis of sexual orientation." 854 P. 2d, at 1284. Also repealed, and now forbidden, are "various provisions prohibiting discrimination based on sexual orientation at state colleges." Id., at 1284, 1285. The repeal of these measures and the prohibition against their future reenactment demonstrates that Amendment 2 has the same force and effect in Colorado's governmental sector as it does elsewhere and that it applies to policies as well as ordinary legislation.

Amendment 2's reach may not be limited to specific laws passed for the benefit of gays and lesbians. It is a fair, if not necessary, inference from the broad language of the amendment that it deprives gays and lesbians even of the protection of general laws and policies that prohibit arbitrary discrimination in governmental and private settings . . . At some point in the systematic administration of these laws, an official must determine whether homosexuality is an arbitrary and thus forbidden basis for decision . . .

We cannot accept the view that Amendment 2's prohibition on specific legal protections does no more than deprive homosexuals of special rights. To the contrary, the amendment imposes a special disability upon those persons alone. Homosexuals are forbidden the safeguards that others enjoy or may seek without constraint. They can obtain specific protection against discrimination only by enlisting the citizenry of Colorado to amend the state constitution or perhaps, on the State's view, by trying to pass helpful laws of general applicability. This is so no matter how local or discrete the harm, no matter how public and widespread the injury. We find nothing special in the protections Amendment 2 withholds. These are protections taken for granted by most people either because they already have them or do not need them; these are protections against exclusion from an almost limitless number of transactions and endeavors that constitute ordinary civic life in a free society.

III

The Fourteenth Amendment's promise that no person shall be denied the equal protection of the laws must coexist with the practical necessity that most legislation classifies for one purpose or another, with resulting disadvantage to various groups or persons. Personnel Administrator of Mass. v. Feeney, 442 U. S. 256, 271–272 (1979); F. S. Royster Guano Co. v. Virginia, 253 U. S. 412, 415 (1920). We have attempted to reconcile the principle with the reality by stating that, if a law neither burdens a fundamental right nor targets a suspect class, we will uphold the legislative classification so long as it bears a rational relation to some legitimate end. See, e.g., Heller v. Doe, 509 U. S. ___, ___ (1993) (slip op., at 6). Amendment 2 fails, indeed defies, even this conventional inquiry. First, the amendment has the peculiar property of imposing a broad and undifferentiated disability on a single named group, an exceptional and, as we shall explain, invalid form of legislation. Second, its sheer breadth is so discontinuous with the reasons offered for it that the amendment seems inexplicable by anything but animus toward the class that it affects; it lacks a rational relationship to legitimate state interests. . . .

The absence of precedent for Amendment 2 is itself instructive; "[d]iscriminations of an unusual character especially suggest careful consideration to determine whether they are obnoxious to the constitutional provision." Louisville Gas & Elec. Co. v. Coleman, 277 U. S. 32, 37B38 (1928).

It is not within our constitutional tradition to enact laws of this sort. Central both to the idea of the rule of law and to our own Constitution's guarantee of equal protection is the principle that government and each of its parts remain open on impartial terms to all who seek its assistance. "Equal protection of the laws is not achieved through indiscriminate imposition of inequalities." Sweatt v. Painter, 339 U. S. 629, 635 (1950) (quoting Shelley v. Kraemer, 334 U. S. 1, 22 (1948)). Respect for this principle explains why laws singling out a certain class of citizens for disfavored legal status or general hardships are rare. A law declaring that in general it shall be more difficult for one group of citizens than for all others to seek aid from the government is itself a denial of equal protection of the laws in the most literal sense. . . .

"[I]f the constitutional conception of 'equal protection of the laws' means anything, it must at the very least mean that a bare . . . desire to harm a politically unpopular group cannot constitute a legitimate governmental interest." Department of Agriculture v. Moreno, 413 U. S. 528, 534 (1973). Even laws enacted for broad and ambitious purposes often can be explained by reference to legitimate public policies which justify the incidental disadvantages they impose on certain persons. Amendment 2, however, in making a general announcement that gays and lesbians shall not have any particular protections from the law, inflicts on them immediate, continuing, and real injuries that outrun and belie any legitimate justifications that may be claimed for it . . . We cannot say that Amendment 2 is directed to any identifiable legitimate purpose or discrete objective. It is a status-based enactment divorced from any factual context from which we could discern a relationship to legitimate state interests; it is a classification of persons undertaken for its own sake, something the Equal Protection Clause does not permit. "[C]lass legislation . . . [is] obnoxious to the prohibitions of the Fourteenth Amendment. . . ." Civil Rights Cases, 109 U. S., at 24.

We must conclude that Amendment 2 classifies homosexuals not to further a proper legislative end but to make them unequal to everyone else. This Colorado cannot do. A State cannot so deem a class of persons a stranger to its laws. Amendment 2 violates the Equal Protection Clause, and the judgment of the Supreme Court of Colorado is affirmed.

It is so ordered.

United States v. *Virginia et al.* 518 U.S.___; 135 L.ed.2d 735 (1996)

By 1996 only two state supported male-only institutions of higher learning were left in the United States. Both were military colleges with long traditions of male-only education. The Citadel in South Carolina agreed to admit women in 1996, and four women entered its fall 1996 class. However, the constitutional issues were not fully addressed until the Supreme Court handed down its decision in the case of United States v. Virginia.

The Virginia Military Institute (VMI) had provided an all-male education since 1800. By 1997 it was the last all-male military college in

the nation. The school authorities believed that the distinctive history and special character of the college justified a single-sex program. Many applications were made to admit women applicants, but until 1997, all had been rejected.

The seven-to-one decision in United States v. Virginia *is a strong endorsement of sexual equality in education. Justice Ruth Bader Ginsburg, who had long been an exponent of more equal treatment for women, wrote the majority decision. The Supreme Court found that the program at VMI was physically and mentally grueling, but it was not inherently unsuitable to women. The state of Virginia could not justify or give good reasons for excluding women from a publicly-supported school.*

On August 18, 1997, VMI opened its doors to women as a result of the decision of the Supreme Court. The officials at VMI had the choice of losing $11 million in state funds or complying with the order of the Supreme Court. They chose to admit women. In the fall of 1997, 31 women were admitted to the freshman class at VMI. Some still attend, in spite of hazing and serious harassment incidents intended to discourage them from continuing.

JUSTICE GINSBURG delivered the opinion of the Court.

Virginia's public institutions of higher learning include an incomparable military college, Virginia Military Institute (VMI). The United States maintains that the Constitution's equal protection guarantee precludes Virginia from reserving exclusively to men the unique educational opportunities VMI affords. We agree.

Parties who seek to defend gender-based government action must demonstrate an exceedingly persuasive justification for that action. E.g., Mississippi Univ. for Women v. Hogan, 458 U. S. 718, 724. Neither federal nor state government acts compatibly with equal protection when a law or official policy denies to women, simply because they are women, full citizenship stature equal opportunity to aspire, achieve, participate in and contribute to society based on their individual talents and capacities. To meet the burden of justification, a State must show "at least that the [challenged] classification serves 'important governmental objectives' and that the discriminatory means employed are 'substantially related to the achievement of those objectives.'" Ibid., quoting

Wengler v. Druggists Mutual Ins. Co., 446 U. S. 142, 150. The justification must be genuine, not hypothesized or invented post hoc in response to litigation. And it must not rely on overbroad generalizations about the different talents, capacities, or preferences of males and females. See, e.g., Weinberger v. Wiesenfeld, 420 U. S. 636, 643, 648. The heightened review standard applicable to sex-based classifications does not make sex a proscribed classification, but it does mean that categorization by sex may not be used to create or perpetuate the legal, social, and economic inferiority of women. . . .

Virginia's categorical exclusion of women from the educational opportunities VMI provides denies equal protection to women . . . Virginia contends that single-sex education yields important educational benefits and that provision of an option for such education fosters diversity in educational approaches. Benign justifications proffered in defense of categorical exclusions, however, must describe actual state purposes, not rationalizations for actions in fact differently grounded. Virginia has not shown that VMI was established, or has been maintained, with a view to diversifying, by its categorical exclusion of women, educational opportunities within the State. A purpose genuinely to advance an array of educational options is not served by VMI's historic and constant plan to afford a unique educational benefit only to males. However well this plan serves Virginia's sons, it makes no provision whatever for her daughters. . . .

Virginia also argues that VMI's adversative method of training provides educational benefits that cannot be made available, unmodified, to women, and that alterations to accommodate women would necessarily be so drastic as to destroy VMI's program. It is uncontested that women's admission to VMI would require accommodations, primarily in arranging housing assignments and physical training programs for female cadets. It is also undisputed, however, that neither the goal of producing citizen soldiers, VMI's raison d'etre, nor VMI's implementing methodology is inherently unsuitable to women. The District Court made "findings" on "gender-based developmental differences" that restate the opinions of Virginia's expert witnesses about typically male or typically female "tendencies." Courts, however, must take "a hard look" at generalizations or ten-

dencies of the kind Virginia pressed, for state actors controlling gates to opportunity have no warrant to exclude qualified individuals based on "fixed notions concerning the roles and abilities of males and females." Mississippi Univ. for Women, 458 U. S., at 725. The notion that admission of women would downgrade VMI's stature, destroy the adversative system and, with it, even the school, is a judgment hardly proved, a prediction hardly different from other self-fulfilling prophecies, see id., at 730, once routinely used to deny rights or opportunities. Women's successful entry into the federal military academies, and their participation in the Nation's military forces, indicate that Virginia's fears for VMI's future may not be solidly grounded. The State's justification for excluding all women from "citizen-soldier" training for which some are qualified, in any event, does not rank as "exceedingly persuasive. . . ."

The remedy proffered by Virginia—maintain VMI as a male-only college and create VWIL as a separate program for women—does not cure the constitutional violation . . . A remedial decree must closely fit the constitutional violation; it must be shaped to place persons unconstitutionally denied an opportunity or advantage in the position they would have occupied in the absence of discrimination See Milliken v. Bradley, 433 U. S. 267, 280. The constitutional violation in this case is the categorical exclusion of women, in disregard of their individual merit, from an extraordinary educational opportunity afforded men. Virginia chose to leave untouched VMI's exclusionary policy, and proposed for women only a separate program, different in kind from VMI and unequal in tangible and intangible facilities. VWIL affords women no opportunity to experience the rigorous military training for which VMI is famed. Kept away from the pressures, hazards, and psychological bonding characteristic of VMI's adversative training, VWIL students will not know the feeling of tremendous accomplishment commonly experienced by VMI's successful cadets.

Virginia maintains that methodological differences are justified by the important differences between men and women in learning and developmental needs, but generalizations about "the way women are," estimates of what is appropriate for most women, no longer justify denying opportunity to women whose talent and capacity place them outside the average description. In myriad respects other than military training, VWIL does not qualify as VMI's equal. The VWIL program is a pale shadow of VMI in terms of the range of curricular choices and faculty stature, funding, prestige, alumni support and influence. Virginia has not shown substantial equality in the separate educational opportunities the State supports at VWIL and VMI. Cf. Sweatt v. Painter, 339 U. S. 629 . . .

The Fourth Circuit failed to inquire whether the proposed remedy placed women denied the VMI advantage in the position they would have occupied in the absence of discrimination, Milliken, 433 U. S., at 280, and considered instead whether the State could provide, with fidelity to equal protection, separate and unequal educational programs for men and women. In declaring the substantially different and significantly unequal VWIL program satisfactory, the appeals court displaced the exacting standard developed by this Court with a deferential standard, and added an inquiry of its own invention, the "substantive comparability" test. The Fourth Circuit plainly erred in exposing Virginia's VWIL plan to such a deferential analysis, for all gender-based classifications today warrant heightened scrutiny. See J. E. B. v. Alabama ex rel. T. B., 511 U. S. 127, 136. Women seeking and fit for a VMI-quality education cannot be offered anything less, under the State's obligation to afford them genuinely equal protection . . . 976 F. 2d 890, affirmed; 44 F. 3d 1229, reversed and remanded.

We therefore affirm the Fourth Circuit's initial judgment, which held that Virginia had violated the Fourteenth Amendment's Equal Protection Clause. Because the remedy proffered by Virginia—the Mary Baldwin VWIL program—does not cure the constitutional violation, i.e., it does not provide equal opportunity.

Glossary
General Bibliography
Table of Cases
Index

Glossary

A

Acquittal: A judicial decision, following a jury verdict, that a person charged with a crime is not guilty.

Adversary system: A system of law, as found in the United States, in which there must be at least two parties competing with each other over a legal matter. In a criminal case the state is always a party on one side, while the accused defendant is the other party. In a civil case the parties may both be private persons or firms. The government itself may also be a party in a civil case.

Affidavit: A written statement of facts made voluntarily that is taken under oath and may be used in a trial.

Affirm: To uphold the decision of any lower court.

Affirmative action: The policy of affording special opportunities or advantages to members of groups that have been the historic victims of discrimination. Taking positive steps to remedy past acts of discrimination.

Amicus curiae: A Latin phrase meaning, "friend of court." A legal brief submitted by a person (or usually a group) not a party to a case, suggesting how a court should decide it. Used extensively in civil rights cases by rights interest groups.

Appeal: A legal procedure for taking a case from a lower court to a higher court in order to review or reverse the lower court decision.

Appellant: The party who seeks an appeal.

Appellee: The party against whom the appeal is sought. The appellant has usually won at the lower court level and is satisfied with its judgment.

Apportionment: The allocation of seats in a legislative body. Apportionment is subject to constitutional limitations guaranteeing essential equality of voting power through representation.

Arraignment: A formal stage in the criminal process at which the defendants are brought before a judge to hear the charges that have been brought against them. A plea in response to those charges is usually made at this stage.

Arrest: The physical act of taking the suspect into custody on suspicion of violating the criminal laws.

Attainder, Bill of: A legislative act that declares a person or a group of persons guilty of a criminal act without a trial.

B

Bail: A security deposit required by a court in serious criminal cases. Bail allows accused persons to be released from jail pending trial.

Bill of Rights: The first ten amendments to the U.S. Constitution, ratified in 1791, which guarantee basic rights and liberties to the people. Originally applied only to federal actions. Only after 1925 was the Supreme Court finally willing to extend the provisions of the Bill of Rights against the states.

Black Codes: Statutes passed in most Southern states after the Civil War. These laws were designed to deny African Americans most of the rights and attributes of citizenship. African Americans were denied the right to sit on juries, to testify against whites in courts, or to attend schools with whites. Many laws went beyond these restrictive provisions to make it easy to jail African Americans.

Boycott: A strategy of combined economic action by refusal to purchase a product or use a service. In 1955 an African American boycott of segregated buses in Montgomery, Alabama, was the first step in a process of direct community action leading to the 1956 Supreme Court decision that declared segregated seating in local transportation unconstitutional.

Brief: A written argument of law presented to a court, usually at an appellate level, which states the legal arguments for a represented party.

Busing: A judicially mandated technique for correcting school segregation. Because of its unpopularity it is used sparingly and almost never across the boundaries between municipalities.

C

Case: A legal dispute or controversy that has been brought to the attention of a court.

Case law: Law that has evolved from prior decisions of courts rather than from specific acts of legislation.

Certiorari, Writ of: The primary method by which cases reach the Supreme Court of the United States. The writ is discretionary and allows the Court to pick and choose which lower court cases it deems appropriate for a full hearing and possible decision.

Charter: In American history, a legal document that grants property in a territory of land, allowing for the government of a new colonial area.

Citizenship: The rights, duties, and privileges that are bestowed by governments on those born in the United States or "naturalized" by law.

Civil case: A suit between two private parties or firms, usually for damages. There is no risk of fines or imprisonment for either party.

Civil liberties (Civil Rights): Those recognized principles of American law that limit the powers of government and also guarantee the privileges of citizenship, such as voting and equality of treatment.

Class action: A lawsuit that is brought on behalf of a group of persons who are similarly involved or injured. Damages are usually sought.

Clear and present danger doctrine: Supreme Court interpretation of the First Amendment free speech guarantee. Laws cannot directly or indirectly restrict freedom of speech unless a particular publication or speech creates a danger that an illegal act actually will be committed as a result of the speech or publication.

Common law: Law that has evolved over time through the decisions of courts. English common law rested upon customs, and American common law borrows from the English to some extent. Legislation always supplants common law.

Concurring opinion: An opinion of a judge that agrees with the result of the majority but is based on different legal reasoning.

Constitutionalism: The belief—particularly strong in the United States—that the government must abide by the provisions of written constitutions.

Contempt: A purposeful failure to follow the orders of a court (civil contempt), or a willful display of disrespect for the court. A judge may punish both. Contempt of Congress may flow from a failure to cooperate with congressional committees.

Criminal case: A case that is based on charges of criminal wrongdoing. The government must bring the charges, and the constitutional protections of the Bill of Rights are afforded to defendants. If the criminal case is won by the government, after establishing proof of guilt beyond a reasonable doubt, the court may impose punishment (usually imprisonment or fines, but even the death penalty may be imposed in the most extreme cases).

D

De facto: Latin for "in fact" or "actual." Sometimes applied to segregation or discrimination situations that are not legally created, but are, nevertheless, burdensome.

De facto segregation: Racial segregation that is not the direct result of law or government policy, but which is nonetheless present in society, whether created by residential patterns, income inequalities, or some other means.

De Jure segregation: Racial or other segregation that is the direct result of a statute, administrative action, or other official policy of government.

De Novo: Latin for "from the beginning." Sometimes the Supreme Court orders a lower court to apply constitutional principles in a fresh trial *de novo.*

Defendant: A party being sued in a civil case or the accused in a criminal case.

Dicta; obiter dicta: Latin phrase signifying that part of a judge's opinion that exceeds the necessary elements to deciding the case. Dicta are not law, only opinion.

Dissenting opinion: A formal written expression of a judge's disagreement with the results of a majority of an appellate court. Dissents are not law; they are efforts to persuade other judges to some day reach a different result.

Distinguish: A process of legal reasoning used by lawyers and judges to show why a particular case that seems to be a precedent really is not applicable to the facts at hand.

District court: The lowest level of federal courts where trials are held and cases of general jurisdiction are usually started within the federal system. Federal district courts are very active in school desegregation issues, reapportionment of voting districts, and prisoners' rights questions.

Docket: The calendar or schedule of cases to be heard by a court.

Double jeopardy: The provision in the federal Constitution that bars criminal trials more than once for the same crime.

Due process: Found in the Fifth and Fourteenth Amendments to the Constitution, but essentially defined by courts as essential conditions of procedural fairness.

E

Electoral college: Persons selected by the voters in each state to cast their ballots in a presidential election. To be strictly accurate, American voters do not directly cast ballots for the president.

Eminent domain: The right of a government to take private property for a public use. Reasonable compensation must be paid for such takings.

Equal protection: A fundamental aspect of American rights derived from language found in the Fourteenth Amendment to the Constitution. Since 1954 it has signified judicial efforts to make the Constitution a device for providing equal treatment for all citizens.

Ex parte: A proceeding in which only one side to a legal dispute is heard.

Ex post facto law: An action made criminal retroactively. Forbidden to American governments in criminal law, but permitted in other kinds of law, such as taxation.

Exclusionary rule: American judges apply the search and seizure requirements of the Bill of Rights in a manner that excludes evidence which has been illegally obtained by law enforcement officials.

F

Fair hearing: Required of government officials for the protection of individual rights. The exact content of a fair hearing depends upon judicial (mostly Supreme Court) interpretation.

Federalism: A system of government that divides powers between a national government and regional (or, as in America) state governments. Under Article VI of the national Constitution, federal laws and treaties are "the supreme law of the land," binding all states and state judges.

Felony: A serious criminal offense, usually punishable by imprisonment for a year or more.

Franchise: The right to vote.

G

Gay rights: The claim of homosexuals to some forms of constitutional protection. Recognized only to a very limited extent by courts and legislatures.

Gerrymandering: Apportionment of voters in districts in such a way as to give unfair advantage to a political party or a racial group.

Glass ceiling: The claim that women are subject to discrimination in promotion to high-level positions in the public or private sector.

Grand jury: A panel of citizens who review the prosecution's evidence in a criminal indictment or charge. They decide whether the evidence presented is sufficient to hold a defendant for a later criminal trial.

H

Habeas corpus: Latin for "you have the body." An ancient writ issued by a judge to correct an unjust detention. The writ declares that a person being held in custody by law enforcement officials should be released.

Harmless error: An error by a court deemed too insignificant to require a change in the decision.

I

Indictment: A document issued by a grand jury in a criminal case that officially charges a defendant with committing a crime.

In forma pauperis: A special status available to indigents who are unable to afford the cost of court fees.

Infra: Simply means below. When found in a judicial opinion it usually refers to a lower court decision.

Injunction: A writ issued by a judge whereby one is required to do or to refrain from doing certain listed acts. Used principally in labor relations matters but also used in civil rights questions.

J

Japanese relocation: During World War II all persons of Japanese ancestry, including American citizens, were forcibly moved from their lands and homes, and placed under military curfew. This extreme measure shows how civil rights can be lost or suspended in wartime.

Jim Crow System: Those various practices and laws that enforced racial segregation after the Civil War. Forms of legal segregation persisted until 1954 in the North as well as in the South.

Judgment of the court: The effective final ruling, not the reasoning of a judicial opinion.

Judicial restraint: A policy of many courts to avoid using its full powers of judicial review.

Judicial review: The authority of a court to declare unconstitutional the laws of a state or federal legislature or the acts of the executive branch of government. A powerful judicial tool available to American judges but used sparingly.

Justiciable: Within the jurisdiction and authority of a court. A court may not hear matters that are not justiciable.

Juvenile delinquency: Offenses against the laws that are not regarded as criminal in nature because of the age of the violator. May also include status offenses, such as truancy or "incorrigibility," which would not be criminal.

K

Kerner Commission: President Lyndon Johnson appointed a biracial and bipartisan Advisory Commission on Civil Disorders following urban riots of the 1960s. The Commission, under its chairman, former Governor Otto Kerner of Illinois, issued its unanimous report in 1968. The Report included the historic statement that "our nation is moving towards two separate societies, one black, one white-separate and unequal."

L

Legislative intent: The supposed real meaning of a statute that may be determined from the legislative history of the measure.

Libel: A false published statement about a person that tends to subject them to public hatred, contempt, or ridicule. A group cannot make a libel claim.

Literacy tests: A practice designed to limit access of minority groups to the polls. Since these tests have often been applied in a discriminatory manner, they may not be used in a voting context. Literacy tests for voting are banned by the Voting Rights Act of 1965.

Litigant: A party to a law suit.

Lynching: Inflicting punishment, usually death by hanging, upon a person without any trial to establish guilt. A form of mob action. African Americans, Asian Americans, Native Americans, and Hispanics have frequently been victims of lynching at various times in the past.

M

Manifest Destiny: The belief held by American expansionists that America was naturally required to expand and dominate much of the Western Hemisphere, creating an "empire of freedom." Land acquisitions from Mexico and Spain were often justified by this claim.

Merits: The basic issues of a law case.

Miranda warning: As a result of the 1966 Supreme Court case of *Miranda* v. *Arizona* police must now read an elaborate warning to an arrested person, informing him of his rights. The purpose is to restrict the use of forced confessions.

Miscegenation: Intermarriage among the races. Laws against miscegenation are unconstitutional.

Motion: A request made to a judge by a party to a lawsuit.

O

Obscenity: Speech or other forms of expression that are not protected by the First Amendment to the Constitution. Such speech lacks any serious literary, artistic, political, or scientific value. Courts differ about the legitimacy of particular statutes that touch on obscenity and attempt to define it.

Opinion of the court: The printed public statement that announces the results of a law case.

Overbreadth doctrine: Simply stated, the doctrine requires that a statute effecting speech be invalidated if its language is fairly capable of being applied in such a way as to punish constitutionally protected speech. Sometimes courts use the doctrine as a way to declare unwise statutes invalid, without reaching the issue of whether the particular speech was protected or not.

P

Peonage: The use of forced labor in bondage to creditors or to debts owed to another. Wage slavery.

Per curiam: An unsigned, collectively written opinion of an appellate court.

Petition: The right granted by the First Amendment to citizens that allows them to inform their representatives of their views and to make pleas before government agencies.

Petitioner: A party who seeks the assistance of a court by filing legal papers.

Plaintiff: The party who initiates a civil case. The government begins all criminal cases.

Police power: A phrase that refers to the power reserved to state governments to pass laws regulating the health, safety, and morals of its citizens.

Poll tax: A practice of limiting access to voting by requiring the payment of a tax as a condition of participation in elections. The Twenty-fourth Amendment prohibits such a tax.

Precedent: The use of prior court opinions to guide current cases. In civil rights leading precedents establish basic rights principles.

Prior restraint: An effort by a government agency to deny publication of controversial material on the ground that it may be harmful. In the United States this kind of censorship is forbidden except in extreme situations, as determined by courts.

Privacy: A debated concept in American law that means, at least, the right to be left alone from the prying eyes of the state or of private citizens. Some also contend that the decision to choose to have an abortion is an aspect of the privacy right.

Procedural due process: The Supreme Court doctrine that forbids any procedure of government that "shocks the conscience" or makes a fair trial impossible.

Prohibition: The sale, manufacture, or transportation of alcoholic beverages was made illegal by constitutional provision between 1920 and 1933. The rapid repeal of this provision shows the unpopularity of the ban.

Public accommodations: Hotels, theaters, swimming pools, parks, and other such places supported by public funds or private facilities usually open to the public. Law prohibits segregation in public accommodations.

R

Racism: The belief that one race is inherently superior to all others, or that some racial groups are inherently inferior to others.

Reapportionment: Periodic redrawing of political boundaries for the purpose of voting representation. Subject to judicial review to ensure equality of treatment.

Reconstruction: The period in American history from about 1866 to 1870 when the newly freed slaves were given some legal, political, and constitutional rights. Unfortunately, this period did not accomplish full equality of treatment.

Redlining An illegal practice of lending institutions that discriminates against poor people living in certain areas.

Remand: The action of an appellate court to return a case to a lower tribunal to reconsider or alter the lower court's decision. Commonly used by the Supreme Court to instruct and inform lower courts.

Restrictive covenant: A legally unenforceable provision in a land deed that prohibits sale to members of certain groups. Formerly used to ban land purchases by members of unpopular groups, including African Americans, Jews, and Hispanics.

Reverse: The action of an appellate court that sets aside the decisions of a lower court. A case may be both reversed and remanded.

Reverse discrimination: The contention by many opponents of affirmative action that preferences for some groups are a form of discrimination against others.

S

School prayers: Because of the First Amendment, formal prayers or Bible readings may not be required in public schools.

Sedition: Any verbal or other nonviolent incitement to resist governmental authority. Sharply limited by the First Amendment freedoms of speech and press.

Segregation: A system of race relations that requires separation of individuals by race or to minimize contacts between races, usually for the purpose of securing dominance of one racial group over another. Segregation by income or class is not unlawful, but racial segregation is unconstitutional.

Self-incrimination: The privilege against self-incrimination derives from English and American history. Located in the Fifth Amendment to the Constitution, it means that a criminal defendant cannot be compelled to testify against himself in a criminal trial. He may remain silent, if he chooses, in a criminal case. Originally intended to protect people against torture and oppression by the state, the privilege has been extended to mean some sort of protection of individual privacy as well as against coerced confessions.

Separation of church and state: A concept derived from the First Amendment to the Constitution which implies that all public activities must be freed of religious preferences. In practice, the Supreme Court is often called upon to draw specific boundaries between church and state in America.

Solicitor General: Justice Department official who represents the national government in all cases before the Supreme Court of the United States.

Standing: The right of an individual or a group to initiate a court case.

Statute: A law enacted by a state legislature or by Congress that is signed by the chief executive or passed over her veto.

Stay: A court order that stops or suspends some form of action. For example, the carrying out of a death penalty may be stayed.

Strict construction: A narrow, and often strict, interpretation of a constitution or of statutes.

Suffrage: The right to vote.

Suspect classification: Supreme Court provides heightened scrutiny of statutes and policies that classify people on the basis of race or ethnicity.

Sustain: To uphold, especially to support the decision of a lower court. Motions may be overruled or sustained, too.

T

Test case: A deliberate effort to challenge a court to interpret a statutory or constitutional provision.

Treason: The only crime defined by the national Constitution. Article III says that treason against the United States shall "consist only in levying war against them, or in adhering to their enemies, giving them aid and comfort."

Treaty: An agreement between two or more nations, states, or sovereign powers. Many Native American rights are claimed to be derived from treaties. Immigration arrangements are sometimes made in treaties. All American treaties must receive the advice and consent of the Senate.

Tribal reservations: Lands of Native Americans bestowed upon them by Congress or created by treaty. Native American laws and customs usually prevail there, although self-governance is limited.

V

Vacate: To void or rescind a prior judicial action.

W

Warrant: A judicial order that must be obtained by police officers to authorize an arrest or a search. Arrests and searches may be made without warrants in special, limited circumstances.

Welfare state: All advanced, industrial states have created some minimum guarantees for the poor, the disabled, the sick, and the needy. To some that use this term, the American government has gone too far in that direction.

White primary: A method of restricting minority voting in the South by limiting access to the Democratic Party to whites only. This practice is illegal and unconstitutional.

Wiretapping: Electronic eavesdropping, which is subject to strict legal limitations.

Women's Liberation: A movement aimed at full legal equality for women started in the 1960s as an outgrowth of the civil rights movement. Leaders were writers Betty Friedan and Gloria Steinem. Betty Friedan founded the National Organization for Women (NOW) in 1966.

Writ: A court order commanding that an action be done or not be done.

General Bibliography

This bibliography is designed to supplement the texts suggested at the end of each chapter. Those who wish to gain a richer grasp of various aspects of American rights should consult the books, articles, and videotapes listed here. Some annotations are given, but each reader will have to make his or her own judgments about these references. It is every reader's privilege to search and find his or her own meaning of rights in America.

A list of leading civil rights organizations is also provided in this section. Readers can contact these organizations, but keep in mind that each has its own agenda. Some are activist groups; others are research oriented. Most publish useful materials, especially the American Civil Liberties Union, which has a lengthy list of guidebooks to civil rights.

The subject matter of American rights is vast and daunting, so some creative selectivity in entries was adopted by the editor to reduce the subject to a manageable scale. The organization adopted in this bibliography is intended not only to support the text, but to emphasize certain other features of American civil rights not discussed in the main chapters. For example, race and race relations are clearly at the heart of many aspects of civil rights in America, and this bibliography allows for independent reading on this important subject. Immigration is also highlighted in this section, as are Native American land and water rights.

Some American rights are so controversial that they have become unstable. For example reproductive rights, as an extension of privacy rights, were first recognized by the Supreme Court in the 1973 decision of *Roe* v. *Wade*. The political, religious, and ethical reactions to the 1973 decision are still being felt. The Supreme Court and state legislatures are currently changing this policy. The issue of abortion and reproductive rights is best studied by using the brief bibliography found here, and by watching for new developments.

Abortion/Reproductive Rights

Baird, Robert M., and Stuart E. Rosenbaum, eds. *The Ethics of Abortion: Pro-Life against Pro-Choice.* 2d ed. Amherst, N.Y.: Prometheus Books, 1993.

Bowers, James R. *Pro-Choice and Anti-Abortion: Constitutional Theory and Public Policy.* Westport, Conn.: Praeger, 1994.

Butler, J., and David Walbert. *Abortion, Medicine, and the Law.* 4th ed. New York: Facts on File, 1992. A lengthy technical exploration of legal-medical issues.

Craig, Barbara H., and David M. O'Brien. *Abortion and American Politics.* Chatham, N.J.: Chatham House, 1993.

Davis, Nanette J. *From Crime to Choice: The Transformation of Abortion in America.* Westport, Conn.: Greenwood Press, 1985. Traces the early development of reproductive rights from a feminist viewpoint.

Dworkin, Ronald. *Life's Dominion: An Argument about Abortion, Euthanasia and Individual Freedom.* New York: Random House, 1994.

Faux, Marian. *Roe v. Wade: The Untold Story of the Landmark Supreme Court Decision That Made Abortion Legal.* New York: Macmillan, 1988.

Goldstein, Leslie F. *Contemporary Cases in Women's Rights.* Madison, Wis.: University of Wisconsin Press, 1994. Places the abortion controversy in the context of women's rights.

Hood, Howard H., ed. *Abortion in the United States: A Compilation of State Legislation.* Buffalo, N.Y.: W. S. Hein Publishers, 1992. Since much of abortion law is in state legislation, this volume and its supplement provide an accurate, if highly legalistic, view of what is really happening.

Jelen, Ted G. *Perspectives on the Politics of Abortion.* Westport, Conn.: Greenwood Press, 1995.

Joffe, Carol. *Doctors of Conscience: The Struggle to Provide Abortion Before and After Roe v. Wade.* Boston: Beacon Press, 1995.

Kamm, Francis M. *Creation and Abortion: A Study in Moral and Legal Philosophy.* New York: Oxford University Press, 1992.

Melton, Gary B., ed. *Adolescent Abortion: Psychological and Legal Issues.* Lincoln, Nebr.: University of Nebraska Press, 1986.

Rubin, Eva. *Abortion, Politics and the Courts: Roe v. Wade and Its Aftermath.* Westport, Conn.: Greenwood Press, 1987.

Rubin, Eva, ed. *The Abortion Controversy: A Documentary History.* Westport, Conn.: Greenwood Press, 1994.

Segers, Mary, and Timothy Byrnes, eds. *Abortion Politics in American States.* Armonk, N.Y.: M. E. Sharpe, 1994.

Staggenborg, Suzanne. *The Pro-Choice Movement: Organization and Activism in the Abortion Conflict.* New York: Oxford University Press, 1994.

Tribe, Laurence H., ed. *Abortion: The Clash of Absolutes.* New York: W. W. Norton, 1992. Good collection by a leading constitutional scholar.

Ezorsky, Gertrude. *Racism and Justice: The Case for Affirmative Action.* Ithaca, N.Y.: Cornell University Press, 1991.

Glazer, Nathan. *Affirmative Action.* New York: Basic Books, 1975. Helped spark the debate against affirmative action.

Lambert, Richard D., ed. *Affirmative Action Revisited.* Newbury Park, Calif.: Sage Publications, 1992. Careful collection of essays on the topic.

Lynch, Frederick R. *Invisible Victims: White Males and Affirmative Action.* New York: Praeger, 1991.

Mezey, Susan Gluck. *In Pursuit of Equality.* New York: St. Martin's Press, 1992. Touches on affirmative action and women but also takes much broader approach to equality.

Nieli, Russell, ed. *Racial Preference and Racial Justice.* Washington, D.C.: Ethics and Public Policy Center, 1991. A positive view of affirmative action.

Sowell, Thomas. *Affirmative Action Reconsidered: Was It Necessary in Academia?* Washington, D.C.: American Enterprise Institute, 1975. Critical of affirmative action policy.

Turner, Ronald. *The Past and Future of Affirmative Action.* New York: Quorum Books, 1990. A guide for personnel offices and lawyers dealing with affirmative action programs.

Witt, Stephanie L. *The Pursuit of Race and Gender Equity in American Academe.* New York: Praeger, 1990.

Yates, Steven. *Civil Wrongs: What Went Wrong with Affirmative Action.* San Francisco, Calif.: Institute for Contemporary Studies, 1994.

Affirmative Action

America, Richard F. *Paying the Social Debt: What White America Owes Black America.* Westport, Conn.: Praeger, 1993.

Bergmann, Barbara. *In Defense of Affirmative Action.* New York: Basic Books, 1996. A defensive argument by an economics professor who believes that discrimination by race and sex is prevalent in America, justifying continuation of such policies.

Blanchard, Fletcher. *Affirmative Action in Perspective.* New York: Springer-Verlag, 1989. Reviews affirmative action policies and programs; reactions to affirmative action; and the justice, merit, and future of the policy.

Carnevale, Anthony. *The American Mosaic.* New York: McGraw-Hill, 1995. A report on the advantages of diversity in the workplace.

Carter, Stephen L. *Reflections of An Affirmative Action Baby.* New York: Basic Books, 1991. Author discusses status of affirmative action and his own experience as a product of affirmative action.

Clayton, Susan D., and Faye G. Crosby. *Justice, Gender, and Affirmative Action.* Ann Arbor, Mich.: University of Michigan Press, 1992. Critical perspectives on women and gender.

Edwards, John. *When Race Counts.* New York: Routledge, 1995. Comparative study of racial preference programs in Britain and the United States.

Bibliographies

Hispanic Information Management Project and the National Chicano Research Network. *Guide to Hispanic Bibliographic Services in the United States.* Ann Arbor, Mich.: Survey Research Center, University of Michigan, 1980. Important, but badly in need of updating.

Hoxie, Frederick E., and Harvey Markowitz. *Native Americans: An Annotated Bibliography.* Pasadena, Calif.: Salem Press, 1991. Good introduction to a large body of literature.

Smith, Dwight La Vern, ed. *Afro-American History: A Bibliography.* Santa Barbara, Calif.: ABC-Clio, 1974. An older source.

Smith, John David, comp. *Black Slavery in the Americas: An Interdisciplinary Bibliography, 1865–1890.* Westport, Conn.: Greenwood Press, 1982. Useful starting point for study of slavery.

White, Phillip M. *American Indian Studies: A Bibliographic Guide.* Englewood, Colo.: Libraries Unlimited, 1995. Narrow but informative.

Bigotry/Violence

Belknap, Michael. *Racial Violence and Law Enforcement in the South.* New York: Garland Publishing, 1991.

———. *Urban Race Riots.* New York: Garland Publishing, 1991.

Christensen, Loren. *Skinhead Street Gangs.* Boulder, Colo.: Paladin Press, 1994.

Cose, Ellis. *Rage of a Privileged Class.* New York: Harper Collins, 1993. Explains the origins of hostile and bigoted attitudes.

Dees, Morris, and Steve Fiffer. *Hate on Trial: The Case Against America's Most Dangerous Neo-Nazis.* New York: Villard Books, 1993. Describes the trials of leaders of the White Aryan Resistance, revealing their attitudes and programs.

Dinerstein, Leonard. *Antisemitism in America.* New York: Oxford University Press, 1992. Detailed history of prejudice against Jews, beginning with anti-Semitism in Europe through the colonial period, the Civil War, the 1930s, and beyond.

Finkelman, Paul, ed. *Lynching, Racial Violence and the Law.* New York: Garland Publishing, 1992.

Flynn, Kevin, and Gary Gerhardt. *The Silent Brotherhood: Inside America's Racist Underground.* New York: 1989. Somewhat dated by recent events, but a good overview.

Jackson, Kenneth T. *The Ku Klux Klan in the City, 1915–1930.* Chicago: I. R. Dee, 1992.

Kronewetter, Michael. *United They Hate: White Supremacist Groups in America.* New York: Walker and Co., 1992.

Lang, Susan. *Extremist Groups in America.* New York: F. Watts, 1990. Examines many of the extremist religious groups, paramilitary groups, and other racist groups. Suggests how they recruit new members and how they may be opposed.

Langone, John. *Spreading Poison: A Book About Racism and Prejudice.* Boston: Little, Brown, 1993. Methods of racist groups revealed.

MacLean, Nancy K. *Beyond the Mask of Chivalry: The Making of the Second Ku Klux Klan.* New York: Oxford University Press, 1993. The social and cultural conditions that led ordinary men to revive the Ku Klux Klan in America.

Madhubuti, Haki R., ed. *Why L.A. Happened: Implications of the '92 Los Angeles Rebellion.* Chicago: Third World Press, 1993. A critical appraisal of contemporary America in the light of the 1992 Los Angeles riots.

National Institute Against Prejudice and Violence. *Prejudice and Violence: An Annotated Bibliography of Selected Materials on Ethnoviolence.* Baltimore: National Institute Against Violence, 1989.

Newton, Michael, and Judy Ann. *The Ku Klux Klan: An Encyclopedia.* New York: Garland Publishing, 1991. Basic reference source.

———. *Racial and Religious Violence in America.* New York: Garland Publishing, 1991. Historic accounts.

Skolnick, Jerome H., and James J. Fyfe. *Above the Law: Police and the Excessive Use of Force.* New York: The Free Press, 1993. A study of the nature of police violence, its practice in America today, and possible remedies to a problem that is undermining minority public confidence in the police.

Thompson, Sharon. *Hate Groups.* San Diego, Calif.: Lucent Books, 1994. A broad overview of this important topic.

United States Commission on Civil Rights. *Bigotry and Violence on American College Campuses.* Washington, D.C.: U.S. Commission on Civil Rights, 1990. Official study of a growing campus problem.

United States Commission on Civil Rights. *Intimidation and Violence: Racial and Religious Bigotry in America.* Washington, D.C.: U.S. Commission on Civil Rights, 1990. A brief restatement of existing statutes and case law.

Vollers, Maryanne. *Ghosts of Mississippi: The Murder of Medgar Evers, the Trials of Byron De La Beckwith, and the Haunting of the New South.* New York: Little, Brown, 1995. Mississippi attempts to confront its violent past and bring a murderer to justice.

Williams, Robert Gooding, ed. *Reading Rodney King/Reading Urban Uprising.* New York: Routledge, 1993. Discusses the events leading up to and following the 1991 Rodney King beating.

Biography and Autobiography

Baldwin, Lewis V. *There is a Balm in Gilead: The Cultural Roots of Martin Luther King, Jr.* Minneapolis: Fortress Press, 1991. Broad biography indicates the grounds for many of Dr. King's beliefs.

Ball, Howard. *The Vision and Dream of Justice Hugo Black.* University, Ala.: University of Alabama Press, 1975. Significant biography of one of the most influential liberal justices to sit on the Supreme Court.

Ball, Howard, and Phillip Cooper. *Of Power and Right: Hugo Black, William O. Douglas and America's Constitutional Revolution.* New York: Oxford University Press, 1985. Explains the role of two liberal justices in transforming the Supreme Court's views on civil rights during the 1960s and 1970s.

Bass, Jack. *Taming the Storm: The Life and Times of Judge Frank M. Johnson, Jr., and the South's Fight Over Civil Rights.* New York: Doubleday, 1993. Judge Johnson took brave and firm stands as a federal district court judge during the 1960s and 1970s.

Black, Hugo. *A Constitutional Faith.* New York: A. A. Knopf, 1968. Black's autobiography is a clear and ringing statement of an absolutist view of the Bill of Rights. Justice Black may have had one of the broadest views of American rights among members of the Supreme Court.

Carson, Clayborne, ed. *The Papers of Martin Luther King, Jr.* Berkeley, Calif.: University of California Press, 1991.

Crawford, Vicki L., Jacqueline Anne Rouse, and Barbara Woods, eds. *Women in the Civil Rights Movement: Trailblazers and Torchbearers, 1941–1965.* Brooklyn, N.Y.: Carlson Publications, 1990.

Davis, Micheal D., and Hunter R. Clark. *Thurgood Marshall: Warrior at the Bar, Rebel on the Bench.* New York: Carol Publishing Group, 1992. The story of America's first African American Supreme Court justice.

Drake, St. Clair, and Horace R. Cayton. *A Study of a Negro Life in a Northern City.* New York: Harcourt, Brace and World, 1995.

Goldman, Roger L. *Thurgood Marshall: Justice for All.* New York: Carroll and Graff Publishers, 1992. Includes recollections of Justice Marshall and a selection of his opinions and dissents.

Irons, Peter. *The Courage of Their Convictions: Americans Who Fought Their Way to the Supreme Court.* New York: Viking Penguin, 1990. A very unusual collection of biographical sketches of those who have pressed the Supreme Court for rulings about their rights. Also shows that interest group support may be needed.

Mills, Kay. *This Little Light of Mine.* New York: Penguin Books, 1993. Biography of Fannie Lou Hamer, a heroine in the voting rights struggle of the 1960s.

Rowan, Carl T. *Dream Makers, Dream Breakers: The World of Justice Thurgood Marshall.* Boston: Little, Brown, 1993. A leading biography by a well-known journalist.

Schwartz, Bernard. *Super Chief: Earl Warren and His Supreme Court—A Judicial Biography.* New York: New York University Press, 1983. Describes the leadership of Chief Justice Earl Warren during the Supreme Court's most active civil rights period.

White, G. Edward. *Justice Oliver Wendell Holmes.* New York: Oxford University Press, 1993. Details the thoughts and concepts of this important judge and legal philosopher while serving on the Massachusetts bench and the Supreme Court of the United States.

Wilkinson, Brenda. *Jesse Jackson: Still Fighting for the Dream.* Englewood Cliffs, N.J.: Silver Burdett Press, 1990. Balanced treatment of an important civil rights leader.

Due Process and Criminal Justice

Beany, W. M. *The Right to Counsel in American Courts.* Westport, Conn.: Greenwood Press, 1972.

Bedau, High, ed. *The Death Penalty in America.* 3d ed. New York: Oxford University Press, 1982. The best introduction to this controversial topic.

Berger, Raoul. *Death Penalties: The Supreme Court's Obstacle Course.* Cambridge, Mass.: Harvard University Press, 1982.

Bodenheimer, David J. *Fair Trial: Rights of the Accused in American History.* New York: Oxford University Press, 1992. Excellent for an overview of a complex set of problems. Supreme Court views have toughened somewhat since this book, but many of the issues still remain unresolved.

Kamisar, Yale. *Police Interrogations and Confessions: Essays in Law and Policy.* Ann Arbor, Mich.: University of Michigan Press, 1980.

La Fave, Wayne. *Search and Seizure: A Treatise on the Fourth Amendment.* New York: Foundation Press, 1978. The leading work on search and seizure. The case law may have changed, but the problems have not.

Laurence, John. *A History of Capital Punishment.* New York: Citadel Press, 1960.

Levy, Leonard. *Origins of the Fifth Amendment.* New York: Oxford University Press, 1968. Definitive work on the original meanings of the Fifth Amendment.

Lewis, Anthony. *Gideon's Trumpet.* New York: Vintage Books, 1966. Inspiring reconstruction of a constitutional law case that expanded the right to counsel in America.

Freedom of the Press

Bollinger, Lee C. *The Tolerant Society: Freedom of Speech and Extremist Speech in America.* Knoxville, Tenn.: University of Tennessee Press, 1973. Still timely discussion of basic American views on free speech.

————. *Images of a Free Press.* Chicago: University of Chicago Press, 1994. Theoretical issues tackled in update of previous book.

Campbell, Douglas S. *Free Press v. Fair Trial: Supreme Court Decisions Since 1807.* Westport, Conn.: Praeger, 1994. Press coverage of trials given a legal, historical treatment.

Carter, T. Barton, et al. *Mass Communications Law in a Nutshell.* St. Paul, Minn.: West Publishing Co., 1994. A highly compressed legal analysis. Libel and slander are emphasized.

Dill, Barbara. *At What Price?: Libel Law and Freedom of the Press.* New York: Twentieth Century Fund, 1993.

Downs, D. A. *Nazis in Skokie: Freedom, Communication and the First Amendment.* Notre Dame, Ind.: Notre Dame University Press, 1985. Explains that extremist groups may speak and parade but points out some limits.

Garry, Patrick M. *Scrambling for Protection: The New Media and the First Amendment.* Pittsburgh: University of Pittsburgh Press, 1994. Scope of First Amendment and the Internet, cable television, and other technological developments.

McCoy, Ralph E. *Freedom of the Press: An Annotated Bibliography, Second Supplement, 1978–1992.* Carbondale, Ill.: Southern Illinois University Press, 1994. Excellent resource base.

McWhirter, Darien. *Freedom of Speech, Press, and Assembly.* Phoenix, Ariz.: Oryx Press, 1995. General statement.

Nerone, John. *Violence Against the Press: Policing the Public Sphere in U.S. History.* New York: Oxford University Press, 1994. A little-known aspect of press freedom.

Rudenstine, David. *The Day the Presses Stopped.* Berkeley, Calif.: University of California Press, 1996. A history of the pivotal Pentagon Papers Case. Still the leading legal basis for press freedom against a claim of government secrecy.

Thaler, Paul. *The Watchful Eye: American Justice in the Age of the Television Trial.* Westport, Conn.: Praeger, 1994.

Freedom of Religion

Alley, Robert S. *School Prayer: The Court, the Congress, and the First Amendment.* Buffalo, N.Y.: Prometheus Books, 1994.

Boston, Rob. *Why the Religious Right is Wrong About the Separation of Church and State*. Buffalo, N.Y.: Prometheus Books, 1993. Should be read with the Buckley book listed below.

Buckley, Thomas. *Church and State in Revolutionary Virginia: 1776–1787*. Charlottesville, Va.: University of Virginia Press, 1977.

Davis, Derek. *Original Intent: Chief Justice Rehnquist and the Course of American Church/State Relations*. Buffalo, N.Y.: Prometheus Books, 1991. Explains the current Supreme Court leader's influential views on the subject and his belief in discovering the original intent of the Founding Fathers.

Flowers, Ronald B. *That Godless Court? Supreme Court Decisions on Church-State Relationships*. Louisville, Ky.: Westminster/John Knox Press, 1994.

Frankel, Marvin E. *Faith and Freedom: Religious Liberty in America*. New York: Hill and Wang, 1994.

Gamwell, Franklin I. *The Meaning of Religious Freedom: Modern Politics and the Democratic Resolution*. Albany, N.Y.: State University of New York Press, 1995.

Haas, Carol. *Engel v. Vitale: Separation of Church and State*. Hillside, N.J.: Enslow Publishers , 1994. Analysis of one of the most significant Supreme Court decisions.

Kauper, Paul G. *Religion and the Constitution*. Baton Rouge, La.: Louisiana State University Press, 1964. Regarded as a classic work on the subject.

Levy, Leonard W. *The Establishment Clause: Religion and the First Amendment*. 2d ed. Chapel Hill, N.C.: University of North Carolina Press, 1994. Highly persuasive explanation by well-known constitutional historian.

Lugo, Luis E., ed. *Religion, Public Life and the American Polity*. Knoxville, Tenn.: University of Tennessee Press, 1994.

Marty, Martin E., ed. *Equal Separation: Understanding the Religion Clause of the First Amendment*. Westport, Conn.: Greenwood Press, 1990.

McWhirter, Darien A. *Separation of Church and State*. Phoenix, Ariz.: Oryx Press, 1994. Brief overview.

Nord, Warren A. *Religion and American Education: Rethinking an American Dilemma*. Chapel Hill, N.C.: University of North Carolina Press, 1994.

Wilcox, Clyde, and Ted G. Jelen. *Public Attitudes Toward Church and State*. Armonk, N.Y.: M. E. Sharpe, 1994.

Freedom of Speech

Barron, Jerome A. *First Amendment Law in a Nutshell*. St. Paul, Minn.: West Publishing, 1993. Really a handbook for law students, but it has accurate, brief statements. Can be used for all First Amendment topics.

Bracken, Harry M. *Freedom of Speech: Words Are Not Deeds*. Westport, Conn: Praeger, 1994. Useful explanation of free speech theories.

Cleary, Edward J. *Beyond the Burning Cross: The First Amendment and the Landmark R.A.V. Case*. New York: Random House, 1994.

Crosier, Louis M., and Jennifer A. Peter, eds. *The Cultural Battlefield: Art, Censorship and Public Funding*. Washington, D.C.: Avocus Publishing, 1995. Discusses government's role in supporting and censoring art.

Easton, Susan M. *The Problem of Pornography: Regulation and the Right to Free Speech*. New York: Routledge, 1994. Unimpassioned approach to a sensitive issue.

Eldridge, Larry D. *A Distant Heritage: The Growth of Free Speech in Early America*. New York: New York University Press, 1994.

Fish, Stanley. *There's No Such Thing as Free Speech, and It's a Good Thing, Too*. New York: Oxford University Press, 1994. As shown in the title, a provocative and accurate statement.

Freedman, Monroe H., and Eric M. Freedman. *Group Defamation and Freedom of Speech: The Relationship Between Language and Violence*. Westport, Conn.: Greenwood Publishing Press, 1994. Explains that the victims of strong speech may be unpopular minorities, but free speech usually wins out over claims of damaging group feelings, unless violence is induced.

Fuson, Harold W. *Telling it All: A Legal Guide to the Exercise of Free Speech*. Kansas City, Mo.: Andrews and McMeel, 1994.

Garvey, John H., ed. *The First Amendment: A Reader*. St. Paul, Minn.: West Publishing, 1992. A reliable collection for beginners in this field.

Gates, Henry, Jr., et al. *Speaking of Race, Speaking of Sex: Hate Speech, Civil Rights and Civil Liberties*. New York: New York University Press, 1994. How to deal with hate speech.

Hentoff, Nat. *Free Speech for me—but not for Thee*. New York: Harper Collins, 1992. Subtitle is descriptive: "How the American left and right relentlessly censor each other."

Lane, Robert W. *Beyond the Schoolhouse Gate: Free Speech and the Inculcation of Values*. Philadelphia: Temple University Press, 1995.

MacArthur, John R. *Second Front: Censorship and Propaganda in the Gulf War*. New York: Hill and Wang, 1992.

Ross, Henry D. *Free Speech and Talk Radio Hosts and Other Pieces*. New York: Capricorn Press, 1994.

Smolla, Rodney. *Free Speech in an Open Society*. New York: Vintage Books, 1992.

Strossen, Nadine. *In Defense of Pornography: Free Speech and the Fight for Women's Rights*. New York: Scribner, 1995. Highly controversial book by a feminist author.

Van Winkle, Harold. *Speaking Freely: Your Right of Free Speech and Its Legal Limitations*. Tampa: Mancorp Publishing, 1994.

Walker, Samuel. *Hate Speech: The History of an American Controversy*. Lincoln, Neb.: University of Nebraska Press, 1994.

History and Theory

Anderson, Terry H. *The Movement and the Sixties*. New York: Oxford University Press, 1993. A thoughtful history of a decade of protest against racial discrimination, the Vietnam War, and women's changing social position.

Belz, Herman. *Equality Transformed: A Quarter-Century of Affirmative Action*. New Brunswick, N.J.: Transaction Publishers, 1991. Describes and criticizes early development of affirmative action programs.

Bolick, Clint. *Unfinished Business: A Civil Rights Strategy for America's Third Century*. San Francisco: Pacific Research Institute for Public Policy, 1990. A forward-looking approach to civil rights.

Branch, Taylor. *Parting the Waters: America During the King Years, 1954–63*. New York: Simon and Schuster, 1989.

Carson, Clayborne, ed. *The Movement 1964–70*. Westport, Conn.: Greenwood Press, 1993.

Cogan, Neil H. *The Complete Bill of Rights*. New York: Oxford University Press, 1993. A definitive collection of nearly all relevant material concerning the origins of the Bill of Rights, tracing every draft and proposal. This is the best available record of the original purposes of the Bill of Rights.

De Varona, Frank. *Hispanic Presence in the United States: Historical Beginnings*. Miami, Fla.: Mnemosyne Publishing, 1993. Points out little-known facts about the long period of Hispanic occupation of the United States, showing the influence of these groups on American history.

Durham, Michael S. *Powerful Days: The Civil Rights Photography of Charles Moore*. New York: Stewart, Tabori and Chang, 1990. Documents civil rights photographic history in the American South from 1958–1963.

Dworkin, Ronald. *Taking Rights Seriously*. Cambridge, Mass.: Harvard University Press, 1982. Regarded as one of the best philosophical approaches to the study of rights.

Fairclough, Adam. *Race and Democracy: The Civil Rights Struggle in Louisiana, 1915–1972*. Athens, Ga.: University of Georgia Press, 1995. This book is the first detailed, comprehensive history of the civil rights movement in Louisiana.

Francione, Gary L. *Animals, Property and the Law*. Philadelphia: Temple University Press, 1995. Powerful argument against existing animal protection laws, which the author finds inadequate.

George, Robert P. *Making Men Moral: Civil Liberty and Public Morality*. New York: Oxford University Press, 1993. Politics can justify restricting liberty in order to maintain public morality.

Glendon, Mary Ann. *Rights Talk: The Impoverishment of Political Discourse*. New York: The Free Press, 1991. Author expresses concern over tendency of social issues to explode into rights issues.

Graham, Hugh Davis. *The Civil Rights Era: Origins and Development of National Policy, 1960–1972*. New York: Oxford University Press, 1990. Discusses the civil rights revolution with respect to the government's task of assuring equal rights.

Grinde, Donald A. *Exemplar of Liberty: Native America and the Evolution of Democracy*. Los Angeles: American Indian Studies Center, 1991. Native Americans had a form of democracy that adds to our understanding. Representative democracy existed among some Native American groups prior to European arrival in America.

Guinier, Lani. *The Tyranny of the Majority: Fundamental Fairness and Representative Democracy*. New York: The Free Press, 1994. Guinier sketches a map to a democracy of all the people, based on just consideration of everyone's views.

Higgenbotham, A. Leon. *In the Matter of Color*. New York: Oxford University Press, 1993. One of the very best accounts of the role of the law in the history of slavery. Shows the early origins of racism in American law.

———. *Shades of Freedom*. New York: Oxford University Press, 1996. Important critical history of American legal decisions regarding race from the seventeenth century to the present. Author is former Chief Judge of United States Court of Appeals, Third Circuit.

Levy, Peter B. *Documentary History of the Modern Civil Rights Movement*. New York: Greenwood Press, 1992. A useful collection.

Licht, Robert A. *The Framers and Fundamental Rights*. Washington, D.C.: American Enterprise Institute, 1991. A conservative interpretation of the meaning and scope of American rights.

Lofgren, Charles. *The Plessy Case*. New York: Oxford University Press, 1987. The *Plessy* case is one of the most controversial cases in American history. It not only denied African Americans fundamental citizenship, it also helped provoke the Civil War and the post-Civil War constitutional amendments.

Maier, Pauline. *American Scripture*. New York: A. A. Knopf, 1997. Professor Maier convincingly demonstrates that the idea of American independence was widely supported by ordinary people. Declarations of independence appeared in many colonies before Thomas Jefferson ever drafted the 1776 document. The Declaration incorporated many commonly held beliefs.

Shull, Steven A. *A Kinder, Gentler Racism? The Reagan-Bush Civil Rights Legacy*. Armonk, N.Y.: M. E. Sharpe, 1993. Assesses impact of presidential statements, actions, and results.

Smith, J. Owens. *The Politics of Racial Inequality*. Westport, Conn.: The Greenwood Press, 1987. An original analysis of the problems of immigrants to America, including the slaves. Shows that white ethnic immigrants have received more favored treatment by the government.

Weisbrot, Robert. *Freedom Bound: A History of America's Civil Rights Movement*. New York: W. W. Norton, 1990.

Wexler, Sanford. *The Civil Rights Movement: An Eyewitness History*. New York: Facts on File, 1993.

Willis, Deborah, and Howard Dodson. *Black Photographers Bear Witness: 100 Years of Social Protest.* Williamstown, Mass.: Williams College Museum of Art, 1989. A moving, vivid testimonial.

Wilson, Reginald. *Thinking About Our Rights: Civil Liberties and the United States.* New York: Walker and Co., 1988. This book outlines the history and development of American civil liberties.

Immigrants

Abowd, John M., and Richard P. Freeman, eds. *Immigration, Trade, and the Labor Market.* Chicago: University of Chicago Press, 1991.

Borjas, George J. *Friends or Strangers: The Impact of Immigrants on the U.S. Economy.* New York: Basic Books, 1990.

———. *Immigration and Welfare, 1970–1990.* Cambridge, Mass.: National Bureau of Economic Research, 1994. Brief but useful.

Bouvier, Leon F. *Peaceful Invasions: Immigration and Changing America.* Lanham, Md.: University Press of America, 1994. Historical treatment of immigration.

Briggs, Vernon M. *Mass Immigration and the National Interest.* Armonk, N.Y.: M. E. Sharpe, 1992.

Briggs, Vernon M., and Stephen Moore. *Still an Open Door? U.S. Immigration Policy and the American Economy.* Washington, D.C.: American University Press, 1994. Questions turn away from open door towards immigrants.

Brimelow, Peter. *Alien Nation: Common Sense about America's Immigration Disaster.* New York: Random House, 1995. Strong attack on generous American immigration policies.

Cose, Ellis. *A Nation of Strangers: Prejudice, Politics, and the Populating of America.* New York: Morrow, 1992.

Daniels, Roger. *Coming to America: A History of Immigration and Ethnicity in American Life.* New York: HarperCollins, 1990. Balanced historical recounting of immigrant life.

D'Innocenzo, Michael, and Josef P. Sirefman, eds. *Immigration and Ethnicity: American Society—"Melting Pot" or "Salad Bowl"?* Westport, Conn.: Greenwood Press, 1992. Essays indicate a search for a new description of immigrants in America.

Dudley, William, ed. *Immigration: Opposing Viewpoints.* San Diego, Calif.: Greenhaven Press, 1990. Designed to set forth opposing views of current immigration policies.

Jasso, Guillermina, and Mark P. Rozenzweig. *New Chosen People: Immigrants in the United States.* New York: Russell Sage Foundation, 1990.

Jones, Maldwyn Allen. *American Immigration.* Chicago: University of Chicago Press, 1990.

Maffi, Mario. *Gateway to the Promised Land: Ethnic Cultures on New York's Lower East Side.* New York: New York University Press, 1995. Description of New York immigrant life earlier in this century.

Mills, Nicolaus, ed. *Arguing Immigration: The Debate over the Changing Face of America.* New York: Simon and Schuster, 1994. Essays give a sense of the issues in current immigration policies.

Palmer, Ransford W. *Pilgrims from the Sun: West Indian Migration to America.* New York: Twayne Publishers, 1995. Describes experiences of a new immigrant group.

Passel, Jeffrey S., and Barry Edmonston. *Immigration and Race in the United States: The 20th and 21st Centuries.* Washington, D.C.: The Urban Institute, 1992. Important outlook for the future, as portrayed by one liberal analytical group.

Reimers, David M. *Still the Golden Door: The Third World Comes to America.* New York: Columbia University Press, 1992. Scholarly treatment of controversial topics.

Rolph, Elizabeth S. *Immigration Policies: Legacy from the 1980s and Issues for the 1990s.* Santa Monica, Calif.: Rand, 1992.

Stave, Bruce M., John F. Sutherland, and Aldo Salerno. *From the Old Country: An Oral History of the European Migration to America.* New York: Twayne, 1994. Stories from the mouths of the European immigrants.

Ueda, Reed. *Postwar Immigrant America: A Social History.* Boston: Bedford Books of St. Martin's Press, 1994.

Walch, Timothy, ed. *Immigrant America: European Ethnicity in the United States.* New York: Garland, 1994.

Winnick, Louis. *New People in Old Neighborhoods: The Role of New Immigrants in Rejuvenating New York's Communities.* New York: Russell Sage Foundation, 1990.

Yans-McLaughlin, Virginia, ed. *Immigration Reconsidered: History, Sociology, and Politics.* New York: Oxford University Press, 1990.

Asians

Barkan, Elliot Robert. *Asian and Pacific Islander Migration to the United States: A Model of New Global Patterns.* Westport, Conn.: Greenwood Press, 1992.

Hein, Jeremy. *States and International Migrants: The Incorporation of Indochinese Refugees in the United States and France.* Boulder, Colo.: Westview Press, 1992. Interesting comparative study.

Hing, Bill Ong. *Making and Remaking Asian America through Immigration Policy, 1850–1990.* Stanford, Calif.: Stanford University Press, 1993. Fine historical treatment of changing policies towards Asian Americans.

Saran, Parmatma. *The Asian Indian Experience in the United States.* Cambridge, Mass.: Schenkman, 1985.

Takaki, Ronald T. *Ethnic Islands: The Emergence of Urban Chinese America.* New York: Chelsea House, 1994.

Hispanics

Busmante, Jorge A., Clark W. Reynolds, and Raul A. Hinojosa, eds. *U.S.-Mexico Relations: Labor Market Inter-*

dependence. Stanford, Calif.: Stanford University Press, 1992.

Calavita, Kitty. *Inside the State: The Bracero Program, Immigration, and the I.N.S.* New York: Routledge, 1992.

DeFrietas, Gregory. *Inequality at Work: Hispanics in the U.S. Labor Force.* New York: Oxford University Press, 1991.

Diza-Briquets, Sergio and Sidney Weintraub, eds. *Determinants of Emigration from Mexico, Central America, and the Caribbean.* Boulder Colo.: Westview Press, 1991.

Gutierrez, David G. *Walls and Mirrors: Mexican Americans, Mexican Immigrants, and the Politics of Ethnicity.* Berkeley, Calif.: University of California Press, 1995.

Heer, David M. *Undocumented Mexicans in the United States.* New York: Cambridge University Press, 1990.

Hondagneu-Sotelo, Pierrette. *Gendered Transitions: Mexican Experiences of Immigration.* Berkeley, Calif.: University of California Press, 1994.

Lowenthal, Abraham F., and Katrina Burgess, eds. *The California-Mexico Connection.* Stanford, Calif.: Stanford University Press, 1993.

Monto, Alexander. *The Roots of Mexican Labor Migration.* Westport, Conn.: Praeger, 1994.

Pachon, Harry, and Louis De Sipio. *New Americans by Choice: Political Perspectives of Latino Immigrants.* Boulder, Colo.: Westview Press, 1994.

Suro, Robert. *Remembering the American Dream: Hispanic Immigration and National Policy.* New York: Twentieth Century Fund Press, 1994.

Native American Land and Water Rights

Alaska Division of State Libraries. *Bibliography of Alaska Native Organizations and Selected References on Alaska Native Land Claims.* Juneau, Alaska: The Division of State Libraries, 1971.

Anaya, S. James. 1994. "Native Land Claims in the United States: The Unatoned-for Spirit of Place." *Cultural Survival Quarterly* 17(4):52–55.

Barsh, Russell L. "Indian Land Claims Policy in the United States." *North Dakota Law Review* 58 (1982): 1–82.

Benedek, Emily. *The Wind Won't Know Me: A History of the Navajo-Hopi Land Dispute.* New York: Knopf, 1992.

Berger, Thomas R. *Village Journey: The Report of the Alaska Native Review Commission.* New York: Hill and Wang, 1985. Reports on land tenure and land claims in Alaska.

Berry, Mary C. *The Alaska Pipeline: The Politics of Oil and Native Land Claims.* Bloomington, Ind.: Indiana University Press, 1975.

Brodeur, Paul. *Restitution: The Land Claims of the Mashpee, Passamaquoddy, and Penobscot Indians of New England.* Boston: Northeastern University Press, 1985.

Brugge, David M. *The Navajo-Hopi Land Dispute: An American Tragedy.* Albuquerque, N.Mex.: University of New Mexico, 1994.

Churchill, Ward. "The Earth is Our Mother: Struggles for American Indian Land and Liberation in the Contemporary United States." In *The State of Native America: Genocide, Colonization, and Resistance.* Boston: South End Press, 1992. The militant position of Native Americans regarding the title to lands in America is stated here.

Cohen, Felix S. "Original Indian Title." *Minnesota Law Review* 32 (1947): 28–59.

Deloria, Vine Jr., and Clifford M. Lytle. *American Indians, American Justice.* Austin, Tex.: University of Texas Press, 1983.

Fixico, Donald. *Termination and Relocation, 1945–1960.* Albuquerque, N.Mex.: University of New Mexico Press, 1986.

Forbes, Jack. "The Public Domain of Nevada and Its Relationship to Indian Property Rights." *Nevada State Bar Journal* 30 (1965): 16–47.

Grinde, Donald A. *Ecocide of Native America: Environmental Destruction of Indian Lands.* Santa Fe, N.Mex.: Clear Light Press, 1995. Discusses the environmental damage inflicted on Native American lands.

Jaimes, M. Annette, ed. *The State of Native America: Genocide, Colonization, and Resistance.* Boston: South End Press, 1992. An informative and comprehensive collection by militant Native Americans, with essays on land and treaty rights, water rights, fishing, and uranium mining.

Johnson, C. Montgomery, and Ann Quantock. *First Our Land, Now Our Treaties: The Story of Washington State's Initiative 465 and Sponsors' Plans to Export It Across America.* Hadlock, Wash.: C. Montgomery Johnson Associates, 1985. Publisher's address is P.O. Box 300, Hadlock, WA 98339.

Jorgensen, Joseph G., ed. *Native Americans and Energy Development II.* Cambridge, Mass.: Anthropology Resource Center, 1984. Key work on subject.

Kammer, Jerry. *The Second Long Walk: The Navajo-Hopi Land Dispute.* Albuquerque, N.Mex.: University of New Mexico, 1980.

Laurence, R. "The Abrogation of Indian Treaties by Federal Statues Protective of the Environment." *Natural Resources Journal* 31 (1991): 859–886.

Lyons, David. "The New Indian Claims and Original Rights to Land." *Social Theory and Practice* 4 (1977): 249–272.

Nagel, Joane. *American Indian Ethnic Renewal.* New York: Oxford University Press, 1996. Provides an excellent overview of the resurgence of American Indian identity, as well as the "red power" movement and federal policy in general.

Parker, Linda S. *Native American Estate: The Struggle over Indian and Hawaiian Lands.* Honolulu, Hawaii: University of Hawaii, 1989.

Scudder, Thayer, and David F. Aberle, et al. *No Place to Go: Effects of Compulsory Relocation on Navajos.* Philadelphia: Institute for the Study of Human Issues, 1982. Discusses the Navajo-Hopi "land dispute."

Shipek, Florence C. *Pushed into the Rocks: Southern Californian Indian Land Tenure, 1769–1986.* Lincoln, Neb.: University of Nebraska Press, 1987.

———. "Indian Land Rights and the Sagebrush Rebellion." *Geographical Review* 72 (1982): 357–359.

Sutton, Imre. *Indian Land Tenure: Bibliographical Essays and a Guide to the Literature.* New York: Clearwater Publishing, 1975. Extensive bibliography, but old.

Sutton, Imre, and Theodore S. Jojola, eds. *Irredeemable America: The Indians' Estate and Land Claims.* Albuquerque, N.Mex.: University of New Mexico Press, 1985.

Tehan, Kevin. "Of Indians, Land, and the Federal Government: The Navajo-Hopi Land Dispute." *Arizona State Law Journal* (1976): 173–212.

Tollefson, Kenneth D. "The Political Survival of Landless Puget Sound Indians." *American Indian Quarterly* 16, no. 2 (1992): 213–235.

Van Ness, John. *Land, Water, and Culture: New Perspectives on Hispanic Land Grants.* Albuquerque, N.Mex.: University of New Mexico, 1987.

Vecsey, Christopher, and William A. Starna, eds. *Iroquois Land Claims.* Syracuse, N.Y.: Syracuse University Press, 1988.

Walker, Deward E., Jr. "Protection of American Indian Sacred Geography." In *Handbook of American Indian Religious Freedom,* edited by Christopher Vecsey. New York: Crossroads Publishing, 1991.

Wallace, Harry B. "Indian Sovereignty and the Eastern Indian Land Claims." *New York University Law School Law Review* 27 (1982): 921–950.

Watts, Tim J. *American Indian Treaty Rights: A Bibliography.* Monticello, Ill.: Vance Bibliographies, 1991.

Wilkinson, Charles F. *American Indians, Time, and the Law: Native Societies in a Modern Constitutional Democracy.* New Haven, Conn.: Yale University Press, 1987.

Wishart, David J. *An Unspeakable Sadness: The Dispossession of the Nebraska Indians.* Lincoln, Nebr.: University of Nebraska, 1994.

Wright, J. B. "Tribes v. States: Zoning Indian Reservations." *Natural Resources Journal* 32, no. 1 (1992): 195–206.

Race and Race Relations

Bell, Derrick. *Faces at the Bottom of the Well: The Permanence of Racism.* New York: Basic Books, 1992. Derrick Bell conveys his progressive ideas regarding racism, which he regards as permanent in the United States.

Brooks, Roy L. *Rethinking the American Race Problem.* Berkeley and Los Angeles, Calif.: University of California Press, 1990.

D'Souza, Dinesh. *The End of Racism.* New York: The Free Press, 1995. Highly controversial book. Dinesh D'Souza insists terrible problems of many African Americans exist not because of racism but because of a dysfunctional black culture.

Dudley, William, and Charles Cozic, eds. *Racism in America.* San Diego, Calif.: Greenhaven Press, 1991.

Early, Gerald, ed. *Lure and Loathing: Essays on Race, Identity and the Ambivalence of Assimilation.* New York: Penguin Press, 1993.

Essed, Philomena. *Understanding Everyday Racism: An Interdisciplinary Theory.* Newbury Park, Calif.: Sage Publications, 1991. Compares discrimination and racism in the Netherlands with that found in the United States. Also relates racism and sex discrimination.

Feagin, Joe R., and Melvin P. Sikes. *Living with Racism: The Black Middle-Class Experience.* Boston: Beacon Press, 1994. One of the more unusual works about racism in America.

Finkenstadt, Rose L. *Face to Face: Blacks in America: White Perceptions and Black Realities.* New York: William Morrow, 1994.

Foner, Philip S., and Daniel Rosenberg, eds. *Racism, Dissent, and the Asian Americans from 1850 to the Present: A Documentary History.* Westport, Conn.: Greenwood Press, 1993. Racism directed at Asians is documented here.

Franklin, John Hope. *The Color Line: Legacy of the Twenty-first Century.* Columbia, Mo.: University of Missouri Press, 1993. Thoughtful views of a prominent historian.

Hacker, Andrew. *Two Nations: Black and White, Separate, Hostile, Unequal.* New York: Macmillan, 1992. The title says it all.

Kennedy, Theodore R. *You Gotta Deal With It: Black Family Relations in a Southern Community.* New York: Oxford University Press, 1980. A still timely account of African American relations with whites in the South.

Loury, Glenn C. *One by One from the Inside Out: Essays and Reviews on Race and Responsibility in America.* New York: The Free Press, 1995. Loury hopes for the equality of opportunity for African Americans, while maintaining the integrity of the democratic system.

McKee, James B. *Sociology and the Race Problem: The Failure of a Perspective.* Urbana and Chicago: University of Illinois Press, 1993.

McLemore, S. Dale. *Racial and Ethnic Relations in America.* 4th ed. Needham Heights, Mass.: Allyn and Bacon, 1994.

Piazza, Thomas, and Paul M. Sniderman. *The Scar of Race.* Cambridge, Mass.: Belknap Press of Harvard University, 1993.

Powell, Thomas. *The Persistence of Racism in America.* Lanham, Md.: Littlefield Adams, 1993.

Ringer, Benjamin B. *Race-Ethnicity and Society.* New York: Routledge, 1989.

Rusk, David. *Cities Without Suburbs.* Washington, D.C.: The Woodrow Wilson Center Press, 1993. Discusses how racial and economic segregation is at the heart of America's urban problem.

San Juan, E. *Racial Formations/Critical Transformations: Articulations of Power in Ethnic and Racial Studies in the United States.* Atlantic Highlands, N.J.: Humanities Press, 1992.

Schlesinger, Arthur Meier. *The Disuniting of America*. New York: W. W. Norton, 1992. Professor Schlesinger, a distinguished historian of Roosevelt's New Deal, deplores the divisive effects of race thinking in America.

Smith, J. Owens, and Carl E. Jackson, eds. *Race and Ethnicity: A Study of Intracultural Socialization Patterns*. Dubuque, Iowa: Kendall/Hunt, 1989.

Sniderman, Paul M., et al. *Prejudice, Politics and the American Dilemma*. Stanford, Calif.: Stanford University Press, 1993.

Steele, Shelby. *The Content of Our Character*. New York: Harper Perennial, 1991. A hopeful view of race relations.

Taylor, Jared. *Paved With Good Intentions: The Failure of Race Relations in Contemporary America*. New York: Carroll and Graf Publishers, 1992.

Terkel, Studs, ed. *Race: How Blacks and Whites Think and Feel About the American Obsession*. New York: New Press, 1992. A best-selling book based upon taped interviews with Americans from many classes and groups.

Thomas, Gail. E. *U.S. Race Relations in the 1980s and 1990s*. Washington, D.C.: Hemisphere Publishing, 1990. An evaluation of race relations in the United States.

Van Horne, Winston A, ed. *Race: Twentieth Century Dilemmas, Twenty-First Century Prognoses*. Milwaukee: The University of Wisconsin System, Institute on Race and Ethnicity, 1989.

Webster, Yehudi O. *The Racialization of America*. New York: St. Martin's Press, 1989.

West, Cornel. *Beyond Eurocentrism and Multiculturalism*. Monroe, Maine: Common Courage Press, 1993. The author explains how and why we should travel beyond Eurocentrism and multiculturalism.

———. *Keeping Faith: Philosophy and Race in America*. New York: Routledge, 1993. West ponders race, culture, politics, and philosophy.

———. *Race Matters*. Boston: Beacon Press, 1993. West discusses critical issues pertaining to African Americans as well as to all Americans as the country charts its future course.

Zack, Naomi. *Race and Mixed Race*. Philadelphia: Temple University Press, 1993. The problems and opportunities of racially mixed families.

Supreme Court Interpretations of Rights

Abernathy, Glenn, and Barbara Perry. *Civil Liberties under the Constitution*. 6th ed. St. Paul, Minn.: West Publishing, 1993. A casebook used in colleges.

Abraham, Henry, and Barbara Perry. *Freedom and the Court: Civil Rights and Liberties under the Constitution*. New York: Oxford University Press, 1994. A well-established textbook. Bibliography is excellent.

Barker, Lucius, and Twiley W. Barker, Jr. *Civil Liberties and the Constitution*. 7th ed. Englewood Cliffs, N.J.: Prentice Hall, 1994. A standard college casebook.

Cohen, William, and David Danielski. *Constitutional Law, Civil Liberty and Individual Rights*. 3d ed. Westbury, N.Y.: Foundation Press, 1994. Fine law school case collection. Contains brief profiles of many justices.

Congressional Quarterly, and Elder Witt. *Supreme Court and Individual Rights*. Washington, D.C.: Congressional Quarterly, 1988. Accurate overview of the topic.

Ducat, Craig, and Harold W. Chase. *Constitutional Interpretation: Rights of Individuals*. 5th ed. St. Paul, Minn.: West Publishing, 1992. Used mainly in law schools. Detailed but accurate.

Graham, Hugh D., ed. *Civil Rights in the United States*. State College, Pa.: Pennsylania State University Press, 1994. Short but stimulating collection.

Kairys, David. *With Liberty and Justice for Some: A Critique of the Conservative Supreme Court*. New York: New Press, 1993. A radical lawyer's viewpoint, which argues that the Supreme Court has neglected the rights of minorities and women and has failed to correct discrimination in America.

Karst, Kenneth L. *Belonging to America: Equal Citizenship and the Constitution*. New Haven, Conn.: Yale University Press, 1989. A famous law professor's views.

———. *Civil Rights and Equality*. New York: Macmillan, 1989. Selections from the standard, *Encyclopedia of the American Constitution*. Each short essay is written by an expert. Most essays focus on racial equality.

King, Richard H. *Civil Rights and the Idea of Freedom*. New York: Oxford University Press, 1992.

Kluger, Richard. *Simple Justice*. New York: Knopf, 1975. The best book on the most important case of the century: *Brown* v. *Board of Education*. Desegregation began there.

Lewis, Anthony. *Make No Law*. New York: Vintage Books, 1992. A popular book that can be read for its free speech significance or as a general introduction to the struggles of the Supreme Court when dealing with presidential claims of national security.

Lively, Donald E. *The Constitution and Race*. New York: Praeger, 1992.

Murphy, Paul L. *World War I and the Origins of Civil Liberties in the United States*. New York: W. W. Norton, 1979. Demonstrates that the Supreme Court's role did not really begin in earnest until after World War I.

Rappaport, Doreen. *Tinker vs. Des Moines: Student Rights on Trial*. New York: Harper Collins, 1993. Places this most important student free speech case into context.

Spann, Girardeau A. *Race Against the Supreme Court: The Minorities in Contemporary America*. New York: New York University Press, 1993.

Voting

American Bar Association. *Now that You are 18*. Chicago: The American Bar Association, 1989. Deals with much more than voting rights.

Ball, Howard. *Warren Court's Conceptions of Democracy*. Madison, N.J.: Fairleigh Dickinson Press, 1971. Shows that the interpretations of this liberal court were influenced by its views of democracy, especially with regard to reapportionment and representation.

Grofman, Bernard, and Chandler Davidson, eds. *Controversies in Minority Voting: The Voting Rights Act in Perspective.* Washington, D.C.: Brookings Institution, 1992.

Guinier, Lani. *The Tyranny of the Majority: Fundamental Fairness in Representative Democracy.* New York: The Free Press, 1994.

Gurin, Patricia, et al. *Hope and Independence: Blacks' Response to Electoral and Party Politics.* New York: Russell Sage Foundation, 1989.

Women: Violence and Harassment

Barnett, Ola W., and Alyce D. LaViolette. *It Could Happen to Anyone: Why Battered Women Stay.* Newbury Park, Calif.: Sage Publications, 1993. Some psychological insights.

Davis, Angela. *Women, Culture and Politics.* New York: Vintage Books, 1990. A radical view, not only about violence.

Dobash, R. Emerson, and Russell Dobash. *Violence against Wives.* New York: The Free Press, 1979. An important earlier work.

———. *Women, Violence and Social Change.* New York: Routledge, 1992.

Dutton, Maryann. *Empowering and Healing the Battered Woman.* New York: Springer, 1992.

Esaguirre, Lynne. *Sexual Harassment: A Reference Handbook.* Santa Barbara, Calif.: ABC-CLIO, 1993.

Gelb, Joyce. *Feminism and Politics.* Berkeley, Calif.: University of California Press, 1989. A leading feminist interpretation.

Ingulli, Elaine D. "Sexual Harassment in Education." *Rutgers Law Journal* 18: 281–342.

MacKinnon, Catherine. *Sexual Harassment of Working Women.* New Haven, Conn.: Yale University Press, 1979. A pioneering work on a rapidly developing problem area.

Martin, Del. *Battered Wives.* New York: Simon and Shuster, 1976.

Walker, Lenore E. *The Battered Woman.* 2d ed. New York: Harper and Row, 1984.

Women's Suffrage

Banner, Lois. *Elizabeth Cady Stanton: A Radical for Women's Rights.* Boston: Little, Brown, 1980.

Gattey, Charles Nielson. *The Bloomer Girls.* New York: Coward-McCann, 1967.

Griffith, Elisabeth. *In Her Own Right: The Life of Elizabeth Cady Stanton.* New York: Oxford University Press, 1984.

Gurko, Miriam. *The Ladies of Seneca Falls: The Birth of the Woman's Rights Movement.* New York: Schocken Books, 1976.

Moynihan, Ruth Barnes, ed. *Second To None: A Documentary History of American Women.* 2 vols. Lincoln, Nebr.: University of Nebraska Press, 1993.

Sherr, Lynn. *Failure is Impossible: Susan B. Anthony in Her Own Words.* New York: Time Books, 1995.

Stone, Lucy. *Loving Warriors: Selected Letters of Lucy Stone and Henry Blackwell, 1853–1893.* New York: Dial Press, 1981.

Prominent Rights Interest Groups

The following organizations are actively involved in one or another aspect of civil rights in America. Any of these groups can supply topical information. Many are actively involved in current litigation, and each has its own viewpoint on civil rights. Contact information is provided here.

American-Arab Discrimination Committee
1731 Connecticut Ave. NW, Ste. 400
Washington, DC 20009
(202) 797-7662

American Civil Liberties Union
132 W. 43d St.
New York, NY 10036
(212) 944-9800
Has nationwide reach.

American Council of the Blind
1010 Vermont Ave. NW, Ste. 1100
Washington, DC 20005
(202) 393-3666

American Foundation for the Blind
11 Penn Plaza, Ste. 300
New York, NY 10001
(212) 502-7648
Fax: (212) 502-7774
Contact: Dennis Brookshire

Americans of Italian Descent
51 Madison Ave., Ste. 2902
New York, NY 10010
(212) 725-5011
4521 Woopdward Avenue
Ridgewood, NY 11385
Dr. Joseph F. Valletti, Executive Director
(718) 456-5641

Amnesty International, U.S.A.
322 8th Ave.
New York, NY 10001
(212) 807-8400
Human rights group has international scope.

Asian American Legal Defense and Education Fund
99 Hudson St., 12th Fl.
New York, NY 10013
(212) 966-5932

Asian Law Caucus, Inc.
468 Bush St., 3d Fl.
San Francisco, CA 94108
(415) 391-1655
Fax: (415) 391-0366

Association for Persons with Severe Handicaps
11201 Greenwood Ave.
Seattle, WA 98133
(206) 361-8870
Fax: (206) 361-9208

Association for the Sexually Harassed
P.O. Box 27235
Philadelphia, PA. 19118
(215) 952-8037

Americans United for Separation of Church and State
8120 Fenton St.
Silver Spring, MD 20910-4781
(301) 589-3707
 Fax: (301) 495-9173

Association on American Indian Affairs
245 5th Ave.
New York, NY 10016
(212) 689-8720
Fax: (212) 645-4692

Balch Institute for Ethnic Studies
18 S. 7th St.
Philadelphia, PA
(215) 925-8090
Contact: Gale Farr, ext. 217

B'Nai Brith
Antidefamation League
823 United Nations Plaza
New York, NY 10017
(212) 490-2525
Concerned with anti-Semitism.

Center for Civil and Human Rights
Notre Dame Law School
Notre Dame, IN 46566
(219) 283-6483
Research center.

Center for Constitutional Rights
666 Broadway, 7th Fl.
New York, NY 10012
Miriam Thompson, Executive Director
(212) 614-6464
Fax: (212) 614-6499
Frequently involved in litigation.

Center for Law and Social Policy
1616 P St. NW, Ste. 550
Washington, DC 20036
(202) 328-5140
Defends rights of the poor and underrepresented.

Center for Women's Policy Studies
2000 P St., Ste. 508
Washington, DC 20036
(202) 872-1770

Center for Women's Studies and Services
908 E St.
San Diego, CA 92101
(714) 233-8944

Child Welfare League of America
440 First St. NW, Ste. 310
Washington, DC 20001-2085
(202) 638-2952
Fax: (202) 638-4004

Children's Defense Fund
122 C St. NW, 4th Fl.
Washington, DC 20001
(202) 628-8787

Chinese for Affirmative Action
17 Walter U. Lum Pl.
San Francisco, CA 94108
(415) 274-6750

Citizen's Commission on Civil Rights
2000 M St. NW, Ste. 400
Washington, DC 20036
(202) 659-5565
Fax: (202) 223-5320

Arthur Fleming, Chairman
Disability Rights Center, Inc.
2500 Q St. NW, Ste. 121
Washington, DC 20007
(202) 337-4119

Disability Rights Education and Defense Fund, Inc.
2212 6th St.
Berkeley, CA 94710
(510) 644-2555
Fax: (510) 841-8645
Contact: Linda D. Kilb

Division of Child Protection
111 Michigan Ave. NW
Washington, DC 20010
(202) 745-4100
Lobbies for social services for neglected children.

Education Law Center, Inc.
155 Washington St.
Newark, NJ 07102
(201) 624-1815
225 S. 15th St.
Philadelphia, PA 19102
(215) 732-6655

Equal Rights Advocates, Inc.
1663 Mission St.
San Francisco, CA 94103
(415) 621-0672
Handles sex discrimination issues.

First Amendment Foundation
1313 W. 8th St., Ste. 313
Los Angeles, CA 90017
(213) 484-6661
Fax: (213) 484-0266
Concerned with FBI and government "repression."

Gray Panthers
1424 16th St. NW, Ste. L1
Washington, DC 20036
(202) 387-3111
Fights for older Americans

Homosexual Information Center
115 Monroe St.
Bossier City, LA 71111-4539
(318) 742-4709

Indian Resource Law Center
601 E St. SE
Washington, DC 20003
(202) 547-2800
Legal group aids Native Americans.

Institute for the Development of Indian Law
c/o Kirke Kickingbird
School of Law
Oklahoma City University
2501 Blackwelder
Oklahoma City, OK 73106

Leadership Conference on Civil Rights
2027 Massachusetts Ave. NW
Washington, DC 20036
(202) 667-1780
Pending civil rights legislation monitored.

Legal Services for Prisoners with Children
1535 Mission St.
San Francisco, CA 94103
(415) 255-7036
Handles custody, visitation, and child support cases.

Lewisburg Prison Project
P.O. Box 128
Lewisburg, PA 17837-0128
(717) 523-1104
Contact: E. Marsh
Bulletins on prisoners' rights.

Martin Luther King, Jr. Center for Social Change
449 Auburn Ave. NE
Atlanta, GA 30312
(404) 524-1956
Center for advocacy and voting rights.

Meiklejohn Civil Liberties Institute
P.O. Box 673
Berkeley, CA 94701
(510) 848-0599
Fax: (510) 848-6008
Contact: Beverly Wilson
Largely a research site.

Mexican-American Legal Defense and Education Fund
634 S. Spring St., 11th Fl.
Los Angeles, CA 90014
(213) 629-2512

Migrant Legal Action Program
2001 S St. NW, Ste. 310
Washington, DC 20009
(202) 462-7744

National Abortion Rights Action League
1101 14th St. NW, 5th Fl.
Washington, DC 20005
(202) 371-0779

NAACP Legal Defense and Educational Fund, Inc.
99 Hudson St.
New York, NY 10013
(212) 219-1900
Elaine R. Jones, Director-Counsel
One of the most active groups in litigation.

National Center for Immigrant's Rights, Inc.
256 S. Occidental Blvd.
Los Angeles, CA 90057
(213) 388-8693

National Center for Lesbian Rights
1663 Mission St., 5th Fl.
San Francisco, CA 94103
(415) 621-0674
Fax: (415) 621-6744

National Center for Youth Law
114 Sansome
San Francisco, CA 04104
(415) 543-3307
Poor children advocates.

National Clearinghouse for the Defense of Battered Women
125 S. 9th St., Ste. 302
Philadelphia, PA 19107
(215) 351-0010
Provides battered women with direct assistance.

National Committee for the Prevention of Child Abuse
332 S. Michigan Ave., Ste. 1600
Chicago, IL 60604
Supports research and prevention.

National Council of La Raza
810 1st St. NE, Ste. 300
Washington, DC 20002
(202) 289-1380
Coalition of Latino groups.

National Council of Senior Citizens, Inc.
1331 F St. NW
Washington, DC 20004
(202) 347-8800

National Emergency Civil Liberties Committee
175 5th Ave., Rm. 814
New York, NY 10010
(212) 673-2040

National Gay and Lesbian Task Force
1734 14th St. NW
Washington, DC 20009
(202) 332-6483

National Housing Law Project, Inc.
122 C St. NW, Ste. 220
Washington, DC 20001-2109
(202) 783-5140
Funded by Legal Service Corp.

National Immigration Project
14 Beacon St., Ste. 506
Boston, MA 02108
(617) 227-9727

National Lawyers Guild
55 Avenue of the Americas
New York, NY 10013
(212) 966-5000
Combines lawyers and law students.

National Organization for Women
1401 New York Ave. NW, Ste. 800
Washington, DC 20005
(202) 331-0066

National Urban League
Equal Opportunity Building
500 E. 62d St.
New York City NY 10021
(212) 310-9000

NOW Legal Defense and Educational Fund
99 Hudson St.
New York, NY 10013
(212) 925-6635
Active women's rights group.

Native American Rights Fund
1506 Broadway
Boulder, CO 80302-6296
(303) 447-8760
Fax: (303) 443-7776
1712 N St. NW
Washington, DC 20036
(202) 785-4166

Polish American Guardian Society
6200 W. 64th St.
Chicago, Illinois 60638
(312) 586-4734

Puerto Rican Legal Defense and Education Fund, Inc.
99 Hudson St., 14th Fl.
New York, NY 10013
(212) 219-3360
Fax: (212) 431-4276

Schomburg Center for Research in Black Culture
New York Public Library
515 Lenox Ave.
New York City, NY 10037
(212) 862-4000

Women for Racial and Economic Equality
198 Broadway, Rm. 106
New York, NY 10038
(212) 385-1103

Women's Law Project
125 S. 9th St., Rm. 401
Philadelphia, PA 19107

Worker's Defense League
218 West 40th St.
New York, NY 10018
(212) 730-7412
Employee protection.

Youth Law Center
1663 Mission St., 5th Fl.
San Francisco, CA 94103
(415) 543-3379

Federal Civil Rights Agencies

Office for Civil Rights (Education)
400 Maryland Ave. SW
Washington, DC 20202
(202) 732-1213

U.S. Department of Health and Human Services (HHS)
National Center on Child Abuse and Neglect
U.S. Children's Bureau
Box 1182
Washington, DC 20013
(202) 245-0910
Fax: (202) 245-6721

Office for Civil Rights (HHS)
330 Independence Ave. SW
Washington, DC 20201
(202) 245-6403

U.S. Department of Housing and Urban Development (HUD)
Office of Fair Housing and Equal Opportunity
451 7th St. SW
Washington, DC 20410
(202) 708-1422
Handles all discrimination issues in housing.

U.S. Department of the Interior
Bureau of Indian Affairs
Public Affairs Office
Washington, DC 20240
(202) 208-7315

U.S. Department of Justice
Civil Rights Division
10th and Penn Avenues NW
Washington, DC 20530
(202) 633-2151, (202) 514-4224

U.S. Department of Labor
200 Constitution Ave.
Washington, DC 20210

Office of Federal Contract Compliance Program:
(202) 523-9475

Women's Bureau: (202) 523-6611

U.S. Commission on Civil Rights
624 9th St. NW
Washington, DC 20245
(202) 376-7700
Maintains directory for federal, state, and local agencies.

U.S. Equal Employment Opportunities Commission
Washington, DC 20507
(202) 663-4900
Fax: (202) 663-6912

Teachers, Librarians

American Library Association
Peggy Sullivan, Executive Director
50 E. Huron St.
Chicago, IL 60611
(312) 944-6780
(800) 545-2433
Fax: (312) 280-3255

American Library Association
Peggy Krug
Office for Intellectual Freedom
(800) 545-2433, ext. 4223

International Association of School Librarianship
P.O. Box 19586
Kalamazoo, MI 49019
Dr. Jean E. Laurie, Executive Director
(616) 343-5728

National Coalition of Education Activists
P.O. Box 405
Rosendale, NY 12472
(914) 658-8115
Fax: (914) 658-3153

Multicultural network.
Network of Educators on the Americas
1118 22nd St. NW
Washington, DC 20037
(202) 329-0137
Fax: (202) 429-9766

People for the American Way
2000 M St. NW, Ste. 400
Washington, DC 20036
Elliot Mincberg, Legal Director
Tends to be quite "progressive," but useful on censorship in schools and libraries.

Selected Videotapes

A brief annotated list of selected quality videotapes is provided in order to assist in the appreciation of rights in America. This list of commercially available videotapes is in chronological, not alphabetical, order. All of the materials listed here have appeared on U.S. television. In some small way they contribute to an understanding of the history and the development of American rights by giving a visual impression and dramatization of American rights. The printed page is still more reliable, and that is what our book is intended to supply. Nevertheless, for newcomers in this field these television productions are a fair starting point. All the videos listed may be acquired from PBS Home Video in Alexandria, Virginia, and the catalog code number is provided.

A1284 *The Native Americans.* Six videocassettes, approximately 4 hours and 30 minutes. The stories of America's original settlers are told in their own words. Included are representatives of the Northeast Nations, the Northwest, the Southeast, the Southwest, and the Great Plains.

A1802 *Pocahontas.* One videocassette, 50 minutes. Popular history dwells on the story of Pocahontas and Captain John Smith, the English explorer. This cassette also reveals Pocahontas to have been a notable stateswoman and peacemaker.

A1827 *Native Lands: Nomads of the Dawn.* One videocassette, 58 minutes. The paths of the early nomads who came to the Americas before the Europeans is revealed in a combination of ritual dance, drama, and storytelling. Although the origins of the Aztecs, Incas, and other South American groups are emphasized, the cultures of other Native Americans are considered.

A1810 *Civil War Legends.* Four videocassettes, 2 hours. An understanding of the Civil War is pivotal to obtaining a grasp of civil rights because it spelled the end of slavery. This production portrays four great leaders of the Civil War: Robert E. Lee, Abraham Lincoln, Stonewall Jackson, and Ulysses S. Grant.

A1842 *Held in Trust: The Story of Lt. Henry O. Flipper.* One videocassette, 60 minutes. General Colin Powell introduces this dramatic recreation of the career of the first African American graduate of West Point Military Academy. Lt. Henry Flipper was a victim of racial prejudice, and was hounded out of the military after being framed on a trumped-up charge of embezzlement.

A1841 *Mississippi, America.* One videocassette, 60 minutes. Actors Ossie Davis and Ruby Dee narrate this powerful documentary about the 1964 Freedom Summer, when a coalition of civil rights activists broke through the racial barriers that had kept Mississippi African Americans from access to the voting booth. This struggle led to the passage of the *Voting Rights Act of 1965.*

A1845 *The Spirit of Crazy Horse.* One videocassette, 60 minutes. This videotape tells the story of the quest of the Sioux Indians to reclaim their ancestral lands in the Black Hills of South Dakota, during the 1960s and 1970s. Narrated by Milo Yellow Hair, a full-blooded Ogala Sioux, the Native American position about their lands is clearly stated.

A1715 *Amerika.* Five videocassettes, 12 hours. This fictional portrayal of a future America features Kris Kristofferson, Christine Lahti, Sam Niell, Robert Urich, and other Hollywood stars. It portrays a nation in which democracy is extinguished and the Bill of Rights ignored by an occupying force that has taken over the United States. The ideals of freedom are pitted against a regime based upon a tyrannical disregard of rights.

PBS has also produced various excellent videotapes about the Supreme Court, but the availability of these materials is uncertain. (PBS Video, in Alexandria, Virginia, should be contacted regarding its list.) One of the finest is a 1992 production entitled: *The Delicate Balance II: Our Bill of Rights,* which was produced by Columbia University in association with television station WNET in New York City. This is a set of five videocassettes, running 320 minutes.

Capital University and Law Center in Columbus, Ohio, has created useful, topical, and lively videotapes on many rights topics.

The American Bar Association in Chicago, Illinois, also produces a number of videotapes that are reliable, although sometimes technical.

The American Civil Liberties Union, in New York City, has produced a number of rights videotapes showing its viewpoint effectively.

C-SPAN has produced some valuable videocassettes. One of the best is a live Forum sponsored by the B'Nai Brith International held on September 9, 1992, which concentrates on hate crimes and the changing views of the Supreme Court.

Internet Resources

Check under the following categories, using various Internet search engines:

Civil rights, Bill of Rights, Civil Rights Division, minorities, free speech, freedom of religion, Supreme Court, race, discrimination, voting, African Americans, Asian Pacific Islanders, Asian Americans, Chicanas, Latinas, Native Americans, American Indians, Hispanics, immigration, abortion, free speech, freedom of religion.

There are many Internet sources dealing with the topic of human rights. The official American version of human rights around the world is the U.S. Department of State's, *Human Rights Practices.* This interesting annual report is found at: **www.usis.usemb.se/human/index.htm.**

The best single source on human rights groups is Human Rights Internet, based in Ottawa, Canada. Their telephone number is (613) 789-7407. Some of their information is on the Internet.

The best Internet address for human rights information generally is: **www.hri.ca.**

The Internet address for the American Civil Liberties Union is **www.aclu.org.**

Table of Cases

T

Texas Education Agency v. *Leeper,* 893 S.W.2d 432 (Tex. 1994), 414

Thomas v. *Review Board, Indiana Employment Division,* 450 U.S. 707 (1981), 335

Tilton v. *Mayes,* 163 U.S. 376 (1896), 233

Timothy W. v. *Rochester, New Hampshire, School District,* 875 F.2d 954 (1st Cir. 1989), 441

Tinker v. *Des Moines Independent Community School District,* 393 U.S. 503 (1969), 411, 457–58, 465, 644–47

Town of Lockport, 430 U.S. 259 (1977), 400

TransWorld Airways v. *Hardison,* 432 U.S. 63 (1977), 466

U

United States v. *Bhaghat Sing Thind,* 43 U.S. 338 (1923), 143

United States v. *Cruikshank,* 92 U.S. 542 (1876), 90

United States v. *Eichman,* 496 U.S. 310 (1990), 341

United States v. *Grace,* 461 U.S. 171 (1983), 368

United States v. *Kagama,* 118 U.S. 375 (1886), 221

United States v. *Kuch,* 288 F.Supp. 439 (D.D.C. 1968), 337

United States v. *New York Times Publishing Company,* 403 U.S. 713 (1971), 341

United States v. *Nixon,* 418 U.S. 683 (1974), 341

United States v. *O'Brien,* 391 U.S. 367 (1968), 341

United States v. *Sandoval,* 231 U.S. 28 (1913), 223

United States v. *Usery,* 116 S.Ct. 2135 (1996), 284

United States v. *Virginia, VMI, et al.* 518 U.S.___; 135 L.ed2d 735 (1996), 50, 445, 659–61

United States v. *Washington,* (Phase I), 496 F.2d 620 (9th Cir. 1974), 236

United States v. *Washington,* 443 U.S. 658 (1979), 236

V

Vernonia School District v. *Wayne Acton,* 115 S.Ct. 2386 (1995), 459

Virginia State Board of Pharmacy v. *Virginia Citizens Consumer Council, Inc.,* 425 U.S. 748 (1976), 364

W

Walker v. *Saurinet,* 92 U.S. 90 (1876), 13

Wallace v. *Jaffree,* 105 S.Ct. 2479, 472 U.S. 38 (1985), 292, 328, 452

Watson v. *City of Cambridge,* 157 Mass. 561 (1893), 440

Wesberry v. *Sanders,* 376 U.S. 1 (1964), 385, 399

West Virginia State Board of Education v. *Barnette,* 319 U.S. 624, (1943), 334, 448–49

Widener v. *Frye,* 809 F.Supp. 35 (S.D. Ohio, 1992), 526

Wisconsin v. *Mitchell,* 508 U.S. 476 (1993), 348–49

Wisconsin v. *Yoder,* 406 U.S. 205 (1972), 290, 335, 410, 446

Wolman v. *Walter,* 433 U.S. 229 (1977), 452

Y

Yick Wo v. *Hopkins,* 118 U.S. 356 (1886), 17, 134

Index

Italicized page numbers refer to illustrations.

A

Abernathy, Ralph, 103
  biography, 104
  and King, M. L., 104
  and Southern Christian Leadership Conference, 104
Abortion, 59–61, 366–68
Access to the ballot, 370–72, 389–91
ACLU. *See* American Civil Liberties Union (ACLU)
Adams, Abigail, 46
Adams, Henry, 113
Adams, John, 46, 243, *437*
Addams, Jane, 50, 304
  and ACLU, 50
  biography, 50
  and labor movement, 68
  and Lincoln, Abraham, 50
Advance directives, 554–56
Affirmative action, 123–25, 126–28, 256–57, 548
  and Civil Rights Division, 124, 127–28
  in employment, 481–83
  Hispanics, 217
  and Johnson, Lyndon, 32
  and other minorities, 127–28
  and reverse discrimination, 126–27
  and women, 62–64
Affordable housing, 499–500
AFL. *See* American Federation of Labor (AFL)
African Americans, 87–130
  and affirmative action, 115, 123–25
  and AFL, 119
  and arrival in the North, 118–19
  civil rights, 21–34, *32*

compared to European immigrants, 106–109
and criminal justice system, 542, *542*
economic experience, 104–128
and economic self-reliance, 107–15
and education, 87
housing, 495
housing discrimination, 511–15
jury trial, 533–34
and Ku Klux Klan, 24–25
labor migration, 116–18
and lack of entrepreneurship pattern, 122–23
and lack of system of protection, 119–21
lynchings, 22, 548
migration, 23–26
mortgage lending, 504–505
and New Deal programs, 111–12, 119
poverty, *33*
pre-1865, 3
and Roosevelt, Franklin, 25, *25*
school desegregation, 425–31
and seniority system, 121
and slave codes, 87
and voter fraud, 81
voting, 28, 29, 87
voting rights, 125, 376, 380–83, *381, 397,* 400–403
World War II, 22, *23,* 27, *27*
Age discrimination, *485,* 485–86
Age Discrimination in Employment Act, 76, 485–86, 514, 620–21
Agnew, Spiro T., 33–34
AIDS and rights, 288, 360
Aid to Families with Dependent Children (AFDC), 296, 560
Alianza Hispano-Americana, 203
Alien and Sedition Acts, 243
Alien Land Law of 1920, 139–40

and racial segregation, 13, 629–31
and school desegregation, 28, 422–31
Washington, Booker T. 113–15, *114*
accomodationist, 306
and Atlanta Compromise, 113
biography, 307
and progressive education, 118–19
Tuskegee Institute, 23
Washington, George, 20
Watergate scandal, 362
Watkins, Arthur, 228
Wattenberg, Ben J, 209
Weaver, Robert, 25
Wehr Steel Corporation, 120–21
Welfare policies, 574–75
Welsh, 14
West Florida, 162
Whistleblowers, 464
White, Byron R., 459–60
White, Jack, 341
White, Ryan, 288
White, Theodore H., 255
White Citizens Council, 303
Whitman, Christine Todd, 500
Wilke, John C., 60
Wilkins, Roy, 322
Wilkinson, Frank, 79–81
William Beaumont Hospital, 556
Willoughby, Charles, 42
Wilson, Edith Bolling Galt, 48
Wilson, Pete, 208
Wilson, William B., 248
Wilson, Woodrow
Native Americans, 226
and women's suffrage, 47, 48, 607
Wiretapping, 527, 528
Wobblies, 68–71
Women's Bureau, 71
higher education, 444–45
Women's Committee of Philadelphia, 69
Women's Equity Action League, 265
Women's Health Center, 367
Women's International Terrorist Conspiracy from Hell
(WITCH), 61
Women's Liberation Union, 61

Women's movement, 63–64
Women's Peace Party, 50
Women's Political Union, 47
Women's rights, 45–64, *52, 53, 54*, 261–70, *261*
and jury duty, *533*
Fourteenth Amendment, 45–46
in military, 659–61
Women's suffrage, *47*, 47–48, 376–78, 607
Women's Suffrage Association, 378
Women's Trade Union Industrial League, 51–52
Wonderlich Intelligence Test, 475
Woolworth lunch counter sit-in, 28
Workplace hazards, 552
World War I
World War II
and African Americans, 118–20
and Chinese, 134–35, 137
Puerto Rican immigration, 183–85
veterans, 73–74
and women, 54
Worldwide Church of God, 466
Wounded Knee, 222, 237
Wright, S. Skelly, 320

Y

Yamoto Colony, 36
Yellow Peril
and Chinese, 137
and Japanese, 35
Yoder, Jonas, 290
Yzaguirre, Raúl, 173, 217

Z

Zedillo, Ernesto, 211
Zinsmeister, Karl, 209
Zionitz, Alvin J., 224
Zion School for the Colored, *94*
Zoning, 495–501
Zonta, 450
Zuni Pueblo, 505